The Gender and Psychology Reader

The Gender and Psychology Reader

EDITED BY

Blythe McVicker Clinchy

AND

Julie K. Norem

New York University Press

NEW YORK AND LONDON

NEW YORK UNIVERSITY PRESS
New York and London

© 1998 by New York University
All rights reserved

Library of Congress Cataloging-in-Publication Data
The gender and psychology reader / edited by Blythe McVicker Clinchy
and Julie K. Norem.
    p.   cm.
   Includes bibliographical references and index.
   ISBN 0-8147-1546-X (hardcover : alk. paper).—ISBN 0-8147-1547-8
(pbk. : alk. paper)
   1. Sex (Psychology)   2. Sex differences (Psychology)   I. Clinchy,
Blythe.   II. Norem, Julie K., 1960–
BF692.2.G4654   1998   97-42572
155.3—dc21   CIP

Manufactured in the United States of America

10 9 8 7 6 5 4 3 2

Contents

PART VII: Contextual Constraints and Affordances

Introduction

Blythe McVicker Clinchy and Julie K. Norem

Assembling this volume was roughly equal parts joy and frustration. The joy came both from the process of collaboration and from being able to discover, read, discuss, and learn, all while virtuously claiming that we were working. The frustration too had many sources: Some of what we read caused us to sigh in despair or shake our heads in exasperation. More importantly, however, we were frustrated by the number of wonderful works we could not include because we did not have space (and we cannot even begin to list them here). We used a number of different criteria to pare down our list. First and foremost, we wanted an eclectic group of papers that were *provocative*—that would stimulate others to think, read, disagree, and discuss further. We chose not to select reports of single studies, because we did not think that any single study would be as useful as the more general papers we include. We did select papers (and organize sections), however, that we thought would provide a context for students to think about and question examples of single studies on gender-related topics.

Though the volume has a psychological focus, the readings are interdisciplinary, with contributions from sociologists, philosophers, and anthropologists. In addition to influential contemporary work, we wanted to include a few "classic" older pieces that offer valuable perspectives on the field. The selections included range from research summaries on particular topics (e.g., gender differences in emotion) to work on development of gendered self-concepts, to discussion of psychology's ambivalence about the study of difference and its failure to systematically consider race, ethnicity, and class. Our concluding chapter considers themes that can be traced through different sections, gaps in current perspectives, and future directions we think might be useful. The book is not intended to be a comprehensive survey of the psychology of gender. It does, however, touch upon most of the significant and controversial underlying issues involved in the study of gender, including methodological issues.

The book is intended for use alone or as a supplementary text for upper-level undergraduate and graduate courses in gender. We have divided the volume into seven broad sections, some of which are further divided into subsections. Though selecting the articles was a daunting task, it was easier than dividing them into sections, because so many of the pieces we chose could reasonably fit into more than one section. This is not surprising, given that the pieces we found most intriguing tended to employ more than one perspective or level of analysis, and thus did *not* fit neatly into any particular, circumscribed category.

Nevertheless, we think there is both coherence and diversity within the sections we have created. Each section can be used independently, without the need for a particular chronological progression. In the introduction to each section we preview some of the major issues considered by the authors included in that section, mention historical controversies relevant to the readings, and point students toward general questions and themes that arise from those readings. Beyond the usefulness of individual sections, we think there is considerable coherence, as well as pedagogical potential, to the entire collection. Many of the points raised in one way by one author are considered from very different perspectives by other authors in different sections, vividly illustrating the power of multiple analyses, as well as the irreducible complexity involved in the study of gender.

As is obvious from our introductions to the various sections and from our concluding chapter, we have opinions and we do not try to hide them. We will introduce ourselves to provide some background for our points of view.

Blythe: I am a white, middle-class, married heterosexual with three sons and three grandchildren. Although I was a committed feminist in my "personal" life, in my early days as a developmental psychologist I had no particular professional interest in women or gender. Inspired by William Perry's (1970) research at Harvard on intellectual development during the college years, my colleague Claire Zimmerman and I decided to conduct a follow-up study at Wellesley, the undergraduate college where we taught. Perry's sample was largely male; ours, perforce, was entirely female, because Wellesley is a women's college. In applying for funds for the project, we claimed that one of our goals was to test the applicability of Perry's developmental scheme on a sample of women, but in truth we had no doubt that it was perfectly applicable, that Perry's was a gender-neutral theory. To some extent, this turned out to be true: We found that we could code most of our interview data in terms of Perry's scheme.

But not quite all of it. We found, as Carol Gilligan found in attempting to fit women's moral considerations into Lawrence Kohlberg's scheme, that the women who spoke to us in this and subsequent research (reported in Belenky, Clinchy, Goldberger, & Tarule, 1986/1997) often spoke in a different key, describing ways of knowing and ways of being that were largely ignored or denigrated in developmental theory and in academic circles generally. At first, when we could not make sense of a woman's perspective in terms of the theory, we just shunted her aside—left her out. But gradually we began to wonder if perhaps something had been left out of the developmental story we had been taught, as well as the methods we had been taught to use in assembling the data to construct that story. This was a wrenching transition for me. After years devoted exclusively to "women's things"—housewifery and child-rearing—I was deeply wedded to the cool professionalism of being a psychologist. Occasionally, I still feel a pinch of nostalgia for that peaceful period before the gender Zeitgeist swept over psychology. Mostly, however, I am thrilled to be a part of it, for I am convinced not only that modern psychology can teach us a great deal about gender, but that our understanding of gender can profoundly alter the discipline of psychology.

Julie: I am a white, middle-class, married heterosexual with one son. Since at least third grade, I have considered myself a feminist. Like Blythe, however, I have not always considered myself a "feminist scholar," and I did not intend to focus on gender in my own research in personality and social psychology. I enjoyed doing traditional experiments and was rather relieved not to consider gender in my work—discussion of gender tended to raise my blood pressure. My professional involvement in the study of gender developed slowly, as I became more and more frustrated with mainstream theory and research in personality and social psychology—especially with the focus on reified structure in personality psychology, and on "disembodied" process in social psychology. Sometimes that frustration was a reaction to specific writings about gender. More often, however, frustration arose from *how* that psychology was typically conducted and what was *not* written, discussed, or considered. Identification with traditional paradigms left me without a language, and thus without a voice, to talk about the kinds of psychological processes I found most interesting. I was forced to study gender in order to learn about language (and ideas) that would allow me to pursue the psychology I wanted to pursue. I believe, based on my own experience, that Abigail J. Stewart is absolutely right in her claim (see chapter 3, this volume) that personality psychology has a great deal to learn from feminist theory. I also believe that some of the most telling gaps in personality theory will not be filled until workers in this field face the need to consider gender systematically in their theory building and theory testing.

We hope that as they think about gender, both instructors and students will find our points of view useful even if they do not agree with them, just as we have learned from those authors with whom we disagree and from our disagreements with each other. We hope that this volume will contribute to the stimulating, exciting, frustrating, infuriating, and absolutely crucial ongoing conversation about gender.

REFERENCES

Belenky, M. F., Clinchy, B. M., Goldberger, N. R., & Tarule, J. M. (1986/1997). *Women's Ways of Knowing.* New York: Basic Books.

Perry, W. G. (1970). *Forms of Intellectual and Ethical Development in the College Years.* New York: Holt, Rinehart & Winston.

Part I

Underlying Epistemological Issues

Recent theory and research on the psychology of gender has been profoundly influenced by developments in epistemological theory. These developments take a variety of forms. Those who call themselves postmodernists, post-structuralists, social constructionists, and contextual relativists (to name just a few possibilities) do not agree in every respect, but all share the view that meanings are *contextual* and that knowledge, being constructed rather than simply discovered, inevitably involves interpretation. As Jane Roland Martin notes in her chapter, "any human or social phenomenon can be understood in countless different ways," depending upon the context in which it occurs and the angle from which it is viewed. No particular understanding can ever be complete, adds Abigail J. Stewart, for it is filtered through "a perspective which is inevitably partial."

From this standpoint there is no such thing as utter objectivity; the knower is inextricably involved in the known, and much that passes for observable "fact" actually involves interpretation. This position is at odds with the objectivist paradigm that, as Laurel Furumoto tells us, came to dominate psychology in the early twentieth century, driving out earlier, more humanistic models. At the heart of that "new scientific psychology," derived from natural science, was a "subject–object split." According to this paradigm, to quote the philosopher Susan Bordo, it is "the otherness of nature" that "allows it to be known" (Bordo, 1986, p. 452), and psychological truth is achieved through quantitative accretion of measurable data by detached, impersonal observers. Furumoto sees this as a "masculine" paradigm, inhospitable to women. Other feminist scholars have suggested that women and people of color may be particularly wary of objectivist theories: Because they themselves have too often been objectified, treated as things, as "other" (Fee, 1981; Jordan, 1985; Keller, 1983), they do not wish to see the human subjects of psychological research treated as faceless objects, devoid of subjectivity.[1] Mindful of the ways in which people in power have "made a pretense of objectivity . . . and have used the claim of objectivity to protect their judgments from rational scrutiny" (Nussbaum, 1994, pp. 60–61), members of oppressed groups have learned to be suspicious of such claims. Although few psychologists would abandon the scientific norm of objectivity, many would see it now as an ideal to be approximated, but rarely if ever utterly achieved: "It is crucial," Evelyn Fox Keller writes, "to distinguish between the objective effort and the objectivist illusion" (1983, p. 134), an illusion that is maintained and reinforced by the "rhetoric of objectivity" (Dillon, 1991, cited by Madigan, Johnson, & Linton, 1995, p. 433) prevalent in mainstream psychological journals, which portrays the authors as models of "neutrality" and "impersonal detachment" who are "conveying objective information about a fixed external reality" (Madigan et al., 1995, pp. 433–434).

Furumoto now believes that the reason she was unable to hear "a distinctly feminine voice" in the early women psychologists she studied was that "since mainstream and masculine became synonymous, those who were counted as contributors—female as well as male—were obliged to employ the same rhetoric." Although this remains largely true, in recent years a more feminine voice has begun to emerge in psychology as well as other disciplines, one that argues for a conception of knowledge grounded "not in detachment and distance, but in closeness, connectedness, and empathy" (Bordo, 1986, p. 455; see also Code, 1991). Such an approach, Keller asserts, need not be considered unscientific. Just as there is no single truth, there is no single science; the history of science reveals a "thematic pluralism" (Keller, 1987, p. 245). There have always been scientists who, rather than attempting to dominate and control the object of their investigations, subordinated themselves to it, "letting the material speak to [them]," as the biologist Barbara McClintock put it, treating the "object" as "subject"—even when, as in McClintock's case, the subject was an ear of corn—and stepping into it instead of stepping back: Keller quotes McClintock as saying "I wasn't outside, I was down there—I was part of the system" (Keller, 1983, p. 141).

Stephanie Riger, Hope Landrine, and Abigail J. Stewart, in their contributions to this volume, argue that psychologists have paid too little attention to the social context in which behavior occurs. The experimental paradigm entails "context-stripping," Riger asserts; by controlling for the effect of "extraneous" factors other than the ones under investigation through procedures such as random assignment to treatment conditions, "psychologists rule out the study of sociocultural and historical factors, and implicitly attribute causes to factors inside the person." Personality psychology's individualistic intrapsychic bias, combined with its search for universal laws, Stewart says, has caused it to ignore political and economic realities, as if everyone in the society had equal opportunities and bore equal burdens. As Riger puts it, "In an ironic reversal of the feminist dictum of the 1960s, when social context is ignored, the political is misinterpreted as personal." Michelle Fine and Susan Gordon (1989) argue that in conventional laboratory experiments "the social relationships and contexts in which women weave their lives are excluded as if irrelevant" (pp. 154–155). If, as is customary, one defines *gender* as a social construct, distinct from biological sex and the sex category to which people are assigned, and if one conceives of gender not as a bundle of intrapsychic predispositions but as "constituted through social interaction," as Candace West and Don H. Zimmerman and other social constructionists do (see chapter 6 of this volume), then it is clear that such practices make it impossible to explore the workings of gender, at least as it operates in "real life."

But the problem of decontextualization goes deeper than this. It is not just that laboratories are sterile, artificial settings lacking in ecological validity and thus rendering behavior "unnatural." It is, as Landrine reminds us, that we *define* behavior as acontextual. Context, in Landrine's view, is not "a mere setting in which behavior occurs"; it is not something outside the behavior that influences it. Rather, context is *part* of the behavior. "The sociocultural, historical, and political context," Landrine says, must be seen as "an integral part of the label for and definition of behavior," rather than "something outside of it, something surrounding it." To call a slave more "dependent" than his master because he shows more groveling "behaviors," without accounting for the difference in power, makes no sense.

Some psychologists who are drawn to these more contextual, interpretive approaches reject conventional scientific methods as useless in the study of psychology in general and of the psychology of gender in particular. However, to us it seems that if knowledge is regarded as perspectival, then there can be no single road to truth, and one is obliged to acknowledge the legitimacy of a multiplicity of methods. To assert otherwise, we believe, is to engage in the "methodological essentialism" that Martin deplores.

NOTES

1. Madigan, Johnson, and Linton (1995) observe that "although the current view is that subjects . . . are anonymous, interchangeable, and distinct from experimenters, this was not always the case. During much of psychology's early history, studies were reported in which participants were explicitly named individuals who were frequently the authors of the report" (pp. 429–43).

REFERENCES

Bordo, S. (1986). The Cartesian Masculinization of Thought. *Signs, 11*, 439–456. Reprinted in S. Harding, & J. F. O'Barr (Eds.) (1987), *Sex and Scientific Inquiry* (pp. 247–264). Chicago: University of Chicago Press.

Code, Lorraine. (1991). *What Can She Know?* Ithaca, NY: Cornell University Press.

Fee, E. (1981). Is Feminism a Threat to Scientific Objectivity? *International Journal of Women's Studies, 4*, 378–392.

Fine, M., & Gordon, S. M. (1989). Feminist Transformations of/Despite Psychology. In M. Crawford & M. Gentry (Eds.), *Gender and Thought* (pp. 146–174). New York: Springer-Verlag.

Jordan, J. (1985). *On Call: Political Essays*. Boston: South End Press.

Keller, E. F. (1983). Women, Science, and Popular Mythology. In J. Rothschild (Ed.), *Machine Ex Dea* (pp. 131–135). New York: Pergamon Press.

Keller, E. F. (1987). Feminism and Science. In S. Harding, & J. F. O'Barr (Eds.), *Sex and Scientific Inquiry* (pp. 233–246). Chicago: University of Chicago Press.

Madigan, R., Johnson, S., & Linton, P. (1995). The Language of Psychology: APA Style as Epistemology. *American Psychologist, 50*, 428–436.

Nussbaum, M. (1994, October 20). Feminists and Philosophy. Review of *A Mind of One's Own: Feminist Essays on Reason and Objectivity*, edited by Louise M. Antony and Charlotte Witt. Boulder, CO: Westview. *New York Review of Books*, 59–63.

Chapter One

Methodological Essentialism, False Difference, and Other Dangerous Traps

Jane Roland Martin

At meetings, workshops, and conferences in the 1980s, feminist scholars became accustomed to hearing women accuse one another of essentialism. In the literature of that period, one regularly read of sightings of feminists in or near the essentialist trap (e.g., Echols 1983, 1984; Eisenstein 1983, xvii–xix; Jones 1985, 367; Alcoff 1988, 411; see also Snitow 1990, 17; Berg 1991). I use the term *accuse* advisedly. If I had called your work or you had called mine essentialist, you or I would not merely have been offering criticism, as we would if we had called that work sketchy or unconvincing or disorganized or badly written or even false (see, e.g., Spelman 1988, 159; Fraser and Nicholson 1990, 20). Of course, not everyone who used the term *essentialist* intended it as a condemnation. Nevertheless, the net effect was to place on the work a seal of disapproval. When in a 1989 conversation about feminist criticism Nancy Miller said, "You don't like to feel in a rank of things racist or sexist," Jane Gallop asked her, "Do they feel worse or better than being accused of being an essentialist?" (Gallop, Hirsch, and Miller 1990, 353; see also de Lauretis 1990, 255). In an interview published in a special issue of *differences* on essentialism, Gayatri Chakravorty Spivak said, "What I am very suspicious of is how anti-essentialism, really more than essentialism, is allowing women to call names and to congratulate ourselves" (Spivak 1989, 128–29).

Just as a chilly classroom climate can have a profound negative impact on women's academic and career development (Hall and Sandler 1982), a chilly research climate can adversely affect the development of feminist theory and research. I am very worried that the accusations of essentialism that feminist scholars directed at one another—and also of ahistoricism, false generalization, and their variants—may have had precisely this result. I am also concerned about the methodological advice given to scholars who sought to avoid these traps.

Those of us who are white academic feminists have recognized the terrible mistake we made in assuming that all the individuals in the world called "women" were exactly like us. Paradoxically, though, our acts of unmasking the differences among women and reveling in them became occasions for imposing a false unity on our research. Condemning essence talk in connection with our bodies and ourselves, we came dangerously close to adopting it in relation to our methodologies.[1] In our determination to honor diversity among women, we told one another to restrict our ambitions, limit our sights, beat a retreat from certain topics, refrain from using a rather long list of categories or concepts, and eschew generalization. I can think of no better prescription for the stunting of a field of intellectual inquiry.

One reason for this regimen of self-denial is that in attempting to steer clear of the traps of essentialism, ahistoricity, and false generalization, feminist theorists fell into opposite but equally dangerous ones. In overcompensating for our failure to acknowledge the differences of race, class, and ethnicity, we tended a priori to give privileged status to a predetermined set of analytic categories and to affirm the existence of nothing but difference. In other words, in trying to avoid the pitfall of false unity, we walked straight into the trap of false difference. Overreacting to the historical gaps in feminist scholarship, we concluded that every scholar must be her own historian, which is to say that in trying to circle around the ahistorical trap we landed in the trap of compulsory historicism. Meanwhile, rejecting one kind of essence talk but adopting another, we followed a course whose logical conclusion all but precludes the use of language.

Ironically, we unwittingly created for ourselves a research climate in which we imposed on our investigations the very thing we condemned—false unity. Equally ironically, in this chilly climate we came to judge women's scholarship by a harsher standard than the one we applied to men's. Furthermore, the routes we charted around the traps of essentialism, ahistoricism, and false generalization exposed us to new pitfalls, methodological dangers that beg for critical examination. At meetings, workshops, and conferences in the 1990s one is told that the debate about essentialism is dead. Yet such pronouncements are troubling insofar as they are made without consideration of the methodological questions at issue or the functions the debate may have served.

The Trap of Essentialism and the Pitfall of Proscribed Categories

Old and New Essentialisms

There may be an intellectual and cultural tradition that views essentialism quite differently from the way my philosophical training taught me to see it.[2] It is fair to say, however, that in Western thought the search for essences goes back at least to Socrates. When he asked, What is justice? What is truth? What is piety? he did not want the answer to take the form of an isolated illustration—for instance, justice is paying your debts—or even a list of examples. He was looking for a general account or definition that would hold true for all cases of justice or truth or piety past, present, and future and for nothing else. Even if it met the requirements of generality, a statement might not be acceptable, however. When Socrates asked a "What is X" type of question, he wanted to know the nature or essence of X, be it justice, truth, or piety, and not merely some accidental property of X.

The troubling epistemological and metaphysical issues surrounding the search for essences have long been recognized and so has the fact that the accidental/essential distinction is unclear. Supposing one discovers a property that all those things that fall into the category justice or into that philosophical favorite, man, have in common, how does one know that the property is essential and not simply accidental? And assuming it is essential, what is its ontological status? Men change over time but man's essence is said to be fixed; every man dies but man's essence is considered eternal. But then, what kind of thing is an essence and what is the relationship between the thing that has an essence, be it justice or man, and particular instances in the real world?

At least in Anglo-American philosophy, long before the postmodern turn, these thorny matters contributed to a retreat from what have been called *de re* accounts of necessity—ones that attribute essential properties directly to things—to *de dicto* accounts that tie attributions of essences to linguistic conventions: that is, from metaphysical inquiries into the nature of justice, truth, and piety to linguistic investigations of the definition or meaning of the terms *justice, truth,* and *piety.*[3] They also explain my own long-standing distrust of essence-talk on whatever level it occurs.

To my everlasting regret, my philosophical training did not inform me that Western culture's thought about women has been premised on essences. The arguments that proceed from assertions about women's nature to conclusions about our subordinate place in society and our domination by men are by now so well-known as to require little comment. Reading back onto our nature the social programs they then claimed to derive from it, philosophers, theologians, and other rational animals have used essence talk to justify their own rule in both the family and the state.

I take it that in discussing "reactionary tendencies" in feminism under the heading "The Politics of Feminist Theory: Against the New Essentialism," Hester Eisenstein in *Contemporary Feminist Thought* was making implicit reference to this discredited project of arguing from our nature to our place in society; that in referring to "a new biologism" according to which "women are superior beings to men, by virtue of their physical identity as female" (1983, xviii), she was pointing out that some feminist theorists have now turned the tables on the men. Whereas proponents of "the old essentialism" attributed to women essential properties very different from and inferior to those possessed by men, these feminist thinkers see women as possessing essential properties different from and superior to men's. And just as the men claimed to derive women's moral, social, and political subordination from the inferior nature they mapped onto us, the women claim to derive our moral, social, and political superiority from the superior nature they assign us. I also understand Eisenstein to say that even though the content of the argument from women's nature has been changed, women are still the ones who stand to suffer. Not only does the historical association between attributions of a female essence and women's imprisonment in the domestic "sphere" raise the specter of a revival of the traditional Western view of women's proper place, but also the discoveries of women's essence that feminists claim to have made are used to support social and political programs inimical to women.

The question remains of whether the new essentialism is as disabling as Eisenstein and others have claimed. Quite clearly, anyone who tries to derive moral, social, political, and cultural conclusions from her new readings of women's essential nature runs the standard risks of *de re* essentialism, namely, attributing to women properties that not all women possess or else mistaking accidental properties for essential ones.[4] In addition, like those men who claimed to derive women's place in society from our nature, Eisenstein may be mapping onto our bodies or our psyches or both the very conclusions she wishes to draw—a form of circular reasoning and a risky project in that it might well encourage others to do likewise. Even if she is not committing this error, her reasoning will be faulty: the argument from women's nature to our social and political superiority—or even to our equality—is no more valid than the one to our social and political subordination.

No programmatic statements—no policies, recommendations, calls to action, or the like—follow from claims about women's essential nature because no conclusions about what ought to be the case follow directly from what is.[5] Thus, if cultural feminism or some other stance that appeals to essences is dangerous for women, the source of the problem is not the essence talk per se but the uses to which it is put.

Biologism

The same can be said of biological talk. Given that both male and female thinkers have attributed to women an essential nature rooted in biology, one might conclude that the search for essences is necessarily a biological quest. But Socrates would not have undertaken his inquiries into the essence of justice and truth if this were the case. Moreover, most Western thinkers who have maintained that rationality is the essence of man have believed in the separation of mind and body. Claiming that reason belongs to the domain of mind and that mind is not material, they have been committed to the view that rationality is not a biological property. Indeed, these thinkers were able to place women beneath men in the Great Chain of Being precisely because they affirmed that men's essential nature is spiritual whereas ours is "merely" biological.

Just as essence talk is not necessarily about biology, biological talk is not necessarily about essences. Insofar as the biological attribute of having blue eyes is not shared by all women, it cannot be considered a defining or essential property of women. And even if all women were blue-eyed, being blue-eyed might be deemed an accidental property. This logical gulf between biological and essence talk contains two important lessons. First, because essences can be attributed to human inventions such as justice and piety, those who say that even our bodies and our sexuality are social constructions are not automatically guaranteed a safe journey around the trap of essentialism. Second, one does not have to purge one's theories of all references to biology in order to avoid it.

To determine which social constructionists and which users of biological talk have actually fallen into the essentialist trap, each case has to be examined on its own merits. But feminist theorists object to biologism—or biological determinism—not principally because it makes reference to biology. They consider it damaging because it purports to derive harmful moral, social, and political conclusions about women from statements about our biology.[6]

Feminist theorists who have expressed concern about the new essentialism have had relatively little to say about the invalidity of inferences from women's essence to our fates (see, however, Pierce 1983 and Trebilcot 1983). They have also paid scant attention to the logical pitfall known as the fallacy of denying the antecedent, which takes the form: if p then q, and not p, therefore not q. Suppose one grants that feminist claims about women's essential nature are false, indeed, that there is no such thing as women's essential nature. It does not follow that the program or programs that supposedly have been derived from our essence are thereby invalidated, for the possibility remains open that they are warranted on other grounds. In committing the fallacy of denying the antecedent, we are not merely being illogical, however. Insofar as we judge either the whole or some part of cultural feminism or any other position invalid without a close examination of its doctrines and their practical implications, we deprive ourselves a priori of access to ideas and programs that might in fact serve us well (see also Schor 1989, 50).

In directing attention to the trap of denying the antecedent, I do not mean to endorse the woman-centered perspective that Eisenstein warned us against or the cultural feminism that according to Linda Alcoff "is founded on a claim of essentialism that we are far from having the evidence to justify" (1988, 421). These may be every bit as dangerous to women as "antiessentialist" feminist theorists have been saying. My point is simply that the cases for or against these stances need to be made in their own right, for the rejection of female essences does not in itself constitute rejection of them.

Masking Difference

While some of the criticisms of essentialism focus on the support that essences seem to lend programs and policies considered inimical to women, others single out the denial of difference or diversity on which essences rest and the consequent illusion of uniformity (e.g., Spelman 1988, 158). The search for the essence of things—the *de re* search, as it might be called—is a quest for unity or commonality. Socrates wanted to know what all the disparate actions that everyone agrees are just have in common. Whether the subject is justice, truth, piety, man, or woman, *de re* essence talk—in fact, all essence talk—focuses on sameness. Indeed, the concern for uniformity is often so pronounced that the diversity that first gives rise to the essence quest is forgotten. It is assumed that if all instances of, for example, justice or woman have one property or a small set of properties in common, they are alike in all respects. This reasoning is obviously invalid, the unity it posits clearly false; it also undermines the very point of essence talk—to locate uniformity in diversity. After all, it is the existence of differences among things that we group together and label that motivates the search for essences in the first place.

There may be occasions when an assumption of total uniformity does not matter. When, however, the subject is woman, false unity can definitely be—undoubtedly has already been—harmful. As the denial by male scholars of differences within the category of human beings has led to the perception that women fall short of the norms of morality and mental health, to cite but two examples, the denial by female scholars of differences among women can cause some women to perceive other women as below standard or abnormal. Damaging self-confidence and destroying trust, the *de re* essentialist trap easily can undermine efforts that aim at unified action.

Feminist scholarship unquestionably stands to gain—already has gained—from the reminder that essence talk masks differences and that this masking can be destructive. Yet the truth of the matter is that this danger is present even when talk of womanhood or woman "as such" is assiduously avoided (see also Riley 1988). Nancy Fraser and Linda Nicholson have criticized those who "rely on essentialist categories such as gender identity" (1990, 32). Others have suggested that both women and gender are essentialist concepts or categories. Insofar as the concern is that these obscure diversity, however, all general terms need to be flagged. Any naming or categorizing tends to call attention to similarities and to neglect differences. In other words, the use of any general term, be it *chair, dog, virtue, mother, family, male dominance,* or *women's subordination,* easily can give rise to the very consequence that feminist scholars have attributed to essence talk. But this, in turn, is to say that the masking of difference or diversity is built into language itself.

One response of feminists to their realization that talk about women masks difference has been to recommend that we substitute talk about specific kinds of women: black women, white women, Asian women, Hispanic women; lesbians, heterosexual women, bisexual women; and so forth. Another response has been to recommend that our categories "be inflected by temporality," that instead of using categories such as gender identity, mothering, or reproduction, we use historically specific ones such as the modern, restricted, male-headed nuclear family (Fraser and Nicholson 1990, 34). Both responses highlight at least some differences, yet in each case the problem of masking diversity recurs at the more specific level of discourse.

Although talk about black women differentiates them from white, Hispanic, and Asian women, it can serve to mask the considerable diversity among black women. And although talk of a historically specific family form differentiates it from other historically specific forms, it too masks diversity.

Granted, the specific terms or categories that feminist theorists recommend mask fewer differences than the general terms they replace.[7] But the argument that more specific categories are therefore better than more general ones can be used against the very terms that feminist theorists have advocated. Just as the category of women masks everything the category black women does and more, the category black women masks everything black Caribbean women does and more. The same is true of the category black Caribbean women in relation to black Jamaican women, of the category black Jamaican women vis-à-vis twentieth-century black Jamaican women, and so on.

Taken to its logical extreme, the argument against general categories like women, gender, mothering, reproduction, and family leaves feminist scholars in the lurch. If categories exist that do not conceal difference, they will be so specific as to stultify intellectual inquiry. Even when a category is so hedged around with qualifications that only one individual falls within it, difference will still be masked: as postmodernism informs us, an individual is different from one time to the next—even from moment to moment—and from one place to another.

Obviously, feminist scholars do not have to travel to the extreme. Acknowledging that whatever categories we use will mask some differences, we can decide to use ones that uncover the differences we consider most important and that best fit our practical and theoretical purposes. *Decision* and *choice* become key words here, for feminist theory and research are practical activities that carry with them heavy responsibilities. While a person engaging in feminist scholarship is guided by both political and intellectual purposes and values, these no more dictate one's theoretical categories than do one's data. Just as different sets of categories will be consonant with a given body of data, alternate conceptualizations will be compatible with a given set of values and purposes. The question of which categories we should choose cannot be answered in advance of inquiry or decided upon once and for all because the contexts of our investigations change over time and so do our interests and purposes. Further, everyone need not choose the same categories. Indeed, if the categories that feminist theorists have been recommending seem to fit some research interests and purposes, the general categories that feminist theorists have told us to shun may turn out to be appropriate to other projects.

Essentialist and Nonessentialist Definitions

Feminist theorists have rejected those categories they call essentialist not merely because existing difference and diversity are obliterated, however. Although women's experiences and social practices differ from culture to culture and across historical periods, the offending categories seem to presuppose some fixed core that all members of the relevant class possess.

The a priori assumption that things that go by the same name share all or even some properties is mistaken. Yet it is equally a mistake to ban categories a priori—to deprive ourselves, in advance of inquiry, to access to conceptual frameworks and ideas that might be fruitful. Denying the existence of different kinds of definitions—or different approaches to definition—the category-banning policy assumes that a concept or category or term that has been given an essentialist definition must always and everywhere be defined in that way. This represents a faulty view of language.

There is no doubt that many of those philosophers who replaced the *de re* search for the essence of things, for example, justice, with a search for definitions of, for example, the term *justice,* assumed that all uses of a given term have something in common. This explains the countless attempts to discover a set of individually necessary and jointly sufficient conditions under which terms such as *justice* are used. But although this *de dicto* enterprise might be said to repeat on the linguistic level features of the Socratic quest for essences, it does not constitute the only valid approach to definition. Consider the proceedings that we call "games," Ludwig

Wittgenstein said. "Similarities crop up and disappear" as we move from one group of games to the next, the result being that "we see a complicated network of similarities overlapping and criss-crossing: sometimes overall similarities, sometimes similarities of detail" (Wittgenstein 1953, par. 66). He called these "family resemblances" (par. 67). Needless to say, Wittgenstein's approach to language does not replicate the *de re* search for essences—nor do approaches to definition that bear a family resemblance to Wittgenstein's.[8]

It is ironic, to say the least, that in keeping their distance from the *de re* essentialist trap—the trap of attributing essences to phenomena such as women, gender, reproduction, and mothering—feminist theorists have fallen into another essentialist pitfall. In labeling certain categories essentialist they have committed themselves to essentialism at the definitional level—what I will call *de definitione* essentialism.[9]

Different kinds of definition are available. Thus, supposing that feminist scholars have been defining *woman, gender identity, mothering,* and so forth, in essentialist ways, it does not follow that the rest of us must. For instance, if, as Fraser and Nicholson have said (1990, 30), Nancy Chodorow mistakenly attributed a common core to all cases of gender identity wherever and whenever they may be found—and I leave open the question of whether she did—we have the choice of eschewing the concept of gender identity as those who fall into the *de definitione* essentialism trap advise or of trying to redefine the concept in a nonessentialist manner. To be sure, no guarantee exists that an adequate definition of a given category or term can be constructed. But the possibility of failure in this endeavor does not vindicate a blanket rejection of the attempt.

The question remains of whether *de definitione* essentialism harms women. Some may also wonder if I am not falling into an essentialist trap by attributing negative properties to all forms of essentialism (see also Fuss 1989, 9). This is not the place to explore the issue of whether essentialism is ever a good policy (Rabine 1989; Spivak 1989) nor to review the claims made by some feminist theorists that certain forms of essentialism are benign (Fuss 1989; Spivak 1989; de Lauretis 1990). Certainly, however, we can expect the *de definitione* essentialist trap to have harmful effects in the long run insofar as it results in the proscription of certain concepts. In any field imagination is at a premium. In a relatively new area, which feminist research is, the free play of imagination is especially important. In addition, in a field as young as ours, the development of diverse and even radically divergent research programs is desirable. I can think of no better way to dampen the creative spirit or to reduce interpretive diversity than to draw up a list of concepts to be avoided at all costs.

The Ahistorical Trap and the Pitfall of Compulsory Historicism

Hiding History

When Fraser and Nicholson recommended that categories like reproduction and mothering be abandoned, they were taking history into account. Historical specificity was their concern, not specificity per se. Calling these categories "ahistorical" and expressing concern that feminist theorists have discussed societal practices such as reproduction and sexuality without investigating their origins, Fraser and Nicholson portrayed ahistoricity as a pitfall every bit as disabling for feminists as essentialism (see also Alcoff 1988; Scott 1988).

Charges of ahistoricity rest on the extraordinarily important insight that phenomena that traditionally have been considered natural, and therefore fixed, are social constructs with histories. The trouble with an ahistorical approach to sexuality, reproduction, gender, mothering, domesticity, and the family, then, is not simply that the resulting account will be incomplete but that findings that actually hold for one time period are apt to be projected onto other or even all time periods.

The warnings to avoid ahistoricity that feminists have posted alongside those about essentialism are by no means redundant. Ahistoricism and essentialism are separate traps: a piece of feminist theory or research can be ahistorical without being essentialist or, conversely, essentialist without being ahistorical. In telling feminist scholars to keep clear of the ahistorical pitfall by using concepts inflected by temporality, feminist theorists, however, have stepped into the *de definitione* essentialist trap. The reasons that have been given for turning our backs on categories such as sexuality, mothering, family, reproduction, and gender identity are by now familiar: because the individual phenomena, practices, institutions—call them what you will—that fall into these categories change over time, no basis or justification exists for referring to them by the same name (see, e.g., Fraser and Nicholson 1990). Assuming that the definitions of general terms can only be essentialist, feminist theorists have turned the flight from ahistoricity into a retreat from a particular set of concepts. Premised as it is on *de definitione* essentialism, such self-denial is unnecessary (see also Rabine 1989, 111). "Transhistorical" uses of concepts need not commit one to *de re* essentialism. To be sure, many past and present human activities bear so slight a resemblance to those things we call, for example, family or mothering that we would not count them as such. Nevertheless, time per se does not determine whether a given categorization is appropriate. We cannot know in advance if some past phenomenon is so similar to or so different from the diverse things we label, for example, family, that the label does or does not apply. Historical research is needed.

Insofar as feminist theorists have decided that certain concepts or categories are unacceptable without undertaking the relevant historical inquiries, they have fallen into the very ahistorical trap that they have been telling us to avoid. Some feminist scholars may well have attributed essential unchanging properties to sexuality, mothering, or other interesting phenomena precisely because they have treated their subject matter ahistorically. Others may by dint of ahistoricity have walked straight into the essentialism *de dicto* pitfall of defining central terms or concepts by reference to a set of necessary conditions. Nevertheless, to determine whether feminist scholars have been ahistorical, one must do more than note which categories they employ. One must see how these are used.

Like nontemporally inflected categories, temporally inflected ones mask diversity. Thus, for example, the category of the modern, restricted, male-headed, nuclear family masks historical change within the modern time period. Moreover, one who uses it could leap recklessly to the conclusion that all modern, restricted, nuclear families are alike or else that they all have been male-headed. Granted, one can defend such concepts by saying that in using them feminists must neither overgeneralize nor make invalid inferences. But this defense can be given in reference to nontemporally inflected categories too. Thus, instead of telling us not to use family, reproduction, mothering, and sexuality because they are ahistorical categories, feminist theorists merely might have told us not to abuse them.

Every Woman Her Own Historian

The strategy of deploying temporally inflected categories is actually one of three paths that feminist theorists have charted around the ahistorical trap.[10] The theorist pursuing the second course traces the history—narrates the story—of whatever her object of inquiry may be, thereby exposing change to view and illuminating the differences this change entails while keeping a respectful distance from the essentialist traps. In contrast, one who follows the third course does not construct narratives but places her objects of study in their historical context by relating them to, for example, contemporaneous institutions, practices, and ideologies. Although this type of historical inquiry no more exposes change to view than does the use of temporally inflected concepts, like the second course, it does help to fill some of those gaping holes in our knowledge.

Yet while we are sorely in need of historical knowledge, the advice that every woman write history delivers us up to the trap of compulsory historicism, a pitfall that does a disservice to the field of feminist theory and research. It is surely important for someone like me who is not a historian to position myself: to acknowledge that as a white, middle-class, heterosexual academic woman I write and think at a particular time from within a particular tradition. But to put the writing of history into the hands of one who probably does not have the knowledge or skill or mind-set to do it well encourages a kind of amateurism that we can ill afford. Worse still, by privileging one disciplinary source of illumination and insight into the phenomena we study, this policy gives short shrift to others and places those trained in disciplines other than history at a definite disadvantage.

Perhaps, however, that women, gender, and other phenomena of interest to most of us are social constructs with histories of their own makes it imperative that every feminist scholar give her work a historical dimension. Yet if something has a history it does not mean that everyone must study it from a historical point of view or that it can only be understood—or only "really" understood—historically. After all, the phenomena that interest us also have biological, linguistic, psychological, sociological, political, economic, and aesthetic dimensions. If we can detach our objects of study from other contexts, why not from the historical? Why, to put it bluntly, is *ahistorical* a term of disapprobation but not *apsychological, asociological, aphilosophical?* Of course, in the name of consistency one could maintain that besides being a historian, every woman must henceforth be her own psychologist, sociologist, philosopher, and so forth. Yet no one has the time, the skills, the education to do it all, and in any case, there always will be more approaches to a given topic of study than are presently dreamed of.

One could also argue that the various perspectives are not all of a piece: that history has a special status in the explanation and understanding of human affairs; indeed, that a historical perspective is so vital to genuine understanding that it must be considered an essential ingredient of all feminist research. The thesis that in the case of social life a historical approach is necessary itself has a history (see, e.g., Rickman 1964). Rather than trace it here, let me just point out that it is one thing to say that historical research into the phenomena that interest feminist scholars is vitally important and that a lot more needs to be done, and quite another to say that there can be no understanding without it. To insist on this latter is to embrace another form of essentialism.[11]

At issue regarding what may be called the trap of methodological essentialism is "the" nature of understanding—a controversial topic if there ever was one. Although many Western philosophers have claimed to know "the" way in which inquiry must proceed and to discern "the" nature of understanding, as I understand understanding, it takes no one single form (Martin 1970, 143–67). Any phenomenon, hence any human or social phenomenon, can be understood in countless different ways. Setting, for example, a practice such as mothering in its historical context is one way of understanding the practice, and tracing its history is another. But perfectly good nonhistorical questions can also yield understanding—for instance, about economic or political or cultural functions mothering serves at the present time, about relationships that obtain between and among the various elements or aspects of mothering now, about ways in which participants in the practice of mothering think, and so on.[12] Of course, none of these ways yields complete or total understanding but, then, neither do historical ways.

Because one can understand a given thing—admittedly, incompletely—without doing historical scholarship, and the cost of compulsory historicism is the loss of valuable kinds of illumination, I conclude that methodological essentialism is a trap best avoided by feminist scholars. I do not mean to minimize the significance and importance of a historical approach. What is not essential can still be vital. Unfortunately, when the historical approach is deemed essential, other equally important ones are all too likely to be sacrificed. It is ironic that at the very moment in history when feminist theorists are reminding feminist scholars to broaden the scope of their research so as to include people unlike themselves, these same feminist theorists are becoming exclusionary in regard to methodology. Instead of encouraging us to tap as diverse a range of potential sources of illumination as possible, they would have us adopt one preferred source.

A pluralistic conception of understanding is surely more consistent with feminism's respect for diversity than an essentialist one. Indeed, even if social phenomena can only be understood if they are set in their historical context or if their histories are traced, or both, it does not follow that every feminist scholar must do such tracing or setting in context. So that our field gains understanding of its objects of study, some of us would be required to do it, but not all—provided we are engaging in a cooperative enterprise. To think otherwise is to fall into the logical pitfall known as the fallacy of division. For even if historical study is after all essential for understanding our subject matter, a division of scholarly labor would be quite compatible with carrying out that study.

The Trap of False Generalization and the Pitfalls of False Difference and Predetermined Categories

The Affirmation of Diversity

The ahistorical trap is disabling not only because history is an important route to understanding. The danger is that we who fall into it will falsely generalize across historical periods. False generalization or universalization does not stem only from ahistoricity, however. In the classic textbook cases time is not even a factor: an inquirer simply generalizes about a whole population on the basis of an unrepresentative sample. This, of course, is what psychologists of the past did when they drew conclusions about human development from all male subjects. It is also what white middle-class women like me do when we assume that our own experiences represent all women's.

According to Eisenstein, by focusing on experiences that participants had in common while deemphasizing the participants' differences, the consciousness-raising groups of the late 1960s and early 1970s led women directly into the pitfall of false generalization (1983, 137). Among the notable feminist thinkers she identified as having been trapped there are Jean Baker Miller, Susan Brownmiller, Mary Daly, and Robin Morgan. Others have reported seeing Shulamith Firestone and Carol Gilligan fall into the same trap and have spotted Chodorow in its vicinity.

That false generalization can be disabling for women is not to be doubted, for racism can be both a cause and a consequence. In *Ain't I a Woman*, bell hooks said, "While it is in no way racist for any author to write a book exclusively about white women, it is fundamentally racist for books to be published that focus solely on the American white woman's experience in which that experience is assumed to be *the* American woman's experience" (1981, 137). In rendering other women invisible, this practice reduces their status "to that of non-person" (hooks 1981, 140) even as it reinforces the view that white women represent the norm. As if this in itself were not sufficiently damaging to both groups of women, the practice is politically harmful in that it separates women who might otherwise form fruitful alliances. hooks is surely right that when, even implicitly, theory and research represent one group of women as Other, the rhetoric of sisterhood will not be capable of binding women together.

To decide if the routes that feminist theorists have designed around this deadly trap are safe, scholars need to know just where in relation to the traps of essentialism the trap of false generalization is located. Although they both deal in generalizations, false generalization and essentialism are distinct phenomena. No doubt one who falsely generalizes may claim to have discovered some essence. But attributions of essential properties need not rest on this mistake; all members of a given class may indeed share some characteristic that can justifiably be said to define them. Moreover, those who generalize falsely need not be committed to essences at all, given that essence talk specifically allows for generalizations that capture nonessential or accidental properties.

I take the reports published in 1974 by anthropologists Michelle Rosaldo and Sherry Ortner of the discovery of cross-cultural universals to have been of this latter sort (Ortner 1974; Rosaldo 1974). Although Rosaldo and Ortner generalized about all known cultures, they made it clear that no necessity was at work, that it was perfectly consistent with their discoveries that cultures could once have existed or might exist in the future in which men did not dominate women, in which public and domestic spheres were not separate and gender specific, in which women were not perceived of as close to nature. I am not qualified to say if their extrapolations were justified. Supposing, however, that they were, these generalizations did not commit Rosaldo and Ortner to essences. And if the generalizations were false, a search for better ones would not have to be essentialist either.

One might think that an obvious way for a feminist scholar to avoid the trap of false generalization would be to improve her sample so that it was more representative. One might also wonder if feminist scholars who conduct empirical investigations could not exercise greater care in the way they report the results of their research, for instance, by the repeated flagging of statistical conclusions. Feminist theorists have, however, given the impression that any attempt to replace a false generalization with a true one—or, rather, any attempt to replace an unwarranted extrapolation with a warranted one—would be misguided.[13] Concluding her book with a discussion of the directions in which feminist theory should be moving, Eisenstein wrote, "First among these would be a retreat from false universalism, and a sensitivity to the diversity of women's experiences and needs" (1983, 141). Fraser and Nicholson ended their essay by saying, "Postmodern-feminist theory would be nonuniversalist" (1990, 34). And according to Alcoff, "Universalist conceptions of female or male experiences and attributes are not plausible in the context of such a complex network of relations" (1988, 412). The burden of messages like these is that to avoid the false generalization trap, feminist scholars must abandon any impulses to universalize we may have even if they are statistical in spirit.

What should feminist scholars be doing instead of generalizing? The advice we have been given is that through the medium of particularistic studies ranging from historical narratives of other times and anthropological reconstructions of other cultures to autobiographies, oral histories, and other accounts of personal experience, we should be focusing on difference and diversity. Twenty years ago no one would have guessed that difference would emerge as the privileged perspective in feminist theory and research and that any attempt to find commonalities among women would be condemned out of hand. After all, in the early phase of the late twentieth-century women's movement it was the discovery that the experience of others was so like one's own that was at once comforting, illuminating, and energizing. Sadly, it has turned out that this presumed discovery was a mere invention. Not only were we generalizing from too homogeneous a sample; we also were assuming that those who are alike in some respects are alike in all. No one can say, however, that having found out how wrong we were, we have been impenitent. Overgeneralizing from the existence of some differences among women to the existence of nothing but difference, we have set a brand new trap for ourselves and have insisted on walking into it.

Susan Bordo has written brilliantly, if briefly, about the a priori affirmation of difference by contemporary feminist theorists. She might have added that from a methodological point of view, no trap is more dangerous for women than the self-made trap of false difference. Cutting us off from the developmental insights of feminist psychologists and denying us the chance to discover even limited cross-cultural and temporal commonalties, it encourages us to construct not just other times and places but also other women as utterly Other.

Of course, black and white women, middle-class and working-class women, Irish and Arab women are different. But just as no two individuals and no two circumstances are alike in every respect, no two are different in every respect; the question of whether all women have one or more attributes or circumstances in common cannot be answered in advance of investigation.[14] Supposing that similarities are found, there is of course no guarantee that they will be important. Nevertheless, as long as there might be commonalties among all women—or among women such as blacks and whites who are now considered to be entirely different—it is at the very least perverse to deny ourselves access to knowledge of them, and quite possibly self-defeating.

Recurrences of Essentialism

Philosophers are often criticized for doing armchair social science. Feminist theorists indulge in this discredited occupation when in rejecting false generalizations about women they conclude that the differences of race, class, and perhaps ethnicity result in nothing but difference. They also engage in it when, in another act of self-denial, they assume without conducting the necessary inquiries that race, class, and ethnicity are the critical differences for women.

After remarking on "the coercive, mechanical requirement that all enlightened feminist projects attend to 'the intersection of race, class, and gender,' " Bordo asked, "What happened to ethnicity? Age? Sexual orientation?" (1990, 139). One might dispute Bordo's assumption that ethnicity and sexual orientation were not on the approved list of variables, but her point is well-taken that the list is incomplete. This is not its only troubling aspect, however. Prior to investigation, how can we be so sure that in a woman's case being a rape victim does not matter as much or more than her race or class? How do we know that, for us, difference does not turn on being fat or religious or in an abusive relationship?

Rightly responsive to charges of racism and classism and accordingly intent on avoiding the pitfall of false generalization, we have constructed alongside the trap of false difference the trap of predetermined categories. That race and class have been considered fundamental variables in research about men scarcely entitles these concepts to the privilege they now enjoy in the study of women. Indeed, just as historical study has been treated as an essential ingredient of good feminist methodology, these constructs are perceived to be essential elements of feminist investigations. To be sure, empirical inquiry may yet prove race and class to be *the* fundamental variables in our case. Because, however, the very categories that we have been assuming a priori to be definitive of our differences may in fact be less significant than some others, we need to find a way between the pitfalls of false generalization and false difference that does not lead into this essentialist trap. We should be looking for one that does not cut us off from the illumination that other categories of analysis might yield.

Even more troubling than the coercive nature of the policy that feminist research must always and everywhere attend to race and class, said Bordo, "is the (often implicit, sometimes explicit) dogma that the only 'correct' perspective on race, class, and gender is the affirmation of difference" (1990, 139). Actually, however, even as feminist theorists have been telling us to lay bare the diversity that exists within the category of women, they have been masking difference and manufacturing unity within the more specific racial and class categories. Regarding being black, for example, as "the" defining property of black women—in other words, falling once again into the *de re* essentialist trap—feminists have lost sight of the myriad ways in which black women differ from one another. Worse still, reasoning that if one property—for example, being black or Asian—is held in common by women, then all properties are, they have compounded the invalid inference that all black or Asian women are utterly different from all white women by the equally fallacious one that all black or all Asian women are absolutely alike.

The reification of difference between recognized categories of women and the inattentiveness to differences within these categories are definitely dangerous for women, for these policies actually construct women who belong to another race or class from oneself as the Other. They also legitimate an analogue in feminist scholarship to the old Separate but Equal segregationist policy. When, not long ago, the male bias of men's scholarship was revealed, feminists responded that once women are brought into the disciplines of knowledge, new narratives and theories have to be constructed. Now that feminist scholarship itself has been charged with race and class bias, our response has been different. Proclaiming in advance the impossibility of constructing adequate "integrated" theories and narratives, feminist theorists have opted for a "different but equal" policy.

Assume that black and white women or middle-class and working-class women are radically different and then there is no point in telling a feminist scholar who has fallen into the trap of false generalization to improve her sample. For given this premise, no matter what she does, the only generalizations she can come up with will be false. The assumption of absolute difference is untenable, however, and the best that can be said about the presumption that when the missing women are finally brought into feminist research scholars must treat them separately—that, in effect, there should be no intermingling of races or classes—is that it is intellectually stifling.

In urging that we do not cut ourselves off from generalizing research I am not condemning studies of difference or indicting ones that segregate categories of women for the purpose of study. On the contrary, I firmly believe that our field has been greatly enriched by work of this very sort. I am also sure that such research might never have been undertaken—or, if undertaken, might not have been published—if in response to charges of false generalization white academic feminist scholars had not acknowledged their mistakes. It is not one or the other kind of scholarship but the either-or approach to understanding social life that I reject here. As long as feminists refuse to accept the underlying premise of those claims that there is something that qualifies as "the" proper mode of understanding or investigating human beings, we can comfortably engage in both ideographic and generalizing projects. That these latter will most likely be statistical, in the broadest sense of this term, goes without saying.[15] I hope it is also clear by now that generalizing projects need not commit us to essentialism.

Improving the Climate and Revitalizing Our Methodology

"So what's at stake in these attacks?" Marianne Hirsch asked when Nancy Miller reported that at a conference on feminist theory she had felt denounced and publicly dismissed (Gallop, Hirsch, and Miller 1990, 352). The students in my feminist theory class asked the same question after reading some recent articles in feminist theory.

Remarking that it is not accidental "that feminists are questioning the integrity of the notion of 'female reality' just as we begin to get a foothold in those professions which could be most radically transformed by our (historically developed) Otherness," Bordo asked, "could feminist gender-skepticism . . . now be operating in the service of the reproduction of white, male knowledge/power?" (1990, 151). I have no doubt that if feminist scholars en masse take the routes around essentialism, ahistoricism, and false generalization that feminist theorists have been mapping, we will reproduce white male knowledge/power and the other varieties of white male power. Rather than explore this eventuality, however, I want to talk about the damage that a chilly climate of feminist research can do and why it is important to honor diversity in the methodological realm as we already honor it in other areas.

In positing a chilly research climate I put forward a hypothesis derived from my own experience and my admittedly limited observations. Lest it be thought that I am falsely generalizing, let me say that I take as empirical the question of just how widespread the phenomenon is. I do not for a moment mean to suggest that the atmosphere in the past decade turned chilly for all feminists. It certainly became far more comfortable than it was for those scholars whose lives and experiences were ignored or misrepresented in the research of the 1970s and 1980s. I am also aware that some scholars who all along have found the climate hospitable have felt no drop in the temperature. Still, a surprising number of people in the audiences to which I have read an earlier version of this article told me—often privately and in highly emotional language—that they had indeed suffered because of the accusations and the acrimony. The comments of some well-known feminist scholars also lend credence to the supposition that many feminist scholars have been experiencing the chill of which I speak.

In a discussion of the direction feminist theory has taken, Evelyn Fox Keller said, "It is almost as if we have sought to defuse the force of external censorship by becoming our own harshest critics" (Hirsch and Keller 1990, 384). But we have not merely become too hard on ourselves. "I feel like a lot of conversations are getting cut off by using the 'club' words—essentialism and things like that," Hirsch said to Miller and Gallop (Gallop, Hirsch, and Miller 1990, 350). "What revisionism, not to say essentialism, was to Marxism-Leninism, essentialism is to feminism: the prime idiom of intellectual terrorism and the privileged instrument of political orthodoxy. Borrowed from the time-honored vocabulary of philosophy, the word essentialism has been endowed within the context of feminism with the power to reduce to silence, to excommunicate, to consign to oblivion," Naomi Schor wrote in the Summer 1989 issue of *differences* (1989, 40).

I do not doubt that it is possible to conduct creative scholarship in an atmosphere of recrimination. I am sure that some women are courageous—or foolhardy— enough to continue to pursue their research programs after being publicly de- nounced. But, as Nancy Miller's own experience taught her, with accusation comes fear: "I also learned to fear other women in a way I hadn't done until that point. If I was polemical, my polemic was with men. In my mind I was writing *for* women against some establishment—institution, theory—that was male. For the first time I thought, 'I am now in a situation where *women* are not going to like what I'm saying' " (Gallop, Hirsch, and Miller 1990, 352).

Some might say that the fear of being given a negative label can be a good thing. Just as it prevents at least some men from harassing women or making sexist or racist remarks, fear may serve to keep white, middle-class feminists from promulgat- ing racist, classist, and other malicious forms of theory. I agree that white, middle- class feminists need constant reminders and close monitoring if we are to stop using the tools of the master. It is also imperative to realize that even as the research climate has been discouraging certain kinds of scholarly work, the attention to differences has allowed other equally important forms to flourish. But I know of no law saying that to make room for one type of feminist scholarship, it is necessary to repudiate other types, no reason why feminists should not strive to establish a warm and welcoming research climate for all. Thus, one must ask in this case, as one should when fear is used to bring children into line, if better ways do not exist to achieve what is wanted. One must also ask what is sacrificed in the process. Where intellectual inquiry is concerned, fear often produces timidity and self-censorship. If in the world of the coeducational college classroom this too frequently translates into a woman's inability to speak up, her increased disposition toward self-doubt, and even a tendency to drop out academically, we can expect it to have analogous consequences in the realm of feminist research.[16]

But suppose that the accusations stop—as, indeed, they now may have. The research climate will not improve if we continue to embrace a double standard. Right now we look tolerantly upon the gravest mistakes and omissions of a Michel, a Jacques, a Jean-François, even as we denounce works by women that contain far less egregious errors. Take Foucault. Does this master's inattention to women, to male domination, to the genderization of power, discourse, reason, knowledge lead femi- nist theorists to dismiss his work? On the contrary, they quite rightly tell us that it is a rich source of understanding and empowerment (Diamond and Quinby 1988). Take Lyotard. Does this man's utter neglect of women and of the workings of gender in both society and social criticism cause feminist theorists to condemn his work? No; they wisely want us to learn from it (Fraser and Nicholson 1990).

Feminists can learn much from Foucault and the others. We need to do some soul-searching, however, about the discrepancy between our cordial treatment of the men's theories and our punitive approach to the women's (see, e.g., Berg 1991, 51).

Many prominent feminist scholars have been accused of essentialism or ahistoricism or false generalization or all three, but perhaps no one has so frequently and from so many quarters been charged with falling into all three traps as Gilligan (see, e.g., Kerber 1986; Nicholson 1986, 105; Scott 1988, 40; Fraser and Nicholson 1990, 32–33; Stacey 1990, 540). I cite the case of Gilligan for illustrative purposes only (see also Bordo 1990, 148–49; Gallop, Hirsch, and Miller 1990, 364). My interest is not in whether Gilligan has fallen into traps but in the double standard by which her work has been judged. For the record, let me also say that I do not for a moment mean to imply that those who have criticized Gilligan's work have intentionally used a double standard. For that matter, Gilligan's critics and those who are tolerant of the mistakes of male thinkers are not necessarily the same individuals. My point is, simply, that a double standard has emerged and that it is not a healthy development.

Upon realizing that the original samples leading to Gilligan's discovery of a different voice (Gilligan 1982) were limited, her readers had ample reason to conclude that she had not demonstrated that women of all races and classes spoke in that different voice. Feminist critics instead convicted her of essentialism and false unity. Knowing that Gilligan was a psychologist, not a historian, readers also had excellent grounds for judging that she had not shown that the different voice existed in historical periods other than our own. Feminist theorists instead condemned her for being ahistorical. Pointing to the various ways in which Gilligan's discovery had still to be confirmed or disconfirmed, feminist scholars could have treated it as a hypothesis. Instead, they left the impression that further research was unnecessary. They implied, if they did not actually say, that Gilligan's ahistorical approach demonstrated the nonexistence of the different voice in other times and that her limited sample proved that the voice was uniquely white and middle class.[17]

Irene Diamond and Lee Quinby have offered the possibility of friendship between feminism and Foucault. Considering his theory illuminating but incomplete, in their introduction to *Feminism and Foucault* they proposed that we explore and fill in the gaps (1988, ix). Compare this constructive approach based on a belief in the possibilities of mutual correction and a fuller understanding with the one feminist theorists have taken toward Gilligan's work.

As an example, in the introductory section of an essay on the moral thinking and behavior of working-class women in nineteenth-century England, Ruth L. Smith and Deborah M. Valenze cited Gilligan only to distance themselves from her research. Claiming that the moral behavior of the women they studied "starkly contrasts with the autonomous moral agent central to liberalism" (1988, 277), that for these women " 'self' was often expressed and experienced as 'jointness' rather than 'oneness' and as mutual rather than atomistic" (278), that the women "risked their reputations and safety in order to satisfy substantive needs for their families and communities" (287), and that in their eyes "dependence—and independence—were closely tied to interdependence" (289), Smith and Valenze might have turned to Gilligan's research for illumination. Or they might have conceived of themselves as exploring and filling in a historical gap in hers. Instead, they were so loath to acknowledge any kinship that although their findings actually gave historical support to Gilligan's hypothesis, in their conclusion they told readers that "her moral theory remains without historical and political context" (297).[18]

"The question I really want to come back to," Hirsch insisted toward the end of the conversation with Gallop and Miller, "is whom does criticism, divisiveness, really hurt? What's the risk?" (Gallop, Hirsch, and Miller 1990, 364). Remarking that "there is no direct relation between being trashed and having career difficulties, suffering in your career," Gallop said, "I can't feel sorry for Carol Gilligan because despite it no longer being cool or sophisticated, Gilligan has an enormous impact. Her books have sold a lot. She's on the cover of the *New York Times Magazine*. All kinds of people who are not on the cutting edge of feminist theory continue to be influenced by her, to use and accept her" (Gallop, Hirsch, and Miller 1990, 365).

Focusing on the damage that Gilligan's career did or did not suffer, the parties to this conversation forgot to ask about the chilling effects the accusations and application of the double standard could have had on her subsequent research and perhaps did have on that of others such as Smith and Valenze. Hirsch stopped to wonder if "the hysteria around her work has prevented many from grappling with the radical potential it has in spite of its problems" (Gallop, Hirsch, and Miller 1990, 365). But the more general topic of the hobbling consequences of a policy that places a Keep Away! sign on certain women's research programs, thus shutting feminist theory and research off from ideas, concepts, methodologies—from intellectual possibilities, if you will—was not addressed.

In the event, the accusations and the application of a double standard after the publication of *In a Different Voice* did not cause Gilligan to abandon her research program. Expanding her database and developing an ever more sensitive methodology, she continued to ask the kinds of questions and to use the categories that exercised so many feminist theorists. In *Mapping the Moral Domain*, Gilligan and her colleagues presented a refined hypothesis that girls and women speak in a different voice along with additional confirming data (Gilligan, Ward, and Taylor 1988; see also Gilligan, Lyons, and Hanmer 1990). Needless to say, a great many questions remain. Did our foremothers speak in that voice? Is that voice so constituted by late-twentieth-century thinking that it was inaccessible to an earlier age? Do rural girls, Chicanas, lesbians, older women speak in it? In Asian and African societies is what Gilligan calls a different voice actually the dominant one? That these questions have not yet been answered, however, does not mean that their answers will disconfirm Gilligan's hypothesis. To suppose that they will is to engage in armchair social science. I fear that in response to the research of many feminist scholars besides Gilligan, many of us have been doing just this.

According to Fraser and Nicholson, "Feminist scholars have come to regard their enterprise more collectively, more like a puzzle whose various pieces are being filled in by many different people than like a construction to be completed by a single great theoretical stroke" (1990, 32). I wish I could agree. But my vision of a collective enterprise is of a research community governed by an open welcoming spirit, one that is as inclusionary on the methodological level as on the personal. It is of people who hold up high standards for themselves and each other but do not demand perfection. And it is of scholars from different backgrounds and with quite different kinds of training who are expert enough to see the mistaken assumptions and the gaps in other women's research, generous enough to give constructive criticism and to recognize the positive contributions contained in the work of others, and wise enough to know that their way of doing research is not the only right way—indeed, that there probably is no single right way or even a short list thereof.[19]

The chilly research climate, whose existence I can vouch for even though its extent remains to be determined, is far from being a welcoming one for diverse methodologies and divergent thought. But let me repeat that I am as concerned about the methodological advice that feminist theorists have been giving one another as about the accusatory language and the double standard. A product of a priori thinking that is itself the product of untenable dualisms, this advice promotes a kind of dogmatism on the methodological level that we do not countenance in other contexts. It rules out theories, categories, and research projects in advance; prejudges the extent of difference and the nonexistence of similarity; and arbitrarily privileges one type of methodology. Happily, to avoid the essentialist traps it is not necessary to eschew general categories or concepts. To steer clear of the ahistorical pitfall we do not have to endorse universal compulsory historicism. To navigate around false generalization we need not forgo generalization. In each case there are alternative paths to take if we choose.

Alternative paths around the well-marked pitfalls do exist and we need to know about them. It would be too cruel an irony if, just when white academic feminists have realized that many of our theories and concepts have excluded other women or masked the diversity among women—and just when we have sought to make amends—we allowed our creative impulses to be stunted and our interests to be redirected by an unwarranted accusation of methodological essentialism. So that ours can be an inclusive and collective enterprise it behooves us to find ways to keep out of the methodological traps and at the same time remain open to intellectual possibilities and receptive to different ideas.

Because my primary concern is the bad advice we have been given, I am deeply disturbed that the "essentialism/antiessentialism debate" is already being regarded as past history and even as something of a bore. For if the debate is laid to rest without critical examination of its presuppositions, the methodological mistakes of the parties to it will all too likely be repeated. If no clear routes around the traps of essentialism, ahistoricism, and false generalization are discerned, some of us will continue to fall into opposite and equally dangerous pitfalls while others of us, thinking we have no choice, will deliberately step into one or another essentialist trap. In addition, although the debate's demise may make the atmosphere less acrimonious, if the faulty advice given is not corrected, generalizing integrative research will continue to be dismissed out of hand.

Besides, we need to ask ourselves if the focus on theory and methodology that characterized discussions about essentialism was an adequate response to the charges of racism and classism that had been leveled against us. Maria Lugones has rightly said that in interpreting the "problem of difference" as a problem for feminist theory, white feminist theorizers have made theory, instead of racism, their main concern (1991, 41). Theory, as hooks has pointed out, can be used "to promote an academic elitism that embraces traditional structures of domination" (1989, 36). "In shifting the focus of crucial feminist concerns about the representation of cultural diversity from practical contexts to questions of adequate theory," Bordo wrote, we are "diverted from attending to the professional and institutional mechanisms through which the politics of exclusion operate most powerfully in intellectual communities" (1990, 136; see also Spelman 1988, 183). Before we put the discussions of essentialism behind, it behooves us to find out whether, and to what extent, they may have functioned as one more form of resistance to the sharing of our power and privilege.

NOTES

An earlier version of this chapter was presented at the Conference on Interdisciplinary Approaches to Knowledge and Gender in June 1991 at the University of Calgary, at the annual meeting of the Society for Women in Philosophy, Eastern Division, in December 1991 in New York, and as the inaugural lecture of the Society for Feminist Philosophy in April 1992 at the University of Massachusetts—Boston. I am grateful to the members of all three audiences as well as to Ann Diller, Hilde Hein, Barbara Houston, Susan Laird, Michael Martin, Beatrice Nelson, Jennifer Radden, and the three anonymous reviewers at *Signs* for their helpful criticisms.

1. I use the pronouns *we* and *ours* intentionally. To do otherwise would amount to falsely distancing myself, as a white academic feminist, from my subject matter. My usage should not, however, be taken to mean that I assume that all feminist theorists are white academics, that all white academic feminist theorists subscribe to the same views, that all white academic feminists have fallen into one or more of the traps under discussion, or that all those who have flagged the traps share the same views. I do not.

2. For rather different analyses of essentialism from the one that follows see, e.g., Fuss 1989; Schor 1989; and de Lauretis 1990. For a critique of Fuss, see Kuykendall 1991.

3. See, e.g., Boyd 1980 for a discussion of *de re* and *de dicto* accounts of necessity or essential properties. See also the discussion of real versus nominal essences by Fuss 1989, 4–5.

4. They also face the metaphysical problems mentioned above. It should be noted that new approaches to *de re* essences such as that employed by Morris 1986 have been designed to try to get around these.

5. Unless, of course, the programmatic conclusion is smuggled into the statement of essence itself.

6. There may be other reasons too. See, e.g., Spelman 1988 and the discussion of "somatophobia" (126–32).

7. In this connection, the problem of how to individuate or count differences does arise, however.

8. See, e.g., Black 1954 and Achinstein 1968. I use "property talk" in relation to definitions broadly here so as to include definitions in terms of relations between or among things.

9. Whereas, e.g., the *de re* variety attributes essential properties to women and the *de dicto* variety attributes essential properties to the definition of the term women, the *de*

definitione variety attributes essential properties to definitions themselves. *De definitione* essentialism can be considered a special case of *de re* essentialism, with definition being the thing to which essential properties are attributed. Alternatively, it can be considered a special case of *de dicto* essentialism, with *definition* the term to which essential properties are attributed. It seems important for analytic purposes, however, to distinguish it from the other two categories.

10. In distinguishing three quite different recommendations, I do not mean to suggest that any given person subscribes to all of them or that one or more of them is endorsed by all those who have flagged the ahistorical trap.

11. I am not taking a stand here on whether one or another feminist theorist actually holds this position. My purpose is not to report sightings of those who have fallen into this trap but to show that there is such a trap.

12. The point I make here does not rule out the possibility that the various functions a practice serves, the relationships that obtain in it, or the ways in which participants think, themselves have histories.

13. Actually, degrees of warrant would be involved here.

14. "As anyone who has taught courses in gender knows, there are many junctures at which, for example, women of color and white women discover profound commonalities in their experience, as well as differences," Bordo commented (1990, 150). In my experience, however, the trap of false difference has placed even the most profound commonalities at risk of being overlooked. In a faculty seminar I attended in the 1980s no one seemed to see—or else no one was brave enough to acknowledge aloud—the very obvious commonality between the experiences reported by a black woman scientist and a white woman scientist. At a feminist colloquium no one objected when the renowned speaker answered a black woman's question by saying that they both knew that she, the speaker, being white, could know nothing about her interrogator's experience.

15. In this category I include probabilistic statements, tendency statements, loose regularities, statements with a ceteris paribus clause, and the like.

16. I wish I could specify these consequences here, but by the very nature of the case I cannot. I do not mean to say that one can never know what would have been done had things been different. But it would surely require sophisticated research techniques of a sort I do not pretend to possess to find out: what inquiries have not been undertaken; what papers have not been written—or, if written, have not been published or, if published, have not been reviewed; what studies have not been pursued—or, if pursued, have not been funded; and so forth.

17. According to information supplied by Gilligan, the original sample included black middle-class women and white working-class women.

18. In contrast, Katzenstein and Laitin 1987 made the case that "Gilligan's portrayal of the female mode of moral reasoning is in part confirmed by the very history and rhetoric of feminist politics" (262).

19. The three anonymous readers of this article for *Signs* and assistant editor Kate Tyler seemed to me to exemplify this process beautifully.

REFERENCES

Achinstein, Peter. 1968. *Concepts of Science.* Baltimore: Johns Hopkins University Press.
Alcoff, Linda. 1988. "Cultural Feminism versus Post-Structuralism: The Identity Crisis in Feminist Theory." *Signs: Journal of Women in Culture and Society* 13(3):405–36.

Berg, Maggie. 1991. "Luce Irigaray's 'Contradictions': Poststructuralism and Feminism." *Signs* 17(1):50–70.

Black, Max. 1954. *Problems of Analysis.* Ithaca, N.Y.: Cornell University Press.

Bordo, Susan. 1990. "Feminism, Postmodernism, and Gender-Skepticism." In *Feminism/ Postmodernism,* ed. Linda J. Nicholson, 133–56. New York: Routledge.

Boyd, Richard. 1980. "Materialism without Reductionism: What Physicalism Does Not Entail." In *Readings in Philosophy of Psychology,* ed. Ned Block, 1:67–106. Cambridge, Mass.: Harvard University Press.

de Lauretis, Teresa. 1990. "Upping the Anti [*sic*] in Feminist Theory." In *Conflicts in Feminism,* ed. Marianne Hirsch and Evelyn Fox Keller, 255–70. New York: Routledge.

Diamond, Irene, and Lee Quinby, eds. 1988. *Feminism and Foucault.* Boston: Northeastern University.

Echols, Alice. 1983. "The New Feminism of Yin and Yang." In *Powers of Desire,* ed. Ann Snitow, Christine Stansell, and Sharon Thompson, 439–59. New York: Monthly Review Press.

———. 1984. "The Taming of the Id: Feminist Sexual Politics, 1968–83." In *Pleasure and Danger,* ed. Carole S. Vance, 50–72. Boston: Routledge & Kegan Paul.

Eisenstein, Hester. 1983. *Contemporary Feminist Thought.* Boston: G. K. Hall.

Fraser, Nancy, and Linda J. Nicholson. 1990. "Social Criticism without Philosophy: An Encounter between Feminism and Postmodernism." In *Feminism/Postmodernism,* ed. Linda J. Nicholson, 19–38. New York: Routledge.

Fuss, Diana. 1989. *Essentially Speaking.* New York: Routledge.

Gallop, Jane, Marianne Hirsch, and Nancy Miller. 1990. "Criticizing Feminist Criticism." In *Conflicts in Feminism,* ed. Marianne Hirsch and Evelyn Fox Keller, 349–69. New York: Routledge.

Gilligan, Carol. 1982. *In a Different Voice.* Cambridge, Mass: Harvard University Press.

Gilligan, Carol, Nona P. Lyons, and Trudy J. Hanmer, eds. 1990. *Making Connections.* Cambridge, Mass.: Harvard University Press.

Gilligan, Carol, Janie Victoria Ward, and Jill McLean Taylor, eds. 1988. *Mapping the Moral Domain.* Cambridge, Mass.: Harvard University Press.

Hall Roberta, and Bernice Sandler. 1982. *The Classroom Climate: A Chilly One for Women?* Washington: Project on the Status and Education of Women, Association of American Colleges.

Hirsch, Marianne, and Evelyn Fox Keller. 1990. "Conclusion: Practicing Conflict in Feminist Theory." In *Conflicts in Feminism,* ed. Marianne Hirsch and Evelyn Fox Keller, 370–85. New York: Routledge.

hooks, bell. 1981. *Ain't I a Woman.* Boston: South End Press.

———. 1989. *Talking Back.* Boston: South End Press.

Jones, Ann Rosalind. 1985. "Writing the Body: Toward an Understanding of l'Ecriture Féminine." In *Feminist Criticism,* ed. Elaine Showalter, 361–77. New York: Pantheon.

Katzenstein, Mary Fainsod, and David D. Laitin. 1987. "Politics, Feminism, and the Ethics of Caring." In *Women and Moral Theory,* ed. Eva Feder Kittay and Diana T. Meyers, 261–81. Totowa, N.J.: Rowman & Littlefield.

Kerber, Linda. 1986. "Some Cautionary Words for Historians." *Signs* 11(2):304–10.

Kuykendall, Eleanor. 1991. "Subverting Essentialism." *Hypatia* 6(3):208–17.

Lugones, Maria C. 1991. "On the Logic of Pluralist Feminism." In *Feminist Ethics,* ed. Claudia Card, 35–44. Lawrence: University Press of Kansas.

Martin, Jane R. 1970. *Explaining, Understanding, and Teaching.* New York: McGraw-Hill.

Morris, Thomas V. 1986. *The Logic of God Incarnate.* Ithaca, N.Y.: Cornell University Press.

Nicholson, Linda J. 1986. *Gender and History.* New York: Columbia University Press.

Ortner, Sherry B. 1974. "Is Female to Male as Nature Is to Culture?" In *Woman, Culture and Society,* ed. Michelle Zimbalist Rosaldo and Louise Lamphere, 67–88. Stanford, Calif.: Stanford University Press.

Pierce, Christine. 1983. "Natural Law Language and Women." In *Philosophy of Woman,* ed. Mary Briody Mahowald, 364–76. Indianapolis: Hackett.

Rabine, Leslie. 1989. "Essentialism and Its Contexts: Saint-Simonian and Post-Structuralist Feminists." *differences* 1(2):105–23.

Rickman, H. P. 1964. "Geisteswissenschaften." In *The Encyclopedia of Philosophy,* ed. Paul Edwards, 3–4:275–79. New York: Macmillan.

Riley, Denise. 1988. *"Am I That Name?"* Minneapolis: University of Minnesota Press.

Rosaldo, Michelle Zimbalist. 1974. "Woman, Culture, and Society: A Theoretical Overview." In *Woman, Culture and Society,* ed. Michelle Zimbalist Rosaldo and Louise Lamphere, 17–43. Stanford, Calif.: Stanford University Press.

Schor, Naomi. 1989. "The Essentialism Which Is Not One: Coming to Grips with Irigaray." *differences* 1(2):38–58.

Scott, Joan Wallach. 1988. *Gender and the Politics of History.* New York: Columbia University Press.

Smith, Ruth L., and Deborah Valenze. 1988. "Mutuality and Marginality: Liberal Moral Theory and Working-Class Women in Nineteenth-Century England." *Signs* 13(2):277–98.

Snitow, Ann. 1990. "A Gender Diary." In *Conflicts in Feminism,* ed. Marianne Hirsch and Evelyn Fox Keller, 9–43. New York: Routledge.

Spelman, Elizabeth. 1988. *Inessential Woman.* Boston: Beacon.

Spivak, Gayatri Chakravorty. 1989. "In a Word: Interview." *differences* 1(2):128–29.

Stacey, Judith. 1990. "On Resistance, Ambivalence and Feminist Theory: A Response to Carol Gilligan." *Michigan Quarterly Review* 29(4):537–46.

Trebilcot, Joyce. 1983. "Sex Roles: The Argument from Nature." In *Philosophy of Woman,* ed. Mary Briody Mahowald, 377–83. Indianapolis: Hackett.

Wittgenstein, Ludwig. 1953. *Philosophical Investigations.* New York: Macmillan.

Chapter Two

Epistemological Debates, Feminist Voices
Science, Social Values, and the Study of Women

Stephanie Riger

Modern scientific methods, invented in the sixteenth century, were not only a stunning technical innovation, but a moral and political one as well, replacing the sacred authority of the Church with science as the ultimate arbiter of truth (Grant, 1987). Unlike medieval inquiry, modern science conceives itself as a search for knowledge free of moral, political, and social values. The application of scientific methods to the study of human behavior distinguished American psychology from philosophy and enabled it to pursue the respect accorded the natural sciences (Sherif, 1979).

The use of "scientific methods" to study human beings rested on three assumptions:

> (1) Since the methodological procedures of natural science are used as a model, human values enter into the study of social phenomena and conduct only as objects; (2) the goal of social scientific investigation is to construct laws or lawlike generalizations like those of physics; (3) social science has a technical character, providing knowledge which is solely instrumental. (Sewart, 1979, p. 311)

Critics recently have challenged each of these assumptions. Some charge that social science reflects not only the values of individual scientists but also those of the political and cultural milieux in which science is done, and that there are no theory-neutral "facts" (e.g., Cook, 1985; Prilleltensky, 1989; Rabinow & Sullivan, 1979; Sampson, 1985; Shields, 1975). Others claim that there are no universal, ahistorical laws of human behavior, but only descriptions of how people act in certain places at certain times in history (e.g., K. J. Gergen, 1973; Manicas & Secord, 1983; Sampson, 1978). Still others contend that knowledge is not neutral; rather, it serves an ideological purpose, justifying power (e.g., Foucault, 1980, 1981). According to this view, versions of reality not only reflect but also legitimate particular forms of social organization and power asymmetries. The belief that knowledge is merely technical, having no ideological function, is refuted by the ways in which science has played

Stephanie Riger, "Epistemiological Debates, Feminist Voices: Science, Social Values, and the Story of Women." *American Psychologist, 47*, pp. 730–740. © 1992 by the American Psychological Association. Reprinted with permission.

handmaiden to social values, providing an aura of scientific authority to prejudicial beliefs about social groups and giving credibility to certain social policies (Degler, 1991; Shields, 1975; Wittig, 1985).

Within the context of these general criticisms, feminists have argued in particular that social science neglects and distorts the study of women in a systematic bias in favor of men. Some contend that the very processes of positivist science are inherently masculine, reflected even in the sexual metaphors used by the founders of modern science (Keller, 1985; Merchant, 1980). To Francis Bacon, for example, nature was female, and the goal of science was to "bind her to your service and make her your slave" (quoted in Keller, 1985, p. 36). As Sandra Harding (1986) summarized,

> Mind vs. nature and the body, reason vs. emotion and social commitment, subject vs. object and objectivity vs. subjectivity, the abstract and general vs. the concrete and particular—in each case we are told that the former must dominate the latter lest human life be overwhelmed by irrational and alien forces, forces symbolized in science as the feminine (p. 125).

Critics see the insistence of modern science on control and distance of the knower from the known as a reflection of the desire for domination characteristic of a culture that subordinates women's interests to those of men (Hubbard, 1988; Reinharz, 1985). Some go so far as to claim that because traditional scientific methods inevitably distort women's experience, a new method based on feminist principles is needed (M. M. Gergen, 1988). Others disagree, claiming that the problem in science is not objectivity itself, but rather lack of objectivity that enables male bias to contaminate the scientific process (Epstein, 1988). The first part of this chapter summarizes feminist charges against standard versions of science; the second part explores three possibilities for a distinctly "feminist" response to those charges: *feminist empiricism, feminist standpoint epistemologies,* and *feminist postmodernism.* (By feminist, I refer to a system of values that challenges male dominance and advocates social, political, and economic equity of women and men in society.)

Bias within Psychology in the Study of Women

Since Naomi Weisstein denounced much of psychology as the "fantasy life of the male psychologist" in 1971, numerous critics have identified the ways that gender bias permeates social science (summarized in Epstein, 1988, pp. 17–45; Frieze, Parsons, Johnson, Ruble, & Zellman, 1978, pp. 11–27; Hyde 1991, pp. 7–15; Lips, 1988, pp. 64–75; Millman & Kanter, 1975; Wilkinson, 1986). For many years, subjects of relevance to women, such as rape or housework, have been considered either taboo topics or too trivial to study, marginal to more central and prestigious issues, such as leadership, achievement, and power (Epstein, 1988; McHugh, Koeske, & Frieze, 1986; Farberow, 1963; Smith, 1987). Women's invisibility as subjects of research extends to their role as researchers as well, with relatively few women in positions of power or prestige in science (Rix, 1990). Even today, women make up only 25 percent of the faculty in psychology departments and only 15 percent of editors of psychological journals (Walker, 1991). When women are studied, their actions often are interpreted as deficient compared with those of men. Even theories reflect a male standard (Gilligan, 1982). The classic example dates back to Freud's (1925/1961) formulation in 1925 of the theory of penis envy.

Over the last two decades, critics have compiled a long and continually growing list of threats to the validity of research on women and sex differences (see Jacklin 1981). For example, a great many studies have included only male samples. Sometimes women are included only as the stimulus, not the subject of study—they are seen but not heard—but conclusions are generalized to everyone (Meyer, 1988). Sex-of-experimenter effects contaminate virtually every area of research (Lips, 1988), and field studies yield different findings than laboratory research on the same phenomenon (Unger, 1981). Multiple meanings of the term *sex* confound biological sex differences with factors that vary by sex (i.e., sex-*related* differences) and are more appropriately labeled *gender* (McHugh et al., 1986; Unger, 1979). Sex is treated as an independent variable in studies of gender difference, even though people cannot be randomly assigned to the "male" or "female" group (Unger, 1979). The emphasis on a "difference" model obscures gender similarities (Unger, 1979); this emphasis is built into the methods of science because experiments are formally designed to reject the null hypothesis that there is no difference between the experimental group and the control group. When a difference is found, it is usually small, but the small size is often overshadowed by the fact that a difference exists at all (Epstein, 1988). A focus on between-gender differences and a lack of attention to within-gender differences reflects a presupposition of gender polarity that frames this research (Fine & Gordon, 1989).

Findings of the magnitude of sex differences have diminished over time, perhaps because of an increasing willingness to publish results when such differences are not significant (Hyde, 1990), or perhaps because of a reduction in operative sex role stereotypes. For example, findings of differences in cognitive abilities appear to have declined precipitously over the past two decades (Feingold, 1988), and researchers have found greater influenceability among women in studies published prior to 1970 than in those published later (Eagly, 1978). Carol Jacklin (1981) pointed out that the more carefully a study is carried out, the less likely it is that gender differences will be found: "With fewer variables confounded with sex, sex will account for smaller percentages of variance. Thus, paradoxically, the better the sex-related research, the less useful sex is as an explanatory variable" (p. 271). The decline in findings of difference suggest either that increasing care in designing studies has eliminated differences that were artifacts of bias, or that historical factors, rather than ahistorical, universal laws, shape behavior, whether of subjects or experimenters. In fact, so many studies find no sex differences that this research might more appropriately be called the study of sex similarities (Connell, 1987).

Psychological research on women often contains another source of bias, the lack of attention to social context. The purpose of the laboratory experiment is to isolate the behavior under study from supposedly extraneous contaminants so that it is affected only by the experimental conditions. The experimental paradigm assumes that subjects leave their social status, history, beliefs, and values behind as they enter the laboratory, or that random assignment vitiates the effects of these factors. The result is to abstract people's action from social roles or institutions (Fine & Gordon, 1989; Parlee, 1979; Sherif, 1979). Instead of being contaminants, however, these factors may be critical determinants of behavior. By stripping behavior of its social context, psychologists rule out the study of sociocultural and historical factors, and implicitly attribute causes to factors inside the person. Moreover, an absence of consideration of the social context of people's actions is not limited to laboratory research (Fine, 1984). In an ironic reversal of the feminist dictum of the 1960s, when social context is ignored, the political is misinterpreted as personal (Kitzinger, 1987).

Ignoring social context may produce a reliance on presumed biological causes when other explanations of sex differences are not obvious, even when the biological mechanisms that might be involved are not apparent (Lips, 1988). Social explanations become residual, although sociocultural determinants may be just as robust and important as biological causes, if not more so (Connell, 1987). Although biological differences between the sexes are obviously important, it is critical to distinguish between biological difference and the social meaning attached to that difference (Rossi, 1979).

Alice Eagly (1987) raised a different objection to experimentation. She disagreed that the psychological experiment is context-stripped, and contended instead that it constitutes a particular context. An experiment typically consists of a brief encounter among strangers in an unfamiliar setting, often under the eye of a psychologist. The question is whether this limited situation is a valid one from which to make generalizations about behavior. To Eagley, the problem is that social roles (such as mother, doctor, or corporation president) lose their salience in this setting, bringing to the foreground gender-related expectations about behavior.

Cynthia Fuchs Epstein (1988) stated that "Much of the bias in social science reporting of gender issues comes from scientists' inability to capture the social context or their tendency to regard it as unnecessary to their inquiry—in a sense, their disdain for it" (p. 44). In psychology, this disdain has at least two sources (Kahn & Yoder, 1989; Prilleltensky, 1989). First, psychology focuses on the person as he or she exists at the moment. Such a focus leads the researcher away from the person's history or social circumstances. Second, the cultural context in which psychology is practiced (at least in the United States) is dominated by an individualistic philosophy (Kitzinger, 1987; Sampson, 1985). The prevailing beliefs assume that outcomes are due to choices made by free and self-determining individuals; the implication is that people get what they deserve (Kahn & Yoder, 1989). Not only assumptions of individualism, but also those of male dominance are often so taken for granted that we are not aware of them. Recognition that supposedly scientific assertions are permeated with ideological beliefs produces, in Shulamit Reinharz's (1985) words, a condition of "feminist distrust." Perhaps one of the most difficult challenges facing social scientists is to disengage themselves sufficiently from commonly shared beliefs so that those beliefs do not predetermine research findings (McHugh et al., 1986).

Feminist Responses to the Criticisms of Science

Challenges to the neutrality of science have long been a concern to those who study women, and have prompted three different reactions among feminists (Harding 1986). Some remain loyal to scientific traditions, attempting to rise above the cultural embeddedness of these traditions by adhering more closely to the norms of science (e.g., Epstein, 1988; McHugh et al., 1986). Others seek to redress the male-centered bias in science by giving voice to women's experience and by viewing society from women's perspective (e.g., Belenky, Clinchy, Goldberger, & Tarule, 1986; Gilligan, 1982; Smith, 1987). Still others abandon traditional scientific methods entirely (e.g., Hare-Mustin, 1991). Philosopher of science Sandra Harding (1986) labeled these three approaches, respectively, feminist empiricism, feminist standpoint science, and postmodernism (see also Morgan's [1983] distinction among positivist, phenomeno-logical, and critical/praxis-oriented research paradigms). Next, I examine the mani-festations of these three positions in the study of the psychology of women.

Feminist Empiricism

The psychologists who identified the problem of experimenter effects did not reject experimentation. Instead, they recommended strategies to minimize the impact of the experimenter (Rosenthal, 1966). Likewise, feminist empiricists advocate closer adherence to the tenets of science as the solution to the problem of bias. From this perspective, bias is considered error in a basically sound system, an outbreak of irrationality in a rational process. Scrupulous attention to scientific methods will eliminate error, or at least minimize its impact on research findings (Harding, 1986). Once neutrality is restored, scientific methods, grounded in rationality, will give access to the truth.

Maureen McHugh and colleagues (1986) presented a set of guidelines for eliminat-ing bias. In addition to obvious corrections of the problems described earlier, other steps can be taken to ensure that the impact of the researcher's values is minimized, such as specifying the circumstances in which gender differences are found (because contexts tend to be deemed more appropriate for one sex than the other) and assessing experimental tasks for their sex neutrality (because many tasks are perceived to be sex linked; Deaux, 1984). The sex composition of the group of participants in research also may affect behavior because individuals act differently in the presence of females or males (Maccoby, 1990). Finally, attention ought to be paid to findings of sex similarities as well as sex differences, and the magnitude of such differences reported.

These suggestions are intended to produce gender-fair research using traditional scientific methods. The assumption is that a truly neutral science will produce unbiased knowledge, which in turn will serve as a basis for a more just social policy (Morawski, 1990). Yet the continuing identification of numerous instances of androcentric bias in research has led some to conclude that value-free research is impossible, even if it is done by those of good faith (Hare-Mustin & Maracek, 1990).

Technical safeguards cannot completely rule out the influence of values; scientific rigor in testing hypotheses cannot eliminate bias in theories or in the selection of problems for inquiry (Harding, 1986, 1991). Hence critics assert that traditional methods do not reveal reality, but rather act as constraints that limit our understanding of women's experiences.

Feminist Standpoint Epistemologies

Feminist empiricism argues that the characteristics of the knower are irrelevant to the discovery process if the norms of science are followed. In contrast, feminist standpoint epistemologies claim that we should center our science on women because "what we know and how we know depend on who we are, that is, on the knower's historical locus and his or her position in the social hierarchy" (Maracek, 1989, p. 372). There are several justifications for this viewpoint (see Harding, 1986). First, some argue that women's cognitive processes and modes of research are different than men's. It has been suggested that a supposedly feminine communal style of research that emphasizes cooperation of the researcher and subjects, an appreciation of natural contexts, and the use of qualitative data contrasts with a supposedly masculine agentic orientation that places primacy on distance of the researcher from the subjects, manipulation of subjects and the environment, and the use of quantitative data (Carlson, 1972; cf. Peplau & Conrad, 1989). Evelyn Fox Keller (1985) attempted to provide grounds for this position in a psychoanalytic view of child development. She argued that the male child's need to differentiate himself from his mother leads him to equate autonomy with distance from others (see also Chodorow, 1978). The process of developing a masculine sense of self thus establishes in the male a style of thinking that both reflects and produces the emphasis in science on distance, power, and control. Keller identifies an alternative model of science based not on controlling but rather on "conversing" with nature.

Keller's (1985) argument that science need not be based on domination is salutary, but her explanation is problematic. She presumes, first, that male and female infants have quite different experiences and, second, that those early experiences shape the activities of adult scientists, but she does not substantiate these claims. The supposedly masculine emphasis on separation and autonomy may be a manifestation of Western mainstream culture rather than a universal distinction between women and men. Black men and women who returned from northern U.S. cities to live in the rural South manifest a relational as opposed to autonomous self-image (Stack, 1986), and both Eastern and African world views see individuals as interdependent and connected, in contrast to the Western emphasis on a bounded and independent self (Markus & Oyserman, 1989). Identifying a masculine cognitive style as the grounds for scientific methods seems to doom most women and perhaps non-White men to outsider status. Furthermore, an emphasis on cognitive style ignores the role played by social structure, economics, and politics in determining topics and methods of study (Harding, 1986). Experimental methods in psychology characterized by control and objectivity are accorded prestige partly because they emulate the highly valued physical sciences (Sherif, 1979). Within social science, the prestige of a study mirrors the prestige of its topic (Epstein, 1988). Sociocultural factors such as these seem more likely as determinants of the shape of science than individual psychology.

A more plausible basis for a feminist standpoint epistemology is the argument that women's life experiences are not fully captured in existing conceptual schemes. Research often equates *male* with the general, typical case, and considers *female* to be the particular—a subgroup demarcated by biology (Acker, 1978). Yet analytical categories appropriate for men may not fit women's experience. Dorothy Smith (1987) argued that women are alienated from their own experience by having to frame that experience in terms of men's conceptual schemes; in Smith's terms they have a "bifurcated consciousness"—daily life grounded in female experience but only male conceptual categories with which to interpret that experience. Starting our inquiries from a subordinate group's experience will uncover the limits of the dominant group's conceptual schemes where they do not fully fit the subordinates (see also Miller, 1986). Accordingly, a science based on women's traditional place in society not only would generate categories appropriate to women, but also would be a means of discovering the underlying organization of society as a whole (see also Code, 1981).

In contrast to traditional social science in which the researcher is the expert on assessing reality, an interpretive-phenomenological approach permits women to give their own conception of their experiences. Participants, not researchers, are considered the experts at making sense of their world (Cherryholmes, 1988). The shift in authority is striking. Yet phenomenological approaches are limited in at least two ways. First, they require that the subjects studied be verbal and reflective (Reinharz 1992); second, they run the risk of psychological reductionism (attributing causation simply to internal, psychological factors; Morawski, 1988).

Carol Gilligan's (1982) theory of women's moral development is the most influential psychological study in this tradition. Her work asserting that women stress caring in the face of moral dilemmas in contrast to men's emphasis on justice has been criticized because other researchers have found no sex differences in moral reasoning using standardized scales (e.g., Greeno & Maccoby, 1986; Mednick, 1989). Gilligan (1986) retorted that women's responses on those scales are not relevant to her purposes:

> The fact that educated women are capable of high levels of justice reasoning has no bearing on the question of whether they would spontaneously choose to frame moral problems in this way. My interest in the way people *define* moral problems is reflected in my research methods, which have centered on first-person accounts of moral conflict. (P. 328)

Although standardized scales might tell us what women have in common with men, they will not reveal the way women would define their own experiences if given the opportunity to do so. The absence (and impossibility) of a comparison group of men in Gilligan's definitive study of twenty-nine women considering abortions raises questions about whether moral orientations are sex linked, however (Crawford, 1989; Epstein, 1988, pp. 81–83).

The feminist standpoint epistemologies aim not simply to substitute "woman centered" for "man centered" gender loyalties, but rather to provide a basis for a more accurate understanding of the entire world. Howard Becker (1967) claimed that "in any system of ranked groups, participants take it as given that members of the highest group have the right to define the way things really are.... Credibility and the right to be heard are differentially distributed through the ranks of the system" (p. 241). Feminist standpoint epistemologies argue that traditional methods of science give credibility only to the dominant group's views. Listening to subordinates reveals the multifocal nature of reality (Riger, 1990). The term *subjugated knowledges* describes the perspectives of those sufficiently low on the hierarchy that their interpretations do not reflect the predominant modes of thought (Foucault, 1980, p. 81). Giving voice to women's perspective means identifying the ways in which women create meaning and experience life from their particular position in the social hierarchy.

Moreover, women (and minorities) sometimes have a better vantage point to view society than do majorities because minority status can render people socially invisible, thus permitting them access to the majority group that is not reciprocated (Merton, 1972). Accordingly, incorporating subordinates' experience will not only "add" women and minorities to existing understandings, it will add a more thorough understanding of the dominant group as well. For example, bell hooks (1984) described African Americans living in her small Kentucky hometown as having a double vision. They looked from the outside in at the more affluent White community across the railroad tracks, but their perspective shifted to inside out when they crossed those tracks to work for White employers. Movement across the tracks was regulated, however: Whites did not cross over to the Black community, and laws ensured that Blacks returned to it.

The arguments for feminist standpoint epistemologies have stimulated rich and valuable portrayals of women's experience. Yet there are problems with a feminist standpoint as the basis for science. First, assuming a commonality to all women's experience glosses over differences among women of various racial and ethnic groups and social classes (Spelman, 1988). The life experience of a woman wealthy enough to hire childcare and household help may have more in common with her spouse than with a poor woman trying to raise her children on a welfare budget. Standpoint epistemology can recognize multiple subjugated groups demarcated by gender, race, social class, sexual orientation, and so on. Yet carried to an extreme, this position seems to dissolve science into autobiography. A critical challenge for feminist standpoint epistemology is to identify the commonalities of subjugated experience among different groups of women without losing sight of their diversity. Moreover, those who are subjugated may still adhere to a dominant group's ideology.

Furthermore, we each have multiple status identities (Merton, 1972). The poet Audre Lorde (1984) described herself as "a forty-nine-year-old Black lesbian feminist socialist mother of two, including one boy, and a member of an interracial couple" (p. 114). Each of these identities becomes salient in a different situation; at times, they conflict within the same situation. The hyphenated identities that we all experience in different ways—Black feminist, lesbian mother, Asian American, and so on—call into question the unity of the category of woman, making it difficult to generalize about "women's experience" (Harding, 1987).

Nonetheless, feminist standpoint epistemologies do not claim that social status alone allows the viewer clarity. Reasonable judgments about whether views are empirically supported are still possible. Rather than proclaiming the one true story about the world, feminist standpoint epistemologies seek partial and less distorted views. These partial views, or situated knowledges, can be far less limited than the dominant view (Haraway, 1988).

Feminist Postmodernism

A number of perspectives, including Marxism, psychoanalysis, and postmodernism, share a challenge to the primacy of reason and the autonomy of the individual. Here I focus on postmodernism and, in particular, poststructuralism, because of its influence on an emerging stream of feminist psychology (e.g., Hare-Mustin & Maracek, 1990; Wilkinson, 1986). A traditional social scientist entering the terrain of poststructuralism at times feels a bit like Alice falling into a Wonderland of bewildering language and customs that look superficially like her own yet are not. Things that seem familiar and stable—the meaning of words, for example—become problematic. What once were nouns (e.g., privilege, valor, foreground) now are verbs. Even the landscape looks different, as words themselves are chopped up with parentheses and hyphens to make visible their multiple meanings. What is most unsettling, perhaps, is the fundamental poststructuralist assertion that science does not mirror reality, but rather creates it (i.e., making science a process of invention rather than discovery; Howard, 1991). Many scientists would agree that an unmediated perception of reality is impossible to obtain, and that research findings represent (rather than mirror) reality. However, they would maintain that some representations are better than others. The traditional scientific criteria of validity, generalizability, and so forth determine how close research findings come to actual truth. In contrast, poststructuralists reject traditional notions of truth and reality, and claim instead that power enables some to define what is or is not considered knowledge. Expressing our understanding of experience must be done through language, but language is not a neutral reflection of that experience because our linguistic categories are not neutral:

> If statements and not things are true or false, then truth is necessarily linguistic: if truth is linguistic, then it is relative to language use (words, concepts, statements, discourses) at a given time and place; therefore, ideology, interests, and power arrangements at a given time and place are implicated in the production of what counts as "true." (Cherryholmes, 1988, p. 439)

Or, as Humpty Dumpty said to Alice in *Through the Looking Glass*:

> "When *I* use a word," Humpty Dumpty said in a rather scornful tone, "it means just what I choose it to mean—neither more nor less."
> "The question is," said Alice, "whether you *can* make words mean so many different things."

"The question is," said Humpty Dumpty," which is to be master—that's all." (Carroll, 1872/1923, p. 246).

The central question in poststructuralism is not how well our theories fit the facts, or how well the facts produced by research fit what is real. Rather, the question is which values and social institutions are favored by each of multiple versions of reality (i.e., discourses). Of critical concern is whose interests are served by competing ways of giving meaning to the world (Weedon, 1987). Feminists of a postmodern bent claim that positivism's neutral and disinterested stance masks what is actually the male conception of reality; this conception reflects and maintains male power interests (Gavey, 1989). As legal scholar Catharine MacKinnon (1987) put it, "Objectivity— the nonsituated, universal standpoint, whether claimed or aspired to—is a denial of the existence of potency of sex inequality that tacitly participates in constructing reality from the dominant point of view" (p. 136). In MacKinnon's view, rather than being neutral, "the law sees and treats women the way men see and treat women" (p. 140). The same criticism can be made about traditional social science in its exclusion, distortion, and neglect of women.

The social constructionist stance, as poststructuralism is known within psychology (K. J. Gergen, 1985), offers a particular challenge to the psychology of women. In contrast to feminist empiricism, the central question no longer asks whether sex or gender differences exist. Knowing the truth about difference is impossible (Hare-Mustin & Maracek, 1990). Varying criteria of differentness can produce divergent findings, for example, when conclusions based on averages contradict those based on the amount of overlap of scores of men and women (Luria, 1986). When an assumed difference is not scientifically supported, the argument simply shifts to another variable (Unger, 1979), and similar findings can be interpreted in opposing ways. Given the impossibility of settling these questions, poststructuralism shifts the emphasis to the question of difference itself (Scott, 1988):

> What do we make of gender differences? What do they mean? Why are there so many? Why are there so few? Perhaps we should be asking: What is the point of differences? What lies beyond difference? Difference aside, what else is gender? The overarching question is choice of question. (Hare-Mustin & Maracek, 1990, pp. 1–2)

One goal of a feminist constructionist science is "disrupting and displacing dominant (oppressive) knowledges" in part by articulating the values supported by alternate conceptions of reality (Gavey, 1989, p. 462). An analysis of contrasting perspectives on sex differences demonstrates the relationship among values, assumptive frameworks, and social consequences. According to Rachel Hare-Mustin and Jeanne Maracek (1988), the received views of men and women tend either to exaggerate or to minimize the differences between them. On the one hand, the tendency to emphasize differences fosters an appreciation of supposedly feminine qualities, but it simultaneously justifies unequal treatment of women and ignores variability within each sex group. The consequence of emphasizing difference, then, is to support the status quo. On the other hand, the tendency to minimize differences justifies women's access to educational and job opportunities, but it simultaneously overlooks the fact that equal treatment is not always equitable, because of differences in men's and women's position in a social hierarchy. Gender-neutral grievance procedures in organizations, for example, do not apply equally to men and women if men are consistently in positions of greater power (Riger, 1991).

Researchers have widely different interpretations of the implications of poststructural critiques for social science methods. Some use empirical techniques for poststructuralist ends. Social constructionists see traditional research methods as a means of providing "objectifications" or illustrations, similar to vivid photographs, that are useful in making an argument persuasive rather than in validating truth claims (K. J. Gergen, 1985). Traditional methods can also help identify varying versions of reality. For example, Celia Kitzinger (1986, 1987) used Q-sort methodology to distinguish five separate accounts of lesbians' beliefs about the origin of their sexual orientation. Techniques of attitude measurement can also be used to assess the extent to which people share certain versions of reality. Rhoda Unger and her colleagues used surveys to assess belief in an objectivist or subjectivist epistemology, finding that adherence to a particular perspective varied with social status (Unger, Draper, & Pendergrass, 1986).

Others propose that we treat both psychological theories and people's actions and beliefs as texts (i.e., discursive productions located in a specific historical and cultural context and shaped by power), rather than as accounts, distorted or otherwise, of experience (Cherryholmes, 1988; Gavey, 1989). Methods developed in other disciplines, particularly literary criticism, can be used to analyze these texts. For example, through careful reading of an interview transcript with an eye to discerning "discursive patterns of meaning, contradictions, and inconsistencies," Nicola Gavey (p. 467) identified cultural themes of "permissive sexuality" and "male sexual needs" in statements by a woman about her experiences of heterosexual coercion (see also Hare-Mustin, 1991; Walkerdine, 1986). A particular technique of discourse analysis, deconstruction, can be used to expose ideological assumptions in written or spoken language, as Joanne Martin (1990) did to identify forces that suppress women's achievement within organizations. Deconstruction highlights the revealing quality not just of what is said, but also of what is left out, contradictory, or inconsistent in the text. Deconstruction offers a provocative technique for analyzing hidden assumptions. Yet it is a potentially endless process, capable of an infinite regress, inasmuch as any deconstruction can itself be deconstructed (Martin, 1990).

The absence of any criteria for evaluation means that the success of accounts of social construction "depend primarily on the analyst's capacity to invite, compel, stimulate, or delight the audience, and not on criteria of veracity" (K. J. Gergen, 1985, p. 272). This raises the possibility that what Grant (1987) said in another context could apply here: "Such theories risk devolving into authoritarian non-theories more akin to religions" (p. 113). The relativism of poststructuralism can be countered, however, by the identification of moral criteria for evaluation (K. J. Gergen, 1985; Unger, 1983). Theory and research can be assessed in terms of their pragmatic utility in achieving certain social and political goals, rather than the allegedly neutral rules of science (Gavey, 1989). However, because feminists disagree about whether celebrating women's difference or emphasizing the similarity of the sexes is most likely to change women's basic condition of subordination (Snitow, 1990), agreement about criteria for evaluation seems unlikely.

What poses perhaps the greatest dilemma for feminists is the view of the subject advocated by poststructuralist theory. Poststructuralists consider the attribution of agency and intentionality to the subject to be part of a deluded liberal humanism, complicit with the status quo. The multiple discourses of selfhood, intentionality, and so forth that are present in our culture compete for dominance; those that prevail constitute individual subjectivity. Social cognition on the part of the individual is channeled into certain ways of thinking that dominate society (although resistance is possible). Those discourses antedate our consciousness and give meaning to our experience, which otherwise has no essential meaning (Weedon, 1987). In contrast, feminist standpoint epistemologies consider individuals to be the active construers of their reality, albeit within a particular social and historical context; women's subjectivity is considered an important source of information about their experience. Poststructuralism's rejection of intentionality on the part of the individual seems to deny the validity of women's voices, just at a time when women are beginning to be heard (see also Hartsock, 1987).

Poststructuralism offers a provocative critique of social science and makes us critically aware of the relationship of knowledge and power. Yet the focus on "problematizing the text" of our disciplines, although admirably self-reflexive, can lead to an inward emphasis that neglects the study of women in society. In a parallel manner, poststructuralism's emphasis on language as determining consciousness can lead to the disregard of other determinants, such as women's position in a social hierarchy (Segal, 1986). Furthermore, Rhoda Unger (1988) identified a dilemma for social scientists who reject traditional empirical methods:

> The attempt to infer cause-and-effect relationships about human behavior using the tools of empiricism is one of the few unique contributions that psychology as a discipline can offer to the rest of scholarship. If such tools may not be used by feminist psychologists there is little likelihood that their insights will be taken seriously by the rest of the discipline. (p. 137)

Feminist foremothers in psychology, such as Helen Thompson (Woolley) and her colleagues, at the turn of this century, used traditional scientific methods to contest social myths about women (Reinharz, 1992; Rosenberg, 1982); they may still serve that purpose today. Poststructuralists would likely retort that the fact that Thompson's insights have had to be repeatedly rediscovered (or, rather, reinvented) demonstrates that power, not truth, determines which version of reality will prevail.

Is There a Feminist Method?

On the basis of multiple critiques of the social sciences, some propose an alternative research method based on feminist values. The lack of consensus on what values are feminist makes this a daunting project, yet many would agree on the need for more interactive, contextualized methods in the service of emancipatory goals (cf. Peplau & Conrad, 1989). A feminist method should produce a study not just *of* women, but also *for* women, helping to change the world as well as to describe it (Acker, Barry, & Esseveld, 1983; Wittig, 1985). Mary Gergen (1988) advocated the following as central tenets of a feminist method (see also Wilkinson, 1986):

1. recognizing the interdependence of experimenter and subject;
2. avoiding the decontextualizing of the subject or experimenter from their social and historical surroundings;
3. recognizing and revealing the nature of one's values within the research context;
4. accepting that facts do not exist independently of their producers' linguistic codes;
5. demystifying the role of the scientists and establishing an egalitarian relationship between science makers and science consumers. (p. 47)

Joan Acker and her colleagues (1983) attempted to implement some of these principles in a study of women who had primarily been wives and mothers and were starting to enter the labor market. Interviews became dialogues, a mutual attempt to clarify and expand understandings. Often friendships developed between researchers and the women in the study. Acker and her colleagues discovered that these methods are not without problems, however. The researcher's need to collect information can (perhaps inadvertently) lead to the manipulation of friendship in the service of the research. Methods that create trust between researchers and participants entail the risk of exploitation, betrayal, and abandonment by the researcher (Stacey, 1988). Acker's study took place over a number of years, and participant's interpretations of their lives were constantly changing in hindsight, raising problems of validity in the research. The desire to give participants an opportunity to comment on researchers' interpretations of the interviews became a source of tension when disagreements arose. The solution to these dilemmas reached by Acker and her colleagues—to report the women's lives in their own words as much as possible—was not satisfactory to the women in the study who wanted more analysis of their experience. Finally, it was difficult to determine if this research experience had an emancipatory effect on participants. Intending to create social change is no assurance of actually doing so.

The conflict between the researcher's perspective and that of the participants in this study raises a critical issue for those who reject positivism's belief in the scientist as expert. Because a feminist method (at least according to the principles listed) assumes that there is no neutral observer, whose interpretations should prevail when those of the researcher and the people under study conflict? Feminism places primacy on acknowledging and validating female experience (Wilkinson, 1986), yet postmodern perspectives challenge the authority of the individual (Gavey, 1989; Weedon, 1987). Consider, for example, Margaret Andersen's (1981) study of twenty corporate wives. She disbelieved their claims of contentment and attributed their lack of feminism to *false consciousness,* a Marxist term meaning that these women identified with (male) ruling class interests against their own (female) class interests. The women wrote a rebuttal rejecting Andersen's interpretation. In response, Andersen revised her position to accept the women's statements of satisfaction with their lives.

Instead of treating them as deluded or insincere, she looked for sources of their contentment in their position in the social hierarchy. Lather (1986, 1988) recommended this kind of dialogic process to avoid imposing on research participants interpretations that disempower them (see also Kidder, 1982). Without it, we grant privilege to the authority of the researcher, even if on postmodern rather than positivist grounds.

Conclusion

Although the strategies intended as a feminist method overcome some of the objections to traditional social science, they raise as many problems as they solve (see Reinharz, 1992). No method or epistemology seems devoid of limitations or perfectly true to feminist values, which are themselves contested (e.g., Jaggar & Struhl, 1978). Feminism is most useful as a set of questions that challenge the prevailing asymmetries of power and androcentric assumptions in science and society, rather than as a basis for a unique method (Reinharz, 1992). Feminism thus identifies "patterns and interrelationships and causes and effects and implications of questions that nonfeminists have not seen and still do not see" (Lorber, 1988, p. 8).

The psychological study of women emerged from the field of individual differences. Dominated by the question of sex differences, this tradition assumes that an inner core of traits or abilities distinguishes women from men (Buss, 1976). Such a conceptualization no longer seems useful. Few gender differences in personality or abilities have been reliably demonstrated (Feingold, 1988; Hyde, 1990), and factors other than individual dispositions influence our behavior (Maccoby, 1990). A more appropriate strategy for the study of women would consider the ways in which gender is created and maintained through interpersonal processes (Deaux & Major, 1987).

From this perspective, gender does not reside within the person. Instead, it is constituted by the myriad ways in which we "do" rather than "have" gender; that is, we validate our membership in a particular gender category through interactional processes (West & Zimmerman, 1987). Gender is something we enact, not an inner core or constellation of traits that we express; it is a pattern of social organization that structures the relations, especially the power relations, between women and men (Connell, 1985, 1987; Crawford & Maracek, 1989): "In doing gender, men are also doing dominance and women are doing deference" (West & Zimmerman, 1987, p. 146). Transsexuals know well that merely altering one's sex organs does not change one's gender. Membership in the category of "male" or "female" must be affirmed continuously through social behavior (see, e.g., Morris, 1974).

Each of the epistemological positions described can contribute to this perspective, despite their contradictions. An interactional conceptualization of gender recognizes that the behavior and thoughts of men and women are channeled into certain sociocultural forms, as poststructuralism claims. As Peter Manicas and Paul Secord (1983) stated:

> Social structures (e.g., language) are reproduced and transformed by action, but they preexist for individuals. They enable persons to become persons and to act (meaningfully and intentionally), yet at the same time, they are "coercive," limiting the ways we can act. (p. 408)

The dominant ideology of a society is manifested in and reproduced by the social relations of its members (Unger, 1989). Unlike poststructuralism, however, an interactional view of gender also acknowledges individual agency in the production and transformation of social forms. Such a perspective would regard the person as an initiator of action and construer of meaning within a context composed not only of varying modes of interpreting the world but also of structural constraints and opportunities (see, e.g., Buss, 1978; Riegel, 1979; Sampson, 1978; Unger, 1983), as standpoint epistemologies claim.

Diverse methods, evaluated by reasonable criteria, are needed to capture the rich array of personal and structural factors that shape women and girls, and in turn are shaped by them. What is critical is that we are aware of the epistemological commitments—and value assumptions—we make when we adopt a particular research strategy (Unger, 1983). Moreover, rather than abandoning objectivity, systematic examination of assumptions and values in the social order that shape scientific practices can strengthen objectivity (Harding, 1991).

Epistemological debates in recent years have shattered the traditional picture of science as neutral, disinterested, and value free and have replaced it with a view of knowledge as socially constructed. Feminists' contributions to this debate highlight not only the androcentric nature of social science, but also its collusion in the perpetuation of male dominance in society. To assume that the multiple voices of women are not shaped by domination is to ignore social context and legitimate the status quo. On the other hand, to assume that women have no voice other than an echo of prevailing discourses is to deny them agency and, simultaneously, to repudiate the possibility of social change. The challenge to psychology is to link a vision of women's agency with an understanding of the shaping power of social context.

REFERENCES

Acker, J. (1978). Issues in the sociological study of women's work. In A. Stromberg & S. Harkness (Eds.), *Women working* (pp. 134–161). Palo Alto, CA: Mayfield.

Acker, J., Barry, K., & Esseveld. J. (1983). Objectivity and truth: Problems in doing feminist research. *Women's Studies International Forum, 6,* 423–435.

Andersen, M. (1981). Corporate wives: Longing for liberation or satisfied with the status quo? *Urban Life, 10,* 311–327.

Becker, H. S. (1967). Whose side are we on? *Social Problems, 14,* 239–247.

Belenky, M. F., Clinchy, B. M., Goldberger, N. R., & Tarule, J. M. (1986). Women's ways of knowing: The development of self, voice, and mind. New York: Basic Books.

Buss, A. R. (1976). Galton and sex differences: An historical note. *Journal of the History of the Behavioral Sciences, 12,* 283–285.

Buss, A. R. (1978). The structure of psychological revolutions. *Journal of the History of the Behavioral Sciences, 14,* 57–64.

Carlson, R. (1972). Understanding women: Implications for personality theory and research. *Journal of Social Issues, 28,* 17–32.

Carroll, L. (1923). *Alice's adventures in Wonderland; and Through the looking glass.* Philadelphia: Winston. (Original work published 1872).

Cherryholmes, C. H. (1988). Construct validity and the discourses of research. *American Journal of Education, 96,* 421–457.

Chodorow, N. (1978). *The reproduction of mothering.* Berkeley: University of California Press.

Code, L. B. (1981). Is the sex of the knower epistemologically significant? *Metaphilosophy, 12,* 267–276.

Connell, R. W. (1985). Theorizing gender. *Sociology, 19,* 260–272.

Connell, R. W. (1987). *Gender and power: Society, the person and sexual politics.* Stanford, CA: Stanford University Press.

Cook, T. D. (1985). Postpositivist critical multiplism. In L. Shotland & M. M. Mark (Eds.), *Social science and social policy* (pp. 21–62). Beverly Hills, CA. Sage.

Crawford, M. (1989). Agreeing to differ: Feminist epistemologies and women's ways of knowing. In M. Crawford & M. Gentry (Eds.), *Gender and thought: Psychological perspectives* (pp. 128–145). New York: Springer-Verlag.

Crawford, M., & Maracek, J. (1989). Psychology reconstructs the female, 1968–1988. *Psychology of Women Quarterly, 13,* 147–165.

Deaux, K. (1984). From individual differences to social categories. *American Psychologist, 39,* 105–116.

Deaux, K., & Major, B. (1987). Putting gender into context: An interactive model of gender-related behavior. *Psychological Review, 94,* 369–389.

Degler, C. (1991). *In search of human nature.* New York: Oxford University Press.

Eagly, A. H. (1978). Sex differences in influenceability. *Psychological Bulletin, 85,* 86–116.

Eagly, A. H. (1987). *Sex differences in social behavior: A social-role interpretation.* Hillsdale, NJ: Erlbaum.

Epstein, C. F. (1988). *Deceptive distinctions: Sex, gender and the social order.* New Haven, CT: Yale University Press.

Farberow, N. L. (1963). *Taboo topics.* New York: Atherton Press.

Feingold, A. (1988). Cognitive gender differences are disappearing. *American Psychologist, 43,* 95–103.

Fine, M. (1984). Coping with rape: Critical perspectives on consciousness. *Imagination, Cognition, and Personality: The Scientific Study of Consciousness, 3,* 249–67.

Fine, M., & Gordon, S. M. (1989). Feminist transformations of/despite psychology. In M. Crawford & M. Gentry (Eds.), *Gender and thought: Psychological perspectives* (pp. 146–174). New York: Springer-Verlag.

Foucault, M. (1980). *Power/knowledge: Selected interviews and other writings, 1972–1977* (C. Gordon, Ed. and Trans.), New York: Pantheon Books.

Foucault, M. (1981). *The history of sexuality: Vol. 1. An introduction.* Harmondsworth, England: Viking.

Freud, S. (1961). Some psychical consequences of the anatomical distinctions between the sexes. In J. Strachey (Ed. and Trans.), *The complete psychological works of Sigmund Freud* (Vol. 19, pp. 248–258). London: Hogarth Press. (Original work published 1925).

Frieze, I. H., Parsons, J. E., Johnson, P. B., Ruble, D. N., & Zellman, G. L. (1978). *Women and sex roles: A social psychological perspective.* New York: Norton.

Gavey, N. (1989). Feminist poststructuralism and discourse analysis: Contributions to a feminist psychology. *Psychology of Women Quarterly, 13,* 459–476.

Gergen, K. J. (1973). Social psychology as history. *Journal of Personality and Social Psychology,* *26,* 309–320.

Gergen, K. J. (1985). The social constructionist movement in modern psychology. *American Psychologist, 40,* 255–265.

Gergen, M. M. (1988). Building a feminist methodology. *Contemporary Social Psychology, 13,* 47–53.

Gilligan, C. (1982). *In a different voice.* Cambridge, MA: Harvard University Press.

Gilligan, C. (1986). Reply by Carol Gilligan. *Signs: Journal of Women in Culture and Society, 11,* 324–333.

Grant, J. (1987). I feel therefore I am: A critique of female experience as the basis for a feminist epistemology. In M. J. Falco (Ed.), *Feminism and epistemology: Approaches to research in women and politics* (pp. 99–114). Binghamton, NY: Haworth Press.

Greeno, C. G., & Maccoby, E. E. (1986). How different is the "different voice"? *Signs: Journal of Women in Culture and Society, 11,* 310–316.

Haraway, D. (1988). Situated knowledges: *The science question in feminism* and the privilege of partial perspective. *Feminist Studies, 14,* 575–599.

Harding, S. (1986). *The science question in feminism.* Ithaca, NY: Cornell University Press.

Harding, S. (1987). Introduction: Is there a feminist method? In S. Harding (Ed.), *Feminism and methodology: Social science issues* (pp. 1–14), Bloomington: Indiana University Press.

Harding, S. (1991). *Whose science? Whose knowledge?* Ithaca, NY: Cornell University Press.

Hare-Mustin, R. T. (1991). Sex, lies, and headaches: The problem is power. In T. J. Goodrich (Ed.), *Women and power: Perspectives for therapy.* New York: Norton.

Hare-Mustin, R. T., & Maracek, J. (1988). The meaning of difference: Gender theory, postmodernism, and psychology. *American Psychologist, 43,* 355–464.

Hare-Mustin, R. T., & Maracek, J. (1990). *Making a difference: Psychology and the construction of gender.* New Haven, CT: Yale University Press.

Hartsock, N. (1987). Epistemology and politics: Minority vs. majority theories. *Cultural Critique, 7,* 187–206.

hooks, b. (1984). *Feminist theory: From margin to center.* Boston: South End Press.

Howard, G. S. (1991). Culture tales: Narrative approach to thinking, cross-cultural psychology, and psychotherapy. *American Psychologist, 46,* 187–197.

Hubbard, R. (1988). Some thoughts about the masculinity of the natural sciences. In M. M. Gergen, *Feminist thought and the structure of knowledge* (pp. 1–15). New York: New York University Press.

Hyde, J. (1990). Meta-analysis and the psychology of gender differences. *Signs: Journal of Women in Culture and Society, 16,* 55–73.

Hyde, J. (1991). *Half the human experience: The psychology of women* (4th ed.). Lexington, MA: Heath.

Jacklin, C. N. (1981). Methodological issues in the study of sex-related differences. *Developmental Review, 1,* 266–273.

Jaggar, A., & Struhl, P. R. (1978). *Feminist frameworks: Alternative theoretical accounts of the relations between women and men.* New York: McGraw-Hill.

Kahn, A. S., & Yoder, J. D. (1989). The psychology of women and conservatism: Rediscovering social change. *Psychology of Women Quarterly, 13,* 417–432.

Keller, E. F. (1985). *Reflections on gender and science.* New Haven, CT: Yale University Press.

Kidder, L. (1982). Face validity from multiple perspectives. In D. Brinberg & L. Kidder (Eds.), *Forms of validity in research* (pp. 41–58). San Francisco: Jossey-Bass.

Kitzinger, C. (1986). Introducing and developing Q as a feminist methodology: A study of accounts of lesbianism. In S. Wilkinson (Ed.), *Feminist social psychology: Developing theory and practice* (pp. 151–172). Milton Keynes, England: Open University Press.

Kitzinger, C. (1987). *The social construction of lesbianism.* London: Sage.

Lather, P. (1986). Research as praxis. *Harvard Educational Review, 56,* 257–277.

Lather, P. (1988). Feminist perspectives on empowering research methodologies. *Women's Studies International Forum, 11,* 569–581.

Lips, H. (1988). *Sex and gender: An introduction.* Mountain View, CA: Mayfield.

Lorber, J. (1988). From the editor. *Gender & Society, 1,* 5–8.

Lorde, A. (1984). *Sister outsider: Essays and speeches.* New York: Crossing.

Luria, Z. (1986). A methodological critique. *Signs: Journal of Women in Culture and Society, 11,* 316–320.

Maccoby, E. E. (1990). Gender and relationships: A developmental account. *American Psychologist, 43,* 513–520.

MacKinnon, C. A. (1987). Feminism, Marxism, method and the state: Toward feminist jurisprudence. In S. Harding (Ed.), *Feminism and methodology: Social science issues* (pp. 135–156). Bloomington: Indiana University Press.

Manicas, P. T., & Secord, P. F. (1983). Implications for psychology of the new philosophy of science. *American Psychologist, 38,* 399–413.

Maracek, J. (1989). Introduction: Theory and method in feminist psychology [Special issue]. *Psychology of Women Quarterly, 13,* 367–377.

Markus, H., & Oyserman, D. (1989). Gender and thought: The role of the self-concept. In M. Crawford & M. Gentry (Eds.), *Gender and thought: Psychological perspectives* (pp. 100–127). New York: Springer-Verlag.

Martin, J. (1990). Deconstructing organizational taboos: The suppression of gender conflict in organizations. *Organizational Science, 5,* 339–359.

McHugh, M., Koeske, R., & Frieze, I. (1986). Issues to consider in conducting nonsexist psychological research: A guide for researchers. *American Psychologist, 41,* 879–890.

Mednick, M. T. (1989). On the politics of psychological constructs: Stop the bandwagon, I want to get off. *American Psychologist, 44,* 1118–1123.

Merchant, C. (1980). *The death of nature: Women, ecology, and the scientific revolution.* New York: Harper & Row.

Merton, R. (1972). Insiders and outsiders: A chapter in the sociology of knowledge. *American Journal of Sociology, 78,* 9–47.

Meyer, J. (1988). Feminist thought and social psychology. In M. Gergen (Ed.), *Feminist thought and the structure of knowledge* (pp. 105–123). New York: New York University Press.

Miller, J. B. (1986). *Toward a new psychology of women* (2nd ed.). Boston: Beacon.

Millman, M., & Kanter, R. (Eds.). (1975). *Another voice: Feminist perspectives on social life and social sciences.* Garden City, NY: Anchor Books.

Morawski, J. G. (1988). Impasse in feminist thought? In M. M. Gergen (Ed.), *Feminist thought and the structure of knowledge* (pp. 182–194). New York: New York University Press.

Morawski, J. G. (1990). Toward the unimagined: Feminism and epistemology in psychology. In R. L. Hare-Mustin & J. Maracek, *Making a difference: Psychology and the construction of gender* (pp. 150–183). New Haven, CT: Yale University Press.

Morgan, G. (Ed.). (1983). Toward a more reflective social science. In G. Morgan (Ed.), *Beyond method: Strategies for social research* (pp. 368–376). Beverly Hills, CA: Sage.

Morris, J. (1974). *Conundrum.* New York: Harcourt, Brace, Jovanovich.

Parlee, M. (1979). Psychology and women. *Signs: Journal of Women in Culture and Society, 5,* 121–133.

Peplau, L. A. & Conrad, E. (1989). Feminist methods in psychology. *Psychology of Women Quarterly, 13*, 379–400.

Prilleltensky, I. (1989). Psychology and the status quo. *American Psychologist, 44*, 795–802.

Rabinow, P., & Sullivan, W. M. (1979). The interpretive turn: Emergence of an approach. In P. Rabinow & W. M. Sullivan (Eds.), *Interpretive social science: A reader* (pp. 1–21). Berkeley: University of California Press.

Reigel, K. F. (1979). *Foundations of dialectical psychology.* San Diego, CA: Academic Press.

Reinharz, S. (1985). Feminist distrust: Problems of context and context in sociological work. In D. N. Berg & K. K. Smith (Eds.), *The self in social inquiry: Researching methods* (pp. 153–172). Beverly Hills, CA: Sage.

Reinharz, S. (1992). *Feminist methods in social research.* New York: Oxford University Press.

Riger, S. (1990). Ways of knowing and organizational approaches to community research. In P. Tolan, C. Keys, F. Chertok, & L. Jason (Eds.), *Researching community psychology* (pp. 42–50). Washington, DC: American Psychological Association.

Riger, S. (1991). Gender dilemmas in sexual harassment policies and procedures. *American Psychologist, 46*, 497–505.

Riger, S. (in preparation). *Psychology of women: Biological, psychological and social perspectives.* New York: Oxford University Press.

Rix, S. E. (Ed.) (1990). *The American woman, 1990–1991.* New York: Norton.

Rosenberg, R. (1982). *Beyond separate spheres.* New Haven, CT: Yale University Press.

Rosenthal, R. (1966). *Experimenter effects in behavioral research.* New York: Appleton-Century-Crofts.

Rossi, A. (1979). Reply by Alice Rossi. *Signs: Journal of Women in Culture and Society, 4*, 712–717.

Sampson, E. E. (1978). Scientific paradigms and social values: Wanted—A scientific revolution. *Journal of Personality and Social Psychology, 36*, 1332–1343.

Sampson, E. E. (1985). The decentralization of identity: Toward a revised concept of personal and social order. *American Psychologist, 40*, 1203–1211.

Scott, J. W. (1988). Deconstructing equality-versus-difference: Or, the uses of poststructuralist theory for feminism. *Feminist Studies, 14*, 33–50.

Segal, L. (1986). *Is the future female? Troubled thoughts on contemporary feminism.* London: Virago.

Sewart, J. J. (1979). Critical theory and the critique of conservative method. In S. G. McNall (Ed.) *Theoretical perspectives in sociology* (pp. 310–322). New York: St. Martin's Press.

Sherif, C. W. (1979). Bias in psychology. In J. A. Sherman & E. T. Beck (Eds.), *A prism of sex: Essays in the sociology of knowledge* (pp. 93–133). Madison: University of Wisconsin Press.

Shields, S. (1975). Functionalism, Darwinism, and the psychology of women: A study in social myth. *American Psychologist, 30*, 739–754.

Smith, D. (1987). *The everyday world as problematic.* Boston: Northeastern University Press.

Snitow, A. (1990). A gender diary. In M. Hirsch & E. F. Keller (Eds.), *Conflicts in feminism* (pp. 9–43). New York: Routledge.

Spelman, E. V. (1988). *Inessential woman: Problems of exclusion in feminist thought.* Boston: Beacon Press.

Stacey, J. (1988). Can there be a feminist ethnography? *Women's Studies International Forum, 11*, 21–27.

Stack, C. (1986). The culture of gender: Women and men of color. *Signs: Journal of Women in Culture and Society, 11*, 321–324.

Unger, R. K. (1979). Toward a redefinition of sex and gender. *American Psychologist, 34,* 1085–1094.

Unger, R. K. (1981). Sex as a social reality: Field and laboratory research. *Psychology of Women Quarterly, 5,* 645–653.

Unger, R. K. (1983). Through the looking glass: No wonderland yet! (The reciprocal relationship between methodology and models of reality). *Psychology of Women Quarterly, 8,* 9–32.

Unger, R. K. (1988). Psychological, feminist, and personal epistemology: Transcending contradiction. In M. M. Gergen (Ed.), *Feminist thought and the structure of knowledge* (pp. 124–141). New York: New York University Press.

Unger, R. K. (1989). Sex, gender, and epistemology. In M. Crawford & M. Gentry (Eds.), *Gender and thought: Psychological perspectives* (pp. 17–35). New York: Springer-Verlag.

Unger, R. K., Draper, R. D., & Pendergrass, M. L. (1986). Personal epistemology and personal experience. *Journal of Social Issues, 42,* 67–79.

Walker, L. (1991). The feminization of psychology. *Psychology of Women Newsletter of Division 35, 18,* 1, 4.

Walkerdine, V. (1986). Post-structuralist theory and everyday social practices: The family and the school. In S. Wilkinson *(Ed.), Feminist social psychology: Developing theory and practice* (pp. 57–76). Milton Keynes, England: Open University Press.

Weedon, C. (1987). *Feminist practice and poststructuralist theory.* New York: Basil Blackwell.

Weisstein, N. (1971). *Psychology constructs the female: Or, the fantasy life of the male psychologist.* Boston: New England Free Press.

West, C., & Zimmerman, D. H. (1987). Doing gender. *Gender & Society, 1,* 125–151.

Wilkinson, S. (1986). Sighting possibilities: Diversity and commonality in feminist research. In S. Wilkinson (Ed.), *Feminist social psychology: Developing theory and practice* (pp. 7–24). Milton Keynes, England: Open University Press.

Wittig, M. A. (1985). Metatheoretical dilemmas in the psychology of gender. *American Psychologist, 40,* 800–811.

Chapter Three

Doing Personality Research
How Can Feminist Theories Help?

Abigail J. Stewart

About twenty-five years ago, a few feminist psychologists raised new questions about how we did research in psychology. Some raised questions about how sex stereotypes influenced clinical diagnosis and practice; others wondered why generalizations were made about human beings when only men participated in the research; still others raised doubts about theories that seemed to be based either on men's lives and experiences, or on fantasies and assumptions about women's lives that were inconsistent with many women's own experiences. Since that time, a great deal of progress has been made, not only in psychology but also in feminist scholarship. However, personality psychology is not keeping pace with contemporary feminist scholarship. While many researchers have incorporated responses to the critiques of the 1970s, we are much less likely to be bringing the insights and perspectives of 1990s feminist theory into our research programs. Although the translation from insight to practice is always tricky, theoretical and epistemological advances in feminist scholarship could lead to improved empirical research in personality.

What Is the Problem Feminist Theories Can Help Solve?

Paradoxically, personality psychology appears simultaneously committed to individualism and universalism. Many observers think this twin commitment precludes serious attention to relationships, contexts, communities, social structure, culture, and history, and at the same time to assume an investment in the status quo. But those are precisely the issues that seem critical to understanding the life experiences and actions of people who historically have been underrepresented in personality psychology, as in other fields: women, people from working-class backgrounds, and people of color, to name a few. To psychologists interested in understanding personality structures and processes in these groups, a field that has no systematic concep-

Abigail J. Stewart, "Doing Personality Research: How Can Feminist Theories Help?" (revision of a paper delivered as invited address at the American Psychological Association 1993 convention). Reprinted with permission.

tion of the socially and culturally structured differences among people, or of the importance and meaning of their different situations, seems painfully inadequate. This felt inadequacy of our discipline to provide a fruitful intellectual environment in turn discourages people with these interests from participating in it.

If personality psychology is to remain a vital, growing discipline, we must expand our intellectual agenda beyond individualism and universalism in ways that are visible and meaningful. One valuable source of ideas about how that expansion might take place is feminist theory. (I am not claiming that it is the best, or only, source of ideas—just a very good one, and one I know.)

It is crucial to note that feminist theory is precisely theory—that is, it is a source of hypotheses and conceptual tools. As such, it can be used by those who find it intuitively appealing. Just as important, it can also be used by those who do *not* experience the present field of personality as limiting, but are willing to try to approach questions differently because of their respect for others who do.

Personality, Individualism, and Universalism

Although individual studies, research programs, and researchers have reached well beyond these notions (see, e.g., Veroff, 1983), the central intellectual agenda of personality psychology, since it was first shaped by Henry Murray and Gordon Allport more than fifty years ago, has been defined by two issues.

First, how do individuals differ from one another? This issue has been taken to encompass personality traits, motives and goals, dispositions to certain emotions or to emotional styles, even tendencies to hold certain kinds of opinions and beliefs. This focus is generally perceived to commit us to the individual as the unit of analysis, and to an individual level of explanation. That is, differences between individuals are generally assumed to result from individual differences in biology or personal experience. It is also generally assumed that the same basic individual differences can be used to describe all people. This issue, then, includes both an individualistic and a universalistic aspect.

Second, how do various characteristics of the individual cohere within a single "personality"? That is, how are persons and personalities organized or structured? This issue can be taken as referring to unique organizations within a single person, or organizations that tend to describe many persons (e.g., in terms of selves, egos, or identities; or hierarchies of motives, etc.) Again, this issue is focused at the individual level, and it is often assumed that the same structuring processes or functions operate in all persons.

At the level of our "big questions," then, personality psychology can reasonably be viewed as committed to both individualism and universalism. In addition, our field is seen as preoccupied with measurement, in the technical domain (in contrast with, say, social psychology's preoccupation with experiments, and developmental psychology's with observation). The theories of measurement that have dominated our field have also assumed universalism (measures should be identical for all people, places, and contexts) and individualism (measures should be taken and their psychometric properties assessed at the individual level).

Feminist Theories and Personality Research

Feminist theories in the 1990s are extraordinarily diverse (see Herrmann & Stewart, 1994). They originate from many disciplines and practices and are aimed at a wide range of problems. Some theories make claims that are incompatible with others; they are not uniformly relevant or useful. One could adopt a particular feminist theoretical perspective—say, "French feminism" based on Lacanian psychoanalysis— and simply recommend that personality research should flow from that perspective. This is a potentially useful way of connecting personality research and feminist theory. Research aimed at testing the propositions contained in the theories of Nancy Chodorow, Carol Gilligan, and Catharine MacKinnon has enriched, and will continue to enrich, our field. But I am arguing for something different—the possibil- ity of finding theoretical tools in feminist theory that can enrich our research, regardless of the perspective from which we are operating or the question we are testing. Such tools would affect both how we frame our research questions and how we answer them.

Reading across different feminist theories, I have identified six broad claims that such theories could lead us to take seriously when we do personality research. I describe these six claims as practices personality researchers could incorporate, in rough chronological order of their emergence within feminist theories beginning in the 1970s.

Look for What Has Been Left Out

Personality researchers should begin by looking for what has been left out in traditional personality research, because features of women's experience have been systematically excluded from the discipline.

Early feminist theorists articulated the ways that male practitioners of the disci- pline had ignored women as research participants, had ignored aspects of women's lives and experience in defining research problems, and had universalized the lives and experience of men (see, e.g., Sherif, 1979). These arguments have led to some changes in research practices in many fields within psychology, including personality. For example, within the motivation research tradition founded by David McClelland (for overviews, see McClelland, 1985; Smith, 1992), early criticisms of the male-based definitions of achievement motivation (Alper, 1974; French & Lesser, 1964) led to formulation of additional constructs, such as the motive to avoid success (Horner, 1972; Fleming & Horner, 1992); differentiation of types of achievement motivation (Veroff, 1977; Gaeddert, 1985); and more equal inclusion of men and women in subsequent research on the affiliation, power (Stewart & Chester, 1982), and especially intimacy motives (McAdams, 1992).

However, many aspects of personality and even of motivation continue to be formulated leaving crucial components out. For example, throughout our literature on human motivation—whether it is focused on largely nonconscious and general motivational systems like the need for achievement, or on conscious goals, strivings, projects, and strategies (for an excellent review see Cantor & Zirkel, 1990)—we have generated rich models of what individuals want and have assumed that desires would translate fairly straightforwardly into realities. We have, in addition, a well-developed understanding of how people react to successes and failures in pursuing what they want—but it is an understanding similarly based on an assumption that everyone has an equal chance of succeeding or failing at getting what they want. We have, then, largely ignored the obstacles that may be in people's way, and that may crucially shape or determine their success in pursuing what they want, may even shape how they define what they want.

By considering what is left out, we can see that we must know not only what people want but what they have with which to pursue it, and what they must overcome in order to get it. A universalistic assumption—that motives will have the same effects for everyone, regardless of resources and obstacles—leaves us with an understanding of motivation too incomplete to inspire research on many important questions. An exciting task lies ahead for motivation researchers—to articulate the connections among what people have, what they want, the obstacles to getting what they want, what actions they can and do take to get what they want, how and why they succeed and fail, and how they understand and react to their successes and failures. In pursuing this integration, Carol Tomlinson-Keasey's recent (1994) reflections on women's lives may be useful. She has argued that many women's life courses are determined not only by the familiar concepts of goal-setting and serendipity (or luck), but by a great deal of improvisation—that is, attempts to find personal satisfaction within situations defined by roles and obligations to others.

Research on motivational problems that began by including what has been left out in the past could focus on when and how individuals faced with certain kinds of obstacles are able to overcome them; on what resources are necessary to support certain motives if they are to find direct expression in satisfying actions; on what obstacles are particularly daunting to what kinds of purposes; on what complex strategies people use to pursue personal goals that others in their environment do not support for them. These kinds of questions would, I think, both enrich our understanding of motivation and engage the interest of some of those currently unexcited about it.

Analyze Your Own Position

Personality researchers should begin by analyzing our own position as it affects our understanding and the research process. Feminist theorists have been among those to argue that all scholarship—all knowledge—begins from a perspective that is inevitably partial (Harding, 1991). Therefore, our own position as educated, middle-class professionals will inevitably influence how we frame our research problems. Often this argument has been used to question highly routinized research practices in the social sciences (see, e.g., Fonow & Cook, 1991; Nielsen, 1990). Some scholars have argued, for example, that a serious consideration of the position of the re-searcher should lead to greater efforts to include research participants in the research process as collaborators—both to avoid abuse of power and to ensure inclusion of the perspective of the research participants in the definition of the research problem (Mies, 1983; Smith, 1987; Fine, 1992).

It is useful to reflect carefully on practices that have become so standard in the field that we do not think much about them. For example, in a particularly thought-ful and original paper, Brinton Lykes (1989) explored what the notion of "informed consent" really implies—among other things, that we, the researchers, have all the power in the situation and must therefore be sure to explain the situation to the participant. She recounted her conversation with a Guatemalan Indian research participant who found this construction implausible and knew that she—the inter-viewee—had the power to tell or not to tell whatever she chose, regardless of the interviewer's beliefs about her own power in the situation.

A variety of implications for our practice can be drawn from taking seriously our position in the research process, but one is critical to personality measurement. One of the assumptions most personality measures make is that answers given to ques-tions mean the same thing no matter who is giving the answer. This assumption is viewed as tenable particularly to the extent that the same measures used with different kinds of people demonstrate the "same" result. But we do not always inquire very deeply into just what differences apparent "sameness" may conceal.

In a study with profound implications for personality researchers, Hope Landrine, Elizabeth Klonoff, and Alice Brown-Collins (1992) asked women to rate seven per-sonality attributes on a seven-point scale: I make decisions easily; I am sensitive to the needs of others; I am feminine; I am assertive; I am independent; I have leadership abilities; I am passive. They also asked the women to circle one of several definitions that best matched what they had in mind when they rated themselves for each of the attributes. Thus, for example, women could indicate that when they rated themselves on the attribute "passive" they had in mind the meaning "Don't say what I really think," "Let people take advantage of me," or "Agree with others when I shouldn't," or "Am, laid-back/easy going."

The authors compared white women with women of color on overall endorsement of the seven attributes. There were no differences between the two groups—evidence for "sameness." However, on four of the seven adjectives there were differences in the *meanings* the women had in mind when they rated themselves. For example, when white women rated themselves as high or low on passivity they most often had "Am laid-back/easy-going" in mind, but women of color most often had "Don't say what I really think" in mind. Moreover, the meaning a woman had in mind when she rated herself was strongly associated with her self-rating. Thus, women of color who defined passive as "laid-back/easy-going" (the preferred definition of white women) rated themselves as less passive then did those who were thinking of passive as "let people take advantage of me."

These results are obviously of enormous importance for personality measurement. They suggest not only that there are systematic differences among women (and, presumably, among men) in the meanings routinely attributed to personality descriptors, but also that the meanings attributed affect the liklihood or degree of self-attribution. Landrine, Klonoff, and Brown-Collins have provided us a wonderful model of a simple addition to many personality measures: a set of alternative meanings the person might have in mind.

It also may be the case that there are systematic differences in attributes. For three of the attributes the women in this study rated, white women and women of color did not indicate different meanings: I make decisions easily; I am independent; I have leadership abilities. All three are characteristics conventionally attributed more to men than women. Of the four attributes where white women and women of color did show differences, three are stereotypically associated with women (I am sensitive to the needs of others; I am passive; I am feminine). It would be interesting to know if there is more within-gender variation in meanings attached to characteristics traditionally associated with one's own gender than with stereotypically cross-gender characteristics. Knowing whether this is so would also help define the implications of this study.

Finally, we do have some measurement approaches—content analysis, Kelly repertory grid techniques, semi-projective and narrative methods, to name a few—that permit research participants to provide enough context for their self- or other-descriptions to permit us to examine what they mean, both as individuals and as members of socially defined groups.

Use Gender as an Analytic Tool

Personality researchers should use the concept of gender as an analytic tool. Historian Joan Scott (1988) recommended the use of gender as a category of analysis. Her point was that historians should pay attention to gender well beyond efforts to include women in narrative accounts of "what happened." Thus, in some circumstances gender may have nothing directly to do with sex or sex differences; it may apply to roles, to metaphors, or to the associations and meanings we attach to behaviors, attributes, feelings, and institutions. The critical point abut using gender as an analytic tool, then, is to recognize that gender is socially constructed and has different meanings in different cultural and historical contexts, as well as for individuals.

There are many examples of personality researchers who have used gender as an analytic tool; even so, we have only scratched the surface of what is possible and significant. Within the broad domain of research on gender-linked personality traits—whether labeled masculinity, femininity, androgyny, or (as more recently) instrumental and expressive traits—some researchers have sought to separate attributed sex from sex-linked personality attributes and examined the different implications of each (see, e.g., Bem, 1974; Spence, 1984; Deaux, 1984, 1985). For example, in a secondary analysis of longitudinal data, Jennifer Aube and Richard Koestner (1992) found that boys who had described themselves at age twelve in terms of undesirable feminine traits and feminine interests had poorer self-reported adjustment at age forty-one; girls who had described themselves in the same terms showed no such effect. This study suggests—as have many others—that characteristics with strong gender associations in the culture as a whole may have very different implications for males and females.

Other research has focused on the more individual concepts of gender that people hold. When Sandra Bem (1993) proposed that some of us are "gender-schematic" while others are not, she was using gender as an analytic tool in a double sense: she was describing the awareness of gender, and at the same time observing that awareness of gender is an individual difference dimension (see Bem, 1981, 1985). Bem 1993) has also argued that in our culture being "gender schematic" includes two processes: gender polarization, or the tendency to attach opposite characteristics to the two sexes and sex roles; and androcentrism, or the tendency to value the perspective and attributes associated with the masculine pole. She suggests the value of contrasting the worldviews of those who perceive the world through the shared "lenses of gender" provided in the culture generally and those who are "gender nonconformists."

Much of the research on "gender constructions," however these are defined, has focused on the views of college students; as a result, what we know about contemporary notions of gender is based on samples of people who are mostly white and mostly middle class. Andrea Hunter and James Earl Davis (1992) explored the meanings of masculinity or "manhood" as articulated by a sample of African-American men who varied widely in age and occupational status. Using a combined interview and Q-sort strategy that allowed the men first to generate and then to sort characteristics according to their importance to men's definitions of manhood, Hunter and Davis found that for these adult black men manhood was defined in four domains: self-determinism and accountability; family connectedness; pride; and spirituality and humanism. Interestingly, characteristics tapped by conventional measures of "masculinity" (ambition, handling crises and stress, etc.) as well as some tapped by conventional measures of "femininity" (being kind and caring, placing needs of others before one's own, etc.) were among those defined as most important to being a man. This research provides a model of an approach that can be used for broadening and deepening our understanding of the gender constructions shared within and across structurally defined groups in our culture, as well as the highly idiosyncratic gender constructions a single individual may hold.

Finally, some research has explored the implications of different life experiences for gendered social roles. In a series of important analyses of her longitudinal study of women college graduates, Ravenna Helson and her colleagues have demonstrated the long-term consequences of gendered adult roles for one cohort of women. In one study, for example, Helson and Picano (1990) asked, "Is the traditional role bad for women?" They showed that in this cohort lifelong sole pursuit of domestic marriage and motherhood roles was associated with lower physical and psychological well-being in middle age than was pursuit of life courses less traditional for white, middle-class women. In related research, Helson, Mitchell, and Moane (1984) showed that living an adult life according to the "social clocks" traditionally associated with masculine occupations or feminine family concerns had an impact on personality in middle age.

In all of these accounts gender is used as an analytic tool to understand differences among people of the same attributed sex—differences in life trajectories, actions, and lenses for looking at the world that are themselves gendered. This research helps show us that many aspects of human experience are "gendered," and that this gendering has consequences; but we have only begun to understand this. For example, a large and influential body of research in personality psychology aims to create a taxonomy of crucial personality traits (see John, 1990, for a review). The numbers and substance of proposed traits differ, but many of them cry out for analysis in terms of gender. According to one account there are five basic personality traits: surgency of dominance; agreeableness; conscientiousness; emotional stability; and openness to experience or culture. While these are not all equally "gendered" constructs, at least three of them (dominance, agreeableness, and emotional stability) make regular appearances on lists of sex-linked personality attributes. (See, e.g., the Bem Sex Role Inventory [BSRI], the Personal Attributes Questionnaire [PAQ], and the masculinity and femininity scales of the Adjective Check List as reported in Lenny [1991]. Interestingly, different features of a fourth—"culture"—are attributed to men and women on the PAQ: "know ways of world" to men and "enjoys art and music" to women. While "conscientiousness" is viewed as "neutral" on the BSRI, "strong conscience" is associated with females on the PAQ.) it is time to explore not merely whether men and women differ on these dimensions, but how these traits themselves reflect and replicate gender in their meanings and consequences.

Gender Is Not (Only) about Difference

In exploring gender as an analytic tool, recognize that gender is not (only) about difference; it is also about dominance or power relations.

Catharine MacKinnon is the feminist theorist most clearly associated with the "dominance" approach to gender. MacKinnon (1987, p. 40) writes:

> On the first day that matters, dominance was achieved, probably by force. By the second, division along the same lines had to be relatively firmly in place. On the third day, differences were demarcated, together with social systems to exaggerate them in perception and in fact, because the systematically differential delivery of benefits and deprivations required making no mistake about who was who. Comparatively speaking, man has been resting ever since. Gender might not even code as difference, might not even mean distinction epistemologically, were it not for its consequences for social power.

Not all feminist theorists agree with MacKinnon that dominance is primary—that is, that it precedes "difference"—but there is consensus that power is a critical aspect of gender requiring analysis. Thus, if we consider the gendered nature of "agreeableness" we notice that subordinates have very different reasons to be agreeable than do dominants. For subordinates, agreeableness may make survival possible; for dominants, it is entirely optional. Perhaps, then, agreeableness has a more secure anchor in temperament for dominants, and is more often shaped by socialization for subordinates. Posing questions about the sources of personality traits without reference to either gender or power will not allow us to know.

Leslie Brody, in a significant program of research on emotion and emotional expressiveness, has demonstrated the importance of gender as power relations. After reviewing findings from a variety of different empirical studies, Brody (1985) concluded that girls "have to adapt to an interpersonal and physical world in which men are more aggressive than they are from a very young age. . . . [I]n order to be safe, females may need to avoid being the object of male aggression" (pp. 50–51). The expression of anger, in particular, is problematic for those who are afraid of the objects of their anger (see Brody and Hall, 1993). Thus Brody (1993) argues that males and females differ not only in emotional expressiveness in general, but in the particularities of their emotional lives. And those differences seem closely related to the fact that females more often than males seek to appease, please, and otherwise avoid harm from threatening others. Bringing together research on emotional expressiveness and emotion recognition, Brody and her colleague Judith Hall (1993) suggest that

> gender differences in emotion are adaptive for the differing roles that males and females play in this culture. Thus, the emotions that women display more of (warmth, happiness, shame, guilt, fear, nervousness) are related to affiliation, vulnerability and self-consciousness, and are consistent with women's lower social status and power, lower physical aggression, and their traditional gender roles including child caretaking and social bonding, which necessitates being able to read the emotion signals of others. Greater male anger, pride, and contempt are consistent with the male role of differentiating and competing with others, in which the goals are the minimization of vulnerability in order to maximize the chances of success. (p. 452)

Bringing together notions of the variability of gender within groups of men and women, Brody and Hall point out that "behavioral gender roles (e.g., the amount of child care individuals do and the types of occupations in which they are engaged) are . . . systematically related to emotional functioning" (p. 453) in ways that replicate overall sex differences. In this case, then, it seems that Brody and Hall are showing, within the domain of emotional experience, how "dominance" might very well precede and shape "difference."

In a very different approach to the implications of dominance and subordination, a number of feminist psychologists have shown that the agency and instrumentality of those in subordinate positions may not be visible if they are observed from the perspective of dominants. Individuals in situations with few resources and many constraints may "take action" in ways that are not as obvious as the actions of dominants. Thus, Michelle Fine (1992) has shown how one rape survivor's refusal of social services was in fact an instrumental step toward her own social network and self-help. Similarly, Brinton Lykes (1982) has shown that in a sample of older black women direct actions were often taken to solve problems that arose in settings with other blacks, but more indirect, apparently "passive" strategies were used in settings that were dominated by whites.

Not only are different strategies employed in different settings to accomplish the same goals, but in addition the same behavior may mean different things among different groups of subordinates, given different cultural histories. For example, historians Evelyn Brooks Higginbotham (1992) and Darlene Hine (1989) have both argued that although "silence" is experienced by white women as reflecting helplessness and passivity (see Belenky, Clinchy, Goldberger, & Tarule, 1986), for African-American women it has often been a self-conscious strategy of concealing feelings and withholding information. Similarly, psychologist Aída Hurtado (1989) has argued that "for white women, the first step in the search for identity is to confront the ways in which their personal, individual silence endorses the power of white men. . . . For women of Color, the challenge is to use their oral traditions for specific political goals" (pp. 848–849).

Hurtado's argument derives from her analysis of the different relations of white women and women of color to white men; she suggests that white women are always in a relation of potential seduction by white men (their value defined by their potential as a sexual partner), while women of color are always in a relation of potential rejection (as inappropriate carriers of a white male's "line"). These different stances or positions in turn provide completely different contexts for the meanings of behaviors of white women or women of color toward white men. Relying on universalistic understandings of behaviors would seriously distort our understanding of what those behaviors mean.

Explore Other Aspects of Social Position

Serious analyses of gender reveal that other aspects of people's social position must also be explored. Sensitized to the power dimension of gender, and moved by evidence of the importance of power relations among women, feminist theorists have increasingly argued that all of the axes of structural power in a culture shape and define gender and personality. In some of the studies discussed earlier we have seen how aspects of race and ethnicity shape personality. Other, less explored aspects of social structure are likely to be equally important.

In some recent research Joan Ostrove has been examining the significance of social class origin for women who attended Radcliffe College in the early 1960s (Stewart & Ostrove, 1993; see also Ostrove & Stewart, 1994). Although this could be thought of as a nearly homogeneous sample of white, middle- or upper-middle-class women, from another perspective it is a sample of white women who came from families that were in fact different: some were working class, some squarely middle class, and some upper class.

Disaggregated in this way, it is possible to show that even in middle age more than three-quarters of the women from working-class backgrounds recalled their experience of Radcliffe as one of deep and painful alienation; about half of the middle-class women also felt alienated at Radcliffe; and virtually none of the upper-class women did. Moreover, when Ostrove examined the ways in which women in these three groups described marriage, she found that the women from working-class families described it as a dangerous institution with the potential to trap them in economic dependence and unfair division of labor; middle-class women described it as an intimate haven in a heartless world; and upper-class women described it as a rather detached collaboration or partnership. These different constructions of marriage, and experiences of themselves at Radcliffe, are surely parts of these women's personalities—parts that are invisible without thinking about their original social class position.

In another important program of research, Deborrah Frable and her colleagues (see, e.g., Frable, Blackstone, & Scherbaum, 1990) has shown that individuals who are "different" from what is socially normative within mainstream U.S. culture— that is, for example, who are homosexual or not white—are more "mindful" in social interaction than those who do not "stand out." Not only did the different, or marginal, people in her studies attend more closely to the perspective of their partners, but their partners also attended more closely to them if their difference was visible. If, however, nonmarginal people interacted with people whose marginality was invisible to them, they "rarely took their partner's perspective, and they remembered little about the situation" (p. 146). Being treated in these ways is surely consequential for personality, but we need to know more about how. Moreover, in her program of research, Frable (1993) is working to separate not only the context-specific and relatively enduring implications of experiencing oneself as different, but to differentiate the consequences of being "merely" different, different in a socially unacceptable way, or "atypical."

Give Up the Search for a Unified Self

Many contemporary feminist theorists would recommend that personality psychologists give up our search for a unified self. This prescription from contemporary feminist theory may seem the most at odds with personality's basic agenda, but I think it is not. The point here is to recognize that individual personalities derive from multiple and conflicting "subject positions." One is rarely either entirely dominant or entirely subordinate. Instead, one is dominant and subordinate along particular dimensions and in particular contexts; therefore, we cannot expect to find in persons a single, unified "self."

Some personality research has in fact recognized the multiplicity of selves in various ways—for example, in Hazel Markus's notion of "possible selves" (Markus & Nurius, 1986) or Patricia Linville's (1985, 1987) notion of self-complexity—without always connecting those multiple selves with the multiple subject positions. The past decade, however, has seen increasing recognition that people may construct more than one kind of self. In particular, a number of scholars—including Brinton Lykes (1985) and Hazel Markus and her colleagues (Markus & Oyserman, 1989; Markus & Kitayama, 1991)—have argued that although American psychology has generally assumed and investigated a highly individuated, autonomous self-concept, it may also be that some people in this culture and others construct a more connected, relationally embedded self. Moreover, these theorists have argued that there may be important cultural and social-structural sources of these different kinds of selves. This research importantly complicates our picture of a single unified self; in fact, Markus and Oyserman (1989) have suggested that perhaps "a self-concept that is rooted in connectedness [is] a more variable or a more complex self because its precise nature depends on relations with diverse other" (p. 120). Lykes (1985) has shown that working-class adults and those who participated in collective organizations were more likely to exhibit a socially embedded self-construction. Moreover, among women, this kind of self-construction was associated with greater involvement in networks of relationships at all ages, and with playing active roles in their communities. Even so, these exciting innovations in research and theory exploring alternative self-constructions have tended to polarize and separate different kinds of still fairly unified selves, even though the measures of those self-constructions might permit exploration of more complexity.

In a rather different line of research, Pat Gurin and her colleagues have explored the consequences of having a stronger or weaker identification with one's social status or "stratum" (Gurin, Miller, & Gurin, 1980; Gurin, 1985). In a study integrating Gurin's work on gender identity with Markus's work on self-schemas, Gurin and Markus (1989) explored some of the complexities and contradictions in women's gender identities. They found—consistent with the self-schema perspective—that overall the centrality of gender in a woman's identity influenced her processing of gender-relevant information. Consistent with a stratum-consciousness perspective, they also found that women who felt they had much in common with other women were more likely to perceive structural causes of gender inequities and to seek collective remedies for them. Interestingly, though, despite the fact that the centrality of gender to identity and the sense of common fate with other women were positively correlated for both groups, and the sense of common fate was associated with a feminist political consciousness for both groups, the centrality of gender to identity had opposite political implications for women in roles traditional or nontraditional for women. Among women in nontraditional roles, the centrality of gender identity was associated with a stronger feminist consciousness, but among women in traditional roles it was associated with stronger acceptance of traditional gender roles. Obviously, these women's enduring role commitments helped shape their identities and give different political meaning to their gender identity. Here, then, is an example of researchers exploring the complexities and different organizations of identities among women.

It is an important theoretical task for personality psychologists to work through the implications of avoiding a search for a unified self for our large integrating constructs, such as "identity" or "ego" or "the" self. One rather practical implication would be for us to stop trying to reconcile different levels of ego development or identity status, as we currently do, by arriving at a single overall summary. Perhaps we should at least sometimes explore the multiplicities of levels we are already recording but often ignoring in our research.

Conclusion

Feminist theories can be mined for insight into improved research practices in personality psychology. These practices can enrich our understanding, while helping us to overcome our traditional individualism and universalism. By following these practices we should be able simultaneously to explore aspects of the motivations, emotions, selves, identities—the *personalities*—of individuals and to take seriously those individuals' social-structural, cultural, and relational contexts.

REFERENCES

Alper, T. G. (1974). Achievement motivation in college women: A now-you-see-it-now-you-don't phenomenon. *American Psychologist, 29,* 194–203.

Aube, J., & Koestner, R. (1992). Gender characteristics and adjustment: A longitudinal study. *Journal of Personality and Social Psychology, 63,* 485–493.

Belenky, M. F., Clinchy, B. M., Goldberger, N. R., & Tarule, J. M. (1986). *Women's ways of knowing: The development of self, voice, and mind.* New York: Basic Books.

Bem, S. L. (1974). The measurement of psychological androgyny. *Journal of Clinical and Consulting Psychology, 42,* 155–162.

Bem, S. L. (1981). Gender schema theory: A cognitive account of sex typing. *Psychological Review, 88,* 354–364.

Bem, S. L. (1985). Androgyny and gender schema theory: A conceptual and empirical integration. In T. B. Sonderegger (Ed.), *Nebraska Symposium on motivation, 1984: Psychology and gender* (pp. 179–226). Lincoln: University of Nebraska Press.

Bem, S. L. (1993). *The lenses of gender.* New Haven, CT: Yale University Press.

Brody, L. R. (1985). Gender differences in emotional development: A review of theories and research. *Journal of Personality, 53,* 102–149.

Brody, L. R. (in press). On understanding gender differences in the expression of emotion. In S. Ablon, D. Brown, E. Khantzian, & J. Mack (Eds.), *Human feelings.* New York: Analytic Press.

Brody, L. R., & Hall, J. A. (1993). Gender and emotion. In M. Lewis & J. Haviland (Eds.), *Handbook of emotions.* New York: Guilford.

Cantor, N., & Zirkel, S. (1990). Personality, cognition, and purposive behavior. In L. Pervin (Ed.), *Handbook of personality: Theory and research* (pp. 135–164). New York: Guilford.

Deaux, K. (1984). From individual differences to social categories: Analysis of a decade's research on gender. *American Psychologist, 39,* 105–116.

Deaux, K. (1985). Sex and gender. *Annual Review of Psychology, 36,* 49–81.

Fine, M. (1992). *Disruptive voices.* Ann Arbor: University of Michigan Press.

Fleming, J., & Horner, M. S. (1992). The motive to avoid success. In C. P. Smith (Ed.), *Motivation and personality* (pp. 179–189). Cambridge: Cambridge University Press.

Fonow, M. M., & Cook, J. A. (1991). *Beyond methodology: Feminist methodology as lived research.* Bloomington: Indiana University Press.

Frable, D. E. S. (1993). Dimensions of marginality: Distinctions among those who are different. *Personality and Social Psychology Bulletin, 19,* 370–380.

Frable, D. E. S., Blackstone, T., & Scherbaum, C. (1990). Marginal and mindful: Deviants in social interactions. *Journal of Personality and Social Psychology, 59,* 140–149.

French, E. G., & Lesser, G. S. (1964). Some characteristics of the achievement motive in women. *Journal of Abnormal and Social Psychology, 68,* 119–128.

Gaeddert, W. P. (1985). Sex and sex role effects on achievement strivings: Dimensions of similarity and difference. *Journal of Personality, 53,* 286–305.

Gurin, P. (1985). Women's gender consciousness. *Public Opinion Quarterly, 49,* 143–163.

Gurin, P., & Markus, H. (1989). Cognitive consequences of gender identity. In S. Skevington & D. Baker (Eds.), *The social identity of women* (pp. 152–172). Newbury Park, CA: Sage.

Gurin, P., Miller, H., & Gurin, G. (1980). Stratum identification and consciousness. *Social Psychology Quarterly, 43,* 30–47.

Harding, S. (1991). *Whose science? Whose knowledge?* Ithaca, NY: Cornell University Press.

Helson, R., Mitchell, V., & Moane, G. (1984). Personality and patterns of adherence and nonadherence to the social clock. *Journal of Personality and Social Psychology, 46,* 1079–1096.

Helson, R., & Picano, J. (1990). Is the traditional role bad for women? *Journal of Personality and Social Psychology, 59,* 311–320.

Herrmann, A., & Stewart, A. J. (1994). *Theorizing feminisms: Parallel trends in the humanities and the social sciences.* Boulder, CO: Westview.

Higginbotham, E. B. (1992). African-American women's history and the metalanguage of race. *Signs, 17 (2),* 251–274.

Hine, D. (1989). Rape and the inner lives of Black women in the Middle West: Preliminary thoughts on the culture of dissemblance. *Signs, 14,* 912–920.

Horner, M. S. (1972). Toward an understanding of achievement-related conflicts in women. *Journal of Social Issues, 28,* 157–176.

Hunter, A. G., & Davis, J. E. (1992). Constructing gender: An exploration of Afro-American men's conceptualization of manhood. *Gender and Society, 6,* 464–479.

Hurtado, A. (1989). Relating to privilege: Seduction and rejection in the subordination of white women and women of color. *Signs, 14 (4),* 833–855.

John, O. P. (1990). The "big five" factor taxonomy: Dimensions of personality in the natural language and in questionnaires. In L. A. Pervin (Ed.), *Handbook of personality: Theory and research* (pp. 66–100). New York: Guilford.

Landrine, H., Klonoff, E., & Brown-Collins, A. (1992). Cultural diversity and methodology in feminist psychology: Critique, proposal, empirical example. *Psychology of Women Quarterly, 16,* 145–163.

Lenney, E. (1991). Sex roles: The measurement of masculinity, femininity, and androgyny. In J. P. Robinson, P. R. Shaver, & L. S. Wrightsman (Eds.), *Measures of personality and social attitudes* (pp. 573–660). San Diego, CA: Academic Press.

Linville, P. W. (1985). Self-complexity and affective extremity: Don't put all your eggs in one cognitive basket. *Social Cognition, 3,* 94–120.

Linville, P. W. (1987). Self-complexity as a cognitive buffer against stress-related illness and depression. *Journal of Personality and Social Psychology, 52,* 663–676.

Lykes, M. B. (1982). Discrimination and coping in the lives of black women. *Journal of Social Issues, 39, (3),* 79–100.

Lykes, M. B. (1985). Gender and individualistic vs. collectivist bases for notions about the self. In A. J. Stewart & M. B. Lykes (Eds.), *Gender and personality: Current perspectives on theory and research.* Durham, NC: Duke University Press.

Lykes, M. B. (1989). Dialogue with Guatemalan Indian women: Critical perspectives on constructing collaborative research. In R. Unger (Ed.), *Representations: Social constructions of gender* (pp. 167–185). Amityville, NY: Baywood.

MacKinnon, C. (1987). *Feminism unmodified: Discourses on life and law.* Cambridge, MA: Harvard University Press.

Markus, H. R., & Kitayama, S. (1991). Culture and the self: Implications for cognition, emotion and motivation. *Psychological Review, 98,* 224–253.

Markus, H., & Nurius, P. (1986). Possible selves. *American Psychologist, 41,* 954–969.

Markus, H., & Oyserman, D. (1989). Gender and thought: The role of the self-concept. In M. Crawford & M. Gentry (Eds.), *Gender and thought* (pp. 100–127). New York: Springer-Verlag.

McAdams, D. P. (1992). The intimacy motive. In C. P. Smith (Ed.), *Motivation and personality* (pp. 224–228). Cambridge: Cambridge University Press.

McClelland, D. C. (1985). *Human motivation.* Glenview, IL: Scott Foresman.

Mies, M. (1983). Towards a methodology for feminist research. In G. Bowles & R. Klein (Eds.), *Theories of Women's Studies.* Boston: Routledge & Kegan Paul.

Nielsen, J. M. (1990). *Feminist research methods.* Boulder, CO: Westview.

Ostrove, J. M., & Stewart, A. J. (1994). Meanings and uses of marginal identities at Radcliffe in the 1960s. In C. Franz & A. J. Stewart (Eds.), *Women creating lives: Identities, resistance, resilience.* Boulder, CO: Westview.

Scott, J. (1988). *Gender and the politics of history.* New York: Columbia University Press.

Sherif, C. (1979). Bias in psychology. In J. A. Sherman & E. T. Beck (Eds.), *Prism of Sex: Essays in the sociology of knowledge* (pp. 93–133). Madison: University of Wisconsin Press.

Smith, C. P. (Ed.) (1992). *Motivation and personality: Handbook of thematic content analysis.* Cambridge: Cambridge University Press.

Smith, D. (1987). Women's perspective as a radical critique of sociology. In S. Harding (Ed.), *Feminism and methodology* (pp. 84–96). Bloomington: Indiana University Press.

Spence, J. T. (1984). Masculinity, femininity, and gender-related traits: A conceptual analysis and critique of current research. In B. A. Maher & W. B. Maher (Eds.), *Progress in experimental research in personality* (vol. 13, pp. 1–97). New York: Academic Press.

Stewart, A. J., & Chester, N. L. (1982). Sex differences in human social motives: Achievement, affiliation and power. In A. J. Stewart (Ed.), *Motivation and society* (pp. 172–218). San Francisco: Jossey-Bass.

Stewart, A. J., & Ostrove, J. (1993). Social class, social change, and gender: Working-class women at Radcliffe and after. *Psychology of Women Quarterly, 17,* 475–497.

Tomlinson-Keasey, C. (1994). My dirty little secret: Women as clandestine intellectuals. In C. Franz & A. J. Stewart (Eds.), *Women creating lives: Identities, resistance, resilience* (pp. 227–248). Boulder, CO: Westview.

Veroff, J. (1977). Process vs. impact in men's and women's achievement motivation. *Psychology of Women Quarterly, 1,* 228–293.

Veroff, J. (1983). Contextual determinants of personality. *Personality and Social Psychology Bulletin, 9,* 331–343.

Chapter Four

Gender and the History of Psychology

Laurel Furumoto

I'm not prepared to insist that there is a need for convergence between history and theory in psychology in a general sense. Instead, what I would like to offer here is a minor case study of what has become for me the siren call of a particular emerging theoretical perspective beckoning to be used as an interpretive framework for revisioning the history of American psychology. In what follows, I will first sketch the background and current status of that theoretical perspective and then illustrate how it can be applied to guide and inform inquiry in the history of psychology by giving two specific examples.

Recent developments in women's history, as well as scholarship in the emerging specialty of men's history, reveal a heightened emphasis on the category of gender in historical analysis. A conference held at Radcliffe College in the spring of 1994 to commemorate the fiftieth anniversary of the Schlesinger Library on the History of Women in America took as its theme "New Viewpoints in Women's History." As one of almost four hundred attendees at that conference, I listened to a group of leading scholars discuss what they saw as some of the larger theoretical and historiographical issues currently affecting the field of women's history. The conferees were in general agreement that it was important and necessary to continue the now well-established tradition of scholarship investigating women's lives and experience. However, time and again speakers also voiced their belief that gender studies, i.e., research that examines femininity and masculinity as historical categories subject to change, would be of signal importance to the future of the field. Alice Kessler-Harris was one of those who stressed the necessity for exploring gender "as a complex and multi-layered system of social organization" in search of answers to what she called the most pressing question confronting women's historians: "how it is that women (whatever their relations to powerful men) have, as a group, so often found access to power elusive" (1994, p. 20).

The new men's history—whose practitioners acknowledge that the impetus for their area came from the burgeoning field of women's history—investigates male gender roles and the social construction of masculinity and considers the question of

Laurel Furumoto, "Gender and the History of Psychology." *History and Philosophy of Psychology Bulletin, 8* (2), pp. 10–16. © 1996 by the History and Philosophy of Psychology Bulletin (Section 25, Canadian Psychological Association). Reprinted with permission.

"where and to what extent gender is an independent variable" influencing social, economic and political processes (Carnes & Griffen, 1990, p. 7). Some recent examples of scholarship in this field include two book-length studies, one of masculinity and male codes of honor in France (Nye, 1993) and the other of transformations in American manhood (Rotundo, 1993), both dealing with roughly the same historical period—from the eighteenth through the early decades of the twentieth century. Interest in men's history has continued to build over the past five years and new titles in the area are multiplying, e.g. Bederman (1995), *Manliness and Civilization: A Cultural History of Gender and Race in the United States, 1880–1917;* Connell (1995), *Masculinities;* Kimmel (1996), *Manhood in America: A Cultural History;* Mosse (1996), *The Image of Man: The Creation of Modern Masculinity.*

Whereas historians of women and of men have recognized "the importance of gender as both tool and a subject of historical analysis" (Carnes & Griffen, 1990, p. 1), this is less true for historians of science. As Marina Benjamin—a feminist author of several articles on eighteenth-century history of science—recently observed, issues of gender have not been given sufficient attention even in the new science criticism, which has tended to overlook the relationship between masculinity and knowledge production.[1] Political, religious, and class interests are assumed to matter in science she maintains, but not gender interests. As Benjamin puts it, "the fact that the majority of the Royal Society's early fellowship was Protestant, for example, has been considered more significant than the fact that the entire fellowship was male" (1993, pp. 7–8).

Yet, there are recent indications that the topic of gender is beginning to attract the attention of at least some historians of science. In May 1995, a conference at the University of Minnesota called "The Women, Gender, and Science Question" attracted scholars from throughout North America to address the question: What do research on the history of women and science, and research on science and gender have to do with each other? Among the sessions at that conference was one concerned with historical analyses of gender and scientific practice which included papers on the medieval foundations of scientific masculinity, the masculine gendering of mathematical analysis in eighteenth-century France, and the defeminizing of botany in England during the eighteenth and nineteenth centuries. In October 1995, the program for the annual meeting of the History of Science Society featured two sessions, both well attended, focusing on gender: "Revisiting Gender, Nature, and the Laboratory" and "Gender and the Pursuit of Knowledge in Early Modern Europe."

What bearing does this emerging theoretical perspective, which insists that gender matters in historical analysis and which regards gender as a historical category relevant to understanding the development of modern science, have on scholarship in the history of psychology? In the past three years, it has prompted a quite radical change in my own thinking about the direction taken by American psychology as the discipline took shape in the first decades of the twentieth century. For the twenty years prior to this revisioning process, I had been studying the history of American psychology focusing on the forgotten women contributors to the field—their work, their lives, their experience. During that time, my scholarship was heavily influenced by developments in the field of women's history and especially the writing of Gerda Lerner.

A question I was often asked about the contributions of the early women psychologists was whether there was anything that marked or distinguished their work as feminine in contrast to the men's contributions to the field. My answer was "no." The women were different in that their work settings were for the most part women's colleges rather than universities, but in terms of the subject matter they studied and the publications they produced, they looked very much like the men in the field. I was later to revise my view on this for at least one of the early women, Mary Whiton Calkins, in regard to the system of self-psychology which she created (Furumoto, 1991). Nevertheless, looking back on this period, I now realize that the way I was thinking about this question presupposed that the psychological canon produced by men was unmarked or gender neutral and what I was searching for in the women's writing was for signs of a different—and more specifically a feminine—voice.

Only recently, after encountering the new gender studies already discussed, did the idea crystallize for me that the psychological corpus was itself gendered through and through and that its gender is predominantly masculine.[2] This is despite the fact that I had always known that most of the research and theory in the field had been produced by men, and that my research in the mid-1980s on the professionalization of psychology in the United States up to World War II had convinced me that the women in the field could best be described as "marginalized."

Although women had been present in the discipline in sizeable numbers from the late nineteenth century and some of them even managed to achieve eminence in their time, those who entered the discipline in its early years were severely restricted in access to academic positions and experienced sharp contradictions between the roles they were expected to fulfil as women on the one hand and as professionals on the other. Moreover, I concluded from my research that between the two world wars a gendered occupational hierarchy took shape in psychology with men predominating "in the higher status, more professionally pure academic realm of the discipline, while women found their place in the lower status, less pure practitioner roles" (Furumoto, 1987, p. 110). If one becomes persuaded, as I have become, that mainstream psychology—dominated by men—expresses a masculine viewpoint, it becomes easier to understand why a distinctly feminine voice is not readily discernible in the work of early women psychologists. Since mainstream and masculine became synonymous, those who were counted as contributors—female as well as male—were obliged to employ the same rhetoric.

But what tangible evidence is there to support the assertion that masculinity came to be embedded in American psychology as it established itself as a discipline in the twentieth century? Here one needs to bring together what historians of men have to say about the transformation of manhood in the late nineteenth century with a gendered approach to women's history and scholarship in the history of psychology. This is obviously a project that is still waiting to be done, and I will only be able to indicate by presenting a pair of examples how a gender model might serve as an interpretive approach to the history of psychology.

My first example examines an early rallying cry by a prominent male psychologist urging that the young discipline style itself an objective, natural science; the second considers the alienation from the discipline exhibited by a woman who was initially attracted to a career in psychology. Both examples, I suggest, can be linked to cultural patterns and ideals of femininity and masculinity in America during the Gilded Age and the Progressive Era.

Historians of men have pointed to what has been called a "crisis of masculinity" in late nineteenth- and early twentieth-century America (Bederman, 1993; Dubbert, 1980; Kimmel, 1987). One historian has described this era as a "time of disunity, of economic depression and labour strife, of immigrant workers and impoverished rural farmers challenging a predominantly Anglo-Saxon Protestant economic and social elite" (Trachentenberg, 1982, p. 16). Additionally, during this period of uncertainty and concern for the social group which psychologists were a part of, changes were occurring in middle-class men's work lives including diminished expectations for substantial career advancement and women's entry into the public sphere. Historian E. Anthony Rotundo (1993) maintains that this era also witnessed the emergence of a new ideal of manliness characterized by strenuous passion and primitive vigor with an emphasis on reasserting dominance. It was personified by the man who was re-elected president in a landslide victory in 1904, and who became one of the era's most acclaimed heroes, Theodore Roosevelt.

During these same years, American psychology was becoming institutionalized as a discipline with the establishment of laboratories and journals and in 1892, the founding of the American Psychological Association. In contrast with the relatively uncontested institutionalization of the discipline in the late nineteenth century, the effort to forge a substantive consensus turned the 1890s into a decade of extensive and rancorous debate (O'Donnell, 1985). There was disagreement among other things over whether psychology could or should become one of the natural sciences and whether it could or should find practical applications.

Eventually, American psychology would be won over by a conception of the discipline which was both scientistic and technologically oriented. A harbinger of that development was an address delivered in 1904 by one of the leading psychologists of the day, James McKeen Cattell, who used the prestigious platform of the St. Louis Exposition to proclaim psychology an objective, quantitative, experimental, and applicable natural science. It was a message warmly received by established men in the field as well as by the next generation of men psychologists (Sokal, 1993). It was also a conception of psychology that mirrored many aspects of the new ideal of manliness which exercised a powerful influence over Cattell and other middle-class men of his time.

For example, there is Cattell's thoroughgoing dismissal of introspection—which he pronounced both unnecessary and scientifically suspect—in his St. Louis address. Claiming most of the research carried out in his laboratory to be "nearly as independent of introspection as work in physics or in zoology" he insisted that "it is usually no more necessary for the subject to be a psychologist than it is for the vivisected frog to be a physiologist" (1904, p. 176). In commenting on Cattell's address, introspection was defined by another prominent psychologist as "the reflective analysis of what goes on in one's own mind" (Angell, 1905, p. 536). In everyday discourse, the term "introspection" would be interchangeable with the terms "reflection" and "contemplation."

Rotundo (1993) observes that in the late nineteenth century, men "began sorting themselves out into hardy, masculine types and gentle, feminine types" (p. 265) and that Cattell's generation "in particular—men born from the 1840s to the 1860s—became preoccupied with the contrast between the strong, assertive man and the gentle contemplative one" (p. 267). In this context, Cattell's disavowal of introspection, or reflective contemplation, may be viewed as stemming not so much from his alleged discovery that introspection was a scientifically undesirable approach to the production of psychological knowledge as from his identification with the new assertive ideal of manhood.

This explanation also fits well with what both Rotundo and Cattell's biographer, Michael M. Sokal, have to say about Cattell's preoccupations and personal style. Rotundo (1993), who targets Cattell as an exemplar of the assertive manly ideal, observes that "like other men of his time Cattell leaned on powerful new cultural types" (p. 267). To illustrate his point, Rotundo presents excerpts from Cattell's personal correspondence that express prominent themes in the newly emerging conception of manhood including fascination with body building and concern for a muscular body image, the idealization of what were commonly agreed to be male "instincts" such as lust and physical assertiveness, and worries that civilization was causing modern men to lose touch with their "animal nature."

Cattell also exhibited a disinclination, indeed aversion, to reflection coupled with an intense predilection for activity, another hallmark of the new masculinity. As Rotundo (1993) notes, middle-class men came to see "action—even unthinking action—as manly" (p. 224). Entertaining the notion that American psychology took on gendered features as its mostly male practitioners struggled to define their discipline in the late nineteenth and early twentieth centuries and that these gendered features were consonant with the new masculine ideal, also helps explain why some women, initially attracted by the idea of a career in psychology, became disenchanted with the field.

Estelle B. Freedman (1996) provides us with an intriguing example of this in her recently published biography of Miriam Van Waters who, after completing her doctorate at Clark in 1913, chose to pursue a career in social service rather than in social science. Freedman, a feminist social historian, became interested in Van Waters as a member of a vanguard—women who entered graduate study in the early twentieth century. While the proportion of doctorates awarded to women rose from 11 percent in 1910 to 30 percent in 1980, women's proportion of college faculty peaked in 1940 at 28 percent and it was not until 1989 that the proportion of women faculty reached 30 percent (Freedman, 1994). Freedman says that she often wondered why, given the influx of women into the ranks of Ph.D. holders, "American women seemed not to persist in the academy" (p. 196).

Factors that have been cited as contributing to the levelling off of the proportion of women in the academy include: discrimination in the universities—especially in the sciences; limited opportunities for women faculty to reproduce themselves, leading to a lack of female role models; and devaluation by research universities of teaching, in which women excelled. While testifying to the ample evidence supporting the claim that a variety of discriminatory practices operated to exclude women from academic careers, Freedman (1994) advances another reason for attrition. She maintains that a close study of the lives of women such as Van Waters who entered graduate study early in the twentieth century "suggests that women sometimes rejected the university as much as it rejected them" (p. 197).

In the case of Miriam Van Waters, who entered Clark University in the fall of 1910 as a doctoral candidate in psychology with G. Stanley Hall as her mentor, a progressive disillusionment with both the fledgling science and her venerable advisor eventually propelled her out of the academic discipline. Born in 1887, the daughter of an Episcopal minister, Van Waters grew up in Portland, Oregon, and later attended the University of Oregon where she completed an undergraduate degree majoring in philosophy. Staying on to work toward a master's degree in philosophy, Van Waters taught psychology classes and began to entertain the idea of an academic career. Acting on the recommendation of one of her professors, Van Waters applied to Clark University in Worcester, Massachusetts, where she was admitted as a doctoral student in psychology and awarded a fellowship.

The founder of Clark University, Jonas Clark, and its first president, the psychologist G. Stanley Hall, were in solid agreement that it should remain the preserve of men. As late as 1909, Hall wrote privately "I am strongly opposed to giving women the slightest foot-hold in the college, even if we could do so under the Founders will" (Freedman, 1996, p. 36). Practical considerations, however, such the loss of possible bequests, led Hall to persuade the Clark trustees in 1910 to allow women to enrol in the graduate programs while courses at Clark College remained open exclusively to men.

Thus, in the fall of 1910, Miriam Van Waters became one of the first women admitted to graduate studies at Clark. At first Van Waters was very enthusiastic about her mentor, characterizing him in one letter to her parents a few months after her arrival as "that clear-thinking, logical man of science" (Freedman, 1996, p. 37). But Van Waters was also beginning to be aware of discrimination at Clark and soon joined together with other university women who sought each other out in response to the hostile climate, "sharing both horror stories and moments of triumph" (Freedman, 1996, p. 41). By February, Van Waters found herself struggling to resist Hall's demands for intellectual conformity and expressing dismay over the blind loyalty of his students. In letters to her mother she complained that Hall used "his tractable students to collect data of all kinds, which later he combines" and that if one did not choose to work on "one of *Dr. Hall's* problems—one got nothing out of him" (Freedman, 1996, p. 46).

Van Waters also found herself at odds with the new scientific psychology— especially with its emphasis on objectivity—preferring the older philosophical school with its broader humanistic approach. Dejected by the knowledge that "a trained psychologist measuring heartbeats in a laboratory experiment in attention, memory, fatigue etc. is rated higher in the modern academic world than the most oracular of living philosophers," Van Waters became convinced that doing a dissertation in psychology depended too much "on one's ability to dissect thoroughly one inch of reality" (Freedman, 1996, p. 46–47). Moreover, she questioned the wisdom of harnessing herself "to some sort of mental peanut, and by much straining and groaning—lift it from the ground' " (Freedman, 1996, p. 47).

In sharp contrast to her progressive disenchantment with Hall and psychology during her first year at Clark, Van Waters found inspiration in reading two recent works of the social reformer and founder of Hull House, Jane Addams, that summarized her approach to social reform through community services. Returning home to spend the summer of 1911 with her family in Oregon provided Van Waters a respite from her struggles with Hall and the opportunity to reexamine her values through talking with her mother about the works of Jane Addams which had impressed her so deeply. Van Waters's mother was also able to express her concerns about Miriam's future and the possibility that her graduate school education might make her "too learned" to serve others (Freedman, 1994, p. 204).

That summer after her first year in graduate school proved to be a turning point for Van Waters. Although she continued to work with Hall for another year before switching advisors and fields—anthropologist Alexander Chamberlain would be her dissertation advisor—she exhibited a more independent stance toward Hall and a more optimistic outlook about her situation and surroundings. In the end her dissertation work with Chamberlain, a politically engaged scholar who like Jane Addams "placed research in the service of social progress" (Freedman, 1996, p. 50), linked Van Waters to the world of social service. Visits to the Boston Juvenile Court while she was working on her dissertation, which included case studies of delinquent adolescent girls, led her to consider career possibilities outside of academia. Following what Van Waters called her "great emancipation" from Clark in 1913, she embarked on a distinguished life-long career devoted to social service—first working in the juvenile court system for two decades and then, from 1932 until her retirement in 1957, serving as superintendent of the Massachusetts Women's Reformatory in Framingham (Freedman, 1994, p. 208).

Freedman (1996) argues that the primary force steering Van Waters away from a career in academic psychology to one devoted to social service can be found in her ties to the nineteenth-century women's reform tradition. Transmitted most directly in Van Waters's case by her mother's influence and by her reading of Jane Addams's work, the female reformers in this movement "spoke a language of gender" (p. xii). Drawing "upon a rhetoric of maternalism, emphasizing women's public roles as mothers," these women worked within "nineteenth-century female voluntary organizations that provided social services to poor women and children" (p. xii). Miriam Van Waters's career, Freedman concludes, illustrates what became of this female reform tradition in the twentieth century. Van Waters—along with others among the new breed of highly educated, socially conscious, professional women—applied her training to movements for social change.

In conclusion, I have attempted in this paper to draw attention to an emerging theoretical perspective that impresses me as a fruitful avenue for historians of psychology to explore. I am not insisting that the gender theoretical approach is the only or even the best way for historians of psychology to go about their work. But I am optimistic about its potential contribution to historical understanding and think that it may prove to be, in the words of one of its practitioners, "truly transformative, making known elements fall together—as in a kaleidoscope—in an entirely new pattern" (Cott, 1990, p. 208).

NOTES

1. There is, of course, an ongoing feminist critique of modern science which emphasizes the importance of gender and gender norms. For example, Evelyn Fox Keller (1992) calls them "silent organizers" of scientific knowledge and scientific practice and claims that their work remains silent to the degree that "norms associated with masculine culture are taken as universal" (p. 17). However, although Keller and other contributors to the feminist critique of science affirm that gender is socially constructed, they have not examined how gender has functioned as a historical category subject to change.

2. Interestingly enough, this is in spite of the fact that I was quite familiar with feminist critiques of science expressing this very idea stretching back at least to Virginia Woolf's statement almost sixty years ago in *Three Guineas*: "Science it would seem is not sexless; she is a man, a father, and infected too" (cited in Harding & O'Barr, 1987, p. 1).

REFERENCES

Angell, J. R. (1905). Psychology at the St. Louis Congress. *The Journal of Philosophy, Psychology, and Scientific Methods, 2,* 533–546.

Bederman, G. (1993). Civilization, the decline of middle-class manliness, and Ida B. Wells's antilynching campaign (1892–94). In B. Melosh (Ed.), *Gender and American history since 1890* (pp. 207–239). London: Routledge.

Bederman, G. (1995). *Manliness and civilization: A cultural history of gender and race in the United States, 1880–1917.* Chicago: University of Chicago Press.

Benjamin, M. (1993). A question of identity. In M. Benjamin (Ed.), *A question of identity: Women, science, and literature* (pp. 1–21). New Brunswick, NJ: Rutgers University Press.

Carnes, M. C., & Griffen, C. (Eds.). (1990). *Meanings for manhood: Constructions of masculinity in Victorian America.* Chicago: University of Chicago Press.

Cattell, J. M. (1904). The conceptions and methods of psychology. *Popular Science Monthly, 66,* 176–186.

Connell, R. W. (1995). *Masculinities.* Berkeley: University of California Press.

Cott, N. F. (1990). On men's history and women's history. In M. C.

Carnes & C. Griffen (Eds.), *Meanings for manhood: Constructions of masculinity in Victorian America* (pp. 205–211). Chicago: University of Chicago Press.

Dubbert, J. L. (1980). Progressivism and the masculinity crisis. In E. H. Pleck & J. H. Pleck (Eds.), *The American man* (pp. 303–320). Englewood Cliffs, NJ: Prentice-Hall.

Freedman, E. B. (1994). Social science or social service? Miriam Van Waters and the dilemmas of graduate education for women in the Progressive Era. In S. Ware (Ed.), *New viewpoints in women's history: Working papers from the Schlesinger Library 50th anniversary conference, March 4–5, 1994* (pp. 196–213). (Available from The Arthur and Elizabeth Schlesinger Library on the History of Women in America, Radcliffe College, 10 Garden Street, Cambridge, MA 02138.)

Freedman, E. B. (1996). *Maternal justice: Miriam Van Waters and the female reform tradition.* Chicago: University of Chicago Press.

Furumoto, L. (1987). On the margins: Women and the professionalization of psychology in the United States. In M. G. Ash & W. R. Woodward (Eds.), *Psychology in twentieth-century thought and society* (pp. 93–113).

Furumoto, L. (1991). From "paired associates" to a psychology of self: The intellectual odyssey of Mary Whiton Calkins. In G. A. Kimble, M. Wertheimer, & C. White (Eds.), *Portraits of pioneers in psychology* (pp. 56–72). Washington, DC: American Psychological Association.

Harding, S., & O'Barr, J. F. (Eds.). (1987). *Sex and scientific inquiry.* Chicago: University of Chicago press.

Keller, E. F. (1992). *Secrets of life, secrets of death: Essays on language, gender, and science.* New York: Routledge.

Kessler-Harris, A. (1994). Reflections on a field. In S. Ware (Ed.), *New viewpoints in women's history: Working papers from the Schlesinger Library 50th anniversary conference, March 4–5, 1994* (pp. 19–28). (Available from The Arthur and Elizabeth Schlesinger Library on the History of Women in America, Radcliffe College, 10 Garden Street, Cambridge, MA 02138).

Kimmel, M. S. (1987). The contemporary "crisis" of masculinity in historical perspective. In H. Brod (Ed.), *The making of masculinities: The new men's studies* (pp. 121–153). Boston: Allen & Unwin.

Kimmel, M. S. (1996). *Manhood in America: A cultural history.* New York: The Free Press.

Mosse, G. L. (1996). *The image of man: The creation of modern masculinity.* New York: Oxford University Press.

Nye, R. A. (1993). *Masculinity and male codes of honour in modern France.* New York: Oxford University Press.

O'Donnell, J. M. (1985). *The origins of behaviorism: American psychology, 1870–1920.* New York: New York University Press.

Rotundo, E. A. (1993). *American manhood: Transformations in masculinity from the Revolution to the modern era.* New York: Basic Books.

Sokal, M. M. (1993). *The man of science in modern America: James McKeen Cattell, 1860–1944.* Unpublished manuscript.

Trachtenberg, A. (1982). *The incorporation of America: Culture and society in the Gilded Age.* New York: Hill & Wang.

Chapter Five

Cultural Diversity, Contextualism, and Feminist Psychology

Hope Landrine

In recent years, psychology as a whole and feminist psychology in particular have focused greater attention on cultural diversity and on the need to integrate such diversity into teaching, theory, research, and practice. There has been an enormous increase in the past ten years in publications reporting ethnic differences on a variety of behaviors relevant to feminist, social, clinical, health, and developmental psychology (Dana, 1993; Goodchilds, 1991; Jones, 1991; Sue, 1991). Although the sheer amount of data on ethnic differences continues to mount, theories regarding those differences have not. Instead, research on ethnic differences remains strikingly atheoretical relative to research on all other topics, including research on gender differences (Jones, 1991). Typically, researchers simply investigate the extent to which ethnic groups differ on some scale or behavior without predicting the nature and direction of those differences and without presenting a theoretical model of why such differences should or would exist. The ensuing ethnic differences are then reported without meaningful theoretical explanation, or with simplistic speculations about the cultures of others (Jones, 1991; Sue, 1991). Reporting ethnic differences without theoretical explanation belittles culture and simultaneously exploits it as a commodity for publication purposes and career advancement in the Zeitgeist of multiculturalism. Reporting ethnic differences with speculative remarks about the cultures of others derides and dismisses culture, and it simultaneously re-"discovers" exotic "natives" and "primitives" whose "difference" maintains the very social arrangements ostensibly challenged by the focus on diversity (hooks, 1992).

Thus, the evidence on ethnic differences continues to mount, and most psychologists take it for granted (rightfully so) that this evidence has important implications for their knowledge and interventions. Simultaneously and nonetheless, however, explanations for the differences have not been forthcoming, and the absence of such theoretical models reflects and perpetuates the marginal status of culture in psychology. Indeed, unlike all other topics in the discipline, ethnicity alone remains without

Hope Landrine, "Introduction: Cultural Diversity, Contextualism, and Feminist Psychology." In H. Landrine (Ed.), *Bringing Cultural Diversity to Feminist Psychology,* pp. 1–20. © 1995 by the American Psychological Association. Reprinted with permission.

theory: There is no general theory of the relation between culture and behavior; there is no unified model of cultural differences; there is no framework for psychologists to use to make sense of the multitude of ethnic differences in the literature (Jones, 1991),and that may be precisely why integrating data on diversity into research, teaching, and practice remains difficult.

The challenge for psychology in this increasingly multicultural society and the major problem that psychologists in the next century must solve is to develop an explicit, theoretical framework through which sociocultural variables and differences will be rendered coherent. I see this as the most important problem for psychology in a multicultural society for three reasons. First, the model through which psychologists understand cultural variables will shape the structure and content of research on cultural diversity for decades to come, just as the implicit, deficit model[1] has in the past. Second, the model through which psychologists understand cultural differences will define the place of culture in psychology and will either justify its current relegation to the periphery or place it squarely in the center of the science. Finally, like the implicit, deficit model before it, the model psychology develops for understanding cultural differences likewise will play a major role in public attitudes toward minorities and in the perception, status, and the treatment of people of color in American society.

Thus, psychology as a whole and feminist psychology in particular need a model for understanding cultural variables, a theory of the relationship between culture and behavior that neither romanticizes cultures nor renders difference deviance. In this chapter I argue that contextualistic behaviorism is one such possible model for psychology as a whole and specifically for feminist psychology. This is because contextualism provides a simple but radical model not only for understanding culture and ethnicity but also for understanding gender. First, I describe the concept and understanding of "behavior" that dominates modern psychology and other social sciences and highlight the manner in which this way of thinking about behavior has hampered the understanding of ethnicity. That approach is then contrasted with the contextualistic approach, and the advantages of the latter are emphasized.

Two Ways of Defining Behavior

There are two ways that one can think about behavior, and both stem from the two radically different definitions of the word *behavior* that B. F. Skinner offered in his classic 1938 book, *Behavior of Organisms*. The first way that one can think about and understand the term *behavior* has been called *mechanistic* (Biglan, Glasgow, & Singer, 1990; Hayes & Hayes, 1992; Morris, 1988; Pepper, 1942), and this view dominates psychology as well as several other disciplines.

Mechanistic Behaviorism

The mechanistic way of conceptualizing behavior is based on Skinner's (1938) definition of behavior as "the movement of an organism or of its parts" (p. 6). Here, behavior is defined as superficial, mechanical movements, and the name for a behavior is based on the precise features of those movements. For example, reading a newspaper is a movement with specific features and therefore is a type of behavior. Not looking someone in the eye is a movement with specific features and is another type of behavior. Being aggressive or being passive likewise are both highly specific sequences of mechanical movements and are additional types of behavior. Behavior is defined and labeled in terms of the precise features of superficial mechanical movements irrespective of the context in which such movements occur. Reading a newspaper is a type of behavior and is the same type of behavior irrespective of the political, social, or cultural context in which it appears. Thus, picking up a newspaper and reading it while riding the subway on one's way to work, and picking up a newspaper and reading it in the middle of a serious discussion with one's significant other on a topic one does not want to hear about are the same behavior, regardless of these different contexts. Certainly, different contingencies surround these two episodes of reading the newspaper; the episodes have different causes or motives and most would agree with that. Nonetheless, the behavior or operant[2] is "reading the newspaper" in both cases. The essence of mechanistic behaviorism then is the assumption that movements have a meaning and a label, and have one and the same meaning and label, regardless of the context in which they are exhibited.

This mechanistic view of behavior dominates psychology, feminist psychology, and most other social sciences, irrespective of whether scholars and clinicians consider themselves to be behaviorists or to have a behavioral theoretical orientation. When researchers study aggression or aggressive behavior, they define that operant as a specific set of superficial, mechanical movements abstracted from their context. When they study depression or depressive behavior, achievement behavior, passive behavior, leadership behavior, risky sexual behavior, or any other behavior, researchers typically mean specific constellations of superficial, mechanical movements that have a label regardless of their context. The name for these various movements is assumed to be inherent in the movements themselves. Behaviors are assumed to have one and only one label and meaning that they carry with them like designer luggage across time, race, ethnicity, gender, social class, age, and international borders.

When one defines and understands behavior as superficial-mechanical movements with an inherent meaning irrespective of context, one produces a multitude of types or categories of behavior out there in the world. This way of thinking produces a social world filled with a multitude of behavioral types—of behavioral shoes that everyone everywhere can and does walk in. From this perspective, then, any person of any culture or ethnicity who engages in the specific set of movements is by definition engaging in the "same behavior" regardless of its different sociocultural contexts. When an African American woman does not look a person in the eye, an Asian American woman does not look a person in the eye, and a European American woman does not look a person in the eye, they are all necessarily engaging in precisely the same behavior. When African American, Asian American, Native American, and European American women make self-belittling remarks, they are all engaging in the same behavior, a priori. Because they are understood as engaging in the same behavior regardless of their different sociocultural contexts, they can be compared; one can compare women of different ethnic groups and ask if they differ in the frequency or prevalence of a specific behavior. The answer often is affirmative.

Implications of Mechanistic Behaviorism

This way of conceptualizing and defining behavior has several serious consequences and implications for understanding culture and ethnic groups. First, the only reason that researchers can compare ethnic groups at all is that they have defined *behavior* as inherently meaningful, superficial, context-free movements. Behavior has to be removed from its sociocultural context and defined and labeled independent of that context in order for people of different ethnic groups—people from different sociocultural and historical contexts—to be compared. All data on ethnic differences in feminist psychology, women's studies, sociology, psychology, public health, and several other disciplines is this kind of data. Evidence of differences in the frequency and prevalence of superficial mechanical movements believed to have the same meaning irrespective of their sociocultural, political, and historical context constitutes knowledge of cultural diversity and of gender differences as well. The first serious consequence of the mechanistic view of behavior then is that it makes ethnic comparisons—and gender comparisons—possible.

In addition, by defining and understanding behavior as movements irrespective of context, the mechanistic view relegates culture and context to the periphery and renders them superfluous. The sociocultural, historical, and political context is not an integral part of the label for and definition of behavior but is instead something outside of it, something surrounding it. Thus, for example, gender stratification (i.e., the sociocultural context of women's powerlessness relative to men) is not part of the label researchers attribute to women's behavior but is instead understood as being outside of women's behavior, as a larger setting in which women's behavior occurs. Movements labeled *dependent*, for example, when engaged in by women or by men, are understood as the same behavior with the same label and meaning, and women's powerlessness does not alter that label for those movements. Women and men can be compared and women "discovered" to engage in dependent behaviors more frequently. Likewise, cultural contexts are not part of the definition and label of the behavior of people of color but instead are understood as being outside of it.

Thus, the mechanistic view creates a bifurcated world of types of behavior on the one hand, and sociocultural contexts from which they can be differentiated on the other. The context is not part of behavior but is instead understood as a place, as a mere setting in which behavior occurs. The context is viewed as a setting that impinges on behavior like a mechanistic force, changing the intensity, frequency, and probability of a behavior, but not the name and meaning of it. When researchers speak of "understanding behavior in its context" (something most endeavor to do), they mean that they invoke the ostensible forces of the context post hoc to explain the frequency or intensity of a behavior understood as exhibited within that context;

the context and its forces nonetheless are conceptualized as being outside of and impinging on behavior and are not part of the name for it. The second serious consequence of the mechanistic view of behavior then is that it relegates the sociocultural, historical, and political context to the periphery of human action by making said context fully independent of the name for or meaning of the type of behavior viewed as merely occurring within it.

Finally, the third consequence of this view is that it creates, it produces ethnic differences and, indeed, gender differences as well. Race, ethnicity, culture, and gender are the most robust and complex of social, cultural, political, and historical contexts. When one defines *behavior* as mechanistic movements irrespective of these contexts, ethnic and gender differences in behavior so defined necessarily are found and exist only by virtue of that definition.

In summary, the mechanistic view of behavior manufactures the ethnic and gender "differences" that it struggles incessantly to explain. This ongoing production of a hierarchy of behavioral differences[3] reproduces and reinforces existing social hierarchies and thus perpetuates the very social arrangements purported to be challenged by the focus on differences. People of color and women are invited and encouraged to speak and write about their differences in a celebration of diversity because the ensuing hierarchy of difference maintains their low statuses. As bell hooks (1990) put it, "[the new] unprecedented support among scholars and intellectuals for the inclusion of [diversity] is a 'celebration' that fails to ask who is sponsoring the party and who is extending the invitations" (pp. 54–55). Diversity, in the current vernacular, is yet another "bandwagon" construct, Mednick's (1989) term for regressive, political constructs in psychological garb that masquerade as liberal, political change.

Thus, the bifurcated world created by the mechanistic behaviorism that dominates social science has not advanced the analysis of gender and culture. Instead, it has reduced the complex, chaotic contexts and positions of gender and culture to superficial, context-free behavioral differences that reinforce racist, patriarchal, and capitalist ideology.

Contextualistic Behaviorism

The alternative way of thinking about behavior has been called *contextualistic behaviorism* or *contextualism* (Biglan et al., 1990; Hayes & Hayes, 1992; Morris, 1988; Rosnow & Georgoudi, 1986). This way of thinking is based on the alternative definition of the term *behavior* that Skinner gave in his 1938 book, and indeed, it appeared on the same page as the mechanistic definition. The alternative definition he gave was that behavior refers to "an organism . . . having commerce with the world" (Skinner, 1938, p. 6). In this definition, behavior is a meaningful exchange with, in, and by virtue of a context. Behavior and its context are a single unit. The operant is not a superficial-mechanical movement irrespective of context but a highly specific act-in-context. The context is therefore part of the name for the behavior, for the act-in-context. Consequently, from this perspective, a movement does not have a single label and meaning but several different labels and meanings, depending on the context in which it appears, because that context is part of what the behavior-in-context is called.

For example, from a contextualistic perspective, picking up a newspaper and reading it on the subway on one's way to work, and picking up a newspaper and reading it when one's significant other raises a topic that one does not want to hear about are *not* the same behavior; they are not both "reading the newspaper" because their contexts are different. The first behavior is "killing time on the subway" or "avoiding the potentially hostile strangers on the subway by not looking at them and pretending to be busy," where the context is part of the name of the behavior. The second behavior is "ignoring one's partner" or "letting one's partner know that one does not want to have this conversation," where the context is again part of the name of the behavior. When defined contextually, these are two different behaviors despite the similarity of the superficial-mechanical movements entailed. These two acts-in-context are responses to (elicited by) different stimuli, are maintained by different consequences, and elicit different responses from others. Thus, most people probably would not respond with anger at their significant other for picking up a newspaper and reading it on the subway on her or his way to work. However, most people probably would respond with some anger at a significant other who picks up a newspaper and reads it in the middle of a serious conversation; picks up a newspaper and reads it at the table during a holiday dinner; picks up a newspaper and reads it in synagogue or church; or picks up a newspaper and reads it while making love. In the psychology of people's everyday lives, they do not label and understand behavior as superficial movements. Instead, people think contextually; they use the context to tell them what the behavior is, what it means, and how to respond. Thus, most people would reject the idea that a partner who picked up a newspaper and started reading it in the middle of a serious discussion was simply, merely "reading the newspaper," and indeed would insist that the behavior was everything but that.

The assumptions of contextualistic behaviorism can now be made explicit. First, from this perspective, behaviors have no inherent label or meaning, no matter how obvious, there-on-the-surface, self-evident, and inherent in superficial-mechanical movements such a label and meaning may appear to be. Instead, the label for a behavior is to be discovered empirically through a careful analysis of the context in which the behavior occurs, with this context as part of the behavior's name. Silence can be "respect for my teachers," "avoiding being hit by my violent husband," or "distrust of outsiders," depending on the social, cultural, and historical context in which the superficial movement "silence" occurs. Not looking someone in the eye can be "showing respect for my elders," "ignoring the speaker," "paying close attention to the speaker," or "avoidance of the Navajo monster 'He-who-kills-with-his-eyes,'" depending on the cultural, historical, and political context of the individual who does not look others in the eye. The name for a behavior is to be discovered empirically by analyzing the context, and the name is given (not by the movement but) in its context.

Finally, the third and most important assumption of contextualism is that superficially similar mechanical movements appearing in different contexts are not the same behavior. They are different behaviors, unless an empirical analysis of their discriminative stimuli, correlates, and contingencies indicates otherwise. As radical as this latter view may seem at first, it has ample empirical support. For example, studies have shown that even among White American couples and families of the 1980s, whether a movement is labeled as hitting, helping, aggression, or affection is contingent, not on the act, but on the structure and form of the relationship in which it occurs, on the context. These labels and meanings are socially constructed and negotiated in relationships. The manner in which these labels are applied to specific movements does not generalize across relationships of various types, such that these labels are by and large independent of the movements themselves (see Gergen & Gergen, 1983; Greenblat, 1983; Harre, 1981; Kayser, Swinger, & Cohen, 1984; Lasswell & Lasswell, 1976; Mummendey, Bonewasser, Loschper, & Lenneweber, 1982; Tedeschi, 1984). Such data suggest that people appear to understand behavior contextually; psychologists' ability to predict and understand behavior, and feminist psychologists' understanding of such gender-related behaviors as aggression, hitting, and helping, can be facilitated by a similar contextual approach.

Implications of Contextualism

The implications of this view for culture are clear. From this perspective, ethnic groups (as well as women and men) engaged in similar superficial movements must be assumed to be engaged in different behaviors, because their sociocultural contexts are different. Ethnic minority groups therefore cannot be compared with European Americans or with each other because there is no common behavior on which to compare them. Ethnic groups (and women and men) cannot be compared unless researchers can demonstrate empirically that the context of the movements, and so the label and meaning of the behavior, is the same. This perspective assumes that there are no ethnic (or even gender) differences in behavior. What researchers have understood to be ethnic or gender differences in the frequency or intensity of a decontextualized, superficial movement are not ethnic or gender differences at all; they are different acts in different contexts.

Contextualistic Analysis and Intervention: Two Examples

How can researchers conduct research or therapists perform clinical work from this perspective? Although somewhat more time-consuming, one can approach behavior contextually by following these four steps. First, begin with the assumption that, when one is observing members of cultures other than one's own, one does not know what kind of behavior one is observing. One does not know what it is called or what it means; one assumes that what the behavior is called and means is an empirical question. Second, examine the sociocultural context of the behavior and gather as much information as possible about the antecedents, contingencies, and correlates of the behavior in that context. Third, use the context to define and label the behavior under investigation as a specific act-in-context. Finally, manipulate and modify the contingencies of the context to create change. I next provide two brief examples of this process to elucidate these points.

Example 1: Gender × Ethnic Differences in Unprotected Anal Intercourse

Recent studies have shown that the prevalence of AIDS among young Latinas is significantly higher than for other Gender × Ethnic groups (e.g., Mays & Cochran, 1988). Other studies (e.g., Singer et al., 1990) have shown that this ethnic difference is in part a function of differences in the frequency of engaging in unprotected anal intercourse (with intravenous drug abusers in particular). This risky sexual behavior appears to be frequent among young, unmarried, heterosexual Latinas, but infrequent among heterosexual women of other ethnic groups. Researchers who have reported this Ethnic × Gender difference in behavior among heterosexual women did not predict such findings and offered no theoretical model of why these differences should or would be found.

The standard, mechanistic-behavioral approach to reducing AIDS among this population would be to define the problematic behavior to be modified in this case as unprotected anal intercourse. By the term *unprotected anal intercourse* one would mean a highly specific sequence of movements that anyone anywhere can engage in, with these movements presumed to have the same label and meaning irrespective of their sociocultural context. In the absence of a theoretical model of the unpredicted ethnic difference in behavior so defined, researchers have resorted to a deficit model in which they have suggested that young Latinas are deficient in information about the risks entailed in this sexual behavior and therefore require culturally tailored AIDS education (e.g., Mays & Cochran, 1988). Yet, other studies have shown that young Latinas are well aware of how AIDS is transmitted. Singer et al. (1990), for example, found that Latinos knew as much about the transmission of AIDS as other ethnic groups. Although Latinos did hold the additional erroneous belief that AIDS could be transmitted through casual contact, they nonetheless knew that unprotected vaginal or anal intercourse with anyone, and with intravenous drug abusers in particular, was dangerous and was a means of transmitting AIDS. They were not deficient in AIDS information.

If the problem is not a lack of information about AIDS transmission, the solution is not to send health educators to Latino communities to provide such information in a culturally sensitive manner. Where, then, does one go from here? How do researchers intervene to change behavior and to save lives by so doing? The traditional, mechanistic-behavioral approach (a) has produced titillating ethnic differences that cannot be explained; (b) has manufactured exotic "primitives" whose cultural "difference" is readily translated as a (sexual) "deviance" that reinforces existing social arrangements and racist ideology; and (c) has left researchers and educators without a way to intervene.

The alternative approach, the contextual approach, begins with the assumption that the name for this behavior is to be discovered empirically through a careful analysis of its context and of its highly contextual contingencies. The first step is to discover what the behavior-in-context is and what it means by observing the behavior and its correlates and consequences, as well as by talking informally to the young Latinas who engage in it. Arguello (1993) and her colleagues at the Center for the Study of Latino Health in Los Angeles did precisely that. What they found was that these young unmarried Latinas (many of whom were gang members) were engaging in anal intercourse in order to maintain their virginity. As unmarried, Roman Catholic, Mexican American women, they wanted to be (and men demanded that they be) virgins when they finally got married, but their boyfriends were demanding intercourse. Anal intercourse was a solution to these contradictory Gender $\times$ Culture demands; it was a way to have intercourse with, yet still remain a virgin for, boyfriends who demanded both in a Culture $\times$ Gender $\times$ Age $\times$ Class context (working-class gang community) where the consequences of failing to meet men's sexual demands are aversive. Condoms were not used because condoms were conceptualized as a means of birth control and birth control is not an issue when intercourse is anal.

When contextually defined, when understood as an act-in-context, the behavior here is not unprotected anal intercourse except in the most superficial way of thinking about complex human beings. For these particular Latinas, the behavior was "trying to maintain virginity for, but still have intercourse with, men who are demanding both," and that surely is not the behavior gay men engage in when they exhibit similar, superficial, mechanical movements. Comparisons across groups on superficially similar movements cannot be made because the acts-in-context are different behaviors and have different meanings. The contingencies that control the behavior also differ for different groups. For these particular Latinas, the contingency was the aversive consequences of losing one's virginity before one is married in a cultural context where women's virginity is valued and the Virgin Mary is a powerful symbol. For these specific Latinas, the consequence of losing one's virginity before marriage was that one may render oneself un-marry-able and bring shame on one's family. That contingency was viewed by Arguello's (1993) sample as more aversive than the possibility of contracting AIDS.

When viewed in its context, there is no need to attribute information deficits to these Latinas. Instead, by defining the behavior contextually as "trying to maintain virginity for and simultaneously have intercourse with men who demand both," the culturally specific contingencies that elicit and maintain this behavior-in-context are obvious, as are several contextualistic and culturally specific interventions entailing manipulating those contingencies. At the simple level, the intervention can stress the need to use condoms without addressing the act-in-context. At a more fundamental level, the intervention must be a feminist one that addresses virginity, the sexual double standard, and young Latinos' control of Latinas' sexuality. Arguello (1993) and her colleagues began doing that in a series of feminist workshops on Virginity as Social Control, Virginity as Oppression, and Who Owns Latinas' Bodies? These workshops are led by feminist, Latina health educators who, like Arguello, are former gang members and so are not only well attended and effective but popular in the community. This intervention has a far greater potential to succeed than a standard AIDS education intervention and is extraordinarily effective according to Arguello's preliminary data.

Feminist workshops on the concept of virginity as a way to reduce AIDS among Latinas occurred to these researchers only because they defined behavior contextually. Such an intervention would be irrelevant to gay men because the act-in-context that they engage in may be superficially similar to, but nonetheless is totally unrelated to, the act-in-context of these Latinas.

Example 2: Gender × Ethnic Differences in Cigarette Smoking among Adolescents

Cigarette smoking is still one of the most preventable causes of illness and death in the United States. Data indicate that 80–90 percent of children and adolescents have smoked at least one cigarette, that 20–40 percent of them are regular smokers, and that smoking as a child or adolescent is the best predictor of being a chronic, regular smoker as an adult (Klonoff, Fritz, Landrine, Riddle, & Tully-Payne, 1994; Landrine, Klonoff, & Fritz, 1994; Landrine, Richardson, Klonoff, & Flay, 1994). Consequently, interventions designed to prevent smoking are typically directed toward children and adolescents (Landrine, Klonoff, & Fritz, 1994). Ethnic, gender, and Gender × Ethnicity differences in the prevalence of cigarette smoking among children and adolescents have been found in which smoking is lowest among ethnic minority boys and girls (who also have a later onset of smoking than European Americans) and highest among European American girls, while steadily decreasing among European American boys. Indeed, despite the plethora of smoking prevention programs in elementary, middle, and high schools, smoking appears to be increasing among European American girls and teenagers alone (Lynch & Bonnie, 1994).

This Gender × Ethnic difference in cigarette smoking was not predicted by the various researchers who have reported it, and little theoretical explanation for why European American girls would smoke more than other groups has been offered. Thus, a way to intervene to decrease and prevent smoking among these girls (a Gender × Culture-Specific program) does not suggest itself. As previously, this is because the behavior has been defined and understood as the superficial, mechanical, decontextualized movement 'smoking," a movement presumed to have the same label and meaning irrespective of the context in which it appears. Smoking is understood as a type of behavior that girls and boys of any ethnicity can and do engage in, and therefore unpredicted Gender × Ethnic differences in behavior so defined have emerged.

The alternative, contextualistic approach is to empirically discover the label for and meaning of this behavior by observing the correlates and consequences of it for the European American girls who engage in it, in their context. Those contextual correlates and consequences can then be modified in a Gender × Culture intervention. Using this approach, Camp, Klesges, and Relyea (1993) discovered that European American girls who smoked also were engaged in chronic, perpetual dieting, were obsessed with their weight and physical appearance, and smoked to reduce and control their appetites, eating, and subsequent weight. Their nonsmoking cohorts, as well as ethnic minority girls and boys and European American boys, did not share these weight concerns and so did not smoke; those who did smoke did not do so for weight reduction and were not on diets.

When approached contextually, the behavior here is not 'smoking," except in the most superficial understanding of these European American girls and teenagers. Instead, the behavior is "one more self-destructive way to keep my weight down." The contingencies maintaining this act-in-context are loss of male attention and affection in response to girls' weight and loss of self-esteem, name-calling, belittling, distancing, ostracism, and other negative responses to girls' obesity in the cultural context of European American teenagers, their parents, their role models, and their culture's messages. These contingencies are viewed as more aversive (in that context) than the destructive health consequences of smoking.

Although Camp, Klesges, and Relyea (1993) did not suggest a new, Gender × Ethnicity-Specific intervention for these girls, such an intervention is obvious. The intervention must be a purely feminist one that focuses on complex issues about weight among European American girls and women and on the self-destructive things that they do (dieting, self-starvation, vomiting, smoking) to control their weight. Such an intervention is likely to be more successful for this specific Gender × Ethnic group than the standard educational intervention that teaches children to resist peer pressure to smoke. This is because peers are only a variable when the behavior is "trying to fit in with my peers and look cool," and that is not the behavior that these girls (or that ethnic minority boys and girls) engage in when smoking (Landrine, Richardson, et al., 1994). Likewise, exercise, something that is not included in standard smoking prevention programs for adolescents, also must be discussed and encouraged as a healthy means of controlling weight, provided that the European American girls in question are actually overweight. This new intervention would be irrelevant to ethnic minority girls and boys who smoke, as well as to European American boys who smoke, because the act-in-context differs for these groups.

Advantages of Contextualism

Rather than obstructing social scientists' understanding of and ability to predict and modify behavior, contextualism facilitates new and deeper understandings and new, more effective interventions. In addition, by defining behavior contextually, social scientists do not manufacture politically functional ethnic and gender differences that can be exploited to maintain the status quo; they do not produce a hierarchy of behavioral difference that justifies existing social hierarchies, and they do not discover primitives whose existence maintains their masters' positions. Contextualism, then, is one possible model for understanding culture and gender. Contextualism argues that the relationship between behavior and its context is a simple one in which culture and context are an essential part of the behavior of all people. The view that the appropriate label for and meaning of behavior is to be found in its sociocultural context is one that has the potential to advance the understanding of all behavior, especially of behavior in various ethnic and gender contexts.

The suggestion that the label for and meaning of a behavior depend on its sociocultural context does not mean that a variety of behaviors do not exist in certain contexts or cultures. I am not suggesting that anal intercourse and cigarette smoking do not exist in certain cultures. Rather, the point is that understanding and interventions are advanced and improved more by viewing smoking and anal intercourse as acts-in-context than by approaching these behaviors mechanistically. Certainly, both the mechanistic and the contextual approach to behavior are viable. However, the mechanistic approach examines the mere surface structure, the grammar of behavior, and simultaneously serves regressive political purposes. The contextual approach examines the deep structure, the syntax of behavior, and thereby challenges ideological representations and exploitation of diversity.

Contextualism and the Future of Feminist Psychology

Data on women's diversity are by and large anomalous insofar as they fail to fit neatly into current conclusions regarding gender differences. In light of that, the major question raised is, Can such anomalous data be integrated into the existing paradigm of feminist psychology and women's studies?

For example, a plethora of studies indicate that the extended, sociocentric experience of the self (and its ethic of care) is the most prevalent way of experiencing the self among people of color (Heelas & Locke, 1981; Landrine, 1992; Shweder & Bourne, 1982). Specifically, data suggest that the extended or sociocentric self characterizes the experiences of Asian American men and women (e.g., DeVos, 1985; Marsella, DeVos, & Hsu, 1985), Native American men and women (e.g., Strauss, 1977), Latino men and women (e.g., Gaines, 1982), and African American men and women in particular (Haraway, 1986; Nobles, 1976; Stack, 1986). Can these data be integrated into a feminist psychology that regards the sociocentric self and its morality as inherently "womanly" experiences that stem from women's unique, early interactions with mothers (e.g., Bordo, 1986, 1990; Chodorow, 1978; Flax, 1986, 1990; Gilligan, 1977; Lykes, 1985)? Can such anomalous data be sprinkled like an exotic spice on textbooks and articles without radically changing the flavor of the assumptions, the issues and styles defined as women's, and therefore the agenda beneath?

I suggest that the answer to these questions is no and yes, depending on the direction that feminist psychology takes in the future. One direction is to retain the paradigmatic assumption that gender by and large can be understood without reference to context and that feminist psychology's knowledge therefore is knowledge of gender per se. If psychologists choose to persist in that belief, then the answer is "no, cultural diversity cannot be integrated into feminist psychology." This is because, to persist in the belief that knowledge that is based almost solely on studies of middle-class, European American women and men is knowledge of gender, while readily admitting that women of color are cultural products, is to render culture exotic, superfluous, and relevant to people of color alone. To persist with such an assumption is to continue the implicit belief that European American cultures are not relevant to the behavior of European Americans. In the context of such beliefs, women and men of color can be understood only as exceptions to feminist psychology's knowledge of gender.

Alternatively, feminists can modify their beliefs. Their paradigmatic assumption can be changed to the view that gender cannot be understood without reference to context. To give this assumption more than the perfunctory nod that it has been afforded, to regard it with a seriousness currently lacking, is to render European American cultures powerful, problematic contexts requiring analysis. Feminists have not yet done so; they have not begun to analyze the role of European American cultures in the gender behavior of European American women and men. The failure to do so is the best empirical evidence that the purpose of focusing on cultural diversity at present is not to analyze and reveal culture in behavior but to manufacture politically functional "differences."

Thus, for example, articles increasingly offer hypotheses regarding the role of the culturally specific values and beliefs of minorities in minority behavior, but similar analyses for European American samples are not conducted, even though the plethora of scales assessing values and politics were standardized on them. Acculturation and ethnic identity scales are increasingly used as measures of cultural context in studies of people of color, but middle-class European American samples are rarely required to complete these as well, although such scales for them exist (e.g., Helms, 1990). Similarly, feminist researchers have begun to address the role of poverty in the behavior of poor women, but have they ever analyzed the role of financial security and privilege in that of others? Indeed, Camp, Klesges, and Relyea (1993) failed to analyze, expose, and render problematic the middle-class European American values, beliefs, and cultural practices surrounding gender and weight that lead young White girls to smoke, vomit, and starve themselves, even though such an analysis was appropriate. Exotic, problematic cultural differences specific to middle-class European Americans are hidden or neglected in favor of a focus on the differences of people of color. European American values of individualism, autonomy, control, and a belief in rights, liberty, the self, self-fulfillment, opposites, and progress have yet to fully be analyzed as the lathe of European American gender, gender differences, and gender politics.

Despite vigorous protests to the contrary, then, feminist researchers do not yet believe that context is truly relevant to understanding gender, for if they did, the European American contexts that characterize most samples would be addressed as the source of their differences from people of color. Likewise, feminist researchers do not yet believe that culture is an integral part of behavior, for if they did, the abundance of studies of gender among European Americans would explore the relevant, explanatory cultural beliefs and practices entailed. Indeed, if feminists truly believed that culture and context were relevant to gender, studies of European American women and men would analyze the extent to which being Jewish, Irish, Italian, or Greek accounts for the variance found within White samples. Consequently, feminist psychologists have yet to relinquish the paradigmatic assumption that they deny embracing, viz., that European American gender is gender per se.

Thus, to bring cultural diversity to feminist psychology requires not only a focus on the cultures of others but a focus on European American cultures. As long as "cultural diversity" means "how those minorities are different" (from whom?), diversity discourse eloquently eludes addressing, yet quietly maintains, existing social arrangements. Until the focus on culture regards European American cultures as being as salient and in need of analysis as the cultures of others, cultural diversity belittles culture while exploiting it. Culture will be regarded with dignity and the sociology of knowledge altered only when European American cultures are treated like all others. As bell hooks (1990) put it, cultural diversity

> is always an issue of Otherness that is not white; it is black, brown, yellow, red, purple even [and thereby is] a discourse on race that perpetuates racial domination. . . . Few . . . scholars are being awarded grants to investigate and study all aspects of white culture from a standpoint of "difference"; doesn't this indicate just how tightly the colonizer/colonized paradigm continues to frame the discourse on race and the "Other"? (pp. 54–55)

Alternatively, then, I also suggest that, "yes, culture can be integrated into feminist psychology," but if and only if all cultures are subjected to a similar analysis, the diversity of cultures of European Americans (lumped together as "White") first and foremost.

Culture is not just an additional variable that demarcates the local limits of otherwise universal gender-related principles and gender differences, nor is it simply an additional, moderating variable whose inclusion will allow researchers to account for a larger percentage of the variance in human behavior. Rather, culture is us, it is each of us, and thus only it can be known, revealed, and discovered in social science. Researchers need to understand that European American culture is the structure and content of feminist psychology and is the only thing that is discovered and revealed in feminist data, constructs, therapies, and theories on gender. Challenging researchers to understand feminist data in this manner argues for and demonstrates the benefits of contextualism as a philosophy of science for a multicultural feminist psychology.

NOTES

1. The term *deficit model* refers to the tendency to interpret ethnic differences as deficits, deviances, pathologies, and problems within minorities (see Jones, 1991).

2. Operants are movements or behaviors that are voluntarily exhibited, as opposed to respondents, which are movements or behaviors that are involuntary (e.g., blinking and other reflexes).

3. The differences researchers discover typically reveal that ethnic minorities, women, the poor, and other subordinate groups have a higher prevalence of behaviors understood to be deviant, pathological, less functional, less healthy, less normal, and the like. Differences discovered always produce a psychological hierarchy in which the Other occupies a lower

status than the dominant group. This psychological hierarchy of difference matches and reinforces existing social hierarchies.

REFERENCES

Arguello, M. (1993, February). *Developing outreach programs for AIDS prevention with Latino youth*. Paper presented at the Institute for Health Promotion and Disease Prevention Research, University of Southern California Medical School, Los Angeles.

Biglan, A., Glasgow, R. E., & Singer, G. (1990). The need for a science of larger social units: A contextual approach. *Behavior Therapy, 21*, 195–215.

Bordo, S. (1986). The Cartesian masculinization of thought. *Signs, 11*, 439–456.

Bordo, S. (1990). Feminism, postmodernism, and gender skepticism. In L. J. Nicholson (Ed.), *Feminism/postmodernism* (pp. 133–156). New York: Routledge & Kegan Paul.

Camp, D. E., Klesges, R. C., & Relyea, G. (1993). The relationship between body weight concerns and adolescent smoking. *Health Psychology, 12*, 24–32.

Chodorow, N. (1978). *The reproduction of mothering: Psychoanalysis and the sociology of gender*. Berkeley: University of California Press.

Dana, R. H. (1993). *Multicultural assessment perspectives for professional psychology*. New York: Allyn & Bacon.

DeVos, G. (1985). Dimensions of the self in Japanese culture. In A. J. Marsella, G. DeVos, & F. Hsu (Eds.), *Culture and the self: Asian and western perspectives* (pp. 141–184). New York: Tavistock.

Flax, J. (1986). Gender as a social problem: In and for feminist theory. *Amerikastudien/American Studies, 31*, 193–213.

Flax, J. (1990). Postmodernism and gender relations in feminist theory. In L. J. Nicholson (Ed.), *Feminism/postmodernism* (pp. 39–62). New York: Routledge & Kegan Paul.

Gaines, A. (1982). Cultural definitions, behavior and the "person" in American psychiatry. In A. J. Marsella & G. M. White (Eds.), *Cultural conceptions of mental health and therapy* (pp. 167–192). London: Reidel.

Gergen, K., & Gergen, M. (1983). The social construction of helping relationships. In J. D. Fisher, A. Nadler, & B. DePaulo (Eds.), *New directions in helping* (Vol. 1). San Diego, CA: Academic Press.

Gilligan, C. (1977). In a different voice: Women's conception of the self and of morality. *Harvard Educational Review, 47*, 481–517.

Goodchilds, J. D. (1991). *Psychological perspectives on human diversity in America*. Washington, DC: American Psychological Association.

Greenblat, C. S. (1983). A hit is a hit is a hit . . . or is it? In D. Finkelhor, R. Gelles, & M. Straus (Eds.), *The dark side of families: Current family violence research*. Beverly Hills, CA: Sage.

Haraway, D. (1986). The curious coincidence of feminine and African moralities: Challenges for feminist theory. In E. Kittay & D. Meyers (Eds.), *Women and morality*. Totowa, NJ: Rowman & Allenheld.

Harre, R. (1981). Expressive aspects of descriptions of others. In C. Antaki (Ed.), *The psychology of ordinary explanations*. San Diego, CA: Academic Press.

Hayes, S. C., & Hayes, L. J. (1992). Some clinical implications of contextualistic behaviorism. *Behavior Therapy, 23*, 225–249.

Heelas, P., & Locke, A. (1981). *Indigenous psychologies: The anthropology of the self*. San Diego, CA: Academic Press.

Helms, J. E. (1990). *Black and white racial identity.* New York: Greenwood.

hooks, b. (1990). *Yearning: Race, gender, and cultural politics.* Boston: Gloria Watkins/South End Press.

hooks, b. (1992). Eating the other. In b. hooks, *Black looks: Race and representation* (pp. 21–39). Boston: Gloria Watkins/South End Press.

Jones, J. M. (1991). Psychological models of race: What have they been and what should they be? In J. D. Goodchilds (Ed.), *Psychological perspectives on human diversity in America* (pp. 3–46). Washington, DC: American Psychological Association

Kayser, E., Swinger, T., & Cohen, R. (1984). Laypersons' conceptions of social relationships. *Journal of Social and Personal Relationships, 1,* 433–458.

Klonoff, E. A., Fritz, J. M., Landrine, H., Riddle, R. W., & Tully-Payne, L. (1994). The problem and sociocultural context of single cigarette sales. *Journal of the American Medical Association, 271,* 618–620.

Landrine, H. (1992). Clinical implications of cultural differences: The referential v. the indexical self. *Clinical Psychology Review, 12,* 401–415.

Landrine, H., Klonoff, E. A., & Fritz, J. M. (1994). Preventing cigarette sales to minors: The need for contextual, sociocultural analysis. *Preventive Medicine, 23,* 322–327.

Landrine, H., Richardson, J. L., Klonoff, E. A., & Flay, B. (1994). Cultural diversity in the predictors of adolescent cigarette smoking: The relative influence of peers. *Journal of Behavioral Medicine, 17,* 331–346.

Lasswell, T., & Lasswell, M. (1976). I love you but I'm not in love with you. *Journal of Marriage and Family Counseling, 38,* 211–224.

Lykes, M. B. (1985). Gender and individualistic v. collectivist bases for notions of self. *Journal of Personality, 53,* 356–383.

Lynch, B. S., & Bonnie, R. J. (1994). *Growing up tobacco free: Preventing nicotine addiction in children and youths.* Washington, DC: Institute of Medicine, National Academy Press.

Marsella, A. J., DeVos, G., & Hsu, F. (1985). *Culture and self: Asian and western perspectives.* New York: Tavistock.

Mays, V. M., & Cochran, S. D. (1988). Issues in the perception of AIDS risk and risk reduction activities by Black and Hispanic/Latina women. *American Psychologist, 43,* 949–957.

Mednick, M. (1989). On the politics of psychological constructs: Stop the bandwagon, I want to get off. *American Psychologist, 44,* 1118–1123.

Morris, E. K. (1988). Contextualism: The world view of behavior analysis. *Journal of Experimental Child Psychology, 46,* 289–323.

Mummendey, A., Bonewasser, M., Loschper, G., & Lenneweber, V. (1982). It is always somebody else who is aggressive. *Zeitschrift für Sozialpsychologie, 13,* 341–355.

Nobles, W. W. (1976). Extended self: Rethinking the so-called "Negro" self concept. *Journal of Black Psychology, 2,* 2–8.

Pepper, S. C. (1942). *World hypotheses: A study in evidence.* Berkeley: University of California Press.

Rosnow, R. L., & Georgoudi, M. (1986). *Contextualism and understanding in behavioral science.* New York: Praeger.

Shweder, R., & Bourne, E. J. (1982). Does the concept of the "person" vary cross-culturally? In A. J. Marsella & G. M. White (Eds.), *Cultural conceptions of mental health and therapy* (pp. 97–137). London: Reidel.

Singer, M., Candida, F., Davison, L., Burke, G., Castillo, Z., Scanlon, K., & Rivera, M.

(1990). SIDA: The economic, social and cultural context of AIDS among Latinos. *Medical Anthropology Quarterly, 4,* 72–114.

Skinner, B. F. (1938). *Behavior of organisms.* New York: Appleton-Century-Crofts.

Stack, C. (1986). The culture of gender: Women and men of color. *Signs, 11,* 321–324.

Strauss, A. S. (1977). Northern Cheyenne ethnopsychology. *Ethos, 5,* 326–357.

Sue, S. (1991). Ethnicity and culture in psychological research and practice. In J. D. Goodchilds (Ed.), *Psychological perspectives on human diversity in America* (pp. 47–86). Washington, DC: American Psychological Association.

Tedeschi, T. (1984). A social psychological interpretation of human aggression. In A. Mummendey (Ed.), *Social psychology of aggression.* Berlin: Springer-Verlag.

Part II

The Study of Difference

Reflecting fluctuating currents in the wider society (Rosenberg, 1992), psychological research has sometimes been guided by the presumption that there are no significant psychological differences between men and women, and sometimes by the presumption that there are. Twenty-five or thirty years ago, it was not unusual for investigators (usually male) to conduct studies using exclusively male samples and then generalize their results to the population at large, implying that they applied to women as well as men.[1] For instance, in constructing his developmental scale of moral judgment, Lawrence Kohlberg drew on the writings of Western male philosophers and on interviews with adolescent and adult males.[2] When in subsequent research women were tested against this standard, their responses were sometimes found to be wanting (inferior to the men's) or uncodable (and thus inaudible).[3] Such results seemed to some to support the suspicions of earlier psychologists (Sigmund Freud and Jean Piaget, for example) that women's grasp of justice was weaker than men's. Similarly, when stimuli that aroused achievement motivation in men failed to do so in women, it was inferred that women had less need to achieve and more "fear of success" than men did. As is so often the case, differences between groups (whether selected on the basis of sex, race, or class) were interpreted as deficiencies among members of the less powerful group or as justifying the status quo: thus, if women fear success, perhaps they should seek therapy or, on the other hand, perhaps they should stay home.

It is small wonder, then, that women psychologists (and most of the gender research was and is conducted by women) began to question the value of research on "sex differences." As Alice H. Eagly points out in her chapter, these researchers often shared the assumption that men and women were fundamentally the same. They had embarked on this research not to demonstrate but to discredit assertions of difference. They hoped that their work would contribute to the cause of equality for women by showing that gender stereotypes were invalid, thus removing any empirical basis for discrimination. This enterprise was problematic from the start, because, of course, one cannot confirm a "no-difference" hypothesis, one can only disconfirm a hypothesized difference—and even this proved to be difficult, because, as Eagly reports, often the data seemed to support rather than refute the stereotypes. Furthermore, if one's aim is to achieve a "gender-blind" society and guarantee true equality, any study of gender differences is likely to seem counterproductive. Roy F. Baumeister (1988), for example, for whom "the ultimate goal is presumably a sex-neutral psychology of people, not separate psychologies of men and women," argues that "by reporting and discussing sex differences, psychology contributes to the persistence of discrimination" (p. 1093). In 1996, lawyers for Virginia Military Institute (VMI) called on "expert witnesses" to evoke "different voice theory" (see Part IV) in support of their case against the admission of women students. After hearing this testimony, a Fourth Circuit judge allowed as "a finding of fact" VMI's claim that "men prefer adversarial environments" while women put "greater emphasis on relationships and cooperation" (Nussbaum, 1997).[4]

In spite of such events, Eagly believes, as Sandra Scarr (1988) puts it, that "cowardice about . . . gender differences will lead us nowhere" (p. 56). Eagly argues that to refrain from investigating gender differences out of fear that our results might lend support to our political enemies is bad science; good scientists stick to the rules of objective inquiry. Opponents of difference research contend, however, that much of this work is not only bad politics but bad science. Until recently, much of the "catalogue of differences" reported in the literature was accumulated in a haphazard fashion, emerging serendipitously from studies without a central focus on gender, "a byproduct," as Ellen Berscheid (1993) says, "of wider and more traditional issues of concern to psychologists" (p. vii). According to some psychologists, when we routinely analyze data for gender differences that were not predicted, while ignoring other equally plausible but less easily ascertainable "subject variables" (classification variables), we seem to be *assuming* that gender makes a difference, rather than *asking* whether it does or not. And, because there were no theoretical grounds for predicting serendipitous findings of difference, there was no good way of interpreting them, especially given the chaos of the catalog, with some investigators reporting gender differences in a particular domain while others did not: a 1974 review of the literature on sex differences in achievement motivation in undergraduate women, for instance, called it a "now-you-see-it-now-you-don't phenomenon" (Alper, 1974).

Critics argue that findings of differences in behavior based on sex category, even when obtained from studies designed to obtain them, are fundamentally uninterpretable; they are "merely descriptive." As Bernice Lott (1996) says, "It is the task of scientific psychology to study the necessary and sufficient conditions under which such culturally-selected behaviors are learned and practiced and not simply to catalogue all the ways in which some members of two groups of people sometimes differ from one another" (p. 155). Sex category, as Baumeister (1988) and others (e.g., Yoder & Kahn, 1993) point out, is not a true independent variable: one cannot randomly assign subjects to one sex category or the other, keeping all other variables constant.[5] Because sex category is a multidimensional variable, composed of a multitude of characteristics and experiences, a finding that men and women differ tells us nothing about why they differ. Is it social status? Hormones? Differential maternal child-rearing practices?[6] One or more or none of the above?

Although findings of gender difference supply little by way of answers, they can serve as useful starting points for elucidating the processes involved. Suppose we find that women are more empathic than men. We might then look for differences in early experiences of boys and girls: for instance, do mothers talk more to their daughters than their sons about feelings? Here, "gender" serves as an initial "proxy" variable. But, some argue, why bother with gender at all? "Why the detour?" Baumeister asks. "One might profitably start by focusing on the true causal variable"

(1988, p. 1094). But when we have little idea of the "true causal variable," as is often the case, cannot gender serve as an initial clue? Perhaps, but if our primary concern is to study how behaviors are learned, rather than whether or not one gender learns them more thoroughly than another (as Lott suggests), then why not begin with the behavior in question rather than with gender? Why not, for instance, divide one's subjects on the basis of their scores on a measure of empathy, ignoring gender, and look for differences between the early experiences of high and low scorers? Lott (1996) cites a study by Mark A. Barnett and colleagues (1980) showing that similar experiences seemed to enhance empathy in both men and women; this being so, to begin with a comparison of men and women does indeed seem to be an unnecessary detour.

But sometimes the conditions under which behaviors are learned and practiced are different for men and women. Although "main effects" of gender tell us little or nothing about process, interactions between gender and other variables can tell us a great deal. For instance, Eleanor E. Maccoby (see chapter 36 of this volume) cites the finding (Jacklin & Maccoby, 1978) that preschool girls, when paired with other girls, were are least as active as boys paired with boys, but when paired with boys, the girls "frequently stood on the sidelines and let the boys monopolize the toys." "Passivity," here, is not a feminine essence but an aspect of girls' behavior in a particular situation. Studies of this sort, as well as the meta-analyses Eagly describes, support Eagly's contention that research on gender differences need not ignore context, as critics have claimed it inevitably does, and that systematic research can reveal the "contextual patterning" that lies beneath the apparent chaos of a catalogue of differences. As Eagly says, these contextual patterns constitute "an invitation to theory building" that might lead us to discover "the necessary and sufficient conditions under which such . . . behaviors are learned and practiced," in Lott's phrase, or, in Candace West and Don H. Zimmerman's (chapter 6 in this volume) more radical social constructivist view, the interactional contexts in which specific gender differences are actually "created."[7]

Nonetheless, findings of difference, even when contextually qualified, remain problematic. Relative differences, often small differences, when reported and re-reported, have a tendency to turn into absolute dichotomies. Consider our description of the results of the Jacklin and Maccoby study in the previous paragraph: we speak of "preschool girls," "the boys," and "the girls," but a statistically significant difference can occur in spite of considerable overlap in scores. We cannot assume *all* "the girls" were less active than their male partners; some may have followed the boys' predominant pattern, and some of the boys may have looked more like the girls. These complexities tend to disappear in the telling, and, especially when the media take up the tale, the exaggeration of gender differences seems almost inescapable.

The underestimation of diversity within gender is as perilous as the overestimation of diversity between genders: "All women are women," writes the philosopher Elizabeth Spelman, "but there is no being who is only a woman" (1988, p. 102). Psychologists (often feminists) have been accused by other psychologists (usually feminists) of ignoring race, class, sexual preference, and other aspects of women's identities and constructing a "normative woman," based on data obtained largely from white, middle-class, well-educated, heterosexual research participants bearing a striking resemblance to themselves. Pamela Reid and Elizabeth Kelly (1994) note that although "feminist researchers have worked diligently for more than 20 years to dispel the assumption that essential human behavior could be represented by one group of humans, that is, men," the same researchers appear to have accepted the notion that the behavior of white, middle-class women can be assumed to be typical of all women (p. 478). Indeed, Reid and Kelly assert that "researchers often wish so strongly to find similarities among differing groups of women that they create them" by selecting homogeneous samples: "For example, when issues of self-esteem, sexual harassment, employment equity, body image, and techniques for therapy are studied, Asian women, African-American women, or Latinas are rarely examined" (p. 479).[8]

Although it is disrespectful of diversity to treat all women as alike, it is also disrespectful to ignore diversity within marginalized groups. For instance, all lesbians may be lesbians—although that phrase is ambiguous, given the variations along the "continuum of lesbian existence" (Rich, 1980)—but no lesbian is only a lesbian. Within any category there is diversity, but without categorization we cannot practice psychology. (We cannot, in fact, even think.) Taken to its logical extreme, as Jane Roland Martin (chapter 1 of this volume) points out, a prohibition against categorization would make it impossible to describe even a single individual, because the "same" individual (especially the postmodern individual) behaves differently at different times in different situations. "Acknowledging that whatever categories we use will mask some differences," Martin concludes, "we can decide to use ones that uncover the differences we consider most important and that best fit our practical and theoretical purposes."

Whenever we compare any two groups (such as men versus women or black women versus white women) we run the risk of treating one of the two, usually the less powerful and prestigious one, as "other," as a deviation from the norm. For this reason, among others, psychologists have increasingly turned to "noncomparative studies." The authors of *Women's Ways of Knowing* (Belenky, Clinchy, Goldberger, & Tarule, 1986/1997), for instance, deliberately chose to listen only to the voices of women, on the grounds that when the male voice intrudes it becomes the standard and the women's voices are heard, if they are heard at all, as deviations from the male voice. Although this work is based entirely on interviews with women, it was widely described as a study of "sex differences," presumably because when gender categories are perceived as binary opposites, as they typically (often unconsciously) are, it is difficult to see why one would speak of "women's" ways of knowing unless to contrast them with men's ways. But much can be learned about gender (or race or class or any other social category) by focusing only upon members of a single category, observing "how they behave within their own social context, not as they exist relative to other groupings who may operate in a different social context" (Yoder & Kahn, 1993, 848).

For instance, Lyn M. Brown and Carol Gilligan's (1992) longitudinal research, carried out in a private school for girls, provides a rich account of the increasing dissociation from themselves and from authentic relationship experienced by a particular group of girls, in a particular social context, as they move from childhood into adolescence. The authors cast their tale in terms of gender (it matters that these are girls), but not in terms of sex differences. Readers of the book may ask, But would it be different for boys? Brown and Gilligan need not and do not answer this question, but their work may provoke others to undertake comparable investigations of the development of boys in specific settings. Such research would be welcome, for in assembling the material for this book we found far richer material of this sort on growing up female than on growing up male.

Studies of exclusively male samples were common in the past, of course, but the results were assumed to apply universally, regardless of gender or context. Feminist critiques of this approach led psychologists to include females in their samples and to analyze their data in terms of gender differences. But the results of "difference research" turned out to be equally problematic for women. In an essay published in 1967, the psychoanalyst Karen Horney asserted that "the psychology of women hitherto represents a deposit of the desires and disappointments of men" (1967, p. 56). Some argue that this is still the case, that the qualities in women that are "discovered" through difference research were put there by men. In an androcentric society (and, at least in the past, as Laurel Furumoto reminds us, an androcentric discipline), men have the privilege of defining the nature of women, and they have defined it in terms of their own interests. For instance, it benefits men to construct women as nurturant and averse to competition, so that women can raise the children and attend to the domestic chores; although many women may accept or even welcome this construction, they did not choose it. We have no idea what a psychology of women would look like in a society where women were considered equal to men.

Our understanding of the psychology of men would also be enhanced by noncomparative studies. When we focus only upon behaviors that distinguish boys and men from girls and women, the picture that emerges is of a "single masculinity," a "hegemonic masculinity" constructed, as R. T. Connell (1987) puts it, "in relation to various subordinated masculinities as well as in relation to women" (p. 183). This creates an ideal that most men fail to attain, leading to "painful, even catastrophic, consequences" (Jefferson, 1994, p. 12), among them, according to Joseph Pleck (chapter 29 of this volume), "self-hatred." Pleck argued in that essay, first published twenty years ago, that "patriarchy is a *dual* system both in which men oppress women, and in which men oppress themselves and other men," and he called for a "systematic examination of the implications of patriarchal culture for men" comparable to the feminist analysis of its implications for women. One effect of patriarchal culture has been the subordination of deviant masculinities. Systematic examination of variations in behavior, attitudes, and experiences among a variety of individual men, in a variety of contexts, might reveal the range of masculinities masked by the hegemonic ideal. We are beginning to see an increase in such research, in the wake of the recent upsurge of interest in the "psychology of men," institutionalized in 1995 as a division of the American Psychological Association.

NOTES

1. One of us remembers that around that time her graduate school advisor advised her to select only men as participants in an experiment she was about to undertake, because "women's responses are too variable," making it difficult to obtain significant results.

2. As will become increasingly apparent to readers wending their way through this book, the use of such terms as "men" and "women" or "male" and "female" is problematic, and so, echoing the French feminist writer Hélène Cixous, we ask that "every time [we] say 'masculine' or 'feminine,' or 'man' or 'woman,' please use as many quotation marks as you need to avoid taking these terms too literally" (1987, p. 1).

3. Whether Kohlberg's scale is biased against women is a matter of controversy. See Gilligan's chapter in this volume, Walker (1984), and Baumrind (1986) for a variety of views.

4. A number of the psychologists cited entered an *amicus curiae* brief arguing that their findings had been misinterpreted.

5. Baumeister admits that this is true of all subject-variables—personality characteristics like introversion–extroversion, for example—but he claims that these are more "precise" than sex category. Readers may or may not agree.

6. Researchers who compare men and women are aware, of course, that gender is not a true independent variable, but when they report global gender differences in behavior they may leave the impression that "gender" *causes* the differences. Although investigators may profess themselves agnostic with respect to the source of the difference, making no claim that biology or early experience have laid down an immutable male and female "essence," this research seems to many to play into an essentialist view of gender as an internal individual characteristic, and to suggest that biological "sex" is involved.

7. West and Zimmerman, however, might not endorse a strategy of comparing males and females.

8. On the other hand, they assert, women of color are selected as a comparison sample to whites, "for investigations of deviant female behavior" such as welfare mothering, teenage pregnancy, homelessness, and criminality (Reid & Kelly, 1994, p. 479).

REFERENCES

Alper, T. (1974). Achievement Motivation in College Women: A Now-You-See-It-Now-You-Don't Phenomenon. *American Psychologist, 29,* 194–203.

Barnett, M. A., Howard, J. A., King, L. M., & Dino, G. A. (1980). Antecedents of Empathy. *Personality and Social Psychology Bulletin, 6,* 361–365.

Baumeister, R. F. (1988). Should We Stop Studying Sex Differences Altogether? *American Psychologist, 43,* 1092–1095.

Baumrind, D. (1986). Sex Differences in Moral Reasoning: Response to Walker's (1984) Conclusion That There Are None. *Child Development, 57,* 511–521.

Belenky, M. F., Clinchy, B. M., Goldberger, N. R., & Tarule, J. M. (1986/1997). *Women's Ways of Knowing: The Development of Self, Mind and Voice.* New York: Basic Books.

Berscheid, E. (1993). Foreword. In A. E. Beall & R. J. Sternberg (Eds.), *The Psychology of Gender* (pp. vii–xvii). New York: Guilford Press.

Brown, L. M., & Gilligan, C. (1992). *Meeting at the Crossroads: Women's Psychology and Girls' Development.* Cambridge, MA: Harvard University Press.

Cixous, Hélène. (1987), Reaching the Point of Wheat, Or, Portrait of the Artist as a Maturing Woman. *New Literary History, 19 (1),* 1–22.

Connell, R. T. (1987). *Gender and Power.* Stanford, CA: Stanford University Press.

Horney, K. (1967). *Feminine Psychology,* ed. H. Kelman. New York: Norton.

Jacklin, C. N., & Maccoby, E. E. (1978). Social Behavior at Thirty-Three Months in Same-Sex and Mixed-Sex Dyads. *Child Development, 49,* 557–569.

Jefferson, Tony. (1994). Theorizing Masculine Subjectivity. In T. Newburn & E. A. Stanko (Eds.), *Men, Masculinities and Crime* (pp. 10–31). New York: Routledge.

Lott, B. (1996). Politics or Science? The Question of Gender Sameness/Difference. *American Psychologist, 51,* 155–156.

Nussbaum, E. (1997, January). The Group. *Lingua Franca,* 22–24.

Reid, P. T., & Kelly, E. (1994). Research on Women of Color: From Ignorance to Awareness. *Psychology of Women Quarterly, 18,* 477–486.

Rich, Adrienne. (1980). Compulsory Heterosexuality and Lesbian Existence. *Signs, 5,* 631–659. Reprinted in E. Abel & E. K. Abel (Eds.), *The Signs Reader: Women, Gender, and Scholarship.* Chicago: University of Chicago Press, 1983.

Rosenberg, R. (1992). *Divided Lives: American Women in the Twentieth Century.* New York: Hill and Wang.

Scarr, S. (1988). Race and Gender as Psychological Variables. *American Psychologist, 43,* 56–59.

Spelman, E. V. (1988). *Inessential Woman: Problems of Exclusion in Feminist Thought.* Boston: Beacon Press.

Walker, L. J. (1984). Sex Differences in the Development of Moral Reasoning: A Critical Review. *Child Development, 55,* 677–691.

Yoder, J. D., & Kahn, A. S. (1993). Working toward an Inclusive Psychology of Women. *American Psychologist, 48,* 846–850.

Chapter Six

Doing Gender

Candace West and Don H. Zimmerman

In the beginning, there was sex and there was gender. Those of us who taught courses in the area in the late 1960s and early 1970s were careful to distinguish one from the other. Sex, we told students, was what was ascribed by biology: anatomy, hormones, and physiology. Gender, we said, was an achieved status: that which is constructed through psychological, cultural, and social means. To introduce the difference between the two, we drew on singular case studies of hermaphrodites (Money 1968, 1974; Money and Ehrhardt 1972) and anthropological investigations of "strange and exotic tribes" (Mead 1963, 1968).

Inevitably (and understandably), in the ensuing weeks of each term, our students became confused. Sex hardly seemed a "given" in the context of research that illustrated the sometimes ambiguous and often conflicting criteria for its ascription. And gender seemed much less an "achievement" in the context of the anthropological, psychological, and social imperatives we studied—the division of labor, the formation of gender identities, and the social subordination of women by men. Moreover, the received doctrine of gender socialization theories conveyed the strong message that while gender may be "achieved," by about age five it was certainly fixed, unvarying, and static—much like sex.

Since about 1975, the confusion has intensified and spread far beyond our individual classrooms. For one thing, we learned that the relationship between biological and cultural processes was far more complex—and reflexive—than we previously had supposed (Rossi 1984, especially pp. 10–14). For another, we discovered that certain structural arrangements, for example, between work and family, actually produce or enable some capacities, such as to mother, that we formerly associated with biology (Chodorow 1978 versus Firestone 1970). In the midst of all this, the notion of gender as a recurring achievement somehow fell by the wayside.

Our purpose in this article is to propose an ethnomethodologically informed, and therefore distinctively sociological, understanding of gender as a routine, methodical, and recurring accomplishment. We contend that the "doing" of gender is undertaken by women and men whose competence as members of society is hostage to its production. Doing gender involves a complex of socially guided perceptual, interactional, and micropolitical activities that cast particular pursuits as expressions of masculine and feminine "natures."

When we view gender as an accomplishment, an achieved property of situated conduct, our attention shifts from matters internal to the individual and focuses on interactional and, ultimately, institutional arenas. In one sense, of course, it is individuals who "do" gender. But it is a situated doing, carried out in the virtual or real presence of others who are presumed to be oriented to its production. Rather than as a property of individuals, we conceive of gender as an emergent feature of social situations: both as an outcome of and a rationale for various social arrangements and as a means of legitimating one of the most fundamental divisions of society.

To advance our argument, we undertake a critical examination of what sociologists have meant by *gender,* including its treatment as a role enactment in the conventional sense and as a "display" in Goffman's (1976) terminology. Both *gender role* and *gender display* focus on behavioral aspects of being a woman or a man (as opposed for example, to biological differences between the two). However, we contend that the notion of gender as a role obscures the work that is involved in producing gender in everyday activities, while the notion of gender as a display relegates it to the periphery of interaction. We argue instead that participants in interaction organize their various and manifold activities to reflect or express gender, and they are disposed to perceive the behavior of others in a similar light.

To elaborate our proposal, we suggest at the outset that important but often overlooked distinctions be observed among *sex, sex category,* and *gender. Sex* is a determination made through the application of socially agreed upon biological criteria for classifying persons as females or males.[1] The criteria for classification can be genitalia at birth or chromosomal typing before birth, and they do not necessarily agree with one another. Placement in a *sex category* is achieved through application of the sex criteria, but in everyday life, categorization is established and sustained by the socially required identificatory displays that proclaim one's <u>membership</u> in one or the other category. In this sense, one's sex category presumes one's sex and stands as proxy for it in many situations, but sex and sex category can vary independently; that is, it is possible to claim membership in a sex category even when the sex criteria are lacking. *Gender,* in contrast, is the activity of managing situated conduct in light of normative conceptions of attitudes and activities appropriate for one's sex category. Gender activities emerge from and bolster claims to membership in a sex category.

We contend that recognition of the analytical independence of sex, sex category, and gender is essential for understanding the relationships among these elements and the interactional work involved in "being" a gendered person in society. While our primary aim is theoretical, there will be occasion to discuss fruitful directions for empirical research following from the formulation of gender that we propose.

We begin with an assessment of the received meaning of gender, particularly in relation to the roots of this notion in presumed biological differences between women and men.

Perspectives on Sex and Gender

In Western societies, the accepted cultural perspective on gender views women and men as naturally and unequivocally defined categories of being (Garfinkel 1967, pp. 116–18) with distinctive psychological and behavioral propensities that can be predicted from their reproductive functions. Competent adult members of these societies see differences between the two as fundamental and enduring—differences seemingly supported by the division of labor into women's and men's work and an often elaborate differentiation of feminine and masculine attitudes and behaviors that are prominent features of social organization. Things are the way they are by virtue of the fact that men are men and women are women—a division perceived to be natural and rooted in biology, producing in turn profound psychological, behavioral, and social consequences. The structural arrangements of a society are presumed to be responsive to these differences.

Analyses of sex and gender in the social sciences, though less likely to accept uncritically the naive biological determinism of the view just presented, often retain a conception of sex-linked behaviors and traits as essential properties of individuals (for good reviews, see Hochschild 1973; Tresemer 1975; Thorne 1980; Henley 1985). The "sex differences approach" (Thorne 1980) is more commonly attributed to psychologists than to sociologists, but the survey researcher who determines the "gender" of respondents on the basis of the sound of their voices over the telephone is also making trait-oriented assumptions. Reducing gender to a fixed set of psychological traits or to a unitary "variable" precludes serious consideration of the ways it is used to structure distinct domains of social experience (Stacey and Thorne 1985, pp. 307–8).

Taking a different tack, role theory has attended to the social construction of gender categories, called "sex roles" or, more recently, "gender roles," and has analyzed how these are learned and enacted. Beginning with Linton (1936) and continuing through the works of Parsons (Parsons 1951; Parsons and Bales 1955) and Komarovsky (1946, 1950), role theory has emphasized the social and dynamic aspect of role construction and enactment (Thorne 1980; Connell 1983). But at the level of face-to-face interaction, the application of role theory to gender poses problems of its own (for good reviews and critiques, see Connell 1983, 1985; Kessler, Ashendon, Connell, and Dowsett 1985; Lopata and Thorne 1978; Thorne 1980; Stacey and Thorne 1985). Roles are *situated* identities—assumed and relinquished as the situation demands—rather than *master identities* (Hughes 1945), such as sex category, that cut across situations. Unlike most roles, such as "nurse," "doctor," and "patient" or "professor" and "student," gender has no specific site or organizational context. Moreover, many roles are already gender marked, so that special qualifiers—such as "female doctor" or "male nurse"—must be added to exceptions to the rule. Thorne (1980) observes that conceptualizing gender as a role makes it difficult to assess its influence on other roles and reduces its explanatory usefulness in discussions of power and inequality. Drawing on Rubin (1975), Thorne calls for a reconceptualization of women and men as distinct social groups, constituted in "concrete, historically changing—and generally unequal—social relationships" (Thorne 1980, p. 11).

We argue that gender is not a set of traits, nor a variable, nor a role, but the product of social doings of some sort. What then is the social doing of gender? It is more than the continuous creation of the meaning of gender through human actions (Gerson and Peiss 1985). We claim that gender itself is constituted through interaction.[2] To develop the implications of our claim, we turn to Goffman's (1976) account of "gender display." Our object here is to explore how gender might be exhibited or portrayed through interaction, and thus be seen as "natural," while it is being produced as a socially organized achievement.

Gender Display

Goffman contends that when human beings interact with others in their environment, they assume that each possesses an "essential nature"—a nature that can be discerned through the "natural signs given off or expressed by them" (1976, p. 75). Femininity and masculinity are regarded as "prototypes of essential expression—something that can be conveyed fleetingly in any social situation and yet something that strikes at the most basic characterization of the individual" (1976, p. 75). The means through which we provide such expressions are "perfunctory, conventionalized acts" (1976, p. 69), which convey to others our regard for them, indicate our alignment in an encounter, and tentatively establish the terms of contact for that social situation. But they are also regarded as expressive behavior, testimony to our "essential natures."

Goffman (1976, pp. 69–70) sees *displays* as highly conventionalized behaviors structured as two-part exchanges of the statement-reply type, in which the presence or absence of symmetry can establish deference or dominance. These rituals are viewed as distinct from but articulated with more consequential activities, such as performing tasks or engaging in discourse. Hence, we have what he terms the "scheduling" of displays at junctures in activities, such as the beginning or end, to avoid interfering with the activities themselves. Goffman (1976, p. 69) formulates *gender display* as follows:

> If gender be defined as the culturally established correlates of sex (whether in consequence of biology or learning), then gender display refers to conventionalized portrayals of these correlates.

These gendered expressions might reveal clues to the underlying, fundamental dimensions of the female and male, but they are, in Goffman's view, optional performances. Masculine courtesies may or may not be offered and, if offered, may or may not be declined (1976, p. 71). Moreover, human beings "themselves employ the term 'expression', and conduct themselves to fit their own notions of expressivity" (1976, p. 75). Gender depictions are less a consequence of our "essential sexual natures" than interactional portrayals of what we would like to convey about sexual natures, using conventionalized gestures. Our *human* nature gives us the ability to learn to produce and recognize masculine and feminine gender displays—"a capacity [we] have by virtue of being persons, not males and females" (1976, p. 76).

Upon first inspection, it would appear that Goffman's formulation offers an engaging sociological corrective to existing formulations of gender. In his view, gender is a socially scripted dramatization of the culture's *idealization* of feminine and masculine natures, played for an audience that is well schooled in the presentational idiom. To continue the metaphor, there are scheduled performances presented in special locations, and like plays, they constitute introductions to or time out from more serious activities.

There are fundamental equivocations in this perspective. By segregating gender display from the serious business of interaction, Goffman obscures the effects of gender on a wide range of human activities. Gender is not merely something that happens in the nooks and crannies of interaction, fitted in here and there and not interfering with the serious business of life. While it is plausible to contend that gender displays—construed as conventionalized expressions—are optional, it does not seem plausible to say that we have the option of being seen by others as female or male.

It is necessary to move beyond the notion of gender display to consider what is involved in doing gender as an ongoing activity embedded in everyday interaction. Toward this end, we return to the distinctions among sex, sex category, and gender introduced earlier.

Sex, Sex Category, and Gender

Garfinkel's (1967, pp. 118–40) case study of Agnes, a transsexual raised as a boy who adopted a female identity at age seventeen and underwent a sex reassignment operation several years later, demonstrates how gender is created through interaction and at the same time structures interaction. Agnes, whom Garfinkel characterized as a "practical methodologist," developed a number of procedures for passing as a "normal, natural female" both prior to and after her surgery. She had the practical task of managing the fact that she possessed male genitalia and that she lacked the social resources a girl's biography would presumably provide in everyday interaction. In short, she needed to display herself as a woman, simultaneously learning what it was to be a woman. Of necessity, this full-time pursuit took place at a time when most people's gender would be well-accredited and routinized. Agnes had to consciously contrive what the vast majority of women do without thinking. She was not "faking" what "real" women do naturally. She was obliged to analyze and figure out how to act within socially structured circumstances and conceptions of femininity that women born with appropriate biological credentials come to take for granted early on. As in the case of others who must "pass," such as transvestites, Kabuki actors, or Dustin Hoffman's "Tootsie," Agnes's case makes visible what culture has made invisible—the accomplishment of gender.

Garfinkel's (1967) discussion of Agnes does not explicitly separate three analytically distinct, although empirically overlapping, concepts—sex, sex category, and gender.

Sex

Agnes did not possess the socially agreed upon biological criteria for classification as a member of the female *sex*. Still, Agnes regarded herself as a female, albeit a female with a penis, which a woman ought not to possess. The penis, she insisted, was a "mistake" in need of remedy (Garfinkel 1967, pp. 126–27, 131–32). Like other competent members of our culture, Agnes honored the notion that there *are* "essential" biological criteria that unequivocally distinguish females from males. However, if we move away from the commonsense viewpoint, we discover that the reliability of these criteria is not beyond question (Money and Brennan 1968; Money and Erhardt 1972; Money and Ogunro 1974; Money and Tucker 1975). Moreover, other cultures have acknowledged the existence of "cross-genders" (Blackwood 1984; Williams 1986) and the possibility of more than two sexes (Hill 1935; Martin and Voorhies 1975, pp. 84–107; but see also Cucchiari 1981, pp. 32–35).

More central to our argument is Kessler and McKenna's (1978, pp. 1–6) point that genitalia are conventionally hidden from public inspection in everyday life; yet we continue through our social rounds to "observe" a world of two naturally, normally sexed persons. It is the *presumption* that essential criteria exist and would or should be there if looked for that provides the basis for sex categorization. Drawing on Garfinkel, Kessler and McKenna argue that "female" and "male" are cultural events—products of what they term the "gender attribution process"—rather than some collection of traits, behaviors, or even physical attributes. Illustratively they cite the child who, viewing a picture of someone clad in a suit and a tie, contends, "It's a man, because he has a pee-pee" (Kessler and McKenna 1978, p. 154). Translation: "He must have a pee-pee [an essential characteristic] because I see the *insignia* of a suit and tie." Neither initial sex assignment (pronouncement at birth as a female or male) nor the actual existence of essential criteria for that assignment (possession of a clitoris and vagina or penis and testicles) has much—if anything—to do with the identification of sex category in everyday life. There Kessler and McKenna note, we operate with a moral certainty of a world of two sexes. We do not think, "Most persons with penises are men, but some may not be" or "Most persons who dress as men have penises." Rather, we take it for granted that sex and sex category are congruent—that knowing the latter, we can deduce the rest.

Sex Categorization

Agnes's claim to the categorical status of female, which she sustained by appropriate identificatory displays and other characteristics, could be *discredited* before her transsexual operation if her possession of a penis became known and after by her surgically constructed genitalia (see Raymond 1979, pp. 37, 138). In this regard, Agnes had to be continually alert to actual or potential threats to the security of her sex category. Her problem was not so much living up to some prototype of essential femininity but preserving her categorization as female. This task was made easy for her by a very powerful resource, namely, the process of commonsense categorization in everyday life.

The categorization of members of society into indigenous categories such as "girl" or "boy," or "woman" or "man," operates in a distinctively social way. The act of categorization does not involve a positive test, in the sense of a well-defined set of criteria that must be explicitly satisfied prior to making an identification. Rather, the application of membership categories relies on an "if-can" test in everyday interaction (Sacks 1972, pp. 332–35). This test stipulates that if people *can be seen* as members of relevant categories, *then categorize them that way.* That is, use the category that seems appropriate, except in the presence of discrepant information or obvious features that would rule out its use. This procedure is quite in keeping with the attitude of everyday life, which has us take appearances at face value unless we have special reason to doubt (Schutz 1943; Garfinkel 1967, pp. 272–77; Bernstein 1986).[3] It should be added that it is precisely when we have special reason to doubt that the issue of applying rigorous criteria arises, but it is rare, outside legal or bureaucratic contexts, to encounter insistence on positive tests (Garfinkel 1967, pp. 262–83; Wilson 1970).

Agnes's initial resource was the predisposition of those she encountered to take her appearance (her figure, clothing, hair style, and so on), as the undoubted appearance of a normal female. Her further resource was our cultural perspective on the properties of "natural, normally sexed persons." Garfinkel (1967, pp. 122–28) notes that in everyday life, we live in a world of two—and only two—sexes. This arrangement has a moral status, in that we include ourselves and others in it as "essentially, originally, in the first place, always have been, always will be, once and for all, in the final analysis, either 'male' or 'female' " (Garfinkel 1967, p. 122).

Consider the following case:

> This issue reminds me of a visit I made to a computer store a couple of years ago. The person who answered my questions was truly a *salesperson*. I could not categorize him/her as a woman or a man. What did I look for? (1) Facial hair: She/he was smooth skinned, but some men have little or no facial hair. (This varies by race; Native Americans and Blacks often have none.) (2) Breasts: She/he was wearing a loose shirt that hung from his/her shoulders. And, as many women who suffered through a 1950s' adolescence know to their shame, women are often flat-chested. (3) Shoulders: His/hers were small and round for a man, broad for a woman. (4) Hands: Long and slender fingers, knuckles a bit large for a woman, small for a man. (5) Voice: Middle range, unexpressive for a woman, not at all the exaggerated tones some gay males affect. (6) His/her treatment of me: Gave off no signs that would let me know if I were of the same or different sex as this person. There were not even any signs that he/she knew his/her sex would be difficult to categorize and I wondered about that even as I did my best to hide these questions so I would not embarrass him/her while we talked of computer paper. I left still not knowing the sex of my salesperson, and was disturbed by that unanswered question (child of my culture that I am). (Diane Margolis, personal communication)

What can this case tell us about situations such as Agnes's (cf. Morris 1974; Richards 1983) or the process of sex categorization in general? First, we infer from this description that the computer salesclerk's identificatory display was ambiguous, since she or he was not dressed or adorned in an unequivocally female or male fashion. It is when such a display *fails* to provide grounds for categorization that factors such as facial hair or tone of voice are assessed to determine membership in a sex category. Second, beyond the fact that this incident could be recalled after "a couple of years," the customer was not only "disturbed" by the ambiguity of the salesclerk's category but also assumed that to acknowledge this ambiguity would be embarrassing to the salesclerk. Not only do we want to know the sex category of those around us (to see it at a glance, perhaps), but we presume that others are displaying it for us, in as decisive a fashion as they can.

Gender

Agnes attempted to be "120 percent female" (Garfinkel 1967, p. 129), that is, unquestionably in all ways and at all times feminine. She thought she could protect herself from disclosure before and after surgical intervention by comporting herself in a feminine manner, but she also could have given herself away by overdoing her performance. Sex categorization and the accomplishment of gender are not the same. Agnes's categorization could be secure or suspect, but did not depend on whether or not she lived up to some ideal conception of femininity. Women can be seen as unfeminine, but that does not make them "unfemale." Agnes faced an ongoing task of *being* a woman—something beyond style of dress (an identificatory display) or allowing men to light her cigarette (a gender display). Her problem was to produce configurations of behavior that would be seen by others as normative gender behavior.

Agnes's strategy of "secret apprenticeship," through which she learned expected feminine decorum by carefully attending to her fiancé's criticisms of other women, was one means of masking incompetencies and simultaneously acquiring the needed skills (Garfinkel 1967, pp. 146–147). It was through her fiancé that Agnes learned that sunbathing on the lawn in front of her apartment was "offensive" (because it put her on display to other men). She also learned from his critiques of other women that she should not insist on having things her way and that she should not offer her opinions or claim equality with men (Garfinkel 1967, pp. 147–148). (Like other women in our society, Agnes learned something about power in the course of her "education.")

Popular culture abounds with books and magazines that compile idealized depictions of relations between women and men. Those focused on the etiquette of dating or prevailing standards of feminine comportment are meant to be of practical help in these matters. However, the use of any such source *as a manual of procedure* requires the assumption that doing gender merely involves making use of discrete, well-defined bundles of behavior that can simply be plugged into interactional situations to produce recognizable enactments of masculinity and femininity. The man "does" being masculine by, for example, taking the woman's arm to guide her across a street, and she "does" being feminine by consenting to be guided and not initiating such behavior with a man.

Agnes could perhaps have used such sources as manuals, but, we contend, doing gender is not so easily regimented (Mithers 1982; Morris 1974). Such sources may list and describe the sorts of behaviors that mark or display gender, but they are necessarily incomplete (Garfinkel 1967, pp. 66–75; Wieder 1974, pp. 183–214; Zimmerman and Wieder 1970, pp. 285–98). And to be successful, marking or displaying gender must be finely fitted to situations and modified or transformed as the occasion demands. Doing gender consists of managing such occasions so that, whatever the particulars, the outcome is seen and seeable in context as gender-appropriate or, as the case may be, gender-*in*appropriate, that is, *accountable*.

Gender and Accountability

As Heritage (1984, pp. 136–37) notes, members of society regularly engage in "descriptive accounts of states of affairs to one another," and such accounts are both serious and consequential. These descriptions name, characterize, formulate, explain, excuse, excoriate, or merely take notice of some circumstance or activity and thus place it within some social framework (locating it relative to other activities, like and unlike).

Such descriptions are themselves accountable, and societal members orient to the fact that their activities are subject to comment. Actions are often designed with an eye to their accountability, that is, how they might look and how they might be characterized. The notion of accountability also encompasses those actions undertaken so that they are specifically unremarkable and thus not worthy of more than a passing remark, because they are seen to be in accord with culturally approved standards.

Heritage (1984, p. 179) observes that the process of rendering something accountable is interactional in character:

> [This] permits actors to design their actions in relation to their circumstances so as to permit others, by methodically taking account of circumstances, to recognize the action for what it is.

The key word here is *circumstances*. One circumstance that attends virtually all actions is the sex category of the actor. As Garfinkel (1967, p. 118) comments:

> [T]he work and socially structured occasions of sexual passing were obstinately unyielding to [Agnes's] attempts to routinize the grounds of daily activities. This obstinacy points to the *omnirelevance* of sexual status to affairs of daily life as an invariant but unnoticed background in the texture of relevances that compose the changing actual scenes of everyday life. (italics added)
> everywhere

If sex category is omnirelevant (or even approaches being so), then a person engaged in virtually any activity may be held accountable for performance of that activity as a *woman* or a *man*, and their incumbency in one or the other sex category can be used to legitimate or discredit their other activities (Berger, Cohen, and Zelditch 1972; Berger, Conner, and Fisek 1974; Berger, Fisek, Norman, and Zelditch 1977; Humphreys and Berger 1981). Accordingly, virtually any activity can be assessed as to its womanly or manly nature. And note, to "do" gender is not always to live up to normative conceptions of femininity or masculinity; it is to engage in behavior *at the risk of gender assessment.* While it is individuals who do gender, the enterprise is fundamentally interactional and institutional in character, for accountability is a feature of social relationships and its idiom is drawn from the institutional arena in which those relationships are enacted. If this be the case, can we ever *not* do gender? Insofar as a society is partitioned by "essential" differences between women and men and placement in a sex category is both relevant and enforced, doing gender is unavoidable.

Resources for Doing Gender

Doing gender means creating differences between girls and boys and women and men, differences that are not natural, essential, or biological. Once the differences have been constructed, they are used to reinforce the "essentialness" of gender. In a delightful account of the "arrangement between the sexes," Goffman (1977) observes the creation of a variety of institutionalized frameworks through which our "natural, normal sexedness" can be enacted. The physical features of social setting provide one obvious resource for the expression of our "essential" differences. For example, the sex segregation of North American public bathrooms distinguishes "ladies" from "gentlemen" in matters held to be fundamentally biological, even though both "are somewhat similar in the question of waste products and their elimination" (Goffman 1977, p. 315). These settings are furnished with dimorphic equipment (such as urinals for men or elaborate grooming facilities for women), even though both sexes may achieve the same ends through the same means (and apparently do so in the privacy of their own homes). To be stressed here is the fact that

> the *functioning* of sex-differentiated organs is involved, but there is nothing in this functioning that biologically recommends segregation; *that* arrangement is a totally cultural matter ... toilet segregation is presented as a natural consequence of the difference between the sex-classes when in fact it is a means of honoring, if not producing, this difference. (Goffman 1977, p. 316)

Standardized social occasions also provide stages for evocations of the "essential female and male natures." Goffman cites organized sports as one such institutionalized framework for the expression of manliness. There, those qualities that ought "properly" to be associated with masculinity, such as endurance, strength, and competitive spirit, are celebrated by all parties concerned—participants who may be seen to demonstrate such traits, and spectators, who applaud their demonstrations from the safety of the sidelines (1977, p. 322).

Assortative mating practices among heterosexual couples afford still further means to create and maintain differences between women and men. For example, even though size, strength, and age tend to be normally distributed among females and males (with considerable overlap between them), selective pairing ensures couples in which boys and men are visibly bigger, stronger, and older (if not "wiser") than the girls and women with whom they are paired. So, should situations emerge in which greater size, strength, or experience is called for, boys and men will be ever ready to display it and girls and women, to appreciate its display (Goffman 1977, p. 321; West and Iritani 1985).

Gender may be routinely fashioned in a variety of situations that seem conventionally expressive to begin with, such as those that present "helpless" women next to heavy objects or flat tires. But, as Goffman notes, heavy, messy, and precarious concerns can be constructed from *any* social situation, "even though by standards set in other settings, this may involve something that is light, clean, and safe" (Goffman 1977, p. 324). Given these resources, it is clear that *any*, interactional situation sets the stage for depictions of "essential" sexual natures. In sum, these situations "do not so much allow for the expression of natural differences as for the production of that difference itself" (Goffman 1977, p. 324).

Many situations are not clearly sex categorized to begin with, nor is what transpires within them obviously gender relevant. Yet any social encounter can be pressed into service in the interests of doing gender. Thus, Fishman's (1978) research on casual conversations found an asymmetrical "division of labor" in talk between heterosexual intimates. Women had to ask more questions, fill more silences, and use more attention-getting beginnings in order to be heard. Her conclusions are particularly pertinent here:

> Since interactional work is related to what constitutes being a woman, with what a woman *is,* the idea that it *is* work is obscured. The work is not seen as what women do, but as part of what they are. (Fishman 1978, p. 405)

We would argue that it is precisely such labor that helps to constitute the essential nature of women *as* women in interactional contexts (West and Zimmerman 1983, pp. 109–11; but see also Kollock, Blumstein, and Schwartz 1985). Individuals have many social identities that may be donned or shed, muted or made more salient, depending on the situation. One may be a friend, spouse, professional, citizen, and many other things to many different people—or, to the same person at different times. But we are always women or men—unless we shift into another sex category. What this means is that our identificatory displays will provide an ever-available resource for doing gender under an infinitely diverse set of circumstances.

Some occasions are organized to routinely display and celebrate behaviors that are conventionally linked to one or the other sex category. On such occasions, everyone knows his or her place in the interactional scheme of things. If an individual identified as a member of one sex category engages in behavior usually associated with the other category, this routinization is challenged. Hughes (1945, p. 356) provides an illustration of such a dilemma:

> [A] young woman . . . became part of that virile profession, engineering. The designer of an airplane is expected to go up on the maiden flight of the first plane built according to the design. He *[sic]* then gives a dinner to the engineers and workmen who worked on the new plane. The dinner is naturally a stag party. The young woman in question designed a plane. Her co-workers urged her not to take the risk—for which, presumably, men only are fit—of the maiden voyage. They were, in effect, asking her to be a lady instead of an engineer. She chose to be an engineer. She then gave the party and paid for it like a man. After food and the first round of toasts, she left like a lady.

On this occasion, parties reached an accommodation that allowed a woman to engage in presumptively masculine behaviors. However, we note that in the end, this compromise permitted demonstration of her "essential" femininity, through accountably "ladylike" behavior.

Hughes (1945, p. 357) suggests that such contradictions may be countered by managing interactions on a very narrow basis, for example, "keeping the relationship formal and specific." But the heart of the matter is that even—perhaps, especially—if the relationship is a formal one, gender is still something one is accountable for. Thus a woman physician (notice the special qualifier in her case) may be accorded respect for her skill and even addressed by an appropriate title. Nonetheless, she is subject to evaluation in terms of normative conceptions of appropriate attitudes and activities for her sex category and under pressure to prove that she is an "essentially" feminine being, despite appearances to the contrary (West 1984, pp. 97–101). Her sex category is used to discredit her participation in important clinical activities (Lorber 1984, pp. 52–54), while her involvement in medicine is used to discredit her commitment to her responsibilities as a wife and mother (Bourne and Wikler 1978, pp. 435–37). Simultaneously, her exclusion from the physician colleague community is maintained and her accountability *as a woman* is ensured.

In this context, "role conflict" can be viewed as a dynamic aspect of our current "arrangement between the sexes" (Goffman 1977), an arrangement that provides for occasions on which persons of a particular sex category can "see" quite clearly that they are out of place and that if they were not there, their current troubles would not exist. What is at stake is, from the standpoint of interaction, the management of our "essential" natures, and from the standpoint of the individual, the continuing accomplishment of gender. If, as we have argued, sex category is omnirelevant, then any occasion, conflicted or not, offers the resources for doing gender.

We have sought to show that sex category and gender are managed properties of conduct that are contrived with respect to the fact that others will judge and respond to us in particular ways. We have claimed that a person's gender is not simply an aspect of what one is, but, more fundamentally, it is something that one *does*, and does recurrently, in interaction with others.

What are the consequences of this theoretical formulation? If, for example, individuals strive to achieve gender in encounters with others, how does a culture instill the need to achieve it? What is the relationship between the production of gender at the level of interaction and such institutional arrangements as the division of labor in society? And, perhaps most important, how does doing gender contribute to the subordination of women by men?

Research Agendas

To bring the social production of gender under empirical scrutiny, we might begin at the beginning with a reconsideration of the process through which societal members acquire the requisite categorical apparatus and other skills to become gendered human beings.

Recruitment to Gender Identities

The conventional approach to the process of becoming girls and boys has been sex-role socialization. In recent years, recurring problems arising from this approach have been linked to inadequacies inherent in role theory *per se*—its emphasis on "consensus, stability and continuity" (Stacey and Thorne 1985, p. 307), its ahistorical and depoliticizing focus (Thorne 1980, p. 9; Stacey and Thorne 1985, p. 307), and the fact that its "social" dimension relies on "a general assumption that people choose to maintain existing customs" (Connell 1985, p. 263).

In contrast, Cahill (1982, 1986a, 1986b) analyzes the experiences of preschool children using a social model of recruitment into normally gendered identities. Cahill argues that categorization practices are fundamental to learning and displaying feminine and masculine behavior. Initially, he observes, children are primarily concerned with distinguishing between themselves and others on the basis of social competence. Categorically, their concern resolves itself into the opposition of "girl/boy" classification versus "baby" classification (the latter designating children whose social behavior is problematic and who must be closely supervised). It is children's concern with being seen as socially competent that evokes their initial claims to gender identities:

> During the exploratory stage of children's socialization ... they learn that only two social identities are routinely available to them, the identity of "baby," or, depending on the configuration of their external genitalia, either "big boy" or "big girl." Moreover, others subtly inform them that the identity of "baby" is a discrediting one. When, for example, children engage in disapproved behavior, they are often told "You're a baby" or "Be a big boy." In effect, these typical verbal responses to young children's behavior convey to them that they must behaviorally choose between the discrediting identity of "baby" and their anatomically determined sex identity. (Cahill 1986a, p. 175)

Subsequently, little boys appropriate the gender ideal of "efficaciousness," that is, being able to affect the physical and social environment through the exercise of physical strength or appropriate skills. In contrast, little girls learn to value "appearance," that is, managing themselves as ornamental objects. Both classes of children learn that the recognition and use of sex categorization in interaction are not optional, but mandatory (see also Bem 1983).

Being a "girl" or a "boy" then, is not only being more competent than a "baby," but also being competently female or male, that is, learning to produce behavioral displays of one's "essential" female or male identity. In this respect, the task of four-to five-year-old children is very similar to Agnes's:

> For example, the following interaction occurred on a preschool playground. A 55-month-old-boy (D) was attempting to unfasten the clasp of a necklace when a preschool aide walked over to him.
> A: Do you want to put that on?
> D: No. It's for girls.
> A: You don't have to be a girl to wear things around your neck. Kings wear things around their necks. You could pretend you're a king.
> D: I'm not a king. I'm a boy. (Cahill 1986a, p. 176)

As Cahill notes of this example, although D may have been unclear as to the sex status of a king's identity, he was obviously aware that necklaces are used to announce the identity "girl." Having claimed the identity "boy" and having developed a behavioral commitment to it, he was leery of any display that might furnish grounds for questioning his claim.

In this way, new members of society come to be involved in a *self-regulating process* as they begin to monitor their own and others' conduct with regard to its gender implications. The "recruitment" process involves not only the appropriation of gender ideals (by the valuation of those ideals as proper ways of being and behaving) but also *gender identities* that are important to individuals and that they strive to maintain. Thus gender differences, or the sociocultural shaping of "essential female and male natures," achieve the status of objective facts. They are rendered normal, natural features of persons and provide the tacit rationale for differing fates of women and men within the social order.

Additional studies of children's play activities as routine occasions for the expression of gender-appropriate behavior can yield new insights into how our "essential natures" are constructed. In particular, the transition from what Cahill (1986a) terms "apprentice participation" in the sex-segregated worlds that are common among elementary school children to "bona fide participation" in the heterosocial world so frightening to adolescents is likely to be a keystone in our understanding of the recruitment process (Thorne 1986; Thorne and Luria 1986).

Gender and the Division of Labor

Whenever people face issues of *allocation*—who is to do what, get what, plan or execute action, direct or be directed, incumbency in significant social categories such as "female" and "male" seems to become pointedly relevant. How such issues are resolved conditions the exhibition, dramatization, or celebration of one's "essential nature" as a woman or man.

Berk (1985) offers elegant demonstration of this point in her investigation of the allocation of household labor and the attitudes of married couples toward the division of household tasks. Berk found little variation in either the actual distribution of tasks or perceptions of equity in regard to that distribution. Wives, even when employed outside the home, do the vast majority of household and child-care tasks. Moreover, both wives and husbands tend to perceive this as a "fair" arrangement. Noting the failure of conventional sociological and economic theories to explain this seeming contradiction, Berk contends that something more complex is involved than rational arrangements for the production of household goods and services:

> Hardly a question simply of who has more time, or whose time is worth more, who has more skill or more power, it is clear that a complicated relationship between the structure of work imperatives and the structure of normative expectations attached to work as *gendered* determines the ultimate allocation of members' time to work and home. (Berk 1985, pp. 195–96)

She notes, for example, that the most important factor influencing wives' contribution of labor is the total amount of work demanded or expected by the household;

such demands had no bearing on husbands' contributions. Wives reported various rationales (their own and their husbands') that justified their level of contribution and, as a general matter, underscored the presumption that wives are essentially responsible for household production.

Berk (1985, p. 201) contends that it is difficult to see how people "could rationally establish the arrangements that they do solely for the production of household goods and services"—much less, how people could consider them "fair." She argues that our current arrangements for the domestic division of labor support *two* production processes: household goods and services (meals, clean children, and so on) and, at the same time, gender. As she puts it:

> Simultaneously, members "do" gender, as they "do" housework and child care, and what [has] been called the division of labor provides for the joint production of household labor and gender; it is the mechanism by which both the material and symbolic products of the household are realized. (1985, p. 201)

It is not simply that household labor is designated as "women's work," but that for a woman to engage in it and a man not to engage in it is to draw on and exhibit the "essential nature" of each. What is produced and reproduced is not merely the activity and artifact of domestic life, but the material embodiment of wifely and husbandly roles, and derivatively, of womanly and manly conduct (see Beer 1983, pp. 70–89). What are also frequently produced and reproduced are the dominant and subordinate statuses of the sex categories.

How does gender get done in work settings outside the home, where dominance and subordination are themes of overarching importance? Hochschild's (1983) analysis of the work of flight attendants offers some promising insights. She found that the occupation of flight attendant consisted of something altogether different for women than for men:

> As the company's main shock absorbers against "mishandled" passengers, their own feelings are more frequently subjected to rough treatment. In addition, a day's exposure to people who resist authority in a woman is a different experience than it is for a man. ... In this respect, it is a disadvantage to be a woman. And in this case, they are not simply women in the biological sense. They are also a highly visible distillation of middle-class American notions of femininity. They symbolize Woman. Insofar as the category "female" is mentally associated with having less status and authority, female flight attendants are more readily classified as "really" females than other females are. (Hochschild 1983, p. 175)

In performing what Hochschild terms the "emotional labor" necessary to maintain airline profits, women flight attendants simultaneously produce enactments of their "essential" femininity.

Sex and Sexuality

What is the relationship between doing gender and a culture's prescription of "obligatory heterosexuality" (Rubin 1975; Rich 1980)? As Frye (1983, p. 22) observes, the monitoring of sexual feelings in relation to other appropriately sexed persons requires the ready recognition of such persons "before one can allow one's heart to beat or one's blood to flow in erotic enjoyment of that person." The appearance of heterosexuality is produced through emphatic and unambiguous indicators of one's sex, layered on in ever more conclusive fashion (Frye 1983, p. 24). Thus, lesbians and gay men concerned with passing as heterosexuals can rely on these indicators for camouflage; in contrast, those who would avoid the assumption of heterosexuality may foster ambiguous indicators of their categorical status through their dress, behaviors, and style. But "ambiguous" sex indicators are sex indicators nonetheless. If one wishes to be recognized as a lesbian (or heterosexual woman), one must first establish a categorical status as female. Even as popular images portray lesbians as "females who are not feminine" (Frye 1983, p. 129), the accountability of persons for their "normal, natural sexedness" is preserved.

Nor is accountability threatened by the existence of "sex-change operations"—presumably, the most radical challenge to our cultural perspective on sex and gender. Although no one coerces transsexuals into hormone therapy, electrolysis, or surgery, the alternatives available to them are undeniably constrained:

> When the transsexual experts maintain that they use transsexual procedures only with people who ask for them, and who prove that they can "pass," they obscure the social reality. Given patriarchy's prescription that one must be *either* masculine or feminine, free choice is conditioned. (Raymond 1979, p. 135, italics added)

The physical reconstruction of sex criteria pays ultimate tribute to the "essentialness" of our sexual natures—as women *or* as men.

Gender, Power, and Social Change

Let us return to the question: Can we avoid doing gender? Earlier, we proposed that insofar as sex category is used as a fundamental criterion for differentiation, doing gender is unavoidable. It is unavoidable because of the social consequences of sex-category membership: the allocation of power and resources not only in the domestic, economic, and political domains but also in the broad arena of interpersonal relations. In virtually any situation, one's sex category can be relevant, and one's performance as an incumbent of that category (i.e., gender) can be subjected to evaluation. Maintaining such pervasive and faithful assignment of lifetime status requires legitimation.

But doing gender also renders the social arrangements based on sex category accountable as normal and natural, that is, legitimate ways of organizing social life. Differences between women and men that are created by this process can then be portrayed as fundamental and enduring dispositions. In this light, the institutional arrangements of a society can be seen as responsive to the differences—the social order being merely an accommodation to the natural order. Thus if, in doing gender, men are also doing dominance and women are doing deference (cf. Goffman 1967, pp. 47–95), the resultant social order, which supposedly reflects "natural differences," is a powerful reinforcer and legitimator of hierarchical arrangements. Frye observes:

For efficient subordination, what's wanted is that the structure not appear to be a cultural artifact kept in place by human decision or custom, but that it appear *natural*—that it appear to be quite a direct consequence of facts about the beast which are beyond the scope of human manipulation. . . . That we are trained to behave so differently as women and men, and to behave so differently toward women and men, itself contributes mightily to the appearance of extreme dimorphism, but also, the *ways* we act as women and men, and the *ways* we act toward women and men, mold our bodies and our minds to the shape of subordination and dominance. We do become what we practice being. (Frye 1983, p. 34)

If we do gender appropriately, we simultaneously sustain, reproduce, and render legitimate the institutional arrangements that are based on sex category. If we fail to do gender appropriately, we as individuals—not the institutional arrangements—may be called to account (for our character, motives, and predispositions).

Social movements such as feminism can provide the ideology and impetus to question existing arrangements, and the social support for individuals to explore alternatives to them. Legislative changes, such as that proposed by the Equal Rights Amendment, can also weaken the accountability of conduct to sex category, thereby affording the possibility of more widespread loosening of accountability in general. To be sure, equality under the law does not guarantee equality in other arenas. As Lorber (1986, p. 577) points out, assurance of "scrupulous equality of categories of people considered essentially different needs constant monitoring." What such proposed changes *can* do is provide the warrant for asking why, if we wish to treat women and men as equals, there needs to be two sex categories at all (see Lorber 1986, p. 577).

The sex category/gender relationship links the institutional and interactional levels, a coupling that legitimates social arrangements based on sex category and reproduces their asymmetry in face-to-face interaction. Doing gender furnishes the interactional scaffolding of social structure, along with a built-in mechanism of social control. In appreciating the institutional forces that maintain distinctions between women and men, we must not lose sight of the interactional validation of those distinctions that confers upon them their sense of "naturalness" and "rightness."

Social change, then, must be pursued both at the institutional and cultural level of sex category and at the interactional level of gender. Such a conclusion is hardly novel. Nevertheless, we suggest that it is important to recognize that the analytical distinction between institutional and interactional spheres does not pose an either/or choice when it comes to the question of effecting social change. Reconceptualizing gender not as a simple property of individuals but as an integral dynamic of social orders implies a new perspective on the entire network of gender relations:

[T]he social subordination of women, and the cultural practices which help sustain it; the politics of sexual object-choice, and particularly the oppression of homosexual people; the sexual division of labor, the formation of character and motive, so far as they are organized as femininity and masculinity; the role of the body in social relations, especially the politics of childbirth; and the nature of strategies of sexual liberation movements. (Connell 1985, p. 261)

Gender is a powerful ideological device, which produces, reproduces, and legitimates the choices and limits that are predicated on sex category. An understanding of how gender is produced in social situations will afford clarification of the interactional scaffolding of social structure and the social control processes that sustain it.

NOTES

1. This definition understates many complexities involved in the relationship between biology and culture (Jaggar 1983, pp. 106–13). However, our point is that the determination of an individual's sex classification is a *social* process through and through.

2. This is not to say that gender is a singular "thing," omnipresent in the same form historically or in every situation. Because normative conceptions of appropriate attitudes and activities for sex categories can vary across cultures and historical moments, the management of situated conduct in light of those expectations can take many different forms.

3. Bernstein (1986) reports an unusual case of espionage in which a man passing as a woman convinced a lover that he/she had given birth to "their" child, who, the lover, thought, "looked like" him.

REFERENCES

Beer, William R. 1983. *Househusbands: Men and Housework in American Families.* New York: Praeger.

Bem, Sandra L. 1983. "Gender Schema Theory and Its Implications for Child Development: Raising Gender-Aschematic Children in a Gender-Schematic Society." *Signs: Journal of Women in Culture and Society* 8:598–616.

Berger, Joseph, Bernard P. Cohen, and Morris Zelditch, Jr. 1972. "Status Characteristics and Social Interaction." *American Sociological Review* 37:241–55.

Berger, Joseph, Thomas L. Conner, and M. Hamit Fisek, eds. 1974. *Expectation States Theory: A Theoretical Research Program.* Cambridge: Winthrop.

Berger, Joseph, M. Hamit Fisek, Robert Z. Norman, and Morris Zelditch, Jr. 1977. *Status Characteristics and Social Interaction: An Expectation States Approach.* New York: Elsevier.

Berk, Sarah F. 1985. *The Gender Factory: The Apportionment of Work in American Households.* New York: Plenum.

Bernstein, Richard. 1986. "France Jails Two in Odd Case of Espionage." *New York Times* (May 11).

Blackwood, Evelyn. 1984. "Sexuality and Gender in Certain Native American Tribes: The Case of Cross-Gender Females." *Signs: Journal of Women in Culture and Society* 10:27–42.

Bourne, Patricia G., and Norma J. Wikler. 1978. "Commitment and the Cultural Mandate: Women in Medicine." *Social Problems* 25:430–40.

Cahill, Spencer E. 1982. "Becoming Boys and Girls." Ph.D. dissertation, Department of Sociology, University of California, Santa Barbara.

———. 1986a. "Childhood Socialization as Recruitment Process: Some Lessons from the Study of Gender Development." Pp. 163–86 in *Sociological Studies of Child Development,* edited by P. Adler and P. Adler. Greenwich, CT: JAI Press.

———. 1986b. "Language Practices and Self-Definition: The Case of Gender Identity Acquisition." *Sociological Quarterly* 27:295–311.

Chodorow, Nancy. 1978. *The Reproduction of Mothering: Psychoanalysis and the Sociology of Gender.* Los Angeles: University of California Press.

Connell, R. W. 1983. *Which Way Is Up?* Sydney: Allen & Unwin.

———. 1985. "Theorizing Gender." *Sociology* 19:260–72.

Cucchiari, Salvatore. 1981. "The Gender Revolution and the Transition from Bisexual Horde to Patrilocal Band: The Origins of Gender Hierarchy." Pp. 31–79 in *Sexual Meanings: The Cultural Construction of Gender and Sexuality,* edited by S. B. Ortner and H. Whitehead. New York: Cambridge University Press.

Firestone, Shulamith. 1970. *The Dialectic of Sex: The Case for Feminist Revolution.* New York: William Morrow.

Fishman, Pamela. 1978. "Interaction: The Work Women Do." *Social Problems* 25:397–406.

Frye, Marilyn. 1983. *The Politics of Reality: Essays in Feminist Theory.* Trumansburg, NY: Crossing Press.

Garfinkel, Harold. 1967. *Studies in Ethnomethodology.* Englewood Cliffs, NJ: Prentice-Hall.

Gerson, Judith M., and Kathy Peiss. 1985. "Boundaries, Negotiation, Consciousness: Reconceptualizing Gender Relations." *Social Problems* 32:317–31.

Goffman, Erving. 1967 (1956). "The Nature of Deference and Demeanor." Pp. 47–95 in *Interaction Ritual.* New York: Anchor/Doubleday.

———. 1976. "Gender Display." *Studies in the Anthropology of Visual Communication* 3:69–77.

———. 1977. "The Arrangement Between the Sexes." *Theory and Society* 4:301–31.

Henley, Nancy M. 1985. "Psychology and Gender." *Signs: Journal of Women in Culture and Society* 11:101–19.

Heritage, John. 1984. *Garfinkel and Ethnomethodology.* Cambridge: Polity Press.

Hill, W. W. 1935. "The Status of the Hermaphrodite and Transvestite in Navaho Culture." *American Anthropologist* 37:273–79.

Hochschild, Arlie R. 1973. "A Review of Sex Roles Research." *American Journal of Sociology* 78:1011–29.

———. 1983. *The Managed Heart: Commercialization of Human Feeling.* Berkeley: University of California Press.

Hughes, Everett C. 1945. "Dilemmas and Contradictions of Status." *American Journal of Sociology* 50:353–59.

Humphreys, Paul, and Joseph Berger. 1981. "Theoretical Consequences of the Status Characteristics Formulation." *American Journal of Sociology* 86:953–83.

Jaggar, Alison M. 1983. *Feminist Politics and Human Nature.* Totowa, NJ: Rowman & Allanheld.

Kessler, S., D. J. Ashendon, R. W. Connell, and G. W. Dowsett. 1985. "Gender Relations in Secondary Schooling." *Sociology of Education* 58:34–48.

Kessler, Suzanne J., and Wendy McKenna. 1978. *Gender: An Ethnomethodological Approach.* New York: Wiley.

Kollock, Peter, Philip Blumstein, and Pepper Schwartz 1985. "Sex and Power in Interaction." *American Sociological Review* 50:34–46.

Komarovsky, Mirra. 1946. "Cultural Contradictions and Sex Roles." *American Journal of Sociology* 52:184–89.

———. 1950. "Functional Analysis of Sex Roles." *American Sociological Review* 15:508–16.

Linton, Ralph. 1936. *The Study of Man.* New York: Appleton-Century.

Lopata, Helen Z., and Barrie Thorne. 1978. "On the Term 'Sex Roles.'" *Signs: Journal of Women in Culture and Society* 3:718–21.

Lorber, Judith. 1984. *Women Physicians: Careers, Status and Power.* New York: Tavistock.

———. 1986. "Dismantling Noah's Ark." *Sex Roles* 14:567–80.

Martin, M. Kay, and Barbara Voorhies. 1975. *Female of the Species.* New York: Columbia University Press.

Mead, Margaret. 1963. *Sex and Temperment.* New York: Dell.

———. 1968. *Male and Female.* New York: Dell.

Mithers, Carol L. 1982. "My Life as a Man." *The Village Voice* 27 (October 5):1ff.

Money, John. 1968. *Sex Errors of the Body.* Baltimore: Johns Hopkins University Press.

———. 1974. "Prenatal Hormones and Postnatal Sexualization in Gender Identity Differentiation." Pp. 221–95 in *Nebraska Symposium on Motivation,* vol 21, edited by J. K. Cole and R. Dienstbier. Lincoln: University of Nebraska Press.

Money, John, and John G. Brennan. 1968. "Sexual Dimorphism in the Psychology of Female Transsexuals." *Journal of Nervous and Mental Disease* 147:487–99.

Money, John, and A. Erhardt Anke. 1972. *Man and Woman/Boy and Girl.* Baltimore: Johns Hopkins University Press.

Money, John, and Charles Ogunro. 1974. "Behavioral Sexology: Ten Cases of Genetic Male Intersexuality with Impaired Prenatal and Pubertal Androgenization," *Archives of Sexual Behavior* 3:181–206.

Money, John, and Patricia Tucker. 1975. *Sexual Signatures.* Boston: Little, Brown.

Morris, Jan. 1974. *Conundrum.* New York: Harcourt Brace Jovanovich.

Parsons, Talcott. 1951. *The Social System.* New York: Free Press.

Parsons, Talcott, and Robert F. Bales. 1955. *Family, Socialization and Interaction Process.* New York: Free Press.

Raymond, Janice G. 1979. *The Transsexual Empire.* Boston: Beacon.

Rich, Adrienne. 1980. "Compulsory Heterosexuality and Lesbian Existence." *Signs: Journal of Women in Culture and Society* 5:631–60.

Richards, Renee (with John Ames). 1983. *Second Serve: The Renee Richards Story.* New York: Stein and Day.

Rossi, Alice. 1984. "Gender and Parenthood." *American Sociological Review* 49:1–19.

Rubin, Gayle. 1975. "The Traffic in Women: Notes on the 'Political Economy' of Sex." Pp. 157–210 in *Toward an Anthropology of Women,* edited by R. Reiter. New York: Monthly Review Press.

Sacks, Harvey. 1972. "On the Analyzability of Stories by Children." Pp. 325–45 in *Directions in Sociolinguistics,* edited by J. J. Gumperz and D. Hymes. New York: Holt, Rinehart & Winston.

Schutz, Alfred. 1943. "The Problem of Rationality in the Social World." *Economics* 10:130–49.

Stacey, Judith, and Barrie Thorne. 1985. "The Missing Feminist Revolution in Sociology." *Social Problems* 32:301–16.

Thorne, Barrie. 1980. "Gender . . . How Is It Best Conceptualized?" Unpublished manuscript.

———. 1986. "Girls and Boys Together . . . But Mostly Apart: Gender Arrangements in Elementary Schools." Pp. 167–82 in *Relationships and Development,* edited by W. Hartup and Z. Rubin. Hillsdale, NJ: Lawrence Erlbaum.

Thorne, Barrie, and Zella Luria. 1986. "Sexuality and Gender in Children's Daily Worlds." *Social Problems* 33:176–90.

Tresemer, David. 1975. "Assumptions Made about Gender Roles." Pp. 308–39 in *Another Voice: Feminist Perspectives on Social Life and Social Science,* edited by M. Millman and R. M. Kanter. New York: Anchor/Doubleday.

West, Candace. 1984. "When the Doctor Is a 'Lady': Power, Status and Gender in Physician–Patient Encounters." *Symbolic Interaction* 7:87–106.

West, Candace, and Bonita Iritani. 1985. "Gender Politics in Mate Selection: The Male-Older

Norm." Paper presented at the Annual Meeting of the American Sociological Association, August, Washington, DC.

West, Candace, and Don Zimmerman. 1983. "Small Insults: A Study of Interruptions in Conversations between Unacquainted Persons." Pp. 102–17 in *Language, Gender and Society,* edited by B. Thorne, C. Kramarae, and N. Henley. Rowley, MA: Newbury House.

Wieder, D. Lawrence. 1974. *Language and Social Reality: The Case of Telling the Convict Code.* The Hague: Mouton.

Williams, Walter L. 1986. *The Spirit and the Flesh: Sexual Diversity in American Indian Culture.* Boston: Beacon.

Wilson, Thomas P. 1970. "Conceptions of Interaction and Forms of Sociological Explanation." *American Sociological Review* 35:697–710.

Zimmerman, Don H., and D. Lawrence Wieder. 1970. "Ethnomethodology and the Problem of Order: Comment on Denzin." Pp. 287–95 in *Understanding Everyday Life,* edited by J. Denzin. Chicago: Aldine.

Chapter Seven

The Meaning of Difference
Gender Theory, Postmodernism, and Psychology

Rachel T. Hare-Mustin and Jeanne Marecek

Conventional meanings of gender typically focus on difference. They emphasize how women differ from men and use these differences to support the norm of male superiority. The overlooking of gender differences occurs as well. Until recently, psychology accepted the cultural meaning of gender as difference, and psychological research offered scientific justification for gender inequality (Lott, 1985a; Morawski, 1985; Shields, 1975; Weisstein, 1971). Theories of psychotherapy similarly supported the cultural meanings of gender (Hare-Mustin, 1983).

The connection between meaning and power has been a focus of postmodernist thinkers (Foucault, 1973; Jameson, 1981). Their inquiry into meaning focuses especially on language and the process of representation. Our concern here is with language as the medium of cognitive life and communication, rather than as the rules by which sentences are strung together. Language is not simply a mirror of reality or a neutral tool (Bruner, 1986; Taggart, 1985; Wittgenstein, 1960; 1953/1967). Language highlights certain features of the objects it represents, certain meanings of the situations it describes. Once designations in language become accepted, one is constrained by them. Language inevitably structures one's own experience of reality as well as the experience of those to whom one communicates.

Language and meaning making are important resources held by those in power. Indeed, Barthes (1957/1972) has called language a sign system used by the powerful to label, define, and rank. Throughout history, men have had greater influence over language than women. This is not to say that women do not also influence language, but within social groups, males have had privileged access to education and thus have had higher rates of literacy; this remains true in developing countries today (Newland, 1979). In addition, more men are published, and men control the print and electronic media (Strainchamps, 1974). The arbiters of language usage are primarily men, from Samuel Johnson and Noah Webster to H. L. Mencken and Strunk and White. Although not all men have influence over language, for those who do, such authority confers the power to create the world from their point of view, in the

Rachel T. Hare-Mustin & Jeanne Maracek, "Gender Theory, Postmodernism, and Psychology." *American Psychologist, 43*, pp. 455–464. © 1988 by the American Psychological Association. Reprinted with permission.

image of their desires. This power is obscured when language is regarded simply as description.

Two recent postmodernist movements, constructivism and deconstruction, challenge the idea of a single meaning of reality and concern themselves with the way meaning is represented. The current interest in constructivism and deconstruction is part of a widespread skepticism about the positivist tradition in science and essentialist theories of truth and meaning (Rorty, 1979). Both constructivism and deconstruction assert that meanings are historically situated and constructed and reconstructed through the medium of language.

In this chapter, we apply postmodernist thought to the psychology of gender. We first take up constructivism. We examine various constructions of gender, and the problems associated with the predominant meaning of gender—that of male–female difference. We then turn to deconstruction. We show how a deconstructive approach to therapeutic discourse can reframe clients' understanding of reality by revealing alternative meanings and thus can promote change. We do not propose a new theory of gender; rather, we shift to a metatheoretical perspective on gender theorizing. Our purpose is not to answer the question of what is the meaning of gender but rather to examine the question.

The Construction of Reality

Constructivism asserts that we do not discover reality, we invent it (Watzlawick, 1984). Our experience does not directly reflect what is "out there" but is an ordering and organizing of it. Knowing is a search for "fitting" ways of behaving and thinking (Von Glaserfeld, 1984). Rather than passively observing reality, we actively construct the meanings that frame and organize our perceptions and experience. Thus, our understanding of reality is a representation, that is, a "re-presentation," not a replica, of what is "out there." Representations of reality are shared meanings that derive from language, history, and culture. Rorty (1979) suggests that the notion of "accurate representation" is a compliment we pay to those beliefs that are successful in helping us do what we want to do.

Constructivism challenges the scientific tradition of positivism, which holds that reality is fixed and can be observed directly, uninfluenced by the observer (Gergen 1985; Sampson 1985; Segal, 1986). As Heisenberg (1952) has pointed out, a truly objective world, devoid of all subjectivity, would be unobservable. Constructivism also challenges the positivist presumption that it is possible to distinguish facts and values; for constructivists, values and attitudes determine what are taken to be facts (Howard, 1985). It is not that formal laws and theories in psychology are wrong or useless, but rather, as Kuhn (1962) asserted, that they are explanations based on a set of social conventions. Thus, whereas positivism asks what are the facts, constructivism asks what are the assumptions; whereas positivism asks what are the answers, constructivism asks what are the questions.

The positivist tradition holds that science is the exemplar of the right use of reason, neutral in its methods, socially beneficial in its results (Flax, 1987). Constructivism, and postmodernism more generally, hold that scientific knowledge, like all other knowledge, cannot be disinterested or politically neutral. In psychology, constructivism, drawing on the ideas of Bateson and Maturana, has influenced epistemological developments in systems theories of the family (Dell, 1985). Constructivist views have also been put forth in developmental psychology (Bronfenbrenner, Kessel, Kessen, & White, 1986; Scarr, 1985), in the psychology of women (Unger, 1983), and in the study of human sexuality (Tiefer, 1987). Constructivist views also form the basis of the social constructionism movement in social psychology, which draws inspiration from symbolic anthropology, ethnomethodology, and related movements in sociology and anthropology (Gergen, 1985).

Theories of gender, like other scientific theories, are representations of reality organized by particular assumptive frameworks and reflecting certain interests. In the next section, we examine gender theorizing in psychology and indicate some of the issues that a constructivist approach makes apparent.

The Construction of Gender as Difference

From a constructivist standpoint, the "real" nature of male and female cannot be determined. Constructivism focuses our attention on representations of gender, rather than on gender itself. The very term *gender* illustrates the power of linguistic categories to determine what we know of the world. The use of gender in contexts other than discussions of grammar is quite recent. Gender was appropriated by American feminists to refer to the social quality of distinctions between the sexes (Scott, 1985). Gender is used in contrast to terms like *sex* and *sexual difference* for the explicit purpose of creating a space in which socially mediated differences can be explored apart from biological differences (Unger, 1979). We still lack an adequate term for speaking of each gender. *Male–female* has the advantage of including the entire life span but implies biological characteristics and fails to distinguish humans from other species. *Men–women* is more restrictive, referring specifically to human adults but omitting childhood and adolescence. We use male–female, as well as men–women, especially when we wish to suggest the entire life span.

Just what constitutes "differentness" is a vexing question for the study of sex and gender. Research that focuses on mean differences may produce one conclusion, whereas research that focuses on range and overlap of distributions may produce another (Luria, 1986). Moreover, the size and direction of gender differences in any particular behavior, such as aggression or helping, will vary according to the norms and expectations for men and women made salient by the setting (Eagly & Crowley, 1986; Eagly & Steffen, 1986). Even more troubling, the very criteria for deciding what should constitute a difference as opposed to a similarity are disputed. How much difference makes a difference? Even anatomical differences between men and women can seem trivial when humans are compared with daffodils or ducks.

Psychological inquiry into gender has held to the construction of gender as difference. One recent line of inquiry reexamines gender with the goal of deemphasizing difference by sorting out "genuine" male–female differences from stereotypes. Some examples include Hyde's (1981) meta-analyses of cognitive differences, Maccoby and Jacklin's (1974) review of sex differences, and Eccles's work on math achievement (Eccles & Jacobs, 1986). The results of this work dispute that male–female differences are as universal, as dramatic, or as enduring as has been asserted (Deaux, 1984). Moreover, this line of inquiry sees the origins of difference as largely social and cultural, rather than biological. Thus, most differences between males and females are seen as culturally and historically fluid.

Another line of inquiry, exemplified in recent feminist psychodynamic theories (e.g., Chodorow, 1978; Eichenbaum & Orbach, 1983; Miller, 1976), takes as its goal establishing and reaffirming differences. Although these theories provide varying accounts of the origins of difference, they all emphasize deep-seated and enduring differences between women and men in "core self-structure," identity, and relational capacities. Other theorists have suggested that gender differences in psychic structure give rise to cognitive differences, for example, differences in moral reasoning and in acquiring and organizing knowledge (cf. Belenky, Clinchy, Goldberger, & Tarule, 1986; Gilligan, 1982; Keller, 1985). All these theorists represent differences between men and women as essential, universal (at least within contemporary Western culture), highly dichotomized, and enduring.

These two lines of inquiry have led to two widely held but incompatible representations of gender, one that sees few differences between males and females and another that sees profound differences. Both groups of theorists have offered empirical evidence, primarily quantitative in the first case and qualitative in the second. Rather than debating which representation of gender is "true," we shift to a meta-level, that provided by constructivism.

From the vantage point of constructivism, theories of gender are representations based on conventional distinctions. Such theories embody one or the other of two contrasting biases, alpha bias and beta bias (Hare-Mustin, 1987). Alpha bias is the tendency to exaggerate differences; beta bias is the tendency to minimize or ignore differences.

The alpha–beta schema is in some ways analogous to that in hypothesis testing. In hypothesis testing, alpha or Type I error involves reporting a significant difference when one does not exist; beta or Type II error involves overlooking a significant difference when one does exist. In our formulation, the term *bias* refers not to the probability of "error" (which would imply that there is a "correct" position), but rather to a systematic inclination to emphasize certain aspects of experience and overlook other aspects. This formulation of bias relates to the idea that all knowledge is influenced by the standpoint of the knower. "Taking a standpoint" has been seen by some feminist theorists as a positive strategy for generating new knowledge (Harding, 1986; Hartsock, 1985). Our use of the term bias underscores our contention that all ideas about difference are social constructs that can never perfectly mirror reality. Alpha and beta bias can be seen in representations of gender, race, class, age, and the like. Here we use the alpha–beta schema to examine recent efforts to theorize about gender.

Alpha Bias

Alpha bias is the exaggeration of differences. The view of male and female as different and opposite and thus as having mutually exclusive qualities transcends Western culture and has deep historical roots. Ideas of male–female opposition are present in Eastern philosophy and in the works of Western philosophers from Aristotle, Aquinas, Bacon, and Descartes to the liberal theory of Locke and the romanticism of Rousseau (Grimshaw, 1986). Women have been regarded as the repository of nonmasculine traits, an "otherness" men assign to women. Alpha bias has been the prevailing view in our culture and one that has also attracted many feminist theorists.

The scientific model developed by Bacon was based on the distinction between "male" reason and its "female" opposites — passion, lust, and emotion (Keller, 1985). Because women were restricted to the private sphere, they did not have knowledge available in the public realm. When women had knowledge, as in witchcraft, their knowledge was disparaged or repudiated. As Keller points out, women's knowledge was associated with insatiable lust; men's knowledge was assumed to be chaste. In Bacon's model of science, nature was cast in the image of the female, to be subdued, subjected to the penetrating male gaze, and forced to yield up her secrets. Our purpose here is not to provide a critique of gender and science, which has been done elsewhere (cf. Keller, 1985; Merchant, 1980), but to draw attention to the long-standing association of women with nature and emotion, and men with their opposites, reason, technology, and civilization (Ortner, 1974).

In psychology, alpha bias can be seen most readily in psychodynamic theories. Freudian theory takes masculinity and male anatomy as the human standard; femininity and female anatomy are deviations from that standard. The Jungian idea of the animus and the anima places the masculine and the feminine in opposition. More recent psychodynamic theories also depict female experience as sharply divergent from male experience. For example, Erikson (1964) holds that female identity is predicated on "inner space," a somatic design that "harbors ... a biological, psychological, and ethical commitment to take care of human infancy" (p. 586) and a sensitive indwelling. Male identity is associated with "outer space," which involves intrusiveness, excitement, and mobility, leading to achievement, political domination, and adventure-seeking. In Lacan's (1985) poststructuralist view, women are "outside" language, public discourse, culture, and the law. The female is defined not by what is, but by the absence or lack of the phallus as the prime signifier. These theories all overlook similarities between males and females and emphasize differences.

Parsons's sex role theory, which dominated the social theories of the 1950s and 1960s, also exaggerates male–female differences (Parsons & Bales, 1955). The very language of sex role theory powerfully conveys the sense that roles are fixed and dichotomous, as well as separate and reciprocal (Thorne, 1982). Parsons asserted that men were instrumental and women were expressive, that is, men were task-oriented and women were oriented toward feelings and relationships. Parsons's sex role theory was hailed as providing a scientific basis for separate spheres for men and women.

Men's nature suited them for paid work and public life; women became first in "goodness" by making their own needs secondary to those of the family and altruistically donating their services to others (Lipman-Blumen, 1984). Parsons believed that separate spheres for men and women were functional in reducing competition and conflict in the family and thus preserving harmony. The role definitions that Parsons put forward became criteria for distinguishing normal individuals and families from those who were pathological or even pathogenic (cf. Broverman, Broverman, Clarkson, Rosenkrantz, & Vogel, 1970).

Alpha bias, or the inclination to emphasize differences, can also be seen in feminist psychodynamic theories such as those of Chodorow (1978), Eichenbaum and Orbach (1983), Gilligan (1982), and Miller (1976). Their emphasis on women's special nature and the richness of women's inner experience has been an important resource for cultural feminism. Cultural feminism is a movement within feminism that encourages women's culture, celebrates the special qualities of women, and values relations among women as a way to escape the sexism of the larger society.

According to Chodorow (1978), boys and girls undergo contrasting experiences of identity formation during their early years under the social arrangement in which women are the exclusive caretakers of infants. Her influential work, which is based on object relations theory, argues that girls' identity is based on similarity and attachment to their mothers whereas boys' identity is predicated on difference, separateness, and independence. These experiences are thought to result in broad-ranging gender differences in personality structures and psychic needs in adulthood. Women develop a deep-seated motivation to have children; men develop the capacity to participate in the alienating work structures of advanced capitalism. Thus, according to Chodorow, the social structure produces gendered personalities that reproduce the social structure. Although Chodorow locates the psychodynamics of personality development temporally and situationally in Western industrial capitalism, much of the work in psychology based on her ideas overlooks this point. Her work is taken to assert essential differences between women and men and to view these, rather than the social structure, as the basis for gender roles (cf. Chernin, 1986; Eichenbaum & Orbach, 1983; Jordan & Surrey, 1986; Schlachet, 1984). In any case, both Chodorow's theory and the work of her followers emphasize differences and thus exemplify alpha bias.

In her study of women's development, Gilligan (1982) harks back to Parson's duality, viewing women as relational and men as instrumental and rational. Her theory of women's moral development echoes some of the gender differences asserted by Freud (1925/1964) and Erikson (1964). She describes female identity as rooted in connections and relationships and female morality as based on an ethic of care. However, unlike Freud, she views women's differences from men in a positive light.

A final example of alpha bias comes from the theories of certain French feminists such as Cixous and Irigaray. They have asserted that differences in the structure of the body and in early childhood experience give rise to differences in language and in the sexual desires of men and women (Donovan, 1985).

Beta Bias

Beta bias, the inclination to ignore or minimize differences, has been less prominent in psychological theory, and thus our treatment of it is necessarily briefer. Until recently, beta bias has gone unnoticed in theories of personality and adult development. Prior to the last decade, most generalizations that psychologists made about human behavior were based on observations of males (Wallston, 1981). The male was the norm against which human behavior was measured, and male experience was assumed to represent all experience. Generalizations about human development based only on the male life course represent a partial view of humanity and overlook the many differences in men's and women's experiences.

Overlooking the social context and differences in social evaluation reflects beta bias. Women and men typically have different access to economic and social resources, and their actions have different social meanings and consequences. Beta bias can be seen in recent social policies and legislation that try to provide equal benefits for men and women, such as comparable parental leave and no-fault divorce (Weitzman, 1985). Beta bias can also be seen in educational and therapeutic programs that ignore aspects of the social context. They groom women for personal or professional success by providing training in what are deemed "male" behaviors or skills, such as assertiveness, authoritative speech patterns, or "male" managerial styles. Such programs make the presumption that a certain manner of speaking or acting will elicit the same reaction regardless of the sex of the actor. This can be questioned (Gervasio & Crawford, 1987; Marecek & Hare-Mustin, 1987). For example, asking for a date, a classic task in assertiveness training, is judged differently for a woman than a man (Muehlenhard, 1983).

Beta bias can also be seen in theories that represent male and female roles or traits as counterparts, as in the theory of psychological androgyny. When the idea of counterparts implies symmetry and equivalence, it obscures differences in power and social value. Bem's (1976) theory of psychological androgyny, which involves the creation of a more "balanced" and healthy personality by integrating positive masculine and feminine qualities, implies the equivalence of such qualities (Morawski, 1985; Worrell, 1978), but in fact, the masculine qualities she includes are more highly valued and adaptive (Bem, 1976). This is not to say that every quality associated with males is regarded as positive. Aggression, for instance, is deplored outside of combat situations.

Beta bias occurs in systems approaches to family therapy such as the systems and structural theories of Haley (1976) and Minuchin (1974). The four primary axes along which hierarchies are established in all societies are class, race, gender, and age. Within families, class and race usually are constant, but gender and age vary. However, family systems theories disregard gender and view generation (that is, age) as the central organizing principle in the family (Hare-Mustin, 1987). In so doing, they ignore the fact that mothers and fathers, though they may be of the same generation, do not necessarily hold comparable power and resources in the family. Systems theories put forward a neutered representation of family life (Libow, 1985).

The Question of Utility

Rather than debate the correctness of various representations of gender, the "true" nature of which cannot be known, constructivism examines their utility or consequences. How do representations of gender provide the meanings and symbols that organize scientific and therapeutic practice in psychology? What are the consequences of representations of gender that either emphasize or minimize male–female difference? The alpha–beta schema affords a framework for discussing the utility of gender theories.

Because alpha bias has been the prevailing representation of gender, we first examine its utility. Alpha bias has had a number of effects on our understanding of gender. The idea of gender as male–female difference and the idea of masculinity and femininity as opposite and mutually exclusive poles on a continuum of personality— as in the Terman-Miles M–F Personality Scale (Terman & Miles, 1936), the Femininity Scale of the California Psychological Inventory (Gough, 1964), and other measures (see Constantinople, 1973)— mask inequality between men and women as well as conflict between them. For example, by construing rationality as an essential male quality and relatedness as an essential female quality, theories like those of Gilligan and Parsons conceal the possibility that those qualities result from social inequities and power differences. Many differences of men and women can be seen as associated with their position in the social hierarchy (Eagly, 1983). Men's propensity to reason from principles may stem from the fact that the principles were formulated to promote their interests; women's concern with relationships can be understood as the need to please others that arises from a lack of power (Hare-Mustin & Marecek, 1986). Typically, those in power advocate rules, discipline, control, and rationality, whereas those without power espouse relatedness and compassion. Thus, in husband–wife conflicts, husbands call on rules and logic, whereas wives call on caring. When women are in the dominant position, however, as in parent–child conflicts, they emphasize rules, whereas children appeal for sympathy and understanding. Such a reversal suggests that these differences can be accounted for by an individual's position in the social hierarchy rather than by gender.

In her interpretations of women's narratives, Gilligan (1982) highlights women's concern with caring and construes it as an essential female attribute. From another point of view, this concern can be seen as the necessity for those in subordinate positions to suppress anger and placate those on whom they depend. In a careful analysis, Hayles (1986) has pointed out that the only female voice that a male world will authorize is one that does not openly express anger.

Feminist psychodynamic theories make assertions of extensive male–female personality differences throughout life. Critics have challenged the idea that a brief period in early life is responsible for broad-ranging differences in men's and women's lives and for gendering all social institutions throughout history (cf. Kagan, 1984; Lott, 1985b; Scott, 1985). Further questions have been raised as to whether changes in patterns of infant caregiving such as Chodorow (1978) and Dinnerstein (1976) have proposed are sufficient to effect social transformation. The alpha bias of feminist psychodynamic theories leads theorists to underplay the influence of economic conditions, social role conditioning, and historical change. Moreover, in focusing on the question of why *differences* exist, feminist psychodynamic theories disregard the question of why *domination* exists.

Alpha bias, the exaggerating of differences between groups, has the additional consequence of ignoring or minimizing within-group variability. Furthermore, out-groups such as women are viewed as more homogeneous than dominant groups (Park & Rothbart, 1982). Thus, men are viewed as individuals, but women are viewed as women. As a result, most psychological theories of gender have not concerned themselves with differences among women that are due to race, class, age, marital status, and social circumstances.

Another consequence of alpha bias is the tendency to view men and women as embodying opposite and mutually exclusive traits. Such a dichotomy seems a caricature of human experience. For example, to maintain the illusion of male autonomy at home and in the workplace, the contribution of women's work must be overlooked. Similarly, the portrayal of women as relational ignores the complexity of their experiences. Rearing children involves achievement, and nurturing others involves power over those in one's care (Hare-Mustin & Marecek, 1986). Gender dichotomies are historically rooted in an era, now past, when the majority of women were not part of the paid labor force (Hare-Mustin, 1988). When gender is represented as dichotomized traits, the possibility that each includes aspects of the other is overlooked.

The autonomy–relatedness dichotomy is not unique; it clearly resembles earlier gender dichotomies, such as instrumentality–expressiveness (Parsons & Bales, 1955) and agency–communion (Bakan, 1966). The idea of man/woman as a universal binary opposition is not a result of faulty definitions, but of prevailing ideology, according to Wilden (1972). He has drawn attention to the way that calling the psychosocial and economic relationships of men and women "opposition" imputes a symmetry to a relationship that is unequal. Furthermore, inequality can only be maintained if interrelationships are denied. The representation of gender as opposition has its source, not in some accidental confusion of logical typing, but in the dominant group's interest in preserving the status quo. The cultural preoccupation with gender difference may be the result (Chodorow, 1979). Dinnerstein (1976) points out that women have been discontent with the double standard, but men on the whole are satisfied with it.

In our opinion, an important positive consequence of alpha bias, or focusing on differences between women and men, is that it has allowed some theorists to assert the worth of certain "feminine" qualities. This has the positive effect of countering the cultural devaluation of women and fostering a valued sense of identity in them. The focus on women's special qualities by some feminists has also prompted a critique of cultural values that extol aggression, the pursuit of self-interest, and narrow individualism. It has furnished an impetus for the development of a feminist social ethics and for a variety of philosophical endeavors (Eisenstein, 1983).

Beta bias, or minimizing differences, also has consequences for understanding gender, but its consequences have received less attention. On the positive side, equal treatment under the law has enabled women to gain greater access to educational and occupational opportunities. This enhanced access is largely responsible for the improvement in some women's status in the last two decades.

Arguing for no differences between women and men, however, draws attention away from women's special needs and from differences in power and resources between women and men. In a society in which one group holds most of the power, seemingly neutral actions usually benefit members of that group, as in no-fault divorce or parental leave. In Weitzman's (1985) research, no-fault divorce settlements were found to have raised men's standard of living 42 percent while lowering that of women and children 73 percent. Another example is the effort to promote public policies granting comparable parental leave for men and women. Such policies overlook the biological changes in childbirth from which women need to recuperate and the demands of breastfeeding, which are met uniquely by women.

Birth is, paradoxically, both an ordinary event and an extraordinary one, as well as the only visible biological link in the kinship system. The failure of the workplace to accommodate women's special needs associated with childbirth represents beta bias, in which male needs and behaviors set the norm.

In therapy, treating men and women as if they are equal is not always equitable (Gilbert, 1980; Margolin, Talovic, Fernandez, & Onorato, 1983). In marital and family therapy, equal treatment may overlook structural inequality between husband and wife. When the social status and economic resources of the husband exceed those of the wife, quid pro quo bargaining as a strategy for resolving conflicts between partners will not lead to equitable results. "Sex-fair" or "gender-neutral" therapies that advocate nonpreferential and nondifferential treatment of women and men to achieve formal equality may inadvertently foster inequality (Marecek & Kravetz, 1977).

Our purpose in examining representations of gender has not been to catalogue every possible consequence of alpha and beta bias but rather to demonstrate that representation is never neutral. From the vantage point of constructivism, theories of gender can be seen as representations that construct our knowledge and inform social and scientific practice. Representation and meaning in language are the focus of deconstruction. We now turn to the ways in which deconstruction can be used to examine the practice of therapy.

Deconstruction

Just as constructivism denies that there is a single fixed reality, the approach to literary interpretation known as deconstruction denies that texts have a single fixed meaning. Deconstruction offers a means of examining the way language operates below our everyday level of awareness to create meaning (Culler, 1982; Segal, 1986). Deconstruction is generally applied to literary texts, but it can be applied equally readily to scientific texts, or, as we suggest, to therapeutic discourse.

A primary tenet of deconstruction is that texts can generate a variety of meanings in excess of what is intended. In this view, language is not a stable system of correspondences of words to objects but "a sprawling limitless web where there is constant circulation of elements" (Eagleton, 1983, p. 129). The meaning of a word depends on its relation to other words, specifically, its difference from other words.

Deconstruction is based on the philosophy of Derrida, who has pointed out that Western thought is built on a series of interrelated hierarchical oppositions, such as reason–emotion, presence–absence, fact–value, good–evil, male–female (Culler, 1982). In each pair, the terms take their meaning from their opposition to (or difference from) each other; each is defined in terms of what the other is not. Moreover, the first member of each pair is considered "more valuable and a better guide to the truth" (Nehamas, 1987, p. 32). However, Derrida challenges both the opposition and the hierarchy, drawing attention to how each term contains elements of the other and depends for its meaning on the other. It is only by marginalizing their similarities that their meaning as opposites is stabilized and the value of one over the other is sustained.

Just as the meaning of a word partly depends on what the word is not, the meaning of a text partly depends on what the text does not say. Deconstructive readings thus rely on gaps, inconsistencies, and contradictions in the text, and even on metaphorical associations, to reveal meanings present in the text but outside our everyday level of awareness. Our intention here is not to provide a detailed explication of deconstruction but to demonstrate how it can be used to understand therapy and gender.

Therapy, Meaning, and Change

Therapy centers on meaning, and language is its medium. A deconstructivist view of the process of therapy draws attention to the play of meanings in the therapist–client dialogue and the way a therapist uses alternative meanings to create possibilities for change. From this standpoint, we examine the therapeutic process as one in which the client asks the therapist to reveal something about the client beyond the client's awareness, something that the client does not know.

Clients in therapy talk not about "actual" experiences but about reconstructed memories that resemble the original experiences only in certain ways. The client's story conforms to prevailing narrative conventions (Spence, 1982). This means that the client's representation of events moves further and further away from the experience and into a descriptive mode. Experience and its description are not the same. The client as narrator is a creator of his or her world, not a disinterested observer.

The therapist's task of listening and responding to the client's narratives is akin to a deconstructive reading of a text. Both seek to uncover hidden subtexts and multiple levels of meaning. The metaphor of therapy as healing is an idealization that obscures another metaphor, that therapists manipulate meanings. These metaphors are not contrary to each other; rather, as part of helping clients change, therapists change clients' meanings (Haley, 1976). Just as deconstructive readings disrupt the frame of reference within which conventional meanings of a text are organized, so a therapist's interventions disrupt the frame of reference within which the client sees the world. Providing new frames imparts new meanings (Watzlawick, Weakland, & Fisch, 1974).

As a multiplicity of meanings becomes apparent through such therapist actions as questioning, explaining, and disregarding, more possibilities for change emerge. The deconstructive process is most apparent in psychoanalysis, but indeed, all therapy involves changing meaning as part of changing behavior.

Gender and Meaning in Therapy

Just as a poem can have many readings, a client's experience can have many meanings. However, as postmodernist scholars have pointed out, certain meanings are privileged because they conform to the explanatory systems of the dominant culture. As a cultural institution whose purpose is to help individuals adapt to their social condition, therapy largely reflects and promulgates privileged meanings. For therapists who bring a social critique to their work, therapy involves bringing out alternative or marginalized meanings. In what follows, we examine certain privileged and marginalized meanings in relation to gender issues, issues that have been the center of considerable debate among therapists and in society at large (Brodsky & Hare-Mustin, 1980).

When we look at Freud's classic case of Dora (Freud, 1905/1963) from a deconstructive perspective, we can see it as a therapist's attempt to adjust the meaning a client attaches to her experience to match the prevailing meanings of the patriarchal society in which she lives. Dora viewed the sexual attentions of her father's associate, Herr K., as unwanted and uninvited. She responded to them with revulsion. Freud framed the encounter with Herr K. as a desirable one for a fourteen-year-old girl and interpreted Dora's revulsion as disguised sexual arousal. When Dora refused to accept Freud's construction, he labeled her as vengeful and the therapy as a failure.

From our vantage point ninety years after Dora's encounter with Freud, the case shows how meanings embedded in the dominant culture often go unrecognized or unacknowledged. Freud evidently viewed Herr K.'s lecherous advances as acceptable behavior, although Herr K. was married and Dora was only fourteen and the daughter of a close family friend. We might surmise that the cultural belief in the primacy of men's sexual needs prevented Freud from seeing Dora's revulsion as genuine.

Freud's analysis of Dora provides an example of how a therapist attempts to reaffirm privileged meanings and marginalize and discourage other meanings. The many meanings of Dora's behavior—and Freud's as well—are evident in the numerous reanalyses, film representations, and critical literary readings of the case.

Conventional meanings of gender are embedded in the language of therapy. Like all language, the language used in therapy can be thought of as metaphoric: it selects, emphasizes, suppresses, and organizes certain features of experience and thus imparts meaning to experience. For example, "Oedipus complex" imposes the complexity of adult erotic feelings onto the experiences of small children and emphasizes male development and the primacy of the phallus. The metaphor of the "family ledger" in family therapy implies that family relations are (or should be) organized as mercantile exchanges and centered on male achievements (Boszormenyi-Nagy & Sparks, 1973).

Therapists can also use language and metaphor to disrupt dominant meanings.

With respect to gender, for example, a therapist may "unpack" the metaphor of "family harmony" and expose the hierarchy by pointing out that accord within the family often is achieved through women's acquiescence and accommodation (Hare-Mustin, 1978, 1987). The stress generated by women's prescribed family roles is marginalized or overlooked (Baruch, Biener, & Barnett, 1987). In unpacking the metaphor of "family loyalty," the therapist may draw attention to the way the needs of some family members are subordinated to those of dominant members in the name of loyalty. Pogrebin (1983) has disrupted such metaphors as "preserving the family," or "the decline of the family," by suggesting that "the family" is a metaphor for male dominance when used in this way.

When the metaphor of "women's dependency" is disrupted, the dependency of men and boys on women as wives and mothers is revealed. Women have traditionally been characterized as dependent, but Lerner (1983) has questioned whether women have been dependent enough, that is, have been able to call on others to meet their needs. The therapist may draw attention to the way men's dependency on women is obscured while women's own dependency needs go unmet.

As we have shown, the resemblance of therapeutic discourse to narrative offers the possibility of using deconstruction as a resource for understanding meaning and the process of therapy. Therapy typically confirms privileged meanings, but deconstruction directs attention to marginalized meanings. Doing therapy from a feminist standpoint is like the deconstructivist's "reading as a woman" (Culler, 1982). The therapist exposes gender-related meanings that reside in culturally embedded metaphors such as "family harmony," but go unacknowledged in the conventional understanding of those metaphors. These examples also show how deconstruction reveals the meanings of gender embedded in the hierarchical opposition of male–female.

Conclusion

Postmodernism makes us aware of connections among meaning, power, and language. A constructivist view of gender theorizing in contemporary psychology reveals that gender is represented as a continuum of psychological difference. This representation serves to simplify and purify the concept of gender; it obscures the complexity of human action and shields both men and women from the discomforting recognition of inequality. Deconstruction focuses attention on hidden meanings in culturally embedded metaphors. Applying deconstruction to the discourse of therapy shows how metaphors also simplify gender by obscuring and marginalizing alternative meanings of gender. From a postmodernist perspective, there is no one "right" view of gender, but various views that present certain paradoxes.

Paradoxes in Gender Theorizing

Paradoxes arise because every representation conceals at the same time it reveals. For example, focusing on gender differences marginalizes and obscures the interrelatedness of women and men as well as the restricted opportunities of both. It also obscures institutional sexism and the extent of male authority.

The issue of gender differences has been a divisive one for feminist scholars. Some believe that differences affirm women's value and special nature; others are concerned that focusing on differences reinforces the status quo and supports inequality, given that the power to define remains with men. A paradox is that efforts to affirm the special value of women's experience and their "inner life" turn attention away from efforts to change the material conditions of women's lives and alleviate institutional sexism (Fine, 1985; Russ, 1986; Tobias, 1986). Another paradox arises from the assertion of a female way of knowing, involving intuition and experiential understanding, rather than logical abstraction. This assertion implies that all other thought is a male way of knowing, and if taken to an extreme, can be used to support the view that women are incapable of rational thought and of acquiring the knowledge of the culture.

There is a paradox faced by any social change movement, including feminism: Its critique is necessarily determined by the nature of the larger social system, and its meanings are embedded in that system. Moreover, feminist separatism, the attempt to avoid male influence by separating from men, leaves intact the larger system of male control in the society. In addition, as Sennett (1980) has observed, even when one's response to authority is defiance, that stance serves to confirm authority just as compliance does. In this regard, Dinnerstein (1976) has suggested that woman is not really the enemy of the system but its loyal opposition.

There is yet another paradox. Qualities such as caring, expressiveness, and concern for relationships are extolled as women's superior virtues and the wellspring of public regeneration. At the same time, however, they are seen as arising from women's subordination (Miller, 1976). When we extol such qualities, do we necessarily also extol women's subordination (Echols, 1983; Ringleheim, 1985)? If subordination makes women "better people," then the perpetuation of women's "goodness" would seem to require the perpetuation of inequality.

The assertion that women are "as good as" men is a source of pride for some women, but it is also a paradox arising from beta bias. Man is the hidden referent in our language and culture. As Spender (1984) points out, "women can only aspire to be as good as a man, there is no point in trying to be as good as a woman" (p. 201). Paradoxically, this attempt at denying differences reaffirms male behavior as the standard against which all behavior is judged.

In conclusion, difference is a problematic and paradoxical way to construe gender. What we see is that alpha and beta bias have similar assumptive frameworks, despite their diverse emphases. Both take the male as the standard of comparison and support the status quo. Both construct gender as attributes of individuals, not as the ongoing relations of men and women, particularly relations of domination. Neither effectively challenges the gender hierarchy. The representation of gender as difference frames the problem of what gender is in such a way that the solution produces "more of the same" (Watzlawick, Weakland, & Fisch, 1974).

The paradoxes we discover when we challenge the construction of gender as difference shake us loose from our conventional thought, revealing meanings that are present but obscured in the dominant view. Contradictions become apparent when we examine the play among meanings and entertain the question of the utility of various representations.

Postmodernism accepts randomness, incoherence, indeterminacy, and paradox, which positivist paradigms are designed to exclude. Postmodernism creates distance from the seemingly fixed language of established meanings and fosters skepticism about the fixed nature of reality. Constructing gender is a process, not an answer. In using a postmodernist approach, we open the possibility of theorizing gender in heretofore unimagined ways. Postmodernism allows us to see that as observers of gender we are also its creators.

REFERENCES

Bakan, D. (1966). *The duality of human existence.* Chicago: Rand McNally.

Barthes, R. (1972). *Mythologies* (A. Lavers, Trans.). New York: Hill & Wang. (Original work published 1957).

Baruch, G. K., Biener, L., & Barnett, R. C. (1987). Women and gender in research on work and family stress. *American Psychologist. 42,* 130–136.

Belenky, M. F., Clinchy, B. M., Goldberger, N. R., & Tarule, J. M. (1986). *Women's ways of knowing: Development of self, voice, and mind.* New York: Basic Books.

Bem, S. L. (1976). Probing the promise of androgyny. In A. G. Kaplan & J. P. Bean (Eds.), *Beyond sex-role stereotypes: Readings toward a psychology of androgyny* (pp. 48–62). Boston: Little, Brown.

Boszormenyi-Nagy, I., & Sparks, G. M. (1973). *Invisible loyalties.* New York: Harper & Row.

Brodsky, A. M., & Hare-Mustin, R. T. (1980). *Women and psychotherapy: An assessment of research and practice.* New York: Guilford.

Bronfenbrenner, U., Kessel, F., Kessen, W., & White, S. (1986). Toward a critical social history of developmental psychology: A propaedeutic discussion. *American Psychologist, 41,* 1218–1230.

Broverman, I. K., Broverman, D. M., Clarkson, F. E., Rosenkrantz, P., & Vogel, S. R. (1970). Sex role stereotypes and clinical judgments of mental health. *Journal of Consulting Psychology, 34,* 1–7.

Bruner, J. (1986). *Actual minds, possible worlds.* Cambridge, MA: Harvard University Press.

Chernin, K. (1986). *The hungry self: Women, eating, and identity.* New York: Perennial Library.

Chodorow, N. (1978). *The reproduction of mothering.* Berkeley: University of California Press.

Chodorow, N. (1979). Feminism and difference: Gender, relation, and difference in psychoanalytic perspective. *Socialist Review, 9*(4), 51–70.

Constantinople, A. (1973). Masculinity–femininity: An exception to a famous dictum. *Psychological Bulletin, 80,* 389–407.

Culler, J. (1982). *On deconstruction: Theory and criticism after structuralism.* Ithaca, NY: Cornell University Press.

Deaux, K. (1984). From individual differences to social categories: Analysis of a decade's research on gender. *American Psychologist, 39,* 105–116.

Dell, P. F. (1985). Understanding Bateson and Maturana: Toward a biological foundation for the social sciences. *Journal of Marital and Family Therapy, 11,* 1–20.

Dinnerstein, D. (1976). *The mermaid and the minotaur.* New York: Harper & Row.

Donovan, J. (1985). *Feminist theory: The intellectual traditions of American feminism.* New York: Ungar.

Eagleton, T. (1983). *Literary theory: An introduction.* Minneapolis: University of Minnesota Press.

Eagly, A. H. (1983). Gender and social influence: A social psychological analysis. *American Psychologist, 38,* 971–981.

Eagly, A. H., & Crowley, M. (1986). Gender and helping behavior: A meta-analytic review of the social psychological literature. *Psychological Bulletin, 100,* 283–308.

Eagly, A. H., & Steffen, V. J. (1986). Gender and aggressive behavior: A meta-analytic review of the social psychological literature. *Psychological Bulletin, 100,* 309–330.

Eccles, J., & Jacobs, J. (1986). Social forces shape math participation. *Signs, 11,* 368–380.

Echols, A. (1983). The new feminism of yin and yang. In A. Snitow, C. Stansell, & S. Thompson (Eds.), *Powers of desire: The politics of sexuality* (pp. 440–459). New York: Monthly Review Press.

Eichenbaum, L., & Orbach, S. (1983). *Understanding women: A feminist psychoanalytic approach.* New York: Basic Books.

Eisenstein, H. (1983). *Contemporary feminist thought.* Boston: G. K. Hall.

Erikson, E. H. (1964). Inner and outer space: Reflections on womanhood. *Daedalus, 93,* 582–606.

Fine, M. (1985). Reflections on a feminist psychology of women. *Psychology of Women Quarterly, 9,* 167–183.

Flax, J. (1987). Postmodernism and gender relations in feminist theory. *Signs, 12,* 621–643.

Foucault, M. (1973). *The order of things.* New York: Vintage.

Freud, S. (1963). *Dora: An analysis of a case of hysteria.* New York: Collier Books. (Original work published 1905)

Freud, S. (1964). Some psychical consequences of the anatomical distinction between the sexes. In J. Strachey (Ed. and Trans.), *Standard edition of the complete psychological works of Sigmund Freud* (Vol. 19, pp. 243–258). London: Hogarth Press. (Original work published 1925)

Gergen, K. J. (1985). The social constructionist movement in modern psychology. *American Psychologist, 40,* 266–275.

Gervasio, A. H., & Crawford, M. (1987). *Social evaluations of assertiveness: A review and reformulation.* Unpublished manuscript, Hamilton College, Clinton, NY.

Gilbert, L. A. (1980). Feminist therapy. In A. M. Brodsky & R. T. Hare-Mustin (Eds.), *Women and psychotherapy: An assessment of research and practice* (pp. 245–265). New York: Guilford.

Gilligan, C. (1982). *In a different voice: Psychological theory and women's development.* Cambridge, MA: Harvard University Press.

Gough, H. G. (1964). *California Psychological Inventory: Manual.* Palo Alto, CA: Consulting Psychologists Press.

Grimshaw, J. (1986). *Philosophy and feminist thinking.* Minneapolis: University of Minnesota Press.

Haley, J. (1976). *Problem-solving therapy.* San Francisco: Jossey-Bass.

Harding, S. (1986). *The science question in feminism.* Ithaca, NY: Cornell University Press.

Hare-Mustin, R. T. (1978). A feminist approach to family therapy. *Family Process, 17,* 181–194.

Hare-Mustin, R. T. (1983). An appraisal of the relationship of women and psychotherapy: 80 years after the case of Dora. *American Psychologist, 38,* 593–601.

Hare-Mustin, R. T. (1987). The problem of gender in family therapy theory. *Family Process, 26,* 15–27.

Hare-Mustin, R. T. (1988). Family change and gender differences: Implications for theory and practice. *Family Relations, 37,* 36–41.

Hare-Mustin, R. T., & Marecek, J. (1986). Autonomy and gender: Some questions for therapists. *Psychotherapy 23,* 205–212.

Hartsock, N. C. M. (1985). *Money, sex, and power: Toward a feminist historical materialism.* Boston: Northeastern University Press.

Hayles, N. K. (1986). Anger in different voices: Carol Gilligan and *The Mill on the Floss. Signs, 12,* 23–39.

Heisenberg, W. (1952). Philosophic problems of nuclear science (F. C. Hayes, Trans.). New York: Pantheon.

Howard, G. (1985). The role of values in the science of psychology. *American Psychologist, 40,* 255–265.

Hyde, J. S. (1981). How large are cognitive gender differences? American Psychologist, 36, 892–901.

Jameson, F. (1981). *The political unconscious: Narrative as a socially symbolic act.* Ithaca, NY: Cornell University Press.

Jordan, J. V., & Surrey, J. L. (1986). The self-in-relation: Empathy and the mother–daughter relationship. In T. Bernay & D. W. Cantor (Eds.) *The psychology of today's woman: New psychoanalytic visions* (pp. 81–104). New York: Analytic Press.

Kagan, J. (1984). *The nature of the child.* New York: Basic Books.

Keller, E. F. (1985). *Reflections on gender and science.* New Haven, CT: Yale University Press.

Kuhn, T. S. (1962). *The structure of scientific revolutions.* Chicago, IL: University of Chicago Press.

Lacan, J. (1985). *Feminine sexuality* (J. Mitchell & J. Rose, Eds.; J. Rose, Trans.). New York: Norton.

Lerner, H. G. (1983). Female dependency in context: Some theoretical and technical considerations. *American Journal of Orthopsychiatry, 53,* 697–705.

Libow, J. (1985). Gender and sex role issues as family secrets. *Journal of Strategic and Systemic Therapies, 4*(2), 32–41.

Lipman-Blumen, J. (1984). *Gender roles and power.* Englewood Cliffs, NJ: Prentice-Hall.

Lott, B. (1985a). The potential enrichment of social/personality psychology through feminist research and vice versa. *American Psychologist, 40,* 155–164.

Lott, B. (1985b). *Women's lives: Themes and variations.* Belmont, CA: Brooks/Cole.

Luria, Z. (1986). A methodological critique: On "In a different voice." *Signs, 11,* 316–321.

Maccoby, E. E., & Jacklin, C. N. (1974). *The psychology of sex differences.* Stanford, CA: Stanford University Press.

Marecek, J., & Hare-Mustin, R. T. (1987, March). *Cultural and radical feminism in therapy: Divergent views of change.* Paper presented at the meeting of the American Orthopsychiatric Association, Washington, DC.

Marecek, J., & Kravetz, D. (1977). Women and mental health: A review of feminist change efforts. *Psychiatry, 40,* 323–329.

Margolin, G., Talovic, S., Fernandez, V., & Onorato, R. (1983). Sex role considerations and behavioral marital therapy: Equal does not mean identical. *Journal of Marital and Family Therapy, 9,* 131–145.

Merchant, C. (1980). *The death of nature: Women, ecology, and the scientific revolution.* San Francisco: Harper & Row.

Miller, J. B. (1976). *Toward a new psychology of women.* Boston: Beacon Press.

Minuchin, S. (1974). *Families and family therapy.* Cambridge, MA: Harvard University Press.

Morawski, J. G. (1985). The measurement of masculinity and femininity: Engendering categorical realities. *Journal of Personality, 53,* 196–223.

Muehlenhard, C. L. (1983). Women's assertion and the feminine sex-role stereotype. In V. Frank & E. D. Rothblum (Eds.), *The stereotyping of women: Its effects on mental health* (pp. 153–171). New York: Springer.

Nehamas, A. (1987, October 5). Truth and consequences: How to understand Jacques Derrida. *The New Republic,* pp. 31–36.

Newland, K. (1979). *The sisterhood of man.* New York: Norton.

Ortner, S. B. (1974). Is female to male as nature is to culture? In M. Z. Rosaldo & L. Lamphere (Eds.), *Women, culture, and society* (pp. 67–87). Stanford, CA: Stanford University Press.

Park, B., & Rothbart, M. (1982). Perception of out-group homogeneity and levels of social categorization: Memory for the subordinate attributes of in-group and out-group members. *Journal of Personality and Social Psychology, 42,* 1051–1068.

Parsons, T., & Bales, R. F. (1955). *Family, socialization, and interaction process.* Glencoe, IL: Free Press.

Pogrebin, L. C. (1983). *Family politics: Love and power on an intimate frontier.* New York: McGraw-Hill.

Ringleheim, J. (1985). Women and the Holocaust: A reconsideration of research. *Signs, 10,* 741–761.

Rorty, R. (1979). *Philosophy and the mirror of nature.* Princeton, NJ: Princeton University Press.

Russ, J. (1986). Letter to the editor. *Women's Review of Books, 3*(12), 7.

Sampson, E. E. (1985). The decentralization of identity: Toward a revised concept of personal and social order. *American Psychologist, 40,* 1203–1211.

Scarr, S. (1985). Constructing psychology: Making facts and fables for our times. *American Psychologist, 40,* 499–512.

Schlachet, B. C. (1984). Female role socialization: The analyst and the analysis. In C. M. Brody (Ed.), *Women therapists for working with women* (pp. 55–65). New York: Springer.

Scott, J. (1985, December). *Is gender a useful category of historical analysis?* Paper presented at the meeting of the American Historical Association, New York.

Segal, L. (1986). *The dream of reality: Heinz von Foerster's constructivism.* New York: Norton.

Sennett, R. (1980). *Authority.* New York: Knopf.

Shields, S. A. (1975). Functionalism, Darwinism, and the psychology of women: A study in social myth. *American Psychologist, 30,* 739–754.

Spence, D. P. (1982). *Narrative truth and historical truth.* New York: Norton.

Spender, D. (1984). Defining reality: A powerful tool. In C. Kramarae, M. Schulz, & W. M. O'Barr (Eds.), *Language and power* (pp. 194–205). Beverly Hills, CA: Sage.

Strainchamps, E. (Ed.). (1974). *Rooms with no view: A woman's guide to the man's world of the media.* New York: Harper & Row.

Taggart, M. (1985). The feminist critique in epistemological perspective: Questions of context in family therapy. *Journal of Marital and Family Therapy, 11,* 113–126.

Terman, L. M., & Miles, C. C. (1936). *Sex and personality.* New York: McGraw Hill.

Thorne, B. (1982). Feminist rethinking of the family: An overview. In B. Thorne & M. Yalom (Eds.), *Rethinking the family: Some feminist questions* (pp. 1–24). New York: Longmans.

Tiefer, L. (1987). Social constructionism and the study of human sexuality. In P. Shaver & C.

Hendrick (Eds.), *Review of social and personality psychology: Vol. 7. Sex and gender* (pp. 70–94). Beverly Hills, CA: Sage.

Tobias, S. (1986). "In a different voice" and its implications for feminism. *Women's Studies in Indiana, 12*(2), 1–2, 4.

Unger, R. K. (1979). Toward a redefinition of sex and gender. *American Psychologist, 34,* 1085–1094.

Unger, R. K. (1983). Through the looking glass: No wonderland yet! (The reciprocal relationship between methodology and models of reality). *Psychology of Women Quarterly, 8,* 9–32.

Von Glaserfeld, E. (1984). An introduction to radical constructivism. In P. Watzlawick (Ed.), *The invented reality: Contributions to constructivism* (pp. 17–40). New York: Norton.

Wallston, B. S. (1981). What are the questions in psychology of women? A feminist approach to research. *Psychology of Women Quarterly, 5,* 597–617.

Watzlawick, P. (Ed.). (1984). *The invented reality: Contributions to constructivism.* New York: Norton.

Watzlawick, P., Weakland, J. H., & Fisch, R. (1974). *Change: Principles of problem formation and problem resolution.* New York: Norton.

Weisstein, N. (1971). Psychology constructs the female. In V. Gornick & B. K. Moran (Eds.), *Woman in sexist society* (pp. 133–146). New York: Basic Books.

Weitzman, L. J. (1985). *The divorce revolution: The unexpected social and economic consequences for women and children in America.* New York: Free Press.

Wilden, A. (1972). *System and structure: Essays in communication and exchange.* London: Tavistock.

Wittgenstein, L. (1960). *Preliminary studies for the "Philosophical Investigations": The blue and brown books.* Oxford: Blackwell.

Wittgenstein, L. (1967). *Philosophical investigations.* Oxford: Blackwell. (Original work published 1953)

Worrell, J. (1978). Sex roles and psychological well-being: Perspectives on methodology. *Journal of Consulting and Clinical Psychology, 46,* 777–791.

Comment

Selective Citation

Julian C. Stanley

Hare-Mustin and Marecek wrote as follows: "Constructivism asserts that we do not discover reality, we invent it. . . . Rather than passively observing reality, we actively construct the meanings that frame and organize our perceptions and experience." This would seem to imply that authors of articles such as theirs construct meanings partly by what they choose to cite, for example, Hyde (1981) but not Stanley and Benbow's (1982) critical comment about it or Benbow and Stanley's (1983) finding of a 13-to-1 gender difference in mathematical reasoning ability. This enabled them to say that the results of the four works they cited "dispute that male–female differences are as universal, as dramatic, or as enduring as has been asserted."

Many writers choose to omit evidence contrary to their beliefs, and the studies by Benbow and Stanley (1980, 1981, 1982, 1983) and Stanley (1987) were omitted in this case. Yes, when viewed from a politics-of-gender perspective there may not be much actual "reality" out there. At least, however, published empirical evidence based on large data sets should be allowed to make its contribution to the jousting.

REFERENCES

Benbow, C. P., & Stanley, J. C. (1980). Sex differences in mathematical reasoning ability: Fact or artifact? *Science, 210,* 1262–1264.

Benbow, C. P., & Stanley, J. C. (1981). Mathematical ability: Is sex a factor? *Science, 212,* 118–119.

Benbow, C. P., & Stanley, J. C. (1982). Consequences in high school and college of sex differences in mathematical reasoning ability: A longitudinal perspective. *American Educational Research Journal, 19,* 598–622.

Benbow, C. P., & Stanley, J. C. (1983). Sex differences in mathematical reasoning ability: More facts. *Science, 222,* 1029–1031.

Hyde, J. S. (1981). How large are cognitive gender differences? *American Psychologist, 36,* 892–901.

Stanley, J. C. (1987, April 24). *Summary of points made about 82 cognitive tests in symposium entitled "Sex differences in cognitive abilities and achievements."* Paper presented at the meeting of the American Educational Research Association, Washington, DC.

Stanley, J. C., & Benbow, C. P. (1982). Huge sex ratios at upper end. *American Psychologist, 37,* 972.

Notes on Postmodernism and the Psychology of Gender

Barnaby B. Barratt and Barrie Ruth Straus

For too long, psychology has pretended that its methods are neutral; thus, it is refreshing to find an article published in the *American Psychologist* that insists on examining the non-neutrality of the system of representations through which inquiry is conducted. Hare-Mustin and Marecek's dual attempt to introduce postmodernist ideas to psychology and to elaborate feminist concerns in relation to the deconstructionist approach to discourse is exciting and commendable. However, confusions in their arguments reveal a miscomprehension of postmodernism that grossly oversimplifies and vitiates its significance. Postmodernist thinking in general, and deconstruction in particular, constitute a critique of the "rationality" that has beguiled science for the past three centuries. Although Hare-Mustin and Marecek recognized that deconstruction is "part of a widespread skepticism about the positivist tradition in science and essentialist theories of truth and meaning," their article does not demonstrate a full grasp of the significance of this radicalism. Deconstruction is more than just an attitude of skepticism; it calls into question the very "rationality" that Hare-Mustin and Marecek end up endorsing. In this way, their work falls short of the goals to which it seems to aspire; thus, despite its appearances, their article does not ultimately succeed in furthering feminist scholarship. We hope the following points will clarify these issues.

1. Hare-Mustin and Marecek's initial introductory remarks about deconstruction are helpful, but their later remarks confuse this highly important and distinctive approach to the study of discourse with a range of familiar hermeneutic techniques, to which deconstruction might more advantageously be contrasted. It is neither precise scholarship nor justifiable in terms of an overall polemical intent to confuse deconstruction with the exegetical pursuit of "hidden meanings," or with methods that generate "alternative meanings" by which to critique and change the prevailing discourse, or with an approach that purports to adjudicate between representations on the basis of some external criterion such as their "utility" or the "interests" they seem to serve. Perhaps these misleading aspects of the article result from the authors' apparent reliance on secondary sources in their discussion of deconstruction. Although they knew deconstruction to be the work of Jacques Derrida, they never specifically cited any of the writings that exemplify his approach (e.g., Derrida, 1967/ 1978, 1972/1981). More remarkably, they did not seem familiar with any of the publications in which Derrida has offered deconstructionist treatments of gender issues (e.g., 1978/1979, 1982). Hare-Mustin and Marecek did not mention some of the best programmatic texts that have already advocated the marriage of deconstruction and feminism (e.g., Meese, 1986; Spivak, 1987), and they did not seem to have read properly the works of many eminent feminists who actually deploy a deconstructive approach in their publications on gender (e.g., Cixous & Clément, 1975/1986; Irigaray, 1974/1985a, 1977/1985b).

2. The authors' scholarship lapses more grossly in their use of the terms *modernism* and *postmodernism*. Contrary to their assertions, *constructivism* cannot, by even

the wildest stretch of imagination, be properly called a postmodernist movement. Considered as the doctrine that subjects "actively construct the meanings that frame and organize . . . perceptions and experiences" and that "reality" is represented (that it is, in a certain sense, invented not discovered), constructivism not only dates at least from the eighteenth century (notwithstanding that twentieth-century psychology has only just learned of it), but also might appropriately be characterized as *the* exemplary movement of modernism. Modernism is, after all, a complex set of metaphysical assumptions about the nature of knowledge (an *episteme*) that privilege the creativity of the agential or authorial (phallocentric) subject in the constitution of meaning. It elaborates an "identitarian" doctrine concerning the unified totality of representations as a system, and it thus upholds the motif of mastery (knowledge as domination, difference as deficit). Postmodernism is a distinctively twentieth-century movement that might aptly be characterized by its critique of constructivism: Although postmodernist thinkers do emphasize the representational condition of reality, their work typically is an attack on the notion of subject-centered reason, on the ontology of being as presence, and on the (phallo) logocentric metaphysics of the epistemic totality as absolute and identitarian. For definitional discussions of modernism and postmodernism, we recommend the works of Reiss (1982, 1988), and Lyotard (1979/1984). We also urge that the works of postmodernist thinkers be *read*: for example, the writings of Georges Bataille, Maurice Blanchot, Emmanuel Levinas, and others have an enormously rich significance for anyone interested in the study of the human mind.

3. The confused and inaccurate account of the intellectual movements that the authors address (modernism, postmodernism, constructivism, deconstruction) is paralleled by their "grasp" of psychoanalysis. It seems tendentious to denounce psychodynamic theories by asserting that they "all overlook similarities between males and females," while later crediting psychoanalytic method as being the "most apparent" example of a deconstructive process in psychotherapy. There are indeed postmodernist thinkers who are psychoanalysts and have used a feminist psychoanalysis precisely in powerful deconstructionist scholarship against patriarchy and the psychological implications of its phallocentric discourse. However, Hare-Mustin and Marecek either omitted these works entirely (e.g., Kristeva, 1986) or cursorily dismissed them on the basis of secondary sources as merely exemplifying "alpha bias" (e.g., Cixous & Clément, 1975/1986; Irigaray, 1974/1985a, 1977/1985b). Also Hare-Mustin and Marecek should know that there are ongoing discussions concerning the dialectical and deconstructive character of psychoanalysis (cf. Barratt, 1984) and concerning the postmodernist character of psychoanalysis (cf. Barratt, 1988, 1989); this is not to deny that much of "psychoanalytic" practice is embedded in modernist and patriarchal assumptions.

4. This brings us to some concluding comments concerning Hare-Mustin and Marecek's own position. Their central thesis seems to be as follows: If gender differences are ignored or minimized ("beta bias"), all experience is represented in terms of the predominant standards of phallocentric ("masculine") discourse, but if gender differences are exaggerated ("alpha bias"), then there is at least some hope that the consequent focus can be used critically against the predominant "masculine"

standards; however, both tendencies ("biases") illustrate that "masculine standards" are indeed predominant in the structuring of our thinking (in exactly what way the authors then infer that *both* tendencies "support the status quo," we will leave aside). This central thesis is, in our view, excellent (although not new). The thesis—with which we are in agreement—is surely that *all* human experiences and understandings are constituted within a representational system that is phallocentric. Such a thesis has important critical implications (even though it should not be taken to imply, in the way that these authors did seem to imply, that we can willingly step outside this system, relinquish its "presuppositions," and change it). But why must Hare-Mustin and Marecek dress up this thesis with the pseudotechnological jargon of "alpha and beta bias"? It does not empower methodology; rather it obfuscates the central requirement for a critical study of discourse, about which Hare-Mustin and Marecek actually seemed confused. The misleading notion they seemed to advance— which runs against the entire current of postmodernist thinking—upholds the potency of subjects to change the discourse system within which their own experiences and understandings are constituted. The authors' interest in nonpsychoanalytic styles of "psychotherapy" that achieve their "utilitarian" effects by techniques of the manipulation of and the mastery of meanings is exemplary here. Techniques based on mastery and manipulation subscribe to the same logic and rhetoric of domination as the oppressive culture they may be designed to oppose. Whatever the liberal "intentionality" of the practitioners, such techniques, operating on thoroughly modernist assumptions, endorse precisely the very system of phallocentric discourse that Hare-Mustin and Marecek seemed to wish to deconstruct. Thus, in this article, under the guise of feminism, the discourse of domination—the episteme of an oppressive "rationality"—and all its profoundly patriarchal values, is once again replicated (cf. Mills, 1987). As a result, Hare-Mustin and Marecek's work is neither postmodernist nor deconstructive and does not advance feminism. Psychology and feminism could indeed benefit from the lessons of both postmodernist criticism and a deconstructive approach; regrettably, Hare-Mustin and Marecek's work has not yet helped to move us in this direction.

REFERENCES

Barratt, B. B. (1984). *Psychic reality and psychoanalytic knowing*. Hillsdale, NJ: Analytic Press.

Barratt, B. B. (1988). Why is psychoanalysis so controversial? Notes from left field! *Psychoanalytic Psychology, 5*(3), 223–239.

Barratt, B. B. (1989). *Knowing and being since Freud's psychology*. Book in preparation.

Cixous, H., & Clément, C. (1986). *The newly born woman* (B. Wing, Trans.). Minneapolis: University of Minnesota Press. (Original work published 1975)

Derrida, J. (1978). *Writing and difference* (A. Bass, Trans.) Chicago: University of Chicago Press. (Original work published 1967)

Derrida, J. (1979). *Spurs: Nietzsche's styles* (B. Harlow, Trans.). Chicago: University of Chicago Press. (Original work published 1978)

Derrida, J. (1981). *Dissemination* (B. Johnson, Trans.). Chicago: University of Chicago Press. (Original work published 1972)

Derrida, J. (1982). Choreographies. *Diacritics, 12,* 66–76.

Irigaray, L. (1985a). *Speculum of the other woman* (G. C. Gill, Trans.). Ithaca, NY: Cornell University Press. (Original work published 1974)

Irigaray, L. (1985b). *This sex which is not one* (C. Porter, Trans.). Ithaca, NY: Cornell University Press. (Original work published 1977)

Kristeva, J. (1986). *The Kristeva reader* (T. Moi, Ed). New York: Columbia University Press.

Lyotard, J-F. (1984). *The postmodern condition: A report on knowledge* (G. Bennington & B. Massumi, Trans.). Minneapolis: University of Minnesota Press. (Original work published 1979)

Meese, E. A. (1986). *Crossing the double-cross.* Chapel Hill: University of North Carolina Press.

Mills, P. J. (1987). *Woman, nature, and psyche.* New Haven: Yale University Press.

Reiss, T. J. (1982). *The discourse of modernism.* Ithaca, NY: Cornell University Press.

Reiss, T. J. (1988). *The uncertainty of analysis: Problems in truth, meaning, and culture.* Ithaca, NY: Cornell University Press.

Spivak, G. C. (1987). *In other worlds: Essays in cultural politics.* New York: Methuen.

Science, Genre, and the New Style: Some Constructive Criticisms

James Walkup

It is a rare topic in the humanities or social sciences that has remained untouched by a new style of thinking that emphasizes close readings of texts, attention to unmentioned assumptions of theories, and a general suspicion of the voice of "disinterested" observation long associated with science. Practitioners of the new style often associate themselves with one of several movements or schools, such as postmodernism, poststructuralism, the new historicism, constructivism, or deconstruction.[1] Hare-Mustin and Marecek show how "two recent postmodern movements, constructivism and deconstruction, . . . can be applied to the psychology of gender." In this comment, the problems I find in this article are treated as a joint function of problems in the authors' presentation and the pitfalls faced by new stylists in the creation of a new genre. Specifically, I criticize simplifications based on the poor use of sources and a failure to apply fully certain insights associated with the new style theory of language. I introduce my comment with some historical antecedents of contemporary interdisciplinary work and conclude with some tentative rules of thumb for new stylists.

My primary goal is to expedite the reception and evaluation of a growing body of theoretical work by critics of mainstream psychology. In the past few years, names associated with these groups, such as Foucault (e.g., 1977) or Derrida (e.g., 1977), appear with increasing frequency in the reference lists of articles in the *American Psychologist.* When I paged through the schedule for Division 24 (Theoretical and Philosophical) at the 1988 meeting of the American Psychological Association (APA), somewhere between 20 percent and 30 percent of the sessions listed paper titles indicating some discussion of these ideas.[2]

As a psychologist with sympathies for the scientific method, who nevertheless shares many of the misgivings voiced by the new stylists about mainstream psychology, I have found my mind divided. At its best, the new style does what a scientific way of thinking should do—it makes it possible to see new connections otherwise obscured by conventional prejudices. At its worst, the new style is a mosaic of clichés with more signification than significance.[3] The question is: How is an interested consumer to distinguish the best from the worst? For the remainder of my comments, I will illustrate what seem to me to be some reasonable standards by applying them to the article by Hare-Mustin and Marecek. Not discussed here are the many points in the article that do not bear on distinctively new style concerns. The authors' interesting proposals for the study of gender, for example, are discussed only insofar as they involve theoretical and methodological issues.

Gender is a particularly promising topic for a new style approach. It is difficult to imagine a psychologist of any philosophical persuasion who would fail to agree that the set of concepts and practices that organize gender identities contains many unexamined, incorrect, and morally undesirable members. Among professionals, there is a strong consensus that at least some conventional assumptions about gender identities—especially those about the identity of women—cry out for a fresh evaluation because they are outmoded or ill-conceived. The authors' choice of a new style approach is therefore especially fortunate because, in this article, one finds exemplified to a high degree a refreshing feature of the new style, a feature with the strongest claim to the interest of the scientist: a refusal to take things at face value.

I believe that this refusal is worth emulating in another domain. When one looks at the avant-gardist rhetoric of the new stylists themselves, one finds that a consistent emphasis on what is new about their project has directed attention away from ancestors of their undertaking and from continuities between their work and the mainstream.

The neglect of historical precedents of the new style tosses out a potential source of common ground that might facilitate much-needed debate between new stylists and others. It is also ironic. The study of the history of science by Kuhn (1972), Toulmin (1972), and others challenged the prevailing preoccupation with normative philosophies of science (the search for demarcation principles, etc.) by insisting on attention to the history and practice of science. This challenge is usually echoed by new stylists. A related irony is that disregard for history can lead to the use of stereotyped representations of doctrines and movements, thus flattening a historically complex series of transformations into a simplified, usually negatively valenced, "thing." This sort of flattening is often condemned by new stylists as a "reification."

Let me be more specific. To a reader familiar with the writings of the logical positivists, the picture sketched by Hare-Mustin and Marecek is a cruel, though all too familiar, distortion.[4] In the past decade or so, I have observed that, when it comes to positivism, a great many psychologists, not just new stylists, resemble the Hatfields—sure the positivist McCoys are bad and that they are against them, but unlikely to have seen one except down the barrel of a gun. In this case, the Hatfield mentality can be clearly seen in the authors' unembarrassed support of their statements by citation of secondary sources hostile to positivism. Even if positivists are bad (a conclusion I regard as much too simple), are they not entitled to have their own words used to condemn them? Anyone who doubts this should ask what his or her reaction would be to a sentence that read "and feminism holds that a woman should put herself ahead of her children" or "feminists reject rational thought," followed by a parenthesis reading: "(Schlafly, 19XX)."

My point here is not, primarily, that such citation is unfair to positivists. It may even be that positivism within psychology has sometimes resembled the stereotype used by Hare-Mustin and Marecek. The problem is that this practice abandons a valuable insight associated with the philosopher Derrida (e.g., 1977), the literary critic Paul de Man (e.g., 1979), and other new stylists: that texts have a certain multiplicity that leaves them open to a diverse set of interpretations that could not have been predicted in advance. To use a new style phrase, texts are sites of struggle. White racists offered Blacks a Christianity of moral obedience and otherworldly longing, only to find that Blacks found in Christian texts a demand that justice flow like a mighty river. Although epistemology is not as morally serious as racism, I find the new style stereotype of positivism even more pernicious in its way because it produces a tendency for people to close books I believe they should open. An unread text has little chance of promoting thought.

Consider the following sentences from a rarely read text, written when all but the most senior new stylists were still children:

> It is not our business to set up prohibitions [regarding methods of expression and of inference], but to arrive at conventions. . . . *In logic, there are no morals.* Everyone is at liberty to build up his own logic, i.e. his own form of language, as he wishes. (Carnap, 1937, pp. 51–52)

This quote came from the logical positivist Carnap's book, *The Logical Syntax of Language.* In his foreword, he noted that

> the first attempts to cast the ship of logic off from the terra firma of the classical forms were . . . hampered by the striving after correctness. Now, however, that impediment has been overcome, and before us lies the boundless ocean of unlimited possibilities. (p. xv)

Here, as in many other positivist works, one finds a rhetoric of boldness and adventure that strongly resembles that of the new stylists. More to the point, one finds a form of constructivism that bears a striking resemblance to that praised by Hare-Mustin and Marecek. By the 1930s, Carnap believed that judgments of truth were relative to a framework, that the choice among frameworks could not be based on correspondence to reality, and consequently, that the decision on which framework to adopt must be based on expedience, fruitfulness, and other pragmatic considerations, considerations similar to those advanced by Hare-Mustin and Marecek in their section titled "The Question of Utility."

At this point, a politically oriented new stylist might object that Carnap's model ignores the connection between frameworks and socioeconomic interests and circumstances. Once again, the new stylist can find this connection passionately articulated a half century ago. Otto Neurath, like Carnap, was a member of the Vienna Circle, which later exercised such an influence on the development of positivist research programs in the United States through the "unity of science" movement and the ideas of Hempel. Like Carnap, Neurath was a dedicated socialist; although in contrast to the more academic Carnap, Neurath had been an active political revolutionary, deeply sympathetic to Karl Marx, who served as an economist for the brief Spartacist government in Munich (Bartley, 1985, p. 50; see also Cohen & Neurath, 1973). In the meetings of the circle, Neurath made war against the view that the acceptance of a philosophical doctrine is chiefly the result of its truth. Rather, he stressed that social and material circumstances condition its acceptance. "Up to this point," Carnap later recalled in an article describing the debates in the circle, "Neurath did not find much opposition. But he went further and often presented arguments of a more pragmatic-political rather than of a theoretical nature for the desirability or undesirability of . . . investigations" (Carnap, 1963, pp. 22–23). So when Hare-Mustin and Marecek argued that "rather than debate the correctness of various representations . . . constructivism examines their utility or consequences," they had much in common with these logical positivists.

My point here is not that Neurath and Carnap had in mind the epistemology later articulated by Rorty (e.g., 1979), or Hare-Mustin and Marecek. I doubt that they did. However, as many new style theorists might remind us, the meaning of ideas is not exhausted by what the authors had in mind. An emphasis on the *impersonal* qualities of meaning is a feature common to figures esteemed by both new stylists (e.g., Foucault, 1977; Jameson, 1971; Wittgenstein, 1953) and more conservative theorists (e.g., Frege, 1949). It is exactly this point that was forgotten when Hare-Mustin and Marecek used the fact that Samuel Johnson, Noah Webster, H. L. Mencken, and Strunk and White were men as evidence to support their contention that language is an instrument of male power, "confer(ring) the power to create the world from their point of view, in the image of their desires." Do the authors imagine for a second that when more women write dictionaries, the exercise of male power through language will as a consequence significantly be diminished? This seems to me as likely as the amelioration of the lot of women in the developing world if Jeanne Kirkpatrick becomes secretary of state. Language may serve the interests of men, but many individual women also serve the interests of men—and can be expected to do so if they come to occupy the slots allocated for "arbiters of language usage." Here we would do well to remember the research of Asch (1956) and Milgram (1975) on the social psychological constraints on autonomy.

Thus far, I have criticized this article for two reasons, a failure to go back to primary sources and a failure to use the implications of the new style theory of language. Both of the problems reappear in the most serious shortcoming of the article, the serious distortion of a discussion of the representational aspect of language in new style epistemology. The misused primary source is Rorty's (1979) *Philosophy and the Mirror of Nature*. The unrecognized implication of new style language theory can be seen in the authors' central explanatory terms, alpha and beta bias.

Rorty's work is introduced in the context of a discussion of constructivism and representation.

> Rather than passively observing reality, we actively construct the meanings that frame and organize our perceptions and experience. Thus, our understanding of reality is a representation, that is, a "re-presentation," not a replica, of what is "out there."

> Representations of reality are shared meanings that derive from language, history, and culture. Rorty (1979) suggests that the notion of "accurate representation" is a compliment we pay to those beliefs that are successful in helping us do what we want to do. (p. 456)

When one turns to Rorty (1979), one does find a detailed discussion of the view that "our understanding of reality is a representation," but the point of that discussion (and the point of the whole book) is that this view should be abandoned. Hare-Mustin and Marecek gave no pages numbers in their reference, and it is not entirely clear if they meant to suggest that Rorty's text endorses the view described in the sentences that precede his name. Perhaps they relied on the sentence on page 10, where Rorty (1979) wrote that, when the work of the philosophers Quine and Sellars is properly extended, it can "show us that the notion of 'accurate representation' is simply an automatic and empty compliment which we pay to those beliefs which are successful in helping us do what we want to do."

For reasons I shall discuss later, I believe that Hare-Mustin and Marecek interpreted this point to mean the following: If our contact with things is mediated by representations, then representations filter, channel, and sometimes distort what things are really like. Thus, first, we need to be alert to possible distortions and second, to realize that representations serve purposes and be on guard against pernicious purposes (e.g., sexism). Hare-Mustin and Marecek seemed to think that the quotation marks around the phrase "accurate representation" are meant to warn us away from the adjective "accurate." For Rorty, and probably for Sellars and Quine, it is the noun "representation" that is questionable.

Rorty (1979) wrote: "We must get the visual, and in particular the mirroring, metaphors out of our speech altogether. To do that we have to understand speech not only as not the externalizing of inner representations, but as *not a representation at all*" (p. 371, emphasis added). I have no space to describe Rorty's alternative approach, but it should be noted that his antirepresentationalism has points in common with positivism.

It is unfortunate that this article might invite a reader to suppose that Rorty endorsed representationalism when he actually attacked it, but this problem is relatively minor when compared with Hare-Mustin and Marecek's evident failure to bring Rorty's point to bear on their own thesis. Early in the discussion of alpha and beta bias, evidence of Rorty's point can be seen when the authors wrote that, in their formulation, "the term *bias* refers not to the probability of 'error' (which would imply that there is a 'correct' position), but rather to a systematic inclination to emphasize certain aspects of experience and overlook other aspects." One wonders what justification there might be for using the term "bias," because they claimed to reject one of its central implications. I suspect they hoped to cash in on the associative connotations of hypothesis testing at the same time they disavowed the epistemology that supports it. They got into trouble three sentences later when they wrote that their use of the term "underscores [their] contention that all ideas about difference are social constructs that can never perfectly mirror reality." They were oblivious to the irony of their words. Rorty's point, underscored in his title, is that a mirror is the wrong image. We should scrap it. However, by placing the adverb *perfectly* before the verb *mirror,* the authors implicitly accepted the image of mirroring reality because they implied it is something a construct can do—either perfectly or imperfectly.

The same complaint can be put another way. Consider how they defined their terms: "Alpha bias is the tendency to exaggerate differences; beta bias is the tendency to minimize or ignore differences." The question is whether, when the reader sees the phrases "exaggerate differences" or "minimize differences," she or he should understand exaggerate and minimize in the ordinary way, as transitive verbs, as verbs that take an object (i.e., the "differences" exaggerated or minimized). If this verbal implication is accepted, one must ask if these differences, these "aspects of experience," are themselves constructed—or are they given? Either reply raises problems for the authors. If the differences are constructed, then the reader is owed an explanation of the contrast between constructing a difference and exaggerating a difference. Why not just construct an exaggerated difference (whatever that may mean)? If the differences are not constructed, why not? Why are they exempt from this general feature of mind?

How did Hare-Mustin and Marecek get into this bind? I have suggested that problems in their use of sources and their failure to accept fully certain implications of new style language theory contributed to their difficulties, but I want to stress that the real source lies elsewhere, in the pitfalls inherent in the search for a new genre. Their troubled use of the term *bias,* for example, seems to result from an unintended adherence to the old-fashioned psychology they have rejected, the psychology that uses common-sense grounds for distinguishing biased representations from correct ones. Their poor use of Rorty's work may result from their attempt to use his concepts in a psychology article. *Philosophy and the Mirror of Nature* is deeply tied to the state of philosophy as a discipline and to its role in culture and the academy. Thus, a certain lack of fit may inevitably result from the attempt to import its ideas into another discipline, a discipline with problems of its own. (For example, when psychologists speak of a subject constructing X or Y, they frequently imply this is an activity, or at least a process—something that has stages, takes place in real time, and so on. Philosophers often mean no more than that X or Y supplies a condition evidently presupposed by experience.) When a term moves from one discipline to another, its meaning may change. This point is important to keep in mind because the use of sources from other disciplines is a common feature of the new style genre (and in my view, a laudable one).

I realize that my predominantly critical remarks can be used as an argument against new style work. That is not my purpose. I endorse the turn to the new style, although I view it with skepticism. What is needed, I believe, is a critical dialogue that will improve new style articles, so that they can find an able and effective voice of their own within psychology. Toward this end, I close with a few suggestions for new style work. Here are a few rules of thumb, based on problems I have encountered in various articles, as well as in my attempts to incorporate new style practices into my own work.

Whenever possible, use one's opponent's words against him or her. Avoid secondary sources, especially hostile secondary sources. Supply context, thus allowing your reader to judge for himself or herself. Watch out for the costs of covering too much ground at once. Avoid "atmospheric" references to stereotypes: Instead, cite representatives of movements mentioned. Do not assume that arguments can be imported wholesale from other fields. Again, context makes a difference.

I am certain this list is incomplete, but it is a start.

NOTES

1. Although partisans of these approaches rightly object to being lumped together (because they have as much, and as little, in common as a Skinnerian and a Hullian behaviorist), I will refer to the larger movement as "the new style."

2. The lower figure is probably the more reliable, especially because I contributed to two of the papers with such titles.

3. Even so central a figure as Christopher Norris, the author of *The Deconstructive Turn* (1983), warned that deconstruction "can all too easily degenerate into a kind of self-admiring game" (p. 3).

4. A more balanced treatment of positivism can be found in Hookway's (1988) book on Willard Quine, which emphasizes certain continuities between Carnap's work and Quine's pragmatism. Hookway's Chapter 2 alerted me to these continuities and to part of the first Carnap passage I cite later.

REFERENCES

Asch, S. (1956). Studies of independence and conformity: A minority of one against a unanimous majority. *Psychological Monographs, 70*(9, Whole no. 416).

Bartley, W. W. (1985). *Wittgenstein* (2nd ed.). LaSalle, IL: Open Court.

Carnap, R. (1937). *The logical syntax of language.* London: Routledge & Kegan Paul.

Carnap, R. (1963). Intellectual autobiography. In P. A. Schlipp (Ed.), *The philosophy of Rudolf Carnap.* LaSalle, IL: Open Court.

Cohen, R., & Neurath, M., (Eds.). (1973). *Otto Neurath: Empiricism and sociology.* Dordrecht: D. Reidel.

Derrida, J. (1977). *Of grammatology* (G. C. Spivak, Trans.). Baltimore: Johns Hopkins University Press.

de Man, P. (1979). *Allegories of reading: Figural language in Rousseau, Nietzsche, Rilke and Proust.* New Haven, CT: Yale University Press.

Foucault, M. (1977). *Language, counter-memory, practice* (D. Bouchard, Ed.). Ithaca, NY: Cornell University Press.

Frege, G. (1949). On sense and nominatum (H. Feigl, Trans.). In H. Feigl & W. Sellars (Eds.) *Reading in philosophical analysis.* New York: Appleton Century Crofts.

Hookway, C. (1988). *Quine.* Stanford, CA: Stanford University Press.

Jameson, F. (1971). *Marxism and form.* Princeton, NJ: Princeton University Press.

Kuhn, T. (1972). *The structure of scientific revolutions* (2nd ed.). Chicago: University of Chicago Press.

Milgram, S. (1975). *Obedience to authority.* Harper & Row.

Norris, C. (1983). *The deconstructive turn: Essays in the rhetoric of philosophy.* New York: Methuen.

Rorty, R. (1979). *Philosophy and the mirror of nature.* Princeton: Princeton University Press.
Toulmin, S. (1972). *Human understanding* (vol. 1). Oxford: Oxford University Press.
Wittgenstein, L. (1953). *Philosophical investigations.* New York: Macmillan.

Thinking about Postmodernism and Gender Theory

Rachel T. Hare-Mustin and Jeanne Marecek

We are pleased to have the opportunity to respond to the comments on our article by Stanley, Barratt and Straus, and Walkup. It allows us to clarify our ideas and seek to understand the ideas of others. Because we have been allotted limited space in which to respond, we have chosen to respond primarily to questions related to the topic of our article, gender theorizing in psychology.

In our article, we examined gender theories from a postmodern standpoint, noting that "difference" has been the primary meaning of gender in psychology. As a heuristic device, we described alpha bias and beta bias as a systematic tendency or "inclination" to emphasize certain aspects of experience and overlook other aspects (see also any standard dictionary). Alpha bias refers to the exaggeration of differences; beta bias refers to the minimizing of differences. Using a deconstructivist lens, we also examined the discourse of therapy to reveal hidden assumptions about gender relations. Finally, we observed that paradoxes in the current constructions of gender impel us to go beyond these constructions.

Having taken a postmodern stance, perhaps we should not be surprised that the comments plunge us back into the jungle with the elephant and the blind men (or women). In all three comments, the authors fault us for not citing certain sources that they regard as central, but interestingly, each comment has a different idea of what should be the main knowledge base on which our argument rests. There is no overlap.

In regard to the sources that an author chooses to cite, we would modify Stanley's statement to say that authors of *all* articles (not just articles "such as theirs") construct meanings by what they "choose to cite." No one cites everything or else our journals would be little more than endless lists of references. Certainly Benbow and Stanley deserve recognition for their work. We would also draw attention to the very careful recent review of cognitive gender differences by Feingold (1988), entitled "Cognitive Gender Differences Are Disappearing."

A deep commitment to deconstruction and psychoanalysis is evident in the analysis of our article by Barratt and Straus. We differ with them on many points, but most important, we do not agree with their central thesis. Many of the points of apparent disagreement can be traced to a difference of definitions. Barratt and Straus limit their definition of *postmodernism* to French poststructuralism, whereas we use the term more broadly to refer to a variety of intellectual movements that express uncertainty about the grounding and methods for interpreting human experience and allow us to think in terms of pluralities and diversities. Our usage is in line with that of others such as Flax (1987), Harding (1986), and Scott (1988b). Similarly, Barratt and Straus restrict the term *deconstruction* narrowly to the critical approach of Derrida. We use the term more generally to refer to the exposure of a concept as ideological or culturally constructed (cf. Alcoff, 1988; Kessen in Bronfenbrenner, Kessel, Kessen, & White, 1986; Poovey, 1988; and Scott, 1988a, who argued for a similar usage). Deconstruction is a project of demystification that makes visible what is required to maintain hierarchy and opposition.

To imply there is one right view, as our critics do, seems to us to be antithetical to the spirit of postmodernism. For us, postmodernist discourse is neither uniform nor homogeneous. Indeed, the idea of theoretical orthodoxy does not fit with a speculative postmodern view. The recent debates in the *American Psychologist* demonstrate that psychologists as well as philosophers can become entangled in arguments about what a particular theorist, such as Heidegger or Husserl, *really* meant. In a similar vein, Barratt and Straus assert that we have not read "properly" the works of certain feminists. Because we have gone to some pains to present the idea that there is no single "proper" reading, we would agree: We have not done what it is impossible to do.

As for jargon, which was mentioned by Barratt and Straus, what can we say? One person's meat is another one's jargon. Because the language of postmodernism may seem convoluted to many psychologists, an issue that concerned us was how to foster clarity while retaining excitement. In trying to present complex ideas clearly, we have found the schema of alpha and beta bias to be a helpful heuristic device. This is not because we embrace a positivist stance but because most psychologists have learned during their doctoral training about the two kinds of error called alpha and beta, the assertion of a difference that has not been found, and the overlooking of one that has been found. Yes, we hoped to "cash in on the associative connotations" of alpha and beta. Exactly so.

Barratt and Straus fault us for omitting the work of French feminists such as Kristeva (1986), Cixous (Cixous & Clément, 1986), and Irigaray (1974/1985a, 1977/1985b), who use psychoanalysis to mount a critique of partriarchy and phallocentric discourse. We did not omit such works unintentionally. Rather, we did not find them helpful to our project, which was to examine gender theorizing in American psychology. Perhaps it is their embeddedness in psychoanalysis that has made French feminist approaches more useful to literary critics such as Meese (1986) and Spivak (1987) than to psychologists in this country. In any case, we would welcome work that applied French feminist thought to gender theorizing in American psychology. We would see such work as complementary, not antithetical, to our own.

We differ from Barratt and Straus in that we see in *both* psychoanalytic approaches and nonpsychoanalytic approaches to therapy a concern with transforming meanings (cf. Frank, 1987). However, we do not characterize efforts to transform meanings as manipulation. Nor would we see "mastery and manipulation" (not our terms) as more characteristic of one approach than another. It seems to us that "manipulation" has become a pejorative term applied to the techniques of those therapists one disagrees with. Further, when we talk about the utility of a particular point of view, we are talking about its consequences. The question is Foucault's question: What interests does a particular representation serve? Nowhere do we use the term Barratt and Straus attribute to us, "utilitarian," which usually refers to the ethical doctrine of the greatest good for the greatest number. Finally, we do not endorse rationality, just as we do not endorse emotionality. We wonder, however, how one can inveigh against either when engaged in this kind of exchange of views.

And what are we to make of Walkup? Throughout his lengthy essay he rewrites our work and then attacks the version he has created. For example, he rewrites our text to attribute to Rorty statements that we clearly attribute to Watzlawick and Von Glaserfeld. Then Walkup rails against our alleged misinterpretation of Rorty's ideas. We refer the reader to the full paragraph of our article rather than that portion of the paragraph that Walkup selects as the basis of his lengthy criticism.

Also, we searched our article for the "cruel distortion" and condemnation of positivism to which Walkup alludes. What we say about positivism is confined to a short passage. The essence of it is as follows:

> It is not that formal laws and theories in psychology are wrong or useless, but rather, as Kuhn (1962) asserted, that they are explanations based on a set of social conventions. Thus, whereas positivism asks what are the facts, constructivism asks what are the assumptions; whereas positivism asks what are the answers, constructivism asks what are the questions. The positivist tradition holds that science is the exemplar of the right use of reason, neutral in its methods, socially beneficial in its results (Flax, 1987).

For those who wish to do battle for or against positivism (as Walkup's references to guns, feuds, opponents, and hostility imply), the history of positivism and the nuances of thought found in a "rarely read text" written more than a "half-century ago" are no doubt pertinent. However, our article concerned not positivism, but the development of and impasses in gender theorizing in psychology, and the new directions afforded by postmodern approaches.

Disciplines often put boundaries around knowledge; that is, they "discipline" thought. Breaking down these boundaries is an important aspect of interdisciplinary work. In our view, there is a value in drawing readers' attention to notable thinkers outside psychology who have influenced postmodern thought. It does not follow that a full exegesis on every influential thinker can or should be provided in a journal article. If that were the requirement, interdisciplinary work would stop, and all scholars except those working in small and arcane fields would be silenced.

It was difficult for us to follow Walkup's manuscript because of the inaccurate dates of some citations, works cited in the text but omitted from the reference list, frequent mention of names such as Quine, Wittgenstein, Marx, Asch, Foucault, Jameson, Sellars, and so on, with no sources (let alone primary sources or page numbers), and his consistent mispelling of one of our names. Although we presume that the journal's editorial staff has now taken care of many of these problems, Walkup's many misreadings make us wonder if he noticed that our article was on "gender," not "genre."

Finally, we do not regard ourselves as "opponents" of Walkup or the "opponents" of others but as colleagues seeking to advance knowledge in psychology. This characterization by Walkup further demonstrates that one can not readily move outside a system of meanings of which one is a part. Scholarly inquiry is not a dispassionate accumulation of truth; it is constituted by social relations. Ultimately, meanings arise from social processes and are expressions of power. It seems to us that the best reply to those who would use scholarship to disparage and confuse is Foucault (1980).

REFERENCES

Alcoff, L. (1988). Cultural feminism and poststructuralism. *Signs, 13,* 405–436.

Bronfenbrenner, U., Kessel, F., Kessen, W., & White, S. (1986). Toward a critical social history of developmental psychology: A propaedeutic discussion. *American Psychologist, 41,* 1218–1230.

Cixous, H., & Clément, C. (1986). *The newly born woman* (B. Wing, Trans.). Minneapolis: University of Minnesota Press. (Original work published 1975)

Feingold, A. (1988). Cognitive gender differences are disappearing. *American Psychologist, 43,* 95–103.

Flax, J. (1987). Postmodernism and gender relations in feminist theory. *Signs, 12,* 621–643.

Foucault, M. (1980). *Power/knowledge: Selected interviews and other writings, 1972–1977.* New York: Pantheon.

Frank, J. D. (1987). Psychotherapy, rhetoric, and hermeneutics: Implications for practice and research. *Psychotherapy, 24,* 293–302.

Harding, S. (1986). *The science question in feminism.* Ithaca, NY: Cornell University Press.

Irigaray, L. (1985a). *Speculum of the other woman* (G. C. Gill, Trans.). Ithaca, NY: Cornell University Press. (Original work published 1974)

Irigaray, L. (1985b). *This sex which is not one* (C. Porter, Trans.). Ithaca, NY: Cornell University Press. (Original work published 1977)

Kristeva, J. (1986). *The Kristeva reader* (T. Moi, Ed). New York: Columbia University Press.

Meese, E. A. (1986). *Crossing the double-cross.* Chapel Hill: University of North Carolina Press.

Poovey, M. (1988). Feminism and deconstruction. *Feminist Studies, 14*(1), 51–65.

Scott, J. W. (1988a). Deconstructing equality-versus-difference: Or, the uses of poststructuralist theory for feminism. *Feminist Studies, 14*(1), 33–49.

Scott, J. W. (1988b). *Gender and the politics of history.* New York: Columbia University Press.

Spivak, G. C. (1987). *In other worlds: Essays in cultural politics.* New York: Muthuen.

Chapter Eight

On Comparing Women and Men

Alice H. Eagly

The practice of comparing the sexes in scientific data has been hotly debated by feminists in recent years. The controversy stems, at least in part, from the failure of the findings of empirical research to tell the story that we hoped that they would. When some of us started studying gender in the late 1960s and early 1970s from a feminist perspective that reflected our commitment to furthering equality between the sexes, we anticipated that research would serve the aims of our social movement. Implicit or explicit in the majority of this work was the expectation that feminists' comparisons of women and men would help to raise women's status by dispelling people's stereotypes about women. Much of our gender research reflected two missions: revealing people's damaging stereotypes and attitudes concerning women (e.g., Broverman et al., 1972); and displaying the absence of stereotypic sex differences in behavior, traits and abilities (e.g., Maccoby and Jacklin, 1974). We hoped to explain women's disadvantaged social position through people's negative stereotypes and attitudes. Our research on sex differences would shatter these stereotypes and change people's attitudes by proving that women and men are essentially equivalent. However admirable our goals, scientific research has presented us with a considerably more challenging set of findings.

Before describing some of the complexities of contemporary research findings, a note on terminology is appropriate. Consistent with ordinary usage in scientific psychology, the term "sex difference" refers in this chapter to any observed difference between females and males, without any implications for the causes of the difference (see Eagly, 1987b). Others prefer the more complex terms "sex-correlated" or "sex-related" for this purpose (e.g., Deaux, 1993; Gentile, 1993). Whether or not the "correlated" or "related" feature is added to the term "sex," using "sex" to mark group membership is consistent with typical dictionary definitions of the term as referring to the division of beings into male and female categories. Moreover, treating sex as a marker variable explicitly departs from the artificial "nature versus nurture" dichotomy furthered by psychologists who attach the term "sex" to biology and the term "gender" to culture (e.g., Unger, 1979). Surely an observed difference should not be labeled a "sex" or "gender" difference, depending on whether psychologists wish

Alice H. Eagly, "On Comparing Women and Men." *Feminism and Psychology, 4,* pp. 513–522. © 1994 by Sage Publications, Ltd. Reprinted by permission of Sage Publications, Ltd.

to think about it as biologically caused or culturally induced. The causation of differences between women and men cannot usefully be addressed merely by labeling observed differences by terms intended to connote particular causal factors. Instead, theoretical understanding of the causes of differences and similarities is an end point of effective scientific research.

The State of the Evidence

Caught up in the passions of our feminist social movement in the 1960s and 1970s, many of us had a simple vision of what empirical research on sex differences would yield. Not anticipating how thoroughly our findings would require us to expand and refine this vision, we created a formidable body of scientific knowledge by comparing women and men on a wide range of measures in many different types of research. As the amount of research grew, integrating it to answer questions about similarities and differences became increasingly difficult as long as authors applied informal, narrative methods to the task of overviewing the field. Beginning in the late 1970s, a methodological revolution occurred in the integration of research findings as psychologists turned to the quantitative techniques known as meta-analysis (see Hyde, 1990).

These more sophisticated and reliable methods of aggregating findings describe differences and similarities on a continuum and thus avoid the artificial dichotomization of research findings as demonstrating either sameness or difference. In order to address the global question of the extent to which the behavior of men and women differs in a domain (e.g., aggression), the meta-analyst thus averages the effect sizes from the individual studies and then interprets their central tendency. This central tendency is located somewhere along a continuum that runs from no difference to large differences and thus does not provide a simple "yes" or "no" answer to the question of whether, in general, men differ from women.

Even more important than this escape from a simplistic debate about "sameness versus difference" is the ability of quantitative syntheses to describe sex differences in each domain by a set of effect sizes, each representing a particular study. The set of effect sizes is ordinarily much more important and informative than their central tendency because the effect sizes vary in magnitude (and often in direction as well). This observed variability in the effect sizes is an invitation to theory-building because the principal job of the meta-analyst is to explain *why* these effect sizes differ—that is, why the magnitude of the sex difference varies across the studies (see Eagly and Wood, 1991).

Contrary to our expectations that quantitative syntheses would challenge stereotypes, the majority of them have conformed in a general way to people's ideas about the sexes (Eagly, 1987b, 1993; Eagly and Wood, 1991). Relevant to the accuracy of gender stereotypes are meta-analyses in which student judges estimated the extent to which men and women would or would not differ in each of the studies that had provided a comparison of men's and women's behavior in a particular domain. The correlations between these estimates, which represented students' gender stereotypes, and the actual behavioral sex differences in the studies, assessed by their effect sizes, were positive and significant (e.g., Eagly and Crowley, 1986, Table 5; Eagly and Karau, 1991, Table 6; Eagly and Steffen, 1986, Table 5). In addition, compelling evidence of the general accuracy of people's gender stereotypes was provided by Swim's (1994) demonstration that subjects' perceptions of differences between the sexes predicted with considerable success the aggregated sex differences that had been obtained in prior quantitative syntheses of research (e.g., on cognitive abilities, non-verbal behaviors, social behaviors such as aggression and helping). Moreover, Swim's respondents tended either to be accurate about the magnitude of sex differences or to underestimate them. There was no tendency for subjects to overestimate the magnitude of differences between female and male behavior. Although the issue of stereotype accuracy invites further analysis (see Judd and Park, 1993), this evidence suggests that lay people, once maligned in much feminist writing as misguided holders of gender stereotypes, may be fairly sophisticated observers of female and male behavior.

It is not surprising that many feminist psychologists have been less than enthusiastic about this new wave of research on sex differences. Feminists had already enjoyed considerable success in shaping a consensus about the triviality of sex differences and the inaccuracy of gender stereotypes, a consensus tailored to serve feminist political goals. Attesting to feminist achievements, these views have become "politically correct" in many circles and strongly influence most textbook presentations, despite a counter-theme in feminist writing emphasizing women's distinctive communal characteristics (e.g., Gilligan, 1982).

When contending with the onslaught of meta-analyzed empirical findings, many feminists have been extremely reluctant to accept the subtlety of conceptualizing differences and similarities along a continuum. The holding action of many feminist psychologists has been to argue for the very small size of virtually *all* sex differences as well as for their inconsistency across studies (e.g., Archer, 1987; Deaux, 1984; Lott, 1991). Feminists have also pointed out the multiple ways that science is socially constructed (e.g., Hare-Mustin and Marecek, 1988, 1990).

Advocates of the small-size position often used percent variance accounted for by sex as an index of effect magnitude and then argued that this number was typically small. However, in the very same year that Deaux (1984) suggested that 5 percent of the variance is an "upper boundary" for the magnitude of sex differences, Hall (1984) reviewed numerous research literatures on non-verbal behavior and found that many such behaviors had average effect sizes that exceeded this boundary, some by substantial amounts (see Hall, 1984, Table 11.1). Other feminist psychologists exhorted scientists to accompany any reports of sex comparisons with the percent-variance "tag" attached to them (McHugh et al., 1986). In the face of methodological writing explaining why the percent-variance metric is easily misinterpreted and why differences that appear small by this metric can have considerable practical importance (e.g., Abelson, 1985; Prentice and Miller, 1992; Rosenthal and Rubin, 1979), the consensus about small size should have been eroded. Also devastating to the small-size verdict are the comparisons that can now be made between meta-analyzed sex comparisons and meta-analyzed findings associated with hypotheses unrelated to gender (see Eagly, 1987b). These comparisons suggest that the magnitudes of sex-difference findings are, on the whole, typical of findings produced in psychological research by manipulating variables experimentally or classifying people by other personal characteristics (e.g., personality attributes). In fact, relative to most other findings in psychology, sex-difference findings in some domains are large (see Ashmore, 1990, Table 19.1; Halpern, 1992, 86–87).

The inconsistencies in the magnitude of sex-difference findings (and sometimes in their direction) are their most challenging feature. This feature was obscured by the traditional practice of comparing findings across studies merely by their statistical significance. Inconsistencies suggested by differing significance levels are illusory to the extent that they reflect differences in studies' statistical power (e.g., in sample size). Comparisons of effect sizes are considerably more informative because effect sizes are independent of studies' sample sizes.

Most of the inconsistencies in effect sizes revealed by quantitative syntheses are explicable in terms of methodological dissimilarities between studies (e.g., differences in measuring instruments or in the social settings or role relationships examined). Between-studies inconsistencies such as these demonstrate the contextual quality of findings—that is, their tendency to differ in magnitude (and sometimes in direction) depending on the particular context in which a behavior is elicited. Quantitative reviewers test hypotheses about the contextual quality of sex-difference findings by calculating statistical models that use studies' contextual features to predict effect sizes. For example, Eagly and Crowley's (1986) synthesis of helping behavior studies examined, among other features, the presence versus absence of an audience of people who could observe research participants' helpful behavior.

It is quite startling to find that psychologists critical of work on sex differences still claim that context is neglected in this work. Perhaps these critics have not actually studied contemporary syntheses of sex-difference findings or have been prevented from understanding these syntheses by technical barriers (e.g., specialized meta-analytic statistics). Claims that context is ignored are inaccurate and may reflect a stereotype based on these critics' reading of pre-1980s research. It is important not only to understand the strong emphasis on context in much contemporary research on sex differences, but also to appreciate that context-dependence is not unique to sex-difference findings. Rather, it is another typical feature of the findings of psychological research. As Rosnow and Rosenthal (1989, 1280) wrote: "there is growing awareness in psychology that just about everything under the sun is context dependent in one way or another." The context-dependence of our empirical findings should encourage us to offer contextually-qualified generalizations about gender, but it should not prevent us from drawing conclusions from our research.

A social constructionist position has frequently been contrasted with a logical positivist position ascribed by some feminists to those researchers who study sex differences empirically (e.g., Mednick, 1991). The feminist message that science is biased appears to be directed to psychologists who are thought to believe that science is objective (see Crawford and Marecek, 1989). However, it would be startling to find a modern social scientist who would fail to agree that science is socially constructed or who would maintain that science is objective or value-free. There are virtually no empirical researchers adopting a feminist perspective who would neglect to scrutinize research for masculinist methodological and theoretical biases. Although it is appropriate to sow uneasiness about science through emphasizing its social construction, science remains a rule-bound set of social activities that provides a powerful tool for examining relations between variables and for testing theories about these relations. Science is ultimately strengthened and improved by feminist psychologists' many analyses of the failures of science to live up to its rules (e.g., Sherif, 1979; Shields, 1975).

Given the rediscovery of the once-banished sex differences, comparing the sexes is newly regarded by some feminists as a possibly dangerous and potentially subversive activity that feminists should avoid. Mednick's (1991) summary of her survey of a selected sample of feminist psychologists suggests that these negative views about research comparing women and men are quite widespread. Given that comparisons of the sexes do not shatter stereotypes in the simple fashion we had hoped, the faint of heart among feminists seem ready to abandon such comparisons. Considerably more palatable to many feminist psychologists is the targeting of our empirical research to study people's ideas about gender—in effect, an emphasis on only the "damaging stereotype" aspect of our original dual-purpose research agenda.

A Recommendation for Action

How should we proceed as feminist scientists? We should not discourage sex-difference research by calling for its censorship and close regulation, as some have done (e.g., Baumeister, 1988; McHugh et al., 1986). Such a closed-minded approach would only undercut the feminist agenda in the long run. Feminist psychologists ought, instead, to consider whether the advantages of fostering comparisons of the sexes outweigh the risks. More radically, we might encourage *all* scientists to share openly their comparisons of male and female research participants. As I have suggested earlier (Eagly, 1987a), comparisons of the sexes might become a routine part of scientific reports, until such time that these reports are merely redundant with established knowledge and therefore no longer of interest. This recommendation does not imply an emphasis on these comparisons in research reports—only that investigators make them accessible for archival purposes.

There are numerous political and scientific arguments in favor of full and open reporting of comparisons between women and men (see Eagly, 1987a, 1990). Fundamentally important is the point that more data would produce a richer and more differentiated picture of gendered behavior and, in particular, would reveal its contextual patterning. This patterning lends itself to understanding the ways in which behavior is constrained by its social context and, in particular, by men's more dominant social position (e.g., Eagly and Crowley, 1986; Eagly and Johnson, 1990; Eagly and Karau, 1991; Eagly and Steffen, 1986; Wood and Rhodes, 1992). Reports of sex comparisons provide a magnificent lens for revealing gender to the extent that many such comparisons are accessible from a wide variety of studies that have established differing social settings and used different methods. Such data sets are a rich lode for theory building (Eagly and Wood, 1991) and belie the criticism that "using sex as a subject variable is essentially atheoretical" (Archer, 1987, 89). Indeed, it is quite puzzling to find that critics of sex-difference research believe that such work is atheoretical. On the contrary, the flowering of theories to explain sex differences and similarities is the most exciting feature of research in the area, especially during the last five or so years.

Although some critics acknowledge the theory-driven quality of contemporary research, they sometimes offer a different and equally puzzling claim—namely, that theories produced to explain sex differences and similarities presume that the causes of differences are inherent in the individual or that they arise from biology or early socialization (e.g., Kahn and Yoder, 1989). On the contrary, feminist social scientists, especially social psychologists, routinely offer theories that stress the shaping of behavior by people's expectations, which are in turn shaped by the roles that women and men play in society and by the social hierarchies within which gender is enacted (e.g., Deaux and Major, 1987; Eagly, 1987b; Ridgeway, 1992). Such theories mesh well with the feminist political commitment to change in social arrangements.

Finally, feminist social scientists should consider the consequences of abandoning research comparing the sexes. Would any other scientists continue this work? Most assuredly the answer to this question is affirmative. Particularly important are the efforts of biologically oriented scientists, whose interest in sex differences is even more intense than that of social scientists in the modern period (e.g., Haug et al., 1993; Hoyenga and Hoyenga, 1993; Kimura, 1992). Although feminism has a voice among biologists and biopsychologists (e.g., Gowaty, 1992; Lancaster, 1991), most biological theories foster interpretations of sex differences as relatively ingrained. For example, sociobiologists and evolutionary psychologists view behavioral sex differences as arising primarily from the differing roles of women and men in reproduction (see Buss, 1989; Buss and Schmitt, 1993; Daly and Wilson, 1983; Kenrick, 1994). Such theories tend to have more troubling implications for feminist political goals.

The most important outcome of sex-difference research is not the placement of sex comparisons along a continuum of magnitude, but the interpretation that scientists give to differences and similarities. To the extent that scientists' interpretations become accepted by the public, they will affect everyday behavior as well as public policy. Feminist theoretical positions would only be weakened by constraints on the reporting of comparisons between the sexes, because it is the rich diversity of findings that allows compelling arguments to be made for these theories. Our comparisons of women and men have turned out somewhat differently than we had anticipated, but we can meet this challenge by providing effective theories of female and male behavior. These theories must withstand rigorous scientific scrutiny.

Feminists be bold! Let us be active, smart scientists who welcome new research findings and who enter the theoretical fray as powerful contenders.

REFERENCES

Abelson, R. P. (1985). "A Variance Explanation Paradox: When a Little Is a Lot," *Psychological Bulletin* 97:128–32.

Archer, J. (1987). "Beyond Sex Differences: Comments on Borrill and Reid," *Bulletin of the British Psychological Society* 40:88–90.

Ashmore, R. D. (1990). "Sex, Gender, and the Individual," in L. A. Pervin (ed.), *Handbook of Personality: Theory and Research,* pp. 486–526. New York: Guilford Press.

Baumeister, R. F. (1988). "Should We Stop Studying Sex Differences Altogether?" *American Psychologist* 42:1092–95.

Broverman, I. K., Vogel, S. R., Broverman, D. M., Clarkson, F. E., and Rosenkrantz, P. S. (1972). "Sex-Role Stereotypes: A Current Appraisal," *Journal of Social Issues* 28(2):59–78.

Buss, D. M. (1989). "Sex Differences in Human Mate Preferences: Evolutionary Hypotheses Tested in 37 Cultures," *Behavioral and Brain Sciences* 12:1–49.

Buss, D. M., and Schmitt, D. P. (1993). "Sexual Strategies Theory: An Evolutionary Perspective on Human Mating," *Psychological Review* 100:204–32.

Crawford, M., and Marecek, J. (1989). "Psychology Reconstructs the Female, 1968–1988," *Psychology of Women Quarterly* 13:147–65.

Daly, M., and Wilson, M. (1983). *Sex, Evolution and Behavior,* 2d ed. Boston: Willard Grant Press.

Deaux, K. (1984). "From Individual Differences to Social Categories: Analysis of a Decade's Research on Gender," *American Psychologist* 39:105–16.

Deaux, K. (1993). "Commentary: Sorry, Wrong Number—a Reply to Gentile's Call," *Psychological Science* 4:125–6.

Deaux, K., and Major, B. (1987). "Putting Gender into Context: An Interactive Model of Gender-Related Behavior," *Psychological Review* 94:369–89.

Eagly, A. H. (1987a). "Reporting Sex Differences," *American Psychologist* 42:756–57.

Eagly, A. H. (1987b). *Sex Differences in Social Behavior: A Social-Role Interpretation.* Hillsdale, NJ: Erlbaum.

Eagly, A. H. (1990). "On the Advantages of Reporting Sex Comparisons," *American Psychologist* 45:560–62.

Eagly, A. H. (1993). "Sex Differences in Human Social Behavior: Meta-analytic Studies of Social Psychological Research," in M. Haug, R. Whalen, C. Aron and K. Olsen (eds), *The Development of Sex Differences and Similarities in Behaviour,* pp. 421–36. London: Kluwer Academic.

Eagly, A. H., and Crowley, M. (1986). "Gender and Helping Behavior: A Meta-analytic Review of the Social-Psychological Literature," *Psychological Bulletin* 100:283–308.

Eagly, A. H., and Johnson, B. T. (1990). "Gender and Leadership Style: A Meta-analysis," *Psychological Bulletin* 108:233–56.

Eagly, A. H., and Karau, S. (1991). "Gender and the Emergence of Leaders: A Meta-analysis," *Journal of Personality and Social Psychology* 60:685–710.

Eagly, A. H., and Steffen, V. J. (1986). "Gender and Aggressive Behavior: A Meta-analytic Review of the Social-Psychological Literature," *Psychological Bulletin* 100:309–30.

Eagly, A. H., and Wood, W. (1991). "Explaining Sex Differences in Social Behavior: A Meta-analytic Perspective," *Personality and Social Psychology Bulletin* 17:306–15.

Gentile, D. A. (1993). "Just What Are Sex and Gender, Anyway? A Call for a New Terminological Standard," *Psychological Science* 4(2):120–24.

Gilligan, C. (1982). *In a Different Voice: Psychological Theory and Women's Development.* Cambridge, MA: Harvard University Press.

Gowaty, P. A. (1992). "Evolutionary Biology and Feminism," *Human Nature* 3:217–49.

Hall, J. A. (1984). *Nonverbal Sex Differences: Communication Accuracy and Expressive Style.* Baltimore, MD: Johns Hopkins University Press.

Halpern, D. F. (1992) *Sex Differences in Cognitive Abilities*, 2d ed. Hillsdale, NJ: Erlbaum.

Hare-Mustin, R. T., and Marecek, J. (1988) "The Meaning of Difference: Gender Theory, Postmodernism, and Psychology," *American Psychologist* 43:455–64.

Hare-Mustin, R. T., and Marecek, J., eds. (1990). *Making a Difference: Psychology and the Construction of Gender*. New Haven: Yale University Press.

Haug, M., Whalen, R., Aron, C. and Olsen, K., eds. (1993). *The Development of Sex Differences and Similarities in Behaviour*. London: Kluwer Academic.

Hoyenga, K. B., and Hoyenga, K. T. (1993). *Gender-Related Differences: Origins and Outcomes*. Boston: Allyn and Bacon.

Hyde, J. (1990). "Meta-analysis and the Psychology of Gender Differences," *Signs: Journal of Women in Culture and Society* 16:55–73.

Judd, C. M., and Park, B. (1993). "Definition and Assessment of Accuracy in Social Stereotypes," *Psychological Bulletin* 100:109–28.

Kahn, A. S., and Yoder, J. D. (1989). "The Psychology of Women and Conservatism: Rediscovering Social Change," *Psychology of Women Quarterly* 13:417–32.

Kenrick, D. T. (1994). "Evolutionary Social Psychology: From Sexual Selection to Social Cognition," in M. P. Zanna (ed.), *Advances in Experimental Social Psychology*, vol. 26, pp. 75–121. San Diego, CA: Academic Press.

Kimura, D. (1992). "Sex Differences in the Brain," *Scientific American* 267(3):118–25.

Lancaster, J. B. (1991). "A Feminist and Evolutionary Biologist Looks at Women," *Yearbook of Physical Anthropology* 34:1–11.

Lott, B. (1991). "Social Psychology: Humanist Roots and Feminist Future," *Psychology of Women Quarterly* 15:505–19.

Maccoby, E. E., and Jacklin, C. N. (1974). *The Psychology of Sex Differences*. Stanford, CA: Stanford University Press.

McHugh, M. D., Koeske, R. D. and Frieze, I. H. (1986). "Issues to Consider in Conducting Non-Sexist Psychological Research: A Guide for Researchers," *American Psychologist* 41:879–90.

Mednick, M. T. (1991). "Currents and Futures in American Feminist Psychology: State of the Art Revisited," *Psychology of Women Quarterly* 15:611–21.

Prentice, D. A., and Miller, D. T. (1992). "When Small Effects Are Impressive," *Psychological Bulletin* 112:160–64.

Ridgeway, C. L., ed. (1992). *Gender, Interaction, and Inequality*. New York: Springer-Verlag.

Rosenthal, R., and Rubin, D. (1979). "A Note on Percent Variance Explained as a Measure of the Importance of Effects," *Journal of Applied Social Psychology* 9:395–96.

Rosnow, R. L., and Rosenthal, R. (1989). "Statistical Procedures and the Justification of Knowledge in Psychological Science," *American Psychologist* 44:1276–84.

Sherif, C. W. (1979). "Bias in Psychology," in J. A. Sherman and E. T. Beck (eds.). *The Prism of Sex: Essays in the Sociology of Knowledge*, pp. 93–133. Madison: University of Wisconsin Press.

Shields, S. A. (1975). "Functionalism, Darwinism, and the Psychology of Women: A Study in Social Myth," *American Psychologist* 30:739–54.

Swim, J. K. (1994). "Perceived Versus Meta-analytic Effect Sizes: An Assessment of the Accuracy of Gender Stereotypes," *Journal of Personality and Social Psychology* 66:21–36.

Unger, R. K. (1979). "Toward a Redefinition of Sex and Gender," *American Psychologist* 34:1085–94.

Wood, W., and Rhodes, N. (1992). "Sex Differences in Interaction in Task Groups," in C. L. Ridgeway (ed.), *Gender, Interaction, and Inequality*, pp. 97–121. New York: Springer-Verlag.

Chapter Nine

New Voices, New Visions
Toward a Lesbian/Gay Paradigm for Psychology

Laura S. Brown

Voices Lost and Found

What does it mean for psychology if the experiences of being lesbian and/or gay male, in all the diversity of meanings that those experiences can hold, are taken as core and central to definitions of reality rather than as a special topic tangential to basic understandings of human behavior, particularly human interactions? After all, just as there is no American Psychological Association division of the psychology of men or of white people, there is no special topic area called heterosexual studies in psychology. "Psychology," the official entity, values those experiences that are white, male, heterosexual, young, middle class, abled-bodied, and North American; thus has the universe of "human behavior" been defined. "Special topics," including lesbian and gay issues, have traditionally been defined as of special interest only, not in the core curriculum in reality or emotionally.

My raising of this essentially feminist question has roots both in personal experience and in a developing line of feminist theory. The personal experience, which was the catalyst for my thinking, has been both primary and most powerful and illustrates the feminist adage that the personal is political as well as theoretical. In 1987, I developed a supposedly untreatable neurological disorder of the voice called spastic dysphonia that left me literally speechless. For three months I had no voice; I experienced in an embodied way the powerlessness of the often-used metaphor of being unable to be heard. But rather than accepting the verdict of Western medical science that my disorder, because neurological, was untreatable, I pursued non-Western medical care: acupuncture and Chinese herbal medicine, cranial osteopathic manipulation, spiritual healing. By deciding to change the point of view from which I understood my disorder, I regained a voice: a new and often fragile one, but a voice, nonetheless. It was a jarring reminder of the importance of not taking the view from the mainstream as the only one there is, and one that intuitively led me to

Laura S. Brown, "New Voices, New Visions: Toward a Lesbian/Gay Paradigm for Psychology." *Psychology of Women Quarterly, 13*, pp. 445–458. © 1989 by Cambridge University Press. Reprinted with the permission of Cambridge University Press.

develop the thought process represented in this work. If I could have a new voice by changing the point from which I understood my problem, could such a new voice not also be raised within psychology, a voice that would reflect another set of my experiences in the world, those of a white North American lesbian?

Concurrent with my personal experiences, a developing line of feminist theory has raised questions about the nature of the observer's perspective in science. Such theory suggests that the pretensions of mainstream science to objectivity, or to encompassing the universe of knowledge and meaning, are in fact evidence of white, androcentric ways of understanding (Harding, 1986; Rose, 1983). Rose and Harding have joined other authors in attempting to redefine the conditions of discourse within the sciences, including psychology and other social sciences, so as to make central and visible the previously excluded experiences of women. These theorists have argued not only for the simple inclusion of women in the discourse, but also that the terms of the discourse be changed, be reinvented, in order to move from an androcentric to a feminist science. Sandra Harding (1986), in particular, has argued that a feminist science would be one in which categories of discourse and understanding would of necessity become destabilized in order to move beyond the deeply internalized structures of Western thinking. Feminist science and social science would ask questions from the female experience.

But let us move beyond that. What happens if what has previously been a conceptual ghetto, even within feminist psychology, is redefined as the center of the universe of understanding? If the ways of knowing and of legitimizing knowledge are opened to understandings that are rooted in the phenomenology of being gay or lesbian in the world, what new voices and visions become available? Does the way in which psychologists explore lesbian and gay issues become transformed by asking such questions? How has psychology so far been shaped through the distorted lens of heterosexist psychological science and practice? Beyond that, what happens if a lesbian/gay paradigm is used as core to psychological science and practice in general? How do psychologists change their understandings of such phenomena as intimacy, parenting, attraction, relationships, or gender, if they make assumptions based in experiences of being lesbian or gay?

In order to begin the process of answering such questions, the assumptions that lie within the questions themselves must be explored. Such questions assume first that current paradigms reflect a heterosexual reality, and second, that it is possible to identify what is meant by lesbian/gay reality in such a way as to address issues from that perspective.

Heterosexism in Psychology

The first assumption is based on the notion that the worldview of North American psychology, besides being biased by sexism, racism, and other exclusionary modal perspectives, views human behavior through the lens of heterosexual experience and is thus inherently heterosexist. What do I mean by that assertion? Concretely, this takes a number of forms. Our knowledge base is heterosexist. That is, it assumes heterosexuality and heterosexual forms of relating as the norm. More precisely, white, middle class, North American, married, Christian, able-bodied heterosexuality is defined as the norm. All other forms of experience are viewed in contrast to the norm. This non-conscious heterosexism manifests in myriad subtle ways; there are "couples," meaning heterosexual couples, and then there are "lesbian and gay couples." There are "families," meaning nuclear, two-heterosexual-parent families, and "lesbian and gay families." And so on, ad nauseum. Even in the field of psychology of women, which has probably contributed more than any other field of psychology toward the movement to deconstruct psychology and dethrone the god of logical positivism (Hare-Mustin & Marecek, 1988), there are "women," and then there are "lesbians," tucked away in our own chapters of the textbooks. Lesbian experiences are seen as unique, offering little to the understanding of the norm. What occurs instead is that we are compared to the norm, in the past to demonstrate our pathology and, more recently, to affirm our normalcy. Or we are simply categorized as an interesting variant of human experience, equal but still separate and always marginal.

This tendency to perceive lesbian and gay issues within the broadest scope of that term as tangential "special topics" robs psychology of much of its ability to understand human behavior. There are certain aspects of lesbian and gay experience which, if made central to all psychological inquiry, would change and expand the ability to comprehend both the intrapsychic and the interpersonal. But to use such a universe as core to hypothesis generation requires answering my second question regarding the definition of lesbian and gay experience.

Defining a Lesbian and Gay Reality

In some ways, this is more complex and problematic than establishing the presence of heterosexism in psychology. This complexity exists largely because there is not one unitary lesbian and gay reality. Instead, there are multiple realities. The experience of being a white lesbian or gay man will be different from that of a lesbian or gay man of color and different within each ethnic group. The lesbian or gay man who comes from an orthodox religious background will be different from those who grew up in more religiously liberal settings. Also, a person's age cohort has a profound impact on the experience of being a sexual minority person, as does age of coming out and past history of overt heterosexual identity such as marriage. Class plays a powerful role in defining the experience and expression of being lesbian or gay. Moreover, North American lesbians and gay men live different realities than do our peers in other countries and cultures. Furthermore, constructions and parameters of gender separate the experiences of lesbians from those of gay men.

Even the concept of sexual orientation is one that is not clearly defined. Although, for the purpose of lesbian and gay rights, we may adhere to the notion that sexual orientation is a fixed and relatively immutable phenomenon, clinically and experientially we are aware that it is a fluid, continuous one, with the words "lesbian" and "gay" encompassing a range of internal experiences and social constructions of attraction, arousal, identity, and affection (Greenberg, 1988; Kitzinger, 1987). Although there is a seductive pull to see ourselves as a unitary, and thus a united group, lesbians and gay men are more diverse than my own first minority group, Jews, where we joke that "if there are two Jews, there are three schuls" (i.e., three opinions). Anyone who has been active in the lesbian and gay community will bear testimony to our variability and the challenges that this can present to the well-meaning gay pride parade organizer. Yet we are a nation of sorts; 10 percent of the U.S. population is larger than the total population of my partner's native country of The Netherlands. And all nations contain a certain amount of diversity.

So, with all that diversity, are there within this "country" of internal experience those elements of being lesbian or gay male that are common to all and can be said to form a "lesbian and gay reality" from which to reconceptualize our study of human behavior? I would like to suggest that those common elements do exist cross-situationally, and that they are in fact central to my movement toward a new vision.

Biculturalism

The first among these common elements is the experience of biculturalism. Lesbians and gay men are always simultaneously participants in both heterosexual experience and lesbian and gay experiences. Our families of origin are usually comprised of heterosexual persons who participate in the privileges and rituals of the dominant heterosexual majority. Many of us have behaved heterosexually during our lifetimes, although we often revise the meaning of these aspects of our histories when we embrace a lesbian or gay identity. We are often very much in the position to "pass" for heterosexual and may experience discomfort with those aspects of ourselves or our peers that conform to cultural stereotypes of the "obvious" lesbian or gay man, while simultaneously cultivating certain aspects of those behaviors in more secure settings (Nestle, 1987). With rare exceptions, all lesbians and gay men must be in both cultures most of the time.

Marie Root (1988), writing on biracial identity development, pointed out that the experience of the biracial person include having both minority and dominant cultures as part of one's family of origin. She suggested that this can lead to a sense of confusion and of non-fit in any context. While a person who is purely one minority group or another may feel free in the process of minority identity development to reject dominant culture, Root pointed out that for the biracial individual such a rejection also implies a rejection of a part of oneself. Biracial individuals are also often in the position of being able to choose to "pass" as members of the dominant culture and may feel ambivalence or distaste for those family members, often siblings and one parent, who are more physically like the devalued minority group and who threaten their passing status. In order to develop a functional biracial identity, the biracial person must develop ways to live within this matrix of complexity, to balance and value the differences that lie within.

Extrapolating from Root's model, it may be that living and developing biculturally, while not unique to lesbian and gay men, is an experience that may create different ways of knowing and understanding oneself and one's reality. A healthy resolution of such conflicts of identity is one that must eschew either/or perspectives on who one is and embrace what is "other" within oneself. Such a successful resolution of a bicultural identity may create a propensity to view things on continua rather than in a polarized fashion. Being able to operate within grey areas and on middle grounds and balancing the demands of two divergent groups that are now internalized self-representations are characteristic of the experience of being gay or lesbian. Walter Williams's (1987) work on sexual identity among Native American cultures provides some confirmation for this idea. He noted that in many Native nations, the persons who occupied the interim space between the genders and whose behavior might be identified as gay or lesbian within white American culture, were perceived as seers, shamans, capable of greater wisdom than their clearly heterosexually defined peers. Different external factors may operate to influence the felt and lived experiences of this bicultural existence, and some lesbians and gay men, for example, lesbians or gay men of color in North America, actually may have multicultural identities.

This experience, like that of the biracial person, is distinct from that of members of racial and ethnic minorities in that even at the most intimate level of family relationships, there will be cultural differences and pulls to participate in the dominant culture in ways that do not exist for members of racial and ethnic minorities whose families share their group membership. The experience of having both self and other within one's identity development creates a singular and potentially powerfully heuristic model for self-understanding. The constant "management of difference" (deMonteflores, 1986) can lead to a rich and distinctive perspective on reality if we are willing to embrace and value it, rather than stigmatize it as not conforming to the dominant norm. The bicultural perspective of lesbians and gay men facilitates an understanding of the rules by which the mainstream culture operates, while simultaneously being able to envision new forms by which the same tasks might be accomplished.

Marginality

A second experience that informs a lesbian and gay reality is that of marginality. Even in the most supportive and accepting of settings, we carry the experience of existential "otherness." For many lesbians and gay men, the first awareness of who we were was simply that vague sense of difference and distance from the rituals of the heterosexual culture, of not understanding what our friends saw in the opposite gender, of watching to see how heterosexual courtship rituals were played out so that we could imitate them and fit in (Adair & Adair, 1978).

Mary Daly long ago pointed out how this "otherness" can allow women to see what is not seen, to know what is forbidden to know, because they are not sanctified as knowers (Daly, 1973). Harding (1986) argued that a feminist epistemology depends upon the valuing of "alienated," "bifurcated," or "oppositional" consciousnesses in theory making. Lesbian and gay male experience reflects this alienated, marginal worldview, no matter how well an individual lesbian or gay man appears to be integrated into the dominant social context.

It is no coincidence that one of the ways that political and religious conservatives attempt to undermine the movement against violence against women and children is to "lesbian-bait" its leadership (Schechter, 1982). In essence, what they are saying is that only a woman who is, as Adrienne Rich (1979) puts it, "disloyal to civilization" will be able to continue to break the patriarchy's silence on its crimes. It's no wonder that any man who attempts to analyze and move beyond the defined male gender roles is called "faggot": who else is enough outside the definition of the role to see alternate possibilities for male existence (Grahn, 1984)? In the catcalls of those who would annihilate lesbians and gay males lie germs of the truth; our experience of the world as outsiders may allow us to see differently, hear differently, and thus potentially challenge the conventional wisdom. We may be freer to see, speak and act other truths, to have, as Judy Grahn says, "another mother tongue."

These other truths can be powerful affirmations of our experience; they can also be frightening challenges to the culture of the mainstream and even to lesbians and gay men who are struggling with our own conflicting desires to both fit in and be who we are. One striking example of the outcomes of empowering our alienated lesbian and gay knowing has been in how we have created our families.

As asked by Dykewomon (1988) in a society caught up in sanctification of "The Family," can there be such a thing as a functional family under patriarchy? While this is also an essential feminist question found early in this wave of the U.S. women's movement in the work of Firestone (1970), lesbians and gay men have put that question into practice by the creation of families that are not patriarchal. Likewise, there may be a specifically lesbian way to raise children (Cooper, 1987), different from the power-unequal norms of the heterosexist family in which age differences are assumed inherently to connote power imbalance. Also challenged is the assumption that biological parents of both genders are necessary for the creation of emotionally healthy children, and the assumption that the only appropriate number of parents is two (Pollack & Vaughn, 1987). These challenges have not been without a price to the lesbian and gay male parents who have lost access to their children of blood or spirit for daring to raise such questions. Yet, many continue to raise them, knowing by looking in from the outside that the current paradigm of "family" cannot be the only one.

Normative Creativity

A final common theme is that of being normatively different and thus creative. In other words, by lacking clear rules about how to be lesbian and gay in the world, we have made up the rules as we go along. For example, in their recent book on lesbian couples, Merilee Clunis and Dorsey Green (1988), discuss how they decided what was normative for lesbian couples. They put it rather simply: if a lot of lesbians seemed to be doing it, this must be the norm. And these norms challenge the dominant notions about what occurs in intimate interpersonal relationships; they question notions about how agency and communion function within a couple, about the healthy expression of dependency needs between adult partners. Simply *being* lesbian or gay has been something we have had to invent for ourselves (Grahn, 1984), since whatever roadmaps the dominant culture offered have been full of wrong turns and uncharted territories. This need to invent for ourselves has been equal parts terrifying and exhilarating (vide the common theme of works on lesbian-and-gay-affirmative therapy regarding the problems due to the lack of clear models for lesbians and gay men). However, those who claim this as a positive and possibly unique aspect of our experience as lesbians and gay men begin to embrace the possibilities for actively deconstructing and re-creating our visions of human behavior far beyond the field of lesbian and gay studies.

In summary, there are three intertwined themes that define, cross-situationally, the experience of being lesbian and gay: biculturalism, with its requirements of juggling, balance, and living in and with ambiguity; marginality, with its perspective that is both outside and within the mainstream; and normative creativity, the ability to create boundaries that will work where none exist from tools that may be only partially suited to the task. If psychologists adopt these as guiding principles for their work, where can and does this lead?

Toward a Lesbian and Gay Paradigm for Psychology

A first and, for those in academic settings, somewhat risky step is to reevaluate the methodologies by which the knowledge base is generated. Mary Ballou (1988) has identified five epistemological perspectives that might be available for studying human behavior and pointed out how they lead to very different types of "revealed truths" when applied to inquiry. If scholars attempt to work from a valuing of the mixed, the ambiguous, the marginal, then it becomes extremely difficult to fit themselves solely within the logical positivist framework dominant in psychology. After all, such a framework assumes that phenomena are either A or B, and that if enough rigor is used in the design and test of a hypothesis, one truth can be found. This has a seductive flavor to it; as Harding (1986) pointed out, the tendency to perceive the universe in logical positivist terms is supported by such a wide variety of institutional and cultural structures that it "cannot be shucked off by mental hygiene and willpower alone" (p. 662). But this tendency must be continuously questioned since an exclusionary paradigm would not fit well with an application of lesbian and gay reality to the study of human behavior.

An alternative approach that draws upon lesbian and gay experience must allow for the use of many methodologies and the possibility of many, even conflicting, answers. A lesbian/gay psychology would be one of many truths, one in which a dialectical tension would constantly operate in such a manner as to stimulate new and wider inquiry. Rather than endless replications of the old, researchers would begin asking the questions not yet raised in the first place and then question further the answers received. If they allow their scholarship to live in as many realities as they do themselves, they find the possibility of many shades of meaning.

This has certainly been the case with my work in the area of psychotherapy ethics. By working from my lived experience as a white lesbian therapist practicing in the context of diverse lesbian communities, I've come to see ethical action as a continuous variable. One is not either ethical or nonethical, but changing and varying degrees of ethical at various levels of affective, cognitive, and behavioral expression during different periods of one's work as a therapist (Brown, 1985, 1987, 1988). I've found that simply having rules about what to do narrowed my thinking and excluded that which had never been considered, thus making it invisible. I've also learned that lesbian and gay male therapists, faced with situations unpredicted and unenvisioned by the ethics codes, have had to be creative in the development of norms that would allow us to behave ethically and yet still live within the realities of our communities (Gonsiorek, 1987; Hayden, 1987; Moss, 1987). For instance, the ethical principle regarding dual relationships (APA, 1981) gives little guidance about what to do when a therapist's former lover becomes lovers with a current client; notwithstanding, if that's what one has to deal with, and more than a few lesbian and gay male therapists have, the ethical principles for it are created along the way. The paradigms for ethical therapy evolving from lesbian and gay experience stress, not rules and regulations, but the relationship of the therapist to her or his community, and the relational context in which therapy takes place. This different perspective has allowed lesbian and gay therapists to both ask and answer questions that cannot even be raised in the conceptual universe of mainstream psychology ethics.

A second implication of adopting a paradigm for psychology that would embrace the themes of lesbian and gay experience would be a continuous reevaluation of taken-for-granted concepts in all aspects of psychology. For example, psychologists usually hold heterosexual couples as a norm simply because of their majority status. But it might be possible that what is normative for lesbian couples is in fact healthy for any intimate pair. In a paper written since her book was published, Dorsey Green (1988) raised this possibility when she discussed the issues of merger, fusion, and contact boundaries in relationships, suggesting that perhaps the merger that a healthy lesbian couple experiences is more normative and functional for intimate pairs than the illusion of autonomy and distance within a relationship that exists, she believed, exists in heterosexual couples simply as an artifact of gender roles. In other words, by taking the position of outsider and suggesting that the emperor in fact has no clothes, we may move psychology toward a deeper and more complex understanding of interpersonal relationships. This movement would have particular significance for the study of behaviors related to sexuality, gender role and identity, intimacy and bonding, and the development of family dynamics. While feminist psychology has commented at length on the problems of the "patriarchal, father-absent family" (Luepnitz, 1988), how might inquiries be expanded by looking first at the functioning of healthy lesbian and gay families?

An analogy can be made here to work that develops non–North American cultural versions of psychology and that generates norms and hypotheses about development from within those cultural contexts. Carla Bradshaw (1988), in a paper on the interface between Japanese psychology and feminist therapy theory, pointed out how even the basic process of personality development is quite different when viewed through the lens of Japanese experience. Bradshaw pointed out that the concepts of dependence and individuation carry strikingly different meaning in Japanese culture from that in North American society and noted how behavior that would be considered pathological or pathogenic here represents normative and functional ways of being.

Similar work is underway in the Philippines to create a "Sikolohiyang Pilipino," Philippine psychology from within a Philippine cultural context (Protacio-Marcelino, 1988). The explicit aim of this work is to strip away North American concepts and ways of seeing from psychological theory and practice. It uses Philippine language and experience to develop an entirely new and different way of seeing and knowing human behavior. For example, Protacio-Marcelino analyzed the notion of "personality" in Western psychology, contrasting it with the eight different terms in Tagalog, one of the primary indigenous languages of the Philippines, that can define "personality" in terms of the context in which the person is found and the relationship of one actor to another. From the point of view of Philippine culture, a person has not one personality, but many, each determined by the relational context in which she or he is acting.

Clearly the diversity that exists within the lesbian and gay population makes the explication of a lesbian and gay psychology a challenging task. Or perhaps not; within any culture, however defined, there must be levels of difference to be accounted for by a psychology of that culture. However, the analogies hold in many ways. Protacio-Marcelino and her colleagues (1988) spoke of how psychology in the Philippines was intellectually colonized by Americans; so, too, is American psychology colonized and dominated by heterosexual experience. By defining norms and terms from within lesbian and gay realities, psychologists ask themselves how these new paradigms might broaden the understanding of heterosexual realities as well.

Finally, by working from within lesbian and gay realities, the study of lesbian and gay issues will and must change. This new approach in no way denigrates that which has been done before and will continue to be done by way of research and practice in the field. Everything that has come before has allowed for the conceptual leaps in this article. But scholars have been constrained by working within the dominant paradigm so that only certain kinds of knowledge are pursued or revealed. To quote Audre Lorde (1984): "The master's tools will never dismantle the master's house," and such a renovation is what many lesbians and gay men in psychology had in mind when, a decade or more ago, we began to challenge the notion of homosexuality as psychopathology.

In challenging that one dearly held tenet of one branch of the tree of the behavioral sciences, we were, in the end, also challenging the whole structure, all of the assumptions that went into creating that idea. It's not certain that we realized that or even would have admitted how radical in fact this apparently simple goal was. To take the word out of the *Diagnostic and Statistical Manual* was simply one aspect of challenging the entire system of thinking that had allowed it to be placed there at all. Thus, the ideas suggested in this article are simply a carrying forward of that action. At the very first APA program on lesbian and gay issues, Barbara Love (1975) suggested that lesbians might be the model of healthy female development. Her paper appealed intuitively to many, but few have yet to follow concretely the direction in which this non-psychologist lesbian activist was pointing: that is, to rearrange the norms and then to go about the business of seeking greater self-knowledge.

Some initial steps have been taken, both in psychology and in related fields of endeavor; the volume *Lesbian Psychologies* (Boston Lesbian Psychologies Collective,

1987) provides an example of what is needed in the behavioral sciences. Some of the most exciting work developing from lesbian and gay paradigms is occurring in philosophy (Hoagland, 1988) and theology (Heyward, 1989). Both Sarah Lucia Hoagland and Carter Heyward proposed epistemologies that flow from the embodied experience of living as lesbians (Hoagland, 1988) or either lesbians or gay men (Heyward, 1989) and provide models that could be used for psychological inquiry as well.

In a paper I gave at APA in 1986 in a symposium on the state of the art in lesbian and gay affirmative psychotherapy (Brown, 1986), I suggested that lesbian and gay therapists were at a point where we needed to ask more complex questions about our work. I believe now that in order to ask those questions in satisfying ways, we need to use a lesbian/gay paradigm to construct the process of inquiry. For instance, one question raised in that earlier paper is "Why are so many lesbians in therapy?" It is now known, thanks to the National Lesbian Health Care Survey, just how high the numbers are: 78 percent of their respondents were current or former therapy clients (Bradford & Ryan, 1987).

To avoid quick and easy answers to this question or answers that reflect the perspectives of the dominant culture on either lesbians or psychotherapy, the questions inside the questions must be asked, that is, create a dynamic tension within psychology. What does therapy mean in a lesbian and gay context? What associations arise to the word, what does it suggest to the sexual minority speaker and hearer, the sentence, "I'm in therapy." Who are the therapists and how do they see their work? Is the therapist, particularly the lesbian or gay male therapist working within their own communities, meaning something different at non-conscious levels by her or his choice of work than does the heterosexual therapist? What is the interaction of being in therapy with other experiences in the world as lesbians or gay men? Are we defining being in therapy as evidence of pathology, which has traditionally been the case? Or have lesbians and gay men re-visioned the meaning of therapy as prima facie evidence of health and health-seeking behaviors, as one useful and appropriate strategy for sanely managing to live in the ambiguity, which, in the final analysis, is the situation for most late twentieth century Americans, not only those of us on the official margin?

This last question is one that quite directly flows from the lesbian/gay paradigm proposed here; that is, it is an outsider question, one that sees strength in what has been called weakness, one that questions that which is taken for granted about the meaning of therapy in society. It is a question about the ritual of therapy that emphasizes how the context gives that ritual place and meaning. These are questions that go beyond the statistics and encourage a search for the meaning given to the experience by culture, context, and living in a particular way. And those are the sorts of questions that psychologists need to ask in all of their work.

In proposing this new voice and vision, I am raising more questions here than I am able to provide answers to. I'm not entirely certain myself of all the concrete implications of the paradigm that I'm suggesting; in writing this article, I have discovered just how much this idea still exists within me preconsciously, felt but unformed. Audre Lorde (1978), in *The Uses of the Erotic,* said that "in order to perpetuate itself every oppression must corrupt or distort those various sources of power within the culture of the oppressed that can provide energy for change." One such source of power is the process of owning and valuing as central one's experience even when the words are lacking in the dominant reality to describe it. My own thinking is still struggling through the muck of that distortion. It is my hope that by taking you with me as I continue that journey, I have set you to thinking, too, and that between us we will give form to what is still only a vague imagining on my part. We can pursue the comfort of the mainstream, or we can search for new voices and visions as psychology moves past its centenary with lesbian and gay psychology finally in place.

REFERENCES

Adair, N., & Adair, C. (1978). *Word is out: Stories of some of our lives.* New York: New Glide/ Delta.

American Psychological Association [APA]. (1981). Ethical principles of psychologists. *American Psychologist, 36,* 633–638.

Ballou, M. (1988, May). *Building feminist theory through feminist principles.* Paper presented at the Seventh Advanced Feminist Therapy Institute Conference, Seattle, WA.

Boston Lesbian Psychologies Collective (Eds.). (1987). *Lesbian psychologies: Explorations and challenges.* Urbana: University of Illinois Press.

Bradford, J., & Ryan, C. (1987). *National lesbian health care survey: Mental health implications.* Richmond: Virginia Commonwealth University Survey Research Laboratory.

Bradshaw, C. (1988; May). *Japanese psychology: What can Eastern thought contribute to feminist theory and therapy?* Paper presented at the Seventh Advanced Feminist Therapy Institute Conference, Seattle, WA.

Brown, L. S. (1985). Power, responsibility, boundaries: Ethical concerns for the lesbian feminist therapist. *Lesbian Ethics, 1,* 30–45.

Brown, L. S. (1986, August). A time to be critical: Directions and developments in lesbian-affirmative therapy. In B. Sang (Chair), *Lesbian and gay affirmative psychotherapy: State of the art.* Symposium presented at the Convention of the American Psychological Association, Washington, DC.

Brown, L. S. (1987, August). Beyond thou shalt not: Developing conceptual frameworks for ethical decision-making. In L. Garnets (Chair), *Ethical and boundary issues for lesbian and gay psychotherapists.* Symposium presented at the Convention of the American Psychological Association, New York, NY.

Brown, L. S. (1988). From perplexity to complexity: Thinking about ethics in the lesbian therapy community: *Women and Therapy, 8,* 13–26.

Clunis, D. M., & Green, G. D. (1988). *Lesbian couples.* Seattle: Seal Press.

Cooper, B. (1987). The radical potential in lesbian mothering of daughters. In S. Pollack & J. Vaughn (Eds.), *Politics of the heart: A lesbian parenting anthology* (pp. 233–240). Ithaca, NY: Firebrand Books.

Daly, M. (1973). *Beyond God the father: Toward a philosophy of women's liberation.* Boston: Beacon Press.

deMonteflores, C. (1986). Notes on the management of difference. In T. S. Stein & C. J. Cohen (Eds.). *Contemporary perspectives on psychotherapy with lesbians and gay men* (pp. 73–104). New York: Plenum Medical.

Dykewomon, E. (1988). Notes for a magazine. *Sinister Wisdom: A Journal for the Lesbian Imagination in the Arts and Politics* [Special Issue on Surviving Psychiatric Assault], 36, pp. 2–6.

Firestone, S. (1970). *The dialectic of sex.* New York: William Morrow.

Gonsiorek, J. (1987, August). Ethical issues for gay male therapists. In L. Garnets (Chair), *Ethical and boundary issues for lesbian and gay psychotherapists.* Symposium presented at the Convention of the American Psychological Association, New York, NY.

Grahn, J. (1984). *Another mother tongue: Gay words, gay worlds.* Boston: Beacon Press.

Green, G. D. (1988, May). *Is separation really so great?* Paper presented at the Seventh Advanced Feminist Therapy Institute Conference, Seattle, WA.

Greenberg, D. (1988). *The construction of homosexuality.* Chicago: University of Chicago Press.

Harding, S. (1986). The instability of the analytical categories of feminist theory. *Signs: Journal of Women in Culture and Society, 11,* 645–664.

Hare-Mustin, R. T., & Marecek, J. (1988). The meaning of difference: Gender theory, postmodernism, and psychology. *American Psychologist, 43,* 455–464.

Hayden, M. (1987, January). *Clinical issues in boundary setting and maintenance.* Paper presented at a conference, Boundary Dilemmas in the Client-Therapist Relationship, Los Angeles, CA.

Heyward, C. (1989). *Touching our strength: The erotic as power and the love of god.* New York: Harper & Row.

Hoagland, S. L. (1988). *Lesbian ethics: Toward new value.* Palo Alto: Institute of Lesbian Studies.

Kitzinger, C. (1987). *The social construction of lesbianism.* London: Sage.

Lorde, A. (1978). *Uses of the erotic: The erotic as power.* Trumansburg, NY: Crossing Press.

Lorde, A. (1984). *Sister outsider.* Trumansburg, NY: Crossing Press.

Love, B. (1975, August). *A case for lesbians as role models for healthy adult women.* Paper presented at the convention of the American Psychological Association, Chicago, IL.

Luepnitz, D. A. (1988). *The family interpreted: Feminist theory in clinical practice.* New York: Basic Books.

Moss, L. E. (1987, January). *The problem of overlapping relationships with clients.* Paper presented at a conference, Boundary Dilemmas in the Client-Therapist Relationship, Los Angeles, CA.

Nestle, J. (1987). *A restricted country.* Ithaca, NY: Firebrand Books.

Pollack, S., & Vaughn, J. (Eds.). (1987). *Politics of the heart: A lesbian parenting anthology.* Ithaca, NY: Firebrand Books.

Protacio-Marcelino, E. (1988, May). *Toward understanding the psychology of the Filipino.* Paper presented at the Seventh Advanced Feminist Therapy Institute, Seattle, WA.

Rich, A. (1979). *On lies, secrets, and silence.* New York: Norton.

Root, M. P. P. (1988, May). *Resolving "other" status: The process of identity development in biracial individuals.* Paper presented at the Seventh Advanced Feminist Therapy Institute, Seattle, WA.

Rose, H. (1983). Hand, brain, and heart: A feminist epistemology for the natural sciences. *Signs: A Journal of Women in Culture and Society, 9,* 73–90.

Schechter, S. (1982). *Women and male violence: The visions and struggles of the battered women's movement.* Boston: South End Press.

Williams, W. (1987). *Spirit and the flesh: Sexual diversity in American Indian culture.* Boston: Beacon Press.

Part III

Gender Embodied

A. Evolving Genders

The chapters in this section consider the biological bases for the categories "male" and "female" and the ways in which distal evolutionary and more immediate biological factors can be considered "causes" of behavior. The psychological characteristics considered range from sexual desire to experience of anger to math ability to gender identity. All of the authors address, in varied forms, the question of what biological sex might have to do with gender.

Anne Fausto-Sterling immediately complicates that question by arguing that sex is anything but the simple, dichotomous category we assume it to be. Though we may find them daunting, we welcome such complications; indeed, complication of some of our traditional questions and assumptions is the overriding goal of this section. As Adrienne Rich (1979) has written, "Truth is not one thing . . . It is an increasing complexity" (p. 187). Each of these pieces illustrates one or more ways in which the relationships among biology and psychology, sex and gender, process and product, nature and culture are multifaceted, bidirectional, intricate, changeable, a function of interpretation, and increasingly complex the further we inquire.

Whether to study difference is not the central issue these authors address. Indeed, they provide substantial argument for why difference questions cannot and should not be avoided. The varied approaches represented here do, however, illustrate ongoing questions about how to study differences, where to look for them, and, especially, how to interpret their implications. For Jerre Levy and Wendy Heller, for example, the question is not simply whether there are anatomical and functional differences between male and female brains, but the ways in which those differences influence different mental processes and outcomes such as spatial performance. Their discussion raises several critical issues and distinctions that are important to keep in mind (and often confounded) when considering sex, gender, and differences.

One of these issues has to do with distinguishing the processes by which a "product" (e.g., a specific behavior, a mental outcome, an emotion) is achieved from the characteristics of that product. Levy and Heller conclude that current evidence supports the idea that there may be some differences in the ways males and females typically process spatial information, and that those differences may stem from the influence of hormones on brain organization and function. They note, however, that different processes may lead to very similar outcomes. (See also Antony S. R. Manstead's discussions of how different underlying processes lead to similar manifest emotions). They also conclude that there is no basis for making sex-based decisions, as opposed to decisions based on individual assessments, in selection of people for tasks that require spatial-reasoning ability.

By making explicit what they see to be the policy implications of the research they review, Levy and Heller confront one of the persistent questions that readers pose when reading about biological differences between (or, as Fausto-Sterling might say, *among*) the sexes: How should knowledge about these differences affect what we expect, or even allow people to do? A prior question, however, might be *why* we expect research on biological influences on behavior necessarily to have implications for anything else.

Evidence about biology is often "heard" in ways that social science research is not. One powerful reason for this is that many people (including members of the media) feel competent to evaluate the results of social science research, weighing survey evidence against their own experience, for example, and confidently rejecting the former if it conflicts with the latter. In contrast, relatively few people feel qualified to evaluate the underlying assumptions, research questions, procedures, and results from "hard" science (or, as we sometimes hear, "real" science) fields, unless they have specialized training in biology, neurology, genetics, or related areas. Our lack of confidence may translate into passively waiting for the authoritative words of scientific experts.

"Real" science is also expected to generate unbiased "real facts," which by definition are indisputable. Once we have a sufficiently comprehensive set of real facts, then surely they will point unerringly to the appropriate policies? This perception of science has been strongly (and in our view, effectively) challenged by many writers on a priori grounds, as well as by striking specific examples from the history of science (e.g., Bleier, 1988); but that does not mean that it is not still influential. Sarah Blaffer Hrdy's chapter serves as an important reminder that the "facts" we discover, uncover, or observe are often as much a function of what we are looking for as they are determined by nature—though she also argues that even a flawed science has advantages over unadulterated ideology.

As with most things, there is a history to our varied reactions to evidence about biology and behavior. Consideration of the effects that the different embodiment of males and females may have on psychological characteristics and behaviors immediately raises the specter of past instantiations of nature/nurture debates, as well as classic questions about mind/body relations. Many of these debates hinge upon assumptions that there is a relationship between anything biological on the one hand, and heredity, inevitability, and immutability on the other. Thus, echoing some reactions to difference research in general, readers may cringe at the idea that human behavior is influenced by human embodiment, because they fear that acknowledging the influence of biology necessarily means rejecting the possibility of social reform and individual change. Culturally, we tend to believe that if a behavior is influenced by biological factors (e.g., genes or hormones), then we are not "responsible" for it and it cannot be influenced by anything else.[1]

Neither belief is true, of course. As Jane Roland Martin noted in chapter 1, biological explanations are not necessarily essentialist. There is ample historical and cross-cultural precedent for expecting individuals to refrain from acting on their feelings, no matter how "natural" they may be: no society exists that does not expect its members to learn to defecate (surely a "natural" urge if ever there was one) only in appropriate places at appropriate times. Moreover, as Sally Mendoza (Mendoza &

Shaver, 1995) has noted, "nature" already requires that we regulate our own "natural" urges, because they themselves may often conflict, such as when both "fight" *and* "flight" seem strongly indicated. Finally, as many theorists have noted, there may be nothing more natural to humans as a species than the tendency to create culture and to live in societies. Indeed, it is possible that the strongest biological mandates our genes carry include using culture as a tool for adaptation.

In his chapter, David M. Buss argues that males and females will be most jealous about different kinds of infidelity, because in our evolutionary past they have faced different selection pressures and risks. Specifically, males should be more jealous of sexual infidelity than of emotional infidelity (because paternal uncertainty means that they risk investing resources in another man's offspring if their mates are sexually unfaithful), while females should be more jealous of emotional infidelity than of sexual infidelity (because if their mates become emotionally attached to another woman, they may divert resources to that woman and her offspring; see Buss & Schmitt, 1993).[2] If this evolutionary account of emotional differences is accurate, however, it certainly does not follow that male violence against women is somehow excusable or justifiable if the perpetrators suspect sexual infidelity, nor that women whose mates fall in love with someone else should be permitted to murder either the mate or the "other woman" with impunity. In other words, even if we come to accept the idea that a particular emotional reaction, or other preference or behavior, is somehow "natural" because it has been influenced by evolution (or genes, or hormones), neither society nor individuals are thereby absolved from determining what we believe to be moral or immoral, or in the interests of the society or against them. To assume otherwise is to fall into a "naturalistic fallacy": As Jane Roland Martin says, (chapter 1 of this volume) "No conclusion about what ought to be the case follows from what is."

If we reject the notion that evidence about the influence of biology on human behavior automatically includes justification for that behavior, we take away some of its special potency in discussions of gender and policy. We are left, however, with residual questions, beliefs, and assumptions about the inevitability and immutability of that influence. Yet it is unlikely that there are many "one-way" transactions between genes or hormones and individual behavior. In other words, although it may be true that there are important ways in which genes, neurotransmitters, and hormones influence behavior, it is equally true that behavior affects the expression of genetic characteristics, the production and action of neurotransmitters, and the production and level of hormones. The assumption that genetic or biological effects are immutable continues to be assailed, as evidence accumulates that the phenotypic expression of virtually all genotypes is influenced by environmental factors (Woodward, 1995). Moreover, for better or worse, our own ability to alter biology through technology (e.g., gene therapies and hormonal supplements) continues to increase.

Just as importantly, showing a relationship between, for example, a particular allele on a particular gene and a particular characteristic or behavior does not mean that one has *explained* that characteristic or that behavior: as Woodward (1995) notes, gene alleles encode proteins, not behaviors. Hypothesizing that males may have evolved to experience more sexual jealousy than females does not help us to explain why one man will respond to his wife's infidelity with physical violence, another will file for divorce, and a third will work toward reconciliation. Understanding and explaining behavior requires knowing about environments and about transactions between individuals and those environments—whether or not the behavior being examined relates to gender.

Without the mythology of inevitability, immutability, and primacy, the study of and controversies about biological influences on gender-related characteristics become both less frightening and more germane to the study of gender. There is wide-ranging consensus that psychology as a field (at least in its best instantiations) has moved far beyond "nature or nurture" questions to complex questions of interactions (Kendrick, 1987), such as: How do genetic predispositions influence the creation of environments? How do external physical environments influence internal hormonal environments? These question are considerably more complex than the questions that have often dominated our thinking in the past. We believe that they also move us closer to truth.

NOTES

1. A notable exception to this pattern of cultural belief can be seen in examination of beliefs about weight and body shape. There is voluminous evidence that weight is strongly biologically influenced, directly via genetics, and indirectly via our bodies' attempts to maintain weight with metabolic setpoints. This evidence is as strong or stronger, and more consistent, than the evidence concerning the heritability of intelligence, or of most personality characteristics. Nevertheless, we tend to believe that weight is under the control of the individual, who bears responsibility (and should accept blame) for being overweight. As a nation, we act on these beliefs by spending literally billions of dollars on various diets, surgeries, and other "treatments" for obesity.

2. There is considerable controversy and conflicting data about this hypothesis. See Buss, Larsen, Westen, 1996; De Steno & Salovey, 1996; Harns & Christenfeld, 1996.

REFERENCES

Bleier, R. (1988). Science and the Construction of Meanings in the Neurosciences. In S. V. Rosser (Ed.), *Feminism within the Science and Health Care Professions: Overcoming Resistance*. Elmsford, NY: Pergamon Press.

Buss, D. M., Larsen, R. J., & Westen, D. (1996). Sex Differences in Jealousy: Not Gone, Not Forgotten, and Not Explained by Alternative Hypotheses. *Psychological Science, 7*, 373–375.

Buss, D. M., & Schmitt, D. P. (1993). Sexual Strategies Theory: An Evolutionary Perspective on Human Mating. *Psychological Review, 100*, 204–232.

DeSteno, D. A., & Salovey, P. (1996). Evolutionary Origins of Differences in Jealousy? Questioning the Fitness of the Model. *Psychological Science, 7*, 367–372.

Harris, C. R., & Christenfeld, N. (1996). Gender, Jealousy, and Reason. *Psychological Science, 7*, 364–366.

Kendrick, D. T. (1987). Gender, Genes and the Social Environment: A Biosocial Interactionist Perspective. In P. Shaver & C. Hendrick (Eds.), *Sex and Gender*. Newbury Park, CA: Sage.

Mendoza, S. P., & Shaver, P. R. (1995). One Rendition of Evolutionary Psychology: A Review of *The Evolution of Desire: Strategies of Human Mating*, by D. M. Buss. *Contemporary Psychology, 40,* 634–635.

Rich, A. (1979). Women and Honor: Some Notes on Lying. In *On Lies, Secrets and Silence: Selected Prose: 1966–78* (pp. 185–194). New York: Norton.

Woodward, V. (1995). Can We Draw Conclusions about Human Societal Behavior from Population Genetics? In E. Tobach & B. Rosoff (Eds). *Genes and Gender VII: Challenging Racism and Sexism: Alternatives to Genetic Explanations.* New York: Feminist Press, CUNY.

Chapter Ten

Gender Differences in Human Neuropsychological Function

Jerre Levy and Wendy Heller

Introduction

Scientific studies of sex differences in cognitive abilities have been stimulated by a long history of popular interest in psychological differences between men and women. According to Anastasi, when Samuel Johnson was asked whether men or women were more intelligent, he replied by asking, "Which man, which woman?" (Anastasi, 1958, p. 453). Johnson's reply highlights the fact that for a very large number of cognitive capacities (e.g., vocabulary, verbal reasoning, the ability to recognize an object from incomplete parts), no consistent sex differences exist. For other cognitive characteristics, the average difference between sexes is very small compared to within-gender variations. As Anastasi (1958) says, "Owing to the large extent of individual differences within any one group as contrasted to the relatively small difference between group averages, an individual's membership in a given group furnishes little or no information about his status in most traits" (p. 453).

We would add that if predictions are derived about an individual's probable success in a particular educational program or occupation based on regressed true scores of psychometric evaluations, the addition of gender to the prediction equation does not improve its accuracy. Claims that feminist aims would be invalidated were science to establish that cognitive sex differences are caused partly or totally by biological factors (e.g., Levin, 1980; see Levy, 1981, for rebuttal) reflect a failure to understand the scientific literature. The scientific findings strongly support the conclusion that an effective use of human talent compels sex-blind evaluations in meeting occupational requirements and the demands of educational programs.

Many psychological investigations have found average differences between human males and females in a variety of cognitive abilities (see Wittig & Petersen, 1979, for review; see Table 10.1). Females perform at a higher average level on tests of verbal fluency, spelling, reading speed, and reading comprehension. Speech and language

Jerre Levy & Wendy Heller, "Gender Differences in Human Neuropsychological Function." In A. Gerall, H. Moltz, & I. L. Ward (Eds.), *Handbook of Behavioral Neurobiology, 11*, pp. 245–274. © 1992 by Plenum Publishing Corporation. Reprinted with permission.

TABLE 10.1
*Average Performance of Females Relative to Males for
Various Cognitive Abilities*

Cognitive ability	Average performance of females (F) relative to males (M)
Verbal fluency	F > M
Spelling	F > M
Reading speed and comprehension	F > M
Social comprehension, understanding emotional information	F > M
Field independence	M > F
Mathematical reasoning	M > F
Comprehension of spatial relations	M > F
Verbal reasoning	F = M
Verbal IQ	F = M
Performance IQ	F = M

fluency develop earlier in girls than boys, and reading disorders are about four or five times more common in boys than girls (see Maccoby & Jacklin, 1974, for developmental studies). Female superiority in the communicative aspects of language does not, however, generalize to the formal manipulation of symbols as characterized by mathematical reasoning, in which males obtain average higher scores. The males' better performance on tests of mathematical reasoning (as distinct from arithmetical calculation) even appears among youngsters whose mathematical talents are at the upper end of the range and among boys and girls who have had equal training and express equal interest in mathematics (Benbow & Benbow, 1984).

The sexes differ not only in aspects of natural and formal language but also in nonverbal processes. Males, on average, perform better than females in understanding and mentally manipulating spatial relations on paper-and-pencil maze tests (Porteus, 1965). Higher performance on spatial tests is correlated with a greater ability of males than females to perceive underlying visuospatial relations in a confusing and conflicting context, an ability that has been called "field independence" (Witkin, Dyk, Faterson, Goodenough, & Karp, 1962/1974). Thus, there is an average male superiority in identifying a simple figure embedded in a more complex one (Embedded Figures Test), setting a rod to the absolute vertical when the rod is surrounded by a tilted frame (Rod-and-Frame Test), and correctly specifying the horizontal water line in a tilted bottle (Morris, 1971; Thomas, Jamison, & Hummel, 1973).

Field independence, though positively correlated with other spatial abilities, is negatively correlated with many personal attributes involved in social interaction. In comparison to field-independent people, field-dependent individuals are more attentive to social sources of information, more open in expressing thoughts and feelings, and more effective in social interactions (see Witkin, Goodenough, & Oltman, 1979, for review). These observations suggest that an increase in field dependence, such as typically seen in women, may reflect a greater use of contextual information. Such sensitivity may be important for social understanding. Females, cross-culturally, are better than men at interpreting the meaning of facial expression and other social, emotional information (Rosenthal, Hall, DiMatteo, Rogers, & Archer, 1979). Women also discriminate fine visual details better than men (Schneidler & Paterson, 1942).

Sex Differences in Human Neuropsychological Organization

In the large majority of right-handers, language functions, including speech, speech comprehension, reading, writing, mathematics, and arithmetic abilities, are mediated predominately by the left cerebral hemisphere. The right hemisphere is specialized for a variety of nonverbal processes, including interpretation of facial expression and emotional information, understanding of spatial relations, and non-verbal representation of sensory experience (see Bradshaw & Nettleton, 1983, for review).

Neither gender is consistently superior to the other in the functions of either hemisphere. The left hemisphere is specialized for verbal fluency, in which females are superior, for mathematical reasoning, in which males are superior, and for verbal reasoning, in which the genders are equal. Similarly, the right hemisphere is specialized for understanding spatial relations, in which males are superior, for interpreting emotional information, in which females are superior, and for imagistic representations of sensory events (in which the genders are equal). Additionally, the genders are equal in Performance IQ (which measures nonverbal intelligence) and in Verbal IQ (which measures verbal intelligence) on the Wechsler Adult Intelligence Scale (Matarazzo, 1972). Brain metabolic activity, as assessed from positron emission tomography (PET), is more strongly correlated with Performance IQ (PIQ) in the right than in the left hemisphere and with Verbal IQ (VIQ) in the left than right hemisphere (Chase et al., 1984). We can conclude, therefore, that the overall level of intelligence of each hemisphere is no different in men and women. Nonetheless, specific processes associated with each hemisphere may not be equally expressed by the sexes.

Sex Differences in the Degree of Functional Brain Asymmetry

In patients with unilateral brain damage, the association between verbal disorders and left hemisphere damage and between nonverbal disorders and right hemisphere damage is stronger in men than in women (Basso, Cupitani, & Monaschini, 1982; Edwards, Ellams, & Thompson, 1976; Inglis, Ruckner, Lawson, MacLean, & Monga, 1982; Kimura & Harshman, 1984; McGlone, 1977, 1980; Messerli, Tissot, & Rodriguez, 1976). The fact that the side of brain damage is more predictive of the nature (verbal and nonverbal) and severity of behavioral deficits in men than it is in women suggests a more symmetrical functional organization in women.

The greater similarity of the female's cerebral hemispheres in cognitive functioning appears to reflect both increases in the functional capacity of the nonspecialized hemisphere and decreases in the functional capacity of the specialized hemisphere. Kimura and Harshman (1984) examined groups of nonaphasic patients with unilateral hemispheric lesions to determine whether cognitive deficits differed for the two sexes. Digit span was significantly depressed in men but not in women with left-side damage, which suggests that the right hemisphere of women may be more involved in digit-span processing than the right hemisphere of men. In both sexes, vocabulary knowledge was deficient following left hemisphere lesions, but only women showed a vocabulary deficit with right hemisphere lesions. Quite possibly, word representation in women is more dependent on contributions from both hemispheres.

Both male and female patients with right hemisphere damage (Kimura & Harshman, 1984) were deficient in their ability to detect a missing portion of a picture (Wechsler Adult Intelligence Scale [WAIS]; Picture Completion subtest), but only men were deficient in copying designs with colored blocks (WAIS; Block Design subtest), in arranging cartoon pictures to tell a story (WAIS; Picture Arrangement), and in putting together simple jigsaw puzzles (WAIS; Object Assembly). The infrequency of deficits in women suggests that the left hemisphere represents and processes nonverbal information to a greater degree than it does in men.

Although these observations suggest that verbal and nonverbal functions are more bilaterally represented in the female than male brain, no evidence indicates that the right hemisphere of women mediates speech. In both genders, speech is entirely dependent on the left hemisphere in about 98 percent of right-handers.

Electrophysiological studies of normal people also suggest that cognitive functions are more symmetrically organized in women than in men. When engaging in laterally specialized tasks, men's α rhythm is suppressed more over the specialized side than women's (see Butler, 1984).

Investigations of normal right-handers responding to lateralized tachistoscopic input have often reported that perceptual asymmetries are smaller in women than in men. Typically, right-handers are faster or more accurate at identifying verbal stimuli in the right visual field/left hemisphere and certain nonverbal stimuli in the left visual field/right hemisphere. Many studies using verbal tasks, however, have revealed that the magnitude of the left hemisphere superiority is smaller in women than men (Bradshaw & Gates, 1978; Bradshaw, Gates, & Nettleton, 1977; Bryden, 1979; Hannay & Malone, 1976; Kail & Siegel, 1978), whereas on nonemotional visuospatial tasks, the right hemisphere superiority is smaller in women than men (Davidoff, 1977; Levy & Reid, 1978; McGlone & Davidson, 1973; Rizzolatti & Buchtel, 1977). It should be noted that many investigations of perceptual asymmetries fail to find gender differences on nonemotional tasks (e.g., Hannay & Boyer, 1978; Kershner & Jeng, 1972; Leehey, Carey, Diamond, & Cahn, 1978; Piazza, 1980). Investigators who have found them, however, consistently report greater asymmetries for men than women (e.g., Bradshaw & Gates, 1978; Rizzolatti & Buchtel, 1977).

The results of the foregoing studies on sex differences in perceptual asymmetries are consistent with those from electroencephalographic studies and from investigations of brain-damaged patients. Two quite distinct explanations can be made for the smaller perceptual asymmetries observed in women. The greater similarity between hemispheres can result, in some cases, from a reduced functional competency of the specialized hemisphere. In other cases, it can be caused by an increased representation of function in the unspecialized hemisphere (see Figure 10.1). Both causes for relative hemispheric similarity have been observed in women. First, in Levy and Reid's (1978) study, a right hemisphere superiority that was observed for both genders

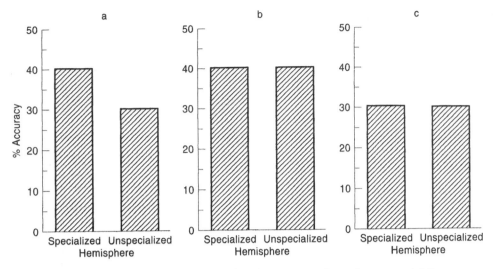

Fig. 10.1. Two possible explanations for a reduced asymmetry in performance. (a) Suppose the typical asymmetry in favor of the specialized hemisphere is 10 percent. A reduced asymmetry can result from (b) an increase in the level of performance by the unspecialized hemisphere or (c) a decrease in the level of performance by the specialized hemisphere.

on a spatial task was smaller for women than men. Since the performance for the two genders was equal for the less specialized left hemisphere, the reduced asymmetry in women had to reflect a relatively poorer performance by the more specialized right hemisphere. The inference is that the right hemisphere of women is less specialized for spatial functions than the right hemisphere of men, resulting in a greater similarity of the left and right hemispheres for females than males. In other words, spatial functions in this case are not more bilaterally represented in women; rather, the right hemisphere of females is only slightly better than the left hemisphere in spatial functions. Failures of women to show spatial disorders with right-hemisphere damage, therefore, may reflect the fact that the right hemisphere was little better than the left hemisphere premorbidly.

For verbal functions, however, the reduced perceptual asymmetry of women compared to men may arise from a much better performance by the less specialized right hemisphere. Thus, in a study by Bradshaw, Gates, and Nettleton (1977), right and left hemisphere performance was similar in women because language functions were well represented in the right side of the brain. In this case, the reduced asymmetry of women compared to men reflects a greater bilateral representation of language, not a reduced competency of the specialized hemisphere. The relatively good language capacities of the right hemisphere could explain cases where women fail to show verbal disorders following left-side damage or do manifest verbal disorders with right-side damage.

A greater hemispheric similarity in women for certain verbal and spatial functions does not imply that the female brain is more symmetrical than the male brain with respect to *all* functions. In fact, Ladavas, Umilta, and Ricci-Bitti (1980) found that women, but not men, had a right hemisphere superiority in identifying facial expressions. The greater symmetry in male performance resulted from a depression of right hemisphere accuracy compared to female performance, not from an enhancement of left hemisphere performance. These results suggest that the male's right hemisphere lacks the emotional specialization of the female's right hemisphere, just as the female's right hemisphere appears to lack the spatial specialization of the male's right hemisphere. On another task requiring interpretation of facial expression, Strauss and Moscovitch (1981) confirmed the results of Ladavas, Umilta, and Ricci-Bitti (1980) with respect to both the lack of asymmetry in men and the depression of right hemisphere performance in men as compared to women. These data are concordant with findings from dichotic-listening tasks, where two different auditory inputs are simultaneously presented to the two ears. When melodic patterns or environmental sounds are presented, both of which have an emotional impact, discrimination is better for the left ear/right hemisphere than for the right ear/left hemisphere. However, the superiority of the right hemisphere over the left is larger for women than men (Piazza, 1980).

We conclude that the female brain is more functionally symmetric than the male brain in verbal and spatial processes and less functionally symmetric in emotional processes. The male's right hemisphere, although differing greatly from the left in its spatial and verbal abilities, is only a little better in interpreting emotional information. In contrast, the female's right hemisphere is much better than the left hemisphere at interpreting emotional information but is only slightly superior in spatial ability. Although the female's right hemisphere, like that of the male, lacks expressive speech capacities, certain receptive language functions may have a relatively high level of representation.

The fact that the genders differ in the degree of similarity of the two hemispheres, in the nature of specializations, and in cognition does not, of course, establish that psychological and neurological sex differences are functionally related. Males, on the average, are taller than females and have shorter hair. Hair length and height are two variables that differentiate males and females, yet, within genders, height is not related to hair length. In contrast, height and weight differentiate the genders, and they also covary within genders. The within-gender covariation establishes that the between-gender difference in one variable can partially explain (depending on the within-gender correlation) the between-gender difference in the other variable. To infer that neurological gender differences are functionally related to psychological gender differences, it is necessary to show that within-gender relations between the two variables correspond to gender relations.

Within-Gender Association between Cognitive Abilities and Perceptual Asymmetries

If the greater similarity of the two hemispheres of female brains for verbal and spatial processes is functionally related to their cognitive abilities, then *within* genders, greater similarity between hemispheres should be associated with decreased spatial abilities and increased field dependence. In line with this expectation are data provided by Oltman, Ehrlichman, and Cox (1977) and Zoccolotti and Oltman (1978), who reported that, within genders, the greater the field dependency the smaller the perceptual asymmetry on lateralized tasks. Further, O'Connor and Shaw (1978) and Oltman, Semple, and Goldstein (1979) found that the electroencephalographic patterns of the two hemispheres were more similar when field dependency scores increased, suggesting that the two hemispheres were more in phase for field-dependent than for field-independent people.

In Zoccolotti and Oltman's (1978) study of males, a tachistoscopically presented letter-identification task yielded better right visual field/left hemisphere than left visual field/right hemisphere performance in field-independent people and no asymmetry in field-dependent people. The lack of asymmetry in field-dependent men was related to unusually high performance by the right hemisphere. This outcome is consistent with the conclusion that field dependency is associated with increased language representation in the right hemisphere. On a nonemotional face recognition task, field-independent people had better right hemisphere than left hemisphere performance, and field-dependent people had no asymmetry. However, in this case, the lack of asymmetry in field-dependent people resulted from unusually poor performance by the right hemisphere. These results suggest that for nonemotional visuospatial functions, the specialized right hemisphere of field-dependent people is inferior to that of field-independent people.

Rapaczynski and Ehrlichman (1979) examined a group of women on a tachistoscopically presented face-recognition task similar to that used in men by Zoccolatti and Oltman (1978). As was the case for males, field-independent women had better right hemisphere performance than left. However, field-dependent women, rather than having no asymmetry, had better left hemisphere performance than right. The performance of the left hemisphere did not differ significantly for the two groups, suggesting that visuospatial function in the left hemisphere was not elevated in field-dependent subjects. Rather, the performance of the right hemisphere was much lower for field-dependent than for field-independent subjects. The field-dependency scores of women in Rapaczynski and Ehrlichman's study were considerably higher than the scores of the field-dependent men in Zoccolatti and Oltman's (1978) study. This may explain why field-dependent women performed better with the left than right hemisphere, whereas field-dependent men showed no asymmetry.

Extreme degrees of field dependency may be associated with a relative failure of right hemisphere specialization for spatial function as a result of an unusually high degree of right hemisphere specialization for emotional or language processes. In such cases, a verbal coding of visuospatial stimuli by the left hemisphere may provide a better representation of information than an imagistic coding by the right hemisphere. Thus, the observations from Rapaczynski and Ehrlichman's (1979) study are not inconsistent with those of Zoccolatti and Oltman (1978), since the field-dependent women in the former were more field dependent than the men in the latter.

Sheehan and Smith (1986) examined a group of boys (ages 11–13) on lateralized verbal and spatial tachistoscopic tests and on verbal and spatial ability tests. For each subject, they derived an index of lateralization, based on the two laterality tasks, and examined the relationship between the degree of hemispheric asymmetry and cognitive ability. The verbal factor score (based on verbal fluency, vocabulary, and verbal reasoning) was unrelated to the degree of lateralization, but the spatial factor score, which included a measure of field independence, was strongly predicted by lateralization. The more similar the hemispheres, the lower the spatial ability. Unfortunately, separate performance scores for each visual field were not presented.

The fact that verbal performance was not related to the degree of hemispheric asymmetry in Sheehan and Smith's (1986) study is not surprising. There is no evidence that the normal female superiority in verbal fluency and the quite minor female superiority in vocabulary (0.12 standard deviation relative to within-gender variation [Matarazzo, 1972]) are related to the greater bilateral representation of language functions in females than males. Further, even if there were a relationship, the small female superiority in vocabulary is only detectable with very large samples, and the genders do not differ in verbal reasoning. Briefly, had females been included in Sheehan and Smith's (1986) sample, it is unlikely that they would have differed significantly from males on the verbal ability measure.

In contrast, the smaller asymmetry scores for spatial tasks observed in females compared to males result from poorer right hemisphere performance. Females are considerably more field dependent than males, and Sheehan and Smith's (1986) spatial ability measure included an index of field independence as well as measures of other spatial processes in which females are inferior to males. Their finding that hemispheric asymmetry declined as spatial ability decreased within males is to be expected if within-gender relationships are the same as between-gender relationships.

Weak lateralization in association with field dependence has also been demonstrated by Dawson (1977), Pizzamiglio (1974), and Pizzamiglio and Cecchini (1971) on verbal dichotic-listening tasks. These latter studies suggest that as the verbal capacities of the right hemisphere increase (which reduce verbal asymmetry), the spatial specialization of the right hemisphere decreases. Such a relationship may be explained by presuming that as the organizational patterns of the right hemisphere become progressively specialized for verbal processing, they would become progressively less specialized for spatial processing.

The various investigations show that the degree of spatial ability and field independence is positively correlated with the magnitude of performance asymmetries between the hemispheres. When studies reported separate accuracy and speed scores for each hemisphere, small asymmetries on verbal tasks were associated with better right hemisphere performance, whereas small asymmetries on spatial tasks were associated with poorer right hemisphere performance.

We can infer that developmental factors that lead to small asymmetries between hemispheres result in reduced spatial abilities and reduced field independence. If reduced spatial specialization of the right hemisphere is associated with increased emotional specialization, then small hemispheric asymmetries should also be associated with enhanced right hemisphere specialization for interpreting emotional information. Not only does this relationship occur between genders, but as discussed, field dependency is associated with social interest and social competence (Witkin et al., 1979). Unfortunately, no studies to date have investigated the relationship between hemispheric asymmetry within genders and emotional and social understanding.

In summary, the within-gender relationships between hemisphere asymmetry and cognitive patterns appear to be the same as the between-gender relationships. We can therefore conclude that, at least to some degree, cognitive differences between men and women are functionally related to gender differences in hemispheric specialization.

Sex Differences in Anterior and Posterior Cortical Organization

Differences in cortical organization of function in normal people can be inferred from patterns of perceptual asymmetries on behavioral tasks. Such differences have also been found in studies of men and women with brain damage. Kimura (1983) found that aphasic disorders were equally common in men with either anterior or posterior left-side lesions. In women, however, aphasia was rarely observed after posterior damage but was as common as in men after anterior damage. In the few female patients who manifested aphasia with damage to the posterior regions, receptive language function was considerably better than in women with anterior lesions. In contrast, males with posterior lesions had poorer receptive functions than those with anterior lesions.

Mateer, Polen, and Ojemann (1982) electrically stimulated regions of the left hemisphere cortex to determine the regions of stimulation that disrupted speech. In 100 percent of both men and women, stimulation of the frontal speech zone blocked the ability of the patient to name an object. Stimulation in a relatively confined area around this zone also disrupted speech in men but never in women. In men, speech was also disrupted with stimulation in any postcentral region of either the middle or superior temporal gyrus or the inferior parietal cortex. In women, however, the only postcentral stimulation that ever interfered with speech was in a highly restricted zone in the posterior portion of the superior temporal gyrus. These studies show that speech functions are more widely distributed in the left hemisphere of men than women.

The Mateer, Polen, and Ojemann (1982) findings are consistent with those of Kimura (1983), since posterior damage in women would be expected to disrupt speech only if the lesion invaded the critical portion identified by Mateer and coworkers. In contrast, for men, speech disorders would be expected with damage to any region of the posterior left hemisphere that included the inferior parietal cortex or any portion of either the middle or superior temporal gyrus.

It is of interest that the large perisylvian cortex, both temporal and parietal, which is important for speech functions in men but not women, includes regions critical for reading. Females are superior to males in reading comprehension and speed (Hitchcock & Pinder, 1974; Schaie & Roberts, 1970), and reading disabilities are much more common in boys than girls (Biller, 1974; Garai & Scheinfeld, 1968). Possibly, much of the female postcentral cortex of the left hemisphere is specialized for skills involved in reading. The comparable regions of males may be specialized more for language in general, including speech and mathematics, but less for reading in particular. Neither reading nor mathematical ability has yet been compared for men and women with posterior left hemisphere damage.

Gender differences in the functional organization of anterior and posterior regions are also present for the right hemisphere. Kimura (1983) found that in male patients, performance on the WAIS Block Design and Object Assembly tasks was equally depressed for those with anterior and posterior damage of the right side of the brain. In female patients, however, performance on these tasks was essentially normal or close to normal with posterior right hemisphere damage and significantly depressed with anterior right hemisphere damage. Clearly, the postcentral regions of the female brain are not without function. As suggested, the postcentral left hemisphere of women may be more highly specialized than the comparable area of men for skills involved in reading. Perhaps the postcentral right hemisphere of females is specialized for interpreting social information, and to a greater extent than is the case for males, just as the posterior right hemisphere of males may be more specialized than that of females for spatial processing.

Although a relationship is present between sex differences in cognition and in the organization of the anterior and posterior cortical regions, its magnitude is relatively small. The sex difference in anterior and posterior cortical organization is profound and larger than the within-gender variation. This relationship stands in dramatic contrast to the small between-gender difference in cognition and hemispheric asymmetry, compared to the large within-gender variance. Factors that generate a massive difference between genders in functional localization in the anterior and posterior portions of the brain do not generate a similarly large gender difference in either cognition or hemispheric asymmetry. The implication is that the structures of neural programs in the two hemispheres of males and females may be quite different yet have quite similar, though not identical, capacities to solve various cognitive problems.

Sex Differences in the Maturation of the Two Hemispheres

Basic patterns of lateral specialization are known to be present even in infancy (Best, Hoffman, & Glanville, 1982; Entus, 1977; Glanville, Best, & Levenson, 1977; Molfese, 1977; Molfese & Hess, 1978). In both male and female infants, the left hemisphere is more responsive to and better able to discriminate verbal stimuli than the right hemisphere, and the reverse holds for musical stimuli. The functional asymmetries present at birth represent different potentialities of the two hemispheres for the development of verbal and nonverbal skills. The differing potentialities, however, do not define either the nature of the verbal and nonverbal processes that will be developed or the degree of functional hemisphere asymmetry that will be present in the adult.

In infantile hemiplegics, in whom one hemisphere is dysfunctional from birth and hemispherectomy is performed in infancy or childhood, the intact hemisphere develops a notable level of bifunctional competence in both the verbal and nonverbal domains. When infantile hemiplegics with left hemispherectomy reach adulthood, speech and other language functions are remarkably normal, and disorders of language can only be detected by rather subtle linguistic tests (Dennis & Kohn, 1975). In infantile hemiplegics with right hemispherectomy, spatial functioning is as good as in normal children up to ten years of age, and the minor disorders that are present are restricted to spatial processes that emerge after age ten (Kohn & Dennis, 1974). Thus, even though at birth the two hemispheres have differing potentialities for the development of verbal and nonverbal abilities, neither hemisphere is committed to any fixed level of adult capacities. Each hemisphere can develop either a highly restricted set of abilities very different from those of the other hemisphere or a broader, more general set of abilities similar to those of the other hemisphere.

As each hemisphere matures, new representational strategies develop, which, in turn, affect its organization and capacities. As Levine (1985) has shown, children under the age of ten fail to show the right hemisphere superiority present in older children and adults for recognizing unfamiliar faces flashed to the lateral visual fields. Performance by the left hemisphere is as good for younger as older children, but performance by the right hemisphere is significantly poorer in younger children. Prior to age ten, the right hemisphere's superior potential for representing unfamiliar faces is not yet established.

Levine (1985) has also shown, however, that even for the youngest children tested (age seven), the right hemisphere is superior, as in older children and adults, for recognizing highly familiar faces of classmates. With sufficient experience, hemispheric potentials can apparently be reached at an earlier age, which illustrates the interactive effects between hemispheric maturity and environmental influences. Thus, the maturity of each hemisphere during development, in interaction with environmental influences, governs both the nature and level of capacities that each hemisphere can display. This conclusion is extremely important in understanding the emergence of adult gender differences in cognition, because evidence is accumulating that the right hemisphere matures faster in males and the left hemisphere matures faster in females.

By three months of age, and possibly earlier, boys and girls differ in the functional reactivity of the two sides of the brain. Shucard and colleagues (1981) examined evoked responses over the two hemispheres to a pair of clicks superimposed over either a music or speech background in three-month-old infants. Regardless of background, girls showed larger responses over the left than right hemisphere, whereas boys had larger responses over the right than left hemisphere. By six months of age (Shucard, Shucard, & Thomas, 1984), male infants continued to show larger right hemisphere evoked responses for either a music-background or a speech-background condition, whereas females showed the adult pattern; i.e., evoked responses to clicks were larger over the left hemisphere with a speech background but larger over the right hemisphere with a music background (Shucard, Shucard, & Thomas, 1977).

The gender differences in evoked response patterns are specific for neutral stimuli (clicks) that are superimposed over a background noise of either speech or music. As stated earlier, newborn boys and girls show the same asymmetry of evoked responses to direct speech or musical stimuli (Molfese, 1977; Molfese & Hess, 1978) and, by a few months of age, the same asymmetry in discriminating speech or musical stimuli (Best et al., 1982; Entus, 1977; Glanville et al., 1977). The basic verbal and nonverbal characteristics of the two hemispheres are present in both genders, as reflected in the electrophysiological response to and discrimination of speech and musical stimuli. However, the click-evoked responses studied by Shucard and colleagues (1981, 1984) in infants index a different aspect of hemispheric function.

When these clicks are superimposed over a complex background, the magnitude of the evoked response will depend on how well the clicks can be discriminated from background complexity. In infants three months of age, possible differences between hemispheres in differentiating clicks from speech or clicks from music are minor compared to hemispheric differences in the ability to discriminate the click signal from *any* complex auditory background. Such differences depend on the functional maturity of the two sides of the brain. Only after a sufficient level of maturity has been achieved by both sides of the brain can the more subtle distinction of signal versus speech or signal versus music affect the asymmetry of evoked responses to the click signal.

The evoked-response studies of Shucard and colleagues (1981, 1984) suggest that the female's left hemisphere and the male's right hemisphere predominate in sensory analysis at three months of age. By six months of age, right hemisphere predominance is still present in males, suggesting a rather pronounced maturational lag of the left hemisphere. The fact that six-month-old female infants show the normal adult pattern of evoked-response asymmetries for speech and music backgrounds demonstrates that at this age, the female's left hemisphere is evidently far advanced in development compared to that of the male. During the first year of life, it appears that the maturational asymmetry in favor of the right hemisphere in males is considerably more pronounced than the maturational asymmetry in favor of the left hemisphere in females.

In support of this inference are findings of Taylor (1969) on adult patients with temporal lobe epilepsy in association with mesial temporal sclerotic (MTS) lesions induced by febrile convulsions. Retrospective histories show that the majority of such patients have their first seizure prior to the first birthday and that the proportion with later onset of the first seizure declines monotonically with age. Thus, the longer an infant and child is seizure-free, the less likely it becomes that an MTS disorder will develop.

Taylor (1969) found that males with left hemisphere lesions were significantly overrepresented among patients with a seizure onset prior to the first year of age. As the age of onset of the first seizure increased, the overrepresentation of males with left hemisphere lesions declined. These observations indicate that during the first year of life, the male's left hemisphere is less mature in its resistance to seizures than the male right hemisphere or either hemisphere of females. No significant difference was found in the frequency of left and right hemisphere lesions in female patients with a seizure onset prior to the first birthday, suggesting that the maturity levels of the two female hemispheres were considerably more similar than those of males. These data support the suggestion that the observations of Shucard and colleagues (1981, 1984) on evoked response asymmetries in three- and six-month-old infants imply a larger discrepancy between the hemispheres of boys (in favor of the right) than of girls.

Maturational asymmetries of the two hemispheres established during infancy continue during the childhood period and can be expected to influence the development of communicative language, symbolic representation, spatial skills, and emotional and social abilities. The kinds of activities in which children engage, the degree of competence they display at various ages for different skills, and the amount of reinforcement they receive are in part determined by how mature the hemispheres are at various stages of development. Environmental factors, in turn, affect the subsequent development and specializations of each hemisphere. Thus, sexual differentiation of cognitive function and hemispheric specialization continues during childhood and is probably heavily influenced by an interaction between the rate of hemispheric maturation and various environmental influences. Studies of children support our suggestion that gender differences in hemispheric maturation, established during the first year of life and present throughout development, condition how boys and girls process incoming information, as we discuss in the next section.

Hemispheric Asymmetries during Childhood

A number of behavioral studies indicate that maturational differences are present in the two hemispheres of school-age boys and girls, especially as reflected in tactile perception by the left and right hands. These gender differences may relate to Conel's finding (cited by Landsdell, 1964) that at four years of age, myelinization of axons for the hand-projection region of the cortex is more complete in the right hemisphere of boys and in the left hemisphere of girls.

Based on Hermelin and O'Connor's (1971) observation that blind readers are more proficient in reading Braille with the left than right hand, Rudel, Denckla, and Spalten (1974) examined the two hands of normal children to determine which was more proficient at learning to associate letters with Braille. In boys, there was no hand asymmetry in the youngest group of seven- and eight-year-olds, but, thereafter, a left-hand (right hemisphere) superiority was evident. For girls, a left-hand superiority only emerged at age eleven, and prior to that age, either no asymmetry or a right-hand (left hemisphere) superiority was detected.

In interpreting these data, it is essential to keep in mind that in adults, Braille configurations are better represented in the right than left hemisphere. This adult right hemisphere superiority depends on the maturity of its specialized representational systems. Prior to such maturation, the representational strategies of the right hemisphere would be as primitive as those of the left hemisphere. The observations of Rudel, Denckla, and Spalten (1974) therefore imply that an adequate maturity of spatial specialization of the right hemisphere for the Braille-letter task was present by age nine in boys but was delayed until age eleven in girls. Thus, the maturity level of the right hemisphere of girls is still behind that of boys during school years.

The fact that boys had a left-hand superiority by age nine does not, however, imply that the male right hemisphere was fully mature by this age. It only implies that, for the particular task given, with its particular level of difficulty, the male right hemisphere was *sufficiently* mature to utilize its specialized capabilities.

Rudel, Denckla, and Hirsch (1977) examined children on a more difficult Braille task than that of Rudel, Denckla, and Spalten (1974), which required the comparing of *two* Braille configurations and deciding whether they were the same. Thus, demands on the specialized spatial abilities of the right hemisphere were greater for this task than for that of Rudel, Denckla, and Spalten (1974). A left-hand superiority on the two-configuration task did not appear until age eleven in boys and age thirteen in girls. Thus, with sufficient task difficulty, it was possible to demonstrate that right hemisphere maturation was still discrepant between boys and girls late in development.

Cioffi and Kandel (1979) compared the left and right hands of boys and girls on cross-modal tactovisual tasks. Tactile stimuli were presented to each hand for simultaneous palpation, and children were then asked to select the matching stimuli from a visual display. In one task, the stimuli were two-letter words formed from plastic letters. At all ages tested (from age seven), performance was superior for the right hand (left hemisphere) in both boys and girls. The absence of a gender difference on the word task is not surprising. Most children learn to read at age six, and at birth both male and female infants show larger evoked responses over the left than right hemisphere to speech stimuli (Molfese, 1977). Even if the male's left hemisphere is less mature than the right, its word-representation capacities would still be expected to exceed those of the right hemisphere by age seven.

On a second task, stimuli consisted of consonant bigrams formed from two plastic letters. This task differs from the first in that the letters did not form words. Nonetheless, they were highly familiar stimuli that could be represented easily either as letter names or as familiar visual images. At all ages, girls showed a right-hand (left hemisphere) superiority, and boys showed a left-hand (right hemisphere) superiority. Overall performance did not differ between genders. Thus, for highly familiar stimuli that could be equally well represented as letter names or as visual images, girls were biased to rely on left hemisphere representation, and boys on right hemisphere representation. These biases may reflect a better linguistic encoding for girls and a better imagistic–spatial encoding for boys.

On a third task, which was developed by Witelson (1976), stimuli consisted of unfamiliar nonsense shapes. On this task, Cioffi and Kandel (1979) found a left-hand (right hemisphere) superiority in both boys and girls from seven years of age on. Although the task was basically spatial in nature, it was evidently much simpler than even the single-configuration Braille task of Rudel, Denckla, and Spalten (1974), since on the Braille task, a left-hand superiority emerged for boys only at age nine, and for girls at age eleven. Apparently, the spatial specialization of the right hemisphere at age seven in both genders was sufficiently mature to provide a better representation of the nonsense stimuli than was possible for the left hemisphere.

In contrast to Cioffi and Kandel (1979), Witelson gave children very extensive practice with the shapes prior to the experimental trials. In principle, at least, such practice would allow children to develop verbal descriptions or even names (e.g., "the house shape") for the nonsense stimuli. In Witelson's study, boys had a left-hand (right hemisphere) superiority at the youngest age tested (age six), whereas girls did not. However, close examination of Witelson's data shows that between ages ten and twelve, the left hand of girls showed an improvement, whereas the right hand did not. As a result, twelve-year-old girls had a left-hand advantage very similar to that of boys. Apparently, by age twelve, the right hemisphere of girls was superior to the left in representing the nonsense shapes, even though extensive practice probably allowed the left hemisphere to develop verbal codes for the nonsense shapes.

We do not believe that Cioffi and Kandel's (1979) observations for girls conflict with those of Witelson (1976). Rather, we suggest that the extensive practice provided by Witelson, but not by Cioffi and Kandel, allowed the left hemisphere of girls to utilize verbal encoding strategies that could be applied to the nonsense shapes. In consequence, the verbal representations of the left hemisphere were as adequate as the spatial representations of the right hemisphere up through age ten. With continued maturation of the right hemisphere, however, its spatial representations by age twelve surpassed the verbal representations of the left hemisphere in their accuracy in stimulus encoding. The lack of any right-hand improvement for girls between ages ten and twelve suggests that by age ten, verbal representation of the inherently spatial stimuli had reached its asymptote.

To summarize, a left-hand (right hemisphere) superiority in discriminating Braille configurations emerges later in girls than boys, and later for both genders as spatial complexity increases. A right-hand (left hemisphere) superiority is present for tactile word discrimination in children as young as seven, and the asymmetry does not differ between genders. However, for consonant bigrams, which are equally amenable to verbal and spatial representation, girls have a right-hand (left hemisphere) and boys have a left-hand (right hemisphere) superiority. Thus, boys are biased to represent stimuli spatially, and girls are biased to represent stimuli verbally.

For tactile nonsense shapes, boys as young as six or seven have a left-hand (right hemisphere) superiority regardless of whether they have been given the opportunity to learn verbal encoding strategies or not. Girls, however, manifest a left-hand (right hemisphere) superiority from age seven onward only if there has been no opportunity to learn verbal representation strategies. When such an opportunity is available, the two hemispheres of girls perform at equal levels up through age ten, although by age twelve the right hemisphere surpasses the left.

The various studies indicate that up to the beginning of adolescence, the right hemisphere is more functionally mature in males than females. They further suggest that when encoding stimuli that are equally well represented by either strategy, girls have a bias to rely on verbal processes of the left hemisphere, and boys a bias to rely on spatial processes of the right hemisphere. In addition, given the opportunity, girls can and do learn to encode inherently spatial stimuli with a verbal strategy. The verbal encoding produces left hemisphere performance as good as right hemisphere performance until the right hemisphere has achieved complete or almost complete maturity. The differing biases of prepubertal boys and girls show that gender differences in hemispheric maturity throughout the developmental period have major effects on how information is processed and represented.

Such biases suggest that during infant and toddler development, verbal communications and interactions between young children and parents would be highly effective in stimulating a left hemisphere development of verbal communicative skills in girls but would be much less effective in boys, since their left hemisphere might not be sufficiently mature to process and encode such information. Since the right hemisphere of girls lags only slightly behind the left, the emphasis on verbal activities might also tend to stimulate the right hemisphere to develop some level of language competency. Simultaneously, skill in understanding nonverbal aspects of social communication and emotion, which go hand in hand with verbal communication, would develop a strong representation in the female right hemisphere. These effects, taking place in preschool years, might influence the subsequent maturation of the female hemispheres and cognitive profiles.

Since the verbal environment is relatively inaccessible to the immature left hemisphere of males at the time when the right hemisphere is maturationally advanced, boys would be expected to center their interest on the physical environment and its mechanics and spatial relations as spatial schemas develop. Their activities would be self-reinforcing and would foster a strong right hemisphere specialization for spatial skills that does not depend on understanding social communications. By the time the left hemisphere becomes sufficiently mature to process verbal communicative information effectively, the right hemisphere would already be committed to a spatial specialization. This might limit the right hemisphere's level of specialization for interpreting social communication, either verbal or emotional.

As it matures, the male's left hemisphere would, of course, develop skill in the communicative aspects of language. However, this communicative understanding might not be reinforced as strongly for boys as for girls, since it was not temporally linked and thereby integrated with the developing specialization in the right hemisphere for emotional information. Further, a high level of spatial specialization in the right hemisphere might encourage the development of a left hemisphere specialization for representing symbolic relations that can be mapped onto the spatial representations of the right hemisphere.

The effects of learning, social interaction, and general environmental stimulation on hemispheric development are dramatically highlighted in the case of Genie, who from the age of eighteen months until thirteen years was confined to a room and had neither social interaction nor the opportunity to learn language (Curtis, 1977). Objects in the room, as well as environmental sights and sounds through an open window, provided sensory stimulation. As an adult, Genie developed a highly defective language that, among other limitations, lacks syntax and function words and is echolalic. Laterality testing shows a deficiency in left hemisphere processing of all stimuli, and electroencephalographic studies reveal severe dysfunctions in left hemisphere activity. On cognitive tests, Genie is profoundly retarded on all left hemisphere processes. In contrast, Genie scores at the ninety-eighth percentile or better on many right hemisphere spatial functions.

Genie's development (Curtis, 1977) reveals not only that her left hemisphere failed to develop in the absence of verbal and social stimulation but that her right hemisphere developed hypernormal spatial abilities. Presumably, Genie's right hemisphere could develop neither a typical female language representation nor a specialization for interpreting nonverbal social and emotional information. The only stimulation available induced a very high level of spatial specialization in the right side of the brain.

In the discussions to follow of the relationships between gonadal hormones in early development and cognition and hemispheric specialization and asymmetry, the foregoing developmental model should be kept in mind. Studies of children and adults with abnormal early hormonal environments strongly suggest that fetal or infant gonadal androgen and estrogen affect the development of the two sides of the brain and, consequently, the development of cognitive abilities. Optimal levels of both androgens and estrogens appear to be necessary for normal neuropsychological development, and departures from the normal range are associated with a variety of cognitive deficits. However, we can relate the effects of hormones to hemispheric maturation rates only by considering the normal gender differences in left and right hemisphere maturation, in the early hormonal environment, in adult cognitive patterns, and in adult specializations of the two hemispheres.

Genetic and Hormonal Effects on Human Neuropsychological Gender Differences

Studies of cognitive patterns in individuals with genetic or hormonal anomalies provide otherwise unattainable information on the effects of abnormal karyotypes and hormonal environments in humans. Two genetic anomalies that have been studied are men with Klinefelter syndrome (XXY) and women with Turner syndrome (XO).

Neuropsychological Profiles in Abnormal Karyotypes

Klinefelter Syndrome. In Klinefelter syndrome (KS), there is an XXY karyotype, but androgen production and testicular development are normal during infancy (Ratcliffe & Tierney, 1982). At puberty, however, the testes begin to degenerate, androgens fail to reach the normal levels, and some physical feminization occurs.

Compared to normal men, KS men have a normal performance IQ but significant and severe disabilities in a wide spectrum of verbal abilities (Netley & Rovet, 1982a, 1987; Nielsen, Sorensen, Theilgaard, Froland, & Johnsen, 1969; Ratcliffe, Bancroft, Axworthy, & McLaren, 1982; Walzer, Graham, Bashir, & Sibert, 1982). Furthermore, in tests of hemispheric lateralization, KS men show depressed performance for the left hemisphere but normal or better than normal performance for the right hemisphere (Netley & Rovet, 1984, 1987).

Netley and Rovet (1987) hypothesized that abnormal functioning of the left hemisphere in KS men could be related to developmental slowing in the rate of cell division prenatally. Developmental slowing in the KS fetus has been inferred from studies of fingerprint patterns, which show an abnormally low total ridge count (Hreczko & Sigmon, 1980; Netley & Rovet, 1987; Penrose, 1967; Valentine, 1969) typically associated with a slow rate of cell division prenatally (Barlow, 1973; Mittwoch, 1973).

Using total ridge count as an index of developmental slowing, Netley and Rovet (1987) found that KS boys with the lowest ridge counts (slowest early development) manifested the lowest verbal IQ and the most abnormal laterality patterns, whereas those with the highest ridge counts manifested the highest verbal IQ and the most normal laterality patterns.

An association between a slowing in the rate of cell division and abnormal left hemisphere development has also been suggested by Geschwind and Galaburda (1987), who argue that excessive androgenic activity is responsible. Although KS infants do not differ from normal infants in plasma androgen levels, it might be the case that KS individuals manifest higher sensitivity to androgen, at least in some tissues, since they have more autoimmune disorders than normal males (Segami & Alarcon-Segovia, 1978). Increased susceptibility to autoimmune disorders has been linked to increased action of androgens, which suppress the development of the "self-versus-other" discrimination of the immune system (see Geschwind & Galaburda, 1987, for review).

Since infant androgen levels are normal in the KS male (Ratcliffe & Tierney, 1982), some other mechanism, such as an increase in the density of androgen receptors, may lead to excessive androgenic action in early development. Further research is clearly needed, however, to identify the hormonal and genetic mechanisms that underlie the neuropsychological findings. Furthermore, although it is evident that left hemisphere functions are severely affected in KS individuals, there are also data suggesting mild impairments in right hemisphere functions (Nyborg & Nielsen, 1981; Serra, Pizzamiglio, Boari, & Spera, 1978). These results must be reconciled with other findings of normal or superior right hemisphere performance on lateralized tasks.

Turner Syndrome. Turner syndrome (TS) is a congenital abnormality in phenotypic females in which one of the two X chromosomes is missing or its short arm is deleted or translocated. The ovaries are typically represented by two dysfunctional streaks of ovarian tissue. In addition to gonadal dysgenesis, these women display a variety of somatic stigmata such as short stature, webbed neck, and skeletal abnormalities. Turner syndrome women can vary greatly in the degree to which they manifest the classical stigmata (Simpson, 1975; Turner, 1960) as well as in the degree to which the gonads are dysfunctional (Grumbach & Conte, 1985; Lippe, 1982). All develop the external genitalia of normal women and are, therefore, reared as such, and some appear in clinics only when they fail to undergo puberty.

As a group of subjects in whom gonadal hormones are essentially absent, TS women have been extensively studied. Originally, TS women were thought to be retarded, based on overall IQ scores (Bekker & Van Gemund, 1968; Turner, 1960). Further research demonstrated, however, that TS women have a normal verbal IQ but very significantly depressed abilities on a wide spectrum of visuospatial tasks, including those in which there is a normal male superiority (e.g., understanding spatial relations) and those in which there is a normal gender equality (e.g., performance IQ, which is standardized to gender equality; see Alexander, Walker, & Money, 1964; Garron, 1977; Money & Alexander, 1966; Shaffer, 1962).

Although verbal IQ is normal in TS women, they show minor and selective disorders of certain verbal functions. First, TS women score lower than normal women in verbal fluency (Heller & Levy, 1986; Money & Alexander, 1966; Waber,

1979). Second, on lateralized verbal tachistoscopic tasks, performance for the right hemisphere does not differ between TS and normal women, but performance for the left hemisphere is significantly lower (Heller & Levy, unpublished manuscript; McGlone, 1985). Heller and Levy (1986) also showed, through an analysis of the pattern of errors, that the depression of left hemisphere performance for TS as compared to normal women was caused by a reduction in linguistic encoding of information (see Levy, Heller, Banich, & Burton, 1983). Heller and Levy (1986) found that verbal fluency was predicted by the level of linguistic encoding of left hemisphere stimuli: as linguistic encoding increased, verbal fluency improved. Verbal reasoning, however, was unrelated to the linguistic encoding of stimuli by the left hemisphere, which indicates that the left hemisphere disorders of TS women may be specific for those verbal processes for which there is a normal female superiority.

On verbal dichotic-listening tests, TS women also have a reduced left hemisphere advantage compared to controls (Gordon & Galatzer, 1980; Netley & Rovet, 1982b; Rovet & Netley, 1983), and in the one study where separate ear performances could be derived (Gordon & Galatzer, 1980), the decreased left hemisphere advantage for TS women resulted from normal right hemisphere performance and depressed left hemisphere performance. The normal right hemisphere performance of TS women on verbal laterality tasks shows that their right hemisphere has no more verbal capacity than the right hemisphere of normal women. The spatial disorders in TS women are therefore not a consequence of an unusual degree of verbal specialization in the right hemisphere.

In brief, TS women appear to have a disorder of right hemisphere spatial function compared to either normal men or women and, in addition, a more selective disorder of certain left hemisphere verbal processes as compared to normal women. Their verbal reasoning does not differ from that of normal men and women, but they have a deficit in verbal fluency compared to normal women and decreased linguistic encoding of verbal stimuli by the left hemisphere. The level of linguistic encoding by the left hemisphere, furthermore, is predictive of verbal fluency.

Some authors have argued that the cognitive differences between TS and normal women are unlikely to be caused by the effects of hormones. They claim that the normal fetal and infant ovaries are inactive and do not contribute to normal female differentiation (see Döhler, 1978; Rovet & Netley, 1982). This view has been challenged, however, by many studies (see Bidlingmaier, Strom, Dorr, Eisenmenger, & Knorr, 1987). The evidence is strong that significant amounts of gonadal hormones (androgens and estrogens) circulate in both sexes during early postnatal life (see MacLusky & Naftolin, 1981), and the first six months of life are associated with fluctuating, and often high, plasma levels of estradiol in girls (Winter, Hughes, Reyes, & Faiman, 1976). Furthermore, the theca interna of fetal ovarian follicles yields the same strong alkaline phosphatase reaction as shown by these cells in ovaries of mature women, a reaction that has been related directly to gonadotropic stimulation and steroidogenesis (Ross & Vande Wiele, 1974). In addition, Bidlingmaier and colleagues (1987) report that gonadal estrogen concentrations in female infants paralleled changes in gonadal morphology. In particular, ovarian weights varied as a function of estrogen concentration, and the biggest ovaries contained multiple macroscopic cysts.

In normal women, a small number of genes are thought to specify gonadal differentiation, with consequent phenotypic sexual dimorphism organized almost exclusively by gonadal products (i.e., androgens, estrogens, Müllerian duct inhibitor; Haseltine & Ohno, 1981). Somatic gene activity in TS women and in normal women is virtually identical, since in normal women a large portion of one of the X chromosomes is inactivated early in embryogenesis (Gordon & Ruddle, 1981). One might argue that if the second X chromosome in normal females is truly inactive, TS women ought to be phenotypically normal. Although most regions are inactivated, two loci that mediate gonadal differentiation escape inactivation (Gordon & Ruddle, 1981).

Therefore, although it is possible that the loss of genetic activity of the second X chromosome acts through a nonhormonal mechanism to produce the cognitive abnormalities of TS women, it seems equally probable that they reflect the lack of gonadal hormones in early development. Evidence that the cognitive differences between TS and normal women may be hormonally mediated is strengthened by studies of individuals with other hormonal disorders, which indicate that cognitive abilities are affected by gonadal hormone status, even in the presence of a normal karyotype.

Neuropsychological Profiles in Abnormal Hormonal Environments

Androgen-Insensitivity Syndrome. Women with the androgen-insensitivity (AI) syndrome have an XY male karyotype and normal androgen production by the testes, but cells are deficient in androgen receptors. Androgen itself, therefore, cannot regulate cell differentiation. The fetus develops female external genitalia, and testicular estrogens induce a feminizing puberty. At puberty the testes are typically removed, and AI women are maintained on estrogen therapy. Their juvenile and adult behaviors are stereotypically feminine (Money, Schwartz, & Lewis, 1984).

Masica, Money, Ehrhardt, and Lewis (1969) assessed verbal and performance IQ in fifteen girls and women from twelve families with a complete testicular feminizing syndrome. With IQs averaged within sets of siblings to provide a single performance and verbal IQ score for each of the twelve families, mean performance IQ was 99.6 and mean verbal IQ was 111.7. The 12.1-IQ-point offset in verbal and performance IQ was significant, and in ten of the twelve cases, verbal IQ exceeded performance IQ. In one case, this was reversed, and in one case, verbal and performance IQs were equal. In a single case report, Spellacy, Bernstein, and Cohen (1965) describe an AI girl whose verbal IQ was 128 and performance IQ was 105.

Unfortunately, neither Masica and colleagues (1969) nor Spellacy, Bernstein, and Cohen (1965) had control groups, and their data therefore can only be compared to standardizations for the population. These standardizations show that for both males and females, the average discrepancy in verbal and performance IQ is zero. The discrepancy shown by AI women, therefore, deviates equally from those of normal females and normal males. Without a matched control group, it is not possible to know whether the verbal–performance discrepancy in AI women was caused by an increased verbal IQ, a reduced performance IQ, or both.

The discrepancy between verbal and performance IQ does indicate, however, that visuospatial and visuomotor abilities are inferior to verbal abilities in AI women. Since these are abilities typically associated with the right hemisphere, these data suggest that right hemisphere function may be impaired relative to left when androgen is depleted or when its actions are prevented.

Idiopathic Hypogonadotropic Hypogonadism. Hier and Crowley (1982) examined verbal and spatial abilities in nineteen men with idiopathic hypogonadotropic hypogonadism (IHH) as compared to nineteen normal men and five men who developed acquired hypogonadotropic hypogonadism following a normal virilizing puberty (postpubertal AHH). These patients have a normal 46,XY karyotype and undergo apparently normal masculinization in utero, a process that is presumably mediated by maternal gonadotropins. Puberty does not occur, however, because of a deficiency in gonadotropin-releasing factor. Depending on the severity of the disorder, the testes vary in size and in androgen production. Thus, in the IHH male, prenatal androgen levels appear relatively normal because of maternal gonadotropins, but androgen levels during infancy are extremely low.

The IHH men in Hier and Crowley's (1982) study all had a normal XY karyotype, a failure of pubertal development by age eighteen, a normal pituitary as inferred from x-ray analysis of the sella turcica, small testes, and defective virilization prior to androgen therapy. They had been withdrawn from androgen therapy for three months prior to psychometric assessment. These men showed a marked decrement in spatial skills compared to both normal men and males who developed the androgen deficiency after puberty. On the Block Design subtest of the Wechsler performance scale, IHH men were a full standard deviation below control subjects. On a test of field independence (Embedded Figures), they required almost twice as long (69.8 seconds) to complete the task as normal men (37.4 seconds) or AHH men (37.8 seconds). Furthermore, in IHH men, testicular volume (which is indicative of androgen production) was uncorrelated with verbal ability but was correlated with spatial ability such that the more severe the androgen deficiency, the greater the spatial deficit. Even when the androgen deficiency was corrected through replacement therapy, spatial ability did not improve.

Equivalent standardized scores were available for the Block Design subtest and the three verbal tests in Hier and Crowley's (1982) study. For the nineteen control and five AHH men, the average verbal ability score was 0.19 standard deviations above the Block Design score (equivalent to 2.8 IQ points). However, for IHH men, the average verbal ability score was 0.84 standard deviations above the Block Design score (equivalent to 12.6 IQ points), which is very similar to the observations of Masica and colleagues (1969) in AI women. Further, the verbal and performance IQs of IHH men (based on a prorated score) were practically identical to those of AI women in the Masica study.

It is relevant to note that in the standardization population, the difference for males between the three verbal tasks that Hier and Crowley (1982) administered and the Block Design subtest is equivalent to 1.28 IQ points in favor of the verbal tasks, and the difference for females is equivalent to 3.15 IQ points in favor of the verbal tasks (Matarazzo, 1972). Thus, the difference for IHH males in favor of verbal performance is not only greater than for the male control subjects but also greater than for females in the standardization population.

The studies reviewed above suggest that right hemisphere spatial functions are more poorly developed in both AI women and IHH men than in normal women. Normal women simply do not show anything like a 12-point IQ discrepancy between verbal and performance IQ or between performance on the three verbal subtests that Hier and Crowley (1982) examined and the Block Design subtest.

Congenital Adrenal Hyperplasia Syndrome. A common androgen disorder in early development is congenital adrenal hyperplasia (CAH), in which the fetal adrenals secrete abnormally high levels of androgen. When detected, usually at birth, medical intervention is typically initiated to normalize adrenal corticoid output. In CAH children, therefore, postnatal androgen status can be within normal limits. Although CAH children have been reported to be masculinized in various emotional and personality variables as compared to control children (see Hines, 1982, for review), investigations of cognitive function have generally found few differences between CAH girls and others.

Early studies that claimed that CAH female subjects possessed higher than normal intellectual function (Dalton, 1968, 1976; Ehrhardt & Money, 1967; Money & Lewis, 1966) were not confirmed when appropriate control samples were used (Baker & Ehrhardt, 1974; McGuire, Ryan, & Omenn, 1975; Perlman, 1973). With respect to specific abilities, Lewis, Money, and Epstein (1968) report that verbal and perfor-mance IQs were equal in CAH subjects, which indicates no selective enhancement or depression of left or right hemisphere functions.

The CAH males and CAH females could not be distinguished from control subjects on any of a set of verbal and spatial cognitive tests (McGuire et al., 1975). In a small sample, Perlman (1973) found that, compared to normal girls, CAH girls performed less well on verbal IQ, on arithmetic tasks, and on Block Design tasks but obtained higher scores in a picture completion task, whereas CAH boys did not differ from normal boys. Perlman's (1973) observations for girls reveal no interpretable pattern and, in addition, conflict with negative outcomes in other studies that used identical tasks.

Two studies report meaningful differences between CAH and normal subjects. In Baker and Ehrhardt's (1974) research, both CAH males and CAH females manifest lower mathematics ability than their unaffected siblings. Resnick and Berenbaum's (1982) research found that CAH girls and women were superior to normal women in spatial tasks for which men are generally superior to women. Thus, Resnick and Berenbaum's female CAH subjects manifested a cognitive masculinization. The relia-bility of Baker and Ehrhardt's and Resnick and Berenbaum's observations can only be determined from future investigations. However, the inferences drawn from the two studies are in opposite directions. Spatial and mathematical abilities are generally positively correlated, which makes it surprising that CAH children were simultaneously deficient in mathematics ability and superior in spatial ability. Conceivably, CAH children are highly variable in cognitive profiles, depending on the severity and timing of the androgen disorder and on their postnatal hormonal status. It should also be noted that the androgen environment to which CAH children are exposed is not that typical of normal males, which consists predominantly of the testicular hormone, testosterone. Adrenal androgens may not be comparable in their effects.

Prenatal Exposure to Diethylstilbestrol. Excessive estrogen levels in early development are present in two conditions. Prenatally, fetuses are exposed to an abnormal estrogen concentration when mothers have been treated with diethylstilbestrol (DES) in an attempt to control a threatened abortion. Postnatally, excessive estrogens accumulate as a result of a disorder of liver metabolism typically, but not always, in association with protein starvation during infancy (kwashiorkor).

Before it was discovered to have many adverse effects on development, DES, a synthetic estrogenic compound, was prescribed to a large number of pregnant women at risk for abortion. Although studies have shown that prenatal exposure of human fetuses to synthetic progestin or estrogen affects various emotional and personality characteristics (see Hines, 1982, for review), most studies have found no effects on cognitive abilities. Reinisch and Karow (1977) differentiated between subjects who had been exposed predominantly to prenatal estrogen versus prenatal progestin and compared the two groups to their siblings on verbal IQ, performance IQ, and verbal, spatial, and attentional cognitive factors. The two groups of affected individuals did not differ, and neither differed from sibling controls on any of the measures. No cognitive effects of abnormal prenatal exposure to estrogen or progestin were reported by Yalom, Green, and Fisk (1973), Kester, Green, Finch, and Williams (1980), or Hines (1981). Hines (1981) reported, however, that DES-exposed women showed a larger asymmetry in favor of the left hemisphere on a verbal dichotic-listening test than did control women, even though she found no cognitive differences between the two groups.

Kwashiorkor. In kwashiorkor excessive estrogens accumulate as a consequence of a disorder in liver metabolism. Even with subsequent diet correction, symptoms of kwashiorkor are resistant to cure, and gynecomastia (breast enlargement) as well as other signs are frequent in the adult man (Davies, 1947).

We are aware of only one cognitive study of men with symptoms of kwashiorkor. Dawson (1966) studied cognitive characteristics of a group of men with gynecomastia and a large control group. Both gynecomastic ($N = 10$) and control ($N = 149$) men were apprentices working at an iron-ore mine in Sierra Leone. The two groups did not differ in general intelligence, but men with gynecomastia were significantly superior on a measure of verbal ability (by 0.40 S.D. relative to within-group variance) and significantly inferior in spatial ability, as indexed by a block design task (by 0.65 S.D. relative to within-group variance) and a test of spatial relations (by 0.75 S.D. relative to within-group variance). The nature of the verbal ability measure is unknown, since Dawson (1966) only says that it is the verbal portion of an intelligence test constructed in terms of the Sierra Leone indigenous culture. The offset in standard units between groups cannot be compared to the typical gender offset, since no data are available for the Sierra Leone culture.

Conclusions and Speculations

The studies reviewed above suggest that in both normal males and females, right hemisphere maturation and the consequent development of spatial abilities may be dependent on stimulating effects of gonadal hormones, particularly androgen but also estrogen, in early development. When gonadal hormones are absent (TS women), depleted (IHH males), or otherwise reduced in potency (AI women), spatial abilities suffer. Furthermore, the results from IHH males suggest that infancy may be a crucial period for these hormonal influences, since prenatal androgens are apparently normal, and androgen replacement therapy in later years did not enhance their spatial abilities. This inference is supported by observations of relatively high levels of plasma gonadal hormones during the first six months of life in normal infants.

Whether androgenic and estrogenic activity is totally absent in infancy or reduced compared to that in normal babies, general verbal intelligence appears to be unaffected. Since men and women do not differ in verbal intelligence, the lack of effects would be expected. However, since TS women are impaired in both verbal fluency and left hemisphere linguistic development, which favor females, the question is raised regarding the possibility that estrogen may have a selective feminizing effect on the development of the left hemisphere. Infant ovarian hormones may have a restricted effect on the development of those left hemisphere specializations that are better organized in women than men. A pattern of better verbal abilities in association with abnormally high estrogen levels during early development in kwashiorkor suggests that estrogen may stimulate left hemisphere development, possibly, in these cases, by inhibiting effects of androgen.

More research is needed to clarify the effects of estrogen versus androgen on development. However, the hypothesis that estrogens act to feminize certain aspects of cognitive function is not without precedent in animal studies, which have shown a number of nonreproductive behaviors to be feminized by estrogen in infancy. Male rats are superior to female rats in complex maze learning, which in part is related to greater open-field activity in females and in part to superior spatial memory in males (see Beatty, 1984). Open-field exploration is more dependent on the left than the right cerebral hemisphere in rats, since it is dramatically reduced after ligation of the left but not the right middle cerebral artery (Robinson, 1979).

Estrogens administered during infancy impair maze learning in male rats (Dawson, Cheung, & Law, 1975), and neonatal ovariectomy reduces open-field activity in females (Blizard & Denef, 1973; Stewart & Cygan, 1980) unless replacement estrogens are given during infancy (Stewart & Cygan, 1980). Stewart and Cygan demonstrated that feminine open-field behavior is preserved in rats ovariectomized during the first days of life if low doses of exogenous estrogen are supplied between the tenth and twentieth postnatal days or either low or high doses are supplied between the twentieth and thirtieth days.

The foregoing data are not consistent with the traditional concept that brain differentiation in mammals follows a feminine pattern unless sufficient levels of androgens are present during initial periods in early development (see Döhler et al. 1984; Toran-Allerand, 1984, for reviews). Similarly, the evidence reviewed from humans suggests that physiological levels of estrogen in infancy may function to feminize certain neurological structures. In particular, the data suggest the possibility that under some circumstances, an absence of estrogen may lead to a lack of feminine development of the left hemisphere.

To summarize our reading of this literature, the various studies are consistent with a model of cortical development in which the right hemisphere is highly dependent on and sensitive to the stimulating effects of gonadal steroids in infancy, and in which the effects of androgen are more potent than the effects of estrogen.

In contrast to the strong steroid dependence of right hemisphere spatial development, we suggest that left hemisphere cortical maturation proceeds in the absence of gonadal steroids in infancy but may be slowed by androgen (as suggested by Geschwind & Galaburda, 1987) and may be stimulated by estrogen. Within the normal range of male and female infant gonadal steroid levels, or when these hormones are depleted, variations in the rate of left hemisphere maturation have no effects on general verbal intelligence, which does not differ between sexes. The normal slowing effects of androgen, under this model, in conjunction with a stimulating effect on the right hemisphere, lead to faster right than left hemisphere development in normal males. This, in turn, results, through interactions with environmental influences, in the typical male pattern of left hemisphere specialization for symbol manipulation in mathematics and reduced verbal communicative skills as compared to females, and to right hemisphere specialization for spatial skills and reduced social–emotional abilities as compared to females.

The foregoing considerations help to explain why within-gender variations in cognition and hemispheric asymmetry are so large compared to between-gender differences in spite of the very large gender difference in infant gonadal steroids. Even minor variations in infant gonadal steroids could lead to major changes in hemispheric maturation rates, so that a fairly large fraction of males have a maturation pattern as feminine as that of the average female, and a similar fraction of females have a maturation pattern as masculine as that of the average male. If, as we argue, hemispheric maturational rates govern adult cognitive profiles, hemispheric specialization, and hemispheric asymmetry, then the average gender difference in these rates underlies cognitive gender differences, and within-gender variations in these rates underlie within-gender cognitive variations. The fact that hemispheric asymmetry and specialization have the same relation to cognition within and between genders then becomes completely comprehensible.

Finally, in spite of the relative gender similarity in hemispheric specialization, hemispheric asymmetry, and cognition, the gender difference in posterior and anterior cortical organization is extremely large, larger than the within-gender variation. Selection pressures demand gender differences in behaviors directly related to reproductive success, but a secondary result is that neural organization in general is regulated by ovarian versus testicular hormones in females and males. The fact that the between-gender difference in cognition is quite small compared to within-gender variations or to the neurological gender difference means, however, that cognitive demands on men and women throughout human evolution differed only to a minor degree. The central problem of evolution was not, therefore, to generate this minor difference in cognition, given an obligatory major difference in male and female neural programs, but was rather to mold the different male and female programs to serve similar cognitive functions. In brief, the observations strongly indicate that similar selective forces acted on the cognitive evolution of men and women to produce a functional convergence of two very different structures of neural programs in the two genders. Although selective pressures could not produce similar patterns of functional localization within the hemispheres in men and women, they could and did produce similar, but not identical, hemispheric maturation rates and functional cognitive capacities.

Thus, we conclude that early gonadal hormones influence the development of gender differences in cognition. However, in spite of such hormonal influences, and the consequent major sex differences in certain aspects of the organization of the cortex, the cognitive functions controlled by the different underlying neural programs are highly similar for men and women.

REFERENCES

Alexander, D., Walker, H. T., Jr., & Money, J. (1964). Studies in direction sense. Turner's syndrome. *Archives of General Psychiatry, 10,* 337–339.

Anastasi, A. (1958). *Differential psychology.* New York: Macmillan.

Baker, S. W., & Ehrhardt, A. A. (1974). Prenatal androgen, intelligence and cognitive sex differences. In R. C. Friedman, R. N. Richart, & R. L. Vande Wiele (Eds.), *Sex differences in behavior* (pp. 33–51). New York: John Wiley & Sons.

Barlow, P. (1973). The influence of inactive chromosomes on human development. *Humangenetik, 17,* 105–136.

Basso, A., Cupitani, E., & Monaschini, S. (1982). Sex differences in recovery from aphasia. *Cortex, 18,* 469–475.

Beatty, W. W. (1984). Hormonal organization of sex differences in play fighting and spatial behavior. In G. J. De Vries, J. P. C. De Bruin, H. B. M. Uylings, & M. A. Corner (Eds.), *Sex differences in the brain, The relation between structure and function, Vol. 61, Progress in brain research* (pp. 315–330). Amsterdam: Elsevier.

Bekker, F. J., & Van Gemund, J. J. (1968). Mental retardation and cognitive deficits in XO Turner's syndrome. *Maandschrift voor Kindergeneeskunde, 36,* 148–156.

Benbow, C. M., & Benbow, R. M. (1984). Biological correlates of high mathematical reasoning ability. In G. J. De Vries, J. P. C. De Bruin, H. B. M. Uylings, & M. A. Corner (Eds.), *Sex differences in the brain, The relation between structure and function, Vol. 61, Progress in brain research* (pp. 469–490). Amsterdam: Elsevier.

Best, C. T., Hoffman, H., & Glanville, B. B. (1982). Development of infant ear asymmetries for speech and music. *Perception and Psychophysics, 31,* 75–85.

Bidlingmaier, F., Strom, T. M., Dorr, H. G., Eisenmenger, W., & Knorr, D. (1987). Estrone and estradiol concentrations in human ovaries, testes, and adrenals during the first two years of life. *Journal of Clinical Endocrinology and Metabolism, 65,* 862–867.

Biller, H. B. (1974). Paternal deprivation, cognitive functioning, and the feminized classroom. In A. Davids (Ed.), *Child personality and psychopathology: Current topics* (pp. 11–52). New York: John Wiley & Sons.

Blizard, D. A., & Denef, C. (1973). Neonatal androgen effects on open-field activity and sexual behavior in the female rat: The modifying influence of ovarian secretions during development. *Physiology and Behavior, 11,* 65–69.

Bradshaw, J. L., & Gates, A. (1978). Visual field differences in verbal tasks: Effects of task familiarity and sex of subject. *Brain and Language, 5,* 166–187.

Bradshaw, J. L., Gates, A., & Nettleton, N. (1977). Bihemispheric involvement in lexical decisions: Handedness and a possible sex difference. *Neuropsychologia, 15,* 277–286.

Bradshaw, J. L., & Nettleton, N. C. (1983). *Human cerebral asymmetry.* Englewood Cliffs, NJ: Prentice-Hall.

Bryden, M. (1979). Evidence for sex differences in cerebral organization. In M. Wittig & A. Petersen (Eds.), *Sex-related differences in cognitive functioning: Developmental issues* (pp. 121–139). New York: Academic Press.

Butler, S. (1984). Sex differences in cerebral function. In G. J. De Vries, J. P. C. De Bruin, H. B. M. Uylings, & M. A. Corner (Eds.), *Sex differences in the brain. The relation between structure and function, Vol. 61, Progress in brain research* (pp. 443–455). Amsterdam: Elsevier.

Chase, T. N., Fedio, P., Foster, N. L., Brooks, R., Di Chiro, G., & Mansi, L. (1984). Wechsler adult intelligence scale performance: Cortical localization by fluorodeoxyglucose F^{18}-positron emission tomography. *Archives of Neurology, 41,* 1244–1247.

Cioffi, J., & Kandel, G. (1979). Laterality of stereognostic accuracy of children for words, shapes, and bigrams: A sex difference for bigrams. *Science, 204,* 1432–1434.

Curtis, S. (1977). *Genie: A psycholinguistic study of a modern-day "wild child."* New York: Academic Press.

Dalton, K. (1968). Ante-natal progesterone and intelligence. *British Journal of Psychiatry, 114,* 1377–1382.

Dalton, K. (1976). Prenatal progesterone and educational attainments, *British Journal of Psychiatry, 129,* 438–442.

Davidoff, J. (1977). Hemispheric differences in dot detection. *Cortex, 13,* 434–444.

Davies, J. N. P. (1947). Pathology of Central African natives; Mulago Hospital post-mortem studies. *East African Medical Journal, 24,* 180.

Dawson, J. L. M. (1966). Kwashiorkor, gynaecomastia, and feminization processes. *The Journal of Tropical Medicine and Hygiene, 69,* 175–179.

Dawson, J. L. M. (1977). An anthropological perspective on the evolution and lateralization of the brain. In S. J. Dimond and D. A. Blizard (Eds.), *Evolution and lateralization of the brain, Vol. 299, Annals of the New York Academy of Sciences* (pp. 424–447). New York: New York Academy of Sciences.

Dawson, J. L. M., Cheung, Y. M., & Law, R. T. S. (1975). Developmental effects of neonatal sex hormones on spatial and activity skills in the white rat. *Biological Psychology, 3,* 213–229.

Dennis, M., & Kohn, B. (1975). Comprehension of syntax in infantile hemiplegics after cerebral hemide-cortication: Left hemisphere superiority. *Brain and Language, 2,* 472–482.

Döhler, K.-D. (1978). Is female sexual differentiation hormone mediated? *Trends in Neuroscience, 1,* 138–140.

Döhler, K.-D., Hancke, J. L., Srivastava, S. S., Hoffman, C., Shryne, J. E., & Gorski, R. A. (1984). Participation of estrogens in female sexual differentiation of the brain: Neuroanatomical, neuroendocrine, and behavioral evidence. In G. J. De Vries, J. P. C. De Bruin, H. B. M. Uylings, & M. A. Corner (Eds.), *Sex differences in the brain. The relation between structure and function, Vol. 61, Progress in brain research* (pp. 99–117). Amsterdam: Elsevier.

Edwards, S., Ellams, J., & Thompson, J. (1976). Language and intelligence in dysphasia: Are they related? *British Journal of Disorders of Communication, 11,* 83–114.

Ehrhardt, A. A., & Money, J. (1967). Progestin-induced hermaphroditism: IQ and psychosexual identity in a sample of 10 girls. *Journal of Sex Research, 2,* 83–100.

Entus, A. (1977). Hemispheric asymmetry in processing of dichotically presented speech and nonspeech stimuli by infants. In S. Segalowitz & F. Gruber (Eds.), *Language development and neurological theory* (pp. 63–73). New York: Academic Press.

Garai, J. E., & Scheinfield, A. (1968). Sex differences in mental and behavioral traits. *Genetic Psychology Monographs, 77,* 169–299.

Garron, D. C. (1977). Intelligence among persons with Turner's syndrome. *Behavioral Genetics, 7,* 105–127.

Geschwind, N., & Galaburda, A. M. (1987). *Cerebral lateralization: Biological mechanisms, associations, and pathology.* Cambridge, MA: MIT Press.

Glanville, B. B., Best, C. T., & Levenson, R. (1977). A cardiac measure of cerebral asymmetries in infant auditory perception. *Developmental Psychology, 13,* 55–59.

Gordon, H. W., & Galatzer, A. (1980). Cerebral organization in patients with gonadal dysgenesis. *Psychoneuroendocrinology, 5,* 235–244.

Gordon, J. W., & Ruddle, F. H. (1981). Mammalian gonadal determination and gametogenesis. *Science, 211,* 1265–1272.

Grumbach, M. M., & Conte, F. A. (1985). Disorders of sexual differentiation. In J. D. Wilson & D. W. Foster (Eds.), *Williams' textbook of endocrinology* (7th ed.). Philadelphia: W. B. Saunders.

Hannay, H., & Boyer, C. (1978). Sex differences in hemispheric asymmetry revisited. *Perceptual and Motor Skills, 47,* 317–321.

Hannay, H., & Malone, D. (1976). Visual field effects and short-term memory for verbal material. *Neuropsychologia, 14,* 203–209.

Haseltine, F. P., & Ohno, S. (1981). Mechanisms of gonadal differentiation. *Science, 211,* 1272–1278.

Heller, W., & Levy, J. (1986). Deficits in left-hemisphere linguistic function in Turner's syndrome. *Society for Neuroscience Abstracts 12,* 1442.

Hermelin, B., & O'Connor, N. (1971). Functional asymmetry in the reading of Braille. *Neuropsychologia, 9,* 431–435.

Hier, D. B., & Crowley, W. F., Jr. (1982). Spatial ability in androgen-deficient men. *New England Journal of Medicine, 306,* 1202–1205.

Hines, M. (1981). *Prenatal diethylstilbestrol (DES) exposure, human sexually dimophic behavior and cerebral lateralization.* Doctoral dissertation, University of California. Los Angeles. *Dissertation Abstracts International, 42,* 423B.

Hines, M. (1982). Prenatal gonadal hormones and sex differences in human behavior. *Psychological Bulletin, 92,* 56–80.

Hitchcock, D. C., & Pinder, G. D. (1974). *Reading and arithmetic achievement among youths 12–17 years as measured by the Wide Range Achievement Test: Vital and health statistics — Series 11 — No. 136.* Washington, DC: U.S. Government Printing Office.

Hreczko, T., & Sigmon, B. (1980). The dermatoglyphics of a Toronto sample of children with XXY, XYY and XXX aneuploides. *American Journal of Physical Anthropology, 52,* 33–42.

Inglis, J., Ruckner, M., Lawson, J. S., MacLean, A. W., & Monga, T. N. (1982). Sex differences in the cognitive effects of unilateral brain damage. *Cortex, 18,* 277–286.

Johnson, M., & Everitt, B (1980). *Essential reproduction.* Boston: Blackwell Scientific Publications.

Kail, R., & Siegel, A. (1978). Sex and hemispheric differences in the recall of verbal and spatial information. *Cortex, 14,* 557–563.

Kershner, J. R., & Jeng, A. G. (1972). Dual functional hemispheric asymmetry in visual perception: Effects of ocular dominance and postexposural processes. *Neuropsychologia, 10,* 437–445.

Kester, P., Green, R., Finch, S. J., & Williams, K. (1980). Prenatal "female hormone" administration and psychosexual development in human males. *Psychoneuroendocrinology, 5,* 269–285.

Kimura, D. (1983). Sex differences in cerebral organization for speech and praxic function. *Canadian Journal of Psychology, 37,* 19–35.

Kimura, D., & Harshman, R. A. (1984). Sex differences in brain organization for verbal and nonverbal functions. In G. J. De Vries, J. P. C. De Bruin, H. B. M. Uylings & M. A. Corner (Eds.), *Sex differences in the brain. The relation between structure and function, Vol. 61, Progress in brain research* (pp. 423–441). Amsterdam: Elsevier.

Kohn, B., & Dennis, M. (1974). Selective impairments of visuospatial abilities in infantile hemiplegics after right cerebral hemidecortication. *Neuropsychologia, 12,* 505–512.

Ladavas, E., Umilta, C., & Ricci-Bitti, P. E. (1980). Evidence for sex differences in right-hemisphere dominance for emotions. *Neuropsychologia, 18,* 361–366.

Lansdell, H. (1964). Sex differences in hemispheric asymmetries of the human brain. *Nature, 203,* 550.

Leehey, S. C., Carey, S., Diamond, R., & Cahn, A. (1978). Upright and inverted faces: The right hemisphere knows the difference. *Cortex, 14,* 411–419.

Levin, M. (1980). The feminist mystique. *Commentary, 70,* 25–30.

Levine, S. C. (1985). Developmental changes in right-hemisphere involvement in face recognition. In C. T. Best (Ed.), *Hemispheric function and collaboration in the child* (pp. 157–191). New York: Academic Press.

Levy, J. (1981). Letter. *Commentary, 71,* 10–11.

Levy, J., Heller, W., Banich, M. T., & Burton, L. A. (1983). Are variations among right-handed individuals in perceptual asymmetries caused by characteristic arousal differences between hemispheres? *Journal of Experimental Psychology: Human Perception and Performance, 9,* 329–359.

Levy, J., & Reid, M. (1978). Variations in cerebral organization as a function of handedness, hand posture in writing, and sex. *Journal of Experimental Psychology: General, 107,* 119–144.

Lewis, V. G., Money, J., & Epstein, R. (1968). Concordance of verbal and nonverbal ability in the adrenogenital syndrome. *Johns Hopkins Medical Journal, 122,* 192–195.

Lippe, B. (1982). Primary ovarian failure. In S. A. Kaplan (Ed.), *Clinical pediatric and adolescent endocrinology* (pp. 269–299). Philadelphia: W. B. Saunders.

Maccoby, E. E., & Jacklin, C. N. (1974). *The psychology of sex differences.* Stanford: Stanford University Press.

MacLusky, N. S., & Naftolin, F. (1981). Sexual differentiation of the nervous system. *Science, 211,* 1294.

Masica, D. N., Money, J., Ehrhadt, A. A., & Lewis, V. G. (1969). I.Q., fetal sex hormones and cognitive patterns: Studies in the testicular feminizing syndrome of androgen insensitivity. *Johns Hopkins Medical Journal, 124,* 34–43.

Matarazzo, J. D. (1972). *Wechsler's measurement and appraisal of adult intelligence* (5th ed.). Baltimore: Williams & Wilkins.

Mateer, C. A., Polen, S. B., & Ojemann, G. A. (1982). Sexual variation in cortical localization of naming as determined by stimulation mapping. *The Behavioral and Brain Sciences, 5,* 310–311.

McGlone, J. (1977). Sex differences in human brain asymmetry: A critical survey. *The Behavioral and Brain Sciences, 3,* 215–263.

McGlone, J. (1980). Sex differences in human brain asymmetry: A critical review. *The Behavioral and Brain Sciences, 3,* 214–263.

McGlone, J. (1985). Can spatial deficits in Turner's syndrome be explained by focal CNS dysfunction of atypical speech laterization? *Journal of Clinical and Experimental Neuropsychology, 7,* 375–394.

McGlone, J., & Davidson, W. (1973). The relationship between cerebral speech laterality and spatial ability with special reference to sex and hand preference. *Neuropsychologia, 11,* 105–111.

McGuire, L. S., Ryan, K. O., & Omenn, G. S. (1975). Congenital adrenal hyperplasia: II. Cognitive and behavioral studies. *Behavior Genetics, 5,* 175–188.

Messerli, P., Tissot, A., & Rodriguez, J. (1976). Recovery from aphasia: Some factors and prognosis. Y. Lebrun & R. Hoops (Eds.), *Recovery in aphasics* (pp. 124–135). Amsterdam: Swets & Zeitlinger.

Mittwoch, U. (1973). *Genetics of sex differentiation.* New York: Academic Press.

Molfese, D. (1977). Infant cerebral asymmetry. In S. J. Segalowitz & F. F. Gruber (Eds.), *Language development and neurological theory* (pp. 21–35). New York: Academic Press.

Molfese, D., & Hess, T. M. (1978). Hemispheric specialization for VOT perception in the preschool child. *Journal of Experimental Psychology, 26,* 71–84.

Money, J., & Alexander, D. (1966). Turner's syndrome: Further demonstration of the presence of specific cognitive deficiencies. *Journal of Medical Genetics, 3,* 47–48.

Money, J., & Lewis, V. (1966). IQ, genetics and accelerated growth: Adrenogenital syndrome. *Johns Hopkins Hospital Bulletin, 118,* 365–373.

Money, J., Schwartz, M., & Lewis, V. G. (1984). Adult erotosexual status and fetal hormonal masculinization and demasculinization: 46,XX congenital virilizing adrenal hyperplasia (CVAH) and 46,XY androgen insensitivity syndrome (AIS) compared. *Psychoneuroendocrinology, 9,* 405–414.

Morris, B. B. (1971). Effects of angle, sex, and cue on adults' perception of the horizontal. *Perceptual and Motor Skills, 32,* 827–830.

Netley, C., & Rovet, J. (1982a). Verbal deficits in children with 47,XXY and 47,XXX karyotypes: A descriptive and experimental study. *Brain and Language, 17,* 58–72.

Netley, C., & Rovet, J. (1982b). Atypical hemisphere lateralization in Turner syndrome subjects. *Cortex, 18,* 377–384.

Netley, C., & Rovet, J. (1984). Hemispheric lateralization in 47,XXY Klinefelter's boys. *Brain and Cognition, 3,* 10–18.

Netley, C., & Rovet, J. (1987). Relations between a dermatoglyphic measure, hemispheric specialization, and intellectual abilities in 47,XXY males. *Brain and Cognition, 6,* 153–160.

Nielsen, J., Sorensen, A., Theilgaard, A., Froland, A., & Johnsen, S. G. (1969). A psychiatric-psychological study of 50 severely hypogonadal male patients, including 34 with Klinefelter's syndrome, 47,XYY. *Acta Jutlandica, 41,* 3.

Nyborg, H., & Nielsen, J. (1981). Spatial ability of men with karyotype 47,XXY or normal controls. In W. Schmid & J. Nielsen (Eds.), *Human behavior and genetics* (pp. 85–106). Amsterdam: Elsevier/North-Holland.

O'Connor, K. P., & Shaw, J. C. (1978). Field dependence, laterality, and the EEG. *Biological Psychology, 6,* 93–109.

Oltman, P. K., Ehrlichman, H., & Cox, P. W. (1977). Field independence and laterality in the perception of faces. *Perceptual and Motor Skills, 45,* 255–260.

Oltman, P. K., Semple, C., & Goldstein, L. (1979). Cognitive style and interhemispheric differentiation in the EEG. *Neuropsychologia, 17,* 699–702.

Penrose, L. (1967). Finger print patterns and the sex chromosome. *Lancet, 1,* 298–300.

Perlman, S. M. (1973). Cognitive abilities of children with hormone abnormalities: Screening by psychoeducational tests. *Journal of Learning Disabilities, 6,* 21–29.

Piazza, D. M. (1980). The influence of sex and handedness in the hemispheric specialization of verbal and nonverbal tasks. *Neuropsychologia, 18,* 163–176.

Pizzamiglio, L. (1974). Handedness, ear preference and field dependence. *Perceptual and Motor Skills, 38,* 700–702.

Pizzamiglio, L., & Cecchini, M. (1971). Development of the hemispheric dominance in children five to ten years of age and their relations with development of cognitive processes. *Brain Research, 31,* 361–378.

Porteus, S. D. (1965). *Porteus maze test: Fifty years' application.* Palo Alto, CA: Pacific Books.

Rapaczynski, W., & Ehrlichman, H. (1979). Opposite visual hemifield superiorities in face recognition as a function of cognitive style. *Neuropsychologia, 17,* 645–652.

Ratcliffe, S. G., Bancroft, J., Axworthy, D., & McLaren, W. (1982). Klinefelter's syndrome in adolescence. *Archives of Diseases of Childhood, 57,* 6–12.

Ratcliffe, S. G., & Tierney, I. R. (1982) 47,XXY males and handedness. *Lancet, 2,* 716.

Reinisch, J. M., & Karow, W. G. (1977). Prenatal exposure to synthetic progestins and estrogens: Effects on human development. *Archives of Sexual Behavior, 6,* 257–288.

Resnick, S., & Berenbaum, S. A. (1982). Cognitive functioning in individuals with congenital adrenal hyperplasia. *Behavior Genetics, 12,* 594–595.

Rizzolatti, G., & Buchtel, H. (1977). Hemispheric superiority in reaction time to faces: A sex difference. *Cortex, 13,* 300–305.

Robinson, R. G. (1979). Differential behavioral and biochemical effects hemispheric infarction in the rat. *Science, 205,* 707–710.

Rosenthal, R., Hall, J. A., DiMatteo, M. R., Rogers, P. L., and Archer, D. (1979). *Sensitivity to nonverbal communication.* Baltimore: Johns Hopkins University Press.

Ross, G. T., & Vande Wiele, R. L. (1974). The ovaries. R. H. Williams (Ed.), *Textbook of Endocrinology* (pp. 368–422). Philadelphia: W. B. Saunders.

Rovet, J., & Netley, C. (1982). Processing deficits in Turner's syndrome. *Developmental Psychology, 18,* 77–94.

Rovet, J., & Netley, C. (1983). Hemisphere specialization in Turner's syndrome. *The INS Bulletin, October,* p. 35. (as cited by McGlone 1985).

Rudel, R., Denckla, M., & Hirsch, S. (1977). The development of left-hand superiority for discriminating Braille configurations. *Neurology, 27,* 160–164.

Rudel, R., Denckla, M., & Spalten, E. (1974). The functional asymmetry of Braille letter learning in normal sighted children. *Neurology, 24,* 733–738.

Schaie, K. W., & Roberts, J. (1970). *School achievement of children as measured by the reading and arithmetic subtests of the Wide Range Achievement Test. Vital and Health Statistics— Series 11—No. 103.* Washington, DC: U.S. Government Printing Office.

Schneidler, G. G., & Paterson, D. G. (1942). Sex differences in clerical aptitude. *Journal of Experimental Psychology, 33,* 303–309.

Segami, M. I., & Alarcon-Segovia, U. S. A. (1978). Systemic lupus erythematosis and Klinefelter's syndrome. *Archives of Rheumatology, 20,* 1565–1567.

Serra, A., Pizzamiglio, L., Boari, A., & Spera, S. (1978). A comparative study of cognitive traits in human sex chromosome aneuploids and sterile and fertile euploids. *Behavior Genetics, 8,* 143–154.

Shaffer, J. (1962). A specific cognitive deficit observed in gonadal aplasia (Turner's syndrome). *Journal of Clinical Psychology, 18,* 403–406.

Sheehan, E. P., & Smith, H. V. (1986). Cerebral lateralization and handedness and their effects on verbal and spatial reasoning. *Neuropsychologia, 24,* 531–540.

Shucard, D. W., Shucard, J. L., & Thomas, D. G. (1977). Auditory evoked potentials of probes of hemispheric differences in cognitive processing. *Science, 197,* 1295–1298.

Shucard, D. W., Shucard, J. L., & Thomas, D. G. (1984). The development of cerebral specialization in infants. R. J. Emde & J. Harmon (Eds.), *Continuities and discontinuities in development.* New York: Plenum Press.

Shucard, J. L., Shucard, D. W., Cummins, K. R., & Campos, J. J. (1981). Auditory evoked potentials and sex-related differences in brain development. *Brain and Language, 13,* 91–102.

Simpson, J. L. (1975). Gonadal dysgenesis and abnormalities of the human sex chromosomes: Current status of phenotypic–karyotypic correlations. *Birth Defects, 11,* 23–59.

Spellacy, W. N., Bernstein, I. C., & Cohen, W. H. (1965). Complete form of testicular feminization syndrome. Report of a case with biochemical psychiatric studies. *Obstetrics and Gynecology, 26,* 499–503.

Stewart, J., & Cygan, D. (1980). Ovarian hormones act early in development to feminize open-field behavior in the rat. *Hormones and Behavior, 14,* 20–32.

Strauss, E., & Moscovitch, M. (1981). Perception of facial expressions. *Brain and Language, 13,* 308–332.

Taylor, D. C. (1969). Differential rates of cerebral maturation between sexes and between hemispheres. *Lancet, 2,* 140–142.

Thomas, H., Jamison, W., & Hummel, D. D. (1973). Observation is insufficient for discovering that the surface of still water is invariantly horizontal. *Science, 181,* 173–174.

Toran-Allerand, C. D. (1984). On the genesis of sexual differentiation of the central nervous system. Morphogenetic consequences of steroidal exposure and possible role of alpha-fetoprotein. In G. J. De Vries, J. P. C. De Bruin, H. B. M. Uylings, & M. A. Corner (Eds.), *Sex difference in the brain. The relation between structure and function, Vol. 61: Progress in brain research* (pp. 63–98). Amsterdam: Elsevier.

Turner, H. H. (1960). Ovarian dwarfism and rudimentary ovaries. E. B. Astwood (Ed.), *Clinical endocrinology, Vol. 1* (pp. 455–467). New York: Grune & Stratton.

Valentine, G. H. (1969). *The chromosome disorders: An introduction for clinicians.* Philadelphia: J. B. Lippincott.

Waber, D. (1979). Neuropsychological aspects of Turner's syndrome. *Developmental Medicine and Child Neurology, 21,* 58–70.

Walzer, S., Graham, J. M., Bashir, A. S., & Sibert, A. R. (1982). Preliminary observations on language and learning in XXY boys. *Birth Defects: Original Article Series, 18,* 185–192.

Winter, J. S. D., Hughes, I. A., Reyes, F. I., & Faiman, C. (1976). Pituitary–gonadal relations in infancy: 2. Patterns of serum gonadal steroid concentrations in men from birth to two years of age. *Journal of Clinical Endocrinology and Metabolism, 42,* 679–686.

Witelson, S. (1976). Sex and the single hemisphere: Right hemisphere specialization for spatial processing. *Science, 193,* 425–427.

Witkin, H. A., Dyk, R. B., Faterson, H. F., Goodenough, D. R., & Karp, S. A. (1974). *Psychological differentiation.* Potomac, MD: Lawrence Erlbaum. (Original work published 1962)

Witkin, H. A., Goodenough, D. R., & Oltman, P. K. (1979). Psychological differentiation: Current status. *Journal of Personality and Social Psychology, 37,* 1127–1145.

Wittig, M., & Petersen, A. (Eds.). (1979). *Sex-related differences in cognitive functioning: Developmental issues.* New York: Academic Press.

Yalom, I. D., Green, R., & Fisk, N. (1973). Prenatal exposure to female hormones: Effect on psychosexual development in boys. *Archives of General Psychiatry, 28,* 554–561.

Zoccolotti, P., & Oltman, P. K. (1978). Field independence and lateralization of verbal and configurational processing. *Cortex, 14,* 155–168.

Chapter Eleven

The Five Sexes
Why Male and Female Are Not Enough

Anne Fausto-Sterling

In 1843 Levi Suydam, a twenty-three-year-old resident of Salisbury, Connecticut, asked the town board of selectmen to validate his right to vote as a Whig in a hotly contested local election. The request raised a flurry of objections from the opposition party, for reasons that must be rare in the annals of American democracy: it was said that Suydam was more female than male and thus (some eighty years before suffrage was extended to women) could not be allowed to cast a ballot. To settle the dispute a physician, one William James Barry, was brought in to examine Suydam. And, presumably upon encountering a phallus, the good doctor declared the prospective voter male. With Suydam safely in their column the Whigs won the election by a majority of one.

Barry's diagnosis, however, turned out to be somewhat premature. Within a few days he discovered that, phallus notwithstanding, Suydam menstruated regularly and had a vaginal opening. Both his/her physique and his/her mental predispositions were more complex than was first suspected. S/he had narrow shoulders and broad hips and felt occasional sexual yearnings for women. Suydam's "feminine propensities, such as a fondness for gay colors, for pieces of calico, comparing and placing them together, and an aversion for bodily labor, and an inability to perform the same, were remarked by many," Barry later wrote. It is not clear whether Suydam lost or retained the vote, or whether the election results were reversed.

Western culture is deeply committed to the idea that there are only two sexes. Even language refuses other possibilities; thus to write about Levi Suydam I have had to invent conventions—*s/he* and *his/her*—to denote someone who is clearly neither male nor female or who is perhaps both sexes at once. Legally, too, every adult is either man or woman, and the difference, of course, is not trivial. For Suydam it meant the franchise; today it means being available for, or exempt from, draft registration, as well as being subject, in various ways, to a number of laws governing marriage, the family and human intimacy. In many parts of the United States, for instance, two people legally registered as men cannot have sexual relations without violating anti-sodomy statutes.

But if the state and the legal system have an interest in maintaining a two-party sexual system, they are in defiance of nature. For biologically speaking, there are many gradations running from female to male; and depending on how one calls the shots, one can argue that along that spectrum lie at least five sexes—and perhaps even more.

For some time medical investigators have recognized the concept of the intersexual body. But the standard medical literature uses the term *intersex* as a catch-all for three major subgroups with some mixture of male and female characteristics: the so-called true hermaphrodites, whom I call herms, who possess one testis and one ovary (the sperm- and egg-producing vessels, or gonads); the male pseudohermaphrodites (the "merms"), who have testes and some aspects of the female genitalia but no ovaries; and the female pseudohermaphrodites (the "ferms"), who have ovaries and some aspects of the male genitalia but lack testes. Each of those categories is in itself complex; the percentage of male and female characteristics, for instance, can vary enormously among members of the same subgroup. Moreover, the inner lives of the people in each subgroup—their special needs and their problems, attractions and repulsions—have gone unexplored by science. But on the basis of what is known about them I suggest that the three intersexes, herm, merm and ferm, deserve to be considered additional sexes each in its own right. Indeed, I would argue further that sex is a vast, infinitely malleable continuum that defies the constraints of even five categories.

Not surprisingly, it is extremely difficult to estimate the frequency of intersexuality, much less the frequency of each of the three additional sexes: it is not the sort of information one volunteers on a job application. The psychologist John Money of Johns Hopkins University, a specialist in the study of congenital sexual-organ defects, suggests intersexuals may constitute as many as 4 percent of births. As I point out to my students at Brown University, in a student body of about 6,000 that fraction, if correct, implies there may be as many as 240 intersexuals on campus—surely enough to form a minority caucus of some kind.

In reality though, few such students would make it as far as Brown in sexually diverse form. Recent advances in physiology and surgical technology now enable physicians to catch most intersexuals at the moment of birth. Almost at once such infants are entered into a program of hormonal and surgical management so that they can slip quietly into society as "normal" heterosexual males or females. I emphasize that the motive is in no way conspiratorial. The aims of the policy are genuinely humanitarian, reflecting the wish that people be able to "fit in" both physically and psychologically. In the medical community, however, the assumptions behind that wish—that there be only two sexes, that heterosexuality alone is normal, that there is one true model of psychological health—have gone virtually unexamined.

The word *hermaphrodite* comes from the Greek names Hermes, variously known as the messenger of the gods, the patron of music, the controller of dreams or the protector of livestock, and Aphrodite, the goddess of sexual love and beauty. According to Greek mythology, those two gods parented Hermaphroditus, who at age fifteen became half male and half female when his body fused with the body of a nymph he fell in love with. In some true hermaphrodites the testis and the ovary grow separately but bilaterally; in others they grow together within the same organ, forming an ovo-testis. Not infrequently, at least one of the gonads functions quite well, producing either sperm cells or eggs, as well as functional levels of the sex hormones—androgens or estrogens. Although in theory it might be possible for a true hermaphrodite to become both father and mother to a child, in practice the appropriate ducts and tubes are not configured so that egg and sperm can meet.

In contrast with the true hermaphrodites, the pseudohermaphrodites possess two gonads of the same kind along with the usual male (XY) or female (XX) chromosomal makeup. But their external genitalia and secondary sex characteristics do not match their chromosomes. Thus merms have testes and XY chromosomes, yet they also have a vagina and a clitoris, and at puberty they often develop breasts. They do not menstruate, however. Ferms have ovaries, two X chromosomes and sometimes a uterus, but they also have at least partly masculine external genitalia. Without medical intervention they can develop beards, deep voices and adult-size penises.

No classification scheme could more than suggest the variety of sexual anatomy encountered in clinical practice. In 1969, for example, two French investigators, Paul Guinet of the Endocrine Clinic in Lyons and Jacques Decourt of the Endocrine Clinic in Paris, described ninety-eight cases of true hermaphroditism—again, signifying people with both ovarian and testicular tissue—solely according to the appearance of the external genitalia and the accompanying ducts. In some cases the people exhibited strongly feminine development. They had separate openings for the vagina and the urethra, a cleft vulva defined by both the large and the small labia, or vaginal lips, and at puberty they developed breasts and usually began to menstruate. It was the oversize and sexually alert clitoris, which threatened sometimes at puberty to grow into a penis, that usually impelled them to seek medical attention. Members of another group also had breasts and a feminine body type, and they menstruated. But their labia were at least partly fused, forming an incomplete scrotum. The phallus (here an embryological term for a structure that during usual development goes on to form either a clitoris or a penis) was between 1.5 and 2.8 inches long; nevertheless, they urinated through a urethra that opened into or near the vagina.

By far the most frequent form of true hermaphrodite encountered by Guinet and Decourt—55 percent—appeared to have a more masculine physique. In such people the urethra runs either through or near the phallus, which looks more like a penis than a clitoris. Any menstrual blood exits periodically during urination. But in spite of the relatively male appearance of the genitalia, breasts appear at puberty. It is possible that a sample larger than ninety-eight so-called true hermaphrodites would yield even more contrasts and subtleties. Suffice it to say that the varieties are so diverse that it is possible to know which parts are present and what is attached to what only after exploratory surgery.

The embryological origins of human hermaphrodites clearly fit what is known about male and female sexual development. The embryonic gonad generally chooses early in development to follow either a male or a female sexual pathway; for the ovo-testis, however, that choice is fudged. Similarly, the embryonic phallus most often ends up as a clitoris or a penis, but the existence of intermediate states comes as no surprise to the embryologist. There are also uro-genital swellings in the embryo that usually either stay open and become the vaginal labia or fuse and become a scrotum. In some hermaphrodites, though, the choice of opening or closing is ambivalent. Finally, all mammalian embryos have structures that can become the female uterus and the fallopian tubes, as well as structures that can become part of the male sperm-transport system. Typically either the male or the female set of those primordial genital organs degenerates, and the remaining structures achieve their sex-appropriate future. In hermaphrodites both sets of organs develop to varying degrees.

Intersexuality itself is old news. Hermaphrodites, for instance, are often featured in stories about human origins. Early biblical scholars believed Adam began life as a hermaphrodite and later divided into two people—a male and a female—after falling from grace. According to Plato there once were three sexes—male, female and hermaphrodite—but the third sex was lost with time.

Both the Talmud and the Tosefta, the Jewish books of law, list extensive regulations for people of mixed sex. The Tosefta expressly forbids hermaphrodites to inherit their fathers' estates (like daughters), to seclude themselves with women (like sons) or to shave (like men). When hermaphrodites menstruate they must be isolated from men (like women); they are disqualified from serving as witnesses or as priests (like women), but the laws of pederasty apply to them.

In Europe a pattern emerged by the end of the Middle Ages that, in a sense, has lasted to the present day: hermaphrodites were compelled to choose an established gender role and stick with it. The penalty for transgression was often death. Thus in the 1600s a Scottish hermaphrodite living as a woman was buried alive after impregnating his/her master's daughter.

For questions of inheritance, legitimacy, paternity, succession to title and eligibility for certain professions to be determined, modern Anglo-Saxon legal systems require that newborns be registered as either male or female. In the U.S. today sex determination is governed by state laws. Illinois permits adults to change the sex recorded on their birth certificates should a physician attest to having performed the appropriate surgery. The New York Academy of Medicine, on the other hand, has taken an opposite view. In spite of surgical alterations of the external genitalia, the academy argued in 1966, the chromosomal sex remains the same. By that measure, a person's wish to conceal his or her original sex cannot outweigh the public interest in protection against fraud.

During this century the medical community has completed what the legal world began—the complete erasure of any form of embodied sex that does not conform to a male–female, heterosexual pattern. Ironically, a more sophisticated knowledge of the complexity of sexual systems has led to the repression of such intricacy.

In 1937 the urologist Hugh H. Young of Johns Hopkins University published a volume titled *Genital Abnormalities, Hermaphroditism and Related Adrenal Diseases*. The book is remarkable for its erudition, scientific insight and open-mindedness. In it Young drew together a wealth of carefully documented case histories to demonstrate and study the medical treatment of such "accidents of birth." Young did not pass judgment on the people he studied, nor did he attempt to coerce into treatment those intersexuals who rejected that option. And he showed unusual even-handedness in referring to those people who had had sexual experiences as both men and women as "practicing hermaphrodites."

One of Young's more interesting cases was a hermaphrodite named Emma who had grown up as a female. Emma had both a penis-size clitoris and a vagina, which made it possible for him/her to have "normal" heterosexual sex with both men and women. As a teenager Emma had had sex with a number of girls to whom s/he was deeply attracted; but at the age of nineteen s/he had married a man. Unfortunately, he had given Emma little sexual pleasure (though *he* had had no complaints), and so throughout that marriage and subsequent ones Emma had kept girlfriends on the side. With some frequency s/he had pleasurable sex with them. Young describes his subject as appearing "to be quite content and even happy." In conversation Emma occasionally told him of his/her wish to be a man, a circumstance Young said would be relatively easy to bring about. But Emma's reply strikes a heroic blow for self-interest:

> Would you have to remove that vagina? I don't know about that because that's my meal ticket. If you did that, I would have to quit my husband and go to work, so I think I'll keep it and stay as I am. My husband supports me well, and even though I don't have any sexual pleasure with him, I do have lots with my girlfriends.

Yet even as Young was illuminating intersexuality with the light of scientific reason, he was beginning its suppression. For his book is also an extended treatise on the most modern surgical and hormonal methods of changing intersexuals into either males or females. Young may have differed from his successors in being less judgmental and controlling of the patients and their families, but he nonetheless supplied the foundation on which current intervention practices were built.

By 1969, when the English physicians Christopher J. Dewhurst and Ronald R. Gordon wrote *The Intersexual Disorders,* medical and surgical approaches to intersexuality had neared a state of rigid uniformity. It is hardly surprising that such a hardening of opinion took place in the era of the feminine mystique—of the post–Second World War flight to the suburbs and the strict division of family roles according to sex. That the medical consensus was not quite universal (or perhaps that it seemed poised to break apart again) can be gleaned from the near-hysterical tone of Dewhurst and Gordon's book, which contrasts markedly with the calm reason of Young's founding work. Consider their opening description of an intersexual newborn:

> One can only attempt to imagine the anguish of the parents. That a newborn should have a deformity . . . [affecting] so fundamental an issue as the very sex of the child . . . is a tragic event which immediately conjures up visions of a hopeless psychological misfit doomed to live always as a sexual freak in loneliness and frustration.

Dewhurst and Gordon warned that such a miserable fate would, indeed, be a baby's lot should the case be improperly managed; "but fortunately," they wrote, "with correct management the outlook is infinitely better than the poor parents—emotionally stunned by the event—or indeed anyone without special knowledge could ever imagine."

Scientific dogma has held fast to the assumption that without medical care hermaphrodites are doomed to a life of misery. Yet there are few empirical studies to back up that assumption, and some of the same research gathered to build a case for medical treatment contradicts it. Francies Benton, another of Young's practicing hermaphrodites, "had not worried over his condition, did not wish to be changed, and was enjoying life." The same could be said of Emma, the opportunistic hausfrau. Even Dewhurst and Gordon, adamant about the psychological importance of treating intersexuals at the infant stage, acknowledged great success in "changing the sex" of older patients. They reported on twenty cases of children reclassified into a different sex after the supposedly critical age of eighteen months. They asserted that all the reclassifications were "successful," and they wondered then whether reregistration could be "recommended more readily than [had] been suggested so far."

The treatment of intersexuality in this century provides a clear example of what the French historian Michel Foucault has called biopower. The knowledge developed in biochemistry, embryology, endocrinology, psychology and surgery has enabled physicians to control the very sex of the human body. The multiple contradictions in that kind of power call for some scrutiny. On the one hand, the medical "management" of intersexuality certainly developed as part of an attempt to free people from perceived psychological pain (though whether the pain was the patient's, the parents' or the physician's is unclear). And if one accepts the assumption that in a sex-divided culture people can realize their greatest potential for happiness and productivity only if they are sure they belong to one of only two acknowledged sexes, modern medicine has been extremely successful.

On the other hand, the same medical accomplishments can be read not as progress but as a mode of discipline. Hermaphrodites have unruly bodies. They do not fall naturally into a binary classification; only a surgical shoehorn can put them there. But why should we care if a "woman," defined as one who has breasts, a vagina, a uterus and ovaries and who menstruates, also has a clitoris large enough to penetrate the vagina of another woman? Why should we care if there are people whose biological equipment enables them to have sex "naturally" with both men and women? The answers seem to lie in a cultural need to maintain clear distinctions between the sexes. Society mandates the control of intersexual bodies because they blur and bridge the great divide. Inasmuch as hermaphrodites literally embody both sexes, they challenge traditional beliefs about sexual difference: they possess the irritating ability to live sometimes as one sex and sometimes the other, and they raise the specter of homosexuality.

But what if things were altogether different? Imagine a world in which the same knowledge that has enabled medicine to intervene in the management of intersexual patients has been placed at the service of multiple sexualities. Imagine that the sexes have multiplied beyond currently imaginable limits. It would have to be a world of shared powers. Patient and physician, parent and child, male and female, heterosexual and homosexual—all those oppositions and others would have to be dissolved as sources of division. A new ethic of medical treatment would arise, one that would permit ambiguity in a culture that had overcome sexual division. The central mission of medical treatment would be to preserve life. Thus hermaphrodites would be concerned primarily not about whether they can conform to society but about whether they might develop potentially life-threatening conditions—hernias, gonadal tumors, salt imbalance caused by adrenal malfunction—that sometimes accompany hermaphroditic development. In my ideal world medical intervention for intersexuals would take place only rarely before the age of reason: subsequent treatment would be a cooperative venture between physician, patient and other advisers trained in issues of gender multiplicity.

I do not pretend that the transition to my utopia would be smooth. Sex, even the supposedly "normal," heterosexual kind, continues to cause untold anxieties in Western society. And certainly a culture that has yet to come to grips—religiously and, in some states, legally—with the ancient and relatively uncomplicated reality of homosexual love will not readily embrace intersexuality. No doubt the most troublesome arena by far would be the rearing of children. Parents, at least since the Victorian era, have fretted, sometimes to the point of outright denial, over the fact that their children are sexual beings.

All that and more amply explains why intersexual children are generally squeezed into one of the two prevailing sexual categories. But what would be the psychological consequences of taking the alternative road—raising children as unabashed intersexuals? On the surface that tack seems fraught with peril. What, for example, would happen to the intersexual child amid the unrelenting cruelty of the school yard? When the time came to shower in gym class, what horrors and humiliations would await the intersexual as his/her anatomy was displayed in all its non-traditional glory? In whose gym class would s/he register to begin with? What bathroom would s/he use? And how on earth would Mom and Dad help shepherd him/her through the mine field of puberty?

In the past thirty years those questions have been ignored, as the scientific community has, with remarkable unanimity, avoided contemplating the alternative route of unimpeded intersexuality. But modern investigators tend to overlook a substantial body of case histories, most of them compiled between 1930 and 1960, before surgical intervention became rampant. Almost without exception, those reports describe children who grew up knowing they were intersexual (though they did not advertise it) and adjusted to their unusual status. Some of the studies are richly detailed—described at the level of gym-class showering (which most intersexuals avoided without incident); in any event, there is not a psychotic or a suicide in the lot.

Still, the nuances of socialization among intersexuals cry out for more sophisticated analysis. Clearly, before my vision of sexual multiplicity can be realized, the first openly intersexual children and their parents will have to be brave pioneers who will bear the brunt of society's growing pains. But in the long view—though it could take generations to achieve—the prize might be a society in which sexuality is something to be celebrated for its subtleties and not something to be feared or ridiculed.

Chapter Twelve

Psychological Sex Differences
Origins through Sexual Selection

David M. Buss

Evolutionary psychology predicts that males and females will be the same or similar in all those domains in which the sexes have faced the same or similar adaptive problems. Both sexes have sweat glands because both sexes have faced the adaptive problem of thermal regulation. Both sexes have similar (although not identical) taste preferences for fat, sugar, salt, and particular amino acids because both sexes have faced similar (although not identical) food consumption problems. Both sexes grow callouses when they experience repeated rubbing on their skin because both sexes have faced the adaptive problem of physical damage from environmental friction.

In other domains, men and women have faced substantially different adaptive problems throughout human evolutionary history. In the physical realm, for example, women have faced the problem of childbirth; men have not. Women, therefore, have evolved particular adaptations that are absent in men, such as a cervix that dilates to 10 centimeters just prior to giving birth, mechanisms for producing labor contractions, and the release of oxytocin in the blood stream during childbirth.

Men and women have also faced different information-processing problems in some adaptive domains. Because fertilization occurs internally within the woman, for example, men have faced the adaptive problem of uncertainty of paternity in putative offspring. Men who failed to solve this problem risked investing resources in children who were not their own. All people descend from a long line of ancestral men whose adaptations (i.e., psychological mechanisms) led them to behave in ways that increased their likelihood of paternity and decreased the odds of investing in children who were putatively theirs but whose genetic fathers were other men. This does not imply, of course, that men were or are consciously aware of the adaptive problem of compromised paternity.

Women faced the problem of securing a reliable or replenishable supply of resources to carry them through pregnancy and lactation, especially when food resources were scarce (e.g., during droughts or harsh winters). All people are descendants of a long and unbroken line of women who successfully solved this adaptive

David M. Buss, "Psychological Sex Differences: Origins through Sexual Selection." *American Psychologist, 50,* pp. 164–168. © 1995 by the American Psychological Association. Reprinted with permission.

challenge—for example, by preferring mates who showed the ability to accrue resources and the willingness to provide them for particular women (Buss, 1994). Those women who failed to solve this problem failed to survive, imperiled the survival chances of their children, and hence failed to continue their lineage.

Evolutionary psychologists predict that the sexes will differ in precisely those domains in which women and men have faced different sorts of adaptive problems (Buss, 1994). To an evolutionary psychologist, the likelihood that the sexes are psychologically identical in domains in which they have recurrently confronted different adaptive problems over the long expanse of human evolutionary history is essentially zero (Symons, 1992). The key question, therefore, is not whether men and women differ psychologically. Rather, the key questions about sex differences, from an evolutionary psychological perspective, are (a) In what domains have women and men faced different adaptive problems? (b) What are the sex-differentiated psychological mechanisms of women and men that have evolved in response to these sex-differentiated adaptive problems? (c) Which social, cultural, and contextual inputs moderate the magnitude of expressed sex differences?

Sexual Selection Defines the Primary Domains in Which the Sexes Have Faced Different Adaptive Challenges

Although many who are not biologists equate evolution with natural selection or survival selection, Darwin (1871) sculpted what he believed to be a second theory of evolution—the theory of sexual selection. Sexual selection is the causal process of the evolution of characteristics on the basis of reproductive advantage, as opposed to survival advantage. Sexual selection occurs in two forms. First, members of one sex can successfully outcompete members of their own sex in a process of intrasexual competition. Whatever characteristics lead to success in these same-sex competitions—be they greater size, strength, cunning, or social skills—can evolve or increase in frequency by virtue of the reproductive advantage accrued by the winners through increased access to more numerous or more desirable mates.

Second, members of one sex can evolve preferences for desirable qualities in potential mates through the process of intersexual selection. If members of one sex exhibit some consensus about which qualities are desirable in the other sex, then members of the other sex who possess the desirable qualities will gain a preferential mating advantage. Hence, the desirable qualities—be they morphological features such as antlers or plumage or psychological features such as a lower threshold for risk taking to acquire resources—can evolve by virtue of the reproductive advantage attained by those who are preferentially chosen for possessing the desirable qualities. Among humans, both causal processes—preferential mate choice and same-sex competition for access to mates—are prevalent among both sexes, and probably have been throughout human evolutionary history (Buss, 1994).

Hypotheses about Psychological Sex Differences Follow from Sexual Asymmetries in Mate Selection and Intrasexual Competition

Although a detailed analysis of psychological sex differences is well beyond the scope of this article (see Buss, 1994), a few of the most obvious differences in adaptive problems include the following.

Paternity Uncertainty. Because fertilization occurs internally within women, men are always less than 100 percent certain (again, no conscious awareness implied) that their putative children are genetically their own. Some cultures have phrases to describe this, such as "mama's baby, papa's maybe." Women are always 100 percent certain that the children they bear are their own.

Identifying Reproductively Valuable Women. Because women's ovulation is concealed and there is no evidence that men can detect when women ovulate, ancestral men had the difficult adaptive challenge of identifying which women were more fertile. Although ancestral women would also have faced the problem of identifying fertile men, the problem is considerably less severe (a) because most men remain fertile throughout their life span, whereas fertility is steeply age graded among women and (b) because women invest more heavily in offspring, making them the more "valuable" sex, competed for more intensely by men seeking sexual access. Thus, there is rarely a shortage of men willing to contribute the sperm necessary for fertilization, whereas from a man's perspective, there is a pervasive shortage of fertile women.

Gaining Sexual Access to Women. Because of the large asymmetry between men and women in their minimum obligatory parental investment—nine months gestation for women versus an act of sex for men—the direct reproductive benefits of gaining sexual access to a variety of mates would have been much higher for men than for women throughout human evolutionary history (Symons, 1979; Trivers, 1972). Therefore, in social contexts in which some short-term mating or polygynous mating were possible, men who succeeded in gaining sexual access to a variety of women, other things being equal, would have experienced greater reproductive success than men who failed to gain such access (see also Greiling, 1993, for adaptive benefits to women of short-term mating).

Identifying Men Who Are Able to Invest. Because of the tremendous burdens of a nine-month pregnancy and subsequent lactation, women who selected men who were able to invest resources in them and their offspring would have been at a tremendous advantage in survival and reproductive currencies compared with women who were indifferent to the investment capabilities of the man with whom they chose to mate.

Identifying Men Who Are Willing to Invest. Having resources is not enough. Copulating with a man who had resources but who displayed a hasty postcopulatory departure would have been detrimental to the woman, particularly if she became pregnant and faced raising a child without the aid and protection of an investing father. A man with excellent resource-accruing capacities might channel resources to another woman or pursue short-term sexual opportunities with a variety of women. A woman who had the ability to detect a man's willingness to invest in her and her children would have an adaptive advantage compared with women who were oblivious to a man's willingness or unwillingness to invest.

These are just a few of the adaptive problems that women and men have confronted differently or to differing degrees. Other examples of sex-linked adaptive problems include those of coalitional warfare, coalitional defense, hunting, gathering, combating sex-linked forms of reputational damage, embodying sex-linked prestige criteria, and attracting mates by fulfilling the differing desires of the other sex— domains that all have consequences for mating but are sufficiently wide-ranging to span a great deal of social psychology (Buss, 1994). It is in these domains that evolutionary psychologists anticipate the most pronounced sex differences—differences in solutions to sex-linked adaptive problems in the form of evolved psychological mechanisms.

Psychological Sex Differences Are Well Documented Empirically in the Domains Predicted by Theories Anchored in Sexual Selection

When Maccoby and Jacklin (1974) published their classic book on the psychology of sex differences, knowledge was spotty and methods for summarizing the literature were largely subjective and interpretive. Since that time, there has been a veritable explosion of empirical findings, along with quantitative meta-analytic procedures for evaluating them (e.g., Eagly, 1995; Feingold, 1990; Hall, 1978; Hyde, in press; Oliver & Hyde, 1993; Rosenthal, 1991). Although new domains of sex differences continue to surface, such as the recently documented female advantage in spatial location memory (Silverman & Eals, 1992), the outlines of where researchers find large, medium, small, and no sex differences are starting to emerge more clearly.

A few selected findings illustrate the heuristic power of evolutionary psychology. Cohen (1977) used the widely adopted d statistic as the index of magnitude of effect to propose a rule of thumb for evaluating effect sizes: $0.20 =$ "small," $0.50 =$ "medium," and $0.80 =$ "large." As Hyde (in press) has pointed out in a chapter titled "Where Are the Gender Differences? Where Are the Gender Similarities?," sex differences in the intellectual and cognitive ability domains tend to be small. Women's verbal skills tend to be slightly higher than men's ($d = -0.11$). Sex differences in math also tend to be small ($d = 0.15$). Most tests of general cognitive ability, in short, reveal small sex differences.

The primary exception to the general trend of small sex differences in the cognitive abilities domain occurs with spatial rotation. This ability is essential for successful hunting, in which the trajectory and velocity of a spear must anticipate correctly the trajectory of an animal as each moves with different speeds through space and time. For spatial rotation ability, $d = 0.73$. Other sorts of skills involved in hunting also show large magnitudes of sex differences, such as throwing velocity ($d = 2.18$), throwing distance ($d=1.98$), and throwing accuracy ($d=0.96$; Ashmore 1990). Skilled hunters, as good providers, are known to be sexually attractive to women in current and traditional tribal societies (Hill & Hurtado, 1989; Symons, 1979).

Large sex differences appear reliably for precisely the aspects of sexuality and mating predicted by evolutionary theories of sexual strategies (Buss & Schmitt, 1993). Oliver and Hyde (1993), for example, documented a large sex difference in attitudes toward casual sex ($d=0.81$). Similar sex differences have been found with other measures of men's desire for casual sex partners, a psychological solution to the problem of seeking sexual access to a variety of partners (Buss & Schmitt, 1993; Symons, 1979). For example, men state that they would ideally like to have more than eighteen sex partners in their lifetimes, whereas women state that they would desire only four or five ($d=0.87$; Buss & Schmitt, 1993). In another study that has been replicated twice, 75 percent of the men but 0 percent of the women approached by an attractive stranger of the opposite sex consented to a request for sex (Clark & Hatfield, 1989).

Women tend to be more exacting than men, as predicted, in their standards for a short-term mate ($d=0.79$). Women tend to place greater value on good financial prospects in a mate—a finding confirmed in a study of 10.047 individuals residing in thirty-seven cultures located on six continents and five islands from around the world (Buss, 1989a). More so than men, women especially disdain qualities in a potential mate that signal inability to accrue resources, such as lack of ambition ($d=1.38$) and lack of education ($d=1.06$). Women desire physical protection abilities more than men, both in short-term mating ($d=0.94$) and in long-term mating ($d=0.66$).

Men and women also differ in the weighting given to cues that trigger sexual jealousy. Buss, Larsen, Westen, and Semmelroth (1992) presented men and women with the following dilemma: "What would upset or distress you more: (a) imagining your partner forming a deep emotional attachment to someone else or (b) imagining your partner enjoying passionate sexual intercourse with that other person" (p. 252). Men expressed greater distress about sexual than emotional infidelity, whereas women showed the opposite pattern. The difference between the sexes in which scenario was more distressing was 43 percent ($d=0.98$). These sex differences have been replicated by different investigators (Wiederman & Allgeier, 1993) with physiological recording devices (Buss et al., 1992) and have been replicated in other cultures (Buunk, Angleitner, Oubaid, & Buss, 1994).

These sex differences are precisely those predicted by evolutionary psychological theories based on sexual selection. They represent only a sampling from a larger body of supporting evidence. The sexes also differ substantially in a wide variety of other ways that are predicted by sexual selection theory, such as in thresholds for physical risk taking (Wilson & Daly, 1985), in frequency of perpetrating homicides (Daly & Wilson, 1988), in thresholds for inferring sexual intent in others (Abby, 1982), in perceptions of the magnitude of upset people experience as the victims of sexual aggression (Buss, 1989b), and in the frequency of committing violent crimes of all sorts (Daly & Wilson, 1988). As noted by Donald Brown (1991), "it will be irresponsible to continue shunting these [findings] aside, fraud to deny that they exist" (p. 156). Evolutionary psychology sheds light on why these differences exist.

Conclusions

Strong sex differences occur reliably in domains closely linked with sex and mating, precisely as predicted by psychological theories based on sexual selection (Buss, 1994). Within these domains, the psychological sex differences are patterned in a manner that maps precisely onto the adaptive problems men and women have faced over human evolutionary history. Indeed, in most cases, the evolutionary hypotheses about sex differences were generated a decade or more before the empirical tests of them were conducted and the sex differences discovered. These models thus have heuristic and predictive power.

The evolutionary psychology perspective also offers several insights into the broader discourse on sex differences. First, neither women nor men can be considered "superior" or "inferior" to the other, any more than a bird's wings can be considered superior or inferior to a fish's fins or a kangaroo's legs. Each sex possesses mechanisms designed to deal with its own adaptive challenges—some similar and some different—and so notions of superiority or inferiority are logically incoherent from the vantage point of evolutionary psychology. The meta-theory of evolutionary psychology is descriptive, not prescriptive—it carries no values in its teeth.

Second, contrary to common misconceptions about evolutionary psychology, finding that sex differences originated through a causal process of sexual selection does not imply that the differences are unchangeable or intractable. On the contrary, understanding their origins provides a powerful heuristic to the contexts in which the sex differences are most likely to be manifested (e.g., in the context of mate competition) and hence provides a guide to effective loci for intervention if change is judged to be desirable.

Third, although some worry that inquiries into the existence and evolutionary origins of sex differences will lead to justification for the status quo, it is hard to believe that attempts to change the status quo can be very effective if they are undertaken in ignorance of sex differences that actually exist. Knowledge is power, and attempts to intervene in the absence of knowledge may resemble a surgeon operating blindfolded—there may be more bloodshed than healing (Tooby & Cosmides, 1992).

The perspective of evolutionary psychology jettisons the outmoded dualistic thinking inherent in much current discourse by getting rid of the false dichotomy between biological and social. It offers a truly interactionist position that specifies the particular features of social context that are especially critical for processing by our evolved psychological mechanisms. No other theory of sex differences has been capable of predicting and explaining the large number of precise, detailed, patterned sex differences discovered by research guided by evolutionary psychology (e.g., Bailey, Gaulin, Agyei, & Gladue, 1994; Buss & Schmitt, 1993; Daly & Wilson, 1988; Ellis &

Symons, 1990; Gangestad & Simpson, 1990; Greer & Buss, 1994; Kenrick & Keefe, 1992; Symons, 1979). Evolutionary psychology possesses the heuristic power to guide investigators to the particular domains in which the most pronounced sex differences, as well as similarities, will be found. People grappling with the existence and implications of psychological sex differences cannot afford to ignore their most likely evolutionary origins through sexual selection.

REFERENCES

Abby, A. (1982). Sex differences in attributions for friendly behavior: Do males misperceive females' friendliness? *Journal of Personality and Social Psychology, 32,* 830–838.

Ashmore, R. D. (1990). Sex, gender, and the individual. In L. A. Pervin (Ed.), *Handbook of personality: Theory and research* (pp. 486–526). New York: Guilford Press.

Bailey, J. M., Gaulin, S., Agyei, Y., & Gladue, B. A. (1994). Effects of gender and sexual orientation on evolutionarily relevant aspects of human mating psychology. *Journal of Personality and Social Psychology, 66,* 1074–1080.

Brown, D. (1991). *Human universals.* Philadelphia: Temple University Press.

Buss, D. M. (1989a). Sex differences in human mate preferences: Evolutionary hypotheses tested in 37 cultures. *Behavioral and Brain Sciences, 12,* 1–49.

Buss, D. M. (1989b). Conflict between the sexes: Strategic interference and the evocation of anger and upset. *Journal of Personality and Social Psychology, 56,* 735–747.

Buss, D. M. (1994). *The evolution of desire: Strategies of human mating.* New York: Basic Books.

Buss, D. M. (1995). Evolutionary psychology: A new paradigm for psychological science. *Psychological Inquiry, 6,* 1–30.

Buss, D. M., Larsen, R., Westen, D., & Semmelroth, J. (1992). Sex differences in jealousy: Evolution, physiology, and psychology. *Psychological Science, 3,* 251–255.

Buss, D. M., & Schmitt, D. P. (1993). Sexual strategies theory: An evolutionary perspective on human mating. *Psychological Review, 100,* 204–232.

Buunk, B., Angleitner, A., Oubaid, V., & Buss, D. M. (1994). *Sexual and cultural differences in jealousy: Tests from the Netherlands, Germany, and the United States.* Manuscript submitted for publication.

Clark, R. D., & Hatfield, E. (1989). Gender differences in receptivity to sexual offers. *Journal of Psychology and Human Sexuality, 2,* 39–55.

Cohen, J. (1977). Statistical power analysis for the behavioral sciences. San Diego, CA: Academic Press.

Daly, M., & Wilson, M. (1988). *Homicide.* New York: Aldine de Gruyter.

Darwin, C. (1871). *The descent of man and selection in relation to sex.* London: Murray.

Eagly, A. H. (1995). The science and politics of comparing women and men. *American Psychologist, 50,* 145–158.

Ellis, B. J., & Symons, D. (1990). Sex differences in sexual fantasy: An evolutionary psychological approach. *Journal of Sex Research, 27,* 527–556.

Feingold, A. (1990). Gender differences in effects of physical attractiveness on romantic attraction: A comparison across five research paradigms. *Journal of Personality and Social Psychology, 59,* 981–993.

Gangestad, S. W., & Simpson, J. A. (1990). Toward an evolutionary history of female sociosexual variation. *Journal of Personality, 58,* 69–96.

Greer, A., & Buss, D. M. (1994). Tactics for promoting sexual encounters. *Journal of Sex Research, 5,* 185–201.

Greiling, H. (1993, June). *Women's short-term sexual strategies.* Paper presented at the Conference on Evolution and the Social Sciences, London School of Economics, London, England.

Hall, J. A. (1978). Gender effects in decoding nonverbal cues. *Psychological Bulletin, 85,* 845–852.

Hill, K., & Hurtado, M. (1989). Hunter-gatherers of the new world. *American Scientist, 77,* 437–443.

Hyde, J. S. (in press). Where are the gender differences? Where are the gender similarities? In D. M. Buss & N. Malamuth (Eds.), *Sex, power, conflict: Feminist and evolutionary perspectives.* New York: Oxford University Press.

Kenrick, D. T., & Keefe, R. C. (1992). Age preferences in mates reflect sex differences in reproductive strategies. *Behavioral and Brain Sciences, 15,* 75–133.

Maccoby, E. E., & Jacklin, C. N. (1974). *The psychology of sex differences.* Stanford, CA: Stanford University Press.

Oliver, M. B., & Hyde, J. S. (1993). Gender differences in sexuality: A meta-analysis. *Psychological Bulletin, 114,* 29–51.

Rosenthal, R. (1991). *Meta-analytic procedures for social research* (rev. ed.). Newbury Park, CA: Sage.

Silverman, I., & Eals, M. (1992). Sex differences in spatial abilities: Evolutionary theory and data. In J. Barkow, L. Cosmides, & J. Tooby (Eds.), *The adapted mind: Evolutionary psychology and the generation of culture* (pp. 539–549). New York: Oxford University Press.

Symons, D. (1979). *The evolution of human sexuality.* New York: Oxford University Press.

Symons, D. (1992). On the use and misuse of Darwinism in the study of human behavior. In J. Barkow, L. Cosmides, & J. Tooby (Eds.), *The adapted mind: Evolutionary psychology and the generation of culture* (pp. 137–159). New York: Oxford University Press.

Tooby, J., & Cosmides, L. (1992). Psychological foundations of culture. In J. Barkow, L. Cosmides, & J. Tooby (Eds.), *The adapted mind: Evolutionary psychology and the generation of culture* (pp. 119–136). New York: Oxford University Press.

Trivers, R. (1972). Parental investment and sexual selection. In B. Campbell (Ed.), *Sexual selection and the descent of man* (pp. 136–179). New York: Aldine de Gruyter.

Wiederman, M. W., & Allgeier, E. R. (1993). Gender differences in sexual jealousy: Adaptationist or social learning explanation? *Ethology and Sociobiology, 14,* 115–140.

Wilson, M., & Daly, M. (1985). Competitiveness, risk taking, and violence: The young male syndrome. *Ethology and Sociobiology, 6,* 59–73.

Chapter Thirteen

Gender Differences in Emotion

Antony S. R. Manstead

Introduction

One of the attributes traditionally ascribed to women, in Western cultures at least, is their greater emotionality relative to men. The Belk and Snell (1986) Beliefs about Women Scale (BAWS) was devised as an objective self-report measure of stereotypes about women. Of the sub-scales assessed by this measure, three were endorsed approximately equally by females and by males as being characteristic of women: "Women have more emotional insight than men"; "Women are more interpersonal than men"; and "Women are less dominating than men." Each of these empirically established beliefs about women maps on to readily recognizable sex stereotypes: that women are "more in touch with their feelings" than men, and are thus more emotionally responsive and sensitive; that women are more oriented towards other persons and are thus better tuned to others' feelings and emotions than men are; and that women are less aggressive than men. The aim of this chapter is to provide a representative review of the evidence pertaining to such beliefs. Are women, indeed, more "emotional" than men? To address this question I shall review evidence under five rubrics:

(1) psychophysiological research;
(2) research on facial expressiveness;
(3) research on subjective experience;
(4) research on emotional behavior (other than facial expression);
(5) research on accuracy in perceiving others' emotional states.

The chapter closes with a set of conclusions that can be drawn from the reviewed evidence.

There are some methodological points that should be made before proceeding to the evidence. The first concerns the magnitude of gender differences. Even where such differences have consistently been found on indices relating to emotion, they tend to be small in absolute terms, typically accounting for less than 5 percent of the

Antony S. R. Manstead, "Gender Differences in Emotion." In A. Gale and M. Eysenck (Eds.), *Handbook of Individual Differences: Biological Perspectives*, pp. 355–387. © 1992 by John Wiley & Sons, Ltd. Reprinted by permission of John Wiley & Sons, Ltd.

variance on the measure in question. It is worth noting that gender differences on cognitive variables, such as verbal and spatial ability, are of an equivalent size (Deaux, 1984). This means, of course, that there is considerable overlap between the distributions of scores of male and female populations on psychological attributes. There is evidence that psychological differences associated with social class are much greater than those associated with sex of subject (Kornbrott, 1986; Newson and Newson, 1986), although such comparative data are not available for measures of emotion.

A related point concerns the reliability of measures of emotion. It is a well-established fact that single measures of any construct are less reliable than multiple measures (Epstein, 1980), although researchers have typically been rather insensitive to this issue. Because the majority of studies in this (as in other) fields of research use single indices of emotion, measured on one occasion and in specific circumstances, it is unwise to attach much theoretical significance to the findings of any one study, or even a small series of studies, especially in view of the fact that the effect attributable to gender is relatively small.

Another related problem concerns the possibility of interactions between sex of subject and other variables. Researchers have not addressed this problem systematically enough, preferring to look for main effects due to sex of subject than for interactions. Yet there are grounds for thinking that sex of subject will interact with, for example, sex of investigator (see Eagly and Carli, 1981; Gale and Baker, 1981; Rumenik, Capasso, and Hendrick, 1977). Thus some effects that are attributed to sex of subject may in fact be due to the interaction of sex of subject with an uncontrolled variable. Alternatively, where researchers fail to find overall gender differences on indices of emotion, it may be that there are significant differences between subsets of male and female subjects.

These are some of the methodological problems that beset the study of differences in the psychological characteristics of males and females (for a fuller discussion, see Archer, 1987). Researchers are beginning to address the first two problems through the use of meta-analytic techniques (Glass, 1976; Rosenthal, 1984). Such techniques are not without their disadvantages; for example, they are relatively insensitive to differences in the quality of the studies across which they integrate. Nevertheless, they also have a number of advantages. These techniques almost invariably involve the computation of measures of effect size, which serves to heighten awareness of the fact that a statistically significant difference may be a small difference in absolute terms. Furthermore, by providing a means of statistically combining the results of many studies, meta-analysis helps to determine whether a difference is robust across specific measurement occasions and circumstances. However, the problem of interaction is one that in general is not being addressed. The difficulty here is that the number of variables with which subject sex could potentially interact is enormous. Although researchers should be guided by theory in their selection of candidate variables, it is a fact that much of the research reviewed in this chapter was not originally conducted in order to test one or other theory of gender differences. As Archer (1987) has noted, "The study of 'sex differences' has its roots in the field of individual differences research and has relied on the fortuitous discovery of statistically significant differences between men and women in studies whose theoretical focus was not concerned with sex differences" (p. 88).

Research Evidence

Psychophysiological Research

Nowhere is the lack of a clear theoretical rationale for the study of gender differences more apparent than in psychophysiological research. There is surprisingly little systematic research on gender differences in psychophysiological response to emotionally arousing stimuli and it is correspondingly difficult to draw clear inferences from those findings that have been reported. Nonetheless, there is the semblance of a consistent difference between males and females across measures of electrodermal and cardiovascular functioning.

As far as *electrodermal responding* is concerned, several studies have found that males exhibit greater skin conductance (SC) responding than females. For example, Graham, Cohen, and Shmavonian (1966) and Shmavonian, Yarmat, and Cohen (1965) reported greater SC responding in males than in females in a classical conditioning procedure involving electric shock. Although Berger (1962) found no gender differences in electrodermal activity among subjects observing another person receiving shocks, Craig and Lowery (1969) found more skin resistance (SR) changes among males than among females when subjects watched others receiving shocks and McCracken (1969; cited in Buck, 1988) found higher SC levels in males than in females among subjects listening to time-compressed speech. It is worth noting that in the latter two studies, males reported a level of distress lower than that reported by females, despite their greater electrodermal responding. Commenting on such findings, Prokasy and Raskin (1973) have argued that females have smaller and/or less frequent electrodermal responses than males in many emotional situations, and that such a difference only becomes manifest after puberty.

Consistent with this conclusion are findings from a series of studies reported by Buck and his colleagues (Buck et al., 1972; Buck, Miller and Caul, 1974; Buck, 1977). In the first two studies cited, adult female subjects tended to be below the median in SC responding whereas adult males tended to be above this median when viewing emotionally loaded color slides. In the third study, involving preschool children, there was no gender difference in SC responding to emotional slides. Also worth noting is a study of crowding reported by Nicosia and colleagues (1979), in which crowded men showed a marked increase in SC over time, whereas crowded women did not.

However, there are exceptions to this general trend for males to exhibit greater electrodermal activity than females. For example, Buck (1972) found that females exhibited greater SC responding than males when subjects were required to administer electric shocks to someone else; and Aronfreed, Messick, and Diggory (1953) also found larger SC responses in females than in males when listening to "unpleasant words."

Evidence of gender differences in *cardiac activity* during emotional stimulation comes mainly from research on aggression. Here the evidence again points to the greater reactivity of male subjects. For example, Cantor, Zillmann, and Einsiedel (1978) found that viewing violent movie excerpts elicited only modest excitatory reactions in females. McLean (1981; reported in Lang, 1984) examined subjects' cardiac responses to two versions of emotional scenarios. In one, subjects simply read a script and were instructed to imagine the scenario as vividly as possible; in the other, the scenario was enacted live as a "mini-drama", using trained actors and involving the subject as a participant observer. One scenario was designed to evoke fear, and concerned a live, poisonous snake; the other was intended to evoke anger, and cast the subject in the role of someone being berated by a tutor for lack of intelligence and poor examination performance. It was found that HR responses to these scenarios depended on their mode of presentation, their emotional content, and the subject's gender and imagery ability. Male good imagers responded more to the fear and anger dramas than did male poor imagers, but female good imagers, while responding much more to the fear scenario, did *not* differ from female poor imagers in response to the anger scenario. Thus female subjects showed reduced cardiac response to stimuli intended to arouse anger. Sapolsky, Stocking, and Zillmann (1977) exposed male and female subjects to a provocation and then gave them the opportunity to aggress either immediately or after a six-minute delay. During this delay period it was observed that females showed greater heart rate deceleration than males, reflecting more efficient physiological recovery from the provocation. It has been argued that such findings reflect the fact that women have learned to minimize the arousing effects of annoying or provocative stimuli (cf. Hokanson, 1970; Zillmann, 1979).

Further evidence of sex differences in cardiovascular responses comes from research on stress. Stimulated by the possible link between such sex differences and epidemiological evidence of sizeable sex differences in risk for coronary heart disease, Stoney, Davis, and Matthews (1987) recently reported a meta-analytic review of all psychophysiological studies reported in English-language journals between 1965 and 1986. The meta-analysis yielded three major findings. First, females had higher resting heart rates (HR) than males, and tended to have higher HR increases during challenge. Second, males had higher resting systolic blood pressure (SBP) than females, and exhibited higher SBP changes during challenge. Third, the males had higher urinary epinephrine responses during stress. The authors note that:

> Taken together, the results provide some support for the hypothesis that men show greater physiological responses during acute behavioural stress than do women. Two caveats should be noted, however. First, the heart rate responses during stress were greater in women than in men, albeit not significantly so. Second, few investigations were available for analysis, and little research in this area has been programmatic (p. 129).

Another aspect of psychophysiological activity in which gender differences have been reported concerns autonomic self-perception. Katkin and his associates (Katkin, Blascovich and Goldband, 1981; Koenigsberg, Katkin and Blascovich, 1981) have studied individual differences in the ability to discriminate one's own heartbeat. In the Katkin procedure subjects are presented with one set of signals that have a fixed, invariant relationship to their own heartbeat, and another set of signals that have a variable relationship to their own heartbeat. The subject's task is to discriminate correctly these two types of signal. In the Katkin, Blascovich, and Goldband (1981) study, male and female subjects received 40 baseline trials followed by 120 trials in which they received veridical feedback on the correctness of their discrimination after each trial. Only male subjects showed any evidence of acquisition of heartbeat discrimination in the course of the feedback trials. The Koenigsberg, Katkin, and Blascovich (1981) study was intended to examine whether the nature of the instructions given to subjects affected acquisition of heartbeat discrimination on 40 "retention" trials conducted after the feedback trials. "Experimental" subjects were given detailed instructions and extensive practice in the discrimination task, while "control" subjects were run under conditions replicating those obtaining in the Katkin, Blascovich, and Goldband (1981) study. Under control conditions male subjects again showed significantly greater acquisition of heartbeat discrimination than did females; under experimental conditions, however, females did not differ from female controls but males performed much worse than male controls and more poorly than either female group. The authors concluded that male and female subjects use different cognitive strategies in learning heartbeat discrimination, such that instructions oriented towards an auditory discrimination strategy undermined the otherwise good acquisition displayed by male subjects while leaving female subjects unaffected.

Research using electromyography (EMG) to assess physiological response to emotional stimuli has generally shown that females exhibit greater facial EMG than males. In a series of studies, Schwartz and his associates (Schwartz, Ahern, and Brown, 1979; Schwartz, Brown, and Ahern, 1980; Schwartz et al., 1976a; Schwartz et al., 1976b; Schwartz et al., 1978) have found that females, by comparison with males, tend to produce greater facial EMG, relative to rest, during affective imagery; to exhibit somewhat higher levels of corrugator activity (possibly indicative of greater sadness or concern) and lower levels of masseter activity (possibly indicative of less anger) during rest; and to generate larger facial EMG patterns when asked to pose overt expressions corresponding to different emotions. As we shall see in the next section of this chapter, these findings are consistent with research examining gender differences in facial expressiveness using different measurement techniques.

Research on Facial Expressiveness

Several studies have examined gender differences in so-called "spontaneous" facial expressiveness. The term "spontaneous" is used here to denote the fact that in such research "sender" subjects' facial reactions to emotional stimuli are covertly recorded (or relayed live via closed-circuit television) in order that other ("receiver") subjects can engage in the task of inferring the nature of the stimulus presented to the sender (e.g., Buck, Miller, and Caul, 1974) or the nature of the sender's emotional response to that stimulus (e.g., Wagner, MacDonald, and Manstead, 1986). For the sake of simplicity, these measures will hereafter be referred to as measures of "sending accuracy."

Consider first those studies involving adult subjects. Here there is consistent evidence that females' spontaneous facial responses to emotional stimuli (typically color slides) are more accurately decoded by receiver subjects, by comparison with males' facial responses (Buck et al., 1972; Buck, Miller, and Caul, 1974; Fujita, Harper, and Wiens, 1980; Gallagher and Shuntich, 1981).

Buck and his associates (Buck, Baron, and Barrette, 1982; Buck et al., 1980) have subjected video-tapes of spontaneous facial expressions to "segmentation analysis," a procedure in which observers are instructed to press a button whenever "something meaningful" occurs. The Buck and colleagues (1980) study found that sending accuracy was positively and significantly associated with the number of segmentation points noted by subjects in relation to the facial expressions of females; this was not the case with males' expressions. Thus the *amount* of "meaningful" facial/gestural activity exhibited by sender subjects is related to their sending accuracy in the case of females but not males.

In the Buck, Baron, and Barrette (1982) study a more detailed analysis of segmentation points was performed, permitting the investigators to assess not just the number of segmentation points, but also the number of *consensual* segmentation points (CPs), where a CP is defined as a one-second period which attracted in excess of one standard deviation above the average number of segmentation points per second given to that video sequence. Obviously, the greater the number of CPs, the more observers agree in their judgment of the location of meaningful behaviors. Furthermore, a second group of observer subjects were shown the same video-tape of facial expressions and told where CPs occurred; for each CP, these subjects had to judge whether it was based on a facial expression on the part of the sender, or related to some other behavior such as head movement or postural change. The percentage of CPs judged to be facial expressions indicates the extent to which consensual judgments of meaningful behavior involve facial expressions. In this study it was found that females' sending accuracy was significantly and positively correlated not only with the number of segmentation points (as in the earlier study) but also with the number of CPs; neither of these correlations was significant in the case of males. However, the percentage of CPs judged to be facial expressions was positively and significantly related to sending accuracy for males but not for females. These findings appear to indicate that sending accuracy, as reflected in the degree to which spontaneous facial expressiveness permits observers to make accurate inferences about the sender's state, is based upon different behaviors in males and females. It seems that among females, sending accuracy is related simply to the amount of meaningful activity, but that among males sending accuracy is related to the extent to which such activity involves facial expressions. As Buck (1984) observes, there appear to be qualitative as well as quantitative differences between males and females with regard to sending accuracy. Why this should be so is as yet unknown, and there is an obvious need for further research on this topic.

What is clear, however, is that the gender difference in spontaneous facial expressiveness observed in adults is not reliably found in infants and children. In two studies of preschoolers, Buck (1975, 1977) found a small gender difference in expressiveness, in that undergraduate receivers were more accurate in guessing the type of stimulus viewed by girls as compared with boys. However, there was no difference between girls' and boys' sending accuracy when the child's mother acted as the receiver. Field (1982) found no reliable gender differences in the facial expressiveness of neonates, and Yarczower and Daruns (1982) also found no gender differences in their study using children aged six or twelve. These failures to find reliable gender differences among children suggest that the differences observed in adults are acquired relatively late in childhood, and may therefore be mediated by sex-role socialization. Consistent with such an interpretation is Buck's (1975, 1977) finding that sending accuracy tends to be inversely related with age among boys, but not girls—suggesting that spontaneous facial expressiveness in boys decreases as they get older.

It is one thing to speculate that gender differences in facial expressiveness are acquired, and quite another to provide evidence concerning the processes by which they are acquired. However, some progress has been made in pinpointing one such process. Malatesta and her colleagues (Malatesta and Haviland, 1982; Malatesta et al., 1986; Malatesta and Lamb, 1987) have been exploring the role played by mothers' modeling of facial expressions and the way in which mothers respond contingently to their infants' facial expressions during the first two years of life. In the Malatesta and Haviland (1982) study, sixty mothers and their three- to six-month-old infants were video-taped during a sixteen-minute play period. Although male and female infants exhibited no significant difference in the type and rate of facial expression change, mothers were found to respond differentially to males and females. Mothers of male infants tended to match their child's expressions with similar expressions of their own, whereas mothers of female infants tended to follow their child's expressions with dissimilar expressions of their own. Mothers showed higher levels of contingent responding (especially contingent smiling) to the smiles of older versus younger male infants. However, the pattern was reversed for female infants, with mothers showing lower contingent responding to older versus younger females.

In the Malatesta and Lamb (1987) study, fifty-eight two-year-olds and their mothers were video-taped during a nine-minute play period and in the "strange situation" developed by Ainsworth and Wittig (1969). Mothers of male infants showed significant matching of infant sadness, unlike mothers of females. On the other hand, mothers of females showed significant matching of a "pressed lip" expression (thought to relate to anger suppression), whereas mother of males tended to ignore this expression. Finally, when infants displayed full anger expressions, mothers of girls tended to ignore such expressions whereas mothers of boys did not.

The notion that such differential responding to male and female infants' expressions may have an impact on the infants' pattern of facial expression is supported by evidence from the longitudinal study reported by Malatesta and colleagues (1986). This research, spanning the period from two to seven months of age, not only found further evidence of differential patterns of contingent responding and modeling on the part of mothers as a function of their infant's gender, but also found evidence that exposure to this differentiated pattern of stimulation in time results in different patterns of expressiveness. For example, modeling by mothers of joy and interest when the infant was five months old was predictive of increases in infant joy and interest expressions two and a half months later.

The painstaking and pioneering research conducted by Malatesta and her associates is in need of replication but it points to the possibility that the ways in which males and females express emotion facially may elicit different reactions from caregivers even at a very early age. However, these differences do not appear to be sufficient in themselves to evoke a clear-cut gender difference in children's facial expressiveness, for as we have seen such a difference does not become reliable until children are into their teens. However, if this differentiated pattern of contingent responding is sufficient over time to provoke subtle differences in infants' facial displays of emotion, consider how much more powerful the more overt socialization effected at later ages, via verbal instruction, is likely to be. It also seems likely that same-sex peer groups will be important agents of socialization from puberty onwards, acting to reinforce behaviors consistent with culturally endorsed sex-roles. Children as young as two to three years attribute to a male doll the characteristic that "he never cries" (Kuhn, Nash, and Bruchan, 1978), and by the time they are aged five to eight children know many of the sex-stereotyped personality traits, including the "feminine" traits of emotionality (Best et al., 1977). Given that overt socialization will tend to incorporate cultural beliefs about the appropriateness of overt emotional displays by males and females, it is hardly surprising that by adulthood males are less expressive than females in their spontaneous facial behavior.

Research on Subjective Experience of Emotion

Gender differences in subjective emotional experience are widely reported in the research literature. For example, questionnaire studies on children and adults tend to find that females experience more fear than males do (see Maccoby and Jacklin, 1974). One difficulty in knowing what to make of such findings is that those who are old enough to provide reliable responses to questionnaires are also sufficiently well socialized to have a fair idea of how appropriate it is for males and females to experience and express various emotions—including fear. Thus it is entirely possible (or even likely) that the way in which males and females respond to such questionnaires will, consciously or unconsciously, be influenced by their knowledge of sex stereotypes. The "greater fear" reported by females may simply reflect their greater willingness to admit to feeling fearful. Indeed, there is some evidence that scores on paper-and-pencil measures of fears and anxieties are inversely related to social desirability scores, indicating that those who report relatively few fears or anxieties tend to score higher on social desirability (Spiegler and Liebert, 1970; Wilson, 1967).

A further problem with questionnaire measures of negative emotionality such as anxiety, as Jahnke, Crannell, and Morrissette (1974) have argued, is that it is difficult—if not impossible—to determine whether differences in the total scores of women and men reflect gender differences in underlying anxiety (or willingness to express anxiety) or are simply an artefact of the sex-typed content of the items included in the questionnaire measure. These authors point out that the Manifest Anxiety Scale, a very widely used self-report measure of anxiety, includes relatively few items that deal with the kinds of anxieties most likely to be experienced by men (such as anxiety over work-related matters). Hill and Sarason (1966) have made a similar point in relation to anxiety scales for children, and Maccoby and Jacklin (1974) suggest that as many as ten of the forty-five items of the General Anxiety Scale for Children are weighted towards fears more likely to be experienced by girls than boys.

Studies of the frequency of affective experience do not suffer from the possible problem of biased item content, but they do potentially suffer from the problem that observed gender differences may simply reflect differential willingness to report affective experience. It is interesting to note, then, that although some studies show that women report themselves as experiencing both positive and negative affect more frequently than men, the gender difference is rather greater in the case of negative affect (Bradburn, 1969; Harding, 1982). Indeed, in a study of over 3,000 British adults, Warr and Payne (1982) found no overall gender difference in how much of the time on the previous day they had felt "pleased with things," but that 18 percent of women experienced "unpleasant emotional strain" on the previous day for about half the time or more, by contrast with 13 percent of men. The fact that gender differences are more reliably found in relation to *negative* emotional experience again raises the possibility that women may simply be more willing than men to confront and express such experience. A similar point applies to the one "non-trivial" gender difference in emotional experience observed in the large-scale cross-national study reported by Scherer, Wallbott, and Summerfield (1986). Respondents were asked about joy, sadness, anger and fear, and with respect to subjective experience the only greater gender difference was that women reported more intense and longer-lasting experiences of *sadness*. One problem with interpreting such findings in terms of differential willingness to express or report negative affect is that women are more likely than men to be homemakers and to be engaged in child care. It is therefore possible that gender differences in reporting dysphoric affect stem partly or wholly from these differences in occupational roles. The average number of aversive events encountered by a woman who is a homemaker and/or mother may simply be greater than those encountered by a man in full-time employment. However, there is some additional evidence that men find it difficult to be open about dysphoric emotional experience. For example, in the research on marital satisfaction reported by Noller (1982), it was found that wives reported that they could often discern that their husbands were upset, but complained that it was difficult to get their husbands to express their feelings and to discuss why they felt upset.

It is worth noting, in passing, the fact that Scherer and his associates found no gender difference with regard to anger experiences, a finding that is consistent with earlier research by Averill (1982). This is interesting because (a) it emphasizes the point that the observed gender difference in negative emotionality does not apply to all negative emotions; and (b) it demonstrates that gender differences in aggressive behavior, which will be discussed below, do not necessarily reflect differences in the subjective experience of anger.

Many psychological disorders have an affective component, so it is worth comparing women's and men's vulnerability to such disorders. Official statistics on psychological disorders should be interpreted cautiously, given that there are grounds for thinking that psychiatric diagnoses might vary according to whether the client is male or female. In a widely-cited study, Broverman and colleagues (1970) examined the possible influence of sex-role stereotypes on clinical diagnosis. Some clinicians were asked to rate a "healthy, mature, socially competent adult person" on a standard questionnaire listing personality traits. Other clinicians were asked to rate a man, also described as healthy, mature and socially competent; and a third group was asked to rate a similarly described woman. It was found that beliefs about what constituted a healthy "adult" were closer to the picture of the healthy male than that of the healthy female. If even a healthy female adult is seen by clinicians as differing from an "ideal" healthy adult, it is possible that women are more readily diagnosed as psychologically disordered than are men. Certainly, women are over-represented in nearly all populations of persons using mental health services (see Cochrane, 1983; Miles, 1987). Archer and Lloyd (1985) report that women represented 58 percent of first admissions to mental hospitals and mental health units in England in 1979. Women are particularly over-represented in certain diagnostic categories: depressive psychosis and involutional melancholia (65 percent); psychoneurosis (66 percent); and senile and presenile psychoses (65 percent). The predominance of women in this last group can be attributed largely to their greater longevity. It should be noted that men are also over-represented in certain diagnostic categories: alcoholic psychosis (65 percent); alcoholism (72 percent); and drug dependence (69 percent). The overall predominance of women among psychiatric populations in the United States is also well established (e.g., Chesler, 1971; Gove, 1978; Guttentag, Salasin, and Belle, 1980), and the general pattern of male and female representation in diagnostic categories is the same as in the UK.

It is clear, then, that women are on average more likely to be diagnosed as suffering from psychoneuroses and depression, two psychological disorders with a strong affective component. Do these higher morbidity rates for women reflect real differences between men's and women's subjective experiences, or do they simply reflect their differential willingness to express emotional problems and/or to seek help for them? Just as with the questionnaire studies of emotional experience mentioned above, a greater readiness on the part of women to admit that they are experiencing negative affect and/or to seek help in alleviating that negative affect may well contribute to the observed gender difference in morbidity. Hammen and Peters (1978) found that reactions to someone enacting a depressed role differed as a function of the person's sex: reactions to the depressed female were less negative than were reactions to the depressed male. Men's awareness of the relative unacceptability of emotional disorders such as depression in males may diminish their readiness to admit to such problems and to seek help in dealing with them. It has been estimated that as much as one quarter of the observed gender differences in psychological disorders could be due to such factors (see Kessler, Price, and Wortman, 1985). Indeed, there is evidence that women more frequently seek help for emotional problems than men do (Phillips and Segal, 1969).

It seems unlikely that the observed gender differences in psychological disorders can be fully accounted for by invoking explanations based on women's greater willingness to acknowledge symptoms and/or to seek help. One possible explanation for such differences is that they reflect different strategies for coping with similar sorts of stressful life events; whereas women's "preferred" coping style is depressogenic in nature, men's "preferred" coping style involves drinking alcohol. Another possibility is one favored by Gove and his colleagues, who have argued that such gender differences reflect real differences in the incidence of psychological disorders in men and women, and that these real differences in turn arise from sociocultural rather than biological factors (Gove, 1978; 1980; Gove and Tudor, 1973). An important basis for the argument that it is sociocultural factors that are responsible for gender differences in psychological disorder is the observation that married women exhibit greater susceptibility to such disorders whereas single, widowed or divorced women do not differ from their male counterparts (Gove, 1972; 1979; 1980). It is therefore reasoned that the social role played by women within marriage is stressful, because it gives rise to greater frustration, more constraint, less reward and ultimately to higher rates of psychological (and physical) illness than does the role played by married men.

It is worth noting, however, that general psychiatric admission rates among married patients in the USA are no longer appreciably higher for women than for men (see Bloom, Asher, and White, 1978). Indeed, admission rates for inpatient facilities are generally higher for males, although those for outpatient facilities are somewhat higher for females (Bloom, Asher, and White, 1978). Even when one compares diagnosis-specific admission rates in different marital status groups, there is relatively little evidence that being married results in greater depression among women than among men (Bloom, 1975). What is not in dispute is the fact that males suffer more than females following marital disruption (separation or divorce: Bloom, Asher, and White, 1978) or bereavement (Stroebe and Stroebe, 1983). Although the fact that males are more adversely affected than females by separation, divorce or bereavement is consistent with Gove's social role hypothesis, there are alternative explanations. For example, males may be less willing or less well placed to elicit social support from others following marital disruption or bereavement (Stroebe and Stroebe, 1983).

A very different approach to the explanation of observed gender differences in psychological disorders is employed by those who emphasize the role of biological factors. Common to the diverse explanations that fall under this general heading is the assumption that sex hormones are important causal agents. For example, it has been suggested that the mood fluctuations experienced by many women premenstrually arise from progesterone deficiency or imbalance (Dalton, 1969; Hamburg and Lunde, 1966). However, direct measurement of levels of progesterone and other hormones such as oestradiol have failed to support such hypotheses. In a review of the evidence, Bancroft and Backstrom (1985) concluded that although there is a prima facie case for considering direct effects of progesterone and oestradiol on CNS activity, it is difficult to account for premenstrual mood changes in terms of varying levels of these two hormones. Furthermore, assessment of the supposedly therapeutic effects of hormonal intervention (e.g., through progesterone injection; Dalton, 1979) shows no evidence of improvement when double-blind procedures are followed (see Bancroft and Backstrom, 1985). Those who favor a more psychological or sociocultural explanation of premenstrual mood changes stress the role of negative beliefs about and attitudes to menstruation, and cognitive biases leading women to attribute to menstruation any negative affect experienced when they believe themselves to be premenstrual (see Parlee, 1988; Ruble and Brooks-Gunn, 1979). Whatever the basis of mood fluctuations during the menstrual cycle, it seems most unlikely that such fluctuations could account for the gender difference in the incidence of depression (see Weissman and Klermann, 1977). Research has also failed to support the notion that post-natal depression stems from hormonal changes at this time, such as the sudden fall in progesterone levels (Weldburn, 1980). Finally, some have argued that women's apparently greater vulnerability to depression at the time of menopause is the result of hormonal change (in this case, the decline in oestrogen levels; Dalton, 1979). However, Weissman (1979) concluded that the menopause is *not* associated with an increase in depression or any other psychological disorder; rather, it seems that depression in middle-aged women may result from factors such as the loss of maternal role (Bart, 1971) or stressful life events such as the death of a loved one (Greene, 1981) that tend to occur at the same general time as the menopause.

To summarize, there is evidence that women may be more inclined than men to experience dysphoric emotions such as fear, anxiety, sadness and depression. It is extremely difficult to determine whether these gender differences accurately reflect phenomenological differences in male and female emotionality but in the case of depression there appears to be some reason to believe that women are more prone than men to experience this type of negative affect. There is no satisfactory evidence that this gender difference has a biological basis. It seems possible that it is a reflection of the peculiar stresses experienced by women in fulfilling role obligations, although there is as yet no evidence that unequivocally supports this explanation.

Research on Emotional Behavior

As Maccoby and Jacklin (1974) have argued, a primary index of emotional disturbance in an infant is that he or she cries. These authors reviewed twenty-one studies of the frequency and duration of crying among children ranging in age from neonates to five-year-olds, with the majority of studies focusing on the first year of life. The findings of these studies show no consistent evidence of a gender difference in frequency or duration of crying.

However, there is some evidence of a gender difference in reactions to frustration. Goodenough (1931) reported that the frequency of anger outbursts in boys and girls was similar up to the age of eighteen months, but that beyond that age the frequency declined for girls and increased for boys. Studies of reactions to frustration tend to suggest that boys react more emotionally than girls do (see Maccoby and Jacklin, 1974). Maccoby and Feldman (1972) found that two-year-old boys were more likely than their female peers to bang on the door through which their mother had departed, when left alone in a strange room. Martin (1981) observed ten-month-old children while their mothers were completing a questionnaire, and noted that boys seemed particularly unwilling to accept the mother's withdrawal of attention, and escalated the intensity of their demands for her attention if she failed to respond. Gunnar (1980) found that when one-year-olds were prevented from controlling a frightening toy, boys were more likely than girls to become distressed.

Further evidence of gender differences in emotional behavior comes from a review reported by Haviland and Malatesta (1981). These authors conclude that boys are more emotionally labile and more easily distressed than girls, at least during infancy. Girls, on the other hand, establish and maintain eye contact more than boys—and this difference appears to be maintained into adulthood. The authors suggest that the greater gazing behavior of infant girls will promote feelings of closeness between mother and daughter, whereas the greater gaze aversion, irritability and inconsolability of male infants is likely to inhibit such feelings. Thus the different signals produced by male and female infants may elicit different responses from caregivers, and these differentiated patterns of response may underlie gender differences in emotional behavior exhibited at later stages of development.

Research on aggressive behavior has in general supported the stereotype that males are more aggressive than females. Before turning to the evidence, it is worth considering more closely what is meant by the term "aggression," and in particular how it relates to emotion. As Archer and Lloyd (1985) have noted, aggression is used sometimes to refer to "assertiveness" and sometimes as meaning "motivation to commit a violent act." These two meanings can be related, these authors go on to argue, "if we regard an assertive person as more ready to commit violent acts if his intentions are frustrated" (p. 126). It is only in the second sense of aggression, i.e., "motivation to commit a violent act" that emotion comes into play, in that anger can motivate and accompany aggressive behavior. Much of the research on gender differences in aggression is not directly concerned with emotions, however. Rather, aggression is measured in terms of overt behavior. Researchers usually observe the incidence of fighting, "rough and tumble play," or destructive acts in children; and the incidence of verbal aggression or the willingness to harm another person (e.g., by administering what are believed to be electric shocks) in adults.

Because aggression may or may not be motivated or accompanied by emotion (see Geen, 1990), this is not the appropriate context in which to review in great detail the research evidence on gender differences in aggression. In any case, the literature has been reviewed comprehensively by others (e.g., Eagly and Steffen, 1986; Frodi, Macauley, and Thome, 1977; Hyde, 1984; Maccoby and Jacklin, 1974, 1980). What follows is therefore a brief overview.

Observational studies of children's behavior typically show boys to be more aggressive than girls (Hyde, 1984). An example of such a study carried out on preschool children is the one reported by Smith and Green (1975). These investigators found that conflicts between boys were more frequent than those between girls or those between boys and girls. Although this finding is typical, it is worth noting that there was greater variation in the incidence of aggression *across* the fifteen nursery schools, day nurseries and play groups studied than between boys and girls *within* these different settings (Henshall and McGuire, 1986). Nevertheless, the direction of the overall gender difference in this study is consistent with that found in other research (Hyde, 1984) and there is very little evidence of a reversal of the typical gender difference, even if one focuses on *verbal* rather than *physical* aggression.

Research on adults has yielded a somewhat less consistent pattern of findings, and it has been argued that this reflects the fact that situational variables become more important determinants of aggressive behavior as age increases (Eagly and Steffen, 1986). The influential review of Frodi, Macauley, and Thome (1977) concluded that the gender difference in aggression is dependent on several other factors, such as the mode of response available to the instigator, the gender of the target person, and emotional arousal. In relation to this last point, Frodi, Macauley, and Thome argued that "women's aggressive behaviour must often be moderated by arousal of aggression anxiety over the propriety of such behaviour. It seems likely that a significant proportion of variation between (and probably within) the sexes can be accounted for by guilt or anxiety avoidance or arousal" (p. 645). Consistent with this argument, Eagly and Steffen (1986) found that women and men think differently about aggression and that these differential beliefs about the consequences of aggressive behavior are important mediators of the gender difference in aggression. More specifically, "Women reported more guilt and anxiety as a consequence of aggression, more vigilance about the harm that aggression causes its victims, and more concern about the danger that aggression might bring to themselves" (p. 325).

Also relevant to this line of argument is a program of research conducted by Hokanson and his colleagues (see Hokanson, 1970). In the context of simulated interaction with a peer, subjects were "attacked" by means of an electric shock administered by their partner. Subjects were free to respond to this attack by pressing one of three buttons: one delivered a shock to the partner; another delivered a reward; and the third delivered neither shock nor reward. A key dependent variable was systolic blood pressure. In males, it was found that recovery from the arousal induced by the partner's attacking behavior was alleviated most rapidly following aggressive (i.e., shock) responses; recovery following non-aggressive responses was as slow as that in a control condition, where subjects were not given the opportunity to respond to the attack. However, females exhibited rapid autonomic recovery regardless of how they responded to the attack. Whichever of the three options they chose, recovery was significantly faster than it was in the control condition.

Commenting on this pattern of findings, Hokanson, Willers, and Koropsak (1968) suggested that "Females undergo a set of learning experiences in which making nonaggressive responses to someone else's aggression is rewarded: in the specific sense of thereby effectively reducing the other person's aversive behaviour, and in the general sense that this behaviour conforms to cultural norms and expectations" (p. 388). To test this speculation, these investigators conducted an experiment involving three phases, during the first and third of which the subject's partner attacked him or her by administering electric shocks on trials determined via a random schedule. The subject could respond to such attacks by delivering a shock or a reward. In the second phase, however, the partner's attacks were contingent upon the sex and behavior of the subject. Females were punished whenever they responded to shock by delivering a reward, and rewarded whenever they responded to shock by delivering another shock. For males this schedule of reinforcement was reversed. The results showed that during the first phase females showed faster autonomic recovery after reacting to shocks by delivering a reward, whereas males recovered faster after responding with a further shock. During the second phase this pattern was reversed, with females recovering more quickly after aggressive responses and males after non-aggressive responses. During the third phase males and females reverted fairly rapidly to the patterns of behavior they exhibited during phase one. These findings are consistent with the view that the way in which an individual responds to annoyance and provocations is at least partly a function of learning (cf. Zillmann, 1979). In many cultures it seems that males and females are taught to react differently, in that annoyance-induced arousal in females dissipates as rapidly or more rapidly when they respond non-aggressively as when they respond aggressively, while such arousal in males dissipates more rapidly following aggressive responses than following non-aggressive responses. To the extent that aggression is a function of autonomic arousal (and there are circumstances under which it is not; see Zillmann, 1979), here is an acquired basis for the "typical" gender difference in aggression.

Archer and Lloyd (1985) point out that although laboratory-based research on adults suggests that the gender difference in aggression is small (albeit significant), a clearer picture emerges from studies of "real life" violence, such as violent crime, in which the perpetrator is almost always male. In the UK, for example, nearly ten times as many men as women are convicted for violence against other persons (*Social Trends*, 1984). It seems clear that willingness to commit violent acts against others is greater in men than in women.

The greater willingness of males to engage in aggressive and violent behavior has attracted some theorists to biologically based explanations that emphasize the role played by sex chromosomes in producing the gender difference. This has been investigated by studying the incidence of the XYY chromosomal pattern in populations of convicted violent criminals. Some reviews of this research (e.g., Kessler and Moos, 1970) have concluded that there is insufficient evidence to support the hypothesized relationship, while others (e.g., Nielsen and Christensen, 1974) conclude that the evidence points to such a relationship. In one of the most exhaustive studies of this issue, Witkin and colleagues (1976) examined XYYs drawn from the general population and compared them with XY controls from the same population. It was found that although XYYs had a higher mean rate of criminal convictions than XY controls, the frequency of crimes of violence was no higher among XYYs than among XYs. Thus the elevated crime rate of XYY males could not be accounted for in terms of aggression; rather, the data suggested that it might be related to low intelligence.

Another biological line of explanation comes from research on the relationship between sex hormones and aggression. There is evidence from studies of non-human species (reviewed by Maccoby and Jacklin, 1974) that prenatal exposure of females to androgens enhances aggressive behavior; that post-natal administration of testosterone to females has a similar effect; and that more aggressive males tend to have higher levels of androgens. Archer and Lloyd (1985) note that much of this research used as subjects rats or mice—species in which the male is known to be more aggressive than the female—rather than gerbils or hamsters, species in which the female is as aggressive as or more aggressive than the male. They also question the relevance of research on rodents to theories about the biological basis of human gender differences in aggression. Nevertheless, Archer (personal communication) suggests that the following comparative argument currently has the most credibility. In a wide range of animals, increased aggressiveness is exhibited by males at puberty or on entering the breeding season, and this increase is likely to be in anticipation of fighting other males over resources necessary to, or useful for, reproduction. Since this makes functional sense over a wide range of animals, it might be worth looking for a similar phenomenon in humans. It remains to be seen whether there is a similar androgen-related effect on aggressiveness in boys at the time of puberty.

In humans, there are two main sources of evidence concerning the relationship between sex hormones and aggression. First, Money and Ehrhardt (1972) have compared girls who for one of a variety of reasons were exposed to androgens prenatally with a "normal" group of girls. This research strategy has also been followed by Reinisch (1981). Second, researchers such as Olweus and colleagues (1980) and Persky, Smith, and Basu (1971) have examined the correlation between testosterone levels and various indices of aggression. Taken at face value, both lines of research tend to support the notion of a relationship between testosterone and aggression, but in each case problems of interpretation arise. In the research on girls exposed to androgens prenatally, it has been argued that the parents of these girls may have treated them differently than they would have treated "normal" girls; that at least some of the girls studied received relatively late surgical correction of genital abnormalities; and that much of the evidence concerning such girls is derived from questionnaires and interviews rather than direct observations of behavior. The research on correlations between testosterone and aggression is obviously vulnerable to the argument that higher levels of testosterone may have *resulted from,* rather than caused, aggressive behavior (cf. Mazur and Lamb, 1980). Such considerations weaken confidence in the conclusion that gender differences in human aggression are biologically caused.

The fact that it is very difficult, if not impossible, to produce evidence that unequivocally supports or refutes the hypothesis that human gender differences in aggression are biologically based is no accident. From birth onwards, boys and girls are treated differently (see Culp, Crook, and Housley, 1983; Smith and Lloyd, 1978; Rubin, Provenzano, and Luria, 1974) and the basis of this differential treatment is the sexual dimorphism that stems from chromosomal and hormonal differences between males and females. Biological and social influences are thus heavily confounded in the normal course of events, with the inevitable result that causal inference is seriously impeded. Even those who argue strongly that biological factors play a key role in determining gender differences in aggression recognize the impossibility of assigning causality in any straightforward manner:

> Women share with men the human capacity to heap all sorts of injury upon their fellows. And in almost every group that has been observed, there are some women who are fully as aggressive as the men. Furthermore, an individual's aggressive behavior is strengthened, weakened, redirected, or altered in form by his or her unique pattern of experiences. All we mean to argue is that there is a sex-linked differential readiness to respond in aggressive ways to the relevant experiences (Maccoby and Jacklin, 1974, p. 247).

Whatever the origin of the gender difference in human aggression, it is worth noting that it is at least partly inconsistent with the cultural stereotype that women are more emotional than men. The inconsistency is only partial in that aggression may or may not be accompanied by anger. Nevertheless, it is curious, as Shields (1987) has observed, that emotion in general is stereotypically associated with female-ness, whereas anger and aggression are stereotypically (and in the case of aggression, at least, to some extent veridically) associated with maleness.

Research on Recognition of Others' Emotions

Studies of the ability to recognize non-verbally communicated affect comprise a fifth area of research on gender differences in emotion. Here, of course, the focus is not on gender differences in the individual who experiences or expresses the emotion, but rather on gender differences in the ability of observers to infer emotion from observations of others' non-verbal behaviors. Are women more accurate than men in decoding the emotional meaning of others' non-verbal behaviors? As Hall (1978) has pointed out, two influential reviews of the literature answered this question in the negative. Maccoby and Jacklin (1974) reviewed several relevant studies and concluded that "neither sex has greater ability to judge the reactions or intentions of others in any generalized sense" (p. 214). Hoffman (1977) arrived at a similar conclu-sion: "when encountering someone in an emotional situation, both sexes are equally adept at assessing how that person feels" (p. 716).

However, Hall (1978, 1984) has conducted meta-analytic reviews of the research literature that point rather convincingly to a different conclusion. In her 1978 review of seventy-five studies published since 1923, Hall found a consistent and statistically reliable tendency for females to be better than males in decoding non-verbal expres-sions. Eighty-four percent of the sixty-one studies in which the direction of the gender difference was reported found a difference in favor of women. From the forty-six studies reporting appropriate statistics, Hall computed that the mean effect size (d; see Cohen, 1977) associated with this gender difference was 0.40 and highly significantly different from zero. Hall (1984) updated this analysis by reviewing 125 relevant studies. Of the ninety-three studies in which the direction of the gender difference was reported, 83 percent favored women, and the mean effect size based on the sixty-four studies reporting appropriate statistics was 0.43. If one considers only those studies in which a statistically significant gender difference was observed, thirty-three of these favored women and only two favored men.

Confidence in the robustness of this gender difference is enhanced by the fact that very similar results emerged from a meta-analysis of 133 studies that were conducted in the course of the development of the Profile of Nonverbal Sensitivity (PONS) test (Rosenthal et al., 1979). (Only eleven of these PONS studies were included in the 125 studies reviewed by Hall [1984], so the analysis of the PONS studies to all intents and purposes constitutes an independent meta-analysis.) Of the 133 PONS studies, 80 percent showed a gender difference favoring females, and the median effect size based on these studies was 0.41.

It is worth noting, however, that very few of the studies included in Hall's meta-analytic reviews were studies of the ability to decode *spontaneous* expression of emotion. As Hall (1978) noted, "the expressive stimuli in these studies were generated in a variety of ways. By far the most common method was to ask the sender or senders to express various emotions, while these expressions were photographed, audiotaped, and so forth" (p. 37). Furthermore, all the expressive stimuli included in the PONS test are of the "posed" variety. This tendency to use posed rather than spontaneous expressive stimuli obviously raises questions about the generalizability of the conclusion that females are better than males in decoding non-verbal cues. Clearly, expressive behavior in everyday social interaction is not always (indeed, is perhaps only rarely) of the posed kind. It is important, then, to consider the extent to which the female advantage in decoding posed non-verbal cues generalizes to spontaneous cues. Some studies of gender differences in decoding spontaneous facial expressions (e.g., Buck et al., 1972; Buck, Miller, and Caul, 1974; Wagner, MacDonald, and Manstead, 1986) have failed to find a significant female advantage. Furthermore, Fujita, Harper, and Wiens (1980) found that although females were significantly better than males at decoding posed expressions, there was no significant gender difference in decoding spontaneous expressions.

A further issue arising from the Hall (1978) meta-analysis relates to the developmental course of the gender difference in decoding non-verbal cues. Hall concluded that the female advantage in judging non-verbal cues does not vary as a function of age. However, Eisenberg and Lennon (1983) have taken issue with this aspect of Hall's analysis. They review the findings of fifteen studies on children's decoding of visual non-verbal cues and note that in only four out of twenty-one comparisons was there a significant or marginally significant difference favoring females, while one comparison revealed a significant male advantage. It is also worth noting that Eisenberg and Lennon review the findings of twenty-three studies of affective role taking, in which children are exposed to another's affective state by means of a story and/or pictures depicting a protagonist in an emotionally arousing situation; here only three studies reported that girls scored significantly higher than boys, while one reported a significant difference in favor of males. On balance, then, there is little evidence to support the view that there are gender differences in the ability of children to recognize emotion in others on the basis of either non-verbal information or pictures and/or stories depicting someone in an emotionally-arousing situation.

A slightly different, but not unrelated, qualification of the general tendency for women to be superior to men in decoding non-verbal cues emerges from research conducted by Rosenthal and DePaulo (1979). They suggested that the female non-verbal decoding advantage might diminish as the non-verbal cues being decoded become less intended and less controllable by the sender. They reasoned that women may be more non-verbally "accommodating" than men, such that although they are more accurate in decoding *intended* cues, they will tend not to "eavesdrop" on non-verbal cues that the sender is not monitoring carefully and may not intend to emit. A key theoretical notion here is that of "leakage," a term coined by Ekman and Friesen (1969) to refer to the way in which some non-verbal behaviors can reveal a person's true feelings even when that person tries to conceal those feelings. Certain non-verbal channels are deemed to be "leakier" in this respect than others. For example, the face is a channel of communication that is typically highly informative about the sender's affective state; however, it is also a channel that can be monitored and controlled by the sender if he or she so wishes. It has been argued that other non-verbal channels, such as the body or the tone of one's voice, will often be more informative about the sender's affect when he or she is attempting to conceal it because these channels are monitored less carefully by the sender and cannot be controlled as effectively as the face. There is a body of empirical evidence confirming that body cues and tone of voice cues are leakier than facial cues (see DePaulo, Zuckerman, and Rosenthal, 1980).

Rosenthal and DePaulo (1979) tested their suggestion about the relatively accommodating decoding style of women in a variety of ways. One of the most persuasive of these was a series of studies of the relationship between the size of the female decoding advantage and the leakiness of the channel being decoded. Here it was found that women's superiority over men systematically declined as the channels became leakier. This is consistent with the idea that women are more accommodating than men in their non-verbal decoding, refraining from accurately decoding the sender's less controllable cues (although there is no evidence that this style is *consciously* deployed). There is some evidence that those who are relatively good at decoding unintended non-verbal cues have less satisfactory personal relationships (Rosenthal et al., 1979), and this was interpreted as showing that "knowing too much" about another person's state may disrupt one's relationship with him or her. If that interpretation is correct, it may be that women's relatively greater advantage in decoding less leaky non-verbal cues is part of their known general tendency to be more interpersonally accommodating than men.

Further evidence to support Rosenthal and DePaulo's thesis comes from research reported by Blanck and colleagues (1981), who examined the developmental acquisition of females' tendency to be non-verbally accommodating. In a cross-sectional study, these investigators showed that with increasing age, females lost their relative advantage in decoding cues from leaky channels, and gained an advantage in decoding cues from less leaky channels. Evidence from a one-year longitudinal study of children aged between eleven and fourteen also showed a tendency for females to lose their relative advantage in decoding leaky cues as they grew older. These findings were interpreted as supporting a socialization hypothesis that females learn to become non-verbally accommodating, presumably because they find that there are social costs in being adept at decoding unintended non-verbal cues and social rewards in being adept at decoding intended non-verbal cues.

On the basis of the research reviewed in this section, it seems reasonable to conclude that adult females have a consistent (albeit fairly small) advantage in decoding others' non-verbal expressions of emotion when these are posed, expressed intentionally, or are expressed in relatively less leaky channels, such as the face; and that this advantage decreases or even disappears when the non-verbal cues are spontaneous, expressed unintentionally, or are expressed in relatively more leaky channels, such as the body or tone of voice. To what extent this pattern of findings can be explained by invoking the argument that females are more non-verbally "accommodating" than males is open to question. First, to subsume all the evidence, one would have to assume that the apparent lack of consistent female advantage in decoding spontaneous facial expressions reflects the fact that such expressions contain more leaky cues than posed expressions. Admittedly, senders are less likely to monitor or control their facial expressions under spontaneous sending conditions, so there are some grounds for thinking that the face—normally regarded as the least leaky non-verbal channel—will be leaky when the expressions are spontaneous, but further research is needed to confirm this assumption. A second reservation concerns the explanatory value of the construct of "accommodatingness." A cynic might argue that this does little more than provide a shorthand description of the observed tendency for the female decoding advantage to be more apparent in some channels than in others. Although the Blanck and colleagues (1981) research suggests that the tendency for females to be non-verbally accommodating is acquired through experience, exactly how this occurs and why it should happen to females but not to males are matters in need of clarification.

Conclusions

In summary, this review of gender differences in emotion indicates:

(1) that males tend to exhibit higher levels of psychophysiological activity than females, with the important exception of facial EMG where the reverse applies;

(2) that females tend to be more facially expressive than males when exposed to emotionally arousing stimuli;

(3) that gender differences in the subjective experience of emotion, while notoriously difficult to interpret, appear to be limited to a tendency for women to experience more dysphoric emotion—a tendency that is echoed by the fact that women are more likely than men to show unipolar depression;

(4) that there is relatively little evidence concerning gender differences in emotional behavior other than aggression, where the evidence is that males are more likely to act aggressively;

(5) that in the realm of non-verbal decoding skills there is a tendency for females to be superior to males.

Any conclusions drawn from this pattern of findings must be tempered by an appreciation of the size of the differences involved. The mean effect size found in the Eagly and Steffen (1986) meta-analysis of the research on adult aggression was 0.29, which corresponds to a point-biserial correlation of 0.14 between gender and aggression. In other words, around 2 percent of the variance in aggressive behavior observed in the studies reviewed by Eagly and Steffen can be accounted for in terms of the gender of the aggressor. The corresponding mean effect size reported by Hyde (1984) in her meta-analysis of the literature on children's aggression was 0.50, but even here just 5 percent of the variance is explained by gender. The mean effect sizes reported by Hall (1978, 1984) in her meta-analyses of the literature on non-verbal decoding skills were around 0.40, which indicates that roughly 4 percent of the variance in measures of such skills is accounted for by decoder gender. The largest gender difference observed in the present review is that associated with unipolar depression, where the mean female-to-male ratio is approximately 2:1 (Nolen-Hoeksema, 1987), but even in this case it is clear that gender is far from perfectly correlated with depression. The general point should be readily apparent: Gender differences in the realm of emotion are generally small even where they have been shown to be consistent across large numbers of studies; they invariably reflect differences between group means in sizeable populations and within these populations there will be substantial numbers of individual males and females whose scores on the measure in question do not reflect the overall mean difference between the groups.

With this in mind, we can turn to a consideration of the extent to which observed gender differences in emotion can be ascribed to biological factors. In the case of *psychophysiological indices,* there is no evidence that directly bears on this question. Although the Prokasy and Raskin (1973) observation that gender differences in electrodermal activity emerge after puberty may suggest that hormonal changes are involved, there is really insufficient evidence to be confident that these differences are confined to post-pubertal subjects and in any case such a pattern could equally well be explained by arguing that it reflects the differential socialization to which boys and girls are exposed. Gender differences in *facial expressiveness* are not reliably observed in infants or children, which casts some doubt on any explanation couched exclusively in genetic terms. On the other hand, there is evidence that male and female infants are exposed to differential socialization with regard to facial expressions, and that such exposure can influence subsequent expressiveness. Biological arguments have often been invoked to account for gender differences in *emotional experience,* and here the commonest type of argument relates to the emotional impact of hormonal fluctuations. However, neither direct assessment of hormonal levels nor double-blind evaluations of hormonal intervention therapy provide adequate support for this view. By contrast, there is some evidence implicating social and psychological factors, such as the conflicting role demands experienced by women (especially married women), the beliefs that women have about biological events such as menstruation and menopause, and the greater (relative to men) willingness of women to confront and express their experience of negative affect. A biological explanation of the observed gender difference in *aggression* commands more support. First, there is some evidence that exposure to androgens increases the likelihood of aggressive behaviour in many species of birds and mammals (and in some fish, amphibians and reptiles)—although the evidence relating to humans is equivocal; second, there is evidence that the gender difference is greater in children than in adults, which is broadly consistent with the view that biological regulation of aggression is overtaken by normative regulation in the course of socialization into adulthood (cf. Eagly and Steffen, 1986). As noted earlier, however, biological and social factors contributing to human aggression are often confounded, which makes assigning causality primarily to one factor or the other difficult, if at all possible. Finally, there is no evidence that the gender difference in *non-verbal decoding skill* is biologically based. Hall (1978) did tentatively suggest that women may be innately predisposed to be sensitive to non-verbal cues or to be rapid learners of their meaning, but as yet there is no evidence to support this argument. Indeed, there is little evidence in children of a gender difference in decoding non-verbal cues. There is also some evidence that the types of non-verbal cues decoded better by females than by males change between childhood and early adulthood, which suggests that non-verbal decoding skills are responsive to social reinforcement; one problem with a socialization explanation, however, is that there is no evidence that males and females receive differential reinforcement for non-verbal decoding.

In general, then, the small but consistent gender differences in emotion reviewed here are currently explained better in terms of social psychological processes than biological processes. However, the lack of programmatic research in many of the areas of research means that there is relatively little evidence that bears directly on issues of causation. Gender differences in emotion (as in other areas) are often not researched for their own sake; rather, they are observed in the course of research conducted chiefly for some other purpose. Serendipitous findings can help to establish whether or not there is a gender difference, but they are most unlikely to constitute evidence relevant to causation.

Given the small effect sizes associated with gender differences in emotion, it is worth reconsidering the value of research specifically focused on these differences. Rather than posing the question "How (or even why) do women and men differ in the realm of emotion?" it might be more productive to focus attention on individual differences in relationships among the different components of emotion, and only then consider whether these individual differences are related to gender. One of the abiding problems in emotion research is the fact that different indices of emotion (psychophysiological, self-report, facial expression, behavioral) are not related to each other in a straightforward manner; moreover, it seems that these relationships vary from individual to individual. For example, it has been argued by various investigators that the repression of overt expression of emotion may result in increased psychophysiological activity. Thus Fowles (1980) showed that behavioral inhibition in humans is associated with increased electrodermal activity; Waid and Orne (1982) have shown that highly "socialized" individuals, whose behavior is more inhibited, exhibit higher SC levels than do their less socialized counterparts; similarly, Hare and his colleagues (see Hare, 1978) have demonstrated that sociopaths, whose behavior is low in inhibition, tend to have lower SC levels than do normal individuals; investigators studying the relationship between spontaneous facial expressiveness and electrodermal activity have often reported negative between-subjects correlations (see Buck, 1979); and Pennebaker and Chew (1985) have demonstrated that the suppression of expressive behavior that is associated with deception is correlated with an increase in electrodermal activity. There are grounds, then, for thinking that inhibition of overt expression of emotion leads to increased psychophysiological activity, and that individuals who chronically suppress emotional expression will tend to be more autonomically reactive than those who do not. Here is a basis for an individual differences analysis of emotion that links two key components of emotion; indeed, other components could be integrated into this analysis if the notion of "expression" were broadened to include any behavioral index of emotion, including self-report. Thus individuals who are willing to express emotion by communicating it to others in the form of uninhibited facial expression, self-report or other behaviors should in theory be characterized by low psychophysiological activity relative to those who are inhibited in expression.

It is also worth noting that a number of researchers have argued that the suppression of emotion can play a causal role in somatic illness (see, e.g., Florin, Freudenberg, and Hollaender, 1985; Malatesta, Jonas, and Izard, 1987; Watson, Pettingale, and Greer, 1984; Wirsching et al., 1982). The fact that individual differences in style of emotional expression have been shown to be associated with illnesses as diverse as asthma, arthritis, eczema and cancer lends further importance to the search for an understanding of the relationships among variables such as temperament, socialization, expressiveness and physiological activity.

It should be apparent that the two broad types of expressive style outlined above appear to map on to what is currently known about gender differences in emotion. With the exception of situations likely to provoke aggression, males tend to be less expressive and more physiologically responsive than females. This is by no means a novel observation (see Buck, 1988) but it has not attracted systematic investigation — perhaps because of the relatively small effect sizes characteristic of gender differences in this area. Progress in understanding might be more rapid if researchers concentrated on specifying the developmental course of individual differences in expressive style, rather than emphasizing group differences between males and females. If, as current research suggests, differential socialization is a key factor underlying gender differences in emotion, these differences are liable to diminish as the socialization of males and females becomes more similar. It therefore seems prudent to develop and test an individual differences model of emotional expressivity without specific reference to gender. Having established the viability of such a model, researchers would be in a position to address the question of gender differences in emotion more coherently.

REFERENCES

Ainsworth, M. D. S., and Wittig, D. S. (1969). Attachment and exploratory behaviour of one year olds in a strange situation. In B. M. Foss (ed.), *Determinants of Infant Behaviour.* London: Methuen.

Archer, J. (1987). Beyond sex differences: comments on Borrill and Reid. *Bulletin of the British Psychological Society, 40,* 88–90.

Archer, J., and Lloyd, B. B. (1985). *Sex and Gender.* Cambridge: Cambridge University Press.

Aronfreed, J. M., Messick, S. A., and Diggory, J. C. (1953). Re-examining emotionality and perceptual defense. *Journal of Personality, 21,* 517–528.

Averill, J. R. (1982). *Anger and Aggression: An Essay on Emotion.* New York: Springer.

Bancroft, J., and Backstrom, T. (1985). Premenstrual syndrome. *Clinical Endocrinology, ,* 313–336.

Bart, P. B. (1971). Depression in middle-aged women. In V. Kornick and B. K. Moran (eds.), *Women in Sexist Society.* New York: Basic Books.

Belk, S. S., and Snell, W. E. (1986). Beliefs about women: components and correlates. *Personality and Social Psychology Bulletin, 12,* 403–413.

Berger, S. M. (1962). Conditioning through vicarious instigation. *Psychological Review, 69,* 450–466.

Best, D. L., Williams, J. E., Cloud, J. M., Davis, S. W., Robertson, L. S., Edwards, J. R., Giles, H., and Fowles, J. (1977). Development of sex-trait stereotypes among young children in the United States, England, and Ireland. *Child Development, 48,* 1375–1384.

Blanck, P. D., Rosenthal, R., Snodgrass, S. E., DePaulo, B. M., and Zuckerman, M. (1981). Sex differences in eavesdropping on nonverbal cues: developmental changes. *Journal of Personality and Social Psychology, 41,* 391–396.

Bloom, B. L. (1975) *Changing Patterns of Psychiatric Care.* New York: Human Sciences Press.

Bloom, B. L., Asher, S. J., and White, S. W. (1978). Marital disruption as a stressor: a review and analysis. *Psychological Bulletin, 85,* 867–894.

Bradburn, N. M. (1969). *The Structure of Psychological Well-Being.* Chicago: Aldine.

Broverman, I. K., Broverman, D. M., Clarkson, F. E., Rosenkrantz, P. S., and Vogel, S. R. (1970). Sex role stereotypes and clinical judgments of mental health. *Journal of Consulting and Clinical Psychology, 34,* 1–7.

Buck, R. (1972). *Relationships between dissonance-reducing behaviour and tension measures following aggression,* Paper presented at the meeting of the Midwestern Psychological Association, Cleveland, 1972.

Buck, R. (1975). Nonverbal communication of affect in children. *Journal of Personality and Social Psychology, 31,* 644–653.

Buck, R. (1977). Nonverbal communication of affect in preschool children: relationships with personality and skin conductance. *Journal of Personality and Social Psychology, 35,* 225–236.

Buck, R. (1979). Individual differences in nonverbal sending accuracy and electrodermal responding: The externalizing-internalizing dimension. In R. Rosenthal (ed.), *Skill in Nonverbal Communication: Individual Differences.* Cambridge, MA: Oelgeschlager, Gunn and Hain.

Buck, R. (1984). *The Communication of Emotion.* New York: Guilford.

Buck, R. (1988). *Human Motivation and Emotion.* (2nd edition). New York: John Wiley & Sons.

Buck, R., Baron, R., and Barrette, R. (1982). Temporal organization of spontaneous emotional expression: a segmentation analysis. *Journal of Personality and Social Psychology, 42,* 506–517.

Buck, R., Baron, R., Goodman, N., and Shapiro, B. (1980). Unitization of spontaneous nonverbal behavior in the study of emotion communication. *Journal of Personality and Social Psychology, 39,* 522–529.

Buck, R., Miller, R. E., and Caul, W. F. (1974). Sex, personality, and physiological variables in the communication of affect via facial expression. *Journal of Personality and Social Psychology, 30,* 587–596.

Buck, R., Savin, V. J., Miller, R. E., and Caul, W. F. (1972). Communication of affect through facial expressions in humans. *Journal of Personality and Social Psychology, 23,* 362–371.

Cantor, J. R., Zillmann, D., and Einsiedel, E. (1978). Female responses to provocation after exposure to aggressive and erotic films. *Communication Research, 5,* 395–412.

Chesler, P. (1971). Women as psychiatric and psychotherapeutic patients. *Journal of Marriage and the Family, 33,* 746–759.

Cochrane, R. (1983). *The Social Creation of Mental Illness.* London: Longman.

Cohen, J. (1977). *Statistical Power Analysis for the Behavioural Sciences.* New York: Academic Press.

Craig, K., and Lowery, H. J. (1969). Heart rate components of conditioned vicarious autonomic responses. *Journal of Personality and Social Psychology, 11,* 381–387.

Culp, R. E., Crook, A. S., and Housley, P. C. (1983). A comparison of observed and reported adult-infant interactions: Effects of perceived sex. *Sex Roles, 9,* 475–479.

Dalton, K. (1969). *The Menstrual Cycle.* New York: Pantheon Books.

Dalton, K. (1979). *Once a Month.* London: Fontana.

Deaux, K. (1984). From individuals to social categories: analysis of a decade's research on gender. *American Psychologist, 39,* 105–116.

DePaulo, B. M., Zuckerman, M., and Rosenthal, R. (1980). Detecting deception: modality effects. In L. Wheeler (ed.), *Review of Personality and Social Psychology, Vol. 1.* Beverly Hills, CA: Sage.

Eagly, A. H., and Carli, L. L. (1981). Sex of researchers and sex-typed communications as determinants of sex differences in influenceability: a meta-analysis of social influence studies. *Psychological Bulletin, 90,* 1–20.

Eagly, A. H., and Steffen, V. J. (1986). Gender and aggressive behavior: a meta-analytic review of the social psychological literature. *Psychological Bulletin, 100,* 309–330.

Eisenberg, N., and Lennon, R. (1983). Sex differences in empathy and related capacities. *Psychological Bulletin, 94,* 100–131.

Ekman, P., and Friesen, W. V. (1969). Nonverbal leakage and clues to deception. *Psychiatry, 32,* 88–105.

Epstein, S. (1980). The stability of behavior: II. Implications for psychological research. *American Psychologist, 35,* 790–807.

Field, T. (1982). Individual differences in the expressivity of neonates and young infants. In R. S. Feldman (ed.), *Development of Nonverbal Behavior in Children.* New York: Springer.

Florin, I., Freudenberg, G., and Hollaender, J. (1985). Facial expressions of emotion and physiologic reactions in children with bronchial asthma. *Psychosomatic Medicine, 47,* 382–393.

Fowles, D. C. (1980). The three arousal model: implications of Gray's two-factor theory for heart rate, electrodermal activity, and psychopathy. *Psychophysiology, 17,* 87–104.

Frodi, A., Macauley, J., and Thome, P. R. (1977) Are women always less aggressive than men? A review of the experimental literature. *Psychological Bulletin, 84,* 634–660.

Fujita, B. N., Harper, R. G., and Wiens, A. N. (1980). Encoding-decoding of nonverbal emotional messages: Sex differences in spontaneous and enacted expressions. *Journal of Nonverbal Behaviour, 4,* 131–145.

Gale, M. A., and Baker, S. (1981). In vivo or in vitro? Some effects of laboratory environments, with particular reference to the psychophysiology experiment. In M. J. Christie and P. G. Mellett (eds.), *Approaches to Psychosomatics.* Chichester: Wiley.

Gallagher, D., and Shuntich, R. J. (1981). Encoding and decoding of nonverbal behavior through facial expressions. *Journal of Research in Personality, 15,* 241–252.

Geen, R. (1990). *Human Aggression.* Milton Keynes: Open University Press.

Glass, G. (1976). Primary, secondary and meta-analysis of research. *Educational Research, 5,* 3–8.

Goodenough, F. L. (1931). *Anger in Young Children.* Minneapolis: University of Minnesota Press.

Gove, W. R. (1972). Sex roles, marital roles, and mental illness. *Social Forces, 51,* 34–44.

Gove, W. R. (1978). Sex differences in mental illness among adult men and women: an evaluation of four questions raised regarding the evidence on the higher rates of women. *Social Science and Medicine, 12,* 187–198.

Gove, W. R. (1979). Sex, marital status, and psychiatric treatment: A research note. *Social Forces, 58,* 89–93.

Gove, W. R. (1980). Mental illness and psychiatric treatment among women. *Psychology of Women Quarterly, 4,* 345–362.

Gove, W. R., and Tudor, J. F. (1973). Adult sex roles and mental illness. *American Journal of Sociology, 78,* 812–835.

Graham, L., Cohen, S., and Shmavonian, G. (1966). Sex differences in autonomic responses during instrumental conditioning. *Psychosomatic Medicine, 28,* 264–271.

Greene, J. G. (1981). Types of life-events in relation to symptoms at the climacterium. *Bulletin of the British Psychological Society, 34,* 187.

Gunnar, M. R. (1980). Control, warning signals, and distress in infancy. *Child Development, 51,* 262–265.

Guttentag, M., Salasin, S., and Belle, D. (eds.) (1980). *The Mental Health of Women.* New York: Academic Press.

Hall, J. A. (1978). Gender effects in decoding nonverbal cues. *Psychological Bulletin, 85,* 845–857.

Hall, J. A. (1984). *Nonverbal Sex Differences: Communication Accuracy and Expressive Style.* Baltimore, MD: Johns Hopkins University Press.

Hamburg, D. A., and Lunde, D. T. (1966). Sex hormones in the development of sex differences in human behavior. In E. E. Maccoby (ed.), *The Development of Sex Differences.* Stanford: Stanford University Press.

Hammen, C. L., and Peters, S. D. (1978). Interpersonal consequences of depression: responses to men and women enacting a depressed role. *Journal of Abnormal Psychology, 87,* 323–332.

Harding, S. D. (1982). Psychological well-being in Great Britain: an evaluation of the Bradburn affect balance scale. *Personality and Individual Differences, 3,* 167–175.

Hare, R. D. (1978). Electrodermal and cardiovascular correlates of psychopathy. In R. D. Hare and D. Schalling (eds.), *Psychopathic Behavior: Approaches to Research.* New York: John Wiley & Sons.

Haviland, J. H., and Malatesta, C. Z. (1981). The development of sex differences in nonverbal signals: fallacies, facts, and fantasies. In C. Mayo and N. Henley (eds.), *Gender and Nonverbal Behavior.* New York: Springer.

Henshall, C., and McGuire, J. (1986). Gender development. In M. Richards and P. Light (eds), *Children of Social Worlds.* Cambridge: Polity Press.

Hill, K. T., and Sarason, S. B. (1966). The relation of test anxiety and defensiveness to test and school performance over the elementary-school years. *Monographs of the Society for Research in Child Development, 31*(2), 1–76.

Hoffman, M. L. (1977). Sex differences in empathy and related behaviors. *Psychological Bulletin, 84,* 712–722.

Hokanson, J. E. (1970). Psychophysiological evaluation of the catharsis hypothesis. In E. I. Megargee and J. E. Hokanson (eds.), *The Dynamics of Aggression: Individual, Group, and International Analyses.* New York: Harper and Row.

Hokanson, J. E., Willers, K. R., and Koropsak, E. (1968). The modification of autonomic responses during aggressive interchange. *Journal of Personality, 36,* 386–404.

Hyde, J. S. (1984). How large are gender differences in aggression? A developmental meta-analysis. *Developmental Psychology, 20,* 722–736.

Jahnke, J. C., Crannell, C. W., and Morrissette, J. O. (1974). Sex differences and the MAS. *Educational and Psychological Measurement, 24,* 309–312.

Katkin, E. S., Blascovich, J., and Goldband, S. (1981). Empirical assessment of visceral self-perception: individual and sex differences in the acquisition of heartbeat discrimination. *Journal of Personality and Social Psychology, 40,* 1095–1101.

Kessler, R. C., Price, B. H., and Wortman, C. B. (1985). Social factors in psychopathology: stress, social support, and coping processes. *Annual Review of Psychology, 36,* 531–572.

Kessler, S., and Moos, R. H. (1970). The XYY karotype and criminality: A review. *Journal of Psychiatric Research, 7,* 153–170.

Koenigsberg, M. R., Katkin, E. S., and Blascovich, J. (1981). The effects of pretraining instructional set on the acquisition and maintenance of heartbeat detection in males and females. *Psychophysiology, 18,* 196–197.

Kornbrott, D. (1986). *Women who excel in maths and science,* Paper presented at Conference on Women and Science and Technology, Lancashire Polytechnic, September, 1986.

Kuhn, D., Nash, S. C., and Bruchan, L. (1978). Sex role concept of two- and three-year-olds. *Child Development, 49,* 445–451.

Lang, P. J. (1984). Cognition in emotion: concept and action. In C. E. Izard, J. Kagan and R. B. Zajone (eds.), *Emotions, Cognition, and Behavior.* New York: Cambridge University Press.

Maccoby, E. E., and Feldman, S. S. (1972). Mother–infant attachment and stranger-reactions in the third year of life. *Monographs of the Society for Research in Child Development, 37*(1), 1–86.

Maccoby, E. E., and Jacklin, C. N. (1974). *The Psychology of Sex Differences.* Stanford, CA: Stanford University Press.

Maccoby, E. E., and Jacklin, C. N. (1980). Sex differences in aggression: a rejoinder and reprise. *Child Development, 51,* 964–980.

Malatesta, C. Z., Grigoryev, P., Lamb, C., Albin, M., and Culver C. (1986). Emotion socialization and expressive development in preterm and full-term infants. *Child Development, 57,* 316–330.

Malatesta, C. Z., and Haviland, J. M. (1982). Learning display rules: the socialization of emotion expression in infancy. *Child Development, 53,* 991–1003.

Malatesta, C. Z., Jonas, R., and Izard, C. E. (1987). The relation between low facial expressivity during emotional arousal and somatic symptoms. *British Journal of Medical Psychology, 60,* 169–180.

Malatesta, C. Z., and Lamb, C. (1987). *Emotion socialization during the second year,* Paper presented at the Annual Meeting of the American Psychological Association, New York, August, 1987.

Martin, J. A. (1981). A longitudinal study of the consequences of early mother–infant interaction: a micro-analytic approach. *Monographs of the Society for Research in Child Development, 46*(3), 1–58.

Mazur, A., and Lamb, T. A. (1980). Testosterone, status, and mood in human males. *Hormones and Behavior, 14,* 236–246.

Miles, A. (1987). *The Mentally Ill in Contemporary Society.* Oxford: Blackwell.

Money, J., and Ehrhardt, A. A. (1972). *Man and Woman, Boy and Girl.* Baltimore, MD: Johns Hopkins University Press.

Newson, J., and Newson, E. (1986). Family and sex roles in middle childhood. In D. J. Hargreaves and A. M. Colley (eds.), *The Psychology of Sex Roles.* London: Harper and Row.

Nicosia, G. J., Hyman, D., Karlin, R. A., Epstein, Y. M., and Aiello, J. R. (1979). Effects of bodily contact on reactions to crowding. *Journal of Applied Social Psychology, 9,* 508–523.

Nielsen, J., and Christensen, A. L. (1974). Thirty-five males with double Y chromosome. *Journal of Psychological Medicine, 4,* 38–47.

Nolen-Hoeksema, S. (1987). Sex differences in unipolar depression: evidence and theory. *Psychological Bulletin, 101,* 259–282.

Noller, P. (1982). Couple communication and marital satisfaction. *Australian Journal of Sex, Marriage and Family, 3,* 69–75.

Olweus, D., Mattsson, A., Schallin, D., and Low, H. (1980). Testosterone, aggression, physical and personality dimensions in normal adolescent males. *Psychosomatic Medicine, 42,* 253–269.

Parlee, M. B. (1988). Menstrual cycle changes in moods and emotions: causal and interpretive processes in the construction of emotions. In H. L. Wagner (ed.), *Social Psychophysiology and Emotion: Theory and Clinical Applications.* Chichester: Wiley.

Pennebaker, J. W., and Chew, C. H. (1985). Behavioral inhibition and electrodermal activity during deception. *Journal of Personality and Social Psychology, 49,* 1427–1433.

Persky, H., Smith, K. D., and Basu, G. K. (1971). Relation of psychologic measures of aggression and hostility to testosterone production in man. *Psychosomatic Medicine, 33,* 265–277.

Phillips, D. L., and Segal, B. E. (1969). Sexual status and psychiatric symptoms. *American Sociological Review, 34,* 58–72.

Prokasy, W., and Raskin, D. (1973). *Electrodermal Activity in Psychological Research.* New York: Academic Press.

Reinisch, J. M. (1981). Prenatal exposure to synthetic progestins increases potential for aggression in humans. *Science, 211,* 1171–1173.

Rosenthal, R. (1984). *Meta-analytic Procedures for Social Research.* Beverly Hills, CA: Sage.

Rosenthal, R., and DePaulo, B. M. (1979). Sex differences in eavesdropping on non-verbal cues. *Journal of Personality and Social Psychology, 37,* 273–285.

Rosenthal, R., Hall, J. A., DiMatteo, M. R., Rogers, P. L., and Archer, D. (1979). *Sensitivity to Nonverbal Communication: The PONS Test.* Baltimore, MD: Johns Hopkins University Press.

Rubin, J. Z., Provenzano, F. J., and Luria, Z. (1974). The eye of the beholder: parents' views on the sex of newborns. *American Journal of Orthopsychiatry, 44,* 512–519.

Ruble, D. N., and Brooks-Gunn, J. (1979). Menstrual symptoms: a social cognition analysis. *Journal of Behavioral Medicine, 2,* 171–194.

Rumenik, D. K., Capasso, D. R., and Hendrick, C. (1977). Experimenter sex effects in behavioral research. *Psychological Bulletin, 84,* 852–877.

Sapolsky, B. S., Stocking, S. H., and Zillmann, D. (1977). Immediate vs. delayed retaliation in male and female adults. *Psychological Reports, 40,* 197–198.

Scherer, K. R., Wallbott, H., and Summerfield, A. B. (1986). *Experiencing Emotion: A Cross-Cultural Study.* Cambridge: Cambridge University Press.

Schwartz, G. E., Ahern, G. L., and Brown, S. L. (1979). Lateralized facial muscle response to positive versus negative emotional stimuli. *Psychophysiology, 16,* 561–571.

Schwartz, G. E., Brown, S. L., and Ahern, G. L. (1980). Facial muscle patterning and subjective experience during affective imagery: sex differences. *Psychophysiology, 17,* 75–82.

Schwartz, G. E., Fair, P. L., Mandel, M. R., Salt, P., Mieske, M., and Klerman, G. L. (1978). Facial electromyography in the assessment of improvement in depression. *Psychosomatic Medicine, 40,* 355–360.

Schwartz, G. E., Fair, P. L., Salt, P., Mandel, M. R., and Klerman, G. L. (1976a). Facial expression and imagery in depression: An electromyographic study. *Psychosomatic Medicine, 38,* 337–347.

Schwartz, G. E., Fair, P. L., Salt, P., Mandel, M. R., and Klerman, G. L. (1976b). Facial muscle patterning to affective imagery in depressed and non-depressed subjects. *Science, 192,* 489–491.

Shields, S. A. (1987). Women, men and the dilemma of emotion. In P. Shaver and C. Hendrick (eds.), *Sex and Gender*. Beverly Hills, CA: Sage.

Shmavonian, B., Yarmat, A., and Cohen, S. (1965). Relations between the autonomic nervous system and central nervous system in age differences in behavior. In A. T. Welford, and J. E. Birren (eds.), *Behavior, Aging, and the Nervous System*. Springfield, IL: Charles C. Thomas.

Smith, C., and Lloyd, B. B. (1978). Maternal behavior and perceived sex of infant. *Child Development, 49*, 1263–1265.

Smith, P. K., and Green, M. (1975). Aggressive behavior in English nurseries and play groups: sex differences and response of adults. *Child Development, 46*, 211–214.

Social Trends (1984). London: HMSO.

Spiegler, M. D., and Liebert, R. M. (1970). Some correlates of self-reported fear. *Psychological Reports, 26*, 691–695.

Stoney, C. M., Davis, M. C., and Matthews, K. A. (1987). Sex differences in physiological response to stress and in coronary heart disease: a causal link? *Psychophysiology, 24*, 127–131.

Stroebe, M. S., and Stroebe, W. (1983). Who suffers more? Sex differences in health risks of the widowed. *Psychological Bulletin, 93*, 279–301.

Wagner, H. L., MacDonald, C. J., and Manstead, A. S. R. (1986). Communication of individual emotions by spontaneous facial expressions. *Journal of Personality and Social Psychology, 50*, 737–743.

Waid, W. W., and Orne, M. T. (1982). Reduced electrodermal response to conflict, failure to inhibit dominant behaviors, and delinquent processes. *Journal of Personality and Social Psychology, 43*, 769–774.

Warr, P. B., and Payne, R. (1982). Experiences of strain and pleasure among British adults. *Social Science and Medicine, 16*, 1691–1697.

Watson, M., Pettingale, K. W., and Greer, S. (1984). Emotional control and autonomic arousal in breast cancer patients. *Journal of Psychosomatic Research, 28*, 467–474.

Weissman, M. M. (1979). The myth of involutional melancholia. *Journal of the American Medical Association, 242*, 742–744.

Weissman, M. M., and Klermann, G. L. (1977). Sex differences in the epidemiology of depression. *Archives of General Psychiatry, 34*, 89–111.

Weldburn, V. (1980). *Postnatal Depression*. London: Fontana.

Wilson, G. D. (1967). Social desirability and sex differences in expressed fear. *Behavior Research and Therapy, 5*, 136–137.

Wirsching, M., Stierlin, H., Hoffman, F., Weber, G., and Wirsching, B. (1982). Psychological identification of breast cancer patients before biopsy. *Journal of Psychosomatic Research, 26*, 1–10.

Witkin, H. A., Mednick, S. A., Schulsinger, F., Bakkestrom, E., Christiansen, K. O., Goodenough, D. R., Hirschhorn, K., Lundsteen, C., Owen, D. R., Philip, J., Rubin, D. B., and Stocking, M. (1976). Criminality in XYY and XXY men. *Science, 193*, 547–555.

Yarczower, M., and Daruns, L. (1982). Social inhibition of spontaneous facial expressions in children. *Journal of Personality and Social Psychology, 43*, 831–837.

Zillmann, D. (1979). *Hostility and Aggression*. Hillsdale, NJ: Erlbaum.

Chapter Fourteen

Raising Darwin's Consciousness
Females and Evolutionary Theory

Sarah Blaffer Hrdy

When people first began seriously to study the behavior of monkeys in their natural habitats, attention of the researchers gravitated to the behavior of adult males. Among most of the group-dwelling terrestrial monkeys (those easiest to study), there were virtually always fewer adult males than females. These males were much larger than females, and their behavior was more boisterous. Male behaviors were more conspicuous, and males were easier to recognize as individuals. But there was more to this research than just a male-oriented focus, for the observational and methodological biases came linked to biases of much older standing—dating back to Darwin, to the nineteenth century generally, and to even older antecedents. Among other things, researchers were enthralled with a powerful theory: Darwin's theory of sexual selection. According to this theory, males actively compete for access to females. In the course of this competition, the stronger male prevails, dooming his rival to relatively fewer reproductive opportunities than the winner will enjoy. Competition between males then led to selection of bigger and more muscular males, so that in the famous example of the Hamadryas baboons, males evolved to be nearly twice as large as females belonging to the same species. Male hamadryas baboons are not only bigger, but far flashier in appearance, endowed with an intimidating mane of hair and a face the color of raw beef steak—as different from the mousey grey-brown females as if they belonged to two different species. Male–male competition was half of Darwin's theory of sexual selection; the other half had to do with female choice, the notion that females by nature will seek to select the single best male as a breeding partner from out of a panoply of competing suitors. As a matter of fact, this part of the theory does not apply very well to monkeys, and particularly not the hamadryas baboon due to certain peculiarities of its breeding system. A female hamadryas baboon is adopted while still a juvenile by an adult male on the make. The male will herd her about for the rest of her life, nipping her on the neck to assure her proximity. But forget those details for a moment, and focus on the central

Sarah Blaffer Hrdy, "Raising Darwin's Consciousness: Females and Evolutionary Theory." In Robert Bellig & George Stevens (Eds.), *The Evolution of Sex: Nobel Conference XXIII*, pp. 161–171. © 1988 by Gustavus Adolphus College. Reprinted by permission of Harper Collins Publishers, Inc.

assumption, that males play the more active role. For the male hamadryas baboon, with his lion's mane and his muscular and domineering disposition, provides the perfect model of a modern sexually selected male. It also happens, however, that the hamadryas case is virtually unique among primates, the only case out of some 175 extant species of primates where we can actually find any sort of clear-cut dichotomy between competitive males and passive females! Instead of the patriarchal hamadryas case, we could just as easily have focused on any of a number of lemur species, species in which females rather routinely dominate males. We could have decided to make an example of the shy and nocturnal owl monkey *(Aotus trivirgatus)*, where males and females cooperate in child care with the male playing the major role in carrying and protecting the infant, or we could have focused on the gentle South American monkeys known as "muriqui" *(Brachyteles arachnoides)*, who specialize in *avoiding* aggressive interactions, or any of a host of other primate species in which we now know that females play an active role in social organization. But the history of primatology did not unfold that way. Instead, until very recently, a hamadryas-like stereotype was taken as the primate norm.

In retrospect it is remarkable that we ever could have believed that selection primarily operated on only one sex, and yet that is precisely the assumption that until recently did underlie many conclusions about primate breeding systems. Consider the treatment of nonhuman primates in a recent textbook in sociobiology. The author describes how male monkeys, such as rhesus macaques, compete among themselves for access to females so that only 20 percent of males are responsible for 80 percent of the breeding, while *all* the females that come into estrus tend to be impregnated. "These data make it clear that only males are directly involved in differential selection among rhesus [monkeys] and probably all the terrestrial and semiterrestiral primates."[1]

A cluster of biases, then—methodological, ideological, and theoretical—contributed to an extraordinary phenomenon: an intellection formulation of primate social organization that lasted for over twenty years and that—based on what we know today—was totally unsupportable. This of course is not the first time that social preconceptions have caused scientists to seriously misinterpret nature, but it is one of the more clear-cut and better documented examples.

To continue this story, but still keep it simple, I will stick to baboons. Let us shift then from the patriarchal hamadryas to a closely related cluster of species known as savanna baboons, which instead of living in harems lives on African savannas in large, multimale troops. These savanna baboons were the first monkeys to be extensively studied, and they were depicted as having a social structure that in many respects was the mirror image of the kind of organization then found in American universities and corporate structures. There was a central male hierarchy in which competing adult males formed alliances with other males in order to maintain high status. Female baboons were viewed as pawns in this game, and sexual access to females was the reward for males successful in maintaining high rank. Whereas males were thought to have almost nothing to do with infants, females were thought to be so absorbed in child care that they had almost no impact on the social structure of the group. What was missing, of course, was any empirical description of the full range of activities of either sex. Lionel Tiger summed up the prevailing opinion: "Primate females seem to be biologically unprogrammed to dominate political systems, and the whole weight of the relevant primates' breeding history militates against female participation in what we call 'primate public life.' " Yet once we begin to examine the actual evidence, few statements could have been further from the truth for any species, except just possibly the hamadryas baboon.

Let's take a closer look, then, at the species which has become anthropology's "type case" for a male-dominated social order. What happened when we identified females as individuals and monitored their behavior over time? The picture changed radically.

The main difference between savanna baboon males and females is not that males are active and females passive, but the fact that females stay in the troop of their birth while males are transients. A male moves every four or five years, and within the troop, his status is in perpetual flux. Typically, a young male leaves his natal troop about the time he matures, and attempts to enter another through a gradual process of insinuating himself into the group. Sometimes a male does this by first forming a friendship with a troop female, who serves as a sponsor for his membership in the group. Male-female friendships are not so much based on dominance as on mutual interactions, such as grooming, in which either sex may take the initiative. That is, not all males are fighting their way into the troop by allying with and defeating other males. Indeed Barbara Smuts, who describes male–female friendships in detail in her recent book *Sex and Friendship Among Baboons*, tells a wonderful anecdote about a female who enters a neighboring troop to lure back with her a particular male to which she seems to have taken a fancy, initiating his entry into her own troop.

Earlier studies that focused on male–male competition for breeding access to females gave us a very skewed picture indeed. Invariably, researchers focused their attention on things like counting the number of copulations for the males so that male–female interactions were usually only recorded when the female was in heat. Instead, Smuts focused on females in all stages of their reproductive cycle. Her analyses revealed that females select and preferentially stay near one or two of the eighteen or so adult males in the troop, and these relationships remain constant through pregnancy and lactation.

Not only are male–female relationships much more reciprocal and complex than previously realized, but there is also much more involvement by males with infants. Once a female baboon gives birth, one or several of her male friends provide various babysitting services for the mother. In terms of actual time spent with the infants, it's rather like the human case: not much. That is, if you are standing on the savanna watching a troop of baboons, you'll see about one male–infant interaction once every nineteen hours. However, the protection offered just by the proximity of these males may be critical for infant survival—particularly for discouraging attacks on the infant either by incoming males who are unfamiliar with the infant's mother, or harassment of the infant and mother by females from competing lineages in the troop.

Once we understand the importance of male involvement with infants, the internal politics of a baboon troop take on new dimensions. Female baboons, for example, actively engage in forging for themselves a network of alliance with different males. In short, there is much more going on than simply males competing with other males. Males are maneuvering for access to females, while females themselves are busily building alliances with males. Both sexes of course are also preoccupied with survival, keeping safe, staying fed, and this leads to another very important set of female activities. Females cooperate with their relatives, their mothers, and grand-mothers, in order to compete with females in other matrilines belonging to their same troop. Competition is for such things as resources and what might be called "living space" or freedom from harassment. The resulting structure from these various female preoccupations turns out to be remarkably persistent and stable.

When two females of different social status approach each other (a dominant female approaches a subordinate or vice versa), you are likely to witness a remarkable performance. The subordinate female greets a dominant female by presenting to her; giving an exaggerated "fear grin," lifting her tail, and jerking a foot back. Even more remarkable is the fact that in an episode like this we can be fairly certain that the main reason this female is dominant is because her mother was.

Not only does there exist a stable hierarchy among females, but it is a very conservative hierarchy, predictable from one year to the next and even one generation to the next; so if baboon social structure is to be understood, relations must be understood.

To make a long story short, then, we completely failed to recognize first the many very active roles females were assuming in troop affairs, and second the many other things—like caring for offspring—that males do.

The collection of data on female behavior from a wide range of species (such as tamarins, lemurs, and woolly spider monkeys) has not only caused us to revise our notion of female nature—to encompass creatures that *are* nurturing—but that are also aggressive, competitive, cooperative, and a wide range of other things. But such data have also forced us to reinterpret the behavior of males.

We have been forced to expand our theoretical constructs to incorporate the full range of selective pressures on both sexes. The assumptions underlying such revised theory are very different from the earlier formulations. For example, by shifting our focus from the production of infants to the survival of infants, we are forced to take account of a whole range of male and female activities that have drastic repercussions on the survival of offspring.

So much for raising of Darwinian consciences. What about the scientific endeavor generally? I have documented just one example of how, for over two decades, researchers in my own field completely misconstrued primate breeding systems because of such bias. The real question is, just how damaging is this?

It seems to me that documenting these biases and starting to look at the world from a female point of view has been terribly valuable in revising history, literature, and even primatology; but it has also contributed to a growing cynicism about science generally, and especially social science. By pointing out the pervasiveness of preconceptions and biases in virtually all scientific and scholarly endeavors, feminist scholars have contributed to a general and quite fashionable challenge currently hurled at science. Given that all scientists are embedded in their cultures and that all research is inevitably informed by cultural bias, the question they ask is: "Can we really *know* anything?"

Clearly, it is unacceptable to permit old biases, once discovered, to persist. It is undeniable that most fields, including history, psychology, and biology, have been male-centered; but the noteworthy and encouraging thing is how little resistance there has been to revisionist enterprises once begun. On the contrary, in fields like sociobiology, there has been something more like a small stampede to study female reproductive strategies so that there exists a real danger that we will now merely substitute a new set of biases for the old ones. According to one emerging revisionist dogma, for example, it is now finally acceptable to say that men and women are different, provided we also specify that women are "cooperative, nurturing, and supportive," not to mention equipped with unique moral sensibilities. Entering the fray from a different perspective, various religious sects would also like to benefit from the current disarray to inject their agendas. Yet there can be no advantage for any scholarly enterprise to specify what can or cannot be found.

In spite of its limitations, scientific inquiry as currently practiced, with all of the drawbacks—including reductionist models, underlying assumptions that have been influenced by cultural context, domination of disciplines by males, and so forth, all the things that gave us several generations of male-biased primatology—science with all these drawbacks is still better than such unabashedly ideological programs that have become advocated in certain religious as well as in some feminist research programs (such as those advocating "conscious partiality"—the notion that since we can't help being biased, let's be biased in an ideologically correct way).

Needless to say, I reject such programs. I accept that the best we can do is to try to remain intellectually independent, to invite multiple inquiries, and to encourage restudies and challenges to current theories. Essentially, then, this is science as currently practiced—inefficient, replete with false starts in need of constant revision—but still better than any of the alternative programs being advocated.

NOTE

1. D. Freedman, *Human Sociobiology* (New York: Free Press, 1979), 33.

Panel Discussion

Maynard Smith: There is a temptation for males to make the comment that, "Well, Darwin was a Victorian and with that background was bound to be somewhat of a male chauvinist, but I'm alright, you know, I'm a decent chap." The following rather sad anecdote about my own scientific career occurred to me. It's trivial, but it's nevertheless quite revealing.

When I was just a beginning scientist, I worked with the fruit fly *Drosophila* which I loved greatly. I was interested in the causes of aging. Why do animals die of old age? One of the things I discovered was that the actual process of laying eggs causes female fruit flies to die sooner than anything else you do to them, even giving them large doses of radiation that stop them from laying eggs. I published this observation and got a lot of credit for it. At the time it never occurred to me to ask if mating could have an effect, good or bad, on the longevity of males. Twenty years later, a young scientist demonstrated that if you allow a male to mate twice a day, he dies young. I don't mean to give you more than one guess as to the sex of the scientist that made this discovery. It was my friend Linda Partridge.

I could have done that experiment painlessly. I didn't say to myself that it would be terrible to discover such a thing and that "I won't do it." So those of us who are absolutely sure that we have no prejudices are almost certainly wrong. It may well be that the prejudices we have, we have because we're men and most scientists are men. They are not, of course, the only prejudices we have, because our color or race can be just as important in how we see the world.

However, the thing that I agree most passionately with was what Dr. Hrdy said towards the end of her lecture. It was this: "Okay, so we are prejudiced. We can try not to be, but we are not going to succeed. We can never be free of our preconceptions." I think there is an obvious way in which we can try to avoid our prejudices and that is to recognize that science is not an activity carried out by a single individual human being. It is a collective activity.

It has been nice to be at this conference with two women who can tell the rest of us to shut up occasionally, and not that it has any effect on me, but it has an effect on others. I think that if we can ensure a sufficiently mixed group of people doing science, we can't get rid of all our prejudices, but at least we will reduce them.

Philip J. Hefner: Dr. Hrdy deals primarily with biases in how data are collected and analyzed. I have heard a lot about the differences between male and female thinking in science, and I wonder if you feel this has an eroding effect on the credibility of science. You know, "Science is just another form of mythology, not much different from theology." "Why should we listen to the scientists?" And so forth.

Hrdy: I think that there has been an erosion in confidence in science. This notion that if all knowledge is relative and everybody is biased, then we can't know anything. The very extreme fringe of the creationist movement takes advantage of those fears to say, "Look, they don't know things any better than we do." I think we are recognizing our fallibility, something the church has been telling us for years.

This objectivity is going to prove to be elusive, and the best we can do is to include in science not just people of both sexes, but also minorities, people who have been oppressed, who know what it feels like to be oppressed, and so forth. Let's say you're studying primate behavior and you are interested in dominance hierarchies. Just how critical is to have someone out there who can identify with the organisms they are studying? For example, the Japanese spend inordinate numbers of pages writing about the phenomena of social ostracism among monkeys. To my knowledge, few American or British primatologists have ever even concerned themselves with the topic of ostracism.

Questions for Further Discussion

1. The scientists have a vested interest in trying to appear unbiased. Have they overstated the self-corecting mechanisms "inherent" in the scientific process?
2. Are there some types of research questions that should not be asked because of the impact their apparent solutions would have on human society?
3. Can you imagine situations where a male researcher would ask different kinds of questions than a female investigator, when the research topic had nothing to do with sex?

B. The Embodied Self

This section focuses both on individuals' reactions to their bodies in particular contexts and life stages, and on societal and cultural constructions of female and male biology and maturation, as they affect individuals' constructions of themselves. Once again, the authors focus not on whether there are differences between males and females, but on the range of experiences among men and women, and the ways in which those actual experiences might conflict with how we are "supposed to" experience ourselves.

One of the interesting, and often forgotten, points that Freud was trying to make when he coined the phrase "anatomy is destiny" is that the *psychological* consequences of having a penis or a clitoris stemmed from what to Freud was the "obviously" greater value and pleasure to be derived from having a penis, its more salient vulnerability, and the pain and devaluation associated with its loss or potential loss. In other words, he believed that the psychological consequences of anatomical distinctions between the sexes were a function of the way we appraise and react to those distinctions. Freud did not hypothesize that there was a direct and uninterrupted causal pathway by which male or female physiology lead to the development of a psychologically masculine or feminine individual. For Freud, "destiny," or the inevitability of psychosexual development, was a function of his conviction that no reasonable person could come up with compelling alternative interpretations of having versus not having a penis. As subsequent thinkers have demonstrated, of course, it is certainly possible to come up with alternative reactions to those differences—as indeed, little girls do all the time (e.g., "Mommy, isn't it a blessing he doesn't have it on his face?" [Tavris & Offir, 1977, p. 155]). Thus, the content of Freud's specific interpretation teaches us about one particular reaction to differences between women's and men's bodies, rather than about a "necessary" or inevitable reaction. The vehemence, both of his insistence on this interpretation, and others' reactions to it, may also teach us something—namely, that although no particular reaction to male and female embodiment is necessarily universal, anatomical and physiological differences between men and women are culturally salient, and thus provide grist for individuals and societies to construct meaning.

The authors in this section consider very different reactions to the fact of our embodiment and its implications for gender and selfhood. Embodiment refers to the idea that as individuals we are "in" bodies—our physical movements are both made possible and restricted by our physical forms; outside of cyberspace, often the first things we perceive about others are aspects of their physical appearance, including, most importantly, their sex.[1] Bodies mean that, at least up until now and in the immediate future, men can neither bear nor nurse children, while some women can.

Bodies mean that some people menstruate during parts of their lives and others do not; some people ejaculate and others do not; some people lactate and others do not; some people have their bodily center of gravity several inches above their navel, and some people have theirs below their navel—and the members of those groups are not randomly distributed across the population.

What the authors in this section are concerned with are the psychological and societal reactions to and consequences of embodiment. They do not consider any particular reaction to embodiment to be universal, inevitable, or independent of society and culture. After all, women who nurse their babies all have experiences involving embodiment that are different from the experiences of men, but they do not necessarily all have the *same* experience. Or, as Joan Chrisler and Karen Levy (1990) argue, many women across a variety of cultures may experience some water retention during the few days before they begin menstruating. Water retention is more likely to be experienced and labeled as a *medical symptom*, however, in a social context that tends to deny cyclic variation and emphasize tight-fitting, tailored clothes and lean female bodies.

In the introduction to the previous section we warned against giving unwarranted primacy to biological influences on human behavior. In this section we hope to provide some counterpoint to the contention that bodies and embodiment are irrelevant to socially constructed gender. It is unlikely that people (in groups and as individuals) will have *no* important reactions to their own and others' embodiment. Different bodies feel different: living in a fit body feels different from living in an unfit body. Different bodies evoke different reactions: thin bodies lead to "halo" effects, while fat bodies are assumed to belong to individuals with a variety of other characterological and behavioral "defects." And the differences between male and female bodies, even if significantly exaggerated by cultural arrangements, are aspects of gender that are noticed by both self and other, across situations, and across our lifetimes.

The chapters in this section all acknowledge the potential power of the "felt experience of biological difference" (Jane Alpert, quoted in Rosenberg, 1992), which both psychologists and feminists have often ignored. In addition, they eloquently discuss the coercive pressure society can exert toward particular interpretations of that "felt experience." As Michelle Fine and Pat Macpherson began to realize, teenage girls may experience their sexuality—and others' responses to it—as a source of power, a source of pleasure, and a source of unwarranted attention, all at the same time, or at different times under varying circumstances. We may feel conflict, both within ourselves and between ourselves and others, over our own and their responses to embodiment. Exploring rather than ignoring our experiences of embodiment promises to enrich our understanding of gender as it is lived by men and women every day.

NOTE

1. Indeed, studies show that gender tends to be noticed first, even relative to race, and even when virtually nothing else is noticed (Grady, 1979).

REFERENCES

Chrisler, J. C., & Levy, K. B. (1990). The Media Construct a Menstrual Monster: A Content Analysis of PMS Articles in the Popular Press. *Women and Health, 14,* 89–104.

Grady, K. E. (1979). Androgyny Reconsidered. In J. H. Williams (Ed.), *Psychology of Women: Selected Readings* (pp. 172–177). New York: Norton.

Rosenberg, R. (1992). *Divided Lives: American Women in the Twentieth Century.* New York: Hill and Wang.

Tavris, C., & Offir, C. (1977). *The Longest War: Sex Differences in Perspective* (2d ed). New York: Harcourt Brace Janovitch.

Chapter 15

Self-Construction
The Gendered Body

Sandra Lipsitz Bem

The Gendered Body

The gendered personality does not exist as pure or disembodied spirit. It is physically embedded in a biological structure, the human body, which is as subject to the processes of androcentric and gender-polarizing self-perception and self-construction as the human personality itself. The construction of the gendered body demonstrates nearly as well as the construction of the gendered personality just how deeply the androcentric and gender-polarizing lenses can shape people's feelings about what is alien to the self and what is not. By the body itself, I mean not just how people look, with and without their clothes on, but also how they function physiologically, how they move around in space, and even how they experience and express their sexual desires.

Consider first people's feelings about how their bodies are supposed to look, even when naked and standing still. Looking through the lens of gender polarization makes people uncomfortable about virtually every feature of their bodies that spontaneously appears more frequently in the other sex. Women with visible hair on their legs and faces and short men with little upper-body muscle development find these features so alien to their sense of self—that is, they feel so much as if these features don't rightfully belong on their particular bodies—that the women use razors, depilatories, and bleaches, and the men use body-building equipment, shoe lifts, and hormone injections to try to manipulate their bodies into conformity with their gender-polarizing vision of who they really are.

This widespread desire to improve on the biological sexual difference by making bodies even more male or female in appearance than nature did attests to just how much of an impact the gender-polarizing lenses can have on the way people perceive and construct their selves; it also suggests that what "normal" gender-polarizers feel about their bodies may be different only in degree (and direction) from what transsexuals feel about their bodies.

Sandra Lipsitz Bem, "Self-Construction: The Gendered Body." In S. L. Bem, *The Lenses of Gender,* pp. 159–167. New Haven: Yale University Press. © 1993 by Yale University Press. Reprinted with permission.

People's feelings about their bodies are never shaped solely by the lens of gender polarization, however. The lenses of androcentrism and gender polarization are always inextricably linked together, which is why males in American society are predisposed to value and affirm the body, whereas females are predisposed to feel ambivalent about—and hence to deny—the body. This asymmetry between the sexes derives from androcentric beliefs: although these beliefs perfectly complement gender polarization in the context of males, they so conflict with gender polarization *and* biology in the context of females that virtually no realizable female embodiment is fully able to satisfy the requirements of both lenses.

With males, the androcentric predisposition to privilege whatever is male and to otherize whatever is female so beautifully harmonizes with the gender-polarizing predisposition to accentuate the natural sexual difference that the male's motivation to affirm and enhance the maleness of his body can only be increased. With females, the interaction of the two lenses has a more paralyzing effect. On the one hand, the lens of gender polarization impels females to accentuate their natural sexual difference so they won't look at all like men. On the other hand, the lens of androcentrism impels them to minimize their natural sexual difference so they won't look very much like women, either.

This androcentric minimizing of the female body has been a part of American culture since at least the 1920s, when women seeking to broaden the boundaries of the female world strapped down their breasts and wore long-waisted dresses to reduce the visibility of their body contours. Although this minimizing of the female body was briefly put aside during the post–World War II era of Marilyn Monroe, motherhood, and the feminine mystique, it returned in full force in the 1970s and 1980s, when the ideal dressed-for-success woman not only wore a man-tailored business suit to work but, underneath that business suit, had so little body fat that few female contours needed to be hidden.

In 1899, Thorstein Veblen speculated in *The Theory of the Leisure Class* that among wealthy people, female beauty is equated with "delicate and diminutive hands and feet and a slender waist" (p. 148) because such features conspicuously display a husband's ability to support a wife who is completely unfit for productive labor. In other words, both "the constricted waist" of Western culture and "the deformed foot" of the Chinese are "mutilations" of the female body that have come to be seen as physically attractive because they visibly demonstrate a husband's "pecuniary reputability" (p. 149).

One aspect of Veblen's analysis is particularly relevant to the question of why female beauty in middle-class America today is so strongly associated with thinness. Just as the corseted waist and the bound foot squeezed women's bodies down to a biologically pathological size, the current ideal of female thinness violates the female body's natural biological tendency to put on adipose tissue—or fat—at every single developmental milestone from puberty to pregnancy to menopause. Besides being inconsistent with the gender-polarizing message that women should not look at all like men, the androcentric equating of female beauty with female thinness is thus also inconsistent with female biology.[1]

Between 1966 and 1970, over 7,500 male and female adolescents were asked in a national survey whether they would rather be heavier, thinner, or about the same (Dornbusch et al., 1984). Consistent with my claim that the lenses of androcentrism and gender polarization predispose males to affirm their bodies and, at the same time, leave females with no biologically realizable embodiment that can satisfy their conflicted vision of what a woman ought to look like, the adolescent boys in this study either became increasingly satisfied with their bodies during the course of their normal sexual development or they stayed the same, whereas the adolescent girls became increasingly dissatisfied with their bodies. Among adolescents at the highest level of sexual maturity, there was thus a vast gender difference, with over 80 percent of the males expressing happiness with their bodies and over 60 percent of the females expressing unhappiness.

The androcentric lens not only makes women ambivalent about the femaleness of their bodies; by thoroughly associating an autonomous self with males, it also creates ambivalence in women about having an autonomous body at all. Even a female body takes up a certain amount of space in the physical world, space that might be seen as rightfully belonging to males and males alone, and it also has the kinds of autonomously motivated needs and urges that only the males in an androcentric world are supposed to have. Accordingly, females are predisposed to position their bodies in ways that take minimal space and to move their bodies in ways that are unintimidating, vulnerable, and accommodating to men rather than in ways that are strong, confident, and interpersonally dominating.[2] Females are also predisposed to feel uncomfortable with almost any overt expression of a physiological need or function. To a woman who is androcentric and gender polarizing, everything from having sexual urges to burping and farting to eating a lot can thus feel as ego-alien as having visible body hair.

This female denial of bodily appetites has taken different forms in different historical periods. In the nineteenth century, for example, it appeared primarily as the suppression of female sexual desire. Today, in contrast, it appears primarily as the suppression of the desire for food—which, in extreme form, becomes anorexia nervosa.[3]

This shift in the form of female self-denial from sex to food should not be seen as implying, however, that sexuality is no longer a critically important context for the self-perception and self-construction of maleness and femaleness. Human sexuality continues to have the particular form that it has in U.S. culture in part because the lenses of androcentrism and gender polarization continue to make whatever is consistent with them seem normal and natural and whatever is inconsistent with them seem alien and problematic. Although this power to shape what feels alien to the self and what feels natural has many consequences in the domain of sexuality, I want to discuss two consequences in some detail: the construction of an androcentric heterosexuality, or the eroticizing of female inequality, and the abhorrence of homosexuality.

Androcentric Heterosexuality

In recent years, an increasing number of Americans have finally begun to acknowledge the epidemic of male violence against women, which feminists have been insistently calling to everyone's attention ever since Susan Brownmiller published *Against Our Will* in 1975. Although the conventional wisdom conceptualizes such violence as the pathological product of a criminal or demented mind, what follows logically from both feminist analysis in general and the cultural analysis in this book in particular is that all forms of female brutalization—including rape and wife beating—are but an exaggeration of the male dominance and the female objectification that have come to seem normal and natural in the context of everyday heterosexuality. Put somewhat differently, the everyday way of experiencing heterosexual desire is itself so shaped by the androcentric and gender-polarizing conception of male dominance as normal and natural, and anything other than male dominance as alien and problematic, that the sexual brutalization of a woman by a man is not just an isolated act, a case of an individual man taking out his psychological problems on an individual woman. It is rather the inevitable cultural by-product of an androcentric heterosexuality that eroticizes sexual inequality.

This eroticizing of sexual inequality can be seen in what most Americans think of as perfectly normal and natural heterosexuality. First, although neither women nor men in American society tend to like heterosexual relationships in which the woman is bigger, taller, stronger, older, smarter, higher in status, more experienced, more educated, more talented, more confident, or more highly paid than the man, they do tend to like heterosexual relationships in which the man is bigger, taller, stronger, and so forth, than the woman.

Second, both women and men see it as normal and natural for the male to play a more dominant or assertive role in a heterosexual encounter and for the female to play a more yielding or accommodating role. They also see it as emasculating for the man and defeminizing for the woman if those assertive and yielding roles are reversed on a regular basis. In normal, everyday heterosexual eroticism, the male is thus supposed to be superior in a wide variety of personal characteristics related to status and to play the dominant role in virtually every aspect of the heterosexual encounter from initiating the date to arranging and paying for the entertainment to guiding the sexual activity.

Finally, both women and men see the female in general and the female body in particular as more the object of male sexual desire than as a desiring sexual subject (or agent). This objectification, which manifests itself in the extraordinary emphasis on a woman's physical attractiveness in American culture, as well as in the almost continuous display of the nude or seminude female body in art, advertising, and the mass media, constitutes an eroticizing of sexual inequality—as opposed to merely a celebrating of female sexuality—because it implicitly imposes a male perspective on the definition of female sexuality. It androcentrically defines women—and predisposes women to define themselves—not in terms of their own sexual desires but in terms of their ability to stimulate and satisfy the male's sexual desires.

It is no accident that American culture has no comparable tradition of displaying the nude or seminude male body. The culture has so completely constructed females and nudes as the objects of male sexual desire that when Americans see a display of a nude or a seminude male body, they instantly assume that it is not a heterosexual woman's object of desire but a gay man's object of desire. This perception, in turn, so arouses their abhorrence of homosexuality that they end up judging the display of the nude male body itself as inherently pornographic.

Given how thoroughly embedded male dominance and female objectification are in even these three "normal" and taken-for-granted aspects of heterosexual desire, it follows that date rape would be a frequent occurrence. After all, when looking through androcentric and gender-polarizing lenses, the man finds it normal and natural to keep pushing for sex even when the woman is resisting a bit, and the woman finds it alien and problematic to assert herself so forcefully and unmistakably that the man will have no choice but to stop what he's doing or use force. Now, however, the norm is so much for men to keep making sexual advances and for women to keep resisting those advances without making a scene or even being impolite that many date rapists do not perceive the sexual intercourse they manage to get as an act of rape.[4]

And if the frequency of date rape is not surprising, given the gender lenses that men and women wear, nor should it be surprising that so many men in American society find violence against women to be so sexually arousing, so affirming of their masculinity, or both, that they brutalize women directly or participate in such brutalization vicariously through violent pornography.

The Abhorrence of Homosexuality

Two interconnected phenomena need to be analyzed next: why Americans in general are predisposed to find homosexual impulses abhorrent and why this abhorrence of homosexuality—which is usually called homophobia—seems to involve males even more than females.[5]

For most of the twentieth century, in psychiatry and the culture at large, homosexuality and heterosexuality have been defined as mutually exclusive sexual orientations; heterosexuality has also been defined as the sine qua non of psychological normality, and homosexuality as proof positive of psychopathology. Prior to the twentieth century, in contrast, homosexuality was conceptualized more as a non-procreative sexual act than as a permanent condition of a person. This didn't mean that the procreation-centered society embraced it as good, but neither was it seen as nearly so central to the self-definition of a male or a female.

Now that homosexuality is considered central to self-identity, however, the gender-polarizing individual is predisposed to see all conformity to the culture's gender scripts as normal and natural and all deviations from the culture's gender scripts as alien and problematic. The gender-polarizing individual is also predisposed to see homosexual deviations as especially problematic, whether in the self or others. This concern about homosexuality is exacerbated by the gender-polarizing concept of a real man or woman, as opposed to a biological man or woman, because that concept makes males and females alike feel tenuous and insecure about their identity as males and females.

These several facets of gender polarization interact in the psyche of the individual to make homosexuality the quintessential threat to one's status as a man or a woman.

More specifically, the gender-polarizing concepts of a real man and a real woman interact with the gender-polarizing vision of homosexuality as a permanent pathology to make even a single homosexual impulse an irreversible threat to normality. No wonder that gender-polarizing males and females are predisposed to repress whatever homosexual impulses they feel and to find abhorrently unnatural whatever homosexual impulses they perceive in others.

This abhorrence of homosexuality implicates males even more than females. Female sexuality in an androcentric society is so defined from a male perspective that the lesbian herself is all but rendered invisible. In addition, the cultural definition of a real man makes males feel much more insecure about the adequacy of their gender than females, for the definition unrealistically requires them not only to suppress every human impulse with even the slightest hint of femininity but also to attain the kind of power and privilege in their social community that will produce respectful deference in women and less powerful men.

This higher level of gender insecurity among males makes the affirmation of maleness much more emotionally charged for men than the affirmation of femaleness is for women; it also predisposes men to engage in two destructive forms of masculinity building that are directly related to homosexuality. First, it predisposes them to suppress virtually all cross-gender impulses, including the desire for physical intimacy with their fathers or their sons. The only exception to this taboo occurs in contexts that are clearly defined by the culture, whether appropriately or inappropriately, as unquestionably masculine, the football field being a prime example. Second, gender insecurity predisposes men to define themselves in terms of their "natural" difference from both women and homosexual men. In some cases, this *psychological* otherizing of the feminine is sufficient to assuage the male's insecurity about being adequately masculine; in more extreme cases, however, more destructive forms of defensive masculinity building are required, including, for example, the dominance of women and the bashing of gay men.

For American men in general, the abhorrence of homosexuality in both themselves and other males is thus produced by their gender-polarizing vision of heterosexuality as normal and homosexuality as pathological, as well as by a defensive need to use their own constructed difference from homosexual men to shore up their own very vulnerable sense of being adequately masculine. None of this is to say, however, that the abhorrence of homosexuality is best conceptualized as a psychological problem, rather than as a cultural one. On the contrary. Even the perpetrators of anti-homosexual hate violence take out their aggressions and their frustrations on gay males and lesbians in particular because these groups have been institutionally otherized in U.S. culture in much the same way that Jews were institutionally otherized in Nazi Germany.

NOTES

1. For the empirical evidence substantiating this inconsistency with biology, see Rodin et al. (1985) and Dornbusch et al. (1984).

2. For research on sex differences in what psychologists call nonverbal behavior, see Mayo & Henley (1981).

3. For a history of female appetite suppression, see Brumberg (1988).

4. For more on date, or acquaintance, rape, see Parrot & Bechhofer (1991) and Warshaw (1988).

5. Many different kinds of evidence document this connection between homophobia and males, including the greater number of laws in the history of Western culture proscribing male homosexuality and the greater amount of attention given to male homosexuality within psychiatric theory. For empirical evidence documenting that males also have more homophobic attitudes than females, see Herek (1988).

REFERENCES

Brownmiller, S. (1975). *Against Our Will: Men, Women, and Rape.* New York: Simon & Schuster.

Brumberg, J. J. (1988). *Fasting Girls: The Emergence of Anorexia Nervosa as a Modern Disease.* Cambridge, MA: Harvard University Press.

Dornbusch, S. M., Carlsmith, J. M., Duncan, P. D., Gross, R. T., Martin, J. A., Ritter, P. L., & Siegel-Gorelick, B. (1984). Sexual Maturation, Social Class, and the Desire to Be Thin among Adolescent Females. *Developmental and Behavioral Pediatrics, 5,* 308–314.

Herek, G. M. (1988). Hererosexuals' Attitudes toward Lesbians and Gay Men: Correlates and Gender Differences. *Journal of Sex Research, 25,* 451–477.

Mayo, C., & Henley, N. M. (Eds.). (1981). *Gender and Nonverbal Behavior.* New York: Springer-Verlag.

Parrot, A., & Bechhofer, L. (Eds.). (1991). *Acquaintance Rape: The Hidden Crime.* New York: Wiley.

Rodin, J., Silberstein, L., & Striegel-Moore, R. (1985). Women and Weight: A Normative Discontent. In T. B. Sonderegger (Ed.), *Nebraska Symposium on Motivation, 1984: Psychology and Gender* (pp. 197–221). Lincoln: University of Nebraska Press.

Veblen, T. (1899/1934). *The Theory of the Leisure Class: An Economic Study of Institutions.* New York: Random House/Modern Library.

Warshaw, R. (1988). *I Never Called It Rape: The Ms. Report on Recognizing, Fighting, and Surviving Date and Acquaintance Rape.* New York: Harper & Row.

Chapter Sixteen

Over Dinner

Feminism and Adolescent Female Bodies

Michelle Fine and Pat Macpherson

> The experience of being woman can create an illusory
> unity, for it is not the experience of being woman but
> the meanings attached to gender, race, class, and age at
> various historical moments . . . that [are] of strategic
> significance.
>
> —Chandra Mohanty, 1987: 39

When we invited four teenagers—Shermika, Damalleaux, Janet and Sophie—for a series of dinners to talk with us about being young women in the 1990s, we could not see our own assumptions about female adolescence much more clearly than we saw theirs. By the end of the first dinner, we could, though, recognize how old we were, how dated the academic literatures were, how powerful feminism had been in shaping their lives and the meanings they made of them, and yet how inadequately their feminism dealt with key issues of identity and peer relations.

Only when we started to write could we see the inadequacies of our feminism to understand the issues of female adolescence they struggled to communicate. In this space of our incredulity, between our comprehension of their meanings and our *in*comprehension of "how they could call themselves feminist," we are now able to see the configuration of our own fantasies of feminism for female adolescents. The revision that is central to feminist process gets very tricky when applied to adolescence, because our own unsatisfactory pasts return as the "before" picture, demanding that the "after" picture of current adolescent females measure all the gains of the women's movement. Our longing is for psychic as well as political completion. Michael Payne (1991: 18) describes the fantasy of the Other: "What I desire—and therefore lack—is in the other culture, the other race, the other gender"—the other

Michelle Fine & Pat Macpherson, "Over Dinner: Feminism and Adolescent Female Bodies." In H. Radtke and H. Stam (Eds.), *Power Gender: Social Relations Theory in Practice*, pp. 219–246. © 1992 by Sage Publications, Ltd. Reprinted by permission of Sage Publications, Ltd.

generation, in our case. In the case of these four young women, to our disbelief, the desired Other is "one of the guys."

Our analyses of power lie revealed and problematic in two intellectual spaces. First we worry about the hegemonic frames that we import as researchers to/on/over their stories (Lather, 1991). And second, in more Foucauldian fashion, we write on *their* strategies of resistance and negotiation with boys and men, girls and women, and the social representations of gender, race, and class that litter their lives (Brodkey and Fine, 1988). We presume that power floats across relations, institutions, and bodies, constructing and resisting asymmetries displayed materially and discursively.

We grew convinced that we needed to construct an essay about these young women's interpretations of and struggles with the discourses of adolescence, femininity, and feminism in their peer cultures. Barbara Hudson explains the incompatibility of femininity and adolescence:

> femininity and adolescence as discourses [are] subversive of each other. All of our images of the adolescent—the restless, searching teen; the Hamlet figure; the sower of wild oats and tester of growing powers—these are masculine figures. . . . If adolescence is characterized by masculine constructs, then any attempt by girls to satisfy society's demands of them qua adolescents is bound to involve them in displaying notably a lack of maturing but also a lack of femininity. (1984: 35)

Adolescence for these four young women was about adventures of males and the constraints on females, so their version of feminism unselfconsciously rejected femininity and embraced the benign version of masculinity that allowed them to be "one of the guys." They fantasized the safe place of adolescence to be among guys who overlook their (female) gender out of respect for their (unfeminine) independence, intelligence, and integrity. For them, femininity meant the taming of adolescent passions, outrage, and intelligence. Feminism was a flight from "other girls" as unworthy and untrustworthy. Their version of feminism was about equal access to being men.

When we scoured the literatures on adolescent females and their bodies, we concluded that the very construction of the topic is positioned largely from white, middle-class, non-disabled, heterosexual adult women's perspectives. The concerns of white *elite* women are represented as *the* concerns of this age cohort. Eating disorders are defined within the contours of what *elite* women suffer (for example, anorexia and bulimia) and less so what non-elite women experience (for example, overeating, obesity). The sexual harassment literature is constructed from *our* age perspective—that unwanted sexual attention is and should be constituted as a crime—and not from the complicated perspectives of young women involved. The disability literature is saturated with images produced by *non-disabled* researchers of self-pitying or embarrassed "victims" of biology, and is rarely filled with voices of resistant, critical and powerfully "flaunting" adolescents who refuse to wear prostheses, delight in the passions of their bodies and are outraged by the social and family discrimination they experience (Corbett et al., 1987; Fine and Asch, 1988; Frank, 1988).

We found that women of all ages, according to this literature, are allegedly scripted to be "good women," and that they have, in compliance, smothered their passions, appetites and outrage. When sexually harassed, they tell "his stories" (Brodkey and Fine, 1988). To please the lingering internalized "him," they suffer in body image and indulge in eating disorders (Orbach, 1986). And to satisfy social demands for "attractiveness," women with and without disabilities transform and mutilate their bodies (Bordo, 1990).

We presumed initially that the three arenas of adolescence in which young women would most passionately struggle with gendered power would include eating, sexuality and outrage. And so we turned to see what these literatures said, and to unpack how race, class, disability and sexuality played with each of these literatures. In brief, within these literatures, we saw a polarizing:

1. Eating disorders appear to be a question studied among elite white women in their anticipated tensions of career vs. mother identities.
2. Sexuality is examined disproportionately as problematic for girls who are black and underprivileged, with motherhood as their primary identity posed as "the problem."
3. Finally, young women's political "outrage" simply does not exist as a category for feminist intellectual analysis.

The literature on adolescent women had thoroughly extricated these categories of analysis from women's lives. So, in our text we decided to rely instead upon the frames that these young women offered as they narrated their own lives, and the interpretations we could generate through culture and class.

Our method was quite simple, feminist and, ironically, anti–eating disorder. We invited the six of us to talk together over pizza and soda, while Sam—Michelle's four-year-old—circled the table. We talked for hours, on two nights two months apart, and together stretched to create conversations about common differences; about the spaces in which we could delight together as six women; the moments in which they bonded together as four young women who enjoy football, hit their boyfriends, and can't trust other girls—Not Ever!; and, too, the arenas in which the race, class and cultural distances in the room stretched too far for these age peers to weave any common sense of womanhood. Collectively, we created a context that Shermika and Sophie spontaneously considered "the space where I feel most safe." We were together, chatting, listening, hearing, laughing a lot and truly interested in understanding our connections and differences, contoured always along the fault lines of age, class, race and culture, bodies, experiences and politics.

But we each delighted in this context differently. For Michelle and Pat, it was a space in which we could pose feminist intellectual questions from our generation— questions about sexuality, power, victimization and politics—which they then turned on their heads. For Shermika (African-American, age fifteen) it was a place for public performance, to say outrageous things, admit embarrassing moments, "practice" ways of being female in public discourse, and see how we would react. For Damalleaux (African-American, age fourteen) it was a place to "not be shy" even though the room was integrated by race, a combination that had historically made her uncomfortable. For Sophie ("WASP," age seventeen), it was a "safe place" where perhaps for the first time, she was not the only "out" feminist in a room full of peers. And for Janet (Korean-American, age seventeen), like other occasions in which she was the only Asian-American among whites and blacks, it was a time to test her assimilated "sense of belonging," always at the margins. In negotiating gender, race/ ethnicity and class as critical, feminist agents, these four women successfully betrayed a set of academic literatures, written by so many of us only twenty years older. Our writings have been persistently committed to public representations of women's victimization and structural assaults, and have consequently ignored, indeed misrepresented, *how well young women talk as subjects*, passionate about and relishing in their capacities to move between nexuses of power and powerlessness. That is to say, feminist scholars have forgotten to take notice of how firmly young women resist— alone and sometimes together.

The four young women began their conversation within this space of gendered resistance. Shermika complained, "Boys think girls cannot *do* anything," to which Sophie added, "So we have to harass them." Shermika explained, "[Guys think] long as they're takin' care of 'em [girls will] do anything they want. And if I'm in a relationship, I'm gonna take care of you just as much as you take care of me. You can't say 'I did this'—No: 'We did this.' ... Guys think you're not nothin'— anything—without them." Janet sneered, "Ego." Shermika recruited her friend into this conversation by saying, "Damalleaux *rule* her boyfriend [Shermika's brother]." Damalleaux announced her governing principle, "Boys—they try to take advantage of you. ... As far as I'm concerned, I won't let a boy own me." Janet provided an example of the "emotionally messed up guys" she encounters: "I didn't want to take care of him. I didn't want to constantly explain things to him. ... I want to coexist with them and not be like their mother. ... It happened to me twice." And Sophie explained: "I'm really assertive with guys [who say sexist stuff]. If they have to be shot down I'll shoot them down. They have to know their place." The four expressed their feminism here as resistance to male domination in their peer relations. They applied the same principle in discussing how they saw careers and marriage, when Michelle asked about men in their future plans. Shermika laid it out in material terms: "I imagine bein' in my *own* house in *my name*. And then get married. So my husband can get out *my house*." Sophie chimed in, "Seriously," and Shermika nodded, "Yes, *very important*. So I won't end up one of them battered women we were talkin' about. I'm not going to have no man beatin' on me." Sophie offered her version: "You have to like be independent. You have to establish yourself as your own person before some guy takes you—I mean. ..." Janet asserted her standard of independence: "I wouldn't follow a guy to college." Their feminism asserted women's independence from men's power to dominate and direct.

Class and cultural differences entered the conversations with their examples of domination and resistance. Shermika's example of guys materially "takin' care" of girls to establish dominance, and Damalleaux's resistance to male "ownership" re- flected the practice of gift-giving as ownership, a norm of their local sexual politics (see Anderson, 1990). Damalleaux explained that *respect* could interrupt this domi- nance structure: "How much respect a guy has for you—especially in front of his friends. ... If a boy finds out you don't care how they treat you, and you don't have respect for your*self* . . . they won't have respect for you." Damalleaux turned to Shermika and said, "You try to teach me." Shermika's talk was full of lessons learned from her mother, and examples of their closeness. "My mom and me like this. Cause she understands." Not talking "*leads* to problems. My Mom tells me so much about life."

Sophie and Janet defined their resistance within their "professional class," peopled by "individuals," not relationships, who suffer from the dilemmas of "independence," typically explained in terms of psychology. Their isolation from their mothers and female friends enabled them to frame their stories alone, as one-on-one battles across the lines of gender and generations.

Ways of Talking: On Cultures of Womenhood

Herein lies a cautionary tale for feminists who insist that underneath or beyond the differences among women there must be some shared identity—as if commonality were a metaphysical given, as if a shared viewpoint were not a difficult political achievement. . . . Western feminist theory has in effect . . . [demanded that] Afro-American, Asian-American or Latin American women separate their "woman's voice" from their racial or ethnic voice without also requiring white women to distinguish being a "woman" from being white. This double standard implies that while on the one hand there is a seamless web of whiteness and womanness, on the other hand, Blackness and womanness, say, or Indianness and womanness, are discrete and separable elements of identity. If . . . I believe that the woman in every woman is a woman just like me, and if I also assume that there is no difference between being white and being a woman, then seeing another woman "as a woman" will involve me seeing her as fundamentally like the woman I am. In other words, the womanness underneath the Black woman's skin is a white woman's, and deep down inside the latina woman is an Anglo woman waiting to burst through the obscuring cultural shroud. As Barbara Omolade has said, "Black women are not white women with color." (Elizabeth Spelman, 1988: 13)

At this moment in social history, when the tensions of race, class and gender couldn't be in more dramatic relief, social anxieties load onto the bodies of adolescent women (Fine, 1988; Halson, 1991). Struggles for social control attach to these unclaimed territories, evident in public debates over teen pregnancy, adolescent promiscuity, parental consent for contraception and abortion, date rapes and stories of sexual harassment, as well as in women's personal narratives of starving themselves or binging and purging towards thinness. For each of these social "controversies," there is, however, a contest of wills, a set of negotiations. Young women are engaged with questions of "being female"; that is, who will control, and to what extent can they control, their own bodies?

Threaded through our conversations at the dining room table, culture and class helped to construct (at least) two distinct versions of womanhood. It became clear that the elite women, for instance, constructed an interior sense of womanhood out of oppositional relations with White Men. They positioned white men as the power group White Men (Baker, 1989), and they positioned themselves in an ongoing, critical, hierarchical struggle with these men. Sophie, for example, often defined her feminism in relation to white boys; instead of "reinforcing guys all the time, I BUST on guys. Because if you don't bust 'em they'll get ahead. You have to keep 'em in their place."

It was quite another thing to hear the sense of womanhood constructed horizontally—still in struggle—by African-American women, situated with or near African-American men. Given the assault on Black men by the broader culture, it was clear that any announced sense of female superiority would be seen as "castrating," and unreconcilable with cross-gender alliances against racism (Giddings, 1984; hooks, 1984). So, the construction of Black womanhood was far less dichotomized and oppositional toward men, and far richer in a sense of connection to community.

In the context of being "deprived" of the traditional (oppositional to White Men) feminine socialization, women of colour, like women of disabilities, may construct womenhoods less deeply repulsed by the traditional accoutrements of femininity, less oppositional to the cardboard White Male, and less assured that gender survives as the primary, or exclusive category of social identity.

Among these four, then, we heard two quite distinct constructions of "being female." From the African-American women, both living in relatively impoverished circumstances, we heard a "womanhood" of fluid connections among women within and across generations; maturity conceived of as an extension of self with others; a taken-for-granted integration of body and mind; a comfortable practice of using public talk as a place to "work out" concerns, constraints and choices; and a nourishing, anchored sense of *home* and *community*. bell hooks describes home as a site of nurturance and identity, *positive in its resistance* to racist ideologies of black inferiority:

> Despite the brutal reality of racial apartheid, of domination, one's homeplace was the one site where one could freely confront the issue of humanization, where one could resist. Black women resisted by making homes where all black people could strive to be subjects, not objects, where we could be affirmed in our minds and our hearts despite poverty, hardship and deprivation, where we could restore to ourselves the dignity denied us on the outside in the public world. (1990: 42)

As the words of Damalleaux and Shermika reveal to us, however, the drawback of this centeredness in community is in its fragility, its contingent sense of the future, terrors of what's "across the border," and the lack of resources or supports for planned upward mobility.

Indeed, when we discussed future plans, Shermika "joked" she would be a custodian or bag lady. She "joked" she would like to be dead, to see what the other world was like. She said she would like to come back as a bird—"Not a pigeon, I hope," said Sophie—"Dove or peacock," Shermika decided, "something nobody be kickin' around all the time." Shermika finally confided—in an uncharacteristic whisper—that she would like to be a lawyer, even the D.A. (district attorney). What Shermika can be—could be—would like to be—and will be—constitutes the terrain of Shermika's and Damalleaux's dilemma. Shermika does not worry that education would de-feminize her, or that her parents expect more or different from her career than she does. She quite simply and realistically doubts she will be able to get all the way to "D.A."

Nevertheless, Damalleaux and Shermika, on the other hand, expressed the connections with and respect for mothers found in Gloria Joseph and Jill Lewis's African-American daughters when they write, "A decisive 94.5% expressed respect for their mothers in terms of strength, honesty, ability to overcome difficulties, and ability to survive" (1981: 94). Shermika's many examples of respect for her mother, and Damalleaux's mother calling her "my first girl" suggest "the centrality of mothers in their daughters' lives" (Joseph and Lewis, 1981: 79). In their stories, active female sexuality and motherhood are everywhere "embodied," while "career" is a distant and indistinct dream, marginal, foreign and threateningly isolated.

In contrast, from the two privileged women, both living in relatively comfortable circumstances, we heard a "womanhood" struggling for positive definition and safe boundaries; a sharp splitting of body and mind; maturity as a dividing of self from family and school to find individual identity; an obsessive commitment to using privacy—in body, thought and conversation—as the only way to "work out" one's problems; all nourishing a highly individualized, privatized and competitive sense of home and community as sites from which they would ultimately leave, unfettered, to launch "autonomous" lives as independent women. Materially and imaginatively these two women recognized an almost uninterruptable trajectory for future plans. Their "womanhood" was built on the sense of *self as exception,* "achievement" meritocratically determining how "exceptional" each individual can prove herself (away) from the group. Self-as-exception, for women, involves "transcending" gender. Rachel Hare-Mustin describes the illusion of gender-neutral, "individualistic" choices:

> The liberal/humanist tradition of our epoch assumes that the meanings of our lives reflect individual experience and individual subjectivity. This tradition has idealized individual identity and self-fulfilment and shown a lack of concern about power. Liberalism masks male privilege and dominance by holding that every (ungendered) individual is free. The individual has been regarded as responsible for his or her fate and the basic social order has been regarded as equitable. Liberal humanism implies free choice when individuals are not free of coercion by the social order. (1991: 3)

The invisibility of women's "coercion by the social order" came out most clearly in Janet's and Sophie's relationships with their working mothers. They did not analyse their mothers' lives for power.

Sophie: "My mom doesn't like her job but she has to work so I can go to college." Janet and Sophie said they were afraid of becoming their mothers, unhappy and overworked in jobs they hate, their workloads doubled with domestic responsibilities. "I fear I might be like her. I want to be independent of her," white middle-class women said of their mothers in the research of Joseph and Lewis (1981: 125). Janet and Sophie said they did not talk much, or very honestly, to their mothers, and did not feel they could ever do enough to gain their mothers' approval. Janet said: "My mother [says] I really have to go to college . . . be a doctor or a lawyer. . . . That's her main goal . . . job security . . . then she wants me to get married and have a nice family ... preferably Catholic. ... Mom's got my life mapped out." Ambition and career "embody" this mother–daughter relationship, in a sense, while the daughter's problems with sexuality and power, and the mother *as woman,* are absent in the relationship Janet describes.

When discussing who they would tell if they had a problem, Shermika immediately said "My mom" and Damalleaux said "I tell Shermika almost everything before I tell my mother." Sophie and Janet agreed only in the negative. It would not be their mothers: "Don't talk to my mom."

Janet: I can't tell my mother anything. If I told her something she would ground me for an entire century.

Sophie: Once you tell them one thing, they want to hear more, and they *pry.* I keep my home life and school—social—life so separate.

Janet: ... I'll be non-committal or I won't tell her the truth. I'll just tell her what she wants to hear.

Sophie: I wish I could talk to my mom. It'd be great if I could.

Shermika: It's the wrong thing to do [not talking], though. ... It always *leads* to problems. My mom tells me so much about life.

Janet said her mother stares at her complexion [her acne] and says, "You're not going to get married, you're not going to have a boyfriend." "I get so mad at her," Janet says. She tells her mother either "I'm leaving, I'm leaving" or "Stop it! Stop it!" Later when Pat asked whether self-respect was learned from her mother, Janet said her self-respect had "nothing to do with my mother. I used to hate myself, partly because of my mother. But not anymore. My mother's opinion just doesn't matter to me." Sophie said,

> My mother ... nitpicks. ... I'm sure it was like her mom [who] never approved anything about her. I get self-respect from my mom because she wants me to respect myself. ... I don't think she respects herself enough. I respect her more than she respects herself. Her mother belittled her so much.

Later Sophie said, "I have the feeling that no matter what I do, it's not enough." Janet said her mother makes her and her sister feel like her mother's "racehorses":

> My mom *lives* through her kids. Two daughters: two *chances.* My sister wants to be an actress and my parents hate that [dykey] way she looks. ... My mom: "You're just not *feminine* enough!" I'm just like, "Mom, grow up!" ... She compares her daughters to everyone else's. [One example is] a straight-A student on top of all her chores. ... I know there's things in her personality that are part of myself. ... We're just like racehorses. ... "My daughter has three wonderful children and a husband who makes a million dollars a year."

Janet and Sophie described their mothers as supports you get over, central to the life these daughters wished to escape, and to revise, in their own futures. Within their liberal discourse of free choice, the inequalities of power determining their mothers' misery were invisible to them—and their own exceptional futures also unquestioned.

The Body: Boundaries and Connections

Over our dinners we created a democracy of feminist differences. That is, all four, as an age/gender cohort, introduced us to the female body in play within gendered politics. These young women consistently recast *our* prioritizing of sex at the center of feminist politics into *their* collective critique of gender politics. Using a language that analyzed dominance and power, they refused to separate sex from other power relations. Perhaps even more deeply Foucauldian than we assumed ourselves to be, they deconstructed our voyeurism with examples of sexuality as only one embodied site through which gendered politics operate. All four shared a distrust of men— "they think they have power." But they also distrusted female solidarity— "they back stab you all the time." Their examples overturned our notions of sisterhood by showing us that both young women and young men proficiently police the borders, and tenets, of masculinity and femininity among today's teens. They are often reminded of their bodies as a public site (gone right or wrong), commented on and monitored by others—male and female. But as often, they reminded us, they forcefully reclaim their bodies by talking back, and by talking feminist. "It'd be harder not to talk," Sophie thinks, "It'd be harder to sit and swallow whatever people are saying."

Resonating much of feminist literature, when these four young women spoke of their bodies, it was clear that they found themselves sitting centrally at the nexus of race, class and gender politics. *Gender* determines that the young women are subject to external surveillance and responsible for internal body management, and it is their gender that makes them feel vulnerable to male sexual threat and assault. *Culture and class* determine how; that is, the norms of body and the codes of surveillance, management, threat, assault, and resistance available to them.

Susan Bordo (1990) writes about body management as a text for "the controlling"/ "controlling the" middle class. Reflecting both elite material status and a pure, interior soul, this fetish of body management, operated by the "normalizing machinery of power," produces a desire to control flesh otherwise out of control, as it positions individuals within an elite class location. The tight svelte body reflects material and moral comfort, while the loose sagging body falls to the "lumpen." Bordo's cultural analysis of the representations and experiences of women's bodies and women's revulsion at sagging fat, captures and yet too narrowly homogenizes what the four young women reported.

Each of the four, as Bordo would argue, was meticulously concerned with her body as the site for cataloguing both her own and others' "list" of her inadequacies. Indeed, each body had become the space within which she would receive unsolicited advice about having "too many pimples," "being too chocolate," "looking chubby," "becoming too thin," "looking like a boy," or in the case of a sister, dressing "very butch." The fetish to control, however, was experienced in ways deeply classed and raced. While the more privileged women were familiar with, if not obsessed by, eating disorders now fashionable among their status peers, the African-American women were quite literally bewildered at the image of a young woman binging on food, and then purging. Therein lies a serious problematic in white feminist literatures—class and culture practices are coded exclusively as *gender,* reinforcing hegemonic definitions of (white) womanhood, while obscuring class/culture contours of the body.

For these women, the female body not only signified a site of interior management vis-à-vis male attention/neglect. It was also a site for gendered politics enacted through sexual violence. Celia Kitzinger (1988), in an analysis of how 2,000 young women and men frame their personal experiences with "unfairness," found that 24 percent of interviewed girls spontaneously volunteered instances of body-centered unfairness, including sexual harassment, rape and/or abuse. So too, violence stories were offered by all four of the young women, each particular to her social context:

> When I got my first boyfriend [he] pressured me to have sex with him. That's why I didn't never go over his house. (Damalleaux)

> I feel safe nowhere. (Sophie)

> When he pulled a gun on me, I said, "This is over." (Shermika)

> I know it's unlikely, but I am terrified of someday being date raped. It's always been something I've been afraid of. (Janet)

For Janet, violence is imagined as possible because of the stories of her friends. For Sophie, violence is encountered as harassment on the street. For Damalleaux and Shermika, violence is encountered or threatened in relations with boyfriends.

> *Michelle:* Is there any place where guys have more power than you?
> *Damalleaux:* In bed.
> *Shermika:* In the street. In the store, when he has all the money.
> *Damalleaux:* And all the guys can beat girls. But I don't think it's true.

> *Michelle:* Are you ever afraid that the hitting will get bad?
> *Shermika:* Yeah, that's why I don't do so much hitting.
> *Damalleaux:* When I go out with a boy I hit him a lot to see if he's going to do anything. . . . You hit me once, I don't want anything to do with you.

> *Shermika:* Sometimes you can get raped with words, though. You feel so slimy.
> . . . The guy at the newspaper stand, I speak to him every morning. Then one day he said, "How old are you? I can't wait till you sixteen." And I told my mom, and she came [with me and told him off]. He lost respect. He didn't give me none. And that day I felt bad, what was I, bein' too loose? . . . You just can't help feelin' like that [slimy].

Liz Kelly offers this definition of sexual violence:

> Sexual violence includes any physical, visual, verbal or sexual act that is experienced by the woman or girl, at the time or later, as a threat, invasion or assault, that has the effect of degrading or hurting her and/or takes away her ability to control intimate contact. (1988: 41)

We found that the fear and/or experience of surviving male violence was indeed central. But its expression was, again, classed and raced. These fears and experiences were deeply traumatic to all the women, and yet the African-American women more frequently and publicly, if uncomfortably, related them in the context of conversation. For the more elite women assaults and fears were privatized and so left relatively unanalyzed, unchallenged and in critical ways "buried." For example, Janet's story of a friend's date rape contrasts radically with Shermika's stories of male violence and female resistance.

Janet: That happened to one of my friends.

Sophie: A date rape?

Janet: Sort of. . . . He'd been pressuring her for a long time, and she's just "no no no no." She's at this party, her [girl] friend says, "Why don't you just do it?" and she says, "Because I don't *want* to." . . . She was drunk, puking. She fell asleep, and the next thing she knows she wakes up and he's on top of her and she's not really happy about it but she didn't do anything about it so she just let it happen. And . . . she was upset about it, she was really angry about it, but there was nothing she could *do* about it? [*Janet's voice rises into a kind of question mark.*] It didn't really bother her, but after that she totally knew who her friends were. . . .

Sophie: She could've done something about it.

Janet: . . . I guess we didn't talk about how she really really felt about it. She seemed really comfortable with it after it. She was upset for while. After she—

Sophie: There's no way she was *comfortable* with it.

Janet: She's dealt with it in a way. She's gotten to the point where it doesn't really make her cry to talk about it.

Earlier in the conversation Sophie complained that the popular crowd got drunk at parties and had one-night stands. Somewhat defensive, Janet said aside to Sophie, "Hey, *I've* done that." Janet's story of the rape included Janet's anger at the girl's girlfriend. "Her *friend* was the hostess of the party and gave her the condoms and told her to go do it." Betrayal by the girlfriend and the boyfriend, a rape Janet calls "sort of" a date rape, in a party situation Janet has been in many times, anger and helplessness, talking about it finally without tears: this worst-case scenario of women's sexuality and powerlessness is "dealt with" by *not* "talk[ing] about how she really felt about it." Janet's story was about the social and interior limits on one girl's control, before and after "sex" she did not want.

In sharp contrast, Shermika offered a story of embodied resistance, through public talk. Michelle asked, "Have you ever been in a relationship where you felt you were being forced to do what you didn't want to do?" Shermika's answer was immediate and emphatic, "Yeah, I quit 'em, I quit 'em." She followed with a story about what happened when she "quit" the boyfriend who was getting possessive:

Shermika: I almost got killed. Some guy pulled a gun on me. . . . He put the gun *to my head.* I said, "You'd better kill me cause if you don't I'm gonna kill you." Then he dropped the gun. . . . I kicked him where it hurts . . . hard, he had to go to the hospital. I was scared. . . .

Janet: What happened—have you ever seen him again?

Shermika: I see him every day.
Michelle: Did you call the cops?
Shermika: Yeah. . . . He had to stay in jail [two weeks] till I decided not to press charges. . . . Don't nobody around my way playin' like that with them guns.

Shermika's examples of male threats and violence all show her and her mother talking back, striking back or disarming the man. The woman is embodied as her own best protector. Shermika followed up her first story (which stunned her audience into awed silence) with a second, another jealous boyfriend: "He told me if I went with anybody else he'll kill me. And he pulled a knife on me . . . 'Stab me. Either way, you ain't gonna have me.' " Later she tells a story about her mother:

> My stepfather and my mother were fightin'—it's the only time they ever fought. And he stepped back and hit my momma with all his might. And he thought she was gonna give up. She stepped back and hit *him* with all *her* might—and he fell asleep. She knocked the mess outta him. He never hit her again.

And another about herself, with her mother as model:

> A guy tried to beat me with a belt, and I grabbed it and let him see how it felt to get beat with that belt. My mom wouldn't even take that.

The scars of actual and/or anticipated sexual violence were clear for each of the young women, and always culturally specific as encounter, resistance and recounting.

As with the violence of gender, the violence of racism on the female body was painfully voiced by the three women of color. Fears of attending a white prep school "where they'll ignore me," stories of fleeing an integrated school after three weeks and retrospective outbursts of anger at being "the only woman of color in my class!' showed a kind of agoraphobia which kept Shermika and Damalleaux in their wholly Black communities, and inversely, created in Janet deep assimilative wishes to disappear into the white suburbs. For Janet the "white church" in her elite suburban neighborhood—not the Korean church her parents attend—was the "safest place" she could imagine.

For Damalleaux and Shermika, the neighborhood and its school are clearly the only safe place. Damalleaux reported that she had lasted three weeks at an integrated school: "It was OK but I didn't feel right. I didn't know anybody. I don't like introducing myself to people, I'm too shy. . . . I came back to the neighborhood school."

Shermika was offered a scholarship to go to a "fancy" private school in a white suburb. When discussing what scares us about the future, Shermika admitted she fears "being neglected. Not fitting in. . . . One time I'm goin' in and nobody likes me." When Michelle asked if that was her fear about the prep school, Shermika said, "Not as far as the people. But I don't like travelling. And I'm not staying on the campus . . . I ain't stayin' away from home, though." By the time of our second interview, Shermika had convinced her mother to delay her going to prep school, from mid-year till the next fall. Shermika said she feared she would not be able to keep her grades up in the new school. Shermika's reliance on non-standard English meant she would have to manage a major cultural shift both academically and socially. Her only envy of Sophie and Janet's school was what she called its "socializing" function, that taught them "how to get along, socialize, fit in, knowin' the right thing to say and do." Shermika said that when she has a job she wants to stay in her neighborhood "where it all happenin' [not] where you won't fit in." Racial identity, segregation and racism combine to reinforce the boundaries of Shermika's and Damalleaux's lives and futures, by defining where and who is "safe."

Shermika evidently decided our dinner table was a "safe" enough place to explore our own racial (and maybe racist) differences. Shermika asked Janet, "Are you Chinese?" and Janet said, "No, Korean," and launched into a story about Japanese racism, including the sale of "Sambo" dolls in Japan, and then a story about a 4,000-year-old hatred of Koreans for the Japanese. Shermika responded, "Well, I don't understand that. I mean, I'm supposed to hate somebody white because somebody I know was a slave?" Then Shermika put race and racism right on our dinner table:

Shermika: I walk into a store and Chinese people be starin' at me. *[Shermika was mistaking Korean for Chinese for the third time.]*

Janet: My *mother* does that — I hate that, my *mother* does it. *[Her mother runs a dry cleaner.]* And I'm just like, "Mom, STOP it."

Damalleaux: I leave [the store].

Janet: How do you feel when you're the only minority in a room?

Damalleaux: I don't care.

Shermika: I make a joke out of it. I feel like a zebra.

Unlike Janet's experience, the assaultive nature of Shermika's and Damalleaux's encounters with the white world had given them little encouragement to isolate themselves among a white majority. Shermika said her "darkness" meant she "looked like a clown" when they put on make-up for her local TV interview about the scholarship program she is in; then her pride and excitement about the video of herself on TV was clouded by family jokes about her dark skin making her "invisible" to the camera. Shermika reported plenty of harassment about her dark skin, from girlfriends and boyfriends, even those as dark as herself. "Chocolate!" was the common, hated term, and Shermika was troubled by its implied racial hierarchy and self-hatred. Atypically, she had no easy "come-back" for that one.

Race in Sophie's (WASP) experience is about being privileged, and feeling harassed for her blonde and blue-eyed good looks. Janet, for instance, annoys Sophie by calling her the "Aryan Goddess." Sophie is harassed on public transportation on her daily commute, where she is in the minority as a white woman (Janet, in contrast, drives from suburb to school). Sophie became exasperated in our interview when she felt targeted for white racism, and said she did not "notice" race half as often as race identified her in public situations in which she is made to represent WASPhood or white womanhood.

Just as these women co-created for us a shared, if negotiated, sense of body politics, they separated along culture lines in their expressed reliance on social connections and surveillance of bodily borders. The African-American women, for instance, detailed deeply textured and relational lives. They not only care for many, but many also care for them. They give much to others, and received much in return, but do not call it volunteer or charity work—simply "what I do." When they receive favors (from mothers and boyfriends), they feel neither "guilty" nor "obligated." Held in a complex web of reciprocal relations, they contribute, easily assured that "What goes around comes around." They resonate the writings of Robinson and Ward:

> Nobles' conception of "the extended self" is seen in the value structure of many black families. Willie (1985) argues that many African American children are encouraged to employ their own personal achievements as a means to resist racism. The importance of hard work and communalism is viewed threefold: as a personal responsibility, as an intergenerational commitment to family, and as a tie to the larger collective. A resistant strategy of liberation, in keeping with African American traditional values, ties individual achievement to collective struggle. We maintain that in the service of personal and cultural liberation, African American adolescent girls must resist an individualism that sees the self as disconnected from others in the black community and, as it is culturally and psychologically dysfunctional, she must resist those who might advocate her isolation and separation from traditional African American cultural practices, values and beliefs. (1991: 94)

The elite women, in contrast, deployed a language of bodily integrity, patrolled borders, social charity, obligation and guilt. As for any favors of gifts or time from mothers and boyfriends, they felt a need to "pay back." Bearing often quite deeply hostile feelings toward their mothers, they nevertheless both feel obligated to repay her sacrifices by fulfilling her expectations, often a professional career in return for a gigantic tuition bill. As vigilantly, they monitor their social and bodily boundaries for what and how much comes in and leaves—food, drink, drugs, exercise, money, sacrifices and gifts. And they give back to community in the form of "charity." They live their connections almost contractually.

Related to these contrasting forms of body-in-relation, these two groups performed quite differently within our *public talk*. That is, they parted sharply in terms of how much they hibernated in privacy, how much they revealed themselves through talk. In numerous instances, the white and Korean teens deferred to a "cultural privacy" in which "personal problems" were rarely aired. "Personal grievances" were typically suffocated. "Personal disagreements" were usually revealed "behind our backs." They often withheld juicy details of life, safe only in diaries or other private writings. Their bodies absorbed, carried and embodied their "private troubles." These elite girls made it quite clear that their strategies for survival were interior, personal and usually not shared. The costs of "privilege," as they revealed them, were in internalizing, personalizing and de-politicizing gender dilemmas. Research makes evident these costs in anorexia, bulimia, depression, "talking behind each other's back" and even the "secrets" of rape or abuse survival stories. Socialized out of using public talk to practice varied forms of womanhood, these women recognized collective gender power struggles, and retreated from women. They embodied their resistance alone, through feminist individualism.

The individualism from which modern feminism was born has much to answer for but much in which to take pride. Individualism has decisively repudiated previous notions of hierarchy and particularism to declare the possibility of freedom for all. In so doing, it transformed slavery from one unfree condition among many into freedom's antithesis—thereby insisting that the subordination of one person to any other is morally and politically unacceptable. But the gradual extension of individualism and the gradual abolition of the remaining forms of social and political bondage have come trailing after two dangerous notions: that individual freedom could—indeed must— be absolute, and that social role and personal identity must be coterminous.

Following the principles of individualism, modern Western societies have determined that the persistence of slavery in any form violates the fundamental principle of a just society. But in grounding the justification in absolute individual right, they have unleashed the specter of a radical individualism that overrides the claims of society itself. To the extent that feminism, like antislavery, has espoused those individualistic principles, it has condemned itself to the dead ends toward which individualism is now plunging. (Fox-Genovese, 1991: 240–41)

In contrast, the African-American women were publicly playful as well as nasty to each other, and about others, "because we love each other." Shermika told wonderful, vivid, outrageous tales, in part to "test" what the others would do, including, we believe, testing whether she was being classified as exotic/sexualized/other/specimen for the white women and the evening's analysis. Their school context made their bodies a matter of public talk. Exposed.

> *Shermika:* I don't like my rear end. Guys are so ignorant. "Look at all that cake."
> *Pat:* Maybe it's their problem.
> *Shermika:* No it *is* my problem. Because you see my butt before you see me.

Public talk could be aggression as well:

> *Damalleaux:* I wouldn't talk to him [a stranger] and he got mad.
> *Shermika:* I hate when they constantly talk to you and they get closer and closer.

The African-American women used and experienced conversation, public disagreements, pleasures and verbal badgerings as ways to "try on" varied ways to be women.

During the second evening the four young women discovered and explored these differences through the metaphor of the "private" and "public" schools they attend.

> *Janet:* I've got a question. At [your school, Shermika] are there kids who are like by themselves? Loners . . . who don't sit with anyone else? . . . who nobody wants to sit with?
> *Shermika:* Yeah but they can't because there's somebody always messin' with 'em, tryin' to get 'em to do something. So if they wanted to be by themselves they couldn't.

> *Janet:* At our school it's so easy to get shut out when you're by yourself.
> *Sophie:* You just kind of — disappear.

Janet: They don't say it [criticism or insult] in front of your face.

Sophie: You insult someone by not considering them. . . . You don't consider their existence . . .

Shermika: . . . Sometimes people need you to tell them how you feel . . .

Janet: . . . for the most part when I'm mad at someone I don't say it to them.

Sophie: Only one on one. You don't say it to them in front of others unless you're joking. It's more private.

Shermika: But if you say it *to* the person, you avoid fights. . . . If they hear you saying it behind their back, they wanna fight.

The four pursued this discovered difference between the "private" and the "public" school.

Shermika: Ain't nothin' private at my school. If someone got gonorrhoea, everyone knows it.

Sophie: Everything's private at my school.

Janet: Cause nobody really cares about each other at our school . . .

Shermika: In our school, when I found out I had cancer, I heard about it on the loudspeaker. And everybody come and offer me help. When you're havin' problems in our school, people talk. That's why they're more mature at my school—excuse me. Say somebody poor, need name brand sneaks, they'll put they money together and give 'em some sneaks. And teachers do that too, if someone need food.

Sophie: We like to pretend that we're good to the neighborhood and socially conscious.

Over time, we came to see that "the facts" of these young women's lives were neither what we had invited them to reveal in our conversations, nor what they were giving us. Rather, we were gathering their interpretations of their lives, interpretations which were roaming within culture and class.

On Good and Bad Girls: Prospects for Feminism

"I consider myself a bad girl," Shermika explained, "but in a good sorta way." Feminist scholars as distinct as Valerie Walkerdine, Carol Gilligan and Nancy Lesko have written about polarizations of good girls and bad ones; that is, those who resist, submit or split on the cultural script of femininity. Gilligan's essay "Joining the Resistance" (1990) argues that at the outset of adolescence, young women experience a severing of insider from outsider knowledge, such that "insider knowledge may be washed away." Gilligan and her colleagues have found that young women at early adolescence begin to submerge their interior knowledge, increasingly relying on "I don't know" to answer questions about self. They say "I don't know" at a rate amazingly greater the older they get—an average of twice at age seven, twenty-one times at age twelve, sixty-seven times at age thirteen. Gilligan and colleagues conclude: "If girls' knowledge of reality is politically dangerous, it is both psychologically and politically dangerous for girls not to know . . . or to render themselves innocent by disconnecting from their bodies, their representations of experience and desire" (1988: 33).

Nancy Lesko (1988) has written a compelling ethnography of gendered adolescents' lives inside a Catholic high school, where she unpacks a "curriculum of the body," mediated by class distinctions. In this school female delinquency was sexualized and "embodied." The genders segregated in high school by class, and created categories of behaviors to hang on to within these class groups. The rich and popular girls at her school paraded popular fashions, spoke in controlled voices, muted their opinions and worked hard at "being nice." If they pushed the boundaries of wardrobe, it was always in the direction of fashion, not "promiscuity." The "burnouts," in contrast, were young women who fashioned their behaviors through smoking and directness. They rejected compulsions towards being "nice" and excelled at being "blunt." Refusing to bifurcate their "personal" opinions and their public stances, they challenged docility and earned reputations as "loose" and "hard" (like Leslie Roman's [1988] working-class women who displayed physicality and sexual embodiment). Social class, then, provided the contours within which a curriculum of the body had its meaning displayed, intensifying within gender oppositions, and undermining possibilities for female solidarity.

Departing somewhat from Gilligan and Lesko, Valerie Walkerdine (1984) sees adolescence for young women as a moment not to *bury* the questioning female "self," but a time in which young women must *negotiate* their multiple selves, through struggles of heterosexuality, and critiques of gender, race and class arrangements. In an analysis of popular texts read by adolescent women, Walkerdine finds that "heroines are never angry; most project anger onto others and suppress it in self, yielding the active production of passivity" (1984: 182). She asks readers to consider that "good girls are not always good, [but] when and how is their badness lived?" Interested in the splitting of goodness and badness we, like Walkerdine, asked these young women that question. When Shermika said, 'I consider myself a bad girl, but in a good sorta way,' she was positioning herself in our collectively made feminist context where *good girls* follow femininity rules, and *bad* girls do not. This good kind of bad girl plays by male rules of friendship, risk, danger and initiative.

Within five minutes of our first meeting, the four girls discovered they all liked (American) football, *playing* football, and they eagerly described the joys of running, catching the ball, tackling and being tackled. Only Janet drew the line at being tackled, citing a "300-pound boy" in her neighborhood. As an explanation for their preferred identities as "one of the guys," football exemplifies "masculine" values of gamesmanship. It is a game with rules and space for spontaneous physicality, with teamwork and individual aggression in rule-bound balance, and with maximum bodily access to others of both sexes, without fear about sexual reputation or reproductive consequences. When asked why they trust and like boys over girls, they cited boys' risk-taking making them more fun, their ability to "be more honest" and not backstab, "be more accepting," "You can tell when a guy's lyin'." "First of all they won't even notice what you're wearing and they won't bust on you." Shermika bragged that all of her boyfriends said they valued her most as a friend, not merely a girlfriend. The behavior, clothing and values associated with such identification with boys and sports suggests both a flight from the "femininity" they collectively described as "wearing pink," "being prissy," "bein' Barbie," and "reinforcing guys all the time"—*and* an association of masculinity with fairness (vs. cattiness), honesty (vs. backstabbing), strength (vs. prissiness, a vulnerability whether feigned or real), initiative (vs. deference or reactionary comments), and integrity (vs. the self-doubt and conflicting loyalties dividing girls). The four's risk-taking behaviors—driving fast, sneaking out at night—reinforced identities as "one of the guys." Such are the Bad Girls.

But being "one of the guys" makes for a contradictory position of self versus "other girls." Sophie mocked the femininity of good girls, at its worst when she said dismissively, "You should sit and wait in your little crystal palace" rather than "chase after guys." This constructed difference between self—the good kind of good girl—and other girls—the bad kind of good girl—is an essential contradiction of identity that all four girls were struggling with. Valerie Hey in her study of adolescent female friendships calls this "deficit dumping" all the "bad" bits of femininity, social and sexual competitiveness, placed upon the "other," that is, other girls (1987: 421). Sophie, like the girls in Hey's study, excepted her best friend along with her self from the generality of femininity: "It's different though with best friends. I mean like girls in general." Shermika likewise excepted Damalleaux when Michelle asked whether *no* other girls were to be trusted. "She a boy," Shermika countered, raising a puzzled laugh. But when Shermika's boyfriend likened her to a bodybuilder when she was running track, she felt ashamed to "feel like a boy . . . like a muscle man."

Sophie confessed ruefully, "I'm certainly no bad girl," and Janet taunted her, "Sophie has a little halo." Certainly Sophie's good grades, good works, politeness, friendliness, trustworthiness, were acceptably "good" to both adults and peers, even if the popular crowd had not approved or welcomed her. "I don't want that image," Sophie told Janet about the halo. Goody-goodyism would be unacceptable to *all* peers. Good-*girl*ism—Sophie's uncomfortable state—seems "good" for her conscience and adult approval, but "bad" for approval by the popular set, whose upper-class drink-and-drug-induced party flirtations and sexual liaisons Sophie disapproves of. The meaning of Sophie's good-girl image is, however, quite class-specific, as Mary Evans describes in her analysis of middle-class schooling, *A Good School*:

> as far as possible a "good" girl did not have an appearance. What she had was a correct uniform, which gave the world the correct message about her—that is, that she was a well-behaved, sensible person who could be trusted not to wish to attract attention to herself by an unusual, let alone a fashionable appearance. (1991: 30–1)

Signalling her acceptance of the career-class uniform, Sophie could not also signal her interest in boys. Indeed, she walked away from her body, except as an athletic court. "Other girls" dressed either "schleppy" (the androgynous or indifferent look) or "provocative." Sophie's neat, "sporty" look—tights and a lean body made her miniskirt look more athletic than hooker-inspired—seems designed to be comfortable and competent as one-of-the-guys while ever-so-casually gesturing toward femininity (no dykey trousers). Her dress is designed to bridge the contradiction of middle-class education and femininity, as Mary Evans describes it in her own schooling in the 1950s:

> To be a successful [prep] school girl involved, therefore, absorbing two specific (but conflicting) identities. First, that of the androgynous middleclass person who is academically successful in an academic world that is apparently gender blind. Second, that of the well-behaved middleclass woman who knows how to defer to and respect the authority of men. (1991: 23)

Feminism has altered, over history, their terms of deference to men, their ability to name sexism and resist. But their feminism does not seem to have revised the categories of "gender" or "body" at all. What seems intact from the 1950s is their terms of respect for the authority of men as superior and normal forms of human being. What seems distinct in the 1990s is that these young women think they have a right to be young men too.

Damalleaux's example of her own good-girlism shares some of Sophie's dilemma of being a good student at the expense of peer popularity. But Damalleaux resolved this tension differently, as Signthia Fordham (1988) would argue is likely to happen among academically talented low-income African-American students:

Damalleaux: I used to be a straight-A girl and now I'm down to Bs and Cs. I used to be so good it's a shame . . .
Pat: What changed?
Damalleaux: I couldn't help it any more. . . . When I got straight As they'd call me a nerd and things. But I'd be happy because my mother would give me anything I want for it. . . . Mom [would say to teasing brothers] "Leave my first girl alone!" . . . [Then] I got around the wrong people, I don't study so much . . .
Pat: Is it uncool to be a girl and get good grades?
Damalleaux: Yes it is. . . . I'll do my work and they'll say "Smarty Pants! Smarty Pants!"

Janet gave an example of "acting stupid" with peers, which seemed to be her manner of flirtation. Sophie pointed out that Janet could afford to because everybody already knew she was smart. Sophie clearly felt more trapped by being a smart and a good girl.

Girls can be good, bad or—best of all—they can be boys. This version of individualized resistance, or feminism, reflects a retreat from the collective politics of gender, and from other women, and an advance into the embattled scene of gender politics—alone, and against boys, in order to become one of them.

On Closings, or, The End of the Second Pizza

We heard these four women struggling between the discourses of feminism and adolescence. Perhaps struggling is even too strong a word. They hungered for a strong version of individualistic, "gender-free" adolescence and had rejected that which had been deemed traditionally feminine, aping instead that which had been deemed traditionally masculine. Delighted to swear, spit, tell off-color jokes, wear hats and trash other girls, they were critical of individual boys, nasty about most girls, rarely challenging of the sex/gender system, and were ecstatic, for the most part, to be engaged as friends and lovers with young men. But we also heard their feminism in their collective refusal to comply with male demands, their wish for women friends to trust, their expectations for equality and search for respect, their deep ambivalence about being "independent of a man" and yet in partnership with one, and their strong yearnings to read, write and talk more about women's experiences among women. They appreciated our creation of a context in which this was possible. "The women of Michelle's place," Shermika called us at the end of one evening, prizing our collectivity by re-using a black woman writer's novel title.

> The public terms of the discourse of femininity preclude the expression of deviant views of marriage, motherhood, and the public terms are the only ones to which girls have access. Part of the task of feminist work with girls is thus, I would suggest, giving girls terms in which to express their experiential knowledge, rather than having to fall back into the stereotyped expressions of normatively defined femininity in order to say anything at all about areas of life which vitally concern them. (Hudson, 1984: 52)

Through critical and collaborative group interview we evolved a form of conversation, what Hudson might call feminist work, with these four young women which allowed us to engage in what we might consider collective consciousness work, as a form of feminist methodology. Our "talks" became an opportunity to "try on" ways of being women, struggling through power, gender, culture and class.

With Donna Haraway's (1989) notion of "partial vision" firmly in mind, we realized that in our talk, no one of us told the "whole truth." We all occluded the "truth" in cultured ways. The conversation was playful and filled with the mobile positionings of all of us women. While we each imported gender, race, class, culture, age and bodies to our talk, we collectively created an ideological dressing room in which the six of us could undress a little, try things on, exchange, rehearse, trade and critique. Among the six of us we were able to lift up what had become "personal stories," raise questions, try on other viewpoints and re-see our stories as narratives through power.

> As a critique of the excesses of individualism, feminism potentially contributes to a new conception of community—of the relation between the freedom of individuals and the needs of society. The realization of that potential lies not in the repudiation of difference but in a new understanding of its equitable social consequences. (Fox-Genovese, 1991: 256)

We could recount together how alone and frightened we have each felt as we have walked, and are watched, down city streets; how our skin tightens when we hear men comment aloud on our bodies; how we smart inside with pain when we learn that other women define themselves as "good women" by contrasting themselves with our feminist politics; how we fetishize those body parts that have betrayed us with their imperfection. Within the safety of warm listening and caring, yet critical talk, we attached each of these "secret" feelings to political spaces defined by culture, class and gender contours of our daily lives. This method moved us, critically and collectively, from pain to passion to power, prying open the ideologies of individualism, privacy and loyalty which had sequestered our "personal stories."

After our last dinner, stuffed and giggly, tired but still wanting just one more round of conversation, we—Pat and Michelle—realized that the four young women were getting ready to drive away. Together and without us. Before, Pat had driven Shermika and Damalleaux to Michelle's and home. But now they were leaving us behind. Stunned, we looked at each other, feeling abandoned. We thought we were concerned about their safety. Four young women in a car could meet dangers just outside the borders of Michelle's block.

We turned to each other realizing that even our abandonment was metaphoric and political. These four young women were weaving the next generation of feminist politics, which meant, in part, leaving us. We comforted ourselves by recognizing that our conversation had perhaps enabled this work. No doubt, individual interviews with each of the four would have produced an essay chronicling the damages of femininity—eating disorders, heterosexual traumas, perhaps some abuse or abortion stories; that is, deeply individualized, depoliticized and atomized tales of "things that have happened to me as an adolescent female." What happened among us instead was that a set of connections was forged—between personal experiences and power, across cultures, classes and politics, and within an invented space, cramped between the discourses of a rejected *femininity,* an individualized *adolescence* and a collective *feminism as resistance.*

> Resistance is that struggle we can most easily grasp. Even the most subjected person has moments of rage and resentment so intense that they respond, they act against. There is an inner uprising that leads to rebellion, however short-lived. It may be only momentary, but it takes place. That space within oneself where resistance is possible remains: It is different then to talk about becoming subjects. That process emerges as one comes to understand how structures of domination work in one's own life, as one develops critical thinking and critical consciousness, as one invents new alternative habits of being and resists from that marginal space of difference inwardly defined. (hooks, 1990: 15)

In our finest post-pizza moment, we—Pat and Michelle—realized that as these women drove off, they were inventing their own feminist legacy, filled with passions, questions, differences and power. We were delighted that we had helped to challenge four young women's versions of individualistic feminism, without solidarity, by doing the consciousness work of our generation. We taught, and relearned, feminism as a dialectical and historical discourse about experience and its interpretations, a collective reframing of private confessions. As we yelled, "Go straight home!" to their moving car, for a moment we felt like the world was in very good hands.

REFERENCES

Anderson, E. (1990). *Streetwise: Race, Class and Change in an Urban Community.* Chicago: University of Chicago Press.

Asch, A., and Fine, M. (1988). "Shared dreams: a left perspective on disability rights and reproductive rights," in M. Fine and A. Asch (eds.), *Women with Disabilities: Essays in Psychology, Culture and Politics*. Philadelphia: Temple University Press, pp. 297–305.

Baker, H. (1989). Personal communication.

Bordo, S. (1990). "Reading the slender body," in M. Jacobus, E. Fox Keller and S. Shuttleworth (eds.), *Body/Politics: Women and the Discourses of Science*. New York: Routledge, pp. 31–53.

Brodkey, L., and Fine, M. (1988). "Presence of mind in the absence of body," *Journal of Education*, 170(3): 84–99.

Corbett, K., with Klein, S., and Bregante, J. (1987). "The role of sexuality and sex equity in the education of disabled women," *Peabody Journal of Education*, 64(4): 198–212.

Evans, M. (1991). *A Good School: Life at a Girl's Grammar School in the 1950s*. London: The Women's Press.

Fine, M. (1988). "Sexuality, schooling and adolescent females: the missing discourse of desire," *Harvard Educational Review*, 58(1): 29–53.

Fine, M., and Asch, A. (1988). "Disability beyond stigma: social interaction, discrimination and activism," *Journal of Social Issues*, 44(1): 3–22.

Fordham, S. (1988). "Racelessness as a factor in Black students' school success," *Harvard Educational Review*, 58(1), 54–84.

Fox-Genovese, E. (1991). *Feminism without Illusions: A Critique of Individualism*. Chapel Hill: University of Carolina Press.

Frank, G. (1988). "On embodiment: a case study of congenital limb deficiency in American culture," in M. Fine and A. Asch (eds.), *Women with Disabilities: Essays in Psychology, Culture and Politics*. Philadelphia: Temple University Press, pp. 41–71.

Giddings, P. (1984). *When and Where I Enter: The Impact of Black Women on Race and Sex in America*. New York: Bantam.

Gilligan, C. (1990). "Joining the resistance: psychology, politics, girls and women." Essay presented as the Tanner Lecture on Human Values, University of Michigan.

Gilligan, C., Wards, J., and Taylor, J. (1988). *Mapping the Moral Domain*. Cambridge, Mass.: Harvard University Press.

Halson, J. (1991). "Young women, sexual harassment and heterosexuality: violence, power relations and mixed sex schooling," in P. Abbott and C. Wallace (eds.), *Gender, Power and Sexuality*. London: Macmillan, pp. 97–113.

Haraway, D. (1989). *Prime Visions: Gender, Race, and Nature in the World of Modern Science*. New York: Routledge.

Hare-Mustin, R. T. (1991). "Sex, lies, and headaches: the problem is power," in T. J. Goodrich (ed.), *Women and Power: Perspectives for Therapy*. New York: Norton, pp. 63–85.

Hey, V. (1987). " 'The company she keeps': the social and interpersonal construction of girls' same sex friendships." Ph.D. dissertation, University of Kent at Canterbury, England.

hooks, b. (1984). *Feminist Theory from Margin to Center*. Boston: South End Press.

hooks, b. (1990). *Yearning: Race, Gender, and Cultural Politics*. Boston: South End Press.

Hudson, B. (1984). "Femininity and adolescence," in A. McRobbie and M. Nava (eds.), *Gender and Generation*. London: Macmillan, pp. 31–53.

Joseph, G., and Lewis, J. (1981). *Common Differences: Conflicts in Black and White Feminist Perspectives*. Boston: South End Press.

Kelly, L. (1988). *Surviving Sexual Violence*. Oxford: Basil Blackwell.

Kitzinger, C. (1988). " 'It's not fair on girls': young women's accounts of unfairness in school." Paper presented at the British Psychological Society Conference, University of Leeds.

Lather, P. (1991). *Getting Smart: Feminist Research and Pedagogy within the Postmodern*. New York: Routledge.

Lesko, N. (1988). "The curriculum of the body: lessons from a Catholic high school," in L. Roman, L. K. Christian-Smith and E. Ellsworth (eds.), *Becoming Feminine: The Politics of Popular Culture*. Philadelphia: Falmer Press, pp. 123–42.

Mohanty, C. (1987). "Feminist encounters: locating the politics of experience," *Copyright*, 1: 39.

Orbach, S. (1986). *Hunger Strike: The Anorectic's Struggle as a Metaphor for Our Age*. New York: Norton.

Payne, M. (1991). "Canon: The New Testament to Derrida," *College Literature*, 18(2): 5–21.

Robinson, T., and Ward, J. V. (1991). " 'A belief in self far greater than anyone's disbelief': cultivating resistance among African-American female adolescents," *Woman and Therapy*, 2(3–4): 87–104.

Roman, L. G. (1988). "Intimacy, labor, and class: ideologies of feminine sexuality in the punk slam dance," in L. Roman, L. K. Christian-Smith and E. Ellsworth (eds.), *Becoming Feminine: The Politics of Popular Culture*. Philadelphia: Falmer Press, pp. 143–84.

Spelman, E. (1988). *Inessential Woman*. Boston: Beacon Press.

Walkerdine, V. (1984). "Some day my prince will come: young girls and the preparation for adolescent sexuality," in A. McRobbie and M. Nava (eds.), *Gender and Generation*. London: Macmillan, pp. 162–84.

Willie, C. V. (1985). *Black and White Families: A Study in Complementarity*. Dix Hill, N.Y.: General Hall.

Chapter Seventeen

Masculinity Ideology and Its Correlates

Joseph H. Pleck, Freya Lund Sonenstein, and Leighton C. Ku

This chapter highlights a relatively neglected research perspective on masculinity and the male gender role: the *masculinity ideology* approach. We first present the construct of masculinity ideology and relate it to other current conceptualizations used in the study of masculinity. We then present some illustrative results from our current research on adolescent males. Finally, we address some methodological and interpretive questions raised by the masculinity ideology perspective and identify future research directions.

Masculinity Ideology: Relationship to Other Constructs

Masculinity ideology refers to beliefs about the importance of men adhering to culturally defined standards for male behavior. This construct derives most directly from a line of research concerning attitudes toward masculinity (Thompson, Pleck, & Ferrera, 1992). Theoretically, it grows out of the "gender-role strain" model for masculinity (Pleck, 1981), as well as the "social constructionist" perspective on men (Brod, 1987; Kimmel, 1987; Kimmel & Messner, 1989).

How Masculinity Ideology Differs from Masculine Gender-Related Personality Traits

Before discussing how masculinity ideology relates to these other constructs, it needs to be clearly differentiated from another concept: masculine gender-related personality traits. The latter refer to the degree to which an individual actually possesses the characteristics expected in men. It is assessed by the masculinity subscales in measures such as the Bem (1974) Sex Role Inventory (BSRI). Lenney's (1991) recent review uses *gender-role orientation* as the generic term for the construct assessed by these measures. However, Spence (1992; cf. Spence, Losoff, & Robbins,

Joseph H. Pleck, Freya L. Sonenstein, & Leighton C. Ku, "Masculinity Ideology: Its Impact on Adolescent Males' Heterosexual Relationships." *Journal of Social Issues, 49* (3), pp. 11–30. © 1993 by the Society for the Psychological Study of Social Issues. Reprinted with permission.

1991) argues that a more descriptive, theoretically neutral label is preferable. Thus we use *masculine gender-related personality traits* as the master term, with *masculine personality traits* and *trait masculinity* as synonyms.

Trait masculinity and masculinity ideology are the two primary masculinity-related constructs used in research. They represent parallel but quite different conceptualizations of "masculinity." In broad terms, the former falls within the trait tradition in personality psychology, whereas the latter derives from the social-psychological and sociological conception of norms. In the former, the essence of masculinity is *being* masculine; in the latter, it is *ideologically endorsing* masculinity. Correspondingly, these two constructs are assessed differently at the individual level — the gender-role orientation conception employs trait measures (or more precisely, measures assessing traits via self-concept ratings), and the masculinity ideology conception uses attitudinal measures concerning endorsement of traditional expectations or standards for males. Thus a "traditional" male, viewed in terms of masculine personality characteristics, actually *has* culturally defined masculine attributes. In contrast, from the perspective of masculinity ideology, the traditional male is one who believes that men *should* have these attributes.

Of the two constructs, trait masculinity has received far more research attention (Lenney, 1991). The nature of gender-related personality traits and how they are psychometrically organized have been interpreted in different ways, ranging from the "gender-role identity"[1] approach dominant in the 1950s and 1960s (Pleck, 1981, 1983) to the variety of perspectives represented in more recent work using the BSRI, the PAQ, and the EPAQ (Lenney, 1991). Although many interpret the M subscales of Spence and Helmreich's (1978) Personal Attributes Questionnaire (PAQ), and Spence, Helmreich, and Holahan's (1979) Extended Personal Attributes Questionnaire (EPAQ) as assessing masculine gender-role orientation, Spence's current work holds that these scale dimensions are best interpreted more narrowly as measures of what their manifest content indicates, namely gender-related instrumental and expressive traits of a desirable nature (Spence, 1992; Spence, Losoff, & Robbins, 1991). For more discussion of ways that trait masculinity measures have been interpreted, see Pleck (1981; Pleck, Sonenstein, & Ku, in press-a). The key point here, however, is that masculinity ideology differs conceptually from masculine gender-related personality traits.

Attitudes toward Masculinity

The construct of masculinity ideology derives most directly from research on attitudes toward masculinity, as assessed by measures such as the Brannon Masculinity Scale (BMS; Brannon, 1985; Brannon & Juni, 1984) and Thompson and Pleck's (1986) Male Role Norms Scale (MRNS) (for reviews, see Beere, 1990; Thompson, Pleck, & Ferrera, 1992). Although the term *attitudes toward masculinity* is widely used as the generic category for these instruments, *masculinity ideology* is a conceptually preferable term for what they assess, for two reasons.

First, the social-psychological conception of attitude actually does not apply well to these measures. *Attitude* generally refers to a person's disposition toward an object or target, primarily on the dimension of favorability. Ordinarily, this disposition should predict some behavior toward that object. To use an example from our own research, adolescent males' attitudes toward condoms predict their use of condoms (Pleck, Sonenstein, & Ku, 1991). This usual conception of attitudes, however, does not fit the available scales for attitudes about masculinity. Masculinity, men, or the male role are not, in the customary sense, the object of the attitudinal disposition, and there is no behavior toward these objects that can be sensibly linked to it. With the exception of Eagly and Mladinic's (1989) work, research on masculinity-related attitudes has not used the classical attitudinal approach.

Second, the more pointed term *masculinity ideology*—better than the neutral term *attitudes toward masculinity*—conveys the significance of what the available scales assess: endorsement and internalization of cultural belief systems about masculinity and male gender, rooted in the structural relationship between the two sexes. Masculinity ideology also connotes better the superordinate nature of the beliefs at issue; they are not just beliefs about a particular social object, but constitute a belief system about masculinity that entails various more specific attitudes and dispositions. Some previous research also provides a precedent for conceptualizing gender-related beliefs as ideologies (e.g., Levinson & Huffman, 1955; Lipman-Blumen, 1972; Mason & Bumpass, 1975).

Masculinity Ideology and Gender-Role Strain

Pleck (1981), synthesizing themes in the contemporary critique of masculinity, formulated a "gender-role strain" model for masculinity. Research has pursued this model in various ways (Eisler & Skidmore, 1987; Komarovsky, 1976; Mason & Bumpass, 1975; O'Neil, Helms, Gable, David, & Wrightsman, 1986). The strain model postulates that cultural standards for masculinity exist, and that socialization encourages men to attempt to live up to them. This process can have three types of negative outcomes for individual males: (a) long-term failure to fulfill male role expectations, with the continuing disjuncture between expectations and one's characteristics leading to low self-esteem and other negative psychological consequences; (b) successful fulfillment of male role expectations, but only through a traumatic socialization process with long-term negative side effects; and (c) successful fulfillment of male role expectations, but with negative consequences because the prescribed characteristics (e.g., low family participation) have inherent negative side effects. These three hypothesized negative effects correspond to three dynamics within male gender-role strain.

We formulate masculinity ideology as playing an essential part in male gender-role strain processes. For example, a male's level of endorsement of traditional masculinity ideology influences the subjective consequences of any existing discrepancies between the male's self-concept and male role standards. It should also influence the extent to which males will attempt to fulfill traditional role expectations in spite of their socialization costs or negative side effects. Pleck (1992) argues that a weakness of his 1981 formulation of male gender-role strain was its lack of attention to processes influencing how psychologically engaged or disengaged males are with traditional male role norms, as a factor influencing role strain outcomes. Thus this chapter seeks to advance the study of masculinity ideology as an essential factor in male gender-role strain. The analyses presented later do so by documenting associations between masculinity ideology and negative side effects.

Social Constructionism and Its Critique of "Sex Role"

"Social constructionism" is a dominant recent theoretical perspective in gender studies (e.g., Hunter College Women's Studies Collective, 1983), and in men's studies (Brod, 1987; Kimmel, 1987; Kimmel & Messner, 1989). As Kimmel and Messner (1989) apply the constructionist perspective to men,

> the important fact of men's lives is not that they are biological males, but that they become men. Our sex may be male, but our identity as men is developed through a complex process of interaction with the culture in which we both learn the gender scripts appropriate to our culture, and attempt to modify those scripts to make them more palatable. (p. 10)

Social constructionism and the concept of gender-role strain are theoretically compatible. Social constructionism's central concept of the learning of gender "scripts" is analogous to the gender-role strain paradigm's equally central concept of gender-role socialization. The concept of masculinity ideology can be easily integrated with social constructionism. Constructionism argues that males act in the ways they do not because of their biological characteristics, but because of the conceptions of masculinity held by their culture. Masculinity ideology is the individual-level construct that links individual males to their culture's construction of masculinity.

Social construction theorists make a pointed critique of what they describe as the "gender-role" model for understanding gender as "ahistorical, psychologically reductionist, and apolitical" (Kimmel, 1987, p. 12). Because parts of this critique potentially apply to the concept of masculinity ideology as well, they should be briefly considered here. One criticism made by Kimmel and other construction theorists is that the idea of "gender role" posits a static, historically and culturally invariant model for each sex, replicated generation after generation, which thus cannot explain how changes in women's and men's behavior occur within individuals or historically.

Actually, two quite different approaches within what Kimmel and other construction theorists label the "gender-role model" need to be distinguished: gender-role *strain* and gender-role *identity*. Construction theorists are arguing against the male gender-role *identity* model (Pleck, 1981), not the gender-role *strain* model. Gender-role identity theorists indeed made these erroneous assumptions of historical and cultural invariance and of automatic intergenerational transmission. Kimmel also links the gender-role model to functionalist sociology, which initially used the term *sex role* to refer to sex role identity (e.g., Parsons & Bales, 1955). Finally, Kimmel cites

Pleck's (1981) analysis of the theory of male gender-role identity as a critique of the gender-role model.

The gender-role strain model is in fact a social constructionist model that predated the term *constructionism*. In gender-role strain theory, gender roles are explicitly *not* assumed to be invariant. In fact, strain theorists use evidence of cultural variations in each sex's behavior as evidence that gender behavior can be understood as role behavior, rather than as a result of biological gender differences. This model clearly conceptualizes gender roles as varying, and empirical research conducted within this model has made some (but not all) dimensions of variation central topics of investigation (e.g., studies of differences associated with wives' employment status).

A second, related criticism made by social construction theorists is that the gender-role model assumes a *single* standard or set of expectations for masculinity, an invalid assumption in light of the differences that exist within cultures. In social constructionism one must not speak of masculinity, but only of masculini*ties*. What role theorists represent as the male role in general is, say constructionists, really only the white heterosexual middle-class male role in the United States at this historical moment. This criticism overlooks the extent to which male gender-role theorists have explicitly argued that male role expectations include several different dimensions, the relative salience of which may vary among individuals and social groups (e.g., Brannon, 1976), and that there are multiple, competing conceptions of masculinity (Pleck, 1976).

The social constructionist criticism implies that one cannot formulate a scale assessing masculinity ideology, because there is not one ideology that is valid for all social groups. In our view, rather than glossing over group differences, measures of masculinity ideology make it possible actually to study them quantitatively, rather than simply to theorize about them. Use of a masculinity ideology scale does not necessitate a theoretical assumption that there is one universal, unvarying standard for masculinity. Rather, the argument is that a particular social construction of masculinity has been widely (though not universally) prevalent in the contemporary United States, which theorists have argued has various kinds of negative concomitants (Brannon, 1976; Doyle, 1989; Franklin, 1984; Pleck, 1976). Though the label has many pitfalls, "traditional" appears to be the best available term for this particular form of the male role (or construction of masculinity) at issue. It is possible to assess similarities and differences among different groups in the prevalence of this conception of masculinity. Researchers can also assess whether endorsing traditional masculinity has the same meaning and correlates among different groups. In these ways, research on masculinity ideology can advance our understanding of masculinity-related dynamics among different groups.

Masculinity Ideology and Adolescent Male Problem Behaviors

We will illustrate the use of the masculinity ideology approach in analyses from our work with the 1988 National Survey of Adolescent Males (Pleck, Sonenstein, & Ku, in press-a). These analyses concern the relationship between masculinity ideology and a group of behaviors known in adolescent research as "problem behaviors": sexual activity, substance use, delinquency, and school problems. One major line of current research on adolescence takes the perspective that a variety of specific deviant or unconventional behaviors are manifestations of a "problem behavior syndrome"; that is, they have common underlying causes and as a result are intercorrelated with each other (Jessor & Jessor, 1977; Ketterlinus & Lamb, in press). In this chapter, the theoretical notion investigated is that in adolescent males one of these underlying causes is adherence to a traditional masculinity ideology. That is, the problematic behaviors shown by many adolescent males are a result of how our society defines masculinity.

This connection may seem obvious and indeed is often expressed informally. For example, in a recent article on the rising sales of malt liquors to young urban males, a youth counselor reports that "the attitude is, 'you're a man if you've got a 40 [ounce bottle] in your hand'" (Deveny, 1992). In a news report, a former male cigarette advertising model who developed lung cancer testified to a legislative committee that the underlying dynamic of the commercials in which he acted was that "we made you believe if you boys smoke, you'll be macho" (Kong, 1992).

Interestingly, the possible connection between masculinity and problem behavior has received little recent research attention. A handful of studies, many using convenience samples of male college students, identify such correlates of masculinity ideology as homophobia, Type A disposition, various behaviors relevant to close relationships, and condom use and attitudes (Bunting & Reeves, 1983; Pleck, Sonenstein, & Ku, in press-b; Snell, Hawkins, & Belk, 1988; Stark, 1991; Thompson, 1990; Thompson, Grisanti, & Pleck, 1985). However, no prior study documents the linkage of masculinity ideology specifically to adolescent male problem behaviors. Even among the large group of studies investigating correlates of the other primary masculinity-related construct, masculine personality traits, only a few have explored their association with problem behaviors (Horwitz & White, 1987; Snell, Belk, & Hawkins, 1987; Thompson, 1990; cf. Spence, Helmreich, & Holahan, 1979; Spence, Losoff, & Robbins, 1991). This relative lack of attention to masculinity in current research on problem behaviors provides an interesting contrast with earlier psychological views. In the 1950s and 1960s, under the influence of what Pleck (1981) labels the "male gender role identity paradigm," it was generally theorized that delinquency among males reflected adolescent males' conflicts or insecurity in sex role identity. However, when this and other lines of research within the male identity paradigm went into eclipse beginning in the mid-1970s, the relationship of masculinity to problem behaviors was generally no longer investigated.

Thus, in addition to arguing for the theoretical and empirical utility of the construct of masculinity ideology, the present study also intends to stimulate new interest in the link between masculinity and problem behaviors from a fresh perspective. The general hypothesis tested here is that among adolescent males, endorsement of masculinity ideology is associated with problem behaviors in four areas: school difficulties, substance use, delinquency, and sexual activity.

Method

Sample

The National Survey of Adolescent Males (NSAM) interviewed 1,880 never-married males aged fifteen to nineteen between April and November 1988. Its sample represented the noninstitutionalized never-married male population aged fifteen to nineteen in the contiguous United States. The sample was stratified to overrepresent black and Hispanic respondents, and in-person interviews averaging seventy-five minutes were completed with 676 young black, non-Hispanic men, 386 young Hispanic men, 755 young white, non-Hispanic men, and 63 respondents in other racial groupings. The response rate for those eligible to be interviewed was 73.9 percent. For other information on the sample, design, and procedures, see Sonenstein and colleagues (1989). Sample weights are available so that distributional results can be estimated for all noninstitutionalized never-married fifteen- to nineteen-year-old males. Analyses of distributions for problem behaviors and attitudes about masculinity use the full sample and are weighted to represent the population. Multivariate analyses use the 1,595 cases with complete data on all measures and are unweighted.

Measures

Masculinity Ideology. This construct was assessed by an eight-item measure. Seven items were adapted from Thompson and Pleck's (1986) Male Role Norms Scale (MRNS), a twenty-six item abbreviated version of the Brannon Masculinity Scale, Short Form (Brannon, 1985). Items were chosen to represent the three factorial dimensions of the MRNS: status (three items), toughness (two items), and antifemininity (two items). Items considered most relevant to an adolescent sample were selected, and wording was simplified or otherwise altered to be more appropriate for this age group. An additional item specifically about sex, a topical area absent from the MRNS, was also included (Snell, Belk, & Hawkins 1986). A guiding principle in the construction of these scales is that, as much as possible, items should refer to men in relation to male standards, rather than comparing men and women. However, one item explicitly concerns the husband-wife relationship, and another, concerning husbands' responsibility for housework, implies this relationship.

An index was derived from the eight items, with an alpha coefficient of .56. Analyses showed that all items contributed to the index, and that omission of any items would not lead to improvement in reliability. Alphas among whites, blacks, and Hispanics were .61, .47, and .54. Although this level of internal reliability is less than ideal, it was considered adequate for use in further analysis. Thompson (1990) reported a coefficient alpha of .91 in a college sample for the twenty-six-item scale from which most of the eight items used in the present study were adapted. The lower reliability found in the present study results from the smaller number of items used.

Most measures of problem behaviors except those concerning sexual activity were composed of items from a short self-administered questionnaire (SAQ) for questions judged to be especially sensitive, which respondents completed and returned to the interviewer in a sealed envelope. For the problem behavior measures, high scores always denote being high on the construct.

School Difficulties. Two items from the SAQ concerning school problems were employed. Males were asked: "Have you ever repeated a grade, or been held back a grade in school?" and "Were you ever suspended from school?"

Alcohol and Drug Use. The SAQ included parallel items for (a) drinking "beer, wine, hard liquor, or any other alcoholic beverage," (b) trying "cocaine or crack," and (c) trying "any other street drugs." For each, respondents were asked whether they had ever done the activity, and if so, how often they had done it during the last twelve months (never, a few times, monthly, weekly, or daily).

Delinquent Activity. Males were asked in the SAQ: "Have you ever been picked up by the police for doing something wrong?" and "Have you ever done something that the police would pick you up for if they had found out?" Those answering positively were asked how often this had happened (once or twice, three to five times, six to ten times, or eleven or more times).

Sexual Activity. Three measures of sexual activity were selected for inclusion in this analysis. Sexual activity status was assessed by the question "Have you ever had sexual intercourse with a girl (sometimes this is called 'making love,' 'having sex,' or 'going all the way')?" Current level of sexual activity was indicated by respondents' reports of the number of different sexual partners they had in the last year; for this analysis, those not sexually active in the last year were assigned a code of zero. These two measures appeared in the interviewer-administered part of the NSAM. Finally, a measure of coercive sex was taken from the SAQ: "Have you ever tricked or forced someone else to have sex with you?"

Sociodemographic and Personal Background Variables. Besides current age, respondents reported the level of education they thought they would ever complete (collapsed to less than high school diploma, high school diploma, some college or vocational school, four years of college, postgraduate). Attendance at religious services at age fourteen was reported in four categories: never, less than once a month, one to three times a month, and once a week or more. Race was coded as black non-Hispanic, white non-Hispanic, Hispanic, and other race, with white non-Hispanic used as the reference category in regression analyses. Respondents estimated their family annual income in one of seven categories (in thousands: 0–10, 10–20, 20–30, 30–40, 40–50, 50–60, and 60+; coded 1–7). Region of the country was coded as the four census regions (North, Midwest, West, and South), with South as the reference category.

Results

Frequency of Problem Behaviors

Difficulties in school were relatively frequent, with 30.1 percent of the sample reporting repeating a grade in school, and 37.8 percent reporting suspension. Moreover, 21.0 percent reported drinking weekly or daily during the last year, and 6.6 percent reported using cocaine or crack in the last year. Among these, most reported cocaine use only "a few times." Use of "other street drugs" in the last year was acknowledged by 17.4 percent. (To a follow-up question, almost 90 percent reported the drug was marijuana.)

More than a quarter, 28.1 percent, had been "picked up" by the police. For most, this occurred only once or twice. A larger proportion, 47.6 percent, acknowledged ever doing something that the police would pick them up for, and 12.4 percent reported such activity six or more times. About 60.4 percent were sexually active. (Sonenstein et al., 1989, provide detailed breakdowns by age and race/ethnicity.) Regarding number of different sexual partners in the last year, 45.1 percent had none, 27.3 percent had one, 15.0 percent had two, 4.8 percent had three, and only 7.6 percent had four or more. For more detail, see Pleck and colleagues (in press-a).

Distributions of the Masculinity Ideology Items and Index. Table 17.1 provides distributional information for the items assessing traditional masculinity ideology. Item distributions may vary not only because of true differences in the rate of endorsement of one aspect of traditional male role expectations compared to another, but also because item wordings may not be precisely equivalent in intensity; because of the latter possibility, differences in means should be interpreted with caution. With this caveat, this sample reported relatively strong endorsement of traditional male role expectations concerning being respected by others, self-confidence, and avoidance of overt femininity (items 1–3, 6). By contrast, the mean levels of endorsement for the items concerning physical toughness and hypersexuality (5, 8) were close to the theoretical midpoint of 2.5. These two items also showed the largest standard deviations. Finally, respondents tended on the average to disagree with the items

TABLE 17.1
Means and Standard Deviations of Masculinity Ideology Items and Index

Item	Mean[a]	S.D.
1. It is essential for a guy to get respect from others.	3.23	.80
2. A man always deserves the respect of his wife and children.	3.53	.71
3. I admire a guy who is totally sure of himself.	3.30	.79
4. A guy will lose respect if he talks about his problems	1.76	.87
5. A young man should be physically tough, even if he's not big.	2.63	1.03
6. It bothers me when a guy acts like a girl.	3.33	.92
7. I don't think a husband should have to do housework.	1.72	.88
8. Men are always ready for sex.	2.13	.96
Traditional male role attitudes index.	2.80	.44

NOTES: Weighted Ns for items = 1,868–1,877; weighted N for index = 1,851.
[a] range: 1–4; 1 = disagree a lot, 2 = disagree a little, 3 = agree a little, 4 = agree a lot.

assessing traditional male role expectations regarding not expressing weakness and not doing housework.

Association between Masculinity Ideology and Problem Behaviors

In these analyses, logistic regression was used to predict the problem behavior measures assessed in dichotomous form, and odds ratios are reported for predictors found to be statistically significant (Morgan & Teachman, 1988). Ordinary least squares regression was used for the problem behaviors assessed on continuous scales. In both sets of analyses, current age, expected level of education completed, frequency of religious attendance at age fourteen, race/ethnicity, current family income, and region of the country were included to control for sociodemographic and personal background factors. Results of the regression analyses of the association between masculinity ideology and problem behaviors are reported in Tables 17.2 and 17.3. Masculinity ideology showed a significant independent association with seven of the ten problem behaviors. Specifically, traditional masculinity expectations were associated with ever being suspended from school, drinking and use of drugs (primarily marijuana), being picked up by the police, being sexually active, number of heterosexual partners in the last year, and coercive sex. Number of partners in the last year was also predicted among the sexually active only; the coefficient for masculinity ideology remained significant (beta = .079, $p < .05$).

Based on factor analyses and reliability analyses not shown in detail here, an index combining the three substance use and the two illegal activities measures was created (alpha = .69), and results paralleled those for the individual problem behavior indicators. In addition, possible interactions between masculinity ideology and race,

TABLE 17.2

Logistic Regression Analyses of Problem Behaviors on Masculinity Ideology and Sociodemographic Factors (N = 1,595)

Predictor	Repeated grade		Suspended		Sexually active		Forced sex	
	Coeff.	Odds ratio	Coeff.	Odds ratio	Coeff.	Odds ratio	Coeff.	Odds ratio
Masculinity ideology	−.026		.398**	1.49	.698**	2.01	.657**	1.93
Age	−.022		.066		.573**	1.77	.212*	1.24
Expected education	−.511**	.57	−.435**	.64	−.126**	.88	−.063**	
Religious attendance at age 14	−.130*	.88	−.142**	.87	−.215**	.81	−.327**	.72
Black[a]	.394**	1.48	.788**	2.20	1.399**	4.05	1.864**	6.45
Hispanic	.340**	1.40	.219		.218		1.491**	4.44
Other race	−.179		.133		−.017		1.981**	7.24
Family income	−.154**	.86	.017		.030		.151	
North[b]	.063		.465**	1.59	−.076		.394	
Midwest	−.620**	.54	.464**	1.59	.127		−.005	
West	−.961**	.38	.403**	1.50	−.278		−.373	
Model chi-square (11 df)	252.72		167.35		313.90		43.73	

NOTES: [a] reference category for race is white.
[b] reference category for region is South.
* $p < .05$; ** $p < .01$

TABLE 17.3

Multiple Regression Analyses of Dichotomous Problem Behaviors as Predicted by Masculinity Ideology and Sociodemographic Factors

(standardized regression coefficients; N = 1,595)

Predictor	Drink alcohol	Use cocaine	Use other drugs	Picked up by police	Police would pick up	Number partners last year
Masculinity ideology	.063*	.020	.064*	.090**	.026	.105**
Age	.215**	.117**	.091**	.077**	.045	.143**
Expected education	−.038	−.092**	−.100**	−.156**	.006	.066
Religious attendance at age 14	−.046	−.089**	−.083**	−.089**	−.051*	−.066**
Black[a]	−.221**	−.100*	−.154**	−.056*	−.200**	.221**
Hispanic	−.078*	.028	.037	.007	−.107**	.012
Other race	−.059	.018	.010	.010	−.044	−.013
Family income	.140**	.017	.047	.042	.121**	.081**
North[b]	.036	.039	.009	.084*	.012	.042
Midwest	.058*	−.010	.041	.145**	.011	.031
West	.002	.061*	.042	.066*	.007	−.016
Adj. R^2	.118	.044	.053	.069	.064	.097

NOTES: [a] reference category for race is white.
[b] reference category for region is South.
*$p < .05$; **$p < .01$

age, and educational expectations were examined, to detect whether the association between traditional expectations and problem behaviors might vary in different sample subgroups. In no case did inclusion of such interaction terms improve model fit. Thus there is no evidence that the association between problem behaviors and masculinity ideology differs among black, white, and Hispanic males.

In the ordinary least squares regression analyses, the size of significant associations observed between masculinity ideology and problem behaviors were modest, with betas ranging from .06 to .11. In the logistic regression analyses, an increment of one scale point (somewhat more than two standard deviations) on the masculinity ideology index was associated with about 50 percent greater odds of being suspended from school and about twice the odds of being sexually active and of ever forcing someone to have sex.

Implications and Issues

Our analysis indicates that adolescent males' problem behaviors are significantly associated with their endorsement of traditional masculinity ideology. The seven problem behavior indicators that demonstrated significant associations with masculinity ideology include at least one measure from each of the four broad areas of problem behaviors investigated here. These results are consistent with other research noted earlier focusing on other theoretical concomitants of masculinity attitudes, such as homophobia, Type A disposition, behaviors relevant to close relationships, and condom use and attitudes.

This analysis does have several limitations. In particular, the measures of problem behaviors utilize only self-reports, and it is not possible to specify the direction of causality: masculinity ideology may be as much a result as a cause of engaging in problem behaviors. But with these limitations acknowledged, these results have important implications from an applied perspective: adolescent males' definitions of masculinity are involved in whether or not they engage in problem behaviors.

Future research on masculinity ideology should address three interpretive or conceptual issues: (a) whether masculinity ideology is empirically distinct from masculine gender-related personality traits; (b) whether masculinity ideology is distinct from attitudes toward women; and (c) similarities and differences in the levels and concomitants of masculinity ideology among different groups, especially racial-ethnic groups.

Is Masculinity Ideology Independent of Masculine Gender-Related Personality Traits?

At the outset of the chapter, we argued that masculinity ideology and masculine gender-related personality traits are fundamentally distinct constructs. However, they could nonetheless be highly empirically correlated. Thus one important issue in evaluating the utility of masculinity ideology is whether it is really empirically different from trait masculinity. Our study did not have both kinds of measures available, so that we cannot estimate this relationship in our own data. In the studies that have both measures, however, the two constructs are generally unrelated (Thompson, Pleck, & Ferrera, 1992). This is consistent with recent reviews suggesting that as a general matter, gender-related attitudes and gender-related personality traits are independent (Archer, 1989, 1990).

As noted earlier, prior research has established that trait masculinity is associated with problem behavior outcomes. Thus it appears that masculinity ideology and masculine personality traits both influence adolescent male problem behaviors (cf. Spence, 1992; Thompson, 1990). It should be noted, however, that the conceptual distance between the problem outcomes considered here and masculinity ideology is greater than the distance between these outcomes and trait masculinity. For example, measures of trait masculinity often include males' self-ratings on aggression, toughness, and risk taking. Finding a relationship between such a measure and, for example, being picked up by the police could be interpreted as simply showing that one indicator of toughness and aggression is correlated with another. However, the association between problem behaviors and beliefs *about* masculinity—for example, between illegal acts and agreeing that males lose respect if they talk about their problems, or that men should not do housework—is far less intuitively obvious. Thus the masculinity ideology perspective hypothesizes a more theoretically ambitious relationship than the masculine personality traits approach.

Is Masculinity Ideology Independent of Attitudes toward Women?

Pleck (1981) argued that masculinity ideology and attitudes toward women are theoretically independent. For example, an individual can hold a liberal attitude toward women (e.g., believing that wives' employment is acceptable) while simultaneously holding a conservative attitude toward masculinity (e.g., viewing boys' playing with dolls as unacceptable). The two attitudes are thus conceptually independent, but what about their empirical relationship? Prior research provides two different answers.

If attitudes toward women are assessed with items concerning the desirability of women adhering to a traditional female role, without comparison to men, or describing relationships between women and men, they are relatively independent of masculinity ideology (Desnoyers, 1988; Thompson & Pleck, 1986). However, if one assesses attitudes toward women, as many scales do, with items concerning whether a behavior is relatively more desirable in women as compared to men, or with items concerning the appropriate relationship between the sexes, then the two attitudes are more related, with within-sex correlations averaging .5 (Riley, 1990; Stark, personal communication, 1991; Thompson, 1990). These latter studies used Spence and Helmreich's (1972; Spence, Helmreich, & Stapp, 1973) Attitudes toward Women Scale (AWS), the majority of whose items compare the sexes. For example, the first item in the AWS short form is "Swearing and obscenity are more repulsive in the speech of a woman than of a man."

Thus two strategies for assessing attitudes toward women give different results concerning the degree of correlation between attitudes toward women and masculinity ideology. We can illustrate this same pattern in our own data. Table 17.4 shows the relationship between masculinity ideology and three measures of gender-related attitudes. The first two are single-item measures first used in national surveys (Mason & Bumpass, 1975). "A working mother can have just as good a relationship with her child as a mother who does not work" assesses an attitude about women fulfilling or not fulfilling a traditional role, without reference to men. The second item, "It is much better for everyone if the man earns the money and the woman takes care of the home and family," is a gender-comparative item. The third measure, adversarial sexual beliefs, is a three-item scale drawn from Burt (1980) assessing the belief that women exploit or use men (e.g., "In a dating relationship, a girl is largely out to take advantage of a guy.") This item thus concerns gender relationships. As indicated in Table 17.4, masculinity ideology is independent of the first item, but strongly related to the other items.

Our interpretation is that gender-comparative items assess what could be better labeled attitudes toward gender roles and relationships. Thus three kinds of gender-related attitudes need to be distinguished: (1) attitudes toward women (narrowly defined, not involving comparison to men), (2) attitudes toward masculinity (also narrowly defined), and (3) attitudes toward gender roles and relationships. The first two are conceptually and empirically independent, but both are conceptually part of, and are empirically correlated with, the third (Pleck et al., 1992).

In other work we have also gone further to show that attitudes toward masculinity have discriminant validity relative to both attitudes toward women and attitudes toward gender roles and relationships. That is, masculinity ideology has stronger associations with theoretically predicted concomitants than do the two other attitudes, and the associations between masculinity ideology and predicted outcomes persist when levels of the two other attitudes are controlled (Pleck et al., 1992, in press-b). Thus there is good evidence that masculinity ideology is independent of

TABLE 17.4

Multiple Regression Analyses of Attitudes toward Women as Predicted by Masculinity Ideology and Sociodemographic Factors (N = 1,624)

Predictor	Working mother can have good relationship	Better if man earns the money, women takes care of family	Adversarial sexual beliefs
Masculinity ideology	.041	.359***	.353***
Age	−.029	−.031	.027
Expected education	−.008	−.171**	.112*
Religious attendance at age 14	−.011	.009	−.017
Sexually active	.053*	−.059*	−.008
Black[a]	.177***	−.073**	.107***
Hispanic	.081**	.001	.064*
Other race	−.131	−.007	.010
Family income	−.026	−.099*	−.123***
North[b]	−.027	.011	−.034
Midwest	−.033	−.010	−.027
West	−.032	−.012	−.010
$F(12, 1611)$	5.564 ***	33.656 ***	38.880 ***
Adj. R^2	.0326	.1945	.2188
Incr. to adj. R^2 due to male role attitudes index	−.0009	.1174 ***	.1130 ***

NOTES: [a] reference category for race is white.
[b] reference category for region is South.
*$p < .05$; **$p < .01$; ***$p < .001$

attitudes toward women. Future research should investigate how masculinity ideology, beliefs about women, and beliefs about gender roles and relationships independently and interactively shape gender-related behavior.

Masculinity Ideology and Racial-Ethnic Similarities and Differences

An especially important issue in the evaluation of masculinity ideology is its application to different populations, especially racial ethnic groups. As we argued above, use of a masculinity ideology scale does not make the theoretical assumption that there is one universal standard for masculinity. Rather, the claim is that a particular version or social construction of masculinity (not all forms of masculinity) has been widely prevalent in contemporary Western society, and this so-called traditional masculinity has various kinds of negative consequences. Masculinity ideology scales attempt to assess belief in this form of masculinity. What do our data indicate about how well this conceptualization applies to different populations?

Although various other comparisons can be made (Pleck et al., 1992, in press-b), the most important comparison is whether masculinity ideology has similar correlates among different groups. The validity concern is whether the scale and its items mean or signify the same thing to males in different groups. For example, saying that men have to get respect might be an expression of traditional masculinity ideology among whites, but not among blacks or Hispanics. There is some precedent for this concern, because 1950s masculinity-femininity scales were criticized for interpreting items like "I would like to be a singer" as revealing feminine gender-role identification among black males, unaware that in the context of black culture this interpretation may be invalid.

One way of addressing this issue is to determine whether masculinity ideology has similar correlates in different subgroups. As noted above, we tested whether the introduction of terms representing the interaction of masculinity ideology with gender led to a significant increment in explained variance in the regression models in Tables 17.2 and 17.3. Applying this formal test, there was no evidence that the association between problem behaviors and masculinity ideology differed among black, white, and Hispanic males. When the association of individual scale items to the outcomes was also examined, the items generally showed the same relationships. Although racial and ethnic differences and similarities in masculinity ideology and its correlates clearly need more research attention, the evidence to date supports the utility of the construct of masculinity ideology in different racial ethnic groups.

Conclusions

Our research supports two general conclusions. First, masculinity ideology is a distinct component of men's involvement with their gender role. It is independent of masculine gender-related personality traits and differs from men's attitudes toward women. Masculinity ideology contributes to our understanding of male behavior independently of these two other constructs. It does so because it addresses the issue of how men understand what their behavior means.

The hypothetical dynamic investigated in the present study—that problem behaviors in adolescent males are related to masculinity—is one that logically applies only to males. However, researchers should consider parallel ways in which traditional feminine ideology promotes some problem behaviors in adolescent females. A good example in the research literature is Fox's (1977) analysis of the "nice-girl dilemma" in adolescent female contraception. Fox argues that in the traditional conception of femininity, the only legitimate excuse for sex prior to marriage is being so uncontrollably in love that one is swept away by passion. Using contraception is inconsistent with this rationalization because it requires advance planning. Thus adherence to the "nice-girl" conception of femininity means not using contraception. Future research should explore the role of feminine ideology in this and other female problem behaviors.

Second, traditional masculinity ideology is associated with male behaviors that have negative consequences. Thus problem behaviors in adolescent males *are* connected to masculinity ideology. Even though masculinity-related dynamics are clearly not the only source of male problem behaviors, their role has been generally overlooked.

The results of our study might inform applied interventions. Some recent research has found cognitive approaches to be effective in youth-oriented interventions. For example, studies have documented positive effects for teen pregnancy prevention programs focusing on modifying pregnancy-related perceptions suggested by the "health beliefs model" (susceptibility to the problem, seriousness of the problem, benefits and costs of preventive action) as influencing preventive health behavior (Eisen, Zellman, & McAlister, 1990). Adolescent violence prevention efforts have employed "cognitive mediation training," attempting to alter beliefs identified as correlates of the use of aggression (Guerra & Slaby, 1990). Based on our results, one component of male youth interventions might focus on attitudes about masculinity. For example, males could discuss specific beliefs about masculinity and discuss whether masculinity is really validated by risk-taking or deviant behavior. Whatever strategy to address masculinity is employed, intervention and prevention efforts targeted to adolescent males might be more effective if they targeted these dynamics to a greater extent than they do now.

Louis Sullivan (1991), while secretary of the Department of Health and Human Services, urged the policy and intervention communities to address the young male "whose manhood is measured by the number of children he has fathered, and the caliber of the gun he carries." The results of our study suggest some possible avenues for doing so. Changing how manhood is measured means changing traditional masculinity ideology.

NOTE

1. In the literature of the 1950s and 1960s, the term was *sex role identity*. To be consistent with contemporary usage, "sex role" has been updated to "gender role" here and elsewhere.

REFERENCES

Archer, J. (1989). The relationship between gender-role measures. A review. *British Journal of Social Psychology, 28*, 173–184.

Archer, J. (1990). Gender-stereotypic traits are derived from gender roles: A reply to McCreary. *British Journal of Social Psychology, 29*, 273–277.

Beere, C. A. (1990). *Gender roles: A handbook of tests and measures*. Westport, CT: Greenwood Press.

Bem, S. L. (1974). The measurement of psychological androgyny. *Journal of Personality and Social Psychology, 42*, 155–162.

Brannon, R. (1976). The male sex role: Our culture's blueprint for manhood and what it's done for us lately. In D. David & R. Brannon (Eds.), *The forty-nine percent majority: The male sex role* (pp. 1–48). Reading, MA: Addison-Wesley.

Brannon, R. (1985). A scale for measuring attitudes about masculinity. In A. G. Sargent (Ed.), *Beyond sex roles* (pp. 110–116). St. Paul, MN: West.

Brannon, R., & Juni, S. (1984). A scale for measuring attitudes about masculinity. *Psychological Documents, 14*, 6. (Ms. 2012).

Brod, H. (Ed.). (1987). *The making of masculinities: The new men's studies*. Winchester, MA: Allen & Unwin.

Bunting, A. B., & Reeves, J. B. (1983). Perceived male sex orientation and beliefs about rape. *Deviant Behavior, 4*, 281–295.

Burt, M. (1980). Cultural myths and supports for rape. *Journal of Personality and Social Psychology, 38*, 217–230.

Desnoyers, R. M. (1988). *The role of religiosity in male sex role attitudes*. Unpublished honor's thesis, Holy Cross College.

Deveny, K. (1992, March 9). Malt liquor makers find lucrative market in the urban young. *Wall Street Journal*, p. A1.

Doyle, J. A. (1989). *The male experience* (2nd ed.). Dubuque, IA: William C. Brown.

Eagly, A., & Mladinic, A. (1989). Gender stereotypes and attitudes toward women and men. *Personality and Social Psychology Bulletin, 15,* 543–558.

Eisen, M., Zellman, G., & McAlister, A. (1990). Evaluating the impact of a theory-based sexuality and contraceptive education program. *Family Planning Perspectives, 6,* 261–271.

Eisler, R., & Skidmore, J. (1987). Masculine gender role stress: Scale development and components factors in the appraisal of stressful situations. *Behavior Modification, 11,* 123–136.

Fox, G. (1977). "Nice girl": Social control of women through a value construct. *Signs: Journal of Women in Culture and Society, 2,* 805–817.

Franklin, C. W. (1984). *The changing definition of masculinity*. New York: Plenum.

Guerra, N., & Slaby, R. (1990). Cognitive mediators of aggression in adolescent offenders: 2. Intervention. *Developmental Psychology, 26,* 269–277.

Horwitz, A. V., & White, H. R. (1987). Gender role orientation and styles of pathology among adolescents. *Journal of Health and Social Behavior, 28,* 158–170.

Hunter College Women's Studies Collective. (1983). *Women's realities, women's choices*. New York: Oxford University Press.

Jessor, R., & Jessor, S. (1977). *Problem behavior and psychosocial development: A longitudinal study of youth*. New York: Academic Press.

Ketterlinus, R. D., & Lamb, M. E. (in press). *Adolescent problem behaviors*. Hillsdale, NJ: Lawrence Erlbaum.

Kimmel, M. S. (1987). Rethinking "masculinity": New directions in research. In M. S. Kimmel (Ed.), *Changing men: New directions in research on men and masculinity* (pp. 9–24). Newbury Park, CA: Sage.

Kimmel, M. S., & Messner, M. (1989). Introduction. In M. S. Kimmel & M. Messner (Eds.), *Men's lives*. New York: Macmillan.

Komarovsky, M. (1976). *Dilemmas of masculinity*. New York: Norton.

Kong, D. (1992, March 12). Same product, different message. *Boston Globe*, p. 35.

Lenney, E. (1991). Sex roles: The measurement of masculinity, femininity, and androgyny. In J. P. Robinson, P. R. Shaver, & L. S. Wrightsman (Eds.), *Measures of personality and social psychological attitudes* (pp. 573–660). New York: Academic Press.

Levinson, D. J., & Huffman, P. E. (1955). Traditional family ideology and its relations to personality. *Journal of Personality*.

Lipman-Blumen, J. (1972). How ideology shapes women's lives. *Scientific American, 226*(1), 34–62.

Mason, K. O., & Bumpass, L. L. (1975). U.S. women's sex role ideology, 1970. *American Journal of Sociology, 80,* 1212–1219.

Morgan, S. P., & Teachman, J. D. (1988). Logistic regression: Description, examples, and comparisons. *Journal of Marriage and the Family, 50,* 929–936.

O'Neil, J. M., Helms, B., Gable, R. K., David, L., & Wrightsman, L. S. (1986). Gender-role conflict scale: College men's fear of femininity. *Sex Roles, 14,* 335–350.

Parsons, T. C., & Bales, R. F. (1955). *Family socialization and interaction process*. Glencoe, IL: Free Press.

Pleck, J. H. (1976). The male sex role: Problems, definitions, and sources of change. *Journal of Social Issues, 32,* 155–164.

Pleck, J. H. (1981). *The myth of masculinity.* Cambridge: MIT Press.

Pleck, J. H. (1983). The theory of male sex role identity: Its rise and fall, 1936–present. In M. Lewin (Ed.), *In the shadow of the past: Psychology portrays the sexes* (pp. 205–225). New York: Columbia University Press.

Pleck, J. H. (1992, August). *Gender role strain, social constructionism, and masculinity.* Paper presented to the American Psychological Association, Washington.

Pleck, J. H., Sonenstein, F. L., & Ku, L. C. (1990). Contraceptive attitudes and intention to use condoms in sexually experienced and inexperienced males. *Journal of Family Issues, 11,* 294–312.

Pleck, J. H., Sonenstein, F. L., & Ku, L. C. (1991). Adolescent males' condom use: Relationships between perceived cost-benefits and consistency. *Journal of Marriage and the Family, 53,* 733–746.

Pleck, J. H., Sonenstein, F. L., & Ku, L. C. (1992). *Attitudes toward the male gender role: Levels, predictors, and discriminant validity in a national sample of adolescent males.* Manuscript under review.

Pleck, J. H., Sonenstein, F. L., & Ku, L. C. (in press-a). Problem behaviors and masculinity ideology in adolescent males. In R. D. Ketterlinus & M. E. Lamb (Eds.), *Adolescent problem behaviors.* Hillsdale, NJ: Lawrence Erlbaum.

Pleck, J. H., Sonenstein, F. L., & Ku, L. C. (in press-b). Masculinity ideology: Its impact on adolescent males' heterosexual relationships. *Journal of Social Issues.*

Riley, D. P. (1990). *Men's endorsement of male sex-role norms and time spent in psychotherapeutic treatment.* Unpublished doctoral dissertation, Boston University.

Snell, W. E., Belk, S. S., & Hawkins, R. C. (1986). The stereotypes about male sexuality scale (SAMSS): Components, correlates, antecedents, consequences, and counselor bias. *Social and Behavioral Sciences Documents, 16,* 9 (Ms. 2746).

Snell, W. E., Belk, S. S., & Hawkins, R. C. (1987). Alcohol and drug use in stressful times: The influence of the masculine role and sex-related personality attributes. *Sex Roles, 16,* 359–373.

Snell, W. E., Hawkins, R. C., & Belk, S. S. (1988). Stereotypes about male sexuality and the use of social influence strategies in intimate relationships. *Journal of Social and Clinical Psychology, 7,* 42–48.

Sonenstein, F. L., Pleck, J. H., & Ku, L. C. (1989). Sexual activity, condom use and AIDS awareness among adolescent males. *Family Planning Perspectives, 21,* 152–158.

Spence, J. T. (1992). Gender-related traits and gender ideology: Evidence for a multifactorial theory. Unpublished manuscript.

Spence, J. T., & Helmreich, R. L. (1972). The Attitudes toward Women Scale: An objective instrument to measure attitudes toward the rights and roles of women in contemporary society. *JSAS Catalog of Selected Documents in Psychology, 2,* 66.

Spence, J. T., & Helmreich, R. L. (1978). *Masculinity and femininity: Their psychological dimensions, correlates, and antecedents.* Austin: University of Texas Press.

Spence, J. T., Helmreich, R. L., & Holahan, C. T. (1979). Negative and positive components of psychological masculinity and femininity and their relationships to self-reports of neurotic and acting out behaviors. *Journal of Personality and Social Psychology, 37,* 1673–1682.

Spence, J. T., Helmreich, R. L., & Stapp, J. (1973). A short version of the Attitudes toward Women Scale (AWS). *Bulletin of the Psychonomic Society, 2,* 219–220.

Spence, J. T., Losoff, M., & Robbins, A. S. (1991). Sexually aggressive tactics in dating relationships: Personality and attitudinal correlates. *Journal of Social and Clinical Psychology, 10,* 289–304.

Stark, L. P. (1991). Traditional gender role beliefs and individual outcomes: An exploratory analysis. *Sex Roles, 24,* 639–650.

Sullivan, L. (1991, May 25). US secretary urges TV to restrict "irresponsible sex and reckless violence." *Boston Globe,* p. 1.

Thompson, E. H. (1990). Courtship violence and the male role. *Men's Studies Review, 7*(3), 1, 4–13.

Thompson, E. H., Grisanti, C., & Pleck, J. H. (1985). Attitudes toward the male role and their correlates. *Sex Roles, 13,* 413–427.

Thompson, E. H., & Pleck, J. H. (1986). The structure of male role norms. *American Behavioral Scientist, 29,* 531–543.

Thompson, E. H., Jr., Pleck, J. H., & Ferrera, D. L. (1992). Men and masculinities: Scales for masculinity ideology and masculinity-related constructs. *Sex Roles, 27,* 573–607.

Part IV

Autonomy and Connection in Relationships

In this section we present three now-classic works first published in the 1970s that launched a "new psychology of women" (Jean Baker Miller) based on "a different voice" (Carol Gilligan), a relational voice clearly audible in the words of women, but underrepresented and undervalued in traditional psychology. Nancy Chodorow's book *The Reproduction of Mothering* (1978) presented a compelling psychoanalytic argument tracing the origins of the male insistence on autonomy and the female's predilection for connection to the child's early relationship with a female caretaker. Proponents of different-voice theory (Gilligan and her associates as well as the authors of *Women's Ways of Knowing* and others) and self-in-relation theory (developed by Miller and her colleagues at the Stone Center at Wellesley College) argued that the discipline of psychology has emphasized and idealized traditional masculine values of autonomy, separation, detachment, and abstraction at the expense of qualities associated with femininity, such as interdependence, connection, attachment, and attention to the concrete and contextual. As a result, the discipline, like the society at large, has promulgated a vision of maturity that, as Miller puts it, is "built on an exceedingly restricted conception of the total human potential."

Although this message was warmly received by thousands of women, within the social sciences it was greeted with some suspicion. As two psychologists wrote,

> Many women readers find that the comments by women quoted in Gilligan's book resonate so thoroughly with their own experience that they do not need any further demonstration of the truth of what is being said ... *intuitively* we feel that Gilligan must be right.... [But] a warning: Women have been trapped for generations by people's willingness to accept their own intuitions about the truth of gender stereotypes. (Greeno & Maccoby, 1986, p. 315).

The charge that the study of gender difference leads to the reification of stereotypes seems to some especially trenchant in regard to this research, because the different voices attributed to men and women so exactly match gender stereotypes. "Haven't we been here before?" asks Katha Pollit. "Indeed we have. Woman as sharer and carer, ... woman as beneath, above, or beyond such manly concerns as law, reason, abstract ideas—these images are as old as time" (1994/1995, p. 44). Such images have pervaded the discipline of psychology as well as the society at large. Sigmund Freud (1925) wrote, "I cannot escape the notion ... that for women the level of what is ethically normal is different from what it is in men. Their superego is never so inexorable, so impersonal, so independent of its emotional origins as we require it to be in men." For Freud, this meant that women had "less sense of justice than men," a conclusion from which, he said, he would not be "deflected by ... the denials of the feminists, who are anxious to force us to regard the two sexes as completely equal in position and worth" (p. 193). Different-voice psychologists *do* regard women as equal to men, of course, but critics fear that to characterize women as they do will lead inevitably to their being seen as inferior, given that in our time and culture, as in Freud's, greater value is placed on rationality and autonomy than on feeling and relationship.

The charge that differences attributed to gender are really due to differences in status also seems especially compelling applied to this strand of research. Katherine Allen and Kristine Baber warn that "uncritical acceptance of women's ways of knowing, being, or doing may naturalize behavior that is actually the consequence of centuries of oppression," behavior that persists only because women continue to occupy subordinate positions, and people in subordinate positions tend to be more adept than their superiors in skills such as role-taking (Allen & Baber, 1992, p. 4).

Orientations toward connection, from this perspective, have no fundamental relation to gender but are instead, in Carol Tavris's words, "artifacts of a power imbalance." (1992, p. 299). Women have not chosen their different voice, says the feminist legal scholar Catherine MacKinnon; it has been foisted upon them. MacKinnon hears it as "the voice of the victim." Given women's unequal status, she says, speaking to Gilligan,

> it makes a lot of sense that we should want to negotiate, since we lose conflicts. It makes a lot of sense that we should want to urge values of care, because it is what we have been valued for. We have had little choice but to be valued this way. . . . It makes a lot of sense that women should claim our identity in relationships because we have not been allowed to have a social identity on our own terms. (MacKinnon, in Marcus et al., 1985, p. 27).

The connected "feminine" voice speaks out of weakness, MacKinnon says, and in a contest with the authoritative "separate" male voice, it is destined always to lose. Relational theories, in her view, not only reify stereotypes of gender difference; they reinforce the gender hierarchy and perpetuate the imbalance of power. Although Miller agrees that women's capacity for connection is partly "a result of their training as subordinates" and that it can be exploited by a dominant partner, she insists that it is nevertheless a "strength."

Joyce Fletcher's (1995) intensive study of a sample of women design engineers who attempted to apply relational practices within a large organization suggests that whether one considers relational thinking to be a strength or a weakness depends on one's standards of success. These practices were effective in getting good work done, but they were not perceived as such by the women's superiors—indeed, were not even perceived as ways of working—and so were not rewarded by appreciation or advancement. Relational practices "get disappeared," in Fletcher's phrase, and the traditional organizational norms of hierarchy and individualism remain in place.[1]

Given findings such as Fletcher's, it is not surprising that many dismiss as "utopian" the notion that people who employ a primarily relational style (at least if they are women) will ever attain positions of power, and some even assert that "Gilligan's perspective serves ultimately to legitimate gender hierarchy within organizations. . . . Women may be in there 'relating' to people, while men will continue to run the corporation" (Auerbach, Blum, Smith, & Williams, 1985, p. 159). The research reported by Susan T. Fiske and Laura S. Stevens (chapter 27 of this volume) is relevant to these issues.

Of course, it is precisely the devaluation of care and connection in the social institutions of this culture (including the discipline of psychology) that drives the work of different-voice psychologists, who have repeatedly maintained that their purpose was not to add to the catalog of gender differences but to bring into psychology and into the wider society a voice that had been muted or missing: "I heard a different voice," Gilligan said, "because I was not comparing women with men. . . . I was comparing women with theory. I said this voice is different from the voice that has been described in the psychology of moral development, in moral philosophy, and in the legal and political system which was sitting all around my work" (Gilligan, in Marcus et al., 1985, p. 38). The women interviewed by Gilligan and Mary F. Belenky (1980) framed the moral dilemma they faced in considering abortion in a fashion that "did not fit the public discussion of abortion in this country" and was not allowable in a court of law (Gilligan, in Marcus et al., 1985, p. 38). They construed the problem not as a contest between the rights of the mother and those of the fetus, pitting one life against another, but in terms of the perspective Gilligan came to call "care": how to respond to the particular needs of the persons involved. Long ago, Jean Piaget asserted that girls, compared with boys, were deficient in "the legal sense" (1965, p. 77); different-voice theorists argue for a "legal sense" that, although different, is not deficient (Menkel-Meadow, 1996).

Different-voice psychologists claim that their aim is to redress a balance by bringing into public discourse a voice that is missing. They do not claim, they say, that this voice is "better" than the prevailing one, but this is the message that is sometimes implied in their writings and often inferred by their readers. These writers are accused of "valorizing" relationship over autonomy, replacing psychology's "individualistic bias" (Guisinger & Blatt, 1994, p. 104) with a relational bias. The "idealized relational self," as Marcia Westkott points out in her chapter, can take on prescriptive power, becoming a feminine ideology that can induce self-hatred in women who fail to meet its criteria and frustration at the repression of desires that violate the criteria.[2]

Most different-voice psychologists believe that to speak in a single voice constricts the development of both men and women. Tony Jefferson (1994) describes how men can be overwhelmed by "a feeling of vulnerability" upon entering a serious emotional relationship in which "the need for and dependence on another is posed most starkly, in direct contradiction to the notions of self-sufficiency and independence central to hegemonic masculinity." Jefferson writes, "It is almost as if to succeed in love one has to fail as a man" (Jefferson, 1994, p. 12). Miller believes that men "struggle to reclaim" the aspects they have disowned, and Sam Osherson suggests that "the vital question may be, How does each gender begin to talk about the disowned parts of self that we project onto the other?" (1996, p. 1143).

The discipline of psychology also seems to be struggling to reclaim aspects of human nature that it has dismissed in the past. Different-voice theorists appear to be part of a growing Zeitgeist aimed at correcting psychology's individualistic bias by placing more emphasis on relational factors. This trend can be seen not only among psychologists concerned with gender, but also those interested in attachment, psychoanalytic object relations, non-Western psychologies, Vygotskian "sociocultural" developmental psychology (e.g., Wertsch, Del Rio, & Alvarez, 1995), modern evolutionary biology, and a host of others.

Anthropologists have taught us that the conception of the mature person as separate, independent, and self-contained is unique to the industrialized West. Other cultures adhere to a more "sociocentric" or "interdependent" ideal. Members of these societies view the self as primarily a self-in-relation, a "fraction" of a whole, rather than complete and self-contained (Sampson, 1988): As Hazel Markus and Shinobu Kitayama (1991) put it, "An interdependent self cannot be properly characterized as a bounded whole, for it changes structure with the nature of the particular social context." Although "within each particular social situation, the self can be differently instantiated," this self is neither powerless nor passive, neither a chameleon nor a clone.

> An interdependent view of self does not result in a merging of self and other, nor does it imply that people do not have a sense of themselves as agents who are the origins of their own actions.[3] On the contrary, it takes a high degree of self-control and agency to effectively adjust oneself to various interpretations. (Markus & Kitayama, 1991, p. 228)

Because issues concerning autonomy and connection, individuality and relatedness, agency and communion pervade so many areas in contemporary psychology, we shall be revisiting them from different perspectives in nearly every section of this volume.

NOTES

1. As the sociolinguist Pamela Fishman has observed, "Since interactional work is related to what constitutes being a woman, with what a woman *is*, the idea that it *is* work is obscured. The work is not seen as what women do, but as part of what they are" (Fishman, 1978, p. 405). Does this imply that relational practices, if used by men, might be perceived as work and might be rewarded?

2. There are signs that the relational self has become a standard, in diluted and distorted form, not only for women but for men too. Men seem to have appropriated to themselves an ersatz version of care and connection that *New York Times* columnist Maureen Dowd (1996) refers to as "pink think." In 1996, she reported sightings of "pink think" at the Democratic National Convention, where politicians made a public show of their intimate (scripted) feelings, and in television coverage of the Olympics, featuring folksy accounts of participants' family life at the expense of covering the competitions.

3. Thus, Bakan's (1966) designation of "agency" and "communion" as two distinctive modes may be misleading.

REFERENCES

Allen, K. R., & Baber, K. M. (1992). Ethical and Epistemological Tensions in Applying a Postmodern Perspective to Feminist Research. *Psychology of Women Quarterly, 16,* 1–15.

Auerbach, J., Blum, L., Smith, V., & Williams, C. (1985). On Gilligan's *In a Different Voice. Feminist Studies, 11,* 149–161.

Bakan, D. (1966). *The Duality of Human Existence.* Boston: Beacon Press.

Chodorow, N. (1978). *The Reproduction of Mothering.* Berkeley: University of California Press.

Dowd, M. (1996, July 12). The Personal Means a Lot These Days. *New York Times,* p. A14.

Fishman, P. M. (1978). Interaction: The Work Women Do. *Social Problems, 25,* 397–406.

Fletcher, J. (1995). Relational Theory in the Workplace. *Work in Progress,* No. 77. Wellesley, MA: Stone Center, Wellesley College.

Freud, S. (1925/1963). Some Psychological Consequences of the Anatomical Distinction between the Sexes. In *Sexuality and the Psychology of Love.* New York: Collier Books.

Gilligan, C., & Belenky, M. F. (1980). A Naturalistic Study of Abortion Decisions. In R. Selman and R. Yando (eds.), *Clinical-Developmental Psychology.* New Directions for Child Development, No. 7. San Francisco: Jossey-Bass.

Greeno, C. G., & Maccoby, E. E. (1986). On *In a Different Voice:* An Interdisciplinary Forum: How Different Is the "Different Voice"? *Signs, 11,* 310–316.

Guisinger, S., & Blatt, S. J. (1994). Individuality and Relatedness: Evaluation of a Fundamental Dialectic. *American Psychologist, 49,* 104–111.

Jefferson, T. (1994). Theorizing Masculine Subjectivity. In T. Newburn & E. A. Stanko (Eds.), *Men, Masculinities and Crime* (pp. 10–31). New York: Routledge.

Marcus, I., Spiegelman, P. J., DuBois, E. C., Dunlap, M. C., Gilligan, C. J., MacKinnon, C. A., & Menkel-Meadow, C. J. (1985). Feminist Discourse, Moral Values, and the Law—A Conversation. Edited transcript of the discussion held on Oct. 19, 1984, at the law school of the State University of New York in Buffalo as part of the James McCormick Mitchell Lecture Series. *Buffalo Law Review, 34,* 11–87.

Markus, H. R., & Kitayama, S. (1991). Culture and the Self: Implications for Cognition, Emotion, and Motivation. *Psychological Review, 98,* 224–253.

Menkel-Meadow, C. (1996). Women's Ways of "Knowing" Law: Feminist Legal Epistemology, Pedagogy, and Jurisprudence. In N. Goldberger, J. Tarule, B. Clinchy, & M. F. Belenky (Eds.), *Knowledge, Difference and Power: Essays Inspired by* Women's Ways of Knowing. New York: Basic Books.

Osherson, S. (1996). The Difficulty of Seeing Men Whole. *Contemporary Psychology, 41,* 1142–1143.

Piaget, J. (1965). *The Moral Judgment of the Child.* New York: Free Press.

Pollit, K. (1994/1995). Marooned on Gilligan's Island. *Reasonable Creatures: Essays on Women and Feminism* (pp. 42–62). New York: Vintage.

Sampson, E. E. (1988). The Debate on Individualism: Indigenous Psychologies of the Individual and Their Role in Personal and Societal Functioning. *American Psychologist, 93,* 15–22.

Tavris, C. (1992). *The Mismeasure of Woman: Why Women Are Not the Better Sex, the Inferior Sex, or the Opposite Sex.* New York: Simon & Schuster.

Wertsch, J. V., Del Rio, P., & Alvarez, A. (1995). *Sociocultural Studies of Mind.* New York: Cambridge University Press.

Chapter Eighteen

Strengths

Jean Baker Miller

Vulnerability, Weakness, Helplessness

Today in psychotherapy a central place is given to feelings of weakness, vulnerability, and helplessness, along with their usual accompaniment, feelings of neediness. These are feelings we have all known, given the long period necessary for maturational development in human beings and, in our society, given the difficulties and lack of support most of us suffer during childhood and indeed in our adult lives. Such feelings are, of course, most unpleasant—in their extreme, they are terrifying—and several schools of psychodynamic thought postulate that they are the root causes of various major "pathologies." In Western society men are encouraged to dread, abhor, or deny feeling weak or helpless, whereas women are encouraged to cultivate this state of being. The first and most important point, however, is that these feelings are common and inevitable to all, even though our cultural tradition unrealistically expects men to discard rather than to acknowledge them.

Two brief examples illustrate this contrast. Mary, a gifted and resourceful young hospital worker with two children, was offered a new and more demanding position. She would lead a team attempting an innovative approach to patient care. It involved greater scope for the team members and for Mary a harder job of coordination and negotiation of the workers' anxieties and difficulties. Mary's immediate reaction was to worry about her ability to carry out the project; she felt weak and helpless in the face of the formidable task. At times, she was convinced she was totally incapable of doing the job and wanted to refuse the offer.

Her worry was in some measure appropriate, for the position of team coordinator was a difficult and demanding one that should be approached only after rigorous self-evaluation. She was, however, extremely able and had demonstrated the abilities necessary for the position. She retained some common feminine problems—having trouble admitting to, and easily losing sight of, her strengths. A clear recognition of her own competence would mean the loss of the weak, little-girl image to which she clung, in spite of its obvious inaccuracy. While some fear about the job seemed justified, her reluctance to relinquish the old image exaggerated the fears.

Jean Baker Miller, "Strengths." In J. B. Miller, *Toward a New Psychology of Women*, pp. 29–47. © 1976, 1986 by Jean Baker Miller. Reprinted by permission of Beacon Press, Boston.

By contrast, a man, Charles, who was also very gifted, had the opportunity to take a higher-level job, and he was very pleased. In its administrative requirements and responsibilities it was similar to Mary's and was equally demanding. Just before he undertook the new job, he developed some fairly severe physical symptoms; characteristically he did not talk about them. His wife, Ruth, however, suspected that they were caused by his anxieties about facing the tasks ahead. Knowing him well, she did not mention the problem directly, but opened up the topic in the only way she felt able. She suggested that it might be a good idea to make some changes in their diet, hours, and general lifestyle. His initial reaction was one of anger; he disparaged her, sarcastically telling her to stop bothering him. Later he admitted to himself, and then to Ruth, that when he feels most uncertain of his abilities and most in need of help, he can react only with anger—especially if anyone seems to perceive his neediness.

Fortunately, Charles is trying hard to overcome the barriers that keep him from acknowledging these feelings. His wife's attempts opened up the possibility of dealing with them. He could not have initiated the process himself. He could not even respond to her initiation immediately, but this time, fairly soon after the fact he was able to catch himself in the act of denying it. Ruth easily might have remained rejected, hurt, and resentful, and the situation could have escalated into mutual anger and recrimination at the very time he was feeling most vulnerable, helpless, and needy.

It is important to note also that Ruth was *not* being rewarded for her strengths. Instead, she was made to suffer for them—by anger and rejection. This is a small example of how women's valuable qualities are not only not recognized but are punished instead. Even in this case, Ruth was not able to state her perceptions openly. She had to use "feminine wiles." Important qualities such as understanding of human vulnerabilities and offerings of help can thus be dysfunctional in relationships as they are presently structured and can make a woman feel she must be wrong.

In no society does the person—male or female—emerge full-grown. A necessary part of all experience is a recognition of one's weaknesses and limitations. That most valuable of human qualities—the ability to grow psychologically—is necessarily an ongoing process, involving repeated feelings of vulnerability all through life. As the example of Charles illustrates, men have been conditioned to fear and hate weakness, to try to get rid of it immediately and sometimes frantically. This attempt, I believe, represents an effort to distort human experience. It is necessary to "learn" in an emotional sense that these feelings are not shameful or abhorrent but ones from which the individual can move on—if the feelings are experienced for what they are. Only then can a person hope to find appropriate paths to new strengths. Along with new strength will come new areas of vulnerability, for there is no absolute invulnerability.

That women are better able than men to consciously admit to feelings of weakness or vulnerability may be obvious, but we have not recognized the importance of this ability. That women are truly much more able to tolerate these feelings—which life in general, and particularly in our society, generates in everybody—is a positive strength. Many adolescent boys and young men especially seem to be suffering acutely from the need to flee from these feelings *before* they experience them. In that sense, women, both superficially and deeply, are more closely in touch with basic life experiences—in touch with reality. By being in this closer connection with this central human condition, by having to defend less and deny less, women are in a position to understand weakness more readily and to work productively *with* it.

In short, in our society, while men are made to feel weak in many ways, women are made to feel weaker. But, because they "know" weakness, women can cease being the "carriers" of weakness and become the developers of a different understanding of it and of the appropriate paths out of it. Women, in undertaking their own journey, can illuminate the way for others.

Until now, women who are already strong in many ways still have had a hard time admitting it. Mary, the woman in the example, illustrates this problem. But even when weakness is real, women can go on to strength and ability once they can convince themselves that it is really all right to let go of their belief in the *rightness* of weakness. Only someone who understands women can understand how this psychic element operates, how widespread and influential the fear of *not* being weak can become, and how persistently it can hang on without being recognized for what it is. It is very difficult for men, with *their fears* of weakness, to see why women cling to it and to understand that it does not, and could not possibly, mean the same thing for women as it does for men.

There is a further social point here. The fact that these feelings are generally associated with being "womanly"—hence unmanly—serves to reinforce the humiliation suffered by the man who has such experiences. Women, in the meanwhile, provide all sorts of personal and social supports to help keep men going and to keep them and the total society from admitting that better arrangements are needed. That is, the whole man–woman interaction thus dilutes the push to confront and deal with our societal deficiencies. We all experience too much danger as we attempt to grow and make our way in the difficult and threatening circumstances in which we live. We all lose in the end, but the loss is kept obscure.

More can be understood of Charles' situation if we ask "what did he really want?" Like many people he wanted at least two things. He not only wanted them, he believed they were essential to his sense of self. He wanted, first of all, to sail through every situation feeling "like a man"—that is, strong, self-sufficient, and fully competent. He required of himself that he always feel this way. Anything less he experienced as a threat to his manliness. Such a requirement is unrealistic in the extreme, for we face repeated challenges in life; we are sure to feel doubts all along.

At the same time that Charles wanted to maintain this image of himself, he harbored the seemingly contradictory wish that his wife would somehow solve everything for him with such magic and dispatch that he would never be aware of his weakness at all. She should do this without being asked; it was essential that he never have to think or talk about his weakness. The fact that Ruth did not instantly accomplish this feat for him was a deep-seated cause of his anger at her.

Instead, she confronted him with an attempt to deal with the problem, and by doing so, she reminded him of his feelings of weakness and vulnerability. But even if she had done nothing, her very presence would have caused him to face the frustration of his wish for total caretaking and problemsolving. This sort of wish is prominent in many people and present to some extent in most. As long as women live under the major prescription that they please and serve men, they will be the objects of such desire. At the same time they will be unable to participate in the free-flowing mutual confrontation and cooperation that can help them and others find ways of growing beyond this stage. The hope is that such wishes can be worked out and integrated on a more satisfactory level as one develops an increasing sense of one's own strengths and an increasing faith in other people. In this task, we need other people all through life, in adulthood no less than in childhood.

Initially, Ruth offered a step in this direction, a wholehearted attempt to help Charles and to struggle together with him. But this he could not accept. His refusal illustrates in a small way how women come to believe they are failures, even in the traditional wifely role. Since a major part of her sense of worth was based on her role as a wife, experiences of this kind could easily have undermined Ruth's self-confidence. She was well prepared to believe that her husband, as the man, was right and that she was wrong. To put this in a shorthand way, if the members of the dominant group—that is, men—claim that they do not have feelings of insecurity, subordinates (women) cannot challenge their claim. Furthermore, it is women's responsibility to supply the needs of the dominant group so that its members can continue to deny these feelings. The fact that such emotions are present in everyone and are intensified by the problems our society creates for all its people makes a difficult situation almost impossible.

With some couples, the mythology may seem to "work." Both partners know what is going on to some extent, and a balance is struck so that the arrangement is sufficiently satisfactory to sustain the status quo. The woman, considering the alternatives that faced her outside of marriage until now, was often willing to accept the situation. Such marriages, however, may create another kind of reaction in women.

In these situations, the women may be very wise in certain ways; but skilled as they are, they really know only half of the story, or perhaps less than half. The woman usually knows well her husband's areas of weakness, and she provides the needed supports. But even though such women may seem to function quite well in a home context, they increasingly develop the pervasive sense that, as keenly as they know the man's weaknesses, he must have an entirely unknown area of strength, some very important ability, that enables him to manage in "the real world." This element in him becomes increasingly foreign for the woman; it takes on the quality of an almost magical ability that men have and women do not.

Women sometimes come to look upon this manly quality as something they must *believe* in; it provides their major sense of support. Many women develop a great need to believe they have a strong man to whom they can turn for security and hope in the world. And, while it may seem improbable, this belief in the man's magical strength exists side by side with an intimate knowledge of the weaknesses to which she caters.

It is not simply that woman are obviously excluded from acquiring experience in the serious world of work, but that they actually come to believe that there is some special, inherent ability, some factor that escapes them and must inevitably escape them. The fact that women are themselves discouraged from serious testing of themselves fosters and deepens the need to believe that men have this special quality. Most women have a lifelong conditioning that induces them to believe this myth.

This very belief is one (but just one) of the expressions that psychiatrists and theorists have perceived as evidence of "penis envy." They may have been encouraged in their perception by the manner in which women talk of this "male quality"—as if it were some sort of magical and unattainable ability. Some men (perhaps those with more self-knowledge than I have generally given them credit for here), knowing that they possess no extraordinary ability women do not share, have settled, for an explanation, on the most noticeable physical difference—the penis.

The truth would seem to be much simpler: that the only thing women lack is practice in the "real world"; this, plus the *opportunity* to practice and the lifelong belief that one has the *right* to do so. Such a simple statement, however, covers a great many complex psychological consequences.

New Paths away from Weakness

The status quo is upset when one *admits* one's weakness publicly. The very fact of acknowledging feelings of weakness and vulnerability is new and original. The next step—the idea that women do not have to *remain* weak—is even more threatening. A hard question is joined when we ask what women can do about moving out of weakness. Here, women immediately run into opposition that can be very severe.

By acknowledging their weakness, women are undertaking, first of all, a vast act of exposure. As soon as women add, "I feel weak now, but I intend to move on from that," they are displaying a great strength, a form of strength that is particularly difficult for men. That is hard enough for men to take, but in addition, women are threatening to remove certain key props from men. It is particularly hard to endure someone's taking props away, but it is even harder if you have pretended all along that you did not need them in the first place.

Although real weaknesses are a problem for every human being, women's major difficulty lies more in admitting the strengths they already have and in allowing themselves to use their resources. Sometimes women already have the necessary resources or they clearly have a basis on which to build. In such instances, anxiety often arises. Indeed, the anxiety is greatly augmented by opposition both from our institutions and from people who are personally close. Women are confronted with obstacles on several levels: not only intrapsychic obstacles from their own pasts—which lead them to fear their strengths—but also obstacles in reality.

But when women begin to perceive forms of strength based on their own life experiences, rather than believing they should have the qualities they attribute to men, they often find new definitions of strength. A nice example of a strength translated into a social form is the patient-advocate system that has been developed by some women's health centers.

Almost everyone knows that confronting the doctor is a fearful prospect. In addition to fears about illness and its possible implications, a visit to a physician often touches off deeper fears of vulnerability, mutilation, and death. Women have recognized that it is very difficult to deal with these fears alone, especially when trying to cope with medical institutions as they are constituted today. In the patient-advocate system, an informed and experienced woman health worker goes along with the woman patient to the clinic or hospital and stays by her side, to speak up, to question, and to challenge. This example illustrates several of the elements to which I am pointing: it is easier for women to openly admit to their fears and, therefore, to identify their needs accurately. It is also easier for them to turn to others and ask for help. Clearly men need this help too. Once women have initiated this procedure perhaps men will adopt it, too—hopefully only as an interim measure until the field of medicine treats all people with greater sensitivity.

Vulnerability in Theory and Culture

As discussed so far, the feelings of weakness, vulnerability, and helplessness may sound commonplace. Our dealing with some of their more obvious implications has perhaps served to obscure their profound importance to the psychology community today. Indeed, current psychiatric thinking places them at the center of most problems. In the jargon of the field they have more impressive names, but the issues of how a person is made to feel vulnerable or helpless and what she/he then tries to do about it is probably the basic issue underlying most modern concerns in psychiatry. In its extreme form such vulnerability can be described as the threat of psychic annihilation, probably the most terrifying threat of all. People will do almost anything to avoid such threats.

There are differences in current psychiatric theory about both the origins of these threats and the form of the reactions they produce. Do they, for example, all originate primarily in separation anxiety in the infant, as John Bowlby postulates?[1] Or do they originate, as the Freudian and other instinct theories propose, because one's instinctual impulses clash with the "real world," leading one to feel weak and vulnerable (in addition to other things)? Whether any current or past theories explain the origins of these feelings adequately, all of them grew out of a culture that has made one sex the embodiment of weakness and the other the embodiment of strength. The new feature is that women are now in a position to open up a new and potentially radically different perspective on this topic.

Psychoanalytic theories, stated simply, hold that one attempts to develop ways to deal with these feelings, mental mechanisms that enable a person to overcome feelings of vulnerability and helplessness. Accordingly, people construct an inner scheme of things by which they believe they will gain satisfaction and safety. The scheme can become very complex and quite rigid too. People often are convinced that they need to relate to the world and people in it in a certain fixed manner, and they may react forcefully if they cannot bring about the desired situation or relationship. One way of describing all psychological problems might be to say that people believe they can be safe and satisfied only if they complete and can force others to complete a certain picture of what they need. If they cannot accomplish this, they feel weak and vulnerable. These feelings are so dreadful that people then push even harder to make their particular schemes come about.

These dreaded feelings—inherent in the human condition—have been associated with women and babies. Both those who *experience* them and those who *respond* to them are covered with derision. Males are "allowed" to have them for only a short period in infancy; after that, they are expected to be virtually done with them for life. Our psychological theories reflect this situation; indeed our very basic model of the human mind is one in which emotional weaknesses are said to be crucially dealt with and almost rigidly fixed in the early years of infancy. This model may have something to do with male culture's attempts to rid men of these experiences.

The second great theme revolves around the relation of other people to these threats. In modern living, the major threats come not from the physical world but from other people; it is people who make us feel vulnerable, from early childhood and on throughout life. If one could turn readily to other people in seeking to deal with these feelings, if one could do this repeatedly with faith and ease, there would be many more chances of productively dealing with life.

Emotions

Emotionality, as part and parcel of every state of being, is even more pervasive than feelings of vulnerability and weakness. In our dominant tradition, however, it has not been seen as an aid to understanding and action, but rather as an impediment, even an evil. We have a long tradition of trying to dispense with, or at least to control or neutralize, emotionality, rather than valuing, embracing, and cultivating its contributing strengths. Most women do have a much greater sense of the emotional components of all human activity than most men. This is, in part, a result of their training as subordinates; for anyone in a subordinate position must learn to be attuned to the vicissitudes of mood, pleasure, and displeasure of the dominant group. Black writers have made this point very clearly. Subordinate groups can use these developed abilities as one of the few weapons available in the struggle with the dominants, and women have often done so. "Womanly intuition" and "womanly wiles" are examples. But, however attained, these qualities bespeak a basic ability that is very valuable. It can hardly be denied that emotions are essential aspects of human life.

Men are encouraged from early life to be active and rational; women are trained to be involved with emotions and with the feelings occurring in the course of all activity. Out of this, women have gained the insight that events are important and satisfying only if they occur within the context of emotional relatedness. They are more likely than men to believe that, ideally, all activity should lead to an increased emotional connection with others. However, psychological and social difficulties have come from the distortions taught to women. Indeed, women have been led to believe that if they act and think effectively they will jeopardize their chances for satisfying emotional experience. Such precepts have led to terrible twists, so that women are made to feel that their strongest assets are really liabilities.

Another aspect is important. Women have been so encouraged to concentrate on the emotions and reactions of others that they have been diverted from examining and expressing their own emotions. While this is very understandable, given the past situation, women have not yet fully applied this highly developed faculty to exploring and knowing *themselves*.

Many women are currently in the process of doing just this in a new way. But to understand thoroughly the situation that still exists for most women, we may return to Ruth. Ruth's experience offers a brief illustration of how strength can be made to seem a weakness. Because of her well-developed ability to attend to emotions, Ruth was more able to grasp the totality of Charles' situation. But the opportunity to let her understanding unfold and to act on it to find a solution was obstructed by her husband's dictum. Ruth retreated, feeling inadequate, a failure, and certain that she must be wrong about the whole thing.

Participating in the Development of Others

There is no question that the dominant society has said, men will do the important work; women will tend to the "lesser task" of helping other human beings to develop. At the outset this dichotomy means that our major societal institutions are *not* founded on the tenet of helping others to develop. All people need help in development at all stages, but it is made to appear as if only children do. This casts both women and children under a pall, with many psychological consequences for children of both sexes. The person most intimately involved in their development is seen as a lesser figure performing a lesser task, even though she is of pre-eminent importance to them. Further, women have had to do this major work without the supports that a culture would give to a task it valued. But the fact is women have done it nonetheless.

Despite all the handicaps, women have a much greater sense of the pleasures of close connection with physical, emotional, and mental growth than men. Growth is one of the—perhaps the—most important, most exciting qualities of being human. Tragically, in our society, women are prevented from fully enjoying these pleasures themselves by being made to feel that fostering them in others is the only valid role for all women and by the loneliness, drudgery, and isolated, noncooperative household setting in which they work.

Participation in others' growth is one of the major satisfactions in psychotherapy. To be part of the experience of another person's struggle to break through to a new and satisfying way of seeing, feeling, or acting is extremely gratifying. Good therapists know that it is the client's own effort, but they also know that they can play an important facilitating part. From this participation, a therapist can derive great pleasure. But this is the same sort of basic activity that women are performing every day.

Women have now stated that helping in the growth of others without the equal opportunity and right to growth for themselves is a form of oppression. In fact, in our unequal situation, the valuable part of women's participation in others' development is in constant danger of degenerating into the provision of mere ego-support or flattery—what Jessie Bernard has described as the "stroking" function.[2] Here again, inequality distorts and negates a valuable ability. Ruth is an example of a woman trying to assist in growth but being pushed toward mere "stroking."

Cooperation

Another important aspect of women's psychology is their greater recognition of the essential cooperative nature of human existence. Despite the competitive aspects of any society, there must be a bedrock modicum of cooperativeness for society to exist at all. (I define cooperative as behavior that aids and enhances the development of other human beings while advancing one's own.) It is certainly clear that we have not reached a very high level of cooperative living. To the extent that it exists, women have assumed the greater responsibility for providing it. Although they may not label it in large letters, women in families are constantly trying to work out some sort of cooperative system that attends to each person's needs. Their task is greatly impeded by the unequal premise on which our families are based, but it has been women who have *practiced* trying.

Take the example of Mary, who was worried about a new, demanding job. If she took the job, she would need a new level of cooperation from her husband, Joe. If he were able to provide it, he would seem a most unusual man. Mary had been giving *him* and the children that kind of cooperative support for years.

Joe may seem to have come out of nowhere at this time. His absence from the discussion until now makes an interesting point. For Joe is, in fact, a "nice guy." He and Mary love and respect each other. "He doesn't stop me from working," says Mary. "He helps me out in a pinch and is often kind and understanding." He does not feel, however, that working out ways to provide the maximum development of everyone in the family is his major responsibility. That is Mary's job.

Women's cooperative tendency, even in the midst of severe psychological problems, was evident in the situation of another couple. Jim was a person with severe problems; he had become addicted to drugs and was progressively deteriorating. His wife, Helen, too, had deep-seated difficulties. After several years spent attacking and diminishing each other, Jim felt he could no longer face anything and he disappeared. In part, he left because he was deeply ashamed of himself and his repeated failure in practically all areas of life. Although trained as a lawyer, he felt by that time that he had nothing left. Helen, on the other hand, though equally ashamed and destroyed, did not leave, much as she, too, may have wished to do so. Although she certainly felt unable to offer anything to anybody, she remained to take care of her three children. As deprived and empty as she herself felt, she hung on in a desperate effort to do whatever she could for them. For a long initial period, she felt it was only her sense of the children's needs that kept her barely moving through the days and surviving through the nights. Eventually, she built many more resources and now says, "I never knew I could be the person I feel today."

Leaving out the long intervening struggle, the point to be made here is that Helen struggled to make something work even though "only the children seemed to have any real reason to live." She still felt the need to engage in some kind of cooperative functioning and a *desire* to do it, even though she could barely manage. The same motivation was not there in any meaningful way for Jim. I have seen examples of this with many other couples.

While men do enter into some forms of concerted endeavor, the prevailing values in the settings in which most men spend their lives make it extremely difficult to sustain it. Moreover, in the family setting, men very early in life acquire the sense that they are members of a superior group. Things are supposed to be done for them by those lesser people who work at trying to do so. From then on, cooperativeness may appear to men as if it were somehow detracting from themselves. To cooperate, to share, means somehow to lose something, or at best, altruistically, to give something away. All this is greatly augmented by men's notions that they must be independent, go it alone, win.

To women, who do not have the same experience, cooperativeness does not have the same quality of loss. In the first place, most women have not been imbued with a spurious sense of advantage over a group of other people.

By saying that women are more practiced in cooperation and that women are at present more able to seek out and enjoy situations that require that quality, I do not mean that women have any greater inherent saintliness, but rather, that life so far has led women to this position. Today, as women try to move on, they are finding not only more necessity but also more desire to consciously struggle for even more cooperation. We all know that women have many competitive aspects, too. Both tendencies exist in each sex but in different proportions. In the past, many women were concerned with competing with each other for men, for obvious reasons. Many women are now trying to turn away from this sort of competition with other women, shifting the balance even further toward cooperativeness.

Creativity

Creativity, taken together with cooperativeness, leads to an overall proposition—and a return to the earlier discussion about psychoanalysis. I have been underlining that psychoanalysis has been pointing out aspects of absolute human necessity; I have said also that these areas of life—such as sexuality and emotional connectedness—are the very realms generally relegated to woman. I should now like to propose that there is yet a third area of absolute human necessity that psychoanalysis has not yet "unearthed" or delineated even as imperfectly as it has defined the issue of sexuality or the nature of basic emotional connections. Not surprisingly, this area has also been denied explicit recognition by the dominant culture. I refer to the absolute necessity of, and the absolute existence in human beings of, the potential for both cooperation and creativity. It is clear that the thwarting of these necessities, the blocking of these needs, produces as many, or more, problems than anything so far delineated in psychodynamics. For emphasis, I will call this consideration the third stage of psychoanalysis.

I am not referring in this context to the creativity in artistic productions by the gifted few but to the intense personal creating that we each must do all through life.

Everyone repeatedly has to break through to a new vision if she/he is to keep living. This very personal kind of creativity, this making of new visions, this continuous struggle, does not usually go on in open and well-articulated ways. But it goes on. Today, we can see this universal process most clearly in women. Women are the people struggling to create for themselves a new concept of personhood; they are attempting to restructure the central tenets of their lives. This effort extends to the deepest inner reaches.

But even in the past, it was women who had to innovate their inner psychological structures in order to survive at all within the dominant culture. Society arranged for, and by, men institutes key social-psychological guidelines and values that are not really applicable to women. (The well-known Broverman study has provided documentation on this point.[3]) Women have grown up knowing the goals most valued for individual development were not to be *their* goals. On the other hand, women do grow and develop. They have constructed an inner person who is different from the person most valued in this society.

Women have always had to come up with a basis for worthiness that is different from that which the dominant culture bestows. They have effected enough of a creative internal transformation of values to allow themselves to believe that caring for people and participating in others' development is enhancing to self-esteem. In this sense, even women who live by all of the old stereotypes are in advance of the values of this society. This does not mean they are therefore recognized and rewarded for their value system. Quite pointedly, they are not; they are made to feel that they are of little worth—"I am only a housewife and mother."

Some women have managed to create other roles for themselves to contribute to their sense of self-esteem. But a woman who has done so has violated a dominant system of values that says she is not worthy; indeed, it implies that there must be something wrong with her for even wanting alternatives. However, any woman who has gone beyond the assigned tasks has already created an inner conception by which she is guided, which sustains her, however imperfectly. Exactly what internal conception each woman creates is often difficult to tease out explicitly. In most cases, such conceptions are not fully stated and clarified in words.

Today, women are struggling to go on from this point to create a new kind of person in a much bolder, more thoroughgoing, and conscious way. In recent years it has become apparent that women must create new conceptions of what it means to be a person if they are to change the day-to-day workings of their lives. When women seriously resist the old internal and external proscriptions and demands they *have* to find new conceptions to live by. They are also the people most stimulated to be imaginative and adventurous.

As women change, they will create severe challenges. To suggest just one, when more women refuse, thoroughly and totally, to allow themselves to be used as objects, either in the grossest commercial form or in the most intimate personal encounter, whom will society then use as objects? If there is no one to use, what kinds of revolutionary personal transformations will the dominant group have to make for itself? Will this not end in liberating some of the creative potential in men?

These are some of the concerns with which women have had to grapple in the past, often in lonely, isolated, and frightening ways. They are now beginning to deal with them in cooperative ways with large numbers of other women. The cooperativeness and creativity that I think exists in all people, that has been essential to all human life, is now being raised to a more conscious level and made explicit.

Women in the past have been led to believe that they had no special contribution to make. If women tried to move beyond the limited assigned area, they felt that they must somehow rush to catch up to, or to catch on to, the dominant group's interests and concerns. It is clear today that there are vast areas in which our dominant society is failing. As women recognize their strengths and as they raise their very own concerns, they can not only progress toward a new synthesis, but simultaneously clarify and make much more obvious the issues central to all human beings.

What about men in all this? Here I would like to return to some of Freud's own last words on the subject, which we can now see in a different light.[4] Freud said that the basic thing that men struggled against is identification with the female, which, a psychoanalyst would immediately have to say, also implies the desire for that identification. I would like to suggest that men struggle not against identification with the female *per se* in a concrete sense, but that men do indeed struggle to reclaim the very parts of their own experience that they have delegated to women. Men, I think, would enjoy great comfort and growth in being able more fully to integrate and reintegrate these parts of themselves. They desire to recapture without shame the experience of their various vicissitudes and struggles, which represent the inevitable problems of growing up and of living with one's total being in our imperfect society; they desire to recapture those parts of themselves which have dreaded and frightening properties for men, but which have been made much more frightening because they have been labeled "female."

As women refuse to become the carriers of some of the central unsolved problems of male-led society, and as women move on to become the proponents of some of the best parts of human potential, we will, I think, create a climate in which men will face the challenge of grappling with their own issues in their own way. Men will be faced with having to deal with their bodily, their sexual, their childish experiences, their feelings of weakness, vulnerability, helplessness, and the other similar unsolved areas. But men can also go on to enlarge their emotional experience and more fully discover their real potential for cooperativeness and creativity. As these areas are no longer "filled in" by women and devalued by a male-led society, men will be forced to confront the ways in which their social forms do not adequately deal with these necessities. They will have to go about finding their own newer and better ways.

It may be useful to summarize the foregoing. I believe that women can value their psychological qualities in a new way as they recognize the origins and functions of these qualities. Eventually, we can hope to place them within a fuller theory of women's development. But even now, we can recognize that women's psychological strengths are not perceived as such by the dominant group.

I do not imply that women should go back into some "nurturing" role. It is the reverse. Women can go on to greatly enlarge their scope and activity, building on a base that is already valuable.

It is possible that this may sound as if I am claiming that women are better because they have suffered more—or that women are more virtuous. I am not addressing this issue. What I *do* see is that our dominant society is a very imperfect one. It is a low-level, primitive organization built on an exceedingly restricted conception of the total human potential. It holds up narrow and ultimately destructive goals for the dominant group and attempts to deny vast areas of life. The falsity and the full impact of this limited conception has been obscured. Significantly, women have now elucidated one large and central part of this impact—precisely because women are the people who receive this impact.

Some of the areas of life denied by the dominant group are relegated and projected onto all subordinate groups, not solely women. This partakes of the familiar scapegoat process. But other parts of human experience are so necessary that they cannot be projected very far away. One must *have* them nearby, even if one can still deny *owning* them. These are the special areas delegated to women. Based on their intimate experiences with them, women feel the problems in these areas most acutely, but they are even further diminished if they mention the unmentionable, expose certain key problems. This proscription has kept women from seeing that they have different desires and ways of living than those recognized and rewarded by the dominant culture. In this, women can indeed be seen to be "ahead" of psychological theory and practice—and of the culture that gave rise to present theory.

NOTES

1. John Bowlby, *Attachment and Loss,* vols. 1, 2, 3 (New York: Basic Books, 1969, 1973, 1980).

2. Jessie Bernard, *Women and the Public Interest: An Essay on Policy and Protest* (Chicago: Aldine-Atherton, 1971).

3. I. Broverman, D. Broverman, et al., "Sex-Role Stereotypes and Clinical Judgments of Mental Health," *Journal of Consulting and Clinical Psychology* 34 (1970), 1–7.

4. Sigmund Freud, "Analysis Terminable and Interminable" (1937), in the *Standard Edition of the Complete Works of Sigmund Freud* (London: Hogarth Press, 1964).

Chapter Nineteen

In a Different Voice
Women's Conceptions of Self and of Morality

Carol Gilligan

The arc of developmental theory leads from infantile dependence to adult autonomy, tracing a path characterized by an increasing differentiation of self from other and a progressive freeing of thought from contextual constraints. The vision of Luther, journeying from the rejection of a self defined by others to the assertive boldness of "Here I stand" and the image of Plato's allegorical man in the cave, separating at last the shadows from the sun, have taken powerful hold on the psychological understanding of what constitutes development. Thus, the individual, meeting fully the developmental challenges of adolescence as set for him by Piaget, Erikson, and Kohlberg, thinks formally, proceeding from theory to fact, and defines both the self and the moral autonomously, that is, apart from the identification and conventions that had comprised the particulars of his childhood world. So equipped, he is presumed ready to live as an adult, to love and work in a way that is both intimate and generative, to develop an ethical sense of caring and a genital mode of relating in which giving and taking fuse in the ultimate reconciliation of the tension between self and other.

Yet the men whose theories have largely informed this understanding of development have all been plagued by the same problem, the problem of women, whose sexuality remains more diffuse, whose perception of self is so much more tenaciously embedded in relationships with others and whose moral dilemmas hold them in a mode of judgment that is insistently contextual. The solution has been to consider women as either deviant or deficient in their development.

That there is a discrepancy between concepts of womanhood and adulthood is nowhere more clearly evident than in the series of studies on sex-role stereotypes reported by Broverman, Vogel, Broverman, Clarkson, and Rosenkrantz (1972). The repeated finding of these studies is that the qualities deemed necessary for adulthood—the capacity for autonomous thinking, clear decision making, and responsible action—are those associated with masculinity but considered undesirable as attributes of the feminine self. The stereotypes suggest a splitting of love and work that relegates the expressive capacities requisite for the former to women while the instrumental abilities necessary for the latter reside in the masculine domain. Yet, looked at from a different perspective, these stereotypes reflect a conception of adulthood that is itself out of balance, favoring the separateness of the individual self over its connection to others and leaning more toward an autonomous life of work than toward the interdependence of love and care.

This difference in point of view is the subject of this essay, which seeks to identify in the feminine experience and construction of social reality a distinctive voice, recognizable in the different perspective it brings to bear on the construction and resolution of moral problems. The first section begins with the repeated observation of difference in women's concepts of self and of morality. This difference is identified in previous psychological descriptions of women's moral judgments and described as it again appears in current research data. Examples drawn from interviews with women in and around a university community are used to illustrate the characteristics of the feminine voice. The relational bias in women's thinking that has, in the past, been seen to compromise their moral judgment and impede their development now begins to emerge in a new developmental light. Instead of being seen as a developmental deficiency, this bias appears to reflect a different social and moral understanding.

This alternative conception is enlarged in the second section through consideration of research interviews with women facing the moral dilemma of whether to continue or abort a pregnancy. Since the research design allowed women to define as well as resolve the moral problem, developmental distinctions could be derived directly from the categories of women's thought. The responses of women to structured interview questions regarding the pregnancy decision formed the basis for describing a developmental sequence that traces progressive differentiations in their understanding and judgment of conflicts between self and other. While the sequence of women's moral development follows the three-level progression of all social developmental theory, from an egocentric through a societal to a universal perspective, this progression takes place within a distinct moral conception. This conception differs from that derived by Kohlberg from his all-male longitudinal research data.

This difference then becomes the basis in the third section for challenging the current assessment of women's moral judgment at the same time that it brings to bear a new perspective on developmental assessment in general. The inclusion in the overall conception of development of those categories derived from the study of women's moral judgment enlarges developmental understanding, enabling it to encompass better the thinking of both sexes. This is particularly true with respect to the construction and resolution of the dilemmas of adult life. Since the conception of adulthood retrospectively shapes the theoretical understanding of the development that precedes it, the changes in that conception that follow from the more central inclusion of women's judgments recast developmental understanding and lead to a reconsideration of the substance of social and moral development.

Characteristics of the Feminine Voice

The revolutionary contribution of Piaget's work is the experimental confirmation and refinement of Kant's assertion that knowledge is actively constructed rather than passively received. Time, space, self, and other, as well as the categories of developmental theory, all arise out of the active interchange between the individual and the physical and social world in which he lives and of which he strives to make sense. The development of cognition is the process of reappropriating reality at progressively more complex levels of apprehension, as the structures of thinking expand to encompass the increasing richness and intricacy of experience.

Moral development, in the work of Piaget and Kohlberg, refers specifically to the expanding conception of the social world as it is reflected in the understanding and resolution of the inevitable conflicts that arise in the relations between self and others. The moral judgment is a statement of priority, an attempt at rational resolution in a situation where, from a different point of view, the choice itself seems to do violence to justice.

Kohlberg (1969), in his extension of the early work of Piaget, discovered six stages of moral judgment, which he claimed formed an invariant sequence, each successive stage representing a more adequate construction of the moral problem, which in turn provides the basis for its more just resolution. The stages divide into three levels, each of which denotes a significant expansion of the moral point of view from an egocentric through a societal to a universal ethical conception. With this expansion in perspective comes the capacity to free moral judgment from the individual needs and social conventions with which it had earlier been confused and anchor it instead in principles of justice that are universal in application. These principles provide criteria upon which both individual and societal claims can be impartially assessed. In Kohlberg's view, at the highest stages of development morality is freed from both psychological and historical constraints, and the individual can judge independently of his own particular needs and of the values of those around him.

That the moral sensibility of women differs from that of men was noted by Freud (1925/1961) in the following by now well-quoted statement:

> I cannot evade the notion (though I hesitate to give it expression) that for women the level of what is ethically normal is different from what it is in man. Their superego is never so inexorable, so impersonal, so independent of its emotional origins as we require it to be in men. Character-traits which critics of every epoch have brought up against women—that they show less sense of justice than men, that they are less ready to submit to the great exigencies of life, that they are more often influenced in their judgments by feelings of affection or hostility—all these would be amply accounted for by the modification in the formation of their super-ego which we have inferred above. (pp. 257–258)

While Freud's explanation lies in the deviation of female from male development around the construction and resolution of the Oedipal problem, the same observations about the nature of morality in women emerge from the work of Piaget and Kohlberg. Piaget (1932/1965), in his study of the rules of children's games, observed that, in the games they played, girls were "less explicit about agreement [than boys] and less concerned with legal elaboration" (p. 93). In contrast to the boys' interest in the codification of rules, the girls adopted a more pragmatic attitude, regarding "a rule as good so long as the game repays it" (p. 83). As a result, in comparison to boys, girls were found to be "more tolerant and more easily reconciled to innovations" (p. 52).

Kohlberg (1971) also identifies a strong interpersonal bias in the moral judgments of women, which leads them to be considered as typically at the third of his six-stage developmental sequence. At that stage, the good is identified with "what pleases or helps others and is approved of by them" (p. 164). This mode of judgment is conventional in its conformity to generally held notions of the good but also psychological in its concern with intention and consequence as the basis for judging the morality of action.

That women fall largely into this level of moral judgment is hardly surprising when we read from the Broverman et al. (1972) list that prominent among the twelve attributes considered to be desirable for women are tact, gentleness, awareness of the feelings of others, strong need for security, and easy expression of tender feelings. And yet, herein lies the paradox, for the very traits that have traditionally defined the "goodness" of women, their care for and sensitivity to the needs of others, are those that mark them as deficient in moral development. The infusion of feeling into their judgments keeps them from developing a more independent and abstract ethical conception in which concern for others derives from principles of justice rather than from compassion and care. Kohlberg, however, is less pessimistic than Freud in his assessment, for he sees the development of women as extending beyond the interpersonal level, following the same path toward independent, principled judgment that he discovered in the research on men from which his stages were derived. In Kohlberg's view, women's development will proceed beyond Stage Three when they are challenged to solve moral problems that require them to see beyond the relationships that have in the past generally bound their moral experience.

What then do women say when asked to construct the moral domain; how do we identify the characteristically "feminine" voice? A Radcliffe undergraduate, responding to the question, "If you had to say what morality meant to you, how would you sum it up?," replies:

> When I think of the word morality, I think of obligations. I usually think of it as conflicts between personal desires and social things, social considerations, or personal desires of yourself versus personal desires of another person or people or whatever. Morality is that whole realm of how you decide these conflicts. A moral person is one who would decide, like by placing themselves more often than not as equals, a truly moral person would always consider another person as their equal . . . in a situation of social interaction, something is morally wrong where the individual ends up screwing a lot of people. And it is morally right when everyone comes out better off.[1]

Yet when asked if she can think of someone whom she would consider a genuinely moral person, she replies, "Well, immediately I think of Albert Schweitzer because he has obviously given his life to help others." Obligation and sacrifice override the ideal of equality, setting up a basic contradiction in her thinking.

Another undergraduate responds to the question, "What does it mean to say something is morally right or wrong?," by also speaking first of responsibilities and obligations:

> Just that it has to do with responsibilities and obligations and values, mainly values. . . . In my life situation I relate morality with interpersonal relationships that have to do with respect for the other person and myself. [Why respect other people?] Because they have a consciousness or feelings that can be hurt, an awareness that can be hurt.

The concern about hurting others persists as a major theme in the responses of two other Radcliffe students:

> [Why be moral?] Millions of people have to live together peacefully. I personally don't want to hurt other people. That's a real criterion, a main criterion for me. It underlies my sense of justice. It isn't nice to inflict pain. I empathize with anyone in pain. Not hurting others is important in my own private morals. Years ago, I would have jumped out of a window not to hurt my boyfriend. That was pathological. Even today though, I want approval and love and I don't want enemies. Maybe that's why there is morality— so people can win approval, love and friendship.

> My main moral principle is not hurting other people as long as you aren't going against your own conscience and as long as you remain true to yourself. . . . There are many moral issues such as abortion, the draft, killing, stealing, monogamy, etc. If something is a controversial issue like these, then I always say it is up to the individual. The individual has to decide and then follow his own conscience. There are no moral absolutes. . . . Laws are pragmatic instruments, but they are not absolutes. A viable society can't make exceptions all the time, but I would personally. . . . I'm afraid I'm heading for some big crisis with my boyfriend someday, and someone will get hurt, and he'll get more hurt than I will. I feel an obligation to not hurt him, but also an obligation to not lie. I don't know if it is possible to not lie and not hurt.

The common thread that runs through these statements, the wish not to hurt others and the hope that in morality lies a way of solving conflicts so that no one will get hurt, is striking in that it is independently introduced by each of the four women as the most specific item in their response to a most general question. The moral person is one who helps others; goodness is service, meeting one's obligations and responsibilities to others, if possible, without sacrificing oneself. While the first of the four women ends by denying the conflict she initially introduced, the last woman anticipates a conflict between remaining true to herself and adhering to her principle of not hurting others. The dilemma that would test the limits of this judgment would be one where helping others is seen to be at the price of hurting the self.

The reticence about taking stands on "controversial issues," the willingness to "make exceptions all the time" expressed in the final example above, is echoed repeatedly by other Radcliffe students, as in the following two examples:

> I never feel that I can condemn anyone else. I have a very relativistic position. The basic idea that I cling to is the sanctity of human life. I am inhibited about impressing my beliefs on others.

> I could never argue that my belief on a moral question is anything that another person should accept. I don't believe in absolutes. . . . If there is an absolute for moral decisions, it is human life.

Or as a thirty-one-year-old Wellesley graduate says, in explaining why she would find it difficult to steal a drug to save her own life despite her belief that it would be right to steal for another: "It's just very hard to defend yourself against the rules. I mean, we live by consensus, and you take an action simply for yourself, by yourself, there's no consensus there, and that is relatively indefensible in this society now."

What begins to emerge is a sense of vulnerability that impedes these women from taking a stand, what George Eliot (1860/1965) regards as the girl's "susceptibility" to adverse judgments of others, which stems from her lack of power and consequent inability to do something in the world. While relativism in men, the unwillingness to make moral judgments that Kohlberg and Kramer (1969) and Kohlberg and Gilligan (1971) have associated with the adolescent crisis of identity and belief, takes the form of calling into question the concept of morality itself, the women's reluctance to judge stems rather from their uncertainty about their right to make moral statements or, perhaps, the price for them that such judgment seems to entail. This contrast echoes that made by Matina Horner (1972), who differentiated the ideological fear of success expressed by men from the personal conflicts about succeeding that riddled the women's responses to stories of competitive achievement.

> Most of the men who responded with the expectation of negative consequences because of success were not concerned about their masculinity but were instead likely to have expressed existential concerns about finding a "non-materialistic happiness and satisfaction in life." These concerns, which reflect changing attitudes toward traditional kinds of success or achievement in our society, played little, if any, part in the female stories. Most of the women who were high in fear of success imagery continued to be concerned about the discrepancy between success in the situation described and feminine identity. (pp. 163–164)

When women feel excluded from direct participation in society, they see themselves as subject to a consensus or judgment made and enforced by the men on whose protection and support they depend and by whose names they are known. A divorced middle-aged woman, mother of adolescent daughters, resident of a sophisticated university community, tells the story as follows:

> As a woman, I feel I never understood that I was a person, that I can make decisions and I have a right to make decisions. I always felt that that belonged to my father or my husband in some way or church which was always represented by a male clergyman. They were the three men in my life: father, husband, and clergyman, and they had much more to say about what I should or shouldn't do. They were really authority figures which I accepted. I didn't rebel against that. It only has lately occurred to me that I never even rebelled against it, and my girls are much more conscious of this, not in the militant sense, but just in the recognizing sense. . . . I still let things happen to me rather than make them happen, than to make choices, although I know all about choices. I know the procedures and the steps and all. [Do you have any clues about why this might be true?] Well, I think in one sense, there is less responsibility involved.

Because if you make a dumb decision, you have to take the rap. If it happens to you, well, you can complain about it. I think that if you don't grow up feeling that you ever had any choices, you don't either have the sense that you have emotional responsibility. With this sense of choice comes this sense of responsibility.

The essence of the moral decision is the exercise of choice and the willingness to accept responsibility for that choice. To the extent that women perceive themselves as having no choice, they correspondingly excuse themselves from the responsibility that decision entails. Childlike in the vulnerability of their dependence and consequent fear of abandonment, they claim to wish only to please but in return for their goodness they expect to be loved and cared for. This, then, is an "altruism" always at risk, for it presupposes an innocence constantly in danger of being compromised by an awareness of the trade-off that has been made. Asked to describe herself, a Radcliffe senior responds:

> I have heard of the onion skin theory. I see myself as an onion, as a block of different layers, the external layers for people that I don't know that well, the agreeable, the social, and as you go inward there are more sides for people I know that I show. I am not sure about the innermost, whether there is a core, or whether I have just picked up everything as I was growing up, these different influences. I think I have a neutral attitude towards myself, but I do think in terms of good and bad. . . . Good—I try to be considerate and thoughtful of other people and I try to be fair in situations and be tolerant. I use the words but I try and work them out practically. . . . Bad things—I am not sure if they are bad, if they are altruistic or I am doing them basically for approval of other people. [Which things are these?] The values I have when I try to act them out. They deal mostly with interpersonal type relations. . . . If I were doing it for approval, it would be a very tenuous thing. If I didn't get the right feedback, there might go all my values.

Ibsen's play, *A Doll House* (1879/1965), depicts the explosion of just such a world through the eruption of a moral dilemma that calls into question the notion of goodness that lies at its center. Nora, the "squirrel wife," living with her husband as she had lived with her father, puts into action this conception of goodness as sacrifice and, with the best of intentions, takes the law into her own hands. The crisis that ensues, most painfully for her in the repudiation of that goodness by the very person who was its recipient and beneficiary, causes her to reject the suicide that she had initially seen as its ultimate expression and choose instead to seek new and firmer answers to the adolescent questions of identity and belief.

The availability of choice and with it the onus of responsibility has now invaded the most private sector of the woman's domain and threatens a similar explosion. For centuries, women's sexuality anchored them in passivity, in a receptive rather than active stance, where the events of conception and childbirth could be controlled only by a withholding in which their own sexual needs were either denied or sacrificed. That such a sacrifice entailed a cost to their intelligence as well was seen by Freud (1908/1959) when he tied the "undoubted intellectual inferiority of so many women" to "the inhibition of thought necessitated by sexual suppression" (p. 199). The strategies of withholding and denial that women have employed in the politics of sexual relations appear similar to their evasion or withholding of judgment in the moral realm. The hesitance expressed in the previous examples to impose even a belief in the value of human life on others, like the reluctance to claim one's sexuality, bespeaks a self uncertain of its strength, unwilling to deal with consequence, and thus avoiding confrontation.

Thus women have traditionally deferred to the judgment of men, although often while intimating a sensibility of their own which is at variance with that judgment. Maggie Tulliver, in *The Mill on the Floss* (Eliot, 1860/1965) responds to the accusations that ensue from the discovery of her secretly continued relationship with Phillip Wakeham by acceding to her brother's moral judgment while at the same time asserting a different set of standards by which she attests her own superiority:

> I don't want to defend myself. . . . I know I've been wrong—often continually. But yet, sometimes when I have done wrong, it has been because I have feelings that you would be the better for if you had them. If *you* were in fault ever, if you had done anything very wrong, I should be sorry for the pain it brought you; I should not want punishment to be heaped on you. (p. 188)

An eloquent defense, Kohlberg would argue, of a Stage Three moral position, an assertion of the age-old split between thinking and feeling, justice and mercy, that underlies many of the clichés and stereotypes concerning the difference between the sexes. But considered from another point of view, it is a moment of confrontation, replacing a former evasion, between two modes of judging, two differing constructions of the moral domain—one traditionally associated with masculinity and the public world of social power, the other with femininity and the privacy of domestic interchange. While the developmental ordering of these two points of view has been to consider the masculine as the more adequate and thus as replacing the feminine as the individual moves toward higher stages, their reconciliation remains unclear.

The Development of Women's Moral Judgment

Recent evidence for a divergence in moral development between men and women comes from the research of Haan (1971) and Holstein (1976), whose findings lead them to question the possibility of a "sex-related bias" in Kohlberg's scoring system. This system is based on Kohlberg's six-stage description of moral development. Kohlberg's stages divide into three levels, which he designates as preconventional, conventional, and postconventional, thus denoting the major shifts in moral perspective around a center of moral understanding that equates justice with the maintenance of existing social systems. While the preconventional conception of justice is based on the needs of the self, the conventional judgment derives from an understanding of society. This understanding is in turn superseded by a postconventional or principled conception of justice where the good is formulated in universal terms. The quarrel with Kohlberg's stage scoring does not pertain to the structural differentiation of his levels but rather to questions of stage and sequence. Kohlberg's stages begin with an obedience and punishment orientation (Stage One), and go from there in invariant order to instrumental hedonism (Stage Two), interpersonal concordance (Stage Three), law and order (Stage Four), social contract (Stage Five), and universal ethical principles (Stage Six).

The bias that Haan and Holstein question in this scoring system has to do with the subordination of the interpersonal to the societal definition of the good in the transition from Stage Three to Stage Four. This is the transition that has repeatedly been found to be problematic for women. In 1969, Kohlberg and Kramer identified Stage Three as the characteristic mode of women's moral judgments, claiming that, since women's lives were interpersonally based, this stage was not only "functional" for them but also adequate for resolving the moral conflicts that they faced. Turiel (1973) reported that while girls reached Stage Three sooner than did boys, their judgments tended to remain at that stage while the boys' development continued further along Kohlberg's scale. Gilligan, Kohlberg, Lerner, and Belenky (1971) found a similar association between sex and moral-judgment stage in a study of high-school students, with the girls' responses being scored predominantly at Stage Three while the boys' responses were more often scored at Stage Four.

This repeated finding of developmental inferiority in women may, however, have more to do with the standard by which development has been measured than with the quality of women's thinking per se. Haan's data (1971) on the Berkeley Free Speech Movement and Holstein's (1976) three-year longitudinal study of adolescents and their parents indicate that the moral judgments of women differ from those of men in the greater extent to which women's judgments are tied to feelings of empathy and compassion and are concerned more with the resolution of "real-life" as opposed to hypothetical dilemmas (1971, p. 34). However, as long as the categories by which development is assessed are derived within a male perspective from male research data, divergence from the masculine standard can be seen only as a failure of development. As a result, the thinking of women is often classified with that of children. The systematic exclusion from consideration of alternative criteria that might better encompass the development of women indicates not only the limitations of a theory framed by men and validated by research samples disproportionately male and adolescent but also the effects of the diffidence prevalent among women, their reluctance to speak publicly in their own voice, given the constraints imposed on them by the politics of differential power between the sexes.

In order to go beyond the question, "How much like men do women think, how capable are they of engaging in the abstract and hypothetical construction of reality?" it is necessary to identify and define in formal terms developmental criteria that encompass the categories of women's thinking. Such criteria would include the progressive differentiations, comprehensiveness, and adequacy that characterize higher-stage resolution of the "more frequently occurring, real-life moral dilemmas of interpersonal, empathic, fellow-feeling concerns" (Haan, 1971, p. 34), which have long been the center of women's moral judgments and experience. To ascertain whether the feminine construction of the moral domain relies on a language different from that of men, but one which deserves equal credence in the definition of what constitutes development, it is necessary first to find the places where women have the power to choose and thus are willing to speak in their own voice.

When birth control and abortion provide women with effective means for controlling their fertility, the dilemma of choice enters the center of women's lives. Then the relationships that have traditionally defined women's identities and framed their moral judgments no longer flow inevitably from their reproductive capacity but become matters of decision over which they have control. Released from the passivity and reticence of a sexuality that binds them in dependence, it becomes possible for women to question with Freud what it is that they want and to assert their own answers to that question. However, while society may affirm publicly the woman's right to choose for herself, the exercise of such choice brings her privately into conflict with the conventions of femininity, particularly the moral equation of goodness with self-sacrifice. While independent assertion in judgment and action is considered the hallmark of adulthood and constitutes as well the standard of masculine development, it is rather in their care and concern for others that women have both judged themselves and been judged.

The conflict between self and other thus constitutes the central moral problem for women, posing a dilemma whose resolution requires a reconciliation between femininity and adulthood. In the absence of such a reconciliation, the moral problem cannot be resolved. The "good woman" masks assertion in evasion, denying responsibility by claiming only to meet the needs of others, while the "bad woman" forgoes or renounces the commitments that bind her in self-deception and betrayal. It is precisely this dilemma—the conflict between compassion and autonomy, between virtue and power—which the feminine voice struggles to resolve in its effort to reclaim the self and to solve the moral problem in such a way that no one is hurt.

When a woman considers whether to continue or abort a pregnancy, she contemplates a decision that affects both self and others and engages directly the critical moral issue of hurting. Since the choice is ultimately hers and therefore one for which she is responsible, it raises precisely those questions of judgment that have been most problematic for women. Now she is asked whether she wishes to interrupt that stream of life which has for centuries immersed her in the passivity of dependence while at the same time imposing on her the responsibility for care. Thus the abortion decision brings to the core of feminine apprehension, to what Joan Didion (1972) calls "the irreconcilable difference of it—that sense of living one's deepest life underwater, that dark involvement with blood and birth and death" (p. 14), the adult questions of responsibility and choice.

How women deal with such choices has been the subject of my research, designed to clarify, through considering the ways in which women construct and resolve the abortion decision, the nature and development of women's moral judgment. Twenty-nine women, diverse in age, race, and social class, were referred by abortion and pregnancy counseling services and participated in the study for a variety of reasons. Some came to gain further clarification with respect to a decision about which they were in conflict, some in response to a counselor's concern about repeated abortions, and others out of an interest in and/or willingness to contribute to ongoing research. Although the pregnancies occurred under a variety of circumstances in the lives of these women, certain commonalities could be discerned. The adolescents often failed to use birth control because they denied or discredited their capacity to bear children.

Some of the older women attributed the pregnancy to the omission of contraceptive measures in circumstances where intercourse had not been anticipated. Since the pregnancies often coincided with efforts on the part of the women to end a relationship, they may be seen as a manifestation of ambivalence or as a way of putting the relationship to the ultimate test of commitment. For these women, the pregnancy appeared to be a way of testing truth, making the baby an ally in the search for male support and protection or, that failing, a companion victim of his rejection. There were, finally, some women who became pregnant either as a result of a failure of birth control or intentionally as part of a joint decision that later was reconsidered. Of the twenty-nine women, four decided to have the baby, one miscarried, twenty-one chose abortion, and three remained in doubt about the decision.

In the initial part of the interview, the women were asked to discuss the decision that confronted them, how they were dealing with it, the alternatives they were considering, their reasons for and against each option, the people involved, the conflicts entailed, and the ways in which making this decision affected their self-concepts and their relationships with others. Then, in the second part of the interview, moral judgment was assessed in the hypothetical mode by presenting for resolution three of Kohlberg's standard research dilemmas.

While the structural progression from a preconventional through a conventional to a postconventional moral perspective can readily be discerned in the women's responses to both actual and hypothetical dilemmas, the conventions that shape women's moral judgments differ from those that apply to men. The construction of the abortion dilemma, in particular, reveals the existence of a distinct moral language whose evolution informs the sequence of women's development. This is the language of selfishness and responsibility, which defines the moral problem as one of obligation to exercise care and avoid hurt. The infliction of hurt is considered selfish and immoral in its reflection of unconcern, while the expression of care is seen as the fulfillment of moral responsibility. The reiterative use of the language of selfishness and responsibility and the underlying moral orientation it reflects sets the women apart from the men whom Kohlberg studied and may be seen as the critical reason for their failure to develop within the constraints of his system.

In the developmental sequence that follows, women's moral judgments proceed from an initial focus on the self at the *first level* to the discovery, in the transition to the *second level,* of the concept of responsibility as the basis for a new equilibrium between self and others. The elaboration of this concept of responsibility and its fusion with a maternal concept of morality, which seeks to ensure protection for the dependent and unequal, characterizes the *second level* of judgment. At this level the good is equated with caring for others. However, when the conventions of feminine goodness legitimize only others as the recipients of moral care, the logical inequality between self and other and the psychological violence that it engenders create the disequilibrium that initiates the *second* transition. The relationship between self and others is then reconsidered in an effort to sort out the confusion between conformity and care inherent in the conventional definition of feminine goodness and to establish a new equilibrium, which dissipates the tension between selfishness and responsibility. At the *third level,* the self becomes the arbiter of an independent judgment that now subsumes both conventions and individual needs under the moral principle of nonviolence. Judgment remains psychological in its concern with the intention and consequences of action, but it now becomes universal in its condemnation of exploitation and hurt.

Level I: Orientation to Individual Survival

In its initial and simplest construction, the abortion decision centers on the self. The concern is pragmatic, and the issue is individual survival. At this level, "should" is undifferentiated from "would," and others influence the decision only through their power to affect its consequences. An eighteen-year-old, asked what she thought when she found herself pregnant, replies: "I really didn't think anything except that I didn't want it. [Why was that?] I didn't want it, I wasn't ready for it, and next year will be my last year and I want to go to school."

Asked if there was a right decision, she says, "There is no right decision. [Why?] I didn't want it." For her the question of right decision would emerge only if her own needs were in conflict; then she would have to decide which needs should take precedence. This was the dilemma of another eighteen-year-old, who saw having a baby as a way of increasing her freedom by providing "the perfect chance to get married and move away from home," but also as restricting her freedom "to do a lot of things."

At this first level, the self, which is the sole object of concern, is constrained by lack of power; the wish "to do a lot of things" is constantly belied by the limitations of what, in fact, is being done. Relationships are, for the most part, disappointing: "The only thing you are ever going to get out of going with a guy is to get hurt." As a result, women may in some instances deliberately choose isolation to protect themselves against hurt. When asked how she would describe herself to herself, a nineteen-year-old, who held herself responsible for the accidental death of a younger brother, answers as follows:

> I really don't know. I never thought about it. I don't know. I know basically the outline of a character. I am very independent. I don't really want to have to ask anybody for anything and I am a loner in life. I prefer to be by myself than around anybody else. I manage to keep my friends at a limited number with the point that I have very few friends. I don't know what else there is. I am a loner and I enjoy it. Here today and gone tomorrow.

The primacy of the concern with survival is explicitly acknowledged by a sixteen-year-old delinquent in response to Kohlberg's Heinz dilemma, which asks if it is right for a desperate husband to steal an outrageously overpriced drug to save the life of his dying wife:

> I think survival is one of the first things in life and that people fight for. I think it is the most important thing, more important than stealing. Stealing might be wrong, but if you have to steal to survive yourself or even kill, that is what you should do. . . . Preservation of oneself, I think, is the most important thing; it comes before anything in life.

The First Transition: From Selfishness to Responsibility

In the transition which follows and criticizes this level of judgment, the words selfishness and responsibility first appear. Their reference initially is to the self in a redefinition of the self-interest which has thus far served as the basis for judgment. The transitional issue is one of attachment or connection to others. The pregnancy catches up the issue not only by representing an immediate, literal connection, but also by affirming, in the most concrete and physical way, the capacity to assume adult feminine roles. However, while having a baby seems at first to offer respite from the loneliness of adolescence and to solve conflicts over dependence and independence, in reality the continuation of an adolescent pregnancy generally compounds these problems, increasing social isolation and precluding further steps toward independence.

To be a mother in the societal as well as the physical sense requires the assumption of parental responsibility for the care and protection of a child. However, in order to be able to care for another, one must first be able to care responsibly for oneself. The growth from childhood to adulthood, conceived as a move from selfishness to responsibility, is articulated explicitly in these terms by a seventeen-year-old who describes her response to her pregnancy as follows:

> I started feeling really good about being pregnant instead of feeling really bad, because I wasn't looking at the situation realistically. I was looking at it from my own sort of selfish needs because I was lonely and felt lonely and stuff.... Things weren't really going good for me, so I was looking at it that I could have a baby that I could take care of or something that was part of me, and that made me feel good ... but I wasn't looking at the realistic side ... about the responsibility I would have to take on ... I came to this decision that I was going to have an abortion [because] I realized how much responsibility goes with having a child. Like you have to be there, you can't be out of the house all the time which is one thing I like to do ... and I decided that I have to take on responsibility for myself and I have to work out a lot of things.

Stating her former mode of judgment, the wish to have a baby as a way of combating loneliness and feeling connected, she now criticizes that judgment as both "selfish" and "unrealistic." The contradiction between wishes for a baby and for the freedom to be "out of the house all the time"—that is, for connection and also for independence—is resolved in terms of a new priority, as the criterion for judgment changes. The dilemma now assumes moral definition as the emergent conflict between wish and necessity is seen as a disparity between "would" and "should." In this construction the "selfishness" of willful decision is counterposed to the "responsibility" of moral choice:

> What I want to do is to have the baby, but what I feel I should do which is what I need to do, is have an abortion right now, because sometimes what you want isn't right. Sometimes what is necessary comes before what you want, because it might not always lead to the right thing.

While the pregnancy itself confirms femininity—"I started feeling really good; it sort of made me feel, like being pregnant, I started feeling like a woman"—the abortion decision becomes an opportunity for the adult exercise of responsible choice.

> [How would you describe yourself to yourself?] I am looking at myself differently in the way that I have had a really heavy decision put upon me, and I have never really had too many hard decisions in my life, and I have made it. It has taken some responsibility to do this. I have changed in that way, that I have made a hard decision. And that has been good. Because before, I would not have looked at it realistically, in my opinion. I would have gone by what I wanted to do, and I wanted it, and even if it wasn't right. So I see myself as I'm becoming more mature in ways of making decisions and taking care of myself, doing something for myself. I think it is going to help me in other ways, if I have other decisions to make put upon me, which would take some responsibility. And I would know that I could make them.

In the epiphany of this cognitive reconstruction, the old becomes transformed in terms of the new. The wish to "do something for myself" remains, but the terms of its fulfillment change as the decision affirms both femininity and adulthood in its integration of responsibility and care. Morality, says another adolescent, "is the way you think about yourself . . . sooner or later you have to make up your mind to start taking care of yourself. Abortion, if you do it for the right reasons, is helping yourself to start over and do different things."

Since this transition signals an enhancement in self-worth, it requires a conception of self which includes the possibility for doing "the right thing," the ability to see in oneself the potential for social acceptance. When such confidence is seriously in doubt, the transitional questions may be raised but development is impeded. The failure to make this first transition, despite an understanding of the issues involved, is illustrated by a woman in her late twenties. Her struggle with the conflict between selfishness and responsibility pervades but fails to resolve her dilemma of whether or not to have a third abortion.

> I think you have to think about the people who are involved, including yourself. You have responsibilities to yourself . . . and to make a right, whatever that is, decision in this depends on your knowledge and awareness of the responsibilities that you have and whether you can survive with a child and what it will do to your relationship with the father or how it will affect him emotionally.

Rejecting the idea of selling the baby and making "a lot of money in a black market kind of thing . . . because mostly I operate on principles and it would just rub me the wrong way to think I would be selling my own child," she struggles with a concept of responsibility which repeatedly turns back on the question of her own survival. Transition seems blocked by a self-image which is insistently contradictory:

> [How would you describe yourself to yourself?] I see myself as impulsive, practical— that is a contradiction—and moral and amoral, a contradiction. Actually the only thing that is consistent and not contradictory is the fact that I am very lazy which everyone has always told me is really a symptom of something else which I have never been able to put my finger on exactly. It has taken me a long time to like myself. In fact there are times when I don't, which I think is healthy to a point and sometimes I think I like myself too much and I probably evade myself too much, which avoids responsibil-

ity to myself and to other people who like me. I am pretty unfaithful to myself . . . I have a hard time even thinking that I am a human being, simply because so much rotten stuff goes on and people are so crummy and insensitive.

Seeing herself as avoiding responsibility, she can find no basis upon which to resolve the pregnancy dilemma. Instead, her inability to arrive at any clear sense of decision only contributes further to her overall sense of failure. Criticizing her parents for having betrayed her during adolescence by coercing her to have an abortion she did not want, she now betrays herself and criticizes that as well. In this light, it is less surprising that she considered selling her child, since she felt herself to have, in effect, been sold by her parents for the sake of maintaining their social status.

The Second Level: Goodness as Self-Sacrifice

The transition from selfishness to responsibility is a move toward social participation. Whereas at the first level, morality is seen as a matter of sanctions imposed by a society of which one is more subject than citizen, at the second level, moral judgment comes to rely on shared norms and expectations. The woman at this level validates her claim to social membership through the adoption of societal values. Consensual judgment becomes paramount and goodness the overriding concern as survival is now seen to depend on acceptance by others.

Here the conventional feminine voice emerges with great clarity, defining the self and proclaiming its worth on the basis of the ability to care for and protect others. The woman now constructs the world perfused with the assumptions about feminine goodness reflected in the stereotypes of the Broverman et al. (1972) studies. There the attributes considered desirable for women all presume an other, a recipient of the "tact, gentleness and easy expression of feeling" which allow the woman to respond sensitively while evoking in return the care which meets her own "very strong need for security" (p. 63). The strength of this position lies in its capacity for caring; its limitation is the restriction it imposes on direct expression. Both qualities are elucidated by a nineteen-year-old who contrasts her reluctance to criticize with her boyfriend's straightforwardness:

I never want to hurt anyone, and I tell them in a very nice way, and I have respect for their own opinions, and they can do the things the way that they want, and he usually tells people right off the bat. . . . He does a lot of things out in public which I do in private. . . . It is better, the other [his way], but I just could never do it.

While her judgment clearly exists, it is not expressed, at least not in public. Concern for the feelings of others imposes a deference which she nevertheless criticizes in an awareness that, under the name of consideration, a vulnerability and a duplicity are concealed.

At the second level of judgment, it is specifically over the issue of hurting that conflict arises with respect to the abortion decision. When no option exists that can be construed as being in the best interest of everyone, when responsibilities conflict and decision entails the sacrifice of somebody's needs, then the woman confronts the seemingly impossible task of choosing the victim. A nineteen-year-old, fearing the consequences for herself of a second abortion but facing the opposition of both her family and her lover to the continuation of the pregnancy, describes the dilemma as follows:

> I don't know what choices are open to me; it is either to have it or the abortion; these are the choices open to me. It is just that either way I don't ... I think what confuses me is it is a choice of either hurting myself or hurting other people around me. What is more important? If there could be a happy medium, it would be fine, but there isn't. It is either hurting someone on this side or hurting myself.

While the feminine identification of goodness with self-sacrifice seems clearly to dictate the "right" resolution of this dilemma, the stakes may be high for the woman herself, and the sacrifice of the fetus, in any event, compromises the altruism of an abortion motivated by a concern for others. Since femininity itself is in conflict in an abortion intended as an expression of love and care, this is a resolution which readily explodes in its own contradiction.

"I don't think anyone should have to choose between two things that they love," says a twenty-five-year-old woman who assumed responsibility not only for her lover but also for his wife and children in having an abortion she did not want:

> I just wanted the child and I really don't believe in abortions. Who can say when life begins. I think that life begins at conception and ... I felt like there were changes happening in my body and I felt very protective ... [but] I felt a responsibility, my responsibility if anything ever happened to her [his wife]. He made me feel that I had to make a choice and there was only one choice to make and that was to have an abortion and I could always have children another time and he made me feel if I didn't have it that it would drive us apart.

The abortion decision was, in her mind, a choice not to choose with respect to the pregnancy—"That was my choice, I had to do it." Instead, it was a decision to subordinate the pregnancy to the continuation of a relationship that she saw as encompassing her life—"Since I met him, he has been my life. I do everything for him; my life sort of revolves around him." Since she wanted to have the baby and also to continue the relationship, either choice could be construed as selfish. Furthermore, since both alternatives entailed hurting someone, neither could be considered moral. Faced with a decision which, in her own terms, was untenable, she sought to avoid responsibility for the choice she made, construing the decision as a sacrifice of her own needs to those of her lover. However, this public sacrifice in the name of responsibility engendered a private resentment that erupted in anger, compromising the very relationship that it had been intended to sustain.

> Afterwards we went through a bad time because I hate to say it and I was wrong, but I blamed him. I gave in to him. But when it came down to it, I made the decision. I could have said, "I am going to have this child whether you want me to or not," and I just didn't do it.

Pregnant again by the same man, she recognizes in retrospect that the choice in fact had been hers, as she returns once again to what now appears to have been missed opportunity for growth. Seeking, this time, to make rather than abdicate the decision, she sees the issue as one of "strength" as she struggles to free herself from the powerlessness of her own dependence:

> I think that right now I think of myself as someone who can become a lot stronger. Because of the circumstances, I just go along like with the tide. I never really had anything of my own before ... [this time] I hope to come on strong and make a big decision, whether it is right or wrong.

Because the morality of self-sacrifice had justified the previous abortion, she now must suspend that judgment if she is to claim her own voice and accept responsibility for choice.

She thereby calls into question the underlying assumption of Level Two, which leads the woman to consider herself responsible for the actions of others, while holding others responsible for the choices she makes. This notion of reciprocity, backwards in its assumptions about control, disguises assertion as response. By reversing responsibility, it generates a series of indirect actions, which leave everyone feeling manipulated and betrayed. The logic of this position is confused in that the morality of mutual care is embedded in the psychology of dependence. Assertion becomes personally dangerous in its risk of criticism and abandonment, as well as potentially immoral in its power to hurt. This confusion is captured by Kohlberg's (1969) definition of Stage Three moral judgment, which joins the need for approval with the wish to care for and help others.

When thus caught between the passivity of dependence and the activity of care, the woman becomes suspended in an immobility of both judgment and action. "If I were drowning, I couldn't reach out a hand to save myself, so unwilling am I to set myself up against fate" (p. 7), begins the central character of Margaret Drabble's novel, *The Waterfall* (1969), in an effort to absolve herself of responsibility as she at the same time relinquishes control. Facing the same moral conflict which George Eliot depicted in *The Mill on the Floss*, Drabble's heroine proceeds to relive Maggie Tulliver's dilemma but turns inward in her search for the way in which to retell that story. What is initially suspended and then called into question is the judgment which "had in the past made it seem better to renounce myself than them" (p. 50).

The Second Transition: From Goodness to Truth

The second transition begins with the reconsideration of the relationship between self and other, as the woman starts to scrutinize the logic of self-sacrifice in the service of a morality of care. In the interview data, this transition is announced by the reappearance of the word selfish. Retrieving the judgmental initiative, the woman begins to ask whether it is selfish or responsible, moral or immoral, to include her own needs within the compass of her care and concern. This question leads her to reexamine the concept of responsibility, juxtaposing the outward concern with what other people think with a new inner judgment.

In separating the voice of the self from those of others, the woman asks if it is possible to be responsible to herself as well as to others and thus to reconcile the disparity between hurt and care. The exercise of such responsibility, however, requires a new kind of judgment whose first demand is for honesty. To be responsible, it is necessary first to acknowledge what it is that one is doing. The criterion for judgment thus shifts from "goodness" to "truth" as the morality of action comes to be assessed not on the basis of its appearance in the eyes of others, but in terms of the realities of its intention and consequence.

A twenty-four-year-old married Catholic woman, pregnant again two months following the birth of her first child, identifies her dilemma as one of choice: "You have to now decide; because it is now available, you have to make a decision. And if it wasn't available, there was no choice open; you just do what you have to do." In the absence of legal abortion, a morality of self-sacrifice was necessary in order to insure protection and care for the dependent child. However, when such sacrifice becomes optional, the entire problem is recast.

The abortion decision is framed by this woman first in terms of her responsibilities to others: having a second child at this time would be contrary to medical advice and would strain both the emotional and financial resources of the family. However, there is, she says, a third reason for having an abortion, "sort of an emotional reason. I don't know if it is selfish or not, but it would really be tying myself down and right now I am not ready to be tied down with two."

Against this combination of selfish and responsible reasons for abortion is her Catholic belief that

> it is taking a life, and it is. Even though it is not formed, it is the potential, and to me it is still taking a life. But I have to think of mine, my son's and my husband's, to think about, and at first I think that I thought it was for selfish reasons, but it is not. I believe that too, some of it is selfish. I don't want another one right now; I am not ready for it.

The dilemma arises over the issue of justification for taking a life: "I can't cover it over, because I believe this and if I do try to cover it over, I know that I am going to be in a mess. It will be denying what I am really doing." Asking "Am I doing the right thing; is it moral?," she counterposes to her belief against abortion her concern with the consequences of continuing the pregnancy. While concluding that "I can't be so morally strict as to hurt three other people with a decision just because of my moral beliefs," the issue of goodness still remains critical to her resolution of the dilemma:

> The moral factor is there. To me it is taking a life, and I am going to take that upon myself, that decision upon myself and I have feelings about it, and talked to a priest . . . but he said it is there and it will be from now on, and it is up to the person if they can live with the idea and still believe they are good.

The criteria for goodness, however, move inward as the ability to have an abortion and still consider herself good comes to hinge on the issue of selfishness with which she struggles to come to terms. Asked if acting morally is acting according to what is best for the self or whether it is a matter of self-sacrifice, she replies:

> I don't know if I really understand the question. . . . Like in my situation where I want to have the abortion and if I didn't it would be self-sacrificing, I am really in the middle

of both those ways ... but I think that my morality is strong and if these reasons—financial, physical reality and also for the whole family involved—were not here, that I wouldn't have to do it, and then it would be a self-sacrifice.

The importance of clarifying her own participation in the decision is evident in her attempt to ascertain her feelings in order to determine whether or not she was "putting them under" in deciding to end the pregnancy. Whereas in the first transition, from selfishness to responsibility, women made lists in order to bring to their consideration needs other than their own, now, in the second transition, it is the needs of the self which have to be deliberately uncovered. Confronting the reality of her own wish for an abortion, she now must deal with the problem of selfishness and the qualification that she feels it imposes on the "goodness" of her decision. The primacy of this concern is apparent in her description of herself:

I think in a way I am selfish for one thing, and very emotional, very ... and I think that I am a very real person and an understanding person and I can handle life situations fairly well, so I am basing a lot of it on my ability to do the things that I feel are right and best for me and whoever I am involved with. I think I was very fair to myself about the decision, and I really think that I have been truthful, not hiding anything, bringing out all the feelings involved. I feel it is a good decision and an honest one, a real decision.

Thus she strives to encompass the needs of both self and others, to be responsible to others and thus to be "good" but also to be responsible to herself and thus to be "honest" and "real."

While from one point of view, attention to one's own needs is considered selfish, when looked at from a different perspective, it is a matter of honesty and fairness. This is the essence of the transitional shift toward a new conception of goodness which turns inward in an acknowledgment of the self and an acceptance of responsibility for decision. While outward justification, the concern with "good reasons," remains critical for this particular woman: "I still think abortion is wrong, and it will be unless the situation can justify what you are doing." But the search for justification has produced a change in her thinking, "not drastically, but a little bit." She realizes that in continuing the pregnancy she would punish not only herself but also her husband, toward whom she had begun to feel "turned off and irritated." This leads her to consider the consequences self-sacrifice can have both for the self and for others. "God," she says, "can punish, but He can also forgive." What remains in question is whether her claim to forgiveness is compromised by a decision that not only meets the needs of others but that also is "right and best for me."

The concern with selfishness and its equation with immorality recur in an interview with another Catholic woman whose arrival for an abortion was punctuated by the statement, "I have always thought abortion was a fancy word for murder." Initially explaining this murder as one of lesser degree—"I am doing it because I have to do it. I am not doing it the least bit because I want to," she judges it "not quite as bad. You can rationalize that it is not quite the same." Since "keeping the child for lots and lots of reasons was just sort of impractical and out," she considers her options to be either abortion or adoption. However, having previously given up one child for adoption, she says: "I knew that psychologically there was no way that I could hack another adoption. It took me about four-and-a-half years to get my head on straight; there was just no way I was going to go through it again." The decision thus reduces in her eyes to a choice between murdering the fetus or damaging herself. The choice is further complicated by the fact that by continuing the pregnancy she would hurt not only herself but also her parents, with whom she lived. In the face of these manifold moral contradictions, the psychological demand for honesty that arises in counseling finally allows decision:

> On my own, I was doing it not so much for myself; I was doing it for my parents. I was doing it because the doctor told me to do it, but I had never resolved in my mind that I was doing it for me. Because it goes right back to the fact that I never believed in abortions. . . . Actually, I had to sit down and admit, no, I really don't want to go the mother route now. I honestly don't feel that I want to be a mother, and that is not really such a bad thing to say after all. But that is not how I felt up until talking to Maureen [her counselor]. It was just a horrible way to feel, so I just wasn't going to feel it, and I just blocked it right out.

As long as her consideration remains "moral," abortion can be justified only as an act of sacrifice, a submission to necessity where the absence of choice precludes responsibility. In this way, she can avoid self-condemnation, since, "When you get into moral stuff then you are getting into self-respect and that stuff, and at least if I do something that I feel is morally wrong, then I tend to lose some of my self-respect as a person." Her evasion of responsibility, critical to maintaining the innocence necessary for self-respect, contradicts the reality of her own participation in the abortion decision. The dishonesty in her plea of victimization creates the conflict that generates the need for a more inclusive understanding. She must now resolve the emerging contradiction in her thinking between two uses of the term right: "I am saying that abortion is morally wrong, but the situation is right, and I am going to do it. But the thing is that eventually they are going to have to go together, and I am going to have to put them together somehow." Asked how this could be done, she replies:

> I would have to change morally wrong to morally right. [How?] I have no idea. I don't think you can take something that you feel is morally wrong because the situation makes it right and put the two together. They are not together, they are opposite. They don't go together. Something is wrong, but all of a sudden because you are doing it, it is right.

This discrepancy recalls a similar conflict she faced over the question of euthanasia, also considered by her to be morally wrong until she "took care of a couple of patients who had flat EEGs and saw the job that it was doing on their families." Recalling that experience, she says:

> You really don't know your black and whites until you really get into them and are being confronted with it. If you stop and think about my feelings on euthanasia until I got into it, and then my feelings about abortion until I got into it, I thought both of them were murder. Right and wrong and no middle but there is a gray.

In discovering the gray and questioning the moral judgments which formerly she considered to be absolute, she confronts the moral crisis of the second transition. Now the conventions which in the past had guided her moral judgment become subject to a new criticism, as she questions not only the justification for hurting others in the name of morality but also the "rightness" of hurting herself. However, to sustain such criticism in the face of conventions that equate goodness with self-sacrifice, the woman must verify her capacity for independent judgment and the legitimacy of her own point of view.

Once again transition hinges on self-concept. When uncertainty about her own worth prevents a woman from claiming equality, self-assertion falls prey to the old criticism of selfishness. Then the morality that condones self-destruction in the name of responsible care is not repudiated as inadequate but rather is abandoned in the face of its threat to survival. Moral obligation, rather than expanding to include the self, is rejected completely as the failure of conventional reciprocity leaves the woman unwilling any longer to protect others at what is now seen to be her own expense. In the absence of morality, survival, however "selfish" or "immoral," returns as the paramount concern.

A musician in her late twenties illustrates this transitional impasse. Having led an independent life which centered on her work, she considered herself "fairly strong-willed, fairly in control, fairly rational and objective" until she became involved in an intense love affair and discovered in her capacity to love "an entirely new dimension" in herself. Admitting in retrospect to "tremendous naiveté and idealism," she had entertained "some vague ideas that some day I would like a child to concretize our relationship . . . having always associated having a child with all the creative aspects of my life." Abjuring, with her lover, the use of contraceptives because, "as the relationship was sort of an ideal relationship in our minds, we liked the idea of not using foreign objects or anything artificial," she saw herself as having relinquished control, becoming instead "just simply vague and allowing events to just carry me along." Just as she began in her own thinking to confront "the realities of that situation"—the possibility of pregnancy and the fact that her lover was married—she found herself pregnant. "Caught" between her wish to end a relationship that "seemed more and more defeating" and her wish for a baby, which "would be a connection that would last a long time," she is paralyzed by her inability to resolve the dilemma which her ambivalence creates.

The pregnancy poses a conflict between her "moral" belief that "once a certain life has begun, it shouldn't be stopped artificially" and her "amazing" discovery that to have the baby she would "need much more [support] than I thought." Despite her moral conviction that she "should" have the child, she doubts that she could psychologically deal with "having the child alone and taking the responsibility for it." Thus a conflict erupts between what she considers to be her moral obligation to protect life and her inability to do so under the circumstances of this pregnancy. Seeing it as "my decision and my responsibility for making the decision whether to have or have not the child," she struggles to find a viable basis on which to resolve the dilemma.

Capable of arguing either for or against abortion "with a philosophical logic," she says, on the one hand, that in an overpopulated world one should have children only under ideal conditions for care but, on the other, that one should end a life only when it is impossible to sustain it. She describes her impasse in response to the question of whether there is a difference between what she wants to do and what she thinks she should do:

> Yes, and there always has. I have always been confronted with that precise situation in a lot of my choices, and I have been trying to figure out what are the things that make me believe that these are things I should do as opposed to what I feel I want to do. [In this situation?] It is not that clear cut. I both want the child and feel I should have it, and I also think I should have the abortion and want it, but I would say it is my stronger feeling, and that I don't have enough confidence in my work yet and that is really where it is all hinged, I think . . . [the abortion] would solve the problem and I know I can't handle the pregnancy.

Characterizing this solution as "emotional and pragmatic" and attributing it to her lack of confidence in her work, she contrasts it with the "better thought out and more logical and more correct" resolution of her lover who thinks that she should have the child and raise it without either his presence or financial support. Confronted with this reflected image of herself as ultimately giving and good, as self-sustaining in her own creativity and thus able to meet the needs of others while imposing no demands of her own in return, she questions not the image itself but her own adequacy in filling it. Concluding that she is not yet capable of doing so, she is reduced in her own eyes to what she sees as a selfish and highly compromised fight

> for my survival. But in one way or another, I am going to suffer. Maybe I am going to suffer mentally and emotionally having the abortion, or I would suffer what I think is possibly something worse. So I suppose it is the lesser of two evils. I think it is a matter of choosing which one I know that I can survive through. It is really. I think it is selfish, I suppose, because it does have to do with that. I just realized that. I guess it does have to do with whether I would survive or not. [Why is this selfish?] Well, you know, it is. Because I am concerned with my survival first, as opposed to the survival of the relationship or the survival of the child, another human being . . . I guess I am setting priorities, and I guess I am setting my needs to survive first. . . . I guess I see it in negative terms a lot . . . but I do think of other positive things; that I am still going to have some life left, maybe. I don't know.

In the face of this failure of reciprocity of care, in the disappointment of abandonment where connection was sought, survival is seen to hinge on her work which is "where I derive the meaning of what I am. That's the known factor." While uncertainty about her work makes this survival precarious, the choice for abortion is also distressing in that she considers it to be "highly introverted—that in this one respect, having an abortion would be going a step backward; going outside to love someone else and having a child would be a step forward." The sense of retrenchment that the severing of connection signifies is apparent in her anticipation of the cost which abortion would entail:

> Probably what I will do is I will cut off my feelings, and when they will return or what would happen to them after that, I don't know. So that I don't feel anything at all, and

I would probably just be very cold and go through it very coldly. . . . The more you do that to yourself, the more difficult it becomes to love again or to trust again or to feel again. . . . Each time I move away from that, it becomes easier, not more difficult, but easier to avoid committing myself to a relationship. And I am really concerned about cutting off that whole feeling aspect.

Caught between selfishness and responsibility, unable to find in the circumstances of this choice a way of caring which does not at the same time destroy, she confronts a dilemma which reduces to a conflict between morality and survival. Adulthood and femininity fly apart in the failure of this attempt at integration as the choice to work becomes a decision not only to renounce this particular relationship and child but also to obliterate the vulnerability that love and care engender.

The Third Level: The Morality of Nonviolence

In contrast, a twenty-five-year-old woman, facing a similar disappointment, finds a way to reconcile the initially disparate concepts of selfishness and responsibility through a transformed understanding of self and a corresponding redefinition of morality. Examining the assumptions underlying the conventions of feminine self-abnegation and moral self-sacrifice, she comes to reject these conventions as immoral in their power to hurt. By elevating nonviolence—the injunction against hurting—to a principle governing all moral judgment and action, she is able to assert a moral equality between self and other. Care then becomes a universal obligation, the self-chosen ethic of a postconventional judgment that reconstructs the dilemma in a way that allows the assumption of responsibility for choice.

In this woman's life, the current pregnancy brings to the surface the unfinished business of an earlier pregnancy and of the relationship in which both pregnancies occurred. The first pregnancy was discovered after her lover had left and was terminated by an abortion experienced as a purging expression of her anger at having been rejected. Remembering the abortion only as a relief, she nevertheless describes that time in her life as one in which she "hit rock bottom." Having hoped then to "take control of my life," she instead resumed the relationship when the man reappeared. Now, two years later, having once again "left my diaphragm in the drawer," she again becomes pregnant. Although initially "ecstatic" at the news, her elation dissipates when her lover tells her that he will leave if she chooses to have the child. Under these circumstances, she considers a second abortion but is unable to keep the repeated appointments she makes because of her reluctance to accept the responsibility for that choice. While the first abortion seemed an "honest mistake," she says that a second would make her feel "like a walking slaughter-house." Since she would need financial support to raise the child, her initial strategy was to take the matter to "the welfare people" in the hope that they would refuse to provide the necessary funds and thus resolve her dilemma:

> In that way, you know, the responsibility would be off my shoulders, and I could say, it's not my fault, you know, the state denied me the money that I would need to do it. But it turned out that it was possible to do it, and so I was, you know, right back where

I started. And I had an appointment for an abortion, and I kept calling and cancelling it and then remaking the appointment and cancelling it, and I just couldn't make up my mind.

Confronting the need to choose between the two evils of hurting herself or ending the incipient life of the child, she finds, in a reconstruction of the dilemma itself, a basis for a new priority that allows decision. In doing so, she comes to see the conflict as arising from a faulty construction of reality. Her thinking recapitulates the developmental sequence, as she considers but rejects as inadequate the components of earlier-stage resolutions. An expanded conception of responsibility now reshapes moral judgment and guides resolution of the dilemma, whose pros and cons she considers as follows:

Well, the pros for having the baby are all the admiration that you would get from, you know, being a single woman, alone, martyr, struggling, having the adoring love of this beautiful Gerber baby . . . just more of a home life than I have had in a long time, and that basically was it, which is pretty fantasyland; it is not very realistic. . . . Cons against having the baby: it was going to hasten what is looking to be the inevitable end of the relationship with the man I am presently with. . . . I was going to have to go on welfare, my parents were going to hate me for the rest of my life, I was going to lose a really good job that I have, I would lose a lot of independence . . . solitude . . . and I would have to be put in a position of asking help from a lot of people a lot of the time. Cons against having the abortion is having to face up to the guilt . . . and pros for having the abortion are I would be able to handle my deteriorating relation with S. with a lot more capability and a lot more responsibility for him and for myself . . . and I would not have to go through the realization that for the next twenty-five years of my life I would be punishing myself for being foolish enough to get pregnant again and forcing myself to bring up a kid just because I did this. Having to face the guilt of a second abortion seemed like, not exactly, well, exactly the lesser of the two evils but also the one that would pay off for me personally in the long run because by looking at why I am pregnant again and subsequently have decided to have a second abortion, I have to face up to some things about myself.

Although she doesn't "feel good about having a second abortion," she nevertheless concludes,

I would not be doing myself or the child or the world any kind of favor having this child. . . . I don't need to pay off my imaginary debts to the world through this child, and I don't think that it is right to bring a child into the world and use it for that purpose.

Asked to describe herself, she indicates how closely her transformed moral understanding is tied to a changing self-concept:

I have been thinking about that a lot lately, and it comes up different than what my usual subconscious perception of myself is. Usually paying off some sort of debt, going around serving people who are not really worthy of my attentions because somewhere in my life I think I got the impression that my needs are really secondary to other people's, and that if I feel, if I make any demands on other people to fulfill my needs, I'd feel guilty for it and submerge my own in favor of other people's, which later backfires on me, and I feel a great deal of resentment for other people that I am doing things for, which causes friction and the eventual deterioration of the relationship. And then I start all over again. How would I describe myself to myself? Pretty frustrated and a lot angrier than I admit, a lot more aggressive than I admit.

Reflecting on the virtues which comprise the conventional definition of the feminine self, a definition which she hears articulated in her mother's voice, she says, "I am beginning to think that all these virtues are really not getting me anywhere. I have begun to notice." Tied to this recognition is an acknowledgment of her power and worth, both previously excluded from the image she projected:

I am suddenly beginning to realize that the things that I like to do, the things I am interested in, and the things that I believe and the kind of person I am is not so bad that I have to constantly be sitting on the shelf and letting it gather dust. I am a lot more worthwhile than what my past actions have led other people to believe.

Her notion of a "good person," which previously was limited to her mother's example of hard work, patience and self-sacrifice, now changes to include the value that she herself places on directness and honesty. Although she believes that this new self-assertion will lead her "to feel a lot better about myself" she recognizes that it will also expose her to criticism:

Other people may say, "Boy, she's aggressive, and I don't like that," but at least, you know, they will know that they don't like that. They are not going to say, "I like the way she manipulates herself to fit right around me." . . . What I want to do is just be a more self-determined person and a more singular person.

While within her old framework abortion had seemed a way of "copping out" instead of being a "responsible person [who] pays for his mistakes and pays and pays and is always there when she says she will be there and even when she doesn't say she will be there is there," now, her "conception of what I think is right for myself and my conception of self-worth is changing." She can consider this emergent self "also a good person," as her concept of goodness expands to encompass "the feeling of self-worth; you are not going to sell yourself short and you are not going to make yourself do things that, you know, are really stupid and that you don't want to do." This reorientation centers on the awareness that

I have a responsibility to myself, and you know, for once I am beginning to realize that that really matters to me . . . instead of doing what I want for myself and feeling guilty over how selfish I am, you realize that that is a very usual way for people to live . . . doing what you want to do because you feel that your wants and your needs are important, if to no one else, then to you, and that's reason enough to do something that you want to do.

Once obligation extends to include the self as well as others, the disparity between selfishness and responsibility is reconciled. Although the conflict between self and other remains, the moral problem is restructured in an awareness that the occurrence of the dilemma itself precludes non-violent resolution. The abortion decision is now seen to be a "serious" choice affecting both self and others: "This is a life that I have taken, a conscious decision to terminate, and that is just very heavy, a very heavy thing." While accepting the necessity of abortion as a highly compromised resolution, she turns her attention to the pregnancy itself, which she now considers to denote a failure of responsibility, a failure to care for and protect both self and other.

As in the first transition, although now in different terms, the conflict precipitated by the pregnancy catches up the issues critical to development. These issues now concern the worth of the self in relation to others, the claiming of the power to choose, and the acceptance of responsibility for choice. By provoking a confrontation with these issues, the crisis can become "a very auspicious time; you can use the pregnancy as sort of a learning, teeing-off point, which makes it useful in a way." This possibility for growth inherent in a crisis which allows confrontation with a construction of reality whose acceptance previously had impeded development was first identified by Coles (1964) in his study of the children of Little Rock. This same sense of possibility is expressed by the women who see, in their resolution of the abortion dilemma, a reconstructed understanding which creates the opportunity for "a new beginning," a chance "to take control of my life."

For this woman, the first step in taking control was to end the relationship in which she had considered herself "reduced to a nonentity," but to do so in a responsible way. Recognizing hurt as the inevitable concomitant of rejection, she strives to minimize that hurt "by dealing with [his] needs as best I can without compromising my own . . . that's a big point for me, because the thing in my life to this point has been always compromising, and I am not willing to do that any more." Instead, she seeks to act in a "decent, human kind of way . . . one that leaves maybe a slightly shook but not totally destroyed person." Thus the "nonentity" confronts her power to destroy which formerly had impeded any assertion, as she consider the possibility for a new kind of action that leaves both self and other intact.

The moral concern remains a concern with hurting as she considers Kohlberg's Heinz dilemma in terms of the question, "who is going to be hurt more, the druggist who loses some money or the person who loses their life?" The right to property and right to life are weighed not in the abstract, in terms of their logical priority, but rather in the particular, in terms of the actual consequences that the violation of these rights would have in the lives of the people involved. Thinking remains contextual and admixed with feelings of care, as the moral imperative to avoid hurt begins to be informed by a psychological understanding of the meaning of nonviolence.

Thus, release from the intimidation of inequality finally allows the expression of a judgment that previously had been withheld. What women then enunciate is not a new morality, but a moral conception disentangled from the constraints that formerly had confused its perception and impeded its articulation. The willingness to express and take responsibility for judgment stems from the recognition of the psychological and moral necessity for an equation of worth between self and other. Responsibility for care then includes both self and other, and the obligation not to hurt, freed from conventional constraints, is reconstructed as a universal guide to moral choice.

The reality of hurt centers the judgment of a twenty-nine-year-old woman, married and the mother of a preschool child, as she struggles with the dilemma posed by a second pregnancy whose timing conflicts with her completion of an advanced degree. Saying that "I cannot deliberately do something that is bad or would hurt another person because I can't live with having done that," she nevertheless confronts a situation in which hurt has become inevitable. Seeking that solution which would best protect both herself and others, she indicates, in her definition of morality, the ineluctable sense of connection which infuses and colors all of her thinking:

> [Morality is] doing what is appropriate and what is just within your circumstances, but ideally it is not going to affect—I was going to say, ideally it wouldn't negatively affect another person, but that is ridiculous, because decisions are always going to affect another person. But you see, what I am trying to say is that it is the person that is the center of the decision making, of that decision making about what's right and what's wrong.

The person who is the center of this decision making begins by denying, but then goes on to acknowledge, the conflicting nature both of her own needs and of her various responsibilities. Seeing the pregnancy as a manifestation of the inner conflict between her wish, on the one hand, "to be a college president" and, on the other, "to be making pottery and flowers and having kids and staying at home," she struggles with contradiction between femininity and adulthood. Considering abortion as the "better" choice—because "in the end, meaning this time next year or this time two weeks from now, it will be less of a personal strain on us individually and on us as a family for me not to be pregnant at this time," she concludes that the decision has

> got to be, first of all, something that the woman can live with—a decision that the woman can live with, one way or another, or at least try to live with, and that it be based on where she is at and other people, significant people in her life, are at.

At the beginning of the interview she had presented the dilemma in its conventional feminine construction, as a conflict between her own wish to have a baby and the wish of others for her to complete her education. On the basis of this construction she deemed it "selfish" to continue the pregnancy because it was something "I want to do." However, as she begins to examine her thinking, she comes to abandon as false this conceptualization of the problem, acknowledging the truth of her own internal conflict and elaborating the tension which she feels between her femininity and the adulthood of her work life. She describes herself as "going in two directions" and values that part of herself which is "incredibly passionate and sensitive"—her capacity to recognize and meet, often with anticipation, the needs of others. Seeing her "compassion" as "something I don't want to lose" she regards it as endangered by her pursuit of professional advancement. Thus the self-deception of her initial presentation, its attempt to sustain the fiction of her own innocence, stems from her fear that to say that *she* does not want to have another baby at this time would be

> an acknowledgment to me that I am an ambitious person and that I want to have power and responsibility for others and that I want to live a life that extends from 9 to 5 every day and into the evenings and on weekends, because that is what the power and responsibility means. It means that my family would necessarily come second ... there

would be such an incredible conflict about which is tops, and I don't want that for myself.

Asked about her concept of "an ambitious person" she says that to be ambitious means to be

power hungry [and] insensitive. [Why insensitive?] Because people are stomped on in the process. A person on the way up stomps on people, whether it is family or other colleagues or clientele, on the way up. [Inevitably?] Not always, but I have seen it so often in my limited years of working that it is scary to me. It is scary because I don't want to change like that.

Because the acquisition of adult power is seen to entail the loss of feminine sensitivity and compassion, the conflict between femininity and adulthood becomes construed as a moral problem. The discovery of the principle of nonviolence begins to direct attention to the moral dilemma itself and initiates the search for a resolution that can encompass both femininity and adulthood.

Developmental Theory Reconsidered

The developmental conception delineated at the outset, which has so consistently found the development of women to be either aberrant or incomplete, has been limited insofar as it has been predominantly a male conception, giving lip-service, a place on the chart, to the interdependence of intimacy and care but constantly stressing, at their expense, the importance and value of autonomous judgment and action. To admit to this conception the truth of the feminine perspective is to recognize for both sexes the central importance in adult life of the connection between self and other, the universality of the need for compassion and care. The concept of the separate self and of the moral principle uncompromised by the constraints of reality is an adolescent ideal, the elaborately wrought philosophy of a Stephen Daedalus, whose flight we know to be in jeopardy. Erikson (1964), in contrasting the ideological morality of the adolescent with the ethics of adult care, attempts to grapple with this problem of integration, but is impeded by the limitations of his own previous developmental conception. When his developmental stages chart a path where the sole precursor to the intimacy of adult relationships is the trust established in infancy and all intervening experience is marked only as steps toward greater independence, then separation itself becomes the model and the measure of growth. The observation that for women, identity has as much to do with connection as with separation led Erikson into trouble largely because of his failure to integrate this insight into the mainstream of his developmental theory (Erikson, 1968).

The morality of responsibility which women describe stands apart from the morality of rights which underlies Kohlberg's conception of the highest stages of moral judgment. Kohlberg (1973) sees the progression toward these stages as resulting from the generalization of the self-centered adolescent rejection of societal morality into a principled conception of individual natural rights. To illustrate this progression, he cites as an example of integrated Stage Five judgment, "possibly moving to Stage Six," the following response of a twenty-five-year-old subject from his male longitudinal sample:

> [What does the word morality mean to you?] Nobody in the world knows the answer. I think it is recognizing the right of the individual, the rights of other individuals, not interfering with those rights. Act as fairly as you would have them treat you. I think it is basically to preserve the human being's right to existence. I think that is the most important. Secondly, the human being's right to do as he pleases, again without interfering with somebody else's rights. (p. 29)

Another version of the same conception is evident in the following interview response of a male college senior whose moral judgment also was scored by Kohlberg (1976) as at Stage Five or Six:

> [Morality] is a prescription, it is a thing to follow, and the idea of having a concept of morality is to try to figure out what it is that people can do in order to make life with each other livable, make for a kind of balance, a kind of equilibrium, a harmony in which everybody feels he has a place and an equal share in things, and it's doing that — doing that is kind of contributing to a state of affairs that go beyond the individual in the absence of which, the individual has no chance for self-fulfillment of any kind. Fairness; morality is kind of essential, it seems to me, for creating the kind of environment, interaction between people, that is prerequisite to this fulfillment of most individual goals and so on. If you want other people to not interfere with your pursuit of whatever you are into, you have to play the game.

In contrast, a woman in her late twenties responds to a similar question by defining a morality not of rights but of responsibility:

> [What makes something a moral issue?] Some sense of trying to uncover a right path in which to live, and always in my mind is that the world is full of real and recognizable trouble, and is it heading for some sort of doom and is it right to bring children into this world when we currently have an overpopulation problem, and is it right to spend money on a pair of shoes when I have a pair of shoes and other people are shoeless. . . . It is part of a self-critical view, part of saying, how am I spending my time and in what sense am I working? I think I have a real drive to, I have a real maternal drive to take care of someone. To take care of my mother, to take care of children, to take care of other people's children, to take care of my own children, to take care of the world. I think that goes back to your other question, and when I am dealing with moral issues, I am sort of saying to myself constantly, are you taking care of all the things that you think are important and in what ways are you wasting yourself and wasting those issues?

While the postconventional nature of this woman's perspective seems clear, her judgments of Kohlberg's hypothetical moral dilemmas do not meet his criteria for scoring at the principled level. Kohlberg regards this as a disparity between normative and metaethical judgments which he sees as indicative of the transition between conventional and principled thinking. From another perspective, however, this judgment represents a different moral conception, disentangled from societal conventions and raised to the principled level. In this conception, moral judgment is oriented toward issues of responsibility. The way in which the responsibility orientation guides moral decision at the postconventional level is described by the following woman in her thirties:

> [Is there a right way to make moral decisions?] The only way I know is to try to be as awake as possible, to try to know the range of what you feel, to try to consider all that's involved, to be as aware as you can be to what's going on, as conscious as you can of where you're walking. [Are there principles that guide you?] The principle would have something to do with responsibility, responsibility and caring about yourself and others. . . . But it's not that on the one hand you choose to be responsible and on the other hand you choose to be irresponsible—both ways you can be responsible. That's why there's not just a principle that once you take hold of you settle—the principle put into practice here is still going to leave you with conflict.

The moral imperative that emerges repeatedly in the women's interviews is an injunction to care, a responsibility to discern and alleviate the "real and recognizable trouble" of this world. For the men Kohlberg studied, the moral imperative appeared rather as an injunction to respect the rights of others and thus to protect from interference the right to life and self-fulfillment. Women's insistence on care is at first self-critical rather than self-protective, while men initially conceive obligation to others negatively in terms of noninterference. Development for both sexes then would seem to entail an integration of rights and responsibilities through the discovery of the complementarity of these disparate views. For the women I have studied, this integration between rights and responsibilities appears to take place through a principled understanding of equity and reciprocity. This understanding tempers the self-destructive potential of a self-critical morality by asserting the equal right of all persons to care. For the men in Kohlberg's sample as well as for those in a longitudinal study of Harvard undergraduates (Gilligan & Murphy, 1977) it appears to be the recognition through experience of the need for a more active responsibility in taking care that corrects the potential indifference of a morality of noninterference and turns attention from the logic to the consequences of choice. In the development of a postconventional ethic understanding, women come to see the violence generated by inequitable relationships, while men come to realize the limitations of a conception of justice blinded to the real inequities of human life.

Kohlberg's dilemmas, in the hypothetical abstraction of their presentation, divest the moral actors from the history and psychology of their individual lives and separate the moral problem from the social contingencies of its possible occurrence. In doing so, the dilemmas are useful for the distillation and refinement of the "objective principles of justice" toward which Kohlberg's stages strive. However, the reconstruction of the dilemma in its contextual particularity allows the understanding of cause and consequence which engages the compassion and tolerance considered by previous theorists to qualify the feminine sense of justice. Only when substance is given to the skeletal lives of hypothetical people is it possible to consider the social injustices which their moral problems may reflect and to imagine the individual suffering their occurrence may signify or their resolution engender.

The proclivity of women to reconstruct hypothetical dilemmas in terms of the real, to request or supply the information missing about the nature of the people and the places where they live, shifts their judgment away from the hierarchical ordering of principles and the formal procedures of decision making that are critical for scoring at Kohlberg's highest stages. This insistence on the particular signifies an orientation to the dilemma and to moral problems in general that differs from any of Kohlberg's stage descriptions. Given the constraints of Kohlberg's system and the biases in his research sample, this different orientation can only be construed as a failure in development. While several of the women in the research sample clearly articulated what Kohlberg regarded as a postconventional metaethical position, none of them were considered by Kohlberg (1976) to be principled in their normative moral judgments of his hypothetical moral dilemmas. Instead, the women's judgments pointed toward an identification of the violence inherent in the dilemma itself which was seen to compromise the justice of any of its possible resolutions. This construction of the dilemma led the women to recast the moral judgment from a consideration of the good to a choice between evils.

The woman whose judgment of the abortion dilemma concluded the developmental sequence presented in the preceding section saw Kohlberg's Heinz dilemma in these terms and judged Heinz's action in terms of a choice between selfishness and sacrifice. For Heinz to steal the drug, given the circumstances of his life (which she inferred from his inability to pay two thousand dollars), he would have "to do something which is not in his best interest, in that he is going to get sent away, and that is a supreme sacrifice, a sacrifice which I would say a person truly in love might be willing to make." However, not to steal the drug "would be selfish on his part . . . he would just have to feel guilty about not allowing her a chance to live longer." Heinz's decision to steal is considered not in terms of the logical priority of life over property which justifies its rightness, but rather in terms of the actual consequences that stealing would have for a man of limited means and little social power.

Considered in the light of its probable outcomes—his wife dead, or Heinz in jail, brutalized by the violence of that experience and his life compromised by a record of felony—the dilemma itself changes. Its resolution has less to do with the relative weights of life and property in an abstract moral conception than with the collision it has produced between two lives, formerly conjoined but now in opposition, where the continuation of one life can now occur only at the expense of the other. Given this construction, it becomes clear why consideration revolves around the issue of sacrifice and why guilt becomes the inevitable concomitant of either resolution.

Demonstrating the reticence noted in the first section about making moral judgments, this woman explains her reluctance to judge in terms of her belief

> that everybody's existence is so different that I kind of say to myself, that might be something that I wouldn't do, but I can't say that it is right or wrong for that person. I can only deal with what is appropriate for me to do when I am faced with specific problems.

Asked if she would apply to others her own injunction against hurting, she says:

> See, I can't say that it is wrong. I can't say that it is right or that it's wrong because I don't know what the person did that the other person did something to hurt him . . . so

it is not right that the person got hurt, but it is right that the person who just lost the job has got to get that anger up and out. It doesn't put any bread on his table, but it is released. I don't mean to be copping out. I really am trying to see how to answer these questions for you.

Her difficulty in answering Kohlberg's questions, her sense of strain with the construction which they impose on the dilemma, stems from their divergence from her own frame of reference:

> I don't even think I use the words right and wrong anymore, and I know I don't use the word moral, because I am not sure I know what it means. . . . We are talking about an unjust society, we are talking about a whole lot of things that are not right, that are truly wrong, to use the word that I don't use very often, and I have no control to change that. If I could change it, I certainly would, but I can only make my small contribution from day to day, and if I don't intentionally hurt somebody, that is my contribution to a better society. And so a chunk of that contribution is also not to pass judgment on other people, particularly when I don't know the circumstances of why they are doing certain things.

The reluctance to judge remains a reluctance to hurt, but one that stems now not from a sense of personal vulnerability but rather from a recognition of the limitations of judgment itself. The deference of the conventional feminine perspective can thus be seen to continue at the postconventional level, not as moral relativism but rather as part of a reconstructed moral understanding. Moral judgment is renounced in an awareness of the psychological and social determinism of all human behavior at the same time as moral concern is reaffirmed in recognition of the reality of human pain and suffering.

> I have a real thing about hurting people and always have, and that gets a little complicated at times, because, for example, you don't want to hurt your child. I don't want to hurt my child but if I don't hurt her sometimes, then that's hurting her more, you see, and so that was a terrible dilemma for me.

Moral dilemmas are terrible in that they entail hurt; she sees Heinz's decision as "the result of anguish, who am I hurting, why do I have to hurt them." While the morality of Heinz's theft is not in question, given the circumstances which necessitated it, what is at issue is his willingness to substitute himself for his wife and become, in her stead, the victim of exploitation by a society which breeds and legitimizes the druggist's irresponsibility and whose injustice is thus manifest in the very occurrence of the dilemma.

The same sense that the wrong questions are being asked is evident in the response of another woman who justified Heinz's action on a similar basis, saying "I don't think that exploitation should really be a right." When women begin to make direct moral statements, the issues they repeatedly address are those of exploitation and hurt. In doing so, they raise the issue of nonviolence in precisely the same psychological context that brought Erikson (1969) to pause in his consideration of the truth of Gandhi's life.

In the pivotal letter, around which the judgment of his book turns, Erikson confronts the contradiction between the philosophy of nonviolence that informed Gandhi's dealing with the British and the psychology of violence that marred his relationships with his family and with the children of the ashram. It was this contradiction, Erikson confesses,

> which almost brought *me* to the point where I felt unable to continue writing *this* book because I seemed to sense the presence of a kind of untruth in the very protestation of truth; of something unclean when all the words spelled out an unreal purity; and, above all, of displaced violence where nonviolence was the professed issue. (p. 231)

In an effort to untangle the relationship between the spiritual truth of Satyagraha and the truth of his own psychoanalytic understanding, Erikson reminds Gandhi that "Truth, you once said, 'excludes the use of violence because man is not capable of knowing the absolute truth and therefore is not competent to punish'" (p. 241). The affinity between Satyagraha and psychoanalysis lies in their shared commitment to seeing life as an "experiment in truth," in their being

> somehow joined in a universal "therapeutics," committed to the Hippocratic principle that one can test truth (or the healing power inherent in a sick situation) only by action which avoids harm—or better, by action which maximizes mutuality and minimizes the violence caused by unilateral coercion or threat. (p. 247)

Erikson takes Gandhi to task for his failure to acknowledge the relativity of truth. This failure is manifest in the coercion of Gandhi's claim to exclusive possession of the truth, his "unwillingness to learn from *anybody anything* except what was approved by the 'inner voice'" (p. 236). This claim led Gandhi, in the guise of love, to impose his truth on others without awareness or regard for the extent to which he thereby did violence to their integrity.

The moral dilemma, arising inevitably out of a conflict of truths, is by definition a "sick situation" in that its either/or formulation leaves no room for an outcome that does not do violence. The resolution of such dilemmas, however, lies not in the self-deception of rationalized violence—"I was" said Gandhi, "a cruelly kind husband. I regarded myself as her teacher and so harassed her out of my blind love for her" (p. 233)—but rather in the replacement of the underlying antagonism with a mutuality of respect and care.

Gandhi, whom Kohlberg has mentioned as exemplifying Stage Six moral judgment and whom Erikson sought as a model of an adult ethical sensibility, instead is criticized by a judgment that refuses to look away from or condone the infliction of harm. In denying the validity of his wife's reluctance to open her home to strangers and in his blindness to the different reality of adolescent sexuality and temptation, Gandhi compromised in his everyday life the ethic of nonviolence to which in principle and in public he was so steadfastly committed.

The blind willingness to sacrifice people to truth, however, has always been the danger of an ethics abstracted from life. This willingness links Gandhi to the biblical Abraham, who prepared to sacrifice the life of his son in order to demonstrate the integrity and supremacy of his faith. Both men, in the limitations of their fatherhood, stand in implicit contrast to the woman who comes before Solomon and verifies her motherhood by relinquishing truth in order to save the life of her child. It is the ethics of an adulthood that has become principled at the expense of care that Erikson comes to criticize in his assessment of Gandhi's life.

This same criticism is dramatized explicitly as a contrast between the sexes in *The Merchant of Venice* (1598/1912), where Shakespeare goes through an extraordinary complication of sexual identity (dressing a male actor as a female character who in turn poses as a male judge) in order to bring into the masculine citadel of justice the feminine plea for mercy. The limitation of the contractual conception of justice is illustrated through the absurdity of its literal execution, while the "need to make exceptions all the time" is demonstrated contrapuntally in the matter of the rings. Portia, in calling for mercy, argues for that resolution in which no one is hurt, and as the men are forgiven for their failure to keep both their rings and their word, Antonio in turn foregoes his "right" to ruin Shylock.

The research findings that have been reported in this essay suggest that women impose a distinctive construction on moral problems, seeing moral dilemmas in terms of conflicting responsibilities. This construction was found to develop through a sequence of three levels and two transitions, each level representing a more complex understanding of the relationship between self and other and each transition involving a critical reinterpretation of the moral conflict between selfishness and responsibility. The development of women's moral judgment appears to proceed from an initial concern with survival, to a focus on goodness, and finally to a principled understanding of nonviolence as the most adequate guide to the just resolution of moral conflicts.

In counterposing to Kohlberg's longitudinal research on the development of hypothetical moral judgment in men a cross-sectional study of women's responses to actual dilemmas of moral conflict and choice, this essay precludes the possibility of generalization in either direction and leaves to further research the task of sorting out the different variables of occasion and sex. Longitudinal studies of women's moral judgments are necessary in order to validate the claims of stage and sequence presented here. Similarly, the contrast drawn between the moral judgments of men and women awaits for its confirmation a more systematic comparison of the responses of both sexes. Kohlberg's research on moral development has confounded the variables of age, sex, type of decision, and type of dilemma by presenting a single configuration (the responses of adolescent males to hypothetical dilemmas of conflicting rights) as the basis for a universal stage sequence. This chapter underscores the need for systematic treatment of these variables and points toward their study as a critical task for future moral development research.

For the present, my aim has been to demonstrate the centrality of the concepts of responsibility and care in women's constructions of the moral domain, to indicate the close tie in women's thinking between conceptions of the self and conceptions of morality, and, finally, to argue the need for an expanded developmental theory that would include, rather than rule out from developmental consideration, the difference in the feminine voice. Such an inclusion seems essential, not only for explaining the development of women but also for understanding in both sexes the characteristics and precursors of an adult moral conception.

NOTES

1. The Radcliffe women whose responses are cited were interviewed as part of a pilot study on undergraduate moral development conducted by the author in 1970.

REFERENCES

Broverman, I., Vogel, S., Broverman, D., Clarkson, F., & Rosenkrantz, P. Sex-role stereotypes: A current appraisal. *Journal of Social Issues,* 1972, *28,* 59–78.

Coles, R. *Children of crisis.* Boston: Little, Brown, 1964.

Didion, J. The women's movement. *New York Times Book Review,* July 30, 1972, pp. 1–2; 14.

Drabble, M. *The waterfall.* Hammondsworth, Eng.: Penguin Books, 1969.

Eliot, G. *The mill on the floss.* New York: New American Library, 1965. (Originally published, 1860.)

Erikson, E. H. *Insight and responsibility.* New York: W. W. Norton, 1964.

Erikson, E. H. *Identity: Youth and crisis.* New York: W. W. Norton, 1968.

Erikson, E. H. *Gandhi's truth.* New York: W. W. Norton, 1969.

Freud, S. "Civilized" sexual morality and modern nervous illness. In J. Strachey (Ed.), *The standard edition of the complete psychological works of Sigmund Freud* (Vol. 9). London: Hogarth Press, 1959. (Originally published, 1908.)

Freud, S. Some psychical consequences of the anatomical distinction between the sexes. In J. Strachey (Ed.), *The standard edition of the complete psychological works of Sigmund Freud* (Vol. 19). London: Hogarth Press, 1961. (Originally published, 1925.)

Gilligan, C., Kohlberg, L., Lerner, J., & Belenky, M. Moral reasoning about sexual dilemmas: The development of an interview and scoring system. *Technical Report of the President's Commission on Obscenity and Pornography* (Vol. 1) [415 060–137]. Washington, D.C.: U.S. Government Printing Office, 1971.

Gilligan, C., & Murphy, M. *The philosopher and the "dilemma of the fact": Moral development in late adolescence and adulthood.* Unpublished manuscript, Harvard University, 1977.

Haan, N. *Activism as moral protest: Moral judgments of hypothetical dilemmas and an actual situation of civil disobedience.* Unpublished manuscript, University of California at Berkeley, 1971.

Haan, N. Hypothetical and actual moral reasoning in a situation of civil disobedience. *Journal of Personality and Social Psychology,* 1975, *32,* 255–270.

Holstein, C. Development of moral judgment: A longitudinal study of males and females. *Child Development,* 1976, *47,* 51–61.

Horner, M. Toward an understanding of achievement-related conflicts in women. *Journal of Social Issues,* 1972, *29,* 157–174.

Ibsen, H. *A doll's house.* In *Ibsen plays.* Hammondsworth, Eng.: Penguin Books, 1965. (Originally published, 1879.)

Kohlberg, L. Stage and sequence: The cognitive-developmental approach to socialization. In D. A. Goslin (Ed.), *Handbook of socialization theory and research.* Chicago: Rand McNally, 1969.

Kohlberg, L. From is to ought: How to commit the naturalistic fallacy and get away with it in the study of moral development. In T. Mischel (Ed.), *Cognitive development and epistemology.* New York: Academic Press, 1971.

Kohlberg, L. *Continuities and discontinuities in childhood and adult moral development revisited.* Unpublished paper, Harvard University, 1973.

Kohlberg, L. Personal communication, August, 1976.

Kohlberg, L., & Gilligan, C. The adolescent as a philosopher: The discovery of the self in a postconventional world. *Daedalus,* 1971, *100,* 1051–1056.

Kohlberg, L., & Kramer, R. Continuities and discontinuities in childhood and adult moral development. *Human Development,* 1969, *12,* 93–120.

Piaget, J. *The moral judgment of the child.* New York: Free Press, 1965. (Originally published, 1932.)

Shakespeare, W. *The merchant of Venice.* In *The comedies of Shakespeare.* London: Oxford University Press, 1912. (Originally published, 1598.)

Turiel, E. *A comparative analysis of moral knowledge and moral judgment in males and females.* Unpublished manuscript, Harvard University, 1973.

Chapter Twenty

Feminism and Difference
Gender, Relation, and Difference in Psychoanalytic Perspective

Nancy Chodorow

> I would go so far as to say that even before slavery or
> class domination existed, men built an approach to
> women that would serve one day to introduce differ-
> ences among us all.
>
> —Claude Lévi-Strauss[1]

In both the nineteenth- and twentieth-century women's movements, it has often been argued that the degendering of society would eliminate male dominance, so that gender and sex would not determine social existence. One approach has sometimes held that "female" virtues or qualities—nurturance, for instance—should be spread throughout society and replace aggression, competitiveness, and so forth; but these virtues are seen as acquired, a product of women's development or social location, and acquirable by men, given appropriate development, experience, and social reorganization. (This approach has at times held that women need to acquire certain "male" characteristics and modes of action—autonomy, independence, assertiveness—again, assuming that such characteristics are acquired.)

Another approach has tended toward an essentialist position, posing male-female differences as innate. Not the degendering of society, but its appropriation by women, with their virtues, is seen as the solution to male dominance. These virtues are uniquely feminine, and usually thought to emerge from women's biology, which is then seen as intrinsically connected to or entailing a particular psyche; or a particular social role, such as mothering; or a particular body image (more diffuse, holistic, nonphallocentric); or a particular sexuality (not centered on a particular organ and its goals; at times, lesbianism). In this view, women are intrinsically better than men and their virtues are not available to men.

In the beginning of the contemporary women's movement, the former view

Nancy Chodorow, "Feminism and Difference: Gender, Relation, and Difference in Psychoanalytic Perspective." *Socialist Review* 46 (July–August 1979): 42–64. © 1979 by Nancy J. Chodorow. Reprinted by permission of Duke University Press.

tended to predominate. More recently, versions of the second view have become much more prevalent and attractive to many feminists (and often to anti-feminists as well). The liberal women's movement continues to hold the first view, as do socialist-feminists. The latter view, in various forms, is held by some radical feminists and lesbian feminists in the United States and is also prevalent among certain segments of the French women's movement.

This paper focuses on the question of gender or sex difference, particularly on thoughts about difference among French theorists. It argues against the essentialist view of difference, and examines the contribution that psychoanalytic theory can make to understanding the question of sex or gender difference. The argument here contrasts with certain readings of psychoanalysis. It criticizes the (Lacan-influenced) views advanced by French theorists of difference like Luce Irigaray, and it contests the claims for Freudian orthodoxy made by most Marxist appropriators of psycho-analysis, such as the Frankfurt School and their followers, or Juliet Mitchell. I argue for another Marxist and feminist appropriation of psychoanalysis, one that stresses the relational ego, rather than the instincts and autonomous ego.

Is gender best understood by focusing on differences between women and men, on women's and men's uniqueness? Should gender difference be a central organizing concept for feminism? My understanding is that "difference" as posed by "The Future of Difference" is absolute, abstract, and irreducible.[2] It is assumed to involve questions of the essence of gender, differences between women and men, each seen as an absolute category.

Gender difference is not absolute, abstract, or irreducible; it does not involve an essence of gender. Gender differences, and the experience of difference, are socially and psychologically created and situated just as are differences among women. Difference and gender difference do not exist as things in themselves: they are created relationally, and we cannot understand difference apart from this relational construction.

Psychoanalysis, by providing a history of the emergence of separateness, differenti-ation, and perceptions of difference in early childhood, clarifies many of the issues involved in questions of difference. It provides a particularly useful means to see the relational and situated construction of difference and gender difference. Moreover, psychoanalysis provides an account of these issues as general psychological issues, as well as issues specific to the question of gender. I will discuss two aspects of the general subject of separateness, differentiation, and perceptions of difference and their emergence. First, I will consider how separation-individuation occurs rela-tionally in the first "me"–"not-me" division, in the development of the "I," or self. I will suggest that we have to understand this separation-individuation in relation to other aspects of development, that it has particular implications for women, and that differentiation is not synonymous with difference or separateness. Second, I will talk about the ways that difference and gender difference are created distinctly, in differ-ent relational contexts, for girls and boys, and, hence, for women and men.

My goal is to reflect upon and help clarify a number of issues relevant to feminist theory and to particular strands of feminist politics. There is now a preoccupation with psychological separateness and autonomy, with individuality, as a necessary women's goal, a preoccupation growing out of many women's feelings of not having distinct autonomy as separate selves in comparison, say, to men. This may find a political counterpart in equal rights arguments based on notions of women as individuals rather than part of a collectivity or social group. And there is also a widespread view that gender differences are essential, that women are fundamentally different from men, and that these differences must be recognized, theorized, and maintained. (This may find a political counterpart in notions that women's special nature will guarantee a good society if we have a feminist revolution.)

Differentiation

Psychoanalysis talks of the process of "differentiation" or "separation-individuation."[3] A child of either gender is born originally with what is called a "narcissistic relation to reality"; cognitively and libidinally it experiences itself as merged and continuous with the world in general, and with its mother or caretaker in particular.

Differentiation, or separation-individuation, means coming to perceive a demarcation between the self and the object world, coming to perceive the subject/self as distinct, or separate from, the object/other. An essential early task of infantile development, it involves the development of ego boundaries (a sense of personal psychological division from the rest of the world) and of a body ego (a sense of the permanence of one's physical separateness and the predictable boundedness of one's own body, of distinction between inside and outside).

This differentiation requires physiological maturation (for instance, the ability to perceive object constancy), but such maturation is not enough. Differentiation happens *in relation* to the mother, or to whomever is the child's primary caretaker. It develops through experiences of the mother's departure and return and through frustration, which emphasizes the child's separateness and the fact that it doesn't control all its own experiences and gratifications. Some of these experiences and gratifications come from within, some from without. If it were not for these frustrations, these disruptions of primary oneness, total holding and gratification, the child would not need to begin to perceive the other, the "outer world," as separate and not an extension of itself. Developing separateness thus involves, in particular, perceiving the mother or primary caretaker as separate and "not-me," where once we were an undifferentiated symbiotic unity.

Separateness, then, is not simply given from birth, nor does it emerge from the individual alone. Differentiation occurs in relationship, separateness is defined relationally: "I" am "not-you." Moreover, "you," or the other, is differentiated. Differentiation involves perceiving the *particularity* of the mother or primary caretaker in contrast to the rest of the world. As the self is differentiated from the object world, the object world is itself differentiated.

From a psychoanalytic perspective, learning to distinguish me and not-me is necessary for a person to grow into a functioning human being. It is also inevitable, since experiences of departure, of discontinuity in handling, feeding, where one sleeps, how one is picked up and by whom, of lack of total relational and physical gratification, are unavoidable. But for our understanding of "difference" in this connection, the concept of differentiation and the processes that characterize it need elaboration.

First, in most psychoanalytic formulations, and in the prevalent understandings of development, the mother, or the outside world, is simply the other, not-me, one who does or does not fulfill an expectation. This perception arises originally from the infant's cognitive inability to differentiate self and world; the infant does not distinguish between its desires for love and satisfaction and those of its primary love object and object of identification. The self here is the infant or growing child, and psychoanalytic accounts take the viewpoint of this child.

However, adequate separation, or differentiation, involves not simply perceiving the separateness, or otherness, of the other. It involves perceiving their subjectivity and selfhood as well. Differentiation, separation, disruption of the narcissistic relation to reality, are developed through learning that the mother is a separate being with separate interests, interests and activities that do not always coincide with just what the infant wants at the time. They involve the ability to experience and perceive the object/other (the mother) in aspects apart from its sole relation to the ability to gratify the infant's/subject's needs and wants; they involve seeing the object as separate from the self *and* from the self's needs.[4] The infant must change here from a "relationship to a subjectively conceived object to a relationship to an object objectively perceived."[5]

In infantile development, this change requires cognitive sophistication and the growing ability to integrate various images and experiences of the mother that come with the development of ego capacities. But these capacities are not enough. The ability to perceive the other as a self, finally, requires an emotional shift and a form of emotional growth. The adult self not only experiences the other as distinct and separate; it also does not experience the other solely in terms of its own needs for gratification and its own desires.

This interpretation implies that true differentiation, true separateness, cannot be simply a perception and experience of self-other, of presence-absence. It must involve two selves, two presences, two subjects. Recognizing the other as a subject is possible only to the extent that one is not dominated by felt need and one's own exclusive subjectivity. Such recognition enables appreciation and perception of many aspects of the other person. Whether we understand differentiation only from the viewpoint of the infant as a self or from the viewpoint of two interacting selves thus has consequences for what we think of as a mature self. If the mature self grows only out of the infant as a self, the other need never be accorded their own selfhood.

The fact that separation-individuation, or differentiation, involves not simply perceiving the otherness of the other, but their selfhood/subjectivity as well, is consequential not only for the development of one's own selfhood, but also for perceptions of women. Hence, it seems to me essential to a feminist appropriation of psychoanalytic conceptions of differentiation. Since women, as mothers, are the primary caretakers of infants, if the child (or the psychoanalytic account) only takes the viewpoint of the infant as a (developing) self, then you get the *mother* only as an object. But from a feminist perspective, perceiving the particularity of the mother must involve according the mother her own selfhood. This is a necessary part of the development process, though it is also often resisted and experienced only conflictually and partially. Throughout life, perceptions of the mother move between perceiving her particularity and selfhood, and perceiving her as a narcissistic extension, a not-separate other whose sole reason for existence is to gratify wants and needs.

Few accounts recognize the import of this particular stance toward the mother. Alice Balint's proto-feminist account is the best I know of the infantile origins of adult perceptions of mother as object:

> Most men (and women)—even when otherwise quite normal and capable of an "adult," altruistic form of love which acknowledges the interests of the partner—retain towards their mothers this naive egoistic attitude throughout their lives. For all of us it remains self-evident that the interests of mother and child are identical, and it is the generally acknowledged measure of the goodness or badness of the mother how far she really feels this identity of interests.[6]

These perceptions, as a product of infantile development, will persist as long as (only) women mother, and they are one major reason why equal parenting is a necessary component of sexual equality. But I think that women, even within the ongoing context of women's mothering, can and must liberate ourselves from such perceptions in our personal emotional lives as much as possible, and certainly in our theorizing and politics.[7]

A second elaboration of psychoanalytic accounts of differentiation concerns the affective or emotional distinction between differentiation or separation-individuation and *difference*. Difference and differentiation are, of course, related to and feed into one another; it is in some sense true that cognitive or linguistic distinction, or division, must imply difference. However, it is possible to be separate, to be differentiated, without caring about or emphasizing difference, without turning the cognitive fact into an emotional, moral, or political one. In fact, assimilating difference to differentiation is defensive and reactive, a reaction to not feeling separate enough. Such assimilation involves arbitrary boundary creation and an assertion of hyperseparateness to reinforce a lack of security in a person's sense of their self as a separate person. But you can be separate from and similar to someone at the same time. For example, you can recognize their subjectivity and humanity as you recognize your own, your *commonality* as active subjects. Or, a woman can recognize her similarity, commonality, even continuity, with her mother, because she has developed enough of an unproblematic sense of separate self. The other side of being able to experience separateness and commonality, however, of recognizing the other's subjectivity, is the ability to recognize difference with a small *d,* differences that are produced and situated historically—for instance, the kinds of meaningful differences among women that I mentioned earlier.

The distinction between differentiation/separateness and difference relates to a third consideration, even more significant for difference and gender difference. Much psychoanalytic theory has centered its account of early infant development on separation-individuation, on the creation of the separate self, on the "me"–"not-me" distinction. There are other ways of looking at the development of self, other important and fundamental aspects to the self. Separation, the "me"–"not-me" division, looms larger, both in our psychological life and theoretically, to the extent that these other aspects of the self are not developed (or theoretically stressed).

Object-relations theory shows that the development of self is not primarily the development of ego boundaries and a body ego.[8] Concomitant with the earliest development of its sense of separate self, the infant constructs an internal set of unconscious, affectively loaded representations of others in relation to its self, and an internal sense of self in relationship emerges. Images of felt good and bad aspects of the mother or primary caretaker, caretaking experiences, and the mothering relationship become part of the self, of a relational ego structure, through unconscious mental processes that appropriate and incorporate these images. With maturation, these early images and fragments of perceived experience become put together into a self. As externality and internality are established, therefore, what comes to be internal includes what originally were aspects of the other and the relation to the other. (Similarly, what is experienced as external may include what was originally part of the developing self's experience.) Externality and internality, then, do not follow easily observable physiological boundaries but are constituted by psychological and emotional processes as well.

These unconscious early internalizations (that affect and constitute the internal quality of selfhood) may remain more or less fragmented, or they may develop a quality of wholeness. A sense of continuity of experience and opportunity to integrate a complex of (at least somewhat) complementary and consistent images enables the emergence of the "I" as a continuous being with an identity. This more internal sense of self, or of "I," is not dependent on separateness or difference from an other. A "true self," or "central self," emerges through the experience of continuity, which the mother or caretaker helps to provide, through not having continually to react to and ward off environmental intrusions and not being continually in need.

The integration of a "true self" that feels alive and whole involves a particular set of internalized feelings about others in relation to the self. These include developing a sense that one is able to affect others and one's environment (a sense that one has not been inhibited by overanticipation of all one's needs), a sense that one has been accorded one's own feelings and a spontaneity about these feelings (a sense that one's feelings or needs have not been projected onto one), and a sense that there is a fit between one's feelings and needs and the mother or caretaker. These feelings all give the self a sense of agency and authenticity.

This sense of agency, then, results from caretakers who do not project experiences or feelings onto the child and who do not let the environment impinge indiscriminately. It results from empathic caretakers who understand and validate the infant's experience as that of a real self. Thus, the sense of agency, which is one basis of the inner sense of continuity and wholeness, grows out of the nature of the parent-infant relationship.

Another important aspect of internalized feelings about others in relation to the self concerns a capacity (or sense of wholeness) that develops through an internal sense of relationship with another.[9] The presence of the primary parent becomes an internal sense of the presence of another who is caring and affirming. The self comes into being here through first feeling confidently alone in the presence of its mother, then through this presence becoming internal. Part of its self becomes a good internal mother. This suggests that the central core of self is, internally, a relational ego, a sense of self-in-good-relationship. The presence or absence of others, their sameness or difference, then becomes something that is not a question of the infant's existing or not. A "capacity to be alone," a relational rather than reactive autonomy, develops because of a sense of the ongoing presence of another.

The senses of agency, of a true self that does not develop reactively, of a relational self or ego core, and of an internal continuity of being, are fundamental to an unproblematic sense of self, and provide the basis of both autonomy and spontaneity. The strength, or wholeness, of the self, in this view, does not depend only or even centrally on its degree of separateness (although the extent of confident distinctness certainly affects and is part of the sense of self). The more secure the central self, or ego core, the less one has to define one's self through separateness from others. Separateness becomes, then, a more rigid, defensive, rather fragile, secondary criterion of the strength of the self and of the "success" of individuation.

This view suggests that no one has a separateness consisting in me–not-me distinctions. Part of myself is always that which I have taken in; we are all to some degree incorporations and extensions of others. Separateness from the mother, defining oneself apart from her (and from other women), is not the only or final goal for women's ego strength and autonomy. In the process of differentiation, leading to a genuine autonomy, people maintain contact with those with whom they had their earliest relationships, where this contact is part of who we are. "I am" is not definition through negation, is not "who I am not." Developing a sense of confident separateness must be a part of all children's development. But once this confident separateness is established, one's relational self can become more central to one's life. Differentiation is not distinctness and separateness, but a particular way of being connected to others. This connection to others, based on early incorporations, in turn enables that empathy and confidence that is basic to the recognition of the other as a self.

What does all this have to do with male-female difference, with gender difference? What we learn from the more general inquiry is that we can only think of differentiation and the emergence of the self relationally. Differentiation occurs, and separation emerges, in relationship; they are not givens. Second, to single out separation as the core of a notion of self and of the process of differentiation may well be inadequate, and it is certainly not the only way to discuss the emergence of self or what constitutes a strong self. Differentiation includes internalization of aspects of the primary caretaker and caretaking relationship.

Finally, we learn that essential attitudes toward mothers and expectations that enter into experiences of women more generally—emerge in the earliest differentiation of self. These attitudes and expectations arise during the emergence of separateness: given that differentiation and separation are developmentally problematic, and given that women are primary caretakers, the mother, who is a woman, becomes and remains for children of both genders the other, or object. She is not accorded autonomy or selfness. Such attitudes arise also from the gender-specific character of the early, emotionally charged, self and object images that affect the development of self and the sense of autonomy and spontaneity. They are internalizations of feelings about the self in relation to the *mother,* who is then often experienced as either overwhelming or overdenying. These attitudes, often unconscious, always with a basis in unconscious, emotionally charged feelings and conflicts, a precipitate of the early relationship to the mother and of an unconscious sense of self, may be more fundamental and determining of psychic life than more conscious and explicit attitudes to "sex differences" or "gender differences" themselves.

This inquiry suggests a psychoanalytic grounding for goals of emotional and psychic life other than separateness and autonomy, for notions that stress our connectedness rather than our separation one from another. Feelings of adequate separateness, fear of merger, are indeed issues for women, because of the ongoing sense of oneness and primary identification with our mothers (and children). A transformed organization of parenting would help women to resolve these issues. However, autonomy, spontaneity, and a sense of agency need not be based on self-other distinctions, on the individual as individual, but can be based on the fundamental interconnectedness, not synonymous with merger, that grows out of our earliest unconscious developmental experience and that enables a nonreactive separateness.[10]

Gender Differences in the Creation of Difference

We are not born with perceptions of gender difference; these emerge developmentally. In the traditional psychoanalytic view, however, when sexual difference is first seen, it has self-evident value: a girl perceives her lack of a penis, knows instantly that she wants one, and subsequently defines herself and her mother as lacking, inadequate, castrated; a boy instantly knows having a penis is better, and fears the loss of his own.[11] This traditional account violates a fundamental rule of psychoanalytic interpretation. When the analyst finds trauma, shock, strong fears, or conflict, it is a sign to look for the roots of such feelings.[12] Freud, because of his inability to focus on the preoedipal years and the relationship of mother to child, could not follow his own rule here.

Clinical and theoretical writings since Freud suggest another interpretation of the emergence of perceptions of gender difference, one that reverses the perception of who experiences the greater trauma and retains only the claim that gender identity and the sense of masculinity and femininity develop differently for men and women.[13] These accounts suggest that for men core gender identity and masculinity are issues in a way that core gender identity and femininity are not for women. Core gender identity here is a cognitive sense of gendered self, that one is male or female. It is established in the first two years, concomitantly with the establishment of the sense of self. Later evaluations of the desirability of one's gender and of the activities and modes of behaving associated with it, or of one's own sense of adequacy at fulfilling gender-role expectation, are built upon this fundamental gender identity. They do not create or change it.

Most people develop an unambiguous core gender identity, a sense that they are female or male. But because women mother, the sense of maleness in men differs from the sense of femaleness in women. Maleness is more conflictual and more problematic. Underlying, or built into, core male gender identity is an early, nonverbal, unconscious, almost somatic sense of primary oneness with the mother, an underlying sense of femaleness that continually, usually unnoticeably, but sometimes insistently, challenges and undermines the sense of maleness.

Thus, because of a primary oneness and identification with his mother, a primary femaleness, a boy's and a man's core gender identity itself—the seemingly unproblematic cognitive sense of being male—is an issue. A boy must learn his gender identity as being not-female, or not-mother. Subsequently, again because of the primacy of the mother in early life and because of the absence of concrete, real, available male figures of identification and love who are as salient for him as female figures, learning what it is to be masculine is also defined as not-feminine, or not-womanly. Because of early-developed, conflictual core gender identity problems and later problems of adequate masculinity, it becomes important to men to have a clear sense of gender difference, of what is masculine and what is feminine, and to maintain rigid boundaries between these. (Researchers find, for example, that fathers sex-type children more than mothers. They treat sons and daughters more differently and enforce gender role expectations more vigorously.)[14] Boys and men come to deny the feminine identification within themselves and those feelings they experience as feminine: feelings of dependence, relational needs, emotions generally. They come to emphasize differences, not commonalities or continuities, between themselves and women, especially in situations that evoke anxiety because they threaten to challenge gender difference or to remind boys and men of their potentially feminine attributes.

Conflicts concerning core gender identity interact with and build upon particular ways that boys experience processes of differentiation and the formation of the self.[15] Both sexes establish separateness in relation to their mother, and internalizations in the development of self are internalizations of aspects of the mother as well. But because the mother is a woman, these experiences differ. Even as children of both sexes are originally part of herself, a mother unconsciously and often consciously experiences her son as more of an other than her daughter and, reciprocally, a son's male core gender identity develops away from his mother. The male's self, as a result, becomes based on a more fixed "me"–"not-me" distinction; separateness and difference as a component of differentiation becomes more salient. The female's self, by contrast, is less separate, involving a less fixed "me"–"not-me" distinction, creating the problems of sense of separateness and autonomy that I mention above.

At the same time, core gender identity for a girl is not problematic in the sense that it is for boys. It is built upon, and does not contradict, her primary sense of oneness and identification with her mother and is assumed easily along with her developing sense of self. Girls grow up with a sense of continuity and similarity to their mother, a relational connection to the world. For them, difference is not originally problematic nor fundamental to their psychological being or identity. They do not define themselves as not-men, or not-male, but as "I, who is female." Girls and women may have problems with their sense of continuity and similarity, if this sense is too strong and they have no sense of a separate self. However, these problems are not inevitable products of having a sense of continuity and similarity, since selfhood does not depend only on the strength and impermeability of ego boundaries. Nor are these problems bound up with questions of gender; rather, they are bound up with questions of self.

What may be problematic in the development of gender identification for girls concerns not the existence of core gender identity (the unquestioned knowledge that one is female) but later-developed conflicts around such an identity, and the identifications, learning, and cognitive choices that this implies. Girls' difficulties in establishing a feminine identity have to do not with the inaccessibility and negative definition of this identity or its assumption by denial, but with the problems that may arise from identification with a negatively valued gender category and with an ambivalent maternal figure, whose mothering and femininity are accessible but devalued, and often conflictual for the mother herself. Conflicts here are conflicts of power and cultural and social value, even as identification and the assumption of core gender identity are straightforward. Such conflicts, I would suggest, arise later in development and are less pervasively determining of psychological life for women than are masculine conflicts around core gender identity and gender difference.

Men's and women's understanding of difference, and gender difference, must thus be understood in the relational context in which these are created, in their respective relation to their mother, who is their primary caretaker, love object, and object of identification, and who is a woman in a gender-organized world. This relational context means that difference, and gender difference, are central for males—one of the earliest, most basic male developmental issues—and not central for females. It gives men a psychological investment in difference that women do not have.

In earliest development, according to psychoanalytic accounts since Freud, it is very clear that males are "not-females"; core gender identity and the sense of masculinity are defined more negatively, in terms of that which is not female, or not-mother, than they are in positive terms. By contrast, it is not the case that females develop as "not-males"; female core gender identity and the sense of femininity are defined positively, as that which is female, or like mother. Difference from males is not so salient. An alternative way to put this is to suggest that developmentally, the maternal identification represents and is experienced as generically human for children of both genders.[16]

Because men have power and cultural hegemony in our society, however, a notable thing happens. Men use and have used this hegemony to appropriate and transform these experiences: both in everyday life and in theoretical and intellectual formulations, men have come to define maleness as that which is basically human, and to define women as not-men. This transformation is first learned in, and helps to constitute, the oedipal transition—the cultural, affective, and sexual learnings of the meaning and valuation of sex differences.[17] Because Freud was not attentive to

yerb

preoedipal development (and because of his sexism), he took this meaning and valuation as a self-evident given rather than a developmental and cultural product.

This transformed interpretation of difference, an interpretation learned in the oedipal transition, is produced by means of masculine cultural hegemony and power. Men are able to institutionalize their unconscious defenses against developmental conflicts that are repressed from consciousness but strongly experienced. This interpretation of difference is imposed on earlier developmental processes, and is not the deepest, unconscious root of either the female or the male sense of gendered self. In fact, the primary sense of gendered self that emerges in earliest development constantly challenges and threatens men and gives a certain potential psychological security, even liberation, to women. The transformed interpretation of difference is not inevitable, given other parenting arrangements and other arrangements of power between the sexes. (It is especially insofar as women's lives and self-conception are male-defined that difference becomes more salient for us, as does differential evaluation of the sexes. Insofar as women's lives and self-conception become less male-defined, differences from men become less salient.) [18]

Evaluating Difference

What are the implications of this inquiry into psychoanalytic understandings of differentiation and gender difference for our understanding of difference and for our evaluation of the view that difference is central to feminist theory?

My inquiry suggests that our own sense of differentiation, of separateness from others, as well as our psychological and cultural experience and interpretation of gender or sexual difference, are created through psychological, social, and cultural processes, and through relational experiences. We can only understand gender difference, and human distinctness and separation, relationally and situationally,[19] as part of a system of asymmetrical social relationships embedded in inequalities of power, in which we grow up as selves, and as women and men. Our experience and perception of gender are processual; they are produced developmentally and in our daily social and cultural lives.

Difference is psychologically salient for men in a way that it is not for women, because of gender differences in early formative developmental processes and the particular unconscious conflicts and defenses these produce. This salience in turn has been transferred into a conscious cultural preoccupation with gender difference. It has also become intertwined with and helped to produce more general cultural notions that individualism, separateness, and distance from others are desirable and requisite to autonomy and human fulfillment.[20] Throughout these processes, it is women, as mothers, who become the objects apart from which separateness, difference, and autonomy are defined.

Ideologies of difference, ideologies that define us as women and as men—and inequality itself—are produced, socially, psychologically, and culturally, by people living in and creating their social, psychological, and cultural worlds. Women participate in the creation of these worlds and ideologies, even if our ultimate power and cultural hegemony are less than those of men. To speak of difference as a final, irreducible concept and to focus on gender differences as central, is to reify and deny those *processes* that create the meaning and significance of gender. To see men and women as qualitatively different kinds of people, rather than seeing gender as processual, reflexive, and constructed, is to reify and deny *relations* of gender, to see gender differences as permanent rather than created and situated.

We certainly need to understand how difference comes to be important, how it is produced, and how it reproduces sexual inequality. But we should not appropriate differentiation and separateness, or difference, for ourselves and take it as given. Feminist theories and feminist inquiry based on the notion of essential difference, or focused on demonstrating difference, ultimately rely on the defensively constructed masculine models of gender that are presented to us as our cultural heritage, rather than creating new understandings of gender and difference that grow from our own politics, theorizing, and experience.

NOTES

1. Quoted in Adrienne Rich, *On Lies, Secrets, and Silence* (New York: W. W. Norton, 1979), p. 84.

2. See, for example, "Women's Exile: Interview with Luce Irigaray," *Ideology and Consciousness* 1 (1977), pp. 57–76; and Monique Plaza, " 'Phallomorphic Power' and the Psychology of 'Woman,' " *Ideology and Consciousness* 4 (1978), pp. 4–36.

3. The work of Margaret S. Mahler, *On Human Symbiosis and the Vicissitudes of Individuation* (New York: International Universities Press, 1968), is paradigmatic here. For a more extended discussion of the earliest development of the self along lines suggested here, see Nancy Chodorow, *The Reproduction of Mothering: Psychoanalysis and the Sociology of Gender* (Berkeley: University of California Press, 1978), chs. 4 and 5.

4. Ernest G. Schachtel, "The Development of Focal Attention and the Emergence of Reality" (1954), in *Metamorphosis* (New York: Basic Books, 1959), provides the best discussion I know of this process.

5. D. W. Winnicott, "The Theory of the Parent-Infant Relationship" (1960), in *The Maturational Processes and the Facilitating Environment* (New York: International Universities Press, 1965).

6. Alice Balint, "Love for the Mother and Mother Love" (1939), in Michael Balint, *Primary Love and Psycho-Analytic Technique* (New York: Liveright, 1965), p. 97.

7. The new feminist/feminine blame-the-mother literature is one contemporary manifestation of failure in such a task. See especially Nancy Friday, *My Mother, My Self* (New York: Dell, 1977). Of course, this is not to ignore or pass over the fact that men have been past masters of such perceptions of women.

8. I am drawing in what follows particularly on the work of D. W. Winnicott and Michael Balint. See Winnicott, *The Maturational Processes*, and *Playing and Reality* (New York: Basic Books, 1971); and Balint, *Primary Love*, and *The Basic Fault: Therapeutic Aspects of Regression* (London: Tavistock, 1968). See also W. R. D. Fairbairn, *An Object Relations Theory of the Personality* (New York: Basic Books, 1952), and Hans Loewald, "Internalization, Separation, Mourning, and the Superego," *Psychoanalytic Quarterly* 31 (1962), pp. 483–504.

9. See Winnicott, "The Capacity to Be Alone" (1958), in *The Maturational Processes*.

10. My interpretation here of differentiation, the self, and the goals of psychic life contrasts with the traditional Freudian view which stresses ego and superego autonomy. For an excellent discussion of questions of ego autonomy and psychic structure, see Jessica Benjamin, "The Ends of Internalization: Adorno's Social Psychology," *Telos 32* (1977), pp. 42–64.

11. See Freud, "The Dissolution of the Oedipus Complex" (1924), *Standard Edition of the Complete Psychological Works* (SE), vol. 19, pp. 172–197; "Some Psychical Consequences of the Anatomical Distinction between the Sexes" (1925), SE, vol. 19, pp. 243–258; and "Femininity" (1933), in *New Introductory Lectures on Psychoanalysis,* SE, vol. 22, pp. 112–135.

12. See Roy Schafer, "Problems in Freud's Psychology of Women," *Journal of the American Psychoanalytic Association,* vol. 22, no. 3 (1974), pp. 459–485.

13. See Robert Stoller, "Facts and Fancies: An Examination of Freud's Concept of Bisexuality," in Jean Strouse, ed., *Women and Analysis* (New York: Grossman Publishers, 1974), and other Stoller writings.

14. For reviews of the social psychological literature on this, see Miriam Johnson, "Sex Role Learning in the Nuclear Family," *Child Development 34* (1963), pp. 319–334, and "Fathers, Mothers, and Sex-Typing," *Sociological Inquiry,* vol. 45, no. 1 (1975), pp. 15–26; and Eleanor Maccoby and Carol Jacklin, *The Psychology of Sex Differences* (Stanford, Calif.: Stanford University Press, 1974).

15. For further discussion see Chodorow, *Reproduction,* ch. 5.

16. Johnson, "Fathers, Mothers," makes this suggestion, and suggests further that the father's masculinity introduces gender difference.

17. See Juliet Mitchell, *Psychoanalysis and Feminism* (New York: Pantheon Books, 1974).

18. The male and female body clearly have relevance for the question of gender difference. We live an embodied life: we live with those genital and reproductive organs and capacities, those hormones and chromosomes, that locate us physiologically as male or female. But, to turn to psychoanalysis once again, Freud's earliest discovery showed that there is nothing self-evident about this biology. How anyone understands, fantasizes about, symbolizes, internally represents, or feels about their physiology is a product of developmental experience in their family and not a direct product of this biology itself. These feelings, moreover, may be shaped by considerations completely apart from that biology. Considerations apart from biology also shape perceptions of anatomical "sex differences" and the psychological development of these sex differences into forms of sexual object choice, mode or aim, into femininity or masculinity as psychoanalysis defines these, into activity or passivity, into one's choice of organ of erotic pleasure, and so forth.

We cannot know what children would make of their bodies in a nongender or nonsexually organized social world, what kind of sexual structuration or gender identities would develop. But it is not obvious that there would be major significance to biological sex differences, to gender difference, or to different sexualities. There might be a multiplicity of sexual organizations, identities, practices, perhaps even of genders themselves. Particular bodily attributes would not necessarily be so determining of who we are, what we do, how we are perceived, who are our sexual partners.

19. See Barrie Thorne, "Gender . . . How Is It Best Conceptualized?" paper presented to the Meetings of the American Sociological Association, San Francisco, August 1978.

20. For a discussion of these general cultural preoccupations and their psychological origins, see Evelyn Fox Keller, "Gender and Science," *Psychoanalysis and Contemporary Thought,* vol. 1, no. 3 (1978), pp. 409–433.

Chapter Twenty-One

Female Relationality and the Idealized Self

Marcia Westkott

For nearly two decades writers on the psychology of women have questioned what they have taken to be the male bias in traditional definitions of psychological health and development. In 1970 Broverman and colleagues charted the terms of what was to become the new feminist critique: their findings showed that clinicians implicitly associated psychological maturity and health with stereotypical male characteristics, but identified normal female traits as the same as those they associated with psychological immaturity or dysfunctioning. The feminist agenda has since been to deconstruct this culturally rooted, professionally accepted equation. The following essay describes the new paradigm that has emerged from this feminist project, analyzes its elaboration in the work of the Stone Center at Wellesley College, and critiques the paradigm from the perspective of Karen Horney.

In 1976 Jean Baker Miller initiated the feminist reevaluation with her thesis that "women have developed the foundations of extremely valuable psychological qualities" (p. 26), but that gender inequality causes these qualities or strengths to go unrecognized or devalued. Among the strengths that Miller identified was "women's great desire for affiliation" (pp. 88–89). Although this female predilection has been a source of women's problems, it can also be, she argued, the basis for important social values. Indeed, Miller concluded her influential book with the hope that it is precisely the affiliative qualities that women have developed—traits that are "dysfunctional for success in the world as it is"—that may be those which are most needed for transforming the world into a more humane place (p. 124).

In 1978 Nancy Chodorow extended Miller's work by proposing that a female affiliative or relational self emerges from a structure of parenting in which mothers treat their sons and daughters differently. Daughters, who are treated as projections of the mother, never fully separate from her and thus come to define themselves as connected to or continuous with others. Boys, who are treated as more separate by their mothers, come to identify themselves as differentiated from others and possess more rigid ego boundaries than their sisters. Thus, "the basic feminine sense of self is connected to the world, the basic masculine sense of self is separate" (Chodorow, 1978, p. 169).

Marcia Westkott, "Female Relationality and the Idealized Self." *The American Journal of Psychoanalysis, 49,* pp. 239–250. © 1989 by Plenum Publishing Corporation. Reprinted with permission.

Like Miller, Chodorow was critical of the social systems that reflect the male psyche, in particular the alienated work world of capitalist societies (Chodorow, 1978, pp. 218–219). But unlike Miller, Chodorow's solution emphasized gender balance rather than a release of women's strengths upon a resisting world. In calling for men to participate equally in parenting, she advocated a realignment that would have "people of both genders with the positive capacities each has, but without the destructive extremes these currently tend toward" (p. 218). Chodorow's androgynous golden mean of individuated but affiliated mothers and fathers nurturing the next generation of balanced children was nevertheless dependent primarily upon a change in *male* behavior. Assuming the public sphere changes for women initiated by the women's movement, Chodorow suggested that it is up to men to complete the rectification of the gender imbalance by engaging in the affiliative, nurturing activities of the private, domestic sphere (p. 218). Thus, like Miller's, Chodorow's solution was one that called for a universal valuing of those relational qualities traditionally identified with women.

Building on both Miller and Chodorow, Carol Gilligan (1982) expanded the theme to the redefinition of moral development. She grounded her work in a critique of Kohlberg's scale of six stages of moral judgment (Kohlberg, 1973), a measurement constructed from interviews with only males, but presumed to be universally applicable. Gilligan noted that females generally made it only to Kohlberg's third level, in which morality is perceived as interpersonal and goodness defined as helping others. She argued that girls and women fall short of the higher levels, where the application of rules and universal principles of justice prevail over concern for specific relationships, not because females are morally deficient but because the scale itself is male-biased and irrelevant to women's own hierarchy of values (Gilligan, 1982, pp. 18–19). Gilligan proposed that women and girls engage in moral judgments according to a different set of imperatives—a "different voice"—from that which men and boys follow: "The moral imperative that emerges repeatedly in interviews with women is an injunction to care, a responsibility to discern and alleviate the 'real and recognizable trouble' of this world. For men, the moral imperative appears rather as an injunction to respect the rights of others and thus to protect from interference the rights to life and self-fulfillment" (p. 100).

Paralleling Chodorow, Gilligan (1982) advocated an integration of both male and female moral perspectives to create an androgynous whole that combines a morality of responsibility to others with a morality of rights and principles (p. 100). Like Miller, Gilligan viewed the devaluation of women's concern for relationships and care for others and the elevation of the male emphasis on individual achievement and autonomy to be "more a commentary on the society than a problem in women's development" (p. 171). Like both Miller and Chodorow, Gilligan proposed to correct the male bias in both psychological models and behavioral norms by valuing the traditional female traits of affiliating with and caring for others.

These works by Miller, Chodorow, and Gilligan have wielded considerable influence on the scholarship about women during the last decade. For example, they have inspired a spate of new studies, including books on women's cognitive development (Belenky et al., 1986), on educational philosophy (Noddings, 1984), and on theories of war (Elshtain, 1987). And the last three volumes of the *Psychology of Women Quarterly* (1986–1988) have included nineteen articles with forty-six references to at least one of the works by Miller, Chodorow, or Gilligan. This subsequent work has filled in the new paradigm of women's psychology that challenges universal models of psychological functioning and development, exposes its male bias, and makes the argument that female characteristics have not only been neglected or devalued, but that they are positive human traits necessary for all people to cultivate.

The quality that has been singled out as most significant is the female relational disposition, variously defined in terms of women's need to affiliate with others, to take care of others, to nurture or mother them, to empathize, to be connected, to relate. This is often contrasted with an opposing psychological makeup that is associated with traditional models of (male) development: the differentiated, individuated self whose maturational goals are autonomy and personal success (for example, Levinson, 1978). The problem of gender inequality is seen to be part of a larger problem in which some privileged groups (notably white, Western males) pursue their own individualistic goals at the expense of other groups (in particular, Third World, people of color, women and children). The solution is a democratization which promotes equal opportunity, equality, and justice; goals which given the conditions of domination require a cultivation of the very devalued traits assigned to women: care, cooperation, empathy, and sense of responsibility for others. The argument is that social and political conditions require that these traditional female traits be universalized as a new ethic of care and cooperation. Men need to learn them, and women need to stop doubting themselves and instead build on their relational strengths to transform the world into their own image (for example, Eisler, 1987).

The most systematic attempt to elaborate the new paradigm is occurring at the Stone Center for Developmental Services and Studies at Wellesley College, which was originally under the directorship of Jean Baker Miller. A group of clinicians and researchers there has assumed the positive value of women's relationality and, through a series of working papers, has explored its implications for both clinical practice (Kaplan, 1984) and an understanding of women's psychology as it relates to such issues as power (J. B. Miller, 1982), work (Stiver, 1983), eating patterns (Surrey, 1984), and violence (Swift, 1987). Mostly, however, the work of the group is united by exploring and developing "the self-in-relation theory" (see especially Surrey, 1985) of female and, by implication, human development.[1]

The Stone Center theory is grounded in an ethical vision in which the self is posited as containing two equally demanding but compatible needs, the need for recognition by *and* the need to understand the other (Surrey, 1983, p. 8). These needs are socially constructed desires, which are created out of the physical and social contexts of mother-child interaction. The realization of the compatible needs is a mutually empathetic relationship. According to Jordan (1983), empathy does not entail a permanent blurring or loss of the self in the other but is based upon a separate sense of oneself that is temporarily relaxed to allow for attunement to the other's meaning systems and feelings (Jordan, 1986, p. 2). Empathy occurs within the framework of intersubjectivity, the disposition to hold "the other's subjectivity as central to the interaction with that individual" (p. 2). In a relationship characterized by mutuality, self and other both express empathy and intersubjectivity, giving and taking in a way that affirms not only self and other individually but also "the larger relational unit" that transcends them (p. 2).

Indeed, maintaining the larger relational unit itself becomes the ultimate end, because it is the condition *sine qua non* that meets the needs of the self. For this reason the emphasis in the theoretical writings of the Stone Center is upon sustaining connection with the other. The self-in-relation abhors and dreads isolation, disconnection, and loss of the other, for this absence produces a fundamental loss of the self. Therefore, because maintaining the relationship is all-important, the two fundamental needs are not equally weighted: recognizing the other as a means of sustaining the relationship is implicitly given greater value than the desire for recognition. If connection is necessary for self-definition, then creating the conditions that keep the other connected becomes the primary personal agenda.

Although Stone Center psychologists routinely mention the importance of the need for "self-empathy" (Jordan, 1984, p. 9), self-growth (J. B. Miller, 1984, pp. 13–14), or personal empowerment (J. B. Miller, 1982, p. 5), they reject the idea of personal desire being met in the absence of relationship. They regard such an individualist concept of motive to be dangerous. According to Jordan (1987), "any system that emphasizes the ascendancy of individual desire as the legitimate basis for definition of self and interpersonal relationship is fraught with the possibility of creating violent relationships based on competition of need and the necessity for establishing hierarchies of dominance, entitlement, and power" (p. 9). The idea of the dangerous individual desire is replaced with a basic relational desire that is by definition informed by "empathy, noncomparativeness, and mutuality ... involving empathetic responsiveness and a sense of compassion in a context of caring for the well-being of others" (Jordan, 1987, p. 9).

How is this deep motive for connection and compassion created? Following most developmental theories, the Stone Center psychologists attribute personality to the early patterns of parent-child, especially mother-child, interaction. According to Jean Baker Miller (1984), the infant, through the interaction with the caretaker, "begins to develop an internal representation of her/himself as a 'being-in-relationship.' This is the beginning of a sense of 'self' which reflects what is happening *between* people ... pick[ing] up the feelings of the other person.... The child experiences a sense of comfort only as the other is also comfortable" (p. 3). The emergent sense of self is one whose core is "attended to by the other(s); and who begins to attend to the emotions of the other(s) ... a self inseparable from dynamic interaction" (p. 4). Human growth is a process of engaging in "progressively complex relationships" (Kaplan and Klein, 1985, p. 3) rather than in separating from caretakers by pursuing goals of autonomy and power. Maturity is defined in terms of "relational competence" (Surrey, 1987, p. 8), "empathy" (Jordan, 1984, p. 3), "clarity in connection" (Jordan, 1987, p. 7), and the ability to create and sustain mutual intersubjectivity (Jordan, 1986, p. 2). This, then, is their maturational ideal: the true relational self, who reflects the earliest human interpersonal experience, realizing its "motive for connection" in mutually empathetic relationships. Relationship is, thus, both the context in which the self develops and the goal for which it strives.

Despite their emphasis on the essential importance of mutuality as the social realization of the self-in-relation, the Stone Center psychologists contend that this goal is rarely attained in adult male-female relationships. The obstacle, argues Miller, is the traditional gender system, which promotes the unrealistic goal of autonomy and "power-over" for men and devalues the truly human activity of relational connectedness and caring as female responsibility (J. B. Miller, 1982, p. 2). The cultural expectation that women, but not men, must care for others closes men off from their humanity, places a lopsided burden upon women, and makes male-female mutuality impossible (J. B. Miller, 1983, pp. 3–5). Men take for granted that women will be caring and empathetic, but they implicitly and explicitly devalue women and refuse to reciprocate. Women, on the other hand, are drawn to relating to the other and caring for him but are neither validated in this role nor given empathetic support and nurturing in response (Stiver, 1984, p. 8).

Like Chodorow, the Stone Center psychologists explain the psychological reproduction of these culturally based gender types as the consequence of the mother's response to sexual differences in her children. Mothers encourage relational dispositions in their daughters and discourage them in their sons. However, unlike Chodorow, who advocates an androgynous balance of these traditional patterns of child rearing, the Stone Center psychologists contend that the mother-daughter pattern of interaction comes closest to promoting the growth of the healthy (i.e., relational) self and should, therefore, be considered the model for all parenting (Surrey, 1985, p. 43; 1987, p. 6).

The developmental theory of the self-in-relation is grounded in the assumption that all infants have an attentiveness to the feeling state of the mother or caretaker. According to Surrey (1985), this disposition is encouraged in daughters but not in sons, because of the mother's "ease with and interest in emotional sharing" with her daughter (p. 4; see also Surrey, 1983, p. 6; J. B. Miller, 1984, p. 4), which does not exist with the son. Consequently, the daughter's mother-attentiveness is reinforced, promoting in her "the basic sense of 'learning to listen,' to orient and attune to the other person through feelings" (Surrey, 1985, p. 4). The mother's continued response of listening, empathizing, and reinforcing the daughter's responses to her creates what Surrey calls the "open relationship" between mother and daughter. This interactive context helps to form the daughter's "increasing ability for mutual empathy" through which the mother and daughter "become highly responsive to the feeling states of the other." Surrey describes the development of this mutuality more fully:

> Through the girl's awareness and identification with her mother as the "mothering one" and through the mother's interest in being understood and cared for, the daughter as well as the mother become mobilized to care for, respond to or attend to the well-being and the development of the other. Moreover, they care for and take care of the relationship between them. This is the motivational dynamic of mutual empowerment, the inherent energizing force of real relationship. It becomes important for the girl to experience validation of her own developing empathetic competence. Thus, mothers empower their daughters by allowing them to feel successful at understanding and

giving support at whatever level is appropriate at a particular period of development. In fact, part of learning to be a "good enough" daughter involves learning to be a "good enough" mother or "empathetic relator" to one's mother and later to other important people. This ongoing process begins to allow for experience and practice in "mothering" and "relational caretaking." (p. 5)

Thus, a girl develops a self-in-relation both through her mother's "ease" in responding to infant female attunement, and through her "expecting empathy and caretaking from [her] daughter" (Surrey, 1983, p. 9). This sense of self that emerges in the daughter is characterized by an "ongoing capacity to consider one's actions in light of other people's needs, feelings, and perceptions" (Surrey, 1987, p. 6). She comes to feel that "maintaining the relationship(s) with the main people in her . . . life is still *the* most important thing" (J. B. Miller, 1984, p. 6). And her "self-esteem is based in feeling that she is a part of relationships and is taking care of relationships" (p. 5) through which she can express empathy, care, and "clarity in connection" with others (Jordan, 1987).

The popularity of the new paradigm, including the work of the Stone Center, reflects the failure of traditional psychologies to meet women's needs and reflect their visions. First, the new approach places a positive value on women's characteristics by turning traditional psychologies upside down. Instead of arguing that women are just as capable or mature or healthy as men, based upon a yardstick derived from male experience, these authors assume a distinct female psychology that has its own unique merits. Whereas traditional psychology once thought of the female as *l'homme manqué*, the new women's psychology now posits the feminine relational traits as *humane superior*. Secondly, by presenting women's psychological traits as ethical dispositions within a worldwide context in which care, empathy, and coopera-tion are so apparently needed, these authors make a powerful argument for the feminization of social life and political structures. Finally, by identifying women's psychological traits as strengths, the writers on the new women's psychology offer individual women hope and a basis upon which to develop their self-worth and inner strength. Women can begin a therapeutic process by tapping resources they already have developed rather than engaging in perpetual self-criticism for not living up to (male-derived) maturational goals that are antithetical to their own deeply rooted dispositions.

However, despite its attempt to rescue the psychology of women from traditional distortions, I believe that the new paradigm inadvertently reproduces these distortions. This occurs through both abstracting traditionally female traits of care and empathy from the larger social contexts in which they are actually cultivated and idealizing those traits as normative for all human beings. The consequence is a narrowing of the idea of women's self-expression and a deepening of expectation that women *should* em-brace these relational and empathetic behaviors. The consequence is a contemporary theoretical justification for traditionally idealized femininity.

This failure of the new paradigm is exemplified in the Stone Center's theoretical writings on female development. Recall that the self-in-relation emerges from a dynamic in which a mother expresses both an ease and interest in emotional sharing with her daughter and a need to be understood and cared for by her daughter. The mother's desire to be cared for is of particular significance because it is the source of the daughter's development of empathy as a permanent feature of her character. The daughter is encouraged to respond to her mother's needs and is rewarded for doing so by receiving in return both care and gratitude.

The Stone Center work celebrates the process through which a daughter learns to be "a 'good enough' mother or 'empathetic relator' to one's mother and later to other people" (Surrey, 1985, p. 5). What is missing from their account is an understanding of the fact that the needs of the infant or child and the needs of the adult are not of the same magnitude, and that the difference in age, capability, and maturation necessarily creates an imbalance in the relationship. Indeed, when one reads the Stone Center formulations of the mother-daughter relationship, one has little indication that this is an interaction between an adult and a child. Their descriptions of the dyad read more like interactions between peers, as if the mutual empathy that is posited as the ideal *adult* engagement is projected back onto the mother-daughter relationship.

The blurring of differences in age, need, and authority between mother and daughter serves to deflect attention from the unique needs of the child and to legitimate the mother's right to have her needs met by her daughter. The Stone Center writers do not question what they describe as "the mother's interest in being understood and cared for" by her daughter (Surrey, 1985, p. 5). Instead, they accept it as a given. This assumption, however, has buried within it a belief that has a profound consequence for explaining the mother-daughter relationship. This belief is that mothers *should* be able to gratify their needs for care and understanding through interacting with their daughters. Instead of questioning this prerogative or placing it in the context of cultural values that foster it, the Stone Center psychologists reproduce it uncritically, implying that it is "natural" or unproblematic. However, by doing so, they close off the possibility for interpreting it as a parent's *use* of her child, a practice which others (e.g., A. Miller, 1981, 1983, 1984) have argued has harmful developmental consequences. Thus, by projecting the model of ideal adult mutuality back on the mother-daughter relationship—a projection which presumes the right of the mother to have her needs met by her daughter—the Stone Center theory mystifies both the real power difference between mother and daughter (which permits a mother to impose her needs) and the possible detrimental consequences of this imposition for the daughter's development.

One of the *sources* of this mystification is the abstraction of the mother-daughter relationship from the wider cultural contexts in which it is actually embedded. The Stone Center writers do describe a cultural context, but they limit discussion of its consequences to adult male-female relationships. According to Jean Baker Miller (1983), traditional gender arrangements are so deeply rooted in male domination and female subordination that mutual empathy between women and men is impossible (pp. 4–5). The Stone Center psychologists provide numerous examples from clinical practice of women struggling with the absence of reciprocal empathy and understanding in their relationships with men (e.g., Jordan, 1984, p. 7; 1986, pp. 8–10; J. B.

Miller, 1986, p. 4). Yet, except for incidental comments that the absence could lead to a mother's overidentification with her children (J. B. Miller, 1972; Stiver, 1986), these writers provide no systematic analysis of the implications of their critique of the gender system for their theory of the mother-daughter relationship.

If they had placed their model of the mother-daughter relationship in the context of the gender system that they criticize, the Stone Center theorists might have interpreted differently their assumption of a mother's need for care and understanding from her daughter. They might have identified the likelihood that a woman who cannot find mutual empathy or care and understanding in her relationships with an adult man might indeed turn to her daughter to meet those needs, not because it is "natural" or "given," but because the mother, too, has internalized the belief that only females are to care for others. This is the cultural devaluation of both women and the socially necessary need for care that, according to Miller, pervades our society (J. B. Miller, 1976). A mother's acting on that belief in her relationship with her daughter is not a failure of mothers *per se*, but an understandable expression of the wider system of values.

Reinterpreted from the perspective of the gendered context of the mother's need for care, the Stone Center model of the mother-daughter bond assumes a different meaning. A mother who turns to her daughter in order to meet her own needs does not create the conditions for the blossoming of the self but instead confounds her own needs for care and recognition with her responsibilities as a caretaker. By turning to her daughter to provide adult mutuality, a mother can, in effect, create a nurturing reversal, seeking care from one who is too young to give it.

This is precisely the kind of contradictory and needy behavior that Karen Horney (1937) argued fosters basic anxiety in a child and results in the child's developing defensive strategies to create a sense of safety (pp. 85–86). From the standpoint of Horney's work, the caring, empathetic qualities that the mother seeks from her daughter and that the daughter offers in return, are not the expressions of an essentially human, relational self, but the protective devices of one who feels that she *must* display these behaviors in order to gain her mother's love and acceptance.

From this perspective, the empathetic qualities of the self-in-relation actually constitute a defensive structure. Hence, I suggest that the self-in-relation is not the authentic self that the Stone Center theorists presume it to be, but the idealized self that Horney associated with self-effacement and living according to others' expectations (Horney, 1937, pp. 119–120; 1950, p. 168). According to this interpretation, the self-in-relation finds acceptance from others through displaying the altruistic qualities of "unselfishness, goodness, generosity, humility, saintliness, nobility, sympathy" that she believes will win her love (Horney, 1950, p. 222). These are the shoulds of her defensive system: doing for others, caring for them, making their needs the sources of her motives, complying with others' demands for recognition. Because her safety lies in appearing empathetic, the self-in-relation needs others to need her as a way of bolstering her self-esteem (Horney, 1937, pp. 109–112). She also needs them to reflect back to her that she is, indeed, her idealized self (Horney, 1945, p. 16). Thus, what Surrey (1987) celebrates as the "motive for connection" (p. 9) is, in effect, a compulsion for confirmation that the self-in-relation is, indeed, empathetic, caring, lovable. As Horney observed, the individual who needs others to mirror herself in this way abhors isolation. She believes that she "is worth as much as ... [she] is liked, needed, wanted or loved" (Horney, 1950, p. 227). Alone, she is cut off from this validation, and therefore, she pursues the company of others with an urgency that makes it feel like the one thing needful in life (p. 229; see J. B. Miller, 1984, p. 6).

From the perspective of Horney's theory, the idealized empathetic self is not only a strategic persona that seeks protective gratitude and admiring confirmation from others; it is also an inexorable inner critic that condemns actual behavior for failing to live up to the proud "shoulds" comprising the ideal (Horney, 1950, pp. 111–112). Failure to be caring enough or sensitive to others' feelings can incur the wrath of the idealized self-image, fostering a compulsion to live up to the shoulds. Nevertheless, one who is dominated by the idealized self cannot escape its wrath. The combination of defensive perfectionism and inevitable shortcomings serves to make anger against the self a permanent feature of character (Horney, 1951). But anger is felt not only because one fails to achieve the ideal, but also because one is forced to repress desires for individual self-fulfillment that violate the relational ideal. The idealized relational self, therefore, perpetuates self-criticism and anger as ongoing intrapsychic processes.

Because the self-in-relation theory idealizes the rational, caring qualities, it obscures the ways in which these idealized qualities themselves create oppressive demands and foster inner rage. Ironically, many of the clinical examples presented in the Stone Center works-in-progress series are of angry or depressed women (e.g., J. B. Miller, 1983; Jordan, 1987, p. 17; Surrey, 1985, p. 13). And usually, the clinical advice is to encourage these women to develop greater "self-empathy" or to meet their own needs (e.g., Stiver, 1983, pp. 9–10; 1984, p. 10; Surrey, 1984, p. 4; 1985, pp. 11–12; Jordan, 1984, p. 9). But because empathy for the other is assumed to be a benign need rather than a compulsive demand, the inner anger that can be generated *by* that demand is never adequately addressed.

The self-in-relation theory, like the paradigm it elaborates, attempts to rescue the psychology of women from traditional distortions by inverting the values ascribed to stereotypically male and female traits. But its solution—hoisting the banner of care and relationality above individual achievement and autonomy—creates another danger for women. As I have argued elsewhere (Westkott, 1986), the expectation that women should be caring and empathetic expresses a deeper cultural belief that men's needs take precedence over women's. The female relational ideal is grounded in, and serves to perpetuate, a context of male privilege. The new paradigm acknowledges this system of male prerogative in adult relationships but fails to understand its deep influence on women's character development. Thus, by celebrating relationality as if its development were free of the effects of female subservience, the new psychology unwittingly advocates an oppressive ideal for women.

NOTE

1. The Stone Center Group has more recently moved away from using the term "self-in-relation" in favor of the term "connection." Nevertheless, the more recent work continues

to build on the earlier theoretical writings on the self-in-relation that posited the development of a core female sense of self connected to or related to others. See, for example, Miller (1988).

REFERENCES

Belenky, M. F., Clinchy, B. M., Goldberger, N. R., and Tarule, J. M. (1986). *Women's Ways of Knowing*. New York: Basic Books.

Broverman, I. K., Broverman, D. M., Clarkson, F. E., Rosenkrantz, P. S., and Vogel, S. R. (1970). Sex-role stereotypes and clinical judgments of mental health. *J. Consult. Clin. Psychol., 34*(1): 1–7.

Chodorow, N. (1978). *The Reproduction of Mothering*. Berkeley: University of California Press.

Eisler, R. (1987). *The Chalice and the Blade*. San Francisco: Harper & Row.

Elshtain, J. B. (1987). *Women and War*. New York: Basic Books.

Gilligan, C. (1982). *In a Different Voice: Psychological Theory and Women's Development*. Cambridge: Harvard University Press.

Horney, K. (1937). *The Neurotic Personality of Our Time*. New York: Norton.

——— (1945). *Our Inner Conflicts: A Constructive Theory of Neurosis*. New York: Norton.

——— (1950). *Neurosis and Human Growth*. New York: Norton.

——— (1951). On feeling abused. *Am. J. Psychoanal., 11:* 5–12.

——— (1967). *Feminine Psychology*. New York: Norton.

Jordan, J. V. (1983). Women and empathy: implications for psychological development and psychotherapy. *Work in Progress* No. 82-02. Wellesley, MA: Stone Center Working Paper Series.

——— (1984). Empathy and self-boundaries. *Work in Progress* No. 16. Wellesley, MA: Stone Center Working Paper Series.

——— (1986). The meaning of mutuality. *Work in Progress* No. 23. Wellesley, MA: Stone Center Working Paper Series.

——— (1987). Clarity in connection: empathic knowing, desire and sexuality. *Work in Progress* No. 29. Wellesley, MA: Stone Center Working Paper Series.

Kaplan, A. G. (1984). Female or male psychotherapists for women: new formulations. *Work in Progress* No. 83-02. Wellesley, MA: Stone Center Working Papers Series.

Kaplan, A. G., and Klein, R. (1985). Women's self development in late adolescence. *Work in Progress* No. 17. Wellesley, MA: Stone Center Working Paper Series.

Kohlberg, L. (1973). Continuities and discontinuities in childhood and adult moral development revisited. *Collected Papers on Moral Development and Moral Education*. Cambridge: Harvard University, Moral Education Research Foundation.

Levinson, D. (1978). *The Seasons of a Man's Life*. New York: Knopf.

Miller, A. (1981). *The Drama of the Gifted Child*. New York: Basic Books.

——— (1983). *For Your Own Good: Hidden Cruelty in Child-Rearing and the Roots of Violence*. New York: Farrar, Straus, & Giroux.

——— (1984). *Thou Shalt Not Be Aware*. New York: Farrar, Straus, & Giroux.

Miller, J. B. (1972). Sexuality and inequality: men's dilemma. (A note on the Oedipus complex, paranoia and other psychological concepts.) *Am. J. Psychoanal., 32:* 147–155.

——— (1976). *Toward a New Psychology of Women*. Boston: Beacon Press.

——— (1982). Women and power. *Work in Progress* No. 82-01. Wellesley, MA: Stone Center Working Papers Series.

———— (1983). The construction of anger in women and men. *Work in Progress* No. 83-01. Wellesley, MA: Stone Center Working Papers Series.

———— (1984). The development of women's sense of self. *Work in Progress* No. 12. Wellesley, MA: Stone Center Working Papers Series.

———— (1986). What do we mean by relationships? *Work in Progress* No. 22. Wellesley, MA: Stone Center Working Papers Series.

———— (1988). Connections, disconnections and violations. *Work in Progress* No. 33. Wellesley, MA: Stone Center Working Papers Series.

Noddings, N. (1984). *Caring: A Feminine Approach to Ethics and Moral Education.* Berkeley: University of California Press.

Psychology of Women Quarterly, Vols. 10, 11, 12 (1986, 1987, 1988).

Stiver, I. P. (1983). Work inhibitions in women. *Work in Progress* No. 82-03. Wellesley, MA: Stone Center Working Paper Series.

———— (1984). The meanings of "dependency" in female-male relationships. *Work in Progress* No. 83-07. Wellesley, MA: Stone Center Working Papers Series.

———— (1986). Beyond the oedipus complex: mothers and daughters. *Work in Progress.* No. 26. Wellesley, MA: Stone Center Working Paper Series.

Surrey, J. L. (1983). The relational self in women: clinical implications. *Work in Progress* No. 82-02. Wellesley, MA: Stone Center Working Paper Series.

———— (1984). Eating patterns as a reflection of women's development. *Work in Progress* No. 83-06. Wellesley, MA: Stone Center Working Papers Series.

———— (1985). Self-in-relation. a theory of women's development. *Work in Progress* No. 13. Wellesley, MA: Stone Center Working Papers Series.

———— (1987). Relationship and empowerment. *Work in Progress* No. 30. Wellesley, MA: Stone Center Working Paper Series.

Swift, C. F. (1987). Women and violence: breaking the connection. *Work in Progress* No. 27. Wellesley, MA: Stone Center Working Papers Series.

Westkott, M. (1986). *The Feminist Legacy of Karen Horney.* New Haven: Yale University Press.

Part V

Engendering Persons

A. Engendering Personality

As Jill G. Morawski notes in her contribution to this section, traditional approaches to masculinity and femininity assumed that these psychological characteristics referred to something that existed within individuals, could be measured, and would correspond with (and was probably caused by) biological sex. They were unprepared for both the difficulties they encountered when they tried to specify what masculinity and femininity are, and how much variation they found *within* the sexes in the characteristics assumed to index masculinity and femininity. Moreover, they found (and current workers continue to find) that individuals differ in the extent to which gender is a defining aspect of their personalities, the ways in which they react to gender-based expectations, and the extent to which they are "gender-typical" in their thoughts, feelings, and behaviors.

Thus, there is an impressive range of individual variation both in gender-related personality characteristics and in the overall salience of gender for different individuals (Bem, 1981; Markus, Crane, Bernstein, & Siladi, 1982). Nevertheless, personalities rarely develop to be "gender-free"—despite the tendency of personality theorists to pay only unsystematic and incomplete attention to gender (see Stewart, chapter 3 of this volume). Even "gender nonconformists," as Sandra Lipsitz Bem points out in her chapter, are in some sense defined by gender, because recognition of their nonconformity requires acknowledgment of the gender norms to which they do not conform. As each of the authors in this section illustrate (and as is echoed in a variety of ways by authors in other sections), gender is a ubiquitous category of thought, experience, and social organization.

Many questions and considerable disagreement remain, however, about how (and how inexorably) gender may become *part of* individuals, in ways that may influence other aspects of their personality (see, e.g., Liam Hudson and Bernadine Jacot's (chapter discussion of intellectual interests and interpersonal style), their understanding of themselves, and their views toward the "other" sex. Individuals (including, as Morawski makes clear, psychologists) encounter *and* incorporate gender-related expectations through their interactions with a very gender-conscious world.

Gendered personality may originate from social (and androcentric) lenses, as Bem argues. We might conceptualize accommodation to the gendered lenses of society as a problem each individual has to "practice" (Thorne & Luria, 1986), as opposed to considering gender as an "essence" to be realized. We can recognize, as Candace West and Don H. Zimmerman argue (see chapter 6 of this volume), that gender may be created in social interaction. Yet even if gendered personality originates to a large extent from "outside" the person, one of the reasons for considering personality is to acknowledge that gender *becomes* part of the individual—something that individuals carry around with them and that affects their thoughts, feelings, and behavior. One reason relationships, institutions, and society at large can so effectively maintain gender is precisely because it becomes inseparable from individuals. Especially if we are interested in changing social relationships, gender norms, institutional behavior, and gender-based expectations, we need to acknowledge the need to address not just what happens "out there," between people and between individuals and institutions, but also what happens "inside": how people develop to "feel" gendered and to think about themselves (and others) as gendered. Put another way that is perhaps more amenable to a social constructionist framework: intrapsychic gender is not just part of the individual, it is part of the context.

REFERENCES

Bem, S. L. (1981). Gender Schemas: A Cognitive Account of Sex-Typing. *Psychological Review, 88,* 354–364.

Markus, H., Crane, M., Bernstein, S., & Siladi, M. (1982). Self-Schemas and Gender. *Journal of Personality and Social Psychology, 42,* 38–50.

Thorne, B., & Luria, Z. (1986). Sexuality and Gender in Children's Daily Worlds. *Social Problems, 33,* 176–190.

Chapter Twenty-Two

Enculturation and Self-Construction
The Gendered Personality

Sandra Lipsitz Bem

Enculturation

Gender schema theory maintains that children in gender-polarizing societies internalize the lens of gender polarization and thereby become gender polarizing (or gender schematic) themselves. This internalized lens, in turn, helps lead children to become conventionally gendered. That is, in imposing a gender-polarizing classification on social reality, children evaluate different ways of behaving in terms of the cultural definitions of gender appropriateness and reject any ways of behaving that do not match their sex.

Gender schema theory contains two fundamental presuppositions about the process of individual gender formation: first, that there are gender lenses embedded in cultural discourse and social practice that are internalized by the developing child, and, second, that once these gender lenses have been internalized, they predispose the child, and later the adult, to construct an identity that is consistent with them. The theory to be presented here retains these presuppositions but elaborates and extends the gender schema account in two important ways.

One way it does so is by adding the lens of androcentrism to the earlier account. Because society is not only gender polarizing but androcentric, the males and females living within it become androcentric and gender polarizing themselves. The inclusion of this second lens dramatically alters the consequences of internalizing the gender lenses. Whereas before, the individual had been nothing more than a carrier of the culture's gender polarization, now the individual is a deeply implicated—if unwitting—collaborator in the social reproduction of male power.

Another way the earlier theory is expanded is in spelling out the processes of enculturation that are presumed to transfer the lenses of androcentrism and gender polarization from the culture to the individual. This model of enculturation is sufficiently general to explain how all cultural lenses are transferred to the individual, not just gender lenses. The analysis of how conventionally gendered women and men are made is thus but a special case of how cultural natives are made. Consistent with this premise, I preface my theoretical analysis of individual gender construction with a more general analysis of the two enculturation processes that are critical to the making of a cultural native: the institutional preprogramming of the individual's daily experience into the default options, or the historically precut "grooves," for that particular time and place, and the transmission of implicit lessons—or metamessages—about what lenses the culture uses to organize social reality.[1]

The Making of a Cultural Native

Preprogramming an individual's daily experience into the default options of a particular culture is apparent in the most superficial analysis of how children have been made into unmistakably different kinds of social beings in different cultures and different historical epochs.[2] Consider the institutionally structured experience of children in modern middle-class America, for example, where everyone from six to sixteen spends seven hours a day, five days a week, forty weeks a year, in rigidly age-segregated classrooms being taught material that frequently has no immediate value to either themselves or anyone else in their communities. Now compare that to the institutionally structured experience of children in a more traditional culture, where skills critical to making a living are learned every day by participating with adults in productive labor and where the child's daily labor—like the adult's—is essential to the economic well-being of family and community.

The point should be clear. The kinds of human beings that children and adults become depend on their daily social experiences; and these social experiences are, in turn, preprogrammed by institutionalized social practices—which are themselves but one embodiment of the same cultural lenses that are also embodied in cultural discourse.

As important as this structuring of daily experience is to the making of a cultural native, however, the less visible process of tacitly communicating what lenses the culture uses to organize reality is equally important. This tacit communication of cultural metamessages about what is important, what is of value, which differences between people and other entities are to be emphasized and which are to be overlooked, which dimensions are to be used in judging how similar or dissimilar people and other entities are in the first place, and so on and so forth, helps to make a cultural native because it nonconsciously transfers the lenses of the culture to the consciousness or the psyche of the individual.

According to the anthropologist Clifford Geertz, the hallmark of a native consciousness is not being able to distinguish between reality and the way one's culture construes reality; in other words, the reality one perceives and the cultural lenses through which one perceives it are "indissoluble" (1983, p. 58). Although this kind of consciousness can sometimes be retained by adults who live in a sufficiently homogeneous society, it can be acquired only by children, who learn about their culture's way of construing reality without yet being aware that alternative construals are possible. In contrast to the adult visiting from another culture, the child growing up within a culture is thus like the proverbial fish who is unaware that its environment is wet. After all, what else could it be?

There are at least two different ways to talk about this nonconscious transfer of lenses from the culture to the child, both of which presuppose that the information to be transferred is embedded within the social practices of the culture. Insofar as social practices communicate metamessages to the child, the acquisition of cultural knowledge can be considered a kind of subliminal pedagogy. Insofar as the child gradually deciphers the meaning embedded in social practices, the acquisition of cultural knowledge can be considered more a matter of picking up information than transmitting it; in this case, the culture itself is more a text to be read—and read by an active, meaning-constructing reader—than a lesson to be taught.

This simultaneous transmission and pickup of information is initiated every time the active, pattern-seeking child is exposed to a culturally significant social practice. Take, for example, the practice of wearing a wristwatch that tells the time to the nearest minute. Simultaneously communicated by this practice and picked up by the child is that time must be quantified precisely and that human behavior must be scheduled precisely. Cultures that tell time by the sun and the seasons communicate a very different conception of social reality.

In real life, social practices cannot be neatly divided into those that prestructure daily experience and those that communicate cultural metamessages. All institutionalized social practices simultaneously do both, as can be seen in the following analysis of how the American middle-class family creates the kinds of radically individualistic people that anthropologists regard as distinctively Western, if not distinctively American.[3]

The process of molding American infants into individualistic American adults begins almost immediately after birth. Although children in many other cultures spend years in close physical contact with their mother—feeding from her breast, being carried on her back, and even sleeping in her bed—American children in families that can afford it are typically put out of their parents' beds and even out of their parents' bedrooms from the start. They are also typically weaned by the time they are one year old. The distinction between self and other is tacitly but forcefully imposed.

Americans structure into their children's daily lives the further notion that this separate self is a privileged entity, with boundaries that should not be violated and with needs, wants, and preferences that should be satisfied if at all possible. Parents communicate that the self has inviolable boundaries by giving children their own bedrooms and knocking on the door before entering, and by giving them diaries—complete with keys—in which to write their private thoughts. They communicate that children's needs, wants, and preferences should be satisfied—and that they *have* needs, wants, and preferences—by asking even toddlers what they want to eat and by responding even to infants as if their every vocalization were the expression of a desire that the parents should try to satisfy. Other, more sociocentric cultures give such rights and privileges to neither children nor adults.

By structuring their social interactions with children in these highly individualistic ways, American parents are doing two things simultaneously. First, they are situating the children in social contexts that will shape them into persons who have strong internal desires and who expect those desires to be satisfied. Second, they are communicating the shared cultural conception of a person.

Not only the American child lives in a social world that treats the individual as if he or she were the fundamental unit of all social life. The American adult lives in a social world that does exactly the same thing.

Consider first, for example, the American institution of "going away to college." Although possible, in principle, for almost any young adult to get an outstanding college education while still living at or near the family home, going to college, for those who can afford it, means going *away* to college. That is, it means being separated geographically, culturally, and psychologically from those with whom the young adult has always shared the bonds of love. The separation of the individual from the family is thus treated as a natural and desirable developmental stage; and connection, as a mark of immaturity and an encumbrance to social mobility.

Consider the American institution of getting married—and then divorced. Although marriage was once seen as a lifetime commitment to be dissolved only in the most extreme circumstances, if ever, it is increasingly seen as a limited partnership to be sustained if and only if it contributes substantially to the growth and development of both partners. Getting a divorce has become easier, not only legally but socially and psychologically as well. Again, separation is the norm, and connection an encumbrance to self-development.

Consider the American institution of going into therapy. So many people who can afford it now seek counseling whenever they experience any sense of dissatisfaction with their lives that some sociologists (like Robert Bellah et al., 1985) see the therapist as a significant cultural figure in late twentieth-century America. From their perspective, the growing prevalence of therapy is significant, in part, because the therapeutic dyad may constitute the kind of self-serving interpersonal relationship that Americans now seek in their personal lives—that is, a relationship that not only makes no demands or moral judgments but that also gives priority to individual self-enhancement rather than to the common good of any larger social unit. Again, connection is desirable if and only if it is not an encumbrance to the individual.

Finally, consider that most fundamental of capitalist institutions—private ownership. Private ownership is so ubiquitous in the daily lives of Americans that even the communal ownership of a neighborhood lawn mower is almost unthinkable. Nor are material things all that Americans have difficulty sharing; even the personal space around the body is treated as if it were private property. This peculiarly American pattern of laying claim to a relatively large amount of personal space is exhibited in face-to-face interactions at international gatherings, where the Americans inch backward to preserve the space around them and their conversational partners from many other cultures inch forward.[4]

Given the highly individualistic social world in which Americans live from the time they are born until the time they die, no wonder that in Tibetan, Americans are known as *nga dangpo,* which roughly means "me-firsters."[5]

The Making of a Gendered Native

Just as American society constructs me-firsters by situating people in a culture whose discourses and social practices are organized around the lens of radical individualism, so, too, does it construct conventionally gendered women and men by situating people in a culture whose discourses and social practices are organized around the lenses of androcentrism and gender polarization. My purpose here is to expose the androcentrism and the gender polarization in some social practices. These social practices program different and unequal social experiences for males and females; they also transfer the androcentric and gender-polarizing lenses of the culture to the psyche of the individual.

The androcentrism of American social practices can be seen most easily in the world of paid employment, where most women are still segregated into occupations which themselves embody the three androcentric definitions of a woman.[6] The androcentric definition of a woman in terms of her domestic and reproductive functions is embodied in those many women's jobs that provide administrative and logistical support to some higher-status male, including secretary, administrative aide, research assistant, paralegal, dental hygienist, and nurse. The androcentric definition of a woman in terms of her power to stimulate or satisfy the male sexual appetite is embodied in jobs that cater to male sexuality directly—prostitute, stripper, and go-go dancer come to mind—as well as in jobs that cater to male sexuality indirectly by emphasizing a woman's sexual attractiveness, including flight attendant, receptionist, and even television news anchorwoman. And the androcentric definition of a woman as an inferior departure from the male standard is embodied in the very definition of what constitutes a normal work life in America: continuous full-time work (with time off only for illness) throughout early and middle adulthood. The definition of full-time work is itself a historical construction, varying—even for men—from something like forty hours or fewer per week for those in "working-class" jobs to a great deal more than forty hours per week for fast-track young professionals in legal practices and financial firms. But whatever the social class of the job, neither the biological fact of female pregnancy nor the cultural and historical fact of female childcare is factored into the definition of a normal work life, which means that women in the world of paid employment are still being forced to cope with social practices (for example, the lack of pregnancy leave and childcare) that were institutionalized at a time when women themselves were still excluded from that world by law.

It should be clear from the discussion of how cultural natives are made that all of these androcentric social practices do two things simultaneously. First, they situate men and women in markedly unequal positions in the social structure, positions where men have much more opportunity than women to earn money, acquire marketable skills, advance in their careers, and wield power. This unequal positioning provides men and women with daily social experiences that, in turn, give rise to drastically different ways of construing reality.

Second, these androcentric social practices communicate to all the participants in the social world, both male and female, as well as to any spectators—children, say, watching representations of that social world in movies or on the television news—that males are the privileged sex and the male perspective is the privileged perspective. That is, these practices communicate that males are the central characters in the drama of human life around whom all action revolves and through whose eyes all reality is to be interpreted. Females, in contrast, are the peripheral, or marginal, characters, defined in terms of their relationship to the central characters. In the words of Simone de Beauvoir, females are the second sex, or the other.

This androcentric message is communicated by many institutionalized social practices. An example is the much-criticized practice of generically using *he, him,* and *man* to include *she, her,* and *woman.* Contrary to what at least some antifeminist pundits (playing on Freud) have condescendingly claimed, the feminist objection to this linguistic convention is not a case of "pronoun envy"; it is a sophisticated critique of a social practice that makes women invisible and treats men as the standard-bearers for the whole species.[7] Another linguistic example is the practice of having a woman take her husband's name and the title Mrs. (Mrs. John Smith) upon marriage. Apart from how androcentric this practice is in form, it gives the father's name to any children that the couple may have and makes it much more important to the couple to have at least one male child—because only a male child can carry on what is euphemistically known as the family name.

Like the androcentrism of the world beyond the family, the androcentrism within the family extends well beyond linguistic convention. In keeping with the androcentric definition of a woman in terms of her domestic and reproductive functions, even the employed wife is thus expected to provide whatever support services her husband requires to earn his living. In keeping with the androcentric definition of a woman in terms of her ability to stimulate and satisfy the male sexual appetite, the wife is also expected to provide her husband with sexual intercourse on demand, which is why the concept of marital rape is so often treated as an oxymoron.

This refusal to acknowledge the reality of marital rape is but one example of how the androcentric privileging of the male has left women with no legal recourse when their husbands abuse them. Still another example is the longstanding policy of the criminal justice system to look the other way when husbands beat their wives.

In some cultures, androcentrism organizes the social practices that impinge on children just as much as it organizes the social practices that impinge on adults, with many more newborn baby girls being killed because of limited resources than newborn baby boys, for example, and with many more school-age girls being denied the kind of an education that would make them literate. In late twentieth-century America, in contrast, where compulsory education and antidiscrimination laws now mandate that girls and boys receive virtually identical formal educations, androcentrism impinges on most children in more subtle ways: school systems treat boys' reading problems more seriously than girls' problems with math and computers, for example, and the culture as a whole treats sissies much more harshly than tomboys. This differential treatment of sissies and tomboys highlights a critically important interaction between androcentrism and gender polarization; we shall return to it below.

Even in late twentieth-century America, however, gender polarization organizes the daily lives of children from the moment a pink or blue nametag is taped to the bassinet to signal the newborn's sex, as it is in almost every American hospital. (In my daughter's case, a pink bow was also taped to her bald head.) Gender polarization continues at home, where parents dress their children in pink or blue, coif them (as soon as possible) with long hair or short, put them into bedrooms decorated with ballet dancers or football players, and tell them in no uncertain terms that they can't wear or play with either this item of clothing or that toy because it's "just for boys" or "just for girls."

Toys and clothes are not the only things defined as inappropriate for one sex or the other; so are a great many natural human impulses. Defined as gender inappropriate for females, for instance, is the desire for autonomy and power; defined as gender inappropriate for males are feelings of vulnerability, dependency, and affection for same-sex others.

Again, all of these gender-polarizing social practices do two things simultaneously. They program different social experiences for males and females, respectively, and they communicate to both males and females that the male-female distinction is extraordinarily important, that it has—and ought to have—intensive and extensive relevance to virtually every aspect of human experience.

Children pick up this gender-polarizing message both from practices that divide reality into masculine and feminine and from certain more subtle aspects of the language. Consider what is being communicated, for example, when a three-year-old is corrected for saying about Grandpa that "she" is eating an apple, or when a four-year-old is taught a song in which "the fingers are ladies and the thumbs are men," or when a five-year-old is taught to keep track of the date by pinning boy paper dolls on the odd-numbered days and girl paper dolls on the even-numbered days. On the surface, these language lessons may be about grammar and body parts and calendars. At the meta level, however, they teach children to look at social reality through a lens that is gender polarizing.

Gender polarization does not end with childhood. During adulthood there is at least as much emphasis on the gender polarization of the body, as well as a strong emphasis on the gender polarization of erotic desire and sexual expression. Males and females alike are all but required to conform to the cultural mandate for exclusive heterosexuality.

This heterosexual mandate is institutionalized in a great number of social practices privileging heterosexuality and marginalizing homosexuality. Examples are (1) the criminalization of same-sex sexual activity, which has been upheld by the Supreme Court as recently as 1986 in *Bowers v. Hardwick;* (2) the denial of the right to marry to gay male and lesbian couples, which also denies them the spousal benefits that accrue to married heterosexual couples, including employment-based fringe benefits, survivorship rights, and legal authority over medical decisions for the partner should he or she become incapacitated by illness or accident; (3) the barring of gay males and lesbians from military service; (4) the refusal of many churches to accept openly gay males and lesbians into their congregations; (5) the organization of almost all postpubescent social life around the heterosexual couple, with dates and dances at the high school and dinner parties in suburbia all but denying the existence of gay male and lesbian relationships; and (6) the similar denial of gay male and lesbian existence by the programming and advertising of the mass media. Although this virtual censorship of same-sex sexuality in the mass media has had to be modified somewhat in the context of the recent AIDS epidemic, news reports and even occasional episodes on sitcoms that are designed to provide information on how the HIV virus is transmitted do not begin to challenge the privileging of heterosexuality as much as a single ad for toothpaste featuring a same-sex romantic couple undoubtedly would.

Besides communicating that the male-female distinction requires attention in all domains of human social life, gender-polarizing social practices also communicate a corollary of that metamessage: that another important distinction is to be made between a *real* male or female and a *biological* male or female. This corollary is first communicated when parents teach children their earliest definitions of male and female.

In a critique of Kohlberg's cognitive-developmental theory, I pointed out that although children as young as three years of age have the capacity to understand that it is biological attributes like the genitalia that define a person as male or female, fully 50 percent of American three-, four-, and five-year-olds are able to distinguish male from female only when those males and females are clothed and coiffed in a fully gender-polarizing way.

From an enculturation perspective, the reason so many young American children pay more attention to hairstyle and clothing than to genitalia is that they have picked up an implicit—if somewhat erroneous—cultural metamessage about what sex is. Americans tend to dress prepubertal males and females differently and to give them different hairstyles—that is, to polarize their physical appearances—precisely so that their sex will be apparent even when their genitalia are hidden from view. Moreover, in supermarkets, on playgrounds, and in every other social context, parents readily identify people as male or female for their children even when they have no specific information about those people's genitalia. In doing these things, adults not only rely on visually salient cultural cues themselves but they also unwittingly teach children a social or cultural definition of sex rather than a biological one.

As I see it, the legacy of learning a social definition of sex lasts long after a child has learned about the special significance of the genitalia as the defining attributes of male and female. Not only does the social definition set up a pattern of behavior that is culturally consistent with whatever sex the child is told he or she is; it also instills in the child the never-to-be-fully-forgotten feeling that being male or female is something to work at, to accomplish, and to be sure not to lose, rather than something one *is* biologically.

If the lifelong pressures and demands of the mutually exclusive cultural scripts did not nourish that germ of an idea, perhaps it would wither and die once the child learned about the genitalia. But because the scripts do nourish it, it grows to become a deeply rooted insecurity, which, in turn, motivates many adults to try to enhance their sense of being either a "real" man or a "real" woman through the kinds of behavioral choices they make in their everyday lives.

This insecurity is profoundly exacerbated by the requirement in a gender-polarizing society that people repress at least some of their most natural human impulses. Polarization of the human impulses exacerbates gender insecurity—as Freud himself would have understood—because no matter how well people manage to keep them under control, those gender-inappropriate impulses not only produce a certain level of conflict and contradiction within the individual psyche; they also constitute an eternal internal threat to the male or female selves that people work so hard to construct and maintain.

In principle, parents could communicate a very different metamessage not only about what sex is but also about when sex matters. They could communicate that sex is a narrowly construed biological concept that does not need to matter outside the domain of reproduction, which is the antithesis of the traditional cultural metamessage that sex matters very much indeed in virtually all domains of human activity. In my own family, I tried to teach my children at the earliest possible age that "being a boy means having a penis and testicles; being a girl means having a vagina, a clitoris, and a uterus; and whether you're a boy or a girl, a man or a woman, doesn't need to matter unless and until you want to make a baby."

Both the liberation that can come from having a narrow biological definition of sex and the imprisonment that can come from not having such a definition are strikingly illustrated by an encounter my son, Jeremy, had when he naively decided to wear barrettes to nursery school. Several times that day, another little boy insisted that Jeremy must be a girl because "only girls wear barrettes." After repeatedly insisting that "wearing barrettes doesn't matter; being a boy means having a penis and testicles," Jeremy finally pulled down his pants to make his point more convincingly. The other boy was not impressed. He simply said, "Everybody has a penis; only girls wear barrettes."[8]

Although the gender-polarizing concepts of a real man and a real woman give both men and women the feeling that their maleness or femaleness is something they must continually construct and reconstruct, rather than something they can simply take for granted, in the context of an androcentric culture it is the males in particular who are made to feel the most insecure about the adequacy of their gender. Androcentrism exacerbates the male's insecurity about his status as a real man in at least two different ways. It so thoroughly devalues whatever thoughts, feelings, and behaviors are culturally defined as feminine that crossing the gender boundary has a more negative cultural meaning for men that it has for women—which means, in turn, that male gender-boundary-crossers are much more culturally stigmatized than female gender-boundary-crossers. At the same time, androcentrism provides such an unreachable definition of what a real man is supposed to be that only a few men can even begin to meet it.

During childhood, the cultural asymmetry between male gender-boundary-crossers and female gender-boundary-crossers can be seen in the merciless teasing of sissies, as opposed to the benign neglect or even open admiration of tomboys. Assymmetry can also be seen in dress and play codes for children: although a girl can now wear almost any item of clothing and play with almost any toy without so much as an eyebrow being raised by her social community, let a boy even once have the urge to try on a princess costume in the dress-up corner of his nursery school, and his parents and teachers will instantly schedule a conference to discuss the adequacy of his gender identity. Although the terms *sissy* and *tomboy* do not apply to adults who have crossed the gender boundary, the asymmetry between male boundary-crossers and female boundary-crossers is as strong as ever for those who have left childhood behind. This is why a woman can wear almost any item of male clothing—including jockey underwear—and be accepted socially, but a man still cannot wear most items of female clothing without being stigmatized.[9]

This heavy-handed suppression of impulses in males that are culturally defined as even slightly feminine—including what I see as the natural impulse to adorn oneself in vibrant colors and silky textures—makes it extraordinarily difficult for many men to acknowledge the existence within themselves of desires that have even the slightest hint of femininity; the layers of their psyches are thus filled with the kinds of repressed impulses that cannot help but constitute a continuous internal threat to the security of their gender identities. Although theoretically, women are also subject to this kind of internal threat, the androcentrism in American culture now allows females to so freely express many impulses that are culturally defined as masculine (including, for example, the impulses to political leadership and athletic mastery) that there are probably not nearly so many repressed masculine impulses in the psyches of women as there are repressed feminine impulses in the psyches of men.

But apart from making gender boundary crossing asymmetrical, androcentrism provides a definition of a real man that is so thoroughly intertwined with being powerful and privileged that it inevitably puts all those millions of men without power and privilege at risk for feeling not just insufficiently powerful and privileged but insufficiently masculine as well. The risk of feeling emasculated—or neutered— is especially intense when a man has to acknowledge a woman who is more powerful or privileged (or even competent) than himself.

This widespread risk to the common man's sense of masculinity might threaten the foundation of an androcentric society if not for two countervailing social practices that enable even those millions of men without power and privilege to feel at least marginally like real men: (1) the historical exclusion of women from positions of public power and the development of a religion and a science presupposing men's natural right, as men, to dominate women, which together enable even those men without power and privilege to confirm at least their male *right* to that power and privilege, and (2) the cultural marginalizing of homosexuals, which enables men without power and privilege to confirm their status as real men by defining themselves not only in terms of their natural difference from all women but also in terms of their natural difference from men who are obviously not real men.

None of this is to say that androcentrism provides a definition of a real woman that is easy for all women to attain. In a culture that androcentrically defines women in terms of their domestic and reproductive functions, women who are unable to have children almost inevitably experience a sense that they are not real women. Moreover, the extraordinary cultural emphasis on a real woman's being sexually attractive to men makes a great many women over forty (or maybe even thirty) worry that their status as real women may be gone forever; it also makes women of every age spend an inordinate amount of time, energy, and money in pursuit of beauty.

Self-Construction

Where androcentric and gender-polarizing social practices so narrowly constrain the roles of women and men that there are few choices, if any, about how to be a woman or a man, the internalized lenses of androcentrism and gender polarization serve exactly the same function in individual gender formation that all internalized cultural lenses serve in creating a cultural native. That is, they make the preprogrammed societal ways of being and behaving seem so normal and natural that alternative ways of being and behaving rarely even come to mind.

A transitional society like the United States, however, makes an almost infinite variety of options available to the individual but then not so subtly communicates that the individual's adequacy as a man or a woman depends on the selection of a limited subset of those options. Here, the internalized lenses of androcentrism and gender polarization so rigorously guide the individual's selection of alternatives that the construction of the self seems to lie as much with the individual as with the culture. This constructed self comprises a gendered personality, a gendered body, an androcentric heterosexuality, and the abhorrence of homosexuality.

The Gendered Personality

I have repeatedly suggested that the social reproduction of male power is aided and abetted by the cultural transformation of male and female into masculine and feminine. In other words, I have argued that the institution of male power depends for its survival on the construction of males and females whose gendered personalities mirror the different and unequal roles assigned to them in the social structure. The assumption here may seem to be that a gendered personality is a static collection of masculine or feminine traits that has already been shaped by enculturation—that it is a finished *product,* so to speak, rather than a psychological *process.* But a gendered personality is both a product and a process. It is both a particular collection of masculine or feminine traits and a way of construing reality that itself constructs those traits.

The collection of masculine or feminine traits that constitute the gendered personality have long been seen as representing two important, if complementary, modes of human functioning. Different theorists have different labels for these modes. According to Talcott Parsons (Parsons & Bales, 1955), masculinity is associated with an "instrumental" orientation, a cognitive focus on getting the job done or the problem solved, whereas femininity is associated with an "expressive" orientation, an affective concern for the welfare of others and the harmony of the group. Similarly, David Bakan (1966) has suggested that masculinity is associated with an "agentic" orientation, a concern for oneself as an individual, whereas femininity is associated with a "communal" orientation, a concern for the relationship between oneself and others. Finally, Erik Erikson's distinction between "inner and outer space" represents an anatomical analogue to a similar psychological distinction between a masculine "fondness for 'what works' and for what man can make, whether it helps to build or to destroy" and a more ethical feminine commitment to "resourcefulness in peacekeeping . . . and devotion to healing" (1968, p. 262).

In the late 1960s and early 1970s, what the many feminist proponents of androgyny were basically arguing was that although instrumental and agentic traits were traditionally reserved for men and expressive and communal traits were traditionally reserved for women, this gender polarization was tragically and unnecessarily limiting human potential, allowing each person only that half of the total personality potential that matched the cultural definitions of gender appropriateness. This limitation might not matter, the argument continued, if all that was at stake was a set of trivial possibilities—like wearing pants or using lipstick—but because everyone was forfeiting a profoundly important way of relating to the world, the limitation was tragic and unnecessary for everyone personally and was, furthermore, worth placing near the center of a feminist revolution.

By the time people reach adulthood, however, it is not just the culture that is limiting them to half their potential. It is also their own readiness to look at themselves through the androcentric and gender-polarizing lenses that they have internalized from the culture and thereby to see every possibility that is consistent with those lenses as normal and natural for the self and every possibility that is inconsistent with those lenses as alien and problematic for the self. In other words, they are limited by their enculturated readiness to constantly ask, "Does this possible way of being or behaving adequately match my culture's conception of a real man or a real woman?" and to answer the question with, "If not, I'll reject it out of hand. If so, I'll consider exploring it further."

To say that the enculturated individual asks this question is not to say, however, that he or she is always—or ever—consciously aware of doing so. More often than not, the culture seems to have tuned the individual's antennae to an androcentric and gender-polarizing station, so they automatically pick up whatever signals that station is sending. Once this tuning is completed, the internalized lenses of androcentrism and gender polarization not only shape how individuals think about the self but also how they feel. Put somewhat differently, the individual's deepest thoughts and feelings about what is alien to the self and what is not alien are shaped by internalized cultural definitions of what a man and a woman ought to be.

The gendered personality, like the gendered culture, thus has a readiness to superimpose a gender-based classification on every heterogeneous collection of human possibilities that presents itself. The gendered personality is more than a particular collection of masculine or feminine traits, then; it is also a way of looking at reality that produces and reproduces those traits during a lifetime of self-construction. This conceptualization of the gendered personality as both process and product is consistent with a longstanding tradition in personality psychology that sees each individual as constructing his or her own unique reality by bringing, say, a particular style of social interaction into all situations. It is also consistent with a longstanding tradition in cognitive psychology that sees human perception itself as a constructive process that always involves some degree of selection, organization, and interpretation on the part of the perceiver.[10]

My empirical research on gender lenses is part of a conceptual challenge to the theoretical tradition of gender polarization in psychology. But the research also comprises an empirical test of the psychological claim being made here that the gendered personality is both process and product. More specifically, the research tests the theory that conventionally gendered women and men *limit themselves* to only half their potential by nonconsciously imposing a gender-based classification on social reality.

The overall strategy of the research was first to identify people who are conventionally gendered—whose self-described traits on the masculinity and femininity scales of the Bem Sex Role Inventory (BSRI) mirror the highly polarized definitions of gender appropriateness in American culture—and then to ask whether these prototypes of masculinity and femininity are significantly more likely than anyone else to organize information on the basis of gender. If so, there is reason to believe that the gendered personality is both process and product, as well as reason to believe that the process itself may be partially responsible for the product. (Because these studies predate my theorizing about androcentrism, they address only the lens of gender polarization.)

In one of these studies, subjects were shown a list of sixty-one words and then asked to recall as many of those words as they could in whatever order the words happened to come to mind. The list included animals, verbs, articles of clothing, and people's first names in random order. Half of the people's names were male and half were female; onethird of the words within each of the other categories had masculine connotations *(gorilla, hurling, trousers)*, one-third had feminine connotations *(butterfly, blushing, bikini)*, and one-third had no gender connotations *(ant, stepping, sweater)*. Research in cognitive psychology has shown that if an individual has stored a number of words in memory in terms of an underlying schema or network of associations, then thinking of one schema-related word enhances the probability of thinking of another. Accordingly, an individual's sequence of recall will reveal runs or clusters of words that are linked in memory by the schema; after thinking of one animal word, for example, he or she is likely to think next of another animal word. Subjects in this study could cluster words either according to semantic category (animals, verbs, clothing, names) or according to gender.

The results showed that conventionally gendered subjects clustered significantly more words by gender than did other subjects. For example, if a conventionally gendered subject happened to recall a feminine animal like a butterfly, he or she was more likely to follow that with another feminine word, such as *bikini*, whereas subjects who were not conventionally gendered were more likely to follow *butterfly* with the name of another animal. (Conventionally gendered subjects were not more likely than others, however, to cluster according to the semantic categories; everyone did that.) As the theory predicted, then, conventionally gendered individuals were more likely than others to organize information in terms of gender—to view reality through the lens of gender polarization (Bem, 1981).

In a study by Deborrah Frable and myself (1985), subjects listened to a group discussion and were then asked to recall who said what. Of interest here was how frequently subjects erroneously attributed statements made by male discussants to other males, rather than to females, and statements made by female discussants to other females, rather than to males. Such within-sex errors indicate that the subject is confusing the members of a given sex with one another, that is, that he or she is noting, sorting, and remembering people on the basis of their sex. The results showed that conventionally gendered subjects were especially likely to do this, revealing once again that their perceptual and conceptual worlds are organized around gender. (A control condition showed that conventionally gendered subjects were not more likely than other subjects to make within-*race* errors; in other words, the effect was specific to gender.)

In a third study (Bem, 1981), the sixty masculine, feminine, and neutral attributes from the BSRI were all projected onto a screen one at a time, and the subject was asked to push one of two buttons, ME or NOT ME, to indicate whether the attribute was or was not self-descriptive. It was found that conventionally gendered subjects responded more *quickly* than others when endorsing gender-appropriate attributes or rejecting gender-inappropriate attributes or rejecting gender-appropriate attributes. This implies that conventionally gendered individuals have a readiness to decide on the basis of gender which attributes to associate and dissociate with their self-concept. It also suggests that when filling out the BSRI, conventionally gendered individuals sort the attributes into equivalence classes on the basis of gender in order to describe themselves.

The next important question is whether the spontaneous use of this classification limits conventionally gendered women and men to that half of their human potential that matches the definitions of gender appropriateness in the culture. To test this hypothesis, a second series of laboratory studies was conducted in which it was asked whether people who describe themselves as conventionally gendered on the BSRI are also significantly more likely than others to restrict their behavior in accordance with cultural definitions of gender appropriateness.

The first study in this series (Bem & Lenney, 1976) demonstrated that conventionally gendered people are more likely than other people to avoid even trivial everyday activities like oiling a squeaky hinge or ironing a cloth napkin if those activities are culturally defined as not appropriate for their sex; furthermore, if conventionally gendered people find themselves in a situation where they must perform such activities, they are more likely than others to report having negative feelings about themselves.

The other studies in the series (Bem, 1975; Bem, Martyna & Watson, 1976) confirmed that this pattern of cross-gender avoidance extends beyond the trivial activities of everyday life to the more profound activities included within the instrumental (or agentic) domain and within the expressive (or communal) domain. Thus, only androgynous women and men managed *both* to stand firm in their opinions when faced with a group unanimously giving an opposing opinion *and* to behave nurturantly toward a baby and a lonely peer. In contrast, conventionally gendered women and men managed to do well only at whichever of these behaviors the culture defines as appropriate for their sex. In other words, conventionally masculine men were independent but not nurturant, and conventionally feminine women were nurturant but not independent.[11]

The conventionally gendered women and men in this program of research represent in purer form all who are enculturated in American society. As such, they serve as a window into the consciousness of the culture as a whole. That cultural consciousness, in turn, includes not just gender polarization but also androcentrism. In real life, it is thus the lenses of androcentrism and gender polarization that together shape perceptions of what feels natural for the self, for other people, and for the social arrangements within the culture.

As an example of how an individual's androcentric and gender-polarizing lenses can shape the perception of other people, consider one of my favorite studies in social psychology. Subjects looking at a photograph of male and female graduate students seated around the two sides and head of a rectangular table rated the group members on leadership and dominance. Consistent with the basic premise that androcentric and gender-polarizing lenses make it seem more normal and natural for a male, not a female, to be in a position of power, it was found that subjects seeing a male seated at the head of the table considered him the leader of the group, but the same benefit of position was not extended to a female seated at the head of the table—she was not perceived as a leader.[12]

As an example of how androcentric and gender-polarizing lenses can together shape the perception of the social arrangements in the culture as a whole, consider the prototypical American view of whether there are now far too many men or just about the right percentage of men in positions of power and influence in American society. Although the gender lenses were able at one time in U.S. history to make even the total legal exclusion of women from such positions hardly worthy of comment, today the lenses not only make the presence of but one woman out of nine on the Supreme Court and one woman out of fifteen in the House and one out of fifty in the Senate seem like a reasonable ratio; they also make the prototypical American blind to the fact that the culture is miscontruing the continued male domination of its social institutions as at least a first approximation of sexual equality. The androcentric and gender-polarizing lenses would not allow the analogous mistake if females dominated those institutions instead of males.

Finally, as an example of how androcentric and gender-polarizing lenses can together shape the perception of what feels natural for the self, consider the observation made plausible by many studies that males and females alike see other males and females, as well as themselves, as subject to one standard of judgment if female and another standard of judgment if male. More specifically, whereas males see themselves and other males as both competent and deserving until proven otherwise (at least if they are white), the burden of proof is on each individual female to demonstrate to herself and to others why she in particular should be seen as either competent or deserving. This burden-of-proof difference is precisely what that social-psychological study showed when it found males—but not females—more likely to be selected as the group leader when they just happened to be seated at the head of the table. This burden-of-proof difference is also what many other empirical studies showed when they found that women underestimate, and men overestimate, the quality of their own performance and, furthermore, that women underreward themselves, and men overreward themselves, for whatever their level of performance actually is.[13]

This androcentric and gender-polarizing way of looking at the self predisposes females to reject any way of being or behaving that treats females as people whose needs, desires, abilities, and interests are to be taken seriously. This includes such things as requesting a merit raise from an employer, submitting an article for publication, competing head on head, or, for that matter, taking one's talents and interests seriously enough in the first place to embark on an important personal project. It also predisposes females to elaborate ways of being and behaving that subordinate their own needs, desires, abilities, and interests to those of the men and the children in their lives.

wage
cnegotiation

In addition to putting females at risk for giving themselves too little priority in relationships with others, this androcentric and gender-polarizing way of looking at the self also puts males at risk for giving themselves too much priority in relationships with others. Specifically, it predisposes males to reject any ways of being and behaving that put them in a subordinate position—a predisposition that is exaggerated whenever the more dominant position is to be held by a woman. It also predisposes males to elaborate any ways of being or behaving that put them in a more dominant or powerful position.

With this whole discussion of androcentric and gender-polarizing lenses as a conceptual backdrop, it is clear that women are culturally predisposed to give themselves much less priority than they rightfully deserve while men are culturally predisposed to give themselves much more priority than they rightfully deserve. It is also clear that on psychological grounds alone, the heterosexual marriage is a perfect breeding ground for inequality because it brings a male assumer of privilege together with a female denier of privilege.

But as powerful as the internalized gender lenses are, and as critical as they are to the self-construction of gendered personalities, it would be wrong to suppose that men's and women's different and unequal ways of being and behaving are created only by acts of self-perception and self-construction. Their ways of being and behaving are simultaneously constructed by the androcentric and gender-polarizing social practices of the culture, which continue to situate males and females in different and unequal positions in the social structure throughout their life cycle. There is thus never just a psychological force responsible for the construction of real men and real women; there is always a structural or situational force operating in the same direction.

NOTES

1. I am indebted to Berger (1963) for suggesting the first enculturation process and to Shweder (1984) for suggesting the second.

2. This theoretical discussion of enculturation has been greatly influenced by Berger (1963), Shweder & LeVine (1984), Geertz (1973, 1983), and Shweder (1984). For more on the social construction of the child, see Edelstein (1983), Kessen (1979), Kessel & Siegel (1983), Tobin et al. (1989), and especially Wartofsky (1983).

3. This discussion of American individualism has been much informed by Bellah et al. (1985), Geertz (1983), Hsu (1985), Ochs & Schieffelin (1984), and Shweder & Bourne (1984).

4. See chapter 10, entitled "Space Speaks," in E. T. Hall (1973).

5. Anne Z. Parker, University of Oregon Geography Department, personal communication.

6. See Connell (1987) for further discussion of these female job types. For more on sex segregation in the workplace generally, see Reskin (1984), Reskin & Hartmann (1986), and Reskin & Roos (1990).

7. For a sample of this feminist critique, see Martyna (1980); for recommendations on alternative forms, see Frank & Treichler (1989).

8. For more on my own analysis of gender-liberated child-rearing, see the final sections of my 1983, 1984, 1985, and 1989 works.

9. For evidence documenting the greater prohibition of cross-gender activity and clothing choice for boys than for girls, see Carter & McCloskey (1983–1984), Fagot (1977, 1985), Fling & Manosevitz (1972), Langlois & Downs (1980), and Stoddart & Turiel (1985). For a provocative analysis of the cultural significance of cross-dressing in history, literature, film, photography, and popular and mass culture, see Garber (1992).

10. The constructivist tradition in personality psychology is exemplified by Allport (1961), Kelly (1955), Bem & Allen (1974), and Caspi, Bem & Elder (1989). For a discussion of other constructivist personality theories, see Bem (1987). The constructivist tradition in cognitive psychology was solidly established as dominant in the field by Ulrich Neisser's 1967 textbook, *Cognitive Psychology.* For a more accessible introduction to Neisser's views, see Neisser (1976). For an extended introduction to this whole perspective, see Glass & Holyoak (1985) and Gardner (1985).

11. For more detailed summaries of these and other empirical studies on the behavioral limitations of conventionally gendered people, see Bem (1978, 1983, 1985). For a more complete discussion of the unconventionally gendered people, who are interesting in their own right but who are not singled out here because of certain theoretical and empirical complexities unrelated to the current argument, see Bem (1985), Frable & Bem (1985), and Frable (1990).

12. The only exception to this pattern was when the members of the group were all male or all female, in which case the benefit of position was extended to anyone seated at the head of the table (Porter & Geis, 1981; Porter et al., 1983).

13. For a good introduction to this research, see pp. 246–249 of Lott (1987) or pp. 129–137 of Matlin (1987). For another good introduction to the general area of feminist psychology, see Unger & Crawford (1992).

REFERENCES

Allport, G. W. (1961). *Pattern and Growth in Personality.* New York: Holt, Rinehart & Winston.

Bakan, D. (1966). *The Duality of Human Existence.* Chicago: Rand McNally.

Bellah, R. N., Madsen, R., Sullivan, W. M., Swidler, A., & Tipton, S. M. (1985). *Habits of the Heart: Individualism and Commitment in American Life.* New York: Harper.

Bem, D. J., & Allen, A. (1974). On Predicting Some of the People Some of the Time: The Search for Cross-Situational Consistencies in Behavior. *Psychological Review, 81,* 506–520.

Bem, S. L. (1975). Sex Role Adaptability: One Consequence of Psychological Androgyny. *Journal of Personality and Social Psychology, 31,* 634–643.

Bem, S. L. (1978). Beyond Androgyny: Some Presumptuous Prescriptions for a Liberated Gender Identity. In J. A. Sherman & F. L. Denmark (Eds.), *The Psychology of Women: Future Directions in Research* (pp. 1–23). New York: Psychological Dimensions.

Bem, S. L. (1981). Gender Schema Theory: A Cognitive Account of Sex Typing. *Psychological Review, 88*, 354–364.

Bem, S. L. (1983). Gender Schema Theory and Its Implications for Child Development: Raising Gender-Aschematic Children in a Gender-Schematic Society. *Signs: Journal of Women in Culture and Society, 8*, 598–616.

Bem, S. L. (1984). From Biology to Feminism: Reply to Morgan and Ayim. *Signs: Journal Women in Culture and Society, 10*, 197–199.

Bem, S. L. (1985). Androgyny and Gender Schema Theory: A Conceptual and Empirical Integration. In T. B. Sonderegger (Ed.), *Nebraska Symposium on Motivation, 1984: Psychology and Gender* (pp. 179–226). Lincoln: University of Nebraska Press.

Bem, S. L. (1987). Gender Schema Theory and the Romantic Tradition. In P. Shaver & C. Hendrick (Eds.), *Review of Personality and Social Psychology* (Vol. 7, pp. 251–271) Newbury Park, Calif.: Sage.

Bem, S. L. (1989). Genital Knowledge and Gender Constancy in Preschool Children. *Child Development, 60*, 649–662.

Bem, S. L., & Lenney, E. (1976). Sex Typing and the Avoidance of Cross-Sex Behavior. *Journal of Personality and Social Psychology, 33*, 48–54.

Bem, S. L., Martyna, W., & Watson, C. (1976). Sex Typing and Androgyny: Further Explorations of the Expressive Domain. *Journal of Personality and Social Psychology, 34*, 1016–1023.

Berger, P. L. (1963). *Invitation to Sociology: A Humanistic Perspective.* New York: Doubleday.

Carter, D. B., & McCloskey, L. A. (1983/1984). Peers and the Maintenance of Sex-Typed Behavior: The Development of Children's Conceptions of Cross-Gender Behavior in Their Peers. *Social Cognition, 2*, 294–314.

Caspi, A., Bem, D. J., & Elder, G. H., Jr. (1989). Continuities and Consequences of Interactional Styles across the Life Course. *Journal of Personality, 57*, 375–406.

Connell, R. W. (1987). *Gender and Power.* Stanford, CA: Stanford University Press.

Edelstein, W. (1983). Cultural Constraints on Development and the Vicissitudes of Progress. In F. S. Kessel, & A. W. Siegel (Eds.). *The Child and Other Cultural Constructions* (pp. 48–81). New York: Praeger.

Erikson, E. H. (1968). Womanhood and the Inner Space. In E. H. Erikson (Ed.), *Identity: Youth and Crisis* (pp. 261–294). New York: Norton.

Fagot, B. I. (1977). Consequences of Moderate Cross-Gender Behavior in Pre-School Children. *Child Development, 48*, 902–907.

Fagot, B. I. (1985). Beyond the Reinforcement Principle: Another Step Toward Understanding Sex Role Development. *Developmental Psychology, 21*, 1097–1104.

Fling, S., & Manosevitz, M. (1972). Sex Typing in Nursery School Children's Play Interests. *Developmental Psychology, 7*, 146–152.

Frable, D. E. S. (1990). Marginal and Mindful: Deviants in Social Interactions. *Journal of Personality and Social Psychology, 59*, 140–149.

Frable, D. E. S., & Bem, S. L. (1985). If You're Gender-Schematic, All Members of the Opposite Sex Look Alike. *Journal of Personality and Social Psychology, 49*, 459–468.

Frank, F. W., & Treichler, P. A. (Eds.). (1989). *Language, Gender, and Professional Writing. Theoretical Approaches and Guidelines for Nonsexist Usage.* New York: Modern Language Association of America.

Garber, M. (1992). *Vested Interests: Cross-Dressing and Cultural Anxiety.* New York: Routledge.

Gardner, H. (1985). *The Mind's New Science: A History of the Cognitive Revolution.* New York: Basic Books.

Geertz, C. (1973). *The Interpretation of Cultures.* New York: Basic Books.

Geertz, C. (1983). From the Native's Point of View: On the Nature of Anthropological Understanding. In C. Geertz (Ed.), *Local Knowledge: Further Essays in Interpretive Anthropology* (pp. 55–70). New York: Basic Books.

Glass, A. L., & Holyoak, K. J. (1985). *Cognition.* New York: Random House.

Hall, E. T. (1973). *The Silent Language.* Garden City, NY: Anchor Press/Doubleday.

Hsu, F. L. K. (1985). The Self in Cross-Cultural Perspective. In A. J. Marsella, G. DeVos & F. L. K. Hsu (Eds.), *Culture and Self: Asian and Western Perspectives* (pp. 24–55). New York: Tavistock.

Kelly, G. A. (1955). *The Psychology of Personal Constructs.* New York: Norton.

Kessel, F. S., & Siegel, A. W. (Eds.). (1983). *The Child and Other Cultural Inventions.* New York: Praeger.

Kessen, W. (1979). The American Child and Other Cultural Inventions. *American Psychologist, 34,* 815–820.

Langlois, J. H., & Downs, A. C. (1980). Mothers, Fathers, and Peers as Socialization Agents of Sex-Typed Play Behaviors in Young Children. *Child Development, 51,* 1237–1247.

Lott, B. (1987). *Women's Lives: Themes and Variations in Gender Learning.* Monterey, CA: Brooks/Cole.

Martyna, W. (1980). Beyond the He/Man Approach: The Case for Nonsexist Language. *Signs: Journal of Women in Culture and Society, 5,* 492–493.

Matlin, M. W. (1987). *The Psychology of Women.* New York: Holt, Rinehart & Winston.

Neisser, U. (1967). *Cognitive Psychology.* New York: Appleton-Century-Crofts.

Neisser, U. (1976). *Cognition and Reality: Principles and Implications of Cognitive Psychology.* San Francisco: Freeman.

Ochs, E., & Schieffelin, B. B. (1984). Language Acquisition and Socialization: Three Developmental Stories and Their Implications. In R. A. Shweder & R. A. LeVine (Eds.), *Culture Theory: Essays on Mind, Self, and Emotion* (pp. 276–320). Cambridge, England: Cambridge University Press.

Parsons, T., & Bales, R. (1955). *Family, Socialization, and Inter-Action Process.* Glencoe, IL: Free Press.

Porter, N., & Geis, F. L. (1981). Women and Nonverbal Leadership Cues: When Seeing Is Not Believing. In C. Mayo & N. M Henley (Eds.), *Gender and Nonverbal Behavior* (pp. 39–61). New York: Springer-Verlag.

Porter, N., Geis, F. L., & Jennings, J. (1983). Are Women Invisible as Leaders? *Sex Roles, 9,* 1035–1049.

Reskin, B. F. (Ed.). (1984). *Segregation in the Workplace: Trends, Explanations, Remedies.* Washington, DC: National Academy Press.

Reskin, B. F., & Hartmann, H. I. (Eds.). (1986). *Woman's Work, Men's Work: Sex Segregation on the Job.* Washington DC: National Research Council.

Reskin, B. F., & Roos, P. A. (1990). *Job Queues, Gender Queues: Explaining Women's Inroads into Male Occupations.* Philadelphia: Temple University Press.

Shweder, R. A. (1984). Anthropology's Romantic Rebellion against the Enlightenment: Or, There's More to Thinking Than Reason and Evidence. In R. A. Shweder & R. A. LeVine (Eds.), *Culture Theory: Essays on Mind, Self, and Emotion* (pp. 27–66). Cambridge, England: Cambridge University Press.

Shweder, R. A., & Bourne, E. J. (1984). Does the Concept of the Person Vary Cross-Culturally? In R. A. Shweder & R. A. LeVine (Eds.), *Culture Theory: Essays on Mind, Self, and Emotion* (pp. 158–199). Cambridge, England: Cambridge University Press.

Shweder, R. A., & LeVine, R. A. (Eds.). (1984). *Culture Theory: Essays on Mind, Self, and Emotion.* Cambridge, England: Cambridge University Press.

Stoddart, T., & Turiel, E. (1985). Children's Concepts of Cross-Gender Activities. *Child Development, 56,* 1241–1252.

Tobin, J. J., Wu, D. Y. H., & Davidson, D. H. (1989). *Preschool in Three Cultures: Japan, China, and the United States.* New Haven, CT: Yale University Press.

Unger, R. K., & Crawford, M. (1992). *Women and Gender: A Feminist Psychology.* New York: McGraw-Hill.

Wartofsky, M. (1983). The Child's Construction of the World and the World's Construction of the Child: From Historical Epistemology to Historical Psychology. In F. S. Kessel & A. W. Siegel (Eds.). (1983). *The Child and Other Cultural Inventions* (pp. 188–215). New York: Praeger.

Chapter Twenty-Three

The Male "Wound"

Liam Hudson and Bernadine Jacot

Step by Step, Our Paths Diverge

To begin with, in the earliest stages of the foetus's growth, only its chromosomes enable us to distinguish female from male. Although they will later develop either into testes or into ovaries, the male and female embryos' gonads are at this stage alike. The male's gonads grow more quickly than the female's, though; and, within a few weeks of conception, the male's are recognizable as testes. In another week or so, specialized cells make their appearance in the male's testes and, triggered by secretions from the placenta, these begin in turn to secrete the sex hormone testosterone. This causes the male's external genitalia to take shape as a penis and scrotum. From other specialized cells in the male's testes, there is also secreted a second hormone. This serves to atrophy the structures that, in the female, will later develop into the fallopian tubes. But it is the action of testosterone, it seems, that is crucial. Without it, the external genitalia of both sexes take the female form.

For the vast majority of mortals, this is the parting of the ways. Thereafter, we are each destined to live inside a body recognized as male or recognized as female. To the extent that our bodies are our fates, this is the point at which these are sealed.

Although there have been dissenting voices, the orthodox view is that the female pattern is the basic one, and that the male pattern is a systematic, genetically programmed variation upon it, triggered by the action of the relevant sex hormones. This is certainly the view taken by Tanner. "The female," he says, "is the 'basic' sex into which embryos develop if not stimulated to do otherwise."[1] It is also the attitude expressed by Stoller:

> The biologic rules governing sexual behavior in mammals are simple. In all, including man, the "resting state" of tissue—brain and peripheral—is female. We can now demonstrate without exception, in all experiments performed on animals, that if androgens in the proper amount and biochemical form are withheld during critical periods in fetal life, anatomy and behavior typical of that species' males do not occur, regardless of genetic sex. And if androgens in the proper amount and form are introduced during critical periods in fetal life, anatomy and behavior typical of that

Liam Hudson & Bernadine Jacot, "The Male 'Wound.'" In L. Hudson & B. Jacot, *The Way Men Think*, pp. 37–58. New Haven: Yale University Press. © 1991 by Yale University Press. Reprinted with permission.

species' males do occur, regardless of genetic sex. We cannot experiment on humans, but no natural experiments (for example, chromosomal disorders) are reported that contradict the general mammalian rule.[2]

For boys, but not for girls, a further surge of testosterone occurs in the six months after birth. Little work has yet been done on the psychological implications of this second surge, but it is a period in which important structures are taking shape in the brain, and in which differential effects on male and female could well arise. Evidence is still sketchy, but there are indications that visual perception in four-, five- and six-month-old girls is superior to that of boys, because, it has been suggested, testosterone inhibits the development of the appropriate cortical tissues in boys.[3]

Our own argument begins with another such parting of the ways. This occurs in infancy, in the two or three years after birth rather than in the months before it; and instead of being anatomical and physiological, it is psychological—a question, that is to say, of individuals' perceptions of who they are and how they relate to the people who constitute their intimate world. Although impossible to locate neatly in time, this shift undoubtedly occurs; and it, too, moves the male away from a pattern which, until then, both sexes have shared. We are by no means the first to notice that this is so. We do seem to be the first, though, to realize how powerfully two-edged the implications of this developmental change are bound to be, and how comprehensively it undermines certain simple-minded beliefs about the paths men and women are subsequently at liberty to follow.[4]

The theoretical background is familiar and is at heart straightforward. As infants, both male and female usually draw primitive comfort and security from their mother or mother-substitute. It is on this intimate, symbiotic relationship with a caring and supportive maternal presence that the subsequent normality of an infant's development depends. As Greenacre says, the foetus "moves about, kicks, turns around, reacts to some external stimuli by increased motion. It swallows, and traces of its own hair are found in the meconium. It excretes urine and sometimes passes stool." Grunberger likens the uterus, accordingly, to "a heavenly, radiant source of bliss and a chamberpot."[5] It is this pre-natal experience of wholly unqualified physical intimacy which is sustained in the symbiotic intimacy between mother and child. Where this bond is lacking, the individual's subsequent competence as an adult is disturbed—for chimpanzees no less than for human beings, as the Harlows' "terry towelling mother" experiments show. In chimpanzees, mating and maternal behavior are disrupted; in humans, it seems to be the capacity to form intimate relationships which is most seriously impaired.[6] It is also in the context of this symbiotic bond with the mother, though, that the infant will first experience pain and frustration: milk that is not instantly forthcoming, griping pains in the stomach, the urge to explore thwarted. The mother, to put the same point in another way, becomes the butt not only of the infant's warmest pleasures but also of its fear and rage.

As well as establishing a position for itself vis-à-vis the emotionally charged features of its world, the infant must also establish a sense of its maleness or femaleness: its gender identity. For the little girl, it is easy to see what is at stake. She remains identified with her mother; the source of all her most potent emotions, positive and negative, pleasurable and painful. As a result, she perceives herself as the same sort of being as her mother, through and through. If, as she probably does, she learns to perceive both her mother and herself as an amalgam of the pleasure-provoking and the pain-provoking, the "good" and the "bad," her sense of herself is to that extent internally fissured. Nevertheless, she remains all of a piece with the creature, her mother, on whom her sense of reality depends. When the little girl moves on to establish for herself an appropriate "object" on whom to focus her desires, she again has her mother available to her as model. She can follow the line of her mother's gaze towards her father and towards other males. The object of her desire is thus a creature inherently unfamiliar to her, even alien, but one whom she addresses from a psychologically coherent foundation.

The male infant's task is dissimilar. As the psychoanalyst Ralph Greenson seems to have been the first to point out, if the little boy is to identify with his father, he must first separate himself imaginatively from his mother—until then, the source of all comfort and security.[7] Greenson describes this as "a special vicissitude." "I am referring to the fact," he says, "that the male child, in order to attain a healthy sense of maleness, must replace the primary object of his identification, the mother, and must identify instead with the father." It is this additional step, he believes, that accounts for the special problems from which the adult male suffers and from which the adult female is exempt.

Dis-identification and Counter-identification

This first step, the one that the little boy takes in order to free himself from his symbiotic connection to his mother, Greenson refers to as *dis-identification*. The subsequent step, independent of the first, and which enables him positively to identify with his father, Greenson calls *counter-identification*. The first establishes the boy's separateness; the second, his maleness. *It is these two developmental processes in combination which we call the male wound.*[8]

With the benefit of hindsight, it is possible to see Greenson's account of the consequences of dis-identification and counter-identification as too limited, but there is no doubting the shrewdness of the insight itself. In order to align himself with his father, the little boy first creates within himself a dislocation; and in as much as he imitates his father's object choice—his desire for women—he must do so with this dislocation as its prior condition.

Initially, while symbiotically connected to their mother, both son and daughter perceive their father as "other." But then, as the male gender identity crystallizes, the son sees that "other" (his father) as "same," and what was "same" (his mother) as "other." That is to say, *the son experiences a reversal—one of similarity-in-difference and difference-in-similarity—which his sister does not.* The elements of this reversal carry a powerful emotional charge; and its form, we are going to argue, is one which will echo and reverberate throughout the male's subsequent experience. If we are right, it is in the light of this reversal that each of the male's later ventures will be cast, his choice of work and imaginative expression no less than the character of his sexual desire.

No one yet knows what causes the male infant to divert his attention from his mother, to dis-identify. It seems likely that, in some way as yet unestablished, he is biologically influenced to do so. For reasons eventually traceable to the intrauterine environment, say, he may be more restless than his sisters, less tolerant of frustration, less attuned to the eye contact on which intimate traffic with his mother depends.[9] Male and female infants, in other words, may be biologically programmed to respond differently to a given maternal regime.

An alternative line of explanation, on which there are several variants, is more transactional. It holds, again for reasons that may be largely biological in origin, that most mothers from the very outset treat their male infants in one way, their female infants in another. There is evidence that mothers, while their babies are still new-born, are more likely to initiate interactions with their daughters than with their sons; and that in these interactions, it is the infant's physical movement which plays a central part in the case of the sons, whereas in the case of daughters it is mutuality of vocalization and gaze.[10] As Hinde and Stevenson-Hinde have stressed, quite small sex differences in biological propensity on the infant's part will in any case be quickly magnified by the mother, whose perception is bound to be influenced by cultural stereotypes of maleness and femaleness, and who is bound, too, to see her son as "other" in a way that her daughter is not.[11]

The child whom the mother sees as "other," it is important to grasp, does actually differ in material ways from his sisters. While boys become larger and stronger than girls, girls mature more rapidly. Halfway through pregnancy, the development of the skeleton is already three weeks more advanced in girls than in boys. At birth the difference in maturation corresponds to four to six weeks of normal growth, and by the time puberty is reached, to two years. This sex difference is common to many mammals and nearly all primates, and while the impact on the body is less than entirely uniform, the "girls earlier" rule has few exceptions. Although both sexes acquire their milk teeth at the same time—one of those few exceptions—the permanent teeth erupt earlier in girls, and the canines by as much as eleven months.[12] We know too that by the sixth or seventh month, girls are beginning to display greater powers of physical co-ordination than boys; and, more specifically, that they are more likely than boys to gain a measure of control over their urinary function.[13] Girls are also quicker to acquire a control over language. At any given stage, their vocabulary is larger than that of boys and they are more articulate. Such differences are bound to be ones that are perceived, at least in part, as ones of responsiveness; of repaying the nurture the mother provides. However subliminally, the small boy will accordingly be perceived as the more intransigent partner in the parent/child relationship, the small girl as the more rewarding (or biddable) one.

An adjacent train of thought expands on this differential perception on the mother's part. Long before her son is in a position to sit up—which he usually does at the age of eight or nine months—and to discover what his own genital apparatus looks like, his mother will be alert to this difference between his anatomy and her own. She may not simply see him as "other," that is to say; she may become erotically invested in his "otherness." It could be this erotic preoccupation, sometimes physically expressed, which hastens her son's disidentification. It does so, it might be argued, because he fears engulfment by his mother; because he is sensitive not just to his mother's erotic investment in him but also to her guilty ambivalence about that investment; or, as classical Freudian theory suggests, because he intuits that his mother's body differs anatomically from his own, and that this discovery creates in him intolerable anxiety.[14]

We do not know which of these explanatory avenues will prove the most satisfactory. Whatever the predisposing circumstances turn out to be, it is clear that Greenson's insight permits three quite different patterns:

- The conventional one, in which the biological male dis-identifies with his mother and counter-identifies with his father;
- The biological male who neither dis-identifies nor counter-identifies; and
- The biological male who dis-identifies but fails to counter-identify.

Of these patterns, it is the first, we are arguing, that yields the "male" male—the man who sees himself as male and acts as a male. The second leads to effeminacy, even in extreme cases to transsexuality—in adulthood, the man who, for all purposes of gender identity, is in substantially the same position as his sister, except that he will somehow have had to accommodate the fact that his own reproductive anatomy and secondary sexual characteristics are unlike his mother's and sister's, and like his father's and brother's. The third yields the male who in adulthood experiences a sense of androgyny or genderlessness.

Granted that no one knows how biology, psychology and culture interact in causing the wound, it would be an error to advance detailed qualifications. Nevertheless, it is easy to see how the effects of dis-identification and counter-identification might arise at later ages than the one we envisage—in adolescence, say, rather than at two or three. Appropriate scenarios can be conjured up. In one, a mother brings up her son alone. When her son is in his early teens, she marries and son and stepfather subsequently establish a close bond. In such cases, the son's sense of himself as male could be real enough, but it may be less deeply rooted, less apparently instinctual, than it otherwise might. He may seem to belong to the first of the patterns just outlined, but in truth more nearly belongs to the second or third.

As one reflects on Greenson's distinction, it becomes clear, too, that other outcomes are possible. These are of special interest in that they help make explicit certain of the assumptions on which the theory of identification rests. Particularly, one can envisage:

- The male child who counter-identifies with his father without first having dis-identified with his mother.

At first sight implausible, such a pattern might arise in a household where the personalities of mother and father are somewhat similar, where both are emotionally distant in their dealings with their son, and where the responsibilities for his nurture are shared. The net effect, from the son's point of view, would be a personality in which the "male" and "female" are weakly etched and poorly differentiated. It is also a pattern, though, that could take a more extreme form. In this, both "male" and "female" characteristics are pronounced, coexisting on the strength of segregations and dissociations that, to the outside eye, are bound to seem arbitrary.

Such outcomes aside, one can also picture:

- The male child who dis-identifies with his mother, but counter-identifies with another woman.

The context for the emergence of such a pattern might be the community in which the care of children is the responsibility of women collectively. Likewise:

- The male child who dis-identifies with his mother, but counter-identifies, subsequently, not with a person but with an emotionally charged idea or symbol: the Fatherland, the Hero (Napoleon), the Leader (Stalin), the Genius (Beethoven or Freud).

Households in which the father is weak or absent form a likely setting for this configuration, likewise cultures where massive coercive pressures are brought to bear on children in the service of a civic ideal.[15] As social psychologists point out, identifications with figures outside the family in any case become increasingly significant as a child grows older, developing both a social identity and the potential for extravagant commitments and loyalties.[16]

The fifth and sixth of these patterns also raise an important issue of interpretation. The common-sense assumption is that the father or father-substitute must be present for counter-identification to occur. Such evidence as we have tends to bear this out. Another train of thought is less literal. It assumes that the maleness at issue is abstract: a property not of individuals but of the disciplines inherent in child-raising and in the child's acquisition of impersonal symbolic skills. Either parent can be seen both as a source of physical and psychological comfort and as the embodiment of authority. On this argument, the male child counter-identifies not with his father, but with those aspects of his parents he intuitively perceives as impersonal (and in that sense "male"). The role of the father, on this view, is essentially confirmatory. He consolidates developmental changes that can take place of their own accord within the confines of the mother/son relationship.[17]

Without doubt, identity and identification are awkward notions, the modeling at issue concerning not just what one does but who one is; not just behavioral patterns and propensities, but states of being. These are precisely the sorts of question with which philosophers, and especially Anglo-Saxon philosophers, have traditionally had difficulty. (In Exodus 3, God appears to Moses in a burning bush and says to him, "I AM THAT I AM." Moses's correct response, the Oxford philosophers of our youth would insist, was "You are that you are *what?*") Practically speaking, there is a distinction between the person's social identity—as a Catholic, or a member of the working class, or a Liverpool fan—and the identifications implicit in the mother/infant relationship, the first being the province of the social psychologist, the second that of the developmental psychologist and psychoanalyst.[18] In the latter, fundamental questions are at issue; ones about what it is that passes between any two people who are emotionally significant to one another. For our intimate relationships commit us not just to propinquity and rational dialogue, but to the non-rational; to a hazardous two-way traffic in unacknowledged desires and fears.[19]

The Costs

One commentator's reassuring conclusion is that "identity is a concept no one has defined with precision, but it seems we can move ahead anyway, because everyone roughly understands what is meant."[20] Our own policy, certainly, rather than compounding difficulties of theory already dense, is to concentrate on consequences rather than causes.

In as much as he sees himself as male and acts as a male, the boy is cut off from the primitive comfort his mother could otherwise provide. It must follow, then—for lack of a better metaphor—that most males differ from most females in terms of what they have "inside" them. Inside most males but not inside most females there must be a species of existential gulf. This, as Greenson and others have pointed out, will act to the male's disadvantage.[21] The male's position is by no means entirely bleak, even so. It consists, in fact, of a pattern of strengths and shortcomings; and it is these we want to explore.

On the debit side, there are two shortcomings to which the adult male is particularly vulnerable:

- Personal insensitivity, and
- Misogyny

The small boy, Greenson's insight enables us to predict, will find it more difficult than his sister to reciprocate affection, and his capacity for empathy will be impaired. He will tend to see those aspects of the world that are unmistakably emotional in black and white terms, either as heaven-on-earth or as unspeakably distasteful. He will be slow, too, to make sense of emotions that conflict; to detect the many shades of grey that separate black from white, and to realize that greys are often blacks and whites intricately mixed. Whatever his strengths elsewhere, in the field of intimate relations the "male" male is bound to be at a disadvantage; even something of a cripple. His ability to experience a relationship as "intersubjective"—as a meeting of experiential worlds—will be curtailed.

In stepping clear of the warm, symbiotic presence of his mother, the small boy may also leave unresolved a sense of loss and resentment; and perhaps, too, the fear of punishment or revenge. A consequence is that there will often exist in the male mind subterranean currents of violently negative sentiment; and that while these will in some cases work themselves out in symbolic form, remote from their source, in others they will focus directly on the female sex and on the female body. We would predict, then, that beneath the surface of his attitudes to the opposite sex the adult male will often betray potently misogynous attitudes and fantasies. Women may well be idealized, and the idea of sexual access to them idealized too. But, at the same time, there may circulate—perhaps just within the range of awareness, perhaps *inone*

beyond it—the vision of women as polluters, beheaders and castrators; creatures to be feared, and in whom, despite appearances, sinister powers reside.

These misogynous preoccupations are expressed stereotypically in Don Juan, the sexual athlete who perceives women as desirable objects, and who ravishes them, but who must make good his escape before the potentially engulfing dangers of sexual intimacy can wreak their havoc. They were also expressed with formidable accuracy during the Renaissance, in the northern, incipiently Protestant, tradition of painting and sculpting the female nude. Where the Italian tradition of Titian and Veronese depicted the nude in idealized terms, the draughtsmen and carvers working north of the Alps explored in minute detail precisely those ambivalences and reversals to which heterosexual desire renders the male subject. Naked rather than nude, the "bulb-like" women and "root-like" men of this northern art, as Kenneth Clark remarks, seem dragged from the protective darkness of the previous thousand years.[22] The alternative convention of the nude thus created is based on different bodily proportions from those established by the Greeks—broader in the hip, narrower in the shoulder, longer, more pear-like in the abdomen. It also dwells on puckers and wrinkles, not on the judicious arrangement of smoothed surfaces and coherent volumes.

Perhaps the definitive statement of this extraordinary vein of invention and discovery is Conrad Meit's carving of Judith and Holofernes. Small and made of alabaster, Meit's *Judith* was produced in the first quarter of the sixteenth century. One commentator speaks of her serene command of space, but finds her eroticism "almost repulsive." Another sees her as "probably the most satisfying" expression of the Renaissance the north ever saw.[23]

At first sight, especially to the eye trained in classical proportions, Judith is grotesque: head and hips too big, rib-cage and breasts too small; the distance from breast to navel twice what we expect it to be. Unathletic, her stomach protrudes and her flesh threatens to sag; a body not only able to bear children but one which has already done so. In her right hand, close to her naked pelvis, she props a massive sword, the handle held abstractedly, very much as if it were an erect penis which was not particularly her concern. In her left hand, held away from her, separated from the sword handle by her lower abdomen and clearly carved vaginal cleft, is Holofernes's bearded head. It is severed; and, holding it by its hair, she is balancing it casually on a plinth. The male has been dismantled, head in one of Judith's hands, sword in the other. As many commentators have noticed, Judith, far from being the grotesque she initially seems, proves on closer inspection to embody an unusually insistent sexual allure. Consequently, the conjunction of sword handle, vagina and severed head could scarcely be more eloquent. Here is the intimation that the male psyche, unlike the female one, is the kind of apparatus which comes apart. Its competences are real—the beard is manly, the sword convincingly massive—but it is subject to collapse when in proximity to the naked female body. It is in physical intimacy with the opposite sex, we are being told, and, more specifically, in sexual intercourse, that such dismantlings of the male psyche take place.[24]

Misogyny, then, is not a feature of the male mind which is simply a byproduct of a narrow-minded upbringing or of sexist biases in education. It is built into the male psyche. Stemming from fears which are a direct consequence of the wound, it lingers in a hinterland where notions of separation and engulfment, erotic excitement and dismay mingle. These fears, obviously, can express themselves in a variety of ways. In a generalized horror of women. In a specific revulsion from sexual intercourse with them, even though their presence is otherwise seen as pleasurable and a reassurance. Or in panic once sexual intercourse with them has been enjoyed. If they are not to be expressed destructively, these are sentiments which must somehow be contained or translated as they were by Meit.

The Benefits

There are, however, more positive consequences in store. Three interest us particularly. These concern:

- The idea of agency—the individual's freedom, that is to say, to act on the world in the light of his own needs and intentions;
- The wound as a constantly replenishing source of psychic energy;
- The notion of abstract passions.

If his search for an alternative focus of identification is successful, the little boy has established for himself, as Greenson points out, a measure of separation. Even more tellingly, he has learnt a primitive lesson which he will not otherwise learn: that of *agency.*[25] Where, in sustaining her gender identity with her mother, the female infant must somehow accommodate whatever frustration is inherent in the relation between them, the male infant discovers that you can reject a source of frustration, and, simultaneously, find a stance independent of it. This discovery will be made at the cost of anxiety, no doubt, and of anxiety's attendant suppressions and repressions; but it is a valuable one, even so. The more "male" the male, the greater the imaginative gulf separating him from his sources of primitive comfort; and the greater that gulf, we would predict, the greater his underlying existential insecurity is bound to be. He is perfectly poised, nevertheless, to heal his wound at one symbolic remove; to use the anxiety his separation provokes in him to create systems of ideas which can stand in the place of lost intimacy, and within which he can strive for coherence and harmony.[26]

Also, being rooted in a primitive separation, the male's energies are in principle inexhaustible. They will last as long as his wound lasts. With them at his command, he can go on for a lifetime searching for order in chaos. Alternatively, he can disrupt the forms of order that already exist—either for the pleasure of disrupting them, or with a view to replacing them with a form of order that is superior and identifiably his own. On this argument, the wound is not just an introduction to the experience of agency. It is an *energy source,* fueling symbolically significant action—typically in fields distant from mothers and fathers, sex and gender. The defining characteristic of such activity is that it is pursued with passion; not for extraneous reasons like profit or status, but as an end in itself. As Anthony Storr has pointed out, conventional psychoanalytic theories tend to define good mental health by equating it with the ability to sustain rich human relationships.[27] But in the "male" male at least, the connections between creativeness, human relationships and mental health are not simple. The biographical evidence—and we shall rehearse what we hope are representative fragments of it later—suggests that the richest relationship many sane and highly creative men establish is with systems of ideas or with pieces of machinery.

From the moment an imagined space opens up between the small boy and his mother, we are suggesting, he is in principle primed to execute within it at least three separate but related sorts of maneuver. As he matures, he can pursue abstract ideas, which are, in a sense, surrogates for his mother, in that they bear a complex symbolic relation to her.[28] He can think about matters, personal or inanimate, in ways that rehearse and celebrate the distance from his mother he has created—he can think, that is to say, in ways that appear objective and dispassionate. And, the possibility of most immediate bearing on our own argument, he can pursue ideas quite unrelated to his mother with the kind of passion he had previously felt towards her. (Notice, we are not saying that the thought processes of the "male" male are distinctively objective. What we are saying is that he has a driven need to use his intelligence on impersonal problems; and that in doing so he can display remorseless powers of application.)[29]

Psychologists' efforts to come to terms with such phenomena have in the past had about them an air of contrivance. They usually suggest either that a biological energy—sex, aggression—has somehow been diverted or "sublimated" into a new channel; or that the motive underlying abstract thought cannot be what it seems; that, after all, it must boil down to ambition, say, or territoriality, or envy, or the desire for access to attractive members of the opposite sex. These explanatory enterprises, it has long been realized, sit uncomfortably with the facts as we know them: the small boy paying rapt attention to his collection of postage stamps; Isaac Newton absorbed to the exclusion of all other considerations by the laws of gravity. In contrast, the idea of the male wound offers a plausible account of just such absorption: that it springs from a dissociative movement of the mind in which the inanimate—things, systems of ideas—acquires the intense emotional significance previously lodged in people, and in which people, stripped of that significance, are treated as though they were things.

It is the wound's capacity to engender fascination with the impersonal that immediately concerns us. For in doing so, it helps makes sense of what, in evolutionary terms, is our species' most conspicuous characteristic: *our capacity for abstract passion*. It explains our ability not merely to think analytically, nor even to think analytically with passionate intensity, but to think analytically and with passionate intensity about topics that have no detectable bearing on our ordinary biological appetites or needs. For the "male" male—and, in explanatory terms, this is crucial point—*such passions will be the more enduringly gratifying the more completely divorced from human relationships they are*. The more abstract their context, the more his enterprises take on a quality that is simultaneously impassioned and aesthetically pure. Nor is there any requirement that the operations the male performs within a framework of objectifying thought will themselves be disinterested in tone and inspiration. On the contrary, what is proposed is that the male can express within this framework—safely and at a distance—any of the impulses an intimate relationship might otherwise have inspired.

At the heart of our account of the psychology of the male imagination, then, is a two-part claim. That, in combination, dis-identification and counter-identification create in the "male" male a sense of agency, allied to a constantly replenishing source of imaginative energy. And that these same processes draw him towards the inanimate—the world of things, mechanisms, abstract ideas and systems within which he operates with the commitment and fervor we might otherwise have expected him to display towards people.[30]

The Intellectual and the Personal

A significant consequence of dis- and counter-identification, we assume, is the existence of complex patterns of linkage and splitting between the nature of a man's work and that of his private life.[31] Often, these linkages and segregations are highly specific. In a study of eminent men in British universities, for example, we found that the humanities, biology and physical science each had their own patterns of marriage, fertility and divorce. Many eminent men in the humanities had remained single, as many as four out of every ten distinguished classical scholars recording themselves as childless. In contrast, nearly all the eminent biological and physical scientists had followed a more conventional pattern, and were married with children.[32] We also found that rates of divorce varied strikingly from group to group, being six times as high, for instance, among eminent physicists as among eminent chemists. The most marked difference of all, though, occurred among the biologists. Those who had risen to eminence through the roles they had played in the fusion of old-fashioned biology with mathematics and the physical sciences—who had helped establish the modern discipline of genetics, for example—were some twenty-five times more likely to divorce than the biologists of the next decade who had implemented these pioneers' discoveries. It seems, in other words, that upheavals in the intellectual and personal spheres echo one another, serious matrimonial disturbance being most common among men in whom intellectual boundaries have been breached. In terms of Kuhn's distinction between "revolutionary" and "normal" science, divorce seems a close concomitant of the first, and to bear only an incidental relation to the second.[33]

The male's dis-identification and counter-identification can be partial or precarious. Where this happens, the abiding preoccupations of the individual in question will deviate significantly from the "male" norm. Some of the most subtle of these deviations arise in science, and, more specifically, in biology. An experimental scientist can approach living subject-matter reductively, with a view to explaining it in terms of mathematics, physics or chemistry. He can work on living forms as a taxonomist; distinguishing, cataloguing, counting. He can explore the living as Darwin did on HMS *Beagle,* hoping to gain access to its hidden laws. He can explore the living as some ecologists do, with a view to conserving and celebrating its variety. Most interesting of all in the present context, he can use biology as a platform from which to attack the human, showing that the distinctive features of our experience—our capacity for love and access to the transcendental—are in principle indistinguishable from those enjoyed by baboon or hamster.

In summary, the male is at liberty to relate the objectifying to the personal in a variety of ways. He can:

- Segregate his experience: on the one side of an invisible dividing line, rapt attention to the impersonal; on the other, the personal acknowledged but left to wither.

Alternatively, he can attempt to knit the personal and impersonal together. If a sustained attempt at integration is made, he may use the impersonal to:

- Attack the personal, and subjugate it; or
- Recreate it in symbolic terms.

The policy the individual adopts will be influenced by the position he occupied within his family as he grew up, and on the nature of the relations with his mother and father he enjoyed—not just his separation from one and his identification with the other, but the terms on which feelings of warmth and hostility within the family were expressed. Of the three options just listed, the first corresponds, in terms of roughest approximation, to the dominant preoccupations of *science and technology*. The second corresponds to the dominant preoccupations of the more fiercely reductive forms of *biology and psychology*. The third corresponds to the dominant preoccupations of the *creative arts*. Between them, in briefest outline, they encapsulate much of the rest of what we have to say.

Even where the long-term effects of dis-identification and counter-identification appear completely secure, hints of instability may nonetheless linger. If they do, the task of shoring up the relevant barricades will continue throughout life. Each venture into the realm of the abstract thus becomes an affirmation of the internal arrangements the wound originally set in place. As distant echoes, each venture may bring with it too the anxieties that thoughts of collapsing defenses and the prospect of re-engulfment provoke. Abstract thought thus becomes a venue for the expression not only of pleasures once associated with symbiotic intimacy, but also of the hostility (and in extreme cases, the panic) engendered by the thought that the symbiotically intimate will not stay in its allotted place. Like "the black tide of mud" that once threatened Freud, and against which his sexual theory was a bulwark, thoughts of excessive intimacy may menace even the most resolutely formal of thinkers, and—like Freud's vision of "occultism"—need repeatedly to be banished with each piece of work undertaken. Threatened access to such thoughts and fantasies may account not only for the combative atmosphere of so much science, but also for its tendency towards internecine rancor, differences in the preferred method of shoring up defenses appearing as dangerous as the incoming tide itself. More tellingly still, it may be the intuitively perceived encroachment of the excessively intimate which serves many (conceivably, all) abstract thinkers as their imaginative trigger, launching each of them on yet another venture into the realm of formal thought.

The Wound's Nature

Later, we are going to illustrate the qualities of the male imagination in more detail. Before we move on, it is important to be clear about the kinds of claim we are making on the wound's behalf, there being the risk that these will seem grandiose and overinclusive.

Our assertions are not ones about biology as destiny any more than they are about the effects of prejudice in a sexist society. As we have outlined it, the wound is a psychological phenomenon; an emergent property of the conjunction of a body with an alert and reflexive intelligence. It takes shape in response to biological realities, that is to say, but, once in being, has an autonomous life, propelling individuals imaginatively along different paths, facilitating heartfelt performance here, stifling it there.[34]

Of the wound we are saying that:

- It is a centrally placed feature of the "male" male's mental architecture;
- It is an energy source—a source of unresolved (and in principle unresolvable) tensions;
- It exerts a formative influence on the imaginative needs the male subsequently experiences;
- It imparts to the expression of those needs a characteristic bias or spin;
- Its action is evidenced by a loose-knit group of tell-tale signs;
- Its influence is of the kind that, in the short term, can often be overridden, but that tends stubbornly to reassert itself over the longer run; and
- Its forms of expression in the adult are protean.

To date, the tendency in psychology has been to propose relatively rigid sequences of developmental phases, and to see such sequences as marked by critical periods, during which learning most naturally and spontaneously occurs. It is also widely assumed, as we ourselves tend to, that the early years are the formative ones; and that it is the qualities acquired early in life that are the warp and weft of the adult personality. To change the metaphor, it is these qualities that seem *ingrained*. To change it again, they become, in the language of the engineer, part of the individual's "spec."

We must be cautious, though. The focus of our own research has been on the academic choices of adolescents, on the career paths of adults, and on the relation of adults' careers to their private lives. Research of this kind teaches an important lesson. It is variousness that characterizes biographical evidence. Whatever the eventual role or accomplishment, there is always, or almost always, more than one antecedent biographical pattern. In the development of adult traits and talents, in other words, one is dealing, as so often in psychology not with one-to-one linkages, but with the action on one another of a variety of causes within a network or lattice, and with the path or trajectory that a series of choices within that lattice creates. So, although the evidence about adults may sometimes yield clear-cut differences between "male" men and genderless or effeminate men, and between men as a whole and women as a whole, such differences are not the only form of evidence compatible with our theory of the wound. Differences of detail and nuance have a bearing on it too. Where stark differences do arise, these indicate not that the relevant options and linkages are themselves stark, but that, for one reason or another, the groups in question have steered consistently different routes though a complex lattice.

A feature of such lattice patterns is that a single point of departure is connected to widely diverse destinations, while closely adjacent destinations can be reached by a wide variety of routes.[35] We each carry our past with us, what is more. A man who follows a career like Truman Capote's will practice the art of the novelist in one way; a man who follows a career like Ernest Hemingway's will practice the same art in another. It is within a model of the mind in which sequences of choices interact and interdepend that our notion of the wound is deployed.

Predictions and Conjectures

If the theory discussed so far is substantially correct, we would expect that the wound's effects:

- Will be stable over broad stretches of the lifespan, not evanescent byproducts of the individual's culture or the social roles he happens to occupy;
- Will express themselves in observable, quantifiable terms among samples of men, and between samples of men and women, as well as in the lives of individuals; and
- Will be resistant to changes in patterns of child-raising and family life.

We would expect, too, that:

- In the lives both of individuals and of groups, the wound's effects will often be characterized by apparently arbitrary inconsistencies and segregations.

The existence of the wound leads us to expect that character traits like misogyny or personal insensitivity will express themselves spontaneously among men whose gender identity is clearly "male." But we are dealing with a system within which migrations and dissociations are the norm. So misogyny could turn out to express itself in different ways, discipline by discipline: in womanizing among poets, say, in celibacy among classical scholars, in high rates of divorce among radically innovative biologists, and in forthrightly sexist prejudice among engineers. Its expression could also alter within a discipline, decade by decade, as the nature of that discipline and recruitment to it change. So while expecting a quality like misogyny to express itself in both the intellectual and the sexual spheres of an individual's life, we remain alert to the possibility that its expression can become localized, specialized. A man may be treacherous in his work, treacherous in his sex life, or treacherous in both alike. Over the years, his mendacious tendencies may spread from his working life to his sex life, or vice versa. They may also migrate. A previously blameless working life may be invaded by the tendency to lie and finagle at just the point when his private life, previously distorted by hostile impulses, at last achieves a more decorous balance.[36]

Despite these propensities for translation and migration, we expect the evidence to reveal, both in its aggregate forms and in detail and nuance, the persistence of certain themes. We would expect the wound to be associated with:

- Segregations of the personal from the impersonal;
- A preoccupation with issues of intellectual control; and
- The conjunction of that control with partisan and aggressive sentiment.

More specifically, we would expect to find the wound associated with:

- Characteristic patterns of cost (misogyny, personal insensitivity) and benefit (agency, imaginative energy, abstract passion);
- Characteristic patterns of career choice; and
- Orderly relations between the first of these patterns and the second.

In terms of style, the "male" cast of mind will:

- Be intolerant of "messy" arguments—i.e., ones that lack formal structure and are, variously, intuitive, empathetic, indeterminate; and
- Emphasize the virtues of dispassion and objectivity (although what is displayed will usually be the exercise of intelligence in the service of enterprises which are partisan and combative, and in that sense impassioned and non-objective).

The existence of the wound also creates expectations of the evidence that are less clear-cut, and that have the status more of conjectures. Particularly, it leads us to expect the existence of "male" formats of thought. These will differ, of course, from field to field, but, in essence, their features are those of the wound itself.[37] The "male" mind should typically show a taste for:

- Arguments cast in terms of dualities and dialectical oppositions (like male/female, conscious/unconscious, mind/body, theory/evidence) and their reconciliations;
- Arguments that depend on the maintenance of conceptual boundaries and segregations (like that between natural sciences and the social ones), and on colonizing forays across such boundaries;
- Arguments (e.g., about classification) that depend on a deep preoccupation with similarities and differences;
- Arguments that are reductive, especially ones that explain the subtly experiential in terms of the prosaic and literal; and
- Arguments centering on ideas—often highly technical—the truth of which is perceived as luminous.

There are also grounds for suspecting, as we have already said, that even the most stable solutions to the dilemmas of dis- and counter-identification contain hints of precariousness; and that, as a consequence, the work of maintaining the wound's dissociations is never quite done. As we shall see, even in the most austerely abstract of "male" thought, traces of the wound's intimately human origin are often detectable, and are perhaps never finally expunged.

NOTES

1. Tanner (1978), p. 56. Rose, Kamin and Lewontin (1984), on the other hand, point to evidence that actively feminizing influences may be at work too.

2. Stoller (1985), p. 74.

3. Held (1989), Geschwind and Galaburda (1987).

4. Keller (1985) follows a train of thought adjacent to our own. A mathematical biophysicist, she was seized—in mid-stride, as it were—by the need to understand the "maleness" of the professional enterprise to which she was committed, and subsequently used psychoanalytic and feminist arguments in doing so.

The terrain where psychoanalysis and feminism meet, it has to be said, is one where a good deal of lambasting goes on. In the 1960s, feminist critics dismissed Freud's views on gender out of hand as sexist. Mitchell (1974) took them to task for failing to read what Freud had written. Chodorow in turn characterized Mitchell as an "apologist"; one who offers "a zealous defence of every claim Freud makes," and who implies that these claims "all have equal empirical and methodological status and are always valid" (1978, p. 141). As Sulloway (1979) demonstrates, Freud saw psychoanalytic theory as an instinct theory, and differences between the sexes as a natural (as opposed to a symbolic) phenomenon. To what extent psychoanalytically minded feminists share these views is now unclear.

5. Greenacre (1952), p. 31, Grunberger (1989), p. 68.

6. Harlow and Harlow (1965), Bowlby (1979), Rutter (1981). Important issues of fact remain unresolved, even so. Little is known about the long-term effects of having several "mothers" rather than a single mother, or a male "mother" rather than a female one. Nor is it clear whether there is a balance to be struck between "too much" mothering and "too little." Arguably, an over-intrusive or enveloping mother does more psychological damage than a neglectful one (Stoller, 1974).

7. Greenson (1968).

8. Bower (1989) and Stern (1985) argue for complex developmental processes early in infancy. Specifically, Stern claims on the basis of child observation that the infant's sense of self is established in stages during the first eighteen months of life, each corresponding to a formative phase: "emergent self" (0–2 months), "core self" (3–6 months), "subjective self" (7–15 months) and "verbal self" (15–18 months). By implication, each of these differentiations of "self" from "other" occurs before—or in parallel with—the establishment of a stable gender identity.

9. Between the ages of three and six months, Stern stresses, infants are already in a position to use their gaze to exert "control over the initiation, maintenance, termination, and avoidance of social contact with the mother; in other words, they help to regulate engagement. Furthermore, by controlling their own direction of gaze, they self-regulate the level and amount of social stimulation to which they are subject. They can avert their gaze, shut their eyes, stare past, become glassy-eyed" (Stern, 1985, p. 21).

10. Rosenthal (1984).

11. Hinde and Stevenson-Hinde (1987).

12. Tanner (1978), p. 58.

13. Greenacre (1952), p. 110.

14. Most psychoanalysts, Stoller (1979, p. 109) contends, follow Freud in believing that "all psychopathology, not just the sexual deviations, results—by such mechanisms as castration anxiety and penis envy in the oedipal conflict—from disturbances in the sense of gender identity, that is of masculinity and femininity."

It is these mechanisms of penis envy and castration anxiety that Chodorow invokes in the context of what we have called the wound. Although she confesses herself uncomfortable with it, she follows the orthodox line: that when the son discovers that his mother lacks a penis, he is seized by castration anxiety, and separates himself from his mother as a result (Chodorow, 1978, p. 107). While we accept that mother/infant relations may be intensely eroticized, we view this part of the orthodox psychoanalytic story with scepticism. Our own view of the wound is unrelated either to castration anxiety or to the idea of the female genitalia as the wound that results when, in fantasy, the male genitalia are cut away. Although our argument belongs to the broad family of psychodynamically inspired ideas, its links with classical Freudian theory are few.

15. See, e.g., Bronfenbrenner's (1970) comparison of the pressures brought to bear on American and Russian school children.

16. Social psychologists (e.g., Tajfel, 1981) see individuals' self-images as having two components: a personal identity and social identities which correspond to each of the groups to which the individual in question belongs. Such theorists assume that whenever individuals join a group, this automatically becomes an "in-group," perceived as superior to any alternatives. Such theorizing is inadequate to cope with the evidence of academic specialization, though. Young physical scientists plainly choose a profession which they themselves continue to perceive in unfavorable terms (Hudson, 1967).

17. Lacan appears to take this view (Bowie, 1987, p. 117). Although attractive, it has an obvious flaw. In as much as both boys and girls are subject to parental authority, it suggests, both will experience themselves as "male"—leaving as determinants of gender identity the relatively superficial questions of noticed similarities and differences of physique, names, ascribed roles, and so on. Rescue is possible; but the difficulty is typical of the puzzles which theories of identification pose.

18. Broadly, psychoanalytic theory admits four sorts of identification: (1) Primary identification—the primitive state which is presumed to exist in the minds of infants before they can discriminate themselves from other people; (2) Secondary identification—the normal developmental process whereby infants model themselves on parents whom they see as separate from themselves; (3) Introjective identification—the process whereby individuals envisage other people (or aspects of those people) as "inside" themselves; and (4) Projective identification—the process whereby individuals envisage themselves as "inside" other people. Primary and secondary identification are uncontentious, at least to the extent that they accord with common sense; but the notions of introjective and projective identification constitute a battle ground.

It is also an assumption of much psychoanalytic theorizing that the infant's early introjective and projective identifications occur in terms which are semantically stereotyped and binary: hence the psychoanalytic shorthand whereby the mother is seen as fragmented in her infant's eyes into "good breast" and "bad breast." It is easy to see how such primitive distinctions could evolve into the categories which structure the stereotypical perceptions of adolescents and adults: "exciting"/"dull," for instance, and "valuable"/"worthless." But while methods of observing mothers and their infants are becoming increasingly sensitive, as Stern's work shows, there is little prospect, ever, of such semantic activity being directly confirmed. To infer it retrospectively from the fantasies of adults is plainly unacceptable, because those fantasies (like the psychoanalyst's theories) could well be shaped by systems of stereotypical perception acquired at a later developmental stage.

19. This traffic in turn permits the "export" from one person to another of complex systems of anxiety and need; hence Erikson's claim that "whatever deep "psychic stimulus" may be present in the life of a young child, it is identical with his mother's most neurotic conflict" (Erikson, 1963, p. 30). There is also the difficulty, as Goffman (1959) has insisted, that so much of our sense of ourselves is dramaturgical.

20. Brown (1986), p. 551.

21. Greenson (1968).

22. Clark (1960), p. 300.

23. Osten and Vey (1969), p. 30; Hibbard (n.d.), pp. 66, 220.

24. See Clark (1960), plate 260; also Hudson (1982), where Meit's image is discussed in more detail.

25. There are female psychologists and psychoanalysts (e.g., Levenson, 1984; Aries and Olver, 1985) who see the absence of an equivalent feat of separation among women as leaving them at a clear disadvantage. Women characteristically have difficulty, they suggest, not only in separating from their parents, but in functioning autonomously within their own adult intimacies. Chodorow reaches the opposite conclusion. She sees the "separateness" of the male rather than the "connectedness" of the female as "problematic" (Chodorow, 1990, p. 120). What women lack, if our own argument is correct, is not a penis but an in-built sense of agency (of which the penis is sometimes assumed to be symbolic). It is this sense which a woman must subsequently construct, and which—especially if her sense of her own femininity is insecure—she may envy.

26. In adopting the idea of a psychic space which opens up between the male infant's sense of himself and his mother, we become heirs to Winnicott's (1971) concept of "potential space." Winnicott envisaged this as an "intermediate area of experience," which serves as model and precursor of imaginative activity among adults. From our point of view, there are nonetheless distinctions to be drawn. Winnicott's potential space is established in the child's mind at a much earlier developmental stage than that created by the wound, and in both sexes alike. We are suggesting, in effect, that under the impact of the male wound potential space takes on a significance which is gender-linked.

Lacan's notion of the *nom-du-père* is pertinent too. "Freud's essential discovery," Lacan believed, was that "man bears otherness within himself'"; that, in the relation of unconscious to conscious, he comes face to face with his own *"excentricité radicale de soi à lui-même"* (Bowie, 1987, p. 118). Lacan follows Freud in taking the Oedipal triad of mother–father–child as given, and assumes that all authority derives from the father: not the actual father, nor even an imagined one, but the symbolic father, *le nom du père*. "The *nom-du-père*, the original Other, introduces a gap between desire and its object(s) which the subject is bounded by, and bound to, throughout his life and at all levels of his experience. This primordial estrangement is by its very nature destined to recur, and be converted, ubiquitously." Again, though, distinctions are necessary. Like Winnicott's potential space, Lacan's *nom-du-père* arises in the first year of life; the wound later. The *nom-du-père* is inseparable from the "Symbolic Order"; the wound relates only indirectly to boy's symbolic capacity. The *nom-du-père* is part of the stock-in-trade of the theoretician who dances; the wound part of that of ones happy to plod.

27. Storr (1988). As Chodorow (1978, p. 177) says, identification among boys and the acquisition of the male role is in any case unlikely "to be embedded in relationship with their fathers or men but rather to involve the denial of affective relationship to their mothers."

28. It is presumably for this reason not only that the earth is perceived as female—"Mother Earth"—but so too are those pre-eminently "male" pieces of machinery, the boat and the motorcar.

29. Keller (1985, p. 158) correctly insists that there is "a world of difference" between the objectivity of the scientist who masters his chosen slice of the natural world and imposes order on it, and that of the scientist—she instances the geneticist Barbara McClintock—who "listens to the material" and develops a feel for it. There is a distinction of principle, in other words, between thought which is objective in the sense that it is abstract or analytic, and thought which is objective in the sense that it is open-minded or dispassionate.

30. The reversal of infantile identity implicit in the wound whereby the father (previously different) is seen as similar, and the mother (previously similar) is seen as different:

SIMILARITY-IN-DIFFERENCE : DIFFERENCE-IN-SIMILARITY

thus leads to a bifurcation of imaginative preoccupation, in which the two components mirror one another:

THINGS-AS-PEOPLE : PEOPLE-AS-THINGS

The step is vital to our argument, and is the first of the three points where our underlying presuppositions show through. It is from this linkage between a reversal of identity and a splitting of imaginative preoccupation that the rest of what we have to say about the male imagination flows. While it is the preoccupation with things-as-people that will dominate our discussion of science and technology, it is the segregation of the two preoccupations—things-as-people and people-as-things—that regulates the male's sexual expression, and does so most clearly in its perverse forms. It is only in the last part of our story, where we discuss the male's distinctive contribution to the creative arts, that, however precariously, these preoccupations with people-as-things and things-as-people are reconciled.

31. The developmental influence of dis- and counter-identification will vary from cost to cost and benefit to benefit. Apparently complex, these interactions are easiest to grasp when tabulated:

		The Developmental Influence of	
		Dis-Identification	Counter-Identification
Costs	Insensitivity	Necessary	Reinforcing
	Misogyny	Necessary	Counteracting
Benefits	Agency	Necessary	Necessary
	Energy Source	Necessary	Irrelevant
	Abstract Passion	Necessary	Reinforcing

This table suggests that the developmental pattern giving rise to abstract passion will also give rise to personal insensitivity—but not to misogyny. Where abstract passion and misogyny do occur in the same man, we would expect the resulting tension to become an organizing principle of the imaginative life of the individual in question (as seems to have been the case for the philosopher Schopenhauer).

32. Hudson and Jacot (1971). These data are derived from *Who's Who*. The samples being large, very high levels of statistical significance were achieved. See also Hudson (1973), where the British evidence is confirmed by American data drawn from the National Surveys of Higher Education, sponsored by the Carnegie Commission.

33. Kuhn (1962).

34. These are effects of the kind which Freud's psychoanalytic colleague Ferenczi labelled "bioanalytic." Winnicott's idea of potential space falls into this category.

Stern (1985, p. 26) argues that, in psychoanalytic theorizing, the psychic apparatus is assumed to operate apart from subjective experience—in terms, for instance, of repression, the mechanisms of defense, the structures of ego and id, and so on—and to yield subjective experience as its by-product. His own account of self-and-other is unique. Stern believes, in that its "main working parts" are the inferred subjective experiences of infants themselves.

Our own impression is that some psychoanalysts are more deeply wedded to the experience-as-by-product view than others: Melanie Klein, say, more than Winnicott. In this respect, nevertheless, we stand with Stern. Once the disjunctions of dis- and counter-identification are in place, there exists, we believe, an apparatus which seeks to resolve perceived consonances and dissonances between emotionally charged alternatives, and does so, not apart from the subjective experience of the individual, but as a centrally placed component of that experience.

35. Lattices are discussed in *Bodies of Knowledge,* in a developmental context; and in *Night Life,* in the context of meaning systems like dreams and poems which are structured but only partially determinate.

36. In making predictions either about individuals or about samples, it follows that simple-minded expectations of the data (like those implicit in the correlation coefficient or the chi-squared test) often have to be abandoned (Hudson, 1977). It is also important to grasp that the differentiation of the pertinent behaviors or perceptions may in practice be sharper within a social group than between groups. In a study of research students and their wives in Edinburgh University, we found the sharpest differences not between those at the extremes of the academic spectrum, but within the discipline of biology, between the "natural historians" and the "physical biologists"—for instance between ecologists and geneticists (Hudson, Johnston and Jacot, 1972).

This study exemplified a further point, itself obvious, but easily overlooked when the time comes to analyze quantitative data. Namely, that a marriage is itself a dynamic system, within which differences can gravitate. Although, in this study, the samples were recruited in terms of the husbands' work, the most pronounced differences proved to be those between the two groups of wives. The "natural historians" had married graduates with whom they conducted dual career marriages; the "physical biologists" had married non-graduates, and their marriages followed the more conventional pattern. The wives even differed in terms of the age at which they had reached sexual maturity; those of the "natural historians" having first menstruated relatively late, those of the "physical biologists" relatively early.

37. The disciplines in which "male" formats are most contentious are those of the midground: philosophy, social science and of course psychology. It is not clear, for example, to what extent Freud's partitioning of the mind between conscious, pre-conscious and unconscious is advantageous, nor how much mileage psychologists can legitimately make out of developmental models clearly divisible into phases: for instance, Freud's view of the imagination as sexual research, in which an anxiety (the infant's misgivings about where babies come from) is subject to resolution in discrete stages (Freud, Standard Edition, 11).

In Derrida, there is the interesting suggestion—one he attributes to Nietzsche—that the process of differentiation implicit in argumentative formats like Freud's is linked to the idea of force (Derrida, 1981, p. 9).

REFERENCES

Aries, E. J. and Olver, R. R., Sex differences in the development of a separate sense of self during infancy, *Psychology of Women Quarterly, 9,* 515, 1985.

Bower, T. G. R., *The Rational Infant,* Freeman, 1989.

Bowie, M., *Freud, Proust and Lacan,* Cambridge University Press, 1987.

Bowlby, J., *The Making and Breaking of Affectional Bonds,* Tavistock, 1979.

Bronfenbrenner, U., *Two Worlds of Childhood,* Russell Sage, 1970.

Brown, R., *Social Psychology, The Second Edition,* Free Press, 1986.

Chodorow, N. J., *The Reproduction of Mothering,* University of California Press, 1978.

Chodorow, N. J., What is the relation between psychoanalytic feminism and the psychoanalytic psychology of women?, in *Theoretical Perspectives on Sexual Difference,* ed. D. L. Rhode, Yale University Press, 1990.

Clark, K., *The Nude,* Penguin, 1960.

Derrida, J., *Positions,* trans. A. Bass, Athlone, 1981.

Erikson, E., *Childhood and Society,* Norton, 1963.

Freud, S., *Leonardo da Vinci and a Memory of his Childhood,* Standard Edition, 11.

Geschwind, N. and Galaburda, A. M., *Cerebral Dominance,* Harvard University Press, 1987.

Goffman, E., *The Presentation of Self in Everyday Life,* Doubleday, 1959.

Greenacre, P., *Trauma, Growth and Personality,* International Universities Press, 1952.

Greenson, R. R., Dis-identifying from mother: its special importance for the boy, *International Journal of Psycho-Analysis,* 49, 370, 1968.

Grunberger, B., *New Essays on Narcissism,* Free Association Books, 1989.

Harlow, H. F. and Harlow, M. K., The affectional systems, in *Behaviour of Non-human Primates,* ed. A. M. Schrier, H. F. Harlow and F. Stollnitz, Academic Press, 1965.

Held, R., Perception and its neuronal mechanisms, *Cognition,* 33, 139, 1989.

Hibbard, H., *Masterpieces of Western Sculpture,* Chartwell, n.d.

Hinde, R. A. and Stevenson-Hinde, J., Implications of a relationships approach for the study of gender differences, *Infant Mental Health Journal,* 8, 221, 1987.

Hudson, L., The stereotypical scientist, *Nature,* 213, 228, 1967.

Hudson, L. Fertility in the arts and sciences, *Science Studies,* 3, 1973.

Hudson, L., Picking winners; a case study in the recruitment of research students, *New Universities Quarterly,* 88, Winter, 1977.

Hudson, L., *Bodies of Knowledge,* Weidenfeld & Nicolson, 1982.

Hudson, L. and Jacot, B., Marriage and fertility in academic life, *Nature,* 229, 531, 1971.

Hudson, L., Johnston, J. and Jacot, B., *Perception and Communication in Academic Life,* Occasional Paper 8, Centre for Research in the Educational Sciences, Edinburgh University, 1972.

Keller, E. F., *Reflections on Gender and Science,* Yale University Press, 1985.

Kuhn, T. S., *The Structure of Scientific Revolutions,* Chicago University Press, 1962.

Levenson, R., Intimacy, autonomy and gender, *Journal of the American Academy of Psychoanalysis,* 12, 529, 1984.

Mitchell, J., *Psychoanalysis and Feminism,* Allen Lane, 1974.

Osten, G. von der and Vey, H., *Painting and Sculpture in Germany and the Netherlands, 1500–1600,* Penguin, 1969.

Rose, S., Kamin, L. and Lewontin, R. C., *Not in Our Genes,* Penguin, 1984.

Rosenthal, M. K., Sex differences in mother-infant interaction during breast feeding in the neonatal period, *Southern Psychologist,* 2, 3, 1984.

Rutter, M., *Maternal Deprivation Reassessed,* Penguin, 1981.

Stern, D., *The Interpersonal World of the Infant,* Basic Books, 1985.

Stoller, R. J., Symbiosis anxiety and the development of masculinity, *Archives of General Psychiatry,* 30, 164, 1974.

Stoller, R. J., The gender disorders, in *Sexual Deviation,* ed. I. Rosen, Oxford University Press, 1979.

Stoller, R. J., *Presentations of Gender,* Yale University Press, 1985.

Storr, A., *Solitude,* Collins, 1988.

Sulloway, F. J., *Freud, Biologist of the Mind,* Basic Books, 1979.

Tajfel, H., *Human Groups and Social Categories,* Cambridge University Press, 1981.

Tanner, J. M. *Foetus into Man,* Open Books, 1978.

Winnicott, D. W., *Playing and Reality,* Tavistock, 1971.

Chapter Twenty-Four

The Measurement of Masculinity and Femininity

Engendering Categorical Realities

J. G. Morawski

When the protagonist of Virginia Woolf's *Orlando* is suddenly transformed from male to female, he/she has minimal difficulty adjusting to a new form. The recent shift from the bipolar, apparently antiquated concepts of masculinity and femininity to one of androgyny, though purportedly a major reformulation, actually intimates a similar facile accommodation. While different in kind, both changes rely on mundane oppositions—those cultural concepts that ordinarily signify masculine and feminine. Both changes constitute fairly undramatic revisions rather than radical transformations.

The study of femininity and masculinity, comprising a massive scientific project across ninety years of experimental psychology, depicts a curious recurrence of these cultural concepts. The research exemplifies the repetition, with minor modifications, of several central stipulations about masculinity and femininity. Conventional literature reviews strive to identify significant advances in gender research, to chart the "breakthroughs" or "discoveries" as it were, but they neglect what is stable and common to the studies. A perspective that acknowledges the repeated similarities is needed to begin to appreciate the virtual reification of the existence, contents, and evaluative dynamics of masculinity and femininity concepts. Such a perspective attends to the procedures through which those stipulations were defended and sustained. It illuminates some of the nonempirical reasons for maintaining certain categorical stipulations about femininity and masculinity and, in turn, intimates how these categories bolstered prescriptions for appropriate social behavior.

The contents of the masculinity and femininity categories are familiar even to those uninitiated into gender-role research. They are constituted by global polarities found in common personality dimensions: instrumental vs. expressive, agentic vs. communal, active vs. passive, independent vs. dependent characteristics. At this level the categories are straightforward and represent nothing more than what is ordinarily

J. G. Morawski, "The Measurement of Masculinity and Femininity: Engendering Categorical Realities." *Journal of Personality,* 53 (2) (June 1985), pp. 196–223. © 1985 by Duke University Press. Reprinted with permission.

meant when one is said to be like a man or woman in our culture. In addition, it is presupposed that the categories are consistent within the individual and that the individual has a sincere desire to manifest them appropriately. The enduring presence of the categories is readily apparent, and in the light of recent feminist studies, so is the unhappy coincidence that the dichotomous personality signifiers indicate behavior norms for social relations between men and women. The present exploration, then, moves beyond these acknowledged conditions in order to locate the means by which scientific psychologists (while avowing an ethos of objectivity, disinterestedness, and impartiality) retained the categories. How, in the face of contradictory empirical findings and of nonobservable postulates, were they sustained? The answer involves more than just revealing unreasonable or unscientific practices, because the assumptions under question were also maintained through normal and legitimate scientific procedures. For their maintenance it was necessary that psychologists occasionally override scientific knowledge as well as the knowledge of ordinary people.

The first section of this study examines the procedures and rhetoric whereby even scientific knowledge was rendered dubious in order to uphold the reality of femininity and masculinity. The second section describes the ways in which psychologists were able to verify the nearly ephemeral gender entities as a psychological *reality* and claim *privileged* access to *observing* and *assessing* that reality. Once this psychological phenomenon was secured, the study of masculinity and femininity seemed to consist simply of healthy competition for the most efficient and elegant assessment techniques. The apparent breakdown of the extended research tradition came primarily through challenges raised by feminist scholarship, and even the subsequent revisions of androgyny theory ultimately proved insufficient to meet those challenges.

The methodology of the present study departs from conventional criticism by looking not at faulty scientific ideas but at how the research practices themselves were constructed to foster certain interests and even to confect certain realities. Historical studies have identified some of the misogynists and androcentric theories in psychology. Yet we must look beyond cranks and heresies to understand how normal scientific practices were integral to the construction and maintenance of an "engendered" psychological reality. The study does not deny the existence of gender differences but rather questions the particular forms ascribed to these differences and the means by which they were sustained. The fact that these practices confirmed the mundane realities of social life, the ethnopsychology of gender categories, makes it surprising that psychologists even had the troubles they did in locating masculinity and femininity.

Discovering Masculinity and Femininity through Science

In his comprehensive review of sex difference research, Havelock Ellis (1894) noted the ideological distortions frequently imposed on the subject. For these ideological biases, Ellis prescribed the remedy of empirical inquiry, particularly the "new" scientific psychology which "lays the axe at the root of many pseudoscientific superstitions" (p. 513). However, he cautioned that science reveals only factual, not potential, conditions, for "our present knowledge of men and women cannot tell us what they might be or what they ought to be, but what they actually are, under the conditions of civilization" (p. 513). Within a decade, numerous American psychologists had taken up the question of sex differences. While acknowledging the precedent of Ellis's work, they professed closer alignment with the empirical spirit of providing what Helen Thompson Woolley (1903) described as the "original investigation" that his study lacked (p. 2). As did many of her cohorts, Thompson Woolley reached somewhat different conclusions than Ellis, for though she admonished pseudoscientific theorizing and anticipated the fruits of objective experimentation, she believed that modifications in social life could or would alter psychological sex differences. With agreement on the correct methods for knowledge acquisition, Ellis and Thompson Woolley disagreed on whether or not the psychology of the sexes might change, or be perfected, with the former betting on nature's desires and the latter on the effects of social organization. Nevertheless, the psychologist's task was not to explore the dynamics of social perfectibility but to better the process of knowledge production. The normative notion of bettering gender arrangements was taken to be another problem altogether.

Thompson Woolley's careful laboratory research resembles a host of similar studies, many of them conducted by women (such as Mary Whiton Calkins, Leta Hollingworth, Catherine Cox Miles, and Margaret Floy Washburn) who, with the new opportunities for higher education, turned to intellectual questions that were not far removed from their own lives (Rosenberg, 1982). Thompson Woolley's dissertation (1903) reported experiments on sex differences in motor, affective, sensory, and intellectual abilities. Within the next three decades hundreds of studies assessed these sex differences as well as those to be found in the association of ideas, color preference, handwriting, remembering of advertisements and moving pictures, motor efficiency, nervous behavior of nursery school children, fear responses, reading speed, credulity regarding fortune telling, stammering, scope of attention, reasoning, and ideals and tastes, not to mention knowledge of psychology after the first course (see Allen, 1927, 1930; Hollingworth, 1916, 1918; Johnson & Terman 1940; Thompson Woolley, 1910, 1914).

The research on the psychology of sex created some confusion because many of the studies reported no or minor sex differences and those finding differences often indicated female superiority. Probably no study equalled the impact of the intelligence research as measured by the new mental tests. In revising the Binet-Simon Intelligence Scale, Lewis Terman (1917) tested 1,000 children and found slight superiority of girls. The results led him to consider why women had not attained eminence and ultimately to suggest that their failure "may be due to wholly extraneous factors." Even before Terman's standardized test, other investigators found few significant sex differences on measures of mental abilities. In her 1914 review of the psychology of sex, Thompson Woolley reported these findings with a cynical conclusion: "On the whole then, girls have stood better than boys in measures of general intelligence. So far as I know, no one has drawn the conclusion that girls have greater native ability than boys. One is tempted to indulge in idle speculation as to whether this admirable restraint from hasty generalization would have been equally marked had the sex findings been reversed!" (p. 365). The reported differences were often so slight that Hollingworth (1918) claimed that any reviewer who restricted himself to reporting sex differences on mental traits would "automatically tend to do himself out of his review. He would have very little to report" (p. 428).

Despite such enthusiasm, the wide-scale operation to attain objective scientific knowledge of the psychology of sex faltered, and by 1930 was mired in complications due to inconsistent findings and a paucity of studies on social factors as well as to professional difficulties of the women psychologists who undertook a substantial amount of the research (see Rosenberg, 1982). Yet, the persistent spirit behind the project was far from exhausted though the problems encountered by experimentalists were serious. For those who had posited the superiority of males on tasks involving general mental ability the ground had fallen away, for the new intelligence tests left their position unsubstantiated. While experimental studies were indicating that males and females diverged on some measures, they gave no coherent explanation of these differences. They ultimately provided no final test of theory—no indication of whether the differences were environmentally or biologically determined. And because a number of variables could not be controlled, the critical experiment to ascertain the respective natures of males and females could not be performed, at least not on conventional ethical grounds. This limitation plagued more than John B. Watson who, in his autobiography claimed "regret" at not having established "a group of infant farms" where various races could be reared under controlled conditions (1936, p. 281), a variation on his earlier proposal for a human laboratory "where squads can be kept at work. Their food, water, sex, and shelter could then be kept under very definite control" (1924, p. 214). In describing these impracticable experiments, some contemplated such perfect controls as Arcady, for their constitution required elimination of all gender-related discrimination (Hinkle, 1920; Thompson Woolley, 1903). What several decades of research apparently had disclosed is that males and females differed on some psychological measures and were similar on others, and that the decisive experiment for ascertaining the essence of gender, while resembling a nonsexist environment, was unfeasible.

The solutions to these problems were of several types. Some psychologists seemed indifferent to the experimental research and proceeded to publish theoretical statements on the psychology of men and women. These researchers frequently intimated that the actualization of psychology as a true science had not yet happened, but they took license as professionals to conjecture, to proffer scientific expertise, on an important psychological and social issue. While lacking experimental evidence, these statements nevertheless represented knowledge of the new "scientific intelligence" as Lippmann (1922) called them, the social scientific experts who had gained a public spotlight during the reform period and later through involvement in the war effort. Thus, G. Stanley Hall (1922) explained that the flapper, rather than exemplifying the demise of femininity in the American woman, actually represented "the bud of a new and better womanhood, and the evolutionary progress of civilization toward maternal femininity." He added, "Our Simon-Binet tests can grade and mark, at least for intelligence, but here they baulk, stammer, and diverge" (p. 780). Watson (1927) identified the dangerous characteristics of modern women which guaranteed that men would opt out of marriage in the next fifty years and suggested behaviorist femininity through careful hygiene for sexual attractiveness. Others turned toward the new "glandular psychology" to learn the final word on masculinity and femininity.

While these respondents exhibited what charitably could be called benign neglect of empirical evidence, others, assured that psychology as science had arrived, stipulated the means for discovering the *real* nature of masculine and feminine. A minor study published in 1922 epitomizes the general logic behind these newer explorations and, therefore, is worthy of extended quotation:

> The mental test seems to have said its utmost on the subject of sex differences, and the results have been on the whole surprisingly at variance with the insistent prejudices of the average man and woman.
>
> When common sense and science clash it is more often science that has the last word, but not always. Occasionally the worm turns, and a supposedly scientific doctrine unacceptable to common sense continues to be scrutinized until a glaring flaw is discovered either in the method or the interpretation of results that led to the doctrine. The history of medicine is strewn with the wrecks of such doctrines, and psychology bids fair to number at least its fair share of derelict 'scientific' notions. . . .
>
> Very much the same may be said of the small differences apparent in the test scores of men and women. So far as these results suggest the interpretation that the mental differences between the two sexes are after all comparatively insignificant, they suggest something that common sense and universal experience refuse to allow. Such results again promise to stand as the mark of the inadequacy of the psychological test to get at the most important features of mental differentiation (Moore, 1922, p. 210).

Moore depicted the important feature of maleness and femaleness in "natural emotional aptitude, of an unyielding innate divergence that predominates the enthusiasms that are to be expected from the two sexes in identically the same environment" (p. 211). He proceeded to test his hypothesis by measuring these "natural aptitudes" as they were expressed in conversations of men and women on Broadway. He found that male-to-male conversations were typically about money and business while woman-to-woman conversations were about persons of the opposite sex. His hypothesis was confirmed.

In addition to natural aptitudes, other researchers looked for maleness and femaleness in such phenomena as levels of "mental energy" (Leuba, 1926), the "unconscious" (Hamilton, 1931), and in "mind" (Jastrow, 1918, p. 303). Jastrow found the intelligence test to be both "partial" and "artificial," claiming that "deeper and more comprehensive are the allied and supporting processes which gave the cutting edge to the instrument, and determine the temper of the mind, the manner and spirit of its use." Real psychological processes corresponding to masculinity and femininity in everyday life are located "in the habitat of deep psychology, where traits are at once subtle and profound. Here the feminine mind, as all minds in the specialized aspects, becomes most revealing" (p. 314). Discontented with the extant empirical research, this last group of psychologists was convinced that the *real* substance of masculinity and femininity existed but not in what was measured by the myriad mental tests.

They argued from the logical premise that *if other* human sciences, notably anatomy, physiology and pathology reveal man as man and woman as woman, then "What reason is there to suspect psychology to enter a dissenting opinion?" (Jastrow, 1918, p. 303).

Producing the Subject of Psychological Science

Given these general trends in psychology, and given the rather audacious ad hoc theorizing without supporting "facts," or without any facts, it appears that some psychologists were engaging in sex role stereotyping. Perhaps they were subjects of a "cultural lag" similar to that which Eagley (1978) detected in some psychologists of a later period. But while investigations of masculinity and femininity seem to have diverged from conventional research practices, perhaps to accommodate particular sex role stereotypes, they also converged with those practices in several revealing ways. They emphasized detached objective observation and the consequential devaluation and even denigration of subjective observations. The ordinary observer or self-observer came to be seen as an incomplete psychologist at best (Watson, 1919; Robinson, 1926); he or she was unable to identify the true causes of behavior (Dashiell, 1928). The image of the incompetent subject gained support not only with the intensified dedication to rigorous objective techniques but also with concurrent assumptions about the complexity and causal interdependence of human actions (Haskell, 1977). The idea of the causal complexity of human action gained adherents throughout the early twentieth century, and it dovetailed with another social assumption adopted by psychology: the increasing human disorder and the consequent need for rational control. While these concerns were voiced in the progressive era (Haber, 1964; Wiebe, 1967) and reinforced with the successes of applied social science in the war effort, they were amplified by psychologists in the 1920s and 1930s (O'Donnell, 1979; Samelson, 1979; Sokal, 1984). Scientists in general showed escalated concern about human ignorance and about the scientists' leadership responsibilities (Kaplan, 1956; Tobey, 1971). For instance Edward Thorndike (1920) suggested that the average citizen, the "half-educated man," should relinquish decision making to the experts.

Similar portraits of human irrationality were depicted by psychologists as were the pleas for scientific, particularly psychological, control (Danziger, 1979; Morawski, 1982, 1983, 1984b). Psychologists became more vocal about their role in bringing social problems under control (Allport, 1924; Angell, 1929; Dunlap, 1920, 1928; Terman, 1922a, 1922b). For many, control became a fundamental component of the definition of psychology: "Ultimately it is a desire to get *control*" (Dashiell, 1928, p. 6). Even the seemingly most detached researchers saw the world in "dire need" of control over human conduct (Hull, 1935, p. 515).

Of the institutions needing control, marriage and family life were thought to be central for they constituted the primary source for individual well-being and for socialization of adjusted adults. Researchers proceeded with several premises: that the family is universal, the nuclear family being the most natural form; that the role of the mother is primary in the socialization of children; and that childrearing failures were to be interpreted as failures of mothers. Intimated in these premises is the preference for studying only adult heterosexual relationships in the context of the nuclear family (Morawski, 1984b).

The shifts in research orientations over the four decades indicate more than innovative conceptual strategies for pursuing an empirical question; they represent an intriguing deviation from mainstream psychology. The conceptual changes proceeded from a search for corporeal differences, then to cognitive and behavioral differences, and eventually to postulates about hidden but salient, nonconscious substrates of masculinity and femininity. To some extent the changes resemble the broader transition from structuralism and introspectionism to behaviorism which was then occurring in American psychology. However, the study of the sexes deviates significantly from that pattern. The rise in behaviorism, although meeting more resistance than is typically believed, involved an extensive exorcism of nonobservable or mentalist phenomena. Even excluding extremists such as John B. Watson and Karl Lashley there was an emerging consensus that psychology consisted of the objective study of observable events. Mind, self, consciousness, and personality traits were like epiphenomena. Personality traits were taken as merely descriptive aspects of more fundamental causal mechanisms since they are, behaviorally speaking, "the individual's characteristic reactions to social stimuli, and the quality of his adaptations to the social features of his environment" (Allport, 1924, p. 101). The ascendency of objective and behavioral psychology foreshortened the search for any real mental mechanisms; even though individual differences research continued, behaviorism challenged the plausibility of interior mental entities such as ethnic and racial traits (Cravens & Burnham, 1971; Samelson, 1978, 1979).

Psychologists' particular interests in the diagnoses and eventual remediation of social disorders provides an important clue to the persistent intrigue with male and female psychological functioning. These interests help explicate the continued discourse on masculinity and femininity which often deviated from current theoretical and methodological trends and disregarded empirical findings. At least hypothetically, standardized tests promised to rectify some of the empirical problems while serving the overall practical interests in control. Hence there ensued a quiet transition from the study of sex differences to the exploration of "masculinity" and "femininity."

The Solution of Terman and Miles

Challenged by the muddled state of masculinity and femininity research and specifically "by the lack of definiteness with respect to what these terms should connote," Lewis Terman and Catherine Cox Miles (1936, p. vi) undertook an extensive project in the early 1920s. They were moved by the questioning of the very existence of such entities which was being made by some psychologists and anthropologists, notably Margaret Mead. Nevertheless, they began with the premise that masculinity and femininity were real. Terman and Miles understood their task to resemble the earlier efforts to eradicate misconceptions about intelligence: like Binet's transformation of intelligence research, they sought "a quantification of procedures and concepts" (p. vi). They believed that despite the failures to determine the origin of sex-related attributes and the inability to attain observer agreement on the content of these attributes, there existed considerable clarity in the composite pictures of femininity and masculinity. Hence, the only assumption Terman and Miles suspended was that about origins; however, like previous researchers they lamented the ethical impossibility of conducting the study, the experimental rearing of infants, that could reveal those origins (p. 464).

Terman and Miles (1936) constructed a test to give "a more factual basis" to ordinary concepts of masculinity and femininity by accumulating test items on which males and females differed (p. 3). A preliminary version of the test was given to members of Terman's group of gifted children, and in this pretesting they observed their first case of a high cross-sex scorer displaying homosexual tendencies, or "sexual inversion." The final product of the psychometric project was a 910-item test with seven subtests: word association, ink-blot association, general information, emotional and ethical attitudes, interests, opinions, and introvertive response. Most subtests were compiled by modifying existing tests on those phenomena according to two criteria: selection of items that best discriminate the responses of males and females, and maximization of the efficiency and economy of test administration. Items were converted to multiple-choice format where two of the response alternatives were feminine and two masculine. Validity was assessed by ascertaining overlap of score distributions for male and female samples and by correlations with independent measures of femininity and masculinity. Since there was no other psychometric measure for ascertaining validity, comparison data were obtained from clinical studies.

The contents of the test perhaps now appear as an intriguing cultural artifact, but it did discriminate successfully between females and males. Scores of the sexes differed on average by 122 points and only about 10 out of 1000 subjects of each sex had scores exceeding the mean of the other sex (Terman & Miles, 1936, p. 371). The Attitude-Interest Analysis Test (AIAT), as the M-F scale was titled to mask its purpose, contains masculine response items such as those requiring negative responses to the questions "Do you like to have people tell you their troubles?", "Do you usually get to do the things that please you most?", "Do you sometimes wish you had never been born?", and "Do you feel that you are getting a square deal in life?" Femininity points are attained by responding negatively to the questions "Do people ever say you are a bad loser?", "Do you feel bored a large share of the time?", and "Were you ever fond of playing with snakes?" Masculinity points are gained by replying that you dislike foreigners, religious men, women cleverer than you are, dancing, guessing games, being alone, and thin women. Femininity points are accrued by indicating dislike for sideshow freaks, bashful men, riding bicycles, giving advice, bald-headed men, and very cautious people.

AIST correlated with only a small number of other personality inventories and poorly with measures of marital adjustment. The scores varied considerably for different age groups (for both sexes, scores declined in older samples), and the test was susceptible to faking. Qualitative comparison of the test results and clinical measures of abnormalities such as homosexuality and female delinquency was more promising: The AIST detected "roughly, degree of inversion of the sex temperament, and it is probably from inverts in this sense that homosexuals are chiefly recruited" (p. 467). Despite its limitations, Terman and Miles endorsed the scale and its potential. Use of the AIST promised to "help clean up the confused notions which are current with regard to what constitutes masculinity and femininity of personality. The fact seems to be that most of us have not acquired the ability to discriminate very clearly the genuinely masculine from the genuinely feminine" (pp. 465–466).

Convinced of the everyday inability to make such discriminations and of the detrimental effects of such judgment errors, Terman and Miles conducted a study on psychologists showing that even professionals, without the use of scientific techniques such as the AIST, were inadequate judges of masculinity and femininity (pp. 454–459). Such findings supported the hypothesis that "the test scores do have behavioral correlates but that ordinary observers lack adeptness in detecting them" (p. 465). The authors confidently anticipated use of the test in clinical diagnosis and in ameliorating familial and marital maladjustments. They refrained from relating their results to the environment-heredity controversy over the origins of sex differences. However, they offered a clear conception of psychological well-being, a model equating mental health with definitive correspondence between psychological and biological sex ascriptions. The subsequent research of Terman and Miles further attests to their interest in relating mental health to gender-based psychological characteristics (Miles, 1942; Terman, 1938).

Production of M-F

Theirs was the first major attempt to assess quantitatively the existence of masculinity and femininity in the psychological realm of temperament and to do so without postulating causality or nature/nurture influences. Terman and Miles had introduced a way of accessing the reality of masculinity and femininity that became a model for constructing scales over the next twenty-five years. Most of the tests shared with their predecessor three assumptions: that masculinity and femininity existed but at a level that could not be readily identified by the ordinary observer; that the attributes were so psychologically charged that subjects had to be deceived of the true nature of the test lest they fake their response in order to appear socially desirable; and that femininity and masculinity were distinct qualities which were somehow related to psychological stability and deviancy, notably homosexuality and familial troubles. The first two assumptions were supported by the popularity of social theories that conceptualized human action as complex, causally interdependent, and beyond the self-knowledge attainable by the ordinary observer. Later investigations confirmed these conjectures when empirical evidence was found to contradict everyday analysis: Psychometric assessments were showing pedestrian attributions of femininity and masculinity to be in error. The third assumption, that of adjustment and mental health, corresponds with the mandates for reconstructing psychology into a more objective behavioral science that would better serve social control. As stated by two psychologists engaged in an extensive study of sex and marriage: "Some of us feel that if we were permitted to train the management, fewer of the exploring children would get hurt, and more of them would find the happiness they are looking for" (Hamilton & MacGowan, 1928, p. 287). Understanding intimate heterosexual relationships, sexuality, and family life comprised a substantial obligation for socially responsible psychologists.

Just as these assumptions directed conceptualizing about the form and location of "gendered" psyches, so Terman and Miles (1936) also indicated their content. In a qualitative analysis of the findings, they described the masculine psyche as adventurous, mechanically and object oriented, aggressive, self-asserting, fearless, and rough, and the feminine psyche as aesthetically and domestically oriented, sedentary, compassionate, timid, emotional, and fastidious. The two composite minds resemble the Victorian sex role schema of separate spheres (Lewin, 1984b, 1984c; Rosenberg, 1982). This reconstituted schema lent certainty to the increasingly fuzzy question of the nature of the sexes, and was similar in content to the one Robert Yerkes (1943) generated from his studies of male and female chimpanzee behavior (see Haraway, 1978). This gender schematization can be contrasted with the concurrent changes in the actual social positions of men and women and the alterations and confusions of gender images and roles (for examples, see Filene, 1974; May, 1980; Showalter, 1978). Given the social conditions of the period, the M-F scale itself may have served more than a taxonomic or descriptive function; it offered prescriptions for a moral order. Here the case of Ernest Hemingway's writing is suggestive. While portraying rigidly sex typed characters in his published fiction, his unpublished works include characters who betray, escape, or eschew conventional gender attributes (Latham, 1977). A somewhat different example of two levels of reality is apparent in writings of John B. Watson in which the strong argument for total conditioning and environmental adjustments were to provide behavior directives primarily for certain classes, including that of women (Harris, 1984). Invoking certainty can appear to arrest the flux of an uncertain social reality. Whatever the intended or unintended prescriptive function of the AIST may have been, and whatever the discrepancy between the test findings and other social indicators may mean, the form and content of the scale are significant, for they came to inform later assessment techniques and normative evaluations.

Reproduction of M-F Inventories

Although the AIST was developed according to a psychometric procedure of selecting test items for their ability to discriminate the criterion groups of men and women, it lacked theoretical coherence due to the variety of psychological phenomena tapped by the subscales. Later attempts to construct M-F instruments often focused on a more specific range of psychological phenomena and were considered in terms of particular personality theories. For instance, in the same year that Terman and Miles published their study, two quite specific inventories were reported, one by Edward K. Strong and the other by J. P. and Ruth Guilford. Strong (1936) prepared a Masculinity-Femininity subscale for his general inventory of vocational interests, the Strong Vocational Interest Blank (SVIB). He reported that although both sexes exhibited more feminine interests with age, sex differences were a major indicator of occupational interest. Strong suspended pronouncement on the origin of these differences, and simply concluded his study by asking, "Are the differences in interest of engineers and lawyers to be found in differences in hormone secretions, or in early attachment to father instead of mother, or in the possession of certain abilities in which the sexes differ?" (p. 65). On the one hand, Strong (1943) cautiously noted that the interests of males and females were more similar than different and that because his inventory also assessed similarities, it was in this sense superior to Terman and Miles's test. On the other hand, he admitted that his inventory was limited in the psychological dimensions it assessed; in the end, he deferred to the findings of Terman and Miles. A later test of occupational preferences also incorporated a M-F subscale (Kuder, 1946).

Guilford and Guilford (1936) attained a sex temperament measure through factor analysis of a test of introversion-extroversion. Guilfords' 101-item Nebraska Personality Inventory contains five factors, one of which is M. Although initially viewing the factor as "masculine-ideal," the investigators chose the "more noncommittal letter M" (p. 121) to signify a factor that was "perhaps masculinity-femininity, or possibly a dominance or ascendance-submission factor" (p. 127). The tentative identification of the masculinity factor later was described with considerable certainty (Guilford & Zimmerman, 1956; Lewin, 1984c). Both the scales of Strong and of the Guilfords, while ostensibly appraising different psychological dimensions, indicated greater aggressiveness, dominance, and fearlessness in males and greater emotionality, subjectivity, and sympathy in females. In both cases checks on external validity were limited and inconclusive.

Masculinity and femininity comprised a subarea of interest in other inventories designed primarily to assess psychological abnormalities. S. R. Hathaway and J. C. McKinley devised the Minnesota Multiphasic Personality Inventory (MMPI) in 1940 to measure traits of importance to the practitioner who "wishes to assay those traits that are commonly characteristic of disabling psychological abnormality" (Hathaway & McKinley, 1951, p. 5). Many of their items were inspired by Terman and Miles's inventory; others were original. The MMPI manual gives no information about the construction of the M-F subscale although other evidence suggests that it was compiled using only a criterion group of thirteen male homosexuals (Lewin, 1984b). In developing a subscale of psychological femininity for the California Psychological Inventory (CPI), Harrison Gough (1952) attempted to create a less obtrusive instrument than the MMPI or SVIB. Gough selected items according to both their differentiation between male and female responses and their subtlety. The resultant fifty-eight true-false questionnaire, containing items like "I am inclined to take things hard," discriminated between males and females but was only moderately successful in identifying psychological abnormalities and in correlating with judgments of trained observers. (Femininity, as interpreted in this scale, is characterized as sensitivity, timidity, compassion, acquiescence, subjectivity, and sentimentality.) A shortened version of the scale, the version that was integrated into the CPI, was examined for cross-cultural validation, accurate identification of adjustment problems, and correlation with other M-F scales; these checks were only moderately successful (Gough, 1966, 1975). A third scale of this type is the M-F subscale of the Depauw Adjustment Inventory (Heston, 1948).

Most of these researchers were concerned that their tests might be susceptible to either faking or reflecting cultural ideals. Yet they typically concluded, as did Guilford and Guilford (1936), that their test was sufficiently complex to elude the acumen or disingenuous calculations of the normal subject. Other researchers were not so readily convinced and sought to eliminate two possible contaminants of the conventional scales: (1) "cultural" biases and (2) the possibility that subjects could deceive testers, and themselves, given the ostensibly common tendency to obscure issues of sex identity. Solution to these problems of cultural and psychological "noise" was sought by testing symbolic representation through projective techniques; symbolic representation was believed to be beyond cultural constraints and the subject's awareness of self. Kate Franck (1946) designed a projective test of M-F based on the subjects' choices of pictures with male or female symbols. This and other studies assumed that normal subjects would prefer opposite sex symbols. The projective study of drawing styles indicated that men close off areas, expand the stimulus, seek unity, and use angular and sharp lines while women leave areas open, elaborate within the stimulus area, and blunt or enclose sharp lines (Franck and Rosen, 1949). Men tend to create objects such as towers, tools, and mechanical vehicles. Women tend to construct vases, windows, flowers, and human figures. Franck and Rosen compared their findings to Erik Erikson's analysis of children's play constructions and to Freudian psychoanalysis; they suggested the universality of symbols, and offered guidelines for evaluating maladjustments in role identification. Other attempts to appraise the "hidden" or "unconscious" of masculinity and femininity identification employed projective devises such as draw-a-person (Caligor, 1951; Machover, 1949), the Thematic Apperception Test (Webster, 1953), and open-ended word association (Goodenough, 1946).

During the forty-year period 1930–1970, projective tests were not the sole means for circumventing cultural artifacts and subject biases. Several researchers adopted rating scales to permit the subject to evaluate self and others; by indirectly assessing social "ideals" or "stereotypes," they could check deviations from those baselines (Berdie, 1959; Reece, 1964). Berdie (1959) claimed that the adjective check list, because it enabled self-other statements, could measure not just "dimensions" of personality but also "processes" including "such things as identification, repression, self-acceptance, and perception" (p. 327). These researchers presumed the primacy of sex role identification for mental health, and that direct behavioral responses which reflect these underlying processes comprised valuable information for clinical practice. Measurement of other behavior indices of masculinity and femininity sometimes (Gray, 1957) though not always (Rosenberg & Sutton-Smith, 1959) linked sex role identification with these elusive or unconscious psychological processes.

The qualitative definitions of masculinity and femininity were consistent among these tests, though quantitative reliability checks did not always confirm such consistency (Constantinople, 1973). The tests were routinely constructed with the three core assumptions originally adopted by Terman and Miles: that masculinity and femininity were unavailable to the ordinary observer, that deception was required to deter the subject's natural tendency toward complicity, and that masculine and feminine traits were indicators of psychological adjustment. But the later scales had added grounds for making more adamant claims. By the late 1930s the idea of psychological femininity and masculinity located beyond the awareness of the person was being corroborated by depth psychology. The works of Freud, Jung, and Erikson, all of which gained popularity during the period, hypothesized that potent gender attributes were nonconscious. In addition, experimental research in general psychology was disclosing the various ways that subjects could bias responses, and these findings prompted attempts to design methods for circumventing such "faking" (Caligor, 1951). Thus, the constructs of masculinity and femininity, concepts which more than one researcher compared to atoms and genes, came to be described as knowable but not without calculated pursuit. Note how the search for the phenomena is described:

> . . . when we come to deal with what is often called the "private world" of the individual, comprising as it does, the feelings, urges, beliefs, attitudes, and desires of which he may be only dimly aware and which he is often reluctant to admit even to himself, much less to others, the problems of measurement are of a very different nature. Here the universe which we wish to assay is no longer overt and accessible but covert and jealously guarded (Goodenough, 1946, p. 456).

The subject typically complicated this search by deceptive behaviors: "A man may be an athlete, may know all about automobiles and fly a plane—and yet be afraid of women. Everyone has known such people, for there are many, who use behavior labeled masculine or feminine by our society to hide their disorientation, often from themselves" (Franck & Rosen, 1949, p. 247).

Other test compilers checked to ensure that subjects' stereotyped ideas about masculinity and femininity did not interfere with the more "subtle" or "true" indices (Nichols, 1962; Reece, 1964). Despite such precautionary circumventions, the constructs of the gender types, when put in verbal form, did not vary much from test to test. Masculine is powerful, strenuous, active, steady, strong, self-confident, with preference for machinery, athletics, working for self, and the external/public life. Feminine is sensitive, compassionate, timid, cautious, irritable, acquiescent, sentimental, preferring artistic and sendentary activities, and the internal/private life. Nevertheless, with the near certainty of the constructs' existence few researchers pronounced on their origins.

Feminist Difference: Complaint or Challenge?

Although problems of validity were occasionally noted, the general techniques of assessing masculinity and femininity were continued until the 1970s. A serious challenge to the tests appeared with Anne Constantinople's (1973) examination of three central postulates: the unidimensionality of femininity and masculinity, their bipolarity, and their definition in terms of sex differences in item-response. She offered convincing evidence of the theoretical vacuity of the masculinity-femininity construct. While Constantinople's critique examined M-F tests specifically, related research on sex and gender further compromised the tests' accepted validity. Theories of sex roles and sex role socialization were criticized for positing conventional norms for appropriate gender behavior (Block, 1973; Carlson, 1972), for making differential evaluations of male and female attributes (Helson, 1972; Rosenberg, 1973), and for assuming temporal stability of gender-linked traits (Angrist, 1972; Emmerich, 1973). These researchers, and those in feminist studies generally, imperiled not only the credibility of M-F scales but the very reality of "masculine" and "feminine."

An expedient solution to the resulting quandary was offered with the concept of androgyny and the accompanying techniques for its assessment. Introduced in 1974, the Bem Sex Role Inventory (BSRI) measured the ideals of masculinity and femininity in a manner enabling comparison of the degree to which an individual rates high on both attributes. It measured the degree to which an individual is "androgynous," and hence psychologically healthy (Bem, 1974, 1977). During the next few years several similar scales were created (Berzins, Welling, & Wetter, 1978; Heilbrun, 1976; Spence, Helmreich, & Stapp, 1975). Initially, the most popular of these androgyny measures, the BSRI, was recognized as successful in predicting gender-related behaviors, in expanding the range of appropriate or healthy responses (Bem, 1974, 1977), and in detecting life-span changes (Maracek, 1979; White, 1979). The concept was expediently adopted to help explain a wide range of human behaviors, especially those for which clear gender differences were found. The scale became a popular tool for explaining activities in the hospital and boardroom, in the school and romantic encounters. The very idea of androgyny was received as a solution to the ostensible "sexism" of talking about masculinity and femininity. In fact, it offered an escape from openly endorsing those gender categories and a new ideal for evaluating behavior (Bem, 1977; Kaplan, 1976; Lee & Scheurer, 1983). That ideal has little if any relevance to psychosexual matters and illustrates a heightened concern with complex cognitive competencies. While the initial M-F scale of Terman and Miles was intended to tap psycho-sexual maladjustments, the androgyny scales exhibit little relation to sexuality (Storms, 1980). Androgyny researchers have tended to eschew consideration of sexuality in favor of correlating androgyny and those complex cognitive styles believed to be essential in, for example, the workplace (see Colwill, 1982).

The concept has also received both empirical and theoretical challenges, some of which fault androgyny research with incorporating the very same presuppositions that it was intended to eliminate. The critics noted that the newer models retain, even if unintentionally, certain values associated with masculine and feminine, and thus contribute to their ossification as universals (Lott, 1981; Hefner & Rebecca, 1979). Associated with these normative stipulations are untenable prescriptions for psychological health (Kenworthy, 1979). For instance, Sampson (1977) indicated how the "self-contained individualism" assumed in the concept of the androgynous person is a dubious yet essentially unquestioned norm. Others noted how the androgyny models neglect negative attributes and gender similarities (Rosen & Rekers, 1980;

White, 1979). And although purportedly sensitive to changes in gender attributes within the individual, these models do not explicate the broader cultural conditions that may mediate or transform these attributes (Kaplan, 1979; Kenworthy, 1979; Sherif, 1982; Worell, 1978). The concept of androgyny has also yielded a questionable record in empirical investigations. The findings of a recent meta-analysis of androgyny research not only confirm some of the theoretical complications but also suggest that neither the BSRI nor the PAQ even adequately predicts psychological well-being (Taylor & Hall, 1982).

The androgyny models were advanced to replace theories that were circumscribed by history and culture; yet they apparently failed to confront their own historically constituted limitations (particularly by assuming transhistorical stability). They renovate rather than replace the rejected presuppositions about the ontology, structure, and desirability of gender concepts (Morawski, 1984a). The criticisms essentially demonstrate that androgyny research proceeded without critical scrutiny of the arguable metatheoretical foundation that subtly guided the entire enterprise of explaining the psychology of gender (Sherif, 1982; Taylor & Hall, 1982; Unger, 1983). Bem (1979) has also come to question the concept. She has suggested that the androgyny concept would sow the seeds of its own destruction by immobilizing the cultural categories of masculinity and femininity and, hence, by undermining its own foundation in those very categories. Bem's (1983) reconsideration of the androgyny construct does acknowledge the historical and cultural processes involved in the construction of gender dichotomies. However, to end the repetitions and sanctioning of a particular reality requires more than acknowledging history. It demands a comprehensive reevaluation of our scientific practices, particularly the reflexivity and empowerment of psychological knowledge.

Repetition in Discoveries

Androgyny research exhibits telling resemblances to the earlier work on femininity and masculinity. Undoubtedly androgyny models no longer prescribe correspondence between biologically ascribed sex and psychologically ascribed gender roles, and they dismiss altogether the issue of sexual deviancy. These "liberating" implications have tended to obscure other qualities of the androgyny scales, most notably their retention of the categorical constructs of femininity and masculinity along with the cultural values associated with them. As such, androgyny may be viewed as extension of an enduring process of pursuing the "real." It forms part of an ostensibly progressive and maybe interminable scientific search for psychological essences by reference to somatic body types, to mind stuff, to personality matter, and eventually to roles and cognitive styles. Androgyny research is part of a pattern whereby appeals to these hypothetical constructs are invoked to locate the hypothetical constructs which were posited initially (those of the masculine and feminine). The process consists of continued indexicality of constructs where, even in the case of androgyny, the idea of gender types is substantiated by indexical relation to previously conjectured constructs. The process in turn engenders objectification and ossification of the constructs. The polarities of masculine and feminine, retaining qualities such as "instrumental" and "expressive" or "agentic" and "communal" action, become fixed, even reified. They come to represent ahistorical entities that potentially can be treated as referents of particular behaviors, traits, or ideals. Masculinity and femininity, then, become symbolic signifiers *and* the signified. Despite the apparent emancipatory implications of the androgyny theories, they, too, are embedded with limiting conditions and valuational underpinnings dictated by these polarities.

A further process operating throughout, by way of protecting the theory from external contamination, might be called "assessment control." There has developed an increasing wariness toward the commonsensical: independent reports or everyday interpretations have become a bias to be minimized or eliminated by implementing deceptive techniques and psychometric complexities. One consequence of this last procedure is the distancing of theory from everyday life. Further, regarding questions of power and privilege, distancing has significant implications for the establishment of norms of conduct. Here we approach the issue of perfectability and must recognize that any conception of betterment—be it of health, working life, or gender arrangements—requires some notion of the good. The masculinity-femininity theorists, purportedly by detaching their conceptual work from social life, have tacitly defined normative objectives by way of reference to an ideal of society and individual behavior within that society. For the earliest theorists the ideals were framed by the nineteenth-century division of labor in both the private and public realms. The test makers of the 1930s and 1940s aligned their ideals with social relations as typified by the nuclear family (hence the concern with marital adjustment, homosexuality, parenting). Their norms were also tied to perceptions of the possible collapse of these social relations. The implicit objectives of the androgyny theorists mirror the virtues of corporate democracy where self-contained individualism and role flexibility (behavioral inconsistency) are desired.

These normative stipulations need not be purposively imposed; their indirect infusion into theoretical work can be seen in the periodic occurrence of unintended reflexivity. The history of gender theorizing illustrates how psychologists' participation in and reflection upon cultural life can affect the primary stipulations in their work (Eagley, 1978; Rosenberg, 1982). Although these occurences were not the focus of the present study, it is clear that research strategies were altered as a consequence of psychologists' experiences of the world wars, suffrage, the feminist movement of the 1960s, and general transitions in public life.

The support given to the idea of androgyny by feminist psychologists raises several obvious questions. Why did feminists not only subscribe to but participate in the reiteration of cultural concepts and consequently endorse the underlying moral edicts? On one level it is apparent how the concept was, in some senses, self-serving: feminist psychologists have been primarily white, professional women who could find in androgyny theory an inspiring model for their own roles in a predominantly male world (not to mention their interests in the desired roles of their male peers). Here may be one case of unintended reflexive thinking. On another level, feminist psychologists may have been vulnerable to the lures of scientific ideals, and to the essentialist psychology that historically underlay the scientific ethos of skeptical empiricism, disinterestedness, and impartiality. Science has been extolled as the primary if not sole technique to work against prejudice and discrimination. Especially for those trained in scientific methods, it is not easy (or sometimes permissible) to acknowledge how scientific rationality itself is fallible (see Lykes & Stewart, 1983); yet the grounds of rationality are derived by social consensus and can be renegotiated and even transformed during normal scientific practice (Knorr-Cetina, 1981; Shapin, 1982). That feminist psychologists throughout the century would entrust their work to the superior rationality of scientific knowledge makes sense (as does the particular faith in psychology with its legacy of social reformism). This adherence is even more comprehensible given the resistance of the discipline to critically confronting the positivist metaphysics and naive realism which has both prefigured our observations of psychological reality as well as foreshortened our understanding of epistemological alternatives.

Toward New Theory

The exploration of masculinity and femininity is but one aspect of the history of gender research, and although highly informative work on the subject is now appearing (Lewin, 1984a; Rosenberg, 1982; Shields, 1975, 1982), further investigation is needed. Such historical ventures, along with those on the history of the actual practices of gender relations, offer correctives to current research (Morawski, 1984a). The history reviewed here suggests a reconsideration of the entire project of developing theory through a critical unpacking of our habits of theorizing and the generation of new theoretical frameworks. Such reconsideration begins with a critical and historical framework. It is critical in the sense of holding that all attempts to establish knowledge claims should be evaluated not simply in terms of empirical confirmation but also in terms of the very criteria of reliable knowledge and rationality that are attributed to the knower (psychologist). It is historical in the sense that knowledge claims must be understood as historical products, as constructions guided by particular interests and problematics. Neither of these provisions necessarily implies any radical relativism (Rorty, 1982, pp. 160–175).

Given this general superstructure, several issues fundamental to constructing gender theory must be considered. Most obvious is the need to take the broader context, and consequently reflexivity, seriously (Unger, 1983). The comprehensive social context must be understood if, borrowing Sherif's (1982) illustrations, we are to understand why the androgynous person may not be a political feminist or how social power relates to gender-linked behaviors. Such contextualist understanding requires sociological, anthropological, and historical studies (Morawski, 1983; Sherif, 1982) and is inescapably political (Parlee, 1979). A corollary is the need for the researcher to undertake critical self-appraisal as well as assessment of the stipulated canons of rationality (Addelson, 1983; Harding, 1984; Jaggar, 1984) and of the social and political facets of his or her work (Buss, 1979; Eagley, 1978; Flanagan, 1981; Sampson, 1977). Masculinity and femininity research demonstrates how the scientific questions of gender necessarily imply political questions in that even the androgyny theorists posit an idealization of society. Mere tacit endorsement of this idealization (in the case of androgyny an idealization where advances in technology and welfare may mitigate the bases for some gender distinctions) harbors debatable stipulations about the kind of world we are promoting.

The second major area of reconsideration concerns replacing conceptions of human nature that have either distorted or impeded research on gender. In light of the history of gender and of psychology generally, it seems prudent if not profitable at least to consider a working conception of human beings *as* human beings. And if we require any metaphors of powers or essences, those atoms of psychological actions, we consider that they be located in the act of the search, in *language* and its context of use. Simply assuming that human beings are active social agents involved with moral ambitions and with the construction of psychological realities generates numerous possibilities for future research. Some contributions in this direction include the study of the phenomenology of gender labeling (Kessler & McKenna, 1978), dialectics of sex role transcendence (Hefner & Rebecca, 1979), alternatives to the orthodox psychoanalytic theories of socialization (Chodorow, 1978; Dinnerstein, 1976; see Steele, in press), and gender styles in moral decision making (Gilligan, 1982). These basic conceptions also imply reappraisal of the conventional modes of assessment control: it is necessary to examine how we empower certain voices (the researcher's) and not others with inordinate privilege, and how we define authority and rationality (Addelson, 1983; Harding, 1984). Whether this empowering is seen as the hegemony of masculine science or as a concomitant of everyday life, in gender research it has profoundly affected theory as well as empirical findings.

These general architectonics simply intimate possibilities for theory construction which are informed by a systematic rereading of the historical record. They address some of the repeatedly evaded temporal, epistemological, and moral dimensions of research. Yet if we choose to participate in generating novel ways of looking at the social world as, at least hypothetically, scientists have sought new ways of viewing the natural world, then we must first audit our inventory of artifactual and conventional beliefs.

REFERENCES

Addelson, K. P. (1983). The man of professional wisdom. In S. Harding & M. B. Hintikka (Eds.), *Discovering reality* (pp. 165–186). Boston: D. Reidel.

Allen, C. (1927). Studies in sex differences. *Psychological Bulletin, 24,* 294–304.

Allen, C. (1930). Recent studies in sex differences. *Psychological Bulletin, 27,* 394–407.

Allport, F. H. (1924). *Social psychology.* Boston: Houghton Mifflin.

Angell, J. R. (1929, April 19). Yale's Institute of Human Relations. *Yale Alumni Weekly* (pp. 889–891).

Angrist, S. (1972). The study of sex roles. In J. M. Bardwick (Ed.), *Readings on the psychology of women* (pp. 101–106). New York: Harper & Row.

Bem, S. L. (1974). The measurement of psychological androgyny. *Journal of Consulting and Clinical Psychology, 42,* 155–162.

Bem, S. L. (1977). On the utility of alternative procedures for assessing psychological androgyny. *Journal of Consulting and Clinical Psychology, 45,* 196–205.

Bem, S. L. (1979). Theory and measurement of androgyny: A reply to Pedhazur-Tetenbaum and Locksley-Colten critiques. *Journal of Personality and Social Psychology, 37,* 1047–1054.

Bem, S. L. (1983). Gender schema theory and its implications for child development: Raising gender-aschematic children in a gender-schematic society. *Signs, 8,* 598–616.

Berdie, R. F. (1959). A femininity adjective check list. *Journal of Applied Psychology, 43,* 327–333.

Berzins, J. I., Welling, M. A., & Wetter, R. E. (1978). A new measure of psychological androgyny based on the Personality Research Form. *Journal of Consulting and Clinical Psychology, 46,* 126–138.

Block, J. H. (1973). Conceptions of sex role: Some cross-cultural and longitudinal perspectives. *American Psychologist, 28,* 512–526.

Buss, A. R. (Ed.). (1979). *Psychology in social context.* New York: Irvington.

Caligor, L. (1951). The determination of the individual's unconscious conception of his own masculinity-femininity identification. *Journal of Projective Techniques and Personality Assessment, 15,* 494–509.

Carlson, R. (1972). Understanding women: Implications for personality theory and research. *Journal of Social Issues, 28,* 17–32.

Chodorow, N. (1978). *The reproduction of mothering: Psychoanalysis and the sociology of gender.* Berkeley: University of California.

Colwill, N. L. (1982). *The new partnership: Women and men in organizations.* Palo Alto, CA: Mayfield.

Constantinople, A. (1973). Masculinity-femininity. An exception to a famous dictum. *Psychological Bulletin, 80,* 389–407.

Cravens, H., & Burnham, J. C. (1971). Psychology and evolutionary naturalism in American thought, 1890–1940. *American Quarterly, 23,* 635–657.

Danziger, K. (1979). The social origins of modern psychology. In A. R. Buss (Ed.), *Psychology in social context* (pp. 27–45). New York: Irvington.

Dashiell, J. F. (1928). *Fundamentals of objective psychology.* Boston: Houghton Mifflin.

Dinnerstein, D. (1976). *The mermaid and the minotaur: Sexual arrangements and human malaise.* New York: Harper & Row.

Dunlap, K. (1920). Social need for scientific psychology. *Scientific Monthly, 11,* 502–517.

Dunlap, K. (1928). The applications of psychology to social problems. In C. Murchison (Ed.), *Psychologics of 1925* (pp. 353–379). Worcester: Clark University Press.

Eagley, A. H. (1978). Sex differences in influenceability. *Psychological Bulletin, 85,* 86–116.

Ellis, H. H. (1894). *Man and woman: A study of human secondary characters.* London: Walter Scott.

Emmerich, W. (1973). Socialization and sex role development. In P. B. Baltes & K. W. Schaie (Eds.), *Life-span developmental psychology: Personality and socialization.* New York: Academic Press.

Filene, P. G. (1974). *Him/her/self: Sex roles in modern America.* New York: Harcourt Brace Jovanovich, 1974.

Flanagan, O. J., Jr. (1981). Psychology, progress, and the problem of reflexivity: A study in the epistemological foundations of psychology. *Journal of the History of the Behavioral Sciences, 17,* 375–386.

Franck, K. (1946). Preference for sex symbols and their personality correlates. *Genetic Psychology Monograph, 33,* 73–123.

Franck, K., & Rosen, E. (1949). A projective test of masculinity-femininity. *Journal of Consulting Psychology, 13,* 247–256.

Gilligan, C. (1982). *In a different voice: Psychological theory and women's development.* Cambridge: Harvard University Press.

Goodenough, F. L. (1946). Semantic choice and personality structure. *Science, 104,* 451–456.

Gough, H. G. (1952). Identifying psychological femininity. *Educational and psychological measurement, 12,* 427–439.

Gough, H. G. (1966). A cross-cultural analysis of the CPI Femininity Scale. *Journal of Consulting Psychology, 30,* 136–141.

Gough, H. G. (1975). *California psychological inventory: Manual* (rev. ed.). Palo Alto: Consulting Psychologists Press.

Gray, S. W. (1957). Masculinity-femininity in relation to anxiety and social acceptance. *Child Development, 28,* 203–214.

Guilford, J. P., & Guilford, R. B. (1936). Personality factors S, E, and M and their measurement. *Journal of Psychology, 2,* 109–127.

Guilford, J. P., & Zimmerman, W. S. (1956). *The Guilford-Zimmerman temperament survey: Manual of instructions and interpretations.* Beverly Hills, CA: Sheridan Supply.

Haber, S. (1964). *Efficiency and uplift: Scientific management in the progressive era, 1890–1920.* Chicago: University of Chicago Press.

Hall, G. S. (1922). Flapper Americana novissima. *Atlantic Monthly, 129,* 771–780.

Hamilton, G. V. (1931). The emotional life of modern woman. In S. D. Schmalhausen & V. F. Calverton (Eds.), *Woman's coming of age* (pp. 207–229). New York: Horace Liveright.

Hamilton, G. V., & MacGowan, K. (1928). Marriage and love affairs. *Harpers, 157,* 277–287.

Haraway, D. (1978). Animal sociology and a natural economy of the body politie. Part I: A political physiology of dominance. *Signs, 4,* 21–36.

Harding, S. (1984). Is gender a variable in conceptions of rationality? A survey of issues. In Carol C. Gould (Ed.), *Beyond domination: New perspective on women and philosophy* (pp. 43–63). Totowa, NJ: Rowman & Allanheld.

Harris, B. (1984). Give me a dozen healthy infants: John B. Watson's popular advice on childrearing, woman, and the family. In M. Lewin (Ed.), *In the shadow of the past: Psychology portrays the sexes.* New York: Columbia University Press.

Haskell, T. L. (1977). *The emergence of professional social science.* Urbana: University of Illinois Press.

Hathaway, S. R., & McKinley, J. C. (1951). *Manual for the Minnesota multiphasic personality inventory* (rev. ed.). Minneapolis: University of Minnesota Press.

Hefner, R., & Rebecca, M. (1979). The future of sex roles. In M. Richmond-Abbott (Ed.), *The American woman: Her past, her present, her future* (pp. 243–264). New York: Holt, Rinehart & Winston.

Heilbrun, A. B., Jr. (1976). Measurement of masculine and feminine sex role identities as independent dimensions. *Journal of Consulting and Clinical Psychology, 44,* 183–190.

Helson, R. (1972). The changing image of the career woman. *Journal of Social Issues, 28,* 33–46.

Heston, J. C. (1948). A comparison of four masculinity-femininity scales. *Educational and Psychological Measurement, 8,* 375–387.

Hinkle, B. M. (1920). On the arbitrary use of the terms "masculine" and "feminine." *Psychoanalytic Review, 7,* 15–30.

Hollingworth, L. S. (1916). Sex differences in mental traits. *The Psychological Bulletin, 13,* 377–384.

Hollingworth, L. S. (1918). Comparison of the sexes in mental traits. *Psychological Bulletin, 15,* 427–432.

Hull, C. L. (1935). The conflicting psychologies of learning—A way out. *The Psychological Review, 42,* 491–516.

Jaggar, A. (1984). Human biology in feminist theory: Sexual equality reconsidered. In Carol Gould (Ed.), *Beyond domination: New perspectives on women and philosophy* (pp. 21–42). Totowa, NJ: Rowman & Allanheld.

Jastrow, J. (1918). The feminine mind. In J. Jastrow (Ed.), *The psychology of conviction* (pp. 280–325). New York: Houghton Mifflin.

Johnson, W. B., & Terman, L. B. (1940). Some highlights in the literature of psychological sex differences published since 1920. *Journal of Psychology, 9,* 327–336.

Kaplan, A. G. (1976). Androgyny as a model of mental health for woman: From theory to therapy. In A. G. Kaplan & J. P. Bean (Eds.), *Beyond sex role stereotypes: Readings toward a psychology of androgyny* (pp. 352–362). Boston: Little Brown.

Kaplan, A. G. (1979). Clarifying the concept of androgyny: Implications for therapy. *Psychology of Women Quarterly, 3,* 223–230.

Kaplan, S. (1956). Social engineers as saviors: Effects of World War I on some American liberals. *Journal of the History of Ideas, 17,* 347–369.

Kenworthy, J. A. (1979). Androgyny in psychotherapy: But will it sell in Peoria? *Psychology of Women Quarterly, 3,* 231–240.

Kessler, S. J., & McKenna, W. (1978). *Gender: An ethnomethodological approach.* New York: John Wiley & Sons.

Knorr-Cetina, K. D. (1981). *The manufacture of knowledge.* New York: Pergamon Press.

Kuder, G. F. (1946). *Revised manual for the Kuder preference record.* Chicago: Science Research Associates.

Latham, A. (1977, October 16). A farewell to machismo. *New York Times,* pp. 52–55, 80–82, 90–99.

Lee, A., & Scheurer, V. L. (1983). Psychological androgyny and aspects of self-image in women and men. *Sex Roles, 9,* 289–306.

Leuba, J. H. (1926). The weaker sex. *Atlantic Monthly, 137,* 454–460.

Lewin, M. (Ed.). (1984a). *In the shadow of the past: Psychology portrays the sexes.* New York: Columbia University Press.

Lewin, M. (1984b). Psychology measures femininity and masculinity. II: From "13 Gay Men" to the instrumental-expressive distinction. In M. Lewin (Ed.), *In the shadow of the past: Psychology portrays the sexes* (pp. 197–204). New York: Columbia University Press.

Lewin, M. (1984c). Rather worse than folly? Psychology measures femininity and masculinity. I: From Terman and Miles to the Guilfords. In M. Lewin (Ed.), *In the shadow of the past: Psychology portrays the sexes* (pp. 155–178). New York: Columbia University Press.

Lippmann, W. (1922). *Public opinion.* New York: Macmillan.

Lott, B. (1981). A feminist critique of androgyny: Toward the elimination of gender attributions for learned behavior. In C. Mayo & N. M. Henley (Eds.), *Gender and nonverbal behavior* (pp. 171–180). New York: Springer-Verlag.

Lykes, M. B., & Stewart, A. J. (1983). Evaluating the feminist challenge in psychology: 1963–1983. Paper presented at the 91st Annual Meeting of the American Psychological Association, Anaheim, CA.

Machover, K. (1949). *Personality projection in the drawing of the human figure.* Springfield, IL: Charles C. Thomas.

Maracek, J. (1979). Social change, positive mental health, and psychological androgyny. *Psychology of Women Quarterly, 3,* 241–247.

May, E. T. (1980). *Great expectations: Marriage and divorce in post-Victorian America.* Chicago: University of Chicago Press.

Miles, C. C. (1942). Psychological study of a young man pseudohermaphrodite reared as a female. In J. F. Dashiell (Ed.), *Studies in personality contributed in honor of Lewis M. Terman* (pp. 209–228). New York: McGraw-Hill.

Moore, H. T. (1922). Further data concerning sex differences. *Journal of Abnormal and Social Psychology, 17,* 210–214.

Morawski, J. G. (1982). On thinking about history as social psychology. *Personality and Social Psychology Bulletin, 8,* 393–401.

Morawski, J. G. (1983). Psychology and the shaping of policy. *Berkshire Review, 18,* 92–107.

Morawski, J. G. (1984a). Historiography as metatheoretical text for social psychology. In K. J. Gergen & M. Gergen (Eds.), *Historical social psychology* (pp. 37–60). New York: Erlbaum.

Morawski, J. G. (1984b). Not quite new worlds: Psychologists' conceptions of the ideal family in the twenties. In M. Lewin (Ed.), *In the shadow of the past: Psychology portrays the sexes* (pp. 97–125). New York: Columbia University Press.

Nichols, R. C. (1962). Subtle, obvious, and stereotype measures of masculinity–femininity. *Educational and Psychological Measurement, 22,* 449–461.

O'Donnell, J. M. (1979). The "Crisis of Experimentalism" in the twenties: E. G. Boring and his uses of historiography. *American Psychologist, 34,* 289–295.

Parlee, M. B. (1979). Psychology and women. *Signs, 5,* 121–133.

Reece, M. (1964). Masculinity and femininity: A factor analytical study. *Psychological Reports, 14,* 123–139.

Robinson, E. S. (1926). *Practical psychology: Human nature in everyday life.* New York: Macmillan.

Rorty, R. (1982). *The consequences of pragmatism.* Minneapolis: University of Minnesota.

Rosen, A. C. & Rekers, G. A. (1980). Toward a taxanomic framework for variables of sex and gender. *Genetic Psychology Monographs, 102,* 191–218.

Rosenberg, B. G., & Sutton-Smith, B. (1959). The measurement of masculinity and femininity in children. *Child Development, 30,* 373–380.

Rosenberg, M. (1973). The biologic basis for sex role stereotypes. *Contemporary Psychoanalysis, 29,* 374–391.

Rosenberg, R. L. (1982). *Beyond separate spheres: Intellectual origins of modern feminism.* New Haven: Yale University Press.

Samelson, F. (1978). From "Race psychology" to "Studies in prejudice." Some observations on the thematic reversals in social psychology. *Journal of the History of the Behavioral Sciences, 14,* 265–278.

Samelson, F. (1979). Putting psychology on the map: Ideology and intelligence testing. In A. R. Buss (Ed.), *Psychology in social context* (pp. 103–167). New York: Irvington.

Sampson, E. E. (1977). Psychology and the American ideal. *Journal of Personality and Social Psychology, 35,* 767–782.

Shapin, S. (1982). History of science and its sociological reconstructions. *History of Science, 20,* 157–207.

Sherif, C. W. (1982). Needed concepts in the study of gender identity. *Psychology of Women Quarterly, 6,* 375–398.

Shields, S. (1975). Functionalism, Darwinism, and the psychology of women. *American Psychologist, 31,* 739–751.

Shields, S. A. (1982). The variability hypothesis: The history of a biological model of sex differences in intelligence. *Signs, 7,* 769–797.

Showalter, E. (Ed.). (1978). *These modern women: Autobiographical essays from the twenties.* Old Westbury, NY: Feminist Press.

Sokal, M. M. (1984). James McKeen Cattell and American psychology in the 1920s. In J. Brozek (Ed.), *Explorations in the history of psychology in the United States* (pp. 273–323). Lewisburg, PA: Bucknell University Press.

Spence, J. T., Helmreich, R., & Stapp, J. (1975). Ratings of self and peers on sex role attributes and their relation to self-esteem and conceptions of masculinity and femininity. *Journal of Personality and Social Psychology, 32,* 29–39.

Steele, R. (in press). Paradigm lost: Psychoanalysis after Freud. In C. Buxton (Ed.), *Points of view in the modern history of psychology.* New York: Academic Press.

Storms, M. D. (1980). Theories of sexual orientation. *Journal of Personality and Social Psychology, 1980, 38,* 783–792.

Strong, E. K., Jr. (1936). Interests of men and women. *Journal of Social Psychology, 7,* 49–67.

Strong, E. K., Jr. (1943). *Vocational interests of men and women.* Palo Alto: Stanford University Press.

Taylor, M. C., & Hall, J. A. (1982). Psychological androgyny: Theories, methods, and conclusions. *Psychological Bulletin, 92,* 347–366.

Terman, L. (1917). *The Stanford revision and extension of the Binet-Simon Scale for Measuring Intelligence.* Baltimore: Warwick and York.

Terman, L. M. (1922a). The control of propaganda as a psychological problem. *Scientific Monthly, 14,* 234–252.

Terman, L. M. (1922b). The psychological determinist, or democracy and the I. Q. *Journal of Educational Research, 6,* 57–62.

Terman, L. M. (1938). *Psychological factors in marital happiness.* New York: McGraw-Hill.

Terman, L. M., & Miles, C. C. (1936). *Sex and personality.* New York: McGraw-Hill.

Thompson Woolley, H. B. (1903). *The mental traits of sex: An experimental investigation of the normal mind in men and women.* Chicago: University of Chicago Press.

Thompson Woolley, H. B. (1910). A review on the recent literature on the psychology of sex. *Psychological Bulletin, 7,* 335–342.

Thompson Woolley, H. B. (1914). The psychology of sex. *Psychological Bulletin, 11,* 353–379.

Thorndike, E. L. (1920). Psychology of the half-educated man. *Harpers, 140,* 666–670.

Tobey, R. C. (1971). *The American ideology of National Sciences, 1919–1930.* Pittsburgh: University of Pittsburgh Press.

Unger, R. K. (1983). Through the looking glass: No wonderland yet! (The reciprocal relationship between methodology and models of reality.) *Psychology of Women Quarterly, 8,* 9–32.

Watson, J. B. (1919). *Psychology from the standpoint of a behaviorist.* Philadelphia: J. B. Lippincott.

Watson, J. B. (1924). *Behaviorism.* New York: Norton.

Watson, J. B. (1927). The weakness of women. *Nation, 125,* 9–10.

Watson, J. B. (1936). Autobiography. In. C. Murchison (Ed.), *A history of psychology in autobiography* (pp. 271–282). Worcester: Clark University Press.

Webster, H. (1953). Derivation and use of the masculinity-femininity variable. *Journal of Clinical Psychology, 9,* 33–36.

White, M. S. (1979). Measuring androgyny in adulthood. *Psychology of Women Quarterly, 3,* 293–307.

Wiebe, R. (1967). *The search for order, 1877–1920.* New York: Hill & Wang.

Worell, J. (1978). Sex roles and psychological well-being: Perspectives on methodology. *Journal of Consulting and Clinical Psychology, 46,* 777–791.

Yerkes, R. M. (1943). *Chimpanzees: A laboratory colony.* New Haven: Yale University Press.

B. Roles and Stereotypes

Individuals become gendered, at least in part, through their encounters with roles and stereotypes, which represent two of the ways societies instantiate expectations about what women and men are like and how they should behave. The authors in this section all consider the dynamics of, consequences of, and reactions to our encounters with gender roles and stereotypes. As noted throughout this volume, gender is particularly powerful as a social category because there are virtually no contexts in which it is irrelevant—gender roles and stereotypes cannot be avoided. And, as Susan T. Fiske and Laura E. Stevens illustrate in their chapter, gender stereotypes are also particularly powerful because in addition to being *descriptive*, they are also *prescriptive:* that is, gender stereotypes include descriptive information of what men and women allegedly are like, but also information about what they are *supposed* to be like. Thus, counter-stereotypical behavior—when the stereotypes concern gender—is likely to be punished. That punishment may come directly from an institution, as in Price Waterhouse's refusal to promote Ann Hopkins because her behavior, while fitting the role of a senior partner, did not fit the stereotype of appropriate femininity (reported by Fiske and Stevens); in the context of interpersonal relationships, as when Child X is initially shunned by its classmates in Lois Gould's fabulous story; and even from within, as when men experience pain and disappointment when they fail to meet internalized male role requirements, as Joseph Pleck points out in his chapter.

These discussions of the power and ubiquity of role expectations and stereotypes, and the consequences of attempts to circumvent or confront them, simultaneously highlight the potential for individuals to act in ways that contradict expectations *and* the extent to which individuals acting alone face powerful opposition. This opposition is not just from other individuals, but from institutions (family, corporations, academic orthodoxies, governments) that are invested in gender arrangements. The intensity of this investment should not be underestimated: witness Price Waterhouse's willingness to act against its own financial interests in order to maintain a conception of appropriate female behavior. First, the company failed to promote someone who was bringing in a great deal of business; then it spent millions of dollars defending its actions in court, only to wind up having to pay further millions when the court's judgment went against it (Fiske and Stevens).

Just as we hope that the pieces included in Part III of the book help to complicate our understanding of biology and gender, the pieces in this section should help to complicate our understanding of how gender is created and maintained by social forces. Explorations of these forces provide a powerful counterpoint to any assumption that change in gender arrangements can be affected at only one level of society

(e.g., in the individual *or* in an institution), or that such change will be uncomplicated or easy.

Nevertheless, for all the complication they add, these pieces also provide a distinctly optimistic note. Rhoda K. Unger illustrates the potential advantages (as well
as the difficulties) of living and working with paradox, including paradoxes about
gender and the study of gender. Gould provides a utopian vision—but a useful one,
in that we need to imagine possibilities in order to pursue them. Jack W. Sattel and
Pleck both suggest exciting new possibilities as they dissect the consequences of
current versions of masculinity. And, after all, Ann Hopkins did succeed (though not
without considerable effort and personal cost) in getting Price Waterhouse to pay for
its gender bias—with, it is important to note, the help of two other powerful
institutions: the American Psychological Association and the United States Supreme
Court. The complexity of these discussions of gender roles and stereotypes exacts a
toll on our attention and understanding; but the rewards of increasing complexity
include both the intellectual satisfaction from the rich portraits of gender that result,
and the increased likelihood that efforts toward social change informed by these
portraits will be effective.

Chapter Twenty-Five

Sex, Gender, and Epistemology

Rhoda K. Unger

It has been argued by Buss (1975) and others that psychology as a discipline tends to alternate between two basic paradigms explaining the relationship between humans and their environment. These two basic conceptual paradigms are: (1) reality constructs the person, and (2) the person constructs reality. Paradigm (1) postulates a model of a reality that is stable, irreversible, and deterministic. It further postulates that this reality is discoverable through the proper application of scientific methodology and that individual differences are a result of the impingement of that reality on the developing organism. This deep structure underlies such diverse schools of thought as behaviorism, psychoanalysis, and sociobiology. These theoretical frameworks do not question that reality exists. They differ merely on the aspects of reality they stress as having the most impact on individual behavior.

Recently, psychology appears to have undergone a "cognitive revolution" (Gardner, 1985; Neisser, 1967). The former paradigm has been replaced by a keen interest in the active role of the individual in constructing his or her own reality. This model postulates that reality is largely a matter of historical and cultural definition (Gergen, 1985). It emphasizes the power of ongoing social negotiation in the creation of individual behavior and is more willing to take a less deterministic view of causality in general. Those who espouse a strong social constructionist viewpoint appear to be more likely to attribute individual differences to chance (nonpredictable or noncontrollable events) and, in the most extreme views, despair of the possibility of any generalizable laws of human behavior at all.

Although the social constructionist viewpoint is much more congenial for feminists in psychology (Unger, 1984–1985), I shall argue that sex and gender pose problems for both paradigms. I shall review briefly some of the major strengths and weaknesses of each in terms of sex and gender research, discuss what I see as some important conceptual and methodological trends in the area, and, lastly, discuss some of my own research and theorizing that bears on attempts to integrate apparently dichotomous views.

Rhoda K. Unger, "Sex, Gender, and Epistemology." In M. Crawford & M. Gentry (Eds.), *Gender and Thought*, pp. 17–35. New York: Springer-Verlag. © 1989 by Rhoda K. Unger. Reprinted with permission.

Reality Constructs the Person

Behaviorism, sociobiology, and psychoanalysis share a commitment to a fixed past as a major determinant of the individual's current behavior. They differ in the phenomena or processes they stress as the most important creators of that past. However, the explanatory power of schedules of reinforcement, genes, or familial psychodynamic processes is based on sometimes unstated assumptions about their connection with basic psychobiological mechanisms.

In these theoretical frameworks, sex is a biological given or an organismic variable. This assumption, of course, is stated explicitly by sociobiologists who assume that current differences between men and women are evolutionarily adaptive and interfered with by society at our peril. This view is most clearly spelled out in the title of the book *The Tangled Wing: Biological Constraints on the Human Spirit* (Konner, 1981).

Classic psychoanalytic theory and even some of its more feminist derivatives, however, also assume psychobiological mechanisms. Biology is introduced by the universal fact of motherhood and the inevitable conflicts produced by the relationship between the custodial parent (almost always the mother) and the developing child. Feminist psychodynamic theories appear to differ from classical Freudian ones by stressing power rather than sexual-erotic mechanisms, and by their belief that the psychodynamic consequences of the basic human family structure are not primarily due to the gender of the chief custodian. They tend to argue that the role of primary childrearer (linked to females, to be sure, by the biological necessity of childbearing) is the major determinant of gender-related differences between the sexes.

Behaviorism seemed to avoid biological assumptions. In its classic form, it tries to avoid the need to utilize variables from any other level of disciplinary discourse. Its essence is to restrict psychology to a few simple, easily observable and categorizable behaviors in order to facilitate the examination of the relationship between behavioral output and its outcomes (so-called reinforcers). In so doing, however, it has limited itself to behaviors that are devoid of much meaning for the human subject — of either sex — and has had to examine these subjects in a controlled environment — a situational context that eliminates any opportunity for the organism to select alternative behaviors. As a "science" that seeks to establish universal "laws of behavior" from an examination of the behavioral similarities between pigeons, rats, and humans, it has had little to say about the similarities or differences between various groups of human beings. In theory, behaviorism has ignored sex as a variable. In practice, even the rats were male.

What, if anything, have we learned about sex and gender from schools of thought emanating from reality-constructs-the-person assumptions? Sociobiologists have compiled a long list of supposed sex differences based on the adaptive value of sex-specific behaviors for the survival of males and females of various species. They have little to say about the rich variability of sex-related behaviors in human cultures of the past and present. And they offer us little in the way of specific mechanisms to explain sex differences (other than their primary notion of relative reproductive economy for mammalian males — who may scatter their plentiful sperm widely —

and mammalian females—who produce relatively few eggs and must cherish their scarce offspring).

Unfortunately, the area of psychology that has had the most to say about sex differences—the subfield of individual differences—is also the area that is most intellectually and historically akin to sociobiology. It has been noted that Galton, the founder of this field, was a strong believer in social Darwinism. He viewed women and colored people as inferior to men and the British (Buss, 1976). The area of individual differences has produced little in the way of a theoretical rationale for its data on differences between various groups and, in fact, has given us little explanation as to why some "causal" variables (such as sex, race, and class) should be studied, whereas others (such as height, physical appearance, or hair color) can be ignored.

The area of individual differences has remained a virtual catalog of behavioral phenomena with the mechanisms left unspecified. Since no systematic theory exists, it has been left to the user of this data base to determine when and why a specific sex difference may be cited. The consequences are obvious when one looks at various introductory textbooks in psychology written by authors with various theoretical perspectives. "Sex differences" in an almost infinite variety of behaviors are cited. There is, however, little consistency in whether or not a particular behavior is cited in different texts, and there is no agreement about what comprises a usable sex difference—in terms of statistical size, generality of occurrence, or cross-situational consistency.

Unfortunately, many early feminists in psychology took this data base seriously (Rosenberg, 1982; Shields, 1975). Early researchers worked to demonstrate that many so-called sex differences could not be verified empirically. Since the list of potential sex differences is potentially infinite, however, they may have spent their lives on issues that later psychologists regard as of no particular importance. The number of possible sex differences is not an important issue in the current feminist agenda. Much more pressing is the issue of how sex difference as a conceptual tool is deployed and manipulated.

Since behaviorism excludes questions about sex and gender entirely, the only other area utilizing this paradigm within which we may look for information is psychodynamic theory. It is noteworthy that this is the area from which feminist scholars outside psychology derive most of their inspiration. It has been largely ignored, however, by the majority of researchers within psychology, who primarily derive from a social psychological framework.

An extensive critique of psychodynamic theories about sex and gender would be tangential to the main thrust of this chapter. I shall therefore limit my discussion to a few remarks about what I see as the major problems of the psychodynamic view of women and men, as well as some benefits feminist social psychologists can derive from the theory. The major problem of the psychodynamic perspective for social psychology is the unexamined psychobiological connections discussed above. It is not clear what causal mechanisms best explain gender differences in the developing child. It is also not clear what role cultural prescriptions about gender-appropriate characteristics for boys and girls, and fathers and mothers, play in the development of such gender-related behaviors as intimacy, relatedness, individualism, or aggression.

Psychodynamic theory roots the individual in a historical time and place. I believe it is this aspect of the theory that makes it attractive to feminist scholars in other academic disciplines. They tend to find the logical positivist underpinning of traditional experimental psychology sterile because they are unwilling to conceptualize human beings devoid of their situational context (Unger, 1983). They also question the morality of the subject-as-object relationship specified by traditional psychology and deny the possibility that researchers can divorce themselves from their subject matter in order to measure human phenomena in an objective manner. They may also resent the arrogance of psychologists in defining themselves as the "measurers" of human beings. While these are all valid criticisms, some of the lack of communication between feminist scholarship and feminist psychology may be attributed to lack of awareness of the former about paradigm shifts within psychology as a discipline. In particular, there appears to be little knowledge about those aspects of the psychology of sex and gender that utilize the "person constructs reality" paradigm.

The Person Constructs Reality

As in the case of the "reality constructs the person" paradigm, there are a number of ways researchers can deal with phenomena having to do with sex and gender using "person constructs reality" assumptions. All these perspectives involve a formulation of human beings as consciously aware individuals who actively select and influence their environment, as well as being influenced by it. This positing of human subjects as agents of their own reality underlies the various perspectives influenced by the "cognitive revolution" within psychology.

In the new psychology of sex and gender, maleness and femaleness are seen as social stimuli that provide valuable information for organizing reality to both actors and observers (Deaux & Major, 1987). Observers use information about sex to determine whether the individual is behaving in a role-consistent manner. Identical male and female behaviors are rarely evaluated similarly, because sex and role are highly confounded in our society. In the absence of disconfirming information, individuals are evaluated in terms of the gender consistency of their behavior. Deviation from normative gender/role prescriptions has a major impact on how the individual is perceived by others. It is difficult to tell, in fact, how often, and to what extent, negative judgments of women's behavior in certain social contexts are due to their role deviance, rather than their gender deviance.

The observer's beliefs about sex as a social reality are confirmed by gender-characteristic styles of self-presentation and by the differential distribution of females and males into roles with divergent degrees of status and power. Individuals may maintain gender-characteristic behaviors because of both intrapsychic needs for self-consistency and pressure from others to behave in a socially desirable manner. Ultimately, the individual may lose sight of distinctions between herself and her role. She may become the person society prescribes.

What evidence supports this theoretical framework for sex as a cognitive variable? The analytic methodology of social psychology is very useful here. For example, it can be demonstrated that sex is a salient social category even under the most impersonal of circumstances and even when it may be useless or counterproductive as a source of information about the person (Grady, 1977). Very few individuals appear to question what makes sex such an apparently useful source of information.

There is evidence, moreover, that people use sex-related information differently, depending on whether they are making judgments about themselves or others (Spence & Sawin, 1985). Males and females also use different categories in evaluating their own gender identity: males use *attributes,* such as strength or size, and females use *roles,* such as mother or wife. Neither group, however, appears to regard either sex or gender as anything other than a simple, unitary, "fact of life."

One of the most difficult questions in understanding sex as a cognitive variable is determining when it is salient for the individual and when it is not. Sex-related effects do not appear in every possible social context. They have a "now you see them, now you don't" quality, which makes analysis difficult (Unger, 1981). Some important work has been devoted to developing typologies of contexts in which sex-related effects appear. A number of intriguing findings have emerged.

First, sex appears to be an important cue for behavior when the individual is a member of a statistically rare category for the social context in which he or she appears. This condition applies to sex both as a self-label (McGuire, McGuire, & Winton, 1979) and as a label used by others (Taylor, Fiske, Close, Anderson, & Ruderman, 1977, cited in Taylor & Fiske, 1978). It is possible that statistical deviance heightens the expectation of role deviance.

Second, sex-related differences in social behaviors appear to be maximized when such behaviors are subject to public scrutiny, as compared to situations in which individuals believe that their behaviors are private and anonymous (Eagly, Wood, & Fishbaugh, 1981; Kidder, Belletirie, & Cohn, 1977). Public behavior appears to conform to sex-stereotypic assumptions much more than does private behavior. What is particularly important about these findings is that they derive from one of the very few methodologies that permit social scientists to manipulate societal norms within a laboratory context. The difference between public and private represents a difference in assumptions about the probability with which others will evaluate one's behavior. For example, males are found to be more concerned with equity and justice in public than in private (Kidder et al., 1977). It is difficult to argue that long-standing personality traits underlie sex-characteristic behaviors that are so easily influenced by social comparisons.

Third, sex-characteristic patterns of behavior can be made to conform to the expectations of others. Laboratory models of the "self-fulfilling prophecy" have demonstrated that gender-linked "personality traits" (such as "sociability") of the target person may be altered by changing the expectations of the individual with whom they are interacting. Effects are produced by manipulating the beliefs of the observer about other gender-relevant characteristics of the target individual, such as her physical attractiveness (Snyder, Tanke, & Berscheid, 1977).

Physical attractiveness is associated with assumptions of further gender-appropriate characteristics for both males and females. Handsome males are seen as particularly likely to possess masculine characteristics, and beautiful females are seen as possessing feminine attributes (Lemay & Unger, 1982). In contrast, lack of attractiveness is associated with perceptions of social deviance in a variety of situational domains. For example, less attractive males and females are seen to be more likely to be campus radicals than are their more attractive counterparts (Unger, Hilderbrand, & Madar, 1982).

Fourth, developmentally and culturally consistent patterns of behaviors directed toward males and females can be identified that may be related to sex-related differences in personality. For example, the most persistent contexts in which females are helped more than males are those involving travel outside the home. (Piliavin & Unger, 1985). Young girls are helped more than boys when they request assistance from their teachers or adult mentors (Serbin, Connor, & Citron, 1978). Interestingly, girls also request more help when they are placed in the kind of structured activities that preschool girls appear to prefer (Carpenter, Huston, & Holt, 1986). Together, these data suggest that social and environmental constraints induce helpless or dependent behaviors in females that are frequently attributed to personality traits or even biological determinants.

Although this kind of constructionist paradigm has produced some very interesting information about sex and gender, there are dangers as well as strengths in the cognitive paradigm. Problems will probably emerge more clearly as the territory is further explored, but a few "traps" are already evident. One major problem is how to distinguish compliance with a gender-prescriptive reality from the actual self as actor. A useful tool in this regard is the methodological distinction between public and private behavior discussed above. One may assume that private behavior is less constrained by social desirability and therefore more closely represents the self as actor.

A more serious problem for cognitive theories about sex and gender involves the search for general laws that regulate behavior. Research has already shown that people use different information about sex and gender to organize their own behavior as contrasted to the behavior of others. Males and females may also use different sources of information to answer identical questions about their gender-relevant attributes (Spence & Sawin, 1985). The "same" information about sex and gender may be used differently by children of different ages (Katz, 1986). We therefore have every reason to believe that such information will also be used differently by individuals of different cultures, social classes, or ethnicities. We must be as wary of overgeneralizing a "female" consciousness as we have been of overgeneralizing from males to females or from the American middle class to everyone else. The search for truly general laws must be conducted with acute attention paid to the influence of transitory contextual variables.

On the other hand, the analysis of reality as individually constructed and highly subjective also carries traps with it. If everyone constructs their own reality, what criteria do we use to test the validity of their constructs? Some personal realities appear to be more functional than others, but utility may come at the cost of the individual's excessive compliance with societal norms. Functional analyses of both intrapsychic and behavioral coping may be greatly influenced by the values of the evaluator (Fine, 1983–1984). Middle-class investigators may too easily blame the victim and ignore the constraints of environments unfamiliar to them.

A focus on events that take place "inside one's head" may also make it easier to ignore external realities that are not under the person's control. For example, current analyses of stereotyping consider stereotypic perception as a normal variant of information seeking and cognitive processing. In a sense, stereotypes offer a kind of cognitive economy for the individual who needs to evaluate information about a wide assortment of different people. Stereotypes provide an easy way to select and remember information about others (Deaux, 1985; Hansen, 1980; Snyder & Uranowitz, 1978). These analyses, however, tend to ignore the fact that this kind of cognitive economy is not helpful to those individuals who are grouped as members of target populations. Nor do social analyses based on information processing explain individual differences in the extent and kind of stereotypes produced. Lastly, our fascination with the more powerful segments of society has produced little work on the consciousness of the victims of prejudice. Faye Crosby's (1982) and Kenneth Dion's (Dion, 1975; Dion & Earn, 1975) excellent work in this area are notable exceptions.

In sum, the "person constructs reality" paradigm as currently applied to sex and gender has both pluses and minuses. It takes a big step forward by providing psychologists with a theoretical rationale for measuring perceptions and cognitions about females and males. It also places explanations for sex-related differences within the framework of social reality rather than physical or biological reality. However, cognitive psychology does not explain how social reality is translated into individual reality. We need to explain when and why people are different as well as when and why they are similar. Some questions that need to be resolved include: Why do perceptions and cognitions about males and females appear to be consistent across a wide variety of times and places? Why do females concur with a social reality that is harmful to themselves as individuals? How do we explain those individuals who appear to be "invulnerable" to sex-characteristic attributions about themselves or others?

There is also a difference between a cognitive and a feminist perspective on sex and gender. Perhaps the greatest danger of a cognitive perspective is that psychologists will come to believe that all the questions about sex and gender can be answered within that paradigm, and we will forget that there are real societal forces that impact on the individual's ability to influence his or her own reality. The major social fact that has been ignored is the differential nature of social power (Unger, 1986). People of some social groups have more ability to impose their definitions of reality than do others. Their definitions influence the extent to which members of oppressed groups make use of resources theoretically available to all (Sherif, 1982). We need to understand how individuals incorporate an inegalitarian reality into their personal identities. But we also need to recognize that society is inegalitarian and that systems as well as individuals must change.

Theoretical and Empirical Work in an Alternative Epistemology

It is important for feminist psychologists to develop theories and to conduct empirical work that takes into account the alternative paradigms discussed earlier and transcends them. In the last few years I have been conducting work in two areas: one on the impact of values on thought and the other—more theoretical—on the nature of the interactive relationship between the person and the social environment. In working empirically and theoretically through these two areas, I have found neither paradigm adequate, and their condition as an "either/or" choice for a feminist conceptual framework is problematic.

This work is by no means complete (if it ever will be), but I want to share some of it here in terms of where I see the work fitting into the psychology of sex and gender, some of the results and problems of trying to work between paradigms, and some of the ironies involved in putting theory into practice. Because I am concerned with the epistemological relationship of this work to the epistemology of psychology, my discussion is less historical than is usually the case. In other words, I present the research questions and ideas in which I am interested in terms of their conceptual meaning for me, rather than in terms of how they represent the "inevitable" progression of the field. Indeed, I argue that psychology's lack of awareness of its own epistemology and its lack of attention to the reflexive connection between researchers and their research account for its inability to achieve a dialectical synthesis between the person and reality.

The Impact of Values on Thought

There is a body of evidence showing that individual researchers within the social sciences espouse different beliefs about the relationship between the person and reality that is similar to the more generic epistemologies discussed above. Not only has psychology shifted back and forth between two alternative epistemologies, but individual psychologists appear to agree predominantly with one or the other of these world views. Various researchers have conferred different terms for these positions, such as nature–nurture (Pastore, 1949), objectivist–subjectivist (Coan, 1979), or, most recently (by analogy to C. P. Snow), psychology's two cultures (Kimble, 1984). These varying epistemological viewpoints appear to be deeply embedded and not consciously attended to by most individuals.

Since feminism has been a major force in the critique of methodology and conceptualization in psychology (Gergen, 1985; Unger, 1983; Wallston, 1981; Wallston & Grady, 1985), it would not be surprising if feminist scholars share an epistemology that differs from others in the field. It is also likely that our epistemology will be consistent with a "person constructs reality" (i.e., social constructionist) framework. On the basis of these hypotheses, I constructed an instrument—the Attitudes about Reality Scale (AAR)—designed to measure epistemological position on a continuum ranging from a strong belief in a logical positivist framework to a strong belief in a social constructionist world view. Beliefs about how the world works were evaluated across a variety of conceptual domains involving such issues as: whether power is personal or social in nature; whether group differences may be best explained by biological or environmental factors; the value and efficacy of individual efforts to change society; and the nature of science and its impact on society (Unger, Draper, & Pendergrass, 1986).

Both feminist scholars (Unger, 1984–1985) and students enrolled in courses on women (Unger et al., 1986) hold more socially constructionist views than comparable others. In sum, they tended to agree with statements indicating that power is conferred by society; that differences between groups can be explained better by environmental than by biological factors; and that science is influenced by cultural values and is not an altogether positive force in the solution of human problems. Feminists also believe that success is not always the result of merit. Although they appear to be aware that individual behavior is constrained by social and cultural forces, feminists paradoxically also strongly agree with statements suggesting that individuals can have an impact on society. In some ways, they seemed to be espousing an inconsistent epistemology—believing that humans are a product of their social reality, while at the same time asserting the ability of the individual to change that reality.

Research in cognitive processes involving sex and gender suggests that neither sex nor gender is used holistically. What is particularly striking is the ability of the individual to process identical information about the self and others differently. For example, we have found enormous differences in agreement with a statement acknowledging sex, race, or class discrimination depending on whether the statement is worded in the first or third person singular (Unger & Sussman, 1986). Women seem to be able to notice the existence of sex discrimination for others, while they deny the relevance of this information to themselves (Crosby, 1982).

Feminists and other social activists appear to be aware that society is unfair and yet believe that they can have an impact on it. This distinction between the self and others probably helps to explain why scores on the AAR do not correlate significantly with traditional measures of internal–external locus of control, which word statements about the relationship between behavior and its outcome in terms of the self. Beliefs about the social construction of reality for others, however, do correlate significantly with a lower belief in the just world (Rubin & Peplau, 1973) and a belief in the social, political, and economic equality of the sexes (Spence & Helmreich, 1978). In contrast, those who believe in more logically positivist explanations about how the world works also show more traditional patterns on these measures; for example, they believe that the world is a fair place, that people get what they deserve, and that traditional gender roles are appropriate and correct.

Not all women are feminists, nor are all feminists female. One of the surprising findings in our studies using the AAR Scale is that when environmental context is held constant (i.e., male and female subjects are selected from the same classes), subject sex differences are far less important than are course differences. In other words, epistemological position is predicted better by the individual's self-selection of what to learn about than by his or her biological or social category.

These data lead to several other interesting questions. How do people develop a social constructionist epistemology? And what is the relationship between social constructionism and the belief in feminism (defined broadly as commitment to the social, economic, and political equality of the sexes)? We have found that social constructionism is significantly correlated to a number of biographical and demographic markers that are consistent with a problematic relationship with American society as a whole. Thus, social constructionists are more likely to be members of a minority religion or espouse no religion at all; they are more likely to be politically liberal; and they are very likely to be found among students who attend college at an untraditionally older age (Unger et al., 1986).

Those who label themselves as feminists appear to have the most socially constructionist views of any group yet tested. These results are consistent with a study of feminist psychologists by Mary Ricketts (1986) using Coan's Theoretical Orientation Scale. She found that feminists were more subjectivist in their views than other women attending conferences on the psychology of women, and that lesbian feminists were the most subjectivist of all. Commitment to various subdisciplines within psychology was less important in predicting epistemological position than were self-assessed ideological and sexual labels.

These findings are difficult to explain except in terms of identification with marginal groups within society. As a pioneering paper by Helen Hacker (1951) asserts, membership in an oppressed group is not the same as membership in a minority group. The awareness that discrimination is due to one's group membership rather than to one's personal failures crucially changes one's perceptions. Social activists appear to be able to maintain a contradictory cognitive schema that acknowledges both social injustice and the efficacy of individual efforts to change society (Forward & Williams, 1970; Sanger & Alker, 1972). Such contradictory belief patterns may be supported by identification with a socially stigmatized group.

Different life experiences appear to be related even to the epistemologies that scholarly researchers develop (Coan, 1979; Sherwood & Nataupsky, 1968). We still know little, however, about the relationship between particular life circumstances and epistemological position. Crosby and Herek (1986) have found, for example, no connection between men's knowledge about the experiences of the women in their lives and their perception of sex inequality. It is possible that different epistemologies lead people to perceive identical circumstances in a different way. The AAR Scale was constructed, in part, as a kind of verbal Rorschach test to get at this question of differing interpretations. Whether one views a "fact" as an enduring truth or a probabilistic statement will probably make a difference in how one responds to an item such as "The facts of science change over time." We are presently conducting research to find out whether people with different epistemologies interpret similar words differently.

These data suggest there is a relationship between personal epistemology and the epistemological frameworks developed by psychologists. Moreover, personal circumstances appear to influence world views in the same way for both scholars and "ordinary people." Since people use the same information to construct conflicting explanatory structures, they may be unaware of the extent to which their subjective realities diverge.

The Relationship between the Individual and Her Social Environment

Research on personal epistemology as well as on the whole field of sex and gender prompts a difficult and crucial question: How does the individual acquiesce in the construction of a reality that is harmful to that individual? It was easier when we could dichotomize society into *us* and *them,* but it is clear that both sexes are part of the reality with which we deal. The question of the extent to which people incorporate the social categories known as norms and roles versus the extent to which people maintain their individuality is one of the basic questions that a true social psychology of people will have to resolve. Circumstances change, but people can also perceive them differently and thus change these circumstances. The processes by which we reconstruct our social categories are fundamental if we are to understand the way individuals produce social change.

In several recent papers, I have discussed the nature of the "invisible" social frameworks that direct behaviors into what we consider to be masculine or feminine traits (Unger, 1985, 1988). A major feature of this theoretical framework is its use of the interpersonal transaction as a unit of analysis rather than the individual alone. In brief, I have argued that stereotypes are a fundamental part of consensual reality, that there are many more cognitively contradictory perceptions of females than males, and that these contradictory perceptions are an important force in shaping gender-characteristic behaviors in our society. I have focused most on the construction of double binds for women, particularly when they step into the world outside the role prescriptions for domesticity. Double binds put the individual at risk regardless of the behavior she manifests. However, since the preferred unit of analysis in our society (as well as within psychology) is the individual, women attribute the inevitable negative consequences of their behavior to themselves rather than to situational constraints. Even our vocabulary for analyzing this kind of social process is miserly compared to our rich vocabulary for documenting every nuance of intrapsychic traits and characteristics.

This theoretical framework is tied to the empirical data on personal epistemology discussed earlier in several ways. First, it places the primary explanation for phenomena related to sex and gender within a social constructionist framework. The terms social and constructionist are both critical here. Individual behavior is defined as meaningless outside a social context, in which both females and males come to share the dominant ideology of a society. This framework posits the dominant ideology, however, as manifested through ongoing relationships, rather than as simply incorporated as a stable aspect of personality within the individual's psyche.

Cognitive mechanisms mediate interpersonal interactions. These mechanisms include: biased perceptions about the sexes, such as the belief that males are more logical than females (Broverman, Vogel, Broverman, Clarkson, & Rosenkrantz, 1972); the ability to screen and remember evidence differentially depending on its consistency with one's cognitive schema (Skrypnek & Snyder, 1982); as well as attributional processes that "explain" sex-related outcomes that are inconsistent with perceptual paradigms in ways that maintain preferred reality. Thus, when women are portrayed as more successful than men, this unexpected outcome is explained by their greater luck, effort, or other unstable cause (Hansen & O'Leary, 1985). Individuals may choose explanations that are harmful to themselves rather than question the social reality of which they are a part. Women's tendency to deny the impact of sex discrimination on themselves while recognizing its impact on other women (Crosby, 1982) illustrates this pattern of thinking.

Second, this theoretical framework acknowledges the difference between the social and "real" self. Individuals, especially those from socially marginal groups, are likely to be isolated within those social contexts in which biased definitions play a large part. They have no opportunity to validate outcomes in terms of the reality of others like themselves and thus have no alternative but to share dominant reality with its value-laden definitions of others in their social category. Distinguishing oneself from others in a devalued category is probably an effective mechanism for defending oneself against depression. This mechanism, however, also ensures that those in a position to change the dominant ideology about members of their group will also be less likely to identify with it.

Development of group consciousness appears to play a crucial role in the formation of a cognitive framework that avoids blaming the victim for her failure to surmount her circumstances (Rosenthal, 1984). This form of consciousness may be facilitated by childhood circumstances that indicate a lack of accord with the dominant values of American society. A social constructionist framework, however, may also lead one to seek information that is consistent with a less meritocratic belief structure. Such information is most likely to be found in situations where people who identify with socially marginal groups are also likely to be found. Hence, biographical background, present information base, and reference group all contribute to our belief structures (Unger et al., 1986).

The Problem of Inconsistency

What are we to make of all this complexity? Clearly, we cannot view sex and gender as holistic concepts, despite the fact that individuals in our society rarely examine their underlying assumptions for either others or themselves (Spence & Sawin, 1985). Assumptions about the sexes are also clearly tied to a complex network of assumptions about how the world works and which strategies are most useful for dealing with that world. Since we pay little attention to our underlying belief structures, we have little opportunity to examine them for inconsistencies or to alter them in the face of conflicting evidence.

Personal epistemology appears to be relatively consistent over a large variety of conceptual domains and fairly stable over time (Unger et al., 1986). People appear to establish systematic belief structures similar to those found among established scholars before being trained in a particular discipline's epistemological assumptions (King, 1980). Social constructionist epistemology appears to be associated with social marginality in such areas as religion and sexual orientation, as well as gender ideology.

Although we have not yet done analyses for other groups, active feminists appear to be able to incorporate an ideology that insists on the possibility of both societal and personal control (Unger, 1984–1985). I would argue that such a paradoxical epistemological position is particularly adaptive to a contradictory reality. Feminists recognize the power of consensually defined social reality, while at the same time recognizing that individuals have the power to evade sex-biased definitions of their behavior. It is possible, for example, that female supervisors may exchange structural criticisms of established corporate policy when among females of equal company rank but frame the same issues in more guarded, individualistic terms when among subordinates or males of any rank. Judith Laws (1975) suggested such a dual consciousness in her early and important work on academic tokenism, but I know of no clear empirical test of this hypothesis. Proof of such contradictory patterns may necessitate the selection of social contexts in which alternative verbal and nonverbal definitional processes apply.

In the examination of the evasion of sex bias, however, the irony of trying to avoid the pitfalls of either logical positivist or constructionist models becomes evident. Social constructionists cannot ignore the fact that the power to define reality is more in the hands of some social groups than others. The governing groups tend to enforce and apply their own epistemological position. Thus the evidence we generate to support the social construction of gender-based reality will be evaluated in terms of both professional and personal epistemology. I have provided data to suggest that feminist epistemology is quite distinct as a constructionist way of looking at the world. Nevertheless, the methods that I have used to demonstrate this point are clearly logical positivist. How am I to deal with this inconsistency?

Scholars in a number of disciplines have attempted to avoid the assumptions of logical positivism by using various deconstructionist techniques. Such methodologies involve letting each person construct her own reality. Personal reality is seen as having no meaning apart from its historical and cultural context or the personal circumstances of the individual's life. Evidence about shared reality is provided through a comparison of shared stories.

This kind of methodology, however, is inconsistent with the desire of most psychologists to find generic predictors of human actions. Feminist social psychologists therefore must live with even more inconsistency than other feminist scholars. Any self-assessment method, as contrasted to psychodynamic or phenomenological approaches, appears to strip behavior from its historical and cultural context. What is the relationship between the response to items on a paper-and-pencil scale and the response to similar issues of effectiveness and merit in the context of personal evaluation? I can measure generic consistency in social constructionist beliefs only by using a measure that may strip these beliefs of their social meaning.

Some of these same kinds of inconsistencies emerge in attempts to analyze the ongoing perceptual dynamics in the relationships between individuals. Double binds are constructed by means of unexamined and contradictory definitions of normative female behavior (Unger, 1988; Wood & Conrad, 1983). They are effective largely because they are invisible to the participants in a social transaction. Not only do we lack a vocabulary to describe these social constraints, but attempts to bring them into awareness will probably cause them to disappear. Ironically, the "Heisenberg principle" is a concept shared with physics that psychologists have been less willing to acknowledge than operationalism or experimental methodology. Physicists recognize that they cannot predict the behavior of single electrons, but psychologists are less willing and less able to abandon the individual. Our apparent inability to deal with the subjective without losing the objective and vice versa is exemplified by psychology's endless cycling between the two basic paradigms with which I introduced this chapter. It has split psychologists into "two cultures" (Kimble, 1984) and threatens to tear apart the field as a unitary discipline.

The Uses of Paradox

It is easy for psychologists to get caught in dualisms (c.f. Coan. 1979, for a list of some of the dualisms uncovered by his Theoretical Orientation Scale). Contradiction, however, may be used to avoid some apparent dichotomies. The person versus situation controversy may be resolved, for example, by noting that persons bring symbolic constraints to situations (in terms of the way they perceive and define the world). These cognitive frameworks influence how they perceive and explain the mechanisms of interpersonal control found within most relationships between the sexes outside the home. We need to integrate findings on contradictory perceptions about men and women and about self versus others in identical circumstances. Unexamined contradictions in such perceptions help explain how people acquiesce to social schemata that are potentially harmful to them.

Similarly, dualisms involving internal versus external causality can be transcended by looking for methods that vary the extent of social coercion in apparently identical behavioral contexts. Private versus public behavior is one method by which societal prescriptions may be varied. Other methods may involve alteration of the "rules" for socially desirable behavior or the imposition of salient stimulus persons who embody particular gender-prescriptive norms. For example, work by Mark Zanna and his associates (von Baeyer, Sherk, & Zanna, 1981) has demonstrated differences in self-presentation style based on women's assumptions about an interview with a sexist or nonsexist employer.

A final duality involves the person versus society. Research on feminist epistemology indicates that a belief in the efficacy of the person may be linked to identification with a reference group whose consensual validation of reality resembles one's own. Some kinds of research questions can be formulated only if we accept the validity of a number of definitions of personal reality and are able to measure the discordance between various constructs. Thus, our American belief in individualism and the meritocracy may be possible only if those who construct this reality benefit from it and are able to discount the realities of others who do not. More communal analyses of social welfare may be easier for those who define human society more inclusively and who find the status quo less personally beneficial or rewarding.

Philosophers value the study of paradox because it prompts questions about the nature of a given belief system that can produce such conceptual "traps." A more familiar analogy for psychology is the study of optical illusions, which are "perceptual paradoxes" in the sense that identical physical stimuli produce several different sensory responses. When we find an optical illusion, we do not question the nature of physical reality. Instead, we analyze neural and perceptual mechanisms to see how the multiple reality is created. Similarly, the study of social paradoxes can lead to a richer conceptualization of what must be known.

Social contradictions exist because people either accept several conflicting definitions about the same person or differ as to when particular definitions should be applied. Psychology lacks the criteria to determine whose definitions are more valid, or even if "validity" has any meaning in consensually defined reality. Our yardsticks cannot be merely methodological—they must be conceptual and moral as well. We need a different, transcendant model for human beings. Perhaps the kind of person who functions best in a socially constructed world is one who can live in each reality as though it were the only one, but who knows that it is possible to stand outside them all.

REFERENCES

Broverman, I. K., Vogel, S. R., Broverman, D. M., Clarkson, F. E., & Rosenkrantz, P. S. (1972). Sex-role stereotypes: A current appraisal. *Journal of Social Issues, 28,* 59–78.

Buss, A. R. (1975). The emerging field of the sociology of psychological knowledge. *American Psychologist, 30,* 988–1002.

Buss, A. R. (1976). Galton and sex differences: An historical note. *Journal of the History of the Behavioral Sciences, 12,* 283–285.

Carpenter, C. J., Huston, A. C., & Holt, W. (1986). Modification of preschool sex-typed behaviors by participation in adult-structured activities. *Sex Roles, 14,* 603–615.

Coan, R. W. (1979). *Psychologists: Personal and theoretical pathways.* New York: Irvington.

Crosby, F. J. (1982). *Relative deprivation and working women.* New York: Oxford University Press.

Crosby, F. J., & Herek, G. M. (1986). Male sympathy and the situation of women: Does personal experience make a difference? *Journal of Social Issues, 42,* 55–66.

Deaux, K. (1985). Sex and gender. *Annual Review of Psychology, 36,* 49–81.

Deaux, K., & Major, B. (1987). Putting gender into context: An interactive model of gender-related behavior. *Psychological Review, 94,* 369–389.

Dion, K. L. (1975). Women's reaction to discrimination from members of the same or opposite sex. *Journal of Research in Personality, 9,* 294–306.

Dion, K. L., & Earn, B. M. (1975). The phenomenology of being a target of prejudice. *Journal of Personality and Social Psychology, 32,* 944–950.

Eagly, A. H., Wood, W., & Fishbaugh, L. (1981). Sex differences in conformity: Surveillance by the group as a determinant of male nonconformity. *Journal of Personality and Social Psychology, 40,* 384–394.

Fine, M. (1983–1984). Coping with rape: Critical perspective on consciousness. *Imagination, Cognition, and Personality, 3,* 249–267.

Forward, J. R., & Williams, J. R. (1970). Internal–external control and black militancy. *Journal of Social Issues, 26,* 75–92.

Gardner, H. (1985). *The mind's new science.* New York: Basic Books.

Gergen, K. J. (1985). The social constructionist movement in modern psychology. *American Psychologist, 40,* 266–275.

Grady, K. E. (1977). *The belief in sex differences.* Paper presented at the meeting of the Eastern Psychological Association, Boston.

Hacker, H. M. (1951). Women as a minority group. *Social Forces, 30,* 60–69.

Hansen, R. D. (1980). Commonsense attribution. *Journal of Personality and Social Psychology, 39,* 996–1009.

Hansen, R. D., & O'Leary, V. E. (1985). Sex-determined attributions. In V. E. O'Leary, R. K. Unger, & B. S. Wallston (Eds.), *Women, gender, and social psychology* (pp. 67–99). Hillsdale, NJ: Erlbaum.

Katz, P. A. (1986). Modification of children's gender-stereotyped behavior: General issues and research considerations. *Sex Roles, 14,* 591–602.

Kidder, L. H., Belletirie, G., & Cohn, E. S. (1977). Secret ambitions and public performance: The effect of anonymity on reward allocations made by men and women. *Journal of Experimental Social Psychology, 13,* 70–80.

Kimble, G. A. (1984). Psychology's two cultures. *American Psychologist, 39,* 833–839.

King, D. J. (1980). Values of undergraduate students and faculty members on theoretical orientations in psychology. *Teaching of Psychology, 7,* 236–237.

Konner, M. (1981). *The tangled wing: Biological constraints on the human spirit.* New York: Harper & Row.

Laws, J. L. (1975). The psychology of tokenism: An analysis. *Sex Roles, 1,* 51–67.

Lemay, M. F., & Unger, R. K. (1982). *The perception of females and males: The relationship between physical attractiveness and gender.* Paper presented at the meeting of the Eastern Psychological Association, Baltimore.

McGuire, W. J., McGuire, C. V., & Winton, W. (1979). Effects of household sex composition on the salience of one's gender in the spontaneous self-concept. *Journal of Experimental Social Psychology, 15,* 77–90.

Neisser, U. (1967). *Cognitive psychology.* New York: Appleton-Century-Crofts.

Pastore, N. (1949). *The nature–nurture controversy.* New York: King's Cross Press.

Piliavin, J. A., & Unger, R. K. (1985). The helpful but helpless female: Myth or reality. In V. E. O'Leary, R. K. Unger, & B. S. Wallston (Eds.), *Women, gender, and social psychology* (pp. 149–189). Hillsdale, NJ: Erlbaum.

Ricketts, M. (1986). *Theoretical orientations and values of feminist psychologists.* Unpublished Ph.D. dissertation, University of Windsor.

Rosenberg, R. (1982). *Beyond separate spheres: Intellectual roots of modern feminism.* New Haven: Yale University Press.

Rosenthal, N. B. (1984). Consciousness raising: From revolution to reevaluation. *Psychology of Women Quarterly, 8,* 309–326.

Rubin, Z., & Peplau, A. (1973). Belief in a just world and reactions to another's lot: A study of participants in the national draft lottery. *Journal of Social Issues, 29,* 73–93.

Sanger, B. P., & Alker, H. A. (1972). Dimensions of internal–external locus of control and the women's liberation movement. *Journal of Social Issues, 29,* 115–129.

Serbin, L. A., Connor, J. M., & Citron, C. C. (1978). Environmental control of independent and dependent behaviors in preschool boys and girls: A model for early independence training. *Sex Roles, 4,* 867–875.

Sherif, C. W. (1982). Needed concepts in the study of gender identity. *Psychology of Women Quarterly, 6,* 375–398.

Sherwood, J. J., & Nataupsky, M. (1968). Predicting the conclusions of Negro–White intelligence research from biographical characteristics of the investigator. *Journal of Personality and Social Psychology, 8,* 53–58.

Shields, S. A. (1975). Functionalism, Darwinism, and the psychology of women: A study in social myth. *American Psychologist, 30,* 739–754.

Skrypnek, B. J., & Snyder, M. (1982). On the self-perpetuating nature of stereotypes about women and men. *Journal of Experimental Social Psychology, 18,* 277–291.

Snyder, M., Tanke, E. D., & Berscheid, E. (1977). Social perception and interpersonal behavior: On the self-fulfilling nature of social stereotypes. *Journal of Personality and Social Psychology, 35,* 656–666.

Snyder, M., & Uranowitz, S. W. (1978). Reconstructing the past: Some cognitive consequences of person perception. *Journal of Personality and Social Psychology, 36,* 941–950.

Spence, J. T., & Helmreich, R. (1978). *Masculinity and femininity: Their psychological dimensions, correlates, and antecedents.* Austin: University of Texas Press.

Spence, J. T., & Sawin, L. L. (1985). Images of masculinity and femininity: A reconceptualization. In V. E. O'Leary, R. K. Unger, & B. S. Wallston (Eds.), *Women, gender, and social psychology* (pp. 35–66) Hillsdale, NJ: Erlbaum.

Taylor, S. E., & Fiske, S. T. (1978). Salience, attention, and attribution: Top of the head phenomena. In L. Berkowitz (Ed.), *Advances in experimental social psychology,* Vol. 11. New York: Academic Press.

Unger, R. K. (1981). Sex as a social reality: Field and laboratory research. *Psychology of Women Quarterly, 5,* 645–653.

Unger, R. K. (1983). Through the looking glass: No Wonderland yet! (The reciprocal relationship between methodology and models of reality.) *Psychology of Women Quarterly, 8,* 9–32.

Unger, R. K. (1984–1985). Explorations in feminist ideology: Surprising consistencies and unexamined conflicts. *Imagination, Cognition, and Personality, 4,* 395–403.

Unger, R. K. (1985). Between the "no longer" and the "not yet": Reflections on personal and social change. First Carolyn Wood Sherif Memorial Lecture. Presented at the meeting of the American Psychological Association, Los Angeles.

Unger, R. K. (1986). Looking toward the future by looking at the past: Social activism and social history. *Journal of Social Issues, 42,* 215–227.

Unger, R. K. (1988). Psychological, feminist, and personal epistemology: Transcending contradiction. In M. Gergen (Ed.), *Feminist thought and the structure of knowledge* (pp. 124–141). New York: New York University Press.

Unger, R. K., Draper, R. D., & Pendergrass, M. L. (1986). Personal epistemology and personal experience. *Journal of Social Issues, 42,* 67–79.

Unger, R. K., Hilderbrand, M., & Madar, T. (1982). Physical attractiveness and assumptions about social deviance: Some sex by sex comparisons. *Personality and Social Psychology Bulletin, 8,* 293–301.

Unger, R. K., & Sussman, L. E. (1986). "I and thou": Another barrier to societal change? *Sex Roles, 14,* 629–636.

von Baeyer, C. L., Sherk, D. L., & Zanna, M. P. (1981). Impression management in the job interview: When the female applicant meets the male (chauvinist) interviewer. *Personality and Social Psychology Bulletin, 7,* 45–51.

Wallston, B. S. (1981). What are the questions in psychology of women? A feminist approach to research. *Psychology of Women Quarterly, 5,* 597–617.

Wallston, B. S., & Grady, K. E. (1985). Integrating the feminist critique and the crisis in social psychology: Another look at research methods. In V. E. O'Leary, R. K. Unger, & B. S. Wallston (Eds.), *Women, gender, and social psychology* (pp. 7–33). Hillsdale, NJ: Erlbaum.

Wood, J. T., & Conrad, C. (1983). Paradox in the experience of professional women. *Western Journal of Speech Communication, 47,* 305–322.

Chapter Twenty-Six

Men, Inexpressiveness, and Power

Jack W. Sattel

Another thing I learned—if *you* cry, the audience won't.
A man can cry for his horse, for his dog, for another
man, but he cannot cry for a woman. A strange thing.
He can cry at the death of a friend or a pet. But where
he's supposed to be boss; with his child or wife, something like that, he better hold 'em back and let *them* cry.
  —John Wayne, in one of his last interviews

Much of the recent commentary on men and sex roles in this society has focused on the inability of males to show affection, tenderness, or vulnerability in their dealings with both other men and women. John Wayne may be dead, but the masculine style stressing silent strength and the masking of emotions is still very much alive. What are the origins and dynamics of such "male inexpressiveness"? How do the strictures against masculine self-disclosure connect to the other roles men and women play in this society?

In their initial thinking about American sex roles, sociologists didn't question the social processes that gave rise to the expectations that men would be relatively unemotional and constrained in the amount of intimacy they displayed and expected from others. For example, in an influential early theoretical statement, Talcott Parsons (1951) assumed the existence of a sexual division of labor in this society whereby men largely do the work of the public sphere (the economy) and women perform the socio-emotional work of the private sphere (the family). Parsons fastened on the fact that the economy demands that action be based upon deliberative, calculated premises which are as free as possible from "contaminating" personal or emotional considerations. Simultaneously, in Parsons's theory, the family—women's specialized domain—serves as respite and haven from the harsh coldness of the economy. For Parsons, learning experiences that shape men into inexpressive ways of relating to others, while reserving for women nurturant and expressive modes of relating, serve nicely to reproduce and perpetuate American institutions.

Jack W. Sattel, "Men, Inexpressiveness, and Power." In B. Thorne, C. Kramerae, & N. Henley (Eds.), *Language, Gender, and Society,* pp. 118–124. © 1983 by Heinle & Heinle Publishers. Reprinted with permission.

Only relatively recently, spurred by the insights of the women's and gay people's movements for change in American institutions, have sociologists begun to rethink the neat link Parsons postulated between what men (and women) are and do in this society. Unfortunately, much of the analysis thus far has focused so narrowly on inexpressiveness as a personality trait of men that one is left with the impression that the problem's solution lies in merely re-educating individual adult men toward their (human) capacity to feel deeply or authentically. In this essay I want to criticize such analyses as fundamentally shallow—the problem, I want to argue, lies not in men's inexpressiveness per se, but in the power and investment men hold *as a group* in the existing institutional and social framework. I am not denying the fact of male inexpressiveness; neither would I deny the destructive consequences inexpressiveness has for individual men and for the tenor of their social relationships (Balswick & Peek, 1971; Jourard, 1971; Farrell, 1974). However, I would deny or certainly argue against an interpretation that fails to connect inexpressiveness to the social and sexual division of labor.

A 1971 article, "The Inexpressive Male: A Tragedy of American Society," typifies a line of argument which has become widespread. The authors, Balswick and Peek, conceptualize male inexpressiveness as a culturally produced personality trait which is simply learned by boys as the major characteristic of their anticipated adult masculinity. Such inexpressiveness is evidenced in two ways: first, in adult male behavior that does not indicate affection, tenderness, or emotion, and second, in men's tendency to not support the affective expectations of others, especially their wives. B.iswick and Peek imply that both boys and men *devalue* expressive behavior in others as non-masculine; the taunts and "put-downs" of expressive or sensitive adolescents are a ready example of how such devaluation enforces a masculine style among men. For Balswick and Peek, the "tragedy" of inexpressiveness lies in the inability of the American male to relate effectively to women in the context of the increasingly intimate American style of marriage; that is, the victim of this tragedy is the American male and the traditional American family.

I think this conceptualization of inexpressiveness has two important weaknesses. First, Balswick and Peek assume that inexpressiveness originates in, and is the simple result of, two parallel and basically equal sex-role stereotypes into which male and female children are differentially socialized:

> Children, from the time they are born both explicitly and implicitly are taught how to be a man or how to be a woman. While the girl is taught to act "feminine", . . . the boy is taught to be a man. In learning to be a man, the boy in American society comes to value expressions of masculinity . . . [such as] toughness, competitiveness, and aggressiveness. (1971, 353–54)

Such an attempt to ground inexpressiveness in socialization overlooks the fact that masculinity is not the opposite of femininity. The starting point for understanding masculinity lies, not in its contrast with femininity, but in the asymmetrical dominance and prestige which accrue to males in this society. Male dominance takes shape in the positions of formal and informal *power* men hold in the social division of labor; greater male prestige includes, and is evidenced by, the greater *reward* which attaches to male than to female activities, as well as the codification of differential prestige in our language and customs (cf. Henley, 1977). What our culture embodies, in other words, is not simply two stereotypes—one masculine, one feminine—but a set of power and prestige arrangements attached to gender. That is what is meant when we talk of this society as being "sexist."

My argument is that one reason little boys become inexpressive is not simply because our culture expects boys to be that way—but because our culture expects little boys to grow up to hold positions of power and prestige. What better way is there to exercise power than *to make it appear* that *all* one's behavior seems to be the result of unemotional rationality. Being impersonal and inexpressive lends to one's decisions and position an apparent autonomy and "rightness." This is a style we quickly recognize in the recent history of American politics: Nixon guarded the assault to his position by "stonewalling" it; Gerald Ford asked us to "hang tough and bite the bullet"; while Edmund Muskie was perceived as unfit for the Presidency because he cried in public.[1]

Keeping cool, keeping distant as others challenge you or make demands upon you, is a strategy for keeping the upper hand. This same norm of political office—an image of strength and fitness to rule conveyed through inexpressiveness—is not limited to the public sphere; all men in this culture have recourse to this style by virtue of their gender. The structural link usually overlooked in discussions of male inexpressiveness is between gender and *power,* rather than gender and inexpressiveness.

There is a second problem with the way Balswick and Peek conceptualize male inexpressiveness. They regard inexpressiveness as the source of communicative barriers between men and women. Balswick has particularly focused on this as *the* problem in contemporary marriages: "men who care, often very deeply, for their wives ... cannot communicate what is really going on in their hearts" (Balswick, 1979: 110). Perhaps, but one of the repeated insights of my students—particularly older women students—is that male inexpressiveness in interpersonal situations has been *used against women* in a fashion Balswick's description fails to capture. Let me share a page of dialogue from Erica Jong's sketch of upper-middle-class sexual etiquette, *Fear of Flying,* to suggest the use of male inexpressiveness to control a situation. The scene is the couple's honeymoon, just after they have returned from a movie:

[She:] "Why do you always have to do this to me? You make me feel so lonely."
[He:] "That comes from you."
"What do you mean it comes from me? Tonight I wanted to be happy. It's Christmas Eve. Why do you turn on me? What did I do?"
Silence.
"What did I do?"
He looks at her as if her not knowing were another injury.
"Look, let's just go to sleep now. Let's just forget it."
"Forget what?"
He says nothing.
"Forget the fact that you turned on me? Forget the fact that you're punishing me for

nothing? Forget the fact that I'm lonely and cold, that it's Christmas Eve and again you've ruined it for me? Is that what you want me to forget?"

"I won't discuss it."

"Discuss what? What won't you discuss?"

"Shut up! I won't have you screaming in the hotel."

"I don't give a fuck what you won't have me do. I'd like to be treated civilly. I'd like you to at least do me the courtesy of telling my why you're in such a funk. And don't look at me that way. . . ."

"What way?"

"As if my not being able to read your mind were my greatest sin. I *can't* read your mind. I *don't* know why you're so mad. I *can't* intuit your every wish. If that's what you want in a wife you don't have it in me."

"I certainly don't."

"Then what is it? Please tell me."

"I shouldn't have to."

"Good God! Do you mean to tell me I'm expected to be a mind reader? Is that the kind of mothering you want?"

"If you had any empathy for me. . . ."

"But I *do*. My God, you don't give me a chance."

"You tune me out. You don't listen."

"It was something in the movie, wasn't it?"

"What, in the movie?"

"The quiz again. Do you have to quiz me like some kind of criminal? Do you have to cross-examine me? . . . It was the funeral scene. . . . The little boy looking at his dead mother. Something got you there. That was when you got depressed."

Silence.

"Well, *wasn't* it?"

Silence.

"Oh, come on, Bennett, you're making me *furious*. Please tell me. Please."

(He gives the words singly like little gifts. Like hard little turds.) "What was it about that scene that got me?"

"Don't quiz me. Tell me!" (She puts her arms around him. He pulls away—she falls to the floor holding onto his pajama leg. It looks less like an embrace than a rescue scene, she's sinking, he reluctantly allowing her to cling to his leg for support.)

"Get up!"

(Crying.) "Only if you tell me."

(He jerks his leg away.) "I'm going to bed."

(1973: 108–9)

The dialogue clearly indicates that inexpressiveness on the part of the male is *not* just a matter of inarticulateness nor even a deeply socialized inability to respond to the needs of others—the male here is *using* inexpression to guard his own position. To not say anything in this situation is to say something very important indeed: that the battle we are engaged in is to be *fought* by my rules and when I choose to fight. Inexpressiveness signals the limits of the discussion and the tactical alignments of the participants.[2] In general, male inexpressiveness emerges as an intentional manipulation of a situation when threats to the male position occur.

I would extend this point to include the expressive quality of men's interaction with other men. In a perceptive article, "Why Men Aren't Talking," Fasteau (in Pleck & Sawyer, 1974) observes that when men talk, they almost inevitably talk of "large" problems—politics or art; cars or fishing—but never of anything personal. Even among equal-status peers, men seldom make themselves vulnerable to each other, for to do so may be interpreted as a sign of weakness, an opportunity for the other to secure advantage. As Fasteau puts it: men talk, but they always need a reason—and that reason often amounts to another effort at establishing who *really* is best, stronger, smarter, or, ultimately, more powerful.

Those priorities run deep and are established early. In Pleck and Sawyer's (1974) collection on masculinity, there is a section dealing with men and sports. Sport activity is important because it is often held out as one area of both authentic and expressive interaction among men. I wonder. Here is an adult male reminiscing about his fourteenth year:

> I take off at full speed not knowing whether I would reach it but knowing very clearly that this is my chance. My cap flies off my head . . . and a second later I one-hand it as cool as can be . . . I hear the applause . . . I hear voices congratulating my mother for having such a good athlete for a son . . . Everybody on the team pounds my back as they come in from the field, letting me know that I've MADE IT. (Peter Candell in Pleck & Sawyer, 1974: 16)

This is a good picture of boys being drawn together in sport, of sharing almost total experience. But is it? The same person continues in the next paragraph:

> But I know enough not to blow my cool so all I do is mumble thanks under a slightly trembling upper lip which is fighting the rest of my face, the rest of being, from exploding with laughter and tears of joy. (Ibid.)

Why this silence? Again, I don't think it is just because our culture demands inexpression; silence and inexpression are the ways men learn to consolidate power, to make the effort appear as effortless, to guard against showing the real limits on one's potential and power by making it all seem easy. Even among males, one maintains control over a situation by revealing only strategic proportions of oneself.

Much of what is called "men's liberation" takes as its task the "rescuing" of expressive capacity for men, restoring to men their emotional wholeness and authenticity. To the extent such changes do not simultaneously confront the issue of power and inexpressiveness, I see such changes as a continuation rather than a repudiation of sexism. Again, let me offer a literary example. In Alan Lelchuk's (1974) novel about academic life in Cambridge, *American Mischief,* there is a male character who has gleaned something from the women's movement. The "John Wayne" equivalent of the academic male may be passé, but if one is still concerned with "scoring" sexually with as many women as possible—which this character is—male expressiveness is a good way of coming on. Lelchuk's character, in fact, tells women fifteen minutes after he meets them that he is sexually impotent, but with the clear insinuation that "maybe with you it would be different. . . ." In this situation the man's skill at dissembling has less to do with handing a woman a "line" than in displaying his weakness or confidences as signs of authentic, nonexploitative male interest. Again, in a society as thoroughly sexist as ours, men may use expressiveness to continue to control a situation and to maintain their position of dominance.

I've tried to raise these points in my discussion thus far: that inexpressiveness is related to men's position of dominance; that inexpressiveness works as a method for achieving control both in male-female and in male-male interaction; and, that male *expressiveness* in the context of this society might also be used as a strategy to maintain power rather than to move toward non-sexist equality. I think my last point is most important. In 1979 Balswick wrote an article based on the conceptualization of inexpressiveness which I've criticized here. Entitled "How to get your husband to say, 'I love you,' " the article was published in *Family Circle*, a mass distribution women's magazine. Predictably, the article suggests *to the wife* some techniques she might develop for drawing her husband out of his inexpressive shell. I think that kind of article—at this point in the struggle of women to define themselves—is facile and wrong-headed. Such advice burdens the wife with additional "emotional work" while simultaneously creating a new arena in which she can—and most likely will—fail.

Sexism is not significantly challenged by simply changing men's capacity to feel or express themselves. Gender relationships in this society are constructed in terms of social power, and to forget that fact, as Andrew Tolson's book, *The Limits of Masculinity* (1977), so nicely points out, is to assume that men can somehow unproblematically experience "men's liberation"—as if there existed for men some directly analogous experience to the politics created by feminist and gay struggles. Men are not oppressed *as men,* and hence are not in a position to be liberated *as men.* This dilemma has prevented—thus far—the creation of a theory (and a language of liberation) which speaks specifically to men. Everyday language, with its false dichotomies of masculinity-femininity/male-female, obscures the bonds of dominance of men over women; feminist theory illuminates those bonds and the experience of women within patriarchy but has little need to comprehend the experience of being male. In the absence of such formulations, masculinity seems often to be a mere negative quality, oppressive in its exercise to both women and men, indistinguishable from oppression per se. What would a theory look like which accounts for the many forms being a man can take? An answer to that question poses not a "tragedy" but an opportunity.

NOTES

1. This link is reflected in the peculiarly asymmetrical rules of socialization in our society which make it more "dangerous" for a boy than for a girl to be incompletely socialized to gender expectations (compare the greater stigma which attaches to the label "sissy" than to "tomboy"). The connection of gender to power is also apparent in data that suggest parents, as well as other adults in the child's world, exert greater social control over boys to "grow-up-male" than girls to "grow-up-female" (Parsons & Bales, 1955).

2. It would be beside the point to argue that women sometimes will also use inexpressiveness in this manner; when they do so, they are by definition acting "unwomanly." A man acting in this fashion is *within* the culturally acceptable framework.

REFERENCES

Balswick, Jack. 1979. How to get your husband to say "I love you." *Family Circle, 92,* 110.

Balswick, Jack & Christine Avertt. 1977. Differences in expressiveness: Gender, interpersonal orientation, and perceived parental expressiveness as contributing factors. *Journal of Marriage and the Family, 38,* 121–27.

Balswick, Jack & Charles Peek. 1971. The inexpressive male: A tragedy of American society. *The Family Coordinator, 20,* 363–68.

Farrell, Warren. 1974. *The liberated man.* New York: Random House.

Henley, Nancy. 1977. *Body politics.* Englewood Cliffs, N.J.: Prentice-Hall.

Jong, Erica. 1973. *Fear of flying.* New York: New American Library.

Jourard, Sidney M. 1971. *Self-disclosure.* New York: Wiley-Interscience.

Lelchuk, Alan. 1974. *American mischief.* New York: New American Library.

Parsons, Talcott. 1951. *The social system* (Chaps. 6 and 7). Glencoe, Ill.: Free Press.

Parsons, Talcott & Robert Bales. 1955. The American family: Its relation to personality and the social structure. In *Family socialization and interaction process.* Glencoe, Ill.: Free Press.

Pleck, Joseph & Jack Sawyer. 1974. *Men and masculinity.* Englewood Cliffs, N.J.: Prentice-Hall.

Tolson, Andrew. 1977. *The limits of masculinity.* New York: Harper & Row.

Chapter Twenty-Seven

What's So Special about Sex?
Gender Stereotyping and Discrimination

Susan T. Fiske and Laura E. Stevens

The Expert Witness: There are general stereotypes of
what people particularly expect men to be like and typically expect women to be like. People typically expect
women to be strong on the social dimensions. Women
are generally expected to be more tender and understanding and concerned about other people, and soft.

The Court: You say that of people who have dealt
with women expect that? People who have dealt with
women in the business context expect that, or are you
talking about people out on the farm?

—*Price Waterhouse v. Hopkins*, 1989, p. 543

People all have their own opinions about gender stereotypes.[1] Consequently, a social
psychologist explaining the well-established research literature may find herself in the
awkward position of disputing or at least elaborating the audience's commonsense
judgments. Although common sense is the natural foil for all of social psychology
given its domain (Kelley, 1992), it is particularly a problem in the field of gender
stereotypes and discrimination, because of the special status of gender. This chapter
addresses what makes sex special, that is, what makes gender-based responses more
vulnerable to commonsense psychologizing than other types of category-based responses, stemming, for example, from race, age, or disability.

We will argue that gender is special (and especially awkward to evaluate in
commonsense terms) because of (a) the heavily prescriptive aspects of gender stereotypes, (b) the inherent power asymmetries implied by gender differences in social
status and average physical size, (c) the intimate communal relationships between
members of the two groups, (d) the sexual and biological context of interpersonal

how is this gender?

✱ Expand!

interactions, and (e) the rapid historical change in the expression of sexism. As an illustration of these points let's begin with two case studies, drawn from the first author's experience as an expert witness. These cases depict superficially different but fundamentally similar cases of gender stereotyping and discrimination.

Tales of Two Women

Lois Robinson worked as a welder in a certain Jacksonville, Florida, shipyard. Jacksonville Shipyards, Inc. (JSI) repairs U.S. Navy and commercial ships in dry dock in what is tough, sometimes dangerous work. The enterprise includes a wide variety of skilled craftworkers: welders, shipfitters, carpenters, electricians, machinists, boilermakers, sheetmetal workers, and more. The atmosphere is heavily identified with the Navy; many of the management had Navy careers before moving to the private sector. Women are less than 5 percent of the JSI work force, and less than half of 1 percent of the skilled craftworkers. What this means from a practical point of view is that there are typically no or few women on any given shift, a minimum of none if business is slow, and a maximum of 8 to 10 out of 150 workers on a busy shift. Most often, there are 1 or 2 women out of 50 to 100 workers on shift, so a woman is likely to be the only woman in the crowd getting on the shipyard buses or at the time clock.

The JSI shipyard has been described as a boy's club, a man's world, and someone even painted "Men Only" on one of the work trailers. (When someone else complained, the sign was painted over, but in a cursory way.) It is perhaps best summarized as an atmosphere with a lot of joking and messing around. For example, one worker put a flashlight in his pants to show how well-endowed horses are; another carved the handle of a tool to resemble a penis, waving it in the faces of the women. There is open hostility to women on the part of a few men: "there's nothing worse than having to work around women; women are only fit company for something that howls." More often, there is simply a great deal of off-color joking (including one often-repeated joke about death by rape). Obscenity and profanity are routine.

Prominent in the visual environment (according to depositions, "every craft, every shop") are many calendars showing women in various states of undress and sexually explicit poses. Comparable magazines are widely shared, and pinups are torn out and posted spontaneously. Decorating various public walls are graffiti, both words and cartoons, with explicit sexual content depicting women. Note that there are of course no pictures, graffiti, or magazines depicting naked men. Note also that the workers are not allowed to bring other magazines on the job, and they are not allowed to post other material that is not work-related.

The few women workers are typically called by demeaning or sexually explicit names (honey, dear, baby, sugar, mamma, pussy, cunt, etc.). They are constantly teased, touched, humiliated, sexually evaluated, and propositioned; the incidents occur "every day all day" involving "all crafts," according to depositions.

Lois Robinson complained about the magazines and calendars, but she was brushed off, all the way up to the highest levels. A manager even pointed out that he had his own pinups. She eventually brought a lawsuit alleging sex discrimination due to sexual harassment in a hostile work environment; she won her case at the trial court level. An appeal by JSI is pending.

Let's move to the boardrooms of a Big Eight accounting firm, Price Waterhouse (PW), where one of the top managers brought in millions of dollars in accounts, worked more billable hours than anyone in that cohort, was well-liked by clients, and was described as aggressive, hard-driving, ambitious. But this exemplary manager was denied partnership because she was not feminine enough. Ann Hopkins was not accepted for partner because of "interpersonal skills problems" that would be corrected, a supporter informed her, by walking, talking, and dressing more femininely.

So trying to be like a man won't get you anywhere ✳

Although the setting was not exactly Jacksonville Shipyards, Inc., it encouraged stereotyping of women in several ways. First, Hopkins was in a firm that had about 1 percent female partners (7 of 662), and she was the only woman out of eighty-eight people proposed for partner that year. The few women managers certainly stood out as women. Second, being a manager in a Big Eight firm is a stereotypically masculine job, calling for tough, aggressive behavior; consequently people think there is a lack of fit between being a woman and being a manager (Heilman, 1983). Third, gender stereotypes are more free to operate on ambiguous criteria, such as judgments of interpersonal skills, than they are on unambiguous counting criteria, such as number of billable hours. PW failed to guard against bias in these subjective judgments by even so minimal an effort as having a written policy against gender-based discrimination. And there were considerable differences of opinion about how to interpret Hopkins's hard-driving managerial behavior. Fourth, the partnership evaluations were based on ambiguous and scant information in many cases; hearsay and casual opinions were given substantial weight. Finally, the firm had no explicit policy against gender discrimination, although it did prohibit discrimination on the basis of age or health in partnership decisions (American Psychological Association [APA], 1989, details these points.)

✳

Ann Hopkins also filed a lawsuit alleging sex discrimination, which she won, even though PW appealed it all the way to the Supreme Court.

What's So Special about Gender in These Cases?

a man could not do this? ?

Could such cases have been brought by a plaintiff who was not a woman (for example, by a man or by a person of color)? The answer is "probably not," and explaining it provides some insight into what is so special about gender. After playing out several alternative scenarios, later sections of the chapter will elaborate the conceptual analysis and provide relevant references. For the moment, simply consider the overall argument.

Imagine the alternative scenario that the Robinson case had been brought by a man of color, alleging racial harassment in a hostile work environment. Legal issues aside, the character of the harassment would have been rather different in several ways, each of which we will spend the rest of the chapter elaborating:

1. The harassment would not have such a prescriptive element. "Be more sexually available," said to a woman, is a more plausible message than "be more musical" or "be more hip," said to an African American.

2. It would not have the same type of power dynamics. Although in both the actual and the hypothetical instance, the target would be vastly outnumbered and perhaps feel physically threatened on that account, there are two important differences: the individual male, white or black, is on average evenly matched on physical power. And the social power is at least theoretically equivalent; an apologist might dismiss sexual harassment as harmless by saying "boys will be boys," but it would be less normative to defend racial hostility by saying "white guys will be white guys." (This is not to say that racial harassment is not often dismissed or minimized as harmless using other stratagems.)

3. Another difference is that the sexual harassers have knowledge and expectations based on their wives, girlfriends, mothers, and daughters, whereas racial harassers are less likely to have intimates or relatives who are members of the targeted group.

4. Yet another major difference lies in the (overt at least) goal of sexual harassment, which supposedly is sexual favors. (Hostility is another possible agenda, shared with other types of harassment.) The double message of sexual harassment is clear: "I am sexually interested in you but I am ignoring your refusal."

5. Finally, the norms against expressing sexism are not the same as the norms against expressing racism. The presence of pictures and messages demeaning to women is far more common than comparable materials demeaning to other groups. People are more defensive about appearing racist than sexist (people react more strongly to being called a racist than a sexist), giving rise to all kinds of subtleties in the expression of racism that do not operate identically in sexism, as we will elaborate later. Thus a charge of racial harassment in the Robinson case probably would have looked quite different in several respects.[2]

Consider the Robinson case again, now from the perspective of a man alleging sexual harassment by women (leaving aside the possibility of sexual harassment by other men). Everything here hinges on power differences, both physical and social. There are three main reasons female sexual harassment is not likely to be as threatening: (a) The average physical size difference favors men. (b) The nature of male and female genital physiology makes it far more plausible for men to genitally rape an unwilling woman than for women to genitally rape an unwilling man. (c) Men have more power in society generally, so they have a broader background of power, against which any particular interaction is set. In short, although a man or a person of color could clearly be harassed on the basis of sexual or racial categories, the nature of the harassment would differ dramatically from sexual harassment because of fundamental features of gender stereotyping. These differences form the themes of our discussion in this chapter.

The dramatically different case of Ann Hopkins also highlights what is so special about gender, but in a superficially quite different setting. Consider the Hopkins case if it were brought by a man of color, praised for his competence but faulted for his interpersonal skills problems. To be comparable, the situation would have to entail a job requiring behavior considered antithetical to the stereotypic expectations (e.g., international sophistication for a stereotypic African American or social improvisation for a stereotypic Japanese American). At the same time, strong social prescriptions would require that the person not display such career-enhancing behavior, at the risk of making the decision makers personally uncomfortable. The tension between job requirements and stereotypic prescriptions would result in the career-oriented target being blamed for interpersonal difficulties. The main issue here is that the prescriptive aspect of racial stereotypes is less salient than that for gender stereotypes, so the racial version of *Hopkins* is less plausible. We will elaborate in a later section.

Finally, consider the Hopkins case from the perspective of a man alleging sex discrimination on the basis of stereotyping of his interpersonal skills. Suppose that he behaved in a "feminine" manner that was suited to his job but not suited to the tastes of his employers. Certainly, the prescriptions are strong against men behaving in stereotypically feminine ways. It is possible to imagine a male nurse, for example, faulted for being a mother hen. But the difference is that most stereotypically feminine behavior is not adaptive in most task settings; it is simply not competent behavior to be stereotypically feminine: emotional, passive, vulnerable, and dependent. Hence the configuration of female gender stereotypic behavior is not valued in the workplace, so few employees aspire to it. Essentially, this brings up the power dimension in yet another form; that is, the workplace values "masculine" traits but suppresses them in women.

The Robinson and Hopkins cases and their hypothetical alternative scenarios illustrate some central features of gender stereotyping that set it apart from other kinds of stereotyping. The next sections address each feature in turn.

Gender Stereotypes Are Heavily Prescriptive

A stereotype has both a descriptive component and a prescriptive component. The descriptive component is composed of the attributes that constitute what people believe the typical group member to be like. For instance, the descriptive component of the female stereotype includes the following attributes: emotional, weak, dependent, passive, uncompetitive, and unconfident (Fiske, Bersoff, Borgida, Deaux, & Heilman, 1991). The prescriptive component of a stereotype is composed of the behaviors deemed suitable for the target group. In other words, prescriptions indicate how a member of the target group "should" behave. For example, the female stereotype includes the following prescriptions: A woman should have good interpersonal skills, she should be passive and docile, and she should cooperate with others.

Although all stereotypes include both descriptive aspects and prescriptive aspects, gender stereotypes are more prescriptive than other stereotypes. The many prescriptions characteristic of gender stereotypes are due in part to the amount of exposure people have to members of both gender categories. While observing and interacting with others, people develop a multitude of complex ideas about how members of each gender category actually do behave and how they would ideally behave. People are then able to incorporate these actual and ideal behaviors and formulate prescriptions or "shoulds" for each gender. These "shoulds" define behavior that is appropriate for members of each gender category (e.g., Terborg, 1977).

On the other hand, many people do not have much experience with the behavior of people in other categories. For example, many European-American people have not observed or interacted with African Americans often enough to have significant knowledge of their behavior. Thus it would be difficult for these people to develop shoulds. However, they could still subscribe to the general descriptive aspect of the African-American stereotype: Blacks are athletic, talkative, religious, and musical (Dovidio & Gaertner, 1986; Stephan & Rosenfield, 1982). The descriptive aspect of a stereotype is more cognitive and could be easily learned from other people (think of all the people who endorse stereotypic descriptions about a category of people with whom they have never interacted). We would argue, however, that the prescriptive aspect of a stereotype is centrally based on experience with the target group.

Not only do people have more experience with gender categories than other categories, people also learn gender categories earlier than other categories. Though children only twenty-four months old have shown gender stereotyping of objects (Thompson, 1975), simple racial classification of black and white dolls does not emerge until around the age of five (Williams & Morland, 1976). In terms of gender stereotypes, by the time children are in preschool and kindergarten they ascribe gender stereotypic labels to toys, activities, and occupations without making many "errors." However, children do not seem to acquire knowledge of gender stereotypic descriptive traits until they are around eight years old. Thus children apparently acquire knowledge of gender roles (i.e., stereotypic prescriptions) before they acquire knowledge of gender attributes (i.e., stereotypic descriptions) (Ruble & Ruble, 1982). Because the prescriptions people develop as a child are held for such a long time, it is likely that they are very strong.

The strength and complexity of the prescriptive aspects of gender stereotypes contribute to their saliency. Overall, gender is a more salient category than other categories. For instance, Fiske, Haslam, and Fiske (1991) found that people are more likely to confuse individuals of the same gender than individuals of the same age, race, role, or name. In addition, Stangor, Lynch, Duan, and Glass (1992) found people were more likely to categorize people according to their sex than their race. Because gender is such a salient category and the many prescriptive aspects are very strong, it follows that the prescriptive aspects of gender stereotypes will be more salient than the weaker prescriptive aspects of less salient categories. Therefore, people should be more likely to notice when a woman breaks with a stereotypic prescription than when, for example, a person fails to "act his or her age," thereby breaking with a stereotypic prescription.

Well-developed gender stereotypic prescriptions or shoulds limit both men's and women's behavior and, when the prescriptions are broken, it is particularly salient to observers. In addition, any behavior that violates gender prescriptions is generally negatively evaluated by others (Nieva & Gutek, 1980). This poses an especially difficult situation for working women. People will notice when working women do not meet the prescriptive demands of the female stereotype. Yet, as noted, these prescriptions are not usually adaptive for women in work settings (Bardwick & Donovan, 1971; Heilman, 1983). For example, if a female lawyer could not make up her mind, tended to behave in a passive and uncompetitive manner with her peers, and had publicly emotional reactions to both professional and personal experiences, she probably would not advance her career. Women are thus in a double bind. Do they behave in a way that will meet the sex stereotypic prescriptive demands to be feminine? Or, do they act competently and aggressively in order to fill job-specific demands? If they work to fill the job-specific demands, they run the risk of being evaluated negatively for displaying behavior antithetical to the stereotypic expectation for women. On the other hand, if they fill the gender-prescriptive demands, they run the risk of being viewed as incapable of having a successful career. Interestingly, both of these scenarios could result in sexual discrimination. In one case, discrimination would result from not behaving like a woman should and, in the other case, from behaving too much like a woman.

In sum, the prescriptive aspects of stereotypes are more central to gender stereotypes than they are to other stereotypes for a number of different reasons. First, people have more experience with members of each gender category than with members of other categories. This experience allows people to develop many complex prescriptions for gender. Second, people begin learning gender prescriptions at a very young age. These prescriptions are strong because they have been with people for so long. Finally, gender prescriptions are more salient than the prescriptions for other social categories. Unfortunately, the centrality and strength of gender prescriptions places working women in a sensitive situation that easily results in sexual discrimination.

Gender Stereotypes Are Based on Dramatic Power Differences

The illustrative hypothetical scenarios presented earlier in the chapter suggested the culturally unusual notion of a man bringing a sexual harassment suit, or a man wanting to behave in a feminine fashion to keep a job, but being prevented from doing so by female colleagues. Power is a core issue defining the implausibility of both hypotheticals. If we define *power* as the asymmetrical control over another person's outcomes (Dépret & Fiske, in press), then because men control a disproportionate share of outcomes valued in society (or at least in the workplace), men have power. It is common wisdom that this is so (e.g., Rohrbaugh, 1979), supported by sample statistics, such as the fact that women comprise a mere 3 percent of the top executive positions, with no increase over the last decade, and earning 72 cents for every dollar earned by men, with wage gaps even in female-dominated professions (Saltzman, 1991).

Sociologists have recognized these phenomena and their impact on gender differences, described in status theories such as expectation states theory (Berger, Conner, & Fisek, 1974; Berger, Fisek, Norman, & Zelditch, 1977). The basic premise is that expected performance (i.e., perceived competence) ranks people in interactions, such that some people's contributions are expected to be more valuable than others. Those higher ranked people (e.g., men, European Americans) are then given more opportunities to contribute, receive deference, and so on (for a recent review and analysis, see Ridgeway & Diekema, 1992). Although this theory is designed to explain gender differences in communication styles, both verbal (Aries, 1987; Smith-Lovin & Robinson, 1992; Wood & Rhodes, 1992) and nonverbal (Ellyson, Dovidio, & Brown, 1992; Hall, 1987; Hall & Veccia, 1992), it also may be expanded to help us understand gender stereotyping.

The higher status of men in general leads to expectations that they will be more competent in general than women. But more specifically, the power and status differences can account for the differential valuing of male stereotypic traits (the competency cluster) and devaluing of female stereotypic traits (the social-emotional cluster), at least in task settings. In fact, the power itself may enable those people in power to define which traits are valuable. Because men have more status and power, their stereotypic traits are viewed as more deserving of respect. Which came first is unclear, but at least some of the variance is due to the power → respect sequence. This is not to say that people do not feel fond of others who display the social-emotional cluster stereotypic of women (Eagly & Mladinic, 1989). They often do, but this fondness may be accompanied by contempt (Kirchler, 1992). Fiske and Ruscher (in press) have argued that people seem to view women simultaneously as likable but also as unworthy of much respect (also see Freeman, 1971). Respect, which translates into rewards in the public marketplace, is differentially awarded to male stereotypic traits precisely because of their association with the group having more power and prestige.

The power and prestige asymmetry can also explain the prescription that women, the stereotypically less competent group, should limit themselves to their stereotypic (less valued) domains of expertise. And, clearly, it explains why men traditionally would not aspire to "feminine" traits, the devalued alternative. Indeed, as more women move into a given field, the status of the field may decline (Touhey, 1974).

In contrast to the status-and-power-differences argument, there is the role theory explanation of gender differences. Eagly (1987) argues that women take on the communal characteristics needed for their traditional roles at home, and men conversely take on the agentic characteristics needed for their traditional roles in the work world. In effect, people are what they do and what other people expect them to be. Both individual and social experience contribute to gender differences. In this analysis, gender roles cause gender differences in behavior, and stereotypes reflect this process. However, this analysis does not account for the devaluing of women more generally in marketplace terms. Role theory does focus squarely on face-to-face interactions as people enact their traditional or nontraditional roles, and the more sociological status theory explanations are incorporating this level of analysis as well (Ridgeway & Diekema, 1992). Power dynamics in specific organizational settings are also important determinants of the extent of stereotyping. So, for example, solo status in an organization encourages stereotyping of individuals from the rare group (B. Mullen, personal communication, May 1992). This is consistent with a power-based explanation, whereby the outnumbered group has less power, and so it is not able to control as many resources. The lack of rewards available from the smaller group in turn decreases the motivation of the larger group to go beyond their initial stereotypes, and it also limits the power of the outnumbered group to alter those stereotypes. The larger, more powerful group in effect defines the norms (Kanter, 1977). Maccoby (1990) suggests that this may cause the disadvantaged group, that is, little girls, to withdraw and create their own subculture.

A final source of power differences results from relative physical size of men and women on average. For example, Dutton (1988) uses this as one among several explanations for the greater seriousness of wife assault than husband assault. This argument of course extends to other types of violence against women by men. It is important to note the physical size issue's contribution to male-female power asymmetries.

Power differences between men and women, then, are based on relative status, expected competence, common roles, relative numbers in the workplace, and average physical size.

Gender Stereotypes Derive Complexity from Close Contacts

Another characteristic of gender stereotypes that separates them from other category-based responses is their complexity. This complexity is derived from the numerous communal relationships between men and women. People have relationships with members of the "opposite" sex every day. Even if people do not have friends or co-workers of the other sex, members of their family are of the other sex. Women have fathers, boyfriends, husbands, and sons; men have mothers, girlfriends, wives, and daughters. Members of no other "minority group" have such routinely close relationships outside their group (Hacker, 1951). The mix of intimacy and discrimination can create profound ambivalence.

Furthermore, people generally have a great deal of time and effort invested in these personal relationships. In fact, some people may consider the behavior of their close friends, family members, and intimates to be the prototypical behavior for other members of the same gender category. They therefore derive expectations for members of the other sex from their personal experiences with these people. Some support for this lies in the fact that men in more egalitarian relationships have less traditional stereotypes of women than men in more traditional relationships (Peplau & Campbell, 1989). Even though these egalitarian partners may have chosen one another because they were each somewhat egalitarian, once in the relationship the expectations of the partners, in particular the male partners, also may have changed to become even more egalitarian.

This variety of close contact with family members, intimates, and friends of the other sex not only affects people's expectations for members of the other sex. It also increases the complexity of gender stereotypes by promoting the use of subtypes. *Subtypes* are "subcategories develop[ed] in response to isolated cases that disconfirm [a stereotype]" (Fiske & Taylor, 1991). For example, a man may have a female cousin who is a very aggressive and competent brain surgeon. She does not fit his female stereotype in many ways. Therefore, he may develop a subtype: female doctors. In essence, he has "fenced off" (Allport, 1954) this family member who disconfirms his more global stereotype of women. In fact, this subtype gives him more information regarding his cousin's dispositions than would the other, broader category (Stangor et al., 1992).

The process of subtyping women is not a recent phenomenon. Women have been subtyped throughout history. Subtypes of women have ranged from love goddesses (e.g., the chivalric notion of the woman on the pedestal) to wholesome mother figures (e.g., the Christian ideal of Mother Mary) to inferior and evil creatures (e.g., the Chinese conception of the feminine nature, the Yin, which is evil and dark) (Rohrbaugh, 1979; Ruble & Ruble, 1982). In the 1970s, research began to address directly these more specific gender subtypes. For instance, Clifton, McGrath, and Wick (1976) discussed two different female stereotypes: "housewife" and "bunny." More recently, Deaux and her colleagues (Deaux, Kite, & Lewis, 1985; Deaux & Lewis, 1984) have also noted specific types of women, many based on job categories.

On the surface, subtyping may appear to be a good process, one that reduces stereotyping. After all, by subtyping, people are recognizing that not all people in a category are the same. For example, there are female doctors, female bunnies, and female leaders. Each of these subtypes has unique characteristics that separate it from the others and, to some degree, from the overall female stereotype. As promising as this line of thinking appears to be, however, it has not proven to be beneficial.

Subtyping or "fencing off" actually allows people to keep their overall stereotype intact (Hewstone, Hopkins, & Routh, 1992; Hewstone, Johnston, & Aird, 1992; Johnston & Hewstone, 1992). By separating people who disconfirm a stereotype into a subtype, people brand these disconfirmatory cases as atypical. If these disconfirmatory cases are considered atypical, they will not affect the overall stereotype because the overall stereotype describes people who are *typical* members of the category.

Interestingly, even the subtypes people form to account for women who disconfirm the stereotype still incorporate gender. Women are not simply doctors or professors. They are *female* doctors or *female* professors. These category labels imply that there is something about being female that is relevant to role performance. One rarely says "male doctor" or "male professor." Moreover, one would think that gender would not be a part of the label of a category developed to classify women who disconfirm the gender stereotype.

So, what would be the best way to disconfirm and, subsequently, to change a stereotype that has a propensity for subtyping? Rothbart and John (1985) argue that disconfirming behaviors will only alter stereotypes if they are associated with people who are otherwise typical group members. In this way the overall category is activated and it is more difficult to subtype. The female fighter pilot who also has a husband, two children, and a big kitchen probably does more to counteract stereotypes than the unmarried female fighter pilot who hates to cook. Change of stereotypes is also promoted if the disconfirming behavior displayed by otherwise typical group members occurs repeatedly in many different settings. This reduces the chance that the disconfirming behavior will be attributed to environmental conditions.

Women who are fighter pilots, rock climbers, and construction workers have under-mined the old stereotype that women cannot do tough, demanding work. More recently, Hewstone and his colleagues have found support for the idea that dispersed inconsistent information promotes more stereotype change than does concentrated inconsistent information (Hewstone et al., 1992; Johnston & Hewstone, 1992).

One would think, with all the experiences shared between members of the two genders, that gender stereotypes would have changed. In particular, in recent years many American women have entered the work force and disconfirmed a number of stereotypic beliefs about women. Yet the basic, core contents of the female stereotype have not changed to any great degree over centuries (for a recent reference, see Eagly & Mladinic, 1989; for a review, see Ruble & Ruble, 1982). Perhaps men who subscribe to the traditional female stereotype think they are "experts" on women's behavior because they have had firsthand experience and they "know" how women should and do act. In other words, these men may have their own prescriptions and descriptions for women's behavior that they think must be appropriate and accurate because they have had many experiences that confirm their ideas. This poses two problems for stereotype change. First, the "experts" may simply refuse to accept that their stereotypes are inaccurate. Second, the group that believes it is an expert on the other group may have a sense of superior status and many studies on intergroup contact have indicated that stereotypes are not likely to change unless the two groups experience contact with one another under conditions of equal status (Stephan & Brigham, 1985).

Finally, the expectations sexual harassers have for people of the opposite sex, which are based on their friends, family members, and intimates, are complex and hard to change. Even sexual harassers who treat their female intimates respectfully are aware of both the more positive aspects of the female stereotype, which may lead to respect, and the more traditional aspects of the stereotype, which may promote harassing behavior in the workplace. Thus, because they have extremely complex and subtyped stereotypes of women, it may be even more difficult to change the stereo-types of "respectful" harassers than those of "consistent" harassers who have less complex and subtyped stereotypes.

On the other hand, racial harassers are less likely to have intimates who are members of the targeted group. Therefore, racial harassers' stereotypes should be less defined and less complex. Thus it may even be simpler to change racial harassers' stereotypes because they do not have a large number of subtypes that would need to be incorporated into the global stereotype. Of course, the problem of promoting equal status between the two groups would still exist.

In sum, gender stereotypes seem more complex than other stereotypes. The two genders share many experiences with one another. These experiences allow people to develop complex expectations for members of the other gender. In addition, this interaction promotes the use of subtypes. Unfortunately, stereotype change for gender stereotypes seems more difficult than for other categories because people have many subtypes for gender categories that would need to be integrated for change to occur.

Gender Stereotypes Derive Universality from Biology

Men and women are biologically fated to intertwined lives. Nevertheless, that very same biology suggests that men and women may want different things from each other, and this is likely to affect their mutual perceptions. The potential impact of sexual biology tells us mostly about the evolution of our ancestors rather than about the social developments since that time or to come in the future. Social change is also part of the evolution of the species. Nevertheless, some evolutionary biological background sheds light on the near universality—but not inevitability—of certain cultural forms, including gender stereotypes.

From this standpoint, men and women regard each other primarily as potential mates, and sex differences in mate preferences suggest some important mismatched goals and stereotypes. Starting from the biological premise that females have more physical investment in each individual child than males do, females should value males who show signs of ability and willingness to invest in joint offspring (Buss, 1988, 1989). This suggests that women will look for men with financial resources. On the other hand, males can maximize their reproductive capability by finding fertile and nurturing females, and this suggests to sociobiologically oriented psychologists that men should value women who appear young and healthy. Other evolutionary sex differences can be similarly analyzed, but the basic contrast lies in women looking for mates showing evidence of resource acquisition and men looking for mates showing evidence of reproductive capacity (Buss, 1988; for a similar analysis, see Kenrick, 1989). Some of these preferences have been confirmed in samples from thirty-seven different cultures (Buss, 1989).

Whatever the merits of the evolutionary argument, it certainly fits with the division of male and female prescriptive stereotypes into a competency cluster for men (indicating the means to resource acquisition) and an attractiveness-nurturance cluster for women (signs of reproductive capacity). If the men in the Jacksonville Shipyard had only appreciated aspects of the women workers other than their reproductive readiness, and if the men at Price Waterhouse had only appreciated other aspects of Ann Hopkins than her apparent lack of nurturance, both environments would have been much more civilized. The women were foolish enough to believe that work was what mattered in the workplace; fortunately, the courts agreed with them, despite human evolutionary proclivities.

Gender Stereotypes Are Historically Situated

Reviewing two decades of research on gender stereotypes (an enterprise not intended here, but see Deaux, 1985; Ruble & Ruble, 1982), one would see a sea-change in the message of the literature then and now. Either our research subjects or our psychological colleagues or both are changing their minds about the content and scope of gender stereotypes. The historical context has shifted from men and women being perceived as opposite sexes to men and women being perceived as overlapping on multiple dimensions and gender stereotypes being fleshed out in multiple subtypes.

Whether we or our subjects are becoming more sophisticated almost does not matter, for some change is accomplished. (Perhaps our biology is not so fixed after all?)

One index of the change is the citation frequency of the classic article by Broverman, Vogel, Broverman, Clarkson, and Rosenkrantz (1972) documenting the content of gender stereotypes. From a steady buildup from 1972 to 1980, with a peak of nearly eighty citations in 1980, the citations dropped to less than half that in 1990 (according to citations listed in the *Social Science Citation Index*). Any article has a similar citation profile, assuming it is cited at all, but this article, as one of the catalysts of the research literature, is intrinsically diagnostic. Although there have been no replications of Broverman and colleagues (1972), there is evidence that people still endorse these gender stereotypes (e.g., Martin, 1987).

Another gender stereotype classic, the Goldberg (1968) study, illustrates the change in the overall message over time. Although the 1968 study seemed to demonstrate that the same work product was evaluated more favorably when attributed to a man than to a woman, the message has become more complex over time (Swim, Borgida, Maruyama, & Myers, 1989). The effect size was larger in studies published during 1968–1973, but not huge even then. Essentially the current message is that stereotyping is a function of many moderator variables, most of which have not been examined in enough detail to conduct a meta-analysis on the moderators. Swim and colleagues suggested several plausible moderators: particular subtypes activated, perceived diagnosticity of information, interaction between stereotype and information, goals or motives of the subject, and task demands.

When one collapses over various moderators, of course, one is averaging over (a) control conditions designed to show the baseline discriminatory effect (i.e., women are evaluated less favorably than comparable men) and (b) experimental conditions designed to eliminate the effect (i.e., the effect goes away if people are motivated to be more careful). It is not surprising then that an overall meta-analysis of the main effect concluded that the effect is small (Fiske, Bersoff, Borgida, Deaux, & Heilman, 1991). The interactions between the basic effect and the proposed moderator variables are being ignored.

One might examine the small main effects for gender and conclude that gender stereotyping has nearly vanished. Some textbook writers indeed are beginning to conclude that gender stereotyping is less of a problem than it used to be. Compare one of the best-selling social psychology texts in 1981: "As we have seen throughout this discussion, sexual stereotypes, and the discriminatory behaviors that accompany them, certainly persist at the present time" (Baron & Byrne, 1981, p. 182); and a decade later: "Together, all these findings point to substantial shifts toward a reduced incidence of sex discrimination in the world of work" (Baron & Byrne, 1991, p. 219). There is clearly some room for optimism at present; however, the experimental research is not an indicator of incidence per se, not being a representative sample survey, but rather having been designed to study moderators and mediators of effects. In other words, current experiments show that stereotyping is a complex process but say little about how frequently it occurs.

An illustration of the role of subtypes in stereotyping serves to indicate the complexity of modern sexism. Ann Hopkins was a victim of gender stereotypes, but certainly not the stereotype that she was passive, incompetent, and emotional. Quite the contrary. And a recent meta-analysis bears (Eagly, Makhijani, & Klonsky, 1992) out the conclusions of the American Psychological Association's amicus brief (APA, 1989) and the Supreme Court:

> Women in leadership positions were devalued relative to their male counterparts when leadership was carried out in stereotypically masculine styles, particularly when this style was autocratic or directive. In addition, the devaluation of women was greater when leaders occupied male-dominated roles and when the evaluators were men. (Eagly, Makhijani, & Klonsky, 1992, p. 3)

In short, one would not expect a main effect such that all women are universally devalued; rather, certain women are devalued when gender-based subtypes interact with the features of a particular work environment.

Elsewhere, Fiske (1989) has argued that these people, who do not match widespread descriptive stereotypes, are faulted on subjective grounds because they make us uncomfortable by violating our notions of how such people should behave. This gives rise to the perception that one is dealing with a "difficult" person, someone who simply does not fit in. The point is that such people are stereotyped and the blame for their problems is laid at the door of their own personal attributes. Hopkins was certainly seen as a difficult person, and Lois Robinson also was faulted for not going along with the locker-room atmosphere. Both were perceived as difficult people.

Besides the increasing complexity of subtypes, gender stereotyping has the potential for another major historical shift. Such a shift has already occurred in the literature on racism, along with changing historical norms. Whereas early research indicated overt, old-fashioned racism (claiming blacks are inferior to whites), more recent efforts have tackled modern racism in several forms (see Pettigrew, 1985, for a review). For example, Sears and his colleagues (Sears, Hensler, & Speer, 1979) argued that people do not want to feel racist, so instead they attack issues symbolic of the out-group; thus, opposing all policies related to busing, affirmative action, welfare, and the like, would indicate symbolic racism. Similarly, Gaertner and Dovidio (1986) described aversive racism: the person's racism is aversive to his or her self-image, so the person behaves in a nondiscriminatory, even reverse discriminatory way, except when the behavior is covert or when there is an acceptable alternative explanation (an excuse) for the discriminatory behavior that would make it appear nonracist. Also, Katz and his colleagues (Katz, Wackenhut, & Hass, 1986) discussed at length the ambivalence and response amplification that may result when people hold simultaneously sympathetic and rejecting attitudes toward an out-group. All of these dynamics seem to us to be plausible accounts of what is beginning to happen with sexism as well; it has not vanished, just become less acceptable in many circles, so it has gone underground. Researchers need to pursue this parallel between modern racism and modern sexism.

Research topics go through a predictable development, and gender stereotyping research is no exception: from the heady days of first discoveries (the more counterintuitive or provocative, the better), to the replications and extensions, to the inevitable dissent, to the moderator variable stage. Gender stereotyping research has clearly arrived at the moderator variable stage. From there, research can fizzle if people decide "there is no there there" (too many contradictions, too many qualifications, too complicated, too limited to one paradigm; whatever the complaint, the result is the same). Alternatively, research at this stage can spin off new theoretical approaches that synthesize previous work. Given the importance and interest value of gender as an enduring feature of the human landscape, we expect that the future will bring synthesis rather than fizzle.

Summary

This chapter has argued that gender-based responses differ from other types of category-based responses in a variety of ways. First, gender stereotypes are heavily prescriptive. People acquire gender categories in the family, before they acquire other categories, and they therefore have more time to develop and motivation to invest in gender prescriptions. Second, gender stereotypes are based on dramatic power differences. Men are not only physically larger than women, but they also control a disproportionate share of the outcomes valued in society. Third, close contact between the two genders increases the complexity of gender stereotypes, and thus gender stereotypes may be characterized by more subtypes than other stereotypes. Fourth, gender stereotypes possess sexual and biological facets that other stereotypes do not have. And, finally, gender stereotypes change as a function of cultural change and scientific advance.

Every one of these distinctive characteristics of gender stereotypes has significant effects on interactions between people. As illustrated in the text of this chapter, they each affected the stereotyping of and discrimination against both Lois Robinson and Ann Hopkins. In addition, these characteristics influence the literature on gender. And, perhaps most importantly, they affect our everyday interactions with our friends, co-workers, relatives, and intimates.

NOTES

1. Technically, the first part of our title should read "What's So Special about Gender?" However, we opted for the more eye-catching "What's So Special about Sex?"

2. We are merely trying to illustrate how sexism is different from racism. We are not saying that sexism is more important or more serious.

REFERENCES

Allport, G. W. (1954). *The nature of prejudice.* Reading, MA: Addison-Wesley.

American Psychological Association Brief for Amicus Curiae in Support of Respondent, *Price Waterhouse v. Hopkins,* 109 S. Ct. 1775 (1989).

Aries, E. (1987). Gender and communication. In P. Shaver & C. Hendrick (Eds.), *Review of personality and social psychology: Sex and gender* (Vol. 7, pp. 149–176). Newbury Park, CA: Sage.

Bardwick, J. M., & Donovan, E. (1971). Ambivalence: The socialization of women. In V. Gornick & B. K. Moran (Eds.), *Woman in sexist society* (pp. 147–159). New York: Basic Books. Reprinted from J. M. Bardwick (Ed.), *Readings on the psychology of women* (pp. 52–58), Harper & Row, 1972.

Baron, R. A., & Byrne, D. (1981). *Social psychology: Understanding human interaction* (3rd ed.). Boston: Allyn & Bacon.

Baron, R. A., & Byrne, D. (1991). *Social psychology: Understanding human interaction* (6th ed.). Boston: Allyn & Bacon.

Berger, J., Conner, T. L., & Fisek, M. H. (1974). *Expectation states theory: A theoretical research program.* Cambridge, MA: Winthrop.

Berger, J., Fisek, M. H., Norman, R. Z., & Zelditch, M., Jr. (1977). *Status characteristics and social interaction.* New York: Elsevier.

Broverman, I. K., Vogel, S. R., Broverman, D. M., Clarkson, F. E., & Rosenkrantz, P. S. (1972). Sex-role stereotypes: A current appraisal. *Journal of Social Issues, 28*(2), 59–78.

Buss, D. M. (1988). Love acts: The evolutionary biology of love. In R. J. Sternberg & M. L. Barnes (Eds.), *The psychology of love* (pp. 100–118). New Haven, CT: Yale University Press.

Buss, D. M. (1989). Sex differences in human mate preferences: Evolutionary hypotheses tested in 37 cultures. *Behavioral and Brain Sciences, 12.* 1–49.

Clifton, A. K., McGrath, D., & Wick, B. (1976). Stereotypes of woman: A single category? *Sex Roles, 2,* 135–148.

Deaux, K. (1985). Sex and gender. *Annual Review of Psychology, 36,* 49–81.

Deaux, K., Kite, M. E., & Lewis, L. L. (1985). Clustering and gender schemata: An uncertain link. *Personality and Social Psychology Bulletin, 11,* 387–397.

Deaux, K., & Lewis, L. L. (1984). Structure of gender stereotypes: Interrelationships among components and gender label. *Journal of Personality and Social Psychology, 46,* 99–1004.

Dépret, E. F., & Fiske, S. T. (in press). Social cognition and power: Some cognitive consequences of social structure as a source of control deprivation. In G. Weary, F. Gleicher, & K. Marsh (Eds.), *Control motivation and social cognition.* New York: Springer.

Dovidio, J. F., & Gaertner, S. L. (1986). Prejudice, discrimination, and racism: Historical trends and contemporary approaches. In J. F. Dovidio & S. L. Gaertner (Eds.), *Prejudice, discrimination, and racism* (pp. 1–34). New York: Academic Press.

Dutton, D. G. (1988). Research advances in the study of wife assault etiology and prevention. *Law and Mental Health.* 161–219.

Eagly, A. H. (1987). *Sex differences in social behavior: A social-role interpretation.* Hillsdale, NJ: Lawrence Erlbaum.

Eagly, A. H., Makhijani, M. G., & Klonsky, B. G. (1992). Gender and the evaluation of leaders: A meta-analysis. *Psychological Bulletin, 111,* 3–22.

Eagly, A. H., & Mladinic, A. (1989). Gender stereotypes and attitudes toward women and men. *Personality and Social Psychology Bulletin, 15,* 534–558.

Ellyson, S. L., Dovidio, J. F., & Brown, C. E. (1992). The look of power: Gender differences and similarities in visual dominance behavior. In C. L. Ridgeway (Ed.), *Gender, interaction and inequality* (pp. 50–80). New York: Springer.

Fiske, A. P., Haslam, N., & Fiske, S. T. (1991). Confusing one person with another: What errors reveal about the elementary forms of social relations. *Journal of Personality and Social Psychology, 60,* 656–674.

Fiske, S. T. (1989, August). *Interdependence and stereotyping: From the laboratory to the*

Supreme Court (and back). Invited address given at the 97th Annual Convention of the American Psychological Association, New Orleans.

Fiske, S. T., Bersoff, D. N., Borgida, E., Deaux, K., & Heilman, M. E. (1991). Social science research on trial: Use of sex stereotyping research in *Price Waterhouse v. Hopkins*. *American Psychologist, 46,* 1049–1060.

Fiske, S. T., & Ruscher, J. B. (in press). Negative interdependence and prejudice: Whence the affect? In D. M. Mackie & D. L. Hamilton (Eds.), *Affect, cognition, and stereotyping: Interactive processes in group perception*. New York: Academic Press.

Fiske, S. T., & Taylor, S. E. (1991). *Social cognition* (2nd ed.). New York: McGraw-Hill.

Freeman, J. (1971). Social construction of the second sex. In M. H. Garskof (Ed.), *Roles women play: Readings toward women's liberation* (pp. 123–141). Belmont, CA: Wadsworth.

Gaertner, S. L. & Dovidio. J. F. (1986). The aversive form of racism. In J. F. Dovidio & S. L. Gaertner (Eds.), *Prejudice, discrimination, and racism* (pp. 61–89). New York: Academic Press.

Goldberg, P. (1968). Are women prejudiced against women? *Transaction, 5,* 28–30.

Hacker, H. M. (1951). Women as a minority group. *Social Forces, 30,* 60–69.

Hall, J. A. (1987). On explaining gender differences: The case of nonverbal communication. In P. Shaver & C. Hendrick (Eds.), *Review of personality and social psychology: Sex and gender* (Vol. 7, pp. 177–200). Newbury Park, CA: Sage.

Hall, J. A. & Veccia, E. M. (1992). Touch asymmetry between the sexes. In C. L. Ridgeway (Ed.), *Gender, interaction, and inequality* (pp. 81–96). New York: Springer.

Heilman, M. E. (1983). Sex bias in work settings: The lack of fit model. *Research in Organizational Behavior, 5,* 269–298.

Hewstone, M., Hopkins, N., & Routh, D. A. (1992). Cognitive models of stereotype change: Generalization and subtyping in young people's views of the police. *European Journal of Social Psychology, 22,* 219–224.

Hewstone, M., Johnston, L., & Aird, P. (1992). Cognitive models of stereotype change: Perceptions of homogeneous and heterogeneous groups. *European Journal of Social Psychology, 22,* 235–250.

Johnston, L., & Hewstone, M. (1992). Cognitive models of stereotype change: Subtyping and the perceived typicality of disconfirming group members. *Journal of Experimental Social Psychology 28,* 260–386.

Kanter, R. M. (1977). *Men and women of the corporation*. New York: Basic Books.

Katz, I., Wackenhut, J., & Hass, R. G. (1986). Racial ambivalence, value duality, and behavior. In J. F. Dovidio & S. L. Gaertner (Eds.), *Prejudice, discrimination, and racism,* (pp. 35–59). New York: Academic Press.

Kelley, H. H. (1992). Common-sense psychology and scientific psychology. *Annual Review of Psychology, 43,* 1–23.

Kenrick, D. T. (1989). A biosocial perspective on mates and traits: Reuniting personality and social psychology. In D. M. Buss & N. Cantor (Eds.), *Personality psychology: Recent trends and emerging directions* (pp. 308–319). New York: Springer.

Kirchler, E. (1992). Adorable woman, expert man: Changing gender images of women and men in management. *European Journal of Social Psychology, 22,* 363–373.

Maccoby, E. E. (1990). Gender and relationships. *American Psychologist, 45,* 513–520.

Martin, C. L. (1987). A ratio measure of sex stereotyping. *Journal of Personality and Social Psychology, 52,* 489–499.

Nieva, V. F., & Gutek, B. A. (1980). Sex effects on evaluation. *Academy of Management Review, 5,* 267–276.

Peplau, L. A., & Campbell, S. M. (1989). The balance of power in dating and marriage. In J. Freeman (Ed.), *Women: A feminist perspective* (pp. 121–137). Mountain View, CA: Mayfield.

Pettigrew, T. F. (1985). New black-white patterns: How best to conceptualize them? *Annual Review of Sociology, 11,* 329–346.

Price Waterhouse v. Hopkins, 109 S. Ct. 1775 (1989).

Ridgeway, C. L., & Diekema, D. (1992). Are gender differences status differences? In C. L. Ridgeway (Ed.), *Gender, interaction, and inequality* (pp. 157–180). New York: Springer.

Rohrbaugh, J. B. (1979). *Women: Psychology's puzzle.* New York: Basic Books.

Rothbart, M., & John, O. P. (1985). Social categorization and behavioral episodes: A cognitive analysis of the effects of intergroup contact. *Journal of Social Issues, 41*(3), 81–104.

Ruble, D. N., & Ruble, T. L. (1982). Sex stereotypes. In A. G. Miller (Ed.), *In the eye of the beholder: Contemporary issues in stereotyping* (pp. 188–252). New York: Praeger.

Saltzman, A. (1991, June 17). Trouble at the top. *U.S. News and World Report,* pp. 40–48.

Sears, D. O., Hensler, C. P., & Speer, L. K. (1979). Whites' opposition to busing: Self-interest or symbolic politics? *American Political Science Review, 73,* 369–384.

Smith-Lovin, L., & Robinson, D. T. (1992). Gender and conversational dynamics. In C. L. Ridgeway (Ed.), *Gender, interaction, and inequality* (pp. 122–156). New York: Springer.

Stangor, C., Lynch, L., Duan, C., & Glass, B. (1992). Categorization of individuals on the basis of multiple social features. *Journal of Personality and Social Psychology, 62,* 207–218.

Stephan, W. G., & Brigham, J. C. (1985). Intergroup contact: Introduction. *Journal of Social Issues, 41*(3), 1–8.

Stephan, W. G., & Rosenfield, D. (1982). Racial and ethnic stereotypes. In A. G. Miller (Ed.), *In the eye of the beholder: Contemporary issues in stereotyping* (pp. 92–136). New York: Praeger.

Swim, J., Borgida, E., Maruyama, G., & Myers, D. G. (1989). Joan McKay versus John McKay: Do gender stereotypes bias evaluations? *Psychological Bulletin, 105,* 409–429.

Terborg, J. R. (1977). Women in management: A research review. *Journal of Applied Psychology, 62,* 647–664.

Thompson, S. K (1975). Gender labels and early sex role development. *Child Development, 46,* 339–347.

Touhey, J. C. (1974). Effects of additional women professionals on ratings of occupational prestige and desirability. *Journal of Personality and Social Psychology, 29,* 86–89.

Williams, J. E., & Morland, K. J. (1976). *Race, color and the young child.* Chapel Hill: University of North Carolina Press.

Wood, W., & Rhodes, N. (1992). Sex differences in interaction style in task groups. In C. L. Ridgeway (Ed.), *Gender, interaction, and inequality* (pp. 97–121). New York: Springer.

Chapter Twenty-Eight

X

A Fabulous Child's Story

Lois Gould

Once upon a time, a baby named X was born. This baby was named X so that nobody could tell whether it was a boy or a girl. Its parents could tell, of course, but they couldn't tell anybody else. They couldn't even tell Baby X, at first.

You see, it was all part of a very important Secret Scientific Xperiment, known officially as Project Baby X. The smartest scientists had set up this Xperiment at a cost of Xactly 23 billion dollars and 72 cents, which might seem like a lot for just one baby, even a very important Xperimental baby. But when you remember the prices of things like strained carrots and stuffed bunnies, and popcorn for the movies and booster shots for camp, let alone twenty-eight shiny quarters from the tooth fairy, you begin to see how it adds up.

Also, long before Baby X was born, all those scientists had to be paid to work out the details of the Xperiment, and to write the *Official Instruction Manual* for Baby X's parents and, most important of all, to find the right set of parents to bring up Baby X. These parents had to be selected very carefully. Thousands of volunteers had to take thousands of tests and answer thousands of tricky questions. Almost everybody failed because, it turned out, almost everybody really wanted either a baby boy or a baby girl, and not Baby X at all. Also, almost everybody was afraid that a Baby X would be a lot more trouble than a boy or a girl. (They were probably right, the scientists admitted, but Baby X needed parents who wouldn't *mind* the Xtra trouble.)

There were families with grandparents named Milton and Agatha, who didn't see why the baby couldn't be named Milton or Agatha instead of X, even if it *was* an X. There were families with aunts who insisted on knitting tiny dresses and uncles who insisted on sending tiny baseball mitts. Worst of all, there were families that already had other children who couldn't be trusted to keep the secret. Certainly not if they knew the secret was worth 23 billion dollars and 72 cents—and all you had to do was take one little peek at Baby X in the bathtub to know if it was a boy or a girl.

But, finally, the scientists found the Joneses, who really wanted to raise an X more than any other kind of baby—no matter how much trouble it would be. Ms. and

Mr. Jones had to promise they would take equal turns caring for X, and feeding it, and singing it lullabies. And they had to promise never to hire any baby-sitters. The government scientists knew perfectly well that a baby-sitter would probably peek at X in the bathtub, too.

The day the Joneses brought their baby home, lots of friends and relatives came over to see it. None of them knew about the secret Xperiment, though. So the first thing they asked was what kind of a baby X was. When the Joneses smiled and said, "It's an X!" nobody knew what to say. They couldn't say, "Look at her cute little dimples!" And they couldn't say, "Look at his husky little biceps!" And they couldn't even say just plain "kitchy-coo." In fact, they all thought the Joneses were playing some kind of rude joke.

But, of course, the Joneses were not joking. "It's an X" was absolutely all they would say. And that made the friends and relatives very angry. The relatives all felt embarrassed about having an X in the family. "People will think there's something wrong with it!" some of them whispered. "There *is* something wrong with it!" others whispered back.

"Nonsense!" the Joneses told them all cheerfully. "What could possibly be wrong with this perfectly adorable X?"

Nobody could answer that, except Baby X, who had just finished its bottle. Baby X's answer was a loud, satisfied burp.

Clearly, nothing at all was wrong. Nevertheless, none of the relatives felt comfortable about buying a present for a Baby X. The cousins who sent the baby a tiny football helmet would not come and visit any more. And the neighbors who sent a pink-flowered romper suit pulled their shades down when the Joneses passed their house.

The *Official Instruction Manual* had warned the new parents that this would happen, so they didn't fret about it. Besides, they were too busy with baby X and the hundreds of different Xercises for treating it properly.

Ms. and Mr. Jones had to be Xtra careful about how they played with little X. They knew that if they kept bouncing it up in the air and saying how *strong* and *active* it was, they'd be treating it more like a boy than an X. But if all they did was cuddle it and kiss it and tell it how *sweet* and *dainty* it was, they'd be treating it more like a girl than an X.

On page 1,654 of the *Official Instruction Manual*, the scientists prescribed: "plenty of bouncing and plenty of cuddling, *both*. X ought to be strong and sweet and active. Forget about *dainty* altogether."

Meanwhile, the Joneses were worrying about other problems. Toys, for instance. And clothes. On his first shopping trip, Mr. Jones told the store clerk, "I need some clothes and toys for my new baby." The clerk smiled and said, "Well, now, is it a boy or a girl?" "It's an X," Mr. Jones said, smiling back. But the clerk got all red in the face and said huffily, "In *that* case, I'm afraid I can't help you, sir." So Mr. Jones wandered helplessly up and down the aisles trying to find what X needed. But everything in the store was piled up in sections marked "Boys" or "Girls." There were "Boys' Pajamas" and "Girls' Underwear" and "Boys' Fire Engines" and "Girls' Housekeeping Sets." Mr. Jones went home without buying anything for X. That night he and Ms. Jones consulted page 2,326 of the *Official Instruction Manual.* "Buy plenty of everything!" it said firmly.

So they bought plenty of sturdy blue pajamas in the Boys' Department and cheerful flowered underwear in the Girls' Department. And they bought all kinds of toys. A boy doll that made pee-pee and cried, "Pa-pa." And a girl doll that talked in three languages and said, "I am the Pres-i-dent of Gen-er-al Mo-tors." They also bought a storybook about a brave princess who rescued a handsome prince from his ivory tower, and another one about a sister and brother who grew up to be a baseball star and a ballet star, and you had to guess which was which.

The head scientists of Project Baby X checked all their purchases and told them to keep up the good work. They also reminded the Joneses to see page 4,629 of the *Manual,* where it said, "Never make Baby X feel *embarrassed* or *ashamed* about what it wants to play with. And if X gets dirty climbing rocks, never say 'Nice little Xes don't get dirty climbing rocks.' "

Likewise, it said, "If X falls down and cries, never say 'Brave little Xes don't cry.' Because, of course, nice little Xes *do* get dirty, and brave little Xes *do* cry. No matter how dirty X gets, or how hard it cries, don't worry. It's all part of the Xperiment."

Whenever the Joneses pushed Baby X's stroller in the park, smiling strangers would come over and coo: "Is that a boy or a girl?" The Joneses would smile back and say, "It's an X." The strangers would stop smiling then, and often snarl something nasty—as if the Joneses had snarled at *them.*

By the time X grew big enough to play with other children, the Joneses' troubles had grown bigger, too. Once a little girl grabbed X's shovel in the sandbox, and zonked X on the head with it. "Now, now, Tracy," the little girl's mother began to scold, "little girls mustn't hit little—" and she turned to ask X, "Are you a little boy or a little girl, dear?"

Mr. Jones, who was sitting near the sandbox, held his breath and crossed his fingers.

X smiled politely at the lady, even though X's head had never been zonked so hard in its life. "I'm a little X," X replied.

"You're a *what?*" the lady exclaimed angrily. "You're a little b-r-a-t, you mean!"

"But little girls mustn't hit little Xes, either!" said X, retrieving the shovel with another polite smile. "What good does hitting do, anyway?"

X's father, who was still holding his breath, finally let it out, uncrossed his fingers, and grinned back at X.

And at their next secret Project Baby X meeting, the scientists grinned, too. Baby X was doing fine.

But then it was time for X to start school. The Joneses were really worried about this, because school was even more full of rules for boys and girls, and there were no rules for Xes. The teacher would tell boys to form one line, and girls to form another line. There would be boys' games and girls' games, and boys' secrets and girls' secrets. The school library would have a list of recommended books for girls, and a different list of recommended books for boys. There would even be a bathroom marked BOYS and another one marked GIRLS. Pretty soon boys and girls would hardly talk to each other. What would happen to poor little X?

The Joneses spent weeks consulting their *Instruction Manual* (there were 249½ pages of advice under "First Day of School"), and attending urgent special conferences with the smart scientists of Project Baby X.

The scientists had to make sure that X's mother had taught X how to throw and catch a ball properly, and that X's father had been sure to teach X what to serve at a doll's tea party. X had to know how to shoot marbles and how to jump rope and, most of all, what to say when the Other Children asked whether X was a Boy or a Girl.

Finally, X was ready. The Joneses helped X button on a nice new pair of red-and-white checked overalls, and sharpened six pencils for X's nice new pencilbox, and marked X's name clearly on all the books in its nice new bookbag. X brushed its teeth and combed its hair, which just about covered its ears, and remembered to put a napkin in its lunchbox.

The Joneses had asked X's teacher if the class could line up alphabetically, instead of forming separate lines for boys and girls. And they had asked if X could use the principal's bathroom, because it wasn't marked anything except BATHROOM. X's teacher promised to take care of all those problems. But nobody could help X with the biggest problem of all—Other Children.

Nobody in X's class had ever known an X before. What would they think? How would X make friends?

You couldn't tell what X was by studying its clothes—overalls don't even button right-to-left, like girls' clothes, or left-to-right, like boys' clothes. And you couldn't guess whether X had a girl's short haircut or a boy's long haircut. And it was very hard to tell by the games X liked to play. Either X played ball very well for a girl, or else X played house very well for a boy.

Some of the children tried to find out by asking X tricky questions, like "Who's your favorite sports star?" That was easy. X had two favorite sports stars: a girl jockey named Robyn Smith and a boy archery champion named Robin Hood. Then they asked, "What's your favorite TV program?" And that was even easier. X's favorite TV program was "Lassie," which stars a girl dog played by a boy dog.

When X said that its favorite toy was a doll, everyone decided that X must be a girl. But then X said that the doll was really a robot, and that X had computerized it, and that it was programmed to bake fudge brownies and then clean up the kitchen. After X told them that, the other children gave up guessing what X was. All they knew was they'd sure like to see X's doll.

After school, X wanted to play with the other children. "How about shooting some baskets in the gym?" X asked the girls. But all they did was make faces and giggle behind X's back.

"How about weaving some baskets in the arts and crafts room?" X asked the boys. But they all made faces and giggled behind X's back, too.

That night, Ms. and Mr. Jones asked X how things had gone at school. X told them sadly that the lessons were okay, but otherwise school was a terrible place for an X. It seemed as if Other Children would never want an X for a friend.

Once more, the Joneses reached for their *Instruction Manual*. Under "Other Children," they found the following message: "What did you Xpect? *Other Children* have to obey all the silly boy-girl rules, because their parents taught them to. Lucky X—you don't have to stick to the rules at all! All you have to do is be yourself. P.S. We're not saying it'll be easy."

X liked being itself. But X cried a lot that night, partly because it felt afraid. So X's father held X tight, and cuddled it, and couldn't help crying a little, too. And X's mother cheered them both up by reading an Xciting story about an enchanted prince called Sleeping Handsome, who woke up when Princess Charming kissed him.

The next morning, they all felt much better, and little X went back to school with a brave smile and a clean pair of red-and-white checked overalls.

There was a seven-letter-word spelling bee in class that day. And a seven-lap boys' relay race in the gym. And a seven-layer-cake baking contest in the girls' kitchen corner. X won the spelling bee. X also won the relay race. And X almost won the baking contest, except it forgot to light the oven. Which only proves that nobody's perfect.

One of the Other Children noticed something else, too. He said: "Winning or losing doesn't seem to count to X. X seems to have fun being good at boys' skills *and* girls' skills."

"Come to think of it," said another one of the Other Children, "maybe X is having twice as much fun as we are!"

So after school that day, the girl who beat X at the baking contest gave X a big slice of her prizewinning cake. And the boy X beat in the relay race asked X to race him home.

From then on, some really funny things began to happen. Susie, who sat next to X in class, suddenly refused to wear pink dresses to school any more. She insisted on wearing red-and-white checked overalls—just like X's. Overalls, she told her parents, were much better for climbing monkey bars.

Then Jim, the class football nut, started wheeling his little sister's doll carriage around the football field. He'd put on his entire football uniform, except for the helmet. Then he'd put the helmet *in* the carriage, lovingly tucked under an old set of shoulder pads. Then he'd start jogging around the field, pushing the carriage and singing "Rockabye Baby" to his football helmet. He told his family that X did the same thing, so it must be okay. After all, X was now the team's star quarterback.

Susie's parents were horrified by her behavior, and Jim's parents were worried sick about his. But the worst came when the twins, Joe and Peggy, decided to share everything with each other. Peggy used Joe's hockey skates, and his microscope, and took half his newspaper route. Joe used Peggy's needlepoint kit, and her cookbooks, and took two of her three baby-sitting jobs. Peggy started running the lawn mower, and Joe started running the vacuum cleaner.

Their parents weren't one bit pleased with Peggy's wonderful biology experiments, or with Joe's terrific needlepoint pillows. They didn't care that Peggy mowed the lawn better, and that Joe vacuumed the carpet better. In fact, they were furious. It's all that little X's fault, they agreed. Just because X doesn't know what it is, or what it's supposed to be, it wants to get everybody *else* mixed up, too!

Peggy and Joe were forbidden to play with X any more. So was Susie, and then Jim, and then *all* the Other Children. But it was too late; the Other Children stayed mixed up and happy and free, and refused to go back to the way they'd been before X.

Finally, Joe and Peggy's parents decided to call an emergency meeting of the school's Parents' Association, to discuss "The X Problem." They sent a report to the principal stating that X was a "disruptive influence." They demanded immediate action. The Joneses, they said, should be *forced* to tell whether X was a boy or a girl. And then X should be *forced* to behave like whichever it was. If the Joneses refused to tell, the Parents' Association said, then X must take an Xamination. The school psychiatrist must Xamine it physically and mentally, and issue a full report. If X's test showed it was a boy, it would have to obey all the boys' rules. If it proved to be a girl, X would have to obey all the girls' rules.

And if X turned out to be some kind of mixed-up misfit, then X should be Xpelled from the school. Immediately!

The principal was very upset. Disruptive influence? Mixed-up misfit? But X was an Xcellent student. All the teachers said it was a delight to have X in their classes. X was president of the student council. X had won first prize in the talent show, and second prize in the art show, and honorable mention in the science fair, and six athletic events on field day, including the potato race.

Nevertheless, insisted the Parents' Association, X is a Problem Child. X is the Biggest Problem Child we have ever seen!

So the principal reluctantly notified X's parents that numerous complaints about X's behavior had come to the school's attention. And that after the psychiatrist's Xamination, the school would decide what to do about X.

The Joneses reported this at once to the scientists, who referred them to page 85,759 of the *Instruction Manual.* "Sooner or later," it said, "X will have to be Xamined by a psychiatrist. This may be the only way any of us will know for sure whether X is mixed up — or whether everyone else is."

The night before X was to be Xamined, the Joneses tried not to let X see how worried they were. "What if—?" Mr. Jones would say. And Ms. Jones would reply, "No use worrying." Then a few minutes later, Ms. Jones would say, "What if—?" and Mr. Jones would reply, "No use worrying."

X just smiled at them both, and hugged them hard and didn't say much of anything. X was thinking, What if—? And then X thought: No use worrying.

At Xactly nine o'clock the next day, X reported to the school psychiatrist's office. The principal, along with a committee from the Parents' Association, X's teacher, X's classmates, and Ms. and Mr. Jones, waited in the hall outside. Nobody knew the details of the tests X was to be given, but everybody knew they'd be *very* hard, and that they'd reveal Xactly what everyone wanted to know about X, but were afraid to ask.

It was terribly quiet in the hall. Almost spooky. Once in a while, they would hear a strange noise inside the room. There were buzzes. And a beep or two. And several bells. An occasional light would flash under the door. The Joneses thought it was a white light, but the principal thought it was blue. Two or three children swore it was either yellow or green. And the Parents' Committee missed it completely.

Through it all, you could hear the psychiatrist's low voice, asking hundreds of questions, and X's higher voice, answering hundreds of answers.

The whole thing took so long that everyone knew it must be the most complete Xamination anyone had ever had to take. Poor X, the Joneses thought. Serves X right, the Parents' Committee thought. I wouldn't like to be in X's overalls right now, the children thought.

At last, the door opened. Everyone crowded around to hear the results. X didn't look any different; in fact, X was smiling. But the psychiatrist looked terrible. He looked as if he was crying! "What happened?" everyone began shouting. Had X done something disgraceful? "I wouldn't be a bit surprised!" muttered Peggy and Joe's parents. "Did X flunk the *whole* test?" cried Susie's parents. "Or just the most important part?" yelled Jim's parents.

"Oh, dear," sighed Mr. Jones.

"Oh, dear," sighed Ms. Jones.

"*Sssh,*" ssshed the principal. "The psychiatrist is trying to speak."

Wiping his eyes and clearing his throat, the psychiatrist began, in a hoarse whisper. "In my opinion," he whispered—you could tell he must be very upset—"in my opinion, young X here—"

"Yes? Yes?" shouted a parent impatiently.

"*Sssh!*" ssshed the principal.

"Young *Sssh* here, I mean young X," said the doctor, frowning, "is just about—"

"Just about *what?* Let's have it!" shouted another parent.

". . . just about the *least* mixed-up child I've ever Xamined!" said the psychiatrist.

"Yay for X!" yelled one of the children. And then the others began yelling, too. Clapping and cheering and jumping up and down.

"*SSSH!*" SSShed the principal, but nobody did.

The Parents' Committee was angry and bewildered. How *could* X have passed the whole Xamination? Didn't X have an *identity* problem? Wasn't X mixed up at *all?* Wasn't X *any* kind of a misfit? How could it *not* be, when it didn't even *know* what it was? And why was the psychiatrist crying?

Actually, he had stopped crying and was smiling politely through his tears. "Don't you see?" he said. "I'm crying because it's wonderful! X has absolutely no identity problem! X isn't one bit mixed up! As for being a misfit—ridiculous! X knows perfectly well what it is! Don't you, X?" The doctor winked. X winked back.

"But what *is* X?" shrieked Peggy and Joe's parents. "*We* still want to know what it is!"

"Ah, yes," said the doctor, winking again. "Well, don't worry. You'll all know one of these days. And you won't need me to tell you."

"What? What does he mean?" some of the parents grumbled suspiciously.

Susie and Peggy and Joe all answered at once. "He means that by the time X's sex matters, it won't be a secret any more!"

With that, the doctor began to push through the crowd toward X's parents. "How do you do," he said, somewhat stiffly. And then he reached out to hug them both. "If I ever have an X of my own," he whispered, "I sure hope you'll lend me your instruction manual."

Needless to say, the Joneses were very happy. The Project Baby X scientists were rather pleased, too. So were Susie, Jim, Peggy, Joe, and all the Other Children. The

Parents' Association wasn't, but they had promised to accept the psychiatrist's report, and not make any more trouble. They even invited Ms. and Mr. Jones to become honorary members, which they did.

Later that day, all X's friends put on their red-and-white checked overalls and went over to see X. They found X in the back yard, playing with a very tiny baby that none of them had ever seen before. The baby was wearing very tiny red-and-white checked overalls.

"How do you like our new baby?" X asked the Other Children proudly.

"It's got cute dimples," said Jim.

"It's got husky biceps, too," said Susie.

"What kind of baby is it?" asked Joe and Peggy.

X frowned at them. "Can't you tell?" Then X broke into a big, mischievous grin. *"It's a Y!"*

Chapter Twenty-Nine

My Male Sex Role—And Ours

Joseph Pleck

When Jimmy was 10, he made his second try to get into a Detroit area Little League, and was turned down. His father, who had been a college football star, was so disappointed that he refused to talk to Jimmy all evening. Later that night, Jimmy swallowed some pills from his parents' medicine cabinet . . .

—Dolores Katz, "Why children attempt suicide,"
Detroit Free Press, February 3, 1974, p. 1A

For some of us the most untrustworthy people in our lives were males of our own age. We've learned, therefore, to be most guarded about ourselves when we're with men our age. . . . Being male has meant being devoured by other males, the way animals are thought to, but really don't. . . .

—*Unbecoming Men*, pp. 59–60.

I know why you fear strong women.
Hate gentle men . . .

—Robin Morgan, *Monster*

I

My first encounter with the male sex role started with sports in grade school. I had very positive anticipations about physical education when I started to go to school. I thought it would be a wonderful thing to learn about my body, and to learn how to do things that I had seen others do, just as I was excited about learning how to read and write, which I had been looking forward to for a long time. But "physical education" was very different from what I expected. At the end of one class, early in first grade, the teacher told us to take our shoes off and to put them in a pile in the center of the gym. Then he mixed all the shoes around, and told us we had to get our shoes back. The catch was that the last person to get his shoes back on would have to do ten pushups. A mad scramble ensued, and I was the last. I don't remember whether I did the ten pushups or not, but I doubt it. Thus began my career in "phys ed."

There was a dodgeball game we played regularly, which had two forms. In the first form, there were two teams, and the idea was to throw the ball at people on the other team. If you hit them, they were out, but if they caught the ball you threw at them, then you were out—the game going on until everyone on one team was out. In the second form, sometimes called "bombardment," or "German" dodgeball, the principle was the same, except that there were no teams, only individuals. With several balls going in a class of thirty, the energy level could get quite high. I was never much good at throwing the ball with any force or accuracy, but I got to be very good at dodging, so my basic strategy was to avoid being hit. But the problem was that I often ended up as one of the last two people in the game. Then the other person would keep throwing the ball at me until I was so worn down and exhausted that I would finally be hit, with the whole class watching this gladitorial contest. This got to be extremely painful, both because I always lost and also because it showed everyone else that I couldn't really throw the ball. I soon learned to let myself get hit about halfway through the game. I learned several things in this game: I learned to be hyper-alert to attacks from other men, and good at dodging them; I also learned that it is extremely important to avoid being conspicuous in the male war of all-against-all.

When I was in the cub scouts in the fifth grade, the big event of the year was a boxing tournament. In my match all I could do was try to defend myself against the other boy hitting me. He hit me a lot, and in spite of the lesson I had learned from dodgeball, I stubbornly refused to be knocked down (perhaps because my parents were there), so mostly I was standing there being hit in the face. Finally the match was over, and the other boy was declared the winner. It was noted approvingly how "tough" I had been in not being knocked down by the blows I received. I don't remember my father saying anything, although he may have.

The most dreadful aspect of sports in school was the daily choosing up of sides for whatever the game was during the lunch period. Whatever it was, I was always picked last. I remember noticing that another boy, who also wasn't very good, had worked it out that he would always be the umpire or referee in these games, and thinking to myself what a brilliant solution this was. The umpire role is one of the few *bona fide* ways to participate in sports without any physical competence. The problem, however, was that there was room for only one umpire. I remember being mad at myself that I hadn't thought of it first. However, in a lot of other situations involving competition with men, I have learned to take safe, noncompetitive "umpire" roles whenever possible.

When I went to high school, things were a little better because there were no longer any lunchtime sports, but I now had physical education every day instead of twice a week. I remember most of all a father-and-son picnic and softball game in my homeroom when I was a freshman. I knew this wouldn't be a good experience, but I was not strong enough to refuse to participate in it, as several other people in the homeroom did. After my father and I arrived, things got right down to business with the softball game. I was the only person on both teams, the fathers and the sons, not to get a hit; I struck out every time. I don't think I have ever felt so ashamed of myself as I felt then, or felt that anyone else was so ashamed of me as my father was then. In the picnic which followed, my father and I avoided each other completely. Driving home with him was excruciating. I didn't attempt anything even remotely athletic on my own initiative for about five years after that experience.

What seems so sad about it now is that my father and I shared in other ways that were important and meaningful. I remember particularly how he liked to walk around the back yard while I played the piano, hearing the sound come through the back porch windows. But none of this mattered during this archetypal Testing of the Sons' Strength before the Fathers of the Tribe. I had failed the test. No matter how else we related to each other, my father and I had to go through a male sex role ordeal that would leave us feeling horrible about each other and ourselves. Why?

At a weekend men's liberation conference last year, we decided to have a volleyball game. The group of us had some decisions about whether we wanted to keep score, and we came up with some interesting ideas about scoring systems that would reward cooperation and sharing instead of competition, both within each team and between the two teams. To my surprise many men seemed threatened and defensive about criticism of competition in sports. The game started up without a clear decision about the scoring system, and it turned out after a while that our side thought we were playing under a cooperative scoring system, while the other side thought we had decided to use the traditional competitive system. In a way, I felt like this had been happening to me all my life. So many times with other men, I thought we were playing cooperatively, and they thought we were playing competitively, and I got hurt sometimes, not so much by what the other men did to me objectively as by their ridicule that I could be so naive as to think that we could really be cooperating.

The other thing that happened during the game was that one man was accidentally hit in the face with the ball, breaking his glasses and shaking him up. This brought back a lot of memories, for it somehow seemed that in every game, someone got hurt like this. What followed was a confusing sequence in which the man was limping off the field trying to make light of how badly he was shaken up, trying to appear strong. At the same time, the other men wanted to reach out to him to help him, but hesitated, partly because the man who was hurt seemed to push it away, but also because they seemed scared of those caring feelings in themselves. Finally the game just started up again.

I've had many discussions with men about competition in sports. Many men say that competition is good because it makes people play harder and better. Though it has a certain plausibility, this argument mystifies what is going on in competition. Competition doesn't "improve" sports; sports provides a vehicle for teaching and reinforcing competition in males. That's why society makes sports a central feature of male upbringing, and that's what males learn from it. Some men say that sports "wouldn't be the same" without competition. They are right.

My experience with sports in school left me hating and feeling distant from my body, something I have really regretted. I always felt like it wasn't *me* who couldn't catch the ball, it was *my body*. Although my body has changed, my experience of it is in many ways much the way it was in grade school. And that experience was not based on any real exploration of my body, any real encounter with its full range of capacities to be strong, or to be coordinated, or to move, let alone to feel, or to give pleasure to myself or others, or to be beautiful. No, that experience of my body was based strictly on how well my body performed certain highly specialized acts of coordination when competing with other men.

More importantly, these experiences left me with a sense of myself as a marginal person, someone who doesn't share the things that are most important to everybody else. I didn't have sports as the major psychological reference point in my life, as nearly every other boy in grade school did, and I did not subscribe to the dominant system of values, images, and symbols it entailed. I saw the world differently from other boys. I identified sports as a major aspect of what I was supposed to be like as a male, which oppressed me because I could not do it, no matter how hard I tried. Sports expressed values about competition and aggression that I knew were awful. And I knew that these perceptions themselves, perhaps even more than my failure at sports itself, made me different from other people.

Recently a women friend told me she thought I would have been happier as a woman, considering the interests and qualities I have. After my initial shock, I asked her whether she hadn't really wanted to be a man at one time or another in her life, because of the relative privilege men have. She said no, she knew all that, but she just didn't think she could stand going through male gym class, no matter what other advantages there were to being a man. After a while, I could see her point.

II

In response to the tremendous pressure I felt from other boys in grade school, by third grade I realized that although I didn't have physical skills, the intellectual skills which I did have would be very important later in life. With them, I thought, I would come out far ahead of the people who were making me so unhappy now. I believe that I came up with this idea all by myself, and I had to believe it in order to survive. It always struck me as unfair that those who weren't any good in school got to say that school was dumb and useless, and that so many other boys would agree with them, while people like me never got to say the same thing about sports.

Though I knew in a general way that education was essential to "making it," I couldn't see any connection between the kinds of things people did in school and the jobs adult males had. I recall thinking during the sixth grade that I had about eleven more years, counting college, in which my life would proceed smoothly because I did so well in school. But then how would I get a job? What was there that I could do after all those years of school that anyone would pay me for?

After a Catholic grade school, I went to a public school which was extremely competitive intellectually. Sports were important in high school, but intellectual performance was also heavily stressed (in the service of the community's status ambitions), so that one could work out a respectable identity by doing well in school. I felt pretty inferior to those who had been in public grade school and junior high system in my area, which was extremely good, much better than the Catholic school I had gone to, and I was anxious about how well I would do. I was placed in a superelitist accelerated program, which flattered me, but also scared me.

In the school's intellectual group, it was important to be creative and artistic as well as intelligent. Because of my intellectual performance, I was able to make a place for myself as a hanger-on of the intellectual-artistic group, but never felt I belonged. I understand now that I was accepted on the condition that I constantly build up the egos of the other people and devalue myself for being so unartistic and for coming from a background that was culturally and intellectually deprived by the standards prevalent in this group. Several people in fact set out to give me "culture," which was no doubt well-intentioned, but which I see in retrospect was extremely patronizing and oppressive.

Anyway, I did well academically in high school, and got some satisfaction from the work I did. In spite of my putting myself down for not being a sculptor or whatever, I felt better about myself than I had felt anywhere before. But the intellectual competition made me anxious, especially as college admission time approached. In some sense, I had turned to intellectual work as a compensation for being terrible at sports, and saw intellectual work as a refuge from the masculine competition and aggression that I knew and hated so much in athletics. But intellectual work became just another arena from that aggression and competition. Although I did well, that competition led to constant, nagging feelings of inadequacy, and distorted my relationship with others.

But my feelings of inadequacy were different from what I had felt earlier in sports. First, I couldn't assume any distance from my feelings of intellectual inadequacy, as I could in sports. I couldn't criticize the system of intellectual competition that made me so anxious (as was so easy for me to do in athletic competition, even if only to myself), because I *believed* in intellectual work. *This* is what I was supposed to be good at, wasn't it? Profoundly as I had been wounded by my failure in sports, at the deepest level I never believed it to be important in the same way that I believed intellectuality to be important.

Second, I had the feelings of inadequacy of someone who was relatively successful, not those of someone who is a complete failure. I was getting enough positive rewards from what I was doing that most of the time I not only repressed or blamed myself for my nagging sense of inadequacy, I also was unaware that those who were not doing well in school hated themselves and deeply resented people like me—just as the boys I felt so inferior to in grade school had been totally unaware of how I felt. In escaping from sports, I had been drawn into a system in which I was relatively successful, in which it was now other people who were made to feel rotten about themselves. In going from grade school to high school, I had graduated from being a total failure as a male to being a member of the great "normal" majority who do

relatively well, while hating themselves and oppressing others. I had been transformed from a self-despising "failed" male to one who simply had normal male self-
hatred and feelings of inadequacy.

III

I hope it's clear that my complaint is not with sports. I know many other men who
were good at sports and terrible in school, and I can see how deeply they were
wounded by it, especially if their parents were middle class. (Relating to women is
another very important area of competition among males, which I don't deal with
here.) I've come to know my body much better in the last few years, and I've
particularly enjoyed regular running. In a post-revolutionary society, there will
certainly be a place for sports—and for intellectual work, too—though neither will
be socially structured the way they are now.

My own personal story, though, does happen to be with sports, and my experiences with it suggest two larger points to me, the first having to do with self-hatred,
and the second with violence. In talks I've had with other men, I've been struck by
how often men will say they enjoyed sports, and never felt critical of them, or hurt
by them, and yet tell of experiences which tell a quite different story. Sometimes they
describe how anxious they felt before games, or how glad they were to be injured so
they wouldn't have to play in particularly crucial ones; or sometimes they tell about
how bad they felt about certain sports they weren't good in. Yet they do not connect
these experiences to their larger feelings about sports.

All this seemed less odd to me when I thought more about my experience in schools.
I would certainly tell most people that I have always enjoyed school. Yet I can remember the insomnia and anxiety attacks I had so often, up to and including finishing my
doctoral dissertation; how in high school and college I was close to having an ulcer, or
how, when teachers would criticize classes I was in for not working hard enough, I was
sure the teacher was talking about me. Other men, too, have described college as a
wonderful intellectual experience for them, and then described times when they were
horribly wounded by tactless and glib criticisms of their work.

These examples illustrate how people can continue to believe in particular social
values in spite of the fact that they are failures according to these values. The social
values in our culture—for masculinity, femininity, beauty, success, normality, and
whatever—are so idealized that all but the tiniest minority of people are failures, to
greater or lesser measure. Yet the majority who are relative failures do not challenge
the legitimacy of the values that adjudge them to be of so little worth. Most people
learn a "false consciousness," an alienation from their own experience, in which they
repress the resentment they would otherwise feel. It is in fact seen as a sign of
maturity *not* to be angry or critical of such social values, instead accepting them
along with one's own failure. How people continue to believe so fervently in values
and norms according to which they can only be failures is an awe-inspiring phenomenon, and surely must be one of the most puzzling questions in understanding
individuals' relationships with society.

The major side effect of this phenomenon is the personal self-hatred which is prevalent to so startling a degree in our society. In their book, *The Adjusted American: Normal Neurosis in American Society,* Gail and Snell Putney point out how each society perceives some social problems as solvable, but others as inevitable and part of the human condition. In some primitive societies, it is thought to be inevitable that the majority of children will die before they reach three or four years of age. Our society would see such a state of affairs as shocking, and take immediate action. However, our society believes that it is an inevitable aspect of the human condition that most people have low self-esteem, and are emotionally crippled by feelings of inadequacy. In my own case, what pains me most about my experience, both early and more recent, is that while I now know that I was and am basically alright, I was so rarely allowed to experience myself as alright—in sports because I was a complete failure, and in intellectual work, because though I performed well, I could never be perfect and live up to my perception of what I was supposed to be.

The basic fact of social organization is that the losers, the people at the bottom of any social system, experience the world very differently than everybody else. The world of the boy who is always picked last in sports is very different from the world of other boys, just as is the world of the boy who is the "dumbest" in his class. It is a terrifying subterranean netherworld, full of hatred and violence which is expressed mostly against the self. If other people really knew and felt what those at the bottom were feeling, it would devastate them.

For the first time, many groups today are challenging the value systems that have oppressed them, and proposing alternate values. "Black is beautiful," "sisterhood is powerful," and "gay is good" are countervalues which are extremely threatening to mainstream society. These counter-values deal directly with a major problem which members of these groups have faced—the problem of believing in, at some level, a white male heterosexual value system in which they are by definition losers and failures. Adherence to these values has generated self-hatred in these groups. Challenging mainstream values, and bringing into awareness this self-hatred and repressed anger, is an extremely painful process, but also a joyful one. The energy of those who stop hating themselves is the most powerful social force that can be unleashed in any society.

Besides self-hatred, the second major theme in my experience with other men is the theme of violence. Male culture is a hostile, devouring culture in which men must adopt an aggressive stance toward the world in order to survive—in spite of all its romanticization by Lionel Tiger and others. As in my grade school dodgeball game, the great secret is to learn how to turn other men's attacks on you to your own advantage. The competitive questions, hostile joking, and clever put-downs of male culture are everyday interpersonal atrocities which are so routinized that we are hardly aware of them, or of how deeply violent they are. To be a man with other men means to always fear being attacked, victimized, exploited, and in an ultimate sense, murdered by other men.

My fear of this violence has been the most paralyzing inhibiter of my relationships with other men. Other men must hate the parts of me that do not conform to the male ideal, the parts of me that show me to be a traitor to my sex. I have had to make myself inconspicuous, and conceal my perception of the world, and especially my perceptions of maleness. However, there have been times when I have been with men who have also been alienated from this culture of male violence. Some of those times, I have felt safe and realized that I could drop my defensive stance, I have literally cried with relief.

IV

We live in a patriarchal, male-dominated culture. The feminist analysis of the effect of patriarchal society on woman is becoming more advanced and sophisticated. But there has been no systematic examination of the implications of patriarchal culture for men, and especially on relationships among men. We need a "sexual politics" of men's relationships with other men, because patriarchy is a *dual* system both in which men oppress women, and in which men oppress themselves and other men.

The dominant theme in men's relationships with other men in our society can be termed "patriarchal competition." This patriarchal competition is not tied to any particular areas of activity, like sports or the military, but in fact pervades nearly every context of encounter among men. Some areas may reveal this competition more explicitly than others, but no area provides a refuge from it. The major effect of competition among men according to patriarchal values is self-hatred, because no man can live up to the ideals he has been socialized to hold for himself about his performance relative to other men. His failure to meet these oppressive standards is experienced as reflecting on the deepest core of his sexual being. Men's need to control and reduce this self-hatred is an extremely powerful motivational force in male behavior. This self-hatred is the mediating link between individual male psychology and the larger sexual politics of masculinity. Patriarchal competition also generates a constant undercurrent of violence among men, physical and psychological, extraordinary and routinized, which men must learn to defend themselves against and to manipulate to their own advantage. In a culture of patriarchal competition among men, which depends so much on hatred toward the self and violence toward others, loving oneself and loving other men are indeed revolutionary acts. . . .

Today, men's liberation exists—not as a movement, exactly, but as an idea. Men's liberation means undoing the effects of patriarchal competition among men and finding out what we can be with each other. I know that one thing I share in common with all other males in our society is that each of us has faced an overwhelming cultural demand to be "a man" in competition with other men—however different have been the arenas in which we have struggled, however successfully or unsuccessfully we have responded to this demand with our unique resources, and most importantly, however much we have been pitted against each other by this very demand. Because of this shared experience, I also have in common with all other men the vision and prospect of men's liberation, a liberation that will at last make it possible for us to be brothers together.

Part VI

Clinical Implications and Applications

The essays in this section deal with problematic behaviors associated with gender that are pervasive in this culture. Ruth H. Striegel-Moore, Lisa R. Silberstein, and Judith Rodin review a large body of research in an attempt to explain the causes of bulimia. They ask, "Why women?" "Which women in particular?" and "Why now?" and attempt to answer these questions from a variety of perspectives, including social, developmental, and clinical psychology, as well as biology. In chapter 1 of this volume, Jane Roland Martin remarked that "any phenomenon can be understood in a variety of ways," and Striegel-Moore and her associates show that the depth of our understanding is vastly increased when "a variety of ways" are brought to bear on the same phenomenon. The complexity they reveal makes it clear that just as there is no single "cause" for bulimia, there can be no single "cure."

Virginia Goldner, Peggy Penn, Marcia Sheinberg, and Gillian Walker take an equally complex look at the problem of male violence against women. They refuse to adopt a reductionist view of male as villain (simply evil) and woman as passive victim (devoid of agency), while at the same time being careful *not* to blame the victim (as in the "she asked for it" view), *nor* to absolve the man from blame. "One level of description or explanation does not exclude another," they say, and "to develop a psychological explanation of violence is not to explain it away." The phenomenon of male violence is complex, but within the complexity, as Sharon Lamb (1996) says, lies the simple moral claim to be free from physical harm. Goldner and her colleagues maintain a "both-and" rather than an "either-or" stance throughout their analysis, observing, for instance, that male violence is both an instrumental and an expressive act, whereas others have insisted that it is one and not the other. In their therapeutic practice, too, they assume a "doubled vision," often choosing to treat the members of a couple together rather than individually, as is more usual in these cases. Rhoda K. Unger (chapter 25 of this volume) recommends that in studying gender psychologists should take "the interpersonal transaction as a unit of analysis rather than the individual alone," and the clinical data obtained from couple therapy seems especially appropriate in this case, since male violence against women is, of course, an "interpersonal transaction."

Stephen J. Bergman and Janet Surrey, dealing with the milder but still troublesome and even more pervasive problem of "impasses" in understanding between men and women, present vivid examples of the interpersonal transactions that occur in their workshops. In observing these interchanges, they, too, try to maintain a doubled vision. Their work grows out of self-in-relation theory (see Part IV), and, as they say, impasses are relational, not individual; they occur between people, not within people. The men and women they describe seem to exemplify the gender differences proposed by self-in-relation theory, with the women asking the men for empathy, while the men feel threatened by the invitation to attend to the women's feelings. This is an example of the "problematic complementarities" (Goldner et al.) that result when men and women look to each other for capacities they have disowned in themselves. Both of these essays offer dramatic evidence of the pernicious effects of rigid gender dichotomization. Both begin to address the question of how, in a therapeutic setting, these categories might be transcended, as men and women learn "to tolerate their disowned similarities." Neither Goldner and her associates nor Bergman and Surrey imagine that such a transformation will be easy to accomplish, for to experience one's self as similar to the "other" gender is not just a cognitive challenge; it is a source of terror, especially, perhaps, for men.

REFERENCES

Lamb, S. (1996). *The Trouble with Blame.* Cambridge, MA: Harvard University Press.

Chapter Thirty

Empathy, Mutuality, and Therapeutic Change
Clinical Implications of a Relational Model

Judith V. Jordan

Concerns about relationships lead many people, particularly women, into therapy in which a primary goal is to expand the experience of what might be called the sense of "real self," particularly in ongoing relationships. Individuals suffering from all sorts of falsifications and distortions of their experiences of self are looking for ways to be known and understood as well as providing that for others. How can we achieve and maintain a sense of contact and connection in which individuals can experience a sense of wholeness which also contributes to the relational unit? The feelings and behaviors that have been shut down to avoid pain, or amplified in order to gain approval, can begin to unfold anew in the therapy relationship. In its broadest sense, therapy offers an opportunity to expand relational presence, providing a sense of realness and contact with one's own inner experience and with the other's subjective experience. The route to this change is through the enhancement of empathy, both for other and for self. For many women, attention to their own inner experience often feels incompatible with attention to other (it is "selfish," "egocentric," "hurtful"); an ethic of caring for others carries the connotation of self-sacrifice or putting oneself last.

The goal in therapy is not to make women divert their attention from the relational context but to provide an opportunity to develop a new integration of self–other experience in which the validity of one's own experience as well as the other's gets acknowledged. This occurs in current real relationship and in memory organization of relationships. Responsiveness to the other as well as awareness of one's own needs—honoring the self—are enhanced. Attention is paid to empathy for self and other.

The elaboration and development of empathy as a means of interacting is central to my work with women in therapy. Many "modern" women initially see their empathic attunement to others as a burden; they wish they could be "more like men"—singleminded, able to "turn off" feelings in the service of logic; they wish all

Judith V. Jordan, "Empathy, Mutuality, and Therapeutic Change: Clinical Implications of a Relational Model." In J. V. Jordan, A. G. Kaplan, J. B. Miller, I. P. Stiver, and J. L. Surrey (Eds.), *Women's Growth in Connection: Writings from the Stone Center,* pp. 283–290. © 1991 Guilford Publications, Inc. Reprinted with permission.

the important areas of their lives, especially love and work, did not feel so intercon-nected, entwined. They have unconsciously, sometimes consciously, adopted the broader cultural values of abstraction, linearity, autonomy, compartmentalization. Unfortunately many therapists share this cultural bias and have devalued empathy as less useful or central than intellectual insight or clarification to the process of change. Both empathy and the therapeutic relationship have been seen as the context within which the important and significant work of interpretation and clarification occur. The Stone Center model suggests in fact that relationship, based on empathic attunement, is the key to the process of therapy, not just the backdrop for it. In therapy informed by a relational model of self we begin to see that there is integrity in the interpenetration of affect and cognition, of self–other boundary oscillation; we see that it produces special tensions and dilemmas, but the presence of these conflicts does not indicate a failure on the woman's part.

A part of her problem is living in a world which cannot clearly acknowledge the important contribution of emotional reaction and interpersonal sensitivity to think-ing, to work, to all aspects of life. Validation of the special tensions of being a person for whom a sense of identity is closely bound to relational context is a part of what I do as a therapist. I have treated numerous women who were previously in treatment, either in individual or couples' work with therapists who did not appreciate this and I have seen the destructive consequences of the therapist's failure to understand this. A brief vignette will illustrate several of these points: C. is a vivacious, attractive, bright forty-year-old divorced lawyer. She came into treatment primarily because of dissatisfaction with an intimate relationship. Her concern with the relationship was pervasive and she had difficulty attending to her professional responsibilities al-though she was "getting by." She blamed herself for not being able to keep her love life separate from her work life, seeing it as a sign of being "out of control" and "too needy." She and the man she lived with had consulted a couples' therapist before she came to me, and at the conclusion of a six-week stint of couples' work she met individually with the therapist who reportedly wondered why she was being so "masochistic" in holding on to a relationship which gave her so much pain and so little gratification. She felt devastated by this and found herself agreeing with the therapist. Now, in addition to feeling the pain of the relationship in which her lover was constantly telling her that she asked for too much intimacy, crowded him emotionally and physically, and told her she was suffering from extreme PMS which made her a "raving bitch," she considered herself a failure because somehow, in being "drawn" to all this pain—masochistic. In fact, what she was engaged by in the relationship were the moments of warmth and sharing, the joint venture of building a "we" together; in the face of his dissatisfaction and disappointment with her, she kept trying to make it better, to make the relationship "work" by adjusting to his demands (with understandably an underlying resentment for which she felt quite guilty). Her dedication to the relationship, her identification with the relationship and her willingness to make internal modifications to better the relationship were viewed by her couples' therapist as masochistic and she felt he must be right.

As we worked together in our therapy to seek other explanations for the unsatis-factory state of affairs, which included a real analysis of why she stayed in the relationship, rather than adopt the sense of blame inflicted on her by the couples' therapist, she began to feel some relief and appreciation of her own feelings and wants. Yes, she felt dependent but, yes, she also felt dependable and giving; and, yes, she was willing to expend considerable energy on trying to establish more mutuality. She came to appreciate the importance of her own giving nature but she also began to accept the limitations of this man's real capacity for intimacy and ultimately the relationship ended; instead of feeling she had "thrown four years down the drain," she was able to retrieve a sense of the integrity of her feelings and actions in the relationship as well as truly grieve for the loss of both a real relationship and hoped-for growth in the relationship. It was an extraordinarily painful process for her but the pain was no longer exacerbated by the persistent self-blame and sense of total personal responsibility and failure that she had felt following the couples' therapy. In working through this loss and appreciating her own capacity to seek connection and relatedness despite it, she in fact experienced a sense of increasing strength and diminishing vulnerability. Thus, although she lost this specific and valued relationship which caused tremendous grief, she gained an awareness of her very real relational capacities which she could now believe would allow her to eventually move forward into new relationships. She came to know these strengths in the therapy relationship itself.

In part, this example demonstrates an increase of what I have called self-empathy. Using Schafer's (1968) tripartite definition of self as "agent" (knower, doer), "object," and "locus," what self-empathy suggests is that the observing, knowing "agent" focuses on some experience (in which the self is experienced as object) in a new, empathic manner. In a broad sense, I am suggesting that how we relate to or make contact with others is a useful model for relating to parts of internal experience. The observing, often judging self can then make empathic contact with the self as object. This could occur in the form of having a memory of oneself in which the inner state at that time has not been fully integrated because it was not acceptable. To be able to observe and tolerate the affect of that state in a context of understanding becomes a kind of intrapsychic empathy, which actually can lead to lasting structural change in relational images and self-representations. The motivational and attitudinal state of nonjudgment and openness, taking an experience seriously, and readiness to experience affect and understanding may contribute to important shifts in the inner experience of troublesome self images.

As a therapist, I have often been moved by seeing the emergence of self-empathy. One patient identified with her critical, punitive father, and spoke of herself in very derogatory terms; one day she was giving an extremely unfavorable description of herself as she went off for her first day of school. In every comment one could hear her harsh, critical father's voice: "I was such an obnoxious little kid. I wanted everyone to pay attention. No wonder my father got so mad." A therapeutic intervention indicating that of course she wanted to feel special as she went out into this new, maybe even scary part of the world at first did not seem to have any impact. Later in treatment, when we were looking at this same incident, however, this woman burst into tears and said, "Suddenly I saw myself as the little girl, so scared and uncertain. My heart just went out to her. I feel it now for her . . . the pain. I feel it now for me.

I couldn't feel it then. But I understand why I was acting that way." It was not simply that she became more accepting and less punitive vis-à-vis certain self representations, although that was an important part of it. But she also actually connected with the affect which had been split off in the memory; both the self as object and the experiencing self were modified by this exchange. And the identification with the critical father was altered in the direction of being less punitive and harsh in her self-judgments. Empathy with self, with the memory of the little girl, increased as rejection and judgment of her decreased. Although there was a momentary increase of anger at the father as he came to be seen as harsh and critical, empathically failing the child, that was not the end point of the process. Rather, as it was worked through, the woman also began to experience a deepened empathy with the father. As she put herself emotionally in the place of each figure, an acceptance of their actions and feelings grew.

Self–other representations change. Both her disappointment and anger at father are an important first step but were she to stop the exploration there, she would simply be left with a negative image of father which does not allow for continued relational elaboration. Movement toward ongoing connection, with both father and others as well, is facilitated when, through empathy, movement toward or with, rather than away from or against, is accomplished. Self–other boundaries are importantly altered here; it is not a self endangered by others and defending against others but a sense of "I" that is more permeable to the "we," more available for relationship.

The therapist plays an important role in enhancing the capacity for self-empathy. First, her empathic attitude and response to the experiences being reported allows for a relaxation of some of the engrained patterns of rejection and judgment on the part of the client. There is a kind of "corrective relational experience" in which the unacceptable is accepted and responded to in a caring, affectively present and reconnected manner. Disowned aspects of self are witnessed and allowed. The therapist models an empathic way of being with painful memories and feelings. By bringing some understanding to bear on the experiencing person from the past (the little girl who was scared, not obnoxious), the therapist assists the patient in both objectifying important value-laden images of the self and paradoxically at the same time, making real affective connections with them. There is room now, however, for new affective-cognitive organization to occur, so old well-worn circuits (obnoxious little kid and disappointed, angry father) give way to new relational organization of the experience (scared little kid and impatient, unempathic father). The patient gains a new image of self as well as a new understanding of the other. The old relational matrix is freshly understood and there is a reorganization of the relational memory. Empathy for both self and other increase through these therapeutic explorations. In some sense, this involves a growth of compassion—for self and other.

Therapy, as I practice it, exists only in so far as empathic attunement occurs between patient and therapist. Mutuality, or more specifically mutual intersubjectivity, the attunement to and responsiveness to the subjective, inner experience of the other, at both a cognitive and affective level, is what the therapeutic enterprise is about. Therapy occurs through the capacity to share in and comprehend the momentary psychological state of another person (Schafer, 1959); it involves the elaboration of an understanding of the person and the relationship which relies on moment-to-moment cognitive-affective contact between patient and therapist. In therapy there are two active members who are both open to change through their participation in this interaction. The relationship that exists is central to the process, whether we talk about transference, "corrective emotional experience," or empathic attunement. The models of relationship as well as the actual manner of relating of the therapist are crucial to the way the therapeutic context influences individual growth. The therapist's appreciation of the ongoing interdependence of human beings leads the therapist to subtly and sometimes directly encourage the ongoing turning to others for support and assistance rather than emphasizing an ultimate state of self reliance and independence.

A model that acknowledges that therapy is a dialogue also recognizes that therapy is characterized by a process of mutual change and impact. Both therapist and patient are touched emotionally by each other, grow in the relationship, gain something from one another, risk something of themselves in the process—in short, both are affected, changed, part of an open system of feeling and learning. There is significant mutuality. It takes courage on both sides to involve themselves in this interaction. But it is in some respects not a fully mutual relationship. In therapy, one individual discloses more, comes expressly to be helped by the other, to be listened to and understood. The patient's self disclosure and expression of disavowed or split off experiences, in a context of nonjudgmental listening and understanding, is a powerful part of the process. In order to facilitate this, there is a contract which puts the patient's subjective experience at the center and there is an agreement to attend to the therapist's subjective experience only in so far as it might be helpful to the patient. The therapist offers herself to be used for the healing. But within this context there is real caring in both directions and is an important feeling of mutuality, with mutual respect, emotional availability, and openness to change on both sides. And the experience of relationship, of mutuality often grows with the therapy. Some therapists feel uncomfortable with the notion of growing through their work with patients; it feels exploitive or too gratifying. That conforms to an old model which suggests that if I benefit, you do not—a scarcity, power, hierarchy model. This is exactly the model that many of our patients carry in their heads, which makes it so hard for them to attend to their own needs. In practice, very often in giving to another we feel enlarged in expanding the relationship and our understanding of it, both members are enriched. If we honor the notion of a relational self, identity anchored in the world of human connection, interaction, and interdependence, and want to assist patients in expanding their sense of personal aliveness and wholeness in relationships, we must be ready to expand our own awareness and openness in the therapy relationship.

Being defined in, valuing, feeling alive through, and growing into relationship does not alter the reality of one's physical separateness in the world; nor does it deny the experience of solitude. But our culture has overemphasized the agentic, individualistic, competitive, lonely qualities of human life; and women have suffered, as their valuing of relationship, their immersion in caring and open need for connection have been denigrated. Yes, it is important that women learn to deal with anger, but it may be more important that they learn they can stay connected in the presence of anger rather than learn to automatically vent their personal frustrations on others without any attention to the impact of these feelings on others (what some would call a male model of anger discharge). And of course women should enjoy the freedom and be encouraged to develop and exercise their creative, intellectual, and self-expressive abilities for their own pleasure as well as for others' benefit. But here, too, it may be more important to find ways to do this which do not necessarily entail the ruthless disregard of others' needs or others' creativity. The reconciliation of self expression and relational enhancement is particularly important for women since so much of our sense of ourselves takes shape in relational contexts. Feeling connected and in contact with another often allows us our most profound sense of personal meaning and reality; at its best, therapy works toward developing and honoring this relational presence.

REFERENCES

Schafer, R. (1959). Generative empathy in the treatment situation. *Psychoanalytic Quarterly, 28* (3), 342–373.
Schafer, R. (1968). *Aspects of internalization.* New York: International Universities Press.

Chapter Thirty-One

Love and Violence

Gender Paradoxes in Volatile Attachments

Virginia Goldner, Peggy Penn, Marcia Sheinberg, and Gillian Walker

As family therapy has widened its scope by bringing social problems like battering, child abuse, and incest into the consulting room, the violent aspects of intimate life have become more visible. This has led to intense debate about how to think about and conduct clinical work with these populations.[4, 6, 8, 10, 11, 14, 20, 21, 25, 28, 30–32, 34]

In an attempt to engage with these issues and, more generally, to make a contribution to the metatheoretical project of incorporating gender into the basic premises of family therapy,[16] we began the Gender and Violence Project at the Ackerman Institute four years ago, and decided to focus on battering. Since we considered this a pilot project in which we would learn about these kinds of relationships through the process of treatment, we worked primarily (but not exclusively) with couples who sought treatment voluntarily, and we intentionally kept the project small so that we could work slowly, carefully, and in depth with each couple. As a result, we consider the ideas in this essay to be the outcome of a truly collaborative process between the four of us and the men and women who have participated in this study.

Our Metaperspectivist Stance

In our thinking about these matters, we have assumed a doubled vision: gender and violence, men and women; and a double stance: feminist and systemic. This layering of perspectives has inclined us toward the view, supported by earlier research, [6, 14] that relationships in which women are abused are not unique but, rather, exemplify in extremis the stereotypical gender arrangements that structure intimacy between men and women generally. Our hope has been that if we could "unpack" the unworkable premises about gender and power that underlie these dangerous relationships, we could interrupt the cycle of violence, and thus make love safer for women

Virginia Goldner, Peggy Penn, Marcia Sheinberg, & Gillian Walker, "Love and Violence: Gender Paradoxes in Volatile Attachments." *Family Process*, 29, pp. 343–364. © 1990 by Family Process Press. Reprinted with permission.

and less threatening to men. Insofar as we have been successful in this effort, we hope we have made a contribution that extends beyond the bleak confines of battering relationships by illuminating something more universal about the structure of male–female attachments.

In our project, we were looking for a description that was consistent with our beliefs as feminists, and simultaneously consistent with our beliefs as systems thinkers and therapists. We tried to get beyond the reductionistic view of men as simply abusing their power, and of women as colluding in their own victimization by not leaving. This description casts men as tyrants and women as masochists, which deprives both of their humanity while simultaneously capturing a piece of the truth.

In order to think more complexly, we decided to test ourselves, to see if it was possible to maintain a "both–and" position when treating couples with this problem. Could we see the problem through both lenses? Would that be helpful in stopping the violence? How would this doubled vision translate clinically? Is conjoint therapy philosophically consistent with our feminist position about battering? Could it be made consistent and still be clinically contraindicated? For which couples would conjoint treatment be helpful, and when?

We knew we would be pulled by the "either/or," either implicitly "blaming the victim" because, in seeing how the woman was implicated in her victimization, we would be inevitably implying that she was responsible for it, or, reciprocally, we were at risk of "constructing a villain" because, in not looking *beyond* the man's abuse of his power, we would not be making contact with the totality of *his* subjective experience.

By selecting couples who wanted to stay together, and treating them in conjoint therapy, we knew the risks. Both professionally and politically, there are many cogent arguments that the use of battering groups for men and support groups for women is the most appropriate treatment strategy.[4, 10, 25, 32, 34] This position makes sense. First, conjoint therapy, by definition, implies that there is a mutual problem to be solved, and this almost inevitably slides into the implication of mutual responsibility for it. This construction of the situation denies and obscures the social reality that the man is more powerful than the woman, and this distortion then falsifies the therapy. If the woman were to act as if she were equal, expressing her opinions and emotions freely, she would put herself in danger after the session. If she protects herself and the fragile relationship that she, for whatever reasons, wishes to maintain, the therapy is inauthentic. On the other hand, there were no well-conceived batterers groups for us to connect with, and the couples who came to us explicitly wanted to be seen conjointly.

These men and women occupied every segment of American society, for example, architects, professors, artists, corporate executives, social workers, small business men and women, chronically unemployed "mental patients" and others with severe social and psychiatric handicaps, and families on welfare. For some clients, this was their first therapy experience generally (or the first for this problem); others had been "through the system," including shelters, groups for batterers, the courts, and so on. In some cases, substance abuse was present and implicated in the violence; in others, drugs and alcohol were not used, or their moderate use did not seem to play a significant role in the problem.

Although these differences obviously shaped our thinking, and our interventive stance and strategy, we found more commonalities than differences with regard to the psychic infrastructure of violence. It is these common themes that we emphasize in this essay.

It was thus, in the context of these kinds of clients and of these ideas and questions, that we began our project four years ago. While we continue to question our thinking and modify our approach, we have clarified and refined many of these early questions and dilemmas. Our working assumptions are summarized below:

1. We begin with the recognition that gender inequality is a social reality and that women who are beaten by men are their victims. At the same time, we believe that reciprocities and complementary patterns in the couple's relationship are implicated in the cycle of violence.

2. At an ethical level, we hold the batterer responsible for the violence and intimidation, and we hold the woman responsible for protecting herself, to the extent that this is possible.

3. We believe that social control is sometimes necessary to stop the violence, and that violence is a criminal act for which legal sanctions are appropriate. However, since we are interested in the psychological dimensions of violence, including the psychological rationalizations for it, our work, whenever possible, is separated from activities of social control.

We also posed for ourselves a moral question: To maintain that violent acts and violent relationships have a psychology, did this once again let batterers "off the hook"? In putting both partners on the same level, since each one has a psychological interior, weren't we making them equal parties to a dangerous relationship we believed was not equal? We decided not.

We decided to maintain a position of "both–and," arguing that one level of description or explanation does not exclude another. To say that violence, domination, subordination, and victimization are psychological, does not mean they are not *also* material, moral, or legal. In other words, to develop a psychological explanation of violence is not to explain it away.

Thus, our attempt to discern and construct meaning in acts of violence does not overrule or substitute for our clear moral position regarding the acts themselves. Violence may be "explainable," but it is not excusable, and it may or may not be forgivable. That is up to the victim. For us, as therapists, what is important is to make sense of the confusing *circumstance* of violence so that the parties caught in its grip can begin to stop it.

One description we find useful, and useful clinically, is to understand male violence as simultaneously an instrumental and an expressive act. Its instrumentality rests on the fact that it is a powerful method of social control. A man can enforce his will and extend his areas of privilege in a relationship by hitting or merely threatening to hit his wife. Eventually he can get his way merely by a shift in his tone of voice or facial expression. In this sense, violence is a strategy of intimidation in the service of male domination, a strategy that a man consciously "chooses." At another level, violence can be understood as an impulsive, expressive act. It is often felt by men to be a regressive experience, the feeling of "losing it." We believe that both are true: that male violence is both willful and impulse ridden, that it represents a conscious strategy of control, and a frightening, disorienting loss of control.

These two ways of seeing are part of a matrix of explanations we rely on as we try to make sense of the quixotic juxtapositions of love and hate, control and dependency, remorse and cynicism, and change and no change in these dangerous relationships.

In the discussion to follow, we will be weaving ideas across four levels of description and explanation: psychodynamic, social learning, sociopolitical, and systemic. The psychoanalytic aspect of our work involves inquiry about ideas, beliefs, and, more deeply, internal representations of self and other, which are sometimes out of awareness but, when elucidated, often seem to constitute the organizing and unworkable premises underlying these couples' fierce attachments. The social learning dimension focuses on how these particular men and women were socialized into their gendered positions in these relationships. At the sociopolitical level, we include all of the external power differentials between men and women, including men's subjective sense of entitlement, privilege, and permission to rule women, and women's subjective belief that they must serve men. Finally, at the systemic level, we are interested in the transactional sequences, especially positive feedback loops, which are the immediate "cause" of the escalations that lead to violence, as well as all the double-binding processes between the couple, the extended families, and the treatment and social-service contexts that constitute the problem-maintaining system.

It is important to clarify the tension between these different stances in our work. As these remarks indicate, we are working within a "both–and" framework, which means we repudiate the stance of the forced choice. It also means that we repudiate the false dichotomies that forced choices dictate. Indeed, what we are trying to do is to push against the boundary definitions of a variety of philosophical stances in order to see how they stretch, what they disallow, and what it means to shift from frame to frame in order to describe most fully the human and therapeutic dilemmas that these couples present to us.

Although a full discussion of these matters lies well beyond the scope of these introductory remarks, we do want to make one point about our process of making distinctions. We have not found too many hard edges. The moves from a constructivist to a feminist stance, or from a systemic to a psychodynamic perspective, do not appear to require the paradigm shifts that the history of these ideas in family therapy would have led us to expect. We feel considerable freedom of movement. This is because we track the clinical process closely, and because, in whatever frame we occupy, we remain sensitive to the same set of issues: the place of language in constructing reality; the position of the observer or observing group that inevitably frames the problem and defines the terms of the problem-maintaining system, the moral limits of relativism, and the attempt to operate with the belief in an "observer-independent world-out-there" without succumbing to a naive, simple construction of "truth." We remain skeptical about essence, universals, and stable meanings, and we believe the layering of these intellectual perspectives is necessary if we are to capture the nuanced complexity of the issues at hand.

In our clinical work, we have borrowed what we liked from other methods and created new strategies as we went along. If there are distinctive elements to this mixture, they include the following: emphasizing the volitional aspects of violence; clarifying the relationship between violence, therapy, and social control in each case; elucidating the contradictory messages each partner may have already received about how to proceed (strong warnings against conjoint therapy from the shelter movement, family pressure to "stay together" or to separate, and so on); deconstructing the psychological interior of the violent episode for both partners; positively describing and then "unpacking" the attachment the couple feels for each other despite the violence; including (when indicated) the family of origin in the treatment to loosen the grip of negative injunctions and loyalty conflicts; seeing each member of the couple separately when we are concerned about the woman's safety and whenever we believe it will further the treatment; and always understanding the dilemmas of both partners in terms of the gendered premises and paradoxes that bind them.

In this essay, the first of a series, we will emphasize the theoretical aspects of our work, and therefore we make reference to these clinical techniques only insofar as they serve to illustrate the ideas we are developing. Moreover, in our attempt to highlight the overdetermined, gender-specific dilemmas that each partner brings to the couple relationship, we have had to shift our written focus from couple transactions to individual narratives. This does *not* mean that we consider an individual's history or psyche more pertinent than a couple's present relational pattern. Rather, we have chosen here to elaborate on those aspects of our thinking that are less familiar than the systemic formulations which do remain central to our work. In subsequent publications, we will describe in more detail the clinical approach summarized above.

A Feminist Relational View of Battering

Using the lens of feminist theory, we have been examining the gender assumptions that inform relationships in which women are physically abused. In analyzing men's violence against their female partners, and women's lack of commitment to their own safety, we hope to make a contribution that illuminates something more universal about the structure of male–female relationships under current social conditions.

We begin our analysis, leaning on twenty years of feminist scholarship, with the formulation that gender is a basic metaphysical category which, in every culture, prescribes an artificial division of the world into masculine and feminine. Most languages are elaborately gendered; all the significant elements of the social, natural, and spiritual world are linguistically differentiated by gender; and the mythologies of most cultures rely heavily on gender symbols. Thus, the construction of gender and of gender difference is not merely a psychological process or a social role; it is also a universal principle of cultural life that manifests itself in the individual psyche, the metaphysical framework, and the ideologies of a society.[33]

In a now classic article, feminist anthropologist Gayle Rubin[26] observed: "The division of labor by sex can be seen as a taboo against the sameness of men and women which divides the sexes into two mutually exclusive categories and thereby *creates* gender. . . . Far from an expression of natural difference, exclusive gender identity is suppression of natural similarities" (p. 180).

This taboo against similarity, and the dread of the collapse of gender difference, operates silently and powerfully in all relations between men and women.[13] The patriarchal structure of power and privilege in society positions men to experience humiliation when gender divisions blur, and positions women for punishment if they claim male prerogatives. *Indeed we have come to think about battering as a man's attempt to reassert gender difference and gender dominance, when his terror of not being different enough from "his" woman threatens to overtake him.*

While such fears are clearly extreme in these men, they are, according to many current theories of gender-identity formation, normatively central to the development of masculinity.[3, 5, 7, 9, 15, 23, 29] Thus, in order to make sense of this kind of male violence, it is necessary to develop an analysis and critique of "masculinity" generally. Although a full discussion of these matters lies well beyond the scope of this essay, the following synopsis of the relevant theorizing is intended to provide a framework for understanding our particular way of formulating the issues.

The contemporary theories of gender-identity development that are compatible with our thinking conceive of "gender" as a deeply internalized psychic structure. They presume that gender acquisition is a process of social learning rather than an expression of natural givens. Moreover, now that researchers have shown that gender identity gets established and consolidated between twelve and thirty-six months,[3] much earlier than had previously been thought, it is becoming clear that the development of the self and the acquisition of gender become fatefully intertwined in early life. In other words, personhood and gender identity develop together, co-evolving and co-determining each other. In this sense, gender is not merely "acquired" by the child but, rather, *creates* the conflict-laden layering of internalized self-representations that *become* the child. As a result, one could no more become "degendered" than "deselfed."[17]

The social context of this psychological process is conceptualized by gender identity theorists (most notably, Nancy Chodorow) in terms of the phenomenon of "asymmetrical parenting." Since women are the primary caretakers of children, both boys and girls must begin the project of becoming a person by defining themselves within the context of their relationship to a single, psychologically gendered woman. This lopsided social arrangement, in which men have traditionally played a marginal role, is considered to have decisive consequences for the creation of gendered personalities.

While the girl's psychic structure develops in relation to someone "just like her," the boy constructs his identity via an experience of difference. Because of the primacy of the mother in early life, and the absence of an equivalently substantial relationship with the father, learning to be masculine comes to mean learning to be "not-feminine." Indeed, as Greenson[15] and others have argued, for boys, this gender difference becomes the vehicle for separating from, and dis-identifying with their mothers. In other words, the boy constructs his sense of himself out of a negative: "I am not like my Mother; I am not female." In the view of most gender-identity theorists, this childhood negation creates problems for the psychological foundation of masculinity, so that when the boy becomes a man, this gender structure is potentially threatened whenever experience calls up echoes of that early maternal bond, that early identification, that early separation. The thinking is that since mother, and later all women, exist as continual reminders of what must be given up to be male, it is not surprising that researchers have found that boys maintain more sharply dichotomous gender divisions than girls,[5] and that fathers have been shown to enforce gender stereotyping much more rigidly than mothers.[18]

By contrast, a woman's identity is forged *within* a feminine relational context and, in a sense, the girl remains part of the mother's psychological space. Gender theorists have argued that this formative female bonding creates the conditions for a woman's empathic orientation, and also for her difficulties in *separating* herself from relationships. Moreover, insofar as the daughter experiences herself as likened to, bonded with, and sometimes virtually *part of* a person of subordinate social rank, she must struggle to claim for herself what her mother was denied: a voice of her own, a mind of her own, a life of her own. Thus, it is not her gender identity that is at risk in her identificatory bond with mother, but her sense of personal power and agency.

Since the girl cannot receive the mantle of power from one who does not have it, she must sometimes settle for "the power behind the throne." This means that the work of becoming female is shaped by the necessity of learning how to become, what Jessica Benjamin[3] has called, an "object of (male) desire," which inevitably must conflict with the task of becoming a subject in one's own right. Instead of being a subject in search of herself, a woman must often transform herself into a "subject-as-object."[7] Not surprisingly, this process of self-betrayal can create its own rebellion.

Given this analysis, men and women under the best of circumstances form attachments in which they must seek in one another the capacities each has lost. This search often results in the problematic complementarities that family therapists encounter in treating couples, and which are often so difficult to change. In our view, it is only when both partners become committed to transcending the rigid categories of gender difference, and can begin to tolerate their disowned similarities, that real change is possible. This would involve, for the woman, reclaiming a sense of her independent subjectivity and establishing or re-establishing her capacity for agency in the world. For the man, the task requires recognition and acceptance of his own dependency needs, and simultaneously learning how to empathize with his mate's subjective experience, with her needs and desires as they exist for her, and not as he defines them.

While such a transformation asks a lot of both partners in ordinarily troubled relationships, it puts a special burden on the man who is violent and the woman whom he abuses. In these circumstances, such a man must tolerate a sense of weakness for perhaps the first time. Since his sense of personal power and psychic autonomy is an illusion that is sustained by denying his dependency needs through controlling his partner, he can become deeply threatened if he begins to see his mate as a person in her own right (who might leave, or disagree, or compete with him). Thus, he may fight against her attempts at independence despite the best of intentions. Indeed, for many of these men, the fear of disintegration, if they sense that the woman may leave them *in any way,* is so great that they will frantically try to regain control by any means necessary.[25]

If the woman is to retain a sense of her entitlement in the face of such intimidation, she must silence the voices from within her and the messages from the culture at large. Everywhere she turns she will hear that she is transgressive if she fails to please him. When she does assert her right to her own experience, her own sexuality, her right to be cared for, he may term her hysterical, extravagant, or insatiable. He may threaten to leave her, thus signaling his social and economic superiority; or he may become violent, thus asserting his physical superiority. She may be confused by his rage because her experience of herself and his view of her are disparate; but she too has been raised in a culture that elevates the male perspective, so she may silence her own mind and submit to his construction of reality even if that means being hit.[1]

Given these temptations, the conjoint therapy of battering must provide a framework for dismantling the powerful gender injunctions that set the terms for such relationships, terms that virtually prescribe male domination and female subjugation.

Gender Premises/Gender Paradoxes

In order to challenge the gender assumptions that we believe provide the legitimation for battering, we have had to refine our thinking about the gendering process. Our theorizing presumes that gender is simultaneously rooted in the biological difference between the sexes, and that the other crucial determinants of gender identity are psychological, cultural, and political. Thus, not only do we take as a given the social learning, sociopolitical and psychoanalytic explanations of gender formation that were articulated earlier in this essay, but we also make a bridge between the psychological and social levels by interpolating a family-systems formulation of the gendering process.

We would argue that not only is gender deeply embedded in the psyche, as the psychoanalysts maintain, but it is also *deeply embedded in the politics of family relations.* Similarly, we believe that ideas about how to be male or female are not simply transmitted from parent to child, as the social learning theorists suggest, but that *these premises become part of the family drama.* Elaborating on the earlier work of Penn[24] and Sheinberg[27] that developed the construct of the family or relationship "premise," we now argue that gender premises, like other passionately held beliefs, create relationship binds and paradoxes across the generations, which are then internalized within the psyche and create for each generation a legacy of insoluble contradictions.

The men and women we see in relationships in which there is battering frequently grew up in families in which these gender dichotomies were rigidly prescribed and exaggerated. Because these gender injunctions were writ large, it has been easier to see the inherent paradoxes that are embedded in the gendering process. For example, one woman's story reads, "Mom doesn't stand up to dad and she seems always silently angry and depressed. But, whenever I get argumentative, she says that I'm 'too masculine' and no man will want me." Or, from a man's story we distill the message he felt *his* mother was sending: "Be strong like your father so that you will be able to protect women like me from men like him." And, from a powerful father to his daughter, "The reason I have to beat your mother is that she 'makes me do it.' If only I were married to someone understanding [like you] we could have a happy home." And from father to son: "You must never be a wimp or feel afraid, but watch out for women. They can do you in. For every Sampson there is a Delilah with scissors."

The contradictions inherent in the conflicting logic of these gender constructions generate paradoxes at all levels of psychic and familial organization. The child not only absorbs these mystifying presentations of filial gender arrangements, but is also enlisted in participating in impossible relationship binds as a function of his or her sex. In other words, the child's sex becomes implicated in the political force field of the family drama.

Thus, the gendered relationship maps that organize both family and psychic life tend to generate untenable coalitions, rivalries, and hierarchies, as well as profound internal confusion. It is, we believe, these overdetermined, internally contradictory, deeply embedded relationship premises, which are always at risk of collapsing under their own weight, that infuse the episodes of violence in the lives of these couples.

In the sections to follow, we will attempt to "unpack" the generational premises and paradoxes about gender identity and gender relations that are implicated in the violence/redemption cycle that characterizes these dangerous relationships.

The Man's Side

Gendered premises about masculinity are rigidly adhered to in the families of the men we have been seeing who are violent toward women. These premises, for example, that men must be stronger than women, and that they must not be sad or afraid, are in direct conflict with psychological reality. Men, like women and children, often feel dependent, scared, sad, and in need of protection. Since the prohibitions against such "feminized" feelings include the man's private sense of himself, and not only his public persona, the psychological task of denial is constant. This is why intimacy can be so dangerous. When the man's terror of not being different enough from "his" woman overtakes him, violence becomes one means of reasserting gender difference and male power.

The injunction against having "unmasculine" feelings is sent to all men through all the channels of the culture. In our clinical work with violent men, we have been tracking the generational transmission of this prohibition and the ways in which it fatefully compromised both the father/son and mother/son relationship.

Looking first at the fathers, we hypothesize that, in these families, the son developed the conviction that his father's love was contingent on his fulfilling a particular definition of masculinity. In one case, for example, the son's connection to his father was predicated on never showing fear, in another it was a readiness to fight back against a perceived insult to the family, in another, never to listen to a woman's opinion, in another, always to use physical force when threatened. The fact that many of the fathers of these men were abusive underlined that father's love was conditional, and that it could be easily transformed into its opposite: some form of brutality. This set the stage for a lifetime of trying to become the man father would at last love and respect.

Because these men grew up believing that they had to be a "man" in order to be worthy of a man's love, they hid their vulnerabilities even from themselves. Their childhood experience with their fathers was so limited and so conditional that it created an intense but deeply buried longing for male connection. However, since cultural prohibitions and particular family dynamics made having an openly de-clared, mutually affirming relationship with father impossible, these men had to make a bond with father symbolically. In other words, instead of "being with" father, they settled for "being like" father. In place of a paternal relationship, they could only substitute a paternal identification.[5]

This solution is itself part of the problem. Ironically, the only way the "fatherless boy" can maintain some sense of being close to his father is by making himself into the kind of "macho man" who disavows his yearning for closeness and denies any need for others. In one couple, Raymond, for example, described his father in what seemed to be an admiring tone, as "a tough guy, tough emotionally and tough physically." Yet, when the therapist asked, "Did you respect that toughness?", he paused and slowly added, "No, I don't think so. . . . I had very little respect for my father, at least outwardly. At least I used to say all the time that I had no respect for him. I'd even tell *him* that. But now I don't know if that's true. . . . These days I wonder, since I'm very much the same style, if I wasn't really, secretly, thinking it was a good thing. However, I *hated* it at the time."

Given a childhood marked by these extreme demands for gender conformity, men like Raymond enter adult relationships with impossible prohibitions ("I must never feel fear, know need, respect a woman's point of view"). Not surprisingly, such premises prove unworkable since, just as when he was a boy, this man still has yearnings and anxieties, and, despite himself, he is quite capable of being deeply "hooked in" to a woman's experience and to see the world through a woman's eyes. Moreover, he is now *in* a relationship with a woman, and the temptations to let his guard down are everywhere.

One solution to this quandary seems to involve arranging for an emotional division of labor in which the woman "carries" the unacceptable feminine feelings for both of them. That way, the needs get met and the feelings expressed, but the man does not experience them as coming from within.[2] Indeed, it is when he is most close to recognizing the feeling as his own that, we believe, he is most tempted to be violent.

Raymond, for example, repeatedly proclaims he will never be a wimp. This premise has resulted in his alienating virtually everyone around him. He is a man without friends, without a job, and with an extremely troubled relationship with his wife and children. He came to marriage therapy after hitting his wife. He was motivated by her threat to leave him if he didn't change. In the course of therapy, we observed that anytime Raymond risked listening to his wife, or being persuaded by her point of view, he argued ferociously. We speculated that it was when he was almost convinced by her opinion, or at the moment that he appeared closest to his "wimp" feelings, that he fought against his wife the hardest.

John developed a different strategy for denying his vulnerabilities in order to maintain some kind of attachment with his harsh father. A young wrestler, he was terrified of the city, but denied his fear by converting it into worry over his wife's safety. This "concern" provided the justification for his not allowing her to go anywhere without him. In time, his preoccupation with her safety resulted in his physically restraining her when she tried to go to work. Thus, the man who had been terrified by the city vanished, replaced by a fearless husband who was protecting his wife from the dangers outside their home.

Because John's parents, especially his father, raised him with the strong injunction never to feel fear, let alone to voice it, we speculated that he feels at risk of losing his psychological connection to his father, which for him is fused with his masculine identity, if he acknowledges feeling frightened. To feel fear raises the feared question, "Am I still a man, a man that father would respect?"

Unfortunately, the mothers of these sons were unable to help them work out a viable relationship with their fathers. In fact, we have observed that it was often one son who was selected to be beaten, and this same son was enlisted by his mother in a coalition against his father's brutality. Ironically, the terms of this coalition reinforced the very values and behavior they were intended to resist. For instance, one son describes the source of pride his mother felt at his being a fighter; another son shares that he knows he was his mother's favorite son because he was more "macho" than his brother; another describes how his mother always protected his brother while encouraging him to fight back.

Thus, in many of our cases, the bond between mother and son existed as a covert coalition in the shadow of the father. To the extent that this was a bond organized around a common experience of subjugation, the boy and his mother had become peers, and occupied the same level of the domestic power hierarchy. Yet, this definition of their relationship is contradictory. The mother, because she is a parent, maintains a senior position in the generational hierarchy while the boy, by virtue of being male in a patriarchal household, is somehow elevated above her.

This paradoxical arrangement put many of these boys in an impossible bind. While still needing their mother's care and protection, they often felt they had to behave as her "little man" in order to lend some kind of credibility to her struggles with father. However, if they bonded too openly with mother, they risked becoming "feminized" in father's eyes, and therefore not "man enough" to win father's approval.

This Gordian knot is tied in many ways, as told by the men in our study. But the common thread is that, as children, these boys felt aligned with their mothers, while wishing they could be close to their fathers. They saw the injustice that mother suffered, and felt, in varying degrees, sympathetically loyal to her, but they craved, nonetheless, to be paired with the powerful, critical father. Thus, these men formed deeply ambivalent, covert attachments to both parents, which they themselves could not fully acknowledge.

Our effort has been to understand if and how these contradictory parental loyalties are implicated in the violence/redemption cycle these men enacted with their mates. To this end, we have developed a line of questioning that separates the strands of meaning, memory, and feeling packed into the explosive moment and its denouement. Although each man and each fight is unique, a paradigmatic relational pattern has suggested itself to us.

The constant oscillation between "feminized" devotion and "macho" domination, which characterizes the stance of these men toward their mates, and which has been so often observed both in the literature and by their confused wives, can be viewed as a conflict of divided loyalty. When they are "protecting" their women, it is as though they re-enact their fateful bond with their one-down mothers, which then must be renounced whenever their mates act independently. This is because, when the woman wants to be separate, she experiences her partner's "protectiveness" as controlling and intrusive. At such moments, the mutually comforting, gendered arrangement of knight and damsel shatters, and a control struggle ensues. The man, momentarily "unhooked" from the romantic bond, now reasserts the "manhood" that symbolically bonds father to son. He goes "on the attack," with the goal of subduing "womanhood" by any means necessary. Thus, Dr. Jeckyll becomes Mr. Hyde, and back again, as the dynamics of these volatile relationships move through their infernal circle.

Deconstructing the Violent Moment

In order to loosen the grip of these dangerous sequences, we have developed an interventive strategy that "deconstructs" the psychological interior of the violence/redemption cycle. Through this process we have found that the violent escalation within each man has many highly condensed, former triggers. When, for example, you see a boy running, you see the simple act of running. However, if you were to draw the act of running, it would be a multipositional rendering of the many and discrete moves packed into the act of running—but it would not be *the* run. Similarly, there are former and discrete relationship conflicts packed into the violent escalation. When a man says, "I just saw black," or "I felt a fire in my veins," the specific conflicts packed into that sentence are unavailable to him because he is "in the run."

Deconstructing the violent moment, or putting into slow motion this high-speed enactment, means fine-graining its precursors. Repetitious questions yield many descriptions that allow the experience of the violent moment to be differently described, thus bringing new meaning to the experience. These new descriptions or language constructions fit themselves around the man's needs, and we hear fragments of old and new relationship conflicts, jumbled ideas, accusing voices, and painful memories, all acting like explosive flack that surrounds a plane on a war mission when any bump may produce an explosion. Repetitiously inquiring about the man's story and carefully separating all its strands encourages him toward a new story, one in which all his feelings may be included.

We have discussed the violent act as a pseudo-solution to a contradiction these men experience when they have feelings they deem unmanly: dependency, fear, sadness, and so on. These are unacceptable feelings in that they do not fit socialized gender premises about masculinity. Indeed, in remembering the escalation that precedes the violent moment, the men often describe an internal struggle between unmanly feelings and macho feelings, which are described as occurring in rapid-fire alternations.

The following example is one in which the therapist deconstructs the moments leading up to a violent explosion. The questions are asked slowly and repetitiously, separating all the man's descriptions, past and present. It is the case of a young wrestler who finds himself far from home, married, estranged from his wife's family, out of work, and dependent on his wife's menial job. His wife has threatened to leave him if he cannot control his violent rages. This particular session follows a twenty-four-hour fight between them. He arrives saying he must have valium "because my head is coming off and I feel like shit!" His wife reports that he held her down, threatened her, and refused to allow her to go to work. Talking with him alone for the first part of the session, he said his anger started the night before when his wife was on the phone with her father.

Th: You overheard that or . . .

John: No, he said it to me on the phone. . . . At the time I didn't say anything because . . . To myself I said, "That's the biggest mistake you'd ever make."

Th: Your father-in-law's voice stayed in your head till the next morning when you prevented L [wife] from leaving? Did you say anything to him that night?

John: I said, "Listen Mr. B., I would never harm your daughter. She's my wife and I love her." He said, "I want you to know if you ever do, I'd make that one phone call." He made me sick when he said that. He shouldn't have said that. If he was going to take a hit on me, he should have never said it because now he's . . .

Th: Was that a big mix of anger and fear you went to bed with that night before you prevented L . . .

John: I'll tell you this, her father is seventy years old. The man is in tremendous condition, healthy as a horse, good-looking, and he's got a lot going for him. If he were fifty, I'd have gone down there and hammered the piss out of him so bad he'd never walk again. I'd have gone down there and wiped the floor with him for threatening my life. Yeah, I was angry.

Th: Do you still have some of the feelings from that phone call?

John: I could run my head through that wall right there, I'm so pissed off at the feelings I have right now, for the way . . . I mean, I just feel . . . Take his two sons! They've never done shit in their life. They walked into their father's business and made it. Me, I was cut for twenty-six stitches; they told me I'd die if I went into the fight. I couldn't breathe through my nose. I got hit for twenty-six stitches in the second round and fought for ten rounds in one-hundred degree heat. I fought for my life, broke both my hands. I mean, I've been fighting for my life. I've been fighting to help my family to have everything and then . . .

His story now includes two families, his wife's and his own. The story of his wife's family torments him because he can't measure up to their social status and his father-in-law has terrified him with his threats of a contract killing. (The family is not to our knowledge in any way connected to "organized crime." Thus, the threat represents, in our view, an empty, intimidating gesture that reflects the father-in-law's own feeling of helplessness and need to appear powerful.) His own story includes desperately trying to fight for his family and not succeeding.

Th: So, before you prevented your wife from leaving for work, were all these ideas mixed up in your head? Feeling rejected by her family and feeling you hadn't done what you wanted to for your own family?

John: (howls)

Th: So, that morning when you got up you were beginning to feel the "fire in your veins"—Is that "fire" a fire about fighting for your life, for your own family and to be a real husband to L and her family?

John: I'm fighting now! I fought all my life to try to help my parents to get a nice home for them, and I have not accomplished that yet. That bothers me. Even though I'm a highly recognized professional, I couldn't turn around and buy bubble gum right now. (howls again)

Th: So, that morning when you got up and you were thinking about these ideas of fighting for your family and against her family's opinion of you, she said she was going to work. And what happened?

John: I said, "Oh no, you're not going to work. You're not going out there when they can shit on you!"

Th: If she has a demeaning job, do you feel you are both brought down? What did she say first?

John: "Oh yes, I'm going." She challenged me! But it wasn't like L challenging me, it was her parents. It was them.

Th: So, although the challenge comes through L, it's really her parents. Are they saying you failed since she has to go to work?

John: I'm twenty-five years old, I'm not thirty-five. Once the challenge is on, I don't care who you are or how many there are. I'll go down. She gets a certain tone in her voice. When I hear it, I hear her old man.

Th: How would you describe it? That tone?

John: It's something that cuts through me like a knife. Her father will *not*, I mean, you can't have a discussion with him because he's right! You're wrong, Jack, you're out like a light. See, this is the way I'm brought up, when you can't handle things, it's that! (leaps up slapping his clenched fist into the palm of his hand) You're not right, Jack, you're out like a light. I don't want to be like that, but the pressure is so strong right now because I'm fighting to turn things around and make things better. And I can't succeed. Its like I'm fighting a losing battle and it's killing me.

Th: So, that morning when you got up feeling scared and angry, you heard her father's voice and felt it was saying that you were disappointing both families. Is that the challenge?

In this conversation, we can hear John struggling with his confusion between his wish to make both families proud of him, and the feeling that they are, in fact, hurting, frightening, and humiliating him. "I try so hard" is a statement of his best image of himself, and also an idea that leaves room for new meanings. He tries so hard to be a proud person who is available to these families, not "the failure" they reject or abuse.

In the course of this deconstruction, we have hardly spoken about his anger toward his wife; the incident involving her is quickly superseded by other voices that seem to be packed like triggers into the escalation. Three prominent voices are involved: his wife's voice, his father-in-law's voice, and his father's voice. These voices embody ideas and issues that John, like many men, is preoccupied with: to bring distinction to one's family, to carve a significant place in the public world, to be recognized by powerful men as powerful, and not to show fear. In sum, they describe his struggle, his fear of failing, and his wish to succeed.

The repetitious listening and tracking of his story allows him to integrate these ideas, all of which had been disconnected from one another and from the overwhelming affects that too often overtake him. By going through the episode in slow motion and "unpacking" his globalized experience of rage, John can begin to confront both the specific issues and the larger themes that ignite his helpless fury. Once he can *see* the pieces, he can start picking them up, one by one, and, if he chooses, he can begin to take charge of his reactivity and his life, piece by piece. He can still choose to be violent when these issues arise, but he can also see that he has a choice, which may then make it easier for him to choose differently, and for his wife to demand that he make a different choice.

The Woman's Side

One of the issues that has preoccupied our thinking has been how to construct an explanation of women's participation in violent relationships. As systems thinkers, we could not be satisfied with descriptions that cast women as hapless victims, and yet we were opposed to lazily constructed narratives of circularity or, worse, of "function of the symptom" notions in which, by some stretch-of-the-imagination reframe, the woman was construed to derive some benefit from her victimization.

In order to include the women in the problem definition, but not to "blame the victim," we have attempted to co-construct with our women clients an explanation of how they were "caught" in the battering situation. More specifically, we wanted to understand why these women did not leave these relationships even when they had the material means to do so, and why they did not seem able to resist the pull of an argument, and often chose to cast the first verbal stone, even when they knew that they were putting their safety at risk.

These questions were not only ours. Often it was the women themselves who

urgently asked for help in understanding why they stayed embroiled in these dangerous relationships. Andrea, for example, says, "I guess basically I would like to find
out what the hell it is that makes me stay. I really don't know. I keep thinking maybe
there's something wrong with me." Wanda puts it this way, "Dick says I blame
everything on him, and that I'm really the crazy one. I mean, I will admit I'm crazy
to stay, but I don't think I'm the crazy one. I might be, but I don't see it."

The mysterious "stickiness" of these relationships was all the more intriguing
when we discovered that these women, contrary to what we had imagined, were not
timid, self-deprecating, fragile victims. They were victims, but they were, in nearly
every case, women of substance who had strong opinions and conveyed a sense of
personal power. Over the past four years, through our process of interviewing, we
have begun to understand this fierce commitment to a man and to a relationship
that seems so destructive.

Our thinking owes much to the revisionist theories of female development and
psychology that have become increasingly influential in recent years.[3, 5, 7, 12, 19, 22, 31]
The central insight in all the new work about women is the idea that women form a
sense of self, of self-worth, and of feminine identity through their ability to build
and maintain relationships with others. This imperative is passed to daughters
from mothers whose view of feminine obligation has been to preserve both family
relationships and the family as a whole, no matter what the personal cost. Thus, the
daughter, like her mother, eventually comes to measure her self-esteem by the success
or failure of her attempts to connect, form relationships, provide care, "reach" the
other person.

Sarah, who as a child was beaten (as was her mother) by an alcoholic father, and
who now is being battered by her husband Mike, put it like this: "From the time that
Mike and I got involved, I got the sense that he was like a hurt child. I felt the best
way of working on our relationship was to try to build him up and make him feel
better about himself." Thus, even in the context of her own victimization, Sarah,
against her own best interests, can humanize her abuser and devote herself to his
care.

With this idea alone we have the beginning of a positive re-description of the
meanings of staying in a bad relationship. For Sarah or women like her, staying put
is not about weak character, morbid dependency, or masochism, but is better understood as an affirmation of the feminine ideal: to hold connections together, to heal
and care for another, no matter what the personal cost. As another woman client put
it, "I stayed for twenty years, even though I knew after a week that it was a mistake,
because 'girls make it work.'" In these terms, staying is what gender pride and self-
respect demand.

Put another way, staying protects the woman against the guilt engendered by
giving up her caretaking role. More specifically, since women learn to be acutely
attuned to the needs of others, their gendered capacity for empathy gives them a
subliminal knowledge of the batterer's fragile dependency. Often this means they
cannot escape the feeling that in leaving they betrayed the terms of the relationship.

As Sophia puts it, "I become confused. I know he's good. I know he can be really bad. But when he's good, he's good. I'm scared if I leave him he'll start thinking 'She's not worth it anyway. Look what she did to me.' " Thus, a woman who walks out must contend with the meanings and consequences of having claimed the male prerogative of putting herself first.

Given that gender prohibitions in the culture at large create a pressure for women to deny their own agency, we were interested in tracking the generational transmission of these injunctions through the stories and memories of the women in our study. It appears that just as battering men tend to come from families in which there was violence, abuse, or exaggerated patriarchal norms, so many of the abused women with whom we have spoken came from families with an excessive patriarchal structure. In many cases, the mothers played extremely subordinate roles to their husbands; in some cases, the gender hierarchy was reversed and the mother appeared to be in the "up" position. But whether the gender hierarchy was conventional or incongruous, the family belief structure held that men should be stronger than and in charge of women. Thus, whether mother's status was elevated or subjugated, these daughters suffered a kind of existential neglect from growing up in families in which women were undervalued, either by a climate of intimidation or by the belief that men *should* subdue women, even if they were unable to do so.

Common to these women's stories is a description of a family that could not abide the daughter making a claim for herself. Daughters grew up with the belief that being loved was contingent upon some kind of self-abnegation. Even though most women, in reconstructing their past, can remember some ways in which their families supported, or at least tolerated, their independent strivings, the women we have interviewed do not seem to regard their past as including such spaces. They describe feeling that they did not count unless they were tending to the needs of others. Indeed, many remember their parents as having been critical of them for not being "giving" enough. They believed the family viewed their independent aspirations as an aberration, and some women recounted stories in which their attempts at differentiation or separation were labeled as destructive or even crazy.

As we explored the relational politics in which these gender prohibitions were enacted, we came to understand better how problematic and contradictory "femininity" had become for the women in our study. Looking first at the mother/daughter relationship, we speculated that the daughters of mothers who were severely subjugated in their marriages were caught in a painful dilemma. They had to construct a feminine identity out of intensely contradictory feelings toward mother: rage and sympathy, contempt and longing, and so on. The problem for such daughters is that, in order to maintain a positive connection to their mothers, they had to become *like* their mothers, and thus accept the very premises about being female that made their mothers victims in the first place, and, in many cases, left them feeling maternally abandoned. This is because the primacy of mother's relationship with her verbally or physically abusive husband meant that her daughter frequently experienced her as powerless, devalued, and depressed. Moreover, mother's preoccupation with father rendered her unable fully to nurture, protect, or value her daughter.

The generational transmission and repetition of this pattern is reflected, once again, by Sarah who, at age thirty-two, has been in three abusive marriages and borne seven children, all but one of whom were left to live with their fathers. Looking back at her life and her choices Sarah remarked, "I'm beginning to realize that mom was probably very much like me as far as her place in the household and with dad. She would totally close off her family, all of them, not be in communication with them, and cater to him, cater to his every need."

Daughters like Sarah were caught in complex triangles. On the one hand, they identified with, and were "lumped" by their fathers with their mothers, who were in the down position. On the other hand, they wanted access to the world of their fathers, who seemed to have the freedom to speak, to rant, to have a life outside the domestic sphere. Moreover, many of these women felt that they were, in some way, preferred by their fathers over their mothers. This, in some cases, was a blatant or implicit incestuous bond; in others, it was simply that their fathers liked their "spunk," even as they tried to subdue them.

Thus, like the men in our study, these women were caught in an impossible loyalty bind. Being loyal to mother meant enduring some kind of social and personal subjugation, while openly choosing their fathers meant betraying their mothers and, in some sense, betraying themselves.

It is against the background of these dilemmas of how to connect and how to be different from their mothers, as well as how to claim male entitlements, that we have come to understand the seemingly crazy behavior of these battered women. In their inability to leave these men, we see the loyal daughter re-enacting mother's stance of submission and upholding femininity's ideal of sacrificial caring. In their unwillingness to resist fruitless and dangerous confrontations with these volatile men, we see the rebellious daughter asserting that she is both different from her mother and militantly opposed to femininity's credo of silence.

Given this contradictory set of impulses and ideals, we make sense of these women's "misguided" compulsion to stay embroiled in impossible relationships by offering the idea that the very ferocity of their involvement is a measure of the ferocity of their drive to expand the culture's definition of feminine affiliation so as to include their own voice. These were women driven to be heard, though the price might be "being hit." They were seeking an intimate attachment that included the emotions usually reserved for men: strong opinions and the right to make one's own needs primary. In their own way, these women were defying what Jean Baker Miller describes as "subservient affiliations,"[22] and were attempting to assert their right to a relationship that included recognition of their own personhood.

Sue puts it this way, "So you ask me why am I in this kind of relationship? John does the same thing that my dad did the whole time I was growing up, which is as soon as I get my own opinion about something, and begin to tell him what that is, he tells me to shut up. John says shut the fuck up; my dad just used to say shut up. As a kid I would keep trying, but dad would scream louder than me, and then I wouldn't bother anymore. With John, I don't care how much he screams, I just keep trying to get my opinion out."

The Alliance

It has been hard to assume that the irrationality of violence has its reasons and that those reasons are powerful enough to hold a couple together in a sometimes fatal attraction. But to react only to the violent "face" of the behavior without viewing its other face, the face of atonement and redemption, is to deny the power of the bond that fully possesses the couple. In the wake of the irrefutable logic that compels the couple to separate, the next wave of that logic breaks, and they are caught in the powerful tides of reaffiliation. This redemptive moment in the couple's cycle, which we are calling "the alliance," is as complexly structured as the violent tide that produced it. Both parts of this cycle must be deconstructed, their elements unpacked and critiqued, if the violence is to stop.

The alliance is a unique aspect of the couple's relationship because it acts to sustain and preserve reconnection after a violent rupture has occurred. It is experienced by both partners as a bond; but, since it is a bond termed by others as shameful, sick, and regressive, it remains a secret, hidden from the world.

The strength of this bond has the potential to defeat the most persuasive shelter or antibattering program: the more outside forces try to separate the couple, the more the bond binds them together. Clearly, neither partner is going to talk openly about their attachment, or even admit their depth of feeling to themselves, when the relationship has been so uniformly stigmatized by others. Since the true nature of the attachment is often a mystery, even from the protagonists themselves, they will remain caught in its grip, common-sense injunctions to separate notwithstanding. Thus, unless this powerful bond is given its due, the relationship will not be visible in all its aspects, and the couple's bond will become a secret coalition against all outsiders, including the therapists.

For these reasons, early in our work with these couples, we listen for any positive descriptions of their relationship, and we encourage those commentaries as part of our therapeutic conversation. Making space for this kind of dialogue takes away the binding power of the secret. This holds a particular value for the woman, since women living in violent relationships often feel their explanations have deserted them. They are confused and shamed by their wish to remain in a situation that is so harmful. Without a self-respecting explanation to hold onto, these women are vulnerable to the popular psychological notions of why women stay in "sick" relationships. These standard, pop clichés always blame the victim, who must accept a definition of herself as masochistic, appallingly weak, or just plain crazy. Generating a different explanation, which offers a more positive description of her participation in the relationship, leaves her with a sense of dignity, which may make it possible for her to choose, eventually, to leave, or to stay on very different terms.

Making the hidden bond our point of entry into the therapy creates a fresh space for discovery, and frees the process from the stereotypical discourse that the couple knows so well and has come to expect from outsiders. While we may include standard behavioral interventions, such as "time out" and safety plans, we invite the couple's curiosity by calling their attention to their attention to their confusion about the relationship. We open space for the woman to tell us that she remains with this man not only because she's too frightened to leave, but also because of an oddly compelling love that she does not understand.

Similarly, the man may be confused by the fact that he brutalizes her and needs to control every aspect of her life. Often, he has a double vision of himself as a decent and good person, and simultaneously as a man who needs to behave viciously, even to destroy the people he loves. But like her, he cannot leave despite the fact that he perceives her power over him to be deeply humiliating.

Through the process of getting to know the underside of these destructive attachments, we have begun to understand what makes them so compelling. The process of unpacking this affectively charged bond into its constitutive elements is a central focus of the therapy. For purposes of this analysis, we will schematize the process even though, in actuality, these elements are psychologically inseparable and conceptually overlapping.

The life stories of these men and women, his and hers, are narratives filled with pain and disappointment. Yet, when the couple tells the story of their relationship, especially how it began, the cloud lifts. It is as though an electrical connection had been made between them, a bond that keeps them attached despite the crazy violence.

Initially, and implicitly, the couple's bond is positioned against their families of origin and against the world at large. Tracing the history of this theme through the reconstructions of both partners led us to speculate that each of them was looking for a magical rescue from the loyalty binds and gender injunctions they experienced in their original families. They were looking for a deus ex machina, and, like many of us, they found it in the extravagant illusions of romantic love. Each partner believed that they had found a perfect match, and together they formed a complementary, reparative bond premised on the fantasy of a yin/yang "fit" between them.

For our purposes, the most intriguing aspect of their initial attraction was the way in which it seemed to represent, at least in part, an attempt to escape the rigid strictures of gender conformity that had been enforced by their families of origin. For the men who had to deny or suppress any sign of need or vulnerability, the relationship represented the chance to reclaim these affects without dishonor. As one man put it, "Alice accepts my weaknesses and my sensitivity. With my mother, I had to be always strong, never weak." And, for the women who were raised to submit and be silent, the relationship gave early dignity to their voice. In Sarah's words, "Mike respects my opinion as no one else has."

This rebellion against oppressive gender codes creates a belief that the relationship is a unique haven from the outside world. The power (and danger) of this illusory escape fantasy is reflected in the observations of Joe and Alice, a couple who have sustained their feeling of specialness despite Alice's two broken ribs.

Joe: Maybe at one level we argue like hell, which is really true, but at another level me and Alice accept each other a hundred percent. She accepts my sensitivity and my weaknesses, unlike my mother, and she's given me free rein to develop according to my own way of developing.

Alice: I don't know why there is a bond between him and me, and not between me and anyone else. I don't know why that's true, except he allowed me to see his weaknesses. Therefore, I don't see him as a threat; even if he hits me I don't really see him as a threat. He allows himself to be vulnerable to me, and I never had that role before, ever. That *set* our relationship. That formed the bond between us, and it's lasted to this day, damaged as it is. That hooked me.

It should be no surprise that this bond, premised on the hope that love can provide reparation for the injuries of the past and freedom from the constraints of the culture, cannot survive the ordinary insults of daily life. A reparative experience is inherently a critique that cannot be sustained. In this case, it is a challenge to family loyalty and to conventional gender dichotomies.

With regard to gender, insofar as the bond is based on an acknowledgment of repressed similarities, the very desire to loosen gender-incongruent prohibitions pushes the man toward an intolerable feeling of similarity to the woman. Eventually, this collapse of difference will become too compromising, and he will have to reassert his masculine difference from her by becoming menacing or even violent.

We can see this turnabout in Joe, who apparently can only tolerate Alice's knowledge of his "weakness" if she devotes herself completely to his care. As he puts it, "One thing I notice that I go through every time I hit her is my intense need for her. . . . When things get to the point that I need her a lot and I can't get her, I *want* her. I want her, that's it. I want her love, I want her attention, and I'll get it. I'll get it no matter what."

Another trigger embedded in the very terms of the couple's bond is the loyalty conflict it engenders with regard to their families of origin. In a sense, they are serving two alliances, one to their family of origin and one to each other. For many couples, the most incendiary situation is when one member of the couple attacks the other's family. At these times, the one whose family is under attack forfeits his or her alliance with the mate, and rallies toward the family of origin. Now the spouse/ally appears as a representative of the outside world, an enemy of the original family.

This seems to be especially true of the men. Many of them describe feeling that they always had to stand up for their families, protecting them from the rest of the world. When the families of these men are compared to other families, it is clear that the family felt itself to "suffer by comparison," that other families had more money, status, background, and education. Several men in our group grew up with family slogans that embody this loyalty mandate: "Don't fool with Kuhl," or "The fighting Fagins"! They describe violent fights on behalf of their families when the family endured insults from outsiders, or when they believed they were perceived by others as inferior, incompetent, or deficient. Yet, while violently defending their families from the slings and arrows of outsiders, they were often the sons most beaten and abused within the family.

The following sequence from an interview with Sue and John illustrates how quickly discussion of these issues can get dangerous.

John: Mother is very quiet and timid.
Sue: His mother never says a damn word about anything.

Th: Is she afraid?

John: Of my father? No, she was just . . .

Sue: Tell her about the times you used to call out to her. You're being beaten up, you're under the bed, being smacked around with a belt, you're calling for your mom who sat and listened to it.

John: I guess she was afraid, obviously she was afraid. Listen, I'd get off this if I were you, because I'm starting to get a little upset.

Given the unworkable premises that underlie the bond that binds these couples, the sudden switch from ally to enemy is understandable. As long as all the blame is placed on mother and father, the adult-child victim can feel rescued by a similarly injured fellow traveler. But this stance is inherently unstable because it is too polarized. The axiom "my partner is good, my family is bad," holds until the partner disappoints or (less likely) the family comes through. Given the either/or structure of this paradigm, the alliances are defined as mutually exclusive, and require a Hobson's choice that can lead to violence.

Our goal is to shift the terms of these competing relationships from "either/or" to "both–and" so that one kind of love does not preclude another. To this end, we challenge the fixity of the negatively described family of origin by exploring alternative, more positive explanations for parental failures, and by opening space for good memories to co-exist with the bad. We also use coaching to change the current parent–child relationship patterns, and, when indicated, we include the family of origin in the therapy sessions.

This work is not only useful in reducing the risk of violence; it also plays a part in freeing the woman from her "addictive" inability to give up the abusive relationship. This is because it addresses the power of the redemptive aspects of the abusive cycle, which keep the woman hypnotized. In the powerful bid for forgiveness that follows a violent episode, the man engages in a dramatic act of reparation, which recaptures the woman's loyalty by implicitly addressing the injuries of childhood as well as the current circumstance.

Irma, for example, reported that her husband's violent physical abuse reminded her, oddly enough, of her mother's verbal and emotional style. Since she had been unable to find a way toward her mother that did not include accepting a disturbingly negative view of herself, she had cut off relations with her entirely. Now, in her relationship with her husband, a man who had hospitalized her twice because of his violent beatings, her most positive image of herself is summoned up when he begs her forgiveness for what he has done, begs her acceptance of his need for her, begs her recognition of his divided nature, and begs her largesse in the face of his remorse. At this moment, as the reaffiliation tide of their alliance is summoned, she feels a profound sense of reparation. As she explored the meaning of this experience and the way it kept her bonded to him against her better judgment, she said, "My mother never changed, never understood how deeply she hurt me, never apologized to me!" Over the course of therapy, which included coaching her to change her relationship (and her beliefs) about her mother, Irma became less vulnerable to her partner's desperate apologies, and eventually left him.

In another case, we were able to loosen the romantic grip of the man's remorse by connecting it to his experience with his father. Through careful questioning, we learned that Kent would drive himself into violence because of a need to "hit rock bottom," after which he could feel truly close to his wife. In pulling apart the strands of this odd paradigm, we learned that the only time he could feel bonded to his father was when he confessed to some major inadequacy or transgression. Then, "Because I was more vulnerable than my father, he would be wonderful. He would make everything feel all right and be like a rock for me." Hearing this, his wife said, "For the first time I understand why he has to push things all the way to physical violence. That's the only way he can feel so completely disgusted with himself that he can take some comfort from me."

Conclusion

In this project we have attempted to penetrate the infrastructure of relationships in which men are violent toward women. We have found that, for these couples, abuse and coercion co-exist with understanding and friendship in a unique and painful way. When the paradoxical terms of this gendered bond are clarified and critiqued, the freedom to change the terms of the relationship or to leave it behind becomes possible.

REFERENCES

1. Anonymous. A battered woman's story: My seduction into abuse. *Journal of Feminist Family Therapy 1* (2): 63–79, 1989.
2. Bayes, M. Wife battering and the maintenance of gender roles: A sociopsychological perspective. In E. Howell & M. Bayes (eds.), *Women and mental health.* New York: Basic Books, 1981.
3. Benjamin, J. *The bonds of love: Psychoanalysis, feminism and the problem of domination.* New York: Pantheon Books, 1988.
4. Bograd, M. Family systems approaches to wife battering: A feminist critique. *American Journal of Orthopsychiatry 54:* 558–568, 1984.
5. Chodorow, N. *The reproduction of mothering.* Berkeley: University of California Press, 1978.
6. Coleman, K. H. Conjugal violence: What 33 men report. *Journal of Marital and Family Therapy 6:* 207–213, 1980.
7. Dimen, M. *Sexual contradictions.* New York: Macmillan, 1986.
8. Sinkelhor, D., Gelles, R. J., Hotaling, G. T., & Straus, N. A. (eds.), *The dark side of families: Current family violence research.* Beverly Hills CA: Sage Publications, 1983.
9. Fogel, G. Being a Man. In G. Fogel, F. Lane, & R. Liebert (eds.), *The psychology of men.* New York: Basic Books, 1986.
10. Geffner, R. *Family violence bulletin.* Tyler: Family Violence Research and Treatment Program, University of Texas at Tyler, see all issues.
11. Giles-Sims, J. *Wife battering: A systems theory approach.* New York: Guilford Press, 1983.
12. Gilligan, C. *In a different voice.* Cambridge: Harvard University Press, 1982.

13. Girard, R. *Violence and the sacred*. Baltimore: Johns Hopkins University Press, 1986.

14. Gondolf, E. Fighting for control: A clinical assessment of men who batter. *Social Casework* 66: 48–54, 1985.

15. Greenson, R. Dis-identifying from mother: Its special importance to the boy. *International Journal of Psychoanalysis 49:* 370–374, 1968.

16. Goldner, V. Feminism and family therapy. *Family Process 24:* 31–47, 1985.

17. ———. Warning: Family therapy may be hazardous to your health. *Family Therapy Networker 9*(6): 18–23, 1985.

18. Johnson, M. Fathers, mothers and sex-typing. *Sociological Inquiry 45:* 15–26, 1975.

19. Jordan, J., & Surrey, J. The self-in-relation: Empathy and the mother-daughter relationship. In T. Bernay & D. Cantor (eds.), *The psychology of today's woman*. Hillsdale, NJ: Analytic Press, 1986.

20. Lane, G., & Russell, T. Second-order systemic work with violent couples. In L. Ceasar & K. Hamberger (eds.), *Treating men who batter: Theory, practice, and programs*. New York: Springer, 1989.

21. Men Stopping Violence. *Confronting male privilege, ensuring woman's survival/safety/rights.* Atlanta, GA, 1989.

22. Miller, J. *Toward a new psychology of women*. Boston: Beacon Press, 1976.

23. Osherson, S. *Finding our fathers*. New York: Free Press, 1986.

24. Penn, P. Feed forward: Future questions, future maps. *Family Process 24:* 299–310, 1985.

25. Pressman, B. Wife-abused couples: The need for comprehensive theoretical perspectives and integrated treatment models. *Journal of Feminist Family Therapy 1*(1): 23–45, 1989.

26. Rubin, G. The traffic in women: Notes on the political economy of sex. In R. Reiter (ed.), *Toward an anthropology of women*. New York: Monthly Review Press, 1978.

27. Sheinberg, M. Obsessions/counter-obsessions; A construction/reconstruction of meaning. *Family Process 27:* 305–316, 1988.

28. Simon, R. (ed.). Special feature: Family violence (several articles). *Family Therapy Networker 10*(3): 20–69, 1986.

29. Stoller, R. *Sexual excitement*. New York: Pantheon Books, 1979.

30. Strauss, M. Sexuality, inequality, cultural norms and wife beating. *Victimology 1:* 54–69, 1976.

31. Swift, C. Women and violence: Breaking the connection. *Stone Center for Developmental Services and Studies* (Wellesley, MA), No. 27, 1987.

32. Walker, L. *The battered woman*. New York: Harper & Row, 1979.

33. Young, I. Is male gender identity the cause of male domination? In J. Treblicot (ed.), *Mothering: Essays in feminist theory*. Totowa, NJ: Rowman and Allanheld, 1984.

34. Yllo, K., & Bograd, M. *Feminist perspectives on wife abuse*. Beverly Hills, CA: Sage Publications, 1989.

Chapter Thirty-Two

Toward an Understanding of Risk Factors for Bulimia

Ruth H. Striegel-Moore, Lisa R. Silberstein, and Judith Rodin

In its end-of-the-year review, *Newsweek* referred to 1981 as "the year of the binge purge syndrome" (Adler, 1982, p. 29). This designation reflected the public's growing awareness of a significant sociocultural phenomenon, namely, the seemingly sudden and dramatic rise of bulimia. One year earlier, bulimia had become recognized as a psychiatric disorder in its own right in the Diagnostic and Statistical Manual of Mental Disorders (DSM-III; American Psychiatric Association, 1980); this development has facilitated standardized assessment. In the last few years there has been a proliferation of literature on bulimia, as researchers and clinicians have attempted to describe the clinical picture of the disorder, to outline treatment approaches, and to identify factors associated with it.

Even though the investigative forays into bulimia have really just begun, it now seems both possible and useful to draw together the current and sometimes disparate existing pieces of knowledge about the disorder and to propose working hypotheses about its etiology. A few efforts have already been made in this direction (Garner, Rockert, Olmsted, Johnson, & Coscina, 1985; Hawkins & Clement, 1984; Johnson, Lewis, & Hagman, 1984; Russell, 1979; Slade, 1982). Our own conceptualization of this disorder both permits better understanding of the risk factors already proposed and implicates additional variables in the etiology of bulimia. We hope that as we delineate possible risk factors of bulimia, it will become clearer where our current knowledge is most lacking and therefore where research is needed. An understanding of etiology will, we hope, also facilitate the clinical treatment of bulimia.

As we think about bulimia and its recent rise, three questions in particular demand attention. First, bulimia is primarily a woman's problem, with research consistently indicating that approximately 90 percent of bulimic individuals are female[1] (Halmi, Falk, & Schwartz, 1981; Katzman, Wolchik, & Braver, 1984; Leon, Carroll, Chernyk, & Finn, 1985; Pope, Hudson, Yurgelun-Todd, & Hudson, 1984; Pyle

Ruth H. Striegel-Moore, Lisa R. Silberstein, & Judith Rodin, "Toward an Understanding of Risk Factors for Bulimia." *American Psychologist, 41*, pp. 246–263. © 1986 by the American Psychological Association. Reprinted with permission.

et al., 1983; Wilson, 1984). Hence, a key factor that places someone at risk for developing bulimia is being a woman. One major question that demands an answer then is, simply, Why women?

Second, it appears that weight concerns and dieting are so pervasive among females today that they have become normative (Rodin, Silberstein, & Striegel-Moore, 1985). An overwhelming number of women currently feel too fat (regardless of their actual weight) and engage in repeated dieting efforts (Drewnowski, Riskey, & Desor, 1982; Garner, Olmsted, & Polivy, 1983; Herman & Polivy, 1975; Huon & Brown, 1984; Mann et al., 1983; Moss, Jennings, McFarland, & Carter, 1984; Nielsen, 1979; Nylander, 1971; Polivy & Herman, 1985; Pyle et al., 1983; Wooley & Wooley, 1984). Despite the prevalence of dieting and weight concerns among women in general, it is still a minority who develop the clinical syndrome of bulimia, thus prompting another essential question: Which women in particular?[2] In our discussion, we will be conceptualizing a continuum ranging from unconcern with weight and normal eating, to "normative discontent" with weight and moderately disregulated/restrained eating, to bulimia (Rodin, Silberstein, & Striegel-Moore, 1985). The question of "which women in particular" can be seen, therefore, as a question of which women will move along this continuum from normative concerns to bulimia.

Third, it is not women in all times and places but rather women of *this* era in Western society who are developing bulimia. Therefore, a third question is, Why now? This question has received very little empirical attention. However, the seemingly sudden and dramatic rise of bulimia over the past few years suggests that we need to consider the possible role of sociohistorical factors.

One critical aspect to the challenge of developing an etiological model of bulimia is the heterogeneity of the women who develop the disorder. Bulimic women differ with regard to their eating behavior and body weight, with some women exhibiting anorexia nervosa as well as bulimia either in the past or at present, others maintaining weight within the normal range, and others currently or in the past being obese (Beumont, George, & Smart, 1976; Garfinkel & Garner, 1982; Garner, Garfinkel, & O'Shaughnessy, 1985; Gormally, 1984; Loro & Orleans, 1981). Bulimic women can be divided into those who purge (by means of vomiting or abuse of cathartics) and those who do not resort to purging as a way of controlling their weight (Casper, Eckert, Halmi, Goldberg, & Davis, 1980; Garfinkel, Moldofsky, & Garner, 1980; Grace, Jacobson, & Fullager, 1985; Halmi et al., 1981). Furthermore, bulimic women vary greatly regarding the nature and extent of associated psychopathology. Some bulimic women do not exhibit any other psychiatric symptoms aside from those subsumed under the diagnosis of bulimia (Johnson, Stuckey, Lewis, & Schwartz, 1982), whereas others show multiple types of psychopathology (Garner & Garfinkel, 1985; Garner, Garfinkel, & O'Shaughnessy, 1985; Hudson, Laffer, & Pope, 1982; Hudson, Pope, & Jonas, 1984; Lacey, 1982; Wallach & Lowenkopf, 1984). The implications of this heterogeneity for identifying risk factors are crucial. A particular risk factor that may be central to the etiology of the disorder in some women may be minor or even irrelevant in the development of bulimia in other women. Furthermore, this heterogeneity argues against unidimensional models of bulimia. Any model of bulimia (e.g., biochemical or addiction models) still must consider the three questions that we are now posing.

The questions—Why women? Which women in particular? Why now?—compose the starting point for our discussion of factors placing individuals at risk for bulimia. These questions compel us to consider bulimia from a range of perspectives—sociocultural, developmental, psychological, and biological. Examining each of these perspectives in turn, we will consider the first two questions in tandem. From each perspective, we must try first to identify factors that might place women at greater risk than men for bulimia and second to understand which women in particular might be at greatest risk. Subsequently, we will consider our third question, Why now?

Sociocultural Variables

Central to an etiological analysis are the sociocultural factors that place women at greater risk than men for bulimia. We and others have reviewed data suggesting that risk increases because our society values attractiveness and thinness in particular, therefore making obesity a highly stigmatized condition (Boskind-White & White, 1983; Garner, Rockert, Olmsted, Johnson, & Coscina, 1985; Hawkins & Clement, 1984; Johnson et al., 1984; Rodin, Silberstein, & Striegel-Moore, 1985; Russell, 1979). Numerous studies suggest that this attitude affects people of all ages and that these social norms are applied more strongly to women than to men (see Rodin, Silberstein, & Striegel-Moore, 1985, for review). We begin the present analysis by asking which women in particular are affected by these sociocultural attitudes regarding attractiveness and weight, and then we suggest other significant social norms, not previously discussed, that may enhance the risk for bulimia in women.

Which Women in Particular?

How might the high value placed on thinness and the stigmatization of obesity in women have a greater impact on some women than on others, thus placing them at greater risk for bulimia? At a basic level, women at greatest risk for bulimia should be those who have accepted and internalized most deeply the sociocultural mores about thinness and attractiveness. In other words, the more a woman believes that "what is fat is bad, what is thin is beautiful, and what is beautiful is good," the more she will work toward thinness and be distressed about fatness. To explore this hypothesis, we developed a series of attitude statements based on these sociocultural values (e.g., "attractiveness increases the likelihood of professional success"). As predicted, bulimic women expressed substantially greater acceptance of these attitudes than nonbulimic women (Striegel-Moore, Silberstein, & Rodin, 1985a). Another study found that bulimic women aspired to a thinner ideal body size than did normal controls (Williamson, Kelley, Davis, Ruggiero, & Blouin, 1985).

But how do women come to internalize these attitudes differently? One source of influence is the subculture within which they live. Although attitudes about thinness and obesity pervade our entire society, they also are intensified within certain strata. Women of higher socioeconomic status are most likely to emulate closely the trendsetters of beauty and fashion (Banner, 1983), and therefore not surprisingly, they exhibit greater weight preoccupation (Dornbusch et al., 1984). Obesity traditionally has been least punished (and of greatest prevalence) in the lower socioeconomic classes (Goldblatt, Moore, & Stunkard, 1965). Although as yet there are no epidemiological studies drawing representative samples across social classes, we would expect that a differential emphasis on weight and appearance constitutes an important mediating variable in a relationship between social class and bulimia.

Certain environments also appear to increase risk. For example, boarding schools and colleges have been thought to "breed" eating disorders such as bulimia (Squire, 1983). Consistent with this hypothesis, one study found a dramatically higher weight gain in freshmen women during their first year in college than in women of similar socioeconomic background who did not go to college (Hovell, Mewborn, Randle, & Fowler-Johnson, 1985). Several factors may account for this observation. As predominantly middle- and upper-class environments, campuses represent those socioeconomic classes at greater risk, as just discussed. Furthermore, as stressful and semiclosed environments, campuses may serve to intensify the sociocultural pressures to be thin. The competitive school environment may foster not only academic competition but also competition regarding the achievement of a beautiful (i.e., thin) body. Women's appearance is of greater importance in dating than is men's (Berscheid, Dion, Walster, & Walster, 1971; Harrison & Saeed, 1977; Janda, O'Grady, & Barnhart, 1981; Krebs & Adinolfi, 1975; Stroebe, Insko, Thompson, & Layton, 1971; Walster, Aronson, Abrahams, & Rottmann, 1966), and we have preliminary evidence that schools in which dating is heavily emphasized have higher prevalence rates of bulimia than schools in which the emphasis on dating is less prominent (Rodin, Striegel-Moore, & Silberstein, 1985).

Other kinds of subcultures also appear to amplify sociocultural pressures and hence place their members at greater risk for bulimia. Prime examples are those subcultures in which optimal weight is specified, explicitly or implicitly, for the performance of one's vocation or avocation. Members of professions that dictate a certain body weight—for example, dancers, models, actresses, and athletes—evidence significantly greater incidence of anorexia and related eating pathology than individuals whose job performance is unrelated to their appearance and weight (Crago, Yates, Beutler, & Arizmendi, 1985; Druss & Silverman, 1979; Garner & Garfinkel, 1978, 1980; Joseph, Wood, & Goldberg, 1982; Yates, Leehey, & Shisslak, 1983). Although fewer data are available regarding the occurrence of bulimia in these subcultural groups, clinical evidence suggests that it has a high incidence level as well (Vincent, 1979). Eating pathology in these professions seems linked not to their stressful nature so much as to their emphasis on weight and appearance (Garner & Garfinkel, 1980), and the pathology typically begins after the person has entered the subculture (Crago et al., 1985).

Comparative studies of athletes would help to shed light on the role of culturally mandated weight and appearance specifications as a risk factor. Our model predicts that a higher incidence of bulimia would be found in sports emphasizing a svelte body—such as gymnastics or figure skating—or attaining a certain weight class—such as wrestling—than in sports where thinness is less clearly mandated, such as tennis or volleyball. The sparse literature on the effects of athletic participation in general on body image is potentially contradictory. On the one hand, research examining self-esteem variables suggests that athletic involvement enhances self-image, sociability, and feelings of self-worth (e.g., Vanfraechem & Vanfraechem-Raway, 1978). On the other hand, studies examining weight and dieting behavior suggest that athletic activity is associated with dissatisfaction with body weight and body image, repeated dieting attempts, and dysphoric episodes (e.g., Smith, 1980). The ways in which a focus on physical strength and skills might affect body image and eating behaviors, as well as the ways in which weight concerns influence exercise patterns, are issues worthy of further study.

The Central Role of Beauty in the Female Sex Role Stereotype

Beauty ideals have varied considerably in Western cultures over the course of past centuries (Banner, 1983; Beller, 1977; Brownmiller, 1984; Rudofsky, 1971), and women have been willing to alter their bodies to conform to each historical era's ideal of beauty (Ehrenreich & English, 1978). It has been proposed that being concerned with one's appearance and making efforts to enhance and preserve one's beauty are central features of the female sex role stereotype (Brownmiller, 1984). Our language reflects the intimate connection between femininity and beauty: The word *beauty,* a derivative of the Latin word *bellus,* was originally used only in reference to women and children (Banner, 1983). This female connotation of the word beauty still exists today: The most recent revision of Webster's dictionary (Guralnik, 1982) lists as one of its definitions of beauty "a very good-looking woman."

Several studies have documented that physically attractive women are perceived as more feminine (Cash, Gillen, & Burns, 1977; Gillen, 1981; Gillen & Sherman, 1980; Unger, 1985) and unattractive women as more masculine (Heilman & Saruwatari, 1979). It has also been shown that the mesomorphic male silhouette is associated with perceived masculinity, whereas the ectomorphic female silhouette is associated with perceived femininity (Guy, Rankin, & Norvell, 1980). Hence, thinness and femininity appear to be linked.

Interestingly, there also appears to be a relationship between certain types of eating behavior and femininity. In one study, women who were described as eating small meals were rated significantly more feminine, less masculine, and more attractive than women who ate large meals, whereas descriptions of meal size had no effect on ratings of male targets (Chaiken & Pliner, 1984). Another study suggested that women may actually restrict their food intake in the service of making a favorable impression on men (Chaiken & Pliner, 1984).

Do dieting behavior and the pursuit of the svelte body thus constitute a pursuit of femininity? For women who endorse the traditional female sex role stereotype, we would conjecture that being attractive and thin are important because, by definition, these attributes figure prominently in the traditional roles and values of womanhood. However, women who have achieved occupational success and have abandoned many traditional dictums for female behavior and roles also, it appears, worry about their weight and pursue thinness (Lakoff & Scherr, 1984). One possible reason is that thinness represents the antithesis of the ample female body associated with woman as wife and mother (Beck, Ward-Hull, & McLear, 1976). A second reason may be found in the women's orientation to success. These women set high standards for themselves, and thinness represents a personal accomplishment. At the same time, thinness may serve an instrumental and somewhat paradoxical end of furthering a woman's success in a man's world, because femininity gives a woman a "competitive edge" (Brownmiller, 1984). It also may be difficult for women to abandon femininity wholesale—and *looking* feminine, even while displaying "unfeminine" ambition and power, may serve an important function in a woman's sense of self as well as in how she appears, literally, to others.

Which Women in Particular?

Given the central role of beauty in the female sex role stereotype and the association of thinness with femininity and beauty, for which women might these dimensions increase the risk of bulimia? It might be expected that those women endorsing the female sex role most strongly would most value and pursue thinness. Clinical impressions of bulimic clients do suggest that these women show stereotypically "feminine" behavior characteristics (e.g., being dependent, unassertive, eager to please, and concerned with social approval); this suggestion leads to the hypothesis that bulimia is the result of a struggle to live up to an ideal of femininity (Boskind-Lodahl, 1976; Boskind-Lodahl & Sirlin, 1977; Boskind-White & White, 1983; Hawkins & Clement, 1984; Johnson et al., 1984). However, studies considering the relationship between bulimia and femininity, at least as measured by current masculinity–femininity scales (Bem, 1974; Spence & Helmreich, 1978), have yielded inconsistent results (Dunn & Ondercin, 1981; Hatsukami, Mitchell, & Eckert, 1981; Katzman & Wolchik, 1984; Norman & Herzog, 1983; Rost, Neuhaus, & Florin, 1982; Williamson, Kelly, Davis, Ruggiero, & Blouin, 1985). Some of these studies show a relationship, and some show no relationship between bulimia and feminine values and behaviors.

Our data suggest one way to understand the conflicting findings on the association between femininity and bulimia. We found that whereas femininity scores on the Personal Attributes Questionnaire (PAQ; Spence & Helmreich, 1978) did not relate to measures of body image and eating pathology, masculinity scores were inversely related to measures of body dissatisfaction and eating pathology (Striegel-Moore, Silberstein, & Rodin, 1985b). Masculinity as measured on the PAQ reflects such traits as being decisive, self-confident, active, and independent; in short, this construct represents a sense of competence and self-confidence. As we will explore later, self-confidence does seem to be inversely related to bulimia, although the causal direction is unclear. Femininity on the PAQ is represented by such traits as being gentle, emotional, and aware of others' feelings; it is interesting but not surprising that the presence of such traits is not consistently predictive of eating pathology.

In a recent article, Spence (1985) argued that the constructs of masculinity and femininity guiding research during the past decade have been inadequately defined. She pointed out that the terms *masculinity* and *femininity* appear to have two distinct and different meanings. First, they have an empirical meaning and are used as labels for specific qualities or events that are perceived as being more closely associated with males or females. Second, they represent theoretical constructs that refer to a person's phenomenological sense of maleness or femaleness. To date, Spence (1985) argued, no valid measure has been developed that captures these constructs. One suggestion for future measures of femininity/masculinity is to include items relevant to physical appearance.

Developmental Processes

A developmental perspective clarifies many issues relevant to our inquiry about the factors placing women at risk for bulimia. In this section we ask what aspects of female development might make women more vulnerable than men, and some women more vulnerable than others, to developing bulimia.

Childhood

Following from our discussion of sociocultural attitudes, it is not surprising that from early childhood girls learn from diverse agents of socialization that appearance is especially important to them as girls and that they should be concerned with it. From their families, little girls learn that one of their functions is to "pretty up" the environment, to serve as aesthetic adornment (Barnett & Baruch, 1980). Young girls learn that being attractive is intricately interwoven with pleasing and serving others and, in turn, will secure their love. Beyond the family environment, schools also teach the societal message. Significantly more of the positive feedback that boys receive from their teachers is addressed specifically to the intellectual aspects of their performance than is true for girls, whereas girls are more often praised for activities related to intellectually irrelevant aspects, such as neatness (i.e., taking care of appearances; Dweck, Davidson, Nelson, & Enna, 1978).

The mass media and children's books also teach girls about the importance of appearance. From their survey of children's readers, Women on Words and Images (1972) revealed that girls in these primers were constantly concerned about how they look, whereas boys never were. Indeed, attending to one's appearance was a major activity for the girl characters, whereas the boys were more likely to solve problems and play hard. Television teaches girls a singular feminine ideal of thinness, beauty, and youth, set against a world in which men are more competent and also more diverse in appearance (Federal Trade Commission, 1978; Lewis & Lewis, 1974; Schwartz & Markham, 1985).

Girls appear to internalize readily these societal messages on the importance of pursuing attractiveness. Developmental studies have documented that girls are more concerned than boys about looking attractive (Coleman, 1961; Douvan & Adelson, 1966). Parents, teachers, and peers all describe girls as more focused than boys on their looks, and children's fantasies and choice of toys also reflect this interest (Ambert, 1976; Nelsen & Rosenbaum, 1972; Oakley, 1972; Wagman, 1967). Whereas boys tend to choose toys involving physical and mechanical activity, girls select toys related to aesthetic adornment and nurturance (Ambert, 1976; Oakley, 1972).

In the mid-1980s bulimia does not appear to be emerging during childhood. However, it is striking how much of the groundwork seems to be laid during these early years. Two kinds of sex differences in self-concept, which will be especially pertinent to our discussion of adolescence, are already evident in grade-school children. First, when asked to describe themselves, girls as young as seven refer more to the views of other people in their self-depictions than do boys (McGuire & McGuire, 1982). For girls more than for boys it seems that self-concept is an interpersonal construct. The implications of this will be considered soon.

Second, although the role of body image in children's self-concepts has not been studied extensively, body build and self-esteem measures have been found to be correlated for girls but not boys in the fourth, fifth, and sixth grades (Guyot, Fairchild, & Hill, 1981). Furthermore, even among these grade-school children, weight was found to be critical in the relationship between body image and self-concept: The thinner the girl, the more likely she was to report feeling attractive, popular, and successful academically. In addition, studies have found that even as children, females are more dissatisfied with their bodies than are males. Although nonobese girls have a more positive attitude than obese girls toward their bodies, they still express more concerns about their appearance than both nonobese and obese boys (Hammar, Campbell, Moores, Sareen, Gareis, & Lucas, 1972; Tobin-Richards, Boxer, & Petersen, 1983). Indeed Tobin-Richards, Boxer, and Petersen (1983) found that perceived weight and body satisfaction were negatively correlated with weight for girls, whereas boys valued being of normal weight and expressed equal dissatisfaction with being underweight or overweight.

Adolescence

Although girls learn from early childhood to be attentive to their appearance and even to worry about their weight, the major developmental challenge that amplifies a variety of risk factors for bulimia is adolescence. We will consider first the physical changes ushered in at puberty, because the extensive biological changes associated with this period render perceptions of the body highly salient in the adolescent's overall self-perceptions. Coming to terms with the vital adolescent question "Who am I?" involves forming a new body image and integrating the new physical self into one's self-concept.

In the context of the current sociocultural norms already described, pubertal development may create a particular problem for girls. Before puberty, girls have 10 percent to 15 percent more fat than boys, but after puberty girls have almost twice as much fat as boys (Marino & King, 1980). The reason is that girls gain their weight at puberty primarily in the form of fat tissue. In contrast, boys' weight spurt is predominantly due to an increase in muscle and lean tissue (Beller, 1977; Tanner, 1978). Given our cultural beauty ideal of the "thin, prepubertal look" for women (Faust, 1983), and the tall, muscular look for men, it is not surprising that adolescent girls express lower body esteem than adolescent boys (Simmons & Rosenberg, 1975) and greater dissatisfaction with their weight (Dornbusch et al., 1984). Whereas physical maturation brings boys closer to the masculine ideal, for most girls it means a development away from what is currently considered beautiful. Consistent with this tenet is the finding that when boys report dissatisfaction with their weight, their discontent is due to a desire to be heavier, whereas girls want to be thinner (George & Krondl, 1983; Simmons & Rosenberg, 1975; Tobin-Richards, Boxer, & Petersen, 1983).

Crisp and Kalucy (1974) and Rosenbaum (1979) found that adolescent girls were highly concerned about their looks and expressed awareness of the great value society places on physical attractiveness in women. These adolescents had a very differentiated view of their own bodies and appraised critically its various components. Interestingly, girls in the Rosenbaum (1979) study judged themselves more harshly than they thought their peers would. And consistent with our review thus far, these girls listed weight as their leading concern about their appearance. In a survey of 195 female high school juniors and seniors, 125 girls reported that they made conscious efforts to restrict their food intake in order to maintain or lose weight (Jakobovits, Halstead, Kelley, Roe, & Young, 1977).

In addition to the concrete physical changes that adolescents undergo, adolescence is clearly an era replete with challenges of both an intrapersonal and an interpersonal nature. The literature of adolescent psychology describes three primary tasks that both male and female adolescents have to master: achieving a new sense of self (involving the integration of accelerating physical growth, impending reproductive maturity, and qualitatively advanced cognitive skills); establishing peer relationships, in particular heterosexual relationships; and developing independence (Aldous, 1978; Blyth & Traeger, 1983; Douvan & Adelson, 1966; Erikson, 1968; Havighurst, 1972; Simmons, Blyth, & McKinney, 1983; Steele, 1980; Tobin-Richards et al., 1983; Wittig, 1983). Our consideration of sex differences in the ways adolescents negotiate these tasks is informed by work on the psychology of gender. Several authors have argued that women define themselves primarily in relation and connection to others, whereas for men, individuation and a sense of agency are more central in forming a sense of self (Chodorow, 1978; Gilligan, 1982; Miller, 1976).

Turning to the first task, it is consistent with Chodorow's (1978) theory that the self-images of adolescent girls seem to be more interpersonally oriented than are those of boys (Carlson, 1965; Dusek & Flaherty, 1981; Hill, Thiel, & Blyth, 1981; McGuire & McGuire, 1982). Girls also appear to be more self-conscious and insecure than boys (Bush, Simmons, Hutchinson, & Blyth, 1978; Hill & Lynch, 1983). Compared to boys, girls seem to worry more about what other people think of them, care more about being liked, and try to avoid negative reactions from others (Simmons & Rosenberg, 1975). Hill and Lynch (1983) argued that, in response to feeling insecure and in an effort to avoid negative evaluation by others, the adolescent girl becomes increasingly sensitive to and compliant with social demands and sex-role-appropriate standards. The strong message to teenage girls regarding the importance of beauty and thinness (as evidenced, for example, in the teen fashion magazines) thus intersects with heightened sensitivity to sociocultural mandates as well as to personal opinions of others. It is not surprising, then, that the adolescent girl becomes concerned with and unhappy about her pubertal increase in fat.

Following from this, we would expect that the second task of adolescence — forming peer relationships, and heterosexual relationships in particular — would also be relatively more problematic for girls than for boys. Studies support this hypothesis (Douvan & Adelson, 1966; Rosenberg & Simmons, 1975). For example, Simmons and Rosenberg (1975) found that girls were more likely than boys to rank popularity as more important than being independent or competent, and these authors found that this emphasis on popularity is correlated with a less stable self-image and a greater susceptibility to others' evaluations. Given that attractive (i.e., thin) females are rewarded in the interpersonal and especially the heterosexual domain, the wish to be popular and the pursuit of thinness may become synonymous in the mind of the teenage girl.

The third task of adolescence, establishing independence, also seems to pose a different challenge to girls than to boys. According to Gilligan (1982), females' relational orientation becomes particularly problematic for them at adolescence, when tasks of separation and individuation emerge. Gilligan reported that adolescent girls conceptualize dependence as a positive attribute, with isolation its polar opposite; however, in a world that views dependence as problematic, the girls often begin to feel confused, insecure, and inadequate.

We can speculate about ways in which the adolescent girl's increasing preoccupation with weight and dieting behavior is tied to the issue of independence. When other aspects of life seem out of control, weight may appear to be one of the few areas that, allegedly, can be self-controlled (Hood, Moore, & Garner, 1982). Because our society views weight loss efforts as a sign of maturity (Steele, 1980), dieting attempts may reflect a girl's desire to show *others*, as well as herself, that she is growing up. Hence, dieting may be a part of, a metaphor for, or a displacement of movements toward independence. Alternatively, the attempts to lose weight may be a refuge from the developmental challenges regarding independence that are posed to the adolescent. Losing weight may represent an effort to defy the bodily changes signaling maturity and adulthood. A successful diet will indeed preserve the prepubertal look, perhaps reflecting a desire to remain in childhood (Bruch, 1973; Crisp, 1980; Leon, Lucas, Colligan, Ferdinande, & Kamp, 1985; Selvini-Palazzoli, 1978).

Adulthood

The themes of adolescence — self-concept, interpersonal relationships, and dependence/independence — clearly continue into the adult years. We will now follow these issues as women enter late adolescence and adulthood and again delineate how these tasks continue to be different for men and women.

First, let us consider the body image of adult women and men. Given a persistent indoctrination into the sociocultural emphasis on female appearance, it is not surprising that women come to use very exact barometers for measuring their own bodies. In a sample of college students, Kurtz (1969) found that women possessed a more clearly differentiated body concept—that is, they discriminated more finely among various features of the body—than men. Similarly, females have clearly defined "templates" of the ideal, extremely thin female figure (Fallon & Rozin, 1985; Fisher, 1964; Jourard & Secord, 1955) and show much less variability than males in their view of acceptable size and weight (Harris, 1983).

With these two images in mind—their own body image and the ideal body image—women measure themselves against the ideal, and most emerge from such comparisons with discrepancies that are viewed as flaws and causes for self-criticism. Fallon and Rozin (1985) asked a sample of men and women to locate their actual figure as well as their ideal figure on a display of different-sized body shapes. For females, there was a significant discrepancy between their current and their ideal figures, with a thinner figure viewed as ideal. For males, there was no significant difference between self and ideal. These sex differences have been found repeatedly in other studies as well (Leon, Carroll, et al., 1985; Striegel-Moore, McAvay, & Rodin, in press; Rodin, Striegel-Moore, & Silberstein, 1985).

There is evidence suggesting that this self–ideal discrepancy may be exaggerated for women, not only because the beauty ideal for women has become increasingly thin, but also because women tend to overestimate their body size. Many studies document women's consistent exaggeration of body size, both of the figure as a whole and of specific body parts—typically the fat-bearing areas such as waist and hips. Importantly, these estimation differences appear specific to female subjects' own bodies, because they accurately judge the size of other people's bodies and of physical objects (Button, Fransella, & Slade, 1977; Casper, Halmi, Goldberg, Eckert, & Davis, 1979; Crisp & Kalucy, 1974; Fries, 1975; Garner, Garfinkel, Stancer, & Moldofsky, 1976; Halmi, Goldberg, & Cunningham, 1977). In a study comparing the estimation errors of men and women, men were significantly more accurate than women in estimates of their own body size (Shontz, 1963).

An issue integrally related to self-concept that has been implicit in our discussion thus far is the association between body image and self-esteem. Many self-concept theories (for an overview, see Harter, 1985) have proposed that dissatisfaction with a particular domain of one's self will result in overall lower self-esteem. In particular, it is argued that the effect of shortcomings in one domain on an individual's general level of self-esteem is determined by the relative importance of that domain in the person's self-definition. Hence, failure to succeed in an area of relatively minor importance to an individual will prove far less damaging to self-worth than inadequacy in a domain of central importance.

Surprisingly few studies have investigated the influence of body image on self-esteem. In studies that have examined this relationship, moderate, significant correlations have been found (Franzoi & Shields, 1984; Lerner, Karabenick, & Stuart, 1973; Lerner, Orlos, & Knapp, 1976; Mahoney, 1974; Secord & Jourard, 1953). Given the greater societal emphasis on attractiveness in women than in men, we would expect physical appearance to have relatively more influence on a woman's general sense of self-esteem than on a man's. Empirical studies, however, have produced conflicting results.

Some studies have supported the tenet that women's body image satisfaction is more highly correlated with self-esteem than is men's (Lerner et al., 1973; Martin & Walter, 1982; Secord & Jourard, 1953), whereas other studies have found the reverse to be true (Mahoney, 1974; Franzoi & Shields, 1984). Perhaps these contradictory findings are due to the fact that body image satisfaction has a different meaning for men and women (Franzoi & Shields, 1984). Several studies have suggested that whereas men tend to see their bodies as primarily functional and active, women seem to view their bodies along aesthetic and evaluative dimensions (Kurtz, 1969; Lerner et al., 1976; Story, 1979).

The relationship between weight, as a particular component of body image, and self-esteem in women deserves further investigation. We conjecture that dissatisfaction with weight relates to chronic low self-esteem and that, in addition, weight plays a role in more short-term and volatile fluctuations of self-esteem. In a large-scale *Glamour* magazine survey, 63 percent of the respondents reported that weight *often* affected how they felt about themselves, and another 33 percent reported that weight *sometimes* affected how they felt about themselves (Wooley & Wooley, 1984).

Thus far, we have been considering adulthood as a single entity. As theory and research on adult development have increased, earlier views of adulthood as a sustained, stable period have been replaced by conceptualizations of the entire life span as part of an ongoing developmental process (Erikson, 1968; Levinson, Darrow, Klein, Levinson, & McKee, 1978; Neugarten, 1969, 1970). Our knowledge of weight concerns, dieting, and bulimia is limited by the relatively restricted range of samples that have been studied: The majority of research has focused on the narrow band between tenth grade in high school and senior year of college. However, some initial observations about later adulthood can be made.

First, puberty is clearly not the only period in a woman's life when her biology will potentiate fat increase. During pregnancy, a healthy woman may gain five to eleven pounds in fat alone (National Research Council, 1970; Hytten & Leitch, 1971; Pitkin, 1976), and it is often the case that many women have difficulty losing adipose tissue after the baby is born (Beller, 1980; Cederlof & Kay, 1970; Helliovaara & Aromaa, 1981). There is some evidence from cross-sectional studies that menopause may be another event in a woman's life that promotes weight gain (e.g., McKinlay & Jeffreys, 1974), although longitudinal studies are needed to confirm this assumption. Although the precise role of sex hormones in weight regulation is still not fully understood, levels of estrogen and progesterone have been related to hunger and food intake (Dalvit-MacPhillips, 1983; Dippel & Elias, 1980).

Women also have a lower resting metabolic rate than men and thus require fewer calories for their life-sustaining functions. This sex difference is due in part to size differences between men and women, but it is also due to the higher ratio of fat to lean tissue in women. Adipose tissue is more metabolically inert than lean tissue and thus contributes to women's lower resting metabolic rate. With aging, sex differences in metabolic rate may actually increase, along with a relatively larger decrease in lean body mass and concomitant increase in fat tissue in women compared to men (Bray,

1976; Forbes & Reina, 1970; Parizkowa, 1973; Wessel, Ufer, Van Huss, & Cederquist, 1963; Young et al., 1961; Young, Blondin, Tensuan, & Fryer, 1963).

Second, it appears that middle age does not free women from assuming that their attractiveness is a key factor in their happiness. In a large-scale study of American couples, Blumenstein and Schwartz (1983) observed that looks continued to be critical well beyond the early years of relationships. In particular, wives were keenly aware of the importance of their appearance to their husbands. Although the authors did not explicitly separate weight from other aspects of appearance, their case reports suggest that weight gain is a central way in which physical appearance changes over time and is a primary cause of concern.

What happens in later life? In a current longitudinal study of people over age sixty-two, we found that the second greatest personal concern expressed by women in the sample, following memory loss, was change in body weight. Weight concerns were rarely expressed by men in the sample (Rodin, 1985). As just described, women tend to become fatter as they age, as a result of biological changes. In addition, some evidence suggests that the process of aging diminishes a woman's perceived attractiveness more than it does a man's (Hatfield & Sprecher, in press), a phenomenon dubbed by Sontag (1972) as the double standard of aging in our society.

In sum, although the data on the topic are sparse, it seems that women's battle with weight, both psychological and physical, lasts a lifetime. Clinically, we find that bulimia can have its onset well after the adolescent and young adult years. From both a clinical and a theoretical viewpoint, the study of women's concerns with weight and eating problems should examine women across the life span.

Which Women in Particular?

Having looked at the developmental trajectory followed by women in general in our society, we now consider which women during their developmental course will be pushed beyond a normative discontent into the disordered eating range.

Timing of development. One developmental factor that may affect risk for bulimia is the timing of biological development. Life-span theory suggests that being "out-of-phase" (Neugarten, 1972) with one's cohorts presents a particular stressor and increases the likelihood of a developmental crisis. Research on puberty has suggested sex differences in the impact of early versus late maturation, which may be important in identifying risk factors for bulimia. Male early developers have been found to be more relaxed, less dependent, and more self-confident. They also enjoy a more positive body image and a greater sense of attractiveness than do late-developing boys (Clausen, 1975; Jones, 1965; Tobin-Richards et al., 1983).

For girls, results on the outcomes of early maturation are less clear. Although early-maturing girls have been found to enjoy greater popularity among male peers (Simmons, Blyth, & McKinney, 1983) and greater self-confidence (Clausen, 1975) than girls who develop on time or later, early-developing girls also have been reported to be less popular among female peers, to experience greater emotional distress, to perceive themselves as less attractive, and to hold a lower self-concept than their peers (Peskin,

1973; Simmons et al., 1983). Furthermore, pubertal growth may carry more explicit sexualized meanings for girls than for boys, and parents may respond to their daughters' signs of early sexual maturation with more fear and subsequent greater protectiveness than to their sons' sexual maturation (Hamburg, 1974; Seiden, 1976).

In terms of body dissatisfaction, early-developing girls seem to be particularly unhappy with their weight (Simmons et al., 1983; Tobin-Richards et al., 1983). This finding is not surprising, given that early-developing girls tend to be fatter than their peers (and tend to remain so once they have completed their pubertal growth). In Simmons et al.'s (1983) sample, weight and body image satisfaction were inversely correlated for all girls, regardless of maturational status. In fact, when weight was corrected for, the differences in body image satisfaction of early-, middle-, and late-developing girls disappeared. Bruch (1981) suggested that early development may be a risk factor in anorexia nervosa. Although there are no empirical data on this issue, we conjecture that maturing faster than her peers may place a girl at risk for bulimia as well.

Personality. From our depiction of female development, it becomes clear that women have a primarily relational orientation. We conjecture that if a woman's orientation toward others' needs and opinions eclipses a sense of her own needs and opinions, she will be at risk for mental health problems in general. Whereas psychiatry has long noted women's vulnerability to hysteria, agoraphobia, or depression, in our current society, women also will be at risk for bulimia. Indeed, clinicians depict bulimic women as exhibiting a strong need for social approval and avoiding conflict, and as experiencing difficulty in identifying and asserting needs (Arenson, 1984; Boskind-Lodahl, 1976; Boskind-White & White, 1983). Initial research has found that bulimic women have higher need for approval than control women (Dunn & Ondercin, 1981; Katzman & Wolchik, 1984) and also score higher on a measure of interpersonal sensitivity (Striegel-Moore, McAvay, & Rodin, 1984).

One question that arises, then, is whether there is a personality profile that places some women at greater risk for bulimia. Although the methodology of assessing personality traits in individuals who already exhibit the clinical syndrome does not permit casual inferences, let us briefly examine the major findings of this line of research. Group profiles of the Minnesota Multiphasic Personality Inventory (MMPI) obtained for bulimic women were found to show significant elevations on the clinical scales Depression, Psychopathic Deviate, Psychasthenia, and Schizophrenia (Hatsukami, Owen, Pyle, & Mitchell, 1982; Leon, Lucas et al., 1985; Orleans & Barnett, 1984; Wallach & Lowenkopf, 1984).

Presenting MMPI data in the form of group profiles ignores the heterogeneity of profiles within a sample. Hatsukami et al. (1982) reported that the two most common codetypes (which together accounted for only 25 percent of their sample) may represent two subgroups of bulimics, one with more obsessive–compulsive problems and the other with addictive behaviors. Importantly, for 20 percent of the bulimic subjects, none of the clinical scales were significantly elevated; it is possible that this represents another subgroup of bulimics who do not show psychopathology in areas other than their eating disorder.

Many researchers have identified one substantial subgroup of bulimic women to be those who also report problems with alcohol or drug abuse (Leon, Carroll, et al., 1985; Mitchell, Hatsukami, Eckert, & Pyle, 1985; Pyle et al., 1983; Walsh, Roose, Glassman, Gladis, & Sadik, 1985). These observations have led some experts to conclude that bulimia is basically a substance-abuse disorder (Brisman & Siegel, 1984; Wooley & Wooley, 1981), with food either one of many substances or the only substance that is abused. A view of bulimia as a substance-abuse disorder is supported by the high incidence of substance abuse found among the members of bulimic women's immediate families (Leon, Carroll, et al., 1985; Strober, Salkin, Burroughs, & Morrell, 1982). We conjecture that the constellation of personality factors that predispose a woman to substance abuse would place her at risk also for bulimia, including an inability to regulate negative feelings, a need for immediate need gratification, poor impulse control, and a fragile sense of self (Brisman & Siegel, 1984; Goodsitt, 1983).

Another characteristic of bulimic women that has attracted considerable attention has been the high prevalence of depressive symptoms (Fairburn & Cooper, 1982; Hatsukami, Eckert, Mitchell, & Pyle, 1984; Johnson & Larson, 1982; Johnson et al., 1982; Katzman & Wolchik, 1984; Mitchell et al., 1985; Norman & Herzog, 1983; Pyle, Mitchell, & Eckert, 1981; Russell, 1979; Wallach & Lowenkopf, 1984; Walsh et al., 1985; Williamson et al., 1985; Wolf & Crowther, 1983). Between 35 percent and 78 percent of bulimic patients have been reported to satisfy the DSM-III criteria for a diagnosis of affective disorder during the acute stage of illness (Gwirtsman, Roy-Byrne, Yager, & Gerner, 1983; Hatsukami et al., 1984; Herzog, 1982; Hudson et al., 1982; Hudson et al., 1984; Pope, Hudson & Jonas, 1983). This high incidence of depressive symptoms in bulimia has led to the hypothesis that bulimia is a variant of an affective disorder. However, these studies were conducted with patients, and such individuals generally report a high incidence of depressive symptoms regardless of the presenting problem (e.g., Kashani & Priesmeyer, 1983; Rabkin, Charles, & Kass, 1983). Furthermore, the symptoms of a major depressive episode or dysthymic disorder and bulimia overlap considerably, a point that has been made with respect to anorexia (Altschuler & Weiner, 1985).

Whether or not bulimia is a type of affective disorder, several possible links between bulimic and depressive symptoms may obtain. There is some evidence that depressive symptoms increase during or after binge eating and purging episodes (Johnson et al., 1982; Johnson & Larson, 1982; Russell, 1979). For some bulimic women, the binge/purge cycle serves a self-punishing purpose (Johnson et al., 1984), which is consonant with the depressive constellation. Alternatively, eating may be an antidote to depression, used as self-medication and self-nurturance. There also may be an association between depression and the onset of the binge/purge cycle. Perhaps when weight-conscious women become depressed, their customary restraint of eating weakens, thus increasing the likelihood of binging. We have described earlier the apparent association between body dissatisfaction and low self-esteem, which is a common marker of depression. At present, the question remains unanswered whether depression is a symptom secondary to bulimia, or whether a depressive syndrome places a woman at greater risk for bulimia.

Behaviorally oriented researchers have begun to examine the possibility that inadequate coping skills constitute a risk factor for bulimia (Hawkins & Clement, 1984). Several clinicians and researchers have argued that a deficit of coping skills renders a bulimic woman less able to deal effectively with stress, and binging is an expression of her inability to cope (Boskind-White & White, 1983; Hawkins & Clement, 1984; Katzman & Wolchik, 1984; Loro, 1984; Loro & Orleans, 1981).

In addition, researchers have found that women who experience more stress are at greater risk for binge eating (Abraham & Beumont, 1982; Fremouw & Heyneman, 1984; Pyle et al., 1981; Strober, 1984; Wolf & Crowther, 1983). We postulate that stress is not a specific risk factor but rather, in concert with the other risk factors we have discussed, may play a role in a woman's likelihood of developing bulimia. Research is needed to determine whether bulimic women, compared with other women, encounter a higher level of life stress, subjectively experience stressors as more stressful, or are less skilled in coping with stress.

Biological Factors

Genetic Determinants of Weight

In attempts to understand bulimia, it is crucial to examine biological and genetic factors. As discussed in the section on development, women are genetically programmed to have a proportionately higher body fat composition than men—a sex difference that appears to hold across all races and cultures (Bennett, 1984; Tanner, 1978), and the differences between the sexes in fatness increases dramatically, on the average, across the life span.

Substantial individual differences in body build and weight are genetically determined. Identical twins, even when reared apart, are significantly more similar in weight than are fraternal twins or siblings (Borjeson, 1976; Bray, 1981; Brook, Huntley, & Slack, 1975; Fabsitz, Feinleib, & Hrubec, 1978; Feinleib et al., 1977; Medlund, Cederlof, Floderus-Myrhed, Friberg, & Sorensen, 1976; Stunkard, Foch, & Hrubec, 1985). Adopted children resemble their biological parents in weight far more than they resemble their adoptive parents (Stunkard, Sorensen, et al., 1985).

One path by which heredity may influence weight is by determining the ways in which food is metabolized. Individual differences in metabolic rate seem to be of great significance in determining the efficiency of caloric expenditure (Rimm & White, 1979). Indeed, even individuals matched for age, sex, weight, and activity level can differ dramatically from each other in the amount of calories they eat while maintaining identical levels of body weight (Rose & Williams, 1961).

Which Women in Particular?

We conjecture that those women who are genetically programmed to be heavier than the svelte ideal will be at higher risk for bulimia than those women who are naturally thin. Clinical and empirical evidence suggests that a woman who is heavier than her peers may be more likely to develop bulimia (Boskind-White & White, 1983; Fairburn & Cooper, 1983; Johnson et al., 1982; Yager, Landsverk, Lee-Benner, & Johnson, 1985).

It has been suggested that in addition to the genetic predisposition to a specific body weight, a predisposition to an eating disorder may be genetically transmitted. Research on this issue is in an early stage, but initial findings suggest familial clustering of eating disorders. Studies have documented a significantly higher incidence of both anorexia nervosa and bulimia among the first-degree female relatives of anorexic patients than in the immediate families of control subjects (Gershon et al., 1983; Strober, Morrell, Burroughs, Salkin, & Jacobs, 1985). Monozygotic twins have a considerably higher concordance rate than dizygotic twins for anorexia (Crisp, Hall, & Holland, 1985; Garfinkel & Garner, 1982; Holland, Hall, Murray, Russell, & Crisp, 1984; Nowlin, 1983; Vandereyken & Pierloot, 1981). Following from this line of research with anorexic women, the question of the inheritability of bulimia now needs to be examined with bulimic patients.

The Disregulation of Body Weight and Eating Through Dieting

A significant number of women, then, face a frustrating paradox: Although society prescribes a thin beauty ideal, their own genes predispose them to have a considerably heavier body weight. Current society promotes dieting as the pathway to thinness, and as we would expect, significantly more women than men report dieting at any time (e.g., Nielsen, 1979; Nylander, 1971). Before age thirteen, 80 percent of girls report that they have already been on a weight-loss diet, as compared to 10 percent of boys (Hawkins, Turell, & Jackson, 1983).

On the basis of studies investigating the physiological changes that occur as a result of dieting, many researchers now believe that dieting is not only an ineffective way to attain long-term weight loss but that it may in fact contribute to subsequent weight gain and binge eating (Polivy & Herman, 1985; Rodin, 1981; Rodin, Silberstein, & Striegel-Moore, 1985; Wardle, 1980; Wooley & Wooley, 1981). A substantial decrease in daily caloric intake will result in a reduced metabolic rate, which thus impedes weight loss (Apfelbaum, 1975; Boyle, Storlien, Harper, & Keesey, 1981; Garrow, 1978; Westerterp, 1977). The suppression of metabolic rate caused by dieting is most pronounced when basal metabolic rate is low from the outset (Wooley, Wooley, & Dyrenforth, 1979). Because women have lower metabolic rates than men, women are particularly likely to find that, despite their efforts, they cannot lose as much weight as they would like. Upon resuming normal caloric intake, a person's metabolic rate does not immediately rebound to its original pace, and in fact, a longer period of dieting will prolong the time it takes for the metabolic rate to regain its original level (Even, Nicolaidis, & Meile, 1981). Thus, even normal eating after dieting may promote weight gain.

Numerous other physiological changes due to food restriction have been reported (Bjorntorp & Yang, 1982; Faust, Johnson, Stern, & Hirsch, 1978; Fried, Hill, Nickel, & DiGirolamo, 1983; Gruen & Greenwood, 1981; Miller, Faust, Goldberger, & Hirsch, 1983; Walks, Lavan, Presta, Yang, & Bjorntorp, 1983). All of these alternations contribute to increased efficiency in food utilization and an increased proportion of fat in body composition. Hence, dieting ultimately produces effects opposite to those intended. In addition to these biological ramifications, dieting also produces psychological results that are self-defeating. Typically, a dieter feels deprived of favorite foods, and when "off" the diet, she is likely to overeat (Herman & Mack, 1975; Polivy & Herman, 1985).

Which Women in Particular?

We propose that a prolonged history of repeated dieting attempts constitutes yet another risk factor for bulimia. Animal research suggests that regaining weight occurs significantly more rapidly after a second dieting cycle than after a first (Brownell, Stellar, Stunkard, Rodin, & Wilson, 1984). We conjecture that those women who have engaged in repeated dieting attempts will be the least successful at achieving their target weights by dieting. These women may be most vulnerable, then, to attempting other weight loss strategies, including purging.

The literature on the physiological and psychological effects of dieting suggests a seemingly paradoxical picture: The more restrictively a person diets, the more likely she or he will be to crave foods (particularly foods not allowed as part of the diet) and to give in to these cravings eventually. Indeed, several studies have found a high correlation between restraint and binge eating (Hawkins & Clement, 1980, 1984; Leon, Carroll, et al., 1985; Striegel-Moore et al., 1985b). From their review of this research, Polivy and Herman (1985) concluded that food restriction may be an important causal antecedent to binging. In support of this view, the clinical literature suggests that in many cases bulimia was preceded by a period of restrictive dieting (Boskind-Lodahl & Sirlin, 1977; Dally & Gomez, 1979; Johnson et al., 1982; Mitchell et al., 1985; Russell, 1979; Wooley & Wooley, 1985).

Affective Instability

Affective instability has been proposed as another biogenetic risk factor of bulimia (Hawkins & Clement, 1984; Johnson, Lewis, & Hagman, 1984; Strober, 1981). It is widely recognized that women have a higher incidence of affective disorders than men. If a predisposition to affective instability increases an individual's risk of bulimia, then it would represent another answer to the questions of both why women rather than men become bulimic and which women in particular.

Several family studies have revealed a high incidence rate of affective disorders among first-degree relatives of bulimic patients (Gwirtsman et al., 1983; Herzog, 1982; Hudson et al., 1982; Hudson et al., 1983; Pyle et al., 1983; Slater & Cowie, 1971; Strober et al., 1982; Yager & Strober, 1985), with one exception (Stern et al., 1984). Studies considering the incidence of bulimia in first-degree relatives of patents with an affective disorder would constitute another test of the hypothesized familial association between affective disorders and bulimia (Altschuler & Weiner, 1985). Two studies addressing this question, however, did not find increased incidence of eating disorders among the first-degree relatives of patients with an affective disorder, a result that argues against a *simple* hypothesis that affective disorders and eating disorders are merely alternate expressions of the same disposition (Gershon et al., 1983; Hatsukami et al., 1984; Strober, 1983; Yager & Strober, 1985). In the absence of twin studies, adoption studies, and sophisticated family aggregation studies, at present no conclusions regarding genetic transmission of bulimia via an affective disorder link can be made.

Family Variables

With a few exceptions (e.g., Boskind-White & White, 1983; Schwartz, 1982; Schwartz, Barrett, & Saba, 1985; Yager, 1982), the bulimia literature has largely ignored the potential role of family characteristics that might predispose some women to bulimia. Prospective studies are completely missing, and there is no comprehensive theoretical framework that would allow delineation of the relevant variables to be included in a prospective investigation of families.

In light of our review, we conjecture that certain family characteristics may amplify the sociocultural imperatives described earlier. For example, we hypothesize that a daughter's risk for bulimia is relatively increased if the family places heavy emphasis on appearance and thinness; if the family believes and promotes the myth that weight is under volitional control and thus holds the daughter responsible for regulating it; if family members, particularly females (mother, sisters, aunts), model weight preoccupation and dieting; if the daughter is evaluated critically by members of the family with regard to her weight; if the daughter is reinforced for her efforts to lose weight; and if family members compete regarding the achievement of the ideal of thinness.

Furthermore, a risk to develop bulimia may derive from how the family system operates. Clinicians have described families with a bulimic member as sharing similarities with "psychosomatic families" (Minuchin, Rosman, & Baker, 1978), including enmeshment, overprotectiveness, rigidity, and lack of conflict resolution. In addition, bulimic patients' families are reported to exhibit isolation and heightened consciousness of appearance, and they attach special meaning to food and eating (Schwartz et al., 1985). Research evaluating these assumptions is still in its infancy (Johnson & Flach, 1985; Kagan & Squires, 1985; Kog, Vandereycken, & Vertommen, in press; Kog, Vertommen, & DeGroote, in press; Sights & Richards, 1984; Strober, 1981).

Why now?

In the final section, we attempt to speculate on what makes bulimia so likely at this particular time. We recognize that ease of diagnosis per se, after inclusion of the disorder in the DSM-III (American Psychiatric Association, 1980), may have contributed to the apparent increase, but we wish to focus on other sociocultural and psychological mediators that contribute to the increased risk of bulimia in this era.

Shift toward Increasingly Thin Standard

In recent years, the beauty ideal for women has moved toward an increasingly thin standard, which has become more uniform and has been more widely distributed due to the advent of mass media. Changes in measurements over time toward increasing thinness have been documented in Miss America contestants, Playboy centerfolds, and female models in magazine advertisements (Garner, Garfinkel, Schwartz, & Thompson, 1980; Snow & Harris, 1985). During the same time period, however, the average body weight of women under thirty years of age has actually increased (Metropolitan Life Foundation, 1983; Society of Actuaries, 1959, 1979).

Lakoff and Scherr (1984) suggested that models on television and in magazines are seen as realistic representations of what people look like, as compared with painted figures who are more readily acknowledged to be artistic creations. Even though the magazine model or television actress has undergone hours of makeup preparation as well as time-consuming and rigorous workout regimens to achieve the "look," her audience thinks that the model's public persona is what she really looks like. Her "look" is then rapidly and widely disseminated, so that the public receives a uniform picture of beauty.

Effects of Media Attention on Dieting and Bulimia

We hypothesize that current sociocultural influences teach women not only what the ideal body looks like but also how to try to attain it, including how to diet, purge, and engage in other disregulating behaviors. The mass-market weight control industry almost prescribes these rituals. For example, the bestseller *Beverly Hills Diet Book* (Mazel, 1981) advocated a form of bulimia in which binges are "compensated" by eating massive quantities of raw fruit to induce diarrhea (Wooley & Wooley, 1982). In addition to the mass media making available what one might call manuals for "how to develop an eating disorder," females more directly teach each other how to diet and how to binge, purge, and starve. Schwartz, Thompson, and Johnson (1981) found that a college woman who purges almost always knows another female student who purges, whereas a woman who does not purge rarely knows someone who does.

A positive feedback loop is thus established: The more women there are with disordered eating, the more likely there are to be even more women who develop disordered eating. We certainly do not mean to imply that psychopathology is merely learned behavior—but we suggest that the public's heightened awareness of eating disorders and a young woman's likelihood of personal exposure to the behaviors may be a significant factor in the increased emergence of eating disorders in the last several years.

We have already noted how family members may model for other members both attitudes and behaviors concerning weight and eating. Interestingly, as Boskind-White and White (1983) described, the women now presenting with bulimia are the daughters of the first Weight Watchers' generation. A question for future study is, What will the daughters of the generation of bulimic women be like?

Fitness

In the past decade, along with the fitness movement, there has been a redefinition of the ideal female body, which is characterized now not merely by thinness but by firm, shapely muscles (while avoiding too much muscularity) as well. Although the possible health benefits from increased exercise are very real, the current emphasis on fitness may itself be contributing to the increased incidence of bulimia. The strong implication is that anyone who "works out" can achieve the lean, healthy-looking ideal and that such attainment is a direct consequence of personal effort and therefore worthy of pride and admiration. Conversely, the inability to achieve the "aerobics instructor look" may leave women feeling defeated, ashamed, and desperate. The pursuit of fitness becomes another preoccupation, compulsion, even obsession for many. Again, we note that women's bodies are predisposed to have a fairly high proportion of fat; indeed, female hormones are disregulated when the percentage of body fat drops below a certain level. The no-fat ideal reflects an "unnatural" standard for many women.

If the pursuit of fitness represents a step even beyond pursuit of thinness, so too does the upsurge of cosmetic surgery. From suction removal of fat to face-lifts, women in increasing numbers are seeking to match the template of beauty with ever more complicated (and expensive) procedures. The message, again, seems to be that beauty is a matter of effort and that failure to attain the beauty ideal makes one personally culpable.

Shifting Sex Roles

Perhaps, ironically, in this era when women feel capable and empowered to pursue success in professional arenas, they have a heightened sense that their efforts should attain success in the domain of beauty as well. It seems that being occupationally successful does not relieve a woman of the need to be beautiful. Indeed, the pursuit of beauty and thinness may sometimes compromise women's success in other domains, for it takes time, attention, and money and is a drain on self-esteem.

In this transitional time of rapidly shifting sex roles, it seems likely that girls more than boys are experiencing the stresses of changing roles, perhaps placing girls at greater risk for psychological distress in general. These changing roles may intersect with all of the risk factors for bulimia we have been discussing and therefore may be an important part of the answer to Why now? The messages communicated to girls are complex and quite often confusing: Work hard at school, but be sure to be popular and pretty; be a lawyer, but be feminine. Little research has been done that can illuminate these kinds of issues. Clinically, we find that bulimic women often express confusion about their roles; an interesting question for research is whether this distinguishes them from other women in general and from other women psychotherapy clients.

Steiner-Adair (1986) studied adolescent girls' images of the ideal woman and their personal goals for themselves and looked at the relationship of these views with performance on the Eating Attitudes Test (EAT), a measure of disordered eating (Garner & Garfinkel, 1979). Interestingly, all girls had a similar picture of the ideal "superwoman" (career, family, beauty), but those girls who saw the "superwoman" as consonant with their own goals had elevated eating pathology scores, whereas the non-eating-disordered girls had more modest goals for themselves. Hence, a girl's ability to put distance between the societal ideal and her own expectations for herself was associated with decreased evidence of eating disturbance. This seems analogous to our findings of a significant correlation between agreement with statements reflecting sociocultural messages regarding attractiveness, and a measure of disordered eating (Striegel-Moore, Silberstein, & Rodin, 1985a). Gilligan (1982) has argued that the process of female development in our androcentric society makes it difficult for girls and women to find and use their own "voice." We would contend that when women instead adopt the socioculturally defined voice and strive to match the unrealistically successful as well as the unrealistically thin public model, the consequences may be unhealthy.

Conclusions

We have tried to understand bulimia and point to important gaps in our knowledge by examining three questions: Why women? Which women in particular? Why now? We addressed these questions by drawing on a diverse literature in social and development psychology, psychology of gender, clinical psychiatry and psychology, and biological psychiatry and medicine. As we conclude our analysis of risk factors in women, it is instructive to ask how men may fit into this picture.

Though significantly fewer men than women currently show evidence of bulimia (a ratio of 1:10), bulimic men do exist and, we hypothesize, will increase in number in the near future. Indeed, bulimic men are an important group to study in the context of our risk factor model, because although men and women may share certain sociocultural, psychological, and biological risk factors, there clearly are gender differences in the variables placing an individual at risk.

Surely our society's fitness consciousness applies to men as much as, and perhaps even more than, to women. It is possible that the sexes pursue fitness for different reasons, with women focusing more on the effects exercise has on physical appearance, whereas men pursue strength and muscularity (Garner, Rockert, Olmsted, Johnson & Coscina, 1985). However, the workout body type for men has become, it seems, a more widely aspired-to ideal, and similarly to women, more and more men today are fighting to ward off the effects of aging on their appearance. As men become more fashion conscious and more weight conscious, we would expect them to diet more. Already, diet soft drinks, light beers, and other diet products are being marketed for a male as well as a female audience. Because men rarely have the long history of dieting efforts that women do, men typically are more successful in their weight-loss efforts. However, if they succumb to repeated cycles of gaining and losing, we hypothesize that these patterns will lead to the same effects in men as they have in women and could therefore potentiate bulimia.

Beyond the general pressure on men to be conscious of physical fitness and appearance that may result in an increased risk for men to develop bulimia, certain male subcultures (similar to female subcultures) emphasize weight standards and thus place certain men at greater risk for bulimia. If our hypothesis is correct that environments that emphasize weight standards foster the development of bulimia, then we would expect to find a higher incidence of bulimia in men who participate in such environments than in men who do not. In fact, initial research does show that athletes such as wrestlers and jockeys evidence higher incidence of bulimia (Rodin, Striegel-Moore, & Silberstein, 1985) than athletes in sports that do not prescribe a certain body weight. Clinical evidence suggests that homosexual men, whose subculture promotes a thin body ideal and a heightened attentiveness to appearance and fashion (Kleinberg, 1980; Lakoff & Scherr, 1984, Mishkind, Rodin, Silberstein, & Striegel-Moore, in press), may also be at increased risk for bulimia (Herzog, Norman, Gordon, & Pepose, 1984).

The present analysis has underscored questions that remain to be investigated. As we conclude, let us briefly outline some of these agendas for future study. Initial research suggests that a description of bulimia as a single entity does not reflect adequately the heterogeneity of the population. In particular, we need diagnostic categories that allow differentiation among subgroups, which would then permit an investigation of the differential relationships among those subgroups and the various risk factors. An additional step involves clarifying the relationships among bulimia, anorexia, and obesity, and the risk factors involved in each of those syndromes. Another question deserving further attention is the place of bulimia in the spectrum of psychiatric disorders in general and in the affective disorders in particular. In addition, we need to understand the risk factors that bulimia may share with other psychiatric syndromes that have been disproportionally represented by women, such as depression and agoraphobia.

Having emphasized the importance of female socialization as a major contributing factor in bulimia, we also need to examine how changes in the female sex role stereotype may affect the incidence of bulimia. Furthermore, reaching an understanding of the risk factors for bulimia in men could help expand and refine our understanding of risk factors in women as well as in men. Finally, although we have focused our attention on identifying factors that place women at risk for bulimia, it will be equally important to delineate variables that serve a protective function.

Another important task is to develop strategies for the prevention of bulimia. Numerous risk factors have been described that do not lend themselves easily to modification. Many have to do with social values and mores. Unfortunately, large-scale social changes are slow and difficult to effect. Other risk factors involve genetic determinants. Even if some factors that lead to bulimia are genetically determined or transmitted, however, the fact that they are expressed as an eating disorder rather than in some other clinical manifestation can be understood only by referring to the present sociocultural milieu and to female sex role socialization practices. As strategies for change in these areas are developed, shifts in the incidence and prevalence of bulimia may be expected to follow.

NOTES

1. At present, there are insufficient data to discuss the etiology of the disorder in the 10% of bulimics who are men. Some of the risk factors specified for women may relate to men as well. Some speculation on what groups of men are most vulnerable will be considered briefly in the last section of the article.

2. Many investigators suggest that eating disorders should be conceptualized as a spectrum spanning anorexia nervosa, bulimia, and compulsive overeating (Andersen, 1983; Szmukler, 1982; Yager, Landsverk, Lee-Benner, & Johnson, 1983). In this relatively early stage of conceptualization, it seems useful to limit our scope to bulimia. However, we will sometimes draw on the existing literature about other eating disorders when relevant. A task for the future is clearly to delineate more precisely the commonalities and differences among the eating disorders and to develop a conceptual framework that integrates them.

REFERENCES

Abraham, S., & Beumont, P. J. V. (1982). How patients describe bulimia or binge eating. *Psychological Medicine, 12*, 625–635.

Adler, J. (1982, January). Looking back at '81. *Newsweek*, pp. 26–52.

Aldous, J. (1978). *Family careers: Developmental change in families.* New York: Wiley.

Altschuler, K. Z., & Weiner, M. F. (1985). Anorexia nervosa and depression: A dissenting view. *American Journal of Psychiatry, 142*, 328–332.

Ambert, A. M. (1976). *Sex structure.* Don Mills, Canada: Langman.

American Psychiatric Association (1980). *Diagnostic and statistical manual of mental disorders* (3rd ed.). Washington, DC: Author.

Andersen, A. E. (1983). Anorexia nervosa and bulimia: A spectrum of eating disorders. *Journal of Adolescent Health Care, 4*, 15–21.

Apfelbaum, M. (1975). Influence of level of energy intake on energy expenditure in man. Effects of spontaneous intake, experimental starvation and experimental overeating. In G. A. Bray (Ed.), *Obesity in perspective* (OBHEW Publication No. NIH 75–708, Vol. 2, pp. 145–155). Washington, DC: U.S. Government Printing Office.

Arenson, G. (1984). *Binge eating. How to stop it forever.* New York: Rawson.

Banner, L. W. (1983). *American beauty.* New York: Knopf.

Barnett, R. C., & Baruch, G. K. (1980). *The competent woman: Perspectives on development.* New York: Irvington.

Beck, J. B., Ward-Hull, C. J., & McLear, P. M. (1976). Variables related to women's somatic preferences of the male and female body. *Journal of Personality and Social Psychology, 34*, 1200–1210.

Beller, A. S. (1977). *Fat and thin: A natural history of obesity.* New York: Farrar, Straus & Giroux.

Beller, A. S. (1980). Pregnancy: Is motherhood fattening? In J. R. Kaplan (Ed.), *A woman's conflict* (pp. 139–158). Englewood Cliffs, NJ: Prentice-Hall.

Bem, S. L. (1974). The measurement of psychological androgyny. *Journal of Consulting and Clinical Psychology, 42*, 155–162.

Bennett, W. I. (1984). Dieting: Ideology versus physiology. *Psychiatric Clinics of North America, 7*, 321–334.

Berscheid, E., Dion, K. K., Walster, E., & Walster, G. (1971). Physical attractiveness and dating choice. A test of the matching hypothesis. *Journal of Experimental Social Psychology, 7,* 173–189.

Beumont, P. J., George, G. C., & Smart, D. E. (1976). "Dieters" and "vomiters and purgers" in anorexia nervosa. *Psychological Medicine, 6,* 617–622.

Bjorntorp, P., & Yang, M. U. (1982). Refeeding after tasting in the rat: Effects on body composition and food efficiency. *American Journal of Clinical Nutrition, 36,* 444–449.

Blumenstein, P. W., & Schwartz, P. (1983). *American couples.* New York: Morrow.

Blyth, D. A., & Traeger, C. M. (1983). The self-concept and self-esteem of early adolescents. *Theory Into Practice, 22,* 91–97.

Borjeson, M. (1976). The aetiology of obesity in children. *Acta Paediatrica Scandinavica, 65,* 279–287.

Boskind-Lodahl, M. (1976). Cinderella's stepsisters. *Signs: Journal of Women, Culture and Society, 2,* 342–358.

Boskind-Lodahl, M., & Sirlin, J. (1977). The gorging-purging syndrome. *Psychology Today, 10,* 50–52, 82–85.

Boskind-White, M., & White, W. C. (1983). *Bulimarexia: The binge/purge cycle.* New York: Norton.

Boyle, P. C., Storlien, L. H., Harper, A. E., & Keesey, R. E. (1981). Oxygen consumption and locomotor activity during restricted feeding and realimentation. *American Journal of Physiology, 241,* R392–397.

Bray, G. A. (1976). *The obese patient.* Philadelphia: Saunders.

Bray, G. A. (1981). The inheritance of corpulence. In L. A. Cioffi, W. P. T. James, & T. B. Van Itallie (Eds.), *Weight regulatory system: Normal and disturbed mechanisms* (pp. 185–195). New York: Raven Press.

Brisman, J., & Siegel, M. (1984). Bulimia and alcoholism: Two sides of the same coin? *Journal of Substance Abuse Treatment, 1,* 113–118.

Brook, C. G. D., Huntley, R. M. C., & Slack, J. (1975). Influence of heredity and environment in determination of skinfold thickness in children. *British Medical Journal, 2,* 719–721.

Brownell, K. D., Stellar, E., Stunkard, A. J., Rodin, J., & Wilson, G. T. (1984). *Behavioral and metabolic effects of weight loss and regain in animals and humans.* Unpublished manuscript, University of Pennsylvania, Philadelphia.

Brownmiller, S. (1984). *Femininity.* New York: Linden Press/Simon & Schuster.

Bruch, H. (1973). *Eating disorders: Obesity, anorexia nervosa and the person within.* New York: Basic Books.

Bruch, H. (1981). Developmental considerations of anorexia nervosa and obesity. *Canadian Journal of Psychiatry, 26,* 212–217.

Bush, D. E., Simmons, R., Hutchinson, B., & Blyth, D. (1978). Adolescent perceptions of sex roles in 1968 and 1975. *Public Opinion Quarterly, 41,* 459–474.

Button, E. J., Fransella, F., & Slade, P. D. (1977). A reappraisal of body perception disturbance in anorexia nervosa. *Psychological Medicine, 7,* 235–243.

Carlson, R. (1965). Stability and change in the adolescent's self-image. *Child Development, 36,* 659–666.

Cash, T. F., Gillen, B., & Burns, D. S. (1977). Sexism and "beautyism" in personnel consultant decision making. *Journal of Applied Psychology, 62,* 301–310.

Casper, R. C., Eckert, E. D., Halmi, K. A., Goldberg, S. C., & Davis, J. M. (1980). Bulimia: Its incidence and clinical importance in patients with anorexia nervosa. *Archives of General Psychiatry, 37,* 1030–1035.

Casper, R. C., Halmi, K. A., Goldberg, S. C., Eckert, E. D., & Davis, J. M. (1979). Disturbances in body image estimation as related to other characteristics and outcome of anorexia nervosa. *British Journal of Psychiatry, 134,* 60–66.

Cederlof, R., & Kay, L. (1970). The effect of childbearing on body weight. A twin control study. *Acta Psychiatrica Scandinavica,* (Suppl.) *219,* 47–49.

Chaiken, S., & Pliner, P. (1984). *Women, but not men, are what they eat: The effect of meal size and gender on perceived femininity and masculinity.* Unpublished manuscript, Vanderbilt University, Nashville, TN.

Chodorow, N. (1978). *The reproduction of mothering: Psychoanalysis and the sociology of gender.* Berkeley: University of California Press.

Clausen, J. A. (1975). The social meaning of differential physical and sexual maturation. In S. E. Dragastin & G. H. Elder, Jr. (Eds.), *Adolescence in the life cycle: Psychological change and social context* (pp. 24–48). Washington, DC: Hemisphere.

Coleman, J. S. (1961). *The adolescent society.* New York: Free Press.

Crago, M., Yates, A., Beutler, L. E., & Arizmendi, T. G. (1985). Height–weight ratios among female athletes: Are collegiate athletics the precursors to an anorexic syndrome? *International Journal of Eating Disorders, 4,* 79–87.

Crisp, A. H. (1980). *Anorexia nervosa: Let me be.* London: Academic Press.

Crisp, A. H., Hall, A., & Holland, A. J. (1985). Nature and nurture in anorexia nervosa: A study of 34 pairs of twins, one pair of triplets and an adoptive family. *International Journal of Eating Disorders, 4,* 5–27.

Crisp, A. H., & Kalucy, R. S. (1974). Aspects of the perceptual disorder in anorexia nervosa. *British Journal of Medical Psychology, 47,* 349–361.

Dally, P. J., & Gomez, J. (1979). *Anorexia nervosa.* London: William Heinemann Medical Books.

Dalvit-MacPhillips, S. P. (1983). The effect of the human menstrual cycle on nutrient intake. *Physiology and Behavior, 31,* 209–212.

Dippel, R. L., & Elias, J. W. (1980). Preferences for sweets in relationship to use of oral contraceptives in pregnancy. *Hormones and Behavior, 14,* 1–6.

Dornbusch, S. M., Carlsmith, J. M., Duncan, P. D., Gross, R. T., Martin, J. A., Ritter, P. L., & Siegel-Gorelick, B. (1984). Sexual maturation, social class, and the desire to be thin among adolescent females. *Developmental and Behavioral Pediatrics, 5,* 308–314.

Douvan, E., & Adelson, J. (1966). *The adolescent experience.* New York: Wiley.

Drewnowski, A., Riskey, D., & Desor, J. A. (1982). Feeling fat yet unconcerned: Self-reported overweight and the restraint scale. *Appetite: Journal for Intake Research, 3,* 273–279.

Druss, R. G., & Silverman, J. A. (1979). Body image and perfectionism of ballerinas: Comparison and contrast with anorexia nervosa. *General Hospital Psychiatry, 1,* 115–121.

Dunn, P., & Ondercin, P. (1981). Personality variables related to compulsive eating in college women. *Journal of Clinical Psychology, 37,* 43–49.

Dusek, J. B., & Flaherty, J. F. (1981). The development of the self-concept during the adolescent years. *Monographs of the Society for Research in Child Development, 46,* 1–67.

Dweck, C. S., Davidson, W., Nelson, S., & Enna, B. (1978). Sex differences in learned helplessness: II. The contingencies of evaluative feedback in the classroom, and III. An experimental analysis. *Developmental Psychology, 14,* 268–276.

Ehrenreich, B., & English, D. (1978). *For her own good: 150 years of the experts' advice to women.* New York: Anchor Press/Doubleday.

Erikson, E. H. (1968). *Identity: Youth and crisis.* New York: Norton.

Even, P., Nicolaidis, S., & Meile, M. (1981). Changes in efficiency of ingestants are a major factor of regulation of energy balance. In L. A. Cioffi, W. P. T. James, & T. B. Van Itallie

(Eds.), *The body weight regulatory system: Normal and disturbed mechanisms* (pp. 115–123). New York: Raven Press.

Fabsitz, R., Feinleib, M., & Hrubec, Z. (1978). Weight changes in adult twins. *Acta Geneticae Medicae et Gemellologiae, 17,* 315–332.

Fairburn, C. G., & Cooper, P. J. (1982). Self-induced vomiting and bulimia nervosa: An undetected problem. *British Medical Journal, 284,* 1153–1155.

Fairburn, C. G., & Cooper, P. J. (1983). The epidemiology of bulimia nervosa. *International Journal of Eating Disorders, 2,* 61–67.

Fallon, A. E., & Rozin, P. (1985). Sex differences in perceptions of body shape. *Journal of Abnormal Psychology, 94,* 102–105.

Faust, M. S. (1983). Alternative constructions of adolescent growth. In J. Brooks-Gunn & A. C. Petersen (Eds.), *Girls at puberty* (pp. 105–125). New York: Plenum Press.

Faust, J. M., Johnson, P. R., Stern, J. S., & Hirsch, J. (1978). Diet-induced adipocyte number increase in adult rats: A new model of obesity. *American Journal of Physiology, 235,* E279–286.

Federal Trade Commission. (1978). FTC staff report on television advertising to children. Washington, DC: Author.

Feinleib, M., Garrison, R. J., Fabsitz, R., Christian, J. C., Hrubec, Z., Borhani, N. O., Kannel, W. B., Rosenman, R., Schwartz, J. T., & Wagner, J. O. (1977). The NHLBI twin study of cardiovascular disease risk factors: Methodology and summary of results. *American Journal of Epidemiology, 106,* 284–295.

Fisher, S. (1964). Sex differences in body perception. *Psychological Monographs, 78,* 1–22.

Forbes, G., & Reina, J. C. (1970). Adult lean body mass declines with age: Some longitudinal observations. *Metabolism, 19,* 653–663.

Franzoi, S. L., & Shields, S. A. (1984). The body esteem scale: Multi-dimensional structure and sex differences in a college population. *Journal of Personality Assessment, 48,* 173–178.

Fremouw, W. J., & Heyneman, E. (1984). A functional analysis of binge episodes. In R. C. Hawkins II, W. J. Fremouw, & P. F. Clement (Eds.), *The binge-purge syndrome* (pp. 254–263). New York: Springer.

Fried, S. K., Hill, J. O., Nickel, M., & DiGirolamo, M. (1983). Prolonged effects of fasting-refeeding on rat adipose tissue lipoprotein lipase activity. Influence of caloric restriction during refeeding. *Journal of Nutrition, 113,* 1861–1869.

Fries, H. (1975). Anorectic behavior. Nosological aspects and introduction of a behavior scale. *Scandinavian Journal of Behavior Therapy, 4,* 137–148.

Garfinkel, P. E., & Garner, D. M. (1982). *Anorexia nervosa. A multidimensional perspective.* New York: Brunner/Mazel.

Garfinkel, P. E., Moldofsky, H., & Garner, D. M. (1980). The heterogeneity of anorexia nervosa. *Archives of General Psychiatry, 37,* 1036–1040.

Garner, D. M., & Garfinkel, P. E. (1978). Sociocultural factors in anorexia-nervosa. *Lancet, 2,* 674.

Garner, D. M., & Garfinkel, P. E. (1979). The Eating Attitudes Test: An index of the symptoms of anorexia nervosa. *Psychological Medicine, 9,* 273–279.

Garner, D. M., & Garfinkel, P. E. (1980). Sociocultural factors in the development of anorexia nervosa. *Psychological Medicine, 10,* 647–656.

Garner, D. M., & Garfinkel, P. E. (Eds.). (1985). *Handbook of psychotherapy for anorexia nervosa and bulimia.* New York: Guilford.

Garner, D. M., Garfinkel, P. E., & O'Shaughnessy, M. (1985). The validity of the distinction between bulimia with and without anorexia nervosa. *American Journal of Psychiatry, 142,* 581–587.

Garner, D. M., Garfinkel, P. E., Schwartz, D., & Thompson, M. (1980). Cultural expectations of thinness in women. *Psychological Reports, 47,* 483–491.

Garner, D. M., Garfinkel, P. E., Stancer, H. C., & Moldofsky, H. (1976). Body image disturbances in anorexia nervosa and obesity. *Psychosomatic Medicine, 38,* 327–336.

Garner, D. M., Olmsted, M. P., & Polivy, J. (1983). Development and validation of a multidimensional eating disorder inventory for anorexia nervosa and bulimia. *International Journal of Eating Disorders, 2,* 15–34.

Garner, D. M., Rockert, W., Olmsted, M. P., Johnson, C., & Coscina, D. V. (1985). Psychoeducational principles in the treatment of bulimia and anorexia nervosa. In D. M. Garner & P. E. Garfinkel (Eds.), *Handbook of psychotherapy for anorexia nervosa and bulimia* (pp. 513–572). New York: Guilford.

Garrow, J. (1978). The regulation of energy expenditure. In G. A. Bray (Ed.), *Recent advances in obesity research* (Vol. 2, pp. 200–210). London: Newman.

George, R. S., & Krondl, M. (1983). Perceptions and food use of adolescent boys and girls. *Nutrition and Behavior, 1,* 115–125.

Gershon, E. S., Hamovit, J. R., Schreiber, J. L., Dibble, E. D., Kaye, W., Nurnberger, J. I., Andersen, A., & Ebert, M. (1983). Anorexia nervosa and major affective disorders associated in families: A preliminary report. In S. B. Guze, F. J. Earls, & J. E. Barrett (Eds.), *Childhood psychopathology and development* (pp. 279–284). New York: Raven Press.

Gillen, B. (1981). Physical attractiveness: A determinant of two types of goodness. *Personality and Social Psychology Bulletin, 7,* 277–281.

Gillen, B., & Sherman, R. C. (1980). Physical attractiveness and sex as determinants of trait attributions. *Multivariate Behavioral Research, 15,* 423–437.

Gilligan, C. (1982). *In a different voice: Psychological theory and women's development.* Cambridge, MA: Harvard University Press.

Goldblatt, P. B., Moore, M. E., & Stunkard, A. J. (1965). Social factors in obesity. *Journal of the American Medical Association, 192,* 1039–1044.

Goodsitt, A. (1983). Self-regulatory disorders in eating disorders. *International Journal of Eating Disorders, 2,* 51–61.

Gormally, J. (1984). The obese binge eater: Diagnosis, etiology, and clinical issues. In R. C. Hawkins II, W. J. Fremouw, & P. F. Clement (Eds.), *The binge-purge syndrome* (pp. 47–73). New York: Springer.

Grace, P. S., Jacobson, R. S. & Fullager, C. J. (1985). A pilot comparison of purging and nonpurging bulimics. *Journal of Clinical Psychology, 41,* 173–180.

Gruen, R. K., & Greenwood, M. R. C. (1981). Adipose tissue lipoprotein lipase and glycerol release in fasted Zucker (fa/fa) rats. *American Journal of Physiology, 241,* E76–E83.

Guralnik, D. B. (Ed.). (1982). *Webster's new world dictionary* (2nd ed.). New York: Simon & Schuster.

Guy, R. F., Rankin, B. A., & Norvell, M. J. (1980). The relation of sex-role stereotyping to body image. *Journal of Psychology, 105,* 167–173.

Guyot, G. W., Fairchild, L., & Hill, M. (1981). Physical fitness, sport participation, body build and self-concept of elementary school children. *International Journal of Sport Psychology, 12,* 105–116.

Gwirtsman, H. E., Roy-Byrne, P., Yager, J., & Gerner, R. H. (1983). Neuroendocrine abnormalities in bulimia. *American Journal of Psychiatry, 140,* 559–563.

Halmi, K. A., Falk, J. R., & Schwartz, E. (1981). Binge-eating and vomiting: A survey of a college population. *Psychological Medicine, 11,* 697–706.

Halmi, K. A., Goldberg, S., & Cunningham, S. (1977). Perceptual distribution of body image in adolescent girls: Distortion of body image in adolescence. *Psychological Medicine, 7,* 253–257.

Hamburg, B. (1974). Early adolescence: A specific and stressful stage of the life cycle. In G. Coelho, D. A. Hamburg, & J. E. Adams (Eds.), *Coping and adaptation* (pp. 101–126). New York: Basic Books.

Hammar, R. D., Campbell, V. A., Moores, N. L., Sarcen, C., Gareis, F. J., & Lucas, B. (1972). An interdisciplinary study of adolescent obesity. *Journal of Pediatrics, 80,* 373–383.

Harris, M. B. (1983). Eating habits, restraint, knowledge and attitudes toward obesity. *International Journal of Obesity, 7,* 271–288.

Harrison, A. A., & Saeed, L. (1977). Let's make a deal: Analysis of revelations and stipulations in lonely hearts advertisements. *Journal of Personality and Social Psychology, 35,* 257–264.

Harter, S. (1985). Processes underlying the construction, maintenance and enhancement of the self-concept in children. In J. Suls & A. Greenwald (Eds.). *Psychological perspectives on the self* (Vol. 3, pp. 137–181). Hillsdale, NJ: Erlbaum.

Hatfield, E., & Sprecher, S. (in press). *Mirror, mirror: The importance of looks in everyday life.* New York: SUNY Press.

Hatsukami, D., Eckert, E., Mitchell, J. E., & Pyle, R. (1984). Affective disorder and substance abuse in women with bulimia. *Psychological Medicine, 14,* 701–704.

Hatsukami, D. K., Mitchell, J. E., & Eckert, E. (1981). Eating disorders: A variant of mood disorders? *Psychiatric Clinics of North America, 7,* 349–365.

Hatsukami, D., Owen, P., Pyle, R., & Mitchell, J. (1982). Similarities and differences on the MMPI between women with bulimia and women with alcohol or drug abuse problems. *Addictive Behaviors, 7,* 435–439.

Havighurst, R. J. (1972). *Developmental tasks and education.* New York: McKay.

Hawkins, R. C. II, & Clement, P. F. (1980). Development and construct validations of a self-report measure of binge eating tendencies. *Addictive Behaviors, 5,* 219–226.

Hawkins, R. C. II, & Clement, P. F. (1984). Binge eating: Measurement problems and a conceptual model. In R. C. Hawkins II, W. J. Fremouw, & P. F. Clement (Eds.) *The binge-purge syndrome* (pp. 229–253). New York: Springer.

Hawkins, R. C., Jr., Turell, S., & Jackson, L. J. (1983). Desirable and undesirable masculine and feminine traits in relation to students' dietary tendencies and body image dissatisfaction. *Sex Roles, 9,* 705–724.

Heilman, M. E., & Saruwatari, L. R. (1979). When beauty is beastly: The effects of appearance and sex on evaluations of job applicants for managerial and non-managerial jobs. *Organizational Behavior and Human Performance, 23,* 360–372.

Helliovaara, M., & Aromaa, A. (1981). Parity and obesity. *Journal of Epidemiology and Community Health, 35,* 197–199.

Herman, C. P., & Mack, D. (1975). Restrained and unrestrained eating. *Journal of Personality, 43,* 647–660.

Herman, C. P., & Polivy, J. (1975). Anxiety, restraint, and eating behavior. *Journal of Abnormal Psychology, 84,* 666–672.

Herzog, D. (1982). Bulimia in the adolescent. *American Journal of Diseases of Children, 136,* 985–989.

Herzog, D. B., Norman, D. K., Gordon, C., & Pepose, M. (1984). Sexual conflict and eating disorders in 27 males. *American Journal of Psychiatry, 141,* 989–990.

Hill, J. P., & Lynch, M. E. (1983). The intensification of gender-related role expectations during early adolescence. In J. Brooks-Gunn & A. C. Petersen (Eds.), *Girls at puberty* (pp. 201–228). New York: Plenum Press.

Hill, J. P., Thiel, K. S., & Blyth, D. A. (1981). *Grade and gender differences in perceived intimacy with peers among seventh-to tenth-grade boys and girls.* Unpublished manuscript, Boys Town Center for the Study of Youth Development, Richmond, VA.

Holland, A. J., Hall, A., Murray, R., Russell, G. F. M., & Crisp, A. H. (1984). Anorexia nervosa: A study of 34 twin pairs and one set of triplets. *British Journal of Psychiatry, 145,* 414–419.

Hood, J., Moore, T. E., & Garner, D. M. (1982). Locus of control as a measure of ineffectiveness in anorexia nervosa. *Journal of Consulting and Clinical Psychology, 50,* 3–13.

Hovell, M. F., Mewborn, C. R., Randle, Y., & Fowler-Johnson, S. (1985). Risk of excess weight gain in university women: A three-year community controlled analysis. *Addictive Behaviors, 10,* 15–28.

Hudson, J. I., Laffer, P. S., & Pope, H. G., Jr. (1982). Bulimia related to affective disorder by family history and response to the dexamethasone suppression test. *American Journal of Psychiatry, 137,* 605–607.

Hudson. J. I., Pope, H. G., Jr., & Jonas, J. M. (1984). Treatment of bulimia with antidepressants: Theoretical considerations and clinical findings. In A. J. Stunkard & E. Stellar (Eds.), *Eating and its disorders* (pp. 259–273). New York: Raven Press.

Hudson, J. I., Pope, H. G., Jr., Jonas, J. M., Laffer, P. S., Hudson, M. S., & Melby, J. C. (1983). Hypothalamic-pituitary-adrenal axis hyperactivity in bulimia. *Psychiatry Research, 8,* 111–117.

Huon, G., & Brown. L. B. (1984). Psychological correlates of weight control among anorexia nervosa patients and normal girls. *British Journal of Medical Psychology, 57,* 61–66.

Hytten, F. E., & Leitch, I. (1971). *The physiology of human pregnancy.* Oxford: Blackwell Scientific Publications.

Jakobovits, C., Halstead, P., Kelley, L., Roe, D. A., & Young, C. M. (1977). Eating habits and nutrient intakes of college women over a thirty-year period. *Journal of the American Dietetic Association, 71,* 405–411.

Janda, L. H., O'Grady, K. E., & Barnhart, S. A. (1981). Effects of sexual attitudes and physical attractiveness on person perception of men and women. *Sex Roles, 7,* 189–199.

Johnson, C., & Flach, A. (1985). Family characteristics of 105 patients with bulimia. *America Journal of Psychiatry, 142,* 1321–1324.

Johnson, C. L., & Larson, R. (1982). Bulimia: An analysis of moods and behavior. *Psychosomatic Medicine, 44,* 341–353.

Johnson, C., Lewis, C., & Hagman, J. (1984). The syndrome of bulimia. *Psychiatric Clinics of North America, 7,* 247–274.

Johnson, C. L., Stuckey, M. R., Lewis, L. D., & Schwartz, D. M. (1982). Bulimia: A descriptive survey of 316 cases. *International Journal of Eating Disorders, 2,* 3–16.

Jones, M. C. (1965). Psychological correlates of somatic development. *Child Development, 36,* 899–911.

Joseph, A., Wood, J. K., & Goldberg, S. C. (1982). Determining populations at risk for developing anorexia nervosa based on selection of college major. *Psychiatry Research, 7,* 53–58.

Jourard, S. M., & Secord, P. F. (1955). Body-cathexis and the ideal female figure. *Journal of Abnormal and Social Psychology, 50,* 243–246.

Kagan, D. M., & Squires, R. L. (1985). Family cohesion, family adaptability, and eating behaviors among college students. *International Journal of Eating Disorders, 4,* 267–280.

Kashani, J. H., & Priesmeyer, M. (1983). Differences in depressive symptoms and depression among college students. *American Journal of Psychiatry, 140,* 1081–1082.

Katzman, M. A., & Wolchik, S. A. (1984). Bulimia and binge eating in college women: A comparison of personality and behavioral characteristics. *Journal of Consulting and Clinical Psychology, 52,* 423–428.

Katzman, M. A., Wolchik, S. A., & Braver, S. L. (1984). The prevalence of frequent binge eating and bulimia in a nonclinical sample. *International Journal of Eating Disorders, 3,* 53–62.

Kleinberg, S. (1980). *Alienated affections: Being gay in America.* New York: St. Martin's Press.

Kog, E., Vandereycken, W., & Vertommen, H. (in press). Towards verification of the psychosomatic family model. A pilot study of 10 families with an anorexia/bulimia patient. *International Journal of Eating Disorders.*

Kog, E., Vertommen, H., & DeGroote, T. (in press). Family interaction research in anorexia nervosa: The use and misuse of a self-report questionnaire. *International Journal of Family Psychiatry.*

Krebs, D., & Adinolfi, A. A. (1975). Physical attractiveness, social relations, and personality style. *Journal of Personality and Social Psychology, 31,* 245–253.

Kurtz, R. M. (1969). Sex differences and variations in body attitudes. *Journal of Consulting and Clinical Psychology, 33,* 625–629.

Lacey, J. H. (1982). The bulimic syndrome at normal body weight: Reflections on pathogenesis and clinical features. *International Journal of Eating Disorders, 2,* 59–66.

Lakoff, R. T., & Scherr, R. L. (1984). *Face value: The politics of beauty.* Boston: Routledge & Kegan Paul.

Leon, G. R., Carroll, K., Chernyk, B., & Finn, S. (1985). Binge eating and associated habit patterns within college student and identified bulimic populations. *International Journal of Eating Disorders, 4,* 43–57.

Leon, G. R., Lucas, A. R., Colligan, R. C., Ferdinande, R. J., & Kamp, J. (1985). Sexual, body-image, and personality attitudes in anorexia nervosa. *Journal of Abnormal Child Psychology, 13,* 245–258.

Lerner, R. M., Karabenick, S. A., & Stuart, J. L. (1973). Relations among physical attractiveness, body attitudes, and self-concept in male and female college students. *Journal of Psychology, 85,* 119–129.

Lerner, R. M., Orlos, J. B., & Knapp, J. R. (1976). Physical attractiveness, physical effectiveness and self-concept in late adolescents. *Adolescence, 11,* 313–326.

Levinson, D. J., Darrow, C. N., Klein, E. B., Levinson, M. H., & McKee, B. (1978). *The seasons of a man's life.* New York: Knopf.

Lewis, C. E., & Lewis, N. A. (1974). The impact of television commercials on health-related beliefs and behavior in children. *Pediatrics, 53,* 431–435.

Loro, A. D. (1984). Binge eating: A cognitive-behavioral treatment approach. In R. C. Hawkins II, W. J. Fremouw, & P. F. Clements (Eds.), *The binge-purge syndrome* (pp. 183–210). New York: Springer.

Loro, A. D., & Orleans, C. S. (1981). Binge eating in obesity: Preliminary findings and guidelines for behavioral analysis and treatment. *Addictive Behaviors, 6,* 155–166.

Mahoney, E. R. (1974). Body-cathexis and self-esteem: Importance of subjective importance. *Journal of Psychology, 88,* 27–30.

Mann, A. H., Wakeling, A., Wood, K., Monck, E., Dobbs, R., & Szmukler, G. (1983). Screening for abnormal eating attitudes and psychiatric morbidity in an unselected population of 15-year old schoolgirls. *Psychological Medicine, 13,* 573–580.

Marino, D. D., & King, J. C. (1980). Nutritional concerns during adolescence. *Pediatric Clinics of North America, 27,* 125–139.

Martin, M., & Walter, R. (1982). Korperselbstbild und neurotizismus bei kindern und jugendlichen [Body image and neuroticism in children and adolescents]. *Praxis der Kinderpsychologie und Kinderpsychiatrie, 31,* 213–218.

Mazel, J. (1981). *The Beverly Hills diet.* New York: Macmillan.

McGuire, W. J., & McGuire, C. V. (1982). Significant others in self-space: Sex differences and developmental trends in the social self. In J. Suls (Ed.), *Social psychological perspectives on the self* (pp. 71–96). Hillsdale, NJ: Erlbaum.

McKinlay, S., & Jeffreys, M. (1974). The menopausal syndrome. *British Journal of Preventive and Social Medicine, 28,* 108–115.

Medlund, P., Cederlof, R., Floderus-Myrhed, B., Friberg, L., & Sorensen, S. (1976). A new Swedish Twin Registry. *Acta Medica Scandinavica* (Suppl. 600).

Metropolitan Life Foundation. (1983). *Statistical Bulletin, 64,* 2–9.

Miller, J. B. (1976). *Toward a new psychology of women.* Boston, MA: Beacon Press.

Miller, W. H., Faust, I. M., Goldberger, A. C., & Hirsch, J. (1983). Effects of severe long-term food deprivation and refeeding on adipose tissue cells in the rat. *American Journal of Physiology, 245,* E74–E80.

Minuchin, S., Rosman, B. L., & Baker, L. (1978). *Psychosomatic families: Anorexia nervosa in context.* Cambridge, MA: Harvard University Press.

Mishkind, M. E., Rodin, J., Silberstein, L. R., & Striegel-Moore, R. H. (in press). The embodiment of masculinity: Cultural, psychological, and behavioral dimensions [Special issue on men's studies]. *American Behavioral Scientist.*

Mitchell, J. E., Hatsukami, D., Eckert, E. D., & Pyle, R. L. (1985). Characteristics of 275 patients with bulimia. *American Journal of Psychiatry, 142,* 482–485.

Moss, R. A., Jennings, G., McFarland, J. H., & Carter, P. (1984). The prevalence of binge eating, vomiting, and weight fear in a female high school population. *Journal of Family Practice, 18,* 313–320.

National Research Council, Food and Nutrition Board, Committee on Maternal Nutrition. National Research Council. (1970). *Maternal nutrition and the course of pregnancy.* Washington, DC: National Academy of Sciences.

Nelsen, E. A., & Rosenbaum, E. (1972). Language patterns within the youth subculture: Development of slang vocabularies. *Merrill-Palmer Quarterly, 18,* 273–285.

Neugarten, B. L. (1969). Continuities and discontinuities of psychological issues into adult life. *Human Development, 12,* 121–130.

Neugarten, B. L. (1970). Dynamics of transition of middle age to old age: Adaptation and the life cycle. *Journal of Geriatric Psychiatry, 41,* 71–87.

Neugarten, B. L. (1972). Personality and aging process. *Gerontologist, 12,* 9.

Nielsen, A. C. (1979). Who is dieting and why? Chicago, IL: Nielsen Company, Research Department.

Norman, D. K., & Herzog, D. B. (1983). Bulimia, anorexia nervosa, and anorexia nervosa with bulimia. *International Journal of Eating Disorders, 2,* 43–52.

Nowlin, N. (1983). Anorexia nervosa in twins: Case report and review. *Journal of Clinical Psychiatry, 44,* 101–105.

Nylander, J. (1971). The feeling of being fat and dieting in a school population: Epidemiologic interview investigation. *Acta Sociomedica Scandinavica, 3,* 17–26.

Oakley, A. (1972). *Sex, gender and society.* New York: Harper & Row.

Orleans, C. T., & Barnett, L. R. (1984). Bulimarexia: Guidelines for behavioral assessment and treatment. In R. C. Hawkins II, W. J. Fremouw, & P. F. Clement (Eds.), *The binge-purge syndrome* (pp. 144–182). New York: Springer.

Parizkowa, J. (1973). Body composition and exercise during growth and development. In G. L.

Rarick (Ed.), *Physical activity: Human growth and development* (pp. 98–124). New York: Academic Press.

Peskin, H. (1973). Influence of the developmental schedule of puberty on learning and ego functioning. *Journal of Youth and Adolescence, 2,* 273–290.

Pitkin, R. M. (1976). Nutritional support in obstetrics and gynecology. *Clinical Obstetrics and Gynecology, 19,* 489–513.

Polivy, J., & Herman, C. P. (1985). Dieting and binging: A causal analysis. *American Psychologist, 40,* 193–201.

Pope, H. G., Jr., Hudson, J. I., & Jonas, J. M. (1983). Antidepressant treatment of bulimia: Preliminary experience and practical recommendations. *Journal of Clinical Psychopharmacology, 3,* 274–281.

Pope, H. G., Jr., Hudson, J. I., Yurgelun-Todd, D., & Hudson, M. S. (1984). Prevalence of anorexia nervosa and bulimia in three student populations. *International Journal of Eating Disorder, 3,* 45–51.

Pyle, R. L., Mitchell, J. E., & Eckert, E. D. (1981). Bulimia: A report of 34 cases. *Journal of Clinical Psychiatry, 42,* 60–64.

Pyle, R. L., Mitchell, J. E., Eckert, E. D., Halvorson, P. A., Neuman, P. A., & Goff, G. M. (1983). The incidence of bulimia in freshman college students. *International Journal of Eating Disorders, 2,* 75–85.

Rabkin, J. G., Charles, E., & Kass, F. C. (1983). Hypertension and DSM-III depression in psychiatric outpatients. *American Journal of Psychiatry, 140,* 1072–1074.

Rimm, A. A., & White, P. L. (1979). Obesity: Its risks and hazards. In G. A. Bray (Ed.), *Obesity in America* (pp. 103–124). Washington, DC: Department of Health, Education, and Welfare.

Rodin, J. (1981). The current status of the internal–external obesity hypothesis: What went wrong. *American Psychologist, 1,* 343–348.

Rodin, J. (1985, June 30). *Yale health and patterns of living study: A longitudinal study on health, stress, and coping in the elderly.* Unpublished progress report. Yale University, New Haven, CT.

Rodin, J., Silberstein, L. R., & Striegel-Moore, R. H. (1985). Women and weight: A normative discontent. In T. B. Sonderegger (Ed.), *Nebraska symposium on motivation: Vol. 32. Psychology and gender* (pp. 267–307). Lincoln: University of Nebraska Press.

Rodin, J., Striegel-Moore, R. H., & Silberstein, L. R. (1985, July). *A prospective study of bulimia among college students on three U.S. campuses.* First unpublished progress report. Yale University, New Haven, CT.

Rose, G. A., & Williams, R. T. (1961). Metabolic studies on large and small eaters. *British Journal of Nutrition, 15,* 1–9.

Rosenbaum, M. (1979). The changing body image of the adolescent girl. In M. Sugar (Ed.), *Female adolescent development* (pp. 234–252). New York: Brunner/Mazel.

Rosenberg, F. R., & Simmons, R. G. (1975). Sex differences in the self-concept during adolescence. *Sex Roles, 1,* 147–160.

Rost, W., Neuhaus, M., & Florin, I. (1982). Bulimia nervosa: Sex role attitude, sex role behavior, and sex role-related locus of control in bulimiarexic women. *Journal of Psychosomatic Research, 26,* 403–408.

Rudofsky, B. (1971). *The unfashionable human body.* New York: Doubleday.

Russell, G. (1979). Bulimia nervosa: An ominous variant of anorexia nervosa. *Psychological Medicine, 9,* 429–448.

Schwartz, D. M., Thompson, M. G., & Johnson, C. L. (1981). Anorexia nervosa and bulimia: The socio-cultural context. *International Journal of Eating Disorders, 1,* 20–36.

Schwartz, L. A., & Markham, W. T. (1985). Sex stereotyping in children's toy advertisements. *Sex Roles, 12,* 157–170.

Schwartz, R. C. (1982). Bulimia and family therapy: A case study. *International Journal of Eating Disorders, 2,* 75–82.

Schwartz, R. C., Barrett, M. J., & Saba, G. (1985). Family therapy for bulimia. In D. M. Garner & P. E. Garfinkel (Eds.), *Handbook of psychotherapy for anorexia nervosa and bulimia* (pp. 280–307). New York: Guilford.

Secord, P. F., & Jourard, S. M. (1953). The appraisal of body-cathexis: Body-cathexis and the self. *Journal of Consulting Psychology, 17,* 343–347.

Seiden, A. M. (1976). Sex roles, sexuality and the adolescent peer group. *Adolescent Psychiatry, 4,* 211–225.

Selvini-Palazzoli, M. (1978). *Self-starvation: From individuation to family therapy in the treatment of anorexia nervosa.* New York: Aronson.

Shontz, F. C. (1963). Some characteristics of body size estimation. *Perceptual and Motor Skills, 16,* 665–671.

Sights, J. R., & Richards, H. C. (1984). Parents of bulimic women. *International Journal of Eating Disorders, 3,* 3–13.

Simmons, R. G., Blyth, D. A., & McKinney, K. L. (1983). The social and psychological effects of puberty on white females. In J. Brooks-Gunn & A. C. Petersen (Eds.), *Girls at puberty* (pp. 229–278). New York: Plenum Press.

Simmons, R. G., & Rosenberg, F. (1975). Sex, sex roles, and self-image. *Journal of Youth and Adolescence, 4,* 229–258.

Slade, P. (1982). Towards a functional analysis of anorexia nervosa and bulimia nervosa. *British Journal of Clinical Psychology, 21,* 167–179.

Slater, E., & Cowie, V. (1971). *The genesis of mental illness.* London: Oxford University Press.

Smith, N. J. (1980). Excessive weight loss and food aversion in athletes simulating anorexia nervosa. *Pediatrics, 66,* 139–142.

Snow, J. T., & Harris, M. B. (1985). *An analysis of weight and diet content in five women's interest magazines.* Unpublished manuscript, University of New Mexico, Albuquerque.

Society of Actuaries. (1959). *Build and blood pressure study.* Washington, DC: Author.

Society of Actuaries and Association of Life Insurance Medical Directors of America. (1979). *Build and blood pressure study.* Chicago, IL: Author.

Sontag, S. (1972). The double standard of aging. *Saturday Review, 54,* 29–38.

Spence, J. T. (1985). Gender identity and its implications for the concept of masculinity and femininity. In T. B. Sonderegger (Ed.), *Nebraska Symposium on Motivation: Vol. 32. Psychology and gender* (pp. 59–95). Lincoln: University of Nebraska Press.

Spence, J. T., & Helmreich, R. L. (1978). Gender, sex roles, and the psychological dimensions of masculinity and femininity. In J. T. Spence & R. L. Helmreich, *Masculinity and femininity* (pp. 3–18). Austin: University of Texas Press.

Squire, S. (1983). *The slender balance: Causes and cures for bulimia, anorexia, and the weight-loss/weight-gain seesaw.* New York: Putnam.

Steele, C. I. (1980). Weight loss among teenage girls: An adolescent crisis. *Adolescence, 15,* 823–829.

Steiner-Adair, K. (1986). The body politic: Normal female adolescent development and the development of eating disorders. *Journal of the American Academy of Psychoanalysis, 14,* 95–114.

Stern, S. L., Dixon, K. N., Nemzer, E., Lake, M. D., Samsone, R. A., Smeltzer, D. J., Lantz, S., & Scrier, S. S. (1984). Affective disorder in the families of women with normal weight bulimia. *American Journal of Psychiatry, 141,* 1224–1227.

Story, I. (1979). Factors associated with more positive body self-concepts in preschool-children. *Journal of Social Psychology, 108,* 49–56.

Striegel-Moore, R. H., McAvay, G., & Rodin, J. (1984, September). *Predictors of attitudes toward body weight and eating in women.* Paper presented at the meeting of the European Association for Behavior Therapy, Brussels, Belgium.

Striegel-Moore, R. H., McAvay, G., & Rodin, J. (in press). Psychological and behavioral correlates of feeling fat in women. *International Journal of Eating Disorders.*

Striegel-Moore, F. H., Silberstein, L. R., & Rodin, J. (1985a, March). *Psychological and behavioral correlates of binge eating: A comparison of bulimic clients and normal control subjects.* Unpublished manuscript, Yale University, New Haven, CT.

Striegel-Moore, R. H., Silberstein, L. R., & Rodin, J. (1985b, August). *The relationship between femininity/masculinity, body dissatisfaction and bulimia.* Paper presented at the meeting of the American Psychological Association, Los Angeles, CA.

Strober, M. (1981). The significance of bulimia in juvenile anorexia nervosa: An exploration of possible etiological factors. *International Journal of Eating Disorders, 1,* 28–43.

Strober, M. (1983, May). *Familial depression in anorexia nervosa.* Paper presented at the meeting of the American Psychiatric Association, New York, NY.

Strober, M. (1984). Stressful life events associated with bulimia in anorexia nervosa. *International Journal of Eating Disorders, 3,* 2–16.

Strober, M., Morrell, W., Burroughs, J., Salkin, B., & Jacobs, C. (1985). A controlled family study of anorexia nervosa. *Journal of Psychiatric Research, 19,* 239–246.

Strober, M., Salkin, B., Burroughs, J., & Morrell, W. (1982). Validity of the bulimia-restrictor distinction in anorexia nervosa. *Journal of Nervous and Mental Disease, 170,* 345–351.

Stroebe, W., Insko, C. A., Thompson, V. D., & Layton, B. D. (1971). Effects of physical attractiveness, attitude similarity, and sex on various aspects of interpersonal attraction. *Journal of Personality and Social Psychology, 18,* 79–91.

Stunkard, A. J., Foch, T. T., & Hrubec, Z. (1985). *A twin study of human obesity.* Unpublished manuscript, University of Pennsylvania, Philadelphia.

Stunkard, A. J., Sorensen, T. I. A., Hanis, C., Teasdale, T. W., Chakraborty, R., Schull, W. J., & Schulsinger, F. (1985). *An adoption study of human obesity.* Unpublished manuscript, University of Pennsylvania, Philadelphia.

Szmukler, G. L. (1982). Anorexia-nervosa: Its entity as an illness and its treatment. *Pharmacology and Therapeutics, 16,* 431–446.

Tanner, J. M. (1978). *Foetus into man: Physical growth from conception to maturity.* Cambridge, MA: Harvard University Press.

Tobin-Richards, M. H., Boxer, A. M., & Petersen, A. C. (1983). The psychological significance of pubertal change. Sex differences in perceptions of self during early adolescence. In J. Brooks-Gunn & A. C. Petersen (Eds.), *Girls at puberty* (pp. 127–154). New York: Plenum Press.

Unger, R. K. (1985). Personal appearance and social control. In M. Safir, M. Mednick, I. Dafna, & J. Bernard (Eds.), *Woman's worlds: From the new scholarship* (pp. 142–151). New York: Praeger.

Vandereyken, W., & Pierloot, R. (1981). Anorexia nervosa in twins. *Psychotherapy and Psychosomatics, 35,* 55–63.

Vanfraechem, J. H. P., & Vanfraechem-Raway, R. (1978). The influence of training upon physiological and psychological parameters in young athletes. *Journal of Sports Medicine, 18,* 175–182.

Vincent, L. M. (1979). *Competing with the Sylph: Dancers and the pursuit of the ideal body form.* New York: Andrews & McMeel.

Wagman, M. (1967). Sex differences in types of daydreams. *Journal of Personality and Social Psychology, 3,* 329–332.

Walks, D., Lavan, M., Presta, E., Yang, M. U., & Bjorntorp, P. (1983). Refeeding after fasting in the rat: Effects of dietary-induced obesity on energy balance regulation. *American Journal of Clinical Nutrition, 37,* 387–395.

Wallach, J. D., & Lowenkopf, E. L. (1984). Five bulimic women. MMPI, Rorschach, and TAT characteristics. *International Journal of Eating Disorders, 3,* 53–66.

Walsh, B. T., Roose, S. P., Glassman, A. H., Gladis, M., & Sadik, C. (1985). Bulimia and depression. *Psychosomatic Medicine, 47,* 123–131.

Walster, E., Aronson, V., Abrahams, D., & Rottmann, L. (1966). Importance of physical attractiveness in dating behavior. *Journal of Personality and Social Psychology, 4,* 508–516.

Wardle, J. (1980). Dietary restraint and binge eating. *Behavioral Analysis and Modification, 4,* 201–209.

Wessel, J. A., Ufer, A., Van Huss, W. D., & Cederquist, D. (1963). Age trends of various components of body composition and functional characteristics in women aged 20–69 years. *Annals of the New York Academy of Sciences, 110,* 608–622.

Westerterp, K. (1977). How rats economize—energy loss in starvation. *Physiological Zoology, 80,* 331–362.

Williamson, D. A., Kelley, M. L., Davis, C. J., Ruggiero, L., & Blouin, D. C. (1985). Psychopathology of eating disorders: A controlled comparison of bulimic, obese, and normal subjects. *Journal of Consulting and Clinical Psychology, 53,* 161–166.

Wilson, G. T. (1984). Toward the understanding and treatment of binge eating. In R. C. Hawkins II, W. J. Fremouw, & P. F. Clement (Eds.), *The binge-purge syndrome* (pp. 264–289). New York: Springer.

Wittig, M. A. (1983). Sex role development in early adolescence. *Theory Into Practice, 22,* 105–111.

Wolf, E., & Crowther, J. H. (1983). Personality and eating habit variables as predictors of severity of binge eating and weight. *Addictive Behaviors, 8,* 355–344.

Women on Words and Images. (1972). *Dick and Jane as victims: Sex stereotyping in children's readers.* (Available from Women on Words and Images, Box 2163, Princeton, NJ 08540)

Wooley, O. W., Wooley, S. C., & Dyrenforth, S. R. (1979). Obesity and women—II. A neglected feminist topic. *Women Studies International Quarterly, 2,* 81–89.

Wooley, S. C., & Wooley, O. W. (1981). Overeating as substance abuse. *Advances in Substance Abuse, 2,* 41–67.

Wooley, S., & Wooley, O. W. (1982). The Beverly Hills eating disorder: The mass marketing of anorexia nervosa. *International Journal of Eating Disorders, 1,* 57–69.

Wooley, S. C., & Wooley, O. W. (1984, February). Feeling fat in a thin society. *Glamour,* 198–252.

Wooley, S. C., & Wooley, O. W. (1985). Intensive outpatient and residential treatment for bulimia. In D. M. Garner & P. E. Garfinkel (Eds.), *Handbook of psychotherapy for anorexia nervosa and bulimia* (pp. 391–430). New York: Guilford.

Yager, J. (1982). Family issues in the pathogenesis of anorexia nervosa. *Psychosomatic Medicine, 44,* 43–60.

Yager, J., Landsverk, J., Lee-Benner, K., & Johnson, C. (1985). *The continuum of eating disorders: An examination of diagnostic concerns based on a national survey.* Unpublished manuscript, Neuropsychiatric Institute, University of California, Los Angeles.

Yager, J., & Strober, M. (1985). Family aspects of eating disorders. In A. Francis & R. Hales (Eds.), *Annual review of psychiatry,* (Vol. 4, pp. 481–502). Washington, DC: American Psychiatric Press.

Yates, A., Leehey, K., & Shisslak, C. M. (1983). Running—An analogue of anorexia? *New England Journal of Medicine, 308,* 251–255.

Young, C. M., Blondin, J., Tensuan, R., & Fryer, J. H. (1963). Body composition studies of "older" women, thirty–seventy years of age. *Annals of the New York Academy of Science, 110,* 589–607.

Young, C. M., Martin, M. E. K, Chihan, M., McCarthy, M., Mannielo, M. J., Harmuth, E. H., & Fryer, J. H. (1961). Body composition of young women: Some preliminary findings. *Journal of the American Dietetic Association, 38,* 332–340.

Chapter Thirty-Three

The Woman-Man Relationship
Impasses and Possibilities

Stephen J. Bergman and Janet Surrey

As the work of the Stone Center (Jordan, Kaplan, Miller, Stiver, & Surrey, 1991), Gilligan (1982, 1989), and others has evolved over the past decade, we have begun to appreciate the different gender-related pathways of psychological development. The stage is set for a crucial dialogue to begin—for men and women to come together to describe and explore the impact of these differences and to struggle not only for equality but for mutuality in relationship. By mutual relationship we refer to what Miller (1986) and Surrey (1985) have described as growth-fostering relationships characterized by mutual engagement, mutual empathy, and mutual empowerment.

As old systems of relationship break down, new visions are called for. The historical roots of the male-female relationship are thousands of years old and are embedded in a patriarchal system which has shaped our institutions, our thinking, and the patterning of our relationships. As we work toward change, we must recognize the weight and depth of this history. Clinically as well as culturally, we see many couples struggling with very similar relational impasses. It is essential for both women and men to move out of a sense of personal deficiency, pathology, or blame—as we are *all* called on to participate in this cultural transformation of the dynamics of relationship. So far there have not been adequate opportunities to work *together* on these challenges.

In an effort to meet this need, we led our first gender workshop in 1988, "New Visions of the Male-Female Relationship: Creating Mutuality." Since then, we have conducted this workshop more than twenty times, and its evolution has involved almost eight hundred people, including men and women clinicians, college and medical students, and couples, in Holland, Istanbul, Turkey, and four-year-olds in an American preschool. Usually the men and women do *not* come in couples, except in workshops designed explicitly for couples. The workshops are designed for specific periods of time, from three hours to three days. Almost without exception, it is the

Stephen J. Bergman & Janet Surrey, "The Woman-Man Relationship: Impasses and Possibilities." *Work in Progress, No. 55,* Wellesley, MA: Stone Center Working Paper Series. © 1992 by the Stone Center Working Paper Series. Reprinted with permission.

first time in their lives that participants have come together with members of the other gender for the purpose of exploring gender differences and relationships.

In this paper we'd like to describe what happens in these workshops and what we are learning about how women and men struggle for mutuality. We believe that the workshops are a microcosm of the larger culture, suggesting contexts for facilitating positive growth and change in relationships. We will also discuss implications and applications for clinical work with individuals and couples.

The workshops were originally designed on the model of relational mutuality—namely, that healthy, growth-enhancing relationships are built on experiences of mutual engagement, mutual empathy, mutual authenticity, and mutual empowerment. In designing the workshops, we were also influenced by political workshops created at the Center for Psychological Study in the Nuclear Age in Cambridge, Massachusetts, to foster Soviet-American relationships. In those workshops *intergroup dialogue* was a central facilitating structure. Constructive conflict and *struggling with difference* are inevitable in relationships. They stimulate growth when the creative tension of *staying with the differences* is supported by the relational context. What Miller has called "waging good conflict" (1976) can lead to growth and enlargement of relationships. The gender workshops are designed to bring out prototypical conflicts and impasses between men and women, and then to offer structures and strategies for breaking through the impasses and for building connection.

Our work up to his point has been primarily with white, middle-class, highly educated men and women, although in most workshops there are members of various ages, sexual preference, race, class, and ethnicity, who have spoken up to represent their different perspectives. We are hoping to find ways to explore more explicitly the impact of diversity on the dynamics of woman-man relationships. The men who have come to these workshops represent a highly select sample—those who will risk doing such work.

Riane Eisler, in her book *The Chalice and the Blade* (1987), calls for the creation of a new form of relationship—moving beyond the power-over, "dominator" model to what she calls the new "partnership" model, which finds its roots in the pre–Bronze Age, prepatriarchal cultures she has studied. Eisler views this evolution as part of a whole paradigm shift, corresponding to new models of science, physics, and biology, as well as shifts toward global awareness.

In our workshops, we emphasize the qualities of creativity which contribute to mutuality. Moving beyond old models of self-development as the basis for healthy relationship, such as consolidating identity, healthy narcissism, assertiveness, or firm ego boundaries—we emphasize the relational and creative qualities which foster growth-enhancing connection. To name a few: curiosity, flexibility, spontaneity, freedom of movement, patience, persistence, humility, playfulness, humor, and also intuition, risk taking, trying out new perspectives and configurations, paradoxical thinking, holding opposites simultaneously, knowing when to hold and when to let go, and openness to change.

The importance of creativity has not yet been fully recognized in the study of human relationships. Like most psychological characteristics, it has been studied primarily in traditionally male realms—the arts and sciences—and not yet in its fundamental forms in daily life and relationships, where women's creativity has often gone unrecognized.

The Workshop

The workshop begins with a discussion of the larger cultural context, and how important we feel it is for peacemaking and global survival. We discuss the range and limits of our own particular experience, and how issues of class, race, age, and heterosexual orientation make significant differences. We also take up the issue of stereotyping, emphasizing that we are working with *group differences* between men and women, cognizant that these will not describe any particular man or woman. Recognizing our own particularities, we begin to articulate a relational perspective on women's and men's psychological development, assuming a basic underlying motive and desire for human connection in both groups. Janet describes the Stone Center relational model of development and the paradigm shift that we will be using in the workshop. This involves a complex model, encompassing a sense of self but also a sense of the other and a sense of relationship, stressing what Stern calls "self-with-other" experiences (1985). Healthy connection implies an awareness of and care for self, other, and the relationship, and none of these can be sacrificed in the search for mutuality. Janet also describes the connections, disconnections, and violations that shape women's experience in this culture, including women's carrying the one-sided responsibility for the care and maintenance of relationships.

Steve then speaks about reframing men's psychological development from this same relational perspective (Bergman, 1991) and describes "male relational dread," a man's sense, in a close relationship, that he is not enough and therefore must withdraw or attack. As one man described it: "When my wife says 'I love you,' my back starts to sweat." It is essential to provide a common language—conflict, connection, mutuality, empathy, power and dread are named and defined and can then be used as the basis for communication throughout the workshop.

In the second phase of the workshop, men and women are asked to go into separate rooms to answer a prepared questionnaire. Then, breaking each larger gender group into smaller groups of three or four, participants are asked to respond to three questions, with one person recording each small group's answers.

The three questions are:

1. Name three strengths the other gender group brings to relationship.
2. What do you most want to understand about the other gender group?
3. What do you most want the other gender group to understand about you?

The rationale for this is to give each gender group the opportunity to give voice to its particular experience and to stimulate respect, curiosity, interest, and empathy for the other group. The answers to these questions later become the basis for the intergroup dialogue.

When the genders separate for the first time to answer the questions, there is a palpable sense of relief—how much easier it is for members of both genders to be with their own!

The women easily form small groups and seek a group process to answer the questions. They readily engage with each other, and Janet observes the clear relational energies and responsive movements, verbal and nonverbal—there is much hand waving and head nodding—all around the room.

The men, while relieved to be with each other away from the women, begin more slowly, starting with jokes and sarcastic banter, often about having to be there. Many have begun the workshop by holding themselves apart, assuming a critical, contemptuous, or bored stance. Actually, many of the men have been brought under some duress by women—as one said, "dragged kicking and screaming." However when they get with the other men, they become enlivened and energetic. Filling out the questionnaire in the small group, frequently each man will first write down his *own* list of answers in silence and then join in compiling his list with other individual lists.

Next, all the women come together into one large group with Janet, and the men with Steve, to share their responses with each other and with each of us. Typically, a strong sense of connection between the women evolves quickly. Often the women talk about how much easier it is to be with other women than in a *mixed* group, how much safer and more confident they feel. They speak of how much anxiety and attention go toward monitoring the men's responses.

The men, when they get together in one large group, are often surprised at how similar their individual responses to the questions are. Hearing that other men share the same thoughts and feelings in their relationships with women is a tremendously important step and helps the men to feel accepted and validated by other men for doing this work—what one man jokingly referred to as "the wimp-work of relation-ship." This men's group eventually becomes energized and cohesive.

We have found that this same-gender group experience is a vitally necessary precursor to the next phase. Janet and the other women are always amazed at the difference in the men when they come back into the mixed gender group, after being together in the men's group: they are no longer stiff or holding back, but energized and curious, and, as Janet once said, "looking so much more *dimensional.*"

Men's Answers to Question 1

"Name three strengths the other gender group brings to relationship." This question is always the *easiest* for the men to answer. Some of the men's answers about women are: nurturance; capacity for feeling; sensitivity; speaking emotional truth; realness; self-revealing; interest in working on relationships; courage to raise issues; ability to deal with more than one thing at a time; capacity to ask for support; seeing both sides of a situation; warmth; tenderness; skill at noncompetitive interaction; women are the "waker-uppers" in relationship; women have more patience with children.

Women's Answers to Question 1

This, the easiest question for the men, is inevitably the most *difficult* question for the women. (Some groups have said, "None.") It is difficult because the women soon realize that some quality of men—say, "objectivity"—may be a strength or not, depending on whether or not it is in the service of the relationship, that is, it depends on "the relational context." Here are some of the women's answers about men's strengths: caretakers; deep loyalties, relationship through action and projects; lifting heavy objects; rational thinking; focusing on one thing at a time; honesty; directness; can let things go and move on; breadwinners; protectors; know how to deal with fear; alliance builders; not so overwhelmed by feelings; strategic; product makers; purposeful; stabilizers of the relationship; killing spiders; their sex-drive; they make us feel frisky about sex; they have internal heaters at night.

Men's Answers to Question 2

"What do you most want to understand about the other gender group?" This question is invariably the *hardest* for the men. The reasons for this are multiple. Women are usually more forthcoming about their experiences, so men have less to ask about. Also, men have been trained away from a curious, open, empathic stance about others and often are concerned that if they ask questions, they won't know how to deal with the emotions stirred up and unleashed. For many men, opening up a connection by asking questions about a woman's experience feels dangerous. As one man said, "I may get caught in an emotional bog"; another, "an emotional swamp." (This "wetland" imagery is quite common.) Men's questions tend to be about women's anger and what women's relational processes are like: "What are you so angry about? What do you want from me? Why do you expand your processes *ad infinitum?* When you're with your friends, how do you know when to end a conversation?—do you ever actually get anywhere? What is it like to be oppressed? How do you come to personalize relational failure to such a degree? What supports you? What is it like to have your cyclical bodily functions? Why is the sharing of feelings so important? How can your emotions be so fluid? How can you do three things at once? Why do you fake orgasm? How to understand your sensitivity to subtle cues, verbal and nonverbal? How do you stay with your feelings so well? How do you care so much without losing your self? What's this intense need in a relationship? Why do women tend to tolerate men's behavior? What's it like to have babies?"

Women's Answers to Question 2

This, the hardest question for men to answer, is invariably the *easiest* for the women, who have many, many questions. One woman answered, "Everything! I've been waiting my whole life to hear this!" The questions women ask of men center on men's fears and vulnerabilities and the effort to understand men's emotional and relational life: "What are men's real fears? Why is it so hard to talk about relationships? How can you disconnect actions from emotions, how can you have sex without being emotionally involved? Why the urgency for sex? What is the burden of needing to be successful? What moves you deeply? Do men feel? If so, how and what? What do sports really mean? What do jokes really mean? What helps men overcome their experience of dread? Why won't men go to doctors? Why won't men stop and ask directions? What are you so afraid of in relationships? Why do you have trouble listening? What is the most effective way to teach the harms of patriarchy? How can we engage men in dialogue? What goes on between men that you don't want women to know about? What is it between sons and their mothers? What happens between receiving a message and sending back your response? How can you put yourself first so much of the time? What would it take to get men to become relational without major bloodletting? What's it like to live in a man's body?"

As the women and men return from their separate groups, we ask them to sit on opposite sides of the room. At this point, there is a lot of anxiety and often anger from the men, who begin to complain about the separation—"in a workshop on relationship you shouldn't separate us!"—and often to question our competence as leaders.

We asked one man, who seemed terribly anxious, what was wrong. He said, "I'm afraid that *something might happen!*"

The women are often leaning forward in their chairs, curious, expectant, and one woman replied, "I'm *hoping* that something might happen!' "

The men experience the face-to-face setup as an invitation to confrontation, possibly leading to disconnection and maybe even physical withdrawal or violence. Compared to being in the men's group, this is a kind of living hell. As one highly motivated, caring man said, with a mournful sigh, "It was so much easier the old way. You didn't have to work so hard."

This intergroup encounter is the most powerful and poignant time in the workshop. Whether we work for two hours or eight hours (depending on the time available), certain predictable impasses and breakthroughs occur.

Almost invariably, the women will ask the men to go first and to read their responses to Question 1, three strengths women bring to relationship. One small group of men will answer hesitatingly, the women will respond enthusiastically, and then ask more questions, wanting to go deeper. At this, the men will experience the women's questions as (to use the language of three different groups) "bullets," "arrows," or "darts" and will start to feel judged as inadequate, under attack, and criticized. Dread is generated, and the men withdraw and fall silent. This stimulates the *Dread/Anger Impasse:* the men retreat, the women begin to get angry and feel abandoned and misunderstood, and then the men either withdraw further or attack the women for being angry. Things stop, dead. After a while the women will read their responses to Question 1, often beginning by saying, "We found it really *difficult* to answer this question." Since this is the easiest question for the men, the men feel *more* criticized, often saying, "You couldn't even come up with *three* strengths?" The women reply, "It depends on how they're used." The men: "You can't even name three without *qualifying* them?" In this hostile atmosphere the men find it hard to grasp that a strength may also be a weakness, *depending on how it's used in relation-*

ship, the relational context. This is a consistent gender difference, often invisible to men. Stuck in the impasse, there follow attempts to avoid further conflict. One man suggested to a woman that she go and listen to herself alone with a tape recorder until she modified her anger to a level to which he could respond. (An example of how women are supposed to go off, get therapy, or read self-help books to change themselves to fix the relationship.) This comment made the impasse worse.

What Is a Relational Impasse?

An *impasse* occurs when a relationship is stuck, static, unmoving, with a sense that it may never move again. Things go dead, each participant retreats into his or her self. Everyone feels the relational space close down, and the closing down closes down more space, and a negative spiral is created; increased dread leads to increased anger leads to increased dread. Things become more polarized, and often fall into more gender-stereotypical behavior, resulting in disconnection and the loss of the possibility not only of contact but also of *working with the conflict.* An impasse Is *relational* in the sense that it cannot reside only in one person or the other, but *in the process* between them — it's not a matter of him or her, but how they are interacting. While there may be a transferential component, the impasse is not mainly transferential, but rather the result of one relational style meeting another, quite different one — the result of everyone's learnings over many years, about what happens in relationship. Yet in the workshops, when individuals and couples start to see that these group impasses are clearly recognizable in their own lives, there is a sense of relief. In our workshops for couples, people often are astonished to hear other couples using their exact same words or phrases.

Another striking gender difference, also mostly invisible to men, is the way that there is a continuous flow toward the group focusing on the *men's* experience. Partly this is because the women keep asking more questions, partly it is because the men do not. Over and over, like the ballast of a ship, the attention tips to what's going on with the men. If you remember, Question 2 — "What do you most want to understand about the other gender?" — was quite difficult for the men to respond to. Again and again we see how, in the end, the problem of mutuality is not only the men's inability to talk about their experience in relationship, but also their disinclination to explore and their difficulty in searching out the women's experience, in asking questions that would open up the relationship, what Jordan, Kaplan, Miller, Stiver, and Surrey (1991) have called "approaches to empathy" or "relational intersubjectivity" or simply "curiosity about the experience of the other, the other's interiority." The process of "trying on the feelings" of the other as a way of knowing and connecting, so essentially familiar to women in relationship, is often foreign to men. In one group, after Steve over and over urged the men to ask the women a direct question about their experience, one man asked, "What do you want from us?" Group observation of whose experience receives the most attention can lead to a constructive discussion of how power imbalances are played out — without any conscious intent.

In addition to the *Dread/Anger Impasse,* two others are invariably present in our workshops, and often in couples, that we can only mention here: the *Product/Process Impasse,* where the women want to keep opening up the process while the men are trying to complete the task. One couple related a conversation they had when they were moving to a new house, carrying a box to the car:

Woman: "It's sad to say goodbye to this house."
Man: "Yeah, but think about where we're going' " (the woman slows down and starts to cry)
Man: "Uh-oh' "
Woman: "Please—can we talk?"
Man: "Not now. We've got to finish this."
Woman: "I really need to talk. I need to know where you are."
Man: (exasperated) "I'm right here. Moving. How can we talk when we're trying to move?"
Woman: "How can you just go about moving without any feeling?"

The third impasse we call the *Power-over/Power-with Impasse,* where the men experience conflict as a threat or an attempt to control, while the women want everyone's voice to be heard and attended to and retreat from what seem like definitive stands. An example, based on one medical student's dilemma brought up in a workshop, is around something as simple as going to dinner:

Woman: "Where shall we go to dinner?"
Man: "Let's go to Miguel's."
Woman: "How about Pintemento?"
Man: "Okay, let's go to Pintemento."
Woman: "But it sounded like you wanted to go to Miguel's."
Man: "No, no, it's okay—let's go where *you* want to go."
Woman: "But I want to go where you want to go too. (pause) Why don't you want to go to Pintemento?"
Man: "I just want to decide."
Woman: "We *are* deciding."
Man: "We're not getting anywhere. (tensely) Let's just make a decision."
Woman: (screaming) "Why are you yelling at me?"
Man: (screaming) "I'm not yelling"

All three impasses may occur in any particular aspect of a relationship. Think, for example, of how any or all of these impasses might get played out around sex.

The Shift to Mutuality

What happens to break through these impasses? What we consistently try to introduce into the process is the value of *staying with conflict* and *staying in connection,* holding to and moving with a sense of "the relationship," the "We," which includes but also transcends the "You" and the "Me." Acknowledging the importance of mutual responsibility for the relationship can be a very new and fresh level of thinking for many people. Sometimes the concept is not easy. We suggested to one man that when he felt like retreating, he think about taking care of the relationship. He replied, "How can I think about the 'We' when I'm thinking about the 'Me'?" We felt he was speaking for all of us.

And yet it is just at the point when the participants are deadened and flattened by the anger and dread and pain of an impasse that to talk not of a particular person but of "the relationship" is of the most use. Those of you who work with couples know that, in the pain and rage of the initial visit, to focus on one—or each—person's failings or pathology is to invite disaster. But when both members of a couple focus on "the relationship," the idea that "the relationship is not working and we are going to address that, together," often brings a sense of relief, movement out of the impasse, away from blame or shame and toward a new sense of possibility.

In an impasse, the polarization and rage can be extreme. One man, enraged, said to a woman, "I've had enough of women's anger, and if I hear the word 'patriarchy' one more time, I'll kill! It's not *me!*" In this kind of impasse, other men and women try to offer emphatic responses to those who have become polarized, and the group begins to find ways of holding the conflict, and the different perspectives, to move toward some enlarged understanding that encompasses the differences. The work stays in the here and now, and, when it moves, stays away from a "self-centered" perspective. We encourage group members to make "I-statements"—speaking from each one's personal experience, beginning a statement with "I feel" or "I think," but we have learned that it is not enough to just "get your feelings out." Participants have to be aware of the effect of their statements on the tenuous web of connection that is being created by the group. "I-statements" made *with awareness of the relational context and an intention to build connection* move the group toward greater clarity and authenticity; "I-statements" made without this awareness and intention solidify the impasse.

The group moves back and forth through power struggles, polarization, emotional reactivity, defensiveness, avoidance tactics, personalizing, and sometimes deep despair, cynicism, grief, and hopelessness about ever getting anywhere—an accurate microcosm of the woman-man relationship! The group also moves in and out of moments of breakthroughs into connection and creative, constructive dialogue and problem solving. An important breakthrough often comes when the men feel supported enough to follow up on their question to the women, "Why are you so angry?" In a recent workshop, this produced the following dialogue:

A woman: "I was really angry at what was going on in the group yesterday. When you asked us to visualize our images of the relationship in the group, I saw a wall of grey steel with the sound of fingernails going down it. You men don't really give a damn about us." (silence from the men; we ask what's going on)

A man: "If we respond, we'll take away her feelings."

The woman: "No, if you're silent you will. We keep having to read your facial expressions, because you don't tell us the truth."

The man: "I guess I just have to let you be angry."

Steve: "Why not *ask* her what *she* wants?"

The man: "What do you want?"

The woman: "I needed to express my anger — I need you to understand that."

A man: "You want me to agree with you?"

Another woman: "She wants a *response,* rather than a sheet of metal." (The men try to respond, but it is difficult and awkward; the women respond to the men's difficulty — the focus is soon back on the men.)

The woman: "You men keep asking me what I want you to do, but again the *focus here isn't on you,* it's on me. I'm asking you to touch into my anger — to connect."

Janet: "She wants you to 'try on' her experience. She's asking for an empathic connection that feels like you're there with her, like you're *interested."*

The man: "It's hard for me to hear your anger when I feel so responsible, but I'll try."

Another man: "I hear you saying *not* to think about it in terms of my self, right? (the woman nods) You know something? — that's a *big* relief' " (much laughter from the group; a sense of real connection and movement)

This shifted the quality of connection dramatically — and lastingly — toward what we call "mutuality." Everyone sensed the shift. The men felt the relational space open up, and the opening up opened up more space — the negative spiral turned positive. No longer feeling dread, the men were able to listen to, be interested in, and respond to the women. Although there was intense conflict, there was relief in the sense of not being alone with it. Different participants offered different perspectives on how to break through the impasse, with various creative solutions being tried. There were several tries which led to disconnections, but *staying present* through the disconnection allowed a better connection to be made. As the men felt the relational space open, they could trust the women more and be more creative in what they said; as the women began to sense this mutual empathy, they began to trust the men more and take greater risks as well. Suddenly we all found ourselves engaged in the process of growth through and toward connection.

As groups begin to work on the impasses together, there develops a sense of shared responsibility and creativity. There follows a distinct moment when it is clear to everyone present that a shift has occurred, the group feels different. In fact *something has happened.* This we have called the "shift into mutuality." We have a sense, so far, that this shift occurs in our workshops, to a greater or lesser extent, depending on how much time we have for the process of mutual empathy to work. It isn't always clear how we got there, yet everyone can recognize the difference: there is an intense *sense of relational presence — people are really there.* In one group, we asked the participants, at the end, to look back and describe the feeling after the shift had occurred. These were some of the words they used: "release, comfort, caring, safety, sharing, peaceful, easy, enjoyment of different styles, hopefulness, mutual nurturance, energizing, movement, insight, softening, appropriate confrontation, dynamic process, clearer recognition of others' experience."

In Stone Center language, we have described mutuality as a *way* of being in relationship—a dialogical, open, changing movement in relationship, where each person can increasingly represent her or his own experience, feelings, and perceptions, and each can move and be moved by the other and by the relationship. This sense of mutually empathic joining is the basis for new power and new action. When men and women get to this place, something truly hopeful has happened. We don't yet know what is possible or what power this *shift to mutuality* between women and men can truly generate!

In the workshops, only after this shift and movement occur can the most difficult subjects be worked on. The issues brought up previously that led to the impasses are often the ones which the group now "goes back over," with a new, fresh sense of really attending, responding, ruthlessly encountering the psychological "facts" without the burden of judgment, without a need to "agree," "disagree," or even "agree to disagree," and with an authentic desire to understand. It's amazing to us how the same questions which had brought hostile silence now bring animated discussion, how dread and anger—in one workshop nicknamed "the Big D" and "the Big A"—can be addressed unflinchingly. Humor is much in evidence, humor not in the service of sublimated aggression, but in the service of connection. Real information begins to be exchanged with real feeling. Real understanding occurs. For example, the men in one group said that one reason they fall silent when they sense a problem in relationship is that they've been taught they have to *fix* problems, and if they can't fix it, they won't say anything at all, won't even acknowledge that the problem exists— "if you don't talk about it, there's no problem."

With the affirmation of shared experience with other men, and freed from a sense of dread about the women's reaction, the men could show their pain about their sense of relational incompetence, and the women could *feel* it. At the same time, the men could appreciate and feel how crazy-making this is for the women. Through this mutually empathic joining—holding both sets of feelings, simultaneously—a creative moment happens, and the relationship can move.

In that same "fingernail-on-steel" group, after the shift to mutuality had occurred, for the first time we heard men describe how it is only in groups with other men that they can begin to be open about the losses in their lives—the loss of relationships with wives, children, and especially fathers. The men talked about how they could *not* be open about grief and loss with women—and then started to do it! As the men spoke of this, the women were leaning forward with exquisite attentiveness. One man said: "All you women are leaning forward, listening really hard, and it's really quiet, like you can't believe that men have grief, or are lonely."

A woman: "Are men lonely?"

The man: "God, don't you *know?*"

Another woman: "I thought so, but we've been waiting a long time to hear it. About a *millennium,* in fact."

Another woman: "I'm drawn toward you, but I'm pulling back too, because I just don't want to take care of you anymore."

The man: "I can understand that. But we're not asking you to take care of us any-more. Just hear it, that's all."

When the groups are working together in this way, we have heard the most extraordinary, honest, sensitive, intelligent, and thoughtful discussions of questions raised by each group about the other. We have discussed sexual differences and impasses, parenting issues, power imbalances, and even sexual abuse by therapists—to name a few. These are the moments that build our faith in the as yet untapped power of mutuality between women and men. Usually, only at the very end of this male-female encounter part of the workshop, with time running out, do we get to Question 3—"What do you most want the other gender group to understand about you?" By the time we get to these answers, the shift to mutuality has occurred, and we ask the men and women just to read their answers through, without discussion. In the quiet, attentive atmosphere, the answers are always not only touching, but healing.

Women's Answers to Question 3

"What do you most want men to understand about you?"

We are not the enemy; even if I'm not clear, I have a point; to know what my experience of disconnection feels like; that conflict is an invitation to engagement which can bring closeness and resolution; conflict does not mean the dissolution of the relationship; how frightening men's power for violence is in limiting women's actions; don't trivialize my experience—go with my female creative process; what it feels like to make 67 cents to the dollar; that my way is not wrong, just different; that we are angry because we are hurt; that my sexuality is far beyond the physical connection; that I just want you to be there; that I am a human being too; we want to share, not take over; that we're not experts at relationships either.

Men's Answers to Question 3

"What do you most want women to understand about you?"

I am not your enemy; how many of my actions are acts of love; my difficulties communicating feelings; my need for solitude; my difficulties in admitting power-lessness and asking for help; that I need space; that I need time; I'm scared too; not to have to censor my maleness; I love competition and play; how I feel about responsibility; the heavy burden placed on men to be successful and not look foolish; that being a son is often difficult; my sense of intrusion that often comes with relationships and my sense of shame for feeling that; I want to change; we care about relationships as much as women do; men are scared of other men too; men have different priorities; the complexity of masculinity; our relational yearnings; our grief over losses; that I will come back after I go away.

In a workshop with college students, where the group encounter had been particu-larly heated and fragmented, after the men had read what they wanted the women to understand about them, one of the women was so moved, she spoke for the group: There's a glow now. You gave us the other half of the string, and now we can make a tie.

The Double Standard on the Road to Mutuality

How does this shift to mutuality occur? At the end of the group encounter, when we have asked participants what *they* think helped the shift to mutuality to occur, these are some of their answers:

We realized we weren't getting anywhere by staying angry.

We felt, somehow, as if we were *seen*, together. Like we'd deeply seen a truth of the way we were treating each other, together.

We got out of the "I" to the "We," out of the authority/submissive role. We got into a movement rather than an obsessing.

We saw the danger of going on like that.

I think when that young lady there said that we were getting nowhere, I felt kind of ashamed, and didn't want any more conflict, and I tried to listen. And then when you bugged us men to respond, eventually we did.

We have seen that there is a "double standard" on this road to mutuality, and that men and women have different work to do on this shared journey. We also recognize that although men deeply feel women's power in relationships, men's power and privilege in the world has the major impact on the search for mutuality. Most frequently, it is the less powerful person or group who is more aware of the lack of mutuality and who initiates the struggle. Members of the more powerful group have different work to do as they begin to take responsibility for change.

Women's Path to Mutuality

1. *The Importance of Sequence.* At this time in our history, many women are feeling angry, despairing, and "tired of taking care of men, of doing all the *work* in the relationship." In the workshops, we have seen over and over how the beginning point of dialogue is around women's anger. Women *want* to hear men's experience but often first need to feel men moving toward them, learning to connect empathically, listening and seeking to understand their experience, especially to understand the origins of their anger. Only after this happens (or even after a slight forward movement is felt) are women able to listen fully to men and appreciate the depth of honesty the men are often able to express in the workshops.

2. *Women Working Together.* The power that results from the women meeting together and building a sense of solidarity and support before the intergroup dialogue is striking. The women often talk together about how different it feels to be among women. When men are present, especially their own partners, they feel more focused on the men's reactions. They notice together how much energy goes into watching the men—one woman called this "ego-tending," another, "hovering," as she was

constantly checking out her husband to make sure that he wasn't either getting hurt, or hurting someone else. Women can validate each other's experience with this monitoring *and* the desire to change.

When the intergroup dialogue begins then, the women are able to offer enormous support to each other. Feeling this support, individual women are more able to effectively represent their experience to the men and to *stay with* their anger and their needs until the men respond. Other women can then relate to the men's confusion and suggest ways they might respond. This work can be done in a group much more easily and effectively than in a dyad.

There are significant divisions that emerge among women, especially around anger at men. We have seen enormous controversy about anger and where it belongs. These differences can be used to create mutuality if they do not lead to a split among women, that functions to resist change and to support the status quo.

3. The Search for New Models of Relationship. Women in the workshops are often seeking a new model of relating to men—struggling to let go of what feels like "compulsive caretaking." The men often respond anxiously when the old forms are challenged, fearing that women are moving away or abandoning them. It is essential for everyone to work together toward a new psychology of a woman–man relationship, where women can stay *with* their own experience *and* hold an empathic connection to the men without feeling they have to "take care of men or the relationship." One woman described this situation as follows:

"It's like on a football field (she was trying to use men's language). We've been way down on your side and now we're going back to our side. We're having a good time together here. But we're still *holding* the relationship with you and are waiting for you to move toward us so we can play the game over the whole field."

This is a very important growth step—envisioning the possibility of different configurations of connection and allowing for different patterns of movement, distance and initiation within connection.

In the workshops, we have seen women shift to an appreciation of men's intelligence and perceptivity once the dialogue really opens up; we have heard women sharing aspects of their own experience in interesting new ways—ways that emerge as women and men begin to create a *shared relational context*. Appreciating and sharing are beautiful examples of Jean Baker Miller's description (1986) of the five outcomes of connection: new energy, an ability to take new action, new knowledge of self and other, an enhanced sense of self-worth, and a desire for more connection. (However, as growth in connection is never linear, such a positive experience can make it even more painful when, in real life, things revert—as they inevitably will—to old ways.) As a next step, many women say they need to examine why they resist and fear really seeing men's emotional vulnerabilities. Women, at this point, also have to face their own limitations and fears in relationship.

As a white, heterosexual woman (and a psychotherapist), I (Janet) am aware that in some other situations I hold the power and privilege. One of the important learnings for me in doing these workshops has been to understand better the *responsibilities* of the more powerful group in the struggle for relational mutuality, and then to apply that to myself—recognizing in other situations my initial blindness, my resistance to doing the work, and that it is up to me to be responsible for listening to the others' experiences, and for initiating change in relationships where I am in the more powerful position.

Men's Path to Mutuality

In our workshops, men "get to mutual" in several steps-steps which may apply to men "getting to mutual" in any relationship, including therapy:

1. *Men Naming Their Relational Experiences.* It's surprising how rarely men have had their experience *named*. To use words like "relational dread," "a desire for connection," and to talk about a paradigm shift to thinking of "the relationship" as a "thing" give men a language which rings true and makes the relational world more real. As one man put it, "You mean we can take 'the relationship' on vacation with us to the Grand Canyon?"

2. *Men Connecting with Other Men.* In our all-male subgroup, a man listens to another man describe in detail what he had always thought of as his own "secret" experiences—for example, "dread." Hearing similarities may wake both men up, making each sharper and clearer, building a base of understanding through an interchange around *similarity.* Men feel a heightened sense of male identity, and male vulnerability, grief, and loss are often themes. Most Robert Bly/"men's movement" gatherings end at this point (Bly, 1990). Yet we see all-male work as a beginning, as a necessary step for the next phase, when men, facing women, are asked to do the uncomfortable and dangerous work, on their creative edges, of opening to women and connecting through difference.

3. *Men Holding Differences in Relationship with Women.* In the arena of relationship, men often feel incompetent, criticized, and defensive. This may lead to men disparaging the idea of "learning from women," or the fear of becoming "soft males" or "feminized men." We have seen the profound differences between women and men, and one of the differences is that *men are often not as aware of the relational differences.* If men are to learn about mutual empathic relationship and the nurturing of relationship, this learning will most likely take place through engagement with differences with women.

But first, men have to *see the differences.* Often, relational events are invisible to men. (After four years of this work, I [Steve] can vouch for this myself.) Men are not as aware of "the relational context" as women, are not as aware of women's attending to men's egos and responding to men's feeling states in relationship, and are not as aware of power imbalances involving the disempowerment of the subordinate gender. (Often, neither men nor women are aware of the gender differences in *relational timing*—women are often quicker than men.) To make these invisible relational facts visible is an essential step in men's learning mutuality—and crucial in working with men in psychotherapy. When these facts are revealed in a supportive environment, with other men seeing them at the same time so that the facts can be felt not as *personal* blindness but as *gender* blindness, men feel a sense of amazement, relief, and curiosity. Women's *relational* power is often frightening to men. For men to *hear* women's experience of diminished *institutional* power, and, further, to *see* that a shift from a power-over to a power-with model would mean not loss of men's power but in fact a further empowerment of all, has enormous implications for the culture and for the society.

Men often translate difference into conflict, and conflict with women can be intense. Men need to learn that they can encounter and hold conflict without something bad happening. Often, at the first sign of difference and conflict, a man may make a "flyswatter" response—trying to crush it. The fear of becoming violent is a prime element of male relational dread.

Men can get stuck in the paralysis of the dread of connection on the one hand, and, on the other, if they are in connection, in the fear of disconnection, of loss. This stuck stance can feel so precarious that men may do everything in their power not to change anything. If, as one man said, "the feeling of peace is when nothing happens," doing and saying nothing can protect a man from the anxious feeling that "something might happen." In relationship, men may be more at home with stasis, with a finished product, and fear process and relational movement. To get to mutual in relationship with women, it is essential that men be supported through conflict, dread, and fear long enough to have the experience of "something good happening."

4. Men Learning Empathy in Relationship with Women. Faced with women's anger, a crucial step for men to take is *to watch other men respond to women,* and *women respond to women, to see how* the process of attending and responding takes place. Men can learn to allow themselves to be moved by the feelings of the other as a way of becoming connected, and to know that it is possible to move in connection without endangering the sense of self.

At an early age men learn that self-worth means being competent at doing things well. In our workshops, men learn more about "doing empathy well." Empathy is "broken down" into its components, and becomes something real, unmysterious, even fascinating. Each component—"attending," "responding," "not being a blank screen," "trying on feelings"—becomes known, and then reassembled. Men learn what it is and how to do it, and then find that they can get better at it and feel valued for it.

Often in our workshops men will say, "But I *have* good relationships with men— me and my buddy can be out fishing for a whole day, and not talk much, but it's a good relationship." And yet men, when asked, will admit that "with my wife, it's different—both of us can really open up and talk. I feel she really understands me." When this happens—and it is almost always with a woman—men recognize how good it feels to be in mutual empathic relationship. This desire for mutuality may be hard to "get to" in men's awareness and may come out directly only at times when it is unalterably lost, or when men, almost despite themselves, find themselves experiencing it, or when they see women having it with their women friends, see that it is missing in their own lives and sense a deep lonely yearning, for connection.

Finally, the question that women often ask is *How do you get men to listen and attend to these matters?* While men may have a deep yearning for connection, a lot stands in the way of starting to learn about it—for about five thousand years "real men" didn't do this. So why do some men open up?

Sometimes, men will be opened up by *a loving relationship* with a woman, or by being a father, or by caring for a sick or dying father or mother or other family member.

Men may also open up through *the pain and suffering in relationship.* As in our workshops, getting to a painful and creative edge of an impasse with a women is often a precursor to a shift to mutuality. Men may have a difficult time *anticipating* relational events, so that often it is only *after* men say or do something to affect someone—or even to hurt someone—that they wake up. Men may have to flee— or damage or destroy—a relationship with a woman in order to really *feel* what they have to lose, and to realize that they want exactly what they are fleeing, or what they have damaged or destroyed. Men's being stuck between dread of connection and fear of loss, and being afraid of engaging in the movement of relationship, may have much to do with men's difficulty in both anticipating *and* recollecting relational events. It is rare that a man will say to a woman, without prompting, "I was thinking about what we were talking about yesterday."

A final way that men may open up to mutuality is *through men's groups.* Men connecting with men may lead to a separatist mentality which merely and archaically makes men more "male" and doesn't propel men toward making mutual connection; or it may lead to the realization that other men are a *resource* in learning to form mutually empathic, mutually authentic, mutually empowering relationships, with both men and women. There is a tremendous power right now in these men's groups. If this power can be *brought into relationship with women and shifted to mutual connection,* we might just be seeing a beginning in the transformation of the millennial pain shared by women and men to shared creative energy. Our workshop with four-year-old girls and boys gives us much hope for these possibilities.

Clinical Applications

There are a number of applications of this model for clinical work that particularly emphasize the value of psychoeducational-process groups for studying and working with gender differences. (Useful educational material may be found in the Stone Center Working Paper series, Gilligan's and her group's writings [1982, 1989], and in Tannen [1990]. An interesting strategy for group therapy would be to alternate meetings of same-gender groups with the larger mixed-gender group. The value of groups is especially important in breaking down "individual pathology" attribution models and breaking out of the terrible isolation many couples experience. Most heterosexual couples lack a community where open exchange and constructive dialogue around relational struggles can take place.

We have developed an application of this workshop specifically for couples. A small group of couples meets on a Friday night and all day Saturday, with a similar format of intergroup dialogue. We also discuss particular strategies and exercises for building connection, and couples leave with commitments to do particular assignments or projects together. We meet again one month later to see how people are applying the principles and to hear the couples report back on their work together. Mutual relationship has great power not only in one individual with another or others, but in one *couple* with another couple or other couples. As one man said to the group of couples, at the end of one workshop, "Your holding your relationships helps us to hold ours." Coleadership is of great value when the work toward mutuality is a vital and ongoing aspect of the coleadership pair. For example, while we are working together as leaders, we "check-in" periodically on the status of our own relationship both privately and in the group.

In the workshops for clinicians and for couples, we suggest particular "relational principles" which help to break through impasses. These principles, derived from the workshops, include: shifting to a relational paradigm; recognition and naming of impasses; early intervention; using a language of "connectors"; staying with difference and conflict; creativity in action; moving through disconnection; letting go and coming back; and appreciating small changes.

We urge couples to map out the dialogue of a particular impasse they experience together (these are usually quite repetitive and fairly easy to choreograph), actually charting out in each line of dialogue what is going on in the woman, what is going on in the man, and what is going on in the relationship. Then, using our relational principles, we ask them to brainstorm ways to alter the dialogue, as a way of preventing or making early interventions in these destructive spirals and creatively changing impasses to breakthroughs. Looking together at their interaction helps couples to move into a space of mutual responsibility for the relationship.

In workshops for clinicians we also suggest particular strategies for building connection that may help clients work on developing relational mutuality. I'll give a few examples.

First we try to *enhance relational awareness.* To help men and women move into a relational paradigm, the use of "we" language is explored. One useful exercise has been to ask both people to close their eyes and *visualize the relationship,* and then to describe to each other the qualities of the relationship. What is the color, texture, sound, of the relationship. How does this change? For one man the texture went from "velvet" to "gravel" in an instant. Another question is "What animal is the relationship like?" One woman described the relationship as "a lioness, with two huge paws around both of us," while her partner saw "a spirited horse with a lot of energy—but it can gallop and get away from you."

Other ways to enhance relational awareness are (1) to have couples do a *relational inventory, together*—an informal assessment of the strengths and weaknesses of their relationship—and (2) to have both people together write a *relational purpose statement*—what is the purpose of the relationship, what are the questions it holds, what are we together to do or to learn. For example, one couple wrote:

"To create a refuge, a safe place for us and children to grow and thrive, to create a place of peace and thus to contribute to the possibility of global peace."

We have noticed striking gender differences in *relational time*—the tempo and rhythm at which women and men attend to and respond to each other. We suggest several ways of bringing awareness to these gender-specific ways of handling relational time, such as the *check-in*, a simple, powerful, and useful exercise. Either person can call for a check-in, which consists of each person giving a brief "I-statement"—"I feel" or "I think." Discussion is not encouraged. As one couple said, "We have to be careful not to let our check-ins degenerate into conversation." Either person can also call for a *check-out*, with the proviso that the one checking out takes responsibility for checking back in, and saying *when* she or he will do this. Another strategy (Bombadieri, 1990) is the *twenty-minute rule*, which ensures but also limits talking about a particularly troublesome subject to twenty minutes per day. This creates a structure where men feel they don't have to take responsibility for setting time limits, while women can feel confident that they can expect full attention and engagement around the issue at hand.

To deal with the process/product impasse, we suggest *choosing a project*—or, better, *two* projects, one from each person's area of interest or expertise—finding a way to create together, whether this is a garden, a song, or a piece of serious writing—and to grow in the process of facilitating and building on each other's strengths.

We also suggest *ground rules for waging good conflict*, including check-ins (each person stating where he or she is in respect to the process of conflict) and check-outs (either person calling for a time out, if the conflict feels stuck, destructive, or abusive.) Some ground rules need to be set in advance.

Couples can find humorous phrases which give perspective to impasses or conflicts, such as one man saying, in the middle of a fierce stuck place, "It's time to throw the garbage," or to find a phrase which, when the relationship seems to be disappearing, will *evoke* it—one couple's was: "We do it *together*."

Conclusion

From our work together over the past few years, we have grown even more cautious and gravely aware of how far we have to go, yet we also feel some hope that there can be creative change, movement, and growth toward mutuality in the woman–man relationship. It is only when we find ways to work together, to find the community and support we need to *participate* in this work, that such movement can take place. Perhaps what is needed is a "Women-*and*-Men's Movement."

Learning to live together creatively, facing into difference—difference of race, class, sexual orientation, ethnicity, and nation—is of vital significance as we move into the twenty-first century. We believe that this work on woman-man relationships is a potential model for the crucial work we all need to undertake, in transforming human impasses to possibilities.

Discussion Summary

After each colloquium presentation a discussion is held. Selected portions are summarized here. At this session Drs. Cynthia Garcia Coll, Judith Jordan, Jean Baker Miller, Robin Cook-Nobles, and Irene Stiver joined Stephen Bergman and Janet Surrey in leading the discussion.

Garcia Coll: As a development psychologist I am interested in how we develop these patterns. Can you talk about your work in other cultures and with four-year-olds?

Bergman: With four-year-olds at a preschool, we used the same format, first asking the boys and girls separately to answer three questions, modified for their level of understanding. Next the boys and girls sat on the floor facing each other.

The boys' answers to Question 1, "What do you like about girls?"
"They like to play what I like to play."
"They always play with me and help me with things."

The girls' answers:
"We like kissing and hugging boys."
"We like when they chase us and tie us up and they thought we were dead and we faked it and then we like sneaking away and getting away."

This is appalling. But then something started to happen. The boys were fidgeting, not paying much attention to the girls, and the girls began to tell a story, together, each adding lines. The story was about how one girl had tricked a wicked baby sitter. Soon the boys were listening wide-eyed. The girls—we realized this later—had found a way to connect.

Then a rather peculiar thing happened. I asked, "When you play a game with the boys, who goes first?" One girl said, "Boys go first." She looked to the other girls, and then, giggling, started to chant, "Boys go first. Boys go first." Soon all the girls were getting into it, "Boys go first. Boys go first." But the hopeful side was that, after this encounter, there was a free-play period in a field. Soon the teacher, astonished, said, "This is amazing! I've never seen this before! The boys and girls are playing together. And there are no more hierarchical patterns among the boys." He pointed out that the girls and boys were running around holding hands—sometimes a foursome would run by—and that the "top boy," the one usually on top of the hierarchy of play, was by himself. No one was really paying much attention to him. It hadn't been at all clear to us what had been going on in the group, but now we could see that something had shifted, and the shift was being incorporated immediately in their more interconnected play.

Surrey: We were in Turkey, a very gender-segregated society, with very few cross-gender interactions except sexual ones, and with very prescribed and male-dominated ways of being. People in Turkey kept on saying "We're very relational, we define ourselves in relation, what we need is more 'self.' " In fact, they were in very patterned relationships—with rigid and specified male and female roles and identities—they were not dynamic, growth-fostering relationships. We saw that the women were beginning to initiate the struggle for change, but that the men were much further behind the men we'd seen in America and seemed much less sensitized to relational matters.

It's a culture where men spend an enormous amount of time together—there's a strong male role and identity in family and society and a richness of male ritual—no "soft males." It's a power-over culture, and that hinders mutuality in relationships. These observations brought to mind some of the issues of the men's movement in this country, where men are trying to create ritual and identity. Perhaps men here are trying to recreate something that could be at odds with building connection.

Question: Can there be other models of healthy relationship besides mutuality, such as a relationship based on action or autonomy? Do men have to "sell out" to women's model of relationship, to mutuality?

Surrey: To me, mutuality simply means always holding an awareness of the other. You can be very active, doing things together or working "independently," but if you are out of touch with the impact of your actions on others, I don't think that's a healthy mode. Mutuality doesn't mean sitting around and talking all the time, it simply means maintaining a sense of self, a sense of the other, and a sense of what's happening in the relationship. You can be halfway around the world from someone and hold that, or you can be in a room with someone and *not* hold it. You could go off for days and write a book, if you negotiated that, and it still could be done with an awareness of the other and of the relationship—these are not mutually exclusive at all. But I do believe that action without awareness of its impact is extraordinarily dangerous and can lead to violence, so I would never say that that's a positive model. It's the same problem with autonomy—independence, creativity, working on your own—all those things are terrific, but never should be done without the awareness of the other and the impact on the relationship.

Bergman: We are not talking about men adopting women's ways; we are talking about both men and women moving to more healthy, human ways. This is not the "feminization" of men, but rather the "relationalization" of men and women both, together.

Stiver: This relates to the effect that the relational model brings to individual work as well as couples work. Whether you're working with a man or a woman, you can always bring the relationship into the work. The focus is to become aware not only of your own experience but to broaden your experience of the important people in your life. Whether I'm working with a man or a woman, I feel the work is more successful when something really changes in their important relationships. It's a dynamic of experiencing a relationship, often for the first time, in a different way.

Miller: It's a good question because sometimes we tend to get caught in old polarities, like relationships versus action or relationships versus something like autonomy. Relationships are very active if they're moving. Also, people can find their greatest sense of themselves, their fullest use of themselves within the context of relationships. In fact, I think people find their fullest selves when they are in a relationship that's moving toward mutuality.

Jordan: If men have been in a position of power-over and that position has brought them benefits, of course they're going to resist any change that will move them out of that position. Men not wanting to do it the "women's way," or selling out to women, is a crucial question because a huge part of male socialization is towards not being like women. The question is: How to present mutuality as having something in it for men? Steve has suggested very clearly that in these workshops men begin to get the sense that mutuality in relationship offers them a way to relieve and deal with their aloneness, their isolation, and their sense of being so armored and cut off.

Question: I'm wondering how your model applies in situations of difference among races, or gays and straights—the issues that arise from prejudice?

Cook-Nobles: I have been thinking about the male-female relationship within the African-American experience. In the groups you have described, one of the questions the men asked the women was "What is it like to be oppressed?" In the African-American experience, because both men and women have experienced oppression, the fear of the loss of the relationship takes on a different meaning qualitatively. The ultimate fear is that the safety net will be taken away if the relationship or the group is broken up. That threat may get in the way of hearing the other person's experience. I think that is some of what has happened in the African-American community's response to the Thomas hearings. In dealing with the dynamics between two people, you are forced to look at the possible effect on the whole community. Will we lose the whole community? Who will be there to take care of us as a group? So you have those within-group conflicts which complicate the process on another level.

Question: I was also thinking of *different* races. How do people of color get members of the dominant race to sit down and recognize that there is a degree of interdependence that makes it worth their while to engage in the kind of intergroup conflict that these workshops address?

Cook-Nobles: I think there's a shift going on in which the minority group is not necessarily trying to get the majority group to sit down, but a shift in which the majority group needs to see its *need* to sit down. I think that's the shift not only in racial minority groups but also in the lesbian and gay community. We have to own the problem together.

Surrey: That was my point about the double standard and the importance to me of learning about initiating and taking responsibility as a white heterosexual woman. Watching men have to learn has helped me enormously.

Question: What about the danger of stereotyping men and women, polarizing into opposites human characteristics which are probably on a continuum rather than dichotomous?

Surrey: What we see really clearly is that the greater the impasse, the more gender stereotypical the behavior; the greater the movement toward mutuality, the more both women and men show the whole range of human characteristics, and the more we see everyone showing more individual, or "personal" behavior—and I believe that that's a microcosm of the larger situation in the society and in the world.

REFERENCES

Bergman, S. (1991). Men's psychological development: A relational perspective. *Work in Progress, No. 48*. Wellesley, MA: Stone Center Working Paper Series.

Bly, R. (1990). *Iron John*. Reading, MA: Addison-Wesley.

Bombadieri, M. (1990). Personal communication.

Eisler, R. (1987). *The chalice and the blade*. New York: William Morrow.

Gilligan, C. (1982). *In a different voice*. Cambridge, MA: Harvard University Press.

Gilligan, C., Lyons, N., & Hanmer, T. (Ed.). (1989). *Making connections: The relational worlds of adolescent girls at Emma Willard School*. Troy, New York: Emma Willard School.

Jordan, J., Kaplan, S., Miller, J., Stiver, I., Surrey, J. (1991). *Women's growth in connection*. New York: Guilford press.

Miller, J. B. (1976). *Toward a new psychology of women*. Boston: Beacon Press.

Miller, J. B. (1986). What do we mean by relationships? *Work in Progress, No. 22*. Wellesley, MA: Stone Center Working Paper Series.

Stern, D. (1985). *The interpersonal world of the infant*. New York: Basic Books.

Surrey, J. (1985). The "self-in-relation": A theory of women's development. *Work in Progress, No. 13*. Wellesley, MA: Stone Center Working Paper Series.

Tannen, D. (1990). *You just don't understand*. New York: William Morrow.

Part VII

Contextual Constraints and Affordances

A. Engendered Worlds

Our everyday worlds are gendered in ways that seem to have little or no basis in biology. Activities in which males and females engage in very similar ways are segregated by gender: for example, males and females frequent separate public bathrooms for the elimination of bodily wastes, boys and girls meet at separate tables in the school cafeteria for the ingestion of food, and women are overwhelmingly over-represented among the ranks of the poor.[1] In this section we explore varying views concerning the causes and consequences of such phenomena and how they should be investigated.

The contributors focus their attention not on matters of individual difference, as is customary in psychology, but on interpersonal and institutional arrangements. Eleanor E. Maccoby summarizes and analyzes the results of a burgeoning literature on gender-segregated peer groups. She reports that children as young as three observed in nursery schools and in laboratory settings choose to play more with same-sex than with opposite-sex peers, suggesting to most observers that early socialization, building perhaps on biological predispositions, leads boys and girls to adopt incompatible styles of play at a very early age. The comment of a four-year-old girl, interviewed about her friendship patterns, seems to support this idea. Asked why she had listed only girls as her best friends in the class, she replied, "Boys don't know how to play."[2] It turned out, however, that this was not the whole story. Later in the interview, the little girl named a boy in the class as her very best friend and most frequent playmate; asked why she had not mentioned him in answer to the earlier question, she replied, "You said in *school*. I don't play with him in *school*. You can't play with boys in *school*." Social norms, as well as personal preference, clearly play a role in gender segregation. The source of the norms is not always clear. Although teachers at this little girl's school prided themselves on their gender-neutral practices, Myra and David Sadker (e.g., 1994) and others have shown that teachers' gender discrimination is often difficult to detect with the naked eye, even when it can be proved to be present. On the other hand, Virginia Paley, an astute and insightful observer of young children and a veteran kindergarten teacher, asserts that "kindergarten is a triumph of sexual self-stereotyping. No amount of adult subterfuge or propaganda deflects the five-year-old's passion for segregation by sex" (Paley, 1984, p. ix).

Once formed, same-sex peer groups serve as "powerful contexts for learning" (Thorne & Luria, 1986, p. 179; see also Thorne, 1994) in which children practice "doing gender": developing and enforcing sex-typed interaction styles similar to those described by the authors in Part IV, the girls behaving in more "connected" (collaborative and democratic) ways and the boys in more "separate" (competitive and hierarchical) ways. Because the groups seem to differ so dramatically in organizational structure and interactional style, some observers refer to them as "separate cultures" or even "separate worlds."[3]

But Barrie Thorne points to problems with the "separate worlds" model similar to those that occur in research on gender differences among individuals (as discussed in earlier sections of this volume, especially Part II). Differences between gender groups tend to be exaggerated and similarities ignored. Although interaction styles such as competition and cooperation are treated as polarities, as if the presence of one precluded the presence of the other, careful observers have detected competition and individual assertiveness as well as cooperation among members of girls' groups (Hughes, 1988; Sheldon, 1992), and cooperation among boys on sports teams is apparent to the most casual observer. Variations within groups, as a function of individual differences and type of activity, have also been overlooked: Marjorie Goodwin (1988) reports, for instance, that girls in the groups she observed relied on collaborative leadership in most of their play, but when playing house a hierarchical structure emerged.

For the writers in this section, the purpose of studying gender-segregated peer groups and other social arrangements is not to accumulate a catalog of (group) differences but to understand the processes involved in forming and maintaining such arrangements. There is a postmodern flavor to these analyses: to quote Jeanne Maracek (1995), commenting on a similar set of essays, "All see gender as neither stable, unitary, nor universal, but rather in flux, multiple, possibly fragmented, and local (i.e., defined in particular situations), 'a play of differences that is always on the move' (Thorne, 1994, p. 90)" (p. 162). From this perspective, in a very real sense, gender is *created* by social institutions "designed for the purpose," as Erving Goffman says. The society sets up situations that "do not so much allow for the expression of natural differences as for the production of the difference itself," for most biological differences between the sexes would not count unless society made them count.[4] Adrienne Rich asserts that even a "sexual preference" for heterosexuality, usually assumed to be determined by biology (a "natural difference") or personal choice, can be the product of social institutions. "I am suggesting," she writes, "that heterosexuality, like motherhood, needs to be recognized and studied as a *political institution*" (1980, p. 637, emphasis in original), and "heterosexuality may not be a preference at all but something that has to be imposed, managed, organized, propagandized, and maintained by force" (p. 648).

One consequence of the "arrangement between the sexes" that serves to maintain that arrangement, Goffman says, is that "women as a disadvantaged group are like maids"; isolated within their own households, they are "somewhat cut off ecologically from congress with their kind." Another factor operating to to maintain the arrangement, Goffman says, is that "women are also separated from one another by the stake they acquire in the very organization which divides them," because "each is yet linked to particular men through fundamental social bonds" that place her "in coalition with her menfolk against the whole of the rest of the world." Goffman's heterosexual bias is evident here, and perhaps also a class and race bias. Lesbians and single mothers are not in coalition with their menfolk, and poor and working-class women and women of color may perceive themselves as having little stake in the prevailing organization.[5] In spite of women's recent advances in the workplace, Goffman's observation that "wherever the male goes, apparently, he can carry a sexual division of labor with him" continues to apply to situations—still widely prevalent—in which executives are male and "support staffs" are female, but it does not apply equally to men in low-status jobs. And as Aida Hurtado points out, although women of all races occupy largely subordinate positions, the form of subordination they suffer is different, white women being subordinated through "seduction" and women of color through "rejection."

Although acknowledging the power of social structures in constraining behavior, none of the writers in this section views these structures as immutable. Terri Apter and Elizabeth Garnsey (1994) write, "When constraints are structural, we are inclined to treat them as if they were solid, as natural forces. . . . Yet social structures are never more than stable patterns of interactions sustained by mutual expectations" (p. 22). The women's movement, beginning with the consciousness-raising groups in the 1970s, in which women engaged in "congress with their own kind," has demonstrated that resistance is possible and that arrangements between the sexes once considered divinely ordained can be disrupted and reconstructed.

NOTES

1. Catharine MacKinnon observes that although capitalism may require "a collection of individuals to occupy low-status, low-paying positions," it is unclear why "such persons must be biologically female" (1979, p. 15).

2. We are indebted to Margaret Potter for this illustration.

3. Katha Pollit (1994/1995) demurs: "The truth is that there *is* only one culture, and it shapes each sex in distinct but mutually dependent ways in order to reproduce itself" (p. 58).

4. The power of even the most irrational gender arrangements to constrain behavior is illustrated by an experiment conducted by members of the psychology department at Trier University in Germany in 1993, who posted signs on public telephone booths saying "For Men Only" and "For Women Only," and then "watched as their countrymen dutifully complied with the new regulation" (Heilbrunn, 1995, p. 10).

5. In some subcultures women are less isolated from one another than in white middle- and upper-class society: The sociologist Patricia Hill Collins reports that African-American women have always been able to count on a "tradition of sisterhood" (1989, p. 768).

REFERENCES

Aster, T., & Garnsey, E. (1994). Enacting Inequality. Structure, Agency, and Gender. *Women's Studies International Forum 17*, 15–22.

Collins, P. H. (1989). The Social Construction of Black Feminist Thought. *Signs, 14*, 745–773.

Goodwin, M. H. (1988). Cooperation and Competition across Girls' Play Activities. In A. D. Todd & S. Fisher (Eds.), *Gender and Discourse: The Power of Talk* (pp. 55–96). Norwood, NJ: Ablex.

Heilbrunn, J. (1995, July 23). The Weight of the Past. Review of M. Fisher, *After the Wall: Germany, the Germans and the Burdens of History. New York Times Book Review*, p. 10.

Hughes, L. (1988). But That's Not *Really* Mean: Competing in a Cooperative Mode. *Sex Roles, 19*, 669–687.

MacKinnon, C. (1979). *Sexual Harassment of Working Women: A Case of Sex Discrimination.* New Haven: Yale University Press.

Maracek, J. (1995). Gender, Politics, and Psychology's Ways of Knowing. *American Psychologist, 50*, 162–163.

Paley, V. G. (1984). *Boys and Girls: Superheroes in the Doll Corner.* Chicago: University of Chicago Press.

Pollit, K. (1994/1995). Marooned on Gilligan's Island. *Reasonable Creatures: Essays on Women and Feminism* (pp. 42–62). New York: Vintage.

Rich, A. (1980). Compulsory Heterosexuality and Lesbian Existence. *Signs, 5*, 631–659. Reprinted in E. Abel & E. Abel (Eds.), *The Signs Reader: Women, Gender and Scholarship.* Chicago: University of Chicago Press.

Sadker, M. & Sadker, D. (1994). *Failing at Fairness: How America's Schools Cheat Girls.* New York: Scribner's.

Sheldon, A. (1992). Conflict Talk: Sociolinguistic Challenges to Self-Assertion and How Young Girls Meet Them. *Merrill-Palmer Quarterly, 38*, 95–118.

Thorne, B. (1994). *Gender Play: Girls and Boys in School.* New Brunswick, NJ: Rutgers University Press.

Thorne, B., & Luria, Z. (1986). Sexuality and Gender in Children's Daily Worlds. *Social Problems, 33*, 176–190.

Chapter Thirty-Four

The Arrangement Between the Sexes

Erving Goffman

1.

In modern industrial society, as apparently in all others, sex is at the base of a fundamental code in accordance with which social interactions and social structures are built up, a code which also establishes the conceptions individuals have concerning their fundamental human nature. This is an oft stated proposition, but until recently its awesomely ramified significance escaped us. The traditional sociological position that sex is "learned, diffuse, role behavior"—fair enough in itself—seemed to have innoculated previous generations of social scientists against understanding instead of allowing the disease to spread. More even than in the matter of social class, these students simply acted like everyone else, blindly supporting in their personal conduct exactly what some at least should have been studying. As usual in recent years, we have had to rely on the discontented to remind us of our subject matter.

It is these issues I want to try to approach, doing so from the perspective of social situations and the public order sustained within them. (I define a social situation as a physical arena anywhere within which an entering person finds himself exposed to the immediate presence of one or more others; and a gathering, all persons present, even if only bound together by the norms of civil inattention, or less still, mutual vulnerability.)

2.

Women do and men don't gestate, breast-feed infants, and menstruate as a part of their biological character. So, too, women on the whole are smaller and lighter boned and muscled than are men. For these physical facts of life to have no appreciable social consequence would take a little organizing, but, at least by modern standards, not much. Industrial society can absorb new ethnic groups bearing raw cultural differences, a year or so of isolating military service for young men, vast differences in educational level, business and employment cycles, the wartime absence of its

Erving Goffman, "The Arrangement between the Sexes." *Theory and Society,* 4, pp. 301–331. © 1977 by Kluwer Academic Publishers. Reprinted with kind permission from Kluwer Academic Publishers.

adult males every generation, appreciable annual vacations, and countless other embarrassments to orderliness. That our form of social organization has any necessary features is, I take it, rather questionable. More to the point, for these very slight biological differences—compared to all other differences—to be identified as the grounds for the kind of social consequences felt to follow understandably from them requires a vast, integrated body of social beliefs and practices, sufficiently cohesive and all-embracing to warrant for its analysis the resurrection of unfashionable functional paradigms. (Perhaps traditional Durkheimian notions work here because in this business we are all priests or nuns and need but be together and a hallowed ground for worship comes to hand.) It is not, then, the social consequences of innate sex differences that must be explained, but the way in which these differences were (and are) put forward as a warrant for our social arrangements, and, most important of all, the way in which the institutional workings of society ensured that this accounting would seem sound. (Indeed, one might argue that the chief consequence of the women's movement is not the direct improvement of the lot of women but the weakening of the doctrinal beliefs that heretofore have underpinned the sexual division of deserts and labor.) In all, one is faced with what might be thought of as "institutional reflexivity"—a newish phrase for an old social anthropological doctrine.

3.

In all societies, all infants at birth are placed in one or in the other of two *sex classes*, the placement accomplished by inspection of the infant's naked person, specifically its genitalia, these being visibly dimorphic—a placement practice not dissimilar to that employed in regard to domestic animals. This placement by physical configuration allows a sex-linked label of identification. (In English, for example, man-woman, male-female, boy-girl, he-she.) The sorting is confirmed at various stages of the individual's growth by still other biological signs, some recognized in the common lore, some (at least in modern society) an elaboration of science, as described, for example, in chromosomal, gonadal, and hormonal findings. In any case, sex-class placement is almost without exception exhaustive of the population and life-long,[1] providing an exemplary instance, if not a prototype, of social classification. Further, in modern society we feel that male-female is one social division that works in full and realistic harmony with our "biological inheritance" and is something which can never be denied, a unique agreement between the immediate understanding of the man in the street and the findings in laboratories. (Thus the layman may be willing to grant Margaret Mead's famous argument about temperament being culturally, not biologically, determined, and moreover that women can quite competently function as dentists, even as firemen, and still further, that [in English] literary bias is present in the convention which establishes "he" before "she," "man" before "woman," "his" before "hers," in phrases which couple the two, allows "man" to stand for humankind, and employs "his" as the proper relative pronoun for semi-indefinite terms such as "individual," male designations clearly being the "unmarked" form; but in making these concessions, he, like Margaret Mead [and myself apparently], sees no reason to deny that the terms "he" and "she" are still entirely adequate as designations of the individuals under discussion.) It should be repeated, then, that by the term "sex-class" I mean to use a category that is purely sociological, that draws on that discipline alone and not on the biological sciences.

In all societies, initial sex-class placement stands at the beginning of a sustained sorting process whereby members of the two classes are subject to differential socialization. From the start, persons who are sorted into the male class and persons who are sorted into the other are given different treatment, acquire different experience, enjoy and suffer different expectations. In response there is objectively overlayed on a biological grid—extending it, neglecting it, countering it—a sex-class–specific way of appearing, acting, feeling. Every society elaborates sex-class in this way, although every society does this after its own fashion. Viewed by the student as a way of characterizing an individual, this complex can be called *gender*; viewed as a way of characterizing a society, it can be called *sexual subculture*. Observe that although gender is almost wholly a social, not biological, consequence of the workings of society, these consequences are objective. An entire population can certainly be unknowing of a particular gender difference, or even falsely opinioned regarding it, yet the difference can still be there, and again, chiefly not because of biology but because of the social experience common to the members of each of the classes.

Every society seems to develop its own conception of what is "essential" to, and characteristic of, the two sex classes, this conception embracing both praised and dispraised attributes. Here are ideals of masculinity and femininity, understandings about ultimate human nature which provide grounds (at least in Western society) for identifying the whole of the person, and provide also a source of accounts that can be drawn on in a million ways to excuse, justify, explain, or disapprove the behavior of an individual or the arrangement under which he lives, these accounts being given both by the individual who is accounted for and by such others as have found reason to account for him. Norms of masculinity and femininity also bear on objective (albeit mainly socially acquired) differences between the sex-classes, but, as suggested, do not coincide with these differences, failing to cover some, misattributing others, and, of course, accounting for a considerable number by means of a questionable doctrine—in our society, a doctrine of biological influence.

Insofar as the individual builds up a sense of who and what he is by referring to his sex class and judging himself in terms of the ideals of masculinity (or femininity), one may speak of *gender identity*. It seems that this source of self-identification is one of the most profound our society provides, perhaps even more so than age-grade, and never is its disturbance or change to be anticipated as an easy matter.

By "sexuality" I will refer to patterns of activity involving sexual stimulation, sexual experience, and the adumbration of inducement to these activities taking a culture-specific form of appearance, dress, style, gesture, and the like. Obviously, much of this sexual practice is sex-class correlated and therefore part of gender. But presumably not all sexuality distinguishes between the sex-classes, being similarly manifest by both. More important, sexuality appears to have a biological life cycle, presumably being very little marked in infancy, very marked in young adulthood, and once again quiescent in later years. This cycle is, of course, manifest through the development and atrophy of the so-called secondary sexual characteristics, of interest here because social ideals regarding masculinity and femininity are often linked to these manifestations. Gender as such, however, has little of a developmental character, except for the pattern in some societies of treating young males as part of the women's group in certain matters; sex-class linked behavior changes through the life of the individual, and in a sequential, patterned way, but not necessarily in response to some unitary inner development. In any case, it should be perfectly clear that gender and sexuality are not the same thing; by my understanding, at least, a seven-year-old boy who manfully volunteers to help his grandmother with her heavy packages is not trying to make out with her.

It seems that *beliefs* about gender, about masculinity-femininity, and about sexuality are in close interaction with actual gender behavior, and that here popular social science plays a part. Discoveries about gender and about sexuality, whether well or badly grounded, are selectively assimilated to normative understandings regarding masculinity-femininity—sometimes quite rapidly—and thus empowered can have a self-fulfilling effect on objective gender behavior. Nonetheless, *beliefs* about gender, about masculinity-femininity, and about sexuality are themselves not part of gender, except to the extent—which can be considerable—that they are differentially espoused as between the sex classes. Each of the two sex-classes supports its own patterns of in-class social relationships, giving rise to such infrastructures as old boy nets, buddy formations, female support systems,[2] and the like.

Two concluding comments of caution. In referring to an attribute of gender, it is easy to speak of matters that are "sex-linked" (or "sex-correlated") in order to avoid the more cumbersome locution, "sex-class linked." And, of course, it is very natural to speak of "the sexes," "cross-sex," "the other sex," and so forth. And so I shall. But this is a dangerous economy, especially so since such glossing fits perfectly with our cultural stereotypes. One should think of sex as a property of organisms, not as a class of them. Thus "secondary sexual characteristics" are attributes associated with sexuality, but it is misleading to speak of these attributes as sex-linked if, in so doing, one means to imply the existence of a class of persons fundamentally defined and definable by matters biological. As suggested, secondary sexual characteristics are indeed, by and large, linkable to sex-class; but each of the two human categories involved has many non-biological attributes and behavioral practices differentially linked to it, too. Underlying this issue, of course, is an even more troublesome one. Given a definition of a category of persons, in this case sex-class, it would seem that *any* apt label we employ to refer to its members—in this case, "men," "women," "male," "female," "he," "she"—can easily come to function as a characterization, symbol, and overall image of the class, a way of constituting one attribute into the jug while other attributes merely fill it.

Second, there is the matter of "traits," "attributes," and "practices." For example, on traditional middle-class playgrounds in America, boys roughhouse more than girls, and roughhousing can be considered as perhaps a practice of the male sex-class. To say here "of the male sex-class" implies that the behavior is somehow not merely encompassed by male bodies severally but also motivated and styled by something from within these several bodies and not, therefore, merely the response of individuals to a formally established ruling. One might want to refer here to a *genderism,* namely, a sex-class linked individual behavioral practice. But take the practice found on school grounds a generation ago of lining up the students outside the doorway in two sex-segregated files before re-entering the school after a recess, presumably so that entrance would be orderly and respectful. Now although such an arrangement certainly "expressed" beliefs about the differences between the sex-classes and was certainly made up of sex-class linked behavior, still, lines formed with one's sex mates cannot easily be treated as a personally encompassed and generated bit of behavior, a genderism. If anything, what one has here is an institutional genderism, a behavioral property of an organization, not a person. *Lining up behavior* might be seen as individually encompassed, but as such ceases to be gender specific, being something that the two classes equally engage in. The lines themselves, it might be added, are a simple—nay, geometric—example of *parallel organization,* an arrangement in which similar efforts or services, similar rights or obligations, are organized in a segregated manner. However, as in the case of the parallel organization which occurs with respect to other binary social divisions—white/black, adult/child, officer/enlisted man, etc.—parallel organization based on sex provides a ready base for the elaboration of differential treatment, these adumbrative elaborations to be seen as consonant and suitable given the claimed difference in character between the two categories. Thus, to revert to the simple example, once children are made to form sex-segregated files, it is a simple matter to rule that the female file enters before the male file, presumably because the "gentler" sex should be given preference in the matter of getting out of the raw outdoors first, and both sexes should be given little lessons on proper regard for gender.[3]

4.

In almost all known societies it seems that sleeping, child-raising, and (to a lesser degree) eating tend to be centered in small establishments, these functions—especially in modern societies—organized around a married, breeding pair; that broadly speaking the social roles of men and women are markedly differentiated, this, incidentally, giving to women the lesser rank and power, restricting her use of public space, excluding her from warfare and hunting, and often from religious and political office; and that more than the male, the female finds her life centered around household duties. This complex of arrangements is a central theme in human social organization, embarrassing the distinction between savage societies and civilized ones. The reason for these facts would be interesting to know, if, in fact, anyone is ever able to uncover them. (Perhaps a factor is that the segmentation that can be built on sex and procreative lines immensely simplifies social organization.) More interesting still is the ideological use to which these facts have been put. For this patterning in societies in general has allowed us to try to account for what occurs in our own industrial world by referring back to what occurs in small, nonliterate societies—indeed gives us some warrant for using the concept of "a society" in the first place—and from there encourages us to keep on going all the way to nonhuman primates and a fundamentally biological view of human nature. My position will be that the lesson that other societies—let alone other species—teach us has not yet been formulated soundly enough to provide us a warranted text to use for instructional purposes, and I propose to restrict myself to the here and now.

If one thinks of women—as I suppose one should—as just another disadvantaged category of persons in modern society, then comparisons with other such categories recommends itself, along with a statement of where women fit on the scale of being treated unfairly. The answer to the latter question sometimes is: not very far down. Women in American society are more or less equal to men in the question of ethnic and social class; whatever these latter properties confer by way of social gain or loss upon men, they do so, too, upon women. So, too, there is considerable equality between the sexes in regard to inheritance, educational opportunity (at least undergraduate), personal consumption of goods, most rights before the law, and the love and respect of their children. Women are disadvantaged in regard to payment for work and grade of work attained, access to certain occupations and certain credit resources, legal practice with respect to name, claims on use of public streets and places. (Some of these disadvantages diminish in the face of modernization and population control policies.) And it might even be claimed that women are advantaged in certain ways: they have generally enjoyed freedom from military conscription, whole or partial exemption from certain kinds of heavy work, preferential courtesies of various kinds—these, too, perhaps diminishing with increased modernization.

This view of the situation of women has some utility in regard to social policy and political action, but for our purposes is too blunt. (The sociologically interesting thing about a disadvantaged category is not the painfulness of the disadvantage, but the bearing of the social structure on its generation and stability.) The issue, then, is not that women get less, but under what arrangement this occurs and what symbolic reading is given to the arrangement.

Given that a basic unit of our society is the domestic establishment with its nuclear family, ideal or fragmented, the whole embedded in a community somewhat homogeneous with respect to class, color, and ethnicity, and omitting incarcerative institutions, one has reason to distinguish two kinds of disadvantaged categories: those that can and tend to be sequestered off into entire families and neighborhoods and those that do not. Blacks are an example of the first; the physically handicapped, the second. Among those disadvantaged categories which are not segregated, women stand rather apart. Other unsegregated categories, such as the blind, the obese, the ex–mental patient, are scattered somewhat haphazardly throughout the social structure. (Relative concentration may occur in a particular ethnic group, age grade, economic level, or sex class, but incidence is still low.) Women are anything but that: they are allocated distributively to households in the form of female children, and then later, but still distributively, to other households in the form of wives. In the first, nature averages out the matter between the two sexes; in the second, law and custom allow only one to a household but strongly encourage the presence of that one.

Women as a disadvantaged group are, then, like maids (and like house servants), somewhat cut off ecologically from congress with their kind. Unlike household staff, however, women are also separated from one another by the stake they acquire in the very organization which divides them. For instead of an employer or master, a woman is likely to have (through the course of her life) a father, a husband, and sons. And these males transmit to her enough of what they themselves possess or acquire to give her a vested interest in the corporation. Defined as deeply different from men, each is yet linked to particular men through fundamental social bonds, placing her in a coalition with her menfolk against the whole of the rest of the world, a coalition, incidentally, which leads her to participate together with a connected male in many social situations. For plainly, here the disadvantaged and the advantaged comprise two perfectly divided halves of the whole society, with similarity in expectations organized within sex-class and bondedness organized across the sexes. (A pretty support for this arrangement is "complementary ritual": a show of affiliation that one spouse extends to a particular female or male will be echoed in what the other spouse displays to the same person; thus the peculiar character of the cross-sex bond can be preserved in the face of third parties.) It is this sort of patterning, as if designed by some juvenile geometer who had read Radcliffe-Brown at too early an age, that presents the sociologically interesting phenomenon—and a remarkable phenomenon it is.

Furthermore, through one ritualized gesture or another, males are very likely to express, albeit fitfully, that they define females as fragile and valuable, to be protected from the harsher things of life and shown both love and respect.[4] Women may be defined as being less than men, but they are nonetheless idealized, mythologized, in a serious way through such values as motherhood, innocence, gentleness, sexual attractiveness, and so forth—a lesser pantheon, perhaps, but a pantheon nonetheless. Moreover, many women—perhaps the vast majority in America even today—are profoundly convinced that however baleful their place in society, the official view concerning the natural characterological differences between themselves and men is correct, eternally and naturally so.

It is these special factors associated with the position of women that make our modern equalitarian world considerably like the most patriarchal you can imagine—a chip off a very old block. And what makes industrial society special is not that our form of economic production little depends on the natural differences between the sexes—it might be very hard to find a society anywhere at any time that actually did—but rather that some of our citizenry no longer believe that women's traditional place is a natural expression of their natural capacities. And without that belief, the whole arrangement between the sex-classes ceases to make much sense. I do not claim that skepticism here will fundamentally alter the arrangement between the sexes, only that if the traditional pattern is sustained, it will be sustained less comfortably.

5.

I have mentioned the obvious fact that women, unlike other disadvantaged adult groups, are held in high regard. Consider now two basic expressions of this condition: the courtship complex and the courtesy system.

1. In our society courtship tends to occur when potential partners are in their late teens and early twenties, this, incidentally, being a time when, on biological grounds, the female maximally fits commercial ideals regarding sexual attractiveness. The female adorns herself in terms of received notions of sexual attractiveness and makes herself available for review in public, semi-public, and restricted places. Males who are present show broadcast attention to females held to be desirable, and await some fugitive sign that can be taken as encouragement of their interest.[5] Routinely, courtship will mean that a male who was on distant terms comes to be on closer ones, which means that the male's assessing act—his ogling—constitutes the first move in the courtship process. And also that decorum will play an important role; for both male and female will act as if she is unaware that she has incurred an assessment (and, if favorable, that she has aroused sexual interest) and that she is not to be importuned if she does not respond with an encouraging act, the male presumably suppressing or displacing his desire. This is not to deny that successful suitors are likely to be those males who did not quite restrict their address to decorous distance-keeping.

The strategic advantage of the male in courtship derives from his ability and right to withdraw interest at any point save perhaps the last ones, that of the female from control of access to her favors, such sequential access being in our society expressive evidence of pair formation. (Power is another matter, deriving from extendable rights in property, social class, and so forth.) The advantages here are not quite balanced because the man also defines such access as evidence of his capacity as a male, and so he has reasons to submit to a female's gatekeeping apart from courtship considerations. (Women get confirmation, too, but the initial show of interest will often do.) But whether the male is interested in courtship or mere seduction, he must pursue the female with attentions and she has the power to lengthen or shorten the pursuit.

Observe that in traditional terms the female's discretion over bestowal can only remain a right insofar as she is successfully secretive about occasions for its use, or is chary about the numbers whom she so honors and the rapidity with which, in the case of any particular successful candidate, she does so. Traditional logic dictates that she bestow her final favors on only one person, and upon him only in response to his having committed himself to supporting her. This practice in turn permits, or at least is very consonant with, two others.

First, she can allow herself to be assessed in terms of nubility because the period for mate selection is geared into her very temporary qualification in this regard. (Thus the harsh fact that she will for many later years be disqualified, and increasingly so, from what she is supposed to be, will be correlated with, and mitigated by, her withdrawal from competition into domesticity, where presumably she will be able to enjoy what she has been able to win during her biologically supported period at play in the courtship game.[6])

Second, one traditional means of encouraging females to keep up the side and not bestow sexual favors too easily, which if done generally might debase the coin, was to define sexuality as dirty and bad, something that is contaminating, something only men want, something, therefore, that destroys good women and creates loose ones. However, the contract to mate was sealed by the female bestowing access rights, a frame for the act which hopefully transformed it into evidence of relationship formation, not easy virtue. She became a mate, not a lay, someone intrinsically pure who had proven vulnerable to but one special man, and this—he could think— because of his own special worthiness. The affirmation of masculinity the male thereby obtained was patently paradoxical; only virginally spirited women desirable as mates could bestow it, but the gift tended to destroy what had been given. In any case, we have here the traditional, standard formula of the respectable classes: he obtains exclusive rights of access and she gets a social place. Of course, for increasing numbers of our population sexual access has ceased to function in quite this way. Sexual license before marriage with someone not destined to be one's spouse is becoming quite routine, and what betrothal brings in these cases, ideally, is exclusive claim, not first claim.

As oft remarked, the courtship system implies that the two sexes will be differently situated in regard to norms of sexual attractiveness. On the face of it, the job of the male is to be attracted and of the female to attract, and similarly, on the face of it, in deciding whom to encourage from among those men who have shown interest, she is likely—it is said—to take into consideration broader matters than mere good looks and youthfulness. As already suggested, the implication is that she (more than he) will be committed to standards of appearance from which age will soon and increasingly cause her to deviate. Note that more so than with men, what a woman inherits socially from her parents cannot prevent her social position becoming precarious should she remain unmarried, in consequence of which she has an added reason to treat unsuitable suitors more and more seriously.

2. As courtship practices provide one expression of the high value placed on women, so the courtesy system provides another. In terms of what interpersonal rituals convey, the belief (in Western society) is that women are precious, ornamental, and fragile, uninstructed in, and ill-suited for, anything requiring muscular exertion or mechanical or electrical training or physical risk; further, that they are easily subject to contamination and defilement and to blanching when faced with harsh words and cruel facts, being labile as well as delicate. It follows, then, that males will have the obligation of stepping in and helping (or protecting) whenever it appears that a female is threatened or taxed in any way, shielding her from gory, grisly sights, from squeamish-making things like spiders and worms, from noise, and from rain, wind, cold, and other inclemencies. Intercession can be extended even to the point of mediating her contacts with officials, strangers, and service personnel. And some of these obligations on the part of the male will extend not merely to females to whom he is personally related, but to any female who comes in sight, that is, to any female

in the gathering in which he happens to find himself, especially if it appears that she is otherwise unattended by a male. This extension to the category as a whole is nicely confirmed by the fact that the manner in which a male proffers a courtesy to his wife can take an impersonal form, one perfectly suited to be shown to any female, and by the fact that minor courtesies can provide males with a defensible reason for involving themselves with attended females not known to them, as when a man momentarily turns from his course of action to light a woman's cigarette, exhibiting through a self-effacing manner that he has no designs on her time or attention and is not to be seen as ambitious, even by her male companion. Another confirmation, pretty as an example but ugly as a fact, is reported in the rape literature;[7] faced with forced attentions from strangers or persons known, and with the failure of other dissuasions, victims tend to beg and plead for mercy, employing the term "please"—a term that presupposes a claim of some sort that one's plight is to be given consideration, a claim that any woman ought to be able to invoke in regard to any man.

3. There appears to be a fundamental interweaving in our public life of courtship and courtesy, with consequences that are important. Obviously the obligation of a male to offer help of one kind and another, to volunteer his own effort as a substitute for that of any neighboring female, is not merely an obligation but also a license. For he can use this obligation selectively as a cover under which to focus his attentions upon attractive women, thus considerably increasing the means available to him to press his pursuit beyond what mere co-participation in a gathering might otherwise provide; for example, she may find herself obliged to convey gratitude, signs of relief, and so forth. He thus facilitates and encourages the female's show of interest in him, should she be of that mind, and may even oblige her somewhat in that direction. Note, courtesies shown by males to desirable females may be preferred with no great expectation or hope that something beyond the contact can come of them; the interaction itself, laced with such joking allusions as the male can muster, provides him a small nibble of sexuality and a small confirmation of his masculinity.

One consequence of this link between courtship and courtesy is the provision of a benign basis for managing those social contacts which might otherwise be competitive or even hostile. Another consequence is that although the standard courtesies accorded females by males tend to be applied fully and with pleasure to the young and pretty, they tend to be applied with increasing reservation as these two properties are wanting. The old and the ugly are thus continuously threatened with not being treated in a manner as befits the human nature their sex-class is supposed to have conferred upon them. And they will have cause to respond by being very careful not to press their case, or demand or intrude to the point where such niceties as are shown them might be withdrawn. (Thus it turns out that "well-dressed," young, attractive females must be very circumspect in public places for one reason, the unattractive for another.)

Another consequence of the mingling of courtship and courtesy bears on the manner in which a female is constrained to conduct herself in mixed gatherings. By acting in a retiring manner, by projecting shyness, reserve, and a display of frailty, fear, and incompetence, she can constitute herself into the sort of object to which a male can properly extend his helping hand, suppressing coarseness in his speech and behavior while doing so. But observe that when the gathering contains men other than her husband, another reason encourages her in this unforthcomingness. Given that males will be watching for encouragement, looking to some lapse in the female's wonted reserve as a sign of this, it follows that any forwardness on her part, any initiative, insobriety, aggressiveness, or direction-giving, can be seen as sexually inviting, a sign, in short, of accessibility.[8] Thus, specific legal or moral sanctions are not ordinarily needed to restrain women in public, only self-interest, but this self-regulation can be seen as a functional consequence, a by-product, of the interworkings of other social definitions.

6.

Now the heart of the matter. It is common to conceive of the differences between the sexes as showing up against the demands and constraints of the environment, the environment itself being taken as a harsh given, present before the matter of sex differences arose. Or, differently put, that sex differences are a biological given, an external constraint upon any form of social organization that humans might devise. There is another way of viewing the question, however. Speculatively one can reverse the equation and ask what could be sought out from the environment or put into it so that such innate differences between the sexes as there are could count—in fact or in appearance—for something. The issue, then, is institutional reflexivity. Consider some examples.

1. Clearly on biological grounds, mother is in a position to breastfeed baby and father is not. Given that recalcitrant fact, it is meet that father temporarily but exclusively takes on such tasks as may involve considerable separation from the household. But this quite temporary biologically grounded constraint turns out to be extended culturally. A whole range of domestic duties come (for whatever reason) to be defined as inappropriate for a male to perform; and a whole range of occupations away from the household come to be defined as inappropriate for the female. Given these social definitions, coalition formation is a natural response to the harsh facts of the world, for only in this way will one be able to acquire what one needs and yet not have to engage in labor that is unsuitable for someone of one's kind. Nor is couple formation required only because of gender constraints on task performance. In public life in general women will find that there are things that should be done for them, and men will find that there are things that they should be doing for others, so once again they find they need each other. (So that just as a man may take a wife to save himself from labor that is uncongenial to him, so she can seek him so as to have the company she needs if she is to make full use of public places.) Thus, the human nature imputed to the male causes him to be dependent on a female connection, and the reciprocal condition prevails for women. Who a male finds he

needs if he is to act according to his nature is just who needs him so that she can act according to hers. Persons as such do not need one another in these ways, they do so only as gender-based identities.

2. Consider the household as a socialization depot. Take as a paradigm a middle-class pair of cross-sexed sibs. The home training of the two sexes will differ, beginning to orient the girl to taking a domestic, supportive role, and the boy to a more widely based competitive one. This difference in orientation will be superimposed on a fundamental quality in many matters that are felt to count. So from the start, then, there will be two basic principles to appeal to in making claims and warranting allocations. One is the equality of sibs and beyond this of participating members— the share and share alike theme realized in its strongest form in many wills and in its most prevalent form in turn-taking systems. The other is the accounting by sex, as when the larger portion at mealtime is given to the male "because he's a boy" or the softer of two beds is allocated to the female "because she's a girl," or a male is accorded harsher negative sanctions than a female because his is the coarser nature and it will take more to get through to him. And these accountings by appeal to gender will never cease to be used as a handy device to rationalize an allocation whose basis is otherwise determined, to exclude a basis of allocation that might cause disgruntlement, and, even more, to explain away various failures to live up to expectations.

All of this is perfectly well known in principle, although not adequately explored in detail. What is not well appreciated is that differently sexed children coming under the jurisdiction of the same parental authority and living much of their early lives in one another's presence in the same set of rooms produce thereby an ideal setting for role differentiation. For family life ensures that most of what each sex does is done in the full sight of the other sex and with full mutual appreciation of the differential treatment that obtains. Thus, whatever the economic or class level and however well or badly off a female sees she is when compared to children in other families, she can hardly fail to see that her male sib, equal to her when compared to children in other families and often equal, too, in regard to ultimate claims upon the family resources, is yet judged differently and accorded different treatment from herself by their parents. So, too, a male sib. Thus from the beginning males and females acquire a way of judging deserts and treatment that muffles (by cross-cutting) differences in class and economic power. However superior the social position of a family may be, its female children will be able to learn that they are different from (and somewhat subordinate to) males; and however inferior the social position of a family may be, its male children will be able to learn that they are different from (and somewhat superordinate to) females. It is as if society planted a brother with sisters so women could from the beginning learn their place, and a sister with brothers so men could learn their place. Each sex becomes a training device for the other, a device that is brought right into the house; and what will serve to structure wider social life is thus given its shape and its impetus in a very small and very cozy circle. And it also follows that the deepest sense of what one is—one's gender identity—is something that is given its initial character from ingredients that do not bear on ethnicity or socio-economic stratification, in consequence of which we all acquire a deep capacity to shield ourselves from what we gain and lose by virtue of our placement in the overall social hierarchy. Brothers will have a way of defining themselves in terms of their differences from persons like their sisters, and sisters will have a way of defining themselves in terms of their differences from persons like their brothers, in both cases turning perception away from how it is the sibs in one family are socially situated in a fundamentally different way from the sibs of another family. Gender, not religion, is the opiate of the masses. In any case, we have here a remarkable organizational device. A man may spend his day suffering under those who have power over him, suffer this situation at almost any level of society, and yet on returning home each night regain a sphere in which he dominates. And wherever he goes beyond the household, women can be there to prop up his show of competence. It is not merely that your male executive has a female secretary, but (as now often remarked) his drop-out son who moves up the hierarchy of alternative publishing or protest politics will have female help, too; and had he been disaffected enough to join a rural commune, an appropriate division of labor would have awaited him. And should we leave the real world for something set up as its fictional alternative, a science fiction cosmos, we would find that here, too, males engage in the executive action and have females to help out in the manner of their sex. Wherever the male goes, apparently, he can carry a sexual division of labor with him.

3. In modern times, mating pairs appear naked to each other and are even likely to employ a bathroom at the same time. But beyond this, the mature genitalia of one sex is not supposed to be exposed to the eyes of the other sex. Furthermore, although it is recognized that persons of both sexes are somewhat similar in the question of waste products and their elimination, the environment in which females engage in this act ought (we in America apparently feel) to be more refined, extensive, and elaborate than that required for males. Presumably out of consideration for the arrangement between the sexes in general, and the female sex-class in particular, it has come to pass, then, that almost all places of work and congregation are equipped with two sets of toilet facilities (a case of parallel organization), differentiated with respect to quality. A case of separate and unequal. Therefore, in very nearly every industrial and commercial establishment, women will be able to break off being exposed to males and their company and retire into an all-female enclave, often in the company of a female friend, and there spend time in toiletry, a longer time presumably, and perhaps more frequently, than males spend in their segregated toilet, and under more genteel environmental conditions. A resting room that is sex-segregated (as many are) may extend this divided realm. There is thus established a sort of with-then-apart rhythm, with a period of the sexes being immersed together followed by a short period of separation, and so on. (Bars, gyms, locker rooms, pool rooms, etc., accomplish the same sort of periodic segregation, but from the male side, the difference being that whereas female redoubts tend to be furnished more genteely than the surrounding scene, male redoubts [at least in the U.S.] are often furnished less prepossessingly than the surround.) This same pattern seems to be extended outward from toilets and resting rooms to larger domains. Large stores

have floors which merge the sexes but also smaller zones which offer one-sex merchandise patronized very largely by that sex alone. Schools provide coeducational classes, punctuated by gym, sports, and a few other activities that are sex-segregated.[9]

All in all, then, one does not so much deal with segregation as with segregative punctuation of the day's round, this ensuring that subcultural differences can be reaffirmed and reestablished in the face of contact between the sexes. It is as if the joining of the sexes were tolerable providing periodic escape is possible; it is as if equality and sameness were a masquerade that was to be periodically dropped. And all of this is done in the name of nicety, of civilization, of the respect owed females, or of the "natural" need of men to be by themselves. Observe that since by and large public places are designed for males (the big exception being large department stores), female facilities have had to be added to ones already established. Predictably, it has been an argument against hiring females that an extra complement of toilet facilities would be necessary and is not available.

Now clearly, if ogling and sexual access is to play the role it does in pair formation in our society, then sequestering of toilet functions by sex would seem to be indicated. And even more clearly, what is thus sequestered is a biological matter in terms of which the sex-classes biologically and markedly differ. But the sequestering arrangement as such cannot be tied to matters biological, only to folk conceptions about biological matters. The *functioning* of sex-differentiated organs is involved, but there is nothing in this functioning that *biologically* recommends segregation; *that* arrangement is totally a cultural matter. And what one has is a case of institutional reflexivity: toilet segregation is presented as a natural consequence of the difference between the sex-classes, when in fact it is rather a means of honoring, if not producing, this difference.

4. Consider now selective job placement. Traditionally in industrial society women have gravitated to, or have been gravitated to, jobs which sustain the note established for them in households—the garment industry, domestic labor, commercial cleaning, and personal servicing such as teaching, innkeeping, nursing, food handling.[10] In these latter scenes, presumably, it will be easy for us to fall into treating the server as someone to help us in a semi-mothering way, not someone to subordinate coldly or be subordinated by. In service matters closely associated with the body and the self, we are thus able to play down the harshness that male servers might be thought to bring.

Women, especially young, middle-class ones, have also, of course, been much employed in clerical and secretarial labor, which work is often defined as a dead-end job to be filled by someone who dresses well and doesn't expect or want to make a career out of the labor. Presumably secretaries are merely marking time until marriage, preferably in a place where opportunity to "meet" men is to be found. In any case, the age and sex difference between secretary and employer allows for some styling in avuncular terms. By removing the relationship from the strict world of business, the superior can suffer being intimately viewed by a subordinate without feeling that he has lost rank by the association. He can also make minor demands beyond the core of the contract, expecting to be seen as someone whose needs should be attended to however varied these might be—as a child would be attended by a mother. In return he can extend family feeling, using a personal term of address (of course asymmetrically), please-and-thank-you brackets around each of the minor discrete services called for, and gallantry in the matter of opening doors and moving heavy typewriters. He can also allow her to use the telephone for personal calls and can respond to pleas for special time off to accomplish the business of her sex.

So, too, one finds in jobs where women "meet the public"—ticket-takers, receptionists, airhostesses, salespersons—that standards of youthful "attractiveness" apply in employee selection. Which practice is, of course, even more marked in selecting women for advertising displays and the dramatic arts. The consequence is that when a male has business contacts with a female, she is more than otherwise likely to be someone whom he might take pleasure in associating with. Again, the courtesy he here extends and receives can carry a dash of sexual interest. (It appears that the higher the male reaches in the hierarchies within business, government, or the professions, the classier will be the women he is required to have incidental dealings with, a sign and symbol of success.)

Finally, note that in almost all work settings established as places for thoroughly masculine labor, one or two women can be found engaged in some sort of ancillary work. It turns out, then, that there are few social settings where males will not be in a position to enact courtesies due to the female sex.

In all, then, one can see that selective employment comes to ensure that males are likely to find themselves rather frequently in the presence of females, and that these women will not only tend to allow a personalization of the contact, but will be relatively young and attractive beyond what random selection ought to allow. In that sense, the world that men are in is a social construct, drawing them daily from their conjugal milieu to what appear to be all-male settings; but these environments turn out to be strategically stocked with relatively attractive females, there to serve in a specialized way as passing targets for sexually allusive banter and for diffuse considerateness extended in both directions. The principle is that of less for more, the effect is that of establishing the world beyond the household as a faintly red-light district where men can easily find and safely enjoy interactional favors. Observe that the more a male contents himself with gender pleasantries—systematically available yet intermittent and brief—the more widely can a preferential category of females be shared by males in general.[11] (Indeed, the traditional dating game can be seen not merely as a means of getting the sexes paired, but as a means of giving a large number of men a little of the company of exemplary women.)

5. Among all the means by which differentiation along sex-class lines is fostered in modern society, one stands out as having a special and an especially powerful influence: I refer to our *identification system,* this involving two related matters, our means of discovering "who" it is that has come into our ken, that is, our placement practices, and our means of labeling what it is we have thus placed.

On the placement side, it is clear that the appearance established as appropriate to the two sexes allows for sex typing at a distance. Although recently this arrangement has developed some potential for error, still the system is remarkably effective at any angle and from almost any distance, saving only that viewing be close enough to allow perception of a figure. Effectiveness of placement by sight is matched by sound; tone of voice alone—as on the phone—is sufficient by and large for sexual identification. Indeed, handwriting is effective, too, although perhaps not as fully as appearance and voice. (Only appreciable differences in age are as effectively betrayed through all three channels; race in America is conveyed through sight and, by and large, through voice but not through handwriting.)

On the naming side, we have a system of terms including proper personal names, titles, and pronouns. These devices are used for giving deference (whether respect, distance, or affection), for specifying who we are addressing or who among those present we are referring to, and for making attributions in written and spoken statements. And in European languages, by and large, except for second-person pronouns, these naming practices inform at least about sex-class, this often being the only matter they do inform about.

Now our placement practices and naming practices, taken together as a single system, serve to define who we are to have dealings with and enable these dealings to proceed; and both sets of practices very strongly encourage categorization along sex-class lines. Right from the very start of an interaction, then, there is a bias in favor of formulating matters in sex-relevant terms, such that sex-class provides the overall profile or container, and particularizing properties are then attributed to the outline by way of specification. This is not a small bias. And note that this identification-naming system is overwhelmingly accounted for by the doctrine that consequent discriminations are only natural, something not to be seen as a product of personal or social engineering but rather as a natural phenomenon.

7.

I have touched on five examples of institutional reflexivity, five features of social organization which have the effect of confirming our gender stereotypes and the prevailing arrangement between the sexes: the sex-class division of labor, siblings as socializers, toilet practices, looks and job selection, our identification system. In all of this an underlying issue has been the biological differences between the sexes. It is that issue to which I return now, especially in the matter of differences in size, strength, and combat potential.

My argument throughout has been the now standard one that the physical differences between the sexes are in themselves very little relevant to the human capacities required in most of our undertakings. The interesting question then becomes: How in modern society do such irrelevant biological differences between the sexes come to seem of vast social importance? How, without biological warrant, are these biological differences elaborated socially? Again the answer will argue for institutional reflexivity.

1. Clearly if hand-to-hand combat could be arranged on every occasion of human contact, the biological difference between the sex-classes would signify, for in such

combat the weaker would have to extend himself to the full to try for a win or to flee for safety, and overwhelmingly in cross-sex contacts, the himself would be a herself. In much of adult life, these trials are ruled out. But they are not ruled out as a source of guiding imagery. Among young males—and males only—training and practice in boxing and wrestling are fairly widespread, if spread shallow. Thus, instead of spluttering on the occasion of a physical challenge, males learn to do something in a somewhat concerted fashion. In any case, one has here a key source of metaphor, the dueling or punch-out format. Men, even middle-class ones, hold themselves ready to have to defend themselves physically (as a defense of self) or attack another (as a defense of loved ones, property, or principles). For middle-class males, at least, this does not mean actual combat, merely a sizing up of situations in terms of this possibility. Before a male becomes openly aggressive, he thus judges the possible outcome in terms of "having it out" and whether he could "handle" the other. (Of course, he will also be concerned about creating a "scene," with its attendant ill fame, entanglements with the police and the courts, cosmetic disarray, etc.) This judgment produces a great deal of circumspection and carefulness and often the erroneous outward appearance that fighting has ceased to be a relevant possibility. But, in fact, the issue is not that the model has ceased to function as a guide, rather that it functions very well.

Corresponding to the role of combat as a source of imagery and style in dealings between men, one finds an image of sexual imposition or force in dealings across sexes. Relationship formation is seen to come from aggressive initiatory activity on the part of males, a breaking down of boundaries and barriers, a pursuit, a pressing of one's suit. (Indeed, fiction affirms a remarkable version—a mythic encapsulation, as it were—portrayed through hands that start by unsuccessfully fighting off a rapist and end by caressing a lover; and it turns out that some actual rapists look, albeit unsuccessfully, to have the fantasy realized.[12]) Thus, the courtship scene, held to express the ultimate nature of the beasts, turns out to be one of the few available contexts in which myths concerning the differences between the sexes can be realized. Basic social facts, then, are not so much carried into this realm as carried out of it.

2. Consider now dimorphism and social situations. Males, being bigger and stronger than females, can, if of a mind, help women out in social situations in regard, say, to things that are heavy or out of reach. Males on the same count can physically threaten present females, as well as come to their aid should others threaten. In all of this, males will have an opportunity of doing and females of showing respect, if not gratitude, for what is done. But observe how social practice has made it possible for men and women to stage these self-confirming scenes.

Men, of course, are trained from childhood in outdoor competencies, mechanical, electrical, automotive, and so forth, just as they very often are given some rudimentary practice in the arts of self-defense. They come then, to social situations with these advantages, just as women come to social situations without them.

Differential size and strength similarly has a social element. Although men on the whole are larger and stronger than women, there is appreciable overlap in the two normal curves. Thus, if present conventions were reversed and if care were taken, a very evident number of couples could contain males shorter than or equal in height to their female companions. But in fact, selective mating ensures that with almost no exceptions husbands are bigger than wives and boyfriends are bigger than their girlfriends. (One has here a prime example of a norm sustained without official or specific social sanction, diffuse unsatisfactory consequences apparently serving to ensure utter uniformity.) Now since our Western society is very considerably organized in terms of couples, in the sense that the two members are often to be found in each other's company (most constantly, of course, in the recreational and domestic spheres), it will be that displays by men to women of physical help and physical threat will be widely possible. The marital bond—whatever else it is—can be seen as having the consequence of more or less permanently attaching an audience directly to each performer, so that wherever the male or female goes, an appropriate other will be alongside to reciprocate the enactment of gender expressions. Pair formation creates a mutually captive audience. Nor does the matter stop with the marital and dating pair. Even temporary clusters at sociable occasions are likely to be recruited so once again the male is in a position to do his show without being embarrassed by the presence of a female who (it appears) is physically endowed to do it better. Observe, too, that the customary age differential between the pairing sexes ensures that, by and large, the male will be more experienced and moneyed than the female, this, too, supporting the show of control he exhibits in social situations.

In sum, early training reinforces what selection by age and height differential establishes, namely, social situations in which men and women can effectively play out the differential human nature claimed for them. Thus, the image can be sustained that all women are muscularly less developed than all men in all respects, a binary division alien to the biological facts; for in fact, physical forcefulness involves several variables which are incompletely correlated, and a line cleanly dividing the two sex-classes cannot be drawn. Yet the patterning of sex-class behavior is such that puny men and robust women mainly suffer the assaultive contingencies associated with their sex-class, not their size.

3. An important feature of the life of the young, especially the male young, in our society is competitive sports and games. This organized vying is presented by adults as a desirable thing, a scene in which youths can work off their animal energies, learn fairness, perseverance, and team spirit, obtain exercise, and sharpen a desire to fight against the odds for a win; in short, a training ground for the game of life. (Thus when boys are given instruction in fighting, the teaching tends to be in a fair contest frame, with rules and referees to see that nothing gets out of hand.) But indeed, one might just as well see these vying frames as the only discoverable way of establishing the world as we claim it to be. So, one could argue, it is not that sports are but another expression of our human (specifically male) nature, but rather that sports are the only expression of male human nature—an arrangement specifically designed to allow males to manifest the qualities claimed as basic to them: strengths of various kinds, stamina, endurance, and the like. In consequence of this early training in sports, individuals can carry through life a framework of arrangement and response,

a referencing system, which provides evidence, perhaps *the* evidence, of our having a certain nature. Adult spectator sports, live and transmitted, ensure a continuous reminder of this contesting perspective.

There is an important point to be made about contests. Fairness is achieved not only by obedience to the rules of the sport, but also by selecting evenly matched opponents or by handicapping superior ones. This ensures that the outcome will be unpredictable and therefore suspenseful. But for an understanding of biological differences, the issue is that even in the put-together world of sports, only very careful selectivity provides the circumstances in which marginal effort will be determinative, when, that is, the full exercise of physical skill, endurance, and strength is necessary. And in sports, circumstances are also presented in which weight, reach, and height are crucial. *It is here, then, that the sort of biological differences that exist between males and females would tell.* But for these differences to tell, these are the arrangements that must be established. Now what one finds increasingly in civil life is that extremely few jobs call on this marginal performance, this stretching of physical capacity. Yet it is just this marginal difference between the strong and the weak, the sturdy and the slight, the tall and the short, that is employed in the doctrine we have concerning work and sex.

4. Another matter to examine is playfulness. In many social circles, the occasions when physical coercion is threatened or applied may be rare indeed. But although the social environment is thus uncooperative in allowing for a show of gender, forcing the use of sporting scenes designed for the purpose, the ad hoc use of playfulness can compensate, ensuring that opportunity for mock moves of physical dominance will abound. Thus between males one finds various forms of horseplay— shoving, pushing, punching, withholding—along with mock contests such as Indian wrestling, spur of the moment races, hand-squeeze trials, and the like. Across sex, males engage in lift-off bear hugs, mock chasing after, coercive holding in one position, grasping of the two small wrists in one big hand, playful rocking of the boat, dunking, throwing or pushing into the water, spraying with water, making as if to push off a cliff, throwing small stones at the body, approaching with snake, dead rat, squid, and other loathsome objects, threatening with electrical shocks of an order they themselves can bear, and other delights.[13] Observe that by unseriously introducing just those threats and pains that he might protect a woman from, a male can encourage her to provide a full-voiced rendition of the plight to which her sex is presumably prone. And, of course, she herself can create the unserious circumstances in which her display of gender will be possible, as when she pummels he who holds her, as if out of hopelessness at having any effect upon the giant that has captured her, or hides her eyes from the terrible things that are being shown on the silver screen while he laughingly watches on, or squeals and turns away from the overexciting finish of a horse race, or runs across the street with her head down and her arms flailing in mock terror over the oncoming traffic, or unsuccessfully attempts to open a jar with a play at straining all her muscular reserve, or gestures abject fear when the phone rings and signals a call that is unwelcome, or gesticulates that walking over

the stones to get to the water is destroying her tender feet, or that the cold is making her shiver like unto little Liza on the ice floe.

5. I have argued that genderisms are not generated by the impact of an unrelenting environment itself, but by an environment in some sense designed for the purpose of this evocation. Observe now that individuals need not wait for the environment to produce those circumstances for which the display of a genderism will provide a usable response. Individuals can apply a format that automatically transforms an environment into one which induces such a display, guaranteeing that something suitable will be found for ritual management. We tend to think of a chivalrous man helping a woman — unacquainted or merely acquainted — to manage a load that is heavy or messy or precariously placed, and therefore we can see him as someone who stands by parentally in case of trouble; but indeed, a male, bent on this sort of gallantry, can search a women-connected scene for the heaviest or messiest or most precarious concern she happens to have, and then volunteer help with what is thus found. This action on his part is then likely to be confirmed by the gratitude she shows for the consideration given her. But, of course, in *every* social situation involving a female (or anyone else) there will be a heaviest, a messiest, and a most precarious concern, even though by the standards set in other settings, this may involve something that is light, clean, and safe. (There is a symmetry here; a female can similarly search the scene for whatever in it is best adapted to release her from an indication of weakness, fear, mechanical incompetence, or, on the other side, give evidence of her capacity to provide minor domestic-like services.)

6. I have suggested that every physical surround, every room, every box for social gatherings, necessarily provides materials that can be used in the display of gender and the affirmation of gender identity. But, of course, the social interaction occurring in these places can be read as supplying these materials also. Participants in any gathering must take up some sort of microecological position relative to one another, and these positions will provide ready metaphors for social distance and relatedness, just as they will provide sign vehicles for conveying relative rank.

More important, the management of talk will itself make available a swarm of events usable as signs. Who is brought or brings himself into the immediate orbit of another; who initiates talk, who is selected as the addressed recipient, who self-selects in talk turn-taking, who establishes and changes topics, whose statements are given attention and weight, and so forth. As with verbal interaction, so also with joint participation in silent projects such as walking together, arranging objects, and the like. For here, too, organization requires that someone make the decisions and coordinate the activity; and again the opportunity is available, often apparently unavoidably so, for someone to emerge as dominant, albeit in regard to trivial matters.

An interactional field, then, provides a considerable expressive resource, and it is, of course, upon this field that there is projected the training and beliefs of the participants. It is here that sex-class makes itself felt, here in the organization of face-to-face interaction, for here understandings about sex-based dominance can be employed as a means of deciding who decides, who leads, and who follows. Again, these scenes do not so much allow for the expression of natural differences between the sexes as for the production of that difference itself.

May I recommend that the capacity to work social situations for what can inevitably be found in them is of considerable importance. When boys and girls are socialized, one of the basic things they learn is this capacity to size up a social situation for what can be expressively wrung from it. This capacity in turn depends upon the culture's idiom of expression, itself fed from several sources, such as — in Western culture — training in the ideally expressive environments of games and contests, imagery drawn from animal lore, residues from military training, and so forth. In consequence, men and women are able to scan any ongoing social activity for means through which to express gender. And, of course, these means do considerable organizational work; as suggested, what becomes involved is the question of who makes the decisions in regard to a multitude of small doings which, pieced together, allow for smooth collaborative activity. Some of this organizational work need not be done. Much of it could be done by celebrating other statuses. But given that this work *is* presently done by an appeal to sex-class, and given that various institutional practices ensure the copresence of men and women, then the question becomes moot as to whether these rituals ought to be seen as a means of celebrating the social structure, or whether the importance of the social structure, at least in its relevant aspects, ought to be seen as that of providing a template for expressive displays which help to organize social situations. (Which is not to say that social structure is somehow a construct or real only as it affects what occurs in face-to-face interaction.)

8.

I have argued that females are a distinctive disadvantaged category in that they alone among these — save only children — are idealized, in Western society as pure, fragile, valued objects, the givers and receivers of love and care, this giving and receiving being, in a way, their office. And I have also pressed a kind of institutional reflexivity, the argument that deep-seated institutional practices have the effect of transforming social situations into scenes for the performance of genderisms by both sexes, many of these performances taking a ritual form which affirms beliefs about the differential human nature of the two sexes even while indications are provided as to how behavior between the two can be expected to be intermeshed. Now consider the politics of these rituals.

First note that the traditional ideals of femininity and the ideals of masculinity are alike in that both sets tend to be supported for the relevant sex by both sexes. At the same time, the ideals are complementary in that the ones held for women are differentiated from the ones held for men and yet the two fit together. Frailty is fitted to strength, gentleness to sternness, diffuse serving to project orientation, mechanical unknowingness to mechanical competencies, delicacy relative to contamination vs. insensitivity to contamination, and so forth. It turns out, then, that a woman could only realize the ideals of femininity by holding herself away from the heat, grime, and competition of the world beyond the household. So these ideals have, then, a political consequence, that of relieving persons who are males from half the competition they would otherwise face. (A similar consequence can be attributed to age-grading and late schooling.) This in no way implies, of course, that a woman has no ability to make her suitors compete for her hand, or make the one to whom she is inclined dance at her attendance to further his suit, but only that this female power is sequestered from the main show. As she herself is. Even those females who are able and willing to trade some of their favors in exchange for special consideration in the work world will find themselves quite differently related to the contingencies of employment than are males, a difference that then continues to mark at least middle-class women off as belonging essentially to a work-alien, private-sphere.

But this sequestering itself is of a special kind. For, as already considered, social organization ensures that men and women will be in one another's presence, women being a disadvantaged group that is not (in modern society) hidden away in bad neighborhoods or in barracks on the outskirts of town. So the difference between the sex-classes will very commonly be something that can be given ritual expression.

Apologists can, then, interpret the high value placed on femininity as a balance and compensation for the substantive work that women find they must do in the domestic sphere and for their subordination in, if not exclusion from, public spheres. And the courtesies performed for and to women during social occasions can be seen as redress for the retiring role they are obliged to play at these times. What could be thought good about their situation, then, seems always to enter as a means of cloaking what could be thought bad about it. And every indulgence society shows to women can be seen as a mixed blessing.

9.

Surely the argument that ours is a sexist society is valid—as it is for societies in general. A considerable amount of what persons who are men do in affirmation of their sense of identity requires their doing something that can be seen as what a woman by her nature could not do, or at least could not do well; and the reverse can be said about persons who are women. Furthermore, some of these doings the individual does in the company of the other sex, an arrangement facilitated by diverse institutional practices, allowing for the dialogic performance of identity—ritual statements by one party receiving ritual answers from the other party, both displays being necessary for the full portrayal of the human nature of the individuals involved. But, of course, in the case of persons who are women, the issue is not merely that they are in a complementary position to persons who are men; the issue is that for women this complementarity also means vulnerability and, in the feelings of some, oppression. In this light, and as an illustration, consider public life.

Wherever an individual is or goes he must bring his body along with him. That means that whatever harm bodies can do, or be vulnerable to, goes along, too. As for vulnerabilities, their source allows us to distinguish two kinds. First, impersonal risks seen as lodged in a setting and not specifically intended for the recipient: physical risks—fire, falling objects, accidental collision, etc.; medical risks due to contagion, poisons, etc.; contamination of body by smell and grime. Second (and our concern here), social risks, those seen as a product of a malefactor's intention. Here central matters are physical assault, robbery, sexual molestation, kidnapping, blocking of passage, breaching of conversational preserves, verbal insult delivered in conversation already established, importunement. Whomsoever an individual is in the presence of, he makes them vulnerable in these ways and they make him vulnerable similarly.

Now the standard feature of all public life—especially that occurring whenever unacquainted individuals come into one another's immediate presence—is that the inclination to exploit the immediate vulnerability of others is suppressed, if not repressed. A folk theory is maintained that indeed persons can be physically close and be of no interest whatsoever to one another, that, for example, not even evaluative assessment of social attributes is occurring. Among the unacquainted, the symbol of this arrangement is civil inattention, the process of glancing at an other to express that one has no untoward intent nor expects to be an object of it, and then turning the glance away, in a combination of trust, respect, and apparent unconcern.

The arrangement under which an individual causes no difficulty and is given none, when both prospects are eminently feasible, is felt to be ensured by devices of social control. The law is one factor (at least it used to be so thought); another, disapproval and moral condemnation by witnesses to the act—in effect, the threat of defaming. In the case of attack on males (or on females by other females) there is also the issue of physical and verbal counterattack, the possibility of getting back in return what had theretofore been suppressed, and getting as good as one gives or better.

It is known, of course, that conventional standards of social control in public places can prove inadequate; if not that, then certainly that individuals can come to believe that this is the case. The consequence is felt insecurity in public places. What I want to consider here, however, is the special relation of females to these circumstances.

As suggested, women are not trained in fighting and moreover are encouraged to employ quite passive means of avoiding fights and to withdraw from such as have begun. Therefore, relative to men under attack, women are less capable and felt to be so. (I suppose it might be said that men must fear being shown up as unwilling to fight, and that women have less to fear in this matter.) It seems also the case that a woman is at a disadvantage in giving insult back in response to attack. She is faced with the dilemma that any remonstrance becomes in itself a form of self-exposure, ratifying a connection that theretofore had merely been improperly attempted. (Surely an insidious trick on the part of social organization.) Also, not socialized into the fighting frame, she can find herself blithely returning an insult—when a man, mindful of possible escalation, might be leery of doing so—which, in turn, evokes a response that cannot be managed by either party. The male recipient of female insult can feel, for example, that his readiness to abjure the use of physical force with females presupposed that females would not press quarrels to the point where a fight would ordinarily be required; finding that this tacit contract has been breached, he may not know what to do, and whatever he does, do it in a troubled and confused way.[14]

But the difference between the sexes in the matter of being vulnerable in public places goes deeper still.

Consider again what an individual can suffer at another's hands in public. There is loss of life, an equal value as between the sexes except perhaps in time of war. There is injury to limbs, presumably also an equal matter, except that bodily disfigurement is perhaps a greater contingency for females than for males. (More important, perhaps, life and limb, being thought to have ultimate value, can be used in coercive exchange, as in "Your money or your life.") There is the disarray of personal front (clothing and appearance), likely in any physical altercation, and here the standards women are obliged to maintain are considerably more strict than those required of men. (After all, for a woman to appear in public with her costume disarrayed can be taken as a sign of accessibility and looseness of morals.) There is expropriation of cash and valuables, men probably having somewhat more to lose of the first, woman of the second.

From this point, the situation of the two sexes sharply differs. Except in prison, men in modern society can't be much threatened by sexual violence nor threatened by physical harm if sexual access is not allowed; women can be. But there is a more subtle and more important difference. As suggested, the courtship process leads the male to press his pursuit, first in finding some reason for opening up a state of talk, and second, in overcoming the social distance initially maintained therein. Breaching of existing distance, partly on speculation, is, then, a standard part of the male's contribution to cross-sex dealings, at least as far as the male is concerned. And it is in the nature of his view of these dealings that they know no season or place; any occasion will do. All good-looking females wherever found are worth a moment's ogling, and this attention also allows for discernment of possible signs of encouragement or (if not that) signs that discouragement is not complete. And men can be easily confirmed in this approach because they know that many of the relationships they do end up having with women began in this way and were not likely to have begun at all had no breaching occurred. Note that women themselves do not take a consistent line here, for just as some will be offended by these overreachings, so others (even as they discourage the interest shown their person) can be inwardly pleased by the delict, seeing in it an indication of their rating, a measure of their "attractiveness." [15]

It follows, then, that females are somewhat vulnerable in a chronic way to being "hassled"; for what a male can improperly press upon them by way of drawing them into talk or by way of improperly extending talk already initiated stands to gain him (and indeed her) a lot, namely, a relationship, and if not this, then at least confirmation of *gender* identity. [16]

In this context, rebuffs on the part of the female carry special contingencies. The issue appears in starkest form, perhaps, in robbery itself, apart from matters of sex. For it turns out that once the robber has broken cover and revealed himself as a wrongdoer, as a culprit committing an indictable offense, such aggressive feelings as he might otherwise have had but suppressed become something he might as well express, having already paid most of the price for such expression. His "wantonly" injuring his victim may, then, be a sign not of special sadistic impulse but rather of what we all might inflict were no penalty (at least no further penalty) to be incurred. Something similar can occur in the case of salutations some men feel impelled to extend to women with whom they are unacquainted. When such overtures are rebuffed, the male finds not only that he is exposed as desiring what he is now judged unworthy of receiving, but also that he has established himself as someone who has attempted to improperly force or extend a communicative contact. Not uncommonly, then, he uses this channel to redefine what he has not been able to obtain, openly conveying insults to she who has denied him.

And one can see why men are not reciprocally subject to molestation by women; for in general, were a woman to press her favors, there would be men who could only stand to gain by accepting. Takers could always be found. And one can see that women have a power men do not much have, that of allowing access to themselves. A wife can thus betray her husband more easily than the reverse, even though he has greater mobility, implying access to a larger number of pastures.

So it is apparent that men and women find themselves quite differently related to public life, its contingencies being very much greater for females than for males, and for reasons that are structurally deep-seated. This difference cuts sharply and cleanly along sex-class lines in spite of the fact that physical potential for assault and for self-defense is by no means so clearly divisible into non-overlapping classes. Plainly, it is for membership sorting that biology provides a neat and tidy device; the contingencies and response that seem so naturally to follow along the same lines are a consequence of social organization.

NOTES

1. It is apparent, of course, that there are cases of temporary misassignment at birth, cases of mixed biological signs (intersexing), and, recently, surgical and social "reassignment." It should be just as apparent that these three classes of cases are exceptional, that they take their significance from the fact that they are exceptional, and that sex-class placement is, relative to all other placements, rigorously achieved.

2. See Carroll Smith-Rosenberg, "The Female World of Love and Ritual: Relations between Women in Nineteenth-Century America," *Signs* 1, 1 (1975), pp. 1–30, especially pp. 9ff.

3. The history of parallel arrangements for the sexes in American society has never been written.

4. Jessie Bernard in *Women and the Public Interest* (Chicago, 1971), pp. 26, 28, provides a version: ascription, diffuseness, particularism, collectivity-orientation, affectivity, passivity in love-making, obedience, submissiveness to commands and rules, dependence, fearfulness, modesty, chastity, bashfulness, maidenly reserve, love of home, restricted outside interests, monogamic inclination, interest in bodily adornment, love of finery, care for babies.

5. "Civil inattention" allows male and female a quick mutual glance. Her *second* quick look can serve as a signal of encouragement to him. Some men have much experience with second looks; other men, practically none. For experimental and field evidence, see Mark S. Cary, "Nonverbal Openings to Conversation," paper presented at the Eastern Psychological Association Meetings, April 18, 1974, Philadelphia, Pennsylvania, and "Talk? Do You Want to Talk?: Negotiation for the Initiation of Conversation between the Unacquainted," Ph.D. dissertation, Department of Psychology, University of Pennsylvania, 1975.

6. Current tendencies in the direction of no-fault, no alimony divorce, defined as liberalization, override this compensatory arrangement, ensuring that at least some women will get the worst of both worlds.

7. For example, Diana Russell, *The Politics of Rape* (New York, 1975), pp. 28, 38, 99, 132, 201, 223.

8. This accounts for some paradoxical facts. Given that men are defined as desiring access to women and women as holding them in check, it would seem that men would have less license to be familiar with women, in the sense of touching, than have women with men. But, I believe, among nonintimates, men touch women more than the reverse. For men have the right, apparently, to have their reachings seen as protective or joking or undemandingly affectionate; the same act performed by a woman to a man could too easily be read as an invitation, an open movement outward, and thus tends to be suppressed. (Here see Nancy Henley, "The Politics of Touch," in *Radical Psychology*, Phil Brown, ed. [New York, 1973], pp. 421–433.) Between men and women who have a socially ratified intimacy, women seem to have the greater license.

The matter extends beyond obvious reachings out like touch to quite passive ways of being exposed. Thus, a woman who carries on or with her a camera, a dog, a book, or almost any object, is providing reasons strangers can use as a basis for initiating a comment to her and is thus in effect exposing herself.

9. Recently, of course, in the U.S.A. there has been public protest against sex segregation of facilities and activities, feminists taking the lead.

10. Harold L. Wilensky, "Women's Work: Economic Growth, Ideology, Structure," *Industrial Relations*, 7, 3 (1968), p. 244: "If they do go on [to graduate school] they overwhelmingly head toward traditionally 'feminine' fields such as art, nursing, education, social work, biochemistry, English, languages, and the humanities."

11. In noting the special functions of sprinkling women selectively in the work scene, one ought to take note also of a parallel process, the placement of large, sleek white men in highly visible executive and political roles where they can serve as representatives of organizations and in its name meet its specialized public.

12. Russell, op. cit.

13. In rural settlements, square dancing used to provide a nicely patterned opportunity for males to swing their partners off their feet, to the accompaniment of squeals of pleasurable fear, all this under the eye of the whole community. Children, of course, are even more subject to playful assaults, such as being thrown into the air and caught, swung by the hands, and so forth. Observe, too, that there are special play environments, such as swimming pools, hay stacks, and the like, which allow a whole cosmos of unserious playful acts, that being one of their functions.

14. The traditional solution was for a male companion of the threatened female to do the fighting for her, constituting himself her champion. In liberated circles this recourse is sometimes disapproved.

15. Some relevant evocations are provided by Doris Lessing, *The Summer before the Dark* (New York, 1973), pp. 180–207.

16. A useful informal literature is available on hassling. See, for example, Gwenda Linda Blair, "Standing on the Corner," *Liberation* 18, 9 (July–August 1974) pp. 6–8; Barbara Damrosch, "The Sex Ray: One Woman's Theory of Street Hassling," *Village Voice*, April 7, 1975, p. 7.

Chapter Thirty-Five

Girls and Boys Together . . . But Mostly Apart
Gender Arrangements in Elementary Schools

Barrie Thorne

Throughout the years of elementary school, children's friendships and casual encounters are strongly separated by sex. Sex segregation among children, which starts in preschool and is well established by middle childhood, has been amply documented in studies of children's groups and friendships (e.g., Eder & Hallinan, 1978; Schofield, 1981) and is immediately visible in elementary school settings. When children choose seats in classrooms or the cafeteria, or get into line, they frequently arrange themselves in same-sex clusters. At lunchtime, they talk matter-of-factly about "girls' tables" and "boys' tables." Playgrounds have gendered turfs, with some areas and activities, such as large playing fields and basketball courts, controlled mainly by boys, and others—smaller enclaves like jungle-gym areas and concrete spaces for hopscotch or jumprope—more often controlled by girls. Sex segregation is so common in elementary schools that it is meaningful to speak of separate girls' and boys' worlds.

Studies of gender and children's social relations have mostly followed this "two worlds" model, separately describing and comparing the subcultures of girls and of boys (e.g., Lever, 1976; Maltz & Borker, 1983). In brief summary: Boys tend to interact in larger, more age-heterogeneous groups (Lever, 1976; Waldrop & Halverson, 1975; Eder & Hallinan, 1978). They engage in more rough and tumble play and physical fighting (Maccoby & Jacklin, 1974). Organized sports are both a central activity and a major metaphor in boys' subcultures; they use the language of "teams" even when not engaged in sports, and they often construct interaction in the form of contests. The shifting hierarchies of boys' groups (Savin-Williams, 1976) are evident in their more frequent use of direct commands, insults, and challenges (Goodwin, 1980).

Fewer studies have been done of girls' groups (Foot, Chapman, & Smith, 1980; McRobbie & Garber, 1975), and—perhaps because categories for description and analysis have come more from male than female experience—researchers have had difficulty seeing and analyzing girls' social relations. Recent work has begun to

Barrie Thorne, "Girls and Boys Together . . . But Mostly Apart: Gender Arrangements in Elementary Schools." In W. W. Hartup & Z. Rubin (Eds.), *Relationships and Development*, pp. 167–184. © 1986 by Lawrence Erlbaum Associates, Inc. Reprinted with permission.

correct this skew. In middle childhood, girls' worlds are less public than those of boys; girls more often interact in private places and in smaller groups or friendship pairs (Eder & Hallinan, 1978; Waldrop & Halverson, 1975). Their play is more cooperative and turn-taking (Lever, 1976). Girls have more intense and exclusive friendships, which take shape around keeping and telling secrets, shifting alliances, and indirect ways of expressing disagreement (Goodwin, 1980; Lever, 1976; Maltz & Borker, 1983). Instead of direct commands, girls more often use directives which merge speaker and hearer, e.g., "let's" or "we gotta" (Goodwin, 1980).

Although much can be learned by comparing the social organization and subcultures of boys' and of girls' groups, the separate worlds approach has eclipsed full, contextual understanding of gender and social relations among children. The Separate worlds model essentially involves a search for group sex differences, and shares the limitations of individual sex difference research. Differences tend to be exaggerated and similarities ignored, with little theoretical attention to the integration of similarity and difference (Unger, 1979). Statistical findings of difference are often portrayed as dichotomous, neglecting the considerable individual variation that exists; for example, not all boys fight, and some have intense and exclusive friendships. The sex difference approach tends to abstract gender from its social context, to assume that males and females are qualitatively and permanently different (with differences perhaps unfolding through separate developmental lines). These assumptions mask the possibility that gender arrangements and patterns of similarity and difference may vary by situation, race, social class, region, or subculture.

Sex segregation is far from total, and is a more complex and dynamic process than the portrayal of separate worlds reveals. Erving Goffman (1977) has observed that sex segregation has a "with-then-apart" structure; the sexes segregate periodically, with separate spaces, rituals, groups, but they also come together and are, in crucial ways, part of the same world. This is certainly true in the social environment of elementary schools. Although girls and boys do interact as boundaried collectivities—an image suggested by the separate worlds approach—there are other occasions when they work or play in relaxed and integrated ways. Gender is less central to the organization and meaning of some situations than others. In short, sex segregation is not static, but is a variable and complicated process.

To gain an understanding of gender which can encompass both the "with" and the "apart" of sex segregation analysis should start not with the individual, nor with a search for sex differences, but with social relationships. Gender should be conceptualized as a system of relationships rather than as an immutable and dichotomous given. Taking this approach, I have organized my research on gender and children's social relations around questions like the following: How and when does gender enter into group formation? In a given situation, how is gender made more or less salient or infused with particular meanings? By what rituals, processes, and forms of social organization and conflict do "with-then-apart" rhythms get enacted? How are these processes affected by the organization of institutions (e.g., different types of schools, neighborhoods, or summer camps), varied settings (e.g., the constraints and possibilities governing interaction on playgrounds vs. classrooms), and particular encounters?

Methods and Sources of Data

This study is based on two periods of participant observation. In 1976–1977 I observed for eight months in a largely working-class elementary school in California, a school with 8 percent Black and 12 percent Chicana/o students. In 1980 I did fieldwork for three months in a Michigan elementary school of similar size (around four hundred students), social class, and racial composition. I observed in several classrooms—a kindergarten, a second grade, and a combined fourth–fifth grade—and in school hallways, cafeterias, and playgrounds. I set out to follow the round of the school day as children experience it, recording their interactions with one another, and with adults, in varied settings.

Participant observation involves gaining access to everyday, "naturalistic" settings and taking systematic notes over an extended period of time. Rather than starting with preset categories for recording, or with fixed hypotheses for testing, participant-observers record detail in ways which maximize opportunities for discovery. Through continuous interaction between observation and analysis, "grounded theory" is developed (Glaser & Strauss, 1967).

The distinctive logic and discipline of this mode of inquiry emerges from: (1) theoretical sampling—being relatively systematic in the choice of where and whom to observe in order to maximize knowledge relevant to categories and analysis which are being developed; and (2) comparing all relevant data on a given point in order to modify emerging propositions to take account of discrepant cases (Katz, 1983). Participant observation is a flexible, open-ended and inductive method, designed to understand behavior within, rather than stripped from, social context. It provides richly detailed information which is anchored in everyday meanings and experience.

Daily Processes of Sex Segregation

Sex segregation should be understood not as a given, but as the result of deliberate activity. The outcome is dramatically visible when there are separate girls' and boys' tables in school lunchrooms, or sex-separated groups on playgrounds. But in the same lunchroom one can also find tables where girls and boys eat and talk together, and in some playground activities the sexes mix. By what processes do girls and boys separate into gender-defined and relatively boundaried collectivities? And in what contexts, and through what processes, do boys and girls interact in less gender-divided ways?

In the school settings I observed, much segregation happened with no mention of gender. Gender was implicit in the contours of friendship, shared interest, and perceived risk which came into play when children chose companions—in their prior planning, invitations, seeking-of-access, saving-of-places, denials of entry, and allowing or protesting of "cuts" by those who violated the rules for lining up. Sometimes children formed mixed-sex groups for play, eating, talking, working on a classroom project, or moving through space. When adults or children explicitly invoked gender—and this was nearly always in ways which separated girls and boys—boundaries were heightened and mixed-sex interaction became an explicit arena of risk.

In the schools I studied, the physical space and curricula were not formally divided by sex, as they have been in the history of elementary schooling (a history evident in separate entrances to old school buildings, where the words "Boys" and "Girls" are permanently etched in concrete). Nevertheless, gender was a visible marker in the adult-organized school day. In both schools, when the public address system sounded, the principal inevitably opened with: "Boys and girls . . . ," and in addressing clusters of children, teachers and aides regularly used gender terms ("Heads down, girls"; "The girls are ready and the boys aren't"). These forms of address made gender visible and salient, conveying an assumption that the sexes are separate social groups.

Teachers and aides sometimes drew upon gender as a basis for sorting children and organizing activities. Gender is an embodied and visual social category which roughly divides the population in half, and the separation of girls and boys permeates the history and lore of schools and playgrounds. In both schools—although through awareness of Title IX, many teachers had changed this practice—one could see separate girls' and boys' lines moving, like caterpillars, through the school halls. In the fourth–fifth grade classroom the teacher frequently pitted girls against boys for spelling and math contests. On the playground in the Michigan school, aides regarded the space close to the building as girls' territory, and the playing fields "out there" as boys' territory. They sometimes shooed children of the other sex away from those spaces, especially boys who ventured near the girls' area and seemed to have teasing in mind.

In organizing their activities, both within and apart from the surveillance of adults, children also explicitly invoked gender. During my fieldwork in the Michigan school, I kept daily records of who sat where in the lunchroom. The amount of sex segregation varied: It was least at the first-grade tables and almost total among sixth graders. There was also variation from classroom to classroom within a given age, and from day to day. Actions like the following heightened the gender divide:

> In the lunchroom, when the two second-grade tables were filling, a high-status boy walked by the inside table, which had a scattering of both boys and girls, and said loudly, "Oooo, too many girls," as he headed for a seat at the far table. The boys at the inside table picked up their trays and moved, and no other boys sat at the inside table, which the pronouncement had effectively made taboo.

In the end, that day (which was not the case every day), girls and boys ate at separate tables.

Eating and walking are not sex-typed activities, yet in forming groups in lunchrooms and hallways children often separated by sex. Sex segregation assumed added dimensions on the playground, where spaces, equipment, and activities were infused with gender meanings. My inventories of activities and groupings on the playground showed similar patterns in both schools: Boys controlled the large fixed spaces designated for team sports (baseball diamonds, grassy fields used for football or soccer); girls more often played closer to the building, doing tricks on the monkey bars (which, for sixth graders, became an area for sitting and talking) and using cement areas for jumprope, hopscotch, and group games like four-square. (Lever, 1976, provides a good analysis of sex-divided play.) Girls and boys most often played together in kickball, and in group (rather than team) games like four-square, dodgeball, and handball. When children used gender to exclude others from play, they often drew upon beliefs connecting boys to some activities and girls to others:

> A first-grade boy avidly watched an all-female game of jump rope. When the girls began to shift positions, he recognized a means of access to the play and he offered, "I'll swing it." A girl responded, "No way, you don't know how to do it, to swing it. You gotta be a girl." He left without protest.

Although children sometimes ignored pronouncements about what each sex could or could not do, I never heard them directly challenge such claims.

When children had explicitly defined an activity or a group as gendered, those who crossed the boundary — especially boys who moved into female-marked space — risked being teased. ("Look! Mike's in the girls' line!"; " 'That's a girl over there,' a girl said loudly, pointing to a boy sitting at an otherwise all-female table in the lunchroom.") Children, and occasionally adults, used teasing — especially the tease of "liking" someone of the other sex, or of "being" that sex by virtue of being in their midst — to police gender boundaries. Much of the teasing drew upon heterosexual romantic definitions, making cross-sex interaction risky, and increasing social distance between boys and girls.

Relationships between the Sexes

Because I have emphasized the "apart" and ignored the occasions of "with," this analysis of sex segregation falsely implies that there is little contact between girls and boys in daily schools life. In fact, relationships between girls and boys — which should be studied as fully as, and in connection with, same-sex relationships — are of several kinds:

1. "Borderwork," or forms of cross-sex interaction which are based upon and reaffirm boundaries and asymmetries between girls' and boys' groups;
2. Interactions which are infused with heterosexual meanings;
3. Occasions where individuals cross gender boundaries to participate in the world of the other sex; and
4. Situations where gender is muted in salience, with girls and boys interacting in more relaxed ways.

Borderwork

In elementary school settings boys' and girls' groups are sometimes spatially set apart. Same-sex groups sometimes claim fixed territories such as the basketball court, the bars, or specific lunchroom tables. However, in the crowded, multi-focused, and adult-controlled environment of the school, groups form and disperse at a rapid rate and can never stay totally apart. Contact between girls and boys sometimes lessens sex segregation, but gender-defined groups also come together in ways which emphasize their boundaries.

"Borderwork" refers to interaction across, yet based upon and even strengthening gender boundaries. I have drawn this notion from Fredrik Barth's (1969) analysis of social relations which are maintained across ethnic boundaries without diminishing dichotomized ethnic status.[1] His focus is on more macro, ecological arrangements; mine is on face-to-face behavior. But the insight is similar: Groups may interact in ways which strengthen their borders, and the maintenance of ethnic (or gender) groups can best be understood by examining the boundary that defines the group, "not the cultural stuff that it encloses" (Barth, 1969, p. 15). In elementary schools there are several types of borderwork: contests or games where gender-defined teams compete; cross-sex rituals of chasing and pollution; and group invasions. These interactions are asymmetrical, challenging the separate-but-parallel model of "two worlds."

Contests. Boys and girls are sometimes pitted against each other in classroom competitions and playground games. The fourth–fifth grade classroom had a boys' side and a girls' side, an arrangement that re-emerged each time the teacher asked children to choose their own desks. Although there was some within-sex shuffling, the result was always a spatial moiety system—boys on the left, girls on the right—with the exception of one girl (the "tomboy" whom I'll describe later), who twice chose a desk with the boys and once with the girls. Drawing upon and reinforcing the children's self-segregation, the teacher often pitted the boys against the girls in spelling and math competitions, events marked by cross-sex antagonism and within-sex solidarity:

> The teacher introduced a math game; she would write addition and subtraction problems on the board, and a member of each team would race to be the first to write the correct answer. She wrote two score-keeping columns on the board: "Beastly Boys" . . . "Gossipy Girls." The boys yelled out, as several girls laughed, "Noisy girls! Gruesome girls!" The girls sat in a row on top of their desks; sometimes they moved collectively, pushing their hips or whispering "pass it on." The boys stood along the wall, some reclining against desks. When members of either group came back victorious from the front of the room, they would do the "giving five" hand-slapping ritual with their team members.

On the playground a team of girls occasionally played against a team of boys, usually in kickball or team two-square. Sometimes these games proceeded matter-of-factly, but if gender became the explicit basis of team solidarity, the interaction changed, becoming more antagonistic and unstable:

> Two fifth-grade girls played against two fifth-grade boys in a team game of two-square. The game proceeded at an even pace until an argument ensued about whether the ball was out or on the line. Karen, who had hit the ball, became annoyed, flashed her

middle finger at the other team, and called to a passing girl to join their side. The boys then called out to other boys, and cheered as several arrived to play. "We got five and you got three!" Jack yelled. The game continued, with the girls yelling, "Bratty boys! Sissy boys!" and the boys making noises—"weee haw" "ha-ha-ha"—as they played.

Chasing. Cross-sex chasing dramatically affirms boundaries between girls and boys. The basic elements of chase and elude, capture and rescue (Sutton-Smith, 1971) are found in various kinds of tag with formal rules, and in informal episodes of chasing which punctuate life on playgrounds. These episodes begin with a provocation (taunts like "You can't get me!" or "Slobber monster!"; bodily pokes or the grabbing of possessions). A provocation may be ignored, or responded to by chasing. Chaser and chased may then alternate roles. In an ethnographic study of chase sequences on a school playground, Christine Finnan (1982) observes that chases vary in number of chasers to chased (e.g., one chasing one, or five chasing two); form of provocation (a taunt or a poke); outcome (an episode may end when the chased outdistances the chaser, or with a brief touch, being wrestled to the ground, or the recapturing of a hat or a ball); and in use of space (there may or may not be safely zones).

Like Finnan (1982), and Sluckin (1981), who studied a playground in England, I found that chasing has a gendered structure. Boys frequently chase one another, an activity which often ends in wrestling and mock fights. When girls chase girls, they are usually less physically aggressive; they less often, for example, wrestle one another to the ground.

Cross-sex chasing is set apart by special names—"girls chase the boys"; "boys chase the girls"; "the chase"; "chasers"; "chase and kiss"; "kiss chase"; "kissers and chasers"; "kiss or kill"—and by children's animated talk about the activity. The names vary by region and school, but contain both gender and sexual meanings (this form of play is mentioned, but only briefly analyzed, in Finnan, 1982; Sluckin, 1981; Parrott, 1972; and Borman, 1979).

In "boys chase the girls" and "girls chase the boys" (the names most frequently used in both the California and Michigan schools) boys and girls become, by definition, separate teams. Gender terms override individual identities, especially for the other team ("Help, a girl's chasin' me!"; "C'mon Sarah, let's get that boy"; "Tony, help save me from the girls"). Individuals may call for help from, or offer help to, others of their sex. They may also grab someone of their sex and turn them over to the opposing team: "Ryan grabbed Billy from behind, wrestling him to the ground. 'Hey girls, get 'im,' Ryan called."

Boys more often mix episodes of cross-sex with same-sex chasing. Girls more often have safety zones, places like the girls' restroom or an area by the school wall, where they retreat to rest and talk (sometimes in animated postmortems) before new episodes of cross-sex chasing begin.

Early in the fall in the Michigan school, where chasing was especially prevalent, I watched a second-grade boy teach a kindergarten girl how to chase. He slowly ran backwards, beckoning her to pursue him, as he called, "Help, a girl's after me." In the early grades chasing mixes with fantasy play, e.g., a first-grade boy who played "sea monster," his arms outflung and his voice growling, as he chased a group of girls. By third grade, stylized gestures—exaggerated stalking motions, screams (which only girls do), and karate kicks—accompany scenes of chasing.

Names like "chase and kiss" mark the sexual meanings of cross-sex chasing, a theme I return to later. The threat of kissing—most often girls threatening to kiss boys—is a ritualized form of provocation. Cross-sex chasing among sixth graders involves elaborate patterns of touch and touch avoidance, which adults see as sexual. The principal told the sixth graders in the Michigan school that they were not to play "pom-pom," a complicated chasing game, because it entailed "inappropriate touch."

Rituals of Pollution. Cross-sex chasing is sometimes entwined with rituals of pollution, as in "cooties," where specific individuals or groups are treated as contaminating or carrying "germs." Children have rituals for transferring cooties (usually touching someone else and shouting "You've got cooties!"), for immunization (e.g., writing "CV" for "cootie vaccination" on their arms), and for eliminating cooties (e.g., saying "no gives" or using "cootie catchers" made of folded paper) (described in Knapp & Knapp, 1976). While girls may give cooties to girls, boys do not generally give cooties to one another (Samuelson, 1980).

In cross-sex play, either girls or boys may be defined as having cooties, which they transfer through chasing and touching. Girls give cooties to boys more often than vice versa. In Michigan, one version of cooties is called "girl stain"; the fourth graders whom Karkau (1973) describes, used the phrase "girl touch." "Cootie queens," or "cootie girls" (there are no "kings" or "boys"), are female pariahs, the ultimate school untouchables, seen as contaminating not only by virtue of gender, but also through some added stigma such as being overweight or poor.[2] *That girls are seen as more polluting than boys is a significant asymmetry, which echoes cross-cultural patterns,* although in other cultures female pollution is generally connected to menstruation, and not applied to prepubertal girls.

Invasions. Playground invasions are another asymmetric form of borderwork. On a few occasions I saw girls invade and disrupt an all-male game, most memorably a group of tall sixth-grade girls who ran onto the playing field and grabbed a football which was in play. The boys were surprised and frustrated, and, unusual for boys this old, finally tattled to the aide. But in the majority of cases, boys disrupt girls' activities rather than vice versa. Boys grab the ball from girls playing four-square, stick feet into a jumprope and stop an ongoing game, and dash through the ares of the bars, where girls are taking turns performing, sending the rings flying. Sometimes boys ask to join a girls' game and then, after a short period of seemingly earnest play, disrupt the game:

> Two second-grade boys begged to "twirl" the jumprope for a group of second-grade girls who had been jumping for some time. The girls agreed, and the boys began to twirl. Soon, without announcement, the boys changed from "seashells, cockle bells" to "hot peppers" (spinning the rope very fast), and tangled the jumper in the rope. The boys ran away laughing.

Boys disrupt girls' play so often that girls have developed almost ritualized responses: They guard their ongoing play, chase boys away, and tattle to the aides. In a playground cycle which enhances sex segregation, aides who try to spot protential trouble before it occurs sometimes shoo boys away from areas where girls are playing. Aides do not anticipate trouble from girls who seek to join groups of boys, with the exception of girls intent on provoking a chase sequence. And indeed, if they seek access to a boys' game, girls usually play with boys in earnest rather than breaking up the game.

A close look at the organization of borderwork—or boundaried interactions between the sexes—shows that the worlds of boys and girls may be separate, but they are not parallel, nor are they equal. The worlds of girls and boys articulate in several asymmetric ways:

1. On the playground, *boys control as much as ten times more space than girls,* when one adds up the area of large playing fields and compares it with the much smaller areas where girls predominate. Girls, who play closer to the building, are more often watched over and protected by the adult aides.

2. *Boys invade all female games and scenes of play much more than girls invade boys.* This, and boys' greater control of space, correspond with other findings about the organization of gender, and inequality, in our society: compared with men and boys, women and girls take up less space, and their space, and talk, are more often violated and interrupted (Greif, 1980; Henley, 1977, West & Zimmerman, 1983).

3. Although individual boys are occasionally treated as contaminating (e.g., a third-grade boy whom both boys and girls said was "stinky" and "smelled like pee"), *girls are more often defined as polluting.* This pattern ties to themes that I discuss later: It is more taboo for a boy to play with (as opposed to invade) girls, and girls are more sexually defined than boys.

A look at the boundaries between the separated worlds of girls and boys illuminates within-sex hierarchies of status and control. For example, in the sex-divided seating in the fourth–fifth grade classroom, several boys recurrently sat near "female space": their desks were at the gender divide in the classroom, and they were more likely than other boys to sit at a predominantly female table in the lunchroom. These boys—two nonbilingual Chicanos and an overweight "loner" boy who was afraid of sports—were at the bottom of the male hierarchy. Gender is sometimes used as a metaphor for male hierarchies; the inferior status of boys at the bottom is conveyed by calling them "girls":

> Seven boys and one girl were playing basketball. Two younger boys came over and asked to play. While the girl silently stood, fully accepted in the company of players, one of the older boys disparagingly said to the younger boys, "You girls can't play."[3]

In contrast, the girls who more often travel in the boys' world, sitting with groups of boys in the lunchroom or playing basketball, soccer, and baseball with them, are not stigmatized. Some have fairly high status with other girls. The worlds of girls and boys are assymetrically arranged, and spatial patterns map out interacting forms of inequality.

Heterosexual Meanings

The organization and meanings of gender (the social categories "woman/man," "girl/boy") and of sexuality vary cross-culturally (Ortner & Whitehead, 1981) — and, in our society, across the life course. Harriet Whitehead (1981) observed that in our (Western) gender system, and that of many traditional North American Indian cultures, one's choice of a sexual object, occupation, and one's dress and demeanor are closely associated with gender. However, the "center of gravity" differs in the two gender systems. For Indians, occupational pursuits provide the primary imagery of gender; dress and demeanor are secondary, and sexuality is least important. In our system, at least for adults, the order is reversed: heterosexuality is central to our definitions of "man" and "woman" ("masculinity"/"femininity"), and the relationships that obtain between them, whereas occupation and dress/demeanor are secondary.

Whereas erotic orientation and gender are closely linked in our definitions of adults, we define children as relatively asexual. Activities and dress/demeanor are more important than sexuality in the cultural meanings of "girl" and "boy." Children are less heterosexually defined than adults, and we have nonsexual imagery for relations between girls and boys. However, both children and adults sometimes use heterosexual language — "crushes," "like," "goin' with," "girlfriends," and "boyfriends" — to define cross-sex relationships. This language increases through the years of elementary school; the shift to adolescence consolidates a gender system organized around the institution of heterosexuality.

In everyday life in the schools, heterosexual and romantic meanings infuse some ritualized forms of interaction between groups of boys and girls (e.g., "chase and kiss") and help maintain sex segregation. "Jimmy likes Beth" or "Beth likes Jimmy" is a major form of teasing, which a child risks in choosing to sit by or walk with someone of the other sex. The structure, of teasing, and children's sparse vocabulary for relationships between girls and boys, are evident in the following conversation which I had with a group of third-grade girls in the lunchroom:

> Susan asked me what I was doing, and I said I was observing the things children do and play. Nicole volunteered, "I like running, boys chase all the girls. See Tim over there? Judy chases him all around the school. She likes him." Judy, sitting across the table, quickly responded, "I hate him. I like him for a friend." "Tim loves Judy," Nicole said in a loud, sing-song voice.

In the younger grades, the culture and lore of girls contains more heterosexual romantic themes than that of boys. In Michigan, the first-grade girls often jumped rope to a rhyme which began: "Down in the valley where the green grass grows, there sat Cindy (name of jumper), as sweet as a rose. She sat, she sat, she sat so sweet. Along came Jason, and kissed her on her cheek ... first comes love, then comes marriage, then along comes Cindy with a baby carriage ..." Before a girl took her turn at jumping, the chanters asked her, "Who do you want to be your boy-friend?" The jumper always preferred a name, which was accepted matter-of-factly. In chasing, a girl's kiss carried greater threat than a boy's kiss; "girl touch," when defined as contaminating, had sexual connotations. In short, starting at an early age, girls are more sexually defined than boys.

Through the years of elementary school, and increasing with age, the idiom of heterosexuality helps maintain the gender divide. Cross-sex interactions, especially when children initiate them, are fraught with the risk of being teased about "liking" someone of the other sex. I learned of several close cross-sex friendships, formed and maintained in neighborhoods and church, which went underground during the school day.

By the fifth grade a few children began to affirm, rather than avoid, the charge of having a girlfriend or a boyfriend; they introduced the heterosexual courtship rituals of adolescence:

> In the lunchroom in the Michigan school, as the tables were forming, a high-status fifth-grade boy called out from his seat at the table: "I want Trish to sit by me." Trish came over, and almost like a king and queen, they sat at the gender divide—a row of girls down the table on her side, a row of boys on his.

In this situation, which inverted earlier forms, it was not a loss, but a gain in status to publically choose a companion of the other sex. By affirming his choice, the boy became unteasable (note the familiar asymmetry of heterosexual courtship rituals: the male initiated). This incident signals a temporal shift in arrangements of sex and gender.

Traveling in the World of the Other Sex

Contests, invasions, chasing, and heterosexually defined encounters are based upon and reaffirm boundaries between girls and boys. In another type of cross-sex interaction, individuals (or sometimes pairs) cross gender boundaries, seeking acceptance in a group of the other sex. Nearly all the cases I saw of this were tomboys—girls who played organized sports and frequently sat with boys in the cafeteria or classroom. If these girls were skilled at activities central in the boys' world, especially games like soccer, baseball, and basketball, they were pretty much accepted as participants.

Being a tomboy is a matter of degree. Some girls seek access to boys' groups but are excluded; other girls limit their "crossing" to specific sports. Only a few—such as the tomboy I mentioned earlier, who chose a seat with the boys in the sex-divided fourth–fifth grade—participate fully in the boys' world. That particular girl was skilled at the various organized sports which boys played in different seasons of the year. She was also adept at physical fighting and at using the forms of arguing, insult, teasing, naming, and sports-talk of the boys' subculture. She was the only Black child in her classroom, in a school with only 8 percent Black students; overall that token status, along with unusual athletic and verbal skills, may have contributed to her ability to move back and forth across the gender divide. Her unique position in the children's world was widely recognized in the school. Several times, the teacher said to me, "She thinks she's a boy."

I observed only one boy in the upper grades (a fourth grader) who regularly played with all-female groups, as opposed to "playing at" girls' games and seeking to disrupt them. He frequently played jumprope and took turns with girls doing tricks on the bars, using the small gestures—for example, a helpful push on the heel of a girl who needed momentum to turn her body around the bar—which mark skillful and earnest participation. Although I never saw him play in other than an earnest spirit, the girls often chased him away from their games, and both girls and boys teased him. The fact that girls seek, and have more access to boys' worlds than vice versa, and the fact that girls who travel with the other sex are less stigmatized for it, are obvious asymmetries, tied to the asymmetries previously discussed.

Relaxed Cross-Sex Interactions

Relationships between boys and girls are not always marked by strong boundaries, heterosexual definitions, or by interacting on the terms and turfs of the other sex. On some occasions girls and boys interact in relatively comfortable ways. Gender is not strongly salient nor explicitly invoked, and girls and boys are not organized into boundaried collectivities. These *"with" occasions* have been neglected by those studying gender and children's relationships, who have emphasized either the model of separate worlds (with little attention to their articulation) or heterosexual forms of contact.

Occasions where boys and girls interact without strain, where gender wanes, rather than waxes in importance, frequently have one or more of the following characteristics:

1. *The situations are organized around an absorbing task,* such as a group art project or creating a radio show, *which encourages cooperation and lessens attention to gender.* This pattern accords with other studies finding that cooperative activities reduce group antagonism (e.g., Sherif & Sherif, 1953, who studied divisions between boys in a summer camp; and Aronson et al., 1978, who used cooperative activities to lessen racial divisions in a classroom).

2. *Gender is less prominent when children are not responsible for the formation of the group.* Mixed-sex play is less frequent in games like football, which require the choosing of teams, and more frequent in games like handball or dodgeball which individuals can join simply by getting into a line or a circle. When adults organize mixed-sex encounters—which they frequently do in the classroom and in physical education periods on the playground—they legitimize cross-sex contact. This removes the risk of being teased for choosing to be with the other sex.

3. There is more extensive and relaxed cross-sex interaction when *principles of grouping other than gender are explicitly invoked*—for example, counting off to form teams for spelling or kickball, dividing lines by hot lunch or cold lunch, or organizing a work group on the basis of interests or reading ability.

4. Girls and boys may interact more readily in *less public and crowded settings.* Neighborhood play, depending on demography, is more often sex and age integrated than play at school, partly because with fewer numbers, one may have to resort to an array of social categories to find play partners or to constitute a game. And in less crowded environments there are fewer potential witnesses to "make something of it" if girls and boys play together.

Relaxed interactions between girls and boys often depend on adults to set up and legitimize the contact.[4] Perhaps because of this contingency—and the other, distancing patterns which permeate relations between girls and boys—*the easeful moments of interaction rarely build to close friendship.* Schofield (1981) makes a similar observation about gender and racial barriers to friendship in a junior high school.

Implications for Development

I have located social relations within an essentially spatial framework, emphasizing the organization of children's play, work, and other activities within specific settings, and in one type of institution, the school. In contrast, frameworks of child development rely upon temporal metaphors, using images of growth and transformation over time. Taken alone, both spatial and temporal frameworks have shortcomings; fitted together, they may be mutually correcting.

Those interested in gender and development have relied upon conceptualizations of "sex role socialization" and "sex differences." Sexuality and gender, I have argued, are more situated and fluid than these individualist and intrinsic models imply. Sex and gender are differently organized and defined across situations, even within the same institution. This situational variation (e.g., in the extent to which an encounter heightens or lessens gender boundaries, or is infused with sexual meanings) shapes and constrains individual behavior. Features which a developmental perspective might attribute to individuals, and understand as relatively internal attributes unfolding over time, may, in fact, be highly dependent on context. For example, children's avoidance of cross-sex friendship may be attributed to individual gender development in middle-childhood. But attention to varied situations may show that this avoidance is contingent on group size, activity, adult behavior, collective meanings, and the risk of being teased.

A focus on social organization and situation draws attention to children's experiences in the present. This helps correct a model like "sex role socialization" which casts the present under the shadow of the future, or presumed "endpoints" (Speier, 1976). A situated analysis of arrangements of sex and gender among those of different ages may point to crucial disjunctions in the life course. In the fourth and fifth grades, culturally defined heterosexual rituals ("goin' with") begin to suppress the presence and visibility of other types of interaction between girls and boys, such as nonsexualized and comfortable interaction, and traveling in the world of the other sex. As "boyfriend/girlfriend" definitions spread, the fifth-grade tomboy I described had to work to sustain "buddy" relationships with boys. Adult women who were tomboys often speak of early adolescence as a painful time when they were pushed away from participation in boys' activities. Other adult women speak of the loss of intense, even erotic ties with other girls when they entered puberty and the rituals of dating, that is, when they became absorbed into the institution of heterosexuality (Rich, 1980). When Lever (1976) describes best-friend relationships among fifth-grade girls as preparation for dating, she imposes heterosexual ideologies onto a present which should be understood on its own terms.

As heterosexual encounters assume more importance, they may alter relations in same-sex groups: For example, Schofield (1981) reports that for sixth-and seventh-grade children in a middle school, the popularity of girls with other girls was affected by their popularity with boys, while boys' status with other boys did not depend on their relations with girls. This is an asymmetry familiar from the adult world; men's relationships with one another are defined through varied activities (occupations, sports), while relationships among women—and their public status—are more influenced by their connections to individual men.

A full understanding of gender and social relations should encompass cross-sex as well as within-sex interactions. "Borderwork" helps maintain separate, gender-linked subcultures, which, as those interested in development have begun to suggest, may result in different milieux for learning. Daniel Maltz and Ruth Borker (1983), for example, argue that because of different interactions within girls' and boys' groups, the sexes learn different rules for creating and interpreting friendly conversation, rules which carry into adulthood and help account for miscommunication between men and women. Carol Gilligan (1982) fits research on the different worlds of girls and boys into a theory of sex differences in moral development. Girls develop a style of reasoning, she argues, which is more personal and relational; boys develop a style which is more positional, based on separateness. Eleanor Maccoby (1982), also following the insight that because of sex segregation, girls and boys grow up in different environments, suggests implications for gender differentiated prosocial and antisocial behavior.

This separate worlds approach, as I have illustrated, also has limitations. The occasions when the sexes are together should also be studied, and understood as contexts for experience and learning. For example, assymetries in cross-sex relation-ships convey a series of messages: that boys are more entitled to space and to the nonreciprocal right of interrupting or invading the activities of the other sex; that girls are more in need of adult protection, and are lower in status, more defined by sexuality, and may even be polluting. Different types of cross-sex interaction—relaxed, boundaried, sexualized, or taking place on the terms of the other sex—provide different contexts for development.

By mapping the array of relationships between and within the sexes, one adds complexity to the overly static and dichotomous imagery of separate worlds. Individual experiences vary, with implications for development. Some children prefer same-sex groupings; some are more likely to cross the gender boundary and participate in the world of the other sex; some children (e.g., girls and boys who frequently play "chase and kiss") invoke heterosexual meanings, while others avoid them.

Finally, after charting the terrain of relationships, one can trace their development over time. For example, age variation in the content and form of borderwork, or of cross and same-sex touch, may be related to differing cognitive, social, emotional, or physical capacities, as well as to age-associated cultural forms. I earlier mentioned temporal shifts in the organization of cross-sex chasing, from mixing with fantasy play in the early grades to more elaborately ritualized and sexualized forms by the sixth grade. There also appear to be temporal changes in same and cross-sex touch. In kindergarten, girls and boys touch one another more freely than in fourth grade, when children avoid relaxed cross-sex touch and instead use pokes, pushes, and other forms of mock violence, even when the touch clearly couches affection. This touch taboo is obviously related to the risk of seeming to *like* someone of the other sex. In fourth grade, same-sex touch begins to signal sexual meanings among boys, as well as between boys and girls. Younger boys touch one another freely in cuddling (arm around shoulder) as well as mock violence ways. By fourth grade, when homophobic taunts like "fag" become more common among boys, cuddling touch begins to disappear for boys, but less so for girls.

Overall, I am calling for more complexity in our conceptualizations of gender and of children's social relationships. Our challenge is to retain the temporal sweep, looking at individual and group lives as they unfold over time, while also attending to social structure and context, and to the full variety of experiences in the present.

NOTES

1. I am grateful to Frederick Erickson for suggesting the relevance of Barth's analysis.

2. Sue Samuelson (1980) reports that in a racially mixed playground in Fresno, California, Mexican-American, but not Anglo, children gave cooties. Racial, as well as sexual inequality may be expressed through these forms.

3. This incident was recorded by Margaret Blume, who, for an undergraduate research project in 1982, observed in the California school where I earlier did fieldwork. Her observations and insights enhanced my own, and I would like to thank her for letting me cite this excerpt.

4. Note that in daily school life, depending on the individual and the situation, teachers and aides sometimes lessened, and at other times heightened sex segregation.

REFERENCES

Aronson, E. et al. (1978). *The jigsaw classroom*. Beverly Hills, CA: Sage.

Barth, F. (Ed.). (1969). *Ethnic groups and boundaries*. Boston: Little, Brown.

Borman, K. M. (1979). Children's interactions in playgrounds. *Theory into Practice, 18,* 251–257.

Eder, D., & Hallinan, M. T. (1978). Sex differences in children's friendships. *American Sociological Review, 43,* 237–250.

Finnan, C. R. (1982). The ethnography of children's spontaneous play. In G. Spindler (Ed.), *Doing the ethnography of schooling* (pp. 358–380). New York: Holt, Rinehart & Winston.

Foot, H. C., Chapman, A. J., & Smith, J. R. (1980). Introduction. *Friendship and social relations in children* (pp. 1–14). New York: Wiley.

Gilligan, C. (1982). *In a different voice: Psychological theory and women's development.* Cambridge, MA: Harvard University Press.

Glaser, B. G., & Strauss, A. L. (1967). *The discovery of grounded theory.* Chicago: Aldine.

Goffman, E. (1977). The arrangement between the sexes. *Theory and Society, 4,* 301–336.

Goodwin, M. H. (1980). Directive-response speech sequences in girls' and boys' task activities. In S. McConnell-Ginet, R. Borker, & N. Furman (Eds.), *Women and language in literature and society* (pp. 157–173). New York: Praeger.

Greif, E. B. (1980). Sex differences in parent-child conversations. *Women's Studies International Quarterly, 3,* 253–258.

Henley, N. (1977). *Body politics: Power, sex, and nonverbal communication.* Englewood Cliffs, NJ: Prentice-Hall.

Karkau, K. (1973). *Sexism in the fourth grade.* Pittsburgh: KNOW, Inc. (pamphlet).

Katz, J. (1983). A theory of qualitative methodology: The social system of analytic fieldwork. In R. M. Emerson (Ed.), *Contemporary field research* (pp. 127–148). Boston: Little, Brown.

Knapp, M., & Knapp, H. (1976). *One potato, two potato: The secret education of American children.* New York: W. W. Norton.

Lever, J. (1976). Sex differences in the games children play. *Social Problems, 23,* 478–487.

Maccoby, E. (1982). *Social groupings in childhood: Their relationship to prosocial and antisocial behavior in boys and girls.* Paper presented at conference on the Development of Prosocial and Antisocial Behavior. Voss, Norway.

Maccoby, E., & Jacklin, C. (1974). *The psychology of sex differences* Stanford, CA: Stanford University Press.

Maltz, D. N., & Borker, R. A. (1983). A cultural approach to male-female miscommunication. In J. J. Gumperz (Ed.), *Language and social identity* (pp. 195–216). New York: Cambridge University Press.

McRobbie, A., & Garber, J. (1975). Girls and subcultures. In S. Hall and T. Jefferson (Eds.), *Resistance through rituals* (pp. 209–223). London: Hutchinson.

Ortner, S. B., & Whitehead, H. (1981). *Sexual meanings.* New York: Cambridge University Press.

Parrott, S. (1972). Games children play: Ethnography of a second-grade recess. In J. P. Spradley & D. W. McCurdy (Eds.), *The cultural experience* (pp. 206–219). Chicago: Science Research Associates.

Rich, A. (1980). Compulsory heterosexuality and lesbian existence. *Signs, 5,* 631–660.

Samuelson, S. (1980). The cooties complex. *Western Folklore, 39,* 198–210.

Savin-Williams, R. C. (1976). An ethological study of dominance formation and maintenance in a group of human adolescents. *Child Development, 47,* 972–979.

Schofield, J. W. (1981). Complementary and conflicting identities: Images and interaction in an interracial school. In S. R. Asher & J. M. Gottman (Eds.), *The development of children's friendships* (pp. 53–90). New York: Cambridge University Press.

Sherif, M., & Sherif, C. (1953). *Groups in harmony and tension.* New York: Harper.

Sluckin, A. (1981). *Growing up in the playground.* London: Routledge & Kegan Paul.

Speier, M. (1976). The adult ideological viewpoint in studies of childhood. In A. Skolnick (Ed.), *Rethinking childhood* (pp. 168–186). Boston: Little, Brown.

Sutton-Smith, B. (1971). A syntax for play and games. In R. E. Herron and B. Sutton-Smith (Eds.), *Child's Play* (pp. 298–307). New York: Wiley.

Unger, R. K. (1979). Toward a redefinition of sex and gender. *American Psychologist, 34,* 1085–1094.

Waldrop, M. F., & Halverson, C. F. (1975). Intensive and extensive peer behavior: Longitudinal and cross-sectional analysis. *Child Development, 46,* 19–26.

West, C., & Zimmerman, D. H. (1983). Small insults: A study of interruptions in cross-sex conversations between unacquainted persons. In B. Thorne, C. Kramarae, & N. Henley (Eds.), *Language, gender and society.* Rowley, MA: Newbury House.

Whitehead, H. (1981). The bow and the burden strap: A new look at institutionalized homosexuality in Native America. In S. B. Ortner & H. Whitehead (Eds.), *Sexual meanings* (pp. 80–115). New York: Cambridge University Press.

Chapter Thirty-Six

Gender and Relationships
A Developmental Account

Eleanor E. Maccoby

Historically, the way we psychologists think about the psychology of gender has grown out of our thinking about individual differences. We are accustomed to assessing a wide variety of attributes and skills and giving scores to individuals based on their standing relative to other individuals in a sample population. On most psychological attributes, we see wide variation among individuals, and a major focus of research has been the effort to identify correlates or sources of this variation. Commonly, what we have done is to classify individuals by some antecedent variable, such as age or some aspect of their environment, to determine how much of the variance among individuals in their performance on a given task can be accounted for by this so-called *antecedent* or *independent* variable. Despite the fact that hermaphrodites exist, almost every individual is either clearly male or clearly female. What could be more natural for psychologists than to ask how much variance among individuals is accounted for by this beautifully binary factor?

Fifteen years ago, Carol Jacklin and I put out a book summarizing the work on sex differences that had come out of the individual differences perspective (Maccoby & Jacklin, 1974). We felt at that time that the yield was thin. That is, there were very few attributes on which the average values for the two sexes differed consistently. Furthermore, even when consistent differences were found, the amount of variance accounted for by sex was small, relative to the amount of variation within each sex. Our conclusions fitted in quite well with the feminist zeitgeist of the times, when most feminists were taking a minimalist position, urging that the two sexes were basically alike and that any differences were either illusions in the eye of the beholder or reversible outcomes of social shaping. Our conclusions were challenged as having both overstated the case for sex differences (Tieger, 1980) and for having understated it (Block, 1976).

In the last fifteen years, work on sex differences has become more methodologically sophisticated, with greater use of meta analyses to reveal not only the direction of sex differences but quantitative estimates of their magnitude. In my judgment, the

Eleanor E. Maccoby, "Gender and Relationships: A Developmental Account." *American Psychologist, 45,* pp. 513–520. © 1990 by the American Psychological Association. Reprinted with permission.

conclusions are still quite similar to those Jacklin and I arrived at in 1974: There are still some replicable sex differences, of moderate magnitude, in performance on tests of mathematical and spatial abilities, although sex differences in verbal abilities have faded. Other aspects of intellectual performance continue to show gender equality. When it comes to attributes in the personality–social domain, results are particularly sparse and inconsistent. Studies continue to find that men are more often agents of aggression than are women (Eagly, 1987; Huston, 1985; Maccoby & Jacklin, 1980). Eagly (1983, 1987) reported in addition that women are more easily influenced than men and that men are more altruistic in the sense that they are more likely to offer help to others. In general, however, personality traits measured as characteristics of individuals do not appear to differ systematically by sex (Huston, 1985). This no doubt reflects in part the fact that male and female persons really are much alike, and their lives are governed mainly by the attributes that all persons in a given culture have in common. Nevertheless, I believe that the null findings coming out of comparisons of male and female individuals on personality measures are partly illusory. That is, they are an artifact of our historical reliance on an individual differences perspective. Social behavior, as many have pointed out, is never a function of the individual alone. It is a function of the interaction between two or more persons. Individuals behave differently with different partners. There are certain important ways in which gender is implicated in social behavior—ways that may be obscured or missed altogether when behavior is summed across all categories of social partners.

An illustration is found in a study of social interaction between previously unac-quainted pairs of young children (mean age, thirty-three months; Jacklin & Maccoby, 1978). In some pairs, the children had same-sex play partners; in others, the pair was made up of a boy and a girl. Observers recorded the social behavior of each child on a time-sampling basis. Each child received a score for total social behavior directed toward the partner. This score included both positive and negative behaviors (e.g., offering a toy and grabbing a toy; hugging and pushing; vocally greeting, inviting, protesting, or prohibiting). There was no overall sex difference in the amount of social behavior when this was evaluated without regard to sex of partner. But there was a powerful interaction between sex of the subject and that of the partner: Children of each sex had much higher levels of social behavior when playing with a same-sex partner than when playing with a child of the other sex. This result is consistent with the findings of Wasserman and Stern (1978) that when asked to approach another child, children as young as age three stopped farther away when the other child was of the opposite sex, indicating awareness of gender similarity or difference, and wariness toward the other sex.

The number of time intervals during which a child was simply standing passively watching the partner play with the toys was also scored. There was no overall sex difference in the frequency of this behavior, but the behavior of girls was greatly affected by the sex of the partner. With other girls, passive behavior seldom occurred; indeed, in girl–girl pairs it occurred less often than it did in boy–boy pairs. However when paired with boys, girls frequently stood on the sidelines and let the boys monopolize the toys. Clearly, the little girls in this study were not more passive than the little boys in any overall, trait-like sense. Passivity in these girls could be understood only in relation to the characteristics of their interactive partners. It was a characteristic of girls in cross-sex dyads. This conclusion may not seem especially novel because for many years we have known that social behavior is situationally specific. However, the point here is that interactive behavior is not just situationally specific, but that it depends on the gender category membership of the participants. We can account for a good deal more of the behavior if we know the gender mix of dyads, and this probably holds true for larger groups as well.

An implication of our results was that if children at this early age found same-sex play partners more compatible, they ought to prefer same-sex partners when they entered group settings that included children of both sexes. There were already many indications in the literature that children do have same-sex playmate preferences, but there clearly was a need for more systematic attention to the degree of sex segregation that prevails in naturally occurring children's groups at different ages. As part of a longitudinal study of children from birth to age six. Jacklin and I did time-sampled behavioral observation of approximately one hundred children on their preschool playgrounds, and again two years later when the children were playing during school recess periods (Maccoby & Jacklin, 1987). Same-sex playmate preference was clearly apparent in preschool when the children were approximately four and a half. At this age, the children were spending nearly three times as much time with same-sex play partners as with children of the other sex. By age six and a half, the preference had grown much stronger. At this time, the children were spending eleven times as much time with same-sex as with opposite-sex partners.

Elsewhere we have reviewed the literature on playmate choices (Maccoby, 1988; Maccoby & Jacklin, 1987), and here I will simply summarize what I believe the existing body of research shows:

1. Gender segregation is a widespread phenomenon. It is found in all the cultural settings in which children are in social groups large enough to permit choice.
2. The sex difference in the gender of preferred playmates is large in absolute magnitude, compared to sex differences found when children are observed or tested in nonsocial situations.
3. In a few instances, attempts have been made to break down children's preferences for interacting with other same-sex children. It has been found that the preferences are difficult to change.
4. Children choose same-sex playmates spontaneously in situations in which they are not under pressure from adults to do so. In modern co-educational schools, segregation is more marked in situations that have not been structured by adults than in those that have (e.g., Eisenhart & Holland, 1983). Segregation is situationally specific, and the two sexes can interact comfortably under certain conditions, for example, in an absorbing joint task when structures and roles are set up by adults, or in nonpublic settings (Thorne, 1986).
5. Gender segregation is not closely linked to involvement in sex-typed activities. Preschool children spend a great deal of their time engaged in activities that are

gender neutral, and segregation prevails in these activities as well as when they are playing with dolls or trucks.

6. Tendencies to prefer same-sex playmates can be seen among three-year-olds and at even earlier ages under some conditions. But the preferences increase in strength between preschool and school and are maintained at a high level between the ages of six and at least eleven.

7. The research base is thin, but so far it appears that a child's tendency to prefer same-sex playmates has little to do with that child's standing on measures of individual differences. In particular, it appears to be unrelated to measures of masculinity or femininity and also to measures of gender schematicity (Powlishta, 1989).

Why do we see such pronounced attraction to same-sex peers and avoidance of other-sex peers in childhood? Elsewhere I have summarized evidence pointing to two factors that seem to be important in the preschool years (Maccoby, 1988). The first is the rough-and-tumble play style characteristic of boys and their orientation toward issues of competition and dominance. These aspects of male–male interaction appear to be somewhat aversive to most girls. At least, girls are made wary by male play styles. The second factor of importance is that girls find it difficult to influence boys. Some important work by Serbin and colleagues (Serbin, Sprafkin, Elman, & Doyle, 1984) indicates that between the ages of three and a half and five and a half, children greatly increase the frequency of their attempts to influence their play partners. This indicates that children are learning to integrate their activities with those of others so as to be able to carry out coordinated activities. Serbin and colleagues found that the increase in influence attempts by girls was almost entirely an increase in making polite suggestions to others, whereas among boys the increase took the form of more use of direct demands. Furthermore, during this formative two-year period just before school entry, boys were becoming less and less responsive to polite suggestions, so that the style being progressively adopted by girls was progressively less effective with boys. Girls' influence style was effective with each other and was well adapted to interaction with teachers and other adults.

These asymmetries in influence patterns were presaged in our study with thirty-three-month-old children: We found then that boys were unresponsive to the vocal prohibitions of female partners (in that they did not withdraw), although they would respond when a vocal prohibition was issued by a male partner. Girls were responsive to one another and to a male partner's prohibitions. Fagot (1985) also reported that boys are "reinforced" by the reactions of male peers—in the sense that they modify their behavior following a male peer's reaction—but that their behavior appears not to be affected by a female's response.

My hypothesis is that girls find it aversive to try to interact with someone who is unresponsive and that they begin to avoid such partners. Students of power and bargaining have long been aware of the importance of reciprocity in human relations. Pruitt (1976) said, "Influence and power are omnipresent in human affairs. Indeed, groups cannot possibly function unless their members can influence one another"

(p. 343). From this standpoint, it becomes clear why boys and girls have difficulty forming groups that include children of both sexes.

Why do little boys not accept influence from little girls? Psychologists almost automatically look to the nuclear family for the origins of behavior patterns seen in young children. It is plausible that boys may have been more reinforced for power assertive behavior by their parents, and girls more for politeness, although the evidence for such differential socialization pressure has proved difficult to come by. However, it is less easy to imagine how or why parents should reinforce boys for being unresponsive to *girls*. Perhaps it is a matter of observational learning: Children may have observed that between their two parents, their fathers are more influential than their mothers. I am skeptical about such an explanation. In the first place, mothers exercise a good deal of managerial authority within the households in which children live, and it is common for fathers to defer to their judgment in matters concerning the children. Or, parents form a coalition, and in the eyes of the children they become a joint authority, so that it makes little difference to them whether it is a mother or a father who is wielding authority at any given time. Furthermore, the asymmetry in children's cross-sex influence with their peers appears to have its origins at quite an early age — earlier, I would suggest, than children have a very clear idea about the connection between their own sex and that of the same-sex parent. In other words, it seems quite unlikely that little boys ignore girls' influence attempts because little girls remind them of their mothers. I think we simply do not know why girls' influence styles are ineffective with boys, but the fact that they are has important implications for a variety of social behaviors, not just for segregation.

Here are some examples from recent studies. Powlishta (1987) observed preschool-aged boy–girl pairs competing for a scarce resource. The children were brought to a playroom in the nursery school and were given an opportunity to watch cartoons through a movie-viewer that could only be accessed by one child at a time. Powlishta found that when the two children were alone together in the playroom, the boys got more than their share of access to the movie-viewer. When there was an adult present, however, this was no longer the case. The adult's presence appeared to inhibit the boys' more power-assertive techniques and resulted in girls having at least equal access.

This study points to a reason why girls may not only avoid playing with boys but may also stay nearer to a teacher or other adult. Following up on this possibility, Greeno (1989) brought four-child groups of kindergarten and first-grade children into a large playroom equipped with attractive toys. Some of the quartets were all-boy groups, some all-girl groups, and some were made up of two boys and two girls. A female adult sat at one end of the room, and halfway through the play session, moved to a seat at the other end of the room. The question posed for this study was: Would girls move closer to the teacher when boys were present than when they were not? Would the sex composition of a play group make any difference to the locations taken up by the boys? The results were that in all-girl groups, girls actually took up locations *farther* from the adult than did boys in all-boy groups. When two boys were present, however, the two girls were significantly closer to the adult than were the boys, who tended to remain at intermediate distances. When the adult changed position halfway through the session, boys' locations did not change, and this was true whether there were girls present or not. Girls in all-girl groups tended to move in the opposite direction when the adult moved, maintaining distance between themselves and the adult; when boys were present, however, the girls tended to move *with* the adult, staying relatively close. It is worth noting, incidentally, that in all the mixed-sex groups except one, segregation was extreme; both boys and girls behaved as though there was only one playmate available to them, rather than three.

There are some fairly far-reaching implications of this study: Previous observational studies in preschools had indicated that girls are often found in locations closer to the teacher than are boys. These studies have been done in mixed-sex nursery school groups. Girls' proximity seeking toward adults has often been interpreted as a reflection of some general affiliative trait in girls and perhaps as a reflection of some aspect of early socialization that has bound them more closely to caregivers. We see in the Greeno study that proximity seeking toward adults was *not* a general trait in girls. It was a function of the gender composition of the group of other children present as potential interaction partners. The behavior of girls implied that they found the presence of boys to be less aversive when an adult was nearby. It was as though they realized that the rough, power-assertive behavior of boys was likely to be moderated in the presence of adults, and indeed, there is evidence that they were right.

We have been exploring some aspects of girls' avoidance of interaction with boys. Less is known about why boys avoid interaction with girls, but the fact is that they do. In fact, their cross-sex avoidance appears to be even stronger. Thus, during middle childhood both boys and girls spend considerable portions of their social play time in groups of their own sex. This might not matter much for future relationships were it not for the fact that fairly distinctive styles of interaction develop in all-boy and all-girl groups. Thus, the segregated play groups constitute powerful socialization environments in which children acquire distinctive interaction skills that are adapted to same-sex partners. Sex-typed modes of interaction become consolidated, and I wish to argue that the distinctive patterns developed by the two sexes at this time have implications for the same-sex and cross-sex relationships that individuals form as they enter adolescence and adulthood.

It behooves us, then, to examine in somewhat more detail the nature of the interactive milieus that prevail in all-boy and all-girl groups. Elsewhere I have reviewed some of the findings of studies in which these two kinds of groups have been observed (Maccoby, 1988). Here I will briefly summarize what we know.

The two sexes engage in fairly different kinds of activities and games (Huston, 1985). Boys play in somewhat larger groups, on the average, and their play is rougher (Humphreys & Smith, 1987) and takes up more space. Boys more often play in the streets and other public places; girls more often congregate in private homes or yards. Girls tend to form close, intimate friendships with one or two other girls, and these friendships are marked by the sharing of confidences (Kraft & Vraa, 1975). Boys' friendships, on the other hand, are more oriented around mutual interests in activities (Erwin, 1985). The breakup of girls' friendships is usually attended by more intense emotional reactions than is the case for boys.

For our present purposes, the most interesting thing about all-boy and all-girl groups is the divergence in the interactive styles that develop in them. In male groups, there is more concern with issues of dominance. Several psycholinguists have recorded the verbal exchanges that occur in these groups, and Maltz and Borker (1983) summarized the findings of several studies as follows: Boys in their groups are more likely than girls in all-girl groups to interrupt one another, use commands, threats, or boasts of authority: refuse to comply with another child's demand; give information; heckle a speaker, tell jokes or suspenseful stories; top someone else's story; or call another child names. Girls in all-groups, on the other hand, are more likely than boys to express agreement with what another speaker has just said, pause to give another girl a chance to speak, or when starting a speaking turn, acknowledge a point previously made by another speaker. This account indicates that among boys, speech serves largely egoistic functions and is used to establish and protect an individual's turf. Among girls, conversation is a more socially binding process.

In the past five years, analysts of discourse have done additional work on the kinds of interactive processes that are seen among girls, as compared with those among boys. The summary offered by Maltz and Borker has been both supported and extended. Sachs (1987) reported that girls soften their directives to partners, apparently attempting to keep them involved in a process of planning a play sequence, while boys are more likely simply to tell their partners what to do. Leaper (1989) observed children aged five and seven and found that verbal exchanges among girls more often take the form of what he called "collaborative speech acts" that involved positive reciprocity, whereas among boys, speech acts are more controlling and include more negative reciprocity. Miller and colleagues (Miller, Danaher, & Forbes, 1986) found that there was more conflict in boys' groups, and given that conflict had occurred, girls were more likely to use "conflict mitigating strategies," whereas boys more often used threats and physical force. Sheldon (1989) reported that when girls talk, they seem to have a double agenda: to be "nice" and sustain social relationships, while at the same time working to achieve their own individual ends. For boys, the agenda is more often the single one of self-assertion. Sheldon (1989) has noted that in interactions among themselves, girls are *not* unassertive. Rather, girls, do successfully pursue their own ends, but they do so while toning down coercion and dominance, trying to bring about agreement, and restoring or maintaining group functioning. It should be noted that boys' confrontational style does not necessarily impede effective group functioning, as evidenced by boys' ability to cooperate with teammates for sports. A second point is that although researchers' own gender has been found to influence to some degree the kinds of questions posed and the answers obtained, the summary provided here includes the work of both male and female researchers, and their findings are consistent with one another.

As children move into adolescence and adulthood, what happens to the interactive styles that they developed in their largely segregated childhood groups? A first point to note is that despite the powerful attraction to members of the opposite sex in adolescence, gender segregation by no means disappears. Young people continue to spend a good portion of their social time with same-sex partners. In adulthood, there is extensive gender segregation in workplaces (Reskin, 1984), and in some societies and some social-class or ethnic groups, leisure time also is largely spent with same-sex others even after marriage. The literature on the nature of the interactions that occur among same-sex partners in adolescence and adulthood is quite extensive and cannot be reviewed here. Suffice it to say in summary that there is now considerable evidence that the interactive patterns found in sex-homogeneous dyads or groups in adolescence and adulthood are very similar to those that prevailed in the gender-segregated groups of childhood (e.g., Aries, 1976; Carli, 1989; Cowan, Drinkard, & MacGavin, 1984; Savin-Williams, 1979).

How can we summarize what it is that boys and girls, or men and women, are doing in their respective groups that distinguishes these groups from one another? There have been a number of efforts to find the major dimensions that best describe variations in interactive styles. Falbo and Peplau (1980) have factor analyzed a battery of measures and have identified two dimensions: one called direct versus indirect, the other unilateral versus bilateral. Hauser and colleagues (1987) have distinguished what they called *enabling* interactive styles from *constricting* or *restrictive* ones, and I believe this distinction fits the styles of the two sexes especially well. A restrictive style is one that tends to derail the interaction—to inhibit the partner or cause the partner to withdraw, thus shortening the interaction or bringing it to an end. Examples are threatening a partner, directly contradicting or interrupting, topping the partner's story, boasting, or engaging in other forms of self-display. Enabling or facilitative styles are those, such as acknowledging another's comment or expressing agreement, that support whatever the partner is doing and tend to keep the interaction going. I want to suggest that it is because women and girls use more enabling styles that they are able to form more intimate and more integrated relationships. Also I think it likely that it is the male concern for turf and dominance—that is, with not showing weakness to other men and boys—that underlies their restrictive interaction style and their lack of self-disclosure.

Carli (1989) has recently found that in discussions between pairs of adults, individuals are more easily influenced by a partner if that partner has just expressed agreement with them. In this work, women were quite successful in influencing one another in same-sex dyads, whereas pairs of men were less so. The sex difference was fully accounted for by the fact that men's male partners did not express agreement as often. Eagly (1987) has summarized data from a large number of studies on women's and men's susceptibility to influence and has found women to be somewhat more susceptible. Carli's work suggest that this tendency may not be a general female personality trait of "suggestibility" but may reflect the fact that women more often interact with other women who tend to express reciprical agreement. Carli's finding resonates with some work with young children interacting with their mothers. Mary Parpal and I (Parpal & Maccoby, 1985) found that children were more compliant to a mother's demands if the two had previously engaged in a game in which the child was allowed to give directions that the mother followed. In other words, maternal compliance set up a system of reciprocity in which the child also complied. I submit that the same principle applies in adult interactions and that among women, influence is achieved in part by being open to influence from the partner.

Boys and men, on the other hand, although less successful in influencing one another in dyads, develop group structures—well-defined roles in games, dominance hierarchies, and team spirit—that appear to enable them to function effectively in groups. One may suppose that the male directive interactive style is less likely to derail interaction if and when group structural forces are in place. In other words, men and boys may *need* group structure more than women and girls do. However, this hypothesis has yet to be tested in research. In any case, boys and men in their groups have more opportunity to learn how to function within hierarchical structures than do women and girls in theirs.

We have seen that throughout much of childhood and into adolescence and adulthood as well, people spend a good deal of their social time interacting with others of their own gender, and they continue to use distinctive interaction styles in these settings. What happens, then, when individuals from these two distinctive "cultures" attempt to interact with one another? People of both sexes are faced with a relatively unfamiliar situation to which they must adapt. Young women are less likely to receive the reciprocal agreement, opportunities to talk, and so on that they have learned to expect when interacting with female partners. Men have been accustomed to counter-dominance and competitive reactions to their own power assertions, and they now find themselves with partners who agree with them and otherwise offer enabling responses. It seems evident that this new partnership should be easier to adapt to for men than for women. There is evidence that men fall in love faster and report feeling more in love than do women early in intimate relationships (Huston & Ashmore, 1986). Furthermore, the higher rates of depression in females have their onset in adolescence, when rates of cross-sex interaction rise (Nolen-Hoeksema, in press). Although these phenomena are no doubt multidetermined, the asymmetries in interaction styles may contribute to them.

To some degree, men appear to bring to bear much the same kind of techniques in mixed-sex groups that they are accustomed to using in same-sex groups. If the group is attempting some sort of joint problem solving or is carrying out a joint task, men do more initiating, directing, and interrupting than do women. Men's voices are louder and are more listened to than women's voices by both sexes (West & Zimmerman, 1985); men are more likely than women to lose interest in a taped message if it is spoken in a woman's rather than a man's voice (Robinson & MacArthur, 1982). Men are less influenced by the opinions of other group members than are women. Perhaps as a consequence of their greater assertiveness, men have more influence on the group process (Lockheed, 1985: Pugh & Wahrman, 1983), just as they did in childhood. Eagly and colleagues (Eagly, Wood, & Fishbaugh, 1981) have drawn our attention to an important point about cross-sex interaction in groups: The greater resistance of men to being influenced by other group members is found only when the men are under surveillance, that is, if others know whether they have yielded to their partners' influence attempts. I suggest that it is especially the monitoring by other *men* that inhibits men from entering into reciprocal influence with partners. When other men are present, men appear to feel that they must guard their dominance status and not comply too readily lest it be interpreted as weakness.

Women's behavior in mixed groups is more complex. There is some work indicating that they adapt by becoming more like men—that they raise their voices, interrupt, and otherwise become more assertive than they would be when interacting with women (Carli, 1989, Hall & Braunwald, 1981). On the other hand, there is also evidence that they carry over some of their well-practiced female-style behaviors, sometimes in exaggerated form. Women may wait for a turn to speak that does not come, and thus they may end up talking less than they would in a women's group. They smile more than the men do, agree more often with what others have said, and give nonverbal signals of attentiveness to what others—perhaps especially the men— are saying (Duncan & Fiske, 1977). In some writings this female behavior has been referred to as "silent applause."

Eagly (1987) reported a meta-analysis of behavior of the two sexes in groups (mainly mixed-sex groups) that were performing joint tasks. She found a consistent tendency for men to engage in more task behavior—giving and receiving informa- tion, suggestions, and opinions (see also Aries, 1982)—whereas women are more likely to engage in socioemotional behaviors that support positive affective relations within the group. Which style contributes more to effective group process? It de- pends. Wood, Polek, and Aiken (1985) have compared the performance of all-female and all-male groups on different kinds of tasks, finding that groups of women have more success on tasks that require discussion and negotiation, whereas male groups do better on tasks where success depends on the volume of ideas being generated. Overall, it appears that *both* styles are productive, though in different ways.

There is evidence that women feel at a disadvantage in mixed-sex interaction. For example, Hogg and Turner (1987) set up a debate between two young men taking one position and two young women taking another. The outcomes in this situation were contrasted with a situation in which young men and women were debating against same-sex partners. After the cross-sex debate, the self-esteem of the young men rose, but that of the young women declined. Furthermore, the men liked their women opponents better after debating with them, whereas the women liked the men less. In other words, the encounter in most cases was a pleasurable experience for the men, but not for the women. Another example comes from the work of Davis (1978), who set up get-acquainted sessions between pairs of young men and women. He found that the men took control of the interaction, dictating the pace at which intimacy increased, whereas the women adapted themselves to the pace set by the men. The women reported later, however, that they had been uncomfortable about not being able to control the sequence of events, and they did not enjoy the encounter as much as the men did.

In adolescence and early adulthood, the powerful forces of sexual attraction come into play. When couples are beginning to fall in love, or even when they are merely entertaining the possibility of developing an intimate relationship, each is motivated to please the other, and each sends signals implying "Your wish is my command." There is evidence that whichever member of a couple is more attractive, or less in love, is at an advantage and is more able to influence the partner than vice versa (Peplau, 1979). The influence patterns based on the power of interpersonal attraction are not distinct in terms of gender; that is, it may be either the man or the woman in a courting relationship who has the influence advantage. When first meeting, or in the early stages of the acquaintance process, women still may feel at some disadvantage, as shown in the Davis study, but this situation need not last. Work done in the 1960s indicated that in many couples, as relationships become deeper and more enduring, any overall asymmetry in influence diminishes greatly (Heiss 1962; Leik, 1963; Shaw & Sadler, 1965). Most couples develop a relationship that is based on communality rather than exchange bargaining. That is, they have many shared goals and work jointly to achieve them. They do not need to argue over turf because they have the same turf. In well-functioning married couples, both members of the pair strive to avoid conflict, and indeed there is evidence that the men on average are even more conflict-avoidant than the women (Gottman & Levenson, 1988; Kelley et al., 1978). Nevertheless, there are still carry-overs of the different interactive styles males and females have acquired at earlier points in the life cycle. Women seem to expend greater effort toward maintaining harmonious moods (Huston & Ashmore, 1986, p. 177). With intimate cross-sex partners, men use more direct styles of influence, and women use more indirect ones. Furthermore, women are more likely to withdraw (become silent, cold, and distant) and/or take unilateral action in order to get their way in a dispute (Falbo & Peplau, 1980), strategies that we suspect may reflect their greater difficulty in influencing a male partner through direct negotiation.

Space limitations do not allow considering in any depth the next set of important relationships that human beings form: that between parents and children. Let me simply say that I think there is evidence for the following: The interaction styles that women have developed in interaction with girls and other women serve them well when they become mothers. Especially when children are young, women enter into deeper levels of reciprocity with their children than do men (e.g., Gleason, 1987; Maccoby & Jacklin, 1983) and communicate with them better. On the other hand, especially after the first two years, children need firm direction as well as warmth and reciprocity, and fathers' styles may contribute especially well to this aspect of parenting. The relationship women develop with young children seems to depend very little on whether they are dealing with a son or a daughter; it builds on maternal response to the characteristics and needs of early childhood that are found in both boys and girls to similar degrees. Fathers, having a less intimate relationship with individual children, treat young boys and girls in a somewhat more gendered way (Siegal, 1987). As children approach middle childhood and interact with same-sex other children, they develop the interactive styles characteristic of their sex, and their parents more and more interact with them as they have always done with same-sex or opposite-sex others. That is, mothers and daughters develop greater intimacy and reciprocity; fathers and sons exhibit more friendly rivalry and joking, more joint interest in masculine activities, and more rough play. Nevertheless, there are many aspects of the relationships between parents and children that do not depend on the gender of either the parent or the child.

Obviously, as the scene unfolds across generations, it is very difficult to identify the point in the developmental cycle at which the interactional styles of the two sexes begin to diverge, and more important, to identify the forces that cause them to diverge. In my view, processes within the nuclear family have been given too much credit—or too much blame—for this aspect of sex-typing. I doubt that the development of distinctive interactive styles has much to do with the fact that children are parented primarily by women, as some have claimed (Chodorow, 1978; Gilligan, 1982), and it seems likely to me that children's "identification" with the same-sex parent is more a consequence than a cause of children's acquisition of sex-typed interaction styles. I would place most of the emphasis on the peer group as the setting in which children first discover the compatibility of same-sex others, in which boys first discover the requirements of maintaining one's status in the male hierarchy, and in which the gender of one's partners becomes supremely important. We do not have a clear answer to the ultimate question of why the segregated peer groups function as they do. We need now to think about how it can be answered. The answer is important if we are to adapt ourselves successfully to the rapid changes in the roles and relationships of the two sexes that are occurring in modern societies.

REFERENCES

Aries, E. (1976). Interaction patterns and themes of male, female, and mixed groups. *Small Group Behavior, 7,* 7–18.

Aries, E. J. (1982). Verbal and nonverbal behavior in single-sex and mixed-sex groups: Are traditional sex roles changing? *Psychological Reports, 51,* 127–134.

Block, J. H. (1976). Debatable conclusions about sex differences. *Contemporary Psychology, 21,* 517–522.

Carli, L. L. (1989). Gender differences in interaction style and influence. *Journal of Personality and Social Psychology, 56,* 565–576.

Chodorow, N. (1978). *The reproduction of mothering.* Berkeley, CA: University of California Press.

Cowan, C., Drinkard, J., & MacGavin. L. (1984). The effects of target, age and gender on use of power strategies. *Journal of Personality and Social Psychology, 47,* 139–1398.

Davis, J. D. (1978). When boy meets girl: Sex roles and the negotiation of intimacy in an acquaintance exercise. *Journal of Personality and Social Psychology, 36,* 68–692.

Duncan, S., Jr., & Fiske, D. W. (1977). *Face-to-face interaction: Research, methods and theory.* Hillsdale, NJ: Erlbaum.

Eagly, A. H. (1983). Gender and social influence. *American Psychologist, 38,* 971–981.

Eagly, A. H. (1987). *Sex differences in social behavior: A social role interpretation.* Hillsdale, NJ: Erlbaum.

Eagly, A. H., Wood, W., & Fishbaugh, L. (1981). Sex differences in conformity: Surveillance by the group as a determinant of male nonconformity. *Journal of Personality and Social Psychology, 40,* 38–394.

Eisenhart, M. A., & Holland, D. C. (1983). Learning gender from peers: The role of peer group in the cultural transmission of gender. *Human Organization, 42,* 321–332.

Erwin, P. (1985). Similarity of attitudes and constructs in children's friendships. *Journal of Experimental Child Psychology, 40,* 470–485.

Fagot, B. I. (1985). Beyond the reinforcement principle: Another step toward understanding sex roles. *Developmental Psychology, 21,* 1097–1104.

Falbo, T., & Peplau, L. A. (1980). Power strategies in intimate relationships. *Journal of Personality and Social Psychology, 38,* 618–628.

Gilligan, C. (1982). *In a different voice: Psychological theory and women's development.* Cambridge, MA: Harvard University Press.

Gleason, J. B. (1987). Sex differences in parent-child interaction. In S. U. Phillips, S. Steele. & C. Tanz (Eds.), *Language, gender and sex in comparative perspective* (pp. 189–199). Cambridge, England: Cambridge University Press.

Gottman, J. M., & Levenson, R. W. (1988). The social psycho-physiology of marriage. In P. Roller & M. A. Fitzpatrick (Eds.), *Perspectives on marital interaction* (pp. 182–200). New York: Taylor & Francis.

Greeno, C. G. (1989). *Gender differences in children's proximity to adults.* Unpublished doctoral dissertation. Stanford University, Stanford, CA.

Hall, J. A., & Braunwald, K. G. (1981). Gender cues in conversation. *Journal of Personality and Social Psychology, 40,* 99–110.

Hauser, S. T., Powers, S. I., Weiss-Perry, B., Follansbee. D. J., Rajapark, D., & Greene, W. M. (1987). *The constraining and enabling coding system manual.* Unpublished manuscript.

Heiss, J. S. (1962). Degree of intimacy and male–female interaction. *Sociometry, 25,* 197–208.

Hogg, M. A., & Turner, J. C. (1987). Intergroup behavior, self stereotyping and the salience of social categories. *British Journal of Social Psychology, 26,* 325–340.

Humphreys, A. P., & Smith, P. K. (1987). Rough and tumble friendship and dominance in school children: Evidence for continuity and change with age in middle childhood. *Child Development, 58,* 201–212.

Huston. A. C. (1985). The development of sex-typing: Themes from recent research. *Developmental Review, 5,* 1–17.

Huston, T. L., & Ashmore, R. D. (1986). Women and men in personal relationship. In R. D. Ashmore & R. K. Del Boca (Eds.). *The social psychology of female–male relations* New York: Academic Press.

Jacklin, C. N., & Maccoby, E. E. (1978). Social behavior at 33 months in same-sex and mixed-sex dyads. *Child Development, 49,* 557–569.

Kelley, H. H., Cunningham, J. D., Grisham, J. A., Lefebvre, L. M., Sink, C. R., & Yablon, G. (1978). Sex differences in comments made during conflict in close relationships. *Sex Roles, 4,* 473–491.

Kraft, L. W., & Vraa, C. W. (1975). Sex composition of groups and pattern of self-disclosure by high school females. *Psychological Reports, 37,* 733–734.

Leaper. C. (1989). *The sequencing of power and involvement in boys' and girls' talk.* Unpublished manuscript (under review), University of California, Santa Cruz.

Leik, R. K. (1963). Instrumentality and emotionality in family interaction. *Sociometry, 26,* 131–145.

Lockheed, M. E. (1985). Sex and social influence: A meta-analysis guided by theory. In J. Berger & M. Zelditch (Eds.), *Status, attributions, and rewards* (pp. 406–429). San Francisco, CA: Jossey-Bass.

Maccoby, E. E. (1988). Gender as a social category. *Developmental Psychology, 26,* 755–765.

Maccoby, E. E., & Jacklin, C. N. (1974). *The psychology of sex differences.* Stanford, CA: Stanford University Press.

Maccoby, E. E., & Jacklin, C. N. (1980). Sex differences in aggression: A rejoinder and reprise. *Child Development, 51,* 964–980.

Maccoby. E. E. & Jacklin, C. N. (1983). The "person" characteristics of children and the family as environment. In D. Magnusson & V. L. Allen (Eds.). *Human development: An interactional perspective* (pp. 76–92). New York: Academic Press.

Maccoby, E. E. & Jacklin, C. N. (1987). Gender segregation in childhood. In H. W. Reese (Ed.), *Advances in child development and behavior* (Vol. 20, pp. 239–288). New York: Academic Press.

Maltz, D. N., & Borker, R. A. (1983). A cultural approach to male–female miscommunication. In John A. Gumperz (Ed.), *Language and social identity* (pp. 195–216). New York: Cambridge University Press.

Miller, P., Danaher, D., & Forbes, D. (1986). Sex-related strategies for coping with interpersonal conflict in children aged five and seven. *Developmental Psychology, 22,* 543–548.

Nolen-Hoeksema, S. (in press). *Sex differences in depression.* Stanford, CA: Stanford University Press.

Parpal, M., & Maccoby, E. E. (1985). Maternal responsiveness and subsequent child compliance. *Child Development, 56,* 1326–1334.

Peplau, A. (1979). Power in dating relationships. In J. Freeman (Ed.), *Women: A feminist perspective* (pp. 121–137). Palo Alto, CA: Mayfield.

Powlishta, K. K. (1987, April). *The social context of cross-sex interactions.* Paper presented at biennial meeting of the Society for Research in Child Development, Baltimore, MD.

Powlishta, K. K. (1989). *Salience of group membership: The case of gender.* Unpublished doctoral dissertation, Stanford University, Stanford, CA.

Pruitt, D. G. (1976). *Power and bargaining.* In B. Seidenberg & A. Snadowsky (Eds.), *Social psychology: An introduction* (pp. 343–375). New York: Free Press.

Pugh, M. D., & Wahrman, R. (1983). Neutralizing sexism in mixed-sex groups: Do women have to be better than men? *American Journal of Sociology: 88,* 746–761.

Reskin, B. F. (Ed.), (1984). *Sex segregation in the workplace: Trends, explanations and remedies.* Washington, DC: National Academy Press.

Robinson, J., & McArthur, L. Z. (1982). Impact of salient vocal qualities on casual attribution for a speaker's behavior. *Journal of Personality and Social Psychology, 43,* 236–247.

Sachs, J. (1987). Preschool boys' and girls' language use in pretend play. In S. U. Phillips. S. Steele, & C. Tanz (Eds.), *Language, gender and sex in comparative perspective* (pp. 178–188). Cambridge, England: Cambridge University Press.

Savin-Williams, R. C. (1979). Dominance hierarchies in groups of early adolescents. *Child Development, 50,* 923–935.

Serbin, L. A., Sprafkin, C., Elman, M., & Doyle, A. (1984). The early development of sex differentiated patterns of social influence. *Canadian Journal of Social Science, 14,* 350–363.

Shaw, M. E., & Sadler, O. W. (1965). Interaction patterns in heterosexual dyads varying in degree of intimacy. *Journal of Social Psychology, 66,* 345–351.

Sheldon, A. (1989, April). *Conflict talk: Sociolinguistic challenges to self-assertion and how young girls meet them.* Paper presented at the biennial meeting of the Society for Research in Child Development, Kansas City.

Siegal, M. (1987). Are sons and daughters treated more differently by fathers than mothers? *Developmental Review, 7,* 183–209.

Thorne, B. (1986). Girls and boys together, but mostly apart, In W. W. Hartup & L. Rubin (Eds.), *Relationships and development* (pp. 167–184). Hillsdale, NJ: Erlbaum.

Tieger, T. (1980). On the biological basis of sex differences in aggression. *Child Development, 51,* 943–963.

Wasserman, G. A., & Stern, D. N. (1978). An early manifestation of differential behavior toward children of the same and opposite sex. *Journal of Genetic Psychology: 133,* 129–137.

West, C., & Zimmerman, D. H. (1985). Gender, language and discourse. In T. A. van Dijk (Ed.), *Handbook of discourse analysis: Vol. 4. Discourse analysis in society* (pp. 103–124). London: Academic Press.

Wood, W., Polek, D., & Aiken, C. (1985). Sex differences in group task performance. *Journal of Personality and Social Psychology, 48,* 63–71.

Chapter Thirty-Seven

Relating to Privilege

Seduction and Rejection in the Subordination of White Women and Women of Color

Aída Hurtado

Each oppressed group in the United States is positioned in a particular and distinct relationship to white men, and each form of subordination is shaped by this relational position. Men of Color and white men maintain power over women, particularly within their respective groups.[1] However, gender alone does not determine either a superordinate or subordinate position. In a highly industrialized society run by a complex hierarchical bureaucracy and based on individualistic competition, many socially constructed markers of group memberships are used to allocate power.[2] Class, ethnicity, race, and sexuality are but a few. As we develop a discourse for discussing our group memberships, as our consciousness about the mechanisms of subordination evolves, and as previously silenced groups begin to speak, we can begin to have a picture of contemporary forms of subordination and their psychological effects.[3]

I focus on the relationships of white women and women of Color to white men, and how these relationships have affected feminists from both groups.[4] The conflicts and tensions between white feminists and feminists of Color are viewed too frequently as lying solely in woman-to-woman relationships. These relationships, however, are affected in both obvious and subtle ways by how each of these two groups of women relate to white men through linkages that Nancy Henley calls "the everyday social relationships that glue together the social superstructure."[5]

The Structural Position of Women in the United States

In the United States, Blacks, Native Americans, Latinos, and some Asian groups are predominantly working class.[6] On every measure of standard of living (income, years of education, household makeup) they are positioned structurally below the white population. This is especially the case for women in these racial and ethnic groups.

Aída Hurtado, "Relating to Privilege: Seduction and Rejection in the Subordination of White Women and Women of Color." *Signs: Journal of Women in Culture and Society, 14 (41),* pp. 833–855, © 1989 by the University of Chicago. All rights reserved. Reprinted with permission.

The common statistical reporting practice of aggregating the socioeconomic statuses of all groups of women hides substantial differences. A recent newspaper article reported that women had reached 70 percent of pay parity with men in 1987.[7] A closer examination of the statistics quoted showed that not only had the headline collapsed differences among women, it had also exaggerated women's gains and so reduced differences between women and men. In fact, as the story that followed shows, in 1987 white women reached 67.5 percent of pay parity with white men, but Black women reached only 61.3 percent, and Hispanic women reached barely 54.8 percent.[8]

White women tend to earn more money than women of Color because as a group they tend to be able to stay in school longer than many women of Color.[9] White women are more likely to finish high school (68 percent, in contrast to 52 percent of Black women, 54 percent of American Indian women, 36 percent of Mexican women, and 39 percent of Puerto Rican women), and graduate from college (13 percent, in contrast to 8 percent of Black women, 6 percent of Native Americans, and 6 percent of Hispanic women). White women therefore earn substantially higher incomes, even though certain groups of women of Color (e.g., Black women) are more likely than white women to stay in the labor force without interruption. In 1985 the median income for women of Mexican descent was $4,556; for Puerto Rican women, $4,473; for Vietnamese women, $4,694; for Japanese women, $7,410; for Pilipina women, $8,253; and for Black women $14,036. That same year, the median income for white women was $15,575.[10] All women experience job segregation, but white women's current educational attainment gives them a brighter future than that of women of Color (with the exception of certain groups of Asian women).[11] In the past few years, the college enrollment of all women fourteen to thirty-four years old has been nearing that of men. Close to half (49 percent) of all graduate students in 1980 were women, compared to less than a third (29 percent) in 1970. Although the graduate school figures do not include a separate category for women of Color, it is safe to conclude that given the high school and college graduation rates quoted earlier, the women who are enrolled in graduate programs are predominantly white women.[12]

Increasingly, women are becoming the sole supporters of their families. The number of single-parent families has almost doubled since 1970; one in five families with children is now maintained by a woman (16 percent of all families in 1985). However, women of Color are more likely than white women to maintain families (44 percent of Black women, 23 percent of Hispanic women, and 23 percent of Native American women, compared to 13 percent of white women). Furthermore, women of Color are more likely to be heads of households living in poverty (52 percent of Black households and 53 percent of Hispanic households, compared to 27 percent of white households), more likely to be divorced (35 percent of Black women compared to 14 percent of white women), and more likely to have larger families (40 percent of Black women, 60 percent of Hispanic women but only 20 percent of white women had four or more people to support). In addition, teenage mothers are more likely to be Black women than white women (58 percent of teenage mothers are Black compared to 13 percent white).[13]

These measures reveal that women of Color stay fewer years in school, have fewer

dollars to spend, and bear more economic burdens than any other group in thi[?]
country. White women also suffer economically, but their economic situation is no[?]
as dire as that of women of Color. More specifically, white women's relationship to
white men (the highest earners in society) as daughters, wives, or sisters gives them
an "economic cushion."[14]

The Exclusion of Women of Color in Feminist Theory

This cushion has influenced the development of feminist writing. Academic production requires time and financial resources. Poverty hampers the ability of all working-
class people, especially racial and ethnic groups, to participate in higher education:
without financial assistance, few low-income and racial/ethnic students can attend
universities; without higher education, few working-class and ethnic/racial intellectuals can become professors. Not surprisingly, therefore, most contemporary published
feminist theory in the United States has been written by white, educated women.[15]
The experiences of other women (including white working-class women) are absent
in much of white academic feminist theory.[16]

Much of feminist theory focuses on the condition of women qua women. Illustrative of this tendency is the book *Feminist Politics and Human Nature* in which Alison
Jaggar presents an impressive and comprehensive review of contemporary feminist
theory. Jaggar acknowledges that feminist theory fails to integrate race into its
analysis of women's subordination. While she laments this failure, she also proclaims
that women of Color have not developed "a distinctive and comprehensive theory of
women's liberation" and that the existing writings are "mainly at the level of description."[17] If she does not dismiss them altogether, Jaggar fits other writings by Black
feminist theorists into her framework for white feminist theory. In doing so, she
glosses over important differences between those feminists of Color and white
feminists, differences that may elucidate the race/class nexus so lacking in white
feminist theory. For example, she notes that "a very few [Black feminists] are radical
feminists, though almost none seem to be lesbian separatists," but she does not
discuss why this is so beyond locating it within choices that white women have
made.[18] So, for instance, Jaggar notes: "Radical feminism . . . was sparked by the
special experiences of a relatively small group of predominantly white, middle-class,
college-educated, American women in the later 1960s. . . . Today, those who are
attracted to radical feminism still tend to be primarily white and college-educated."[19]
Jaggar also fails even to speculate about why Black feminists might be reluctant to
separate from Black men while simultaneously recognizing their gender subordination.

Recently, white feminist theorists have begun to recognize the theoretical implications of embracing diversity among women. White feminist theory is moving beyond
biological determinism and social categoricalism to a conception of gender as a
process accomplished through social interaction.[20] Rejecting the binary categorization of "man" and "woman," this new conceptualization opens up the possibility of
diversity among women and men and the possibility of many feminisms.[21] However,

despite these advances, white feminist theory has yet to integrate the facts that for women of Color race, class, and gender subordination are experienced simultaneously and that their oppression is not only by members of their own group but by whites of both genders.[22] White feminist theorists have failed to grasp fully what this means, how it is experienced, and, ultimately, how it is fought.[23] Many white feminists do have an intellectual commitment to addressing race and class, but the class origins of the participants in the movement as well as their relationship to white men has prevented them, as a group, from understanding the simultaneity of oppression for women of Color.[24]

The Historical Context

Before the Civil War nearly all white women advocates of equal rights for women were committed abolitionists. However, as bell hooks indicates, this did not mean they were all antiracist.[25] White abolitionists did not want to destroy the racial hierarchy or provide broad citizenship rights to freed slaves. Instead, they were motivated by religious and moral sentiments to take a stand against slavery as an institution.[26] Because many white abolitionists were not antiracist, working relationships between Black and white activists were sometimes strained. When it was expedient, white women in the abolitionist movement would compare their plight to that of the slaves. Elizabeth Cady Stanton, speaking before the New York State Legislature in 1860 stated: "The prejudice against Color, of which we hear so much, is no stronger than that against sex. It is produced by the same cause, and manifested very much in the same way. The Negro's skin and the woman's sex are both prima facie evidence that they were intended to be in subjection to the white Saxon man. The few social privileges which the man gives the woman, he makes up to the (free) Negro in civil rights."[27] Stanton, unfortunately, cast her argument in terms that pitted white women against Black men in a competition for privileges that erased Black women altogether.

The strained bonds between Black and white women involved in the fight for equal political rights finally ruptured after the Civil War. When only Black men received the vote, Black and white activists together decried the exclusion of women's right, but their protests took different forms. Black suffragists did not abandon Black men; white suffragists quickly abandoned Black women.[28] White women's right advocates like Elizabeth Cady Stanton, who had never before argued woman suffrage on a racially imperialistic platform, in 1869 stated her outrage at the enfranchisement of Black men: "If Saxon men have legislated thus for their own mothers, wives and daughters, what can we hope for at the hands of Chinese, Indians, and Africans? . . . I protest against the enfranchisement of another man of any race or clime until the daughters of Jefferson, Hancock, and Adams are crowned with their rights."[29]

Black suffragists could not afford such disengagement from their group. Instead, many Black women leaders of the time fought for the just treatment of all people with the recognition that women of Color experienced multiple oppressions because of their gender, race, and class. Black women suffragists struggled with white suffragists to obtain women's right to vote as they fought against lynchings, poverty, and segregation.[30] In 1893 Anna Cooper addressed the Women's Congress in Chicago and eloquently outlined the position many other Black activists were advocating at that time:

> We take our stand on the solidarity of humanity, the oneness of life, and the unnatural-ness and injustice of all special favoritisms, whether of sex, race, country, or condition. ... Least of all can women's cause afford to decry the weak.... Not till the universal title of humanity of life, liberty, and the pursuit of happiness is conceded to be inalienable to all; not till then is woman's lesson taught and woman's cause won—not the white woman's not the black woman's, not the red woman's, but the cause of every man and of every woman who has writhed silently under a mighty wrong.[31]

Racial conflict emerged in the suffrage movement for many reasons, the most important of which was the white women's privileged relationship to white men. Elizabeth Cady Stanton, Susan B. Anthony, and Lucy Stone were all married to prominent white men who supported them during their involvement in political work, while Black activists such as Sojourner Truth, Ida B. Wells, and Ellen Craft were at birth *owned* by white men.[32] Despite the abolition of slavery, the difference between the relationship of white women to white men and of women of Color to white men has persisted to the present. The conflict that this difference causes between contemporary white feminists and feminists of Color is but a replay of old divisions that are perpetuated with amazing consistency. Like their political ancestors, contemporary feminists of Color do not attribute their oppression solely to their gender and are reluctant to abandon the struggle on behalf of their racial/ethnic group. The largest organization of Chicana academics (Mujeres Activas en Letras y Cambio Social) explicitly states their class and ethnic solidarity: "We are the daugh-ters of Chicano working class families involved in higher education. We were raised in labor camps and urban barrios, where sharing our resources was the basis of survival.... Our history is the story of working people—their struggles, commit-ments, strengths, and the problems they faced.... We are particularly concerned with the conditions women face at work, in and out of the home. We continue our mothers' struggle for social and economic justice."[33]

Rejection versus Seduction

Sojourner Truth, speaking at the Women's Rights Convention in 1851, highlighted the crucial difference between women of Color and white women in their relationships to white men. Frances Dana Gage, the presiding officer of the convention, describes Sojourner Truth marching down the aisle to the pulpit steps where she addressed her audience:

> At her first word there was a profound hush ... "That man over there say that women needs to be helped into carriages, and lifted over ditches, and to have the best place everywhere. Nobody ever helps me into carriages, or over mud-puddles, or gives me any best place!" And raising herself to her full height, asked, "And ain't I a woman?

Look at me! Look at my arm!" (and she bared her right arm to the shoulder, showing her tremendous muscular power). "I have ploughed, and planted, and gathered into barns, and no man could head me! And ain't I a woman? I could work as much and eat as much as a man—when I could get it—and bear the lash as well! And ain't I a woman? I have borne thirteen children and seen them most all sold off to slavery, and when I cried out with my mother's grief, none but Jesus heard me! And ain't I a woman?"[34]

Now, as then, white middle-class women are groomed from birth to be the lovers, mothers, and partners (however unequal) of white men because of the economic and social benefits attached to these roles.[35] Upper-and middle-class white women are supposed to be the biological bearers of those members of the next generation who will inherit positions of power in society. Women of Color, in contrast, are groomed from birth to be primarily the lovers, mothers, and partners (however unequal) of men of Color, who are also oppressed by white men.[36] The avenues of advancement through marriage that are open to white women who conform to prescribed standards of middle-class femininity are not even a theoretical possibility for most women of Color. This is not to say that women of Color are more oppressed than white women but, rather, that white men use different forms of enforcing oppression of white women and of women of Color. As a consequence, these groups of women have different political responses and skills, and at times these differences cause the two groups to clash.

Women of Color came to the United States either through slavery (e.g., Blacks), conquest of their homeland (e.g., Chicanas, Puerto Ricans, American Indians, Pilipinas), or through forced and semi-forced labor migration (e.g., Japanese, Chinese). Unlike European immigrants who become culturally and linguistically assimilated within two generations, these groups of women constitute racially distinct groups. Thus even if a Black career woman were to marry a white professional man, her offspring would *not* inherit the power positions accorded to white sons and daughters of the same class. Indeed, some argue that being one-half Black is a greater stigma than having remained within the subordinate group's boundaries.[37] However, if a working-class white woman were to marry a white professional man, her offspring would automatically acquire the privileged position of the father. In certain circles, a white woman's humble beginnings are a source of pride because they reaffirm the dominant hegemonic belief in the availability of equal opportunity.

White men need white women in a way that they do not need women of Color because women of Color cannot fulfill white men's need for racially pure offspring. This fact creates differences in the *relational position* of the groups—distance from and access to the source of privilege, white men. Thus, white women, as a group, are subordinated through seduction, women of Color, as a group, through rejection. Class position, of course, affects the probability of obtaining the rewards of seduction and the sanctions of rejection. Working-class white women are socialized to believe in the advantages of marrying somebody economically successful, but the probability of obtaining that goal is lower for them than for middle-or upper-class white women. Class position affects women of Color as well. Although rejected by white men as candidates to reproduce offspring, middle-class women of Color may be accepted

into some white middle-class social circles in the well-documented role of token.[3]
Class privilege functions to one degree or another regardless of race, and white
privilege functions to one degree or another regardless of class.[39]

The Dual Construction of Womanhood

For the most part, white feminist theory has difficulty elucidating the condition of
women of Color because much of this theorizing takes the categories of "women"
and "men" as "in no need of further examination or finer distinction."[40] There is an
implicit biological determinism even in the works of those theorists who have
rejected it.[41] When Sojourner Truth, baring her muscular arm, asked "ain't I a
woman?" the reply might not have been obvious, even though she had borne thirteen
children. The answer to her question involves defining *woman*. The white women in
the room did not have to plough the fields, side by side with Black men, and see
their offspring sold into slavery, yet they were clearly women. Sojourner Truth had
worked the fields, and she had borne children; but she was not a woman in the sense
of having the same experiences as the white women at the meeting.

The definition of *woman* is constructed differently for white women and for
women of Color, though gender is the marking mechanism through which the
subordination of each is maintained.[42] White women are persuaded to become the
partners of white men and are seduced into accepting a subservient role that meets
the material needs of white men. As Audre Lorde describes it: "White women face
the pitfall of being seduced into joining the oppressor under the pretense of sharing
power. This possibility does not exist in the same way for women of Color. The
tokenism that is sometimes extended to us is not an invitation to join power: our
racial 'otherness' is a visible reality that makes it quite clear. For white women there
is a wider range of pretended choices and rewards for identifying with patriarchal
power and its tools."[43]

The patriarchal invitation to power is only a pretended choice for white women
because, as in all cases of tokens, their inclusion is dependent on complete and
constant submission. As John Stuart Mill observed: "It was not sufficient for [white]
women to be slaves. They must be willing slaves, for the maintenance of patriarchal
order depends upon the consensus of women. It depends upon women playing their
part ... voluntarily suppressing the evidence that exposes the false and arbitrary
nature of man-made categories and the reality which is built on those categories."[44]

The genesis of the construction of *woman* for Black women is in slavery. During
slavery, Black women were required to be as masculine as men in the performance of
work and were as harshly punished as men, but they were also raped.[45] Many Black
women were broken and destroyed, but the majority who survived "acquired qualities considered taboo by the nineteenth-century ideology of womanhood."[46] As
Davis puts it: "[Black women's] awareness of their endless capacity for hard work
may have imparted to them a confidence in their ability to struggle for themselves,
their families, and their people."[47]

White men perceive women of Color primarily as workers and as objects of sexual power and aggression. Their sexual objectification of women of Color allows white men to express power and aggression sexually, without the emotional entanglements of, and the rituals that are required in, relationships with women of their own group.[48] In many ways the dual conception of woman based on race—"white goddess/black she-devil, chaste virgin/nigger whore, the blond blue-eyed doll/the exotic 'mulatto' object of sexual craving"—has freed women of Color from the distraction of the rewards of seduction.[49] Women of Color "do not receive the respect and treatment—mollycoddling and condescending as it sometimes is—afforded to white women."[50]

Identity Invention versus Reaffirmation of Cultural Roots

A prominent theme in the activities of the white feminist movement has been the deconstruction of patriarchal definitions of gender in order to develop women's own definitions of what it means to be a woman.[51] This is similar to the process of decolonization that minority groups underwent in the 1960s.[52] In both instances, socially stigmatized groups have reclaimed their history by taking previously denigrated characteristics and turning them into positive affirmations of self.[53] For example, radical feminism glorifies the menstrual cycle as a symbol of women's capacity to give birth, while Black Liberation uses skin color in the slogan "Black is Beautiful."[54]

White women are at a greater disadvantage than women of Color in reclaiming their identity—or perhaps it is more accurate to say, in inventing their identity. Unlike people of Color, who can refer to a specific event in history (e.g., slavery, military conquest) as the beginning of their subordination, white women in the United States have always been subordinated to men, and hence their dependency is not the result of a specific historical event or social change.[55] People of Color in the United States retain the memory of the days before slavery or conquest: they share that past, a tradition, and sometimes a religion or culture.[56]

White feminists have to uncover a history and simultaneously define what they want to become in the future. With patriarchal ideology so deeply ingrained, it is difficult for white feminists to reconstruct gender in adulthood.[57] Existing academic paradigms, emanating from male culture and distorting women's experience, are virtually useless for this task.[58] With few academic, historical, and cultural paths to follow, white feminists have nevertheless undertaken the task of redefining gender. It is to their credit that white feminists have succeeded in building feminist theory and in obtaining concrete political results when they started with little more than an intuitive dissatisfaction with their subordination.[59]

As part of their subordination, most white women have been denied equal participation in public discourse with white men.[60] Shirley Ardener argues that (white) women are socialized in the "art of conversation" while (white) men are trained in the more formal "art of rhetoric" or the "art of persuasion."[61] Socialization to a feminine mode of discourse deprives white women of a political medium through which to voice and define their oppression.[62] In 1963, Betty Friedan called this the "problem that has no name" because white middle-class women's discontent did not fit into the categories of the problems already named (by men).[63] In the late 1960s consciousness-raising groups were formed not only to delineate women's discontent but also to develop a discourse for discussing it.[64]

Despite their exclusion from participation in the "manufacturing of culture," white women have not been segregated from the "makers of culture"—white men.[65] White middle-class women's relational position to white men has given them at the very least a spectator's seat. For example, Dorothy E. Smith relates how women who become mathematicians generally discover mathematics by accident in "sharing a brother's lessons, the interest of a family friend, the paper covered with calculus used to paper a child's room—some special incident or relation which introduced them to the territory of their art."[66] Elizabeth Cady Stanton was exposed to the white man's culture by her father, a prominent, conservative judge, who taught her law and supported her obtaining a high school diploma at the age of sixteen.[67]

Most women of Color are not groomed to be the parlor conversationalists that white women are expected to be. Working-class women of Color come from cultures whose languages have been barred from public discourse, as well as from the written discourse, of society at large. Many people of Color speak varieties of English (e.g., Black English) not understood by most white people. Nonetheless, people of Color often excel in verbal performance among their own peers. They embrace speech as one medium for expression. Older women are especially valued as storytellers with the responsibility to preserve the history of the group from generation to genera-tion.[68] Patricia Hill Collins argues that a rich tradition of Black feminist thought exists, much of it produced orally by ordinary Black women in their roles as mothers, teachers, musicians, and preachers.[69] This oral tradition celebrates the open and spontaneous exchange of ideas. The conversation of women of Color can be bawdy, rowdy, and irreverent, and in expressing opinions freely, women of Color exercise a form of power.

What this means is that, for white women, the first step in the search for identity is to confront the ways in which their personal, individual silence endorses the power of white men that has robbed them of their history. For women of Color, the challenge is to use their oral traditions for specific political goals.

The Public/Private Distinction

The public/private distinction that exists among the white middle class devalues "women's work" done in the home and arbitrarily upgrades men's work performed in the public sphere.[70] Throughout the history of the white feminist movement in the United States, white women have gained political consciousness about gender oppression by examining their personal lives. They have realized that what happens in the intimacy of their own homes is not exempt from the political forces that affect the rest of society.[71] The contemporary notion that "the personal is political" identi-fies and rejects the public/private distinction as a tool by which women are excluded from public participation while the daily tyrannies of men are protected from public scrutiny.

Yet the public/private distinction is relevant only for the white middle and upper classes since historically the American state has intervened constantly in the private lives and domestic arrangements of the working class. Women of Color have not had the benefit of the economic conditions that underlie the public/private distinction. Instead the political consciousness of women of Color stems from an awareness that the public is *personally* political.[72] Welfare programs and policies have discouraged family life, sterilization programs have restricted reproduction rights, government has drafted and armed disproportionate numbers of people of Color to fight its wars overseas, and locally, police forces and the criminal justice system arrest and incarcerate disproportionate numbers of people of Color.[73] There is no such thing as a private sphere for people of Color except that which they manage to create and protect in an otherwise hostile environment.

The differences between the concerns of white feminists and those of feminists of Color are indicative of these distinct political groundings. White feminists' concerns about the unhealthy consequences of standards for feminine beauty, their focus on the unequal division of household labor, and their attention to childhood identity formation stem from a political consciousness that seeks to project private sphere issues into the public arena.[74] Feminists of Color focus instead on public issues such as affirmative action, racism, school desegregation, prison reform, and voter registration—issues that cultivate an awareness of the distinction between public policy and private choice.

Because white feminists focus on politicizing the personal, their political consciousness about gender oppression emerges primarily from examining everyday interactions with men. As Nancy Henley observes, as wives, secretaries, or assistants to white men, white women are physically integrated around centers of power, which makes it necessary for powerful white men to have "frequent interaction—verbal and nonverbal—with women."[75] These frequent interactions promote and reinforce white women's socialization to docility, passivity, and allegiance to white men, so that white woman experience an individualized and internalized form of social control.[76] As a result, the white feminist movement is the only political movement to develop its own clinical approach—feminist therapy—to overcoming oppression at the interpersonal level.[77]

In contrast, other oppressed groups in American society "are often physically separated, by geography, ghettos, and labor hierarchies, from power centers."[78] People of Color, as a group, do not have constant familial interactions with white men, and social control is exerted in a direct and impersonal manner. Instead of developing a culturally specific therapy, ethnic and racial political movements in the United States fight vehemently against the use of therapeutic treatments which depoliticize and individualize their concerns by addressing social problems as if they emerged from the psychology of the oppressed.[79]

These differences in political approaches reflect differences in women's relational position to white men. When white middle-class women rebel, they are accused of mental illness and placed in mental institutions.[80] When people of Color rebel, they are accused of violence and placed in prisons.[81] This difference in treatment is related to the distance of each group from the center of power.

Political Socialization and Survival Skills

Women of Color are marginalized in U.S. society from the time they are born. Marginalization is not a status conferred on them as they step outside the confines of ascribed roles, but as Audre Lorde poignantly describes, it is a condition of their lives that is communicated to them by the hatred of strangers. A consciousness of this hatred and the political reasons behind it begins in childhood:

> I don't like to talk about hate. I don't like to remember the cancellation and hatred, heavy as my wished-for death, seen in the eyes of so many white people from the time I could see. It was echoed in newspapers and movies and holy pictures and comic books and Amos 'n' Andy radio programs. I had no tools to dissect it, no language to name it.
>
> The AA subway train to Harlem. I clutch my mother's sleeve. . . . On one side of me a man reading a paper. On the other, a woman in a fur hat staring at me. Her mouth twitches as she stares and then her gaze drops down, pulling mine with it. Her leather-gloved hand plucks at the line where my new blue snowpants and her sleek fur coat meet. She jerks her coat closer to her. I look. I do not see whatever terrible thing she is seeing on the seat between us—probably a roach. But she has communicated her horror to me. It must be something very bad from the way she is looking, so I pull my snowsuit closer to me away from it, too. When I look up the woman is still staring at me, her nose holes and eyes huge. And suddenly I realize there is nothing crawling up the seat between us: it is me she doesn't want her coat to touch. . . . No word has been spoken. I'm afraid to say anything to my mother because I don't know what I've done. I look at the sides of my snowpants, secretly. Is there something on them? Something's going on here I do not understand, but I will never forget it. Her eyes. The flared nostrils. The hate.[82]

Experiences such as these force women of Color to acquire survival skills as early as five years of age.[83] Many children of Color serve as the official translators for their monolingual relatives in disputes with companies and agencies unresponsive to poor, working-class people. Early interaction with the public sphere helps many women of Color to develop a public identity and the political skills to fend off state intervention. Women of Color do not have the rewards of seduction offered to them. Relatively few get a high school diploma, even fewer finish college, and only an infinitesimal number obtain graduate degrees.[84] Most women of Color have to contribute to the economic survival of their families, and therefore their commitment to obtaining an education, acquiring economic independence, and practicing a profession are part of economic survival.[85] In addition, the low-income status of most women of Color means that they must acquire survival skills such as sustaining informal networks of support, practicing alternative forms of health care, and organizing for political and social change.[86]

By comparison, the childhoods of many white middle-class feminists were protected by classism and racism. As a consequence, many do not acquire their political
consciousness of gender oppression until they become adults.[87] Lacking experience
in challenging authorities and white men in particular, white feminists often seem
surprised at the harshness with which the power structure responds to threat, and
they do not have well-developed defenses to fend off the attacks. They often turn
their anger inward rather than seeing it as a valid response.[88] In planning political
actions some adopt white men's approaches, others reject them totally.[89] White
liberal feminists, for instance, have had a significant impact at the macro-level
because they have adopted the bureaucratic language and sociopolitical rules that are
congenial to the power structure.[90] White radical feminists reject men's approaches
and are successful at the micro-level of interaction in developing modes of political
organizing that are consensual and nonhierarchical.[91]

In contrast, the political skills of feminists of Color are neither the conventional
political skills of white liberal feminists nor the free-spirited approaches of white
radical feminists. Instead, feminists of Color train to be urban guerrillas by doing
battle every day with the apparatus of the state.[92] Their tactics are not recorded or
published for others to study and are often misunderstood by white middle-class
feminists. One basic tactic is using anger effectively.[93]

> Women of color in America have grown up within a symphony of anger, at being
> silenced, at being unchosen, at knowing that when we survive, it is in spite of a world
> that takes for granted our lack of humanness, and which hates our very existence
> outside of its service. And I say symphony rather than cacophony because we have had
> to learn to orchestrate those furies so that they do not tear us apart. We have had to
> learn to move through them and use them for strength and force and insight within
> our daily lives. Those of us who did not learn this difficult lesson did not survive. And
> part of my anger is always libation for my fallen sisters.[94]

The loss of children is one of the main reasons for the anger felt by many women
of Color. There is a contemporary ring to Sojourner Truth's words, "I have borne
thirteen children and seen them most all sold off to slavery."[95] Drugs, prison,
discrimination, poverty, and racism continue to deprive women of Color of their
children at alarming rates in contemporary U.S. society. These losses and their
meaning for the survival of future generations often distinguish the concerns of
feminists of Color from those of white women. "Some problems we share as women,
some we do not. You fear your children will grow up to join the patriarchy and
testify against you, we fear our children will be dragged from a car and shot down in
the street and you will turn your backs upon the reasons they are dying."[96]

These differences in childhood experiences with racism and classism, in the
necessity of developing survival skills, and in using anger create conflict between
white feminists and feminists of Color. "When women of Color speak out of the
anger that laces so many of our contacts with white women, we are often told that
we are 'creating a mood of hopelessness,' 'preventing white women from getting past
guilt,' or 'standing in the way of trusting communication and action.' ... One

woman wrote, 'Because you are Black and Lesbian, you seem to speak with the moral authority of suffering.' Yes I am Black and Lesbian, and what you hear in my voice is fury, not suffering. Anger, not moral authority. There is a difference."[97]

Implications for Political Mobilization

Clearly, whether women are subordinated by white men through seduction or rejection, the results are detrimental to women's humanity. Advantages gained by women of Color because of their distance from white men amount to nothing more than the "deformed equality of equal oppression [to that of men of Color.]"[98] The privileges that white women acquire because of their closeness to white men give them only empty choices. As a seventy-three-year-old Black woman observes: "My mother used to say that the black woman is the white man's mule and the white woman is his dog. Now, she said that to say this: we do the heavy work and get beat whether we do it well or not. But the white woman is closer to the master and he pats them on the head and lets them sleep in the house, but he ain't gon' treat neither one like he was dealing with a person."[99] Seen as obstinate mules or as obedient dogs, both groups are objectified. Neither is seen as fully human; both are eligible for race-, class-, and gender-specific modes of domination.[100] In a patriarchal society, all women are oppressed and ultimately that is what unites them.

Neither a valid analysis of women's subordination nor an ethnically and racially diverse feminist movement is likely to emerge if white middle-class feminists do not integrate their own privilege from association with white men into their analysis of gender subordination. This requires an awareness that their subordination, based on seduction, has separated them from other women who are subordinated by rejection. This separation can be bridged, but white women must develop a new kind of consciousness and renounce the privilege that comes from their relationship to white men.

If women of Color are to embrace a feminist movement then they, too, must expand their consciousness of gender oppression. They, too, must understand differences in the dynamics of seduction and rejection and, in particular, that seduction is no less oppressive than rejection. Gloria Anzaldua, a Chicana activist and scholar, advocates a consciousness that simultaneously rejects and embraces—so as not to exclude—what it rejects. It is a *mestiza* consciousness that can perceive multiple realities at once:

> It is not enough to stand on the opposite river bank, shouting questions, challenging patriarchal, white conventions. A counterstance locks one into a duel of oppressor and oppressed; locked in mortal combat, like the cop and the criminal, both are reduced to a common denominator of violence. The counterstance refutes the dominant culture's views and beliefs, and, for this, it is proudly defiant. . . . But it is not a way of life. At some point, on our way to a new consciousness, we will have to leave the opposite bank, the split between the two mortal combatants somehow healed so that we are on both shores at once, and, at once, see through serpent and eagle eyes. . . . The possibilities are numerous once we decide to act and not react.[101]

The experiences of women of Color in U.S. society expose other aspects of patriarchal society that are only beginning to emerge in feminist theory and feminist political action. It is only through feminist theory's integration of a critique of the different forms of oppression experienced by women that a progressive political women's movement can grow, thrive, and last.

NOTES

1. A word about ethnic labels used in this paper. I use people of Color to refer to Chicanos, Asians, Native Americans, and Blacks, all of whom are native minorities. Therefore, I capitalize Color because it refers to specific ethnic groups. I also capitalize Black following the argument that it refers not merely to skin pigmentation but to a "heritage, a social creation, and often a personal identity in ways at least as meaningful as do ethnic identities which are conventionally capitalized" (see Barrie Thorne, Cheris Kramarae, and Nancy Henley, eds., *Language, Gender, and Society* [Rowley, Mass.: Newbury House, 1983], vi). On the other hand, *white* is left in lowercase letters because it refers not to one ethnic group or to specified ethnic groups but to many.

2. Erika Apfelbaum, "Relations of Domination and Movements for Liberation: An Analysis of Power between Groups," in *The Social Psychology of Intergroup Relations,* ed. William G. Austin and Stephen Worchel (Monterey, Calif.: Brooks/Cole Publishing, 1979), 188–204.

3. R. W. Connell, "Theorizing Gender," *Sociology* 19, no. 2 (May 1985): 260–72, esp. 264.

4. By women of Color I mean nonwhite women, especially Blacks, Latinas (e.g., Chicanas, Puerto Ricans), Native Americans, and Asian Americans (e.g., Japanese, Chinese, Pilipina, Vietnamese). I do not include Jewish women because their historical and cultural experience is different from the women of Color I describe. Jewish women merit a separate analysis, perhaps within the context of the discussion of the heterogeneity among white feminists. Women worldwide share commonalities; however, there are very important cultural and economic differences that should not be ignored. I focus on women in the United States in order to understand the differences between white women and women of Color in this country. What the implications of my analysis are for women elsewhere is for them to decide.

5. Nancy Henley, *Body Politics: Power, Sex, and Nonverbal Communication* (New York: Simon & Schuster, 1986), 21. In discussing these linkages my language emphasizes differences—differences *among* women but also the different relationships between various groups of women and white men. I do not mean to imply that these groups are thought of as undifferentiated categories. I acknowledge diversity within them as I examine, for purposes of this paper, the more important problem of the differences in relationship that white women and women of Color have to white men. Readers from the social sciences will recognize this problem in analysis of variance terms in which internal diversity must be considered in order to know if two (or more) groups differ from each other. Although differences *within* groups are intrinsic to the statistical decision about differences *between* groups, we social scientists can be faulted for using language at times that implies that merely statistically different categories are unitary and universal. This tendency fosters essentialist thinking about social categories when in fact members of categories always vary in the extent to which they possess prototypic features of the category. See E. H. Rosch for a discussion of psychological research on categories and Joan W. Scott for a discussion of the need for feminists to find a way of analyzing constructions of meaning and relationships of power that call "unitary, universal

categories into question" (E. H. Rosch, "Natural Categories," *Cognitive Psychology* 4, no.
[1973]: 328–50; Joan W. Scott, "Gender: A Useful Category of Historical Analysis," *American Historical Review* 91, no. 5 [1986]: 1053–75, and "Deconstructing Equality-versus-Difference Or, the Uses of Poststructuralist Theory for Feminism," *Feminist Studies* 14, no. 1 [1988]: 33–51, quote on 33).

6. Asian Americans, *as a group,* are stereotyped as the "model minority," a group to be emulated by less successful people of Color. However, close examination of the statistics of achieved attainment indicates that the structural integration of different Asian groups (e.g., Japanese, Pilipino, Vietnamese, Chinese) is at best uneven and at worst deceptive. Scholars in Asian American studies have highlighted the importance of taking into account bases of stratification such as gender, foreign-born versus U.S.-born nativity, language competency in English, the geographical distribution of the Asian population within metropolitan areas of high income/high cost-of-living locales (e.g., San Francisco, Los Angeles, Hawaii, and New York), historical wave of immigration, and number of wage-earning family members. These factors in combination paint a very different picture of Asian American advancement, especially for women. For example, most Asian Americans (especially women) are overqualified, as measured by formal education, and underpaid when compared to their white male counterparts. For presentations of the intricacies of measuring the structural position of Asian Americans, see Bob H. Susuki, "Education and the Socialization of Asian Americans: A Revisionist Analysis of the 'Model Minority' Thesis," *Amerasia Journal* 4, no. 2 (1977): 23–51; Deborah Woo, "The Socioeconomic Status of Asian American Women in the Labor Force: An Alternative View," *Sociological Perspectives* 28, no. 3 (July 1985): 307–38; Amado Cabezas and Garry Kawaguchi, "Empirical Evidence for Continuing Asian American Income Inequality: The Human Capital Model and Labor Market Segmentation" (paper presented at the Fourth Asian American Studies Conference of the Association of Asian American Studies, San Francisco State University, March 19–21, 1987).

7. "Women Reached 70% of Pay Parity with Men in '87," *San Jose Mercury* (February 2, 1988).

8. I use the word Hispanic only when the source cited uses that label and does not list figures for individual Latino groups. For accuracy I use the ethnic/racial labels used in the original sources. I cite data separately for different groups of women when available.

9. Cynthia M. Taeuber and Victor Baldisera, *Women in the American Economy,* U.S. Bureau of the Census, Current Population Reports, Series P-23, no. 146 (Washington, D.C.: Government Printing Office, 1986).

10. Joseph J. Salvo and John M. McNeil, *Lifetime Work Experience and Its Effect on Earnings: Retrospective Data from the 1979 Income Survey Development Program,* U.S. Department of Commerce, Bureau of the Census, Current Population Reports, Series P-23, no. 136 (Washington, D.C.: Government Printing Office, 1984).

11. Asian women as a group have an impressive educational attainment record. However, while education facilitates mobility among Asian American women, a large proportion of them continue to be in clerical or administrative support jobs. For example, in 1980, close to a third of native-born Pilipinas who were college educated continued to be in clerical administrative support jobs. Deborah Woo indicates that for Asian American women: "Education improves mobility but it promises less than the 'American Dream.' For Asian women, it seems to serve less as an opportunity for mobility than a hedge against jobs as service workers and as machine operatives or assembly workers—the latter being an area where foreign-born Asian women are far more likely than their Anglo male or female counterparts to concentrate.

The single largest category of employment here is as seamstresses or 'textile sewing machine operators' in garment factories" (Woo, 331–32).

12. Taeuber and Baldisera, 13–15.

13. Ibid., 9–10.

14. Phyllis Marynick Palmer, "White Women/Black Women: The Dualism of Female Identity and Experience in the United States," *Feminist Studies* 9, no. 1 (1983): 151–70, esp. 162. Given these data, when I discuss feminists of Color I will treat them as working class unless I specifically mention otherwise. When I discuss white feminists, I will treat them as middle class. Labels are not easy to assign because of the complexity of human experience and because of the insidious and changing nature of subordination. My purpose is not to provide neat categories to be used regardless of social context but rather to provide a framework for discussion by defining the different positions of these groups of women to white men. I believe this will help us to understand the differences between women of Color and white women in general, and feminists in particular.

15. bell hooks, *Ain't I a Woman? Black Women and Feminism* (Boston: South End Press, 1981).

16. Gloria I. Joseph and Jill Lewis, eds., *Common Differences: Conflicts in Black and White Feminists' Perspectives* (New York: Anchor, 1981).

17. Alison Jaggar, *Feminist Politics and Human Nature* (Totowa, N.J.: Rowman & Allanheld, 1983), 11.

18. Ibid., 11.

19. Ibid., 83–84.

20. R. W. Connell, *Gender and Power: Society, the Person and Sexual Politics* (Stanford, Calif.: Stanford University Press, 1987), esp. 140, 264; Candace West and Don H. Zimmerman, "Doing Gender," *Gender and Society* 1, no. 2 (June 1987): 125–51, esp. 126.

21. Leslie Wahl Rabine, "A Feminist Politics of Non-Identity," *Feminist Studies* 14, no. 1 (Spring 1988): 11–31, esp. 19.

22. Aída Hurtado, "Chicana Feminism: A Theoretical Perspective" (paper presented at the Third International Conference on the Hispanic Cultures of the United States, Barcelona, Spain, June 7–10, 1988).

23. Patricia Hill Collins, "Learning from the Outsider Within: The Sociological Significance of Black Feminist Thought," *Social Problems* 33, no. 6 (December 1986): 14–32.

24. Palmer (n. 14 above), esp. 154.

25. hooks, *Ain't I a Woman?* (n. 15 above), esp. 124.

26. Catharine Stimpson, "Thy Neighbor's Wife, Thy Neighbor's Servants': Women's Liberation and Black Civil Rights," in *Woman in Sexist Society: Studies in Power and Powerlessness,* ed. Vivian Gornick and Barbara K. Morgan (New York: Basic, 1971), 452–79.

27. Elizabeth Cady Stanton, Susan B. Anthony, and Matilda Joslyn Gage, eds., *History of Woman Suffrage,* 2d ed. (Rochester, N.Y.: Susan B. Anthony, 1889), 1:456–57.

28. hooks, *Ain't I a Woman?* esp. 127; Angela Y. Davis, *Women, Race and Class* (New York: Random House, 1981), esp. 76–77.

29. Elizabeth Cady Stanton, Susan B. Anthony, and Matilda Joslyn Gage, eds., *History of Woman Suffrage* (Rochester, N.Y.: Charles Mann, 1887), 2:222.

30. Louise Daniel Hutchinson, *Anna Cooper: A Voice from the South* (Washington, D.C.: Smithsonian Institution Press, 1982); Dorothy Sterling, *Black Foremothers: Three Lives* (New York: McGraw-Hill, 1979); Ida B. Wells, *Crusade for Justice: The Autobiography of Ida B. Wells,* ed. Alfreda M. Duster (Chicago: University of Chicago Press, 1970).

31. Hutchinson, 87–88.

32. Sterling.

33. Adeljiza Sosa-Ridell, ed., *Mujeres Activas en Letras y Cambio Social, Noticiera de M.A.L.C.S.* (Davis: University of California, Davis, Chicano Studies Program, 1983).

34. Stanton, Anthony, and Gage, eds., 1:115–17.

35. Simone de Beauvoir, *The Second Sex* (New York: Random House, 1952), xxiv; Audre Lorde, *Sister Outsider* (Trumansburg, N.Y.: Crossing Press, 1984), 118–19.

36. Limitations of space preclude a discussion of the relationship between women of Color and men of Color. Women of Color have started to portray eloquently the solidarity as well as conflict between women and men of Color. For an especially insightful analysis on Chicanas, see Beatriz Pesquera, "Work and Family: A Comparative Analysis of Professional, Clerical, and Blue-Collar Chicana Workers" (Ph.D. diss., University of California, Berkeley, 1985); Denise Segura, "Chicanas and Mexican Immigrant Women in the Labor Market: A Study of Occupational Mobility and Stratification" (Ph.D. diss., University of California, Berkeley, 1986); Patricia Zavella, *Women's Work and Chicano Families: Cannery Workers of the Santa Clara Valley* (Ithaca, N.Y.: Cornell University Press, 1987). Suffice it to say that men of Color are also influenced by the different conceptions of gender that depict women of Color as less feminine and less desirable than white women (see Gloria I. Joseph, "White Promotion, Black Survival," in Joseph and Lewis, eds. [n. 16 above]; and bell hooks, *Feminist Theory from Margin to Center* [Boston: South End Press, 1984]). This is a form of internalized oppression that people of Color have to address—one that I believe has been belabored in the last twenty years. It must ultimately be resolved by men of Color rather than by women (see Albert Memmi, *The Colonizer and the Colonized* [New York: Orient Press, 1965]; and Eldridge Cleaver, *Soul on Ice* [New York: McGraw Hill, 1968]).

37. Malcolm X with the assistance of Alex Haley, *The Autobiography of Malcolm X* (New York: Ballantine, 1973); W. E. B. Du Bois, *The Souls of Black Folk* (Millwood, N.Y.: Kraus-Thomson Organization, 1973).

38. Apfelbaum (n. 2 above), esp. 199; Thomas F. Pettigrew and Joanne Martin, "Shaping the Organizational Context for Black American Inclusion," *Journal of Social Issues* 43 (1987): 41–78.

39. Elizabeth Higginbotham, "Race and Class Barriers to Black Women's College Attendance," *Journal of Ethnic Studies* 13 (1985): 89–107.

40. Connell, "Theorizing Gender" (n. 3 above), esp. 264.

41. Ibid., 56–57, identifies Nancy Chodorow's *The Reproduction of Mothering: Psychoanalysis and the Sociology of Gender* (Berkeley and Los Angeles: University of California Press, 1978); and Juliet Mitchell's *Woman's Estate* (Harmondsworth: Penguin, 1971), as examples of feminist theory with implicit biological assumptions about gender.

42. West and Zimmerman (n. 20 above), 125–377, esp. 145.

43. Lorde, 118–19.

44. As quoted by Dale Spender, *Man Made Language* (London: Routledge, Chapman & Hall, 1980), 101–2.

45. Davis (n. 28 above), esp. 5.

46. Ibid., esp. 11.

47. Ibid., 11. As the United States expanded to the west by colonizing native peoples and importing labor, other women of Color experienced similar treatment. Marta Cotera documents that among the martyrs and victims of social injustice were such women as Juanita of Downiesville, California, who was lynched in 1851, Chipita Rodriguez, who was the only woman to be executed in Texas, and countless other Chicanas who were killed by Texas Rangers during their raids on Chicano communities (see Marta Cotera, *Chicana Feminism* [Austin, Texas: Information System Development, 1977], esp. 24).

48. Adrienne Rich, *On Lies, Secrets and Silence: Selected Prose 1966–1973* (New York: Norton, 1979), esp. 291–95; hooks, *Ain't I a Woman?* (n. 15 above), esp. 58; Palmer (n. 14 above), esp. 156.

49. Rich, esp. 291.

50. Joseph (n. 36 above), esp. 27.

51. Chodorow (n. 41 above); Nancy Friday, *My Mother/Myself: The Daughter's Search for Identity* (New York: Delacorte, 1982).

52. Apfelbaum (n. 2 above), esp. 203.

53. Ibid.; Henri Tajfel, "Social Identity and Intergroup Behavior," *Social Science Information* 13 (1974): 65–93.

54. Jaggar (n. 17 above), esp. 94–95; Tajfel, esp. 83.

55. de Beauvoir (n. 35 above), esp. xxi.

56. Ibid.

57. hooks, *Feminist Theory from Margin to Center*, esp. 47–49.

58. Dorothy E. Smith, "A Peculiar Eclipsing: Women's Exclusion from Man's Culture," *Women's Studies International Quarterly* 1 (1978): 281–95, esp. 293.

59. Betty Friedan, *The Feminine Mystique* (New York: Penguin, 1963), esp. 11.

60. Smith, esp. 281.

61. Shirley Ardener, *Perceiving Women* (New York: Wiley, 1975).

62. Spender (n. 44 above), esp. 78–79.

63. Friedan, esp. 15.

64. Spender, esp. 92–94.

65. Smith, esp. 282.

66. Ibid., 284.

67. Davis (n. 28 above), esp. 48–49.

68. Tomás Ybarra-Fraustro, "When Cultures Meet: Integration or Disintegration?" (Stanford University, Department of Spanish, Stanford, Calif., 1986, typescript); Beth Brant, cd., *A Gathering of Spirit: Writing and Art of North American Indian Women* (Montpelier, Vt.: Sinister Wisdom Books, 1984).

69. Collins (n. 23 above), esp. 80.

70. Joseph and Lewis, eds. (n. 16 above), esp. 33–35.

71. Friedan (n. 59 above), esp. 326–32.

72. I owe this insight to Candace West, personal communication, October 25, 1986.

73. Joseph (n. 36 above), esp. 20; Craig Haney, "The State of Prisons: What Happened to Justice in the '80s?" (paper presented at the American Psychological Association Meetings, Los Angeles, California, August 1985).

74. See, for instance, Susie Orbach, *Fat Is a Feminist Issue* (New York: Paddington, 1978); Heidi Hartmann, "The Unhappy Marriage of Marxism and Feminism: Towards a More Progressive Union," in *Women and Revolution,* ed. Lydia Sargent (Boston: South End Press, 1981), 18; Chodorow (n. 41 above); and Spender (n. 44 above).

75. Henley, *Body Politics* (n. 5 above), 15.

76. Ibid.

77. Nancy Henley, "Assertiveness Training: Making the Political Personal" (paper presented at the Society for the Study of Social Problems, Boston, Mass., August 1979), esp. 8.

78. Henley, *Body Politics,* 15.

79. William Ryan, *Blaming the Victim* (New York: Pantheon, 1971).

80. Charlotte Perkins Gilman, *The Yellow Wallpaper* (New York: Feminist Press, 1973); Barbara Ehrenreich and Deirdre English, eds., *For Her Own Good: 150 Years of the Experts' Advice to Women* (Garden City, N.Y.: Anchor, 1978).

81. Alfred Blumstein, "On the Racial Disproportionality of United States Prison Popula tions," *Journal of Criminal Law and Criminology* 73 (Fall 1983): 1259–81.

82. Lorde (n. 35 above), 147–48.

83. Joseph (n. 36 above), esp. 32–33, 40; Cherrie Moraga and Gloria Anzaldua, eds., *This Bridge Called My Back: Writings by Radical Women of Color* (Watertown, Mass.: Persephone, 1981).

84. Segura (n. 36 above).

85. Pesquera (n. 36 above).

86. Brant, ed.; Robert T. Trotter III and Juan Antonio Chavira, *Curanderismo: Mexican/American Folk Healing* (Athens: University of Georgia Press, 1981); Áida Hurtado, "A View from Within: Midwife Practices in South Texas," *International Quarterly of Community Health Education* 8, no. 4 (1987–88): 317–39; Pesquera.

87. Friedan (n. 59 above), esp. 73–94.

88. Carol Tavris, *Anger: The Misunderstood Emotion* (New York: Simon & Schuster, 1982), esp. 25–45.

89. Jaggar (n. 17 above), esp. 197, 286–87.

90. Ibid., 197.

91. Joyce Trebilcot, "Conceiving Women: Notes on the Logic of Feminism," *Sinister Wisdom*, no. 11 (Fall 1979), 43–50.

92. Moraga and Anzaldua, eds.

93. Lorde (n. 35 above), esp. 129; hooks, *Feminist Theory from Margin to Center* (n. 36 above); Moraga and Anzaldua, eds. (n. 83 above); Gloria Anzaldua, *Borderlands—La Frontera* (San Francisco: Spinsters/Aunt Lute, 1987), esp. 15–23.

94. Lorde, 119.

95. Stanton, Anthony, and Gage, eds. (n. 27 above), 1:117.

96. Lorde, 131–32.

97. Ibid., 130.

98. Davis, "Reflections on the Black Women's Role in the Community of Slaves," *Black Scholar* 3, no. 4 (December 1971): 3–15, quote on 8.

99. As quoted by Collins (n. 23 above), 17.

100. Ibid., esp. 18.

101. Anzaldua, 78–79.

B. Achievement in Context

Psychology's treatment of the "problem" of women's achievement has a fascinating history, deserving of a section of its own. Initially the problem was defined rather simply: psychologists merely needed to elucidate the specific ways in which women were intellectually inferior to men, in order to "explain" their obvious lack of achievement in male spheres. Some psychologists and physicians expected—and went to great lengths in their attempts to find—measurable differences in brain size between men and women that would account for the obvious absence of high-achieving women across a variety of public domains (see Shields, 1975). Others (following the failure of the brain size approach) assumed that slightly more subtle intellectual deficits could be found that would explain women's lower achievement (e.g., see J. G. Morawski's discussion in chapter 24 of this volume). When, even after impressive contortions, research failed to confirm that women were innately less intelligent than men, psychologists turned to explanations that focused on motivation and interest. For Freud, female underachievement was "proof" of his hypothesis that women had stunted superegos and were less motivated to and less able to sublimate (turn their unacceptable impulses into socially desirable action) than men. Researchers interested in psychological masculinity and femininity (again, see Morawski) could account for female underachievement by defining achievement/agency as unfeminine: thus, women—even if they have the necessary intellectual potential—are simply not interested in masculine-type achievement, unless they are unfeminine.

Achievement in women has been a "problem" even for researchers who were studying high-achieving women—a problem residing primarily in the women themselves. For researchers working in Henry Murray's tradition and studying "need for achievement," for example, women's responses on Thematic Apperception Test measures of need for achievement were disconcertingly inconsistent with those of men. Motivational conflict in women (e.g., "fear of success"; see Horner, 1972) was invoked as one explanation of that inconsistency, while research continued on the "normal" need for achievement as measured in male subjects. Subsequent theorizing typically ignored the fact that the results upon which the theory was based applied only to males (Sassen, 1980).

As the presence of women across a number of formerly all-male fields has gradually increased, many psychologists continue to address the "problem" of women's achievement. Some researchers still maintain that the lack of women in some fields (especially engineering and other math-intensive disciplines) is due to innate deficits in ability (Benbow, 1988). In contrast, the authors included in this section focus on the ways in which achievement is often discouraged, made more difficult, made more conflictual, or made more interpersonally complex for women than for men (see chapter 3 of this volume). Some authors discuss the ways in which conflicts about particular kinds of achievement (particularly in "masculine" endeavors involving mathematics) are manifest intrapsychically. The current approaches tend to differ from previous ones, however, in that while they acknowledge the intrapsychic influences that tend to keep girls and women away from particular endeavors, they emphasize the interpersonal, social, and cultural origins of those influences, and of the forces that tend to maintain them.

The "problem" of women's achievement has turned into a multiplicity of problems: Should the focus of women's achievement be on individual efforts, or on societal change? Can women achieve within traditional, hierarchical structures without capitulating to or perpetuating those structures? How are women held to different standards than men, by themselves and by men? Does individual achievement necessitate sacrifice of relational goals, and if so, are women willing to pay the cost?

We are excited about the the reframing of the "problems" of women's achievement according to particular contexts and relationships. The focus has shifted from the assumption that these problems have their origin in female "nature," to the assumption that they are located within past and present societal expectations of women (including the expectations that girls internalize) and the relationships between women and various societal institutions. While applauding this shift in focus, however, we pause to note that it is still primarily *women's* achievement that is "problematized." We look forward to the day when societal arrangements between work, home, individual achievement, personal relationships, and the development of individual potential are "problematized" in terms of the development and life satisfaction of women, men, and society at large.

REFERENCES

Benbow, C. P. (1988). Sex differences in Mathematics Ability in Intellectually Talented Preadolescents: Their Nature, Effects, and Possible Causes. *Behavioral Sciences, 11,* 169–232.

Horner, M. S. (1972). Toward an Understanding of Achievement-Related Conflicts in Women. *Journal of Social Issues, 25,* 157–175.

Sassen, Georgia. (1980). Success Anxiety in Women: Constructivist Interpretation of Its Source and Significance. *Harvard Education Review, 50* 13

Shields, S. A., (1975). Functionalism, Darwinism, and Psychology of Women. *American Psychologist, 30,*

Chapter Thirty-Eight

Gender Role Stereotypes, Expectancy Effects, and Parents' Socialization of Gender Differences

Jacquelynne S. Eccles, Janis E. Jacobs, and Rena D. Harold

Gender differences in academic and occupational choices persist despite efforts at affirmative action in schools and occupational settings (Eccles, 1987). These differences are especially marked in areas associated with mathematics, physical science, technology, sports, clerical/office work, and education (Eccles, 1989; Steinkamp & Maehr, 1984). The differences are particularly dramatic among students enrolled in vocational education programs. For example, in 1978, only 12 percent of high school students enrolled in technical vocational training courses were female while the vast majority of the students enrolled in office training programs were female (Eccles & Hoffman, 1984).

Why is this so? Several authors have suggested that gender differences in self-perceptions play a critical role (see Eccles, 1987; Eccles & Hoffman, 1984). Specifically, gender differences in self-perceptions of their abilities may lead females and males to select different educational training programs, and to aspire to different occupations. The existence of gender differences in early adolescents' views of their own abilities in mathematics, for example, is well documented (e.g., Eccles-Parsons, 1984; Eccles, Adler, & Meece, 1984; Eccles-Parsons et al., 1983). In general, young women rate their math ability lower than young men. They also express less interest than their male peers in studying mathematics and in entering math-related professions. Less research has been done in other domains, but evidence is emerging that gender differences exist there as well. For example, females in grades 6–12 rate themselves as more competent in English than do their male peers (Eccles, Wigfield, et al., 1989). Similarly, males rate their athletic competence higher than do females (Eccles, Wigfield, et al., 1989; Eccles & Harold, 1988).

Many explanations have been suggested for these differences in self-perceptions (for reviews see Eccles-Parsons, 1984; Eccles, 1987; Eccles & Hoffman, 1984). This chapter focuses on one possible cause: parents' gender-differentiated expectations. If

Jacquelynne S. Eccles, Janis E. Jacobs, & Rena D. Harold, "Gender Role Stereotypes, Expectancy Effects, and Parents' Socialization of Gender Differences." *Journal of Social Issues*, 46 (2), pp. 183–201. © 1990 by the Society for the Psychological Study of Social Issues. Reprinted by permission.

parents hold gender-differentiated perceptions of, and expectations for, their chil
dren's competencies in various areas, then, through self-fulfilling prophecies, parent:
could play a critical role in socializing gender differences in children's self-perceptions, interests, and skill acquisition.

Two types of evidence are necessary to establish the effects of parents' gender-differentiated expectations: First, one must demonstrate that parents hold gender-differentiated perceptions of their children's competencies in various domains. Next, one must
show that these gender-differentiated perceptions have an impact on the children's
self-perceptions that is independent of the impact of the children's actual performance
levels on both the children's and the parents' perceptions of the children's competence
(see Jussim, 1989, for discussion of this mode of proof). There is good evidence of both
of these effects for mathematics. Parents of adolescents who are junior high school
aged hold gender-differentiated views of their children's math competence. Furthermore, these gender-differentiated parental beliefs appear to mediate the association between the adolescents' gender and their confidence in their math competence even
after controlling for independent indicators of the adolescents' prior mathematical
competence (Eccles-Parsons, 1984; Eccles & Jacobs, 1986; Eccles-Parsons, Adler, & Kaczala, 1982). Interestingly, the gender-differentiated perceptions of the parents in these
studies exist even though their female and male children do equally well in math on
both their school grades and their performance on standardized tests (Eccles-Parsons
et al., 1982). Thus, the expectancy effects demonstrated in these studies are not due to
perceiver accuracy, and the parents' gender-differentiated expectations for their children's competence in math do appear to facilitate the emergence of gender differences
in the children's perceptions of their own competence in mathematics.

New Sources of Data

Do these results replicate and generalize to other domains? Yes! We now have
evidence of similar effects for different aged children and in two new activity
domains (English and sports). These findings are described in the remainder of the
chapter. They are drawn from two major, ongoing longitudinal studies involving
approximately 2,100 families, both of which were done in suburban communities in
Michigan. Children were recruited through the schools in fourteen different school
districts, with all children in eligible classrooms being asked to participate. In each
study, between 80 percent and 95 percent of the children contacted agreed to
participate. Family participation was solicited after the children were recruited, and
all families of participating children were asked to join the study. In each study,
between 70 percent and 80 percent of the families solicited agreed to participate.
Questionnaires, interviews, and standardized aptitude measures were used in both
studies. The children and adolescents were tested at school, whereas the parent data
were collected via mailed questionnaires. Actual participation rates for the children
averaged 80 percent or better; participation rates for the parents averaged between
60 percent and 70 percent depending on the district and the wave of data collection.
Study 1 (the Michigan Study of Transitions at Adolescence) is a seven-year longitu-

.linal study of adolescent development in the context of the family and the school. In 1983, approximately 2,000 early adolescents were recruited into this study when they were in the sixth grade. About 1,500 of their families agreed to participate as well, and these families have been participating in the study since then. The data reported in this paper were collected in the fall and spring of the adolescents' sixth-grade school year (1983–84).

Study 2 (the Michigan Study of Middle Childhood) is a four-year longitudinal study of the development of children who are elementary school aged, again in the context of the family and the school. In 1986, approximately 600 children and their families were recruited into this study, when the children were either in kindergarten, first, or third grade. These families have been participating annually in the study since that time. The data reported in this paper were collected in the spring and summer of the first year of the study (1987).

Parents in both studies were asked a series of questions regarding their perceptions of their children's competency, and their expectations for their children's performance, in three domains: math, English, and sports. Previous studies had indicated the importance of tapping parents' perceptions of their children's competency with several different constructs. Consequently study 1 used 7-point Likert scales to assess the following parent perceptions: (a) child's current competence (2 items: perceived current level of ability and perceived current level of performance), (b) difficulty of domain for child (2 items: perceived difficulty and amount of effort necessary to do well), (c) child's natural talent (1 item), (d) future performance expectations in math and English courses (1 item in each domain), and (e) future career performance expectations in careers requiring good skills in math and English (1 item in each domain). Similar scales and items were used in study 2. These scales have been used in other studies, and their reliability and validity are reported in several articles (e.g., Eccles-Parsons et al., 1983; Eccles et al., 1984; Eccles, Jacobs, et al., 1989). To test for gender differentiation in these perceptions, ANOVAs were run on each dependent measure using the child's gender as the independent variable. The results are summarized in Table 38.1.

Gender role stereotyped differences were clear in both studies in English and sports. Parents of daughters rated their child as more competent in English than parents of sons and vice versa for sports. The pattern for mathematics depended on the age of the child being judged. There was no gender of child effect on the parent's perceptions of younger children's mathematical competence (study 2); in contrast, a gender of child effect was beginning to emerge in the reports of the mothers of sixth graders. We know from our previous studies that the gender of child effect in the math domain is stronger and more consistent among parents of junior and senior high school students.

Possible Origins of Gender Role Stereotyping in Parents' Perceptions

Many explanations have been offered to account for the gender role stereotyping of ratings of males' and females' competencies in various domains. The most critical

TABLE 38.1
Gender-of-Child Effects on Parents' Perceptions

	Domains								
	Math			English/reading			Sports		
Variables	Girls' mean	Boys' mean	F	Girls' mean	Boys' mean	F	Girls' mean	Boys' mean	F
Adolescent Transition Study[1]									
Parent perception of current competence	5.45	5.40	<1.00	5.65	4.99	101.71***	4.84	5.22	25.75***
Parent perception of task difficulty	4.10	3.80	12.10***	3.73	4.24	39.20***	3.77	3.47	13.21***
Parent perception of natural talent	4.76	5.01	9.85*	5.03	4.51	46.76***	4.22	4.87	59.76***
Parent perception of future performance	5.36	5.34	<1.00	5.59	5.02	74.99***			
Parent perception of performance in career	5.17	5.42	11.17***	5.41	4.87	54.91***			
Parent perception of importance	6.38	6.50	9.21**	6.34	6.34	<1.00	3.80	4.10	12.90***
Middle Childhood Development Study[2]									
Parent perception of current competence	5.38	5.34	<1.00	5.67	5.27	10.28***	4.50	4.98	16.41***
Parent perception of task difficulty	2.08	2.02	<1.00	1.64	2.01	8.33**	2.57	2.15	11.77***
Parent perception of natural talent	5.01	5.15	1.45	5.41	5.11	7.00**	4.31	4.74	12.35***
Parent perception of future performance	5.99	5.91	<1.00	6.36	5.95	19.13***	5.02	5.52	19.91***
Parent perception of importance	6.26	6.46	8.12**	6.65	6.63	<1.00	4.20	4.72	20.00***

NOTE: [1] Mothers of 6th graders, approximate N = 900. [2] Parents of kindergarteners, 1st, and 3rd graders, approximate N = 500.

* p < .05
** p < .01
*** p < .001.

issue for this chapter is the extent to which parents' stereotyped perceptions of their children are either accurate, or are a reflection, at least in part, of perceptual bias. This is a very difficult issue to settle because no consensus has been reached on what criteria should be used to assess the accuracy of gender role stereotypes. It is clear that parents' perceptions of their children's competence in academic subjects are highly correlated with teachers' ratings of the children's competence, and with various indicators of the children's performance and achievement, such as school grades and standardized test scores (Alexander & Entwisle, 1988; Eccles-Parsons et al., 1982). But are their gender role stereotyped perceptions an accurate reflection of true gender differences in either talent or competence? This question is difficult to answer because females and males are treated so differently by their parents and peers from very early in their lives. Consequently, it is impossible to get a good indicator of natural talent that is uninfluenced by the processes associated with gender role socialization—the very processes being described in this chapter.

For example, can it be concluded that parents' gender role stereotyped perceptions of their six-year-old children's talent in sports are accurate if the male children perform better than the female children on a standardized test of athletic skill at this age? Not really, because it is quite likely that the female and male children have already had different opportunities to develop their athletic skills. The best that can be done at this point is to use the strategy proposed by Jussim (1989). This strategy involves assessing the extent to which the perceiver's judgments are related to the variables of interest (in this case the child's gender) after controlling more objective indicators of the children's actual performance level. If they are, then efforts should be made to identify possible mediating cognitive processes to account for the biased portion of these perceptions (i.e., the portion not due to actual differences in the performance levels of girls and boys).

The mathematics domain provides the most fully developed example of this logic at present. In both our own work (see Eccles-Parson et al., 1982; Eccles & Jacobs, 1986) and the work of Entwisle and her colleagues (see Alexander & Entwisle, 1988), parents' perceptions of their children's competence in mathematics have been found to be influenced by their children's gender, independent of the children's actual performance in mathematics. Comparable patterns of results are emerging for the domains of English and sports (e.g., Jacobs & Eccles, 1990). Thus it appears that something other than overt performance is influencing the formation of parents' perceptions of their children's competence in both math and sports. What might these factors be, and do they generalize to domains other than mathematics? Three possible explanations seem especially relevant to the expectancy-effects perspective being outlined in this chapter. First, there may be a true sex difference in the children's aptitude, but girls may compensate by working harder than boys in order to do just as well. Second, aptitude differences may be minor or nonexistent, but parents may attribute their children's performance to different causes, leading them to different conclusions regarding their female children's versus their male children's "talent." Third, parents may generalize their category-based gender role stereotypes to their target-based judgments of their own children's competence. Evidence for each of these three possible explanations is discussed below.

Real Gender Differences in Children's Aptitude and Effort

Attributional theorists have studied how people make inferences regarding a target person's talent. According to these theorists (e.g., Weiner, 1974), adults believe that performance is a joint function of aptitude and effort. Consequently, adults take into consideration indicators of both objective performance and effort in forming an impression of a particular target's "aptitude." To the extent that perceivers believe that one target worked harder than another to achieve the same level of performance, they will conclude that the first target has less true "aptitude" for the activity than the second target, even though the two targets are performing at the same level.

This analysis has possible implications for understanding parents' gender-differentiated perceptions of their children's talent in various activities. For instance, some people have argued that there is a true gender difference in children's aptitude for mathematics and that females compensate for their lower levels of aptitude by working harder than boys to master mathematics. How can one evaluate the validity of this suggestion? One way is to compare the performance of females and males on a specific task that is considered to be more closely related to aptitude, and less closely related to effort, than are school grades. If gender differences appear on this task in a population in which there are no gender differences in math course grades, then one might conclude that there is a true aptitudinal difference that is being overcome by a gender difference in effort. Evidence reported by Benbow and Stanley (1980) is consistent with this interpretation. They found that gifted boys scored higher than gifted girls on standardized tests, and they concluded that the boys had more natural aptitude for math than the girls. Unfortunately, they did not measure effort or prior exposure to mathematics, and thus we cannot rule out the possibility that the gender differences on these "aptitude" tests were due to gender differences in experience (see Eccles & Jacobs, 1986). In addition, although there is a reliable gender difference on standardized tests of math "aptitude" among the gifted, the evidence of such differences among more normally distributed samples is much less reliable, and the differences are much smaller whenever they are obtained (Eccles-Parsons, 1984; Hyde, Fennema, & Lamon, 1990).

Furthermore, several findings from our previous work (e.g., Eccles-Parsons et al., 1982; Eccles & Jacobs, 1986) cast doubt on the notion that girls compensate for lower levels of aptitude with hard work. First and foremost, we found no gender differences on either standardized tests of math aptitude or on school math grades in this sample. Second, the boys and girls reported spending equal amounts of time on their math homework and schoolwork (Eccles & Jacobs, 1986). Finally, the teachers of the boys and girls in this sample did not report any gender differences in these children's talent for mathematics (Eccles-Parsons, 1984). Nonetheless, there was a significant gender of child effect on the parents' ratings of how difficult math was for their child (Eccles-Parsons et al., 1982). This pattern of findings makes it unlikely that the gender of child effect found for these parents' confidence in their children's competence was due primarily to a "real" gender difference either in math talent or in the amount of work the children had invested in mastering mathematics. Although these explana-

.ions may be true in some populations, the Eccles-Parsons and colleagues (1982) study suggests that a child's gender can affect parents' confidence in their child's math competence even when effort and ability are controlled. Since comparable studies have not been done in the domains of English and sports, the validity of the effort/compensation argument cannot be assessed at this point in these domains.

Parents' Causal Attributions

A second plausible explanation for the effect of child's gender on parents' ratings grows out of attribution theory. According to Weiner (1974), perceptions of another's competence depend on the casual attributions made for the person's performance. If parents of boys make different attributions for their children's math performance than do parents of girls, it would follow that these parents should develop different perceptions of their children's math competence. In a test of this hypothesis, Yee and Eccles (1988) found that parents of boys rated natural talent as a more important reason for their child's math successes than did parents of girls. In contrast, parents of girls rated effort as a more important reason for their child's math successes than did parents of boys. In addition, to the extent that the parents attributed their child's success in mathematics to effort, they also rated their child as less talented in mathematics. Conversely, to the extent that they attributed their child's success in mathematics to talent, they also rated their child as more talented in mathematics. Thus, it appears that the gender role stereotyped attributions parents make for their children's performance may be important mediators of the parents' gender role stereotyped perceptions of their children's math competence. The data from study 1 provide a direct test of this conclusion.

Mothers in study 1 were asked to imagine a time when their child did very well in mathematics and then to rate, on a 7-point Likert scale, the importance of the following six possible causes in determining the success experience: natural talent, effort, task ease, teacher help, parent help, and current skill level. Consistent with the findings of Yee and Eccles (1988), significant gender of child effects were obtained on two of the attributions: natural talent and effort. To test the mediation hypothesis, a series of regression analyses was conducted on those mothers' perceptions that yielded a significant gender of child effect in mathematics (see Table 38.1). According to Baron and Kenny (1986), support for a mediational hypothesis consists of demonstrating that the relationship between variables A and C is reduced or eliminated when the hypothesized mediating variable B is entered into the regression equation. We used a path-analytic procedure to test this effect. The results for math are illustrated in Figure 38.1. Consistent with the mediational hypothesis, the significant relationship of child's gender to the relevant parent perception variables (i.e., parents' perceptions of the child's natural math talent, the difficulty of math for their child, and their expectations regarding the child's likely future success in both math courses and a math-related career) disappeared once the relationship between the child's gender and the parents' attributions for the child's math success to either talent or

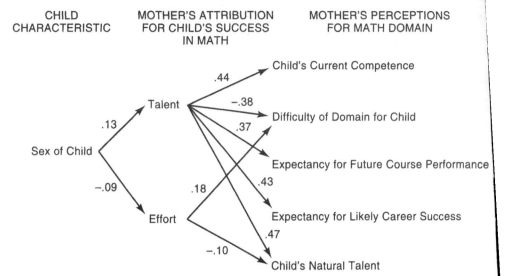

Fig. 38.1. Mediational effects of mothers' attributions for their children's success in mathematics. Standardized regression coefficients for the significant paths ($p < .01$) appear on each path.

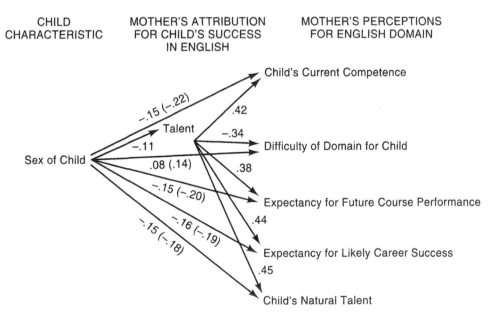

Fig. 38.2. Mediational effects of mothers' attributions for their children's success in English. Standardized regression coefficients for the significant paths ($p < .01$) appear on each path. Zero-order correlations are included in parentheses after the coefficients for those gender-of-child effects that remained significant after mothers' attributions were entered into the regression equations.

effort were controlled. Furthermore, either one or both of these two causal attributions were significantly related to all five parent perceptions.

Comparable results for the talent attribution emerged in both the English and sport domains. The English results are illustrated in Figure 38.2. As predicted, children's gender influenced their mothers' casual attributions, which in turn influenced the mothers' perceptions of, and expectations of, their children.

These data provide good preliminary support for the hypothesized biasing effect of causal attributions on parents' perceptions of their children's competencies. However, it is important to note that these beliefs are all highly interrelated, and the data are correlational in nature. The consistency of the findings across domains suggests that the relationships are reliable, but the causal direction of the relationships is still at issue. The longitudinal analyses necessary to pin down the predominant causal directions of influence among these various beliefs are just beginning. Preliminary analyses suggest that parents' perceptions of their children's competence at time 1 influence causal attributions made at both time 1 and time 2. Furthermore, these analyses suggest that parents' causal attributions for their children's performances prior to time 2 affect the parents' perceptions of their children's competence at time 2. Finally, the impact of children's gender on parents' perceptions of their children's competence at time 2, in both math and English, appears to be mediated, at least in part, by parents' perceptions of their children's competence at time 1 and by parents' causal attributions of their children's successes in these two domains. These preliminary findings add support to our conclusion that gender of child differences in parents' causal attributions for their children's successes in each of these domains contribute to the gender role stereotyped bias we find in their perceptions of their children's competencies in each of these domains.

Parents' Gender Role Stereotypes

But why do parents make different causal attributions for boys' and girls' successes in math, English, and sports? This question brings us to the next explanation for parents' gender-differentiated confidence in their children's competence. Both Eccles-Parsons (1984) and Jacobs and Eccles (1985) suggest that this difference in causal attributions, as well as the gender of child differences in parents' confidence in their children's competencies in various domains, may be due, in part, to the impact of category-based gender role stereotypes on parents' perceptions of their own children's competence. In particular, this hypothesis states that parents' gender role stereotypes regarding the extent to which males or females, in general, are likely to be more talented in a particular domain will influence their perceptions of their own child's ability in this domain, leading to a distortion in the parents' perceptions of their children's abilities in the gender role stereotyped direction. Essentially, we are predicting that parents' perceptions of their children's ability in any particular domain will depend partially on the parents' gender role stereotypes regarding ability in that domain, and that this effect will be significant even after controlling for the children's actual level of competence in the domain.

Before presenting evidence to support these hypotheses, it is important to put them in the broader context of research on the link between category-based beliefs and target-based beliefs. Although there has been very little study of this link in families, or as a developmental phenomenon, there has been quite a bit of relevant research in social psychology. Two basic views have emerged. Work in the field of stereotyping and expectancy effects has repeatedly documented the impact of the perceiver's category-based beliefs (stereotypes) on the perceiver's perceptions of specific members of the social category (e.g., Darley & Gross, 1983; Duncan, 1976). In contrast, work in the area of social judgment has pointed to the power of individuating information to override the impact of stereotypical beliefs on perceptions of specific individuals (e.g., Locksley, Borgida, Brekke, & Hepburn, 1980). Numerous studies have attempted to resolve the discrepancy between these two perspectives. These studies have documented a variety of factors that influence the extent to which social perceptions are influenced by the perceiver's stereotypic beliefs or by individuating information the perceiver has received about the target (e.g., Higgins & Bargh, 1987; Hilton & Fein, 1989; Rasinski, Crocker, & Hastie, 1985). Hilton and Fein (1989) concluded:

> Social judgment is not uniformly dominated by either categorical information or by individuating information. Perceivers do not always ignore individuating information nor do they always suspend their stereotypes when individuating information is available. Instead, the results indicate that social judgment involves a dynamic interplay between the category-based expectations of the perceiver and the information that is available from the target. (p. 208)

What do these conclusions indicate about the probability that parents' gender role stereotypes will affect their perceptions of their own children's abilities? This is a complicated question. On one hand, parents have ample opportunity to get individuating information about their children's abilities in specific subject areas. And evidence suggests that when individuating information about an individual is both readily available and clearly diagnostic about the characteristic being evaluated, perceivers are likely to attend primarily to this individuating information and to ignore their stereotypic beliefs (Hilton & Fein, 1989). This suggests that parents' gender role stereotypes should have little or no impact on their perceptions of their children's abilities.

On the other hand, the strongest support for expectancy effects typically occurs in naturalistic settings with naturally occurring beliefs and perceptions (Jussim, 1986). In addition, categorical beliefs or stereotypes have their largest effect "when categorical information can disambiguate the diagnostic meaning of individuating information" (Hilton & Fein, 1989, p. 210). Families are clearly naturalistic settings; and parents' gender role beliefs and perceptions of their children's abilities are naturally occurring social cognitions. In addition, work in attribution theory (e.g., Weiner, 1974) suggests that achievement-related outcomes are ambiguous as to their cause, and earlier in this chapter we documented that parents' causal attributions for their children's competencies in gender role stereotyped domains are affected by their children's gender. These facts suggest that parents' category-based gender role stereotypes might affect their perceptions of their own children's competencies.

We know of no previous studies that have tested this hypothesis. As reported earlier, parents do hold gender-differentiated views of their children's academic and nonacademic abilities. These beliefs are also more gender differentiated than are objective indicators of the children's actual performance in these domains (e.g., Alexander & Entwisle, 1988; Eccles, Jacobs, et al., 1989; Eccles & Harold, 1988; Jacobs & Eccles, 1985). These studies, however, did not examine the actual relationship between parents' gender role stereotypes and their perceptions of their own child's ability. The critical issue is not whether parents, on the average, give gender-differentiated estimates of their children's abilities. Instead, the issue is whether parents who endorse the culturally dominant gender role stereotype regarding the distribution of talent between males and females distort their perception of *their own children's* abilities in a direction that is consistent with the gender role stereotype *to a greater extent* than parents who do not endorse the cultural stereotype. Evidence from both studies 1 and 2 supports this hypothesis for mothers. (The data from the fathers have not yet been analyzed.)

In study 2, the mothers were asked at time 1 who they thought were naturally better at mathematics, English, and sports—boys, girls, or neither. In a separate questionnaire they also rated on a 7-point Likert scale how much natural talent their child had in each of these three domains, and how difficult (or easy) each of these domains was for their child. In each domain, we tested the significance of the interaction of the child's gender with the parents' category-based gender role stereotypes in predicting the parents' ratings of their own child's competency. All six interactions were significant (Eccles, Wigfield, et al., 1989).

The results for mathematics were particularly interesting (see Fig. 38.3). As Table 38.1 demonstrated, on the average, the gender of their child did not affect these mothers' perceptions of their child's math talent. However, the gender of their child did affect their ratings of the child's natural talent in math when it was considered in interaction with their category-based gender role stereotype of mathematical competence. As predicted, mothers who believed that males are naturally more talented in mathematics displayed a significant gender of child effect in their ratings of their children's math ability. Their ratings of their children were consistent with their category-based stereotype. In contrast, the gender of child effect was not significant for mothers who believed that males and females are equally likely to be naturally talented at mathematics. Similar gender role stereotypic effects characterized the mothers' reports for both sports and English. Although it is possible that these effects are due to the impact of target-based information on the mothers' category-based gender role stereotypes, the extreme stability of gender role stereotypes across time in a variety of populations makes this an unlikely alternative interpretation (Rothbart, 1989).

Jacobs (1987) explored these effects in the domains of math and sports more fully in the data from study 1. Using path-analytic techniques, she tested the significance of the interaction between the child's gender and the mother's category-based gender role stereotypes in predicting mothers' perceptions of their children's ability, controlling for the effect of an independent indicator of the children's actual ability level (the teacher's rating of the children's ability). The interaction term was scored such

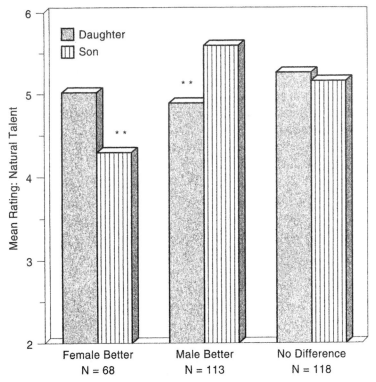

Fig. 38.3. Interactive effects of mothers' gender role stereotypes and child's gender in predicting mothers' rating of own child's natural talent in math (**$p < .01$).

that a positive coefficient indicated that the mother was distorting her impression of her child in the gender role appropriate direction. For instance, if she was talking about a boy child, her rating of her child's ability was higher than what would have been predicted using only the teacher's rating; it was the opposite for a girl child.

Jacobs's results for math are illustrated in Figure 38.4, and rather comparable findings emerged for the sports domain. Once again the data were consistent with our hypothesis, for the interaction term was significant and the coefficient was positive for both math and sports. Thus, to the extent that these mothers endorsed the traditional gender role stereotypic belief that males are naturally better in math and sports than are girls, they distorted their perception of their children's competence in these domains in the gender role stereotypic direction. In addition, consistent with the findings of Eccles-Parsons and colleagues (1982), the mothers' perceptions of their children's competence in each domain had a significant impact on the children's own self-perceptions, even after the children's actual performance in each domain (i.e., the teacher's rating) was controlled.

These data provide clear evidence of the processes associated with expectancy effects. Given the power of individuating information and the large amount of such

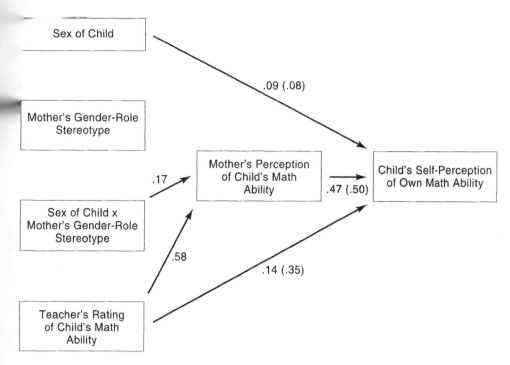

Fig. 38.4. Moderating effect of mothers' gender role stereotypes on the impact of child's gender in predicting mothers' rating of own child's competence in math and child's self-perception of own math ability. Standardized regression coefficients for the significant paths ($p<.01$) appear on each path. Zero-order correlations are included in parentheses after the coefficients for those gender-of-child effects that remained significant after mothers' ratings were entered into the regression equations.

information that parents are exposed to as their children grow up, we would not expect the biasing effects to be large—and they are not. Nevertheless, although the effects are not large, they are both reliable and consistent across different activity domains. Finally, they do appear to influence the development of the children's own self-perceptions in a manner consistent with the self-fulfilling prophecy hypothesis.

Conclusions

We have argued that gender differentiation in parents' perceptions of their children's abilities in various domains results, in part, from processes associated with perceptual bias and expectancy effects. In particular, we hypothesized that both parents' causal attributions for their children's successes, and parents' category-based gender role stereotypes, would lead to perceptual bias in their impressions of their children's competencies in gender role stereotyped activity domains. Current findings from two ongoing longitudinal studies, as well as results from our previous work, support these hypotheses. As one would expect, parents' perceptions of their children's competencies in math, English, and sports are strongly related to independent indicators of their children's actual competence in these domains. Nevertheless, the evidence clearly indicates that parents' perceptions of their children's competencie in math, English, and sports are also influenced by their children's gender, and by the parents' gender role stereotypic beliefs about which gender is naturally more talented in these domains. Furthermore, the evidence supports the conclusion that these influences are independent of any actual differences that might exist in the children's competencies. Thus, it appears that perceptual bias is operating in the formation of parents' impressions of their children's competencies in gender role stereotyped activity domains.

Let us consider this from a self-fulfilling prophecy view concerning the socialization of gender differences in children's competencies in various activity domains. Proponents of such a view would argue that these differences in parents' perceptions of their children's competencies set in motion a train of events that ultimately create the very differences the parents originally believed to exist (see Eccles & Hoffman, 1984). Elsewhere, we have identified one mechanism through which such a process might be mediated: the children's self-perceptions. We have argued that children's self-perceptions and task-perceptions influence the choices children make about their involvement in various activities (see Eccles-Parsons et al., 1983). In particular, children should spend more time engaged in activities that they think they are good at, and that they value and enjoy.

We have now documented these relations in the domains of math and sports, with a variety of findings not reported in this article. In math, we have demonstrated that decisions regarding course enrollment in high school are directly, and powerfully, influenced by adolescents' confidence in their math ability and by the value they attach to developing math skill (Eccles et al., 1984). In sports, we have demonstrated that the gender difference in the amount of free time sixth graders spend engaged in athletic activities is mediated by gender differences in the adolescents' confidence in their athletic ability and in the value they attach to participating in athletic activities (Eccles & Harold, 1988). We have also shown that gender differences in adolescents' self-perceptions are mediated, at least in part, by the gender role stereotyped bias in their parents' perceptions of their competencies in various activities. Together, these results support the conclusion that processes involving self-fulfilling prophecies contribute to the socialization of gender differences in the domains of mathematics and sports.

But, specifically, how do parents' gender role stereotyped perceptions of their children's competencies influence the children's self-and task-perceptions? We are just beginning to study this issue. Figure 38.5 illustrates the theoretical model we are testing. Essentially, we believe that parents' gender role stereotypes, in interaction with their children's gender, affect the following mediators: (a) parents' casual attributions for the children's performance, (b) parents' emotional reactions to their children's performance in various activities, (c) the importance parents attach to their children acquiring various skills, (d) the advice parents provide their children regarding involvement in various skills, and (e) the activities and toys parents provide for their children. In turn, we predict that these subtle and explicit mediators influence development of the following child outcomes across various gender role

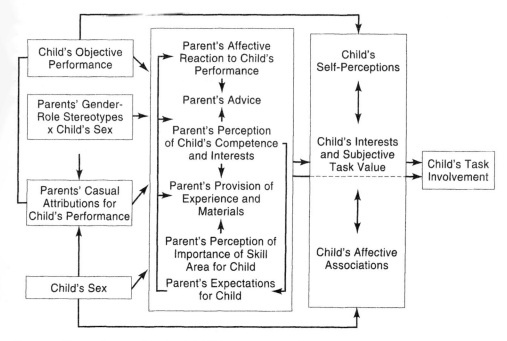

Fig. 38.5. Theoretical model of self-fulfilling prophecy effects in the family.

stereotyped activity domains: (a) children's confidence in their abilities, (b) children's interest in mastering various skills, (c) children's affective reactions to participating in various activities, and (d) as a consequence of these self-and task-perceptions, the amount of time and type of effort that children end up devoting to mastering and demonstrating various skills. Empirical work assessing these various causal links is now under way.

In the end, these differences in self-perceptions and skills influence the type of jobs and activities that females and males seek out and qualify for. If our society rewarded female-typed and male-typed activities and job choices equally, this consequence might not be as problematic as it now is. But this is not the case in this society, particularly with regard to job salaries and status. As a consequence of making female-typed occupational choices, females reduce their earnings potential significantly (see Eccles, 1987), and this fact puts them at substantially greater risk than males for all of the negative social consequences associated with low income and poverty.

REFERENCES

Alexander, K. L., & Entwisle, D. R. (1988). Achievement in the first two years of school: Patterns and processes. *Monograph of the Society of Research in Child Development, 53* (2, entire issue).

Baron, R. M., & Kenny, D. A. (1986). The moderator-mediator variable distinction in social psychological research: Conceptual, strategic, and statistical considerations. *Journal of Personality and Social Psychology, 51,* 1173–1182

Benbow, C. P., & Stanley, J. C. (1980). Sex differences in mathematical ability: Fact or artifact. *Science, 210,* 1262–1264.

Darley, J. M., & Gross, P. H. (1983). A hypothesis-confirming bias in labeling effects. *Journal of Personality and Social Psychology, 44,* 20–33.

Duncan, B. L. (1976). Differential social perception and attribution of intergroup violence: Testing the lower limits of stereotyping Blacks. *Journal of Personality and Social Psychology, 34,* 590–598.

Eccles, J. S. (1987). Gender roles and women's achievement-related decisions. *Psychology of Women Quarterly, 11,* 135–172.

Eccles, J. S. (1989). Bringing young women to math and science. In M. Crawford & M. Gentry (Eds.), *Gender and thought: Psychological perspectives* (pp. 36–58). New York: Springer-Verlag.

Eccles, J. S., Adler, T., & Meece, J. (1984). Sex differences in achievement: A test of alternative theories. *Journal of Personality and Social Psychology, 46* 26–43.

Eccles, J. S., & Harold, R. (1988, October). *Gender differences in participation in sports.* Paper presented at American Association for Applied Sport Psychology meeting, New Hampshire.

Eccles, J. S., & Hoffman, L. W. (1984). Socialization and the maintenance of a sex-segregated labor market. In H. W. Stevenson & A. E. Siegel (Eds.), *Research in child development and social policy* (Vol. 1, pp. 367–420). Chicago: University of Chicago Press.

Eccles, J. S., & Jacobs, J. E. (1986). Social forces shape math attitudes and performance. *Signs, 11,* 367–380.

Eccles, J. S., Jacobs, J. E., Harold-Goldsmith, R., Jayaratne, T., & Yee, D. (1989, April). *The relations between parents' category-based and target-based beliefs: Gender roles and biological influences.* Paper presented at Society for Research on Child Development meeting, Kansas City, MO.

Eccles, J. S., Wigfield, A., Flanagan, C., Miller, C., Reuman, D., & Yee, D. (1989). Self-concepts, domain values, and self-esteem: Relations and changes at early adolescence. *Journal of Personality, 57,* 283–310.

Eccles-Parsons, J. (1984). Sex differences in math participation. In M. L. Maehr & M. W. Steinkamp (Eds.), *Women in Science* (pp. 93–138). Greenwich, CT: JAI Press.

Eccles-Parsons, J., Adler, T., Futterman, R., Goff, S., Kaczala, C., Meece, J., & Midgley, C. (1983). Expectations, values and academic behaviors. In J. T. Spence (Ed.), *Achievement and achievement motivation* (pp. 75–146). New York: Freeman.

Eccles-Parsons, J., Adler T., & Kaczala, C. (1982). Socialization of achievement attitudes and beliefs: Parental influences. *Child development, 53,* 310–321.

Higgins, E. T., & Bargh, J. A. (1987). Social cognition and social perception. *Annual Review of Psychology, 38,* 369–425.

Hilton, J. L., & Fein, S. (1989). The role of typical diagnosticity in stereotyped-based judgments. *Journal of Personality and Social Psychology, 57,* 210–211.

Hyde, J. S., Fennema, E., & Lamon, S. J. (1990). Gender differences in mathematics performance: A meta-analysis. *Psychological Bulletin, 107,* 139–155.

Jacobs, J. E. (1987). *Parents' gender role stereotypes and perceptions of their child's ability: Influences on the child.* Unpublished dissertation, University of Michigan, Ann Arbor.

Jacobs, J. E., & Eccles, J. (1990). *The influence of parent stereotypes on parent and child ability beliefs in three domains.* Unpublished manuscript, University of Michigan, Institute for Social Research, Ann Arbor.

Jacobs, J. E., & Eccles, J. S. (1985). Gender differences in math ability: The impact of media reports on parents. *Educational Researcher, 14,* 20–25.

assim, L. (1986). Self-fulfilling prophecies: A theoretical and integrative review. *Psychological Review, 93*, 429–445.

ussim, L. (1989). Teacher expectations: Self-fulfilling prophecies, perceptual biases, and accuracy. *Journal of Personality and Social Psychology, 57*, 469–480.

Locksley, A., Borgida, E., Brekke, N., & Hepburn, C. (1980). Sex stereotypes and social judgment. *Journal of Personality and Social Psychology, 39*, 821–831.

Rasinski, K. A., Crocker, J., & Hastie, R. (1985). Another look at sex stereotypes and social judgments: An analysis of the social perceiver's use of subjective probabilities. *Journal of Personality and Social Psychology, 49*, 317–326.

Rothbart, M. (1989). *The stability of gender and ethnic stereotypes.* Paper presented at University of Colorado.

Steinkamp, M. W., & Maehr, M. L. (Eds.). (1984). *Women in science, Vol. 2: Advances in motivation and achievement.* Greenwich, CT: JAI Press.

Vetter, B., & Babco, E. (Eds.). (1986). *Professional women and minorities.* Washington, DC: Commission on Professionals in Science and Technology.

Weiner, B. (1974). *Achievement motivation and attribution theory.* Morristown, NJ: General Learning Press.

Yee, D., & Eccles, J. S. (1988). Parent perceptions and attributions for children's math achievement. *Sex Roles, 19*, 317–333.

Chapter Thirty-Nine

Feeling Like a Fraud

Peggy McIntosh

Not so long ago in Wisconsin at the Wingspread Center I attended a conference on women's leadership in higher education. Seventeen women in a row spoke from the floor during a plenary session and all seventeen started their remarks with some kind of apology or disclaimer. The self-deprecating comments ranged from "I just wanted to say ..." to "I have just one point to make ..." to "I never thought about this before, but ..." through "I really don't know what I'm talking about, but here goes!"

Ironically enough, all of us had been funded to attend the conference because we supposedly knew something about Women's Leadership. Yet we seemed to share a feeling of illegitimacy when speaking in front of women like ourselves. The apologies started me on a new train of thought which led to this talk on "Feeling Like a Fraud."

I find that this title triggers a flash of recognition in both male and female friends and colleagues. For many, it calls up a familiar feeling—the feeling that in taking part in public life one has pulled the wool over others' eyes; that one is in the wrong place, and about to be found out; that there has been a colossal mistake in the selection and accreditation process which the rest of the world is about to discover. One dreams recurrently, as I do, that one has been exposed as "not belonging," or as having "gotten in" under false pretenses. In my case, someone from Harvard University calls to say they have found out I never took the Ph.D. qualifying exam in German. Or one feels like a play actor, a hypocrite, a stager of charades, or like sixteen personalities without a common center. One feels illegitimate in doing something, or appearing as something; one feels apologetic, undeserving, anxious, tenuous, out-of-place, misread, phony, uncomfortable, incompetent, dishonest, guilty. Many women and men I know seem to share these feelings. But some research and much observation suggests they are especially severe in women, both in chronic life-long forms and in acute forms in particular situations.

I think we need to take a double look at the phenomenon of feeling like a fraud. I will discuss it here from two apparently opposed points of view. I suggest *both* that we mustn't let the world make us feel like frauds, *and* that we must keep alive in ourselves that sense of fraudulence which sometimes overtakes us in public places. I suggest that on the one hand feeling like a fraud indicates that we have, deplorably,

Peggy McIntosh, "Feeling Like a Fraud." *Work in Progress, No. 18*, Wellesley, MA: Stone Center Working Paper Series. © 1985 by the Stone Center Working Paper Series. Reprinted by permission.

nternalized value systems that said most people were incompetent and illegitimate in the spheres of power and public life and authority. But then on the other hand, I suggest that when we apologize in public, we are at some level making a deeply wise refusal to carry on the pretense of deserving and feeling good about roles in conventional and oppressive hierarchies. I think that most feelings of personal fraudulence need to be analyzed politically and deplored, especially feelings of fraudulence in lower caste people. But on the other hand, I also think that feeling like a fraud is conducive to social and political *change,* and that some forms of it should be applauded and developed in us, so that we become better at spotting fraudulence in, and trying to alter, the forms of our culture.

You may be wondering which of these sides I will come out on. I am coming out on both sides. My talk is like a Moebius strip. On one side it says, "We must not let them make us feel like frauds." And on the other side it says, "Let us continue to spot fraudulence in the roles we are asked to play." And when I twist over this strip which has two "opposing" sides and join it together again as a circle, I have the Moebius strip phenomenon. You run your finger along the surface. Without changing sides, you cover all surfaces of the twisted circle of tape. In the end your finger comes back to the very spot it began without having changed sides. I feel that the two kinds of argument I am making here are similarly, so to speak, both "on the same side."

Let me give some more specific examples of the feelings of fraudulence which I am talking about. In students it often takes these forms. "The Admissions Committee made a mistake. I don't belong here." Or "I got an A on this paper. *So he didn't find me out.*" Or "I got a B on this paper. So he found me out." Or "I got a C on this paper. He really found me out." All three reactions to the grade are variants on the same feeling that one was an imposter to begin with as author of the paper. Or in reaction to the comment: "You made your points beautifully in this paper," the student may think, "It can't be true. I can't even remember what I said." Or a student who works on a committee may be praised by the Dean for her organizational skill, and think guiltily of the mess on the desk which the Dean hasn't seen. Analogously, a person feeling like a fraud when told that someone likes her will feel "Then, he must be a jerk." Or, if told she is beautiful, will think only of her faults. Likewise, a graduate student, told that she has written "the definitive work" and will very likely have a brilliant defense, is likely to think that it is all a colossal mistake, and that she couldn't "defend" a guppy. When a letter of recommendation states: "Ms. X is one of the brightest students I have taught in the last 15 years," Ms. X is likely to think, "What a pushover! But, how long can I keep fooling her?" When a commencement speakers says "Medicine will be better off with people like you entering the field," the graduates are likely to think, "These speakers are all hypocrites." If an executive says, "She has set her goals high and has met them in a truly professional way," the employee may feel, "This is no picture of me. I just hold the office together. I just talk to people, for goodness sake." The book reviewer may say, "This book is a pathbreaking study," while the faculty member feels, "No, I just cobbled my term papers together into a book of essays because I want to get tenure." Within life in general, one may feel like a fraud speaking in meetings, calling in to a talk show, writing to the newspaper, being praised, telling people what one thinks, claiming to know anything, being called an expert, taking a strong point of view, putting one's head up in any public place, having opinions, and, most terrifying of all, having one's opinions taken seriously.

I have begun to touch on the tip of the iceberg for a few rather privileged people in rather academic and elite situations. There are myriad other examples from spheres of experience which are more widely shared in terms of class and race and culture. But I notice as I think through feelings of fraudulance that they seem to me not to occur in some areas of life. I pat our cat and the cat purrs. I don't feel like a fraud. It's not the same as getting an A on a paper. When I bring home chocolate chip mint ice cream, the kids' appreciation doesn't throw me into a panic about who I am. I think that being praised for a good spaghetti sauce or for finding a bargain is not so unnerving as being praised for giving a speech.

I do not think that it is simply the public nature of certain activities which makes us feel fraudulent. Kiyo Morimoto of the Bureau of Study Council at Harvard/Radcliffe has said that a majority of the incoming freshmen feel that they were admitted to the college by mistake. Feeling fraudulent can infect lives even within not-very-public situations.

I have come to think of it this way. The more hierarchical the activity or institution, and the higher up we go in it, the greater our feelings of fraudulence are likely to be. People feel fraudulent especially when ascending in hierarchies in which by *societal definition* they do not belong at the top of the pyramid. I call hierarchies pyramidal because most resemble mountains, with far less room at the top than on the bottom. On the top there is less territory but more power, more money, more press, more praise, and more prizes. On the bottom is far more territory and more people, but less of the powers and privileges. Women and lower caste or minority men are especially few in the tops of the hierarchies of money, decision making, opinion making, and public authority, in the worlds of praise and press and prizes, the worlds of the so-called geniuses, leaders, media giants, "forces" in the culture. Women are not considered, for example, to be actors in real history, but only in women's history. Our perspectives are not featured in mainstream psychology, but only in "Psychology of Women" courses. We are featured not on the front page, but in the Living section of the newspapers. And so on and so forth through the curricular and noncurricular matrix (or should I say patrix?) of our lives. And so when we rise up in hierarchical worlds, while socialized to feel that we *shouldn't* be there, it is not surprising if we appear to ourselves to be fraudulent. "If this is 'one of the best colleges in the country,' then I don't belong here." "He thinks I am wonderful? Then he must be a loser." "She said I argued brilliantly? Then I fooled her." I think most people who feel like frauds have internalized systems of seeing which say most people are not valid and don't belong in the worlds of worth, distinctiveness, excellence, authority, creativity, opinion, or forceful expressiveness, positive or negative.

In recent discussions, people have used terms such as the "imposter syndrome" in "high-achieving" women. They talk about some of the problems I have been discussing, and especially about executive or highly-placed women's feelings of tenubusness and illegitimacy in their careers. Very often such discussions turn to parental attitudes, particularly parental attitudes toward girl children, and some say that when parents supported nontraditional career aspirations in girls, this correlated with fewer feelings of being an imposter.

I like the phrase "imposter syndrome." This is very useful. I also admire the work of Irene Stiver (1982) on this subject. But I think that it does not make sense to start with a unit like the nuclear family to try to account for the imposter syndrome. The unit to study, though it is much harder to study than the individual family with its individual actors, should be the whole society. Most people receive messages from *every* side, *throughout* the culture, that they are not legitimate in places of authority, not legitimate wearing the white coat, not legitimate behind the podium with the presidential seal, not legitimate as a female or minority male within frameworks of the boardroom, the corporate executive office, the banking industry, the Defense Department, in the worlds of making and shaping technology, opinion, and policy. Adults' failures of nerve may relate, of course, to specific attitudes in specific parents. While our own parents may have failed to encourage, for example, nontraditional career aspirations in women, the society as a whole reinforced in a thousand ways that failure to encourage anyone to challenge the hierarchical winners-and-losers arrangements of the whole culture.

We have some remedies for the feeling of personal fraudulence. Particularly in the United States and over the last two decades, we have been introduced to courses on assertiveness training and confidence building, and, for some of us, also courses in public speaking, or workshops in surviving interviews. We have won greater chances at athletics, and now more women than before are developing an ability to compete in athletic situations with confidence and self-respect and enjoyment. These correctives help some women and men to feel that they are not frauds, and that they are, on the contrary, competent, whole, entitled, and legitimate, both as private persons and as public speakers and actors.

In addition, exposure to mentors and to role models apparently helps to create a feeling of competence and of being sponsored and encouraged in high places by those who "ought to know" our worth. I have benefitted very much from some of the correctives mentioned above, and especially from two courses in public speaking given by the wonderful Merelyn Jacobs of Dartmouth College who told us, "Say what you want your audience to know. They have come all this distance to hear you, and you owe it to them to get to the point." Such advice helped her listeners to cut down on the apologies. But such remedies do not go beyond the first way of seeing feelings of fraudulence. They help only to correct the problem as I have outlined it so far, that we feel like frauds because we were socialized to think we do not belong high in hierarchies, and that most feelings of fraudulence come when one is rising in—or appearing to rise in—hierarchical territory, by taking the pulpit, or taking the podium, or taking the front of the class, or taking a position in the news—taking positions which the world associates with people of merit and importance. The higher we go in those hierarchical structures, the more likely we are to feel, hollowly and in our inner selves, that we do not belong and the more we are likely to ask, "What am I doing here?" Assertiveness training *can* help us to look around and check out the people around us, and then say, "I am here because I have as much right to this podium as anyone else, as much competence in this presidency as anyone else see around me." This translates into "I may be a fraud, but I am *no more fraudulent than the next person.*"

Now suddenly, the plot thickens. Is the next person fraudulent? This question leads to my second perspective on feeling like a fraud. Here we move into territory where assertiveness training and speech workshops may be of no help. The next person behind that podium is, yes, very likely to be playing a role which entails fraudulence, pretense, imposter behavior. And it has less to do with that individual than with the roles which develop out of the public *requirements* at the tops of hierarchies as now constructed.

I now shift from the Moebius strip message "We must not let them make us feel like frauds" to the other Moebius strip message which is contiguous yet apparently opposite: "Let us continue to spot fraudulence in the roles we are made to play in the hierarchies of power." And here I want to tell a story about a woman colleague in a large United States research university who dared, figuratively speaking, to move in public from one side of the strip to the other. Her university was holding a faculty-wide debate on whether affirmative action guidelines for hiring should also be followed for decisions about tenure and promotion. The heated meeting on this important subject included all of the undergraduate and graduate school faculties. I was not there, but I heard that, one after another, white male faculty members stood up to say they had their doubts; when it came to promotion and tenuring, the university had to be on guard against *mediocrity,* and not let down its high standards, and that when it came to giving people a lifetime vote of confidence, one couldn't just take "any old person" and give that vote of confidence—one must make a financial investment in excellence. The woman psychologist to whom I am grateful stood up and said, "I am hearing a lot of talk about excellence. But then I look around me and I see a lot of mediocre men. For me the real test of affirmative action will be whether or not I can stand up here in twenty years and see equal numbers of mediocre women and mediocre men." She called the men on their claim to excellence, on their equation of power with merit.

This relates to my second perspective on feeling like a fraud. We feel fraudulent, I think, partly because we know that usually those who happen to get the high titles and the acclaim and the imagery going with them are not "the best and the brightest," and *we don't want to pretend to be so either.* When we entertain nagging thoughts about whether we belong or deserve to be at the podium, or in the boardroom, or tenured, or giving an interview to a newspaper, or earning a good salary for what we like to do, we may be deeply wise in feeling anxious and illegitimate and fraudulent in these circumstances. Those men who feel the same way in such settings may be deeply wise as well, for the public forms and institutions tend to demand that one appear to be an authority figure, an expert, "the best." The forms require that one appear to be a person who sets goals and knows how to meet them, a "leader" who is superior in certain qualities over those who are "followers." The public forms and institutions insisting on these images do require fraudulent behavior of us, and they will turn us into frauds if we accept the roles as written. The roles are dishonest and people who arc still in touch with their humanity and with their frailty will properly feel fraudulent in them. What the public roles entail and promote are usually not those qualities we have really specialized in ourselves. What the systems reward in us rarely corresponds to what we are really good at, and most humane in being.

This point brings me back to the conference of women who appeared to disown their own ideas when they took the floor. When seventeen women in a row apologize, then perhaps we should listen to what they are saying, particularly when the seventeen apologists are known as "leaders" but are not acting like them. We need to listen to what they tell us about *the way they want to lead*. My first response was to think that these apologetic women were testimony to women's incompetence. And that *is* the world's judgment on them. But an alternative way of listening to them, on the assumption that women *are* competent, brings out a message their behavior delivers, which is not that they can't stand behind the podium, but that they can't stand the podium. And in their apologies these women were, let us say, trying to change the forms of public speaking to make them less fraudulent, less ridiculous, less filled with pretense. Conventions of public speaking entail many uses of rhetoric; effective rhetoric requires that one speaker persuades a group of followers. What if a person at a conference simply wants to put new ideas on the table? She may begin by saying, "You may not agree with this, but . . ." In this apparent apology, she is creating an opening which is nonrhetorical, and her words accomplish several important ends. "You may not agree with this, but . . ." This opening not only acknowledges the presence of the Other; it also postulates the engagement of the Other in what is going on (as they say in literature, it postulates reader response). It also acknowledges the validity of the Other's ideas. "You *may not* agree with this, but . . ." and it creates a tentative tone, a conversational matrix, a sense of give and take. As I see it, this opening acknowledges and strengthens the social fabric before it can be torn by rhetoric. It says, "I am not taking the floor from you. I recognize you are there. I am trying to make this more like a conversation than like a speech." The woman who says, "I have just one point to make . . ." is saying also "I don't want to interrupt the flow," or perhaps "I am not saying this in opposition to what has already been said . . ." Research has indicated that girls in playgrounds often break up a game rather than having it disintegrate into conflicts over rules. The woman speaker who says, "I really don't know what I'm saying, but here goes!" inspires neither confidence nor respect in the boardrooms of corporate America; but she is not pretending, and perhaps we need more of her in the boardrooms. At any rate, I find I want to make the case for some of the apologies I heard as refusals to pretend, refusals to be a fraud, refusals to carry through with the rhetorical conventions of public speaking, or writing, or performance in which one must pretend to be a strong man overcoming others, or a woman strongly identified with white males' functions and rules for power and success.

I wish to return now to undergraduate students' feelings of fraudulence, of feeling guilty and out of place. "The Admissions Committee made a mistake. I don't belong here." If one insists on defining certain colleges as "the best," any intelligent woman will feel that no one has done the tests to know whether either the college or she *can* be called "the best." It's a valid doubt. When she gets an A on a term paper, beyond the idea that "this means he didn't find me out" is this idea: An A is a grade absolutely better than B. Even when used together (in A − /B +), there is a slash between to show they are not the same grade. But is the student with the A *absolutely* better than the others who took that exam and who scored lower? A woman down the hall may have studied all month, never having had a course in this subject before, and have gotten a B. Another may never have really understood what was going on, but her questions really showed others what the course was about. Let's say she got a C. Our "A student" may not have done any work until the last two days, and then crammed all night. That puts her up, away from the others, on a pedestal. Does she belong there? A woman may say to herself, "He thinks I am beautiful. But I hate that Beauty Queen stuff; I won't get trapped by it." Or, "They call me an expert. That's because they don't know any better. They probably don't know who the experts *are* on this subject. I certainly don't." Or, "They call me a pathbreaker. But I don't think of myself as breaking paths. I think and write." It seems to me that the absoluteness of hierarchical rankings and ratings and of the existing metaphors of originality or strength contain many elements of fraudulence. For women, especially, this absoluteness, and those metaphors of pathbreaking and being expert don't correspond to our complex sense of the web of circumstances in which we are born, circumstances in which our lives do not have trajectories and goals, but are, rather, threads in the fabric of circumstance, only partly of our own social and emotional weaving.

We resist, in other words, the building of pedestals, and the awarding of titles which we feel are not quite appropriate and which separate us from others like ourselves and which imply that we are self-sufficient or independent loners. And this resistance is healthy for us and others. Or, rather, it can be seen both as good and bad for us, but as good for the whole society.

A colleague told me that she attended a conference in which, in the relaxed aftermath, students began to ask the visiting professors, all of whom were women, how they came to their public lives and their academic fields. One woman, in examining her past, put her distinguished present down mostly to the circumstance that she had been rich. Another, examining her past, put her distinguished present down mostly to the circumstance that she had been poor. And a third put her success down to the fact that she entered the library and the books that interested her more or less fell on her head. None of the women acknowledged her own competence or excellence or enjoyment of her field. None said, "I liked the field; I read the books; I understood them; I got my papers in on time; I became competent; I saw new possibilities; I add to the world; people appreciate my work and I do, too." These women were perhaps then, let's say, deplorably modest, rejecting credit for themselves. But on the other hand, I would say they were applaudably honest. From one point of view, they were all feeling rather like frauds as "success stories," or "notable women," so they put their lives down to circumstances. On the other hand, they were feeling a fraudulence attaching, as I think, to the myths of self-realization which go this way: "I came up from nothing, rags to riches, from pink booties to briefcase on Wall Street. I did it all myself. I knew what I wanted and I was self-reliant. You can be, too, if you set your sights high and don't let anything interfere; you can do anything you want." Now, it seems only honest to acknowledge that that is a myth. When women refuse to take sole credit for their mid-life status and insist on mentioning circumstances of birth and color and wealth and regional and ethnic setting and rejecting the pretenses of the pedestal and the podium, they are doing something that the whole society needs. We need it, in other words, in our highest policy-makers, this sense of how circumstances of birth and status and social network more than individual selves bear on life outcomes. False pictures imply that the individual is the unit of actualization in this culture, and that self-actualization is the main business of all competent people. But most of human life is bound up in collective and social and private experience which is not linear and not filled with clear upward trajectories and not identified with the aspirations of white, upwardly mobile men. Most of human sensibility is not covered by what authoritative experts tell us because their frameworks for thought are often wrong, and are in fact, fraudulent when they claim to cover all of us.

What, then, should we teach students about feeling like a fraud? First, that it is a feeling taught to us. Second, that this teaching is no accident. Third, that it is not good for us to feel like frauds insofar as that feeling perpetuates hierarchies. And fourth, that in another sense, it is good for us to feel like frauds insofar as that feeling may help us to undermine hierarchies. I advocate in this a *double vision*, as I do in virtually all other kinds of work with students and in the society at large. We need a double vision both of what the dominant culture stands for, and of what we lower caste people who are undervalued can develop in the way of a critique of the dominant culture. Within the dominant culture, people who can't deliver the goods from behind the podium will look incompetent. Therefore, we need to get over the socialized feeling of being a fraud and stand behind that podium and deliver the goods. This is learning the present ways of power. But, alternatively, it is constructive for the whole society if we question why there must be a podium, and ask whether the town meeting or the Quaker meeting or the March on Washington weren't perhaps better experiments in public speaking. Only when we examine the difference between the conversation and the speech can we suggest that world leaders try conversation.

Let me turn now to the linguistic aspect of feelings about fraudulence in writing. When one writes a paper on virtually any subject, one is likely to begin with a complex of myriad ideas that constitute what William James called "a buzzing, blooming confusion." But one must choose among these ideas in order to put a paper together, because the rules for the sentence and the paragraph are very arbitrary. The rules insist on beginnings, middles, and ends. Within the sentence, conventions of grammar dictate that the subject act on the object through the verb. Moreover, traditional conventions of expository writing insist on something still more autocratic, that one make a case which is cohesive and clear, an argument which has no holes in it, a position from which one can take on all comers and defend one's self. This assumption about what writing is, the making of a case against the fancied attacker, permeates our teaching of writing from the expository courses through the graduate student's defense of the thesis, which is a kind of king-on-the-mountain in which you take on all attackers of your small piece of territory. It's silly, isn't it, that the paper must make a "watertight," "unimpeachable" argument, mu: make "points," and be like the world of boxing or dueling, holding off imagine attackers. The rules surrounding formal writing leave sensitive people with a feeling that the finished paper makes a statement which is fraudulent. Those who want to use language for other purposes are uneasy with the praise which comes with using language for making arguments. A student who says "I am such a fraud; I can't write this paper" will tend toward self-censorship or silence, and she needs help against those feelings. A student who says that one is, after all, a fraud in writing this kind of paper is in better shape. She knows life doesn't come in sentences; life doesn't come in paragraphs. And although institutions are encouraging her to use the expository essay as a kind of combination attack and defense mechanism, she wants to find alternative uses of language. I think we need to help students to have both states of mind. First, we need to help them get past the feeling that they are *more* fraudulent than anyone else, and help them get past the feeling that everyone else in the class is really writing a first-rate argument, whereas they are blocked individually. Second, we need to help them to project some of their feeling of fraudulence onto societal forms. They should be encouraged to see that the public forms of our lives are a construct for organizing us, and that they particularly serve to keep the present economic, political, racial, and sexual hierarchies in place. Students as actors can gradually change those forms as they use and become successful in them. So the student may wisely repudiate that pinnacle-shaped A in the terms in which it was offered to her, as praise, for example, for "winning" argumentation. She may keep her own rich sense of connection which the subject nevertheless gave her before she wrote the "winning" paper on it, and which may enrich her life as she tries to write new scripts for her own public performance.

Likewise, students can be helped to get high grades or prizes for successful debating, learning to make a point against all comers. We need also to teach them to see fraudulence inherent in the conventions of debate, in that you become a polished expert in making the case for the side you have been assigned, rather than making a case for what you may perceive as the truth. Students need to be helped to see there is a reason why they can accept "You are good to talk to" more easily than "This is the best paper I have had in fifteen years." The letter and the conversation as forms have less of fraud in them; they don't force us into authoritativeness and gross simplification.

My husband, on hearing me work through these ideas, said, "You're saying that those who don't think they are fraudulent are the real frauds." Yes. We have been socialized to feel like frauds but have developed some strengths in the midst of that fact, and because of that fact. Those who were socialized to feel absolutely entitled have made a habit of fraudulent behavior in proportion as they have internalized the view of themselves as the best and the brightest. So our task is complex. When a student says "I get so nervous talking in class," I think we need first to point out that she/he was set up to get nervous: Hierarchies are disempowering, and nearly all people are socialized so that they *will* feel like failures in public and need help to feel confident. At the same time, students are right deeply to mistrust what anyone says authoritatively, including themselves. We need that tentativeness in high places. We

heed it in the Pentagon, in the White House, and in makers of public policy. We
need that conversation, that ability to listen, to have a nonrhetorical, a relational self.

I hope we can move students from "My voice should not be heard at all" to "I
don't like the official tone I am forced to take in those situations; it misrepresents
me" through "What *other* voice can I find to convey not an autonomous, self-
confident me (which doesn't exist), but the self-in-relation, not coercive, and not
deceptive, but social?" If we give students a double vision of social reality, I think
they can learn both the language of power, which we use standing at the podium and
delivering those straight sentences, and the language of social change, which suggests
alternate visions of how to use power.

Women and others who have been disempowered are not all able to bring our
truths to light yet. Many such people tend to apologize. But in doing so we are
creating a voice which, though sounding tentative, has the seeds for the future in it.
When we say, "You may not agree with this, but . . . ," we are creating an atmosphere
of *detente*, peace, negotiation-making tentativeness, rather than using the podium for
the violent act of bringing everyone over to our side. Perhaps, then, we women
should be seen as canary birds testing for the carbon monoxide poison in the
atmosphere. When seventeen women in a row apologize, there may be something
wrong with the air in the nonapologetic world. Our habit of smelling the poison in
the air and trying not to add to the poison can be seen as a strength, not a weakness,
creating a healthier kind of atmosphere. The fraudulent-feeling people in the culture
are perhaps our best canary birds. When they begin to keel over, we know we are
really in trouble—that the air around them does not have enough life-sustaining
oxygen. Those situations in which they sense the poison in the air most clearly are
those situations connected with grades, titles, promotions, public accreditation, and
public pronouncements, in the hierarchies which have the clearest absolute ranking
systems, with a clear demarcation between winners and losers.

So, "which of these things do you want?" says the mind seeking only one vision.
As I have said, I want two things at once: to mitigate apology which reinforces
hierarchy, and to intensify revisionary tentative behavior, so that we see and criticize
fraudulent forms and customs in the expert, the leader, the "self-made" man, the
"self-reliant" person, the self-righteous American certain that God is on our side,
and that He intends us to be a winner. We need more training in seeing the public
presences of winners and authority figures as personae, fraudulent actors in high
places, and in bringing the material of the private consciousness into public life, as
feminists are already trying to do on so many fronts.

My theory of two ways of seeing fraudulence should be put here against my theory
of the psyche and of the society in general. I see both our individual psyches and the
whole society as having the shape of a broken pyramid, with a kind of geological
fault running more or less horizontally through the center and dividing the top part
from the lower part. The public and competitive functions of our psyches are
contained in the top part of the pyramid, and the most ordinary, lateral, everyday
business of simply getting along "without accomplishing anything" is, in my view, at
the base of the psyche, and of civilization, and of the pyramid which I am drawing
here.

All institutions and psyches have both public, competitive functions and, underlying these and making them possible, a substructure of the ordinary work of upkeep, maintenance, and making and mending of the social fabric. At the tops of the pyramids are concentrated money, power, and decision-making functions, and in the very much wider base are the more ordinary functions which have either no visibility at all in most of what we read and do and think and are told, or very little visibility and have seldom been named and identified. The grain in the public part of the psyche and in the public part of our institutions is vertical and contains many ladders to promotion, "success," praise, and prizes. The hidden prescription under these competitive functions of personality and society is that you win lest you lose, because those alternatives are seen to be the *only* alternatives: *Either* you are on your way up, or you're on your way down, falling toward the bottom. One wouldn't want to be on the bottom, so it is assumed one will be striving toward what the world calls the top—that is, toward "accomplishment," "achievement," "success," defined as leading to individual power. In the lateral functions of the psyche and of the society occur the experiences of washing the dishes and patting the cat, and having talks with one's friends, and earning enough money to put the bread on the table, and getting the bread on the table, and washing the dishes, and loving those who cannot help us "get anywhere." These are the functions of answering the phone, of driving home at night, of being a person intimately involved with others for the sake of the involvement. They are not what the world would call the functions of achievement or success. They have instead to do with survival. The hidden prescription in this basis of our institutions and our psyches is that one works for the decent survival of all because therein lies one's own best survival. This is not an altruistic prescription; you don't simply work for others, but you live *with* others because that is one of the impulses and conditions we were born to. One finds one's development through the development of others. One develops, as the researchers here have defined it, a self-in-relation (Miller, 1984; Surrey, 1984).

Now, unfortunately, the functions represented by the top parts of my broken pyramids have been projected onto white males born to circumstances of cultural power, and the functions of the psyche and the institutions which I place at the base of the pyramids have been projected onto women and lower caste males. Much research is now showing, of course, that women aren't so happy with that assignment—that projection onto us—of all of the lateral functions of survival, nor men with the projection onto them of the world of winning versus losing—a world which has only two alternatives: yes/no; right/wrong; top/bottom; win/lose; self/other; success/failure.

By now it is clear to you that the first type of feeling like a fraud occurs chiefly in these top-level public functions of self and society. If one has internalized the view that only the win/lose value system and version of reality are real, women at the podium (or lower caste men) will feel fraudulent, since by definition they are losers trying to act like winners in occupying the podium. If, however, we have educated our students and ourselves to a double vision, to both the public functions of psyche and society and the hidden, lateral functions of psyche and society, the survival functions, then we can see feeling like a fraud as something else again. In its second aspect, the feeling of fraudulence is the *critique* of the vertical from these lateral parts of the personality, objecting both that the vertical behavior is partial and misrepresents us and that the lateral realities which are the ground of our humanity are not honored in the culture's value system or its most conventional praise.

My view of curriculum change superimposed on this diagram goes this way. In Phase I you study womanless History. In Phase II, women in History, but only as exceptions, and still on History's terms. In Phase III, women are seen as a problem, anomaly, or absence in History, as a problem for historians and also for the society, as victims, the oppressed, the losers, or the incompetent. Then one moves further to that main work of women which has been assigned to us—finding one's self through the development of others, and then one is doing Phase IV: Women *As* History, redefining history so as to make us central. In Phase V we will have History Redefined and Reconstructed to Include Us All. Now once one has come to see the traditional lives of women as just as real as the rest of what history has named, and more plentiful, why then everything shifts. The feeling of fraudulence at that point is seen to arise out of the sense that all people are interconnected, and that in no absolute way is one student different from the one down the hall who studied for weeks, or the roommate who never really understood the course. Each of us has done something that cannot be absolutely ranked. When we resist that ranking system that awarded us the A, because of our consciousness of the lateral functions of life and personality, then we are resisting fraudulence in a way that may become useful to the whole society.

Now what do I mean by that? According to my dream of the next hundred years, we can, if we live that long, bring into public life with us our sense of the now-named and reconstituted surviving functions, and we can call into question and change the behavior of those who see the world only in terms of winners and losers. And, of course, we need this work on a global scale to keep from blowing ourselves up. We can see already that so much of public performance is based on rules of acting and image-building, and we can spot the inaccuracy of the hierarchies in that they are not the meritocracies they claim to be. We know that our consciousness coming out of the survival aspects of personality can help us encourage the whole society not to pretend to be what it isn't. The pluralistic version of reality that comes out of seeing women *as* history—and that means all women, not just a few white women—also conduces to a kind of foreign policy which says that the Russians and we and the Chinese are equally valid people. The seventeen apologies come from this deeper level, and if we will *listen* to them and *learn* from them, they will bring revisionary strength to the whole culture. The apologies suggest that most leaders are poseurs, and that the "top" is *not* the top. I think Alice in Wonderland was right when she said to the Court, "You are nothing but a pack of cards!" Wise people go behind the screen and perceive the Wizard of Oz as the little shriveled man. Until we see the authoritative forms *as forms,* we will continue to deny those parts of ourselves that have no words, that don't come in paragraphs and chapters and footnotes; we will be forced to deny the woolgatherer, the conversationalists, the imaginer, the lover of women and lower caste men, the one who likes people and joins with them without necessarily "achieving" anything. The world of neighborhoods and of human communities is the world of survival. If the public world becomes more honest, it may help us invent a form of podium behind which honest people don't have to apologize for their connectedness to others.

I wish to end with the apology, which is not *only* an apology, which might have introduced my talk. I appreciate the invitation to speak in this colloquium series. I am not an expert in women's development. I am only an observer, but you thought I might be a resource for the series. In the same way, in your Stone Center work you invite us all, and not just the experts, in on a process. You show us not a finished theory, but a *process of reaching a theory,* a process of reseeing women and renaming some of our apparent weaknesses as potential or actual strengths. Your work in reconstruing and reconstructing enabled me to do some work, personal as well as public, which goes into my observations tonight. Your work, I think, can help us convert "feeling like a fraud" into resisting fraudulence and pressures toward fraudulence which originate outside of us in absolute, hierarchical systems and in definitions of our strengths as weaknesses. To this audience I want to say that I do see myself as a amateur observer, very limited, merely human, narrowly circumstanced and therefore half blind in observing all of what I have described. But also I would like to ask whether it wouldn't have been good for us all if every *expert* lecturer, every general, and every leader had demonstrated an ability to appreciate the process of living more than the products of success and victory. Wouldn't it have made quite a difference to ourselves and to human life in our time?

Discussion Summary

After each colloquium lecture, a discussion is held. Selected portions are summarized here. In this session, Dr. Janet Surrey joined in leading the discussion.

Question: Don't you think it's more important for women to try to build their self-confidence by learning to be competent in the way the world does operate at this time?

McIntosh: For numbers of women that may be satisfying. I really cannot judge for any one person. However, I've found that for a great many women that isn't enough. They know that there are other parts of themselves, parts which the major institutions of the world, as they operate, do not recognize as existing and valid. I believe it is important to recognize these parts and their importance for all people.

For example, if I am trying to help a student write a speech and I want to help her do things in ways that will be valued according to the standards of our major institutions, I would take her speech and scratch out all of the apologies. But, if I'm trying to help a student see the systemic factors which create fraudulence in the roles we're asked to play, I'd go back and put all the apologies back in, helping her to see the wisdom of her apologies, and applauding her resistance to a fraudulent tone in writing.

It's important to recognize that we have large parts of our personalities which will feel uncomfortable according to the rules of the "vertical world." And we have strengths which come from the "nonvertical world." Women can be held back if we don't recognize this for each other.

Comment: I wonder if we can describe this as a need for different ways of operating in different situations. For example, in a seminar with students, it may be better to take an "apologetic" view, saying, for example, "You may disagree, but let me ask you what you think about this explanation . . . " You are then saying you don't know everything and inviting an exchange. But if I have to meet with the president of my university because he is doing something that I think is not good for the women at the university, I would not want to apologize for what I'm about to say.

McIntosh: That is a very valuable way to extend this discussion. As I hear it, you're suggesting a kind of "taxonomy" of varying situations.

I've talked about this topic really in a very rough "first cut" way. We probably need to work out a much more specific taxonomy of apology.

Surrey: It may be useful to know that we have to work in these different modes and in different kinds of settings, at least at this time in history. For myself, I find it important to work within a workplace which operates very much in the ways that you say are generally valued in public life. It's important to know this reality because it is the way the world operates and it is so powerful. However, it is very important for me to work and be with groups of women—and sometimes men, too—who value the "lateral" parts of life. Even if the dominant world does not recognize these parts of life, it is essential that we keep recognizing their value for each other.

McIntosh: At this time we do have to recognize the existence of these two worlds, so to speak. It means we have a kind of double consciousness or double vision. While it's complicated, I feel that it helps us to provide for these parts of life which are really essential to our psychological well-being.

Comment: Despite what is happening in actuality, what is "invented" by those at the top is going to be the construction that's put on everything—including the explanations about everything that goes on in the lateral parts of life. There's good reason to believe, then, that most explanations of the lateral life are not likely to be valid representations.

McIntosh: I agree, especially since if you think only in terms used at the top, you're not likely to have a well-developed "double vision": you really won't have seen everything from *within* the lateral world. Your account of it will be that of a person who has looked down at the surface of the water in the Caribbean rather than snorkeling in it. The life underneath can't be guessed from the surface.

Comment: I'm thinking of the world as a place in which power is very real. The people in power are not going to act on a basis derived from the recognition of the importance of those lateral parts of life. Perhaps we should begin to think in terms of effective transitional forms—ways of building some bridges between these two realms. Are there ways that we could think about creating such forms?

McIntosh: Power is there all the time in all situations. It's there in the family, too, yet within that political setting we try to recognize that everyone has her or his needs, and try to find the ways to meet them. At least we project this as a valid way to be within the family. Is this, then, perhaps a "transitional form?"

When I talk about the aim being the "decent survival of us all," that means granting recognition to everyone's needs in all of life, including public life. If you make that your stated aim, then you work toward that and you cannot simply work toward a win-lose, one up-one down way of being. You become "transitional," again.

We are just not yet attuned to bringing this value system into all of the situations in the world, in public life; to say, for example, that the secretaries really keep everything going at times. If their work were recognized as equally important or sometimes more important than what the "top" people do, our forms in public life would be very different.

Yes, I think we should work on devising more transitional forms which may help us to move this comprehensive sense of meeting everyone's needs into more parts of our life in the world.

Comment: I think it's dangerous to talk this way about the "bottom" or lateral parts of life. It's important not to romanticize this. It really represents what oppression has done to us, to women and other people who have been made disadvantaged.

McIntosh: I agree it is dangerous to romanticize. But I don't see these lateral parts of life only as those phenomena produced by oppression. I'm describing *functions*—the differing kinds of sustaining fuctions that are needed in all societies but also within everyone's life and personality; I'm saying that we would all be better off if we recognized the crucial validity of these functions of making and mending the personal and social fabric. They do not result simply from our being victimized.

The oppression—and the misunderstanding—come when these parts are devalued and then projected on to women and lower caste people *only.*

It's important for all of us, female and male, to fulfill ourselves in the lateral parts of our personalities.

Comment: I think it's important, too, to point to the illusions of those who operate at the top or only in the vertical mode. It's really clear if you look at a great many of the people who are at the top in institutions that are said to be leading institutions, that they are flawed in many ways.

The people who are most fraudulent may be those who would never be able to consider really asking themselves if they are fraudulent, as you said.

McIntosh: Yes, and you remind me, too, of Elizabeth Dodson Gray's book, *Patriarchy as a Conceptual Trap,* which is very valuable in helping us see that whole point.

Comment: When you were talking, I was thinking that you were talking a great deal about students. I think there is an important age factor. I have been talking to older women, really old, in their eighties or seventies. In the whole way that they talk they do not seem to feel like frauds. They seem to have come to a certain resolution.

McIntosh: That is very encouraging to hear. Perhaps they have seen what really counts for themselves and for others, and what doesn't, and they have gained the courage to state it more openly, and live in a less divided way.

REFERENCES

Dodson Gray, E. (1982). *Patriarchy as a conceptual trap.* Wellesley, MA: Roundtable Press.

Miller, J. B. (1984). The development of women's sense of self. *Work in Progress, No. 12.* Wellesley, MA: Stone Center Working Papers Series.

Stiver, I. (1982). Work inhibitions in women. *Work in Progress, No. 3.* Wellesley, MA: Stone Center Working Papers Series.

Surrey, J. (1984). The "self-in-relation": A theory of women's development. *Work in Progress, No. 13.* Wellesley, MA: Stone Center Working Papers Series.

Chapter Forty

Rethinking Psychological Theory to Encompass Issues of Gender and Ethnicity
Focus on Achievement

Amy J. Dabul and Nancy Felipe Russo

What accounts for differences in achievement among people? Why do some people persist in their efforts to achieve despite great odds, whereas others retreat at the sign of difficulty? Why does a person persevere in some situations but not in others? Questions such as these have long intrigued psychologists. But for decades, researchers predominately defined and examined achievement issues in terms of men and boys (e.g., McClelland, 1961). Fortunately, the second wave of the women's movement in the 1970s proved to be an important catalyst for the development of new scholarship on women's careers and achievement (Betz, 1993; Green and Russo, 1993; Mednick and Thomas, 1993; Nieva and Gutek, 1981).

Also during this period, researchers with an interest in achievement theory began to explore attributional processes in earnest. Causal attributions are the explanations that people give for the causes of behavior—behavior of others and of themselves—in order to make sense out of their worlds. Attributions have been found to influence everyday decisionmaking, with far-reaching consequences for success, well-being, and life satisfaction in a variety of personal, educational, and professional domains (Forgas, Bower, and Moylan, 1990; Fry and Ghosh, 1980; Weiner, 1985). Thus, attribution theory has potential for helping us understand how the meanings that we give to our behaviors can affect the strength of our motivation for and satisfaction with our achievements.

However, we contend that attribution theory has not realized its potential for illuminating why some, but not all, people are motivated to persist in the face of obstacles. The reason for this failure is that attribution theory, like most research on achievement motivation, does not sufficiently incorporate the role of context and culture in its analyses. Yet the same behavior might have different meanings in different contexts and for people of different cultures. Specifically, we believe that

Amy J. Dabul and Nancy Felipe Russo, "Rethinking Psychological Theory to Encompass Issues of Gender and Ethnicity: Focus on Achievement." In Karen Fraser Wyche and F. J. Crosby (Eds.), *Women's Ethnicities: Journeys through Psychology*, pp. 183–199. © 1996 by Westview Press. Reprinted by permission of Westview Press.

ttribution theory, like most American psychology, has viewed the world through a ens of individualism.

This chapter falls into four parts. We first selectively review earlier research on ıchievement attributions. Next, we turn to cross-cultural issues, identifying work on cultural constructions of the self that raises questions for attribution theory and research. We then elaborate a new model of achievement and specifically of achievement attributions. Our model, based on the first author's (AJD's) conceptualizations developed under the guidance of the second author (NFR), moves away from individualistic assumptions and reflects a multilevel approach to the issue of achievement. We conclude by reflecting on how our own experiences and backgrounds enter into our understandings of achievement and of achievement accounts among individuals of diverse cultural identities and in varying contexts.

Attribution and Achievement

Traditional attribution research has suggested that achievement attributions are related to affect as well as performance. That is, attributions to internal causes (ability and effort) are considered to increase feelings of pride in success, whereas attributions to external causes are not (McFarland and Ross, 1982; Weiner, Russell, and Lerman, 1978). In essence, the assumption has been that particular attributions will lead to particular affective evaluations, with some attribution patterns considered more "adaptive" than others (the most adaptive patterns being those most often used by individualistic males). Thus, attributing internal causes to success and external causes to failure (called a self-serving bias) is considered to produce the most ego-enhancing and favorable affective and performance outcomes. The reverse pattern, attributing external causes to success and internal causes to failure (called the self-derogating bias), is considered to lead to unfavorable affect and future performance.

One problem with the traditional approach is that it does not produce consistent results for women and men and across cultures. For more than a decade, scholars have noted inconsistent relationships between achievement attributions and behavior across gender (e.g., Frieze, Whitley, Hanusa, and McHugh, 1982; Mednick and Thomas, 1993; Travis, Phillippi, and Henley, 1991). For example, women often demonstrate self-derogating attributions while still maintaining levels of objective achievement comparable to that of men (Erkut, 1983; Gitelson, Petersen, and Tobin-Richards, 1982). Originally, explanations of gender inconsistencies focused on factors related to research designs and settings. Deaux's early work is typical in this regard. For example, Deaux and Emswiller (1974) hypothesized that observers would attribute the success of a target who completed a gender-consistent task to skill, but the success of a target who completed an opposite-gender task to luck. However, they found that regardless of whether the task was masculine or feminine, in general, successful men were more likely to be perceived as skillful, and successful women were more likely to be perceived as lucky.

Recent examinations of gender, attributions, and achievements have focused less on methodological artifacts and more on "real-world" contextual factors. Consider a study conducted by Russo, Kelly, and Deacon (1991) of 200 males and 42 females in senior positions in public administration. Contrary to simplistic conventional wis dom, these researchers did not find that men made internal and stable attribution for their successes while women assigned their successes to good luck or hard work Rather, Russo and colleagues found that both women and men in the sample generally explained their achievements in terms of a combination of hard work and ability—a combination the researchers labeled the Alger factor after Horatio Alger. Both women and men, furthermore, attributed some of the successes of their col leagues to the Alger factor. But they also clearly perceived the importance of profes sional contacts. In fact, the women believed that professional contacts explained more about the variations in success of their male colleagues than did ability and hard work. Acknowledging the issue of context brings us to a fascinating and disturbing observation. Achievement attributions have typically been studied in situations where individuals compete against each other. Perhaps without intending it, and certainly without identifying it as such, researchers have tended to reproduce in their laboratories the individualism that is so much a part of the larger society.

What happens if one adopts a more complex, multilevel perspective, one that incorporates an interpersonal lens in the analysis? When intergroup contexts have been studied, group-related attributions become critical in explaining individual performance. For example, Chambers and Abrami (1991) reported that team out comes in a cooperative learning setting influenced subsequent individual achieve ment. Group attributions were as important to future success as attributions to individual behavior. Similarly, Croxton and Klonsky (1982) found that team attribu tions were used just as often to explain individual success as were self-attributions. These findings suggest that expanding the definition of achievement settings beyond the traditional individualistic competitive model may provide greater understanding of the achievement attribution process.

Research has also shown that the highly individualistic and often competitive values traditionally endorsed in U.S. culture do not necessarily lead to the most favorable achievement outcomes. Indeed, as Spence (1985) has noted, the extreme individualism of the West may ultimately prove destructive at both local and global levels. Viewing the self as totally distinct from others is neither universal nor univer sally considered good.

Looking across Cultures

Although there may be many aspects of the self that differ across individuals and cultures, a value orientation that reflects the level of collectivism or individualism present in a culture has particular implications for understanding achievement. Whether a culture operates with collectivistic or individualistic values has to do with the degree to which the self is viewed as connected with others or as disengaged from others. This value orientation is thought to be important at both the group level (comparing cultures with one another) as well as at the individual level (comparing individuals within cultures with one another). At the group level, this distinction is referred to as individualism-collectivism (Hofstede, 1980; Triandis et al., 1986, 1988), although the cultural labels of cooperation-competition (Mead, 1934, 1967) and collaterality-individualism (Kluckhohn and Strodtbeck, 1961) have also been used. At the individual level, the terms independent and interdependent are often used (Markus and Kitayama, 1991). Allocentrism-idiocentrism, individual-relational, and personal-collective are other labels that have also been used to refer to similar psychological constructs at the individual level. Here we will refer to individualism-collectivism when referring to the group or cultural level and independent-interdependent when referring to the individual level.

The distribution of cultures into collectivistic and individualistic categories has to do with the emergence of certain themes that occur consistently within a culture. These themes have been studied and measured by a variety of researchers (Hofstede, 1980; Hui and Triandis, 1986; Triandis, Leung, Villareal, and Clack, 1985). A few of the important distinctions are the way behavior is regulated within a culture, the level of connectedness between individuals, the way that individuals are taught to perceive and define themselves, and the goals or tasks that individuals in that culture are expected to reach. In individualistic cultures, the individual tends to be the unit of analysis. In other words, behavior is regulated primarily by the individual, and personal goals take precedence and are largely unrelated to group goals. The major task in individualistic cultures is to reinforce internal attributes of the self (Kitayama, Markus, and Kurokawa, 1994; Markus and Kitayama, 1991). Individuals strive toward independence and uniqueness, seeing themselves as separate entities from the group (Dumont, 1965; Lukes, 1973). Western cultures, primarily North American and European cultures, are usually considered to be individualistic (Singelis, 1994; Triandis, 1983; Triandis et al., 1988).

Alternatively, in collectivistic cultures, the group is the primary unit of analysis. The individual is guided by group goals and cooperation is the desired pattern of social behavior. Fitting in with the group and preserving group harmony while downplaying internal attributes is the primary cultural task. Individuals perceive themselves as appendages of the in-group and changes to the self are thought to occur primarily through interpersonal relationships. Collectivistic tendencies have been found in Asian (Bond, 1988; Kondo, 1990; Lebra, 1993; Triandis, 1983), Hispanic (Marin and Triandis, 1985; Triandis, 1983), and African (Boski, 1983) cultures. It is important to note that individualism and collectivism have been represented as a continuum, such that some cultures can be identified as highly individualistic or collectivistic and others can be identified as falling somewhere in between. For example, Boski (1983) examined three different tribal divisions in Ethiopia and found that these groups varied greatly in levels of collectivism and individualism even though they were relatively close in geographic proximity.

Diversity is found within as well as across cultural groups. An independent construal of the self is characterized by an emphasis on personal freedom, expression, and independence (Johnson, 1985; Markus and Kitayama, 1991; Miller, 1988). The individual defines himself or herself as separate from the social context and works to reaffirm internal attributes. In contrast, those with a more interdependent view of the self emphasize the importance of social relationships and the maintenance of

TABLE 40.1
Summary of Key Differences betwen an Independent and an Interdependent Construal of Self

Feature compared	Independent	Interdependent
Definition	Separate from social context	Connected with social context
Structure	Bounded, unitary, stable	Flexible, variable
Important features	Internal, private (abilities, thoughts, feelings)	External, public (statuses, roles, relationships)
Tasks	Be unique	Belong, fit in
	Express self	Occupy one's proper place
	Realize internal attributes	Engage in appropriate action
	Promote own goals	Promote other's goals
	Be direct: "Say what's on your mind"	Be indirect: "Read other's mind"
Role of others	Self-evaluation: others important for social comparison, reflected appraisal	Self-definition: relationships with others in specific contexts define the self
Basis of self-esteem [a]	Ability to express self, validate internal attributes	Ability to adjust, restrain self, maintain harmony with social context

[a] Esteeming the self may be primarily a Western phenomenon, and the concept of self-esteem should perhaps be replaced by self-satisfaction or a term that reflects the realization that one is fulfilling the culturaly mandated task.
SOURCE: Markus and Kitayama (1991), p. 30. Used by permission.

interdependence and group harmony (DeVos, 1985; Miller, 1988). A summary of the key differences between these construals of the self at the individual level, as characterized by Markus and Kitayama (1991), is presented in Table 40.1.

Attaining success, in the sense of achieving the primary tasks emphasized in a culture, is different in different cultures. By definition, in individualistic cultures, being unique and standing out is important for positive cultural evaluation (unless you are female, where a norm of modesty may prevail). In collectivistic cultures, maintaining group harmony and fitting in are viewed as the primary cultural tasks that lead to favorable evaluations of the self. Given these differences, value orientations at both the individual and cultural levels would be expected to affect definitions of achievement, attributions for achievement, and affective responses to attributions.

Cross-Cultural Studies of Attributions and Achievements

For more than two decades, researchers have reported linkages between interpersonal factors and achievement that differ across ethnic groups. For example, Hawaiians (Gallimore, 1974; Gallimore, Weiss, and Finney, 1974) and Japanese (DeVos, 1985) have been found to associate achievement more with affiliation than competitive, individualistic goals. Mexican Americans and African Americans score higher on needs for family achievement and lower on needs for academic achievement than do their Anglo counterparts (Ramirez and Price-Williams, 1976). We know from early research that individuals from collectivistic cultures are more likely to use context-bound or relational attributions than individuals from individualistic cultures (Miller, 1984; Schweder and Bourne, 1982). But do self-derogating attributions undermine achievement of individuals in collectivistic cultures? We suggest not. For

example, following success, Japanese individuals show an attributional pattern opposite to the traditional individualistic prediction but have no decrement in achievement motivation and behavior (Kashima and Triandis, 1986). In another study, Black
individuals who demonstrated a more "self-defeating" attributional pattern than
White individuals actually expected to perform better in the future, showing greater
persistence and expectations for future success (Whitehead and Smith, 1990). Clearly,
models that consider the interaction between the internal self-structure and aspects
of the external social structure are needed if understanding of the attribution process
across gender, ethnicity, and culture is to be obtained.

Developing a New Model

Researchers have also expressed concern with the failure of psychological theories to
recognize the individual as existing within a network of social groups (e.g., Miller
and Prentice, 1994; Sherif, 1979; Spence, 1985; Zaccaro, Peterson, and Walker, 1987).
The level of analysis in achievement contexts may be an important factor for several
reasons. First, achievement goals and motivations may differ from context to context.
For example, an athlete who competes in an individual sport, such as golf, where
performance outcomes are independent of others, may adopt different motivational,
attributional, and affective strategies than an athlete who is a member of a basketball
team and whose performance outcome is dependent on the performance of others.
Second, because of the differential role of the group in collectivistic and individualistic cultures, this factor may interact with the value orientation of the self discussed
previously. Taken in combination, these two factors highlight the importance of the
role of both the individual as well as the social context in the explanation of social
behavior.

Work on achievement attribution has direct, practical application. Findings in the
attributional literature have been used to develop interventions designed to train
individuals to discard maladaptive causal perceptions and adopt self-enhancing attribution patterns. "Reattribution" training programs have involved token reinforcement or self-instructional cognitive interventions (e.g., Henker, Whalen, and Hinshaw, 1980; Renshaw, 1990). These programs rest on the assumption that modesty
interferes with the motivation to succeed. However, for individuals who hold interdependent self-construals, the values associated with modesty may be the values that
provide the motivation for future performance. Training individuals from collectivistic cultures to engage in self-enhancing attributions may undermine their achievement by disengaging achievement values from those associated with social support.
In addition, reattribution training programs may unintentionally contribute to value
conflicts in interdependent individuals who must struggle between a construal of the
self that promotes self-effacement and the imposed self-enhancing attributional style.
This discomfort may also lead to decrements in motivation. The development of
different attribution training programs for independent and interdependent individuals may be a way of validating both attribution patterns, by retaining the values that
may lead to future persistence and task performance.

In AJD's comprehensive examination, chaired by NFR, she set about to develop model that would indeed include both individualistic and interpersonal dimension of achievement (Dabul, 1994). She developed an alternative, multilevel framewor for understanding achievement attribution behavior that recognizes roles for the se and the social context in the attribution process (see Table 40.2). The extent to whic an individual has an independent or interdependent self-construal is crossed witl three levels of analysis—personal, interpersonal, and intergroup—creating a theo retical matrix. Within each cell of the matrix, a variety of predictions may be mad regarding motivational, attributional, and affective components. For example, ar independent individual in an intergroup context may show a tendency to be moti vated by the desire for personal enhancement, may make group-serving attributions, and may experience self-focused emotional responses. These predictions are specific to this cell in the matrix. Using her model, she can make affective, cognitive, and attributional predictions across cells that can be empirically tested. Areas of attribu tion research that have received heavier attention as well as those areas that remain underdeveloped both theoretically and empirically become illuminated when viewed through the lens of this framework. We have developed several research projects, including AJD's dissertation, to explore how aspects of her model might help us to understand both self-and social attributions. We believe that the ways that we understand and interpret the causes of (i.e., give meaning to) our behavior and that of others is a primary guiding element in how we construct and interact with our culture. In addition to work examining the self-attributions of individuals across gender and ethnicity, we are also interested in looking at how individuals who may not fit the individualistic cultural mold are perceived by our larger society. We emphasize the importance of recognizing that our gender and ethnicity serve as stimulus variables, and perceptions by others can ultimately determine our achieve ment opportunities and experiences through complex avenues.

One of our current projects that seeks to explore those avenues focuses on the costs and benefits associated with holding collectivistic values in the workplace. Are individuals who are perceived as having collectivistic values at a disadvantage? If so, how is that disadvantage manifested?

For our study we created a series of vignettes describing a company employee who had been identified as the most productive employee during a three-month period. Background information for the employee varied. In some cases, the employee was described as having independent values (e.g., stressing the importance of individual goals, workplace competition, and self-promotion); in some cases the employee was described as having interdependent values (e.g., stressing the importance of group goals, cooperation, and modest responses to achievement). In addition, sometimes the employee was described as male, sometimes female, and sometimes the gender was not specified. We then asked 160 male and 160 female Anglo college student participants to place themselves in the role of a company executive and assess the likelihood of assigning various workplace tasks and rewards to the successful em ployee. These tasks and rewards ranged from increasing social contacts with the employee to recommending the employee for advancement opportunities.

We found that the type of activities and rewards assigned were influenced by the perceived value orientation of the target employee. The good news was that independent and interdependent individuals were equally likely to be assigned workplace rewards leading to individual job advancement (e.g., they received support for a promotion, were given increased work responsibilities). The bad news was that interdependent employees were also significantly more likely to be assigned socioemotional leadership tasks for the group that do not lead toward job advancement (e.g., organizing the company picnic, mediating disputes between other employees). This interaction is presented in Figure 40.1.

We suspect that the differential assignment of socioemotional tasks to employees perceived as having collectivistic values is a contributor to the "glass ceiling effect," given the individualistic norms of the typical workplace. In other words, if collectivistic individuals become engaged in time-consuming interpersonal tasks that are not important in the workplace, they have less time to spend on the tasks that are necessary for upward advancement in that context. Although this data set has not been fully analyzed and our ultimate aim is to obtain data from actual managers, this one finding provides a compelling demonstration of the complexity of the path between the perceptions of others and one's path to success in traditional contexts. These data suggest that although it may appear that even if both people with independent and interdependent values are equally valued as people and similarly rewarded for their workplace performances, the additional tasks that interdependent individuals—whether they be men or women—may be expected to perform in the workplace could undermine their chances for job advancement.

We selected this specific finding to give a concrete example of what is coming out of our broader perspective because it demonstrates the interrelationship between our intellectual work and our daily experience. We are high achievers who hold collectivistic values. As such, we are more sensitive to the fact that women are asked to do time-consuming socioemotional tasks that are not "counted" in the academic context and then they are "punished" for not publishing enough. For example, we have seen several instances of young assistant professors (women and minorities) being asked to be on committees or to become involved in university activities who were then negatively evaluated for not publishing as much as those who focused on developing their personal research programs. We marvel at the attribution that such individuals "can't get it together to do research" so they focus on service. We believe that such events occur in diverse circumstances and for diverse individuals who hold interdependent values that have diverse origins, including gender and ethnicity. We are interested in exploring the exquisite double bind for individuals with interdependent values who are asked to do socioemotional tasks that take away time from "real work" of publishing and who will be punished no matter how they respond. At the personal level, we believe that the knowledge that we gain from our work will ultimately make us better teachers and mentors (in the service of our interdependent values). At the political level, we believe that knowledge about the interpersonal dimensions of achievements will enable us to redesign educational and occupational settings to enable individuals of diverse value orientations and skills to achieve success.

TABLE 40.2

A Dimensional Framework of Achievement Attributions Based on the Social Context and Personal Value Orientation

	Level of Analysis		
	Personal	Interpersonal	Intergroup
Independent/individualistic value structure			
Motivation/goal structure	Accuracy/improvement Mastery Personal enhancement	Self-enhancement Superiority over others Success versus failure Strongest motivational context for independent individuals	Competition between groups Success versus failure Self-enhancement via group membership
Attributions	Self-serving attributional bias	Self-serving attributional bias	Group-serving attributional bias
Affective responses			
Success	Pride-competence	Pride, competence	Pride, competence
Failure	Frustration, anger	Frustration, anger	Frustration, anger
Interdependent collectivistic value structures			
Motivation/goal structure	Social obligations of duty	Group goals become individual goals Maintenance of social relationships	Acceptance versus rejection Cooperation, group harmony Strongest motivational context for interdependent individuals
Attributions	Self-effacing attributional bias	Self-effacing attributional bias	Group-effacing attributional bias
Affective Responses			
Success	Gratitude, thankfulness	Gratitude, thankfulness	Gratitude, thankfulness
Failure	Shame/guilt-related constructs	Shame/guilt-related constructs	Shame/guilt-related constructs

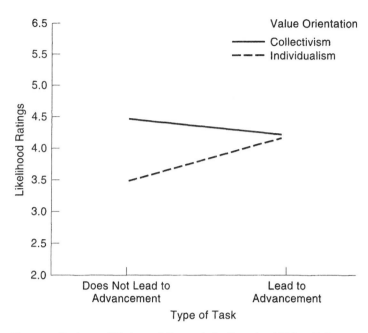

Fig. 40.1. Ratings of Tasks and Rewards by Perceived Value Orientation of Target Employees.

Making Research Part of Our Lives

The opportunities for scholarship and advocacy around women's achievement created by the second wave of the women's movement in 1970 laid the groundwork for the development of interests that have led to our collaboration. Nancy Felipe Russo (NFR) "grew up" professionally during that period, devoting a substantial portion of her career to conducting research and developing action programs to understand issues related to women, achievement, and work and to promote women's advancement (Russo, 1994, and Russo and Cassidy, 1983, present information about some of these activities). These experiences led her to have an intense interest in the relationship of gender and ethnicity to achievement and how the meanings of our achievement-related experiences may differ depending on other gender-and ethnic-related values that we may hold (Russo, Kelly, and Deacon, 1991). The work reported in this chapter reflects the convergence of those interests with those of Amy Dabul around ethnic identity, gender, and achievement.

Amy J. Dabul (AJD) attributes her interest in studying the psychology of ethnicity and gender to her childhood experiences as a biracial female. The feelings of marginality and exclusion associated with simultaneous membership in multiple social categories has led to an ongoing interest in understanding the links between gender and ethnicity and the ways in which dual minority status may influence achievement. Much of her earlier graduate work focused on the perceptions of ethnic individuals with multiple social identities (Saenz and Dabul, 1994; Saenz, Dabul, and Nassar, 1995). More recently, however, her work has evolved to reflect a growing interest in the creation of psychological models that consider both gender-related and cultural aspects of achievement. As she prepares to leave graduate school and begin her academic career she feels fortunate to be "growing up" professionally during a time in which the importance of this kind of work is beginning to be recognized and supported.

We believe that our gender and ethnicity have affected the research topics that interest us, the questions we ask, and the way that we test those questions in multiple and complex ways. The knowledge that we seek reflects our scientific, social, and personal agendas and is intended to serve multiple purposes. In the interest of contributing to science, this research enables us to think more complexly about gender and ethnicity in achievement domains. It does more than fill a gap in the existing literature on how meanings of achievement behavior are influenced by gender and ethnicity: It charts a course for future research needed to attain a multilevel understanding of the relationship of achievement attributions that encompasses diverse cultural values and contexts. In keeping with our social agenda, this research seeks to promote the achievement of women and ethnic minorities by increasing understanding of the links between achievement attribution patterns and achievement behavior in diverse ethnic groups. We believe that current attribution training programs may hinder the achievement progress of women and ethnic minorities and undermine their own purpose by contributing to inequities in achievement outcomes. Thus, promoting understanding of achievement attributions in such populations may be critical for reducing biases in intervention programs. Finally, at a personal level, we hope that learning about how diverse populations respond in achievement settings will increase our effectiveness as mentors and teachers. We recognize that we play an active role in constructing the social context in our classrooms and in our individual relationships with students, and we have made a personal commitment to promote an atmosphere that is conductive to success for all students.

This work is not without its costs, however. Because much of our work is driven by the questions we believe are most important to address with respect to the real-world experience of women and ethnic minorities, these are not always the questions that are the quickest and easiest to study. Obtaining research participants with diverse backgrounds is often difficult. For example, even when academic achievement is the type of achievement of interest and student attributions are relevant, it may be difficult to recruit sufficient numbers of ethnic research participants. Further, when studying achievement behavior, college samples are not likely to produce a sufficient range of differing achievement levels and attributional styles. For example, ethnic minorities attending college are likely to have cultivated achievement strategies that are necessary for success in individualistic academic contexts and may not be similar to their noncollege cohorts. When access to real-world samples is obtained, as in the Russo, Kelly, and Deacon (1991) study, the use of randomized experimental designs may not be feasible without destroying the phenomenon that one is studying. This can make publication of results in traditional journals—the ones needed for tenure—more difficult.

Despite the difficulties associated with this research, the knowledge that we hope to gain and put to practical use far outweighs the potential costs, and it is one of the reasons that our working relationship has been and continues to be productive. We both share a desire to promote the study of the psychology of women and ethnic populations by understanding the way in which the social context shapes our experience. By our engaging in this research, the underlying message is that the psychological experiences of individuals that stem from their experience as a social being and member of multiple, crosscutting groups are important, valuable, and central to psychological theory.

These values have become part of the mentoring process, contributing to AJD's experience of graduate training as both validating and empowering. The incorporation of interdependent values, and a movement away from traditional mentoring styles that emphasize inequitable power structures, have not only led to an interpersonally enjoyable relationship for us but have contributed to our high level of productivity as a research team. Our experiences provide a living example of how interdependent values may contribute to the overall effectiveness and productivity of workplace activities.

At the same time that we recognize and value the interdependence that we see as a basic human need found in all people, we do not aim to homogenize the members of all social groups. We also recognize and value the fact that each person is an individual, with a unique perspective. As psychologists, we see our task as constructing new models that will help us understand the ways that multiple factors interact and result in both commonality and diversity in perspectives across time, place, and person. This too is reflected in our working relationship. Although we value our collaboration, we also value diversity of perspective and independence of thought—which makes for stimulating discussions and two-way learning. Arizona State University is fortunate in having some of the top people in their fields, and AJD has been encouraged to work with a variety of faculty members and to learn all the skills needed to conduct an independent research program. This independence, in turn, has enhanced the productivity of our collaboration. For example, her learning about multivariate analyses and new methods of multiple regression that were developed after NFR left graduate school has been particularly helpful and has enabled NFR to acquire knowledge of new statistical techniques rapidly and painlessly.

By the time you read this, our official adviser-student relationship will have ended, but our ability to learn from each other and continue to collaborate will not. We plan to continue research—individually and collectively—aimed at extending attribution theory and research to include the interpersonal side of achievement. More important, we hope to generate knowledge that can be used to construct contexts at school, at work, and in the community that support achievement of individuals in all their diversity.

REFERENCES

Betz, N. (1993). Women's career development. In F. L. Denmark and M. A. Paludi (Eds.), *Psychology of women: A handbook of issues and theories* (pp. 627–684). Westport, CT: Greenwood Press.

Bond, M. H. (1988). Finding universal dimensions of individual variation in multicultural studies of values: The Rokeach and Chinese value surveys. *Journal of Personality and Social Psychology, 55,* 1009–1015.

Boski. P. (1983). A study of person perception in Nigeria: Ethnicity and self versus other attributions for achievement-related outcomes. *Journal of Cross-Cultural Psychology, 14,* 85–108.

Chambers, B., and Abrami, P. C. (1991). The relationship between student team learning outcomes and achievement, causal attributions, and affect. *Journal of Educational Psychology, 83,* 140–146.

Croxton, J. S., and Klonsky, B. G. (1982). Sex differences in causal attributions for success and failure in real and hypothetical sport settings. *Sex Roles, 8,* 399–409.

Dabul, A. J. (1994). The influence of independent and interdependent self-orientations on achievement attribution: A framework for understanding attribution processes across gender and cultural lines. Unpublished manuscript.

Deaux, K., and Emswiller, T. (1974). Explanations of successful performance on sex-linked tasks: What is skill for the male is luck for the female. *Journal of Personality and Social Psychology, 29,* 80–85.

DeVos, G. A. (1985). Dimensions of the self in Japanese culture. In A. Marsella, G. DeVos, and F. L. K. Hsu (Eds.), *Culture and self* (pp. 149–184). London, England: Tavistock.

Dumont, L. (1965). The modern conception of the individual: Notes on its genesis. *Contributions to Indian Sociology, 8,* 13–61.

Erkut, S. (1983). Exploring sex differences in expectancy, attribution, and academic achievement. *Sex Roles, 9,* 217–231.

Forgas, J. P., Bower, C. H., and Moylan, S. J. (1990). Praise or blame? Affective influences on attributions for achievement. *Journal of Personality and Social Psychology, 59,* 809–819.

Frieze, I. H., Whitley, B. E., Jr., Hanusa, B. H., and McHugh, M. (1982). Assessing the theoretical models for sex differences in causal attributions for success and failure. *Sex Roles, 8*(4), 333–343.

Fry, P. S., and Ghosh, R. (1980). Attributions of success and failure: Comparison of cultural differences between Asian and Caucasian children. *Journal of Cross-Cultural Psychology, 11,* 343–363.

Gallimore, R. (1974). Affiliation motivation and Hawaiian-American achievement. *Journal of Cross-Cultural Psychology, 5,* 481–491.

Gallimore, R., Weiss, L. B., and Finney, R. (1974). Cultural differences in delay of gratification: A problem of behavioral classification. *Journal of Personality and Social Psychology, 30,* 72–80.

Gitelson, I. B., Petersen, A. C., and Tobin-Richards, M. H. (1982). Adolescents' expectancies of success, self-evaluations, and attributions about performance on spatial and verbal tasks. *Sex Roles, 8,* 411–419.

Green, B. L., and Russo, N. F. (1993). Work and family roles: Selected issues. In F. L. Denmark and M. A. Paludi (Eds.), *Psychology of women: A handbook of issues and theories* (pp. 685–720). Westport, CT: Greenwood Press.

Henker, B., Whalen, C. K., and Hinshaw, S. P. (1980). The attributional contexts of cognitive intervention strategies. *Exceptional Educational Quarterly, 1,* 177–193.

Hofstede, G. (1980). *Cultures' consequences: International differences in work-related values.* Beverly Hills, CA: Sage.

Hui, C. H., and Triandis, H. C. (1986). Individualism-collectivism: A study of cross-cultural researchers. *Journal of Cross-Cultural Psychology, 17,* 225–248.

ohnson, F. (1985). The western concept of self. In A. Marsella, G. DeVos, and F. L. K. Hsu (Eds.), *Culture and Self*. London, England: Tavistock.

Kashima, Y., and Triandis, H. C. (1986). The self-serving bias in attributions as a coping strategy: A cross-cultural study. *Journal of Cross-Cultural Psychology, 17*, 83–97.

Kitayama, S., Markus, H. R., and Kurokawa, M. (1994). Cultural views of self and emotional experience: Does the nature of good feelings depend on culture? Unpublished manuscript.

Kluckhohn, F. S., and Strodtbeck, F. L. (1961). *Variations in value orientations*. Evanston, IL: Row, Peterson.

Kondo, T. (1990). Some notes on rational behavior, normative behavior, moral behavior, and cooperation. *Journal of Conflict Resolution, 34*, 495–530.

Lebra, T. S. (1993). *Above the clouds: Status culture of the modern Japanese nobility*. Berkeley, CA: University of California Press.

Lukes, S. (1973). *Individualism*. Oxford, England: Basil Blackwell.

Marin, G., and Triandis, H. C. (1985). Allocentrism as an important characteristic of the behavior of Latin Americans and Hispanics. In R. Diaz-Guerrero (Ed.), *Cross-cultural and national studies in social psychology* (pp. 85–104). Amsterdam, Netherlands: North-Holland.

Markus, H. R., and Kitayama, S. (1991). Culture and the self: Implications for cognition, emotion and motivation. *Psychological Review, 98*, 224–253.

McClelland, D. C. (1961). *The achieving society*. New York, NY: Free Press.

McFarland, C., and Ross, M. (1982). Impact of causal attributions on affective reactions to success and failure. *Journal of Personality and Social Psychology, 43*, 937–946.

Mead, G. H. (1934). *Mind, self, and society*. Chicago, IL: University of Chicago Press.

Mead, M. (1967). *Cooperation and competition among primitive people*. Boston, MA: Beacon.

Mednick, M. T., and Thomas, V. G. (1993). Women and the psychology of achievement: A view from the eighties. In F. L. Denmark and M. A. Paludi (Eds.), *Psychology of women: A handbook of issues and theories* (pp. 585–626). Westport, CT: Greenwood Press.

Miller, D. T., and Prentice, D. A. (1994). The self and the collective. *Personality and Social Psychology Bulletin, 20*, 451–453.

Miller, J. (1984). Culture and the development of everyday social explanation. *Journal of Personality and Social Psychology, 46*, 961–978.

Miller, J. (1988). Bridging the content-structure dichotomy: Culture and the self. In M. Bond (Ed.), *The cross-cultural challenge to social psychology*. Newbury Park, CA: Sage Publications.

Nieva, V., and Gutek, B. (1981). *Women and work: A psychological perspective*. New York, NY: Praeger.

Ramirez, M., and Price-Williams, D. R. (1976). Achievement motivation in children of three ethnic groups in the United States. *Journal of Cross-Cultural Psychology, 7*, 49–60.

Renshaw, P. (1990). Self-esteem research and equity programs for girls: A reassessment. In J. Kenway and S. Willis (Eds.), *Hearts and minds: Self-esteem and the schooling of girls*. London, England: Falmer Press.

Russo, N. F. (1994). The evaluation of a feminist psychologist, advocate, and scholar. In P. Kellar (Ed.), *Academic careers: Career decisions and experiences of psychologists* (pp. 105–119). New York, NY: Lawrence Erlbaum.

Russo, N. F., and Cassidy, M. (1983). Women in science and technology. In I. Tinker (Ed.), *Women in Washington: Advocates for public policy*. Sage Yearbooks in Women's Policy Studies, 7, 250–262.

Russo, N. F., Kelly, R. M., and Deacon, M. (1991). Gender and success-related attributions: Beyond individualistic conceptions of achievement. *Sex Roles, 25*, 331–350.

Saenz, D. S., and Dabul, A. J. (1994). The effects of physical attractiveness on attribution and social categoricalization: Across-race comparison. Manuscript submitted for publication.

Saenz, D. S., Dabul, A. J., and Nassar, R. (1995). Perceptions of biracial targets as a function of their self-labels: Similarity can be costly. Manuscript submitted for publication.

Schweder, R. A., and Bourne, E. J. (1982). Does the concept of person vary cross-culturally? In A. J. Marsella and G. M. White (Eds.), *Cultural conceptions of mental health and therapy* (pp. 257–291). Dordrech, Holland: D. Riedel.

Sherif, C. W. (1979). Bias in psychology. In J. A. Sherman and E. T. Beck (Eds.), *The prism of sex: Essays in the sociology of knowledge.* Madison, WI: University of Wisconsin Press.

Singelis, T. M. (1994). The measurement of independent and interdependent self-construals. *Personality and Social Psychology Bulletin, 20,* 580–591.

Spence, J. (1985). Achievement American style. *American Psychologist, 12,* 1285–1295.

Travis, C., Phillippi, R. H., and Henley, T. B. (1991). Gender and causal attributions for mastery, personal, and interpersonal events. *Psychology of Women Quarterly, 15,* 233–249.

Triandis, H. C. (1983). *Allocentric vs. idiocentric social behavior: A major cultural difference between Hispanic and Mainstream* (Tech. rep. No. ONR-16). Champaign, IL: University of Illinois, Department of Psychology.

Triandis, H. C., Bontempo, R., Betancourt, H., Bond, M., Leung, K., Brenes, A., Georgas, J., Hui, C. H., Marin, G., Setiadi, B., Sinha, J. B. P., Verma, J., Spangenberg, J., Touzard, H., and de Montmollin, G. (1986). The measurement of etic aspects of individualism and collectivism across cultures. *Australian Journal of Psychology, 38,* 257–267.

Triandis, H. C., Bontempo, R., Villareal, M. J., Asai, M., and Lucca, N. (1988). Individualism and collectivism: Cross-cultural perspectives on self-ingroup relationships. *Journal of Personality and Social Psychology, 54,* 323–338.

Triandis, H. C., Leung, K., Villareal, M. J., and Clack, F. L. (1985). Allocentric versus idiocentric tendencies: Convergent and discriminant validation. *Journal of Research in Personality, 19,* 395–415.

Weiner, B. (1985). An attributional theory of achievement motivation and emotion. *Psychological Review, 92,* 548–573.

Weiner, B., Russell, D., and Lerman, D. (1978). Affective consequences of causal ascriptions. In J. H. Harvey, W. J. Ickes, and R. F. Kidd (Eds.), *New directions in attribution research, Vol. 2.* Hillsdale, NJ: Erlbaum.

Whitehead, G. I., and Smith, S. H. (1990). Causal attributions of blacks and whites. *Journal of Social Psychology, 130,* 401–402.

Zaccaro, S. J., Peterson, C., and Walker, S. (1987). Self-serving attributions for individual and group performance. *Social Psychology Quarterly, 50,* 257–263.

Chapter Forty-One

A Plea for Epistemological Pluralism

Blythe McVicker Clinchy

Labouvie-Vief, Orwoll, and Manion (1995) have performed an important service in delineating the narratives of mind that pervade our culture and weave their way into developmental theory and research. In my own work, I have been both perpetrator and victim of the dualisms they describe—polarities of mind and body, intellect and emotion, male and female, individual and society. Although my aim was to be part of the solution—the dissolution of polarities—my work seemed often to become part of the problem. Too often, we feminist psychologists succeed in reifying the very dualisms we are trying to deconstruct or transcend. Bem's (1974) "androgyny" construct, for example, defined as a combination of stereotypically masculine and feminine traits, was an attempt to bridge the two poles, but because it is constituted by conventional images of masculinity and femininity, it actually preserves them (Morawski, 1994). In this commentary I describe some of the ways in which developmental research, including my own, has become entangled in the myths described by Labouvie-Vief and her colleagues. I realize that this is an unorthodox approach, that commentaries are usually composed in a critical analytic mode, but if one shares the conviction that it is important to "liberate mind's other pole," as Labouvie-Vief and her co-authors put it—the pole involving narrative and subjectivity—one must start somewhere.

My part of the story concerns the concepts of "connected" and "separate" knowing that Belenky, Goldberger, Tarule and I began to explicate in *Women's Ways of Knowing* (1986). Separate knowing is the approach defined by the "masculine" pole, by Bruner's (1985) "paradigmatic" mode—a set of detached, impersonal, objective, critical, and analytic procedures for arriving at truth. Zimmermann and I (Clinchy and Zimmermann, 1985) stumbled upon what we now call connected knowing while searching for evidence of what we now call separate knowing. The context was a longitudinal study of epistemological development among undergraduate women. This research was based on a scheme describing "intellectual and ethical development during the college years" devised by Perry (1970) based on a longitudinal study of Harvard students, most of them male. Although the sequence of epistemological positions Perry drew from his unstructured interviews resonated with our impres-

Blythe McVicker Clinchy, "A Plea for Epistemiological Pluralism." Adapted from "Commentary." *Human Development, 38*, pp. 258–264. © 1995 by Karger AG, Basel. Reprinted with permission.

sions of college students' development, it was necessarily schematic. By interviewing students around questions and quotations relevant to the scheme, we hoped to elaborate and articulate it. In a proposal written at the time, we said that we wanted to test the applicability of Perry's scheme to a later cohort of undergraduate women at a small liberal arts college, but in fact we were interested not in testing the theory but in furthering its development, and gender was of no real concern. We did not expect to find sex differences. We studied women because they were the only gender attending the college where we taught. In its inception, then, our work was "gender-blind."

Some of our questions were designed to assess whether or not students had acquired an appreciation of critical thinking, a component of Perry's position 4. For example, we asked them to respond to a statement made by another student that seemed to provide evidence of critical thinking:

> As soon as someone tells me his point of view, I immediately start arguing in my head the opposite point of view. When someone is saying something, I can't help turning it upside down.

Some students responded warmly to the quotation. For instance, one said:

> I do that a lot. I never take anything someone says for granted. I just tend to see the contrary. I like playing devil's advocate, arguing the opposite of what somebody's saying, thinking of exceptions to what the person has said or thinking of a different train of logic.

Quite a few students, however, rejected the quotation. For instance, one woman said that when she disagreed with someone she didn't start arguing in her head; instead she started trying to imagine herself in the person's situation:

> I sort of fit myself into it in my mind and then I say. "I see what you mean." There's this initial point where I kind of go into the story, you know? And become like Alice in Wonderland falling down the rabbit hole.

Another student said:

> When I have an idea about something, and it differs from the way another person's thinking about it, I'll usually try to look at it from that person's point of view, see how they could say that, why they think they're right, why it makes sense.

It took us a long time to hear what these women were saying. Entrapped by the polarities, we assumed that they were simply revealing an incapacity for logical reasoning. We maintained this assumption even in the face of responses such as this one:

> If you listen to people and listen to what they have to say, maybe you can understand why they feel the way they do. There are reasons. They're not just being irrational. When I read a philosopher I try to think as the author does. It's hard, but I try not to bias the train of thought with my own impressions. I try to just pretend that I'm the author. I try to really just put myself in that person's place and feel why is it that they believe this way.

Ultimately, as responses such as these accumulated, especially as my colleagues and I went on to interview a more diverse sample of women (Belenky et al., 1986), we began to suspect that these women were describing a distinctive mode of processing, one that was personal rather than detached, subjective rather than objective, concrete rather than abstract, and intimate rather than distant. Among ourselves, we referred to it ironically as "position 4F," indicating that the mode failed to meet the standard for Perry's position 4 thinking, "4F" being the designation given potential draftees judged unfit for U.S. military duty because of physical or mental defects. In this case, "F" referred also to the stereotypically feminine (passive, receptive, relational) nature of the mode. Thus, gender polarities shaped our interpretations, causing us to impose a gender difference where we had not expected to find one and to make a judgment of inadequacy that we did not wish to make. Our work thus reified and reinforced the polarity myth.

At the same time, however, 4F was the thin edge of the wedge that would deconstruct the dichotomy. Although the 4F label marked the mode as less adequate than Perry's position 4, it marked it also as distinct from and perhaps superior to Perry's position 3 (multiplism, which, in revised form, we came to call subjectivism) (Belenky et al., 1986). Subjectivists rely on their own intuitive reactions as the source of truth. Locked in their own subjectivity, they evince polite tolerance for views that differ from their own, but they do not attempt to actively explore these views; they simply and spontaneously react. They operate according to a "makes-sense epistemology" (Perkins, 1991, p. 99), accepting ideas that strike them as intuitively right (usually those that accord with their own prior beliefs), and rejecting those that do not. In contrast, those categorized as 4F suspend their own disbelief and deliberately and effortfully try to enter into ideas that seem not to make sense, in order to ascertain how they might make sense.

The writer Peter Elbow helped us to see that 4F might be considered an alternative to critical thinking rather than an inferior procedure for arriving at truth. Elbow (1973) distinguishes between two such procedures. In playing the "doubting game," according to Elbow, you look for what's wrong with a given point of view. In playing the "believing game" you say yes to it and look for what's right about it. In the words of one of our interviewees, "I try to look for pieces of the truth in what the person's saying . . . sort of collaborate with them." Elbow's believing game, like our 4F, later rechristened as "connected knowing," is uncritical, but it is not unthinking.

While separate knowing clearly belongs to the masculine *logos*, it is subjectivism, not connected knowing, that belongs to the feminine *mythos*. Connected knowing partakes of both modes and fits neatly into neither. Although it is receptive, it is by no means passive. Although it is a personal, relational way of knowing ("You should treat the text as if it were a friend"), it is not egocentric. It is in a sense objective, although not in the usual sense. Connected knowers, like separate knowers, get out from behind their own eyes, but rather than taking the disinterested stance of an impartial observer "from no position in particular" (Shweder, 1986, p. 172), they adopt the perspective of a particular other. Finally, although connected knowing, like subjectivism, makes use of emotion and intuition as guides to understanding, it is not limited to the irrational. It relies on narrative, rather than argument, as a mode of discourse, but narrative is used as a collaborative way of thinking—thinking with rather than against, the position one is examining, and using storytelling as a way not just of illustrating but of developing concepts (Bruner, 1986, 1992; Cazden and Hymes, 1978).

In positing connected knowing, we intended to make a modest assault on the dichotomies Labouvie-Vief and colleagues describe. But the power of gender myths is such that connected knowing, like the concept of "care," has persistently been assimilated to the feminine pole and misinterpreted as passive, mindless, and nice. The philosopher Noddings (1986) says that she has become resigned to the fact that when she proposes that education be founded upon an ethic of care, defined as "a faithful search for understanding of the subjective aspects of experience" (pp. 501–502), she will be heard as saying that "the solution of education's problems lies rather simply in our being nicer to each other," an interpretation that "has always posed a special problem for women" (p. 506). There are disturbing possibilities, here, as to the role played by gender. Most of the philosophers and psychologists who have made the case for care are women (Gilligan et al., 1988; Martin, 1992; Noddings, 1986; but see Blum, 1990], and there is some evidence that women are more likely than men to espouse an ethic of care (Gilligan et al., 1988; but see Ford and Lowery, 1986) and a connected way of knowing (Mansfield and Clinchy, 1990, 1991, 1992). Some argue that these are intrinsically powerless modes that women, as victims of oppression, are forced to adopt, but it is equally possible that these modes are seen as powerless simply because women use them, just as so-called "powerless" modes of speech, such as qualifiers, are often perceived as powerless only when uttered by women (Bradley, 1981).

My colleagues and I may have unwittingly colluded in the misunderstanding of connected knowing, not only by being women (for which we can hardly be blamed), but also by labeling and defining the two modes in contrasting terms. Unlike Gilligan, who was careful to define each mode in its own terms (care being not necessarily unjust, and justice being not necessarily uncaring), we fell victim to the "dogma of the inseparability of the two poles" (Labouvie-Vief et al, 1995), treating the two modes in some respects as mirror images of each other. Because we defined separate knowing in terms that placed it squarely in the realm of *logos,* connected knowing, in contrast, could easily be drawn into the realm of *mythos* and thus dismissed. Or, as has also occurred, connected knowing could be declared the "good" way of knowing, with separate knowing dismissed as a hostile strategy aimed only at inflating the self and diminishing the other. The latter tactic, of course, reflects just another romantic revolution in which the hierarchy is not transcended but "merely stood on its head," as Labouvie-Vief and co-authors put it.

Labouvie-Vief and her colleagues look forward to a "reconciliation of the polarities," and they suggest that in fact reconciliation sometimes occurs on the part of individuals in the latter part of the life course. Whether or not reconciliation can occur probably depends on which aspects of the polarities are under consideration. Whether or not reconciliation does occur in the course of individual development is largely unknown, given the paucity of relevant research, especially longitudinal research. In our own research on approaches to conflict, we find a few people who report using an integrated approach to disagreement, one involving a complex orchestration of connected and separate procedures; nearly all of these subjects are well into adulthood. Leadbeater (1988), analyzing dialogues of same-sex pairs of adolescents and adults conversing about an issue upon which they disagreed, found such an integrated approach among some of her pairs of both genders. These were the only pairs who, while not always resolving the conflict, often reconstructed their positions in the course of the conversation. Other pairs—all of them female—listened politely but failed to assert their own positions and so avoided conflict. A third group—consisting entirely of males—used an assertive, critical style which, while acknowledging the conflict, failed to deal with it productively. We do not know how the more successful participants acquired their genderless style, but their performance is evidence that for some modes of processing, the "playful cooperation" envisioned by Labouvie-Vief and her colleagues can occur.

This may not be the case, however, for all modes. Bruner (1986) doubts that the narrative and paradigmatic modes can be "fused"—in his words, "the two (though complementary) are irreducible to one another" (p. 11). Cohn (1987) provides an extreme example of their incompatibility. Comparing two descriptions of the aftermath of a nuclear attack, one drawn from the graphic autobiographical narratives of survivors of the bombing of Hiroshima (Matsubara, 1985), the other from a memo prepared for a seminar of "defense intellectuals." Cohn writes:

> There are no ways to describe the phenomena represented in the first with the language of the second. Learning to speak the language of defense analysts is not a conscious, cold-blooded decision to ignore the effects of nuclear weapons on real live human beings, to ignore the sensory, the emotional experience, the human impact. It is simply learning a new language, but by the time you are through, the content of what you can talk about is monumentally different, as is the perspective from which you speak. (p. 705)

Cohn learned the new language while spending a year as a participant observer at a university center for defense strategy. It was not an "additive process" she says: it was "transformative."

> I found . . . that the better I got at engaging in this discourse, the more impossible it became for me to express my own ideas, my own values. I could adopt the language and gain a wealth of new concepts and reasoning strategies—but at the same time as the language gave me access to things I had been unable to speak about before, it radically excluded others . . . The language does not allow certain questions to be asked or certain values to be expressed. (p. 708)

Unable to speak about her concerns, Cohn soon found it difficult even to think about them: "I could go for days speaking about nuclear weapons without once thinking about the people who would be incinerated by them" (p. 709). When Cohn tried to speak the concrete, connected language she preferred, the men treated her as "ignorant or simple-minded or both" (p. 708).

A similar fate can befall anyone whose ways of speaking and knowing are at variance with the norms of an institution's "discourse community" (Cazden and Hymes, 1978), even when the "abnormal" ways are as appropriate to the task at hand as the normative ones. Turkle and colleagues (Turkle and Papert, 1990; Turkle, 1984) supply a case study of this phenomenon. In a computer programming class composed of first-year college students, they identified two gender-related (but not gender-exclusive) approaches to programming. "Planners" use a top-down, hierarchical, rule-driven, impersonal approach, while "bricoleurs" (a term borrowed from Lévi-Strauss) use a concrete, associative, interactive approach. They are like writers who do not use an outline but start with one idea, associate it to another, and find a connection with a third.

> The bricoleur resembles the painter who stands back between brushstrokes, looks at the canvas, and only after this contemplation, decides what to do next. . . . For planners, a program is an instrument for premeditated control; bricoleurs have goals, but set out to realize them in the spirit of a collaborative venture with the machine. (Turkle and Papert, 1990, p. 136)

Bricoleurs resemble connected knowers: they "tend to treat the computer as much like a person as they can" (Turkle and Papert, 1990, p. 149) — "as if it were a friend," one that they can "sort of collaborate with."

To Turkle and Papert, the two approaches appeared equally valid, their final products indistinguishable. The computer culture, however, regards bricolage as inferior to planning. "While the computer supports epistemological pluralism, the computer culture does not" (Turkle and Papert, 1990, p. 150). When a student said she wanted to build her program from the bottom up, starting with the smallest details, the teacher laughed at her, saying she "shouldn't confuse herself with what was going on at that low level." Bricoleurs are aware that their approach is not respected; after describing her style, one woman said, "Keep this anonymous. I know it sounds stupid" (p. 152).

This lesson may be learned in childhood. Turkle and Papert (1990) found similar programming styles and similar norms among elementary-school children. A boy of nine, overhearing a classmate speaking of "getting down inside the computer," sneered, "That's baby talk. . . . I am not in the computer. I'm just making things happen here." It is sad to see such polarities in place at such an early age, especially when at a yet earlier age there does seem to be some fusion of modes, rather like the ancient "undifferentiated unity" Labouvie-Vief and colleagues describe. For the children in Paley's (1990) kindergarten class, for instance, narrative and paradigmatic do seem to be fused. In constructing their stories, the children create rules. Paley's descriptions of how the children "invent the premises" and go on to explore "the logical consequences of their positions" (Paley, 1990, p. 26) led Feldman (1992) to suggest that "it is in the context of narrative that the power for logical thinking first emerges" (p. 75). A fusion of modes appears also in the "double-voiced discourse" observed by Sheldon (1992) among preschool girls, an approach to conflict in which the speaker, while pursuing her own agenda, simultaneously maintains the perspective of other members of the group. For some of these girls, the self-assertive voice will disappear, and the approach will evolve into the merely nice, conflict-avoidant style of the adolescent girls observed by Leadbeater. Brown and Gilligan (1992) tell a version of that story.

Entangled in the myths Labouvie-Vief and her co-authors have described, developmental psychology has shared the cultural assumption that concrete, connected thinking is "baby talk," a childish way of knowing worth exploring only among the very young and the mentally disabled. The field of culture and cognition (Shweder, 1980) has been more hospitable than most, perhaps because these more personal modes seem more appropriate when applied to persons. But investigations of everyday cognition indicate that concrete thinking is effective in other contexts, too. From her study of workers in a dairy, for instance, Scribner (1984) concluded that "progression from the particular and concrete to the general and abstract, from 'context-bound' to 'context-free' intellectual activity" (p. 40) certainly occurs. Yet, "an opposite process may be simultaneously occurring . . . in the direction of mastery of the concrete" (p. 40). Turkle and Papert (1990) believe that their work "supports a perspective that encourages looking for psychological and intellectual development within rather than beyond the concrete and suggests the need for closer investigation of the diversity of ways in which the mind can think with objects rather than the rules of logic" (p. 143).

Because concrete thinking has been relegated to the inferior pole, development within the concrete may be difficult to discern. In some contexts, it may even masquerade as development beyond the concrete. Turkle and Papert (1990) doubt that their undergraduate bricoleurs will develop into planners, but they may learn to look like planners. One student said that she had "turned herself into a different kind of person," and another that she had learned to "fake it" in order to succeed (p. 135).

To investigate development within the concrete, we must listen with respect to people we have rarely attended to, especially those whose epistemologies are at variance with the norms of the ruling class in the society and the discipline— "ordinary African-American women," for example, who, according to Collins (1989), put their faith in the "wisdom" or "mother wit" that emerges from concrete experience rather than in the academic abstractions that turn people into "educated fools who would take a gun to a cockroach" (p. 759). We must venture into settings in which people are working at tasks that allow, encourage, or even demand the use of concrete thinking. And we must take seriously the need for epistemological pluralism in our own discipline, respecting and rewarding the labor-intensive methods of inquiry that embody the kind of concrete, contextual thinking we are trying to understand.

REFERENCES

Belenky, M. F., Clinchy, B. M., Goldberger, N. R. & Tarule, J. M. (1986). *Women's ways of knowing.* New York: Basic Books.

Bem, S. B. (1974). The measurement of psychological androgyny. *Journal of Consulting and Clinical Psychology, 42,* 155–162.

Blum, L. (1990). Universality and particularity. In Schrader, D. (Ed.), *The legacy of Lawrence Kohlberg (New directions for child development, Vol. 47,* pp. 59–69). San Francisco: Jossey-Bass.

Bradley, P. H. (1981). The folk linguistics of women's speech: An empirical examinatio Communication Monographs, 48, 73–90.

Brown, L., & Gilligan, C. (1992). Meeting at the crossroads Cambridge, MA: Harvard Universit Press.

Bruner, J. S. (1985). Narrative and paradigmatic modes of thought. In Eisner, F. (Ed.). Learnin and teaching the ways of knowing (84th yearbook of the National Society for the Study o Education, pp. 97–115). Chicago: University of Chicago Press.

Bruner, J. S. (1986). Actual minds, possible worlds. Cambridge, MA: Harvard University Press.

Bruner, J. S. (1992). The narrative construction of reality. In Beilin, H. & Pufall, P. (Eds.) Piaget's theory: Prospects and possibilities (pp. 229–248). Hillsdale, NJ: Erlbaum.

Cazden, C. & Hymes, D. (1978). Narrative thinking and story-telling rights: A folklorist's clue to a critique of education. Keystone Folklore Quarterly, 22, 21–36.

Clinchy, B. McV. & Zimmerman, C. (1985, July). Connected and separate knowing. Paper presented at a symposium on Gender differences in intellectual development: Women's ways of knowing, at the eighth biennial meeting of the International Society for the Study of Behavioural Development, Tours, France.

Cohn, C. (1987). Sex and death in the rational world of defense intellectuals. Signs: Journal of Women in Culture and Society, 12, 687–718.

Collins, P. H. (1989). The social construction of Black feminist thought. Signs, 14, 745–773.

Elbow, P. (1973). Writing without teachers. London: Oxford University Press.

Feldman, C. (1992). On reading Paley. Quarterly Newsletter of the Laboratory of Human Cognition, 14, (3), 73–77.

Ford, C. F. & Lowery, C. R. (1986). Gender differences in moral reasoning: A comparison of the use of justice and care orientations. Journal of Personality and Social Psychology, 50, 777–783.

Gilligan, C. (1982). In a different voice. Cambridge, MA: Harvard University Press.

Gilligan, C., Ward, J. V. & Taylor JMcL. (Eds.) (1988). Mapping the moral domain. Cambridge, MA: Harvard University Press.

Labouvie-Vief, G., Orwoll, L., & Manion, M. (1995). Narrative of mind, gender, and the life course. Human Developments, 38, 239–257.

Leadbeater, B. J. (1988). Relationship processes in adolescent and adult dialogues: Assessing the intersubjective context of conversation. Human Development, 31, 313–326.

Lyons, N. (1983). Two perspectives on self, relationships and morality. Harvard Educational Review, 53, 125–145.

Mansfield, A., & Clinchy, BMcV. (1990, April). Young women's ways of knowing: A longitudinal study of epistemological development in different domains of knowledge over the college years. Paper presented at a symposium on Life Cycle Perspectives on Knowing: Implications for Teaching and Learning, at the annual meeting of the American Educational Research Association, Boston.

Mansfield, A. F., & Clinchy, B. McV. (1991, April). On achieving faith in the power of one's own mind: A longitudinal study of epistemological development in college women. Research display presented at the biennial meeting of the Society for Research Child Development, Seattle, WA.

Mansfield, A., & Clinchy, B. McV. (1992, May). The influence of different kinds of relationships on the development and expression of "separate" and "connected" knowing in undergraduate women. Paper presented as part of the symposium, Voicing relationships, knowing connection: Exploring girls' and women's development, at the 22nd annual symposium of the Jean Piaget Society, Montreal.

Martin, J. R. (1992). *The schoolhome: Rethinking schools for changing families.* Cambridge, MA: Harvard University Press.

Matsubara, H. (1985). *Cranes at dusk.* Garden City, NY: Dial Press.

Morawski, J. G. (1994). *Practicing feminisms, reconstructing psychology.* Ann Arbor, MI: University of Michigan Press.

Noddings, N. (1986). Fidelity in teaching, teacher education, and research for teaching. *Harvard Educational Review, 56,* 496–510.

Paley, V. G. (1990). *The boy who would be a helicopter.* Cambridge, MA: Harvard University Press.

Perkins, D. N., Farady, M. & Bushey, B. (1991). Everyday reasoning and the roots of intelligence. In Voss, J. F., Perkins, D. N., & Segal, J. W. (Eds), *Informal reasoning and education.* Hillsdale, NJ: Erlbaum.

Perry, W. (1970). *Forms of intellectual and ethical development in the college years.* New York: Holt, Rinehart, & Winston.

Scribner, S. (1994). Toward a model of practical thinking at work. *Quarterly Newsletter of the Laboratory of Comparative Human Cognition, 6 (1–2),* 37–42.

Sheldon, A. (1992). Conflict talk: Sociolinguistic challenges to self-assertion and how young girl meet them. *Merrill-Palmer Quarterly, 38,* 95–118.

Shweder, R. A., (1986). Divergent rationalities. In Fiske, D. W., & Shweder, R. A. (Eds.), *Metatheory in social science: Pluralisms and subjectivities* (pp. 163–196). Chicago: University of Chicago Press.

Turkle, S. (1984). *The second self: The computer and the human spirit.* New York: Simon & Schuster.

Turkle, S., & Papert, S. A. (1990). Epistemological pluralism: styles and voices within the computer culture. *Signs, 16,* 128–157.

Coda
In-Conclusion . . .

Blythe McVicker Clinchy and Julie K. Norem

In assembling this collection we were struck by how much theory and research in the psychology of gender has "grown up," how much more sophisticated and complex it has become in the course of the last couple of decades. In particular, we were impressed by the progress many authors have made in moving beyond the simplistic dualisms (male/female, masculine/feminine, nature/nurture, family/work, rational/ emotional, feminist/scientific) that so often pervade our thinking about gender. Indeed, the absence of dualistic thinking became a criterion for us in selecting the readings for this volume. We believe that the works included represent (though certainly do not exhaust) some of the very best work being done on gender. We find these pieces provocative, insightful, compelling, and challenging—even when we may not agree with a particular position or argument.

At the same time, however, as we scoured different literatures, we found considerable evidence that dualistic thinking about gender is by no means dead; it is still too often the norm or the default, both in the field and in the world. Moreover, the professional discourse sometimes exacerbates the problem: too often, we react to one anothers' propositions and analyses by presuming inherent, dichotomous categories in which one value is right and one is wrong, even attributing good or evil intentions (or at least professional competence or incompetence) to those who hold "right" or "wrong" positions. Based on our own reactions to the work we *did not* include, we thought it might be useful to end this volume with a discussion of some of the ways in which particular dualisms have been and continue to be useful, and some of the ways in which they can be misleading and potentially destructive.

Dualistic thinking is not peculiar to the psychology of gender; it pervades all areas of psychology (as it does all areas of Western thinking). But where gender is concerned, either-or thinking seems inescapable: for instance, when we obey the injunction in the *Publication Manual of the American Psychological Association* to avoid nonsexist language and write "he or she" (where once we might have written "he"), we construct a dichotomy. Our language compels us to posit two sexes, although Anne Fausto-Sterling (chapter 11 of this volume), echoing Virginia Woolf's earlier assertion that "two sexes are quite inadequate" (1929/1989, p. 88), argues for the existence of at least five. The question of "how many sexes" is not just a taxonomical issue, equivalent to, say, the identification of subspecies of tulips. Like most issues having to do with gender, for many people it has political, even moral implications. As we have seen, male and female, masculine and feminine are prescriptive as well as descriptive categories; they name the ways in which men and women not only do but *should* behave, and the dichotomy persists partly because various groups are strongly invested in preserving it, especially when it is defined in terms of sexuality. To take a trivial but telling example, in August 1996 an official of the National Grange, a farmers' organization, condemned the United Nations Conference on Women for defining five genders (female heterosexuals, male heterosexuals, female homosexuals, male homosexuals, and transsexuals) as genders based on "social classification" rather than biology (Ide, 1995).[1] In fact,. however, a binary scheme simplifies the biological category of "sex" as well as the social category of "gender." Scientists such as Fausto-Sterling and Mary Parlee (in press) argue convincingly that the notion of two sexes is based more on ideology than biology, that "sex," as well as gender, is "comprised of multiple components" (e.g., chromosomal configurations, gonadal structure, hormonal profiles, genitalia), and that current constructions of sex capture only two of the many patterns that can be found in nature. Indeed, thinking of sex in terms of taxonomies obscures the extent to which continuous variation at multiple levels is often the norm in nature. As Parlee writes:

> Variation in nature is often not well captured by dichotomous categories of the sort scientists construct when they focus on sex and gender *differences.* Research on "sex differences" and "gender differences" rests on the assumption that variations observed in sex-and gender-related phenomena are best conceptualized with a binary classification scheme: "male/female" for sex. . . . Potential information is lost, however, when patterns are treated as exceptions to a dichotomy rather than as positive instances of gender-related phenomena in which biological and cultural influences are combined in particular ways. . . . [O]ur understanding of neuroendocrine effects on brain development and behavior would be advanced if research questions concerning "sex differences" (a notion which *assumes* dichotomies) were reframed as questions about the causes and consequences of—developmental variations in the biological structures and functions involved in sexual—reproduction. (Parlee, in press)

Testosterone and Behavior

As an example of the ways in which dichotomies can frame thinking, consider the relationship between testosterone and behavior. This is not intrinsically a sex or gender question: testosterone is present in both sexes. Nevertheless, testosterone levels are correlated with possession of testes versus ovaries, which is correlated (though not perfectly) with chromosomal sex; both chromosomal sex and hormone-related physiology are correlated (though not perfectly) with sex-class (i.e., what we typically refer to as males and females). Male/female provides a convenient and reasonable initial heuristic methodology to use in looking for testosterone effects on behavior and behavioral effects on testosterone level. In contrast to many other sex differences, the mean level of testosterone difference between males and females is substantial: after puberty, the distributions are non-overlapping, although they over lap prenatally and are virtually identical at birth (Rollins, 1996). Testosterone, indeed is often considered to be a "male hormone," even though it is present in both male and females and can have some similar effects in both (e.g., lower voices, increased facial and body hair, and increased muscle mass in humans).

Data from several species (e.g., rats, marmosets, rhesus monkeys) suggest that "masculinization" of the brain results from exposure to testosterone prenatally or during critical periods (depending on the species), and that this masculinization affects behavior—primarily mounting behavior and the amount of within-sex versus between-sex aggression, which is associated with attempts to mount (e.g., Dixson, 1993; Goy, Bercovitch, & McBrair, 1988). Masculinization of genetic females often leads to more mounting behavior, and lack of masculinization in genetic males (during critical periods) often leads to lordosis (presentation to receive mounting) or lack of mounting. It is unclear what implications these results have for consideration of human behavior: human sexual behavior, though it sometimes includes physical acts that are in some general morphological sense similar to mounting and lordosis, is certainly not closely analogous to rat mounting behavior.

It is even more difficult to see what relevance these data might have for differences in math performance among male and female humans. (Rats don't do math.) Yet these data are often part of ongoing attempts to demonstrate that male/female corresponds to mathematical ability/lack of ability. Research on the presumed brain-masculinizing effects of testosterone, primarily in fetal rats, led Norman Geschwind and his colleagues to argue that testosterone slows the development of the left hemisphere in genetic males, leading to right-hemisphere dominance, which in turn leads to superior spatial and (consequently) mathematical ability (Geschwind & Behan, 1982; Geschwind & Galaburda, 1987; see also Kolata, 1983). This conclusion was drawn despite the fact that mathematical ability requires coordination of both logical "left-brain" functions and aspects of spatial "right-brain" functions. In what has become a well-known story—at least among feminist psychologists—Ruth Bleier attempted to publish a failure to replicate (based on 500 human fetal brains), but was rejected by the same journal (*Science*) that published Geschwind and Peter Behan's work (Bleier, 1988), and has never subsequently gained attention commensurate with that received by the work she so effectively challenges.

Other workers continue to pursue with enthusiasm the study of male/female difference in math performance. Among the best known work in this area is that of Camilla Benbow and Julian Stanley (1980), who emphasize that the male/female difference in the upper reaches (prodigy/genius level) of math ability is much greater than it is at other points in the distribution. Benbow (1988) argues that sex differences in highly advanced mathematical reasoning may have physiological determinants.

These data and arguments get assimilated into an almost impenetrable system of beliefs that includes the assumption that some abilities are particularly male, that some professions are justifiably male-dominated (e.g., see Boswell, 1985, on children's beliefs about who can do math), and that the gender attributed to performance and profession simply reflects clear biological differences caused by male hormones. As ne example of this assimilative process, consider how data from "anomalous" cases ire considered. Individuals with Turner's syndrome (born XO—i.e., missing the second sex chromosome) have notably low spatial and mathematical abilities (e.g., Money & Erhardt, 1982). These individuals are always categorized as females based on external, feminized genitalia at birth, following the assumption that nature's default is female, even though those with Turner's syndrome have no second X chromosome, no "female" hormones, and no female reproductive organs. Their lack of mathematical ability fits neatly into description of them as "hyper-feminine," which encompasses (though does not explain) their interest in personal adornment and rather extreme compliance and passivity. In turn, this understanding fits neatly into the assumption that lack of testosterone caused their low mathematical ability— thus supporting the presumed maleness of that ability. Meanwhile, there is now evidence that treatment with "female" hormones (estrogen/gestagen) leads to significant increases in mathematical and spatial ability for these "girls" (Nyborg, 1984). In other words, we could consider low math ability in these individuals to be a result of lack of femaleness—though that is not really what we are advocating—rather than a result of lack of maleness generally, or testosterone specifically.

Other researchers have pursued different tracks, less dominated by the assumption that differences in math performance and testosterone will cleanly and neatly map onto the male/female dichotomy. Looking at within-sex variation, in addition to between sex differences, researchers have found equivocal evidence for a relationship between testosterone level and ability on some (but not all) mathematical and spatial ability tasks among men and women (Christiansen & Knussmann, 1987; Gouchie & Kimura, 1991; Shute, Pellegrino, Hubert & Reynolds, 1983). This evidence is not easily assimilated into a model in which a male/female dichotomy is used to support arguments about superior male math performance. Some studies find that *lower* testosterone is associated with better spatial ability (on some tasks) in men, while others find that *higher* testosterone is associated with better mathematical reasoning in men. The same studies that find lower testosterone associated with lower spatial ability in men also find that *higher* testosterone is related to better spatial ability in women (which might suggest a curvilinear model). There is no association between testosterone and mathematical reasoning in women, and no study suggests that male math prodigies are high in testosterone relative to other males.[2] Moreover, recent evidence shows that sex differences in the highest levels of math performance are not cross-culturally consistent: in China, for example, which has a very different system for teaching math, there are no gender differences in math performance (Halpern, 1992).

Pursuing the math performance difference, we discover that gender differences in math performance do not appear until after puberty. Testosterone increases in boys at puberty, so that finding may support a relationship between testosterone and math ability and performance. After puberty, girls take fewer math classes and are less interested in math relative to boys, but that finding is initially neutral with respect to our hypothesis that there is a relationships between testosterone and math. Ability may drive preferences and interests. However, variables such as teacher attention and, as Jacquelynne S. Eccles, Janis E. Jacobs, and Rena D. Harold (chapter 38 of this

volume) report, mothers' beliefs about their children's math ability (and the exten
to which mothers hold traditional beliefs about gender) account for much of th
variance in math performance. Also, changes in girls' preferences and interest
precede any differences in ability or performance. Indeed, girls who drop out o
math have often performed better than many boys who do not (Eccles et al., 1985)
Most of the variation in math performance, both among girls and between girl
and boys, can be accounted for by social and cultural influences on interests and
preferences.[3]

In sum, then, there is no clear evidence that any relationship between mathematical ability and testosterone accounts for the gender difference in SAT scores, choice
of engineering careers, or any other related phenomena. To the extent that researchers have shown clear relationships between hormone levels and math performance,
those relationships appear to differ for men and women, and *causal* pathways remain
largely unspecified. Yet it is still frequently argued in textbooks, educational videos,
and other venues that biological maleness and femaleness somehow account for
gender differences in math performance, even in the face of evidence that those
differences can be overcome by training and have, in fact, decreased substantially
over the past thirty years (Feingold, 1988). In other words, investment in the male/
female dichotomy must be driving this enterprise, rather than an interest in the
effects of testosterone on behavior.

Testosterone and Aggression

More briefly, consider the related research topic of aggression and testosterone. One
can amass both animal and human data to show that many kinds of aggression
(especially physical aggression) are more frequent among males than females. If one
stopped there, however—assuming that the male/female differences in some sense
accounted for or established the testosterone–aggression relationship—one would be
on shaky ground, as with the testosterone–math relationship. (Interestingly, the rat
mounting/lordosis behavior is cited as evidence for both relationships).

Studies showing that violent criminals have higher testosterone levels than other
criminals (e.g., Dabbs, Frady, Carr, & Besch, 1987) are easily assimilated to the
assumption that male hormones cause male behavior (and male/female differences);
after all, they appear to suggest that having even more male hormones causes even
more of the male behavior—in this case, aggression. These ideas have been widely
touted, usually without the corollary that those relationships were only found among
men of low socioeconomic status (Dabbs & Morris, 1990). Belief in the intrinsic
"maleness" of aggression was further bolstered by early evidence that XYY males
(individuals who might be thought "hyper-male" because of their extra male chromosome) were overrepresented in prison populations relative to nonprison populations (Nanko, Saito, & Makino, 1979). Further research, virtually ignored by the
media, compared XYY men to Klinefelter's syndrome men, who are XXY, slightly
feminized physiologically, and also overrepresented in prison populations (Witkin et
al., 1976, cited in Unger & Crawford, 1995). This work found that both groups were

ower in intelligence and education than XY men. Controlling for intelligence, there was no difference in criminality rates among XYY, XXY, and XY men. (Even in the initial study, the XYY were not overrepresented among *violent* criminals, a detail that was lost in the rush to use these data to confirm the maleness–aggression connection.)

Rather than fall back on the male/female difference, aggression researchers moved beyond the differences between sexes to look within sexes—that is, they viewed variation within sex as at least as important to account for as sex difference. They have thus found that testosterone levels are affected by behavior—for example, they are higher after winning a fight than before, and winners typically have higher levels than losers (in humans and some other species). This is true (though not as marked) in females as well as males, and is not restricted to physical aggression—for example, both male and female trial lawyers have higher testosterone after winning a case. Also, on average trial lawyers have chronically higher testosterone levels than corporate lawyers (Dabbs, Alford, Fielden, in press). The evidence that testosterone and behavior have reciprocal effects (i.e., that behavior, social interactions and their outcomes are influenced by *and* influence testosterone levels) is voluminous, both in humans and in nonhuman species (Archer, 1996).

The focus on male/female difference in this research serves as a useful starting point, and it may have significant methodological advantages to the extent that the phenomena of interest are correlated with the classification of male/female (i.e., comparing males and females is an easy way to screen for relatively higher versus lower levels of testosterone). However, the assumption that one is learning anything about the mechanisms underlying the phenomena simply by observing their correlation with male/female is potentially misleading and scientifically unjustifiable—even in sex difference research, correlation does not mean causation. Neither testosterone nor aggression are intrinsically male, no matter how intertwined they may become with our conceptions of maleness. Considering either testosterone or aggression as fundamentally part of maleness contributed to the misleading interpretation of the evidence about XYY individuals. The compelling evidence that testosterone influences aggression and that aggressive behavior influences testosterone levels comes from looking at within-male (and within-female) variations—that is, from looking beyond the male/female dualism and resisting the temptation to regard either aggression or testosterone as fundamentally male.

Biology and the Psychology of Gender

All this is not to suggest that we should abandon research on biological influences on behavior. We do not share the "somatophobia" that Elizabeth V. Spelman (1988, p. 126) has noted among students of gender. The problem is not that researchers were looking for biological influences on behavior; rather, it was their overreliance on or investment in difference as reified in an artificial dualism. Nor does finding biological differences between males and females necessitate (or even suggest) that we adopt essentialist interpretations *or* policy—though the biological/cultural dualism is often inappropriately equated with essentialism/constructivism. Even if most women wei shown to have "innately" poorer math ability than most men (which is not eve remotely the case), this would not justify the political stance that women as a clas should be excluded from math-related opportunities, or that remedial efforts shoul not be attempted, or any other repression. (After all, when some studies suggested lower verbal ability, on average, among boys, the reaction was to fund massive remedial reading programs.)

We recognize that much of the somatophobia in gender studies is based in part on the ugly history of misuse of supposedly "scientifically established" biological differences to justify personal and institutionalized inequality and injustice. However, it seems naive to think that those whose social, political, or religious agendas resist change in the status quo (or advocate more sex stratification) will be significantly crippled without such data. Rather, those who are motivated to explore gender fully should welcome research into the sophisticated and complex interactions among biological levels of analysis (e.g., chromosomes and hormones) and between biology and culture.

Another reason often offered against pursuing biological levels of analysis is the mistaken assumption that biological influences on behavior are somehow more essential and less potentially changeable than other influences. As we argued in the introduction to Part III, we do not believe this view is justified. Moreover, there is no reason to think that research that focuses on nonbiological factors necessarily wins converts from proponents of essentialist positions. One example of the ways in which evidence about cultural influences does not necessarily argue against more biologically based explanations comes from looking at the reaction of some evolutionary psychologists to evidence about social and cultural influences on gender roles. Rather than find that evidence a challenge to the position that the different evolutionary tasks facing males and females has led to different mate selection strategies among men and women, they interpret cultural reinforcement of gender role differences in mating strategies as a *reflection* of innate tendencies, and/or refer to the "co-evolution" of individuals and culture (e.g., Archer, 1996; Buss, 1994).[4]

The reactions of various groups to (unreplicated) research that allegedly shows brain structure differences between male homosexuals and male heterosexuals perfectly illustrates how evidence about biology can be used by those motivated to use it. Some groups herald that evidence because they believe it will challenge those who oppose gay rights. They believe that "scientific proof" that being gay is a consequence of brain structure, not a "choice," will nudge religious and other groups toward greater acceptance of homosexuals, even though it is probably at least as likely that those groups will respond by continuing to condemn homosexual behavior. (Catholics in favor of a celibate priesthood, after all, have never found suggestions or evidence that priests have "natural" sexual urges very compelling counterarguments to their position.) Other groups fear that the discovery of brain structure (or other biological) differences between gays and straights could lead to attempts to develop technologies to "fix" gays. We are not arguing that those fears are unfounded, only that those motivated to use the evidence that way will pursue their cause regardless of the evidence.

The Individual and the Social

As we have seen, some feminist social scientists argue that all research and theory concerning gender differences is based on and contributes to essentialist doctrine by exaggerating differences between men and women and minimizing differences among women, and by focusing exclusively on intrapsychic rather than social factors. In an influential article subtitled "Stop the Bandwagon, I Want to Get Off," Martha Mednick spoke for many when she criticized "different-voice" research as scientifically unsound and politically dangerous. "An intrapsychic emphasis," she wrote, "places the burden of change *entirely* on the person and does not lead scientific inquiry to an examination of cultural, socio-economic, structural, or contemporaneous situational factors that may affect behavior" (1989, p. 1120). Mednick seems to recognize that she may be overstating her critique and replicating the polarization she decries, for at this point she inserts a footnote: "I am here decrying dichotomous thinking and exaggeration of gender differences, but I want to be careful not to fall into the same trap. The focus on intrapsychic factors is perhaps less exclusive than I have indicated" (1989, p. 1120).

We think that Mednick (like Rachel Hare-Mustin and Jeanne Maracek, and others) does exaggerate the dichotomy she deplores. Different-voice researchers did not claim that the "women's voices" they heard were installed at birth or shortly thereafter, that they were immutable, that those voices were unaffected by external factors, or that all women spoke in a single common voice while all men spoke in a different common voice. In fact, they presented data showing a substantial number of individuals (men and women) exhibiting both "care" and "justice" orientations to moral judgment (Gilligan & Attanucci, 1988) and both "separate" and "connected" approaches to conflict (Clinchy, 1996), demonstrating that these modes, while distinctive and gender-related, are neither mutually exclusive nor gender-exclusive. Critics of this work see it, essentially, as "gender-polarizing," to borrow Sandra Bem's term, but the polarities may be lodged in the critics' eyes as well as or even instead of in the work they are scrutinizing. "When I hear my work being cast in terms of whether women and men are really (essentially) different or who is better than whom," Carol Gilligan writes, "I know that I have lost my voice, because these are not my questions" (Gilligan, 1993, xiii).

Gilligan and others wished to repair an omission (perhaps "exclusion" would be a more accurate term) in psychological theory and in the society, by bringing into public consciousness a way of seeing, speaking, and knowing that emphasized attachment and interdependence rather than detachment and autonomy. One of us (BC), an author of *Women's Ways of Knowing*, recalls being puzzled by the accusation that she and her coauthors had ignored "cultural" or "social-economic" factors, for the project was born out of the suspicion that institutions in this society, particularly its educational institutions, crippled the minds and spirits of women. Writers grouped under the "different-voice" label shared the conviction that, lacking that voice, this society is, as Jean Baker Miller (chapter 18 of this volume) put it, "a low-level, primitive organization built on an exceedingly restricted conception of the total human potential." In bringing a different voice into the public domain, these writers hoped to contribute to the demise of this organization. It seemed both inaccurate and unjust to accuse those who held such a vision of focusing only on the intrapsychic.

But, informed by the analyses of thoughtful psychologists such as Hope Landrine, we have learned to see justice in these accusations; the work does now seem to us insufficiently contextual. In *Women's Ways of Knowing*, for instance, the cultural context is present, but only "as a place, as a mere setting in which behavior occurs"; ways of knowing were not presented as "acts-in context" (Landrine, chapter 5 of this volume). When a woman said that she relied on her gut reactions rather than external authorities as a source of truth, her epistemological position was labeled "subjectivist," regardless of whether she was an eighteen-year-old undergraduate from an elite college speaking of her approach to the interpretation of poetry, or a poor, undereducated, middle-aged mother of five explaining how she had found the courage to leave her husband after twenty-five years of abuse. Because their words were the "same," they were given the same name. The authors of *Women's Ways of Knowing* were trained in developmental psychology, a discipline which, like personality psychology (as described by Stewart in chapter 3 of this volume) rests upon assumptions of individualism and universality, and these assumptions doubtless played a role in shaping their construction of the data. They knew, of course, that the same words in the mouths of such differently situated women could not possibly have quite the same meaning; they knew (though none of them could have articulated it so clearly) that, as Landrine says, "behavior and its context are a single unit." At the time, however, it was the commonalities in women's responses across wide variations in age, socioeconomic status, ethnicity, and educational background that were so striking. Women researchers and clinicians in the late 1970s and 1980s, listening to their women "subjects" and "patients," often experienced the sort of communion and solidarity that, a decade earlier, they had discovered in their "consciousness-raising" groups. As Jane Roland Martin (chapter 1 of this volume) remarks, who would have thought, in those heady early days of the women's movement, that "difference would emerge as the privileged perspective in feminist theory and research and that any attempt to find commonalities would be condemned out of hand." Looking for commonalities among women did not seem at the time politically dangerous; it seemed politically necessary. Now, our consciousness raised on matters of diversity as well as solidarity, we think it is both. Although we would still argue that it is useful to open psychology's conversation to two voices instead of the single voice that once prevailed, we agree that the dichotomy masks a plurality, that the effort to include has resulted in excluding those voices that do not "fit" either category. We also think that work such as *Women's Ways of Knowing* and Laurel Furumoto's analysis (see chapter 4 of this volume) point to the ways in which modes of inquiry and social institutions can be considered gendered, even when performed by and populated by both males and females. Gender is not necessarily about "sex differences."

We would argue, in addition, that there is no reason to believe that to the extent this work does focus on the intrapsychic, it places the "burden of change *entirely* on individuals," as Mednick asserts and many imply. This position seems to beg quesions both about the origins of intrapsychic factors and about the reciprocal and merging relationships between intrapsychic and sociocultural factors.

Some psychologists come close to arguing that gender is a function of nothing but the context in which it occurs, that individual traits, motives, or predispositions have nothing to do with it. More than twenty-five years ago, Naomi Weisstein made such a claim in a groundbreaking article with the audacious title "Psychology Constructs the Female," in which she excoriated the "myth of sex-organ causality" perpetrated by clinicians who offered no evidence in its support, and asserted that "psychology has looked for inner traits when it should have been noting social context." "Compared to the influence of the social context within which a person lives," Weisstein wrote, "his or her history and traits, as well as biological make-up, may simply be random variations, noise superimposed on the true signal that can predict behavior" (1971, p. 135).

Although the static introduced by postmodernism now makes it difficult for some of us to detect any "true signal," many psychologists share Weisstein's belief in the importance of situational factors, some of them arguing that gender is not merely socially acquired but socially constructed at both the interpersonal and the institutional level. Candace West and Don H. Zimmerman (chapter 6 of this volume), for instance, maintain that gender is not something we are or have, but something we do. "We argue that gender is not a set of traits, nor a variable, nor a role, but the product of social doings of some sort," they write. "We claim that gender itself is constituted through interaction. . . . Doing gender means creating differences between girls and boys and women and men, differences that are not natural, essential, or biological." Gender in this sense is not something that individuals bring to a situation. It is not a product of the past; it emerges in the present.

We find the sociological evidence and analysis of gender as social construction quite compelling. Erving Goffman and Barrie Thorne (see chapters 34 and 35 of this volume, respectively) among others, show how social arrangements invite us— indeed compel us—for no good intrapsychic or biological reason to "do gender." Teachers call us "boys" and "girls" and line us up separately to go to lunch; sporting events are contrived to force marginal differences between the physical abilities of males and females to count.

Emphasis on the power of social arrangements in shaping behavior serves as a welcome counter to the assumption that there exists some constellation of psychological characteristics that can and should be identified as fundamentally male, in contrast with some set of deficits or opposite characteristics that are female. Despite cogent critiques from J. G. Morawski (chapter 24 of this volume) and others, and the lessons revealed by Bem's (1993) exceedingly useful and self-reflective attempts to wrestle with these constructs over several years, these assumptions persist among psychologists engaged in the investigation of gender. For example, inspired or piqued by feminist analyses of femininity, numerous researchers have turned their attention to examination of masculinity, and often, to reconstruction, or construction of some form of "new" masculinity. Many of these efforts are remarkable for the extent to which they leave unexamined the dual assumptions that (1) there is something

essentially or fundamentally masculine that needs to be defined (or reasserte(
reclaimed, championed, encouraged, etc.); and (2) that whatever that something i;
it should be defined by contrast to "opposite" characteristics in women, or in term
of characteristics that women do not "possess."[5]

While occasionally acknowledging that masculinity may vary among gays an(
nonwhite males, and that men may vary in how masculine they are, the search fo:
essential maleness—for the psychological characteristics that allow men to demonstrate that, whatever they are, they are certainly not women!—continues with great
vigor. Other writers (e.g., Nancy Chodorow and other object-relations theorists) have
commented on this need for men—as individuals—to differentiate themselves from
women, and on the ubiquity of the assumption that maleness needs to be constructed, instructed, socialized, or "realized," as opposed to femaleness, which is
assumed simply to exist (e.g., Gilmore, 1990; Lederer, 1968; Ortner, 1974). We will not
comment extensively on this need, except to reiterate an observation that has been
made by others: to the extent that maleness needs to be constructed and maintained
(through initiation, ritual, devaluation of femaleness) by cultural forces, it cannot be
construed as an essential (innate and immutable, as opposed to important or necessary) part of maleness or male embodiment.

Starting with the assumption of a masculine/feminine dichotomy may have advantages. As an analytical tool it seems useful as one tries to understand the intrapsychic
motivation to establish one's masculinity. This dualism, however, like the others we
consider, can also potentially limit our thinking if we do not use it cautiously and
tentatively.

For example, it can be useful to contrast male inexpressiveness (as a component
of stereotypical masculinity) with female expressiveness. Jack W. Sattel (chapter 26 of
this volume) uses the contrast very well to illustrate how inexpressiveness can relate
to power. Noting the correlation between power and male/female, and inexpressiveness and male/female, he is able to compellingly describe a relationship between
power and inexpressiveness, including how that relationship can, ironically, lead to
male *expressiveness* being used as a tactic. Sattel does not stop there, though; he also
considers how inexpressiveness can be a power-related tactic among males, thus
adding to our understanding of male–female relationships, male–male competition,
and power dynamics generally.   ·

Joseph Pleck (chapter 29 of this volume) also considers inexpressiveness, not as
intrinsically male, but as a part of the ideal of maleness. By making this distinction
(as opposed to adopting the inexpressive-male/expressive-female dichotomy), he is
able to consider the costs to both men and women of men's inexpressiveness (and its
corollaries—the assumption that women have two dangerous powers: the power to
express men's feelings and thoughts for them [and the obligation to do so], and the
power to express thoughts and feelings that might negate a given man's claim to
masculinity).

In contrast, analyses of male inexpressiveness that get stuck in the male/female
difference also seem to get stuck in the male deficit (and correlated "females need to
understand or cure") model. They assume inexpressiveness as part of maleness, not

is something that varies among males in both degree and function, as a tool that maintains conceptions of maleness, or as an ongoing aspect of relationships.

Both Pleck and Sattel transcend the male/female (masculinity/femininity) dualism in their analyses of inexpressiveness. The next step in our understanding depends on our ability to avoid considering their positions in terms of a dualism. We do not want to ask, Who's right? Is male inexpressiveness a tactic to achieve and maintain power, or is it a male deficit that puts (somewhat different) pressures on both males and females? Is it a consequence of institutionalized power, or an individual difference variable? To understand male inexpressiveness (and inexpressiveness in general) we need to be able to understand it as both a tactic and a deficit—and even as a skill—as well as a reflection of differential status and power. That is, one may have to learn how to be inexpressive, which probably occurs simultaneously with *not* learning how to be expressive (assuming we conceive expressiveness as something more than just letting every thought and emotion show without modulation or articulation—and given that women's expressiveness is often in the service of articulating men's thoughts and feelings, this seems an appropriate assumption). As one learns to be inexpressive, capacity for expressiveness may atrophy, so that sometimes an expressive deficit model may be an appropriate characterization for inexpressiveness. At the same time, once one has learned to be inexpressive, one may use that inexpressiveness as a tactic—one that is potentially very powerful, though not without costs.[6] Finally, both formal and informal institutions may assume, expect, reward, require, and use male inexpressiveness.

Following Landrine's analysis, we are reminded that inexpressiveness has no inherent meaning—and no gender! Rather, its meaning derives from the context, including the relationship in which one is inexpressive. Landrine's own work on the differences between white and African-American women's interpretations of "passive" illustrates this point: the black women in her sample frequently defined passive as "not speaking one's mind"—a surface behavior that we might label inexpressive. It is doubtful, however, that any analysis would consider it masculine. And without close examination of the relationships (the context) in which this particular kind of passivity or inexpressiveness is manifest, we would be apt to miss its use as a survival tactic and its relationship to differences in power.

Erving Goffman (chapter 34 of this volume) also provides excellent examples of this point, as he considers how *female* inexpressiveness can be a protective strategy in the face of the pervasive threat of male approach and intrusion. His example also suggests the limits of equating inexpressiveness with maleness: if women are inexpressive in order to guard against undesired male approach, or in response to racism, but expressive in order to maintain desired (or required) relationships, it seems unlikely that inexpressiveness per se can be considered as male, and expressiveness per se as female.

In sum, as Rhoda K. Unger (chapter 25 of this volume) says, neither Paradigm 1 ("reality constructs the person") nor Paradigm 2 ("the person constructs reality") is sufficient. What is required is a "dialectical synthesis" of the two: reality constructs the person as the person constructs reality as reality constructs the person, and so on. The social and cultural context invites us to behave in gendered ways, but, as Joan Luciarello says, "context is constructed by the interpreter" (1995, p. 9). Individu als select from the environment that portion that allows them to achieve, maintain reinforce and reconstruct, produce and reproduce their gendered identities. Ac cording to several contributors to this volume, for instance, men in particular must work unremittingly to achieve the unattainable standards of "masculinity ideology" (Pleck, Sonenstein, & Ku chapter 17 of this volume). These standards and the motive to achieve them, surely in some sense "intrapsychic," drive them to carve out of the environment tasks and relationships that permit them to act out their role: thus, a man bent upon demonstrating his strength and chivalry plucks from the crowd the frailest female with the heaviest parcel and offers his help. Individuals collaborate with social arrangements in the construction of gender, although rarely consciously, and often to their own disadvantage, as Unger and Pleck remind us. Ultimately, as Henry Murray (1938) put it decades ago when describing personality development: "Much of what is *inside* the organism was once *outside*" (p. 40), or, as Gordon Allport (1961) put it, motives become "functionally autonomous." Bem's "gendered lens" resides in the eyes of the individual as well as the society, and the two reinforce each other.

Difference and Dominance

Although Anne Fausto-Sterling (chapter 11 of this volume) envisions a utopia in which parents, like the ones the Bems tried to be and those that Lois Gould (chapter 28 of this volume) portrays, might feel free to raise a child as a gender-neutral or even intersexual being, she does not pretend that in a culture as gender-polarized as ours, the transition to utopia will be smooth. For instance, she asks, "What bathroom would s/he use?" Although, as Goffman points out, males and females manage to use the same facilities in the privacy of their homes, Americans have decreed that in public, bathrooms must be segregated by sex. Why? Biology cannot explain this phenomenon, any more than it can explain why boys and girls in school separate for activities such as walking and eating, for as Goffman observes, males and females "are somewhat similar in the question of waste products and their elimination."

Restrooms for men and women are not just separate, they are unequal. Goffman claims that women's restrooms are superior, "more refined, extensive, and elaborate" than the ones provided for males. We do not know what evidence he has for this claim, but it seems unlikely that he acquired it through direct experience, whereas we, on the basis of firsthand experience, know that it is not always the case. On a recent visit to a major league baseball park, one of us (BC) had occasion to visit the restroom. As she tells the story:

> Finding that there were two men's rooms but no women's room on the level where we were seated, I was forced to descend to a lower level, where I found one women's room (as well as two more men's rooms), with a long line of women waiting to enter. These long lines are a familiar phenomenon, but always before I had interpreted the

phenomenon in exclusively "intrapsychic" individual terms, both biological and social in origin: women, I assumed, made longer stays in restrooms, in order to deal with menstrual matters (biological) and to apply cosmetics (social). It had not occurred to me that there were fewer restrooms for women, let alone to speculate that if my analysis was correct perhaps there should be *more* restrooms for women than men. In effect, as happens all too often in cases of gender discrimination, I blamed the victims.

Still, perhaps one could justify the inequality as a "natural expression" of the fact that more men than women attend baseball games. A comment overheard from a neighbor in line suggested, however, that this construction might be too simple— bathroom arrangements might be a *cause* as well as a consequence of the fact that more men than women go to ball games: "Boy oh boy," she said, as the agonizing wait continued, "It'll be a long time before I go through this again!" It turns out, too, that the male advantage in distribution of restrooms is not limited to masculine-typed settings, for at least as many women as men attend the theater, and, according to the *New York Times,* the men's restrooms in New York theaters are uniformly larger than the women's.

These restroom phenomena clearly demand an analysis in terms not just of difference, but of dominance. Indeed, it is possible that if status were not involved, restrooms and other artifacts of the social scene might not be segregated by sex. In Catharine MacKinnon's view (as Abigail J. Stewart reports in chapter 3) dominance precedes difference: "Gender might not even code as difference," she writes, "might not even mean distinction epistemologically, were it not for its consequence for social power" (MacKinnon, 1987, p. 40). Christine Delphy (1984, p. 144) argues that even "sex" (as we know it) would not exist were it not for status: "The hierarchy of the division of labor is prior to . . . the sexual roles which we call gender. Gender in its turn *created* anatomical sex, in the sense that the hierarchical division of humanity into two transforms an anatomical difference (which in itself is devoid of meaning, like all physical facts) into a category of thought." A world that respected multiple rather than dichotomous sexualities, Fausto-Sterling writes, "would have to be a world of shared powers."

In focusing on the question of "why *differences* exist," according to Rachel T. Hare-Mustin and Jeanne Maracek (chapter 7 of this volume), psychologists "disregard the question of why *domination* exists." They are among numerous psychologists who suggest that differences attributed to "gender" may actually be due to status: if women could shed their subordinate status they would no longer value care and connection over autonomy. Get rid of dominance, and difference, too, will disappear.[7] As evidence for this view, Mednick (1989) cites Brenda Major's finding that "when men and women are in the same high-prestige jobs, their values are identical, and their behavior is similar" (p. 1120).

Research such as Major's, as well as experimental studies in which the effects of gender are observed when occupational role is experimentally manipulated, enhance our understanding of the ways in which status and gender interact, but they do not demonstrate that differences between men and women are "nothing but" differences in status—that, as Susan T. Fiske and Laura S. Stevens (chapter 27 of this volume) put it, "there is no there there." A high-level position is a particular context; Major finding is that in that particular context, there is no evidence for gender difference in certain values. This is useful information, and it should lead us to investigat whether the same is true in other contexts. It is worth noting, too, that high-leve positions constitute, for women, a *very* special context: few women find themselve in such positions. And, this being so, high-level positions are not identical context for men and women; to be one of the 11 percent of the tenured faculty at Harvard who are female is not the same as to be one of the 89 percent who are male. In conducting research we can select (or, in the case of experiments, contrive) special, artificially "clean" conditions, and it is useful to do so, so long as we remember that these conditions are selected or contrived and do not necessarily reflect conditions in the real world. For most women, subordination is part of what it means to be a woman. To isolate gender and status in our research, treating them as "independent variables," can be a useful heuristic, but in the real world gender and power (like race and power) are not independent of each other; they are inextricably intertwined, and research into their relationship should be used to complicate our understanding of the way gender works, rather than to reduce gender to "nothing but" a matter of status.

In omitting any role for the individual, some sociological accounts seem as deterministic and pessimistic (with regard to social change) as the overly individualistic accounts that represent gender as set in utero or at an early age. As we noted in our introduction to Section A of Part VII, it is important to remember that individuals can and do on occasion change their minds in ways that lead them to disrupt the arrangements between the sexes. For instance, women, often with daughters in tow, have begun to storm the men's restrooms in New York theaters; as a result, carpenters are already at work expanding the facilities. Moreover, failing to acknowledge the individual leaves us unable to hear the cries of men such as those in Stephen J. Bergman and Janet Surrey's groups (chapter 33 of this volume), who complain "I am not the patriarchy." In some sense, that has to be true. As an institution with a long and sordid history, the patriarchy clearly affects each individual. Yet, we cannot ignore the possibility of individuals working to distance themselves from that structure, which is after all an emergent one that cannot be reduced to individuals. We can acknowledge the potential agency of the individual without losing sight of the reality of inequality and the need for social change; in fact, it is necessary to do so. As Stephanie Riger (chapter 2 of this volume) says, "The challenge to psychology is to link a vision of women's agency with an understanding of the shaping power of social context."

Directions for Research

As we struggle to transcend the confines of abstract dualisms, our new conceptions of gender seem to some to call for new methods. For instance, if gender is constructed and reconstructed in relationships, then it makes sense to take "the interperonal transaction as a unit of analysis rather than the individual alone," as Unger suggests, whether in the laboratory; in clinical settings, as in the work of Virginia Goldner and her colleagues (chapter 31 of this volume) and Stephen J. Bergman and Janet Surrey (chapter 33 of this volume); or in the field, as in Thorne's (1994) "participant observations" of where, when, and how boys and girls come together and move apart.

On the other hand, we need not discard all traditional methods of investigation and analysis. Sophisticated research designs and statistical techniques, as well as concepts and procedures commonly taught in undergraduate methods courses (convergent validity, statistical interaction, moderator variables, programmatic research) enable us to construct complex, contextual understandings of gender that go far beyond simple lists of mean differences between males and females.

Individual psychologists are not obligated to learn and apply a multitude of methods, just as all of us need not try to be historians or sociologists or philosophers (see Martin, chapter 1 of this volume). But instead of dismissing the results of alien research strategies, we can make use of them. Psychologists of an interpretive-phenomenological bent who are skeptical of the "truths" revealed through conventional scientific methods can still adopt such findings as illustrations, using them, as Stephanie Riger (chapter 2 of this volume) suggests, to enhance the "believability" of their narratives. More traditional psychologists, devoted to the pursuit of "paradigmatic" rather than "narrative" truth, in Jerome Bruner's (1985) terms, can treat the "findings" of the interpretive-phenomenological school as hypotheses and subject them to tests, rather than condemning them as based on "bad data" or no data. And, while remaining rightly wary of the danger of "dissolving science into autobiography," as Riger puts it, they can incorporate individual case material, as well as group data, into their reports. They can also consider carefully the relation between the two—for example, the degree to which the overall results can and do illuminate the behavior of individuals.

We are arguing here for "pluralistic conceptions of understanding," in Martin's words. Instead of treating divergent points of view as alien "others," we advocate an intersubjective approach in which, starting with the assumption that a given theoretical or methodological orientation might have some value, one tries at least to tolerate and if possible to understand it rather than dismiss it, while also maintaining a critical eye. This sort of double vision is not easy to achieve. It is the "mestiza" consciousness Áida Hurtado (chapter 37 of this volume) describes: "a consciousness that simultaneously rejects and embraces—so as not to exclude—what it rejects." Sometimes the conflicting paradigms exist within rather than between psychologists, and sometimes, as with Peggy McIntosh's "Moebius strip" (chapter 39 of this volume), they turn out to be only apparently at odds, actually "on the same side." Sometimes what seemed to be an "either-or" turns out to be a "both-and."

Consider, for example, the case of a study in which women who are interviewed about their experiences as employees of a corporation report that they have encountered no discrimination on the basis of gender. On the one hand, cognizant of the degree to which psychologists in the past have relied on their own "objective" observations and dismissed the subjective accounts of their naive "subjects" (Moraw ski and Steele, 1991), researchers want to believe the women and take their words a face value. On the other hand, they are aware of the problem of "false consciousness" unknown to herself, the interviewee may be mouthing the views of the dominan party. If, however, one abandons the notion that there is a single truth, and tha either the interviewer knows more than the interviewee or vice versa, one can se that both the interviewee and the interviewer simply have access to *different version* of reality, and one can look for avenues leading to both versions.

Of course, dualisms cannot always be dissolved, and paradigms may remain incommensurable. In many such cases, however, we think that rather than choosing between them, it may be advisable to stay with the contradiction, to embrace the paradox. Unger (chapter 25), after a wonderfully candid ironical account of the way in which she uses logical positivist methods to demonstrate a constructivist view of the world, concludes: "Perhaps the kind of person who functions best in a socially constructed world is one who can live in each reality as though it were the only one, but who knows that it is possible to stand outside them all."

There is room for a multiplicity of approaches and voices in the psychology of gender, and we have tried to represent that multiplicity in this book. Some of the authors we included speak in declarative, assertive tones, while others sprinkle their chapters with qualifications and expressions of uncertainty. Some adopt an adversarial stance, others a seductively friendly approach; some speak personally ("I believe ... feel ... wonder"), others in a more objective manner ("Research indicates. . .). Some of our authors tell stories; others make logical arguments and produce statistical charts; some do all three. All such speakers are welcome, as long as we remember that this is a conversation, not a duel in which one asserts one's authority by annihilating the opposition, and that it is important—as "research indicates" many little girls know—to keep the conversation alive and vigorous and developing. We were especially drawn to those writers who portray the study of the psychology of gender as a process and hesitate to take definitive stands, treating even their most cherished assumptions and observations as merely provisional "truths." This is not to say that psychologists engaged in the study of gender should lack moral and political convictions about their subject. The passionate desire for social justice that has drawn many psychologists into this field has also lent energy and power and imagination to their work.

William Perry (1970) describes two sorts of conviction. There is conviction that comes from a dualistic epistemology in which one believes one's own position is absolutely right and any position that disagrees absolutely wrong. In contrast, there is a different kind of conviction that comes from "commitment within relativism." At that position, one recognizes that knowledge may never be certain or absolute, and that the "truth" revealed depends upon the perspective one takes. Nevertheless, individuals are responsible for the positions they adopt, however tentatively, and for acting on the implications of those positions, while remaining open to other points of view. In other words, we are not arguing that we all should "just get along," or that everyone should be nice. Rather, we invite the passion, but hope for a conversation in which there is passionate *listening*, as well as passionate speech.

NOTES

1. The National Grange's fears appear to have been unfounded. According to Ide (1995), the Conference's Draft Platform for Action mentioned only two genders, women and men, thus preserving the dichotomy.

2. These correlations, of course, do not demonstrate causal relationships. One might imagine, for example, that testosterone is related to math via an indirect pathway in which aggressiveness influences free-ranging play, which in turn promotes spatial ability, which in turn increases math ability. Alternatively (or even additionally), one might hypothesize that testosterone is related to math via assertiveness in getting help and attention in math-related activities. And, of course, the pathways of influence need not be the same for males and females.

3. It is too early to rule out prenatal testosterone or other biological factors as influences on the development of genius-level math ability. The main point here is that whatever those factors may be, they are unlikely to be related to "maleness," or to account for differences between men and women within most of the distribution of performance. Also, little more than cursory study has been given to sociocultural factors that influence identification of prodigies, and there is reason to believe that the current male to female ratio (roughly 13:1) of math prodigies represents some inadequate sampling of young girls (Martell, Lane, & Emrich, 1996).

This focus on parental, social, and cultural influences does not mean that we ignore the intrapsychic. These influences act on children's beliefs about themselves and math and help shape children's interests and preferences, which are intrapsychic. See further discussion of the external/internal dichotomy below.

4. We are not arguing that this is necessarily inappropriate—indeed, the concept of co-evolution is extremely important.

5. They also often include the corollary assumptions that (a) it is very hard to be a man, and (b) codifying the fundamentally masculine allows women to better understand this difficult male reality, which they need to do in order to better forgive, compensate, and so forth.

6. Archer (1996) describes the "absence of inexpressiveness" among women, providing a new example of a deficit-model description of women.

7. Such arguments sometimes seem to imply that this would be a good thing—that the values and behaviors of subordinates are inferior to those of superordinates, and that women's ways of knowing are wimpy ways of knowing. Some feminists, of course, argue just the opposite—that views from the margin or from the bottom are especially "privileged" with respect to truth, although they do not provide access to the privileges of power and wealth and prestige. Nadya Aisenberg and Mona Harrington (1988) offer accounts of academic women who suffered vicissitudes in their careers partly because their attitudes toward scholarship and research deviated from the dominant traditions of the academy. Their views were, in this sense, maladaptive, but perhaps the academy would have benefited if it had been able to adapt to the women's ideas. It is well to remember that, as Simone de Beauvoir (1976) says, some "feminine qualities [which] have their origin in our oppression . . . should be preserved after our liberation" (p. 153).

REFERENCES

Aisenberg, N. & Harrington, M. (1988). *Women of Academe: Outsiders in the Sacred Grove.* Amherst: University of Massachusetts Press.

Archer, J. (1996). Sex Differences in Social Behavior: Are the Social Role and Evolutional Explanations Compatible? *American Psychologist*, 51, 909–917.

Allport, G. W. (1961). *Pattern and Growth in Personality*. New York: Holt, Rinehart & Winston

Bem, S. L. (1993). Gender-Schema Theory and Its Implication for Child Development Raising Gender-Aschematic Children in a Gender-Schematic Society. In M. R. Walsh (Ed.), *The Psychology of Women: Ongoing Debates*. New Haven: Yale University Press.

Benbow, C. P. (1988). Sex Differences in Mathematical Reasoning Ability in Intellectually Talented Preadolescents: Their Nature, Effects, and Possible Causes. *Behavioral and Brain Sciences*, 11, 169–232.

Benbow, C. P., & Stanley, J. C. (1980). Sex Differences in Mathematical Ability: Fact or Artifact? *Science*, 210, 1262–1264.

Bleier, R. (1988). Science and the Construction of Meanings in the Neurosciences. In S. V. Rosser (Ed.), *Feminism within the Science and Health Care Professions: Overcoming Resistance*. Elmsford, NY: Pergamon Press.

Boswell, S. L. (1985). The Influence of Sex-Role Stereotyping on Women's Attitudes and Achievement in Mathematics. In S. F. Chipman, L. R. Brush, & D. M. Wilson (Eds.). *Women and Mathematics: Balancing the Equation* (pp. 175–198). Hillsdale, NJ: Erlbaum.

Bruner, J. S. (1985). Narrative and Paradigmatic Modes of Thought. In E. Eisner (Ed.), *Learning and Teaching the Ways of Knowing* (84th Yearbook of the National Society for the Study of Education, pp. 97–115). Chicago: University of Chicago Press.

Buss, D. M. (1994). *The Evolution of Desire: Strategies of Human Mating*. New York: Basic Books.

Chipman, S. F., & Thomas, V. G. (1985). Women's Participation in Mathematics: Outlining the Problem. In S. F. Chipman, L. R. Brush, & D. M. Wilson (Eds.). *Women and Mathematics: Balancing the Equation* (pp. 1–24). Hillsdale, NJ: Erlbaum.

Christiansen, K., & Knussmann, R. (1987). Sex Hormones and Cognitive Functioning in Men. *Neuropsychobiology*, 18, 27–36.

Clinchy, B. (1996). Connected and Separate Knowing: Toward a Marriage of two Minds. In N. R. Goldberger, J. M. Tarule, B. Clinchy, & M. F. Belenky (Eds.), *Knowledge, Difference, and Power: Essays Inspired by Women's Ways of Knowing* (pp. 205–247). New York: Basic Books.

Dabbs, J. M., Alford, E. C., & Fielden, J. A. (In press). Trial Lawyers: The Blue-Collar Workers of the Law. *Journal of Applied Social Psychology*.

Dabbs, J. M., Frady, R. L., Carr, T. S., & Besch, N. F. (1987). Saliva Testosterone and Criminal Violence in Young Adult Prison Inmates. *Psychosomatic Medicine*, 49, 174–182.

Dabbs, J. M., & Morris, R. (1990). Testosterone, Social Class, and Antisocial Behavior in a Sample of 4,462 Men. *Psychological Science*, 3, 209–211.

de Beavoir, S. (1976). Interview by Alice Schwarzer, *Marie-Claire*, October. Reprinted in E. Marks & I. de Courtivron, *New French Feminisms* (pp. 151–153). New York: Schocken Books.

Delphy, C. (1984). *Close to Home*. Amherst: University of Massachusetts Press.

Dixson, A. F. (1993). Effects of Testosterone Propionate upon the Sexual and Aggressive Behavior of Adult Male Marmosets (Callithrix Jacchus) Castrated as Neonates. *Hormones and Behavior*, 27, 216–230.

Eagly, A. H. (1987). *Sex Differences in Social Behavior: A Social Role Interpretation*. Hillsdale, NJ: Erlbaum.

Eccles, J. S., Adler, T. F., Futterman, R., Goff, S. B., Kaczala, C. M., Meece, J. L., & Midgley, C. (1985). Self-Perceptions, Task Perceptions, Socializing Influences, and the Decision to Enroll in Mathematics. In S. F. Chipman, L. R. Brush, & D. M. Wilson (Eds.). *Women and Mathematics: Balancing the Equation* (pp. 95–122). Hillsdale, NJ: Erlbaum.

eingold, A. (1988). Cognitive Gender Difference Are Disappearing. *American Psychologist, 43,* 95–103.

Geschwind, N., & Behan, P. (1982). Left-Handedness: Association with Immune Disease, Migraine and Developmental Learning Disorder. *Proceedings of the Natural Academy of Science, 79,* 5097–5100.

Geschwind, N., & Galaburda, A. M. (1987). *Cerebral Lateralization: Biological Mechanisms, Associations, and Pathology.* Cambridge, MA: MIT Press.

Gilligan, C. (1993). *In a Different Voice: Psychological Theory and Women's Development* (2nd ed.). Cambridge, MA: Harvard University Press.

Gilligan, C., & Attanucci, J. (1988). Two Moral Orientations. In C. Gilligan, J. V. Ward, & J. M. Taylor (Eds.), *Mapping the Moral Domain.* Cambridge, MA: Harvard University Press.

Gilmore, D. D. (1990). *Mankind in the Making: Cultural Concepts of Masculinity.* New Haven: Yale University Press.

Gouchie, C. T., & Kimura, D. (1991). The Relationship between Testosterone Levels and Cognitive Ability Patterns. *Psychoneuroendocrinology, 16,* 323–334.

Goy, R. W., Bercovitch, F. B., & McBrair, M. C. (1988). Behavioral Masculinization Is Independent of Genital Masculinization in Prenatally Androgenized Rhesus Monkey. *Hormones and Behavior, 22,* 552–571.

Halpern, D. F. (1992). *Sex Differences in Cognitive Abilities* (2d ed.). Hillsdale, NJ: Lawrence Erlbaum.

Ide, (1995, August 30). Grange Condemns Women's Conference. *Times Argus, 100 (142);* pp. 1, 8.

Kolata, G. (1983). Math Genius May Have a Hormonal Basis. *Science, 222,* 1312.

Lederer, W. (1968). *The Fear of Women.* New York: Harcourt Brace Jovanovich.

Luciariello, J. (1995). Mind, Culture, Person: Elements in a Cultural Psychology. *Human Development, 38,* 2–18.

MacKinnon, C. (1987). *Feminism Unmodified: Discourses on Life and Law.* Cambridge, MA: Harvard University Press.

Martell, R. F., Lane, D. M., & Emrich, C. (1996). Male-Female Differences: A Computer Simulation. *American Psychologist, 51,* 157–158.

Mednick, M. T. (1989). On the Politics of Psychological Constructs: Stop the Bandwagon, I Want to Get Off. *American Psychologist, 44,* 1118–1123.

Money, J., & Erhardt, A. (1982). *Man and Woman, Boy and Girl.* Baltimore: Johns Hopkins University Press.

Morawski, J. G., & Steele, R. S. (1991). The One or the Other? Textual Analysis of Masculine Power and Feminist Empowerment. *Theory and Psychology, 1,* 107–131.

Murray, H. A. (1938). *Explorations in Personality.* New York: Oxford University Press.

Nanko, S., Saito, S., & Makino, M. (1979). X and Y Chromatin Survey among 1,581 Japanese Juvenile Delinquents. *Japanese Journal of Human Genetics, 24,* 21–25.

Nyborg, H. (1984). Performance and Intelligence in Hormonally Different Groups. In G. J. deVries, J. P. L. de Bruyn, H. B. M. Uylings, & M. A. Corner (Eds.), *Sex Differences in the Brain: The Relation between Function and Structure* (pp. 491–508). New York: Elsevier.

Ortner, S. (1974). Is Female to Male as Nature Is to Culture? In M. Rosaldo & L. Lamphere (Eds.) *Women, Culture and Society* Standford: Standford University Press.

Parlee, M. (in press). Gender Differences: Nature or Nurture? Psycho-Social Aspects. In U. Holbreich (Ed.), *Gonadal Hormones, Sex, and Behavior.* New York: American Psychiatric Press.

Perry, W. (1970). *Forms of Intellectual and Ethical Development in the College Years.* New York: Holt, Rinehart, and Winston.

Rollins, J. H. (1996). *Women's Minds/Women's Bodies: The Psychology of Women in a Biosoci* *Context.* Upper Saddle River, NJ: Prentice-Hall.

Shute, V. J., Pellegrino, J. W., Hubert, L., & Reynolds, R. W. (1983). The Relationship betwee Androgen Levels and Human Spatial Abilities. *Bulletin of the Psychonomic Society, 21,* 465 468.

Spelman, E. V. (1988). *Inessential Woman: Problems of Exclusion in Feminist Thought.* Boston Beacon Press.

Thorne, B. (1994). *Gender Play: Girls and Boys in School.* New Brunswick, NJ: Rutgers University Press.

Unger, R., & Crawford, M. (1995). *Women and Gender: A Feminist Psychology.* New York: McGraw-Hill.

Weisstein, N. (1971). Psychology Constructs the Female, or The Fantasy Life of the Male Psychologist. In V. Gornick & B. K. Moran (Eds.), *Women in Sexist Society,* pp. 133–146. New York: American Library.

Witkin, H. A., Mednick, S. A., Schulsinger, F., Bakkestron, E., Christiansen, K. O., Goodenough, D. R., Hirschhorn, K., Lundsteen, C., Owen, D. R., Philip, J., Rubin, D. B., & Stocking, M. (1976). Criminality in XXY and XYY Men. *Science, 93,* 547–555.

Woolf, V. (1929/1989). *A Room of One's Own.* New York: Harcourt Brace Jovanovich.

Index

About the Editors

Blythe McVicker Clinchy is a professor of psychology at Wellesley College, where she teaches courses in research methodology and in child and adult development. She received her A.B. from Smith College, her M.A. from the New School for Social Research, and her Ph.D. in human development from Harvard University. She is a coauthor of *Women's Ways of Knowing* (Basic Books, 1986, 2d ed. 1997) and a coeditor of *Knowledge, Difference and Power* (Basic Books, 1996). Her research focuses on the evolution of conceptions of knowledge, truth, and value in males and females from early childhood through adulthood and the implications of this development for the practice of education from nursery school through college. She is particularly interested in "connected" and "separate" approaches to knowledge, which appear to be gender-related, although not gender-exclusive.

Julie K. Norem is an associate professor of psychology at Wellesley College, where she teaches courses in personality, gender, self-concept, and research methodology. She received her A.B. from the University of Chicago and her Ph.D. in personality psychology from the University of Michigan in Ann Arbor. She is past associate editor of the *Journal of Research in Personality*, and current associate editor of the *Personality and Social Psychology Review*. Her research focuses on the motivated cognitive strategies individuals develop as they pursue personal goals and on the ways self-knowledge influences goal pursuits and changes over time.